April 2013

To The Long Term Care Community,

Best wishes for good health and happiness!

OPTIMAL
AGING MANUAL

YOUR GUIDE FROM EXPERTS IN MEDICINE, LAW, AND FINANCE

OPTIMAL
AGING MANUAL

YOUR GUIDE FROM EXPERTS IN MEDICINE, LAW, AND FINANCE

EDITED BY

KEVIN W. O'NEIL, MD, FACP

RENNO L. PETERSON, JD

ISBN 0-9753441-0-2
Library of Congress Control Number: 2004109343

Publishers and managing editors: Kevin W. O'Neil, MD, FACP
    and Renno L. Peterson, JD
Composition and Design: Cynthia Mason and Doug Bell
Illustrator: Adam Carlson
Photographer: Mary McCulley (refer to colophon)
Proofreader and Indexer: Julie Cleveland
Printed and bound through: Asia Pacific Offset, China

Optimal Aging LLC
1605 Main Street, Suite 700
Sarasota, FL 34236
941-308-0037
optimalaging.com

 Kevin and Renno dedicate this book to their families whose love and support made it possible.

Maryrose, Kevin Jr., Paul, and Rory O'Neil
Karen, Drew, and Eric Peterson

Success usually comes to those who are too busy to be looking for it.

—*Henry David Thoreau*

A TRIBUTE TO ART LINKLETTER

These words by Thoreau are no more aptly applied than to the life of Art Linkletter. Born in 1912, Art Linkletter has packed much more than 90 years of living into his one life. Two of his television shows entertained multiple generations. *House Party* ran on CBS television and radio for 25 years, and *People Are Funny* ran on NBC television and radio for 19 years. *Kids Say the Darndest Things* was the number-one bestseller for two consecutive years and is one of the top 14 bestsellers in American publishing history. *Old Age Is Not for Sissies* was also a national bestseller and demonstrates his concern and interest in the problems of aging.

In *A Child's Garden of Misinformation,* Art said, "The four stages of man are infancy, childhood, adolescence and obsolescence." Yet actions speak louder than words, and Art has shown by his example that one's later years can be a time of major productivity and significance. He served on President Nixon's National Advisory Council for Drug Abuse Prevention, the Presidential Commission to Improve Reading in the United States, and President Reagan's Commission on Fitness and Physical Education. He was named Ambassador to Australia and Commissioner General to the 150th Australian Anniversary Celebration by President Reagan. He has won two Emmy Awards, including the lifetime achievement award, and received four Emmy nominations. He has received 10 honorary doctorate degrees.

Yet, like so many successful people, Art Linkletter has had his share of setbacks and sorrow, including the death of a child. However, he has turned these difficult and sad experiences into a means to grow personally and to help others. He once said, "Things turn out best for the people who make the best out of the way things turn out." Life is not always fair, and all of us will shed a fair amount of tears. Art Linkletter is a shining example of how overcoming adversity can lead to blessings that we could not have imagined.

Now in his 90s, Art Linkletter is far from idle. In fact, he has been and continues to be a staunch advocate of issues important to seniors. He is currently the Chairman of the Board of the Center on Aging at UCLA. He is also chairman of the board of the French Foundation for Alzheimer's Research, which raises millions of dollars for grants to promising graduate research scientists who might be unable to obtain grants from other national organizations. He is President of United Seniors of America (USA), an organization committed to financial matters which directly impact seniors such as Social Security, Medicare, and prescription drug costs. He continues to lecture extensively and write books related to successful aging. His next book, *How to Make the Best of the Rest of Your Life,* will be ready for publication in the winter of 2004.

The editors and authors of *Optimal Aging Manual* would like to thank Art Linkletter for his support for this project and most importantly for being the person he is—a man who has made a difference in the lives of so many people, young and old.

KEVIN W. O'NEIL, MD, FACP

RENNO L. PETERSON, JD

TABLE OF CONTENTS

TRIBUTE VI

PREFACE X

ACKNOWLEDGMENTS XIV

INTRODUCTION 1

SECTION I YOUR BODY 2

01 THE SKIN 6
Barbara A. Gilchrest, MD and Daniel S. Loo, MD

02 THE EYES 20
Peter J. Kelly, MD and Kevin W. O'Neil, MD

03 HEARING 32
Peter S. Roland, MD and Michelle Caruso Marcincuk, MD

04 THE NOSE 48
Kevin W. O'Neil, MD

05 ORAL HEALTH 58
Kenneth Shay, DDS, MS

06 THE LUNGS 86
Raymond D. Hautamaki, MD

07 THE HEART 106
Tarek Helmy, MD and Nanette K. Wenger, MD

08 THE ARTERIES AND VEINS 138
Russell H. Samson, MD

09 THE GASTROINTESTINAL SYSTEM 156
Gregory L. Eastwood, MD

10 THE KIDNEYS 188
Allen R. Nissenson, MD and Ruth L. Wintz, MD

11 THE PROSTATE 208
Winston Barzell, MD

12 MALE SEXUAL FUNCTION 240
Jayant Dey, MD

13 FEMALE SEXUAL FUNCTION 254
Deborah J. Lightner, MD

14 URINARY INCONTINENCE 264
Rodney A. Appell, MD

15 GYNECOLOGY 276
Vincent G. Stenger, MD

16 BONES, MUSCLES, AND JOINTS I 294
J. Desmond O'Duffy, MD

17 BONES, MUSCLES, AND JOINTS II 318
Robert Seebacher, MD and Samuel Hoisington, MD

18 THE SPINE 418
Ashvin Patel, MD

19 OSTEOPOROSIS 438
Silvina Levis, MD

20 HORMONES, THE ENDOCRINE SYSTEM 448
Mark Shepherd, MD

21 THE NERVOUS SYSTEM 490
Maurice Hanson, MD

22 INFECTIONS 506
Jack L. LeFrock, MD

23 THE BLOOD SYSTEM 530
John Garton, MD

24 CANCER 552
Sarah Hoffe, MD

SECTION II SPECIAL HEALTH ISSUES 566

25 MENTAL HEALTH 570
Susan Maixner, MD and Karyn S. Schoem, MSW

26 MEMORY 602
Bruce E. Robinson, MD and Kathleen Houseweart, MBA

27 ALCOHOL ABUSE 620
Melinda S. Lantz, MD

28 NUTRITION AND DIET 626
Linda Bobroff, PHD, RD, LD/N

29 OBESITY 642
Monica Mathys, Pharm D.

30 REHABILITATION 652
Masayoshi Itoh, MD, MPH and Mathew H. Lee, MD, MPH

31 FALLS 688
Adriana Bida, MD and Edmund Duthie, MD

32 PAIN 688
Marcos Fe-Bornstein, MD

33 DRUG THERAPY 714
Monica Mathys, PharmD

34 COSMETIC SURGERY 726
Braun H. Graham, MD

35 TRAVEL 736
Kevin W. O'Neil, MD

36 SLEEP AND EXERCISE 750
Kevin W. O'Neil, MD

37 ALTERNATIVE MEDICINE 764
Kevin W. O'Neil, MD

38 YOU AND YOUR DOCTOR 774
David R. Stutz, MD

39 END-OF-LIFE CARE 788
Kevin W. O'Neil, MD

40 BEREAVEMENT AND CAREGIVING 802
Christine A. Cauffield, PhD

41 SPIRITUALITY AND HEALTH 822
Susan H. Mcfadden, PhD

42 LONG TERM CARE 832
Kathleen Houseweart, MBA

43 ELDER ABUSE 842
Kathleen Houseweart, MBA

SECTION III LEGAL AND FINANCIAL ISSUES ISSUES 850

44 ESTATE PLANNING 854
Renno L. Peterson, JD and Robert A. Esperti, JD

45 HOW TO TALK YOUR PARENTS ABOUT THEIR MONEY, HEALTH, AND ESTATE PLANNING 886
Susan K. Bradley, CFP

46 STAYING IN YOUR HOME 900
John Schaub

47 LIFE INSURANCE 910
E. Michael Kilbourn, CLU, CHFC

48 INSURANCE PRODUCTS FOR LONG-TERM CARE 944
Carlos C. Whaley

49 RETIREMENT PLANNING 962
Scot W. Overdorf, JD, CPA

50 PERSONAL ANNUITIES DU JOUR 1006
Richard W.D. Buff, JD, CLU

51 INVESTING FOR RETIREMENT 1028
David C. Partheymuller, CFP, CEP

52 LONGTERM CARE AND MEDICAID 1052
Ira Stewart Wiesner, JD

53 HANDLING LEGAL ASPECTS OF DISABILITY AND DEATH 1064
J. David Kerr, JD

APPENDIX A 1098

APPENDIX B 1100

APPENDIX C 1104

MEDICAL GLOSSARY 1112

LEGAL GLOSSARY 1147

INDEX 1154

Old age is like everything else. To make a success of it, you've got to start young.
—*Fred Astaire*

PREFACE

Getting older isn't always easy. To add insult to injury, getting older is also complicated. Which medicines do we take for what ails us? Which kinds of insurance do we need and which kinds do we need to get rid of? Which medical procedures are available and what do they mean? How do we face the death of those who are close to us—and then face our own mortality?

America is truly in an age boom. The fastest-growing segment of our society is the group over 85 years of age, and the rest of us are catching up all too quickly. Most of us do not want to simply live longer. We also want to live well. We want our so-called golden years to be healthy, and we want our financial and legal affairs to be in order. Research has shown that relatively few people have taken the time to organize their affairs. How often have you heard about someone dying without a will? Do you know someone whose family was devastated financially because of an untimely death or a disability? Now think about yourself. Who will make decisions for you if you are sick and incapable of making them yourself? Do you, your family, and your friends really understand the issues that must be faced?

As a geriatrician for over 27 years and an estate planning attorney for over 30 years, we have had the privilege of treating and planning for thousands of older people and their families. We have shared their hopes and fears, their tragedies and triumphs. We know the issues they face.

We also know that it is hard to fathom all the medical, legal, and financial issues that aging presents. Unfortunately, there is a lack of a comprehensive, easy-to-understand resource that gives guidance for these issues. It is this lack of a resource that motivated us to make *Optimal Aging Manual* a reality.

This book is aimed primarily at baby boomers and their parents. *Optimal Aging Manual* is intended to be a single resource on the cutting edge of the information and knowledge required to age as well as is possible. It has been quite an undertaking, and we are proud of the effort taken by a number of wonderful people.

Like so many things, this book started out as a dream. Kevin had been practicing internal medicine and geriatrics for 27 years. Often, he found himself in conversations with his patients, not only about their health but also their plans for the future. Questions about how they had planned for disability or terminal illness were often met with blank stares. It was obvious that many people had simply not considered these possibilities. Kevin wished he had a resource for his patients that would cover not only the common health challenges that they would face as they got older but also the important legal and financial aspects of aging. Care of the older person requires that all these issues be considered. Although he found some books that covered these topics, he wanted a manual that covered the topics in sufficient depth. He also wanted beautiful illustrations and photographs to accompany the text.

The dream gave way to an idea. Kevin contacted Renno, who had dedicated his whole career to estate planning. Renno and his partner had written many books on estate planning, disability, and wealth preservation. After Kevin shared his feelings, Renno began vibrating with excitement. And so the concept for this book took form—doctors, lawyers, and financial professionals coming together to help educate the public about the important issues that a person faces as he or she gets older.

Since no one person can be an expert in every area of medicine, law, or finance, we wanted to find recognized experts in each of the areas that would be covered in our book. We started making phone calls to colleagues and friends. The reception we had was tremendous. Nearly every physician, lawyer, and financial or insurance expert that we contacted was excited about the concept and willing to contribute. The only professionals who declined our invitation were those who already had too much on their plate.

We wanted this book to be an indispensable resource for important information, but we also wanted it to be attractive. We sought illustrations and photographs that reflected the essential information in the text. Serendipitously, one of Kevin's patients put him in contact with Dr. Christine Cauffield, author of Chapter 40 on bereavement and caregiving. Christine was immediately excited. She arranged a meeting with Dr. Larry Thompson, the president of the Ringling School of Art and Design in Sarasota, Florida, a world-renowned institution that has produced some of the finest artists, designers, illustrators, and photographers in the United States and many other countries. From that meeting, a relationship evolved that brought the expertise of our authors together with the creative talents of the Ringling School faculty and students. Under the direction of the head of the Ringling School Design Center, Jennifer Mumford, gifted senior students (now graduates!) Doug Bell and Cynthia Mason developed the layout and design for the book. Adam Carlson did the illustrations. Mary McCulley, a Ringling School alumnus, did most of the photography. Their enthusiasm for the project and their immense talent are reflected in the final product.

Once we put this superb team together, we thought we had it made, but life is full of surprises. It was not as simple as we had hoped. Editing a book of this magnitude was difficult, not only because of the breadth of the material but because it was written by so many authors, each having a different manner of expression. Time was also a factor for our authors. They are all successful professionals, having busy practices of their own. They had to work on this writing project with all their other activities, so it was very hard to meet deadlines.

In addition, we were trying to edit and design the book while it was being written. In hindsight, it would have been better to wait until we had an edited manuscript before we used the talents of the Ringling

School. However, the students who wanted to participate in the project were seniors. We wanted their assistance before they graduated.

The wonderful part of this difficult process was that we all learned together. Mistakes were made; tasks were done and redone. At times, decisions had to be made about design, content, and editing. The two of us would listen to all the alternatives and try to accommodate everyone. Sometimes we went with a traditional approach, and other times we went with some not so traditional ideas. Any criticism of the final product should be directed at us, because in the end we made all of the decisions.

We were also faced with privacy issues. We wanted to include real stories about real people. In some cases, we obtained permission to include true situations. In others, because of these privacy issues, we decided to change names and facts to preserve privacy. We did retain the essence of the point being made. And to drive home important issues, we used a compilation of facts about patients and clients. In every case, the situations and stories are accurate in that they reflect portrayals of realistic cases.

To really highlight the importance of *Optimal Aging Manual*, we wanted a spokesperson who was respected and recognized for contributions to the care of the elderly, and we could think of no one better suited than Art Linkletter. Kevin contacted Mr. Linkletter's staff, hoping to be able to discuss the idea with Mr. Linkletter. Amazingly enough,

he was willing to talk to Kevin. Mr. Linkletter was very interested in the concept, and after reviewing several chapters, he agreed to write some very kind words about *Optimal Aging Manual*. We were so proud of his words that we put them on the back cover. Mr. Linkletter has been an inspiration to both of us.

We believe that this book will help you no matter where in life you are. Although the material is oriented to those over 50, it will benefit you even if you are younger and want to learn what you can do to reduce your risk for problems later on. If you are caring for an aged parent and want to understand the problems he or she is experiencing, reading *Optimal Aging Manual* is a great first step.

We wish you happiness, health, and prosperity as you or someone you care about grows older. It is a journey that is not always pleasant, but by having more knowledge, it is a journey that can be improved exponentially.

Kevin W. O'Neil

KEVIN W. O'NEIL, MD, FACP

Renno Peterson

RENNO L. PETERSON, JD

ACKNOWLEDGMENTS

This book would not be possible without the collaboration of many people. First of all, we would like to thank Kevin's wife, Maryrose, and Renno's wife, Karen, who often see too little of their husbands due to the nature of their medical and law practices. Their understanding and support for this project was unwavering, and many times they spurred us on when we thought the sheer magnitude of this project was overwhelming.

Kevin would like to especially thank his partners in medical practice, Dr. Robert Marcantonio, Dr. Eric Weiner, and Dr. J. Anthony Murat. They assumed Kevin's hospital practice so that he could have a more reasonable schedule in office practice, allowing him to spend time writing his own chapters for *Optimal Aging Manual* and editing the manuscripts for the medical chapters. Special thanks are also due to his office staff and especially his medical assistant of 20 years, Alane Couse, for their understanding and cooperation when it came to the numerous adjustments and disruptions in the office schedule. Kevin also would like to thank the CEO of First Physicians Group, Dr. Brad Lerner, for allowing him flexibility in the scheduling of his duties.

We thank Dr. Duncan Finley, CEO of Sarasota Memorial Hospital, as well as the wonderful staff at Sarasota Memorial Hospital, for their support of this project by allowing our illustrators and photographers to disrupt some of their normally busy days in caring for patients. We thank the radiologists, especially Dr. Steven Morse and Dr. Richard Lichtenstein, and radiology staff, especially Deborah Bohanon and Barbara Foley, of Sarasota Memorial Hospital for permitting us to use X-rays and images from their archives to illustrate important points in this book. We thank Dr. David Siegel and the staff of the Comprehensive Rehabilitation Unit of Sarasota Memorial Hospital for devoting almost a whole Saturday to allow our photographer to shoot photos for this book.

Renno would like to thank Melissa Lord, his longtime assistant, without whom he could not function. A special thank you to Renno's partner of 30 years, Bob Esperti, for his always great support, as well as David Cahoone, Renno's other law partner and colleague.

Words cannot adequately express the great appreciation we have for the many great people at the Ringling School of Art and Design in Sarasota, Florida for the time and commitment they gave to this project. Dr. Larry Thompson, the President of the Ringling School, captured the spirit of the project at our first meeting. Jennifer Mumford, the Director of the Design Center at the Ringling School, assembled a talented group of senior students (now graduates!) who put their hearts and souls into this book. She wanted this book not only to be educational, but beautiful. Mission accomplished! And for this, we especially thank Cindy Mason and Doug Bell, talented graphic designers who are responsible for the layout and design of the book. It is said that a picture is worth a thousand words. Our gifted illustrator, Adam Carlson, has proved that. The collaboration with the Ringling School was made possible because of the enthusiasm and excitement of two wonderful people, Jack Swanson and Dr. Christine Cauffield (author of Chapter 40) from Sarasota, Florida.

Special thanks to Mary McCulley, a Ringling School alumnus, for her magnificent photography and to Margery Floyd for the many great ideas she had for promoting this book.

Last, but not least, we give a big thanks to the contributing authors who put in a huge amount of work, with no assurance of success, just because they believed.

Kevin W. O'Neil

KEVIN W. O'NEIL, MD, FACP

Renno Peterson

RENNO L. PETERSON, JD

INTRODUCTION

We have tried to make using *Optimal Aging Manual* as simple as possible. It is a long book, but it is not designed to be read from cover to cover. *Optimal Aging Manual* is a reference book, allowing its readers to quickly find information about important issues.

Optimal Aging Manual, like Caesar's Gaul, is divided into three parts. Part I addresses health issues of the body. Part II discusses lifestyle, such as obesity, nutrition, mental issues, and other sensitive and important challenges. Part III is a survey of the legal and financial concerns that are particularly unique as people age.

If you are looking for specific information, use the index. In it, you will find a comprehensive array of terms and topics. The index will direct you to the page or pages that contain that term or topic.

Throughout each part, we use tables, charts, illustrations, interesting and inspiring stories, and photographs to help readers better understand some complex material. In some chapters, some illustrations or photographs are not specifically mentioned in the text. Each part has its own introduction, which gives more specific guidance and information as to how that part is structured and how to most effectively use the material.

We have included separate glossaries for medical terms and legal and financial terms to allow readers to have quick access to the sometimes complex words that are associated with medicine, law, and finance. As you read a chapter, words that are in **bold blue** type are a glossary term. This special type is used only when the words first appear in a chapter. Thereafter, the term is in the same type as the rest of the text.

The end of each chapter is summarized with "What You Need to Know," the important highlighted points made in the chapter. After the summary, each author has included a section entitled "For More Information," which is a list of institutions, companies, books, articles, and/or websites that are helpful resources on the issues covered in the chapter.

Even with over 1,000 pages, our authors had to be general in their discussions. Please remember, *Optimal Aging Manual* is not a substitute for seeing a physician, lawyer, or financial professional. The chapters are to help readers get a fundamental understanding of the common issues and terminology associated with the medical, legal, and financial aspects of growing older. Use *The Optimal Aging Manual* as a guide as you seek out professional help.

We live in a fast-changing world. New concepts arise daily. New drugs are introduced, and others become obsolete or are found to be ineffective. The politicians are always tinkering with laws concerning estate planning, taxation, insurance, retirement plans, and investing. Since a great deal of time can pass between the time an author writes a chapter and the time a book comes out, some information in *Optimal Aging Manual* may be outdated. That is why you should verify all the information in the book with a professional.

To keep you on the cutting edge, *Optimal Aging Manual* has its own website. To get up-to-date information on all the topics discussed in this book, please visit

WWW.OPTIMALAGING.COM

You know you are getting old when all the names in your black book have M.D. after them.

—*Arnold Palmer*

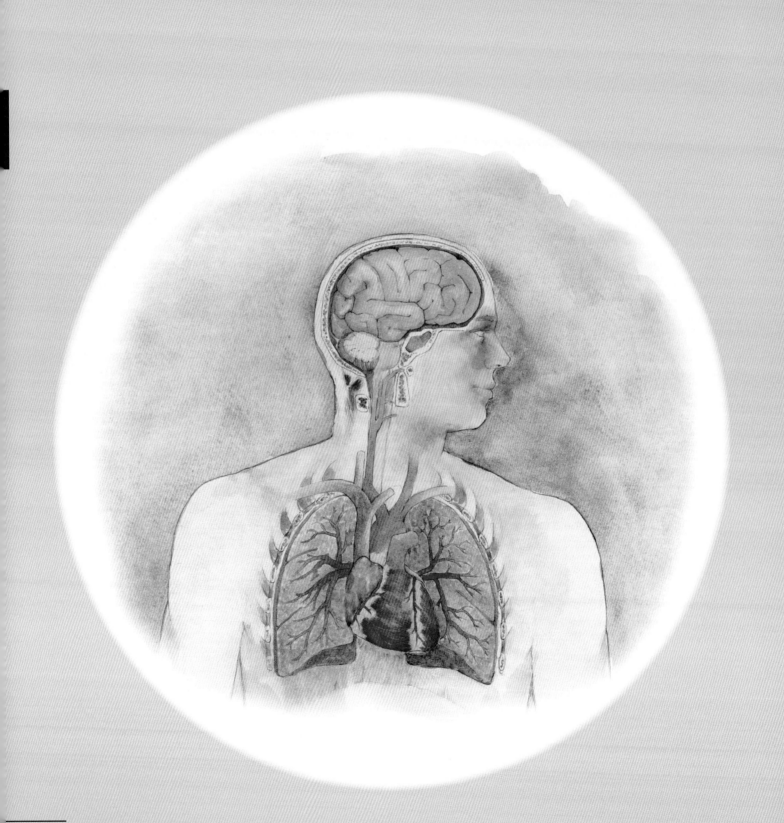

YOUR BODY

Aging is an inevitable part of life, but isn't it interesting how our perspective on aging changes as we get older? Remember, when you were five years old, how you couldn't wait until your next birthday? Didn't it seem like an eternity from one year to the next? Most of us couldn't wait until we turned 16 and could get behind the wheel of a car. And 21! Now I'm "legal"!

Maturity has a way of changing our feelings about the progression of the years. Most of us get married and have children. Did it astonish you when you took your first "child" to college? Where did the years go? I recall telling my wife not to make a scene when we were about to leave our son at college. She did fine. When he gave me a big hug and put his head on my shoulder, a flood of memories came back from his childhood days. I was the one who lost it.

When we hit 40 and 50, we might want to put the brakes on. We realize that we are getting older, whether we like it or not. Hopefully, we have had good health habits, and we are enjoying the fruits of our labors. Some of us, however, will get sick for no good reason. Some diseases strike people who have done all the right things. On the other hand, some of us have not taken such good care of ourselves. The development of hypertension, diabetes, or coronary artery disease may have given us a wake-up call. Sadly, we may have even lost a friend or two.

As we grow older, our health can and should become a major focus of our lives. Without our health, we can't do many of the things we really want to do.

Some of us regret that we did not start taking care of ourselves sooner. As Mickey Mantle said, "If I knew I was going to live this long, I'd have taken better care of myself." In our early adult years, so many things competed for our attention as we tried to make a living—marriage, children, job, social, and community responsibilities—that many of us didn't take the time to take care of our bodies. We may have put on too much weight and exercised seldom or not at all.

In our later years, difficult decisions may be thrust upon us. There have been amazing technological advances in medicine. People are living longer despite serious medical problems. There may come a time when you, a parent, or a spouse has to make a decision about treatment that you are not anxious to have. One of my patients, a widower in his mid-80s, was confronted with the prospect of dialysis for kidney failure. His children brought him to his appointments, and arrangements had been made with a surgeon to place an access for his dialysis treatments. Since he had a serious heart condition as well as diabetes and circulatory problems, I asked him whether he really wanted to go through dialysis. He looked surprised and asked, "Hell, Doc, do I really have a choice?" I reassured him that his body was his and only he could make the decision about whether he wanted to go through with it. I explained the benefits and the risks of treatment, as well as his prognosis if he refused dialysis. He responded, "Doc, I have had a good life. I really don't want to live the rest of my life tied to a

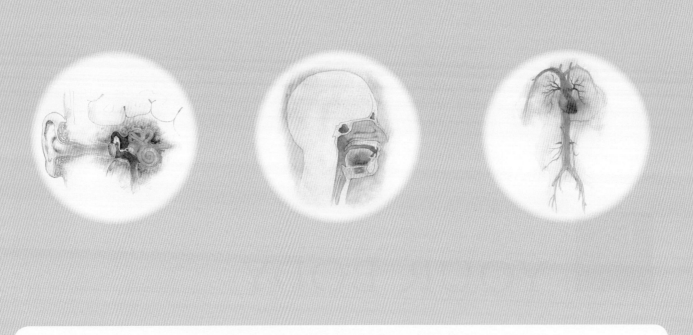

damn machine. I am glad I have a choice. Let's cancel it." We discussed his decision with his children, and they accepted his wishes. I told them there is no such thing as a right or wrong decision in these situations. Harry had a reasonably comfortable life for the next 6 months. As his kidney failure progressed, he became weaker. Hospice helped the family with his care at home, and he died peacefully a few months later.

Making such decisions requires good information about the proposed treatment, the expected results, and the potential complications. The options need to be discussed, and the persons affected should be allowed to make their own decision if they are competent to do so. In addition, these may not be either-or decisions. Some people may start dialysis or chemotherapy for cancer but then decide that their quality of life is worse than they anticipated. In these situations, you have the right to stop the treatment.

Various theories of aging have been printed in magazines and books. These explore the genetic and environmental influences that affect the aging process. Research has given us amazing insights into "normal aging" and the processes that lead to disease, disability, and death. The reality is that we are living longer than our ancestors did. This increased longevity can be explained by the fact that most of us are taking better care of ourselves. In addition, scientific and medical research has taught us to avoid those things that are injurious to our health, and breakthroughs have occurred that have had a major impact on the

prognosis of those with infectious diseases, heart disease, and cancer.

Our purpose in this part of *Optimal Aging Manual* is not to turn you into a doctor but to give you practical information so that you can understand the aging of your body. No matter where you are in life, the following pages can help. Although you and I both know that serious diseases will strike some of us, you will find in Part One measures that you can take to minimize the adverse consequences of aging. You will learn what you need to do to reduce your risks, as well as what can be done if you or a loved one is affected.

PART ONE is broken down into individual organ systems. You will learn what is considered normal or abnormal aging for that particular system. Our authors present information that will make it easier for you to understand what your own doctor tells you. This information does not replace what your own doctor tells you based on your own unique circumstances. You will learn about the diagnosis and treatment of disorders that are common in midlife and later. Those conditions that predominantly affect younger people or have their onset at a younger age are not considered.

Each chapter introduces you to the doctor(s) who will be your guide as you explore the information about the system being discussed. Technical terms in the chapter are in **bold blue** print when they first

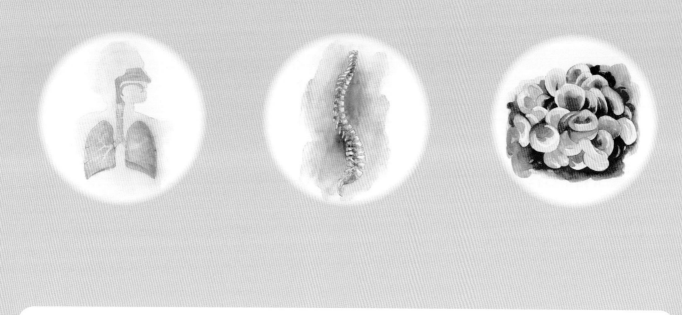

appear. Not only are they explained in the text, but you can also look up the definitions in the medical glossary at the end of the book. Drugs have generic and brand names. The first time the drug appears in a chapter, the generic name is in small capital letters. The brand name has its standard capitalization and its remaining letters are in small capitals. Appendix C includes the generic names of drugs, as well as the corresponding brand names and uses. The illustrations help you understand concepts presented in the text. Case stories, which demonstrate important points, are presented from the perspective of a doctor ("Doctor's Diary"), a patient ("My Story"), a nurse ("Nurse's Notes"), or a family member or friend ("Family Journal"). Names have been changed to ensure confidentiality. Some cases may actually be composites from the author's memory. The point is that these cases are intended to illustrate what is being discussed in the chapter. At the end of each chapter you will find "What You Need to Know," which summarizes the key points from the chapter. If you want additional information, visit the websites or write to the organizations noted in "For More Information."

My hope is that the knowledge you acquire in this section about the aging of your body will help you prepare for or deal with your older years. Perhaps you will realize that you have some unhealthy habits and make some lifestyle changes in order to avoid more serious problems later on. Maybe you have already been affected by one of the conditions described and want to understand it better. I am confident that the information provided by these experts will help you in many ways and that you will find this a valuable reference source for years to come.

Kevin W. O'Neil

KEVIN W. O'NEIL, MD, FACP
MARCH 26, 2004

Wrinkles should merely indicate where smiles have been.

—*Mark Twain*

THE AUTHORS

01

DANIEL S. LOO, MD, is an associate professor in the Department of Dermatology at the Boston University School of Medicine. He went to medical school at the State University of New York at Stony Brook. He completed his internship at the University of Rochester and his residency at the University of Michigan Medical Center. He received an award from the Michigan Dermatological Society in 1996 for the outstanding resident clinical science research paper. He is also the recipient of the Outstanding Teacher of the Year Award (1999–2000) and the Amal K. Kurban Career Development Award (2002–2004) from the Department of Dermatology at the Boston University School of Medicine.

BARBARA A. GILCHREST, MD, is a professor in and chair of the Department of Dermatology at the Boston University School of Medicine. Dr. Gilchrest graduated from Harvard Medical School and did her medical internship and residency on the Harvard service at Boston City Hospital. She completed her dermatology residency and a fellowship in Photomedicine at Massachusetts General Hospital. Highlights from her professional career include being president of the Women's Dermatologic Society from 1987–1988 and on the American Academy of Dermatology Board of Directors, 1995–1999; member of the Institute of Medicine, National Academy of Science, 1998–; president of the Society for Investigative Dermatology, 1999–2000; and president of the Association of Professors of Dermatology, 2002–2004.

01 | THE SKIN

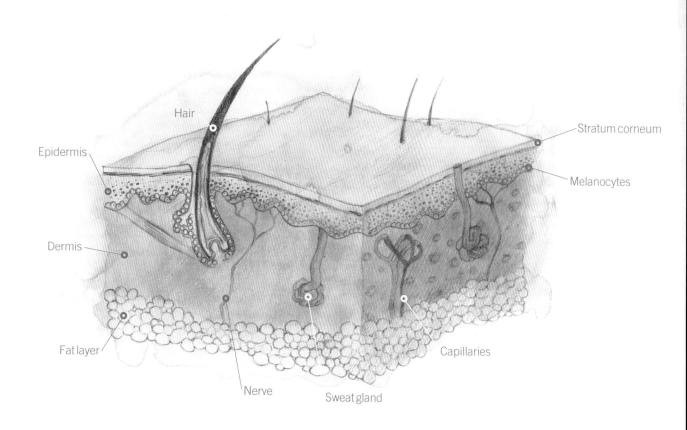

(figure 1-1)

Getting under your skin. Your skin is composed of three layers: the epidermis, dermis, and fat layer. The skin protects you from injury, but like your other organs, it is very active metabolically. It helps control your body temperature and helps fight infection.

The active form of vitamin D, which is important in calcium regulation, is produced in the skin when you are exposed to sunlight. If you live in a climate where you have little sunlight, you may need to take a vitamin D supplement.

Skin problems are among the most common reasons for us to visit a doctor. Billions of dollars are spent each year on antiaging products that promise to reduce wrinkles. Cosmetics are marketed to hide age spots. Numerous lubricating lotions are marketed to treat dry skin. Plastic surgeons attempt to erase some of the common signs of skin aging.

SKIN CHANGES

There are certain common skin changes that occur with aging, such as wrinkles, bruising, age spots, cherry angiomas, and skin tags. Figure 1-2 shows the differences between young and older skin.

Wrinkles result from cumulative sun exposure which damages elastic fibers of the skin (see Figure 1-3, in the Photo Gallery at the end of this chapter). These fibers allow the skin to stretch and retract. When damaged, skin loses its elasticity, becoming lax and wrinkled. Sun avoidance, wearing long-sleeve shirts and broad-brimmed hats, and daily application of sunscreen SPF 15 or greater is the best way to prevent further wrinkles. Very fine wrinkles can be reversed or improved with over-the-counter (OTC) creams containing retinol or prescription TRETINION 0.05% (such as RENOVA). Improvement may be seen after several months of treatment. Cigarette smoking also damages elastic fibers resulting in more wrinkles. Studies have confirmed that cigarette smokers have more wrinkles than persons their age who don't smoke.

Bruising, called purpura, results from the thinning of the skin and the fragility of underlying blood vessels (see Figure 1-4). This is most commonly found on the backs of the hands and forearms. Even the most minor trauma, pressure, or friction can cause purpura. For most patients, these bruises appear to occur spontaneously, as no prior trauma can be recalled. If you are taking aspirin, nonsteroidal anti-inflammatory drugs (ALEVE, MOTRIN), or steroids (PREDNISONE), the chance of bruising is higher as these medications increase the risk of bleeding and slow down

(figure 1-2)

Comparison between (a) normal and (b) older skin. As we age, there is a marked flattening of the junction between the epidermis (the most superficial layer of skin) and the dermis (see arrows). The "anchoring" of the epidermis to the dermis decreases and makes the skin more fragile and susceptible to injury. The dermis contains the supporting structures of the skin. The decreased dermal thickness and blood supply, with aging, contribute to poorer wound healing as we get older.

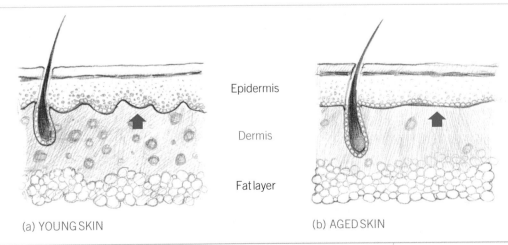

Epidermis

Dermis

Fat layer

(a) YOUNG SKIN

(b) AGED SKIN

wound healing. Conscious avoidance of trauma, pressure, or friction is the only way to minimize purpura. There are no creams or vitamins that can prevent them.

Age spots, also known as *liver spots* or solar lentigos, are caused by increased pigment production in response to sun exposure (see Figure 1-5). These brown, flat spots are safe and unrelated to skin cancer. Protective clothing and sunscreens can help reduce development of additional liver spots. Prescription creams such as tretinoin 0.05% (Renova) or bleaching agents (hydroquinone) can improve the appearance of age spots. Liquid nitrogen and lasers are other treatment options that can only be provided by your physician. As these spots are benign, most health insurance plans will not cover these treatments.

As shown in Figure 1-6, cherry angiomas are benign red growths that commonly dot the trunk of most people as they get older. Such growths may become larger and more numerous as you age. No treatment is required, but some individuals like to have them removed for cosmetic reasons.

Skin tags may be found on the skin under the arm, around the neck, or in the groin area, usually in overweight individuals (see Figure 1-7). No treatment is required, but some people decide to have them removed for cosmetic reasons. Some studies have suggested an association between numerous skin tags and colon polyps.

SKIN DISORDERS

This chapter helps you identify common skin and nail disorders that may affect us as we age. Each disorder discussed includes a definition, description, and simple OTC treatments, as well as noting when you should see a doctor. A summary of preventive health practices to keep your skin healthy is included in the boxes toward the end of this chapter.

Although psoriasis is a common skin disorder and may cause significant disability in the elderly, it generally has its onset at a younger age and is therefore not included here. The reader may obtain information on this topic from the section "For More Information," at the end of the chapter.

BENIGN KERATOSIS

Description: A benign keratosis (seborrheic keratosis) is a common growth on the skin of an adult. Keratoses range in size from 0.5 to 2 cm. Their color can vary from light brown to dark brown. A keratosis often has a rough, wartlike surface and is usually located on a person's chest, back, abdomen, head, or neck (see Figure 1-8).

Treatment: Most benign keratoses do not produce symptoms and do not require treatment. There is no OTC therapy for a keratosis. They may be unsightly, however; and although most insurance companies do not cover their removal because they are harmless and unrelated to skin cancer, many simple cosmetic office procedures can remove selected keratoses.

Alternatively, if you have a keratosis that is painful, bleeding, breaking down, or rapidly growing, you should see your primary care doctor or dermatologist for diagnosis and treatment, if indicated.

CYST

Description: A cyst is an enclosed sac filled with thick cheese like material, representing dead skin cells. They are skin-colored or yellow deep lumps that occur on the trunk, scalp, or face (see Figure 1-9). Occasionally there may be an opening to the skin surface that permits the cheesy material to be squeezed out.

Treatment: Most cysts are harmless and do not require treatment. There is no OTC treatment for a cyst. As noted for keratoses, however, cysts may be treated for cosmetic reasons using simple office procedures. If you have a cyst that breaks open, or becomes red, tender, or painful, it may be infected and you should see your primary physician or dermatologist.

WARTS

Description: Warts are viral infections of the skin. They are skin-colored or brown bumps 5 to 15 mm in size with a rough warty surface that occur commonly on the hands and feet (see Figures 1-10 and 1-11).

Treatment: OTC treatment includes salicylic acid (the active ingredient in aspirin) that comes in a liquid solution or special tape. Solutions *(Compound W, Dr. Scholl's Wart Remover)* may be applied to the warts once a day for months. Special tape *(Mediplast plasters, Duofilm patch, Trans-Ver-Sal)* is cut to fit over the wart and left in place for 24 hours. This is repeated daily. Warts respond to these treatments by getting smaller in size over weeks to months.

If you have a wart, you can see your primary doctor or dermatologist before trying OTC treatments. Office procedures to treat warts usually work faster than OTC treatments do.

DOCTOR'S DIARY

Bob M., 63, plays tennis or works out six days a week. Bob came to my office with an itchy red groin rash and cracking and peeling of the skin between his toes. Bob was shocked when I told him that the groin rash was related to the foot problem. I told him that he had athlete's foot and that the fungus responsible for it was being transmitted to his groin when he was drying himself after showering. I suggested that he dry himself with his towel from head to toe and not go back to other areas of the body and use a fresh towel every day. I prescribed an antifungal cream available over the counter for three weeks. Bob felt much better within a week, and his rash completely cleared within two weeks. I suggested that he use an antifungal powder on his feet after showering to avoid future outbreaks.

KEEPING HEALTHY SKIN

If you have a problem with dry skin or live in a climate that is cold and dry, limit the use of soaps to the body folds (such as your neck, armpits, and groin) while showering and apply a moisturizer, such as Cetaphil or Lubriderm, daily.

Sun exposure causes wrinkles and eventually skin cancer. Avoiding the sun, wearing long-sleeve shirts and broad-brimmed hats, and applying daily an application of sunscreen of SPF 15 or greater to exposed areas (such as your face, neck, forearms, and hands) will help minimize your risk. Avoid tanning products and tanning.

ATHLETE'S FOOT

Description: Athlete's foot *(tinea pedis)* is a fungal infection of the foot. It is characterized by white peeling skin on the sole of the foot and between the toes (see Figures 1-12 and 1-13). It is often itchy and can spread to the groin causing "jock itch." Skin cracking between the toes is dangerous, as it can permit serious bacterial infections to start.

Treatment: Antifungal creams *(Lotrimin or Tinactin twice a day, Lamisil AT once a day)* are available OTC in pharmacies. You should use them for at least three weeks. When applying creams, be sure to cover the sole and sides of your feet, toes, and between the toes. Long-term use of an antifungal powder is then advised to prevent recurrence. If there is no improvement after using the OTC antifungal creams for three to four weeks, see your primary care doctor or dermatologist.

ONYCHOMYCOSIS

Description: *Onychomycosis* is a fungal infection of the toenail that causes a yellow discoloration and thickening of the skin underneath the nail, or a separation of the nail from the underlying skin. Less commonly, the fingernails may be involved, as shown in Figure 1-14.

Treatment: The antifungal creams listed in the above section "Athlete's Foot" can help limit the spread of fungus to other nails, but they will not cure the problem. If you desire to clear the toenail fungus, it is important to make an appointment with a dermatologist. Psoriasis of the nail beds can be indistinguishable from toenail fungus; therefore, a scraping of the nail is required to examine under the microscope. If the test is positive for fungus, three to four months of an oral antifungal medication is the most effective treatment, although many insurers will not reimburse for treating what they consider a cosmetic problem. In addition, some of these treatments may be contraindicated if you have serious medical problems such as liver disease.

DRY SKIN

Description: Resulting from the decreased production of natural oils, *dry skin* (xerosis) becomes red with fine flaking and cracks, as shown in Figures 1-15 and 1-16. The skin feels tight, dry, and itchy. Indoor heat and low humidity combined with hot showers and overuse of soaps result in dryness and cracking of the skin. This occurs most commonly during the winter months.

Treatment: Increasing humidity in your environment, for example, by using a humidifier, is helpful. Limit use of soap only to your neck, armpits, groin, and buttocks, and rinse off quickly. Most importantly, towel dry after bathing or showering, and immediately apply moisturizer *(Cetaphil cream, Amlactin, Aquaphor healing ointment, Lubriderm)* to the skin daily. If you still feel itchy despite use of moisturizers, try hydrocortisone 1% cream applied twice a day.

If the above measures are not effective, see your primary care doctor or dermatologist.

DANDRUFF

Description: *Dandruff (seborrheic dermatitis)* is flaking and itching of the scalp associated with yeast. This produces noticeable fine flakes in the hair, often with redness of the scalp, and itching (see Figure 1-17). This may sometimes involve the eyebrows and center of the face producing an unsightly scaly rash, but dandruff is usually quite responsive to the treatments noted below.

Treatment: Special shampoos *(Head & Shoulders, Selsun Blue, Nizoral 1%)* may be applied to your scalp every day for a week and then decreased to once or twice a week to maintain improvement. Massage lather into your face briefly before rinsing.

If the above shampoos are not effective, see your primary care doctor or dermatologist. Certain prescription shampoos applied twice a week are usually effective.

ADULT ACNE

Description: *Adult acne* (rosacea) is redness, flushing, and pimples on the face of older persons. The pimples and redness involve the nose, cheeks, forehead, and chin (see Figure 1-18). Some people have only flushing or dilated blood vessels.

Treatment: Anything that may increase the skin temperature of the head and neck can trigger redness and flushing. This includes sunlight, hot showers, exercise, alcohol, hot beverages, and spicy foods. Avoid these triggers and apply sunscreen SPF 15 or greater each day.

For pimples, see a dermatologist for prescription creams or antibiotics. Visible blood vessels can be treated with a laser or electrocautery, but such treatment is considered cosmetic.

ALLERGIC CONTACT REACTION

Description: *Allergic contact reaction* (contact dermatitis) is an allergic reaction to a substance that touches the skin and causes an itchy rash. Poison ivy is an example. The initial area of contact may develop water blisters that are extremely itchy (see Figure 1-19).

Treatment: Avoiding the known allergic substance will limit the spread of the rash and allow affected areas to heal over two weeks or so. Hydrocortisone 1% cream may provide some relief from the itching.

If the itch is severe or the rash is spreading, see your primary doctor or dermatologist. Potent steroid creams or steroid pills are often required to get this allergic reaction under control.

DRUG ALLERGY

Description: Drug allergy that involves the skin is a rash that has a sudden onset usually, but not always, during the first two weeks of starting a new medication. The most common medications are antibiotics (AMPICILLIN, AMOXICILLIN, TRIMETHOPRIM–SULFAMETHOXAZOLE), nonsteroidal anti-inflammatory drugs (IBUPROFEN), seizure medication (PHENYTOIN, CARBAMAZEPINE), and high blood pressure pills (CAPTOPRIL, DILTIAZEM).

Red bumps or hives begin on the trunk (see Figure 1-20) and spread to the arms and legs. The rash may be itchy.

Treatment: Sarna lotion or hydrocortisone 1% cream, available OTC, applied two to three times a day may help relieve itching.

If you suspect that the rash is related to a new medication, call your doctor immediately to discuss stopping the medication.

SHINGLES

Description: Shingles *(herpes zoster)* is a skin rash due to reactivation of prior chickenpox infection. (See also Chapter 22.) Water blisters are grouped together on a red base and located on either the right or left side of the body (see Figures 1-21 and 1-22). The rash follows the distribution of a nerve and may occur anywhere from the face to the feet. The blisters are usually preceded by pain on the affected side. Sometimes this can cause diagnostic confusion for a physician, since the pain may mimic that of other conditions, such as a heart attack, gallbladder attack, appendicitis, or even a herniated lumbar disc. The diagnosis becomes obvious once the rash develops. Even after the rash has healed, some patients may experience chronic pain in the same area (postherpetic neuralgia).

Treatment: OTC treatment includes *Domeboro* (salt solution) soaks, which can speed the drying up of the blisters, and application of *Bacitracin* or another antibiotic ointment, which can prevent bacterial superinfection of raw areas.

If you think you have shingles, call your doctor or dermatologist. Prescription oral antiviral medication, if taken within three days of onset of the rash, can reduce acute pain, accelerate healing, prevent scarring, and reduce the risk of developing chronic pain. If taken after three days, it will be less effective.

SCABIES

Description: Scabies is a severely itchy rash caused by a mite that lives on the skin. Close body contact is the most common way of getting it. Itching involves the entire body but is most severe where mites are numerous. These areas also develop bumps and blisters. People with scabies can spread the mite to other persons via close contact.

Treatment: OTC treatment is not available. If you experience itching that keeps you awake at night, see your doctor or dermatologist for evaluation and treatment.

PRESSURE SORE

Description: A pressure sore, also known as a *bedsore* or *pressure ulcer,* is a breakdown of skin that occurs over bony areas (most commonly the lower back, buttocks, heels, knees, and ankles) as a result of constant pressure. Patients that are bedridden, or have spinal cord injuries or diabetes are at higher risk. Initially, there is a redness of the skin that eventually breaks down resulting in loss of the top layer of skin and then an ulcer (as shown in Figure 1–23).

Treatment: If you or a family member is bedridden or otherwise debilitated spending long periods of time in the same position (sitting or lying on your back), it is important to change position every few hours to avoid pressure sores. Soft pads can be placed over bony prominences, and a special air cushion or mattress can help distribute weight evenly. If there is breakdown of the skin, application of an antibiotic ointment *(Bacitracin, Polysporin, Triple Antibiotic)* and covering the area with a nonstick bandage will help to prevent infection.

If you have a pressure sore or high-risk area of persistent redness where there is pressure on the skin, see your primary doctor or other health care professional.

SKIN CANCER

Description: Skin cancer is a result of the cumulative sun-exposure you had since childhood. Although most skin cancers are not life threatening, if left untreated they can locally invade the fat, muscle, and bone. Rarely do they spread to other areas of the body. The exception is melanoma, cancer of the pigment cells, which is fatal unless treated early. Most skin cancers occur on sun-exposed sites (face, neck, scalp, back of the hands) and sometimes the trunk and legs. They may appear as red scaly patches

HOW TO DO A SKIN SELF-EXAM

You can improve your chances of finding skin cancer promptly by performing a simple skin self-exam regularly.

The best time to do this self-exam is after a shower or bath. You should check your skin in a well-lighted room using a full-length mirror and a hand-held mirror. It's best to begin by learning where your birthmarks, moles, and blemishes are and what they usually look like. Check for anything new: a change in the size, texture, or color of a mole or a sore that does not heal.

Check all areas, including the back, the scalp, between the buttocks, and the genital area.

- Look at the front and back of your body in the mirror; then raise your arms and look at the left and right sides.
- Bend your elbows, and look carefully at your palms, forearms (including the undersides), and upper arms.
- Examine the back and front of your legs. Also look between your buttocks and around your genital area.

- Sit and closely examine your feet, including the soles and the spaces between the toes.
- Look at your face, neck, and scalp. You may want to use a comb or a blow dryer to move hair so that you can see better.

By checking your skin regularly, you will become familiar with what is normal. If you find anything unusual, see your doctor right away. Remember, the earlier skin cancer is found, the better the chance for cure.

Source: Courtesy of the National Cancer Institute.

01

or slowgrowing bumps that are painful or tender and have a tendency to break down and bleed. Skin cancers do not heal by themselves. Dark spots that are changing in size, shape, or color may be melanomas. The mnemonic *abcd* characterizes the key features of melanomas: moles that are *asymmetric,* have irregular *borders,* demonstrate *color* change, or measure greater than 6 mm in *diameter.* (See Figure 1-24 for a comparison between a normal mole and a melanoma.)

Treatment: Daily application of sunscreen SPF 15 or greater may help you reduce the risk of skin cancer, even in people with ample past sun exposure.

See your primary doctor or dermatologist if you have a mole that is changing in size, shape, or color or if you have a spot that does not heal, is painful or tender, or breaks down and bleeds. Careful inspection, and a biopsy if necessary, can determine whether this spot is skin cancer or a benign growth. If you have had skin cancer in the past, it is prudent to have a skin examination annually even if you do not detect worrisome spots, because your statistical risk of developing a new skin cancer is substantial.

■

WHAT YOU NEED TO KNOW

▶ Most skin disorders are benign, and the following ones will improve with the suggested OTC treatments:

- Warts
- Athlete's foot
- Dry skin
- Dandruff

▶ Other skin disorders are more serious and can cause pain, itching, discomfort, and suffering:

- Allergic contact reaction
- Drug allergy
- Shingles
- Scabies
- Pressure sore
- Skin cancer

▶ If you think you have one of these conditions, contact your primary physician or dermatologist.

FOR MORE INFORMATION

▶ American Academy of Dermatology
888-462-3376
Web: www.aad.org

▶ National Cancer Institute
800-422-6237
Web: www.nci.nih.gov

▶ National Institute on Aging
800-222-2225
Web: www.nih.gov

PHOTO GALLERY

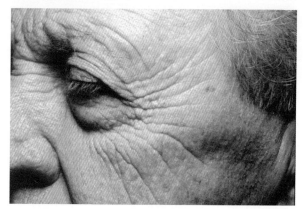

(figure 1-3)
Wrinkles of the face.

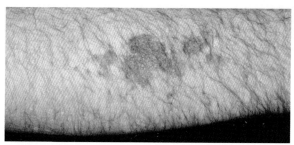

(figure 1-4)
Purpura (bruising) of the back of the forearm.

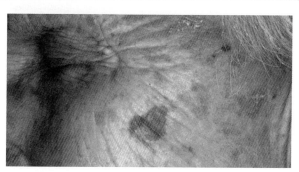

(figure 1-5)
Liver spots (solar lentigos) are brown and flat.

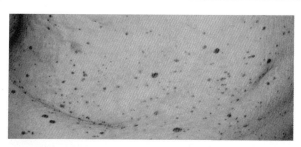

(figure 1-6)
Cherry angiomas are benign red growths.

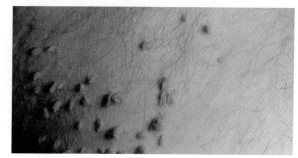

(figure 1-7)
Skin tags.

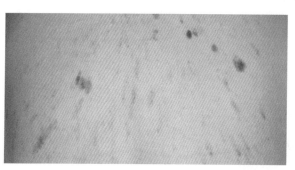

(figure 1-8)
A benign keratosis on the back is brown and raised and may have a warty surface.

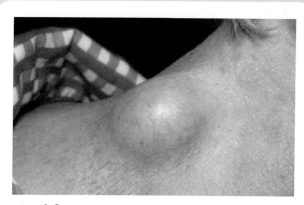

(figure 1-9)
Cyst on the neck appears as a deep lump.

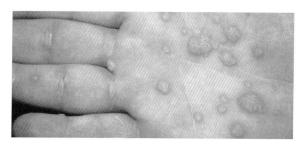

(figure 1-10)
Warts on the palm are bumps with a rough surface.

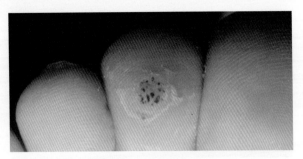

(figure 1-11)
A wart, with characteristic brown dots, on the toe.

(figure 1-15)
Dry skin (xerosis) with early cracking.

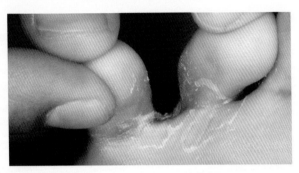

(figure 1-12)
Athlete's foot begins as dry peeling skin between the toes.

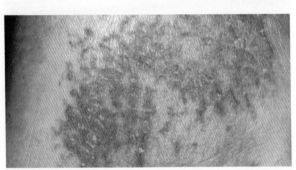

(figure 1-16)
Dry skin on the top of the foot leads to cracks and fissures.

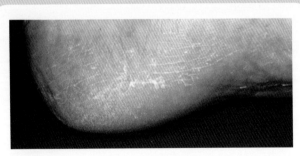

(figure 1-13)
Athlete's foot which has spread to the sole of the foot and heel.

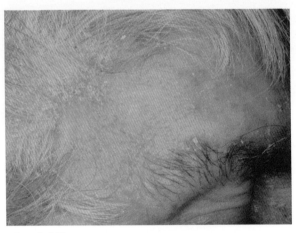

(figure 1-17)
Dandruff is a redness of the scalp with white scales.

(figure 1-14)
Fingernail fungus is yellow with thickening of skin underneath the nail.

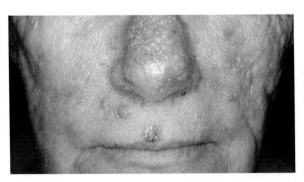

(figure 1-18)
Adult acne with redness and pimples of the central face.

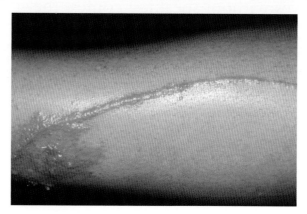

(*figure* 1-19)
Contact dermatitis from poison ivy with linear water blisters at the area of contact with the plant. (Courtesy of Dana Sachs, MD)

(*figure* 1-20)
Drug allergy with red bumps on the trunk usually occurs within 2 weeks of starting a new medication. (Courtesy of Melvin Lu, MD)

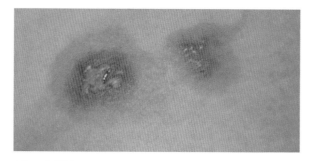

(*figure* 1-21)
Shingles of the right shoulder commonly burns and stings.

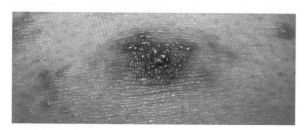

(*figure* 1-22)
Shingles is made up of grouped water blisters on a red base.

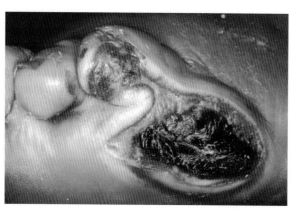

(*figure* 1-23)
Pressure sore (or bedsore): breakdown of the skin due to prolonged pressure.

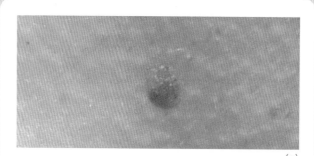

(a)

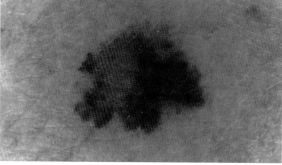

(*figure* 1-24)   (b)
Normal mole versus a melanoma. (a) Note the smooth border and uniform pigment of the benign mole; (b) note the irregular border and variable pigmentation of a melanoma.

The face is the mirror of the mind, and eyes without speaking confess the secrets of the heart.

—*Saint Jerome* (A.D. *374–419*)

THE AUTHORS

02

PETER J. KELLY, MD, graduated from the University of Notre Dame and the Georgetown University School of Medicine. He did his ophthalmology residency at Tufts–New England Medical Center where he is now a clinical instructor of ophthalmology. He is a fellow of the American Academy of Ophthalmology and a member of the American Academy of Cataract and Refractive Surgeons. He practices in Palmer and Ludlow, Massachusetts, and has made frequent trips to Haiti as a medical missionary teaching the eye surgeons there the latest surgical techniques for eye diseases. He is helping to coordinate medical volunteers for a hospital in Haiti.

KEVIN W. O'NEIL, MD, FACP, graduated from Boston College magna cum laude and the Georgetown University School of Medicine. He did his internship at the Washington Hospital Center and his internal medicine residency at the University of Massachusetts Medical Center. He was an assistant professor in the Department of Internal Medicine at the University of Massachusetts Medical Center until moving to Sarasota, Florida, in 1984. He is currently an assistant professor of medicine at the University of South Florida College of Medicine. He is board-certified in internal medicine and holds a Certificate of Added Qualifications in Geriatric Medicine. He is a fellow of the American College of Physicians and a member of the American Geriatrics Society. He practices with the First Physicians Group in Sarasota and is on the staff at Sarasota Memorial Hospital and Doctors Hospital.

02 | THE EYES

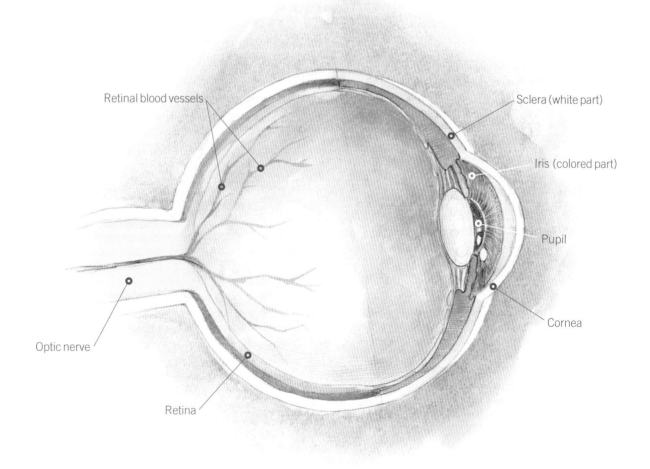

Retinal blood vessels

Sclera (white part)

Iris (colored part)

Pupil

Cornea

Optic nerve

Retina

(figure 2-1)
The anatomy of your eye.

Most of us will retain reasonable visual acuity into our older age. Although we may complain that our arms are not long enough to see the restaurant menu clearly, we compensate with "readers," prescription eyeglasses, or contact lenses. Aging is associated with changes in our vision and in the structure of the eye; however, the incidence of eye disorders increases significantly as we get older. Distinguishing between normal aging and diseases of the eyes and eyelids can be difficult for us. If one eye is functioning normally, we can lose most of the vision in the other eye and not be aware that there is a problem.

Probably the single most important test to evaluate the eyes is a test of visual acuity, or eyesight. Although most of us have an eye doctor, many individuals do not. Some people may not have ready access to an eye doctor, especially if they live in rural environments or if they are homebound due to frailty or reside in a nursing home. Primary care physicians (doctors who specialize in family practice, internal medicine, or geriatrics) may use a Snellen chart or a **Rosenbaum Pocket Vision Screener** to evaluate eyesight in those persons who may not already have an eye doctor (see Figure 2-2). The second most important test is a test for the pressure within the eye to screen for *glaucoma*. Although there are instruments for a primary care doctor to check eye pressure, they are seldom used because of the need to instill eyedrops and sterilize the instrument properly. An eye doctor often uses a device that can easily measure eye pressure painlessly.

An eye doctor may be an **optometrist** or an ophthalmologist. An optometrist can check your eyes for diseases and prescribe eyeglasses. An **ophthalmologist** is a medical doctor who did special training in eye disease and can also perform surgery on the eye such as cataract removal.

THE AGING EYE

The most obvious changes that most of us see in the older person's eyes involve the eyelids and the external parts of the eye. The eyes may look "sunken" in the eye sockets due to shrinkage of fat behind the eye. The

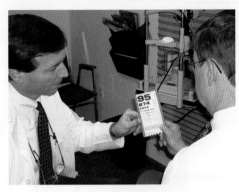

(figure 2-2)

Rosenbaum Pocket Vision Screener.

(figure 2-3)

Baggy eyes are caused by fat from the eye socket dropping into the loose skin around the eye.

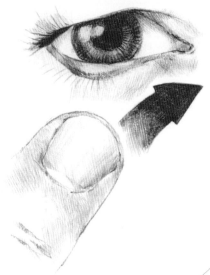

(figure 2-4)

Wipe toward the nose if you experience tearing due to your eyelids turning out.

(figure 2-5)

Eye doctor performing a slit-lamp exam.

fat that is left often slips into the tissue around the eye, which has become less firm due to aging of the skin. This causes the "baggy eyes" (see Figure 2-3), for which many of us would like to see a plastic surgeon. The eyelids may turn out (ectropion) or turn in (entropion). When they turn out, the normal drainage system for the tears is disrupted. This can result in tears spilling down the cheeks. Those who are affected by this will often resort to wiping the tears away with a handkerchief. If they wipe towards the side of the face, this can aggravate the problem since this pulls the drainage system further away. It is best to wipe toward the corner of the eye near the nose, as shown in Figure 2-4. When they turn in, the eyelashes may hit against the eye and cause irritation. Both these conditions may require surgery on the eyelids to correct the problem.

The margins of the eyelids may occasionally become crusted and red, a condition called blepharitis. It may cause itching and a burning sensation. It can sometimes lead to the development of a stye. It is usually a chronic condition and may respond well to gently scrubbing of the eyelids with warm water and application of baby shampoo. If infection is also present, your eye doctor may prescribe an antibiotic ointment.

The eyes may become drier as we get older. This is especially true in postmenopausal women and suggests that estrogen deficiency plays a role in older women. There are two types of tears: a thin film that normally lubricates the eye and the larger "crocodile" tears that occur when we get emotional. With aging, the thin film may be deficient and the eye compensates by forming the crocodile tears. Paradoxically, the eyes become wetter because they are actually drier! Symptoms may include a gritty or burning sensation in the eyes, increased sensitivity to wind, light, or smoke. An eye doctor can diagnose dry eye with a special instrument called a *slit lamp* (see Figure 2-5) or by measuring tear production with filter paper (Schirmer's test). The treatment is the use of artificial tears four times a day. They may need to be used for at least two weeks before improvement is noted. Occasionally they may need to be used every one or two hours when awake, in which case preservative-free tears should be used to avoid irritation from the preservative. When tear supplements do not control the symptoms, your ophthalmologist can insert plugs in your tear duct openings so that your natural tears will be conserved and artificial tears will last longer. More severe symptoms can be associated with Sjögren's syndrome (pronounced Show-gren's), a disease of the body's immune system that can cause dry eyes and dry mouth. Some medications such as diuretics and antihistamines may also cause dry eyes, and you should discuss this with your doctor if you are experiencing these symptoms.

The blue, brown, green, or hazel part of your eye is called the iris. As we age, a whitish ring (arcus senilis) composed of lipid (fat) deposits may form in the clear part of the eye called the cornea. Although this can be considered normal for the older person (see Figure 2-6), it can occasionally be found in younger persons and should prompt an investigation for cholesterol and triglyceride disorders.

The *sclera* is the white part of the eye, but may develop a yellow or gray hue as we get older due to deposition of lipids and pigments. Occasionally an unsightly growth of connective tissue called a pinguecula (pronounced pin-gwek-you-la) can develop adjacent to the iris usually on nasal side of the eye. It has no serious significance and can be left alone. (See Figure 2-7a.) A pterygium (pronounced ter-ij-ee-um), on the other hand, is a triangular patch of tissue that extends over the cornea toward the pupil and may have an adverse impact on vision. (See Figure 2-7b.) Surgery may be required.

The aging lens develops increased density due to a decrease in its water content. This makes the lens less able to change shape to accommodate nearby objects in the field of vision. This accounts for the fact that it is difficult for most of us in midlife and beyond to read print unless we hold it at arm's length or use reading glasses. The term for this is presbyopia, and it tends to become worse as we age.

The gelatinous material that fills the eyeball is called the vitreous humor. As we age this gelatinous material liquifies. The solid pieces of gel float in the liquid and produce "floaters." If the vitreous pulls away from the *retina,* flashing lights may be noticed. It is important that individuals who experience these symptoms see their eye doctor as these symptoms may also occur with the more serious condition of *retinal detachment* (discussed below in the section "Retinal Detachment").

In the remainder of this chapter, we discuss some of the common eye conditions associated with aging.

CATARACT

The best way to describe a cataract is to use the analogy of a camera. The eye has a lens that focuses light onto the retina, just as a camera has a lens that focuses light on the film. A cataract is a clouding of the lens of the

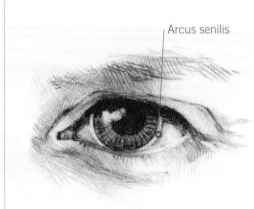

Arcus senilis

(figure 2-6)

Arcus senilis is a white ring that may form around the clear part of your eye (cornea).

(figure 2-7)

(a) A pinguecula and (b) a pterygium.

(a)

(b)

eye (see Figure 2-8). The amount and location of the cloudiness within the lens can vary, and this will determine the severity of the symptoms. You may not be aware that a cataract is present if the cloudiness is not near the center of the lens.

Cataracts affect nearly one out of seven Americans and are the most common cause of visual loss in the elderly. However, it is the most treatable. Symptoms may include blurred vision, frequent change in eyeglass prescriptions, glare or sensitivity to light, difficulty with night vision, double vision in one eye, requiring more light to read, or yellowing of colors. Cataracts do not cause pain or irritation. They do not cause a "film" over the eye. Overusing the eyes does not cause cataracts, and cataracts do not cause permanent damage to the eyes.

Recent studies have shown an association between cataracts and exposure to sunlight (mainly blue light), smoking, and poor nutrition. However, many people develop cataracts but have none of these risk factors. Although exposure to ultraviolet (UV) light does not explain cataracts in many persons, it seems reasonable to use a hat with a brim and sunglasses to reduce exposure to UV light. Persons with diabetes are more likely to develop cataracts. Although some medications such as steroids can cause or accelerate cataract formation, they usually need to be used for several years. Direct injuries to the eye and other eye surgery can sometimes cause the development of cataracts.

Diagnosis of a cataract requires a thorough examination by an eye doctor since other conditions that affect the retina or optic nerve (the nerve that sends signals to the brain so that images on the retina can be interpreted properly) may cause visual loss. In addition, some individuals may have these other conditions as well as the cataracts. If these other conditions are severe, removing the cataract may not improve the vision. Cataracts associated with aging usually progress slowly over a period of years. Cataracts may occur in young people and are often associated with eye trauma, steroid use, or diabetes. These cataracts may progress rapidly over a few months. It is not possible to predict how quickly cataracts will develop in any given person.

Cataracts can only be treated by surgical removal. There is no such thing as a "ripe" cataract. There are two criteria for cataract surgery. The first and most important is that the cataract is interfering with your daily activities, such as reading, driving, cooking, watching television, or sewing. The second is that your vision has decreased to 20/50 or worse. (This fraction is a method of measuring your visual acuity. The first number is the distance in feet at which the test is conducted. The second number is the distance at which a normal eye should be able to read the letters. Thus, if at 20 feet from the Snellen wall chart, you can only read the numbers at which a normal eye could read from 50 feet, your acuity would be 20/50. Normal acuity is 20/20.)

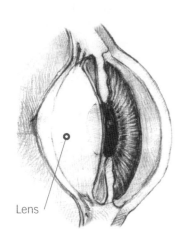

(figure 2-8)

Cataracts form on the lens.

Lens

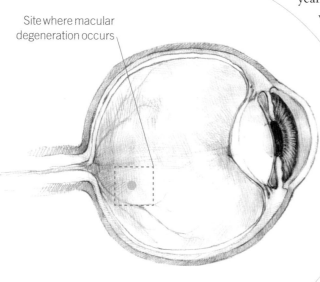

Site where macular degeneration occurs

(figure 2-9)

The macula is the site in the retina where your central vision is located.

WHAT'S NEW?

The Age-Related Eye Diseases Study (AREDS), sponsored by the National Eye Institute, has shown that vitamin supplements slow down the progression of certain types of dry macular degeneration. The vitamins used in this study were vitamin E, vitamin C, beta-carotene, and the minerals zinc and copper. Your ophthalmologist will be able to determine if you would benefit from these supplements. He or she may wish to confer with your primary care physician since some supplements can cause problems. For example, vitamin E must be used cautiously for patients on warfarin (Coumadin). Beta-carotene in high doses may actually increase the risk of lung cancer in cigarette smokers.

Cataract surgery is considered the most successful surgery performed. Over 1.4 million people have cataract surgery each year in the United States, over 95% without complications. The operation is an outpatient procedure usually performed under local anesthesia at an outpatient surgical center. The surgeon removes the cataract with ultrasound *(phacoemulsification)* using a microscope and microsurgical instruments. Lasers are not used to remove cataracts. The lens that is removed is replaced with an **intraocular lens** (an artificial lens).

In about 20% of persons having cataract surgery, the capsule that supports the new lens becomes cloudy and requires laser surgery to open it and restore clear vision. The postoperative recovery period is about two weeks, during which time eyedrops are used. Most individuals can return to all but the most strenuous activities.

MACULAR DEGENERATION

Our analogy of a camera is also useful in explaining **macular degeneration**. Remember that the retina is like the film of a camera (see Figure 2-9). The **macula** is the central part of the retina. If your camera film is damaged, your pictures will be distorted or blank. Similarly, since macular degeneration affects the central part of the retina, only the center of your vision is dark or blurred. Peripheral vision is not affected, so it is important to remember that macular degeneration does not result in total blindness. You will continue to have useful vision and be able to take care of yourself. If you are registered as legally blind, it means your corrected vision has decreased to 20/200 or worse in your better eye. It does not mean you are totally blind.

Macular degeneration is often classified as "dry" and "wet." The dry type affects 90% and is related to degeneration of cells in the macula. Leaking blood vessels are responsible for the wet type.

If you have or are developing macular degeneration, you will experience decreased vision for both near and far objects. Straight lines or surfaces may appear curved or crooked. You may have blank areas in your central vision that cause difficulty with reading or sewing.

Macular degeneration is definitely age-related since it is the most common cause of legal blindness in people over the age of 50. Recent studies have suggested that certain nutritional deficiencies and exposure to blue light may play a role. The disease is more common in women, smokers, and those who have relatives with the disorder.

An eye doctor can often diagnose the condition before symptoms appear by examining the retina after dilating the eye with drops. The dry type is characterized by thinning of the retina and the wet type by growth of abnormal blood vessels, which leak fluid and bleed into the retina. Visual loss occurs more rapidly with the wet type. An *Amsler grid* may be used for diagnosis and monitoring of your disease.

Laser treatment has shown to be useful in certain forms of wet macular degeneration, especially in conjunction with an injected dye called Visudyne. Your doctor can determine if you are a candidate after performing a fluorescein angiogram, a test where special pictures are taken after the injection of a dye in order to determine the location of abnormal blood vessels.

Low-vision aids, such as special lenses or large-print books, help you compensate for macular degeneration. More expensive electronic devices are also available that magnify print and pictures. It is important to know that using your eyes will not hurt them further.

GLAUCOMA

Glaucoma is caused by elevated pressure within the eye that damages the optic nerve. The pressure in your eye is not the same as your blood pressure. The intraocular pressure is created by the balance between the production and drainage of a fluid called aqueous humor. This fluid, which is different from tears, circulates inside the front portion of the eye. A small amount is produced constantly, and an equal amount flows out through a microscopic drainage system called the trabecular meshwork (see Figure 2-10). If the drainage system does not function properly, the fluid pressure in the eye increases, and this pressure in turn causes compression and damage to the optic nerve. Since the optic nerve carries the images we see to the brain, damage to the optic nerve creates blind spots in peripheral vision and usually goes undetected until significant injury to the nerve has occurred.

Open angle glaucoma is the most common type of glaucoma and does not produce any symptoms or warning signs in the early stages. Peripheral vision becomes more restricted and eventually "tunnel" vision develops. If you would like to understand what it is like to have advanced glaucoma, make a fist and look through the center of your fist. Ultimately, if you were not treated, you would go totally blind.

Angle closure glaucoma (sometimes called *narrow angle glaucoma*) produces symptoms that most people associate with

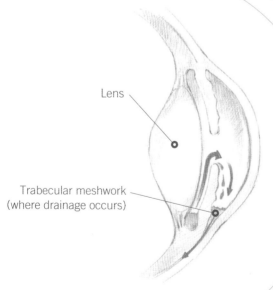

Lens

Trabecular meshwork
(where drainage occurs)

(figure 2-10)

The trabecular meshwork is the site of problems in persons with open angle glaucoma.

glaucoma. These symptoms include blurred vision, nausea and vomiting, severe eye pain and redness, headaches, and rainbow-colored halos around lights. This type of glaucoma is an emergency. Failure to treat this aggressively can result in blindness within a matter of one or two days. Angle closure glaucoma is caused when the iris (the colored portion of your eye) completely blocks the drainage area causing the intraocular pressure to rise very rapidly.

Risk factors for glaucoma include age, African-American ancestry, relatives with glaucoma, and previous eye injuries. Since most of us will have no symptoms with the early stages of glaucoma, it is important to have regular eye examinations with an eye doctor. This will involve not only a check for the intraocular pressure, but an examination of the drainage area of your eye and the optic nerve.

Open angle glaucoma is initially treated with eyedrops. If they do not effectively control the pressure, then laser surgery and possibly even surgery in the operating room may be required. Angle closure glaucoma, the less common form, is first treated with laser to relieve the blockage and then eyedrops may be added to control the pressure.

RETINAL DETACHMENT

The *retina* is the innermost lining of the eye and extends from the back of your eye to the iris. A hole or tear can develop in the retina for a variety of reasons. If untreated, fluid can leak into the hole or tear and cause the retina to detach from its underlying support. As the retina detaches, you can lose your peripheral vision and ultimately your central vision. Retinal detachments affect 1 out of 10,000 people in the United States each year. They may occur at any age, but more often occur in middle-aged and older people. Rarely, the condition may be hereditary, and occasionally may be associated with tumors of the eye, severe inflammation, or diabetes. Some people may be at greater risk: nearsighted persons, those with a history of previous eye trauma, people who have other diseases of the retina, and those who have had other eye surgery especially cataract surgery.

The first symptoms of retinal detachment are "floaters" and "flashes." Floaters look like moving specks or spots in the field of vision. You may see a shower of black spots with lightning like flashes in the periphery of your vision. If untreated, you may develop a black curtainlike obstruction of your peripheral vision above, below, or from the sides. If it progresses further, you will lose your central vision.

Diagnosis requires that an ophthalmologist dilate your eyes with drops and examine the retina. This may require that you be placed in a *supine* (lying down) position with the eye doctor pressing on the eye to see the entire retina. If there is excessive bleeding that obscures the eye doctor's view, a retinal detachment can also be detected by ultrasound.

A retinal hole or tear can be treated in the office with laser therapy or *cryotherapy* (freezing). This can be done with eyedrops for anesthesia and is usually very successful. Progression to a retinal detachment requires more extensive treatment in the operating room.

MY STORY: FRANK B., 80

I was reading the morning newspaper and suddenly noticed sparks of light out of the corner of my eye. I also noticed some black spots. I felt panic and contacted my eye doctor who suggested I come to the office immediately. The examination confirmed a retinal tear, and my doctor successfully treated me with laser surgery in the office. He emphasized the importance of early diagnosis and treatment.

RELATED DISEASES

DIABETES

Diabetes can cause damage to the blood vessels in the retina, which, as you recall from our earlier discussion, is like the film of a camera. The damaged blood vessels can leak fluid and blood. If this affects the central part of the retina (macula), your vision will become blurred and diminished. This is called "background" diabetic retinopathy. As these blood vessels become more damaged, they close off and lead to the growth of new fragile blood vessels. These fragile vessels may result in significant bleeding which can cause severe and sudden loss of vision. This is called "proliferative" diabetic retinopathy. You may need to avoid aspirin and other blood thinners and limit your physical activity. The blood is reabsorbed within three to six months. If the blood does not reabsorb adequately, the doctor will suggest that you undergo a surgical procedure.

All diabetics should have regular eye examinations by an ophthalmologist. You can discuss the frequency of these visits with the doctor, but most likely they will be more frequent if retinopathy is already present. It may be necessary to have a fluorescin angiogram to determine the extent of the retinopathy and whether it needs treatment.

Clinical studies have suggested that the better you control your blood sugar, the longer it will take for diabetic retinopathy to develop. Coexisting conditions, such as *hypertension*, can increase the speed with which diabetic retinopathy develops and may worsen its severity. A class of medications called angiotensin-converting enzyme (ACE) inhibitors has been shown to be especially useful for diabetics with high blood pressure. Recent research also suggests that these medications may protect against retinopathy, as well as kidney damage, in diabetics even if they do not have high blood pressure. A small percentage of patients may experience a cough or other side effects with ACE inhibitors, in which case a newer class of drugs called angiotensin receptor blockers (ARBs) can be tried. Ask your primary care doctor if one of these medications is appropriate for you if you are not already on one.

The mainstay of treatment for established retinopathy is laser photocoagulation. This closes off the leaking blood vessels in order to preserve or improve vision. The part of the retina that is stimulating the growth of the new blood vessels is destroyed. Although most people are anxious about laser treatment, you can be reassured that it is not painful. It does not require any special preoperative testing or postoperative restrictions. It is done in the ophthalmologist's office, with usually only eyedrops being required for anesthesia.

OTHER DISEASES

Since the eye requires the coordination of the brain and nervous system as well as the circulatory system, disorders that involve these systems may cause problems with the eye. For example, infectious endocarditis is a disorder of the heart valves that causes bacteria to "seed" the bloodstream (see Chapter 22). Blindness can result if the eye is involved. Similarly, *atherosclerosis* may cause *plaque* in the carotid arteries that can lead to small clots traveling to the eye and causing transient or permanent blindness. Temporal arteritis is an inflammatory disease of the blood vessels that may involve the retinal circulation and cause blindness. It is discussed in Chapter 16, since it may be associated with polymyalgia rheumatica, which causes stiffness and aching of muscles predominantly of the shoulders and hips.

■

WHAT YOU NEED TO KNOW

▥ There are many changes that occur in our eyes as we get older. Many of these are normal, but sometimes these changes can be difficult to distinguish from serious diseases. Regular examinations by an eye doctor can help identify diseases early so that treatment can be started to avoid vision loss.

▥ Cataracts affect nearly one out of seven Americans and are the most common cause of visual loss in the elderly. However, cataracts are the most treatable cause of visual loss.

▥ Macular degeneration is definitely age-related, since it is the most common cause of legal blindness in people over the age of 50. Although it is not curable, there are measures that can be taken to compensate for the visual loss. Vitamins may play some role in slowing the progression of some forms of macular degeneration.

▥ Glaucoma is diagnosed by measurement of eye pressure and by examination of the eye. There may not be any early symptoms, but early detection and treatment can help prevent vision loss.

▥ Diabetes may cause significant eye problems. All diabetics should have regular examinations with their ophthalmologist.

FOR MORE INFORMATION

▥ National Eye Institute
2020 Vision Place
Bethesda, MD 20892
301-496-5248
Web: www.nei.nih.gov
The National Eye Institute provides an extensive list of eye organizations.

The reason we have two ears and only one mouth, is that we may hear more and speak less.

—*Zeno (335–264 B.C.)*

THE AUTHORS

03   *Michelle Marcincuk, MD*

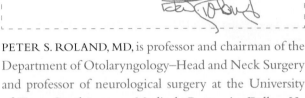

MICHELLE CARUSO MARCINCUK, MD, is originally from Long Island, New York. She attended college in Boston at the Massachusetts Institute of Technology (MIT) and graduated from medical school at Columbia University. She completed a residency in Otolaryngology–Head and Neck Surgery at the University of Texas–Southwestern Medical Center in Dallas. Currently, she is in private practice in Fort Worth, Texas, where she practices all aspects of otolaryngology and serves as a clincal assistant professor for the University of Texas–Southwestern Otolaryngology Department. She has published several articles in medical journals and an online serial textbook on topics within the field of general otolaryngology.

PETER S. ROLAND, MD, is professor and chairman of the Department of Otolaryngology–Head and Neck Surgery and professor of neurological surgery at the University of Texas–Southwestern Medical Center in Dallas. He is chief of pediatric otology at the Children's Medical Center. Dr. Roland received his medical degree from the University of Texas Medical Branch at Galveston and did his otolaryngology (ear, nose, and throat) residency training at Penn State University. Dr. Roland spent 4 years in the U.S. Navy stationed at Bethesda Naval Hospital in Bethesda, Maryland. During his tour in the Navy, he was on the faculty of the Uniform Services, the University of Health Sciences and served as a consultant to the National Institutes of Health. Following his tour in the Navy, Dr. Roland spent a year in fellowship training at the E.A.R. Institute in Nashville, Tennessee, specializing in otology, neurotology, and skull base surgery. The author of over 90 scientific articles on ear surgery, hearing loss, balance disturbance, facial nerve injury, acoustic neuroma, and tumors of the skull base, he has a special interest and extensive experience in the area of cochlear implantation.

03 | HEARING

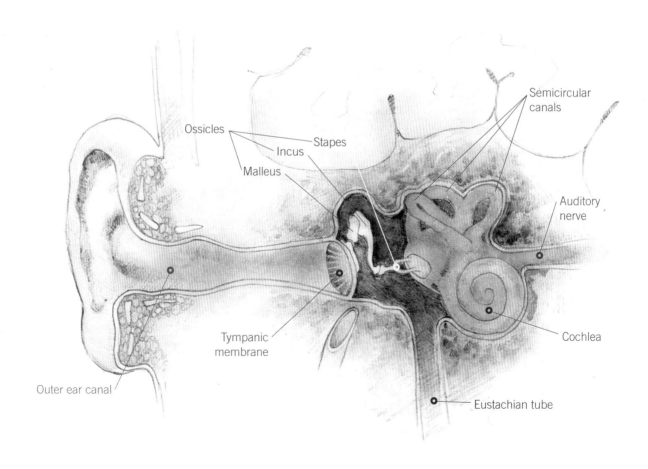

(figure 3-1)
Anatomy of the ear.

Normal hearing requires the funneling of sound vibrations from the environment through your external ear canal (outer ear) to the tympanic membrane (eardrum). (See Figures 3-1 and 3-2.) The vibrations are transmitted from the eardrum to the small bones of the middle ear (ossicles). There are three middle ear bones (the malleus, incus, and stapes) and the transmission of sound through this "chain" of bones provides a small amount of amplification. The third bone, the stapes, then produces a pistonlike movement in the fluids of the cochlea, a snail-shaped organ in the middle ear. The fluid wave produced by the movement of the stapes passes along the cochlear duct and bends the small hairs of the cells lining the duct (hair cells). When these hairs are bent, they trigger the nerve to send an electrical impulse to your brain along the auditory nerve (hearing), which goes from the inner ear to the brain. The nerve impulses are then carried to the conscious area of the brain where they are interpreted as the sounds you hear (e.g., a person's voice, music, or a telephone ring). Note that hearing loss can be caused by a problem in any part of the ear.

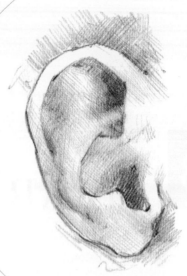

(*figure* 3-2)

The structure of the outer ear is ideally suited to funnel sound vibrations into the inner ear.

HEARING LOSS

Hearing loss is the most common medical problem in people over 65 years of age. It is a common subject for jokes about the elderly, but for those affected, it is no laughing matter. It can have profound effects on one's daily living and may be dangerous. The manifestations of hearing loss are variable. While some people with hearing loss will not be able to hear conversations, others will hear a conversation but not be able to understand the words being spoken. Hearing loss can interfere with the ability to use the telephone, present safety issues for those unable to hear alarms or oncoming traffic, affect a person's ability to participate in social activities, and lead to a sense of isolation.

Hearing loss has many causes. Some causes are treatable and even preventable, while others are not. Certain types of hearing loss are more common in older people than in the younger population. This chapter covers the diagnosis, causes, treatment, and prevention of hearing loss.

DIAGNOSING HEARING LOSS

The accurate diagnosis of hearing loss is very important. This diagnosis involves not only recognizing that a hearing loss is present but also measuring the severity and particular type of hearing loss. These distinctions are important because they affect the treatment options available.

Hearing loss may first be recognized by the person affected (see Figure 3-3). However, often it is an individual's family and friends who first notice that a hearing problem is present. In either case, once a hearing

DOCTOR'S DIARY

Mary Q., 67, is confronted by her three daughters, all of whom tell her that she is difficult to communicate with and that they have become increasingly frustrated trying to talk to her. Mary does not feel that her hearing is impaired, but agrees to a hearing test. The hearing test shows a high frequency hearing loss. She is quite resistant to hearing aids because she regards them as a sign of infirmity. I explain to her that indeed she will not like the hearing aids, but that she will be able to hear more and that it will be easier to communicate with her. At the end of a 30-day trial period, she agrees that several things are now easier for her to do wearing the hearing aids. She tells me that her family is pleased, and she has found that it is easier to communicate with them. She still does not like them but does feel that the benefit is worth the inconvenience.

03

(figure 3-3)

Ask yourself the following questions. If you answer yes to three or more of these questions, you could have a hearing problem and may need to have your hearing checked by a doctor.

YES	NO	
		Do I have a problem hearing on the telephone?
		Do I have trouble hearing when there is noise in the background?
		Is it hard for me to follow a conversation when two or more people talk at once?
		Do I have to strain to understand a conversation?
		Do many people I talk to seem to mumble or not speak clearly?
		Do I misunderstand what others are saying and respond inappropriately?
		Do I often ask people to repeat themselves?
		Do I have trouble understanding the speech of women and children?
		Do people complain that I turn the TV volume up too high?

loss is first recognized, it is important to bring this to the attention of a hearing professional, such as an otolaryngologist (a physician specializing in disorders of the ears, nose, and throat) or audiologist (a practitioner who specializes in the evaluation of hearing and balance disorders). There are several steps involved in the evaluation of hearing loss.

HISTORY

One of the most important tools in understanding a person's hearing loss is to understand the history of the problem. The time course of the hearing loss is very important; specifically, did the loss appear suddenly, or has it worsened slowly over time? One may be asked about other symptoms that can be associated with the hearing loss, such as ringing in the ears or the presence of dizziness or a spinning sensation. A family history of hearing loss is important, as is a thorough medical history of the individual with the hearing loss. Sometimes hearing loss is present in only one ear, although often times it affects both ears. A history of trauma to the head or ears, a history of ear surgery in the past, and a history of prior ear disease are all important clues in diagnosis. Finally, it is very helpful when seeking the advice of a doctor to have a list of current and recent medications on hand, as hearing loss can sometimes be related to medication use. These historical factors are very important clues in helping identify the cause of the underlying hearing loss. The cause of the hearing loss, in turn, ultimately determines the best method of treatment.

PHYSICAL EXAM

A thorough exam of the head and neck, including the ears, nose, mouth, and throat, will be performed. The ears are examined with an otoscope (shown in Figure 3-4), a tool used to look at the outer ear canal and the eardrum. The physical exam also includes an evaluation of eye movement, facial muscle movement, and some simple balance tests.

Tuning forks: Tuning forks are two-pronged instruments that produce a musical note when struck. They are commonly used to help identify the particular type of hearing loss that is present. The tuning forks are placed in various positions on the head, and the individual is asked questions about the sounds that are heard. The tests are quick and painless.

Hearing test: An audiogram is a hearing test that measures the type and severity of hearing loss. It measures how loud a tone of a specific pitch must be for an individual to hear it. These measurements are made in each ear individually for a variety of different pitches. High tones, low tones, and the tones in between are assessed.

A normal audiogram is illustrated in Figure 3-5a. Audiograms are plotted on a graph. The horizontal line, or x axis, on the top of the graph represents frequency, or pitch, measured in hertz (Hz). The frequencies are listed from left to right in sequentially ascending pitches. The lowest frequency on this graph is 250 Hz. This is a very low pitch that would, for example, correspond to the low hum of a truck engine. The highest frequency on this graph is 4000 Hz. The high-pitched ring of a telephone would be an example of a noise corresponding to this frequency.

The vertical, or y axis of the graph represents amplitude, or loudness, of sound measured in decibels (dB). The amplitude progresses from very soft sounds at the top of the graph to sequentially louder levels of sound at the bottom of the graph. For reference, normal conversational speech occurs between 40 and 60 dB. Soft noises, such as the sound of a light wind rustling through the leaves of a tree, would create sounds between 0 and 10 dB. Airplane engines roar at amplitudes of about 100 to 110 dB.

Two lines are plotted on the graph, one for each ear. The lines represent the softest sound each individual ear can hear at each individual pitch. The amplitude of these sounds is called a threshold. The normal range of tone thresholds in adults is from 0 to 25 dB. This is illustrated by the lines in Figure 3-5a, which remain between 0 and 25 dB for each frequency. As hearing loss increases, the threshold at which sounds are first heard also increases—in other words, sounds must be louder to be perceived by the ear.

It is important to understand that thresholds may be very different from one frequency to another. Thus, it is possible to have hearing loss for only certain frequencies but not for others. Some patterns of hearing loss are associated with certain diseases or causes of hearing loss. For example, when a factory worker is exposed to years of loud noise on the job, he or she may develop "high-frequency" hearing loss over time. In this situation, low-frequency hearing may be relatively normal.

(*figure* 3-4)

An otoscope is the instrument used to examine the ear canal and eardrum.

(figure 3-5)

Audiograms showing (A) normal hearing, (B) mild hearing loss in both ears, and (C) severe hearing loss in the right ear.

(A) An illustration of a normal audiogram. The right ear is represented by a line connecting thresholds marked by "**R**". The left ear is represented by a line connecting thresholds marked by "**L**". Notice that the thresholds for every frequency are within 25dB.

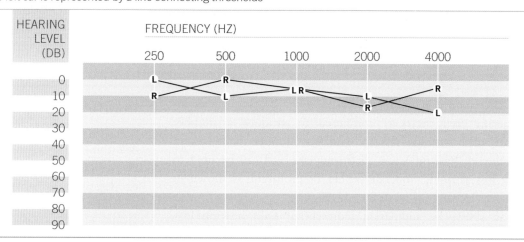

(B) An illustration of an audiogram showing mild hearing loss in both ears. The right ear is represented by a line connecting thresholds marked by "**R**". The left ear is represented by a line connecting thresholds marked by "**L**". Notice that the thresholds for every frequency are between 26 and 40dB.

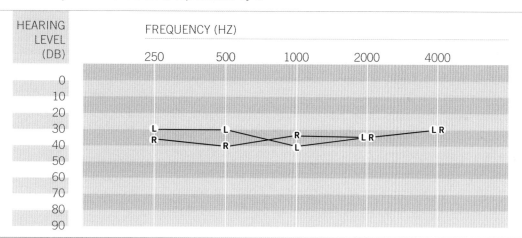

(C) An illustration of an audiogram showing severe hearing loss in the right ear. The right ear is represented by a line connecting thresholds marked by "**R**". The left ear is represented by a line connecting thresholds marked by "**L**". Notice that the thresholds for the right ear are between 71 and 90dB while the thresholds for the left ear are normal.

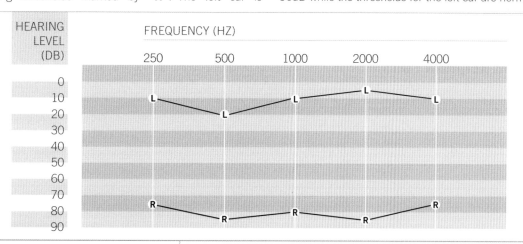

(table 3-1)

CLASSIFICATION OF HEARING LOSS ACCORDING TO PURE TONE AVERAGES.

CLASSIFICATION	PURE TONE AVERAGE (IN DB)
Normal hearing	0–25
Mild loss	26–40
Moderate loss	41–55
Moderately severe loss	56–70
Severe loss	71–90
Profound loss	Greater than 90

Once an audiogram is plotted, an average of the hearing thresholds at several specific frequencies is computed to produce a number called the **pure tone average (PTA)**. This is a number that gives an overall estimation of hearing across all frequencies, and can be used to grade hearing loss as mild, moderate, severe, or profound, as shown in Table 3-1.

Figure 3-5b shows an audiogram representing mild hearing loss, whereas Figure 3-5c shows severe hearing loss. Notice on Figure 3-5c the hearing loss is only in one ear.

It is important to remember that the PTA is only an average, and that some frequencies will be heard at a lower threshold and some at a higher threshold than the PTA. It is also important to realize that the hearing loss measured in decibels does not correlate with a percentage of hearing loss. For example, an individual with a PTA of 20 dB has not lost 20% of his or her hearing. In fact, this individual has what is considered normal hearing and has not lost any functional hearing.

Some primary care physicians may use screening audiograms to determine which individuals should be referred for more thorough testing. Other physicians may make referrals based on history and physical exam alone. Once the determination is made to seek a referral, an individual may be sent to an otolaryngologist or an audiologist. Otolaryngologists and audiologists work closely together in the evaluation, diagnosis, and treatment of hearing loss. Complete **audiometry** includes the testing of hearing thresholds, as described above, and the measurement of one's ability to understand spoken words and the mobility of the eardrum. Word understanding is measured separately because some people with hearing loss can hear sounds quite well but are unable to clearly understand the individual words being spoken.

CAUSES OF HEARING LOSS

There are two basic types of hearing loss that can occur. **Conductive hearing loss** is caused by a blockage of sound transmission as the sound vibrations move from the ear canal, through the eardrum, and finally through the ossicles (or hearing bones) located in the middle ear (see Figure 3-6). These structures are responsible for physically moving sound vibrations to the inner ear. When blockages occur, sounds cannot reach the sensing organ of the inner ear, called the cochlea. **Sensorineural hearing**

TINNITUS: IS THERE HELP?

Tinnitus is the name given to noises heard in the ear when there is no obvious external cause. The sound may be described as a ringing, buzzing, roaring, hissing, or a variety of other noises. Although most of us have experienced these symptoms transiently at one time or another, as many as 10 million Americans experience them continuously. Often it can very difficult to overcome, and in many cases no cure can be found. Some people resort to using masking noises such as background music or listening to the sounds of falling rain or breaking waves on an audiotape or CD. However, it is important to have a medical evaluation to look for possible causes of tinnitus such as ear wax, hearing loss, infections, and certain drugs including aspirin, caffeine, and alcohol.

Less commonly, tinnitus can have a more serious cause including strokes, brain tumors, and aneurysms. Other symptoms such as headaches, pulsating in the ears, unsteadiness, or nausea and vomiting are commonly associated with more serious sources. A doctor can determine if tests such as CT or MRI scans are warranted. The American Tinnitus Association has very helpful information on their website listed in the For More Information section at the end of this chapter.

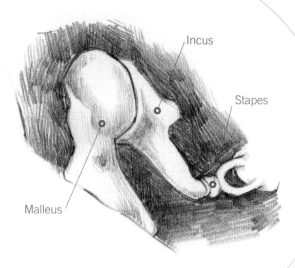

(figure 3-6)

The bones of the middle ear are named after their appearance. Malleus, the largest of these bones, means "hammer" although it looks more like a club; incus, the middle bone, means "anvil"; and stapes, the smallest, means "stirrup."

loss, on the other hand, is due to an abnormality of the cochlea or the auditory nerve, two neural components of the inner ear which sense the sounds brought to the inner ear by the conductive apparatus, change the vibrations of sound into electrical signals, and bring these electrical signals to the brain via nerve fibers. These two types of hearing loss can occur in isolation, or they may occur together, resulting in a mixed hearing loss.

CONDUCTIVE HEARING LOSS

Several problems can lead to conductive hearing loss.

Cerumen impaction: Cerumen, commonly referred to as earwax, is a frequent cause of hearing loss in older adults. When cerumen accumulates in the ear canal, it can cause a blockade to the transmission of sound into the middle and inner ear. Although cerumen builds up over time, the onset of hearing loss from a cerumen impaction may be sudden. This is because even when earwax blocks 90% of the ear canal, hearing may be normal. Once the blockage reaches 95%, however, significant hearing loss may occur. A change from a 90% to a 95% occlusion of the ear canal can occur suddenly and simply be due to a shift in the position of the earwax (as can occur with manipulation by a cotton-tipped applicator, hearing aid insertion, or finger) or by exposure of the cerumen to water (which can cause the cerumen to hydrate and expand like a sponge).

This problem is more common in older people due to the physiologic changes that occur in ears as we age. For example, the glands in the ear canal that produce cerumen undergo age-related changes, which lead to a decrease in the production of the watery component of earwax. Overall, this leads to harder, drier cerumen that is not easily expelled from the ear canal by natural mechanisms. In addition, men tend to have more prominent hairs in the outer ear canal. With age, these hairs become longer, thicker, and coarser, causing them to trap the dry cerumen in the ear canal more easily.

Exostoses and osteomas: Exostoses and osteomas are benign bony growths of the external ear canal. They can lead to hearing loss due to the blockage of sound transmission to the middle and inner ear. In addition, they can trap cerumen, skin cells, and debris in the deeper portions of the ear canal, which can also act as a blockade to sound waves, and can act as a target for chronic infection. Exostoses occur after the ear canal has been repeatedly exposed to cold air or water. They usually occur in both ears simultaneously and generally are found in multiples rather than as a single growth. Osteomas, on the other hand, are benign, noncancerous bony tumors of the ear canal that usually occur in isolation and in only one ear. Treatment, involving surgical removal, is recommended only when the growths cause symptomatic blockage of the ear canal, leading to significant conductive hearing loss, retention of debris, or chronic infection. Surgical removal is generally successful, and recurrence is uncommon.

03

Tympanic membrane perforation: A *tympanic membrane perforation* is a hole in the eardrum (see Figure 3-7). Such holes can be caused by middle ear infections, sudden extreme changes in air pressure (such as experienced during scuba diving), or by trauma to the head or ear canal. Perforations can lead to hearing loss in two ways. First, a perforation may cause the eardrum to be ineffective in moving sound from the ear canal to the hearing bones in the middle ear. This causes sound energy to be lost in transmission, which in turn causes a hearing loss. Second, certain types of perforations are at risk for developing cholesteatoma (a cystlike accumulation of squamous, or skin, cells in the middle ear behind the ear drum). Cholesteatomas can lead to hearing loss by their tendency to enlarge and erode bone or simply by filling up the air space in the middle ear, surrounding the hearing bones, and acting like a mechanical blockade to sound transmission.

Surgical repair of a perforation is indicated when it causes a significant conductive hearing loss, produces chronic ear drainage or infection, or presents a risk for the development of cholesteatoma. As long as an individual is in good general health, advanced age is not a contraindication for surgical repair of tympanic membrane perforations.

Middle ear effusions: Middle ear effusion refers to the development of persistent fluid in the middle ear, behind the eardrum. Older adults may develop middle ear effusions due to poor functioning of the eustachian tube. The eustachian tube is a tube that connects the middle ear and the back of the throat. It opens and closes during swallowing in order to normalize the air pressure in the middle ear. When the eustachian tube does not open properly, air is not able to enter the middle ear and fluid develops instead (see Figure 3-8). This fluid accumulates in the middle ear because it has no way to drain if the eustachian tube is not functioning. When the eustachian tube does not close properly, secretions from the back of the nose and throat can reflux up the tube into the middle ear, leading to inflammation and effusion. Middle ear fluid can lead to significant conductive hearing losses at all pitches.

Treatment of middle ear fluid may involve curing the underlying condition, such as allergies, which can contribute to the abnormal functioning of the eustachian tube. If such medical therapies are unsuccessful, tiny tubes may be placed through the eardrum to allow ventilation and drainage of the air space in the middle ear. Finally, some persistent fluid collections, which do not resolve with medical treatment, warrant an evaluation to discover the cause of the eustachian tube dysfunction. This workup may include endoscopy (using a small fiberoptic camera to visualize the back of the nose and throat) and special radiologic imaging.

(figure 3-7)

Tympanic membrane (the eardrum).

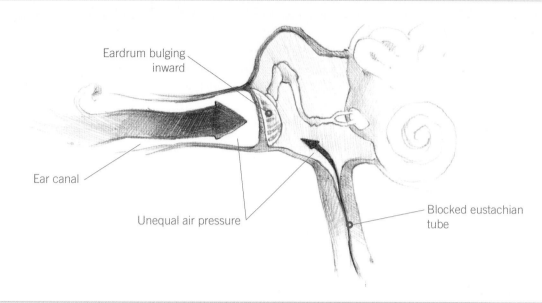

(figure 3-8)
If the eustachian tube becomes blocked, pressure builds up in the middle ear and can produce an earache. You may have had this problem when you had a cold.

Eardrum bulging inward

Ear canal

Unequal air pressure

Blocked eustachian tube

SENSORINEURAL HEARING LOSS

Sensorineural hearing loss can occur suddenly, over the course of minutes to hours or may be slowly progressive over months to years. The time course of hearing loss is often a clue as to the cause of the hearing loss. In addition, certain patterns of hearing loss on audiograms correlate with different causes of hearing loss. The following section describes the most common causes of both sudden and progressive sensorineural hearing loss.

SUDDEN SENSORINEURAL HEARING LOSS

Viral cochleitis: Viral cochleitis refers to a viral infection of the cochlea, the neural sense organ in the inner ear in which mechanical sound from the outer and middle ear is transmitted into an electrical sound stimulus brought to the brain by the hearing nerve. This is the most common reason for a sudden sensorineural hearing loss. The viruses that cause these types of infections are the same viruses that lead to upper respiratory tract infections. In fact, about half the individuals who develop this type of hearing loss have a concurrent viral respiratory infection. The majority of people with this type of hearing loss will have spontaneous return of hearing without the need for medical or surgical intervention. However, there are some individuals who will have a permanent hearing loss after such an infection. Those whose hearing loss is focused in the higher frequencies (pitches), those with associated balance problems, and those with extreme hearing loss have a lower chance of spontaneous recovery. Because of this variable outcome, some physicians will choose to treat individuals with a short course of oral steroids to maximize their chances of recovery, although the scientific evidence for the effectiveness of steroids is inconclusive.

Perilymph fistula: A **perilymph fistula** refers to a break or tear in one of the membranes of the inner ear. These injuries are occasionally spontaneous, but are usually caused by a direct blow to the head (such as that sustained in a fall) or from trauma to the inner ear caused by extreme changes in pressure (such as experienced during high-altitude flying, scuba diving, or heavy lifting). The result is often hearing loss in combination with vertigo. Such tears may close without intervention after several days of bed rest. If the symptoms persist, surgical intervention aimed at closing or plugging the tears may cure the problem.

Vascular occlusive disease: *Vascular occlusive disease* is a generalized form of atherosclerosis, or hardening of the arteries. When the artery responsible for bringing oxygen and nutrients to the inner ear becomes blocked, the sensory nerve endings in the cochlea can suddenly die. This is analogous to the death of heart muscle cells during a heart attack when the arteries to these areas become blocked. Although there is no specific test to confirm that this is the cause of an individual's hearing loss, it is thought to be a relatively uncommon cause of sudden sensorineural hearing loss. There is no proven treatment to restore hearing once this problem has occurred; however, certain medications aimed at opening the blood vessels and thinning the blood may be given in an attempt to minimize the blockage.

Autoimmune disease: Some underlying medical conditions can involve the hearing organs. **Autoimmune diseases** are those disorders in which the body's immune system reacts against itself. For example, rheumatoid arthritis, systemic lupus erythematosus, polyarteritis nodosa, relapsing polychondritis, and Wegener's granulomatosis are some of the autoimmune diseases that may include sensorineural hearing loss as one of their symptoms. There are some blood tests which can differentiate between these diseases. Once the cause of hearing loss has been established to be an autoimmune disease, the treatment of the hearing loss ultimately depends on treating the underlying disease.

Ménière's disease: **Ménière's disease** is caused by a fluid imbalance of the inner ear. It has four characteristic symptoms including sensorineural hearing loss which may fluctuate in severity, a sense of fullness in the ear, ringing in the ear, and a spinning sensation. The symptoms may be episodic, lasting from hours to days with a period of relief between episodes. Treatment of Ménière's disease includes a salt-restricted diet and **diuretic** medications to prevent fluid retention. When medical therapy fails to control the symptoms, there are several surgical procedures available to address severe cases of this disease.

Tumors: Tumors of the hearing nerve, the skull bones surrounding the middle and inner ear, the nerves adjacent to the hearing nerve, and the brain may all be potential causes of sudden sensorineural hearing loss. Such tumors are almost always benign and most commonly affect the hearing in only one ear. They are diagnosed by **magnetic resonance imaging**—a specialized form of radiologic imaging—in conjunction with a history,

RICHARD'S STORY

Richard B., 72, reports during his annual examination that he has developed significant hearing loss in his right ear compared to his left. His doctor orders an audiogram (hearing test), which confirms a severe hearing loss in the right ear and a milder hearing loss in the left ear. Richard is referred to an otolaryngologist who orders a MRI scan that shows a small benign tumor called an acoustic neuroma on the hearing nerve on the right side. Weighing the risk and benefits of surgery, radiation, or observation, the ear specialist and Richard decide that the small benign tumor be observed with serial MRI scans. MRI scans are obtained every year over the next 6-7 years, and no growth in the size of the tumor is noticed. Richard's hearing, however, continues to deteriorate in the right ear. He tries a hearing aid but does not find it helpful. He continues to get along normally using only the hearing in his left ear.

(figure 3-9)

HOW LOUD IS TOO LOUD?

Know which noises can cause damage. Wear ear plugs when you are involved in a loud activity.

(DB)	ACTIVITY
40	Refrigerator humming
50	
60	Normal conversation
70	
80	City traffic noise
90	Lawn mower, motorcycle: *Prolonged exposure to any noise above 90 decibels can cause gradual hearing loss.*
100	Woodshop: *No more than 15 minutes unprotected exposure recommended.*
110	Chainsaw: *Regular exposure of more than 1 minute risks permanent hearing loss.*
120	Boom cars, snowmobile
130	
140	Rock concerts, firecrackers

(Courtesy of National Institute of Deafness and Other Communication Disorders).

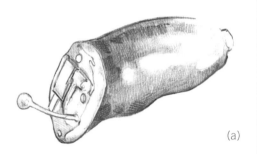

(a)

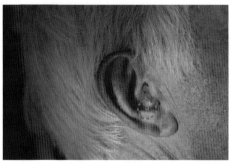

(b)

(figure 3-10)

(a) CIC hearing aids fit completely in the ear canal. (Note: This is a magnified view). (b) The only portion of the hearing aid that protrudes from the ear canal is the small clear plastic ball (circled) that acts as a pull tab to remove the aid from the canal. Red and blue colors helps denote the right from the left aid.

physical exam, and an audiogram. Treatment of these lesions depends on many factors, including the type, location, and size of tumor.

PROGRESSIVE SENSORINEURAL HEARING LOSS

Noise-induced hearing loss: Hearing loss caused by noise exposure is a common problem in older adults (see Figure 3-9). The development of this type of hearing loss depends on accumulated noise exposure over time (generally years), and the severity of the loss is proportional to the intensity and duration of this exposure, as well as to the genetic susceptibility of the individual. It most commonly affects the higher frequencies, including those at which speech occurs. There is no medical or surgical treatment for this type of hearing loss; however, hearing aids may play an important role in the hearing rehabilitation of these individuals.

Presbycusis: **Presbycusis** refers to sensorineural hearing loss caused by the aging process of the hearing apparatus. It generally affects both ears and the underlying cause is unknown. There are factors which are thought to contribute to presbycusis, including atherosclerosis, noise exposure, exposure to certain drugs or medications, and certain dietary and genetic factors. The treatment of this type of hearing loss depends on rehabilitation with hearing aids or cochlear implants.

TREATMENT OF HEARING LOSS

HEARING AIDS

Hearing aids are the treatment of choice for many older patients with sensorineural hearing loss. Delivering amplified sounds to the ear canal, hearing aids are available in many different styles. Some hearing aids can be placed completely within the ear canal (CIC aids), which make them nearly invisible to the casual observer (see Figure 3-10). In the ear (ITE) hearing aids fill much of the ear canal and the bowl of the outer ear, similar to the appearance of putty ear plugs (see Figure 3-11). Others fit behind the ear (BTE), consisting of a unit which rests behind the ear that is attached to an ear mold in the outer ear (see Figure 3-12). The microchips for these devices are quite similar; however, each style differs in the battery life, size of control dials, amplification capacity, durability, cosmetic appeal, and cost. In general, the larger the hearing aid, the larger the dials and controls, the softer the ear mold, the greater the amplification capability, the longer the battery life, and the less the acoustic feedback.

Many new digital hearing aids can be programmed to selectively amplify only those pitches that the patient has trouble hearing. These types of programmable hearing aids are particularly well suited for individuals with hearing loss in the high frequencies, often manifest by difficulty with conversational speech in the presence of a high level of background noise.

HEARING AID FITTING

Individuals considering hearing aids should see an otolaryngologist or an audiologist for an evaluation. Individuals with hearing loss in both ears are candidates for hearing aids in both ears. Using hearing aids in both ears creates a better sense of sound localization, greater understanding of speech in noisy environments, and an improved ability to discriminate spoken words. The only drawback to using two hearing aids is the extra cost involved in purchasing a second aid.

When only one ear is fitted with a hearing aid, the better-hearing ear should be fitted. This allows the individual to approach normal hearing as closely as possible in at least one ear.

Regardless of the style of hearing aid chosen, proper fitting of the components to the individual ear is important to maximize the function of the hearing aid while minimizing the feedback.

Finally, it is important for any individuals considering hearing aids to have a realistic understanding of what hearing aids will do for them. Hearing aids rarely return hearing to normal. However, they can significantly improve one's ability to understand spoken words and to hear speech in noisy environments. In addition, a person's lifestyle will help determine how useful a hearing aid will be in daily life. Those who live quiet lives and have few social encounters or work-related interactions will benefit from hearing aids much less than those who maintain active social or professional lives. Finally, motivation is a key factor in the successful use of hearing aids.

COCHLEAR IMPLANTS

Cochlear implants are sometimes referred to as "bionic ears" (see Figure 3-13). Whereas conventional hearing aids transmit amplified sounds into the ear canal, similar to a loudspeaker in the ear, cochlear implants transform sound energy into electrical impulses. These electrical impulses are delivered directly to the hearing nerve through electrodes that are surgically implanted into the hearing canals of the cochlea in the inner ear.

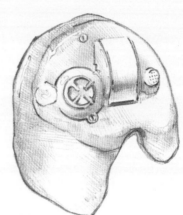

(figure 3-11)

ITE aids are larger than CIC aids (Figure 3-10) because they occupy not only the ear canal but also the bowl of the external ear. However, they do not have components which rest outside of the ear like BTE aids (Figure 3-12).

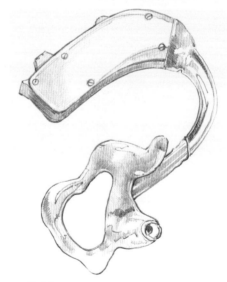

(figure 3-12)

A BTE hearing aid has is composed of an elliptical, flesh-colored piece that rests behind the ear (it contains the battery and electronic components) and clear tubing that leads to a clear piece that rests in the external part of the ear. Sound is transmitted from the receiver behind the ear through the tubing and directed to the eardrum.

Cochlear implants are available for individuals with very severe or profound hearing loss. They may restore functional hearing to those who acquired normal speech and language skills prior to losing their hearing. Some individuals even regain the ability to communicate over the phone.

Cochlear implants require a surgical procedure for implantation. Once implanted, individuals must undergo multiple programming and training sessions to customize the electric characteristics of the implant and to learn how to use it. These sessions are mandatory to derive significant benefit from the implant. In addition to the motivation and dedication involved, cochlear implants involve a significant financial expense which is often, but not always, covered by medical insurance.

CONCLUSION

Hearing loss in older adults is a common problem, but prevention is always an option (see Table 3-2). There are many causes of hearing loss in older persons, and accurate diagnosis requires a thorough investigation by history, physical exam, and appropriate testing. Although age-related hearing loss (presbycusis) is a very common cause, it should only be diagnosed after other potential causes have been ruled out. Some forms of hearing loss are treatable, either medically or surgically. Other forms can be improved with the use of hearing aids. Treatment can lead to an improvement in one's productivity and quality of life.

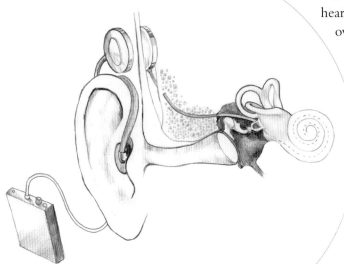

(figure 3-13*)*

Cochlear implants have two main components. One component is external to the ear and functions as the sound receiver, and it communicates with the internal component, which is comprised of strings of electrodes surgically implanted in the hearing canals of the inner ear.

(table 3-2*)*

RECOMMENDED PREVENTIVE HEALTH PRACTICES TO AVOID HEARING LOSS

BY THE PATIENT	BY THE DOCTOR
Avoid using cotton-tipped applicators to clean the ear canal.	Check ears at routine visits.
Have routine professional ear cleanings if predisposed to earwax.	Ask about hearing at routine visits.
Seek medical attention when a hearing loss is first noticed.	Refer to otolaryngologist for evaluation of persistent effusions, significant hearing loss, sudden hearing loss, hearing loss complicated by abnormalities of the ear, and for microscopic ear exams and cleaning.
Seek routine follow-up once hearing aids are prescribed.	
Avoid exposure to loud noise.	Stress importance of lifestyle modifications to preserve hearing and avoid damage to the hearing organs (e.g., avoid excessive noise exposure).

WHAT YOU NEED TO KNOW

▶ Hearing loss is the most common medical condition in persons over 65 years of age.

▶ You may not be the first one to recognize your hearing loss: A spouse, relative, or friend may bring it to your attention.

▶ Proper diagnosis of the cause of the hearing loss requires examination by a physician.

▶ Do not use cotton-tipped applicators to clean your ears! This may push earwax further into the ear canal and pack it down so that it is more difficult to remove. Even worse, you can accidentally perforate your eardrum.

▶ Be aware of the noise level in your environment. Excessive noise can damage your hearing.

▶ If you have hearing loss, tell your family and friends so that they can help you. Suggest that they face you and speak more clearly. They do not need to shout. Eliminate background noise from television and radios if possible. In restaurants or at social functions try to sit in quieter places.

FOR MORE INFORMATION

▶ National Institutes of Health
301-496-4000
Web: www.nih.gov

▶ National Institute on Deafness and Other Communication Disorders
800-241-1044
Web: www.nidc.nih.gov

▶ National Institute on Aging
800-222-2225
Web: www.nia.nih.gov

▶ American Tinnitus Association
800-634-8978
Web: www.ata.org

▶ American Academy of Audiology
8300 Greensboro Drive, Suite 750
McLean, VA 22102-3611
Voice/TTY: 703-610-9022
800-AAA-2336
Fax: 703-790-8631
E-mail: info@audiology.com
Web: www.audiology.com

▶ American Academy of Otolaryngology–Head and Neck Surgery
One Prince Street
Alexandria, VA 22314
703-836-4444
TTY: 703-519-1585
Fax: 703-683-5100
E-mail: webmaster@entnet.org
Web: www.entnet.org

▶ American Speech-Language-Hearing Association
10801 Rockville Pike
Rockville, MD 20852
301-897-5700, 800-638-8255
TTY: 301-897-0157
Fax: 301-571-0457
E-mail: actioncenter@asha.org
Web: www.asha.org

▶ House Ear Institute
2100 West Third Street
Los Angeles, CA 90057
213-483-4431
TTY: 213-484-2642
Fax: 213-483-8789
E-mail: webmaster@hei.org
Web: www.hei.org

■ Laurent Clerc National Deaf Education Center

KDES PAS-6

800 Florida Avenue, NE

Washington, DC 20002

202-651-5051

TTY: 202-651-5052

Fax: 202-651-5054

E-mail: clearinghouse.infotogo@gallaudet.edu

Web: clerccenter.gallaudet.edu

■ Self Help for Hard of Hearing People

7910 Woodmont Avenue, Suite 1200

Bethesda, MD 20814

301-657-2248

TTY: 301-657-2249

Fax: 301-913-9413

E-mail: national@shhh.org

Web: www.shhh.org

Smell is a potent wizard that transports you across thousands of miles and all the years you have lived.

—Helen Keller

THE AUTHOR

04

KEVIN W. O'NEIL, MD, FACP, graduated from Boston College magna cum laude and the Georgetown University School of Medicine. He did his internship at the Washington Hospital Center and his internal medicine residency at the University of Massachusetts Medical Center. He was an assistant professor in the Department of Internal Medicine at the University of Massachusetts Medical Center until moving to Sarasota, Florida, in 1984. He is currently an assistant professor of medicine at the University of South Florida College of Medicine. He is board-certified in internal medicine and holds a Certificate of Added Qualifications in Geriatric Medicine. He is a fellow of the American College of Physicians and a member of the American Geriatrics Society. He practices with the First Physicians Group in Sarasota and is on the staff at Sarasota Memorial Hospital and Doctors Hospital.

04 | THE NOSE

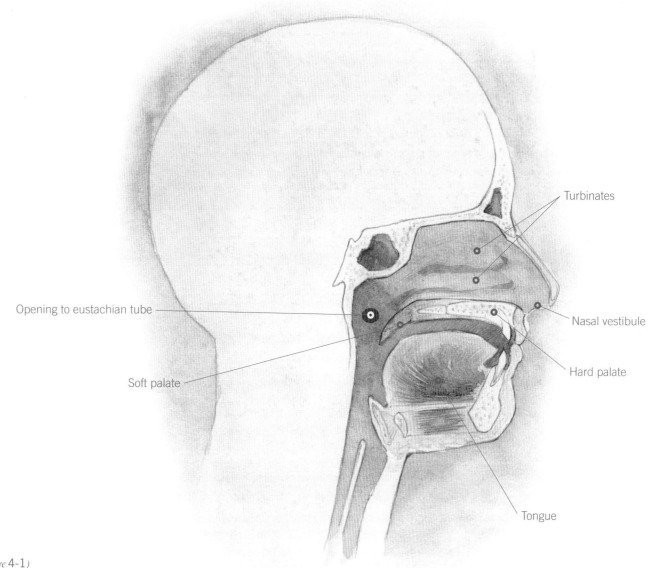

Turbinates

Opening to eustachian tube

Nasal vestibule

Soft palate

Hard palate

Tongue

(figure 4-1)
Side view of the inside of the nose and throat.

Has the aroma of a roasted turkey or a freshly baked pumpkin pie ever transported you back in memory to a Christmas or Thanksgiving long ago? Such is the power of smell to evoke memories. Your sense of smell can provide pleasure but can also warn you of danger. Most of us seldom think of the nose and its function unless a cold or a nosebleed reminds us. However, the nose, the olfactory system (our system for smelling), the sinuses, and the nasal passages serve an important role. Not only does the nose harbor the system responsible for our sense of smell, but the nose also serves to warm, humidify, and purify air on its journey to our lungs. As we age, conditions and diseases that may have minor or serious consequences more commonly affect the nose and the nasal passages.

AS PLAIN AS THE NOSE ON YOUR FACE

Although sharing the same anatomical structure (as shown in Figure 4-1), noses come in all shapes and sizes. Some prominent people are easily recognized by a distinctive nose. Jimmy Durante's nickname was the great "Schnozzola," and Bob Hope was affectionately called "Ski nose." Many people have spent small fortunes to improve their looks with "nose jobs" (rhinoplasty). Some of the major developments in plastic surgery over the years have come from attempts to reconstruct noses injured in accidents or war. Yet most of us don't give the nose a second thought until something goes wrong.

The outside of the nose is composed of skin and cartilage. Therefore, anything that can go wrong with them can go wrong with the nose. Since the nose is an extension of the face, it is more likely to get sunburned. Years of sun exposure make it a likely site for development of skin cancers, including basal cell carcinoma, squamous cell carcinoma, and melanoma. You can reduce your risk by using a sunblock, SPF 15 or greater, and wearing hats.

Adult acne (rosacea) and *seborrheic dermatitis* affect the nose and the surrounding skin of the face. These are benign conditions that can be managed with special creams prescribed by your doctor. Severe recurrent bouts of rosacea can make the nose look large and bulbous, a condition called rhinophyma but more commonly recognized as "rum nose" or "brandy nose." The fact that alcohol can aggravate this condition is probably how it received its more familiar names.

Diseases and conditions that affect the nasal cartilage, the flexible and rubbery part of the nose, are relatively common. Early detection of skin

(figure 4-2)

"Saddle nose" is a deformity caused by destruction or damage to the nasal cartilage.

THEN AND NOW

Rhinoplasty ("nose job") is a common operation performed by plastic surgeons. Although practiced in ancient times, plastic surgery in America did not really start until 1827 when Dr. John Peter Mettauer performed an operation for cleft palate. Much of what we have since learned in plastic surgery has come from the misfortunes of those injured in war. Techniques that have been developed to repair gunshot and shrapnel wounds, as well as burns, have offered new hope to trauma and burn victims. Reconstructive procedures help babies with congenital deformities, and microsurgical techniques allow amputated body parts to be reattached.

04

cancer is important since it may extend to the cartilage if not treated early enough. This can cause significant disfigurement and the need for reconstruction. Mohs' surgery is a technique that attempts to limit the extent of removal of normal tissue, but it requires a longer time since the dermatologist has to carefully examine small sections of skin. If any residual cancer is noticed, he or she has to go back and remove more of the diseased tissue until all the surgical margins are free of cancer.

One of the most commons surgical procedures performed by an otolaryngologist (ear, nose, and throat, or ENT, specialist) is for a deviated nasal septum. The nasal septum is the cartilage that divides your nose into the right and left nostrils. A deviated septum can make it difficult to breath through one side of the nose and may be especially troublesome if the affected individual has a cold, allergies, or nasal polyps.

In years past, syphilis was not an infrequent cause of "saddle nose" (see Figure 4-2). The cartilage over the bridge of the nose collapsed, giving it a saddle appearance. Today, saddle nose is observed more frequently with trauma or other diseases. In the United States, some diseases that relatively rarely affect the nasal cartilage include Wegener's granulomatosis, leprosy, tuberculosis, and relapsing polychondritis. Today, cocaine has been associated with perforations of the nasal septum, but it is not commonly seen in the elderly.

The nasal cartilage is attached to the *nasal bone* and the *maxilla* (the upper jawbone), as shown in Figure 4-3. The nasal bone is the part of the skull that the nosepiece of our eyeglasses or sunglasses rests against. Trauma to this area is not uncommon, often related to sports injuries but even the occasional fist to the nose. Fractures of the nasal bones may require surgery if the fragments do not align properly.

(figure 4-3)

The nasal cartilage and facial bones.

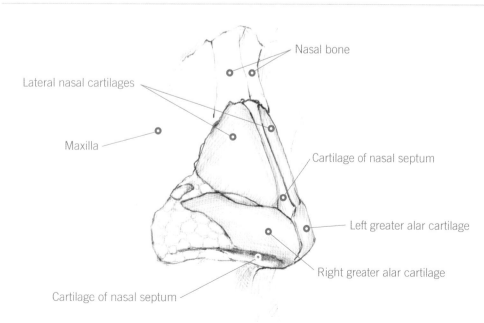

Nasal bone

Lateral nasal cartilages

Maxilla

Cartilage of nasal septum

Left greater alar cartilage

Right greater alar cartilage

Cartilage of nasal septum

EVERYBODY'S DOING IT

Care must be exercised when trimming nose hairs and cleaning nasal debris. Picking the nose and injuring the internal tissues of the nose can lead to serious infections. Since the veins that drain into the nose extend back to the brain, this can potentially lead to infections of the brain itself. Nose hairs should be trimmed with blunt-tipped scissors manufactured specifically for that purpose or with electronic nose-hair trimmers. Never pull out nose hairs. Crusted debris or nasal discharge should be removed by blowing the nose with a handkerchief or nasal tissue. Frequent nose-picking can erode the cartilage in the nasal septum and cause a perforation.

Nasal vestibulitis is a common infection about the nostrils. Often it is related to *Staphylococcus aureus.* It is characterized by redness, swelling, and pain about the nostrils. It can be triggered by nose picking, too frequent blowing of the nose, or excessive cleaning or rubbing of the nose with tissues or a handkerchief. It may require treatment with oral or topical antibiotics. Folliculitis occurs when the nose hairs are involved. This will usually respond to oral or topical antibiotics. Less frequently, a small abscess, called a *furuncle,* may develop at the base of an infected hair follicle. Antibiotics and application of moist heat may expedite healing and provide symptom relief. Due to the venous drainage of the nose, it is not recommended to surgically drain a furuncle.

A dangerous practice among many older people is the use of Vicks or other petroleum-based products in their nose. The warnings for these products explicitly state that they should not be used within the nostrils—and for good reason. When lying down or during sleep, this material may drain down the throat and into the lungs causing an inflammatory reaction mimicking pneumonia or even cancer. If you have problems with nasal congestion or breathing through your nose, tell your doctor. He may prescribe medication or have you see an ENT specialist to make sure there is not a more serious cause for the problem.

WHEN THE NOSE DOESN'T KNOW

The nose contains special cells that allow us to smell. Smell is very important to us. Look at the billions of dollars spent on perfumes and fragrances throughout the world. Some smells can be pleasant, bringing back wonderful memories. Other smells may be quite unpleasant and make us want to avoid a place or situation. Smells may stimulate our appetite or make us sick. They can make us excited or repulsed. Smells may even warn us of danger, such as the smell of smoke in a burning building or propane from a leaking stove line. Interestingly, our sense of smell can adapt quite readily. Ask any doctor or nurse, and you will learn that they don't recognize the familiar "hospital smell" that you experience. This adaptation certainly makes life livable for those who live next to rubber plants or paper mills.

<aside>
MY STORY: MARK H., 62

I used my nail scissors to cut my nose hairs for years. A few months back, I accidentally cut the inside of my nose. A few days later, my nose was sore, and then it became red, hot, and swollen. I took some ibuprofen, but then I started getting a fever. Now I was nervous. I called Dr. Johnson and he saw me right away. When I told him my story, I thought he would go ballistic. He told me that infections around the nose are serious because they can spread through the blood to the brain. I couldn't believe it when he told me I had to be admitted to the hospital to be started on intravenous antibiotics. Fortunately, everything went well and the infection resolved. The first thing I did when I left the hospital is invest in an electronic nose hair trimmer. It was a small price to pay to avoid such a serious problem.
</aside>

What happens when the sense of smell is lost or diminished? Do you remember the last time you had a cold? Did food seem uninteresting? The next time you eat, pinch your nostrils. What does the food taste like? It makes a difference, doesn't it? There is a complex interplay between taste and smell that produces the flavor of the food that we eat. (See Dr. Shay's discussion in Chapter 5.)

Aging itself is associated with significant changes in smell. The special cells located in the nose are called olfactory cells, shown in Figure 4-4. Most clinical studies have shown that these cells become less sensitive with aging. Flavor enhancers may help, but some elderly persons may salt their food more. This can cause problems if they have high blood pressure or congestive heart failure. Falls can cause head injuries that damage these nerve cells resulting in anosmia (loss of smell). Diseases commonly associated with aging such as Alzheimer's disease, Parkinson's disease, and cancer may be associated with decrease in smell sensitivity. This can lead to loss of appetite and malnutrition. A fascinating finding in one clinical study was that smell might be a more potent predictor of persons who will later develop Alzheimer's disease than sophisticated neuropsychological tests are.

Some common medical treatments may affect smell and taste. These include drugs, especially those used in chemotherapy for cancer, and radiation. Certain nutritional deficiencies can play a role. Vitamin supplements can be helpful if deficiencies exist. Zinc sulfate may be useful even when zinc levels are normal. Food preparation can be helpful by altering the color and texture of foods. Chewing slowly and thoroughly allows more time for the olfactory cells and taste buds to appreciate what is presented to them.

Certain precautions are important for older persons due to the decrease in smell sensitivity with aging. Spoiled food can cause serious illness. It may not be possible for you to recognize when food has gone bad. Therefore, be careful about leftovers. If you are not sure about them, throw them away or have someone who has a normal sense of smell check them for you. Smoke detectors are important. Have them placed in every room of your house. Use an electric stove rather than a gas stove. If this is not possible, get a commercial gas detector. If you use propane gas, place the detector near the floor since propane is heavier than air. If you use natural gas, place the detector on the ceiling since natural gas is lighter than air.

DRIP, DRIP

A frustrating problem for many older persons is nasal drip. The condition that is usually responsible is called rhinitis. This can be seen in younger persons as well. Allergies are a common cause *(allergic rhinitis),* but some people may have symptoms all year long *(perennial or nonallergic rhinitis).* Some persons are prone to a condition called *gustatory rhinitis,* which

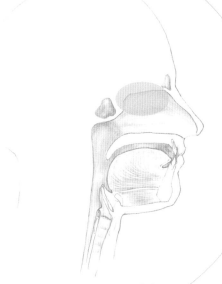

(figure 4-4)

The olfactory area (highlighted) contains specialized cells that are important for our sense of smell.

means that the nasal congestion and dripping are worse when eating hot or spicy foods. An unusual cause of chronic nasal drip is injury to the skull. Fractures through certain parts of the skull may cause a dripping of spinal fluid through the nose. If a nasal drip developed after a fall or head injury, it is important to let your doctor know.

Many people resort to using over the counter (OTC) antihistamines or nasal sprays, but this can be dangerous as you get older. Antihistamines may have adverse effects on sleep and may cause sedation, thus increasing the risk of falls and injuries. Men often have enlarged prostates as they get older, and many antihistamines may affect bladder function. A serious complication is urinary retention, which may require catheterization and hospitalization. Topical nasal sprays such as Afrin and Neo-Synephrine may give some immediate relief, but chronic use can lead to dependency. These sprays cause a constriction of the blood vessels in the lining of the nose that helps relieve symptoms of congestion initially, but when they wear off, the blood vessels dilate and a rebound phenomenon occurs. The congestion and dripping get worse, and more spray is needed. Thus, a vicious cycle is established.

Certain drugs can cause rhinitis. These may include angiotensin-converting enzyme inhibitors, beta-blockers, GABAPENTIN (NEURONTIN), CLONIDINE, nonsteroidal anti-inflammatory drugs, aspirin, and estrogen. Some men have reported nasal congestion with SILDENAFIL (VIAGRA).

If you are troubled with a nasal or postnasal drip, talk with your doctor. There are a variety of options. Corticosteroid steroid sprays reduce the inflammation in the nasal passages, and the absorption through the lining of the nose into the bloodstream is minimal. Most can be taken once a day. They are expensive. IPRATROPIUM (ATROVENT) nasal spray may be helpful as a drying agent. It has also been approved for treatment of rhinitis associated with the common cold. It requires administration two or three times daily. AZELASTINE (ASTELIN) has been useful in allergic and nonallergic rhinitis. Two sprays twice a day are given in each nostril. In situations where the nasal membranes have thinned out *(atrophic rhinitis)* resulting in dryness, crusting, and bleeding, saline solutions or Ayr gel may be tried. In some cases, the newer generation antihistamines may be tried. Generally, these are less sedating and safer in the elderly than the OTC antihistamines. They include CETIRIZINE (ZYRTEC), DESLORATADINE (CLARINEX), and FEXOFENADINE (ALLEGRA). LORATADINE (CLARITIN) is now available without a prescription. MONTELUKAST (SINGULAIR), a drug used for asthma, has been approved for treatment of allergic rhinitis. Its mechanism of action is different from the antihistamines. Immunotherapy (allergy shots) may be helpful for those with allergic rhinitis but do not have a role in the many older persons with nonallergic rhinitis. Common sense would dictate avoiding odors, fumes, dusts, and other environmental irritants. Cigarette smoking or exposure to smoke should be avoided.

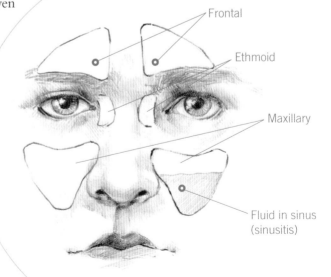

Frontal

Ethmoid

Maxillary

Fluid in sinus (sinusitis)

(figure 4-5)

The sinuses.

I HAVE A HEADACHE

A headache in the older person may have many causes. New onset of headaches in the elderly requires a thorough investigation by a physician. One cause may be an infection of the sinuses. Sinuses are cavities within the bones of the forehead and cheeks (see Figure 4-5). Sinusitis is an inflammation of the sinuses that can be caused by viruses, bacteria, fungi, or allergies. Nasal polyps caused by allergy or infection can block the drainage pathways of the sinuses leading to infection. Acute sinusitis often causes pain and tenderness over the sinus affected. Thus, frontal sinusitis may cause pain over the forehead. Maxillary sinusitis will cause pain over the cheekbones and in the teeth, and ethmoid sinusitis produces pain behind the eyes. Antibiotic therapy is required for infectious sinusitis. If the infection is slow to resolve or symptoms are getting worse, special sinus scans and consultation with an ENT specialist may be required.

Chronic sinusitis is diagnosed if there are frequent recurrences of sinusitis or a sinus infection lasts more than three months. A prolonged course of antibiotics may be required. In refractory cases, surgery may be necessary to allow the sinuses to drain properly. Polyps can be removed if they are blocking the sinus passages. Serious forms of sinusitis caused by fungi can occur in persons whose immunity is compromised by cancer, diabetes, and AIDS. Such fungi include *Mucormycosis, Candida,* and *Aspergillus.*

BLOOD!

Nosebleeds *(epistaxis)* are always a source of alarm. They occur if the lining of the nose gets irritated and the blood vessels underneath break open and bleed. When the bleeding originates from the front part of the nose, it is called an *anterior* nosebleed. When it occurs in the back part, it is called a *posterior* nosebleed. Posterior bleeds tend to be mores serious. They may bleed more, and locating the site of bleeding can be difficult. Often the blood will drip down the back of the throat.

Nosebleeds can be caused by nose picking, vigorous blowing, or injury to the nose or skull. Colds, sinusitis, and rhinitis may make the nasal membranes more fragile and vulnerable to bleeding. A very dry environment may be responsible. In the elderly, uncontrolled hypertension and drugs, such as WARFARIN (COUMADIN) and aspirin, might make a person more susceptible to nosebleeds. Less commonly, nosebleeds may be triggered by serious diseases such as *nasopharyngeal carcinoma* (cancer of the nasopharynx), tuberculosis, hemophilia, and leukemia. Since clotting factors are made in the liver, liver failure caused by cirrhosis may be associated with nosebleeds.

Anterior nosebleeds can usually be managed with simple measures. Often they will resolve on their own, although many people try pinching the nostrils for several minutes or placing ice packs on the nose. The individual should sit up and tilt the head forward. This will reduce the amount of bleeding down the back of the throat. If bleeding persists, you may need to go to the emergency room or see your doctor to have the nose packed. Occasionally application of silver nitrate or *electrocautery* (a special electric instrument) is used to stop a bleeding vessel. After these procedures, it is best to avoid heavy lifting, bending over, or vigorous blowing of the nose.

Posterior nosebleeds may require packing, but some cases are severe enough to require admission to an intensive care unit for close monitoring. These nosebleeds require packing and referral to an otolaryngologist. Sometimes special balloons are used to compress the blood vessel that is causing the bleeding. If these measures are unsuccessful, invasive procedures or surgery may be required.

A MASQUERADE THAT COULD PROVE SERIOUS

Nasopharyngeal cancer involves the upper part of the throat. Interestingly, it does not seem to be associated with use of tobacco products or with alcohol abuse as are most other cancers of the head and neck. It occurs more commonly in persons of Asian and Chinese ancestry. Exposure to the *Epstein-Barr virus* may play a role. This is the same virus that causes mononucleosis. Fortunately, nasopharyngeal cancer is relatively uncommon in the United States.

Symptoms that should prompt further evaluation include headaches, recurrent nosebleeds, persistent sore throat, problems with hearing or speaking, pain or ringing in the ears, or a lump in the nose or neck. As you can see, these symptoms can occur with other less serious disorders of the head and neck. The key point is that you should see your doctor if these symptoms are persisting or getting worse. Special tests such as CT scans or MRI may be necessary to aid in diagnosis. Consultation with an otolaryngologist is necessary. An otolaryngologist may use a flexible fiberoptic instrument called a *nasopharyngoscope* to examine the nose and throat. A definitive diagnosis requires biopsy of the tumor (seeFigure 4-6).

Prognosis depends on the size of the tumor and how much it has spread to surrounding structures or to lymph nodes. Small cancers can usually be cured with radiation treatments. Even locally advanced cancers can achieve a relatively high cure rate with combinations of radiation, chemotherapy, and surgery. The prognosis is poor for cancers that have spread to lymph nodes and distant sites.

Other cancers may infrequently involve the nasal cavity and sinuses. Only rarely do melanomas, cancers of the pigment-containing cells of the skin, involve the nasal cavity. Sarcomas are cancers of the muscle or connective tissue. Midline granuloma is a rare and lethal malignancy; death is usually a result of spread to the brain and nervous system, infection, or bleeding complications.

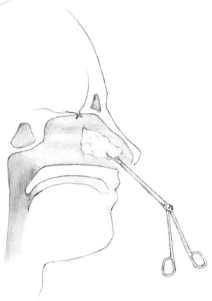

(figure 4-6)

Biopsy of a nasal tumor.

WHAT YOU NEED TO KNOW

▶ Problems with the nose are common with aging. Such skin disorders as sunburn, seborrheic dermatitis, and skin cancer commonly affect the nose as we age. Injury, cancer, and several other diseases can affect the nasal cartilage, the rubbery and flexible part of the nose.

▶ Infections of the nostrils (nasal vestibulitis) or the hair follicles within the nose can be serious. Topical and/or oral antibiotics may be necessary. Avoid picking the nose, pulling out nose hairs, or using sharp instruments to trim nose hairs.

▶ Diminution or loss of smell can be dangerous. It may be difficult to appreciate when food has spoiled. Be careful about leftovers, or have someone whose smell is intact check them for you. Install smoke detectors throughout your house. Use an electric stove, if possible. Get a commercial gas detector if you use propane or natural gas.

▶ Rhinitis is the most common cause of nasal drip and postnasal drip. Effective therapies are available. Avoid using OTC sprays that constrict the nasal blood vessels on a chronic basis. They may lead to dependency.

▶ Sinusitis may be a cause of headache in the elderly. There are many possible causes, and any new onset of headaches requires investigation.

▶ Nosebleeds can have many causes. Minor nosebleeds from the front part of the nose usually will resolve spontaneously. Bleeding in the back (posterior) part of the nose may require evaluation in an emergency room or by an otolaryngologist. Recurrent nosebleeds require evaluation by your doctor.

04

FOR MORE INFORMATION

▶ NIDCD Information Clearinghouse
One Communication Avenue
Bethesda, MD 20892
800-241-1044
TTY: 800-241-1055
E-mail: nidcdinfo@nidcd.nih.gov
Has information on smell disorders.

▶ Indoor Air Quality Information Clearinghouse
(IAQ INFO)
P.O. Box 37133
Washington, DC 20013
800-438-4318
E-mail: iaqinfo@aol.com
Web: www.epa.gov/iaq/iaqinfo.html

▶ NCI's Cancer Information Service (CIS)
800-422-6237
TTY: 800-332-8615

It [toothache] may be numbered among the worst tortures, the patient must abstain entirely from wine, and at first even from food.

—*Aurus Census 25 B.C. – 50 A.D.*

THE AUTHOR

05

KENNETH SHAY, DDS, MS, graduated from the UCLA School of Dentistry in 1982. He completed residency training in the care of medically compromised patients at the Milwaukee Veterans Affairs (VA) Medical Center, after which he was in private practice in Chicago. He returned to Milwaukee for a two-year fellowship in geriatric dentistry. Following completion, he directed that and related programs at the Milwaukee VA for nearly 10 years, during which he earned a graduate dental degree and was on the faculty at the Marquette University School of Dentistry and the Medical College of Wisconsin. He relocated to Ann Arbor, Michigan, in 1993 to direct the dental clinic at the Ann Arbor VA and to join the faculty of the University of Michigan School of Dentistry. Since 1999 his responsibilities for the VA have extended beyond dentistry and well beyond the Ann Arbor area: he is presently responsible for overseeing and coordinating all geriatric programs (nursing home, home care, hospice, etc.) for a four-state region of the VA. He has served as the president of the American Society for Geriatric Dentistry and as the chairman of the Federation of Special Care Organizations in Dentistry and is the designated speaker on geriatric oral health issues for the Council on Dental Practice of the American Dental Association.

05 | ORAL HEALTH

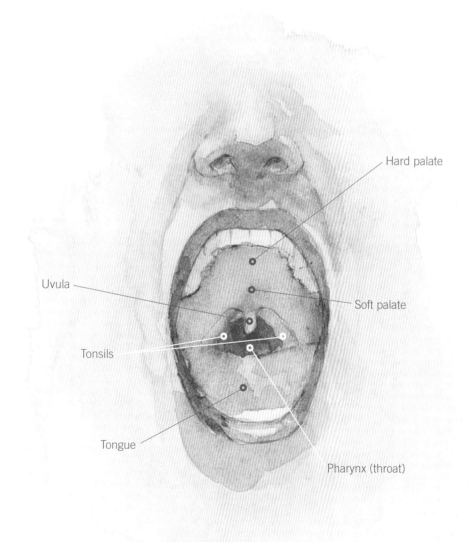

Hard palate

Uvula

Soft palate

Tonsils

Tongue

Pharynx (throat)

(figure 5-1)
The mouth.

Who can deny that the mouth is a very important part of your body, regardless of your age? Your first contact with the world is when your mouth opens wide to cry. The next is when you use your lips and tongue to take nourishment. Studies show that infants' first recognition of another human is through their mothers' smiles. As a child matures, the mouth becomes the origin of more complex communication—talking. All the nutrients responsible for the rapid growth from child to adult pass through the mouth, where the food is prepared for digestion and is an important and repeated source for visceral and emotional pleasure. The mouth is used for that most basic yet most important gesture of human affection, the kiss.

Because the mouth is so important for key aspects of life like eating, communicating, and experiencing pleasure, problems that affect the mouth can dramatically interfere with our lives. When it hurts to chew or swallow, we may fail to eat an adequate diet, missing essential nutrients and transforming a vital source of pleasure into one of pain. Oral disease is often accompanied by unpleasant appearance, tastes, smells, and other sensations, which can interfere with our self-image, our desire to be with others, and the desire of others to be with us.

That is why keeping the mouth healthy is critical for overall health regardless of a person's age. With advancing age, a growing array of factors arises to make oral health more challenging to maintain. This chapter reviews what the older person needs to know and needs to do to keep his or her mouth in top condition. It begins by discussing the ways in which the teeth, the gums, and the other tissues of the mouth change over the lifetime. It reviews the most common oral diseases—decay, gum disease, missing teeth, dry mouth—and goes into detail about how they can be prevented and how they may be treated if they have already occurred, through fillings, root canal, crowns, bridges, implants, and dentures. It explores how medications and nutrition can play very important roles in

(figure 5-2)

Schematic diagram of dental and periodontal anatomy.

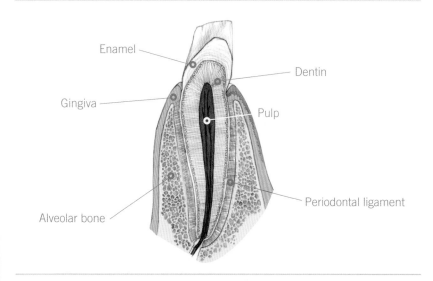

Enamel

Dentin

Gingiva

Pulp

Periodontal ligament

Alveolar bone

preserving—and destroying—the health of the mouth. And it examines some oral problems that are less common but still frequently encountered in persons of advancing age, like diseases of the soft tissues and glands of the mouth, taste and smell disorders, and jaw joint pain.

THE CHANGING MOUTH

A discussion of how people's mouths change as they age needs to begin by clarifying the terms that describe the teeth (see Figure 5-2).

The part of the tooth most visible in the mouth is covered with a very hard, translucent substance called **enamel,** which surrounds the **dentin.** Although enamel is almost pure crystal (a form of calcium phosphate), dentin is more like bone, with lots of microscopic channels (**dentinal tubules**) running through it. The part of the tooth not visible because it is in the **alveolar bone** of the jaw is covered by **cementum,** which is very similar to dentin but lacking the tubules. In the center of each tooth is the **pulp,** which contains nerves and blood vessels surrounded by a single layer of cells responsible for making more dentin: the **odontoblasts.** The tissue that holds the tooth in the alveolar bone is termed **periodontium,** and it consists of the **gingiva** (the part closest to the tooth where the tooth emerges from the alveolar bone) and the **periodontal ligament,** which is a paper-thin, gristly "shock absorber" between the alveolar bone and the cementum on the outside of the root.

The aging of teeth occurs internally and externally. Internally, the odontoblasts constantly secrete chemicals that add dentin to the walls of the **pulp chamber**—the space in the dentin where the pulp resides. The effect of this deposit, over years and decades, is similar to paint that coats the inside of a paint bucket that is never thoroughly washed: layers multiply in the bucket, and over time, the bucket can't hold as much as before. In other words, the internal aging of the tooth involves the pulp chamber gradually shrinking in volume. With a smaller chamber, there is less need for a blood supply, and with less blood supply the nerves slowly reduce in number and send fewer impulses to the brain. This process occurs at different rates in different people, but the direction of change is always the same: the older a person is, the less sensitive the teeth are to hot, to cold, to decay, and to pain. This can be a very troublesome change if the primary reason a person goes for dental care is because he or she feels discomfort, because through aging, a person usually experiences very little dental pain, even when large cavities form or large pieces of teeth break off.

The external aging of teeth is more visible but less significant to oral health. Because enamel is crystalline, years of chewing and eating very cold and very hot foods has caused microscopic cracks in the enamel, and these often appear as very fine "fracture lines." The underlying dentin becomes darker as it ages, and because enamel is almost clear, this change makes teeth grow more yellowish as they age. A lifetime of chewing causes wear on the biting surfaces, flattening the teeth to varying degrees (from slightly to severely) and often exposing the underlying yellow dentin in areas (Figure 5-3). Years of brushing have usually smoothed the nonbiting sides of teeth so that they appear smoother (Figure 5-4).

DOCTOR'S DIARY

Rudy W. was an 81-year-old retired contractor who slipped on the ice and ended up having a hip replacement. A widower, he agreed to convalesce in a nursing home where staff could assist him with bathing and dressing and meal preparation until he was able to move around on his own. The facility adhered to the policy that all residents were required to be offered a dental examination within the first two weeks of admission. Rudy W. had his own dentist but hadn't been to see him for several years since nothing hurt, so he agreed to be examined.

He was quite surprised when I told him that several of his teeth had deep cavities. One of the biggest holes was on the backside of a molar, underneath a gold crown. When I showed him the X-ray, Rudy W. remarked, "That's where the sandwich goes!" When asked to explain, he recounted how he always cleaned the food off his partial dentures after a meal, just like his dentist told him—but that whenever he had a sandwich, he'd find himself nibbling on pieces of the sandwich minutes after he had rinsed. That was a big hole—and he'd never felt a thing.

I described how the teeth grew less and less sensitive with advancing age—and how this process was even more profound in teeth, like the molar, that had large restorations on them. I was even able to use Rudy W.'s lack of sensation to carefully remove extensive decay without harming the nerve, by having Rudy alert me when drilling he didn't feel suddenly started to be felt.

(figure 5-3)

Severely worn incisal (biting) edges of lower front teeth, revealing the differences in color of the different layers of teeth (enamel on the outside, then dentin that has filled the top of the pulp space).

ORAL PROBLEMS

The diseases that affect the mouth are pretty much the same in advanced age as in youth. But because some gum diseases and decay cause destruction of tissues that can not be regenerated, their effects are more profound as a person ages—simply because those processes have been deteriorating the tissues for a longer period of time. This section starts by clarifying how the major tissues of the mouth—the teeth, gums, mucosa (the lining of the mouth), and glands—fall prey to disease. But it ends by pointing out how the causes of oral problems in an older mouth that are the hardest to solve are really not diseases of the mouth at all but are due to other problems elsewhere in the body (diabetes, arthritis, depression, stroke, and dementia) or drugs taken to address nonoral diseases.

CARIES

Dental decay (dentists call it caries) occurs when germs (bacteria) on the tooth surface give off acid for a long enough time that a hole is eaten through the enamel. Bacteria in the mouth number in thousands of billions. Different varieties (several hundred have been identified) live and multiply in different oral environments: the tongue, the saliva, the cheek, the gums, and so on. Some species adhere to tooth surfaces (and form a sticky substance called plaque), especially surfaces that are not regularly cleaned by brushing or chewing. There they dissolve microscopic amounts of enamel whenever there is sugar available for them to transform into acid. Between times of sugar availability, the saliva in the mouth repairs the dissolved areas through the reverse of the process (Figure 5-5). But over weeks, or months, or years of this sort of back-and-forth exchange, if the repair phase is less than the damage done by the bacteria, a hole (a cavity) forms in the tooth. In time the process progresses into the

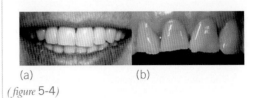

(a)   (b)

(figure 5-4)

Examples of the differing appearances of (a) young and (b) old teeth. The older teeth are darker because the underlying dentin has darkened as the person has aged, and the darker color shows through the translucent enamel. The enamel of the older teeth have a particularly shiny appearance because the surface has been repeatedly polished by daily brushing. The bottom edges of the older teeth are ragged and translucent because the biting surfaces of the teeth have been worn away from the back due to years of abrasion from chewing. Younger teeth are lighter-colored and show more surface texture, and the bottom edge is rounded and relatively unworn.

(figure 5-5)

Schematic representation of the chemical balance between the tooth surface and the fluids of the mouth: (a) represents the calcium phosphate crystals of the tooth surface and the dissolved calcium and phospate in solution. (b) If the acidity rises (for instance, due to plaque bacteria ingesting sugar and then excreting lactic acid), some of the surface crystals release calcium and phosphorus into the oral fluids. (c) Healthy saliva and oral hygiene have resulted in a drop in acidity, and the calcium and phosphorus return to the tooth surface. (d) But if the acidity remains high and/or if the episodes of acidity outnumber the episodes of reduced acidity, the loss of calcium and phosphorus from the tooth into the oral fluids progresses more broadly and deeper into the tooth, eventually forming a cavity.

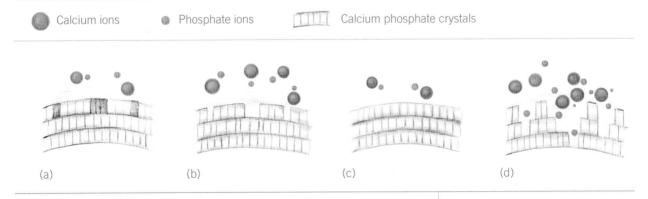

Calcium ions   Phosphate ions   Calcium phosphate crystals

(a)   (b)   (c)   (d)

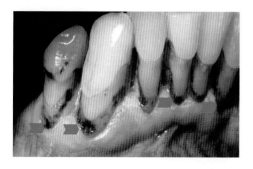

(figure 5-6)

Root caries (severe). Prior periodontal disease has destroyed bony attachment and gingiva, and now decay (arrowheads) can attack the exposed root areas.

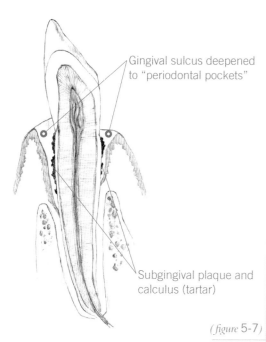

Gingival sulcus deepened to "periodontal pockets"

Subgingival plaque and calculus (tartar)

(figure 5-7)

Schematic of a cross section of a tooth that has experienced damage to its periodontal support due to periodontitis. The presence of bacterial plaque initially resulted in swelling and a bleeding tendency in the gingiva. If host defenses are insufficient, the subgingival bacteria begin to trigger chemicals that dissolve periodontal attachment and alveolar bone. This deepens the gingival sulcus into a periodontal pocket. The pocket is too deep to be cleaned by toothbrushing, and additional bacterial colonies form, continuing the likelihood for the destructive processes to continue.

underlying dentin. Here the destruction accelerates because the dentin is less dense than enamel. If nothing is done to stop the decay (like cleaning out the cavity and putting a filling in it; by the tooth breaking off and making the hole more accessible to the protective effects of saliva; or by the tooth being removed altogether), it will progress until it reaches the pulp chamber. When this occurs, the tissues of the pulp begin to die. In an older person whose pulp nerves have diminished or disappeared, there may be little or no discomfort whatsoever. But in a younger person, this is the cause for extreme sensitivity or excruciating toothache. Yet regardless of whether symptoms are present or not, bacteria inside the pulp chamber have access to the bone and to the bloodstream. Decay in an older person, left untreated because it does not hurt, can thereby become the source of abscesses and infections in the jaw, heart, lungs, joints, kidneys, and brain.

Caries in an older person does not always begin in the enamel. For reasons described in more detail below, it is increasingly likely as a person ages that enlarging areas of root beyond the gum line are exposed to plaque and therefore the threat of caries. The cementum that covers roots is not as smooth as enamel, making it easier for bacteria to stick to the root surface and harder for them to be effectively brushed off it. For these reasons, root caries is a form of caries seldom seen except in older persons (Figure 5-6). Root caries is particularly concerning because it not only tends to progress into a tooth more rapidly than caries that initiates in the enamel but also attacks an area of the tooth that is closer to the pulp chamber.

GUM DISEASES

An entirely different set of bacteria prefers to live on the tooth surface tucked under the gingiva in the gingival sulcus. The bacteria that form this subgingival plaque do not cause decay, but if subgingival plaque remains undisturbed for more than about a day, the gingiva becomes inflamed: swollen, red, and prone to bleeding when brushed. This condition is called gingivitis, and it subsides as soon as the plaque is cleaned away, by either a thorough brushing or through a cleaning at a dentist's office. Under some conditions, not yet perfectly understood, the body reacts to particular species of the subgingival plaque with a form of inflammation that affects not just the gingiva but the entire periodontium (Figure 5-7). The process erodes the periodontal ligament and alveolar bone and is termed periodontitis. Only tiny amounts of these tissues are lost during any one episode of inflammation. But the lost attachment tissues do not regenerate, so a person who repeatedly experiences this process over a lifetime will eventually lose a measurable amount of bone around the tooth, even to the extent that the tooth may become loose or be lost entirely. Because the aggregated tissue loss is often less severe, however, it is common for older individuals—who have had the longest time to be exposed to episodes of this sort of inflammation—to have teeth with parts of the roots exposed. This is the origin of an old-fashioned expression for aging: "growing long in the tooth" (Figure 5-8).

There are several undesirable consequences of periodontitis. One is that teeth that have experienced loss of their supporting bone become much more difficult to clean. This is so because areas once occupied by gingiva are now uncovered and can entrap food debris and bacteria. Special devices and persistence are necessary to keep these areas free of plaque—these are discussed shortly. Another consequence is that the exposure of root areas makes a person prone to attack by root caries. A third consequence of periodontitis, often caused by some of the dental treatments employed to control the disease, is extreme sensitivity to cold and to sweets in the exposed and treated root areas (although this is not often a problem for older adults because of the relative insensitivity of their dental nerves). A fourth consequence is foul-smelling breath, or **halitosis**. The chemicals produced during the tissue destruction of periodontitis cause a distinctive, unpleasant, mothball-type odor in those experiencing the active stage of disease. The fifth consequence of periodontitis is the most serious: loss of a tooth or teeth. This is usually preceded by the affected teeth shifting position or alignment over a period of months or years, eventually becoming so loose that they can be easily moved with the tongue.

Another concerning aspect of periodontitis is still not fully established yet quite alarming in the possibilities it suggests. Several lines of evidence indicate that when the bacteria that cause periodontitis enter the bloodstream, chemicals released by the body in response lead to the development of serious cardiovascular and cerebrovascular (**stroke**) disease. This is still controversial, with preliminary studies still both supporting and refuting the theory.

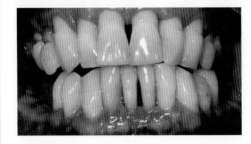

(figure 5-8)

Clinical appearance of teeth and gum tissues with periodontitis.

TOOTH LOSS

Tooth loss is much less common among older persons today than it was just a few decades ago. As recently as 1957, about two-thirds of Americans over age 75 did not have any teeth remaining, but today about two-thirds in that age group have some or many or all of their teeth. Teeth are lost largely due to decay and periodontitis, so attention to preventing or treating these diseases early in their course is the key to keeping your teeth for a lifetime. Once a tooth has been lost it will remain missing for the rest of a person's life; missing one or several teeth is quite common among people of advanced age.

Tooth loss may have only minor or very significant effects on a person's health. Thorough chewing requires teeth, which means that people who are missing some of their teeth end up swallowing their food in larger, less well-chewed pieces. Studies suggest this does not impair nutritional benefit of the food, but it may be a cause for stomach discomfort and

(table 5-1)

MEDICATIONS THAT CAUSE DRY MOUTH

Over 400 drugs can cause dry mouth. Advise your doctor if you are experiencing dry mouth that is troublesome. The following are drugs that are frequently prescribed and that can be associated with dry mouth:

GENERIC NAME	BRAND NAME
alprazolam	Xanax
amitriptyline	Elavil
beclomethasone	Beclovent, Beconase
carbidopa/levodopa	Sinemet
codeine/ acetaminophen	Tylenol #3
cromolyn sodium	Gastrocrom
cyclobenzaprine	Flexeril
diazepam	Valium
diphenhydramine	Benadryl
doxepin	Sinequan
dicyclomine	Bentyl
flavoxate	Urispas
fluoxetine	Prozac
hydrochlorothiazide	Hydrodiuril
hydrocodone/ acetaminophen	Vicodin
hyoscyamine	Levsin, Cystopaz
Isosorbide	Isordil
nortriptylilne	Pamelor
oxybutinin	Ditropan
oxycodone	OxyContin, Percocet, Tylox
penicillin VK	Pen-Vee K
prednisone	Deltasone, Sterapred
prochlorperazine	Compazine
promethazine	Phenergan
propoxyphene/ acetaminophen	Darvon
scopalamine	Transderm-Scop
sertraline	Zoloft
tolterodine	Detrol
triamterene/HCTZ	Dyazide, Maxzide

In addition, many over-the-counter preparations may cause dry mouth.

For example, anitihistamines, such as diphenydramine (Benadryl) and chlorpheniramine (ChlorTrimeton), and decongestants, such as pseudephedrine (Sudafed), used for colds and allergics are also frequently associated with dry mouth.

choking. As a result, people missing some or all of their teeth generally start to avoid foods that are more difficult to chew, such as fresh fruits and vegetables, nuts, and dense bread. When a tooth is lost but the space is not filled in with some sort of dental replacement, the teeth behind the space can, over a period of months or years, begin to lean into the space. This in turn creates sheltered surfaces around the "leaning" teeth that are difficult to clean and that become prone to decay and gum disease.

Even if the space that remains after a tooth is lost is filled with an artificial tooth or teeth, the teeth surrounding the space are put at increased risk for more dental disease. This is because artificial teeth always introduce new surfaces into the mouth that can collect plaque and that can interfere with the body's own defenses and processes for minimizing those deposits. This is not meant to imply that the most common appliances for replacing missing teeth—bridges (which are intended to be permanent) and partial dentures (which are meant to be removed at least daily for cleaning)—are not beneficial. But it does explain why, once a tooth is lost, the adjacent, remaining teeth are often the next to go.

DRY MOUTH

Dry mouth is a frequent complaint among older adults. The perception of a dry mouth, termed xerostomia, is an important and concerning symptom, because saliva is one of the most effective and important defenses against oral disease. Healthy saliva is loaded with calcium, which works to reverse the beginnings of caries. Healthy saliva has many other chemicals that promote healing, fight bacteria, initiate digestion, lubricate the mouth for chewing, speaking, and swallowing, and keep the acidity of the mouth to a minimum. If saliva is absent or diminished, these functions are impaired, leading to higher rates of decay and gum disease, halitosis, difficulty eating, and oral infections and sores.

Because saliva is so critical, it is worth making the distinction that the flow of this important fluid does not diminish just because a person ages but rather as a result of some medicine or disease. A dry mouth, even due to a new medicine, needs to be brought to a doctor's and a dentist's attention (see Table 5-1 for list of medicines that commonly cause dry mouth). The doctor needs to be encouraged to identify a different medicine—one that will address the process for which the prescription was originally written but without the dry mouth side effect. The dentist needs to know about the dry mouth to start the patient on a more robust anticaries program, usually involving frequent home applications of a fluoride gel and dietary counseling and possibly more frequent dental checkups.

OUTSIDE THE MOUTH

A description of causes of oral problems in the elderly would be incomplete if it did not include factors outside the mouth: diet, diseases, and medicines.

Diet: Diet is strongly associated with dental decay. Sugar in the diet feeds the bacteria that cause decay. Saliva washes away the sugar and dilutes the acids the bacteria produce, but the longer sugar stays in the mouth, the longer is the interval during which the plaque can produce acid. This is why it is important to brush the teeth as soon as possible after a meal. And this is why sticky forms of sugar, like caramel and pastries, can be particularly harmful if a person is not diligent with oral hygiene. Unfortunately, desserts and other sweet goodies are often much more available to seniors for a variety of reasons. Often social events and activities at seniors' centers include desserts. Retired people may spend more time at home than they did when they were working, and homes usually contain treats for visitors and special occasions.

Diseases: Several diseases commonly encountered as people age are associated with threats to oral health. *Diabetes* affects nearly one in ten older Americans. People with diabetes have more difficulty fighting infections in general, and periodontal diseases are definitely infections. Diabetics tend to get gingivitis and periodontitis more readily, and more seriously, than people not afflicted with the disease. And recent evidence shows that periodontitis interferes with a diabetic's ability to control his or her blood sugar, resulting in a sort of vicious cycle. *Arthritis* affects over half the Americans over age 65. If it affects the hands, the ability to hold a toothbrush or to use dental floss may be impaired. If arthritis affects the shoulder or elbow, the strength, flexibility, and endurance needed to effectively clean the mouth may be impaired. *Stroke* may impede oral care in much the same way or force a person to use their nondominant hand to perform oral hygiene. *Depression* is the most common psychiatric diagnosis in people over age 65. Someone who is depressed usually overlooks the activities needed to take care of oneself, such as bathing, eating, and cleaning the teeth. A common complaint associated with depression is dry mouth, which was described earlier as an unhealthy, high-risk oral state, particularly so if the mouth is not kept clean. People with *dementia* (Alzheimer's and other forms) typically lose the ability to care for themselves entirely, and the effects of this neglect do not spare the mouth.

Medications: Medications can have serious effects on the health of the mouth in several ways, three of which are mentioned here. The most common way was discussed earlier: the most frequently reported side effect of medications is xerostomia, or dry mouth. There is no single mechanism through which xerostomia occurs, and so a broad variety of drugs can have this troubling effect. Secondly, sores may form in the mouth when certain medications are first prescribed (Figure 5-9). The skin covering the inside of the mouth, the mucosa, is the most rapidly regenerating tissue of its type in the body. For this reason, slight changes in the body's chemistry often are reflected by temporary flaws in the tissue, which then can appear as painful oral ulcerations. Finally, several specific medications (PHENYTOIN [DILANTIN] for seizures; CYCLOSPORINE [IMURAN] after an organ transplant; and the calcium channel blockers prescribed for cardiovascular disease, e.g., NIFEDIPINE, [PROCARDIA]) can cause a very severe and rather unsightly (and unhygienic) growth in the gum tissue in

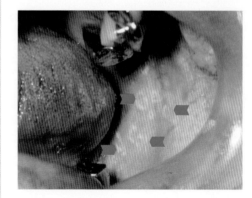

(figure 5-9)

Example of mucosal lesions (arrowheads) caused, in this case, by a prescription of hydrochlorothiazide for management of hypertension.

a quarter to a half of the people receiving the drug. This change, termed **gingival hyperplasia** (Figure 5-10), can be avoided by keeping the teeth free of plaque before the condition develops.

MOUTH CARE

There are three lifestyle components for keeping the mouth healthy: good oral hygiene, a diet that limits sweets (described in the previous section), and regular examinations by a dentist.

ORAL HYGIENE

The first component, good oral hygiene, needs to be focused on keeping the mouth free of plaque. This is true regardless of your age, but as the years pass, several features combine to make daily oral hygiene more challenging. It has already been pointed out that a lifetime's exposure to periodontitis may result in teeth in advanced age that appear to be longer, that have exposed root areas, or that appear crowded (Figure 5-11). Teeth that have been lost may be replaced by fixed or removable artificial teeth (bridges and partials), which represent new areas on which plaque forms. Older mouths are more likely to have less saliva, due to drugs and diseases, and saliva is critically important for fighting plaque and reversing some of its effects. But someone of any age who is motivated to keep his or her teeth throughout life will find the time, and the techniques, that will get the job done.

The most important tool for oral hygiene is the toothbrush. There is a great deal of science to toothbrushing, involving the stiffness and lengths of the bristles, how they are arranged, whether they have rounded ends or not, and how many of them are there. Toothbrush handles have evolved tremendously in the past 15 years, so that many now feature ergonomic design, grips, nonskid surfaces, and flexibility that prohibit the exertion of too much force.

What matters most in a toothbrush is *using it*. If it feels good to you, use it. If feeling good is accomplished with something that costs a dollar, there is little reason to spend more. If you like fancier, prettier, more gadget-laden devices and, by spending more, you have more motivation to brush your teeth, get the *latest model*. This goes for electric toothbrushes as well: if they are not used, they won't do a better job of cleaning your teeth than a popsicle stick. But if you like the feeling of using an electric and you like the way your teeth feel and the way the hygienist compliments you on your teeth and gums when you go for a checkup, that's what counts.

Using a brush correctly involves brushing each tooth, and each surface of each tooth. The bristles should be angled at about 45 degrees to the teeth and placed with their ends right along the gumline, and the head of the brush should describe small circles as you push the bristles toward the tooth. You should feel the bristles work under the gumlines and between the teeth. Once the brush has described two to four circles over one tooth, you can move to the next tooth. Start at one end of one jaw, and when you have done the whole jaw on the lip side, repeat the process on the

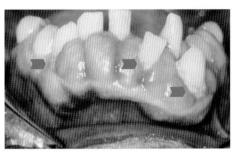

(figure 5-10*)*

Gingival hyperplasia (severe). A number of drugs will stimulate exaggerated and often irreversible gingival growth in response to poor oral hygiene (plaque deposits indicated by arrowheads). This particular patient had been taking felodipine, a calcium channel blocker, for about eight months, without any particular attention being paid to his teeth either by himself or his physician. Other calcium channel blockers may have this effect to varying, usually more modest, degrees. Additional classes of drugs associated with this gingival effect are phenytoin (prescribed for seizures) and cyclosporine (prescribed to prevent organ rejection after transplant).

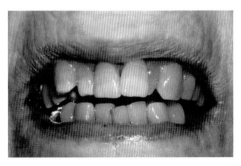

(figure 5-11*)*

As a person ages, the teeth are very slowly pushed forward in the mouth. A typical result is that the front teeth begin to have a crowded or crooked appearance even if the teeth were straight in youth.

tongue side, and then cover both sides of the other jaw in the same way. You will need to switch your grip a bit and just use the tip of the brush to clean the tongue side of your top and bottom front teeth and to get behind your back top teeth.

When you brush correctly, you will probably need to replace your brush every month or two. As soon as a brush has bristles that are no longer standing in neat rows, it is time for a new one.

Toothpaste is important in several ways. First, its taste masks the less pleasant taste and odor of plaque. When an experiment provides two groups of people with different toothpastes for several months—one group gets toothpaste with flavor and the other gets toothpaste that is identical in every way except *without* flavor—the flavor group brushes much longer and does a better job of removing plaque. Toothpaste also has some gentle abrasives that help polish stains off the teeth, sort of the difference between scrubbing a sink with a washcloth versus using cleanser. Toothpastes also usually have an ingredient that works like a detergent, helping to loosen adherent plaque. In recent years, toothpastes are increasingly offered with a "buffet" of possible additional ingredients: ones that may lighten teeth (these products may not be effective in lightening teeth that are darkened by age); antibacterial agents that reduce plaque and/or reduce halitosis; and chemicals that desensitize healthy teeth that are reacting uncomfortably to cold, hot, or sweets.

The most important ingredient of toothpaste, however, is something that has been available since the mid-1950s, and has utterly transformed the dental profession and the dental health of the developed world: fluoride. Fluoride encourages the chemical reaction that reverses decay. When you use a fluoride toothpaste, the fluoride stays in your mouth for several minutes, assisting the saliva to deliver calcium back into the teeth. Teeth that are cleaned with fluoride toothpaste end up being much more resistant to being dissolved by acid produced by plaque. Fluoride toothpaste and fluoride in drinking water have helped people of all ages keep their teeth at an unprecedented rate. Fluoride is available in toothpaste in several forms, but the ingredients are essentially all equally effective. You cannot make a mistake in selecting a toothpaste, as long as it contains fluoride. You can make a mistake, however, by missing out on benefiting from fluoride by deliberately selecting a product that does not contain it, or by using no paste, or by using salt or baking soda. None of these does harm to the teeth, and with good brushing technique, you will be able to clean the teeth effectively. But fluoride really *prevents* dental decay, and it is readily available in almost every flavor imaginable—why bend over backward to avoid a good thing?

Dental floss is a hygiene product that effectively cleans the sides of teeth (like a squeegee cleaning water off a window) where they touch each other and beneath the adjacent gum line. The use of floss is not nearly as popular as toothbrushing, because flossing takes extra time, it is somewhat messy, it can be uncomfortable, and many people have difficulty mastering the manually challenging technique. In older people with "long" teeth, it

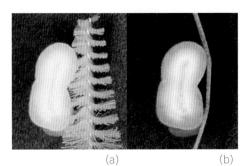

(a)   (b)

(*figure* 5-12)

A cross section of a tooth root, showing how the sides of roots have concave shapes that are difficult to clean. (a) "Interproximal" cleaning devices are capable of cleaning along these surfaces, once the roots are exposed, in a way that (b) floss cannot.

is questionable that it even is as effective as it is in younger people, because the roots of teeth (which are exposed when a tooth looks long) usually have slight concavities along their sides. That means floss cannot clean the whole side of a tooth root the way it can the enamel-covered part of the tooth. A very useful compromise is the use of "interdental cleaners." These are small cone- or cylinder-shaped brushes that fit on handles, and can be gently worked between teeth and underneath bridges to keep all surfaces clean (Figure 5-12). The brush tips are so small that they may wear out quickly and require replacement several times each month.

Mouthwash is not a necessary part of daily oral hygiene. A few products have high alcohol content and other ingredients that are antibacterial. But saliva will dilute, in a few minutes, most of these effects, casting doubt on manufacturers' claims to the contrary. Halitosis has its origins in processes that are not addressed by mouthwash, like inadequate oral hygiene, or a sinus or lung infection, or components in the diet. Using mouthwash to address chronic oral malodor will only be effective for a matter of minutes before the underlying source overpowers the progressively diluted mouthwash. Some rinses specifically contain fluoride, but extensive study has demonstrated that the effect of the additive in this delivery form, while helpful, is minor.

If an older adult starts experiencing an increased rate of decay, or is suddenly faced with a situation that is expected to lead to increased decay (such as receiving radiation or chemotherapy, which can cause severe xerostomia, or following a stroke that interferes with the ability to hold and manipulate a toothbrush), many dentists will prescribe stronger fluoride rinses than can be purchased without a prescription; or they will prescribe a fluoride gel to apply to the teeth. Both of these have demonstrated positive effect when used according to directions. In both cases, the teeth need to be brushed in the usual manner, with toothpaste, before using the fluoride product. This is so even for so-called brush-on gels, which are not toothpaste and will be unable to have their greatest impact unless the teeth are first thoroughly cleaned.

DENTAL OFFICE

The third requirement for a lifetime of oral health is regular visits to the dentist, who can spot problems early on, before little bits of decay turn into broken teeth, root canals, or extractions, and before a little bit of bleeding gums from gingivitis has cost you a tooth or several teeth.

Waiting to see the dentist until you perceive a problem is like holding off checking your oil until the engine freezes—sure, now you know for sure that you've got a problem, but it is a much bigger deal (and expense) than just adding another quart. By the time most people are in their 50s, pain in the mouth represents a process that is now so advanced that the time and expense involved in fixing it is many times more than it has to be, if it can even be fixed at all. This is because the teeth themselves no longer have the internal "early warning device" they had when you were younger, as discussed previously.

Dentists check your teeth for decay and make sure that fillings and crowns are still sound. The condition of the gums and the alveolar bone are assessed. If you have a denture, the dentist makes sure the gum on which it rests is healthy and that the denture teeth bite against each other and or your natural teeth in the most effective way. An extremely important part of every older person's dental checkup is an exam for oral cancer, discussed in greater detail in the section "Oral Cancer." Precancerous mucosa is not difficult to spot if you know what to look for, but most physicians have never been trained to recognize the disease. If only to be sure the soft tissues of the mouth are healthy, everyone should have a thorough oral exam by a dentist at least annually. Twice a year is recommended for those who still occasionally get decay or build up lots of plaque. Patients who have experienced significant periodontitis or have dry mouths may need to come in for thorough cleaning of the teeth three or even four times each year.

In addition to a person receiving a thorough cleaning once or more frequently each year, the dental office treats the results of dental decay. If the decay is detected soon enough, it can often be treated with chemicals that restore the missing calcium to the tooth. These can be applied in the office or as part of a home-care routine. If the decay is more advanced, some sort of filling or other restoration is probably necessary. When you are younger, most decay affects teeth that do not yet have fillings. As you age, there is a greater chance that decay affects teeth that already have one or more fillings. Eventually a tooth gets to the point that it can no longer be filled because there is so little real tooth left. If this happens, the dentist will likely recommend a crown (also called "cap"). This is usually a two-appointment procedure and costs five to ten times as much as a filling because of the time, material, and laboratory expense involved.

Dentists have an increasingly "realistic" set of materials with which to restore teeth. Patients who are dissatisfied by the appearance of dark metal fillings in their back teeth may achieve a much more attractive smile by replacing silver fillings with tooth-colored ones. But a few precautionary notes are in order. First, despite periodic episodes of publicity to the contrary, no dental material lasts as long or has been so thoroughly tested for possible toxic effects as dental amalgam—silver fillings. Claims of curing arthritis or multiple sclerosis by replacing silver fillings with plastic or porcelain ones are fraudulent and unfounded, and have been the basis for countless successful criminal and civil litigations. Second, as lifelike as the plastic and porcelain techniques are, they usually cost two to three times as much but last only five years or less, versus 20 or more for amalgam.

If decay has proceeded to the extent that the dental pulp is encountered when the dentist is removing decay, the tooth will need a root canal. The dentist needs to widen the hole into the pulp chamber and to remove all the pulp. The inside of the chamber is then carefully filed clean all the way to the end of the roots with tiny files, and then the space is filled with an inert material. Nine out of ten root canals cause the patients little to no discomfort during and after the procedure. But that tenth one,

DOCTOR'S DIARY

I first met Edwin S., who was 86 and healthy, when he wanted me to do something about his smile, which made him look like a jack-o'-lantern: every other top tooth was missing and his remaining teeth twinkled with gold. An examination of Edwin S.'s mouth revealed a number of old but intact gold restorations, several teeth broken off at the gumline, and lots of decay. The gums were healthy, and the teeth were clean. I suggested removing his remaining upper teeth and making him an upper plate and a lower partial denture.

Edwin S. was appalled: "Dentures? But I've taken care of my teeth all my life!"

On further questioning, it became clear that his life had gone on hold when, nine years earlier, his wife was diagnosed with Alzheimer's disease. Since that time his entire existence had revolved around her: managing all the household duties while attending to her increasingly difficult needs. With all these demands, he had completely overlooked himself—and his teeth had taken a beating. His wife had since passed away, and he had resumed taking proper care of himself—but some dental damage was already done.

I admitted that I had jumped to an erroneous conclusion, assuming that an older man with a deteriorated teeth would prefer to settle for a quick, less costly plan. I then suggested a more involved and expensive treatment that included some root canals and bridges.

Three months and many appointments later, Edwin S.'s reconstruction was complete. That spring, my assistant showed me an article in the local newspaper, describing a volunteer transportation program for seniors that Edwin S. "and his fiancé" had started. There was Edwin S. with a lovely white-haired lady on his arm, both of them smiling broadly!

---

which is usually the one made necessary because the patient came in with toothache, is the uncomfortable experience that gives root canals their rather unsavory reputation.

Replacements for missing teeth made out of elephant tusk and gold wire have been unearthed in 2400-year-old Etruscan ruins, and dentists continue to develop new and ingenious methods for helping patients who have lost teeth. Removable dentures are the least costly way of putting teeth back when the natural ones are missing. If natural teeth are present on both sides of a toothless space, a fixed bridge may be fabricated (by means, and with results, that have improved significantly over the last 2400 years). The most recent approach for replacing a tooth that has been lost is an implant, in which a machined cylinder of titanium is surgically inserted into a hole drilled in the alveolar bone and allowed to "integrate" with the bone beneath the gum for several months. A tiny window of gum is then removed from atop the implant, and a second piece of metal, which will now poke through the gum, is attached firmly onto the implant. A false tooth, bridge, or denture can then be anchored to that second piece of metal.

Implants are quite expensive, but when properly planned and placed, they have a very high success rate. One of the most reliable predictors for a successful implant is the experience of the person who provides the care, so do some investigating before you undertake this treatment. And if you decide to get an implant, always work *first* with the dentist who will actually complete the final restoration, not with the dentist (or oral surgeon or other specialist) who places the implant. This is crucial for an optimal outcome, because the dentist who plans the whole sequence of treatment will have taken factors into account—such as location of other teeth or implants, the bite, the space between the jaws, and where the artificial tooth or teeth will sit relative to the gum and to each other, that those who are not going to be completing the restoration may not be as concerned about.

DENTURES

Shakespeare described the "last scene" of life (i.e., old age) as the time when one is "sans teeth, sans eyes, sans taste, sans everything" (As You Like It, act 2, scene 7). But as has been pointed out earlier, the stereotype of aging that includes being toothless is out of date. More than two-thirds of Americans over age 75 have some, many, or all of their teeth.

And yet about a third of them, and a lower but still unacceptable proportion of American adults in their 40s, 50s, and 60s, make up the approximately 10 to 15 million denture wearers in this country. About two-thirds of these individuals have no natural teeth at all. Approximately 90 to 95% of those choose to wear artificial replacements—complete dentures. What should you expect from a denture? Why can't you just buy one out of a catalog? How well should you expect them to work? How long should they last? What is the best way to care for them?

Dentures need to look right and they need to work right. Looking right means having the approximate shape and color of a mouthful of teeth that are positioned in the mouth in a natural-looking way. Working right is trickier. Dentures have to conform to the inside of the mouth so that the forces of chewing are not borne by one or two spots on the jaws but can be distributed all along the jaw. A bottom denture needs to keep out of the way of the tongue, lips, and cheeks yet stay put over the gums while bathed in saliva. To accomplish all this, a denture needs to be as big as possible, to keep from sliding into places it does not belong, and also as small as possible, to avoid getting moved around by the muscles. A top plate needs to fit the roof of the mouth as closely as possible so that it defies gravity and stays up. The top and the bottom plates need to position the jaws the correct distance apart, and they have to be oriented correctly in relation to each other and to the face, so that the chewing muscles can work properly.

To accomplish all this, everything about the denture must be custom-made for each mouth: the fit of the gums, the position and color and shape of the teeth, and the way they bite. The fabrication of dentures usually begins with the dentist obtaining a three-dimensional replica of the mouth. This is accomplished by placing over the upper or lower jaw some soft material that then becomes stiff due to temperature or chemical changes (an impression). The impression comes out of the mouth and is filled with plaster, which sets to yield a strong replica of the jaw (the master cast), and the process is repeated for the other jaw. The second step in making a denture records how far apart the two jaws need to be (bite registration), and how they relate side to side, again with some soft material that becomes harder. The dentist then affixes the upper and lower master casts, held together by the bite registration, onto a device that will permit the casts to move in relation to each other much as jaws do. Then, using preformed, individual, artificial teeth (that are startlingly realistic in appearance), the dentures are sculpted out of wax (the trial denture). The trial denture is placed in the mouth and adjusted until it looks and feels acceptable. At this point, a laboratory procedure is employed to replace the wax portion of the trial denture with denture plastic.

Dentures do an excellent job of looking like teeth. And when fabricated properly they make it easier to speak, because the tongue and lips do not have to reach as far to make many of the speech sounds like f and v and s. But chewing can be another matter. Most people do very well eating with dentures after a period of practice. But studies going back more than a century consistently show that people who have dentures prefer softer foods and need to cut their food into smaller pieces just because chewing is not as effective as with natural teeth. There are several reasons that eating can be less successful with dentures. One is that the lower denture usually moves a bit during chewing so the tongue, which should be moving the biggest food pieces onto the teeth where they can get chewed, is instead kept busy holding the denture still. Another reason is that dentures sit on your gums, and gums are really not designed to withstand the forces that are involved in chewing. Imagine if, instead of walking on your feet, which are designed for the purpose and fairly well padded on the bottom, you had to walk everywhere on your knees. Knees are not intended for this, and they certainly are not padded for the stress. Like knees, gums consist of thin, tough skin attached to the bone with very little padding, and they can only take so much pressure. As a result, the forces that natural teeth can exert in chewing are from 5 to 50 times as strong as the forces that people with dentures can exert—just like the difference between how far you can walk on your feet and how far you could walk on your knees. But except in unusual circumstances, people with dentures still function much better than people without teeth who do not have, or do not use, dentures.

An important problem that occurs over time with dentures is that these lifelike appliances are inert: they do not grow or change over time, unlike our bodies. When a tooth is extracted, the purpose for the alveolar bone that held the tooth is gone, and so, over months and years, the bone goes away too. Studies have shown that even decades after a person has had their teeth extracted, the alveolar bone continues to diminish, ever so slightly, with every passing year. As a result, dentures generally loosen in time, and have to be modified or even replaced periodically. Some lucky people manage successfully for 20 years or longer with the same false teeth; others start experiencing difficulties after a matter of months. It is because dentures do not last forever, and usually do not work as well as teeth, even when new, that dentists usually try to put off removing all of a person's teeth as long as possible.

When time has passed and a set of dentures no longer fits as well as it once did, it is time to see the dentist. The dentist will determine whether the denture can be adjusted to improve the fit or whether the denture can be relined (the surface of the denture that sits against the gums is replaced with a new layer that fits the gums intimately), or will need to be replaced. You might be able to buy a little time with denture adhesives, which are very effective at helping hold dentures securely in the mouth. Adhesives are good products and dramatically improve the chewing ability of dentures even when the dentures are new and fit perfectly. But a denture that used to work well without adhesive, but now needs adhesive to keep it from moving or dropping, merits evaluation. There are products other than adhesives, also purchased at drug stores (and invariably in the same section of the store as adhesives), that claim to "reline" dentures or "cushion" them, but these products are harmful to your mouth and to the denture: they bond to the denture surface, they degrade in a matter of days or weeks, and then the denture is ruined. If a material cannot be rinsed or brushed out of a denture on a daily basis, don't buy it!

Daily oral care is not just for the teeth and gums. Dentures build plaque just like teeth do, although denture plaque contains different germs. Most dentures are made from a very hard but rather porous plastic called polymethylmethacrylate, which looks like Swiss cheese under the microscope. The tiny holes fill with germs of the yeast *Candida albicans,* and the particles cannot be dislodged just by rinsing or brushing. Commercial cleansing agents are very effective at sanitizing dentures and thereby preventing a reaction in tissue that contacts the denture. A teaspoon of household bleach in a cup of water works too, but not as well as the "fizzy" commercial products unless the denture has been thoroughly scrubbed first (Figure 5-13). If your denture has shiny silver metal as part of its structure, you want to avoid keeping the denture in the soaking solution for longer than about 10 minutes, or the metal will darken over time. All denture-cleansing agents can severely burn the inside of your mouth if not thoroughly rinsed away before the denture is inserted. Finally, if you use adhesive, always be sure to clean all the material out of the denture before adding more. Warm water makes this easier, and makes it easier to remove any adhesive that is adhering to your gums as well.

Two final suggestions. First, your gums should get a break from dentures at least a few hours every day, to give the gums a rest and to allow them to benefit from the healthful effects of unrestricted access to saliva and oxygen. For most people, sleeping without their dentures is the easiest way to do this. Second, while the dentures are out of the mouth, they should remain in water and then be thoroughly cleaned before being put back into the mouth. Deposits on the dentures become much more difficult to remove if they dry onto the plastic.

OTHER ORAL CONDITIONS

The teeth, the lack of teeth, the gums, and a dry mouth make up the majority of problems that bring people to the dentist office. But the largest area of your mouth—the tissue that covers your lips, cheeks, tongue, palate, and the floor of your mouth—is also prone to a wide variety of disorders, ranging from trivial to life threatening and from painless to agonizing. Because it is relatively straightforward to examine your own mouth, using a flashlight and the bathroom mirror, it is useful to have an understanding of the common disorders that affect the mouth. It is even a good idea to regularly examine all you can of your mouth, even if you do not perceive you have a problem, much like women are encouraged to examine their breasts or men their testes.

ORAL CANCER

It probably does not come as a surprise that the most deadly disease that can affect the mouth is **oral cancer**. Cancers of the lips, tongue, floor of mouth, cheeks, and upper throat (oropharynx) are found in about 30,000 Americans each year, and 95% of these cases occur in people over age 50. About 8000 Americans die from oral cancer annually. Oral cancer is actually more common, and deadlier, than cancers of the cervix, ovaries, testes, stomach, kidneys, or liver. In general, men are twice as likely as women to have oral cancer, and about 8 times as likely to have lip cancer.

If oral cancer is found early, while it is small and has not spread, the proportion of people who will survive for 5 years is much higher than for most cancers. But if the cancer is only discovered after it has spread to lymph nodes or other tissues, the survival rate is poor, and the surgical

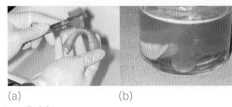

(a)   (b)

(figure 5-13)

Dentures need to be thoroughly cleaned at least daily. (a) Use of a denture brush is effective for removing debris, although cleaning should always be done over a towel or a sink filled with water to prevent damage to the denture if it is accidentally dropped. The toothpaste used for natural teeth should not be used with a denture brush because products designed to polish dental enamel will dull and eventually wear away denture materials. (b) The most thorough method for cleaning a denture is to leave it in a dilute bleach or commercial soaking agent for about 20 minutes. The chemicals in either solution are able to disinfect tiny pits in the surface of the denture in a manner that a brush cannot.

(figure 5-14)

Two examples of oral cancer. Typical characteristics are a red or mixed red and white appearance, a hard texture, and a disturbance in the normal contours of the tissue (arrowheads). Spontaneous bleeding is not unusual in advanced cases.

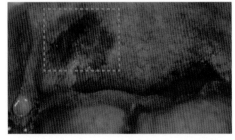

(figure 5-15)

A red patch, or erythroplakia, is a very concerning sign and requires immediate assessment by a health professional.

and radiation treatments employed often leave victims disfigured and dysfunctional. This is the reason it is so important to have regular dental examinations, whether or not you believe you have a dental problem and whether or not you have teeth. Physicians as a rule are not trained to examine the mouth, so failing to get regular dental attention raises the likelihood that any oral cancer that forms will only be found when it has progressed to a point that can only bring about an unhappy ending.

Oral cancer is very strongly associated with smoking tobacco, chewing tobacco, and drinking alcohol while smoking tobacco. Avoiding these habits is the best prevention for oral cancer. Smokers and other users of tobacco should be particularly vigilant about seeing a dentist at least yearly, to optimize the likelihood that any cancer that does form will be discovered while it is still small and relatively curable.

Identifying oral cancer in the early stages requires some familiarity with the range of afflictions that can affect the mouth. But routinely looking in your mouth will soon permit you to recognize when something appears that was not there before, which is really what a dentist is looking for whenever an exam is performed. The key to finding something that does not belong is a sharp transition in color, from pink to red, with no transition zone, for instance (Figure 5-14). Another clue is if something that looks funny is not mirrored on the opposite side of the mouth. A third clue is a swelling under the skin that feels hard and as if it cannot be wiggled around.

If a patch of red or white (or mixed red and white) mucosa is detected in the mouth, and one of the other clues (or both) also is true, then you should seek a professional opinion from a dentist, oral surgeon, or ear-nose-throat doctor *without delay* (Figure 5-15). The professional will know whether you have just been cautious but have no need to worry—or whether a small sample of the tissue (biopsy) needs to be removed for inspection under the microscope. But immediate attention is vital—oral cancer can advance rapidly.

ORAL DISEASES

Other oral diseases that commonly occur, cause discomfort, and have characteristic appearances, include candidiasis, herpes simplex, herpes zoster, aphthous stomatitis, and lichen planus.

Candidiasis, a population explosion of one of the yeast organisms that is found in smaller numbers in half to two-thirds of the population under normal conditions, can take one of several appearances. It can look like small, white, "cottage cheeselike" spots that are easily scraped off (leaving a red, raw surface underneath) the cheeks, inside of the lips, palate, or throat (Figure 5-16). This is usually associated with recently receiving an antibiotic or saliva-reducing medication, both of which reduce the normal population controls on oral yeast. Or candidiasis can be a sore, reddened area that occurs only where a denture sits against the palate—behind the denture the mucosa looks normal (Figure 5-17). Not surprisingly, this form is most commonly associated with a denture that is not kept clean, is

---

FAMILY JOURNAL: MY TWO AUNTS

A merry 90-year-old, Theresa W. lived with her younger sister, Madeline P., age 88. The sisters spent two to four days each week at the local senior center. Lately, however, Theresa W. had been less enthusiastic about going or being in public, because a persistent unpleasant taste in her mouth caused her to have offensive breath. Even worse, her dentures, which have worked perfectly well since she got them two years ago, had become wobbly, and she was afraid they'd pop out while she was talking or eating.

Since her dentist of over 40 years retired, Theresa W. got a referral from her physician and went to see the young dentist. After examining her, the dentist asked, to her embarrassment, whether she recently had a urinary tract infection. She said yes but that antibiotics had cleared it up. He explained that the drugs had changed the balance of germs in her mouth and that she now had a yeast infection, which gave her the bad taste and made her dentures loose. He prescribed a rinse and strongly recommended that she remove her dentures each night. This was contrary to what her previous dentist had told her, but she agreed.

Within a few days the bad taste disappeared, but the dentures remained loose. She returned to the dentist who explained that her habit of wearing the plates all night had caused her gums to swell. Now that they were not swollen but healthy, it was a good time to reline the plates. She agreed and was very pleased with the result.

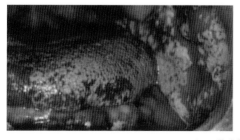

(*figure* 5-16)

Thrush is an infection by the yeast organism *Candida albicans*. The whitish areas are easily rubbed off, revealing red, irritated tissue underneath that easily bleeds. The mouth may be sore, and a persistent unpleasant taste may be present, or the infected person may be unaware of the infection.

not being kept out of the mouth long enough daily, does not fit properly, or a combination of these. Candidiasis can also appear as painful, oozing cracks in the corners of the mouth (Figure 5-18). This condition, called **angular cheilitis**, is usually due to the use of dentures that really need to be replaced. With the gradual loss of the bone on which the dentures rest, the nose and chin slowly get closer and closer over the years (Figure 5-19). As a result, the fold at the corner of the mouth stays moist as the skin sits on itself.

Angular cheilitis can be treated without anything being done to the dentures, but without new dentures to reposition the chin and the nose back to where they would be if natural teeth were present, the infection will return again and again. Unlike oral cancer, candidiasis is usually not very serious, unless the infected person has some problem with the immune system, like AIDS or leukemia, or is undergoing chemotherapy for cancer. Management of the condition is accomplished through the use of one or more of a variety of rinses, salves, or pills. Persons who have dentures should be particularly fastidious about denture hygiene during treatment for candidiasis, in order to limit the likelihood for recurrence.

The appearance of a lesion of **herpes simplex**, commonly known as a "cold sore," is probably not a surprise to an older person. This is because people are usually infected with this virus as children or young adults, and then for the rest of life they periodically experience localized eruptions of the virus. People who are afflicted by herpes simplex learn that the appearance of sores follows a strict pattern. Usually one to three days before anything appears on the lips, gums, or the roof of the mouth, an itching feeling is present at the site where a sore will appear. When something becomes visible, it is usually multiple, small, circular, yellowish blisters with red outlines that, within a day or two, have opened and combined to form an irregular, raw uncomfortable sore (Figure 5-20). The sore resolves in a week or so but in the meantime is teeming with the virus. Because the virus is highly contagious, someone with a herpes simplex sore needs to refrain from kissing. As with candidiasis, herpes simplex is only serious for people with compromised immune systems; for everyone else, it is an uncomfortable annoyance but little more. If a drug called ACYCLOVIR is taken as soon as the symptoms of the sore appear, the lesion will be less severe and will heal more quickly. But it will still continue to recur sporadically, there is presently no solution for getting it to stop altogether.

Herpes zoster, commonly known as **shingles**, is caused by the same virus as chicken pox. The virus resides in a large nerve and periodically causes pain and sores along the distribution of that nerve. Shingles most commonly affects the chest, back, or abdomen, beginning with tingling and pain followed a few days later with blisters that open and then crust. But it may affect one of the nerves that serves the mouth and face, and if it does, the resulting discomfort can be so severe as to interfere with eating. A characteristic of herpes zoster, whether on the body or the mouth, is that it is restricted to one side of the body or the other, it seldom if ever

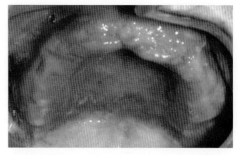

(figure 5-17)

The roof of the mouth affected by an unclean denture or one that is seldom or never removed. The tissue may or may not be sore and may bleed if only minor pressure is exerted on it. Most cases of denture stomatitis like this are caused by the yeast organism *Candida albicans.*

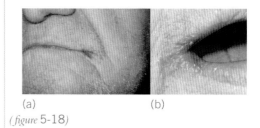

(a)   (b)

(figure 5-18)

(a) Angular cheilitis, usually caused by the yeast *Candida albicans,* is commonly found in persons whose nose and chin are closer than they were before their teeth or dentures wore down. (b) With the mouth overclosed, the corners of the mouth stay moist and become more prone to infection by this common oral organism.

(figure 5-19*)*

When the nose and the chin get closer because teeth or dentures have worn out, the person often looks as if he or she is sticking the chin forward. This is because the lower jaw travels forward as it closes, making the chin appear more prominent.

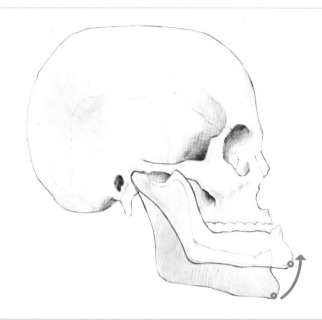

crosses the midline. Herpes zoster responds to acyclovir as well, in terms of limiting the extent and duration of discomfort. But as with herpes simplex, shingles is a condition that comes, goes, and comes back again and again unpredictably.

Aphthous stomatitis is commonly referred to as "canker sores." Like herpes simplex sores, they come, get better, and then reappear some time later. But there the similarity stops. Herpes affects lips and tissues that do not move around, like the roof of the mouth or the gums. Aphthous ulcers attack the inside of the lips, the inside of the cheeks, and the sides of the tongue. Herpes lesions begin as small blisters and coalesce into irregular, raw patches. Aphthous ulcers are generally round and do not feature a blistered stage (Figure 5-21). Herpes lesions are viral and quite contagious, whereas the actual cause for aphthous ulcerations is unclear, and they are not transmissible. There are many folk remedies that are purported to relieve the discomfort of aphthous ulcerations, and most claim to make the sores disappear in 7 to 10 days. If the lesions are just left alone, they will heal themselves, in about 7 to 10 days, so you can decide for yourself about the worth of your Great Aunt Millicent's surefire cure.

Lichen planus is not nearly as common as the other oral disorders described, but it is not rare and can be mistaken for an early stage of oral cancer. For this reason, lichen planus is usually biopsied when first noted and periodically thereafter, to ensure that it is not a malignancy. Lichen planus may cause itchy, silvery, scaly areas on the knees and elbows, but it is most common in the mouth. Oral lichen planus has two different presentations. The more common is painless and appears on the inside of the cheeks and/or lips or floor of the mouth as vaguely reddish areas

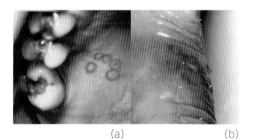

(a)   (b)

(figure 5-20*)*

The very earliest appearance of a herpes simplex sore, also called a cold sore. These small, distinct blisters will soon burst and blend together into an irregular, oozing, extremely sensitive and very infectious lesion. Their occurrence is limited to (a) the roof of the mouth, (b) the outside of the lips, and (not shown) areas of the gums adjacent to the teeth.

with spidery white internal lines (Figure 5-22). The less common form features large, painful red and white blisters in the same areas (Figure 5-23). Lichen planus comes and goes over years; times of flare-up seem associated with increased stress in the person's life. Lichen planus is observed more commonly in diabetics than in nondiabetics. Painful oral lichen planus responds very well to a week's course of steroids of steadily decreasing dosage.

SALIVARY GLAND DISORDERS

The importance of saliva to the health and comfortable function of the oral cavity has already been covered in some detail. The fact that salivary flow does not diminish just because a person gets older has also been stressed. It has been pointed out earlier that medications typically prescribed for diseases that are more common in the elderly are the leading cause for dry mouth in older people. But they are not the only cause for this serious dysfunctional state.

To gain a better understanding of disturbances to saliva flow, we first need to understand how the process works in health. Saliva is mostly produced by three pairs of glands: the parotid, the sublingual, and the submandibular. The *parotids* are located in front of and slightly below the ear, and introduce their saliva into the mouth through ducts high up in the cheek (Figure 5-24). The ducts are covered by a little flap of skin, and if you look in the right place while pushing on your cheek, you can actually see the saliva flow out. The *submandibular* and *sublingual glands* are located beneath the lower jaw and beneath the tongue, respectively, and introduce their fluids from small ducts in the floor of the mouth. The most prominent pair of these ducts is on either side of the tough, fibrous band that runs between the floor of the mouth and the underside of the tongue. The ducts are easily seen just above the floor of the mouth when you touch your tongue to the roof of the mouth (Figure 5-25). About 10% of the saliva in your mouth, however, is produced by "minor salivary glands"—dozens of small clusters of saliva-producing cells that are located on the inside of the lips, cheeks, and the roof of the mouth (Figure 5-26).

Saliva is produced in a two-stage process. In the first stage, fluid is drawn from blood that feeds the gland. The second stage begins when that fluid travels from where it was pulled from the blood to where it actually enters the mouth. The "plumbing" along which the fluid travels is not passive, but actually adds and removes various chemicals. The fluid that is formed in the first stage can either be very watery (serous saliva) or very thick and rich in protein (mucinous saliva). The parotid gland excretes only serous saliva and does it predominantly during eating (or preparing to eat). The parotid gland is fairly inactive during sleep. The other salivary glands of the mouth excrete a mixture of serous and mucinous saliva. During sleep they are less active but not as inactive as the parotid.

Medications that cause dry mouth do so in a variety of ways. They may reduce blood flow to the gland or interfere with the transport of water from the bloodstream into the gland. They can change the composition of the fluid that is formed in the initial step or can modify how that initial

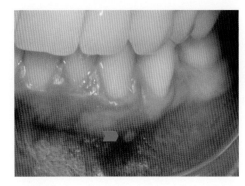

(figure 5-21)

Aphthous ulcers (arrowhead), also called "canker sores," only appear on parts of the mouth covered by very thin skin (mucous membrane), such as the side or tip of the tongue, the floor of the mouth, and the inside of the lips and cheeks.

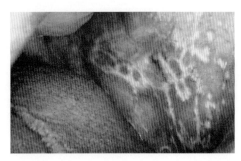

(figure 5-22)

Lichen planus is a dermatological condition that is actually found more frequently in the mouth than on the elbows or knees (the most common extraoral sites). Patients complain of soreness or hypersensitivity in the area of the mouth lesions. The mouth lesions will resolve on their own, but a steroid medication may hasten relief.

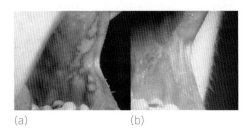

(a)   (b)

(figure 5-23)

(a) A more severe form of lichen planus in which blisters form, leaving raw, painful wounds behind. While these sores will resolve in time, the pain to the patient may interfere with eating unless some medicine is used to facilitate healing and/or to relieve the pain. (b) After one week of steroid treatment.

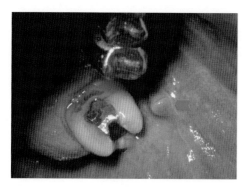

(*figure* 5-24)

Saliva from the largest salivary glands, the parotids, which are located in front of the ears, enters the mouth through Stensen's duct—a little hole in the cheek covered by a flap of tissue, opposite the upper second molar (arrowheads).

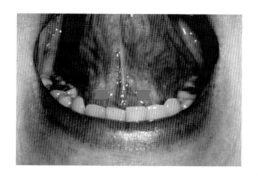

(*figure* 5-25)

Saliva from the paired submandibular glands flows into the mouth from a distinctive bulb of tissue beneath the tongue (arrowheads).

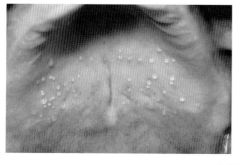

(*figure* 5-26)

This image, in a patient with no teeth, shows droplets of saliva formed by the palatal salivary glands.

fluid is altered as it travels through the gland. Whenever the composition of saliva is altered, its properties are altered as well. Sometimes if a patient complains of a dry mouth, objective measurement of saliva fails to show that the glands are underproducing. But if the composition of saliva is altered, the oral environment feels different, and this is often interpreted as dryness even if fluid is present.

In addition to drug-induced xerostomia, there are four other salivary gland diseases of note. The most common is the mucocele, which is due to the blockage of a minor salivary gland, much like a pimple is due to blockage of an oil gland in the skin. Saliva continues to be produced even if the outflow is blocked, resulting in a discrete, rubbery swelling, most commonly on the lower lip. The swelling likely has a pale bluish look (Figure 5-27) and is usually not painful. In most cases a mucocele will resolve itself, just as a pimple does. In some cases a small incision is needed to remove the gland.

The major salivary glands (parotid, etc.) can have small, hard obstructions in them, just like the bladder, the *gall bladder, and the kidneys.* The most telling symptom of *salivary stones* is that the patient is unaware of them until he or she is preparing to eat, whereupon the increased production of saliva raises pressure within the gland behind the obstruction, causing pain. Salivary stones can sometimes be removed without surgery through exploration of the gland by fine wires.

More than 95% of oral cancers—the oral cancers that have already been described—are cancers formed in mucosal tissue, which are termed squamous cell tumors. But the other 5% form from glandular tissue and are called *adenomas* or adenocarcinomas, depending on whether they are benign or malignant, respectively. Tumors can form from any of the major or minor glands. Tumors usually impair salivary flow because the excess tissue they constitute does not have either the function or the structure of the gland.

Normally salivary flow keeps oral bacteria from getting into the gland, since to do so would involve "swimming upstream." But if a person's salivary flow is slowed or stopped due to medications of some other cause, it is not uncommon for a parotid gland to become infected by oral bacteria that enter the gland and multiply there. This is termed parotitis (the same term used for mumps, which is caused by a virus, however), and it can cause high fever and pain and necessitate a hospitalization. Treatment will involve antibiotics and hot compresses to the gland.

A connective tissues disorder termed Sjögren's syndrome causes severely dry mouth in about three million Americans, most of whom are female and age 50 or above. Sufferers also have very dry eyes and one of the systemic connective tissues disorders, such as rheumatoid arthritis, scleroderma, or lupus erythematosus. The dry mouth and dry eyes are caused by destructive invasion of the salivary and lacrimal (tear-duct) glands by inflammatory cells for reasons that remain unclear.

TASTE AND SMELL DISORDERS

Dentists generally have relatively little involvement with taste and smell disorders, but because of the prominent role that the mouth plays in both of these senses, because both are often considered to be impaired to some extent in advanced age, and because oral malodor is undeniably an olfactory assault (on others) that arises from the mouth, some comments are included here.

It has been recognized, and repeatedly confirmed, that the sense of smell becomes less acute as one grows older. This is particularly true for males, but the diminished ability to discern subtle odors, and to identify an odor, is characteristic of aging of both genders. This deterioration of the sense of smell in older persons has been offered as a compelling reason for older persons to be particularly careful that the smoke detectors in their homes are fully functional; for older persons to discard leftover meals that are more than a few days old in order to minimize the likelihood for accidentally eating spoiled food; and for older persons to avoid gas appliances when electrical alternatives are available, in order to be spared the disastrous consequences of an undetected natural gas leak.

The sense of smell can also be affected by diseases and medications. Everyone has had the experience of being unable to smell due to a head cold. Many people complain of an unpleasant smell if they have a sinus infection. Drugs prescribed to an older person that cause a dry mouth may account for an unpleasant odor being detected because the environment of the mouth is not being regularly flushed by saliva.

The effect of aging on taste perception is much more complex than the effect of age on *olfaction* (the sense of smell). First, let us first clarify what is meant by "taste." Taste is generally described as the sensation consisting of sweet, salt, bitter, and sour that is perceived by the tongue and communicated to the brain. Note that when we speak of the taste of a steak or the taste of pastry, we are actually describing much more than saltiness, sweetness, bitterness, or sourness. We are perceiving the taste, true, but also the temperature, consistency, texture, odor, and even the sound associated with consumption of the food. This composite sensation is termed "flavor," and it is much more complex than taste alone.

The effect of aging on taste (not flavor) perception has been extensively studied. Several conclusions can be reasonably drawn from the findings. First, the ability to tell the difference between distilled water and water to which a tiny amount of taste has been added *(taste threshold)*, truly diminishes as one ages. More relevant to daily situations, however, is the finding that concentrations of taste that are closer to what we experience when eating *(suprathreshold levels)* are just as readily identified by old people as by young ones. And yet, when asked to "scale" different concentrations of a taste ("Is that just *somewhat* salty or *really* salty?"), growing older seems to diminish the degree to which taste intensity is perceived. This has been cited as a possible reason older people may oversalt their food or prefer particularly sweet desserts (if either of these is even true).

(figure 5-27)

The ducts (openings) for minor salivary glands can easily become blocked (arrowheads). If this occurs, saliva rich in thick mucin backs up behind the blockage and causes a swelling, termed a mucocele, in the affected tissue.

Taste perception is unquestionably affected by medications and by some diseases. Several medications—among them penicillamine, lithium, and ferrous sulfate—are infamous for causing an unpleasant taste in the mouths of those that use these drugs. In addition to these medications, any drug that impairs salivary flow is likely to interfere with taste, and even with smell, as described above. Whenever the mouth is dry, taste perception is impaired because the cells that perceive taste *(taste buds)* are located at the bottom of little wells in the tongue. Molecules that give rise to the different taste sensations must be in liquid to reach those cells. In a dry mouth there is no liquid; and the wells themselves become clogged with debris that would otherwise be washed away.

Let's finish this section by getting back to *flavor.* There is a generality that people lose their ability to taste as they grow older. We have learned that this is true in terms of taste thresholds; in terms of the perceived intensity of a taste for a given concentration; and in that so many medications impair taste perception either due to their own effects or their effects on salivary flow. But we also have clarified that when people speak colloquially of taste, they may actually mean flavor. And flavor really does seem to diminish as one ages: taste perception may be impaired in several ways, as just described; the olfactory sense unquestionably declines and may be further affected by medications and xerostomia; the extensive use of dentures among people of advanced age, compared to all other age groups, will limit the surface area of oral mucosa available for sensing temperature and texture and consistency characteristics in food; and even the sound associated with eating may suffer in association with the widespread hearing loss that is encountered with advancing age.

Are people then doomed as they age to perceive their meals as an endless parade of bland, monotonous, odorless, and tasteless excuses for cuisine? Hardly! First, not all the diminished perceptions are experienced by everyone. Second, even if some degree of diminished perception is unavoidable, quitting smoking and steering clear of smokers will reduce the profoundly deleterious impact of smoke on taste and smell. Third, there are taste and smell-enhancers that are commercially available and can be added to meals for those who sense the need. And last, remember that the flavor of something is more than the taste, or the taste and the smell. Food can be very visually appealing, can present a variety of textures and temperatures, and can evoke pleasant memories, and therefore, can still offer a broad palate of delicious flavors, even if the taste and smell may not be as evocative as they once may have been.

JAW JOINT

The human jaw joint—the temporomandibular joint (TMJ)—is unique in the human body in two ways. First, it is the body's only "joint system," in that the right and left sides are unable to move independently of one another. The second way in which each joint is unique is that it is actually two joints in one. Each TMJ features a cartilage prominence (condyle) that sits in a cup-shaped depression *(fossa)* on the underside of the skull

(*figure* 5-28)

(a) Each jaw joint (both the right and left) is actually two joints. (b) One joint on each side (the "condylar joint") accounts for opening the mouth about 12 mm or less and consists of the condyle of the mandible rotating against a flattened disc of fibrocartilage that in turn rests against the bottom of the temporal bone. (c) As the mouth opens wider, the condyle continues to rotate as the second joint on each side (the "temporal joint") begins to move: the fibrocartilage moves forward and downward against the underside of the temporal bone. When a person moves the jaw from side to side, the condylar joint rotates on one side as the temporal joint translates on the other.

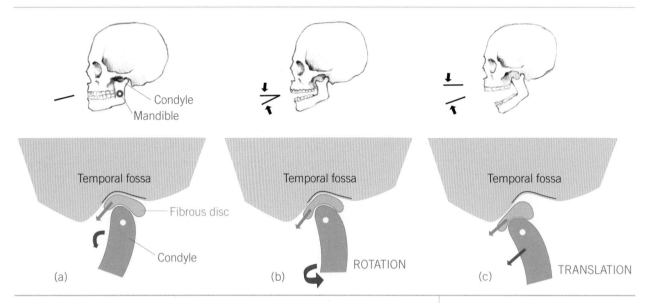

(a)   (b) ROTATION   (c) TRANSLATION

(Figure 5-28). Between the condyle and the fossa is a small pillow *(disc)* of fibrous cartilage. When the mouth first opens, the disc stays in the fossa, and the upper surface of the condyle rotates against the underside of the disc. But as the mouth opens wider, the disc begins to move downward and forward, out of the fossa. At this point, the joint is represented by sliding of the disc–condyle complex along the undersurface of the skull. The full range of jaw movements we make are combinations of these two *(rotation* and *translation),* made doubly complex by different motions on left and right sides. For example, when you chew on your left teeth, the right joint translates back and forth, but the left condyle stays in the fossa and rotates. But if you bring your bottom jaw forward (to bite off a thread, for instance) both sides must translate.

The TMJs are constantly in use. Every time you swallow—and you do that about 1500 times every day—your teeth come together. Add to that how many times you chew at each meal and how much your jaw moves as you talk your way through a day and, if you chew gum, the additional activity there. If you consider the effect of decades of that kind of repetitive movement, there is little wonder that pain in the jaw joints is frequently brought to dentists' attention.

Studies show arthritis commonly attacks the TMJs, and we know arthritis is very common in advanced age. People of advanced age have a greater likelihood than younger adults to have lost teeth, which can lead to imbalance between the chewing muscles and the TMJs. But interestingly enough, the major age group that voices complaints about the TMJ and chewing muscle pain is the group in their 20s through 50s; after that, it is pretty uncommon for a patient to bring it up.

05

The most likely explanation for the lack of complaints about TMJ problems among senior citizens concerns how people perceive pain. Pain is a physical symptom, but its severity is moderated according to the person's perception of its significance. A child perceives an injection as painful because it looks frightening and because most children, thankfully, have not had to experience much pain and therefore have little to compare the sensation to. An adult in her eighties may have given birth to several children; been through surgeries, strains, sprains, burns, cuts, bruises and automobile accidents; and may be taking one or more analgesics to keep her current arthritic pain at bay. Between the pains she has endured already, and the medication she continuously benefits from, some stiffness in the cheeks may not even be noticed or, if noticed, may not be ascribed as anything more than "another ache and pain of aging."

This is not meant to dismiss the significance of problems of the TMJs. Indeed, people who are unable to open their jaws fully because of joint pain or who have blinding headaches attributed to their TMJs or can not chew anything harder than scrambled eggs or bite anything thicker than a slice of toast genuinely suffer and present significant diagnostic and therapeutic challenges to the attention of dentists, neurologists, and oral surgeons. But a diminished sense of pain, or a diminished sense of importance ascribed to the sensation that someone else might call pain, seems to be the reason for the relative infrequency of TMJ complaints among people of advanced age despite the widespread presence of observable damage in the jaw joints.

If an older person experiences discomfort in one or both TMJs, the management is straightforward and generally effective, and very similar to the management of any painful joint. An anti-inflammatory drug such as IBUPROFEN, NAPROXEN, or aspirin should be started and continued at the recommended dosage schedule. The joint should be rested, meaning, "keep away from crunchy French bread and chewing gum and shouting at sports events until it feels better." Apply ice. If the joint particularly hurts when your teeth come together, place cotton balls between your back teeth so that you can rest your bottom jaw without it being forced into a painful position by the way it lines up with your bottom teeth. If these measures fail to provide relief within 24 hours, consult a dentist—but you probably won't need to!

A FINAL COMMENT

Medicare does not cover dental care, and most senior citizens are not lucky enough to have dental insurance. This means that the lion's share—over 90%—of the dental care paid for by Americans over age 65 years comes right out of their pockets. Can it possibly be worth the expense?

That is a personal decision. People who have retained most of their teeth throughout their lifetimes likely consider the $50 to $100 spent twice a year on an examination and a cleaning to be a good investment against the $400 root canals, the $600 crowns, and the $800 partial dentures, to say nothing of the $2000 bridges or the $10,000 implants.

Even those who have had to lose teeth and replace them have clearly made the decision that the money is well spent if they can feel better about how they look, how they talk, and how much more they can enjoy themselves when they eat.

Most people eat three meals and swallow up to 1500 times each day. The sources for pain from diseased teeth diminish as you age, which is good news. But what are the sources for pleasure in the last decades of life? Friends, lovers, meals, and family figure highest on most surveys of older persons. As such, comfort and security while eating and talking and laughing are reported to be important priorities during the golden years. If they are for you, take the time and, as required, the expense, to make sure your mouth stays healthy!

■

WHAT YOU NEED TO KNOW

▶ The dental diseases that are likely to affect you as you age are the same ones that affect people of all ages, but with increasing age you may not get the warning signs you're accustomed to, until it is too late. With advancing age, teeth generally become less sensitive, so waiting until you experience a dental problem may result in problems that are beyond fixing.

▶ Growing old does not mean you will lose your teeth. Teeth are lost mainly due to decay and gum disease, both of which can be prevented through daily oral care, following some basic nutritional guidelines, and regular visits to the dentist.

▶ Growing old also does not mean your mouth should seem dry. A dry mouth is an unhealthy situation, because saliva is your most important internal defense against dental disease. A dry mouth most commonly occurs as a side effect of medicines given for other problems, like high blood pressure, anxiety, or depression. Unless you bring this problem to your doctor's attention and request that you be prescribed medicines that don't have this effect on your mouth, you will have more difficulty keeping your mouth healthy.

▶ Regular dental visits are important whether you have your own teeth or not. This is because oral cancer survival is more likely when the disease is discovered early, but less likely if the disease has spread and has already come to a patient's attention before treatment starts. People with teeth need a professional exam to prevent, identify, and treat tooth and gum problems; and people with dentures can get the best function from their appliances if they are properly adjusted and the tissues they rest on are healthy.

▶ Oral health is important not only for keeping your teeth but also for keeping you healthy overall. A healthy mouth is necessary for maintaining an interesting and varied diet. Dental disease is not always limited to the mouth because bacteria often spread through the bloodstream. Diabetes is more difficult to control if a person also suffers from untreated gum disease. There is growing evidence that gum disease may contribute, over time, to development of diseases of the blood vessels like heart attack and stroke.

FOR MORE INFORMATION

▶ **Laclede, Inc.**
www.laclede.com
"For over 20 years, Laclede has led in the development of biological products which utilize the body's natural defense systems for the prevention and treatment and gum disease due to dry mouth. Laclede continues to pioneer new biological approaches that can help the body strengthen its defenses against harmful pathogens." "Healthwatch" with consumer information; directory of products and where to find them, state by state.

▶ **Crest Healthy Smiles (Proctor & Gamble)**
www.cresthealthysmiles.com
The company is committed to improve oral health nationwide by enhancing access to and involving communities in oral health education.

▶ **Oral Health America**
www.oralhealthamerica.org
"Oral Health America is the only national, independent 501(c)3 organization dedicated to improving oral health for all Americans."

When you can't breath, nothing else matters.

—The American Lung Association

THE AUTHOR

06

RAYMOND DEAN HAUTAMAKI, MD, FCCP, graduated from the University of Florida College of Medicine. He completed his residency in internal medicine and his fellowship in pulmonary and critical care medicine at the Washington University School of Medicine in St. Louis. He is a fellow of the American College of Chest Physicians. He is currently researching the role of certain proteins in emphysema. He resides in Sarasota, Florida, where he serves as a consultant in pulmonary medicine and critical care medicine at Sarasota Memorial Hospital and Doctors Hospital.

06 | THE LUNGS

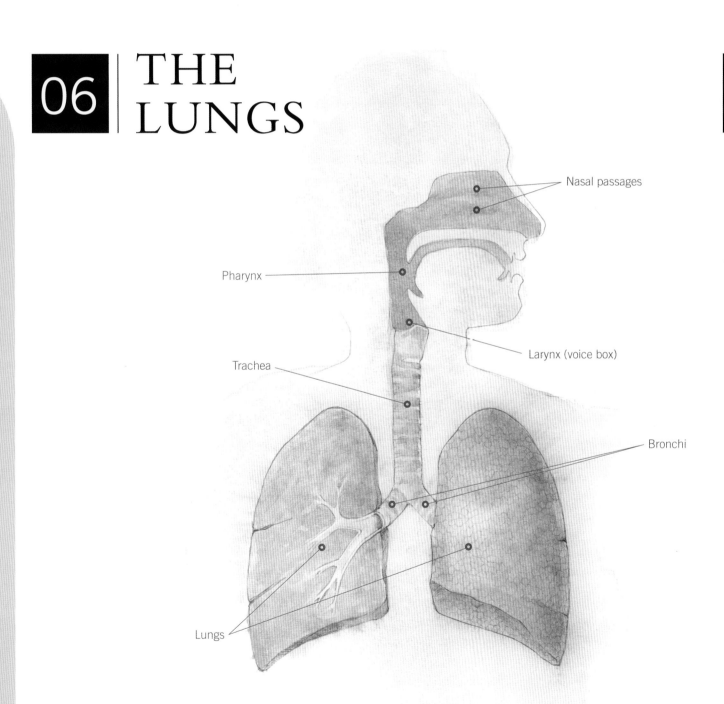

Nasal passages

Pharynx

Larynx (voice box)

Trachea

Bronchi

Lungs

(figure 6-1)
The respiratory system.

NORMAL LUNG STRUCTURE AND FUNCTION

The lungs are a part of the respiratory system (breathing system) within your body. They provide several important functions, the most important of which is the exchange of carbon dioxide for oxygen. Carbon dioxide is a waste product of your body's metabolism and is eliminated by exhaling the gas out of your lungs. Oxygen is critical for cells in your body to function and is delivered to the bloodstream when you inhale. The inability to transfer these gases effectively results in illness and possibly death. The lungs also play a role in filtering out unwanted substances in the blood through tiny blood vessels, as well as producing chemical substances that are involved with the body's control of blood pressure.

The respiratory system is not limited to the lungs but includes several other structures, shown in Figure 6-1. These structures include the nasal passages, sinuses, larynx, trachea, bronchial tubes, lung tissue, pleural cavity (chest cavity), and chest wall. The chest wall is in part responsible for breathing. It consists of the spine, ribs, sternum (breastbone), and muscles connecting all these structures. The respiratory muscles drive the expansion of the chest. The respiratory muscles include muscles of the neck, the intercostal muscles (rib muscles), diaphragm, and abdominal muscles. The chest cavity is airtight and has a small amount of fluid within the cavity to provide lubrication during the movement of the lungs. Air that is inhaled travels through the nose passing between the vocal cords then into the main windpipe called the trachea. The trachea then splits into two main bronchial tubes called the left and right mainstem bronchi, which lead into the left and right lung respectively. The right lung is separated into three lobes, and the left lung has two lobes. Each lobe has several smaller segments within it. Each segment has its own bronchial tube leading into it along with its corresponding blood vessels. The bronchi as they lead deeper into the lung become smaller until they become bronchioles. The bronchioles then lead into the air sacs called alveoli. It is at the level of the alveoli that oxygen moves across the air sac lining into the capillaries and carbon dioxide leaves the blood vessels and is exhaled out of lungs (see Figure 6-2).

Your lungs are in direct contact with the environment through breathing and are exposed to numerous chemicals, fumes, dusts, pollens, and infectious agents including viruses, bacteria, and funguses. These agents can cause significant acute and chronic diseases of the lungs. Acute infections of the lung range from simple acute bronchitis (infection of the bronchial tubes) to severe pneumonia (infection of the lung tissue). Certain occupations may expose an individual to environmental dusts (coal dust, silica, asbestos, grain dust, etc.) and can have a significant impact on lung function and may predispose to chronic scarring or malignant tumors of the lungs. The overall effects of aging on respiratory function are quite complex and the lungs have considerable reserve as you age. Studies on large populations of healthy individuals confirm that there is a decline in lung function as one ages. This loss in lung function with aging appears to be relatively constant. This loss, however, is relatively small in terms of

(figure 6-2)

The alveoli (air sacs). (a) The air that is breathed in eventually moves from the bronchioles into the alveoli. (b) At the level of the alveolus, oxygen moves across the air sac lining into the capillaries, and carbon dioxide leaves the blood vessels and is exhaled out of the lungs.

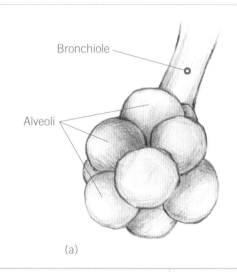

Bronchiole

Alveoli

(a)

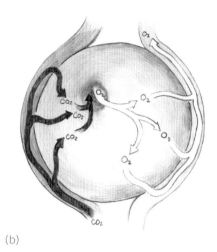

(b)

overall lung capacity. Unless an individual is affected by chronic diseases of the lung or chronic exposures to environmental pollution, the normal functional and structural changes to the lungs as we age typically are not significant enough to cause true breathing impairment and therefore has minimal impact on our overall health.

Your ability to exercise is dependent upon multiple factors including the function of the lungs, heart, and muscles of your body. Exercise is quite variable for each individual and may range from performing simple activities of daily living which would include grooming, bathing, and feeding oneself to performing rigorous aerobic exercise. As you age your capacity to perform certain exercises based upon measurement of oxygen consumption by the body at maximal exercise declines by 10% per decade. In highly trained subjects the decline is approximately 6% per decade. In sedentary individuals the decline is primarily due to a reduction in the pumping strength of the heart. However, sedentary individuals over the age of 60 who initiate a structured vigorous exercise program can significantly improve their exercise capability and performance. This should not be done though without proper evaluation and guidance from one's physician.

CHRONIC OBSTRUCTIVE PULMONARY DISEASE

Chronic obstructive pulmonary disease (COPD) refers to a diverse group of chronic lung disorders. They all have in common narrowing of the bronchial tubes, which results in the obstruction of airflow through the lungs. The three common disorders are emphysema, chronic bronchitis, and asthma. COPD is a common disease and affects over 14 million people in the United States. Approximately 6% of the total U.S. population is affected by the disorder. It is the fourth leading cause of death in adults and is the second leading cause of disability. Chronic bronchitis and asthma are the most common of the conditions, followed by emphysema. Mortality rates from COPD dramatically increase with advancing age and reach their peak at around 85 years of age. Chronic bronchitis and asthma tend to be dispersed evenly among all ages. However, emphysema is a disease among the elderly population, with 60% of all cases occurring in individuals over the age of 65.

COPD is caused primarily from cigarette smoking in about 90% of cases. Fewer than 10% of cases are due to other causes, including occupational dust exposure, air pollution, secondhand smoke, and alpha 1-antitrypsin deficiency. Alpha 1-antitrypsin deficiency is an inherited form of emphysema and results in the reduced production of a protein that protects the lung from destruction. If they smoke, these individuals will show evidence of emphysema at a much earlier age in life, typically in their 50s. There may be a history of lung disease within the family. A simple blood test can measure the protein level to determine if a patient has this condition. In patients with significantly low protein blood levels and impaired lung function, replacement of the protein by weekly infusions can be performed.

Chronic bronchitis is condition that is diagnosed based upon the symptoms of a chronic cough with sputum (material expectorated from the air passages) production. *Chronic bronchitis* is defined as a chronic productive cough for three months in each of two successive years in which other causes have been excluded. In patients with a productive chronic cough with normal lung function testing, simple chronic bronchitis is diagnosed. However, those individuals with abnormal lung function have chronic obstructive bronchitis and make up the majority of patients with COPD. *Emphysema* is defined as the permanent and irreversible destruction of lung tissue and the enlargement of air sacs. The walls of the air sacs lose their elasticity through the loss of the elastic fibers in the lung, and the air sacs gradually enlarge. As the lungs enlarge or overinflate, they flatten the diaphragm muscles and make it more difficult for the respiratory muscles to work. The bronchial tubes become less elastic, and consequently they become narrow and collapse when the patient exhales thus causing obstruction of airflow (see Figure 6-3). Individuals with severe COPD may also accumulate higher blood levels of carbon dioxide and reduced blood oxygen levels.

Asthma is characterized by inflammation of the lining of the bronchial airways with constriction of the airways, a condition that is partially reversible. Although attempts have been made, a more specific definition is currently lacking within the medical community. A common chronic disease, asthma affecting all ages in our society from the very young to the elderly. Although there is some overlap of symptoms with chronic bronchitis and emphysema, the distinction is important to make from these other two diseases. Most individuals are younger and are nonsmokers. The exercise tolerance and lung function of a person with asthma typically return to nearly normal in between flare-ups of the disease. This is in contrast to patients with chronic bronchitis and emphysema. Asthma may

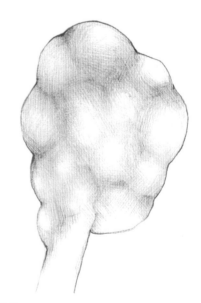

(figure 6-3)

Destruction of the air sacs and enlargement of the walls in emphysema.

(figure 6-4)

Individual doing spirometry.

be associated with other conditions, including allergies, hay fever, nasal polyps, or allergic rhinitis. Symptoms of asthma include cough, wheezing, shortness of breath, and chest tightness. These symptoms may be made worse by such triggers as exercise, weather changes, seasonal allergens, respiratory infections, smoke, air pollution, and medications. Allergens include house dust, animal dander, pollens, and dust mites. Medications that can precipitate asthma symptoms include aspirin, nonsteroidal anti-inflammatory drugs, and beta-blockers.

Diagnosis of these chronic lung disorders is made by a physician taking a complete history. Important information includes frequency of symptoms, duration, and severity. Specific triggers that may precipitate worsening symptoms should be sought out. A detailed occupational history should be obtained to determine specific environmental exposure to dusts, fibers, fumes, or chemicals, and a smoking history should be taken, including the duration and number of packs consumed daily. The physician should perform a complete physical examination.

Pulmonary function tests measure several aspects of lung function. Spirometry measures how much air you can take into your lungs and then how fast you can blow the air out (see Figure 6-4). There are other specific

(figure 6-5)

These pictures show how a lung tumor looks different on (a) chest X-ray compared to (b) CT scan.

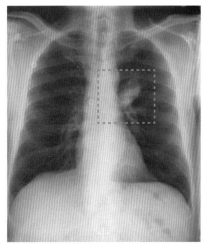

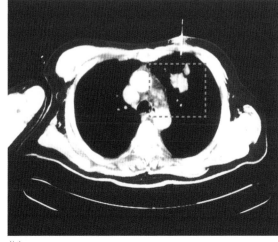

(a)   (b)

tests for the amount of air you exhale and how much air is left in your lungs after breathing out. This measurement is termed *lung volumes*. The **diffusion capacity** is a measure of the ability of gases to diffuse from the air sacs into the pulmonary blood vessels. A complete pulmonary function test is an outpatient procedure and is performed in the physician's office or hospital respiratory department. A qualified respiratory therapist performs the test, which takes approximately 45 minutes. Other testing may include the assessment of one's oxygen levels with a finger probe, called a **pulse oximeter**. In some cases a sample of blood from an artery in the wrist will be taken to measure directly the levels of oxygen and carbon dioxide in the blood. This test is called an **arterial blood gas (ABG)**. Other possible tests are chest X-rays or, if more in-depth images of the lungs are required, a CT scan of the chest (see Figure 6-5).

Treatment begins with smoking cessation if the individual is still an active smoker. There are several methods to provide assistance in becoming smoke-free, such as nicotine replacement therapy, which will significantly improve the rate of smoking cessation to approximately 25% at six months. Nicotine replacement comes in several forms including nicotine gum, nicotine patches, and nicotine inhaler. Individuals with coronary artery disease should avoid these products since nicotine replacement may make their condition worse. BUPROPION HYDROCHLORIDE (ZYBAN or WELLBUTRIN) is an oral tablet that has been shown to be as effective as nicotine replacement for smoking cessation. The most important factor is a strong motivation to quit the use of tobacco products if one is to remain smoke-free for an extended period of time. Although long-term relapse rates remain high, success is possible with the right attitude and support. Medicare has initiated a program called the "Healthy Aging Stop Smoking Program." If you live in one of seven states that has been targeted for this program, Medicare will provide reimbursement for counseling by your doctor as well as coverage for medications, such as Zyban or the nicotine patch, which can help quit smoking. The program is a scientific research project to help determine which interventions are most effective and cost-effective in helping seniors quit smoking. If you smoke and have made the decision to quit, ask your doctor if you qualify. Hopefully, coverage will be extended to all smokers who would like to quit.

Air pollution poses a major threat to both healthy individuals and especially those patients with chronic lung diseases. The **air quality index (AQI)** is the standard system that state and local air pollution control programs use to inform the public about air pollution levels. When air pollution reaches a certain level, it is advisable for certain groups to avoid prolonged outside exposure. These groups include the very young, elderly, and patients with chronic lung diseases. Air pollution levels are measured daily in major metropolitan areas and are announced usually through local media. The AQI breaks air pollution levels into six categories, each of which has a name, an associated color, and advisory statement, as shown in Table 6-1.

Your home environment should be free of smoke, fumes, and dust. Proper ventilation and adequate air conditioning are important in a household with patients who suffer from chronic lung disease. Keep animals out of the bedroom of an asthmatic to avoid prolonged exposure to animal dander, a major allergen. Wash bedding materials in hot water (at least 130°F) to eliminate dust mites, another common allergen. Your home environment is as important as the outdoor air quality, if not more, since we spend a significant amount of time within our residences.

Several classes of medications are available for the treatment of individuals with COPD. The medications come in a variety of forms: metered dose inhalers, dry powder, nebulized solutions, oral tablets, and intravenous. The class of drugs called **bronchodilators** work by relaxing and opening the airways to provided relief from shortness of breath and wheezing. They may also increase movement of the cilia to help clear mucus from the air passages. Some bronchodilators may act quickly, but their effects wear off quickly as well. These drugs include ALBUTEROL, METAPROTERENOL, TERBUTALINE, and PIRBUTEROL. These drugs have been the mainstay in treatment for COPD and also provide immediate relief of symptoms during a severe attack. Another class of drugs takes 60 to 90 minutes to work and typically lasts six to eight hours. The only drug available in this class in the United States is IPRATROPIUM (ATROVENT). It comes either in a metered dose inhaler or nebulized solution. The long-acting medications, SALMETEROL and FORMOTEROL, provide similar benefits

(table 6-1)

THE SIX CATEGORIES OF THE AIR QUALITY INDEX

NAME		ASSOCIATED COLOR		ADVISORY STATEMENT
Good	▶	Green	▶	Best-quality air; no limitations on outside time exposure.
Moderate	▶	Yellow	▶	Unusually sensitive individuals should limit prolonged outdoor exertion.
Unhealthy for sensitive groups	▶	Orange	▶	Children, the elderly, people with lung disease, and active adults should limit prolonged outdoor exertion.
Unhealthy	▶	Red	▶	Members of sensitive groups should avoid prolonged outdoor exposure; everyone else should limit prolonged outdoor exertion.
Very unhealthy	▶	Purple	▶	Members of sensitive groups should avoid outdoor exertion; everyone else should limit outdoor exertion.
Hazardous	▶	Maroon	▶	Everyone should avoid all outdoor exertion.

as the short acting but last approximately 12 hours. The long-acting bronchodilators should never be used in a respiratory emergency.

The benefits of inhaled corticosteroids in asthma has been well documented. Since inflammation of the bronchial airways is the central problem in asthmatics, corticosteroids can be helpful in reducing the inflammation and swelling in the airways. They also can reduce mucus production and decrease the sensitivity of the airways to inhaled irritants and allergens. Inhaled steroids have become the treatment of choice to control symptoms and improve lung function in patients with asthma, and they have minimal side effects compared to tablet forms of steroids, which can result in significant morbidity with long-term use. Inhaled corticosteroid drugs include FLUTICASONE, BUDESONIDE, FLUNISOLIDE, TRIAMCINOLONE, and BECLOMETHASONE. Oral steroid tablets include PREDNISONE, METHYLPREDNISOLONE, and PREDNISOLONE. The use of oral or intravenous steroids is typically reserved for those patients experiencing a severe flare-up of their asthma or require hospitalization for an asthma attack.

Leukotriene modifiers are another class of medication used primarily in asthmatics. They can provide some improvement in asthmatic symptoms and in improved airflow through the lungs. The exact place for these drugs in the management of chronic asthma remains to be established, and there is currently no recommendation for their use in patients with chronic bronchitis or emphysema.

Surgical treatments for patients with severe emphysema include *lung transplantation* and *lung volume reduction surgery*. Lung transplantation is reserved for those patients with very severe disease, but transplantation is not done for people over 70 because of the paucity of organ donors. It is preferred to transplant those who have a more prolonged life expectancy. Lung volume reduction surgery (LVRS) is the partial removal of the diseased lung, typically the upper parts, in the hope of improving airflow through the lungs and restoring the diaphragm to a more normal position. This surgical treatment is currently being evaluated in patients with emphysema in a large clinical trial within the United States.

Several nontraditional therapies have arisen for the treatment of emphysema. Patients desperate for a "cure" will seek unproven treatments advertised in magazines, newspapers, and on the internet. Currently there is no known cure for emphysema. Unfortunately, patients are lured into believing marketed testimonials that are advertised for profit-making purposes only. The infusion of hydrogen peroxide into a vein in the body is one of these practices. There are no scientific data to support the use of this substance in patients with COPD. As well, certain advertised vitamin supplements to promote lung health are unproven. Patients must be cautioned not to expose themselves to unproven remedies that can be costly, ineffective, and possibly harmful.

Depending upon the severity of COPD, an individual may require oxygen either intermittently or continuously throughout the day. Using oxygen increases the amount of oxygen in the blood. Breathing

(figure 6-6)

Oxygen being delivered from a portable container via a nasal cannula.

prescribed oxygen may help reduce shortness of breath and prevent other complications associated with low oxygen levels. Oxygen is not addictive and has virtually no side effects. Patients should use the exact level of oxygen prescribed by the physician for specific activities, whether it be used for sleeping, walking, or exercise. The several forms of oxygen include compressed oxygen, an oxygen concentrator, and liquid oxygen. Depending upon the person's condition and level of activity, the physician and oxygen company will work with individual and family to find the right form of oxygen. Most people requiring oxygen wear flexible plastic tubing around their face, with a nasal cannula delivering the oxygen into the nasal passageways. Oxygen is available in a compressed tank, which come in various sizes: the smaller portable tanks being used for walking if outside the home and the larger tanks if the patient is at home (see Figure 6-6). A meter and a regulator are attached to the tank to control the flow of oxygen. Liquid oxygen comes in a container that holds the liquid form of oxygen at a very low temperature (−297°F). The liquid is filled into a portable container so the person can remain as active as possible. An oxygen concentrator is a machine that concentrates oxygen from the air. This machine runs on electricity and is usually kept in an area of the home with a good supply of air. It should never be placed in a closet or under the bed. This form of oxygen is used at night when the person is sleeping.

Oxygen is flammable, and all flame sources should be kept away from all forms of oxygen by at least three meters. No one should smoke in a home that has supplemental oxygen in place.

Individuals with COPD benefit from structured exercise programs specifically designed for their needs. The programs consist of supervised pulmonary exercises that alleviate some the symptoms of shortness of breath and improve exercise performance. Activities include stationary cycles, treadmill walking, swimming, or bicycling. Upper body strengthening exercises begin with light weights, starting usually at 200 to 400 grams, and gradually increase to a desired level. Exercise helps tone muscles so they use less oxygen and do not fatigue as readily. Exercise results in better sleep quality, improved appetite, and reduced stress levels. Persons with COPD should also have a pneumonia vaccine every five to eight years and an annual influenza vaccine. They are advised to contact their physicians at the first signs of a cold or respiratory infection. Although there is no definitive cure for COPD, one can perform numerous interventions to help improve respiratory symptoms and the overall quality of life.

OBSTRUCTIVE SLEEP APNEA

Obstructive sleep apnea (OSA) is a common disorder with estimates that approximately 1 to 4% of the population is affected. *Obstructive* refers to the blockage of airflow that may occur at any level in the upper airway, starting at the nose and extending to the lower throat. The term *apnea* refers to the cessation of breathing. Excessive daytime sleepiness is the most common symptom of individuals with OSA. These individuals typically have a history of snoring, and their bed partners report periodic pauses in their breathing. Other symptoms that are associated with OSA include dry mouth, chronic sore throat, fatigue, morning headaches or confusion, intellectual impairment, personality changes, and impotence. Risk factors for sleep apnea include increased age, alcohol consumption, obesity, hypothyroidism, acromegaly, use of sedatives or sleeping medication, and being a male.

On physical examination these persons may be noted to have an elevated blood pressure, a short thick neck, nasal blockage, a large tongue, low hanging soft palate, enlarged tonsils or adenoids, displacement of the jaw bone, or an enlarged uvula. A "crowded airway" of the oral cavity is often described by the physician. The cause of upper airway obstruction is complex and may occur at any point from the nose to the voice box. In OSA an obstruction to airflow occurs during sleep resulting in the narrowing or complete closure of the airway. The pharynx, or base of the throat, is abnormal in size and collapsibility. This tube narrows during certain stages of sleep, and the airway collapses. Partial collapse results in snoring, and complete closure results in apnea. There continues to be an attempt to breathe by the respiratory center of the brain, but no air reaches the lungs. During this apnea episode the individual undergoes an arousal or waking up period for the return of sufficient opening of the pharynx and relief of the obstruction. The person may not consciously recall waking up, but deep sleep is interrupted and as a result the individual does not feel rested upon awakening.

Complications of OSA are related to the loss of mental alertness due to sleep deprivation and cardiovascular complications. Several studies have shown that patients with severe sleep apnea are at two to seven times higher risk for having a motor vehicle accident. Patients can become so sleep deprived, due to fragmentation of their sleep, that they fall asleep at the wheel of the car, with tragic results. The risk of cardiovascular events remains unknown, but most published studies report an increased incidence of elevated blood pressure both in the lung circulation, called pulmonary hypertension, and in arterial blood pressure, which is the more common form of high blood pressure. There is also the potential for worsening of blood flow to the heart and brain in patients with coronary heart disease and cerebrovascular disease. A useful screening for the risk of OSA includes four variables: (1) hypertension, (2) increased neck circumference or collar size, (3) habitual snoring, and (4) observed episodes of nighttime gasping or choking. These variables, if combined, clearly increase the likelihood of an individual having OSA.

Most individuals will be referred to a sleep medicine specialist for evaluation. If the physician suspects obstructive sleep apnea, the person will most likely undergo a sleep test referred to as a polysomnogram. Polysomnography, or sleep study, is usually performed overnight in a specialized sleep lab designed to extensively monitor a subject's breathing patterns, oxygen levels, and quality of sleep (see Figure 6-7). The test is performed over one to two evenings, after which the physician reviews all the data to come to a specific diagnosis.

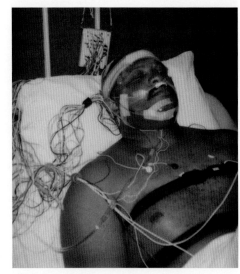

(figure 6-7)

A sleep laboratory.

The treatment of OSA begins with identifying patients with the disease. Eliminating reversible factors that may contribute to the disease include treating low thyroid levels (hypothyroidism), cessation of sedatives and alcohol, and a structured weight loss program or diet. Surgical treatment includes tracheostomy, a surgical procedure placing a small tube in the windpipe at the base of the neck. This in the past was the preferred treatment for patients. It bypassed the blockage and resulted in complete relief of the obstruction and symptoms. However, this procedure is reserved for the most severe of cases due to its risks of complications and psychological impact on the patient. Uvulopalatopharyngoplasty (UPPP) is a surgical procedure designed to remove redundant tissue from the throat. Unfortunately, this procedure is successful only 50% of the time in reducing apneas and improving oxygen levels. Other newer surgical techniques involve removing a portion of bone from the jaw and pulling it forward to advance the tongue off the back of the throat.

Nonsurgical treatments include weight loss in those who are obese. In some individuals the loss of a significant amount of weight dramatically improves their symptoms and may reverse the apnea problem altogether. Positional therapy involves positioning the patient off the back or elevating the head to reverse the obstructive condition. Medications to treat OSA may include a nonsedating tricyclic antidepressant or the selective serotonin reuptake inhibitors (SSRIs). Oral appliances may be used to treat OSA. These devices resemble a retainer that repositions the tongue so that the tongue does not fall back on the back of the throat and does not block the airway. The definitive treatment for OSA in most people today is with nasal continuous positive airway pressure (CPAP). A CPAP nasal mask is applied over the nose, and pressurized air flows from a small machine that attaches to the nasal mask (see Figure 6-8). The pressure of the machine is adjusted to the level needed to overcome the obstruction in the individual's airway. Many people find it difficult to use these devices for extended time periods. This is due to dryness of the throat, facial discomfort, claustrophobia, and noise levels. Long-term compliance is at best around 40 to 60%. Bilevel positive airway pressure (BiPAP) may allow patients to overcome the blockage with a lower pressure setting and thus improve overall compliance in use of the machine.

Humidification systems can also be added to the machine to reduce complaints of a dry throat. With these different treatment options available, the patient and sleep specialist can select the most appropriate therapy on the basis of the individual's severity of symptoms and results of the sleep study. Mild OSA patients can start with weight loss if needed, positional therapy, or an oral device. If unsuccessful, a trial of CPAP may be advised. For those with moderate to severe OSA, nasal CPAP or BiPAP is probably the most effective treatment along with trying to lose weight. Those with moderate to severe OSA who cannot tolerate the CPAP or BiPAP device may want to explore the surgical options that are available. One should not make these decisions without the help and guidance of a sleep medicine specialist.

(figure 6-8)

Use of a continuous positive airway pressure mask.

LUNG CANCER

Lung cancer is the most common malignant tumor in men worldwide. Approximately 16% of all malignant tumors are due to lung cancer and account for 28% of all cancer deaths. In the United States, lung cancer is the leading cause of cancer deaths in both men and women, accounting for 31% of cancer deaths in men and 25% of cancer deaths in women in the year 2000. Approximately 164,000 individuals in the United States will die each year from lung cancer. The main cause of lung cancer is due to smoking tobacco. There is a direct relationship in the development of lung cancer and the amount of exposure to cigarette smoke, as measured by the number of cigarettes smoked, the duration of smoking in years, the age of initiation of smoking, the depth of inhalation, and the tar and nicotine levels in the cigarettes smoked.

Although smoking contributes to approximately 90% of all lung cancers, several occupational and environmental exposures will lead to an increased risk in the development of a lung tumor. Such occupational risks include exposure to asbestos, ionizing radiation, radon, arsenic, nickel compounds, mustard gas, iron or steel founding, and chromium-containing compounds.

Many attempts have been made in the past to develop an effective screening tool to detect lung cancer before the patient has any symptoms. Presumably detecting tumors at an early stage would lead to an improved survival benefit. Annual X-ray exam of the chest in smokers has not been found to be effective in several screening studies in regards to long-term survival. The use of a screening CT scan of the lungs is currently being evaluated, but much more work needs to be done before any conclusions can be drawn.

Over 90% of the patients will have symptoms at the time they are seen by a physician. Respiratory symptoms may include a persistent cough, blood in the sputum, shortness of breath, chest pain, wheezing, or hoarseness. Other more systemic symptoms may include weight loss, loss of appetite, fevers, or chronic weakness. The vast majority of patients are diagnosed with advanced disease by the time they have symptoms from their cancer.

THEN AND NOW

In the 1800s, lung cancer was seldom reported. In those years, gentlemen smoked cigars. Cigarettes were a later invention. The scraps in the cigar factories were scooped up, rolled in paper, and smoked, generally by those of lesser means. Since it take years for lung cancer to develop and is related to length of exposure, the increased occurrence of lung cancer cases wasn't really appreciated until after World War I.

In subsequent years, more studies confirmed the relationship between cigarette smoking and lung cancer. By 1962, the United States Surgeon General reported that cigarette smoking definitely causes lung cancer. Today, lung cancer is the leading cause of cancer death.

NURSE'S NOTES

William S., 69, came to our emergency room with a cough that had lasted three months. He was a nice man who looked quite anxious. He had noticed occasional streaks of blood in his phlegm, as well as shortness of breath with intermittent wheezing when he was sleeping on his back. He had lost approximately 10 pounds over the previous month. He had smoked two packs of cigarettes per day for over 40 years.

I felt very bad when the doctor showed me his chest X-ray. It showed a 6-cm mass in the left lung, undoubtedly cancer. CT scans showed spread to his liver as well as two tumors in his brain. A biopsy of the lung mass confirmed small cell carcinoma. Mr. S. was depressed but was hopeful that he would get a response from his treatments. He said that he had some children in the area that would help him through this. He was referred to an oncologist for cancer treatment.

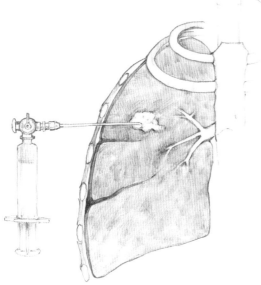

(figure 6-9)

A needle biopsy of a lung tumor.

The evaluation of an individual with suspected lung cancer begins with the referral to a lung specialist called a pulmonologist. To diagnose the cancer, a biopsy is usually performed. A biopsy involves removal of a small piece of the tumor. The biopsy of the lung tumor can be performed by several different techniques. The most common procedures for biopsy are fiberoptic bronchoscopy or CT scan–directed needle biopsy (see Figure 6-9). Both these procedures are performed in the hospital but usually on an outpatient basis. A fiberoptic bronchoscopy is performed under light sedation in a procedure room of the hospital. A flexible fiberoptic scope is passed through the nose or mouth. Then special forceps are passed through the scope to biopsy the lung tumor. In some cases, the patient may have the tumor biopsied under a CT scan with a needle being passed through the chest wall and into the tumor.

Other potential procedures for obtaining a sample of the abnormal tissue are mediastinoscopy or video–assisted thoracoscopic lung biopsy. Both are surgical procedures performed by a thoracic surgeon. These procedures require general anesthesia. A mediastinoscopy requires a small incision above the breastbone through which the surgeon removes lymph nodes from the center part of the chest cavity called the mediastinum. A video–assisted thoracoscopic lung biopsy requires the insertion of several scopes into the chest cavity. The chest cavity is inspected and samples of tissue are removed under direct visualization with the assistance of the video cameras. After the samples of the tumor have been obtained, they are then examined under the microscope by a pathologist (a physician who specializes in the interpretation of tissue biopsies). Usually it takes three to five days for the final results to become available. Once the diagnosis has been confirmed by the biopsy, the physician may then recommend a positron emission tomography (PET) scan. This is a scan of the body that helps detect tumors in other parts of the body. The scan involves injection of a radioactive glucose or sugar through a vein into the body. Tumors tend to accumulate more of the compound and will produce an abnormal spot on the scan's pictures. The PET scan helps determine if the tumor has spread to other parts of the chest cavity, usually lymph nodes, or if it has spread to other organs in the body. Common sites of spread include the liver, adrenal glands, bones, or brain.

Lung cancer causes some cells in the lung to grow out of control. These cancer cells grow at a much faster rate than normal cells. The cancer cells are a different shape and often larger than are normal cells of the lung. The cancer cells can directly grow into other parts of the lungs and surrounding tissues. They can also spread through the bloodstream or lymphatic channels to other parts of the body. This process is termed metastasis. Lung cancers are divided into two major categories, non-small cell and small cell carcinoma. The vast majority of cases of lung cancer are due to non-small cell carcinoma. Small cell has also been called "oat cell" carcinoma due to the tumor cells resembling oats under the microscope.

Non-small cell carcinoma is staged on the basis of an international system called the TNM system. The staging system is a process to measure how advanced the cancer is within the body. The *T* represents tumor characteristics, including the size, location, and direct tumor growth into vital body structures. The *N* represents lymph nodes that are involved with cancer cells. Lymph nodes are found throughout the body, including the lungs and chest cavity. Tumor cells can spread either to lymph nodes within the same side of the chest that the tumor is located or outside this location to the center of the chest or to the opposite side of the chest. The *M* is for metastases, which is the spread of tumor into major organs, including brain, liver, adrenal glands, bones, and the other lung. Combining the TNM information provides the physician with the stage of the cancer. The four stages arc I, II, III, and IV. Stage I is the earliest and provides the best chance of long-term cure. Stage IV is the most advanced and has a dismal survival rate of less than 20%.

Small cell carcinoma makes up approximately 20% of the cases of lung cancer. In general, when patients with small cell carcinoma are initially evaluated by the physician, the vast majority of them, over 70%, will have cancer that has spread outside the lung and chest cavity. This type of lung cancer may grow and spread faster than does non-small cell lung cancer. Patients are separated into *limited stage* small cell and *extensive stage* small cell. Limited stage includes those patients who have the tumor confined to one side of the chest cavity. All others fall into extensive stage disease. The median survival for patients with limited disease averages 20 months. In those with extensive disease median life expectancy is approximately seven to ten months. This tumor often is very sensitive to chemotherapy.

Most patients undergoing **chemotherapy** will receive a combination of drugs to treat the cancer. Drugs used in the treatment of small cell carcinoma of the lung include CYCLOPHOSPHAMIDE, ADRIAMYCIN, VINCRISTINE, ETOPOSIDE, CISPLATIN, and CARBOPLATIN. In patients with limited disease many will be treated with a combination of chemotherapy and chest irradiation. The three-year survival rates for limited stage small cell have climbed to 20 to 30% with combined chemotherapy and irradiation. The outlook for patients with extensive disease unfortunately is far worse than for patients with limited disease. Median survival is approximately seven to nine months. The drugs cisplatin and etoposide remain the commonest choice for combination chemotherapy for patients with extensive disease. Patients who have had a complete response after initial treatment have a 50% risk of developing spread of tumor to their brain. In attempt to prevent this, radiation to the brain is given after a complete remission.

Surgery provides the best chance for overall survival in patients with non-small cell carcinoma. Unfortunately, less than 25% of patients are considered suitable for curative removal of their tumor. Surgical or

DOCTOR'S DIARY

Jane K., 75, sustained a right hip fracture after slipping outside her home. She was taken by ambulance to our hospital, and then she underwent surgery to repair the fracture. She was initially doing well, but then on the third day after surgery she developed severe shortness of breath in association with severe sharp knifelike pain in the right upper chest. The chest pain worsened when she took a deep breath.

Her orthopedic surgeon requested that I see her. When I arrived, she was in severe distress with labored breathing. A chest X-ray showed a small amount of fluid under the right lung. I ordered a CT angiogram of the chest, which showed a pulmonary embolus (blood clot) within the right upper and lower lobe pulmonary arteries.

I immediately started her on intravenous heparin and oxygen, and I transferred her to a monitored bed. She gradually improved and was able to go the rehabilitation unit after she was adequately anticoagulated with warfarin.

aggressive radiotherapy may cure only 10 to 15% of all patients with non-small cell carcinoma. Approximately 85 to 90% of patients with non-small cell carcinoma will have or will develop advanced disease and eventually die of their tumor. The vast majority of patients will receive treatment with **radiotherapy** or chemotherapy. Treatment will depend upon the stage of the cancer and the patient's overall health. If the patient has adequate lung function and has no other major medical problems precluding surgery, those patients with earlier stage disease, including stage I and II, will benefit from surgical removal of the lung containing the tumor. In those patients who have inadequate lung function due to chronic lung disease, chest irradiation and possible chemotherapy are the treatments of choice. In some limited groups of patients with more advanced disease, that is, stage IIIa, there may be a role for preoperative chemotherapy followed by surgical resection of the lung. Otherwise, those patients with advanced stages of disease (stage IIIa/b and stage IV) are treated with either chemotherapy, radiation, or both, depending upon the specific patient situation.

Lung cancer is a very common disease within our society. However, you can substantially reduce your risk by elimination of tobacco products. Everyone should be encouraged by health care providers to stop smoking. Educating our youth regarding the significant health risks associated with smoking is essential. These simple acts alone could save over 100,000 lives per year in our country. Although improvements in surgical and medical treatments for this devastating disease are being made, the need for these treatments can be reduced if more people quit smoking.

PULMONARY EMBOLISM

A pulmonary embolism is a blood clot that detaches from a lower leg or upper arm vein and lodges in and obstructs the circulation of the lung (see Figure 6-10). The clot within the blood vessels of the lung causes significant symptoms and may result in death. This is one of the most common acute pulmonary disorders diagnosed among hospitalized patients. The annual incidence rate for pulmonary embolism is 69 per 100,000 individuals. The vast majority of pulmonary emboli arise within the deep veins of the upper thighs and pelvis. The formation of blood clots in those parts of the body is fostered by reduced flow of blood, inheritable or acquired conditions that "thicken" the blood, or blood vessel abnormalities like **varicose** veins or injuries to the veins.

Conditions predisposing one to the development of blood clots in the legs or lungs include obesity, prolonged distance travel, immobilization (paralysis or confinement to bed or chair), cancer, inflammatory bowel disease, previous

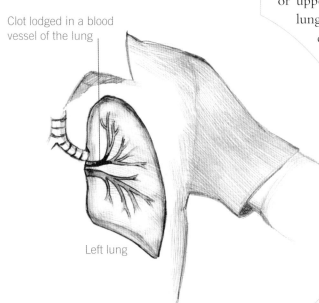

Clot lodged in a blood vessel of the lung

Left lung

(figure 6-10)

A pulmonary embolism is a clot that travels from the veins of the legs or arms and lodges in the lungs.

blood clots, congestive heart failure, heart attacks, strokes, pregnancy or after delivery, varicose veins, fractures of the legs or hips, estrogen use, and surgery. A few of the surgical procedures that tend to carry a higher risk for blood clot formation are operations on the hip or knees and abdominal or pelvic operations. Blood factors, such as deficiencies of protein C, protein S, and antithrombin III, can increase the risk of developing blood clots. Protein C, protein S, and antithrombin III are the body's natural blood thinners. Elevated blood clotting levels of *Factors V* or *VII* make the blood too thick, predisposing it to blood clot formation. The most common hereditary blood abnormality for blood clots in the legs or lung are associated with an abnormal gene called Factor V Leiden.

The symptoms of pulmonary embolism typically occur rather suddenly: shortness of breath, pleurisy (sharp knifelike pain in the chest), coughing, leg swelling, coughing up blood, palpitations in the chest, and wheezing. Patients may display rapid breathing and a rapid heart rate on physical examination. Usually, the lung examination reveals no abnormal sounds on listening to the chest with a stethoscope. Infrequently physicians may hear a pleural friction rub (a grating sound comparable to two pieces of leather rubbing over each other) over the lower chest. Examination of the legs may detect an enlargement of one calf greater than the other, skin redness over the affected leg, or a firm area like a "knot" behind the leg or knee. X-rays of the chest are invariably normal or reveal only nonspecific findings. Therefore, other imaging studies are required. Oxygen levels are usually low in patients who have sustained a pulmonary embolus. However, in some patients the oxygen levels may be normal. The D-dimer is a blood test that measures a by-product of the body's own "clot-dissolving" system, and it may be elevated in patients who have a blood clot in the leg or lungs. However, limiting its usefulness, this test may be positive in other conditions. The D-dimer is used to exclude the diagnosis of a pulmonary embolus or deep vein thrombosis if the blood test is normal.

Several imaging tests are available to detect blood clots in the lungs of patients. A CT angiogram of the lungs is a CT scan but with specific attention to the blood vessels of the lungs by using intravenous contrast. The CT angiogram is noninvasive and has minimal complications. A ventilation-perfusion (VQ) scan is a nuclear medicine study performed to view the blood flow and airflow throughout the lungs. The VQ scan is able to provide some degree of likelihood of a blood clot being in the lung. The pulmonary angiogram is the most definitive test for the diagnosis of a blood clot in the lung. This is an invasive test; the radiologist directs a catheter through a vein in the patient's groin and into the main blood vessels of the lungs. Intravenous dye is injected, and pictures are taken to detect the blood clots. There are several tests to detect blood clots (deep vein thromboses) in the legs: venogram, ultrasound of the legs, or impedance plethysmography (IPG). Ultrasound and IPG are noninvasive tests and are preferred over the invasive venogram.

06

Approximately one-third of deaths from pulmonary embolism occur within one hour of symptoms, and the diagnosis is not suspected in over 50% of the patients. The overall mortality in untreated patients is as high as 30% but dramatically drops to around 6% with appropriate treatment. If the diagnosis is suspected or established, treatment begins immediately with a "blood thinner." (Actually these medications do not thin the blood but inhibit the blood from clotting.) Patients will receive heparin either intravenously or subcutaneously for the first five to seven days of treatment. In some instances if the blood clots are very large and affecting the patient's heart function or significantly lowering blood pressure, two treatment options exist. One is the use of powerful drugs to break down the blood clots more rapidly, and they are called thrombolytic drugs. These "clot busters" have a substantially increased risk of bleeding complications, including bleeding into the brain. The second option is the surgical removal of the blood clots, called a pulmonary embolectomy, reserved for life-threatening circumstances that call for the rapid removal of the blood clot. Pulmonary embolectomy is an uncommon procedure and is only utilized in the most extreme cases.

WARFARIN (COUMADIN), an oral tablet, is started during the hospital stay, while the patient is still on the heparin, and will become the treatment of choice once the patient is discharged from the hospital. Coumadin's ability to thin the patient's blood is measured by a blood test called the international normalized ratio (INR). A normal INR is 1.0, and the goal for patients on Coumadin for pulmonary emboli is between 2.0 and 3.0. Under 2.0 the patient's blood is not thin enough, and over 3.0 the blood is too thin and increases the patient's risk for bleeding. Most patients with a deep vein thrombosis or with pulmonary emboli are treated for 6 months with Coumadin. This helps resolve and prevent recurrence of the blood clots. In some patients treatment may be longer or lifelong, depending upon physician recommendations.

In those patients who are unable to tolerate blood thinners due to bleeding or other conditions, a device can be placed in the major vein leading from the lower legs and pelvis to the lungs in order to prevent additional blood clots from entering the lung circulation. These devices go by different names but are in general referred to as inferior vena cava (IVC) filters. Sometimes they are called "umbrella" filters since they resemble a rain umbrella (see Figure 6-11). The spokes of the umbrella go into the wall of the blood vessel. Small holes in the umbrella allow blood to get through but not blood clots. The inferior vena cava is the large vein in which the device is placed. A vascular surgeon or an interventional radiologist usually performs the procedure.

There has been a significant reduction in preventing blood clots from developing in hospitalized patients through the use of

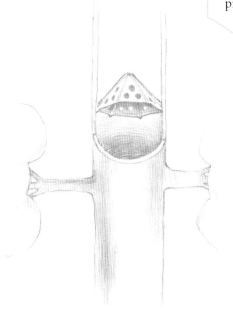

(figure 6-11*)*

An umbrella, or IVC filter, in the inferior vena cava.

preventative measures along with a heightened awareness by the medical profession. Fortunately there continues to be advances in the diagnosis and treatment of this disease that will make it easier for the physician to identify those patients more effectively and provide simpler treatment options in the future.

■

WHAT YOU NEED TO KNOW

▶ Avoid environmental and occupational dust since they may result in lung disease. Always wear protective masks if you work in an environment with dust or fiber particles.

▶ A regular exercise program at any age improves your health and overall well-being.

▶ Smoking is the cause of lung cancer and COPD in most cases. If you smoke, ask your doctor to help you quit. There are effective medications and other aids to help you.

▶ If you are 65 or older, get the pneumonia vaccine and an annual flu vaccine. If you have COPD, you should have a pneumonia vaccine every five to eight years and an annual flu vaccine.

▶ Sleep apnea is a common disorder in older persons. Let your doctor know if you snore or feel sleepy and tired frequently.

▶ Lung cancer is the number one cause of cancer deaths in the United States. Go to your physician if you experience a chronic cough or hoarseness, shortness of breath, expectoration of blood, or chest discomfort. These may be the first symptoms of lung cancer.

▶ Pulmonary emboli are blood clots that form in the lower leg or upper arm veins and travel into the lung circulation. Important risk factors for developing pulmonary emboli include obesity, prolonged travel, bedridden state, estrogen use, surgery or injury to the lower extremities, stroke, major abdominal or pelvic operations, and cancer. There are measures that can be taken to reduce the chance of developing pulmonary emboli in high-risk individuals.

FOR MORE INFORMATION

▶ American Lung Association
61 Broadway, 6th Floor
New York, NY 10006
212-315-8700
Web: www.lungusa.org

▶ National Heart, Lung, and Blood Institute
NHLBI Health Information Center
P.O. Box 30105
Bethesda, MD 20824
301-592-8573
TTY: 240-629-3255
Fax: 301-592-8563
E-mail: nhlbiinfo@rover.nhlbi.nih.gov
Web: www.nhlbi.nih.gov

> To resist the frigidity of old age one must combine the body, the mind, and the heart—and to keep them in parallel vigor one must exercise, study, and love.
>
> —*Karl von Bonstetten*

THE AUTHORS

07

TAREK HELMY, MD, went to medical school at Cairo University–Faculty of Medicine, where he graduated with honors. He did his medicine residency and cardiology fellowship at the University of Texas Medical Branch in Galveston and went on to complete an interventional cardiology fellowship at New England Medical Center–Tufts University in Boston. He is an assistant professor at Emory University School of Medicine and the medical director of the cardiac catheterization laboratory at Grady Memorial Hospital.

NANETTE K. WENGER, MD, MACP, FACC, FAHA, is professor of medicine in the Division of Cardiology at the Emory University School of Medicine. She is chief of cardiology at Grady Memorial Hospital and a consultant to the Emory Heart and Vascular Center. Dr. Wenger is a past president of the Society of Geriatric Cardiology and editor of the *American Journal of Geriatric Cardiology.* Listed in *Best Doctors of America,* Dr. Wenger has been an author or coauthor of over 1000 scientific and review articles and book chapters.

FADI ALAMEDDINE, MD, received his doctor of medicine from the American University of Beirut in Lebanon in 1997. He completed an internal medicine residency at Emory University Hospital in Atlanta, where he is a cardiology fellow. His awards include the Best First-Year Resident Award from the Department of Internal Medicine Residency Program at Emory (1999) and the certificate of excellence given by the Emory Medical School Class of 2001. Dr. Alameddine is certified by the American Board of Internal Medicine.

IBRAHIM HANNA, MD, received his doctor of medicine from the American University of Beirut before joining the internal medicine residency program at Emory in 1998. He is a cardiology fellow at Emory University. His awards include Best Third-Year Resident from the Department of Internal Medicine Residency Program at Emory, and Outstanding Teaching Resident Award given by the Emory University School of Medicine senior classes of 1999 and 2001. Dr. Hanna was certified by the American Board of Internal Medicine in 2002.

07 | THE HEART

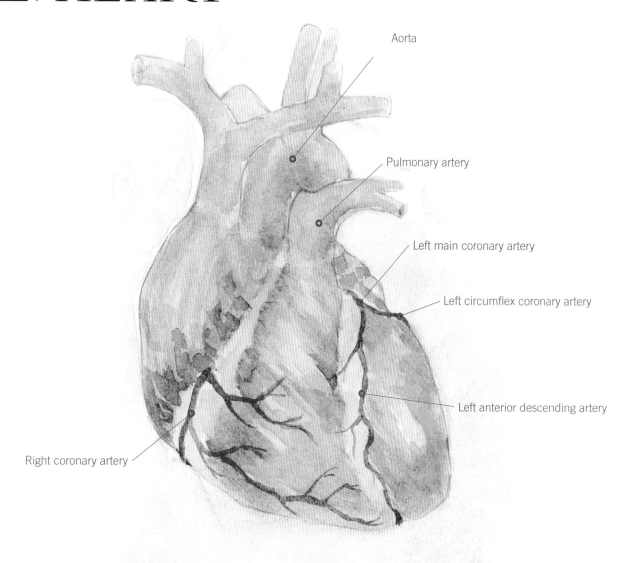

Aorta

Pulmonary artery

Left main coronary artery

Left circumflex coronary artery

Left anterior descending artery

Right coronary artery

(figure 7-1)
The heart and coronary arteries.

Aging is associated with a dramatic increase in heart disease. Coronary artery disease, which causes heart attacks, is the leading cause of death in the United States. More than 80% of deaths from heart disease in the United States occur in persons over 65 years old.

The manifestations of cardiovascular disease may be very different as we grow older. This is related to physiological changes in the *cardiovascular system* (heart and blood vessels) that occur with aging, the coexisting medical conditions commonly seen in older people, and the decreased tolerance that the elderly usually have to illness. As you will see later in this chapter, an older person may not have chest pain or other typical symptoms even if a heart attack is taking place.

Research studies that help decide the best treatments and expected results are limited in the elderly since older persons were deliberately excluded. Although applying the same general approach to both older and younger persons seems reasonable in most cases, the physician has to consider other factors. How well does this person function physically and mentally? Which other medical conditions or medications could complicate this treatment? How well will this person tolerate this medicine or procedure? The benefits of various therapies and interventions must always be weighed against the risks.

LET'S TAKE A JOURNEY

Imagine that you are a red blood cell and that you have just given your oxygen to the leg muscles so those muscles can work properly. You need to go back to the lungs in order to get more oxygen to repeat the cycle. The blood vessels that bring blood back to the heart are called veins and those that carry blood away from the heart are called arteries. You will eventually end up in the inferior vena cava, the large vein that brings blood from the lower body to the right atrium (see Figure 7-2). If you had come from the arms or head, you would end up in the superior vena cava.

As you enter the right atrium, you are initially held back from entering the right ventricle by a valve, which acts like a trapdoor, called the tricuspid valve. When the right atrium contracts, it squirts you into a larger chamber called the right ventricle. You notice the tricuspid valve has muscular anchors called papillary muscles. The valve looks like a parachute. The strings that lead from the valve to the papillary muscles are called chordae tendineae. They help the valve open and close properly. When the right ventricle contracts, the tricuspid valve closes to prevent backflow of blood, and you are ejected through the pulmonic valve into the pulmonary artery.

Arteries usually carry oxygenated blood, but since you haven't been to the lungs yet to pick up your oxygen supply, you are oxygen-poor. Finally, you reach the lung and circle around the small air sacs by which you pick up your oxygen supply and your color becomes redder and healthier. You leave the lungs through the pulmonary veins and travel back to the heart.

You enter the left atrium and are held back from the left ventricle for a brief moment by the mitral valve. The left atrium then contracts and propels you into the left ventricle, the largest and most powerful pumping chamber in the heart. You notice that the mitral valve has a similar structural appearance to the tricuspid valve. Suddenly, you are shot out of the heart through the aortic valve and back into circulation. This time rather than going to the legs, your mission brings you to the brain, and you marvel at the wonders of this intricate human machine.

(figure 7-2)
The interior of the heart.

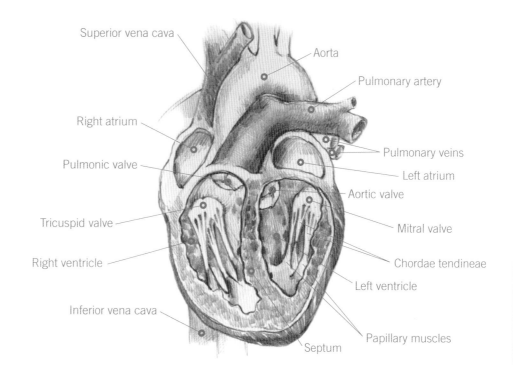

Superior vena cava
Aorta
Pulmonary artery
Right atrium
Pulmonary veins
Pulmonic valve
Left atrium
Aortic valve
Tricuspid valve
Mitral valve
Right ventricle
Chordae tendineae
Left ventricle
Inferior vena cava
Papillary muscles
Septum

CHANGES IN THE CARDIOVASCULAR SYSTEM

The normal aging process takes its toll on your cardiovascular system. This includes changes in the *myocardium* (heart muscle), the heart's own natural *pacemaker and conduction system* (the "electrical system"), and the blood vessels.

VASCULAR SYSTEM

Vascular (blood vessel) changes include mainly an increase in stiffness of the arteries throughout the body, leading to a rapid rise in pressure during systole (when the heart contracts) and a rapid decline in pressure during diastole (when the heart relaxes). The elevated blood pressure leads to detrimental effects on such organs as the heart, brain, and kidneys. It may also accelerate the process of atherosclerosis (hardening of the arteries) and accentuate progression of aneurysms (balloonlike weakening in the walls of blood vessels).

The rise in the blood pressure increases the work that the heart's main pumping chamber, the left ventricle, has to do (see Figure 7–2). If you pump weights, your muscles will get bigger because they are pushing against resistance. Similarly, if pumping against the resistance of stiff arteries, your heart muscle thickens and gets bigger. This is called left ventricular hypertrophy. However, this is not a desirable condition for the heart, since the thickened muscle may not allow the heart to fill properly with blood. Eventually the constant strain may actually cause the heart to get weaker. Either of these situations can result in congestive heart failure (CHF), a condition in which the heart can no longer keep up with the body's blood and oxygen demands; this is discussed in the section "Congestive Heart Failure."

HEART CHANGES

With age there is a decrease in the stretching capability of the left ventricle mainly due to thickening of the heart muscle and decreased elasticity of the heart. Imagine that you are making two water balloons. The first is a thin-walled balloon; the second has a very thick wall. The first balloon will fill and distend easier than the second. Similarly, your heart fills with blood and distends more easily when you are younger. In addition, your maximal heart rate (beats per minute) and maximal aerobic capacity decrease as you age. All these effects may limit your exercise tolerance as you get older. However, you can limit these adverse effects by keeping up a regular aerobic exercise program, such as walking, running, swimming, bicycling, or rowing. If you have not engaged in these types of activities, check with your doctor first. You may need to start slowly, or your doctor may suggest an exercise evaluation prior to commencing these activities.

With aging, we become more dependent on the contribution of the small upper chambers of the heart (the atria) to help fill the ventricles (the larger pumping chambers) with blood. If the left atrium (LA) does not function properly, the filling of the left ventricle is impaired, and symptoms of congestive heart failure may result. This can occur with atrial fibrillation, in which the atria quiver rather than beat in a regular coordinated fashion so that the ventricles fill poorly.

Disease of the heart valves may also occur with aging. Calcific aortic stenosis is a narrowing of the valve between the left ventricle and aorta due to degeneration and thickening of the valve leaflets (see Figure 7-3). It causes obstruction to the flow of blood out of the heart. It should always be considered in patients with angina, shortness of breath, and fainting.

Sclerosis is a thickening of valvular leaflets and may occur without significant narrowing of the valve opening. *Valvular regurgitation* is the

(figure 7-3)

Aortic stenosis is a narrowing of the opening of the aortic valve. Notice the normal aortic valve when (a) closed and (b) open. (c) The calcified aortic valve becomes thickened and rigid. (d) The calcified valve has restricted, motion (stenosis) when open. Notice the smaller separation of the leaflets in the calcified valve when open.

NORMAL VALVE   CALCIFIED VALVE

(a) Closed   (b) Open   (c) Closed   (d) Open

(figure 7-4)

The heart's electrical wiring (the conduction system). A signal travels from the SA node in the right atrium and spreads to the left atrium, causing the upper chambers to contract and, consequently, pushing blood into the ventricles. The electric signal travels via special pathways to a relay station, called the AV node, which temporarily delays the impulse before sending it through the electrical pathway to the ventricles called the bundle of His. This delay allows the ventricles to fill with blood. The signal then travels down the bundle of His, which divides into the right and left bundle branches. The signal spreads to the ventricles, stimulating them to contract and eject blood to supply the rest of the body.

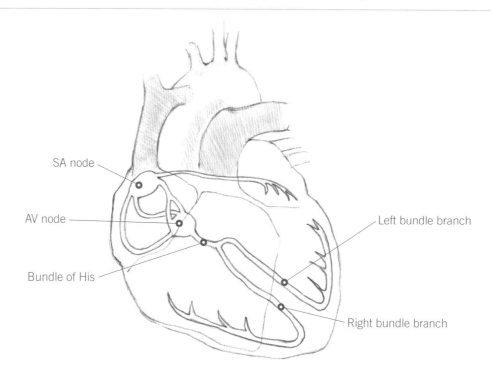

SA node

AV node

Bundle of His

Left bundle branch

Right bundle branch

backflow of blood through a leaky heart valve. Trace to mild regurgitation is commonly seen in older patients, but more severe degrees of regurgitation are also quite common and require meticulous medical attention and occasionally surgical treatment.

CONDUCTION SYSTEM

Your heart has its own pacing system that allows it to beat in a regular fashion, usually between 60 and 100 beats per minute. When you exercise, your heart responds to the need for more blood to bring oxygen to your muscles by increasing its rate to as much as 120 to 160 beats per minute. However, older age is associated with an increased incidence of problems in the heart's *conduction system* (see Figure 7-4). As such, the elderly are prone to develop problems with slow or fast heart rates from disorders of the electrical system, SA node, the AV node, or both. Several heart rhythm disturbances are discussed in the section "Arrhythmias and Conduction Abnormalities."

ATHEROSCLEROSIS

PREVALENCE

Atherosclerosis is often called "hardening of the arteries." It is caused by the buildup of bloodstream fats in the wall of the blood vessels. Normally

(figure 7-5)

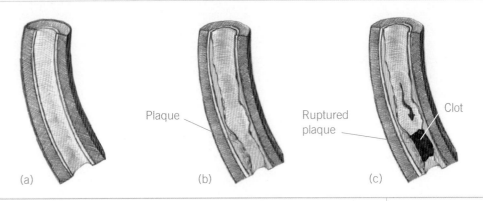

the inside lining of a blood vessel is smooth, but atherosclerosis leads to the development of irregular bumps composed of fat, fibrous tissue, and occasionally calcium (see Figure 7-5). These bumps are called plaque. If the plaque buildup is severe, it can actually block the flow of blood in the blood vessel. Atherosclerotic coronary heart disease is the most prevalent cardiac disease of the elderly. There are estimated 3.6 million elderly persons with coronary artery disease, and it accounts for about two-thirds of all deaths in older persons in the United States.

Atherosclerosis begins early, often in the teenage years or earlier. It is a progressive disease over time. Some individuals, especially those with multiple coronary risk factors (see Table 7-1), may have symptoms in their 20s or 30s. Others may have symptoms in midlife. However, those over 65 account for 83% of all cardiovascular deaths.

Atherosclerotic disease is not only more severe as we get older, but it is also more diffuse. This means that elderly persons who have a heart attack often have disease in areas other than where the heart attack occurred. This places them at higher risk for complications. It also limits options since procedures that restore blood flow, such as coronary angioplasty and coronary bypass surgery, may not adequately correct blood flow problems in other areas of the heart.

SEX DIFFERENCE

The incidence of coronary artery disease is greater in young and middle-aged men than in women due to a possible "protective" effect of female hormones. This difference diminishes in women around the time of the menopause and is abolished by the 80s.

CAUSES OF ATHEROSCLEROSIS

The initial event in atherosclerosis is injury to the endothelium, the cells that line the inside of the blood vessels. The factor most described is hypercholesterolemia (elevated blood cholesterol). The "bad cholesterol" is low-density lipoprotein (LDL) cholesterol. It diffuses from the bloodstream into the wall of the coronary arteries. Special white blood cells, called *macrophages,* respond to the injury caused by the LDL.

(table 7-1)

MAJOR RISK FACTORS FOR CORONARY ARTERY DISEASE

Family history of premature coronary artery disease*	Male
High blood pressure	Advanced age
High blood cholesterol	Obesity
Cigarette smoking	Physical inactivity
Diabetes mellitus	

*Less than 55 years old in men and 65 years old in women.

They ingest the LDL and become bloated and foamy. Eventually this leads to development of an atherosclerotic plaque, a thickened area filled with a cheesy material composed of fat, smooth muscle cells, fibrous tissue, and calcium.

There are two types of plaque. Stable plaque has a small lipid (fatty) core and is covered by a thick fibrous cap. This is typically the lesion that causes stable, slowly progressive angina (chest discomfort due to coronary artery disease). Unstable plaque is the more dangerous type; it consists of a large lipid core covered by a thin fibrous cap. The core of this type of plaque is rich in substances that can make blood readily clot. The inflammatory process at the edges, or "shoulder," of the plaque leads to the release of digestive enzymes, which dissolve the fibrous cap and cause the plaque to rupture. The rupture exposes the core to the circulating blood and allows a thrombus (clot) to form. *Coronary thrombosis* is the major cause of heart attacks and other unstable coronary syndromes. Interestingly, many of these heart attacks occur at sites where the plaque blockage is less than 70%! This is due to rupture of an unstable or vulnerable plaque.

CORONARY ARTERY DISEASE

SYMPTOMS

Chest pain is the most common symptom of significant coronary artery disease. It is usually described as tightness or pressure in the chest, typically brought on by exertion or emotion and relieved by rest or nitroglycerin (a tablet that can be dissolved under the tongue or a spray that can be squirted in the mouth to relieve angina). The pain may radiate to the neck, jaw, and arms or back and sometimes is associated with shortness of breath, nausea, vomiting, and sweating (see Figure 7-6). Pain caused by myocardial ischemia (inadequate coronary blood flow) is referred to as angina (or angina pectoris).

If angina is of new onset, rapidly progressing in intensity or duration, or occurring at rest, the presentation is called acute coronary syndrome (ACS), or *unstable angina.* It is important to remember that angina may have unusual features in the elderly patient and may predominately manifest as fatigue or shortness of breath occasionally occurring even at rest, especially in sedentary patients. Some persons may have no symptoms at all. This is called *silent ischemia.* These individuals warrant therapy, since revascularization (restoring blood flow by angioplasty or bypass surgery) of patients with silent ischemia has been shown to improve survival.

(figure 7-6)

The typical location and pattern of radiation of angina pectoris. Symptoms related to coronary disease include pain in the chest that can sometimes spread to other areas. Upset stomach, profuse sweating, and cold clammy skin can occur. It is important to realize that atypical pain and locations can occur with heart attacks, especially in the elderly. In fact, many older patients may have none of these symptoms. Unusual shortness of breath may be an indication of a problem and should be reported to the doctor.

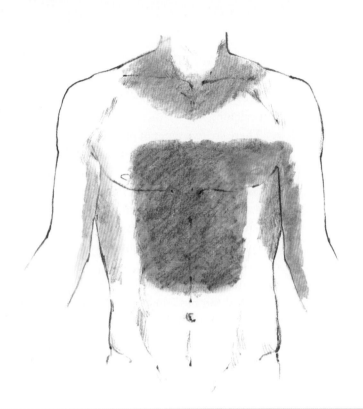

Often physicians will suggest noninvasive testing (see below) of persons with multiple risk factors for coronary artery disease, even if they have no symptoms.

EVALUATION OF PATIENTS

Patients with angina should be evaluated by their physician. Initial evaluation includes a thorough history and physical exam, an electrocardiogram (ECG or EKG), and cardiac enzymes (blood tests). This evaluation will include an assessment of coronary risk factors that might need treatment, such as high blood pressure, high blood cholesterol, obesity, and diabetes. Further evaluation either by noninvasive stress testing or cardiac catheterization is performed at the discretion of the cardiologist.

MANAGEMENT OF ACUTE CORONARY SYNDROMES

Initial medical therapy includes aspirin, nitroglycerin, heparin (an intravenous "blood thinner") and a beta-blocker, and probably a statin. These medicines should be used with caution especially in the elderly patient with low blood pressure or diseases of the conduction system.

Other medications may be appropriate depending on the vital signs and electrocardiogram.

Further management could invoke one of two strategies. The first is considered more aggressive since it involves cardiac catheterization (a dye test to outline the coronary arteries) and possibly angioplasty or bypass surgery depending on the results. This early invasive strategy is supported by several studies that suggest overall outcomes are improved.

The second strategy, the conservative approach, is a reasonable alternative. Patients are observed until blood tests that monitor injury to the heart indicate improvement and symptoms resolve; then a stress test is performed prior to discharge. If the stress test indicates a low risk, patients can be managed medically. If the stress test indicates a large area of heart muscle in jeopardy, patients should proceed to cardiac catheterization. Cardiac catheterization is also preferred for patients with a depressed function of the left ventricle (the main pumping chamber of the heart), even after resolution of anginal symptoms.

MANAGEMENT OF STABLE ANGINA

Due to the high prevalence of coronary artery disease in the elderly, a large number of elderly patients will have stable angina, which means that their symptoms are triggered only by exertion or excitement and are usually promptly relieved by rest or nitroglycerin. These patients have either been managed with medicines or have undergone coronary revascularization, and their symptoms are well controlled. Stable angina may slowly progress requiring adjustments in the medical regimen. It is important to rule out any precipitating causes for worsening of stable angina, such as anemia, hyperthyroidism (an overactive thyroid gland), uncontrolled high blood pressure or low blood pressure, rhythm disturbance, and infection.

Patients who have stable symptoms and whose stress test indicates a low-risk status for serious events should be maintained on medical therapy, given the higher risk of revascularization in elderly patients. Medical therapy should include aspirin, beta-blockers, angiotensin-converting enzyme (ACE) inhibitors, lipid-lowering agents, nitrates, and/or calcium channel blockers. Elderly patients should be followed closely for any side effects or toxicity of medical therapy. This includes slow heart rate, various degrees of conduction abnormalities, low blood pressure, liver or kidney problems, and occasionally mental status changes. The drugs often need to be started at lower dosages and gradually increased. Patients with progressive symptoms should be evaluated by a stress test or directly by cardiac catheterization to evaluate the severity of blockages in the coronary arteries; a decision regarding revascularization is considered accordingly.

ACUTE MYOCARDIAL INFARCTION

A myocardial infarction (MI), often called a *heart attack,* means literally "heart muscle death (see Figure 7-7)." It results from sudden rupture of an atherosclerotic plaque and blockage of blood flow. In 70% of the cases, the plaque does not totally block the vessel. Usually the degree of *stenosis* (narrowing) is less than 70%, but the rupture of the plaque triggers clotting of blood. The artery becomes occluded by a blood clot adhering to the ruptured plaque.

A heart attack will usually cause chest pain, but symptoms can vary considerably especially in elderly patients or diabetics. Some persons may have sudden onset of shortness of breath, shoulder or jaw pain, sudden change in behavior or mental status, extreme fatigue, or fainting. In elderly patients, symptoms of MI usually occur at rest rather than with exertion, and some older persons have no symptoms at all! Given these unusual presentations, the diagnosis of MI can be missed. In large studies, 38 to 60% of patients, whose electrocardiogram showed a previous heart attack, reported that they never had any symptoms that they thought were related to a heart attack. The elderly also have an increased occurrence of non-Q wave myocardial infarction (NQMI). Non-Q wave MI means that a heart attack has occurred without causing a typical ECG abnormality. This can make it difficult to diagnose previous MI in the elderly. There is a dramatically increased mortality from heart attack in the elderly. This can be attributed to atypical symptoms during a heart attack limiting early recognition and treatment, other coexisting medical problems, and the fact that many elderly people do not seek medical attention right away. Moreover, the prognosis for an unrecognized heart attack is as serious as a typical heart attack that produces symptoms. The mortality is sixfold higher for the 75–84 age group and eightfold higher for those over 85 compared to the 55–64 age group. This is due at least in part to preexisting medical conditions, such as hypertension, diabetes mellitus, COPD, chronic kidney disease, congestive heart failure, prior heart attack, and poor overall reserve and function of other body systems.

Area of heart muscle death (myocardial infarction)

(figure 7-7)

Myocardial infarction: a heart attack.

MANAGEMENT OF ACUTE MYOCARDIAL INFARCTION

The goal of therapy for a heart attack is reestablishment of blood flow in the blocked coronary artery. This is achieved by using **thrombolytic therapy** ("clot busters") or urgent cardiac catheterization and angioplasty.

(figure 7-8)

Clot busters are used in the treatment of a heart attack if the ECG shows significant elevation of the ST segment. (a) normal ECG (b) ECG showing ST segment elevation.

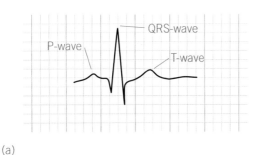

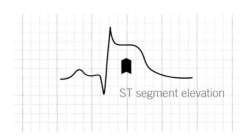

(a)   (b)

(figure 7-9)
Coronary angioplasty.

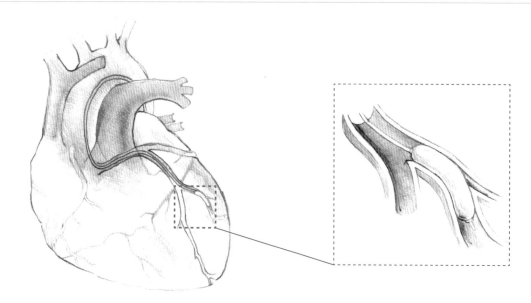

Clot busters are used in a heart attack if the electrocardiogram shows significant ST-segment elevation (see Figure 7-8). Best results are seen when given within six hours of onset of symptoms. This can be a real challenge in the elderly since the typical symptoms of a heart attack may not be present. This can delay the diagnosis of a heart attack or make it difficult to determine when the heart attack started; thus, the benefit of thrombolytic therapy can be decreased or even rendered useless for some elderly patients.

Contraindications to using clot busters include recent stroke, any history of bleeding inside the head, or any active internal bleeding such as a bleeding ulcer. There are some other relative contraindications, such as recent major surgery, significant high blood pressure, blood disorders, and more than 12 hours since onset of symptoms. A cardiologist or emergency department physician weighs the benefits against the risks of administering these drugs in those situations.

Unfortunately, patients older than 75 years of age were excluded from the early studies of thrombolytic therapy. However, considerable data suggest comparable benefit in young and older patients up to age 75 years of age, with a mortality benefit even greater in patients of 65 to 75 years than in younger patients. Data for patients older than 75 years of age are controversial due to the high risk of cerebral hemorrhage (bleeding into the brain) in this age group. However, age by itself should not be considered an exclusion criterion for thrombolytic therapy, and the cardiologist will make a decision whether or not to use it on the basis of all factors involved.

Angioplasty (opening a blocked blood vessel with a balloon catheter with or without placement of a stent, as shown in Figure 7-9) is another strategy to manage a heart attack. Angioplasty has been shown to be more effective in reestablishing flow in the blocked artery than has thrombolytic therapy. It is associated with a decreased incidence of major bleeding, especially brain hemorrhage, which makes angioplasty an attractive strategy in patients over 75 years of age.

Since the availability of angioplasty is limited to centers with around-the-clock catheterization laboratories with surgical backup, it is a limited alternative to thrombolytic therapy in some settings. Recent studies suggest that it may be feasible to withhold thrombolytics and transfer patients to another center for angioplasty if the anticipated transfer time is within three hours. Ongoing studies are examining the safety and efficacy of "facilitated" angioplasty, in which a lower dose of thrombolytics is given prior to transfer for angioplasty. Limited studies suggest that performing urgent angioplasty may be safe without surgical backup in the same center.

Patients in cardiogenic shock (circulatory collapse), complicating a heart attack, have been shown to benefit from an early invasive strategy and revascularization, up to the age of 75; patients older than 75 years of age do not appear to benefit from an early invasive strategy.

Long-term therapy commonly used following a heart attack include aspirin, beta-blockers, ACE inhibitors, and statins, all of which have been shown to improve survival. A recent study supports the addition of CLOPIDOGREL (PLAVIX) to the medical regimen following acute coronary syndromes. There was a significant reduction in the risk of death, stroke, and another heart attack. Nitroglycerin may be used for relief of angina.

The introduction of these new therapies over the last two decades has resulted in a substantial decline in death and disability following heart attack, but complications remain higher for older patients. Future research exploring new treatments will be specifically evaluating their impact on

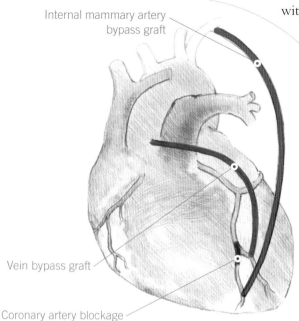

Internal mammary artery bypass graft

Vein bypass graft

Coronary artery blockage

(figure 7-10)

Coronary bypass surgery. The grafts bring blood to the coronary arteries beyond the blocked area, thus "bypassing" the blockage.

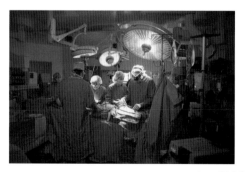

(figure 7-11)

Heart surgical team performing a coronary by-pass operation. *(Courtesy of Sarasota Memorial Hospital).*

older persons. Hopefully this will improve outcomes for the older person with coronary artery disease. However, it is never too late to practice good preventive medicine (see "Health Tips").

CORONARY REVASCULARIZATION

Patients with unstable coronary syndromes who have a high-risk stress test or who are not responsive to medical therapy should be considered for coronary angiography and revascularization. Coronary angiography is a dye test to image the coronary arteries. It involves inserting a small catheter in a blood vessel in the groin and then advancing the catheter to the heart. This test helps the cardiologist find the blockages. In some cases, the cardiologist can open the blocked artery with a balloon catheter (angioplasty) and often insert a stent to prevent the renarrowing of the artery. In more severe cases, the cardiologist will ask a heart surgeon to do bypass surgery. The heart operation is called a coronary artery bypass graft (CABG), shown in Figures 7-10 and 7-11. You may hear some doctors call it a "cabbage." It requires taking small segments from a chest artery and/or from the leg veins to bypass a blocked coronary artery.

Older patients tend to have a higher prevalence of coronary disease that involves all three coronary arteries and the *left main coronary artery.* The coronary blockages are often calcified. This makes revascularization procedures more difficult and risky, especially if other medical conditions are present (diabetes, high blood pressure, congestive heart failure, chronic kidney diseases). Clinical studies suggest that CABG is superior to medical therapy in patients with left main coronary disease and in patients with three-vessel disease if the left ventricular function is impaired.

Angioplasty has been shown to be equally effective to bypass surgery in terms of survival, except in diabetic patients with three-vessel disease where bypass surgery appears to be superior. The best approach to disease that involves the first part of the *left anterior descending coronary artery (LAD)* is still controversial. There is a reasonable body of data to support both angioplasty and bypass surgery. Patients who undergo angioplasty have a higher rate of repeat procedures for renarrowing of the blocked artery, but the rate of stroke, heart attack, and death in the hospital is less compared to bypass surgery. Advanced age, again, substantially increases the risk of death and disability for both bypass surgery and angioplasty.

CONGESTIVE HEART FAILURE

Congestive heart failure (CHF) is the leading cardiac cause for hospitalization and health expenditure in the United States today. With the improvement of cardiac therapies over the last decade and increased survival of cardiac patients, we have seen a marked increase in the number of patients with congestive heart failure, especially the elderly.

One of the main causes for congestive heart failure is weakness of the heart muscle that impairs its pumping function. One of the most common causes is ischemia (poor blood flow) and heart muscle death. After a heart attack, the amount of damage to the left ventricle determines how well the heart pumps. This will determine the symptoms and severity of congestive heart failure. As our management for heart attacks becomes more aggressive, there are more survivors of heart attacks, but they may develop congestive heart failure from the damaged heart muscle.

Cardiomyopathy is the term given to diseases that primarily affect the heart muscle. Cardiomyopathy with poor pump function in the elderly can also be caused by longstanding hypertension (high blood pressure), alcohol excess, and disease of the heart valves. *Myocarditis* (inflammation or infection of the heart muscle), metabolic disorders, and genetic diseases are less commonly seen in the elderly population.

The main manifestations of congestive heart failure are symptoms of fluid overload, including shortness of breath *(dyspnea)* on exertion, shortness of breath when lying down *(orthopnea),* sudden shortness of breath at night requiring sitting up at the side of the bed in order to breath better *(paroxysmal nocturnal dyspnea),* and lower extremity swelling *(edema).* Symptoms of poor cardiac output include poor exercise tolerance and easy fatigue. Chest pain due to increased stress on the heart muscle is

(table 7-2)

NEW YORK HEART ASSOCIATION CLASSIFICATION SCHEME TO ASSESS SYMPTOM SEVERITY RELATED TO CONGESTIVE HEART FAILURE

CLASS	DESCRIPTION	SYMPTOM SEVERITY
I	Patients with cardiac disease but without resulting limitations of physical activity. Ordinary physical activity does not cause undue fatigue, palpitations, shortness of breath, or angina pain.	None to mild
II	Patients with cardiac disease resulting in slight limitation of physical activity. They are comfortable at rest. Ordinary physical activity results in fatigue, palpitations, shortness of breath, or angina pain.	Mild to moderate
III	Patients with cardiac disease that results in marked limitation of physical activity and causes fatigue, palpitations, shortness of breath, or angina pain.	Moderate to severe
IV	Patients with cardiac disease that results in inability to carry on any physical activity without discomfort. Symptoms of cardiac insufficiency or of anginal syndrome may be present even at rest. If any physical activity is undertaken, discomfort is increased.	Severe

Source: The New York Heart Association.

not uncommon. A palpitation is a beating of the heart that is perceived by the patient. It may feel like a thump in the chest. Some patients may feel that their heart is racing or beating irregularly. They may be due to heart rhythm disturbances, which are not uncommon in congestive heart failure.

The New York Heart Association has developed a classification scheme that helps assess the severity of a person's symptoms related to congestive heart failure (see Table 7-2). It may also be helpful in monitoring response to treatment or progression of the disease.

It is sometimes difficult to pinpoint a specific cause for the above-mentioned symptoms in the presence of other diseases that may involve the lungs, kidneys, and so forth. On examining a patient, a doctor will look for physical findings that suggest congestive heart failure. Tests that may help the doctor with the correct diagnosis include heart enzymes, a chest X-ray, and echocardiography (ultrasound examination of the heart). Recently, a blood test called brain natriuretic peptide (BNP) has become available that may be useful in some situations.

Patients with congestive heart failure may exhibit distended neck veins due to poor return of blood back to the heart, crackling noises in the lungs due to fluid buildup, cold clammy extremities, and swelling of the feet and legs (see Figure 7-12). The heartbeat may be rapid, and there may be a murmur related to backflow of blood through the tricuspid or mitral valves. In severe cases the patient may have a very low blood oxygen level and may need to be placed on a mechanical ventilator.

Management of congestive heart failure involves primarily defining and treating the causes. Any precipitating factors, such as uncontrolled high blood pressure, anemia, heart rhythm disturbances, infections, increased dietary salt intake, and medical noncompliance, should also be addressed. Medical therapy for congestive heart failure has significantly changed over the past few years. Medicines called ACE inhibitors have been a major advance and have been shown to improve survival and symptoms. They may also benefit patients with impaired pump function even before the development of actual symptoms. Beta-blockers, specifically CARVEDILOL (COREG) and METOPROLOL (LOPRESSOR, TOPROL-XL), improve symptoms and survival in congestive heart failure patients. SPIRONOLACTONE (ALDACTONE) has also been shown to decrease death and disability in patients with severe heart failure symptoms. Although spironolactone is a diuretic agent, the dose used in the clinical trials that showed a benefit was lower than the usual diuretic dose, which indicates that there are other modes of action to explain the benefit seen in that trial. Management of fluid balance with the use of diuretics, and fluid and sodium restriction, is important to control symptoms. Data on the benefit of DIGOXIN (LANOXIN, DIGITEK) for patients with a normal heart rhythm is controversial. Some patients who are stable on digoxin seem to get worse if it is withdrawn. Most of the benefit of digoxin is related to the control of symptoms. Although survival is not improved, patients on digoxin had improved exercise tolerance and decreased number of hospitalizations.

(figure 7-12)

A patient with congestive heart failure often has shortness of breath and has to sit up to breathe more comfortably.

Data suggest a gender difference in the benefit of digoxin with improved outcomes for men but increased death rates for women.

Hypertrophic cardiomyopathy is caused by increased thickness of the left ventricular muscle and occasionally by enlargement of the septum (the muscular tissue that separates the right and left ventricles) leading to obstruction of the blood flow out of the left ventricle (see Figure 7-13). Hypertrophic cardiomyopathy is common in the elderly population; about 30% of cases are over 60 years of age. Clinical symptoms include dizziness, fainting, fatigue, shortness of breath, and chest pain. Episodes of severe and sudden fluid buildup in the lungs called "flash" *pulmonary edema,* may occur. It is usually triggered by a sudden rise in blood pressure, onset of heart rhythm irregularity or fluid overload, and generally requires *intubation* (insertion of a breathing tube) and use of a mechanical ventilator. Increased left ventricular stiffness and impaired filling of the left ventricle with blood when the heart relaxes contribute to this condition. Hypertrophic cardiomyopathy is usually treated with medications.

Restrictive cardiomyopathy is uncommon. It is characterized by stiffness of the muscle of the heart and impairment of filling of the heart with blood during diastole. It can be caused by *amyloidosis* (a disease in which an abnormal protein accumulates in body tissues), *hemochromatosis* (an iron storage disease), *sarcoidosis* (a disease in which nodules called *granulomas* infiltrate various tissues of the body), and radiation to the chest. Medical therapy is limited, and there is no surgical treatment.

VALVULAR HEART DISEASE

AORTIC STENOSIS

Aortic stenosis (narrowing of the aortic valve) is a common disease of the elderly. The majority of cases are due to calcification of a tricuspid (three cusps or leaflets) aortic valve. Symptoms associated with severe aortic stenosis include shortness of breath that is worse with exertion and chest pain or angina. Aortic stenosis is one of the important causes of **syncope** (fainting) in the elderly patient. Syncope was initially thought to be due to decreased output of blood from the heart with severe narrowing of the aortic valve, but recently a **vasodepressor reflex** has been proposed as an alternative mechanism. The high pressure generated in the left ventricle as it contracts against a narrowed opening causes a drop in blood pressure and heart rate. Heart rhythm problems and sudden death are also common in individuals with severe aortic stenosis. Symptoms usually progress fairly rapidly in elderly patients, and once symptomatic, only 50% of patients will survive five years. Therefore, urgent valve replacement surgery is required once symptoms develop.

To evaluate a person with aortic stenosis, a doctor will gently palpate the carotid pulse in the neck. Due to the obstruction to flow of blood

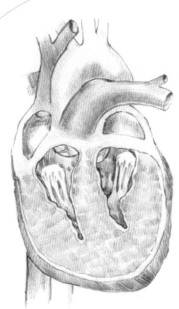

(figure 7-13)

Hypertrophic cardiomyopathy. Notice the thickness of the heart muscle walls compared to Figure 7-2.

FAMILY JOURNAL

My sister Ann is 72. She had rheumaic fever when she was 10 years old.
Ann did pretty well most of the years that we were growing up. She had a heart murmur and had to take antibiotics any time she went to the dentist. She was told that the rheumatic fever had affected two of her heart valves, the mitral and aortic valves.

On a recent visit, Ann told her cardiologist that she was getting more short of breath with exertion and nearly passed out on one occasion. He did an echocardiogram, which showed that the aortic valve had become seriously narrowed and that Ann needed valve replacement surgery.

Her aortic valve was replaced and her mitral valve was repaired. Although she was uncomfortable for several weeks, she is doing much better now. She still needs to take antibiotics before dental work, but she has noticed that she can do more and has more energy.

THEN AND NOW

The first heart valve replacement was done in 1952 by heart surgeon Charles Hufnagel of the Georgetown University School of Medicine. He replaced a diseased aortic valve with a plastic valve. Diseased valves today may be replaced with pig or cow valves or with artificial mechanical valves. Due to clotting risks, mechanical valves require long-term use of anticoagulants.

(figure 7-14)

Patient having an echocardiogram.

by the narrowed aortic valve, the pulse may rise more slowly, but this is less typical in older persons than in younger ones. A harsh whooshing noise called a **murmur** is heard with a stethoscope over the left upper chest, and the murmur may radiate to the neck arteries. The second heart sound, which correlates with the closure of the aortic valve, is often muffled and may even be absent in severe cases. The stiff valve does not close properly, and therefore the normal crisp sound that occurs when the valve closes is diminished or absent. An extra heart sound called a *gallop* (which resembles the galloping sound of a horse) is usually heard when the normal heart rhythm is present. The gallop is produced by vibrations in the heart muscle when the left atrium contracts and forces blood into the left ventricle. To appreciate what a "gallop rhythm" sounds like, tap two fingers one after the other. This resembles the normal heart sounds. Then add a third finger. This mimics the gallop sound. Sometimes even a fourth sound can be heard. Go ahead and tap with four fingers. Do you notice the similarity to a galloping horse?

Echocardiography can evaluate the severity of aortic stenosis noninvasively with great accuracy (see Figure 7-14). The actual degree of narrowing and the pressure gradient across the valve can be assessed. Surgical intervention should be guided by the onset and progression of symptoms in the presence of severe aortic valve narrowing. Cardiac catheterization should be performed to evaluate the coronary arteries prior to valve surgery. About half the patients undergoing aortic valve replacement surgery will also require coronary bypass surgery, which increases the risk of the surgery. The mortality for valve replacement surgery, as you might expect, is higher for older patients. Since *bioprosthetic valves* ("pig valves") have been shown to deteriorate slower in older patients, the choice between a mechanical and a pig valve depends on the age of the patient and also on the risk of long-term anticoagulation. Mechanical valves require long-term anticoagulation with WARFARIN since clots may occur on these valves. These clots can travel to the brain circulation and cause strokes. All patients with prosthetic heart valves require antibiotic treatment when undergoing certain dental or surgical procedures to guard against infection of the heart valve (infectious endocarditis).

Aortic balloon valvotomy is a procedure in which a catheter with a balloon is used to open a narrowed aortic valve. It has no role in the long-term management of aortic stenosis, and is rarely used to stabilize critically ill patients until they can have surgery.

AORTIC REGURGITATION

Aortic regurgitation (AR) is the backflow of blood through the aortic valve when the heart relaxes after a contraction (see Figure 7-15). It has many causes, but the most common include *myxomatous degeneration* (a genetically determined deterioration in the valve), *infective endocarditis* (infection of the heart valve), rheumatic heart disease, high blood pressure, and *congenital bicuspid valve* (two valve leaflets instead of three) being the most common. Other causes include trauma, *aortic dissection* (a tear in the lining of the aorta), and syphilis. Aortic regurgitation causes volume overload of the left ventricle, which over time and depending on the severity of the regurgitation will cause the ventricle to dilate with progressive worsening of the pump function.

In the early stages, aortic regurgitation is well tolerated with preserved exercise tolerance, especially in younger patients. As the disease progresses, symptoms of heart failure become more pronounced. When listening with a stethoscope, a doctor will hear a characteristic murmur when the heart is relaxed due to the backflow. Often this murmur is heard best next to the *sternum (breastbone)* with the patient sitting up and leaning forward. The force and high volume of blood ejected with each heartbeat may actually cause the head to nod. Sometimes a noise like a pistol shot can be heard over the femoral arteries (located near the groin).

Medical therapy is aimed at reducing the workload of the heart with salt restriction, diuretics, digoxin, and ACE inhibitors. Prophylactic antibiotics are given for dental or medical procedures to prevent infection of the abnormal valve. NIFEDIPINE (PROCARDIA, ADALAT) may delay the need for surgery in patients with severe aortic regurgitation and preserved pump function. Aortic valve replacement surgery should be considered in patients with severe aortic regurgitation and depressed pump function or a dilated left ventricle.

Sudden aortic regurgitation is usually caused by trauma, aortic dissection, or infective endocarditis. The abrupt volume overload to a noncompliant ventricle results in sudden fluid buildup in the lungs and severe shortness of breath. Of interest, the typical murmur heard in persons with long standing aortic regurgitation is often not heard in this setting. Doctors will look for other clues from the examination. The diagnosis of aortic regurgitation can be reliably made by echocardiography, which also provides information on left ventricular size and pump function.

MITRAL REGURGITATION

Mitral regurgitation is the backflow of blood through the mitral valve when the heart pumps. Common causes for mitral regurgitation in the elderly population include rheumatic heart disease, myxomatous degeneration (disruption of the connective tissue) of the leaflets, mitral valve prolapse, infective endocarditis, and damage to the structures that support the valve *(papillary muscle and chordae tendineae)*. This is another form of volume overload on the left ventricle, since the blood that flows back into the left atrium is added to the normal blood volume that the left atrium ejects into the left ventricle with every heartbeat. This causes a continual strain of the left ventricle and eventually it wears out, producing symptoms of heart failure. The volume of blood that regurgitates also affects the left atrium. The left atrium gets bigger, and finally lung congestion develops.

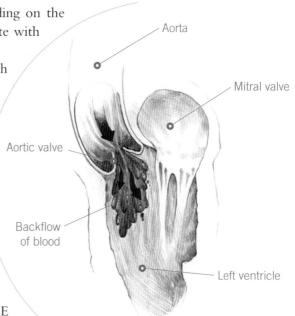

Aorta

Mitral valve

Aortic valve

Backflow of blood

Left ventricle

(*figure* 7-15)

Aortic regurgitation.

The clinical course of chronic mitral regurgitation is usually a benign one. Patients do fairly well until deterioration of left ventricular function occurs. Early symptoms are usually fatigue and weakness. The onset of some rhythm disturbances can affect the contraction of the atria. This can precipitate heart failure since the ventricles will not fill with blood as well. In the advanced stage, congestive heart failure occurs, causing fluid buildup in the lungs and shortness of breath.

Persons with mitral regurgitation may have a prominent impulse over the chest wall that can actually be felt. A doctor will put a hand over the left side of the chest and may notice a "lifting" sensation. The characteristic murmur is heard over the left lower chest wall and radiates to the left armpit. Echocardiography is very important in the diagnosis of mitral regurgitation. It provides information about the severity of the mitral regurgitation, as well as the left ventricular function and size. It can also define the leaflets involved, the probable cause of mitral regurgitation, and the condition of the leaflets and their supporting structures. This information is important to assess the feasibility of valve repair or reconstruction.

Occasionally a heart attack or a heart valve infection may cause the sudden onset of severe mitral regurgitation. This will cause sudden shortness of breath due to fluid buildup in the lungs *(pulmonary edema)* or possibly very unstable vital signs. This is usually a result of injury to the papillary muscles, malfunction of the valve itself, or tearing of the chordae tendineae. Patients are severely ill and require emergency surgery.

Medical therapy for chronic mitral regurgitation consists of diuretics, proper fluid balance, and medications to reduce heart work. Mitral valve surgery is indicated when severe heart failure symptoms develop or when there is an increase in the left ventricular size or a decrease in the left ventricular *ejection fraction* (the amount of blood the left ventricle ejects with each contraction) to less than 60%. Better results are achieved when surgery is performed before severe left ventricular dysfunction occurs.

Mitral valve repair is superior to valve replacement because it preserves the supporting structures and tends to better preserve left ventricular function. It also avoids the issue of long-term anticoagulation. Mitral valve replacement is indicated when valve repair is technically not possible. The choice of a mechanical or a bioprosthetic valve depends on the age of the patient and the risk of anticoagulation. Mortality for mitral valve replacement surgery ranges between 10 and 14%. When combined with bypass surgery, in cases where the mitral regurgitation is due to poor blood flow from coronary artery disease, the mortality increases to 20 or 30%, especially in patients over 80 years old. Emergency surgery for acute severe mitral regurgitation carries a very high mortality, especially if combined with bypass surgery in patients who are having a heart attack.

MITRAL STENOSIS

Mitral stenosis (MS) is a narrowing of the mitral valve that impedes blood flow from the left atrium to the left ventricle. It is less commonly seen in the elderly. It is usually caused by previous rheumatic fever but can be due to progressive calcification of the *mitral annulus* (the ring structure around the valve that supports the valve leaflets). Symptoms are usually stable unless atrial fibrillation occurs. This may lead to symptoms such as shortness of breath and cough. Sometimes coughing up blood can occur.

Medical treatment involves control of the heart rate and diuretics. Balloon valvuloplasty, in which a balloon catheter is used to dilate the narrowed mitral valve, is now the first choice of intervention in suitable patients. It is far less invasive than surgery, yet the results are comparable. Mitral valve replacement surgery may still be indicated in severely symptomatic patients who have other problems, such as a stiff calcified valve, that disqualify them for valvuloplasty.

If you have a heart valve disorder or have had valve replacement surgery, you should receive antibiotics to prevent an infection of the valve when having dental, urological, or gastrointestinal procedures. Make sure your dentist or hygienist is informed, even if you are just having your teeth cleaned. Your doctor will select the antibiotic regimen that is most appropriate for you.

CARDIOVASCULAR RISK REDUCTION

HYPERLIPIDEMIA

Hyperlipidemia means elevated cholesterol, triglycerides, or both. The National Cholesterol Education Program (NCEP) has released a report recommending no upper-age limit for lipid-lowering drug therapy in patients with coronary artery disease or at increased risk for coronary disease. Clinical studies have unequivocally demonstrated that treatment of hyperlipidemia reduces adverse cardiovascular events. Fortunately, hyperlipidemia can be treated with therapeutic lifestyle changes (diet and exercise) and perhaps use of medication. The importance of diet

HEALTH TIPS

The following checklist points out ways to reduce your risk:

- Follow a diet reduced in saturated fats and cholesterol (see Chapter 28).
- Keep weight under control (see Chapter 29 for weight tables and ways to reduce).
- Do regular or aerobic exercises for at least 20 to 30 minutes 3 or 4 times per week. Suggested activities include walking, running, swimming, bicycling, and rowing. Check with your doctor before initiating these activities if you have been sedentary.
- Stop smoking (see Chapter 6 for ways to help you quit).
- Keep alcohol intake less than one or two drinks per day. There is no problem with abstinence.
- Make sure your blood pressure is under control (less than 140/90 or, if you are a diabetic, less than 130/

80). Work with your doctor to get your numbers under control. This may require medicines.
- Make sure you are checked periodically for diabetes. If you are a diabetic, strive to get your hemoglobin A1C (glycohemoglobin) less than 7 and preferably less than 6.5.
- Work with your doctor to get your cholesterol level under control. Your doctor may want to start you on medicines if you have any risk factors or if you have a strong family history of heart disease. You may need to take medicine if you have already had heart problems, even if your cholesterol is normal.

(table 7-3)

CLASSIFICATION OF LDL, HDL, AND TRIGLYCERIDES

LDL (MG/DL)	
Less than 100	Optimal
100–129	Near optimal
130–159	Borderline high
160–189	High
Greater than or equal to 190	Very high
HDL (MG/DL)	
Less than 40	Low
Greater than or equal to 60	High
TRIGLYCERIDE (MG/DL)	
Less than 150	Normal
150–199	Borderline high
200–499	High
Greater than or equal to 500	Very high

is often underappreciated. Many people prefer to take a pill than to change ingrained habits. Even if medication is necessary to reach optimal cholesterol and triglyceride levels, diet may allow use of lower dosages and thus reduce the potential for adverse side effects. Chapter 28 offers useful guidelines for your diet, and Chapter 29 can help you if you are overweight. Increased physical activity can help in many ways including helping you maintain a good body weight.

The third report of the expert panel on detection, evaluation, and treatment of high blood cholesterol in adults (ATPIII) constitutes the updated guidelines for cholesterol testing and management. Although you may have heard that you should have a cholesterol lower than 200, the total cholesterol does not tell the whole story. Knowing the level of HDL and LDL is important. This will require a blood test called a *lipoprotein profile.* Table 7-3 classifies LDL ("bad" cholesterol), HDL ("good" cholesterol), and triglycerides.

The first step in deciding whether or not your bad cholesterol needs to be lowered depends on the assessment of other risk factors you may have:

- Cigarette smoking
- High blood pressure (greater than or equal to 140/90 or on blood pressure medicine)
- Low HDL cholesterol (less than 40 mg/dL)
- Family history of premature coronary heart disease (less than 55 years old for a male first-degree relative; less than 65 years old for a female first-degree relative)
- Age (men over 45 years old; women over 55 years old)

Diabetes is considered a coronary heart disease (CHD) equivalent, which means that diabetics need to be treated as if they already have coronary

(table 7-4)

LDL AND TREATMENT CONSIDERATION

RISK CATEGORY	LDL GOAL (MG/DL)	LDL LEVEL AT WHICH TO INITIATE LIFESTYLE CHANGES	LDL LEVEL AT WHICH TO CONSIDER DRUG THERAPY
CHD or CHD risk equivalents (10-year risk greater than 20%)	Less than 100	Greater than or equal to 100	Greater than or equal to 130 (100–129: drug optional although your doctor may want to be more or less aggressive with treatment based on other factors)
Two or more risk factors (10-year risk < 20%)	Less than 130	Greater than or equal to 130	10-year risk 10–20%: greater than or equal 130 (10-year risk less than 10%: greater than or equal to 160)
Zero or one risk factor	Less than 160	Greater than or equal to 160	Greater than or equal to 190 (160–189: LDL-lowering drug optional)

artery disease. Other CHD equivalents include peripheral arterial disease, abdominal aortic aneurysm, and symptomatic carotid artery disease (TIA or stroke). A HDL cholesterol greater or equal to 60 counts as a negative risk factor; its presence removes one risk factor from the total count.

In addition, there are formulas your doctor can use to calculate your risk of having a heart attack within 10 years (10-year risk). If you are interested in learning more about this, you can write for more information to the National Heart, Lung, and Blood Institute (NHLBI) Health Information Center at P.O. Box 30105, Bethesda, MD 20824, or call 301-592-8573. You can also visit the NHLBI website at www.nhlbi.nih.gov.

Once your risk factors and your 10-year risk are calculated, decisions about proper treatment can be made. Table 7-4 summarizes the LDL goal and when treatment should be considered.

Many clinical trials have confirmed that statin drugs can significantly lower the risk of heart attack and stroke. Statins are the drugs of first choice for those with high or less than optimal LDL cholesterol levels. In fact, the statins have protective effects above and beyond cholesterol lowering, and many physicians recommend a statin to their patients with diabetes or other risk factors even if their LDL cholesterol is normal. These drugs are among the safest drugs developed, and most patients tolerate them without adverse effects. However, exceptions do occur, and your doctor may request that you have periodic blood tests and that you report any unusual muscle pain or flulike symptoms.

Another class of cholesterol-lowering drug blocks absorption of cholesterol from the intestine. The first drug of this class, EZETIMIBE (ZETIA) was approved by the FDA in November 2002. Ezetimibe should be considered an adjunct to statin therapy in patients where the LDL cholesterol reduction is suboptimal.

HYPERTENSION

Hypertension has usually been defined as a systolic (upper number) blood pressure greater than 140 and a diastolic (lower number) blood pressure greater than 90. Hypertension does not mean that the affected individual is overstressed. Some of the calmest people may have severe hypertension, and some very anxious individuals may have perfectly normal blood pressure. Some people may have an increase in their blood pressure when they are nervous, a phenomenon that doctors see quite often in their offices ("white coat hypertension"). In addition, even 140/90 may be too high a blood pressure for some people. Diabetics have a much higher risk for coronary artery disease and other vascular problems. Therefore, it is recommended for diabetics to have their blood pressure be less than 130 over 80.

How the blood pressure (BP) is taken is also important. Generally, it is recommended to place the blood pressure cuff on the left arm while the patient is sitting on the examination table. However, some elderly individuals may have atherosclerosis in the arteries of the left arm that makes the left-arm reading unreliable. It is best that readings be taken from both arms initially, and that the arm with the higher reading be used for BP measurements. In addition, standing BP measurements, especially in those on medications, can be useful to make sure there is not a profound drop in BP with upright position (orthostatic hypotension). Orthostatic hypotension can be associated with dizziness, falls, or even fainting upon standing.

With advancing age, systolic blood pressure gradually increases while diastolic blood pressure peaks around 40 or 50 years of age, then decreases because of impaired elasticity of the blood vessels. This accounts for the common finding of *isolated systolic hypertension* (high systolic blood pressure and normal diastolic blood pressure) in the elderly. As recently as the 1970s, the prevailing medical opinion was to ignore elevated BP in the elderly, even though epidemiologic data demonstrated the age-related risk of coronary artery disease as a result of hypertension. Into the 1980s many physicians still did not believe that antihypertensive drugs could improve outcome in the elderly despite abundant data from clinical trials. It is now generally accepted that effective treatment of isolated systolic or combined systolic and diastolic hypertension can reduce the death and disability from coronary artery disease. Although previous hypertension studies failed to include a large proportion of patients greater than 80 years of age, a new study is expected to enroll all its patients in that age group. An analysis of data collected from multiple studies of patients over 80 years of age suggested that treatment significantly reduced the risk of strokes, heart attacks, and congestive heart failure.

Many studies have demonstrated certain risk factors underlying hypertension. These risk factors can be divided into two groups: factors that cannot be modified, such as age, gender, ethnicity, and genetic factors, and factors that can be modified and in this way decrease or even prevent hypertension. These modifiable risk factors include:

- *Weight.* A relation between body mass and arterial pressure is well established. Chapter 29 explains how to calculate your body mass index (BMI). If you have hypertension and are overweight, significant improvement in your blood pressure can result from weight loss.

- *Salt intake.* Salt restriction can result in significant blood pressure reduction. Your doctor can guide you as to what level of sodium intake is appropriate. Remember that certain foods are highly salted, such as processed meats, some soups, dill pickles, soy sauces, mustard, and ketchup. You can order a free copy of the *Facts about the DASH* [Dietary Approaches to Stop Hypertension] *Eating Plan* (NIH Publication 03-4082) from the NHLBI or view it online on its website.

- *Alcohol.* Numerous investigations have established a close association between excess alcohol consumption and hypertension. However, a small quantity of alcohol (less than 1 ounce per day) might actually reduce arterial pressure. Until more research is available, you should not start drinking, if you don't drink, just because of some possible health benefit. If you drink, you should limit alcohol consumption to one to two drinks per day. If you drink more than this, you need to reduce your intake. Talk with your doctor if this is a problem for you.

- *Potassium intake.* Most studies suggest an inverse relation between potassium intake and blood pressure. Therefore, it appears that increased potassium in your diet can be recommended for prevention of hypertension. Some dietary sources of potassium include apricots, bananas, raisins, orange juice, baked potatoes, and lima beans.

- *Coffee intake.* The incidence of hypertension was higher in coffee drinkers than nondrinkers in some studies. However, the rise in blood pressure was generally transient. Modest consumption of coffee and other caffeinated beverages is generally acceptable, unless your doctor advises otherwise because of other health reasons.

- *Exercise.* Most studies have confirmed that increased physical activity was associated with reduced arterial pressure. Therefore, aerobic or endurance exercise is recommended to reduce or prevent hypertension.

- *Smoking.* Both systolic (the upper number) and diastolic (the lower number) blood pressure are increased after a single cigarette, and heavy smokers consuming two to three packs per day may have increased arterial pressure most of the time. Cessation of smoking is extremely important.

Beta-blockers and diuretics are currently recommended as first-line agents in the drug treatment of hypertension. In fact, diuretic use was associated with better blood pressure control and less orthostatic hypotension (drop in blood pressure on standing) which forms, by itself, a decent short-term goal upon initiation of blood pressure drugs. Low doses of thiazide diuretics are among the most effective and well-tolerated treatments of hypertension. They are also among the simplest, safest, and least expensive medicines available. Diuretics generally should be the foundation of therapy. Those individuals who do not achieve adequate blood pressure control with a diuretic, or who have compelling indications for other agents, should remain on the diuretic along with whatever other drugs they need. Of course, individual patient characteristics need to be taken into consideration. For example, severe sulfa allergy or urinary incontinence may preclude use of diuretics. Beta-blockers usually are avoided in asthmatics, although recent studies suggest that some beta-blockers that act preferentially on the cardiovascular system and less significantly on the respiratory system may be safe in those with mild to moderate asthma.

Initially ACE inhibitors were recommended as standard therapy only for patients who suffered a heart attack that caused weakening of the heart. However, an important research study called the Heart Outcomes Prevention Evaluation (HOPE) compared an ACE inhibitor called RAMIPRIL (ALTACE) with a placebo, and there was a 22% reduction in adverse cardiovascular events with ramipril. For this reason, ACE inhibitors should be considered for all high-risk patients. They may also be considered first-line therapy for those with hypertension who cannot tolerate diuretics or beta-blockers. In addition, there is now strong evidence that ACE inhibitors should be part of the blood pressure-lowering regimen for persons with diabetes and/or kidney disease. Since diabetics have such a high risk for vascular and kidney disease, many physicians will prescribe an ACE inhibitor even if these persons do not have high blood pressure.

Achieving normal blood pressure with medication in the elderly can sometimes be very difficult. Those with very high systolic BP may be quite resistant to medications, and occasionally three or more medications may be required. Concern has been raised that adverse effects of these medications could potentially outweigh the benefits, and therefore your doctor must evaluate the potential benefits of lowering blood pressure versus the risks of multiple medications.

The seventh report of the Joint National Committee (JNC) on the prevention, detection, evaluation, and treatment of high blood pressure stresses the importance of aggressive treatment earlier in life to prevent the complications of hypertension later on. The cardiovascular risk from systolic hypertension begins at a systolic blood pressure of 115 and increases thereafter. The risk from diastolic hypertension begins with a diastolic blood pressure of 75. You may be surprised to learn that individuals who have normal blood pressure at age 55 have a 90% likelihood of developing high blood pressure in the next 25 years. The new goal for blood pressure is 120/80 or less. This new goal will significantly reduce our risk for heart attacks, heart failure, stroke, and kidney disease. Clearly, action to control blood pressure is essential and a challenge we must all accept.

In summary, hypertension is present in the majority of elderly. Clinical studies have confirmed that there is a definite relationship between hypertension and cardiovascular risk. Thus far, clinical studies have not been aimed at the very old (over 80 years). New studies will explore the benefits versus the risks of blood pressure-lowering therapy. Clinical data shows considerable benefit of decreasing LDL cholesterol and blood pressure levels to improve as well as extend quality of life in the elderly population. The magnitude of delay in progression of atherosclerotic disease in response to therapy is still unknown. The cost-effectiveness of screening in the elderly population as well as the groups that would benefit the most from screening needs to be further studied. Although many preventive and treatment strategies with demonstrated efficacy in younger patients are relevant in the older age group, careful attention must be paid to the influence of concomitant illnesses and the unique physiological changes that occur as we get older. Physicians must consider how the changes that occur in the body of an elderly person will affect the way medications are handled. The impact of therapy on survival and the quality of life is essential in treating older persons.

ARRHYTHMIAS AND CONDUCTION ABNORMALITIES

ATRIAL FIBRILLATION

Atrial fibrillation is a disorganized rapid and irregular beating of the atria. Rather than contracting in a regular fashion, the atria quiver. Therefore, the atria do not pump blood into the ventricles properly, and the output of blood from the heart can be decreased. This can generate a variety of symptoms that usually include shortness of breath, tiredness, and palpitations. However, the individual response to atrial fibrillation is quite variable. Some patients remain asymptomatic, while others may be disabled by the symptoms. The strategies used to control the symptoms include the restoration and maintenance of sinus rhythm or the control of the ventricular rate, with large studies showing similar efficacy of both approaches.

Atrial fibrillation is a common abnormality of the heart rhythm. A doctor can usually recognize it on physical examination by a very irregular and rapid pulse; however, in some cases where the heart's conduction system does not function properly, the heart rate may be normal or even slow. The electrocardiogram (ECG) shows the absence of P waves, which represent the activity of the atria, and a grossly irregular ventricular response (represented by the QRS *complex;* see Figure 7-16). Its incidence increases with age, affecting 1% of persons older than 60 years. Atrial fibrillation occurs more commonly among males and those with underlying cardiovascular disease, stroke, and diabetes. The abnormal rhythm can be intermittent *(paroxysmal atrial fibrillation)* or permanent. Occasionally, atrial fibrillation can be caused by *hyperthyroidism* (an overactive thyroid gland), which can be determined by a simple blood test.

The prognosis of atrial fibrillation depends on the clinical setting in which it occurs. *Lone atrial fibrillation* is defined as atrial fibrillation that occurs in patients less than 60 years old without evidence of structural heart disease or hypertension. Studies show no adverse effect on mortality, and the rate of stroke is comparable or only slightly higher than that of the control population. Conversely, older patients with atrial fibrillation in the setting of hypertension, structural heart disease, or a prior stroke or transient ischemic attack (TIA) have a significantly higher risk of death and *thromboembolic* (blood clots) events. Since blood does not move well in the quivering atria, it may clot. If the clot breaks off, it can travel to other areas of the body. The most feared complication is a stroke, but other serious problems can occur if a clot lodges in the arteries to the legs, kidneys, and so forth.

Many studies have assessed the risk–benefit ratio of anticoagulation with warfarin or treatment with aspirin in patients with atrial fibrillation. Warfarin is clearly superior. The guidelines of the American College of Cardiology and the American Heart Association recommend the use of warfarin in patients with chronic or intermittent atrial fibrillation. The adequacy of anticoagulation is monitored with a blood test called an international normalized ratio (INR). The therapeutic range is 2 to 3. This test can be done with a finger-stick blood sample and the result reported immediately.

Atrial fibrillation can sometimes be converted to a normal rhythm *(sinus rhythm)* with a relatively low–intensity electrical shock *(cardioversion)* or chemically using a variety of drugs called *antiarrhythmics*. The decision to use electrical cardioversion or antiarrhythmic drugs is made by the cardiologist depending on the clinical situation. Cardioversion with a defibrillator is administered after light sedation and is generally well tolerated. It does not immediately result in normal atrial contractions despite the restoration of sinus rhythm. As such it is recommended to anticoagulate patients for a duration of 3 to 4 weeks following a successful cardioversion. Anticoagulants should also be administered for 4 weeks prior to a planned cardioversion, unless there is clear documentation that atrial fibrillation has been present for less than 48 hours. Another validated strategy is to obtain a *transesophageal echocardiogram (TEE)*. This examination requires sedation, and an ultrasound probe is placed in the esophagus in order to get better images of the left atrium than can be obtained with standard echocardiography. If no blood clots are identified in the left

(figure 7-16)

(a) ECG tracing of a normal sinus rhythm. The P-wave represents the electric impulse that causes contraction of the atria. The QRS complex correlates with the activation of the ventricles. The T-wave represents the period when the ventricle gets ready for the next cycle. Notice the regular rhythm.

(b) ECG of a person in atrial fibrillation. Notice the irregular and rapid rhythm and the absence of P-waves due to the lack of normal atrial activation and contraction.

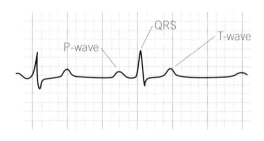

(a)

(b)

atrium, cardioversion is performed and anticoagulation is maintained for 4 weeks. Many experts recommend long-term anticoagulation.

Other approaches to atrial fibrillation include the control of the heart rate with beta-blockers, calcium-blockers, or digoxin. Other techniques may include AV nodal modification and pacemaker insertion, catheter ablation techniques, and implantation of atrial defibrillators. The *maze procedure* is an "open heart" surgical procedure in which small incisions are made in both atria to block the chaotic impulses that occur in atrial fibrillation. The purpose is to channel the impulses to follow the normal electrical pathways from the atria to the ventricles.

Many elderly patients tolerate atrial fibrillation without therapy because of concomitant conduction system disease. Although the atria may beat rapidly or quiver, the ventricles may have a normal or even slow rate. In these patients cardioversion can result in prolonged periods of *asystole* (no heartbeat) secondary to prolonged recovery of the *SA node* (the heart's own pacemaker). As such the risk of the cardioversion should be weighed against the benefit of achieving sinus rhythm.

VENTRICULAR ARRHYTHMIAS

Ventricular arrhythmias encompass abnormal rhythms ranging from isolated *premature ventricular complexes (PVCs; also known as ventricular premature beats, or VPBs),* to ventricular tachycardia, flutter, and fibrillation. See Figure 7-17.

Premature ventricular complexes increase in frequency and complexity with age, especially in patients who develop structural heart disease. PVC importance and how they are treated are dependent on the clinical setting in which they occur.

Ventricular tachycardia consists of a run of three or more ventricular complexes in a row, usually at a rate greater than 120 complexes/minute. The tachycardia is called sustained if it lasts longer than 30 seconds or is associated with unstable vital signs requiring treatment. Otherwise it is referred to as nonsustained ventricular tachycardia. When the rate is faster than 200 beats/minute and the tracing resembles the sine wave on an oscilloscope, the tachycardia is called *ventricular flutter.* If the ventricular activity is fragmented and chaotic without evidence of organized electrical activity on the electrocardiogram, the rhythm is called ventricular fibrillation. Ventricular fibrillation results quickly in death unless immediate measures are taken to abort it.

Ventricular tachycardia can have different causes but usually signals a serious underlying heart disease. It may occur at the time of a heart attack or can occur weeks to months later. In general, the incidence of ventricular tachycardia increases with the increasing severity of the heart disease. It accounts for half the deaths in patients with severe ischemia due to coronary artery disease or in those with weak "baggy" hearts *(dilated cardiomyopathy).*

Because sudden death from malignant ventricular arrhythmia still accounts for a sizable proportion of all cardiovascular mortality, a substantial amount of effort has been invested into identifying diagnostic, prognostic, and therapeutic strategies to prevent its occurrence. Certain diagnostic studies may be very helpful. Measurement of the left ventricular pump function (ejection fraction) can be done by echocardiogram, special heart scans, or cardiac catheterization. *Signal-averaged electrocardiography* is a special type of ECG in which a computer analyzes a single QRS complex, so the cardiologist can determine if there are abnormal electrical impulses that would indicate a higher risk of ventricular rhythm disturbances. *Electrophysiology testing (EPS)* has played an important role in the diagnosis and treatment of ventricular arrhythmias. Occasionally, the cardiologist will deliberately trigger the abnormal heart rhythm to see which drugs can help prevent it.

Another option for the treatment of serious ventricular rhythm disturbances is an *implantable cardiac defibrillator (ICD)*. These devices are surgically implanted in the chest wall. They recognize the abnormal heart rhythm and deliver a shock to the heart to restore the normal rhythm. A cardiologist will decide whether drug therapy or an ICD is most appropriate after evaluating the patient and the test results.

BRADYARRHYTHMIAS AND PACEMAKERS

Older age has been associated with an increased incidence of dysfunction of the heart's natural pacemaker, the *sinoatrial (SA) node*. Problems that result may include sinus bradycardia (slow pulse rate), sinus arrhythmia (irregular pulse), sinoatrial arrest (the SA node fails to send electrical impulses to the atria) and sick sinus syndrome. Sick sinus syndrome is characterized by chaotic atrial activity, and the heart rate may be persistently slow or

(figure 7-17)

VENTRICULAR ARRHYTHMIAS
(a) Ventricular premature beats (VPB), (b) ventricular tachycardia and (c) ventricular fibrillation.

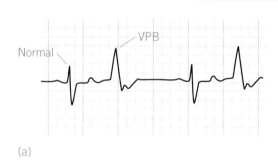

Normal

VPB

(a)

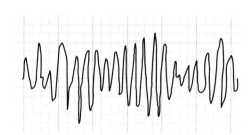

(b)

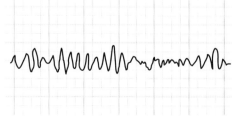

(c)

The first pacemakers were external with a wire leading into a vein and into the heart. The battery life was only a few years. Today, pacemakers are implanted under the skin and their battery life can be up to 20 years. Naturally, like any mechanical device, early failures can occur, so persons with pacemakers need regular check-ups to test the battery.

Pacemakers were first developed to treat very slow heart rates but now can be used to successfully terminate certain types of rapid heart rhythms. A recent exciting indication has been in patients with advanced heart failure with marked conduction abnormalities and lack of response to optimal medical therapy. Clinical studies have shown a significant improvement in New York Heart Association class, quality of life scores, and exercise tolerance with implantation of a biventricular pacemaker. This pacemaker has wires going to both the right and left ventricles, and may help improve the heart's performance. The improvement has persisted for 12 months of follow-up so far, providing encouragement for the use of this therapy in patients with severe cardiomyopathy. Emerging applications of pacemaker therapy also include selected persons with sleep apnea.

rapid heart rates may alternate with slow heart rates *(tachycardia-bradycardia syndrome)*. In some cases, there may be no symptoms. However, it may be a cause of fainting and dizziness due to the slow heart rates, in which case a pacemaker is required. Medications to control the rapid heart rates may cause a profound drop in the pulse rate, necessitating a pacemaker as well.

The electrical conduction through the *atrioventricular node (AV node)* is also affected by increasing age. This can cause delays in the electrical impulse reaching the ventricles, resulting in a condition called heart block. Heart block is graded as first, second, and third degree, depending on the severity of the disturbance. First-degree block is common and seldom provokes symptoms. No treatment is necessary. In second-degree heart block, some impulses do not reach the ventricles. Depending on the symptoms produced, a pacemaker may be required. Third-degree heart block is associated with a complete block of the impulses from the atria to the ventricles. Consequently, another pacemaker in the heart takes over, usually in the AV node or the ventricles. Often those with third-degree heart block will experience dizziness, fainting, or fatigue. Usually a pacemaker is required.

■

WHAT YOU NEED TO KNOW

■ Heart disease is the leading cause of death in both men and women in the United States.

■ The prevalence of cardiovascular disease increases with age. Persons 65 years or older account for over 80% of deaths from heart disease in the United States.

■ The symptoms of heart disease may be different in older persons than in the younger population. It is important to have regular examinations with your physician, and be sure to report any unusual tiredness, shortness of breath, or tightness or heaviness in your chest.

■ If you experience symptoms suggesting a heart attack, call 911. (If you are not sure if your symptoms are related to a heart problem, call your doctor's office for instructions.) Do not go to your doctor's office. Do not drive yourself. Do not ask your wife, neighbor, or a friend to drive you to the hospital. Paramedics are expertly trained to handle these emergencies.

■ Preventing heart disease often requires lifestyle changes. Weight should be kept within established guidelines. Smoking should be avoided. Alcohol consumption should be limited to no more than one or two drinks per day. Do some type of aerobic exercise for 20 to 30 minutes, three or four times a week. Walking, swimming, and bicycling are especially beneficial for older individuals. Controlling your blood pressure and cholesterol is important, even in advanced age. Your doctor will work with you to establish proper goals for your blood pressure and cholesterol numbers.

FOR MORE INFORMATION

■ American Heart Association
7272 Greenville Avenue
Dallas, TX 75231
800-242-8721
Web: www.americanheart.org

■ National Heart, Lung, and Blood Institute
NHLBI Health Information Center
P.O. Box 30105
Bethesda, MD 20824
301-592-8573
TTY: 240-629-3255
Fax: 301-592-8563
E-mail: nhlbiinfo@rover.nhlbi.nih.gov
Web: www.nhlbi.nih.gov

Only a minority of patients with peripheral arterial disease complain of symptoms . . . many patients are elderly . . . and consider their symptoms a part of growing old; therefore, they do not seek medical advice.

—*Transatlantic Inter-Society Consensus (TASC) Working Group*

THE AUTHOR

08

RUSSELL H. SAMSON, MD, graduated from the University of Witwatersrand Medical School in South Africa. He completed his residency in surgery and fellowship in vascular surgery at the Albert Einstein College of Medicine and Montefiore Medical Center in New York. He is certified by the American Board of Surgery and holds a Certificate of Special Competency in Vascular Surgery. He was associate professor of surgery at the Albert Einstein College of Medicine prior to moving to Sarasota, Florida, where he now resides. He is a member of all the major vascular societies, including the prestigious Society for Vascular Surgery. He was president of the Florida Vascular Society. He is on the editorial board of the journal *Vascular and Endovascular Surgery,* an editorial reviewer for the *Journal of Vascular Surgery,* and an associate editor for the sixth edition of *Rutherford's Textbook of Vascular Surgery,* the leading textbook in the field. A prolific author, he lectures throughout the world on topics in vascular surgery.

THE ARTERIES AND VEINS

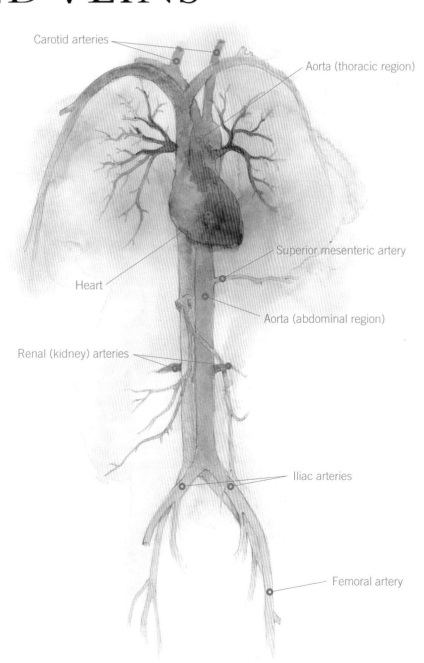

Carotid arteries

Aorta (thoracic region)

Heart

Superior mesenteric artery

Aorta (abdominal region)

Renal (kidney) arteries

Iliac arteries

Femoral artery

(figure 8-1)
The arterial system.

The circulatory system is the part of the body that carries blood. It includes the heart, which pumps the blood, and the blood vessels (arteries and veins), through which the blood circulates. The arteries carry the fresh oxygenated blood from the heart, and the veins carry the old blood back to the heart and lungs (see Figure 8-1).

This chapter first concentrates on disorders of the peripheral arterial system, which includes the arteries of the arms and legs, brain, intestines, kidneys, and abdomen. Since these areas are away from the heart, they are also known as the *peripheral arterial system,* and disorders of these blood vessels are grouped under the term *peripheral arterial disease (PAD).* Some physicians use the term *peripheral vascular disease (PVD).* However, truly speaking, this would imply veins as well. However, veins tend to develop very different problems and so are dealt within a separate section later in this chapter.

Diseases of the arteries are the number-one killer of the elderly since arterial blockages cause heart attacks and strokes. This fact is generally well known, but few realize that the main cause of arterial disease, or hardening of the arteries *(atherosclerosis),* affects all the arteries in the body. Because of this, hardening of the arteries can also cause such diverse problems as high blood pressure, kidney failure, discomfort while walking, and sudden death. In this chapter we deal with these less well known but equally important results of hardening of the arteries, that is, its effects on arteries outside of the heart.

Problems with veins are seldom major unless blood clots form in them. This condition is discussed in Chapter 6. However, the veins of the legs are prone to develop unsightly blue bulges, referred to as *varicose* and *spider veins.* We deal with these problems in this chapter, but readers should be aware that they are significantly different from those caused by arterial diseases.

ARTERIES

PERIPHERAL ARTERIAL DISEASE

Normally the lining of arteries is smooth. However, as one ages, a condition may develop that results in a buildup of fat and calcium in the wall of the artery. The lining becomes irregular, and ultimately the artery can be blocked off. Also, little pieces of this abnormal fatty buildup can break loose and get carried down the artery to lodge elsewhere in the system, causing a blockage at that site. This is called an embolism. The build up of fat, cholesterol, and calcium is called plaque, and the condition is called atherosclerosis, or "hardening of the arteries." When it occurs in the arteries outside the heart and brain, we refer to it as peripheral arterial disease (PAD). In general PAD refers to all arteries outside the heart. However, by common usage it has come to refer to arterial disease of the extremities (i.e., the legs and arms), and this is what this section describes.

Atherosclerosis: Plaque starts to build up in arteries when low-density lipoprotein (LDL), the bad bloodstream fat, gets into the artery wall

(figure 8-2)

Blood vessel: (a) normal and (b) blocked with plaque.

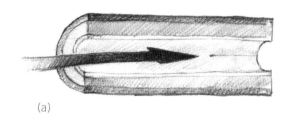

(a)

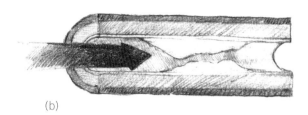

(b)

(see Figure 8-2). Special white blood cells called macrophages ingest the LDL and become bloated and foamy. Muscle cells in the artery wall start to overgrow, and fat and calcium build up in the spaces between the cells. Eventually bleeding into the artery wall can also occur, which can rapidly result in a blocked artery. At any time, but especially when there is a large buildup of plaque, pieces of plaque or blood clot can break loose to cause blockage farther down the arterial system.

We do not know the causes of atherosclerosis. However, certain risk factors will increase the probability that it will develop:

- High cholesterol levels
- High triglyceride levels
- Smoking
- High blood pressure (hypertension)
- Diabetes
- Family history of PAD or heart disease
- Obesity
- Lack of exercise

Atherosclerosis also affects other blood vessels, although it does seem to affect some more than others. It is important to realize that atherosclerosis is a generalized disease and affects all arteries. Thus a patient with PAD may well have coronary artery disease putting that individual at risk for angina or a heart attack (see Chapter 7). If the carotid arteries to the brain are involved, the person may also be at risk for a stroke. If it blocks the kidney arteries, high blood pressure and kidney failure can result. All patients with PAD should seek medical attention to evaluate these other areas.

Other arterial diseases: Other diseases affect arteries too, but these seldom begin in the elderly. They usually involve conditions in which the body starts fighting its own arteries, much like rheumatoid arthritis has the body fighting its own joints and bones.

These conditions are also quite rare and seldom result in major complications such as stroke or limb loss. Two such conditions are *systemic lupus erythematosus* and *polyarteritis nodosa* (diseases of the body's immunity that causes inflammation and damage to some arteries).

DIAGNOSING PAD

In most patients PAD is silent and causes no symptoms. However, when the arteries to the legs become significantly narrowed or blocked, certain telltale symptoms occur. The first and most important symptom is claudication. **Claudication** is a cramping pain, dull ache, or sense of tiredness in the calves or buttocks when one walks a specific distance, but the pain goes away when one stops walking and rests. It comes on again when one resumes walking, usually after reaching the same distance (provided one walks at the same speed).

If the blockage becomes severe, pain may occur even at rest. This is usually noticed at night upon lying down to go to sleep. In bed the patient no longer has gravity helping the blood travel down to the feet, which start to hurt. Patients often remark that the pain eases somewhat after they get out of bed and stand. This is an important symptom since it implies very severe impairment to blood flow. If untreated, **gangrene** or death of the toes or feet can eventually result. Similarly, cuts or scrapes may not heal and also lead to loss of part of the limb.

On examining a patient who has PAD, a doctor may discover any of the following:

- Absent pulses in the foot or leg
- A noise in the artery caused by turbulent blood flow (called a bruit)
- Cool temperature of the foot or leg
- Pale color when the foot is elevated
- Decreased hair or tissue fat
- Open sores or black areas of gangrene

TESTING FOR PAD

Nowadays simple painless tests can be performed to diagnose PAD. Not involving needles or dye, these tests are usually done in a vascular lab. Since the quality of these labs is variable, it is important to request that your test be performed in a lab that is accredited by the Intersocietal Commission on the Accreditation of Vascular Labs (ICAVL).

The simplest test is called the **ankle/brachial index (ABI)**. Using a **Doppler** that is a special handheld device much like an electronic **stethoscope**, a technician compares the blood pressure in the ankle to that in the arm. In normal legs the ankle pressure and the arm pressure should be the same, and the ABI should equal 1. If the patient has PAD, the leg arteries are blocked and so the pressure at the ankle falls. This results in an ABI of less than 1.

In order to get a picture of the blockage site, very advanced machines using ultrasound can painlessly and noninvasively produce images showing the blood vessels and the blood flowing through them. This process is a little like radar. The test is called a **duplex** or **ultrasound scan**.

Alternatively, high-powered magnets can be used to produce pictures of body parts and blood vessels. These tests are expensive but completely safe. There is hope that in the future they may replace the need for arteriograms. However, they cannot be used in patients who have steel implants, such as pacemakers. Some patients also become **claustrophobic** in the scanners.

Blood vessels do not show up on regular X-rays. Accordingly, in an **arteriogram** (also called an **angiogram**) the doctor will insert a needle into the artery and inject a special dye. This will allow detailed pictures of the inside of the arteries. The needle is usually inserted via the groin or **femoral artery**. A sensation of heat often accompanies the dye injection; however, local anesthesia and sedation is used to eliminate pain. The procedure usually takes about half an hour. After it has been completed, the patient is required to lie flat for about four hours in order to prevent bleeding. The procedure is performed in an X-ray facility, often in a hospital. It is rare that an arteriogram is necessary for diagnosis, since this can usually be achieved by noninvasive tests. The arteriogram is generally reserved to help plan some form of intervention.

PREVENTING PAD

Atherosclerosis cannot be completely prevented or cured, but by limiting the following risk factors, you can slow its progress and, in some cases, actually reverse the blockages:

- *Smoking:* All forms of tobacco products are harmful and should be avoided.
- *Diet:* Reduce the intake of cholesterol and saturated fats found in meat, shellfish, and dairy products as well as certain plant oils such as coconut, palm oil, and cocoa (chocolate).
- *High blood pressure:* Hypertension aggravates PAD. It is important that blood pressure is well controlled. A family doctor, internist, or cardiologist usually does this. Some antihypertensive medications, known as **ACE inhibitors,** may reduce the incidence of atherosclerosis.
- *Medications:* **Statins,** niacin, and **fibrates** may reduce cholesterol.

Diabetics should be especially aware of PAD and keep their **diabetes** well in control. Also, diabetics are prone to developing infections and open sores in the feet. Combined with poor circulation, this can become an even more serious problem. Accordingly it is imperative that diabetics takes special care of their feet to prevent foot injuries by observing the following:

- Avoid going barefoot, even at home.
- Wear well-fitting shoes.
- If starting new shoes, wear them for a short time only and reassess to ensure that they are not causing blisters.
- Wash and dry your feet thoroughly but do not soak them so much that they wrinkle.
- Do not expose your feet to extreme temperatures or harmful chemicals.

- Inspect your shoes to ensure that there are no harmful objects inside the shoe.
- Inspect your feet daily for sores or injuries. Diabetics often have a decreased sensation, and so you may not realize that there is a problem area in your foot.
- Treat feet as if they were made of fine crystal. Seek good foot care on a regular basis.
- Whenever possible, have a **podiatrist** cut your toenails. If a podiatrist is unavailable, cut the nails straight across, no shorter than the length of the toe.
- Do not treat calluses or **bunions** yourself.

TREATING PAD

Although no medications can totally reverse PAD, some people will benefit with medication that lowers their cholesterol and consequently improving some blockages. Usually an internist, family doctor, or cardiologist will prescribe these. None of these medications makes plaque go away, nor do they help new arteries grow. They may, however, have some beneficial effects.

PENTOXIFYLLINE (TRENTAL) has been used for many years. We are not sure how it works although it is suggested that it makes the red blood cells "slippery." This allows the cells to go through blockages more efficiently, and this may be why people can walk farther when they are on this medication. It is taken three times a day with meals.

CILOSTAZOL (PLETAL) is a new medication. Again we do not know why it works, but clinical trials suggest it may be more effective than Trental in improving walking distance. Serious side effects can occur in patients with heart failure, so they should not be on it. Pletal can also interact with other medications, especially PRILOSEC (a heartburn medication), some antifungals, and ERYTHROMYCIN. Grapefruit should be avoided. Cilostazol is taken twice a day before meals.

Aspirin has not been shown to improve symptoms or complications from PAD. However, it has been shown to decrease the incidence of heart attack and stroke in patients with PAD and so should be used in most patients with this condition. The dose prescribed is 81 to 325 mg per day. Increasingly, doctors prefer the lower dose.

CLOPIDOGREL (PLAVIX), like aspirin, decreases the stickiness of normal blood elements called platelets, which are responsible for some of the complications of atherosclerosis like blood clots, heart attack, and stroke. In some patients who are especially prone to heart attack, Plavix may be preferred to aspirin. It is usually taken once a day.

Chelation: A chemical "treatment," chelation has been around for a long time. It involves intravenous injection of a chemical that will supposedly take calcium out of the plaque. However, there is so much calcium in bones that there will always be calcium in the body to go into the plaque. Clinical studies have failed to show any benefit from chelation, and insurers will not pay for its use.

Exercise: Many studies have shown the benefit of exercise. Exercise will not only improve stamina but also reduce the risk of heart attack and stroke. Walking, swimming, and bicycling are good aerobic exercises that most older persons can perform. However, if you have been sedentary or if you have multiple medical problems, talk with your doctor before initiating a more intense exercise program (see Chapter 36); you should not undertake increased exercise without the evaluation and approval of a medical doctor.

PROCEDURES FOR PAD

In some patients PAD must be treated invasively, which means either surgery or endovascular procedures.

Endovascular procedures: Endovascular procedures, by which the artery is treated from the inside, are only minimally invasive. Endovascular procedures include balloon angioplasty, stents, laser treatments, and lytic treatments (dissolving clots from within the artery by using special "clot-buster" medications). It should be realized that these procedures are still invasive in that a needle, wire, or balloon has to be inserted into the artery. Furthermore, complications can occur that may be serious. On the other hand these are generally rare, and most patients can go home within 24 hours of the procedure.

Balloon angioplasty can be performed for short areas of narrowing. A balloon is threaded into the artery and inflated, thus breaking the plaque and widening the artery. The balloon is then removed. After balloon angioplasty some arteries will tend to collapse again. A stent is a small metal scaffold that is placed into the artery to prevent this narrowing (see Figure 8-3). Unfortunately, in some patients the body forms scar tissue inside the stent, and this scar can also block the artery again.

Sometimes blood clots can form on plaque and cause a sudden deterioration of the circulation. In some patients the doctor can pass a catheter into the clot and clean the clot out with a special medication. This process is referred to as thrombolytic therapy.

Surgical procedures: The simplest surgical procedure is known as an endarterectomy. Here the surgeon cores out the plaque from the artery

(figure 8-3)

Balloon angioplasty opens a blocked blood vessel; a stent keeps the vessel open afterward.

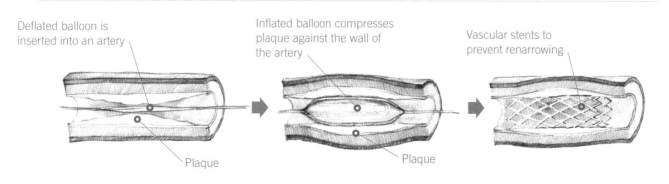

Deflated balloon is inserted into an artery

Plaque

Inflated balloon compresses plaque against the wall of the artery

Plaque

Vascular stents to prevent renarrowing

wall and stitches the artery back together again. This is the procedure of choice to clean out the carotid arteries for the prevention of stroke.

If a piece of the artery or a blood clot from the heart breaks loose and gets carried down the bloodstream, it can block an artery. This is referred to as an *embolism*. The surgeon can sometimes remove this by passing a catheter with a balloon down through the clot and then pulling the clot out again with the balloon inflated. This is known as an **embolectomy**.

A **bypass** is the most common form of surgery performed for PAD involving the legs. The surgeon may use an artificial artery or take the patient's own leg or arm vein and use it as an artery replacement. Incisions are made in the leg, and the new artery is sewn above the blockage and then around the blockage to a good portion of artery beyond the blockage (see Figure 8-4). The original artery is left in place.

Success rates: The success rates of endovascular and standard surgical procedures are very variable. They depend on how bad the blockage is, where the blockage is located, the effects of the blockage, and the general health of the patient. Results may also differ on the basis of the expertise of the surgeon. It is generally recommended that patients seek the help of board-certified vascular surgeons. Do not be afraid to ask your doctor the expected outcome for your particular case. Also, after you have one of these procedures, long-term follow-up care by your surgeon is mandatory, so that the progress of the procedure can be monitored and problems prevented.

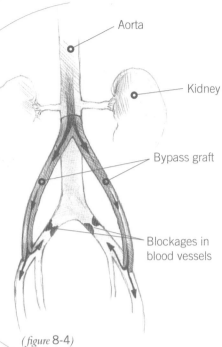

(*figure* 8-4)

A vascular bypass uses a vein or synthetic graft to allow blood to go around a blockage in a blood vessel.

ANEURYSMS

If an artery weakens, it will sometimes bulge out and expand. This enlarged area is called an **aneurysm**. In most cases aneurysms are associated with atherosclerosis, but the exact cause is not fully explained. In rare instances aneurysms can occur following trauma to the artery or infections of the bloodstream. Aneurysms can affect any artery in the body but usually occur in specific sites. The commonest site is in the abdominal **aorta**, the large artery that carries blood from the heart through the abdomen to the legs. Such an aneurysm is called an abdominal aortic **aneurysm** (see Figure 8-5). Aneurysms less commonly occur in the branches of the aorta that go to the legs (the **iliac arteries**) and in the legs themselves where they enlarge the **popliteal artery** behind the knee.

The main risk of an aneurysm is that it can rupture, resulting in profuse bleeding and often death. Sometimes an aneurysm will fill with a blood clot that can break loose and cause a blockage in the arterial circulation "downstream." Accordingly, an abdominal aortic aneurysm can be a "time bomb in the abdomen." Such aneurysms cause more than 10,000 deaths annually in the United States, and many of these deaths would have been preventable by early diagnosis and treatment. Approximately 50,000 patients undergo surgery for abdominal aortic aneurysm in the United

States alone every year. Once the aneurysm has ruptured, the chance of dying is 80 to 90%; therefore, there are clear-cut reasons to screen for this problem.

INCIDENCE OF ANEURYSMS

Aneurysms usually start to appear in a person around the age of 50 years. After age 65 a man has a approximately a 7% risk of developing an abdominal aortic aneurysm, whereas a woman has less than a 1% risk. By 80 years, the risk is up to 10% for a male versus 2% for a female. A person's risk is also increased if a parent, brother, or sister has or had an abdominal aortic aneurysm.

Since aneurysms are usually associated with atherosclerosis, it is not surprising that most people who develop aneurysms are the same ones at risk for atherosclerosis (see the list of risk factors presented earlier in the section on "Atherosclerosis").

DIAGNOSING ANEURYSMS

Aneurysms enlarge slowly over a period of years. In theory, this means they can be discovered before they cause problems. Unfortunately, aneurysms frequently produce no symptoms that would prompt a person to seek medical attention before they leak or rupture. But they can often be diagnosed at a regular physical examination. For example, an abdominal aneurysm often feels like a tender, throbbing lump under the abdominal wall, and the patient or an examining doctor may discover the pulsating mass. Even if the lump cannot be felt, the doctor can often hear suspicious sounds of turbulent blood flow through a stethoscope placed on the abdomen.

When an examining doctor discovers suspicious signs of an abdominal aneurysm, an abdominal X-ray or ultrasound examination may reveal its size and location. More advanced tests, like a CT scan or MRI, are usually included in the diagnostic workup. Some vascular specialists recommend that ultrasound, a simple, quick, noninvasive test, be used to screen people at high risk for an abdominal aortic aneurysm. Once an aneurysm has been diagnosed, an arteriogram may be required to plan treatment.

Screening is quite justified. In the United Kingdom, more than 15,000 volunteers were screened for abdominal aortic aneurysms, and there was a subsequent 55% reduction in the incidence of ruptured aneurysms. Unfortunately, in the United States, Medicare will not pay for screening tests. However, if the treating physician suspects that an aneurysm is present in an individual patient, Medicare will ensure the test is ordered to confirm or rule out the diagnosis.

TREATMENT

There is no medical treatment for aneurysms. Once starting to grow, an aneurysm will not ever get smaller again. In general people with small

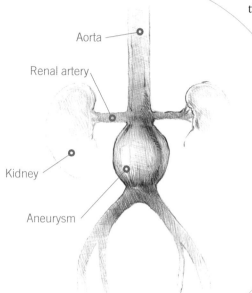

Aorta

Renal artery

Kidney

Aneurysm

(*figure* 8-5)

Abdominal aortic aneurysm.

FAMILY JOURNAL

My husband Robert G., 76, went to his doctor for a physical examination. He has been treated for high blood pressure for many years, and he developed diabetes within the last two years. He smoked a pack of cigarettes a day for 45 years but quit five years ago. His doctor advised him that he had several risk factors for an abdominal aortic aneurysm. Bob has a "pot belly" and his doctor advised him that it would be difficult to feel an aneurysm on physical examination since the aorta sits in the back of the abdomen. The doctor suggested that Bob have an ultrasound of his abdomen. He was sent to a vascular laboratory, and we were flabbergasted when his doctor advised him that he had a 6-cm aneurysm of the abdominal aorta. Thankfully, it was found before it ruptured, and he had successful surgery. He is trying to lose weight and get more exercise.

aneurysms are encouraged to control blood pressure and treat conditions that may accelerate atherosclerosis. Smoking must be curtailed, but exercise, other than heavy weightlifting, need not be restricted. There is some experimental work being performed to see whether drugs, such as beta-blockers or some antibiotics, may slow abdominal aortic aneurysm growth, but as yet results have not been encouraging.

There are two methods to repair aneurysms and both involve surgery.

Open surgical repair: The traditional treatment for an abdominal aortic aneurysm is a surgical procedure performed under general anesthesia. An incision is made in the abdomen, and the surgeon opens the aneurysm and sews in place a vascular graft to replace the diseased artery (see Figure 8-6). In skilled hands, this procedure can be performed with a mortality of 2%. Patients stay approximately five days in the hospital. They convalesce at home for one week and normally recover fully by six weeks. Although very rare, complications such as gangrene of the legs, kidney failure, need for a colostomy, pneumonia, and even paralysis can occur. Because this is major surgery, heart attacks may also—but unusually—complicate the operation. For this reason it is sometimes recommended that patients have a cardiology checkup, which may include a stress test, prior to surgery. In some men sexual dysfunction can occur. This may rarely be impotence, but in some men a condition known as retrograde ejaculation can result. This implies that vaginal penetration and orgasm still can be achieved, but the semen ejaculates into the bladder rather than externally. This can result in infertility. It is important to note, however, that once the abdominal aortic aneurysm is repaired by open surgery, it is rare that any lasting problems or need for further intervention will occur.

Endovascular repair: In this new, less invasive technique of endovascular repair, a catheter, or small tube, is inserted into the arteries through a small incision in the groin. Under X-ray guidance, a vascular endograft is delivered through the catheter and placed inside the aneurysm. This endograft fits snugly into the normal artery above and below the aneurysm and forms a new pathway for the blood to flow, thus excluding the aneurysm, which then usually begins to shrink. Patients go home the next day and frequently are able to resume normal activity by 1 week. It is expected that mortality will be less than that for standard surgery, but as yet this has not been conclusively proved. Such complications as gangrene of the leg, claudication, kidney failure, need for colostomy, pneumonia, paralysis, or heart attack can result from this procedure; however, sexual dysfunction should not occur. Unfortunately, not all patients are candidates for this type of procedure. The vascular surgeon must evaluate each patient on a case-by-case basis, and approximately 10% of the patients may require a further procedure at some stage in the future to fix problems that develop over time with the graft or the aneurysm. Because

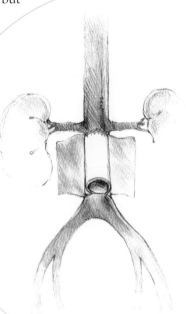

(figure 8-6)

Repair of an abdominal aortic aneurysm.

endovascular repair is a new procedure, long-term surveillance of the patient must be performed usually by means of a CT scan or ultrasound. A few patients have ruptured the abdominal aortic aneurysm despite an apparently successful procedure.

Recommendations: The risk of aneurysm rupture for aneurysms less than 5 cm is quite small. There is not much benefit for surgical intervention for aneurysms of that size. Once the aneurysm reaches 5 cm, the risk of rupture may be approximately 10% per year. Under such circumstances most surgeons would advise the repair of the aneurysm unless the patient has prohibitive medical risks against treatment. Although the endovascular treatment is safer than standard surgery, most surgeons would still favor withholding this treatment until the aneurysm reaches 5 cm.

CAROTID ARTERY DISEASE AND STROKE

A stroke, or **cerebrovascular accident (CVA),** is the sudden death of brain tissue, resulting in symptoms that last over 24 hours. It is usually caused by a vascular problem, either a bleeding artery or vein in the brain or a blockage in an artery that supplies blood to the brain tissue. If the symptoms subside within 24 hours, the patient is said to have suffered a **transient ischemic attack (TIA).** A stroke or TIA may involve one or more of the following symptoms:

- Numbness on one side of the body
- Weakness, paralysis, or loss of coordination on one side of the body
- Drooping on one side of the face or mouth
- Blindness or loss of part of the vision in one eye that typically is described as like a shade being drawn over the eye (which has a medical term, called **amaurosis)**
- Loss of speech or garbled speech
- Inability to write or understand writing
- Episodes of memory loss
- Loss of consciousness

The most common cause of stroke or TIA is a blockage in the internal carotid artery. There are two carotid arteries, one on each side of the neck (see Figure 8-7). These are the main arteries to the brain. Atherosclerotic plaque commonly develops in these arteries at the point at which they divide into the artery to the brain (the **internal carotid artery**) and the artery to the face (the **external carotid artery**). Plaque can decrease blood flow to the brain and hence a TIA or stroke by narrowing the artery or by breaking loose and blocking an artery in the brain itself.

TESTING FOR CAROTID PLAQUE

If a patient has carotid plaque, the doctor may hear a noise in the neck called a *bruit*. A TIA or stroke is also often evidence. However, most often the plaque does not produce symptoms even if detected by a noninvasive test called a *duplex scan*. Patients who may benefit from one of these tests

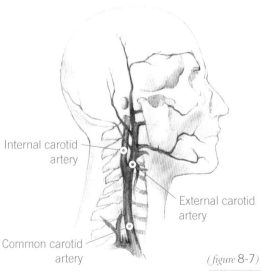

Internal carotid artery

External carotid artery

Common carotid artery

(figure 8-7)

The carotid circulation.

are those at risk for atherosclerosis. (See the list presented earlier in the section "Atherosclerosis.")

Duplex scans, arteriograms, and other tests, described earlier in the section "Detecting PAD," are also used to diagnose carotid plaque. Figure 8-8 shows a duplex scan in progress.

MEDICATION FOR STROKES

There are no medications that can make the plaque disappear although in some patients strict control of cholesterol can reduce plaque.

However, some TIA and strokes are due to blood clots from the plaque dislodging into the brain. These blood "clots" are aggregations of small blood cells called *platelets*. Using medication to make blood "slippery," such as aspirin, may prevent this aggregation and subsequent TIA or stroke. Newer, more effective medications are being added every year, such as AGGRENOX and PLAVIX. In patients with moderate plaque, these medications should be considered. However, side effects can occur, and patients should discuss the risk-benefit balance with their doctor.

PROCEDURES FOR PLAQUE

Carotid endarterectomy: The surgical procedure to remove plaque (carotid endarterectomy) is the most common vascular operation in the United States, with over 100,000 being performed annually. Although endarterectomy is usually quite safe, some patients will suffer a stroke, nerve damage, or heart attack from the procedure. Accordingly, the benefits of this procedure will depend greatly on the skill of the surgeon. It is imperative that the potential patient asks their surgeon about his or her experience with this procedure. National statistics suggest that the stroke rate approximates 3 to 5% and the heart attack rate 1%. However, many board-certified vascular surgeons should be able to achieve stroke rates of approximately 1% and a heart attack rate of 0.5%.

A major study of stroke risk has been conducted under the auspices of the National Institutes of Health. This study concluded that surgery is more effective than is medication and should be considered for patients who have had a TIA or recovered stroke and a blockage of greater than 70%. A second study performed by the Veterans Administration also suggests that some patients, especially men who have an asymptomatic blockage of greater than 60%, should be considered for endarterectomy.

Carotid endarterectomy can be performed under general or local anesthesia and takes about an hour. The plaque is cut out of the artery and the artery repaired. Most patients are sent to a regular ward following surgery and are discharged the next morning. There is very little discomfort. Normal activity can be resumed, but heavy exercise and driving is limited for one week. Thereafter, a full return to normal activity is encouraged, including activities such as golf. Most patients will continue taking aspirin after the procedure. Follow-up duplex scans will be performed on a six-month basis to assess the small chance of recurrent plaque or scar tissue that can narrow the artery again. This occurs significantly in about 4% of patients.

(*figure* 8-8)

Carotid artery scan. (*Courtesy of Sarasota Memorial Hospital*).

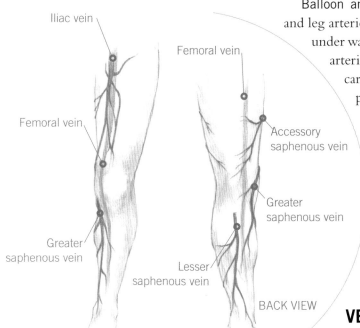

Iliac vein

Femoral vein

Femoral vein

Accessory
saphenous vein

Greater
saphenous vein

Greater
saphenous vein

Lesser
saphenous vein

BACK VIEW

FRONT VIEW

(figure 8-9)

The veins of the left leg.

Balloon angioplasty: Balloon angioplasty of coronary heart arteries and leg arteries has been proved to be effective. Consequently, studies are under way to see whether this technique can be applied to the carotid arteries, but it is important to realize the difference in risk if the carotid arteries are treated in this manner. If a small piece of plaque breaks loose and goes into the brain, a fatal stroke can result. At present the early results suggest, not surprisingly, that angioplasty carries a higher risk of stroke than does surgical endarterectomy. Advances in techniques may improve results, but currently angioplasty is considered experimental and should only be performed as part of an ongoing National Institutes of Medicine study trial. On occasion, however, it may be beneficial for patients who would be at increased risk from surgery. These include patients who have had radiation treatment for neck cancer.

VEINS

Veins are blood vessels that carry blood back to the heart. The leg contains two sets of veins, the deep veins inside the muscle and the superficial veins that lie just under the skin (see Figure 8-9). The two main superficial veins are the greater or long saphenous vein, which runs up the inside of the thigh and calf, and the small or lesser saphenous vein, which runs up the back of the calf. There are also innumerable superficial veins that drain into these two veins. Valves in the veins prevent the blood from falling back to the feet if a person is standing.

VARICOSE VEINS

If the valves are weak or break, blood collects in the veins in the lower legs. The pressure of this blood distends the veins, making them bulge and become tortuous. If this occurs to the veins in the superficial system, we refer to them as varicose veins (see Figure 8-10). Varicose veins can be located anywhere but are usually found in the legs.

The cause of varicose veins remains unknown. Standing for long periods of time may contribute to varicose veins. As women are affected more often than men are, female hormones may play a role. A strong family history of varicose veins could be a factor.

Pain associations: Many patients with varicose veins remain symptom-free or, at most, have a sense of fullness and discomfort after standing for a long time. Some varicose veins may become painful during a woman's menstrual period. Swelling of the ankles, itching, and bleeding are much less common symptoms.

Open sores (ulcers) of the ankle region can result from varicose veins although this is atypical. Usually, this problem only occurs if

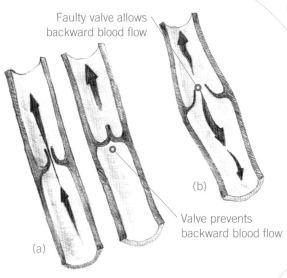

Faulty valve allows backward blood flow

(b)

(a)

Valve prevents backward blood flow

(figure 8-10)

(a) Normal vein (b) Varicose vein.

the patient also has leaking valves in the deep veins of the leg, a condition referred to as chronic venous insufficiency, or stasis dermatitis. The treatment for these ulcerations involves compression to squeeze the blood back to the heart. This involves the use of special wraps or surgical stockings, such as the Jobst UlcerCare.

Other patients ultimately develop serious swelling and a brown discoloration of the lower ankle. This complication is more commonly the result of a previous phlebitis (blood clot) in the veins. Sometimes phlebitis can occur in a varicose vein. Unlike such blood clots in the deep veins of the leg, superficial phlebitis in a varicose vein usually does not pose a risk to the patient's health (see Figure 8-11).

Preventing varicose veins: Varicose veins cannot be prevented if a person is predisposed to getting them by, for example, having a family history of varicose veins, standing for long periods of time, or being obese or pregnant. However, one may help alleviate the discomfort caused by varicose veins by avoiding prolonged standing or controlling weight. A person can also try simple exercises, such as, if standing, flex the feet or stand on toes two or three times per minute. At home one can try elevating legs above the heart for a half hour two or three times a day.

(figure 8-11)

Blood clot in a leg vein.

SPIDER VEINS

Spider veins are not true varicose veins; rather, they are large and unattractive skin capillaries. Most people seek treatment of spider veins for cosmetic reasons.

PROCEDURES FOR VARICOSE AND SPIDER VEINS

Most blood flow takes place in the deep veins, whereas varicose veins involve the superficial system. Therefore, treatment to remove the veins is very safe. Even the main saphenous veins can be removed without any functional impairment. This is the reason why these veins are used by vascular and heart surgeons as artificial arteries for coronary or leg artery bypass operations.

Varicose veins and spider veins can be treated by a large variety of procedures: stripping, microphlebectomy, saphenous vein ligation, radiofrequency ablation, laser ablation, injection sclerotherapy, and PhotoDerm light.

Stripping used to be the standard method of treatment for varicose veins. These days it is very rarely required. In this procedure the entire saphenous vein is removed. The procedure requires general anesthesia and a few days of recuperation. It is generally reserved for patients who have such severe varicose veins that they develop discoloration or ulceration of the skin at the ankle or if the visible varicose veins are the saphenous itself. All these circumstances are unusual. Some surgeons will always remove this vein as part of vein treatment, whereas others will try to spare it so that it can possibly be used by heart or vascular surgeons in the future as an arterial substitute.

Also known as *ambulatory stab avulsion phlebectomy (ASAP),* microphlebectomy is a simple procedure by which varicose veins are removed through 2-mm incisions (see Figure 8-12). No stitches are necessary. Surgery is performed on an outpatient basis under local anesthesia, and scarring is minimal or nonexistent. Results are immediate, and normal activity can be resumed promptly. Procedures take from 15 minutes to two hours.

Sometimes the main superficial vein, the saphenous vein, has a leaking valve. In order to get maximum benefit of other vein treatments, this vein must be tied. This procedure, known as *saphenous vein ligation,* is performed in an outpatient surgery center under local anesthesia with or without mild sedation. The incision is only about 25 mm long and is placed just above the groin crease so that it cannot be seen. Plastic surgery techniques with absorbable stitches are used to close the incision. It takes 20 minutes, and patients can return to normal activity immediately. It does not result in any pain, and the stitches are absorbable.

Radiofrequency ablation (VNUS) involves passing a catheter into the saphenous vein under local anesthesia. The tip of the catheter is then heated by radiofrequency waves, and this heat causes the vein to close down and eventually disappear. In a somewhat similar fashion, laser ablation (EVLT or ELVS) destroys the saphenous vein by the use of heat. A tiny laser light fiber is inserted into the vein under local anesthesia, and the laser light heats the inside of the vein, which likewise causes the vein to close down and disappear. Both procedures can be performed in a doctor's office, and the patient can usually return to normal function the same day. However, some patients may feel some discomfort for a few days after either procedure. Since both are new procedures, long-term outcome (one to three years) is still not well described. However, short-term results appear to be as good as saphenous vein ligation.

Injection sclerotherapy is the injection of an irritant solution into the varicose vein. The solution causes the vein walls to "stick together." Blood flow is routed to other veins, and the body absorbs the varicose vein. For two days after spider vein treatment and three weeks after varicose vein treatment, stockings are worn to compress the vein walls together during the healing phase.

A new treatment to obliterate spider veins, PhotoDerm light can also removing age spots, tattoos, and unwanted hair. A special machine uses brief bursts of intense light to destroy the vein wall. Although the procedure is advertised as painless, most patients state that it feels like they are being hit by a rubber band. It is best for treating very small veins or those left over after injection therapy.

New techniques have made the treatment of varicose and spider veins very safe. Although life-threatening complications such as blood clots or allergic reactions are theoretically possible, they are exceedingly rare. After vein injections, troublesome brown staining may result. Sometimes tiny

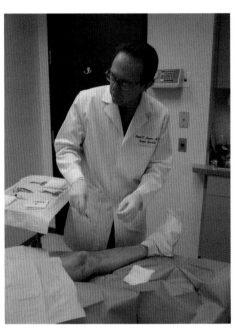

(figure 8-12*)*

Dr. Samson removing varicose veins by microphlebectomy.

new spiders in the form of a blush can occur. Both of these can be treated, but in some cases they may be permanent. A very rare complication is a painful open sore at the injection site that may heal with a pale scar. PhotoDerm can burn the skin or decrease the amount of pigment in the skin causing pale marks. Microphlebectomy may be followed by a painful superficial, if not dangerous, inflammation of the saphenous vein. Radiofrequency and laser ablation can also cause loss of sensation on the inside of the leg by inadvertently damaging the sensation nerve that runs alongside the saphenous vein.

Before you undergo treatment, the doctor should explain all side effects and discuss potential risks with you, and it is important for patients to realize that over time spider or varicose veins will probably return. However, these usually can be readily removed on an outpatient basis.

■

WHAT YOU NEED TO KNOW

▶ Arterial diseases (especially heart attacks and strokes) are the number-one killer of the elderly.

▶ Atherosclerosis is the process of hardening of the arteries, and the major risk factors include lack of exercise, being overweight, high cholesterol and/or triglyceride levels, cigarette smoking, high blood pressure, diabetes, and a family history of heart or circulatory disease.

▶ Your primary care physician can assess your risks for diseases of the circulation. An office examination and simple laboratory tests can be used, and a treatment plan can be established to reduce your risks.

▶ Diagnosis of arterial diseases may involve noninvasive tests such as measurements of the blood pressure differences between the arms and legs, ultrasound, or MRI. Invasive testing (arteriogram) is generally reserved for those who are being evaluated for surgery or angioplasty.

▶ Medications and exercise may play a role in reducing symptoms and preventing progression of arterial diseases. Your primary physician can decide which measures are most appropriate for you.

▶ Chelation therapy is expensive, and numerous clinical studies have shown it to be of no benefit. This treatment should be avoided.

▶ Diseases of the veins are unrelated to arterial disorders and, except for blood clots, are generally not life- or limb-threatening. In most patients treatment is for cosmetic reasons.

▶ Varicose veins have many different treatments. A patient should seek a physician who can offer all the treatment options.

▶ If you have a more severe circulatory disease, your primary physician will refer you to a vascular surgeon who can decide which invasive strategy is most appropriate for you.

WHAT YOU NEED TO KNOW

▶ Managing Editor

VascularWeb
900 Cummings Center, Suite 221-U
Beverly, MA 01915
Web: www.vascularweb.org

Mind and body are not independent. . . . For there are not two processes, and there are not two entities; there is but one process . . . one entity . . . in reality an inextricable mixture and unity of both . . . they are one.

—*Baruch Spinoza, 17th century philospher, (paraphrased by Will Durant, The Story of Philosophy, 1954)*

THE AUTHOR

09

GREGORY L. EASTWOOD, MD, is a professor of medicine and the president of the State University of New York (SUNY) Upstate Medical University in Syracuse, New York, since 1993. He received his medical degree from Case Western Reserve University School of Medicine. He completed his residency in internal medicine at the Hospital of the University of Pennsylvania, and he was a NIH Research Fellow in Gastroenterology at the Boston University Medical Center. He was assistant professor of medicine at Harvard Medical School from 1974 until 1977; professor of medicine and director of the Division of Gastroenterology at the University of Massachusetts Medical Center from 1977 to 1989; and dean of the Medical College of Georgia from 1989 to 1992.

He has written more than 70 journal articles and 50 book chapters, and is the author of the *Core Textbook in Gastroenterology*, coauthor of the *Manual of Gastroenterology*, and editor of *Premalignant Conditions of the Gastrointestinal Tract*. A popular speaker at numerous medical conferences, Dr. Eastwood is a member of Alpha Omega Alpha (medical honor society) and the first honorary member of the Japanese Society of Gastroenterology.

THE GASTROINTESTINAL SYSTEM

09

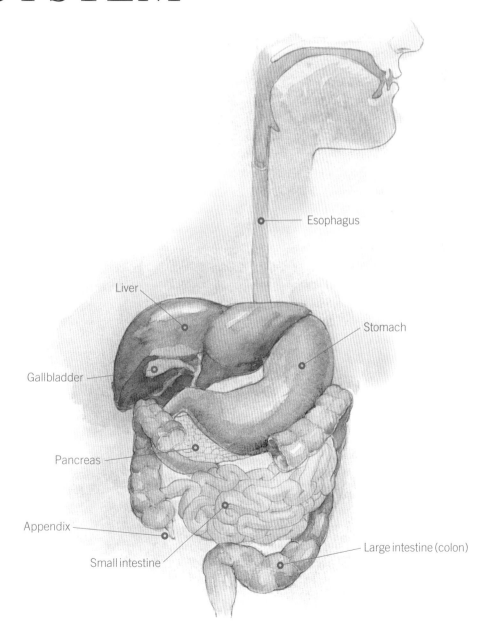

Esophagus

Liver

Stomach

Gallbladder

Pancreas

Appendix

Small intestine

Large intestine (colon)

(figure 9-1)
Gastrointestinal system.

Everyone has had a digestive disease of one kind or another. It may have been a self-limiting bout of "intestinal flu" or indigestion or a more serious condition, such as peptic ulcer disease or cancer of the colon. Regardless of your experience, as you get older, the likelihood that you will experience a problem with some aspect of your digestive system increases, just as is the case with many other systems as we age.

When I first meet medical students, I try to make two initial points that I believe are particularly applicable to the consideration of digestive disorders, although they also apply to all doctor-patient interactions. First, as Spinoza reminds us, the mind and body are not separate, and they influence each other profoundly. Second, the perspectives of a patient and a physician are different. (But they also influence each other profoundly!) A doctor's orientation is in terms of disease categories; a patient knows that he or she is not feeling right, and may explain that by describing pain or some other symptom. Both physicians and patients are better off if the physician can consider the patient simultaneously from the patient's perspective and from the position of a trained and experienced clinician. In this chapter I discuss with you some of the common disorders of the digestive system, largely from your perspective (see Figure 9-1).

TASTE, SMELL, FOOD, AND AGING

Flavor is the complex interaction of smell and taste. Almost half the people over age 65 have some diminution in smell or taste, which may affect appetite. The number of taste buds decreases with age, and some medications can interfere with taste. Appetite can also be diminished by illness and mood. In addition, poor fitting dentures, swallowing disorders, neurological conditions such as Parkinson's disease, inability to prepare meals, irregular sleep habits, or unavailability of food can all contribute to poor nutrition and reduced consumption.

Attention to food preferences and preparing tasteful foods may counteract loss of taste or smell and improve appetite. Certainly, improvement in health, treatment of mood disorders, correction of denture problems, and preparing tasty, healthy meals will all contribute to better nutrition and enjoyment of eating. The importance of nutrition and diet is discussed more fully in Chapter 28.

SWALLOWING DIFFICULTIES

To understand why people sometimes have difficulty swallowing, it is useful to understand the process of swallowing. The main players in the process are the throat (pharynx) and the esophagus, which is a muscular tube that runs from the throat through the middle of the chest to the stomach. Swallowing begins when solid or liquid material is moved to the back of the throat by the tongue. This initiates an automatic sequence that includes contraction of the throat muscles, relaxation of a muscular ring at the top of the esophagus *(upper esophageal sphincter),* and a series of contracting waves *(peristalsis)* that propel the swallowed material down the esophagus. Another muscular ring *(lower esophageal sphincter)* at the junction of the esophagus and stomach then relaxes momentarily to allow the material to pass into the stomach.

Subtle changes in the process of swallowing can occur with aging. Bad teeth can result in poorly chewed food that is difficult to swallow. Neurological conditions can affect the coordination of the throat muscles in the initiation of swallowing. Although the function of the esophagus itself remains normal in healthy seniors, several causes of swallowing difficulty increase in prevalence with age, such as diabetes, which may affect the muscular contractions, and cancer of the esophagus, which obstructs the passageway. Pills can lodge in the esophagus if they are taken with insufficient water or if there is a swallowing disorder. Also, flow of saliva and swallowing normally are decreased during sleep, so medications should be taken well before bedtime or with plenty of water.

People who have a problem with the initiation of swallowing typically cough or expel food through their mouth or nose. Sometimes they suck material into their windpipe and develop irritation of the windpipe, chronic cough, or pneumonia. This usually is related to a disorder of the muscles of the throat or their nerve supply. Sometimes chronic throat infections can do the same thing.

The more common type of swallowing disorder is the sensation that food or fluids have difficulty passing down the esophagus or that they actually stick *(dysphagia)*. The reasons for this range from disorders of the muscle and nerve supply of the esophagus, such as diabetes or muscular spasm, to things that obstruct the esophagus, such as cancer or benign stricture. Sometimes severe irritation of the lining of the esophagus from reflux of stomach contents or from infections can cause dysphagia.

A physician should evaluate symptoms of difficulty in swallowing. Even the transient sensation of food sticking could indicate a benign constriction or the first signal of a tumor. Possible diagnostic procedures include a barium swallow X-ray test; an *esophageal motility* test, which measures the muscular activity of the esophagus; and a direct examination of the esophagus (and incidentally the stomach and upper intestine) through a fiberoptic endoscope. (See the section "Gastrointestinal Endoscopy," below.)

HEARTBURN, GASTROESOPHAGEAL REFLUX, AND HIATAL HERNIA

Nearly everyone has experienced heartburn from time to time, that burning sensation in the chest, usually attributed to overeating or spicy foods and sometimes associated with drinking alcohol or smoking.

The medical explanation of heartburn is that materials in the stomach—acid, digestive enzymes, food—reflux up into the esophagus, irritating the lining of the esophagus and causing pain. Sometimes people also experience regurgitation of food and fluids. These phenomena, heartburn and reflux symptoms, go by the term gastroesophageal reflux disease (GERD), which now appears in the press and advertisements.

The reason that stomach contents reflux into the esophagus is probably related to inefficiencies in the lower esophageal sphincter. Its main function is to keep things in the stomach, but alcohol, smoking, and fatty food (many "spicy" foods also contain a lot of fat) can weaken the sphincter. Also, increased abdominal pressure, such as occurs from overeating, can overcome the sphincter's ability to keep food where it belongs, in the stomach.

Commonly, heartburn and reflux symptoms are attributed to a *hiatus hernia*. The esophagus normally enters the stomach through a small hole *(hiatus)* in the **diaphragm**, which is the large, flat, transverse muscle that separates the chest cavity from the abdomen and is important in breathing. A **hiatus hernia** occurs when a portion of the upper stomach protrudes up through the diaphragm into the chest (see Figure 9-2). The prevalence of hiatus hernia increases with advancing age. Traditionally, hiatus hernia has been thought to predispose one to gastroesophageal reflux. Medical scientists now believe that the major reason for reflux is an incompetent sphincter and a hiatus hernia by itself does not cause reflux. Evidence to support this is the observation that many people have a hiatus hernia but have no reflux symptoms. However, a hiatus hernia can serve as a reservoir for stomach contents that can then be refluxed into the esophagus. So if someone has reflux symptoms, a hiatus hernia may make the condition worse.

The reflux of acid and other stomach contents into the esophagus may cause more than pain. It can irritate the lining of the esophagus, resulting in inflammation or bleeding. The healing response to the inflammation can be variable. Usually, the esophagus heals by regenerating the normal lining. Other times, a benign stricture or scar develops, which can narrow the passageway and cause food to stick.

One potentially serious consequence of chronic gastroesophageal reflux is the development of **Barrett's epithelium**. To understand Barrett's epithelium, it is necessary to understand the characteristics of the normal lining of the esophagus and of the stomach. The lining of the esophagus is called stratified squamous epithelium, which is comprised of flat cells piled on top of each other and similar in appearance to skin under a microscope. At the junction of the esophagus with the stomach, this lining changes abruptly to one that is comprised of glandular cells (columnar epithelium), which is characteristic of the stomach. Further, a form of columnar epithelium lines the entire remaining gastrointestinal tract from stomach, through small intestine, to colon and rectum. These two types—squamous and columnar—are easily distinguishable in biopsies of the esophagus and stomach when viewed under the microscope.

In some people, the healing process in the esophagus in response to chronic reflux results in a change of the lining from squamous to columnar, that is, similar in appearance (but not identical) to what is found in the

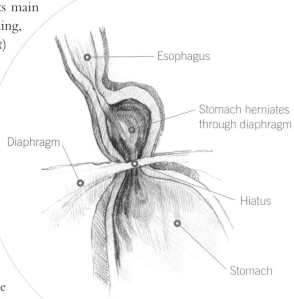

(figure 9-2)

Hiatus hernia: The hiatus is the opening in the diaphragm through which the esophagus passes on its way to the stomach. A hiatus hernia results from a portion of the stomach pushing through the hiatus into the chest cavity.

stomach or in the intestines. Norman Barrett, a British surgeon, described this condition about 50 years ago, and his name has been associated with it ever since (see Figure 9-3). Although Barrett's epithelium itself is a benign condition and most patients with Barrett's epithelium never develop esophageal cancer, the condition is a risk factor for esophageal cancer. Thus, once Barrett's is identified, most doctors recommend a surveillance program, which usually includes periodic endoscopy and biopsy, the frequency of which depends on the type of Barrett's and other risk factors.

Treatment of ordinary heartburn and reflux symptoms includes antacids and medications that inhibit acid production by the stomach. When symptoms do not respond to treatment or recur frequently or if there is difficulty swallowing, a diagnostic test is in order. This could be a barium swallow X-ray test or an endoscopy. A barium swallow X-ray is not a reliable way to diagnose reflux, but it can show strictures and other abnormalities in the esophagus, stomach, and *duodenum* (the upper intestine). Endoscopy allows direct inspection of the esophagus, stomach, and duodenum, as well as the opportunity to take biopsies for subsequent microscopic examination. This is the only practical way that Barrett's epithelium is diagnosed.

INDIGESTION

Indigestion is usually meant to indicate unpleasant symptoms after eating, but it is a nonspecific concept. Symptoms of indigestion are often those of heartburn or gastroesophageal reflux, described above. Or they may connote peptic ulcer disease or gallbladder disorders. Uncommonly, they signal the onset of more serious disorders, such as cancer of the stomach, pancreas, or gallbladder. Most frequently, indigestion means nothing at all, except perhaps a bad meal or transient stress.

Here is a partial list of disorders that can be associated with indigestion.

- Gastroesophageal reflux
- Peptic ulcer disease
- Gallstones and gallbladder disorders
- Pancreatitis
- Cancer of the esophagus, stomach, colon, pancreas, or gallbladder
- Coronary artery disease
- Diarrheal disorders
- Irritable bowel syndrome
- Inflammatory bowel disease (ulcerative colitis, Crohn's disease)
- Abdominal angina (pain after eating due to poor intestinal blood flow)

Indigestion afflicts all age groups, but inasmuch as the prevalence of several of these conditions increases with age (in particular, cancer, heart disease, and abdominal angina), older folks may develop new symptoms of indigestion.

Barrett's epithelium

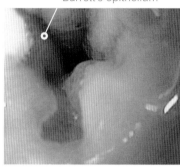

(a)

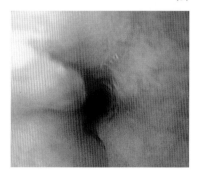

(b)

(*figure* 9-3)

Note the difference in the lining of (a) Barrett's esophagus compared to (b) a normal esophagus.

Most people who experience indigestion endure the symptoms or try antacids or some other over-the-counter (OTC) remedy. Clearly, when symptoms persist or are accompanied by other signs or symptoms, such as loss of weight, vomiting, bleeding, persistent pain, difficulty swallowing, fever, or jaundice (yellow eyes), see your doctor.

PEPTIC ULCER DISEASE

Peptic ulcer disease is a general term that describes injury to the lining (mucosa) of the esophagus, stomach, or duodenum caused by the action of hydrochloric acid and pepsin, a digestive enzyme (see Figure 9-4). Both hydrochloric acid and pepsin are secreted by parietal cells in the lining of the stomach. The mucosal injury can be discrete holes or divots, in which case they are called ulcers, or multiple erosions and inflammation, which is called *esophagitis, gastritis,* or *duodenitis,* depending on the location. Other agents, such as alcohol, bile acids (which can reflux from the duodenum into the stomach and esophagus), and certain medications, including aspirin and the so-called nonsteroidal anti-inflammatory drugs (NSAIDs), such as IBUPROFEN, can injure the mucosa by themselves and certainly can augment the injury caused by acid and pepsin. Cigarette smoking seems to aggravate the development of peptic ulcer, perhaps by interfering with the normal mechanisms that protect most people against the harmful effects of acid and pepsin. Over the past two decades, a bacterium called *Helicobacter pylori* has been implicated in the development of peptic ulcers. Although *H. pylori* infects the stomachs of the large majority of patients who have benign duodenal and gastric ulcers, many other people harbor *H. pylori* without apparent ill effects.

Acid secretion typically diminishes with age, and about 25% of people over age 65 have little or no detectable stomach acid. This does not interfere substantially with normal digestion and would seem to lessen the risk of older people developing peptic ulcer disease. However, the increased use of aspirin and certain other arthritis medications in older people raises the possibility that mucosal injury will occur. In fact, people over age 60 who use NSAIDs are at five times the risk of developing a gastrointestinal complication compared to those who do not use the drugs. Other risk factors for the development of NSAID-related injury include past history of peptic ulcer disease or gastrointestinal bleeding and possibly smoking.

Despite these observations, most older people tolerate arthritis medications well. Taking the medication with food decreases the chance of harmful effects. Upset stomach or other symptoms attributed to NSAIDs may respond to antacids or acid-suppressing medications. Also, not all arthritis medications harm the stomach. Table 9-1 shows some common arthritis drugs according to their ability to cause stomach injury.

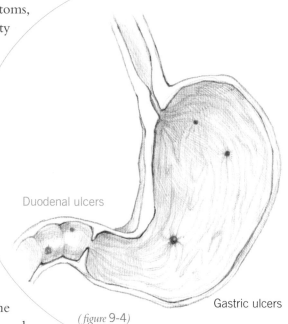

Duodenal ulcers

Gastric ulcers

(figure 9-4)

Note the difference in location of gastric and duodenal ulcers: Gastric ulcers involve the stomach. Duodenal ulcers involve the first part of the small intestine.

(table 9-1)

ABILITY OF COMMON ARTHRITIS DRUGS TO CAUSE STOMACH INJURY

POSSIBLE STOMACH INJURY	LITTLE OR NO STOMACH INJURY
Aspirin	Acetaminophen (Tylenol)
Ibuprofen (Motrin, Advil)	Celecoxib (Celebrex)
Naproxen (Naprosyn)	
Clinoril (Sulindac)	
Indomethacin (Indocin)	
Tolmetin (Tolectin)	

The classic symptoms of peptic ulcer disease—pain in the upper abdomen on an empty stomach that is relieved by food or antacids—are familiar to most of us. However, ulcer pain may be muted in older people or poorly localized, causing confusion with heart disease and other abdominal disorders, such as gallbladder disease, pancreatic disease, irritable bowel syndrome, and cancer of the stomach, pancreas, or *biliary system*. A minority of ulcer patients have bleeding, vomiting, or weight loss.

The definitive diagnosis of peptic ulcer disease requires that an ulcer or erosions be identified by a barium swallow X-ray test or by endoscopy. Many times, mild symptoms are treated without initially ordering one of these tests. However, if symptoms persist or there is severe pain or bleeding, an X-ray examination or endoscopy is indicated.

Treatment of peptic ulcer disease typically includes antacids or acid-suppressing drugs. When *H. pylori* is suspected, antibacterial drugs are added. Conventional wisdom says that diet plays a role in the treatment of peptic ulcer disease. However, several controlled studies have indicated that rigid dietary restrictions are of little or no benefit in healing peptic ulcers that are not complicated by bleeding, obstruction, or perforation. In fact, most foods, including conventional "spicy" foods, cause no direct injury to the stomach. Thus, patients are advised to eat what they want, but because food intolerances are unique to each person, one would be foolish to continue to eat foods that are known to cause discomfort.

The comments above about food, however, do not pertain to alcoholic beverages. Alcohol does injure the stomach lining and should be avoided or restricted in accordance with a doctor's advice when treating peptic

THEN AND NOW

For many years, stress and acid were felt to be the cause of ulcers. Milk diets and avoidance of spicy foods was recommended. Sometimes it is hard to let go of old beliefs. Look how many years it took for people to be dissuaded of the notion that the earth is flat. Doctors too may be slow to accept new things. When Drs. Robin Warren and Barry Marshall from Australia proposed in 1983 that ulcers were caused by a bacterium called *Helicobacter pylori,* their research was greeted with skepticism. It was not until 1996 that the FDA approved the first antibiotic treatment for ulcers. The following year witnessed a national campaign by the Centers for Disease Control to educate physicians that ulcers could be cured with antibiotics ulcer disease. Also, smokers should try to stop smoking because of the negative effects that smoking has on peptic ulcer disease.

The large majority of peptic ulcers are not cancerous. For practical purposes, all duodenal ulcers are benign. However, most gastric cancers occur in people over age 60, and sometimes they ulcerate, mimicking stomach ulcers. Also, some ulcers in the esophagus are associated with cancer in Barrett's epithelium (discussed in the section "Heartburn, Gastroesophageal Reflux, and Hiatal Hernia," above). Thus, further examination, which usually means endoscopy and biopsy of the ulcer, is indicated in gastric and esophageal ulcers.

ABDOMINAL PAIN

Physical pain is not a simple affair of an impulse, traveling at a fixed rate along a nerve. It is the resultant of a conflict between a stimulus and the whole individual.
— *René Leriche (1879–1955)*

Dr. Leriche must have had a bit of the philosopher Baruch Spinoza in him. (See the epigraph at the beginning of this chapter.) Abdominal pain is a good example of the interaction of mind and body. Who has had abdominal pain and not been a little worried or preoccupied with it?

Abdominal pain affects all age groups, but in older people abdominal pain may signify certain conditions that are less likely to be found in younger individuals. Also, coexisting conditions may aggravate the discomfort. Perhaps equally important, pain can alter lifestyle and mood.

Some of the nomenclature of abdominal pain may be useful to understanding it and in interacting with physicians, nurses, and other caregivers. Is the pain acute or chronic, mild or severe, localized or diffuse? What provokes the pain? What relieves it? Acute pain usually connotes both rapidity of onset and increased severity. Chronic pain is typically long-lasting, but may be fluctuating and usually is less severe. Doctors also want to know the location of the pain and whether it radiates somewhere. For example, the pain of acute gallbladder disease can be felt in the right upper abdomen and radiates straight through to the back under the right shoulder blade, although there are many exceptions.

Here is a list of some of the characteristics of abdominal pain:

- Duration (acute, chronic)
- Intensity (mild, severe)
- Quality (dull, sharp, intermittent, constant, burning)
- Radiation
- Associations (with eating, defecation, body position, something else)
- What relieves the pain?
- Location

To localize the pain, different systems are used to partition the abdomen into sections (see Figure 9-5). One common sense system is simply to

MY STORY: JAMES P., 58

I love jogging. I have been getting up early and running 10 miles almost every day for the last 20 years. I have run in several marathons. As I have gotten older, my joints were getting more stiff and sore. Ibuprofen helped get me going in the morning, and I was taking 2-3 before I ran. I had been doing that for about eight months, when one morning I felt some pain in my upper belly. Before long, the pain became excruciating, and I was bent over in pain. My wife brought me to the emergency room, and by the time I got there I was in agony. Test showed I had a perforated ulcer, probably due to my taking ibuprofen on an empty stomach for so long. I was taken immediately to the operating room where the ulcer hole was repaired.

I am jogging again, but I take only acetaminophen; no more ibuprofen or other drugs in that class.

(figure 9-5)

The terms for abdominal surface anatomy help doctors describe the location where pain occurs and may help determine the cause of abdominal pain.

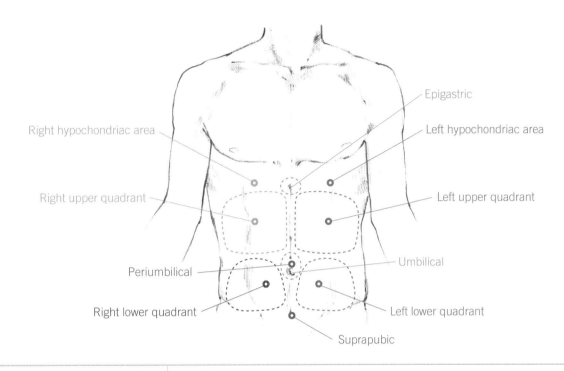

Epigastric

Right hypochondriac area

Left hypochondriac area

Right upper quadrant

Left upper quadrant

Periumbilical

Umbilical

Right lower quadrant

Left lower quadrant

Suprapubic

divide the abdomen into quadrants: *right upper quadrant (RUQ), right lower quadrant (RLQ), left upper quadrant (LUQ), and left lower quadrant (LLQ).* Additional terms are *epigastric* (the upper midabdomen, literally "over the stomach"), *periumbilical* (around the belly button), *suprapubic* (lower midabdomen, literally "above the pubic bone"), and left and right *hypochondriac areas* ("under the ribs"). The latter gives rise to the vernacular term hypochondriac, meaning someone who "bellyaches" or is a constant complainer.

Abdominal pain is further categorized into visceral, somatic, and referred. *Visceral* pain is usually poorly localized and less intense. It is caused by rapid distention, stretching, or traction of an abdominal organ or the tissues that attach the intestines to the abdominal wall *(mesentery).* Interestingly, the stomach and bowel can be cut without causing pain, as demonstrated by the taking of biopsies without the perception of pain, unless the bowel is pulled or stretched in the process. *Somatic* pain is usually sharper and more focused and occurs when the lining of the abdomen is inflamed or the abdominal wall is involved with a hernia, inflammation, or a mass. *Referred* pain is pain that is felt at some location other than the inciting cause. An example is the pain that is felt in the right shoulder if the underside of the right diaphragm is irritated by a liver abscess or the fluid that leaks from a perforated duodenal ulcer. This is because the nerve supply of the shoulder and diaphragm has a common origin during embryonic development (the early development from a cell to a differentiated human being).

You can see from Table 9-2 that abdominal pain has many sources. Although several diagnoses have typical characteristics (e.g., appendicitis is associated with an initial midabdominal discomfort advancing to more severe RLQ pain; acute gallstones with RUQ pain radiating to the back; and ruptured aortic aneurysm with rapid onset back pain), there is sufficient overlap and variability that even experienced clinicians are sometimes uncertain.

The identification of the cause of abdominal pain depends on a careful history, physical examination, knowledge of associated conditions, and, sometimes, diagnostic tests. You should see your doctor for anything more than trivial or transient discomfort.

(table 9-2)

CAUSES OF ABDOMINAL PAIN

URGENT	LESS URGENT	DECEPTIVE
Aortic aneurysm*	Diabetic neuropathy*(nerve damage)	Myocardial infarction* (heart attack)
Blockage of blood supply to an organ*	Gastroenteritis	Pulmonary embolus (blood clot in the lung)
Appendicitis	Peptic ulcer	Adrenal insufficiency (also called Addison's disease)
Perforation of an abdominal organ	Hepatitis	
Ectopic pregnancy (pregnancy in the tubes leading from the ovary to the uterus)	Peritonitis (inflammation of the lining of the abdomen)	Shingles (herpes zoster)
	Pancreatitis	Acute pyelonephritis (kidney infection)
Abscess (liver, pancreas, elsewhere)	Inflammatory bowel disease (ulcerative colitis or Crohn's disease)	Pneumonia
Ruptured liver or spleen	Pelvic infections	Injury to the testes
	Inflammation of the lymph nodes within the abdomen	Familial Mediterranean fever (a rare disease)
	Kidney stones	Porphyria (a rare disease)
	Uterine fibroids	
	Ovarian cyst	
	Endometritis (inflammation of the lining of the uterus)	
	Diverticulitis (inflammation of "pockets" in the colon)	
	Skeletal muscle spasm or tear	
	Abdominal or inguinal (groin) hernia	

*Indicates conditions more likely in older people. However, all these conditions can occur in older people, except for ectopic pregnancy.

FLATULENCE, GAS, AND BELCHING

My wind exploded like a thunderclap,
. . . Iaso blushed a rosy red
And Panacea turned away her head
Holding her nose; my wind's not frankincense.
  —*Aristophanes (ca. 450–ca. 388 B.C.)*

The subject of intestinal gas has been imbued with an aura of humor and triviality since antiquity. Yet to the multitude of people who complain of gas, many of whom are seniors, their symptoms are neither humorous nor trivial. Further, the complaint of gas has no uniform connotation. To one person, too much gas may mean frequent belching. Another may regard the amount of *flatus* passed as signifying too much gas. Still another may attribute abdominal discomfort to gas. Despite these ambiguities, much is known about the sources, composition, and clinical relevance of intestinal gas.

Studies have indicated that a normal person passes between 500 and 2000 ml (between 2 cups and 2 quarts) of flatus per day. The frequency of passing flatus is also quite variable, ranging up to 20 passages per day.

Five gases—nitrogen, oxygen, carbon dioxide, hydrogen, and methane—make up more than 99% of the total volume of intestinal gas, but their proportions vary widely from one person to another. All these gases are odorless. The gases that impart the characteristic bad odor to flatus are present in only trace amounts. These gases include ammonia, hydrogen sulfide (rotten-egg smell), and volatile amino acids and short-chain fatty acids. Despite their low concentration, these gases are easily sensed by the normal human nose, which can detect noxious gases in concentrations as low as 1 part per 100,000,000. However, many older people develop partial loss of smell, and their ability to perceive noxious odors is thus diminished. (*Warning:* Be careful where you pass gas. Even though you may not smell it, others might!)

Nitrogen, the major bowel gas, comes predominantly from air that is swallowed along with food and drink. Several milliliters of ambient air may accompany each normal swallow. Some foods themselves contain air, such as fresh apples, which may be composed of up to 25% air. Nitrogen also diffuses from the bloodstream into the bowel.

DID YOU KNOW?

The gas normally present in our intestines expands during air flight since the plane's cabin has a lower atmospheric pressure than at sea level. This can cause abdominal cramping and pain, as well as some discomfort for you as a passenger—as well as those around you! If you have experienced these problems with air travel, it is best to avoid foods that are "gas producers." These include beans and other legumes, pectin-containing fruits such as apples, and carbonated beverages such as soda drinks and beer.

Oxygen also enters the digestive system via swallowed air. However, intestinal bacteria largely consume swallowed oxygen. Some oxygen in flatus may diffuse into the bowel from the blood.

Carbon dioxide is produced in large amounts in the duodenum and upper small intestine during the normal digestive process by the neutralizing chemical reaction of bicarbonate with hydrochloric acid from the stomach and fatty acids and amino acids, which are products of digestion. Ingestion of soda, beer, and other carbonated drinks provides an external source of carbon dioxide, which is either burped or passed into the intestine. Most carbon dioxide from these sources is absorbed into the blood stream and excreted by the lungs. The carbon dioxide in flatus is derived largely from bacterial action on intestinal contents.

Hydrogen primarily comes from the action of bacteria on carbohydrates in the intestine. Certain vegetables, such as beans and other legumes, contain complex carbohydrates that cannot be completely digested and are metabolized by bacteria. People who are lactase-deficient, that is, deficient in the intestinal enzyme that splits the sugar lactose found in milk, ice cream, and other milk products, also typically produce large amounts of gas, mostly hydrogen, when they consume lactose-containing foods. This contributes to the abdominal cramping and excess flatus that lactase-deficient people experience. Lactase deficiency occurs normally in a high proportion of adults in certain ethnic groups, such as African Americans, Asians, Inuit, and South and Central Americans. Older Caucasians also sometimes develop mild to moderate lactase deficiency.

Methane production by intestinal bacteria has several interesting aspects. The flammability of the flatus of certain people has been recognized for years. Eyewitness reports have verified this phenomenon in fraternity houses and other convivial gatherings. (This can be dangerous and should not be tried.) Only about one-third of adults produce methane; the remaining two-thirds produce little or no methane. Whether or not a person is a methane producer appears to be determined early in childhood, which may be related to the colonization of the intestine of babies and young children by the intestinal bacteria of their parents.

The clinical consequences of gas are several. Burps and belches result from swallowed air. People who complain of burping may swallow excess amounts of air with food and drink, may swallow air as a nervous habit, or may be unusually aware of normal amounts of air in their stomach or esophagus. Occasionally, burping is a sign of something more serious, such as gallbladder disease or obstruction of the stomach or duodenum. Belching fecal-smelling gas may be due to chronic overgrowth of bacteria in the stomach or a fistula between the stomach and colon, which is a rare complication of cancer of the stomach or transverse colon.

People who experience recurrent abdominal cramps or bloating sometimes attribute those symptoms to gas. However, studies have shown that in such individuals the volume and composition of intestinal gas are usually normal. Rather, what seems to be wrong is a heightened sense of pain in response to normal amounts of gas, as well as abnormalities in the *motility* of the intestine, that is, in the way the gas is accommodated and moved along the intestine. Of course, cramps and bloating can signify more serious conditions, and the possibilities include many of the things considered above in the section "Abdominal Pain." Treatment of the symptoms depends on the underlying disorder. Cramps and bloating sometimes respond to dietary changes, bulking agents such as psyllium, or other medications. Unfortunately, the symptoms do not often respond to treatment, and a specific, treatable cause is not found, leaving some to suffer from "nervous bowels" or a similar designation, such as irritable bowel syndrome.

Increased amounts of flatus can result from the gas produced by bacterial action on food. Thus, elimination from the diet of certain high-probability offenders, such as legumes, and other dietary manipulations are common treatments. Some people have specific food intolerances, the most common being lactose. Sometimes excessive flatus accompanies a disorder of the small intestine, such as *sprue* (also called *celiac disease,* which is caused by a sensitivity to gluten, a constituent of wheat).

The evaluation and treatment of complaints of gas are often difficult and unrewarding. An experienced physician of yesteryear summed up the approach to the patient with gas in a manner that cannot be improved.

> *Physician, when thy patient grieves of gas,*
> *Heed, allow ye not that 'plaint to pass.*
> *Inquire further into belching, or pain abdominal*
> *Or, perchance, the ignominy of flatulence phenomenal.*
> *Simple reassurance may suffice.*
> *If not, consider dietary advice.*
> *Despair ye not if all is naught.*
> *Alas, a cure is seldom wrought.*
> *—Eastwood the Elder*

CONSTIPATION AND FECAL INCONTINENCE

> *I have finally come to the conclusion that a good reliable set of bowels is worth more to a man than any quantity of brains.*
> *—Henry Wheeler Shaw (1818–1885)*

Although age alone does not seem to alter intestinal digestive and absorptive functions or normal bowel muscular activity, many elders do experience irregularity of bowel function and constipation. Problems with bowel function, both constipation and incontinence, are more likely in people who live in nursing homes or chronic care facilities than in those who live at home. Wherever it occurs, constipation can be attributed to a combination of limited physical activity and diminished intake of fluid, fiber, and complex carbohydrates. Incontinence can be incapacitating and may be related to diarrhea, poor anal sphincter tone, a debilitating illness,

(table 9-3)

FUNCTIONAL CONSTIPATION*

CONSTIPATION ONE OF SEVERAL SYMPTOMS	DISORDERS WHICH CAN CAUSE CONSTIPATION
Irritable bowel syndrome (may have alternating constipation and diarrhea, sometimes with cramps)	Endocrine-metabolic condition, such as diabetes, hypothyroidism, low potassium, high calcium, and pregnancy
Diverticular disease of the colon	Bowel obstruction from tumor, stricture, or postoperative scarring
Disorders of bowel muscle function, such as myotonic dystrophy and systemic sclerosis (scleroderma)	Disorders that cause painful defecation, such as proctitis (rectal inflammation) and anal fissure
	Disorders of the nerve supply to the bowel, such as Hirschsprung's disease, multiple sclerosis, and Parkinson's disease
	Medications that inhibit bowel activity, such as antidepressants and opiates

*Due to unknown factors or decreases in physical activity and dietary changes.

or, paradoxically, chronic constipation with impaction of stool (stool wedged in the colon so that it is difficult to move).

Constipation is difficult to define because of the wide variation in normal bowel habits, although you certainly know it when you have it. Thus, a functional definition is simply a decrease in frequency or increase in difficulty in passing stool compared to what you think is normal.

The economic cost of constipation is impressive. In the United States, more than $300 million is spent annually on laxatives. Additional costs of unknown magnitude are incurred in the evaluation of patients for underlying disorders that may predispose to constipation.

Constipation is a symptom, not a disease. Thus, it may develop for any of a number of reasons. Table 9-3 presents a partial list of causes.

Evaluation of constipation takes into consideration whether it is recent or chronic and associated with symptoms, such as pain, weight loss, and bleeding. If a specific cause of constipation is found, treatment of that disorder may alleviate the constipation. General measures include changes in lifestyle and diet and use of medications.

Some people simply do not take the time to have a bowel movement. The brain can inhibit the urge to defecate and that is what happens when busy schedules and other priorities intervene. Simply recognizing the urge to have a bowel movement and acting on it may be the first step for many constipated people in achieving a normal bowel habit. A program of mild exercise, such as walking, may be helpful.

Increasing dietary fiber may help. The average daily intake of crude fiber in U.S. adults is about 4 grams, which is roughly one-fifth of the fiber intake of some native Africans, who typically have four or five bulky stools a day. Dietary fiber can be increased by eating fruits, vegetables, potato skins, and bran-containing foods. Sometimes it is easier to take unprocessed bran, 1 to 2 tablespoons a day, or a commercial fiber product. Bran or a fiber supplement should be mixed in water or juice before ingestion. Increasing water intake to 1 or 2 liters a day augments

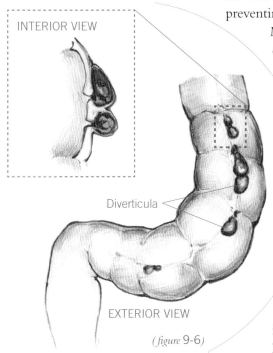

INTERIOR VIEW

Diverticula

EXTERIOR VIEW

(figure 9-6)

Diverticulosis: A diverticulum is a pocket in the wall of the intestine. Often, such "pockets" produce no symptoms. Diverticulitis occurs when they become inflamed, usually producing pain in the left lower abdomen that can vary from mild to severe.

the beneficial effects of fiber. Increasing dietary bran may also help in preventing colon cancer and gallstones.

Most people with chronic constipation have had ample experience with laxatives. Sometimes a vicious cycle develops: First, constipation is relieved by laxatives. Then, because the bowel is empty, the person perceives no urge to defecate and becomes concerned about not having a bowel movement. Resumption of laxatives perpetuates the cycle. Try to avoid the chronic use of laxatives. One gentle laxative is mineral oil, although the taste is unpleasant. The initial dose is 1 tablespoon before bed. If that is ineffective, the dose can be increased in 1-tablespoon increments up to a maximum of 4 tablespoons. There are precautions, however, in using mineral oil. It should be avoided in someone who might *aspirate* (i.e., breath) it into their windpipe and lungs, so mineral oil must be used cautiously or not at all in older people with swallowing difficulties or who are demented. Also, chronic mineral oil ingestion may interfere with the normal absorption of fat-soluble vitamins.

Fecal impaction, which is a firm, immovable mass of stool in the rectum or lower colon, typically develops in elderly, immobile people. Treatment consists first of the doctor, nurse, or caregiver attempting to break up the mass manually, by means of digital rectal examination. If that is unsuccessful, the impaction can sometimes be evacuated by enemas. Oral mineral oil may be useful if there is no risk of aspiration. Occasionally, the mass must be removed through the rectum under anesthesia.

The key to managing constipation and complications such as impaction is to prevent them in the first place by careful attention to diet and fluid intake, exercise, and the rational use of laxatives. Colonic lavage (flushing the colon with water), used by some people in the hope of purging toxins and impurities from the colon, has no scientific basis and may, in fact, be harmful. Colonic lavage is not recommended for the treatment of constipation.

DIVERTICULOSIS

The term **diverticular disease** customarily refers to complications of diverticula of the colon, although diverticula can occur anywhere in the digestive tract from esophagus to rectum (see Figure 9-6). Colonic diverticula are very common in the United States and the prevalence

STOPPAGE AHEAD

Millions of dollars are spent every year on laxatives and advertisements for laxatives. Unfortunately, little information is given on the dangers of long-term use of laxatives. Prolonged use of stimulant-type laxatives may actually diminish the tone in the muscles of your colon, thereby compounding the problem. You may get into a viscous cycle where you have to take these laxatives more frequently, and you end up dependent on them. Breaking a "laxative habit" can be difficult, but your doctor can help you. Ask your doctor which products are safe for you to use.

increases with age. About 30% of the population has colonic diverticula by age 60, and the prevalence increases to about 80% of 80-year-olds. The development of diverticula also is associated with a diet that is low in fiber. Although the large majority of people with diverticula remain without complications, symptomatic diverticulosis is a common condition in older people because of the high prevalence of diverticula.

Several of the terms associated with colonic diverticula and their complications have caused confusion or have been misused. A *diverticulum* is a single outpocketing from the bowel. Note the Latin singular, neuter ending *-um*. Several outpocketings are *diverticula,* not "diverticuli" or "diverticulae." The mere presence of a diverticulum or diverticula is called *diverticulosis,* which is not usually associated with symptoms and does not imply an abnormal condition. *Diverticulitis* has two meanings: inflammation in one or more diverticula and a clinical syndrome characterized by fever and abdominal pain. *Diverticular disease* is a general term to describe symptoms attributed to diverticula.

Patients with diverticular disease typically complain of chronic or intermittent lower abdominal pain. Accompanying symptoms may include infrequent bowel movements, constipation, and flatulence. Other conditions that need to be considered include irritable bowel syndrome, colon cancer, Crohn's disease, and urologic and gynecologic disorders. Development of severe pain, accompanied by fever and the signs of acute illness, raises the likelihood of diverticulitis. Diverticula also are a cause of lower gastrointestinal bleeding in older people, which usually is not accompanied by pain (see the section "Gastrointestinal Bleeding," below). This bleeding occasionally can be massive, requiring multiple transfusions and even emergency surgery.

If symptoms are mild, diagnostic studies may include a barium enema X-ray test, sigmoidoscopy, or colonoscopy. When symptoms are acute or severe, blood and urine tests, plain X-ray examination of the abdomen, and ultrasonography may be indicated.

Treatment of mild or chronic symptoms includes a high-fiber diet and sometimes medications to relax the bowel. Cathartic laxatives should be avoided. Patients with acute diverticulitis usually require hospitalization and receive antibiotics and intravenous fluids. Sometimes surgical removal of the offending portion of bowel is necessary.

JAUNDICE

Jaundice is a yellowing of the eyes and skin that is due to elevated levels of *bilirubin* in the blood. A high blood level of bilirubin is not harmful after the first several weeks of life. However, elevated bilirubin is often a sign of a serious disorder and, in some cases, may be accompanied by elevated *bile salts,* which, like bilirubin, are secreted by the liver and may cause generalized itching.

Bilirubin is formed in the liver from the breakdown products of red blood cells and then is secreted into the bile. Thus, there are multiple causes of jaundice, but the major categories are excessive breakdown

(figure 9-7)

Note the difference between (a) the normal liver and (b) the contracted nodular liver of cirrhosis.

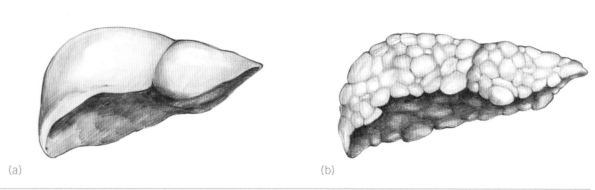

(a)

(b)

of red blood cells (hemolysis), disorders that affect the liver itself, and obstruction of the bile ducts.

Hemolysis can overwhelm the ability of the liver to form and secrete bilirubin, and the result is a functional backup of bilirubin in the blood. A number of conditions cause hemolysis, including certain blood cancers and other blood disorders, enlargement of the spleen, some infections, and medications. Nearly any liver disorder, ranging from acute toxic injury to inflammation *(hepatitis)* to chronic scarring *(cirrhosis)* can cause jaundice. So-called obstructive jaundice results from the obstruction of the bile ducts by gallstones or cancer of the liver, bile ducts, or pancreas. Several of these conditions are discussed in the following sections.

HEPATITIS, ALCOHOLIC LIVER DISEASE, AND CIRRHOSIS

Hepatitis means inflammation of the liver, which can be acute, intermittent, or chronic. Cirrhosis is a chronic condition of the liver in which there is a progressive sequence of damage to liver cells, regeneration, scarring, distortion, and diminution of liver function (see Figure 9-7). Sometimes conditions that cause hepatitis lead to cirrhosis. Although the common causes of hepatitis affect all age groups, because the development of cirrhosis takes years to decades, cirrhosis occurs more often in people over age 50. Also, certain drugs adversely affect the liver, and inasmuch as older people take more medications, they are at more risk of drug-related liver injury.

The most common causes of acute hepatitis are viruses and toxins, including drugs and alcohol. Occasionally certain metabolic disorders, leukemias, and lymphomas can affect the liver in a manner that is similar to hepatitis. The viruses that cause hepatitis have an alphabet soup nomenclature—A, B, and C are the most common, but D and E are described as well. Other viruses, such as Epstein-Barr virus and cytomegalovirus are unusual causes of acute hepatitis. Hepatitis A is acquired by ingesting contaminated water or food, and typically is a mild disease. B and C viruses, transmitted by blood and intimate contact, usually cause more severe disease and may lead to chronic liver disease, including cirrhosis and liver cancer.

The liver is the great metabolic factory of the body, both manufacturing new products and detoxifying harmful agents and drugs. Sometimes a toxin can overwhelm the ability of the liver to metabolize it, and transient or permanent damage to the liver ensues. Common toxins include carbon tetrachloride, phosphorus, mushroom and other plant poisons, and drugs. Older people use or come in contact with many drugs or chemical agents, such as ACETAMINOPHEN (TYLENOL), certain anesthetics, some arthritis medications, some antibiotics, some cholesterol-lowering drugs, and some anticancer drugs. Although the benefit of these agents often exceeds the risks, monitoring by your physician is required. If you take acetaminophen, your daily dose should not exceed 4 grams per day. Lower doses may be required if you take other medications. Check with your doctor if you are unsure. Even herbal products that are used as health aids, such as comfrey, germander, chaparral leaf, and certain teas, can cause liver injury in some people.

Hepatitis can be "subclinical," meaning that the insult to the liver is mild and symptoms of malaise (generally not feeling well), mild fever, headache, or loss of appetite may be ignored or attributed to something else. When these symptoms are more severe and are accompanied by jaundice—yellowing of the eyes and skin—the diagnosis of hepatitis, or some other acute injury to the liver, is likely. An accurate history of exposure plus diagnostic blood tests may give a specific diagnosis.

The widespread use of alcohol and its integration into everyday life perhaps lessen the perception that it can be a dangerous liver toxin. Alcohol is quickly absorbed across the lining of the stomach and intestine (which it can injure in the process) into the bloodstream. It then passes through the liver where it is detoxified on successive passages. Alcohol can cause direct damage to liver cells, which is manifested as acute fatty changes in the cells. This is considered a reversible condition. Higher doses of alcohol generate inflammation in the liver. As the inflammation heals, regenerative nodules of liver cells and fibrous scars develop, which eventually becomes cirrhosis. The loss of liver cells leads to diminished liver function, both in manufacturing clotting factors and other important metabolic products and in detoxifying harmful substances. The nodules and scarring distort liver architecture and impede blood flow through the liver (see Figure 9-8). This leads to the development of alternative pathways for blood around the liver (e.g., varicose veins in the esophagus that may bleed, visible veins on the abdomen, large hemorrhoids) and accumulation of fluid in the abdomen (ascites).

What is a safe amount of alcohol to drink? Because of wide variations in tolerances to alcohol, no specific amount can be recommended. However, studies have shown that an average of one or two drinks a day (i.e., one or two beers, glasses of wine, or mixed drinks) confers about

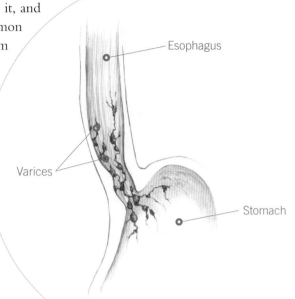

Esophagus

Varices

Stomach

(*figure* 9-8)

Usually due to severe liver disease, esophageal varices are dilated (varicose) veins of the esophagus.

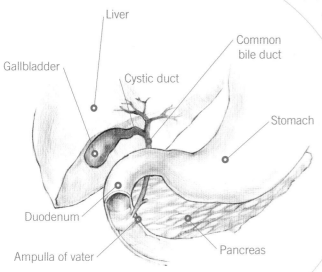

Liver

Gallbladder

Cystic duct

Common bile duct

Stomach

Duodenum

Ampulla of vater

Pancreas

(figure 9-9)

Gallbladder and biliary system: Bile from the liver passes into the intestines to aid in digestion. The gallbladder serves as a reservoir where bile is concentrated.

an optimal balance between the beneficial effects of alcohol in helping to prevent coronary artery disease and the harmful effects of alcohol on the liver and rest of the body. This is not an encouragement to begin drinking two glasses of wine a day if you do not drink alcohol. Being a teetotaler is not considered a health hazard!

One of the serious complications of either acute or chronic liver failure is the development of hepatic **encephalopathy**, a condition characterized by confusion, disorientation, deteriorating mental state, and, sometimes, convulsions and coma. The disorder is incompletely understood but is related to the inability of the liver to detoxify substances that are absorbed through the intestine and that interfere with brain and nerve function. Most patients need to be hospitalized, and treatment is aimed at clearing the digestive tract and maintaining the patient in anticipation that liver function will recover.

Cirrhosis clearly can be a consequence of many years of high intake of alcoholic beverages. Cirrhosis can also result from other things that cause ongoing inflammation or severe damage to the liver. These include viral hepatitis, drug-induced hepatitis, certain metabolic conditions (e.g., *hemochromatosis, Wilson's disease,* and *alpha-1 antitrypsin deficiency),* chronic bile duct obstruction, and chronic malnutrition. In addition to the complications of poor liver function described above, cirrhosis of any origin is a risk factor for the development of primary liver cancer. Thus, the onset of new pain, jaundice, or other unexplained symptom in a person with known chronic liver disease or cirrhosis is reason to consider liver cancer.

GALLSTONES

About 25 million people in the United States have gallstones. Although gallstones affect people of all ages, the prevalence increases with age. About one-third of people over age 80 have gallstones, but most do not know it. Other risk factors include heredity, pregnancy, obesity, diabetes, elevated blood fats, and being a female. Also, certain ethnic groups, including some native Americans, have a high prevalence of gallstones.

The major site of gallstone formation is the gallbladder, which is a collapsible bag roughly the size and shape of a pear and capable of holding about 4 tablespoons of bile (see Figure 9-9). Bile originates in the billions of liver cells and is secreted into tiny canals that converge to form progressively larger bile ducts, which eventually form a single large bile duct called the **common bile duct**. The gallbladder is connected by a narrow corkscrew tube (**cystic duct**) to the common duct shortly after the bile duct system leaves the liver. While a person eats, hormones are liberated from the duodenum that stimulate gallbladder contraction. This sends bile out the cystic duct, down the common duct, and into the upper small intestine. New bile formation by liver cells is increased during meals. This bile comes directly through the biliary duct system into the intestine, bypassing the gallbladder. Bile contains bile salts, which aid in the absorption of fats, and bicarbonate, which creates an optimal environment for digestive enzymes to work and helps neutralize the stomach acid that comes into the upper intestine. Because the liver detoxifies substances and gets rid of waste products, bile also contains things that have nothing to do with digestion.

Gallstones are classified into pigment stones and cholesterol stones, on the basis of whether biliary pigment or cholesterol predominates. In the United States, cholesterol stones are most common. The formation of cholesterol gallstones is a complex process that is related to the inability of bile salts to make cholesterol dissolve completely in the bile. When the bile sits in the gallbladder and the concentration of cholesterol further increases, cholesterol precipitates and forms stones in the gallbladder over months to years.

Gallstones remain "silent" in many people; that is, they do not cause symptoms and may be discovered incidentally during an abdominal ultrasound examination or surgery for some other reason. Symptoms attributed to gallstones vary widely from heartburn, bloating, flatulence, and nonspecific abdominal pain to acute abdominal pain. Whether the milder symptoms are due to irritation of the gallbladder lining or alteration of gallbladder contraction by gallstones is sometimes difficult to determine. However, severe pain in the right upper quadrant or midupper abdomen, radiating to the back under the right shoulder blade or to the shoulder, in the presence of documented gallstones, leaves little doubt that the gallstones are responsible. These symptoms are caused by obstruction of the cystic duct by a gallstone and consequent distention of the gallbladder. Sometimes gallstones traverse the cystic duct into the common duct where they can obstruct the flow of bile. This causes not only pain but jaundice. Both cystic duct and common duct obstruction can be accompanied by fever and signs of systemic illness. Sometimes gallstones obstruct the lower end of the common duct below the junction of the pancreatic duct, causing obstruction of the pancreatic duct and so-called gallstone pancreatitis.

Abdominal ultrasound is a good and relatively comfortable way to diagnose gallstones. Other tests that are occasionally used are *computerized tomography (CT)* and endoscopic retrograde cholangiopancreatography (ERCP). ERCP involves visualizing the biliary and pancreatic duct systems by positioning an endoscope in the duodenum and threading a catheter into the opening of the common duct.

If symptoms are due to gallstones in the gallbladder, removing the gallbladder is usually curative. Traditional open surgery is very successful. Over the past 15 years, *laparoscopic cholecystectomy,* which uses fiberoptic tubes and small incisions, has been perfected for uncomplicated situations. Impaction of a stone in the cystic duct or common duct usually requires conventional surgery, although some common duct stones can be removed via ERCP.

(figure 9-10)

Pancreatic cancer: The head of the pancreas is very close to the common bile duct. Cancer of the head of the pancreas may block the bile ducts and cause jaundice (yellowing of the skin).

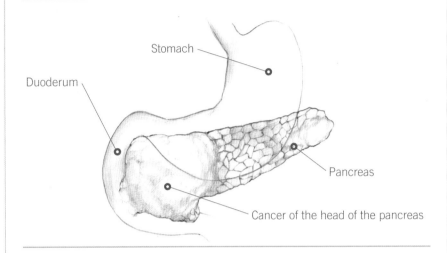

PANCREATIC CANCER

The pancreas is predominantly a digestive organ that secretes enzymes into the duodenum at mealtime. Most pancreatic cancers arise in the tissues that generate these digestive enzymes and are called **adenocarcinomas** (see Figure 9-10). Scattered throughout the pancreas are tiny islands of endocrine cells that secrete insulin and other endocrine substances. Sometimes cancers of these endocrine cells develop and reveal themselves by the actions of the hormones they secrete. The comments that follow deal with the more common variety of pancreatic cancer, adenocarcinoma.

Cancer of the pancreas occurs predominantly in older people and, unfortunately, is very lethal. This is partly because the signs and symptoms of pancreatic cancer are subtle and the disease usually has progressed before it is detected. Men are slightly more likely than are women to develop pancreatic cancer. Other risk factors include cigarette smoking and possibly a high fat diet. Although coffee has been implicated in the past, there is no conclusive evidence for that.

The early symptoms of pancreatic cancer are typically vague, including abdominal discomfort, poor appetite, nausea, weight loss, and sometimes psychological depression. Later, back pain and jaundice may develop because of the effects of the tumor on adjacent structures. You should check with your doctor if you experience these symptoms or signs, particularly if they are new. Also, unexplained acute pancreatitis or recent onset of diabetes may signal a cancer of the pancreas.

The diagnosis of pancreatic cancer can be made by CT scan, ultrasound, ERCP (see the section "Gastrointestinal Endoscopy," below), or, occasionally, exploratory surgery. Treatment, depending on the stage and whether the tumor obstructs the bile duct, includes surgical resection or bypass of the tumor, chemotherapy, and ERCP catheter placement to keep the bile duct open.

(table 9-4)

CAUSES OF GASTROINTESTINAL BLEEDING

UPPER GASTROINTESTINAL BLEEDING	LOWER GASTROINTESTINAL BLEEDING
Bleeding from the nose or lungs that is swallowed and vomited	Cancer* or polyp of the colon
Esophagus: tear, esophagitis, ulcer, varices (distended veins)	Diverticulosis*
	Ischemia (poor blood flow) of small intestine or colon*
Stomach: gastritis, ulcer	Arteriovenous malformation*
Duodenum: duodenitis, ulcer	Fistula between aortic aneurysm and intestine*
Cancer of esophagus, stomach, duodenum	Hemorrhoids
Bile ducts, usually due to cancer	Anal fissure (tear in the tissue around the anus)
Fistula (abnormal connection) between aortic aneurysm and intestine*	Inflammatory bowel disease (ulcerative colitis, Crohn's disease)
	Antibiotic-associated colitis
	Radiation colitis
	Brisk bleeding from an upper GI source (appears as lower GI bleeding)

* Occurs most often in people over age 60.

GASTROINTESTINAL BLEEDING

Bleeding from the gastrointestinal (GI) tract occurs in all age groups, although certain causes, such as colon cancer, bleeding from a diverticulum, ischemic colitis (low blood flow), and colonic arteriovenous malformations (AVMs) (abnormal growth of blood vessels), are almost always found in people over age 60. Advanced age decreases the outlook for acute GI bleeding from any cause, as do associated medical conditions, such as heart disease, chronic lung disease, renal insufficiency, and blood disorders, all of which are more likely in older people. Also, ingestion of aspirin, certain other arthritis medications, and alcohol can cause bleeding from the stomach or aggravate existing bleeding.

GI bleeding is classified as upper or lower in origin because the presenting signs frequently are characteristic of either an upper or a lower GI source. Table 9-4 shows some of the numerous causes of GI bleeding.

If blood sits in the stomach for several minutes, the action of gastric acid quickly forms dark particles that resemble coffee grounds. Vomiting of red blood or coffee ground–appearing material usually signifies a source of bleeding in the esophagus, stomach, or duodenum, but can occasionally result from swallowed blood from the nose or respiratory tract. Passage of red or maroon-colored stool usually indicates a source in the rectum or colon. An important exception is profuse bleeding from the upper GI tract, such as a ruptured esophageal vein or an ulcer that

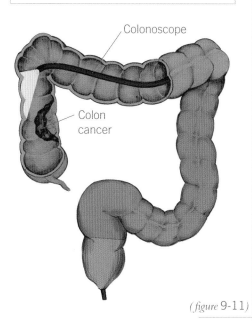

Lower rectum (10%)

Rectum, sigmond, and descending colon (55%)

Cecum, Ascending, Transverse colon (35%)

Colonoscope

Colon cancer

(figure 9-11)

Since colon cancer can occur anywhere in the colon, more and more physicians are recommending colonoscopy to evaluate and screen patients for colon diseases. Cancers in the ascending (as depicted here) and transverse colon are beyond the reach of a sigmoidoscope. The relative frequency of colon cancer in the various portions of the colon are noted in parentheses.

has eroded a vessel, in which case a large volume of blood passes rapidly through the digestive tract. Any sign of GI bleeding, upper or lower, is reason to consult a physician.

The evaluation of GI bleeding includes blood tests to assess the blood loss and check on the status of kidney and other organ function. Electrocardiograms and chest and abdominal X-rays are common. Specific tests include barium contrast X-ray studies of the upper and lower GI tract. In acute bleeding, upper GI endoscopy or colonoscopy are usually performed, both to make a diagnosis and, in some instances, to treat the bleeding source. Most hospitalized patients receive nothing by mouth, are given intravenous fluids, and, sometimes, blood, and may have to swallow a tube that is passed through the nose and down the back of the throat into the stomach, where it is used to suction blood and monitor recurrent bleeding after initial bleeding has stopped.

Most causes of acute bleeding are identified and treated effectively. The mortality from GI bleeding in otherwise healthy patients is less than 5%. However, associated liver, heart, or lung disease or some other systemic illness significantly increases the chance of complications and mortality.

PREVENTING COLON CANCER
THE KILLER WE DON'T MENTION IN POLITE COMPANY

While there are several chronic diseases more destructive to life than cancer, none is more feared.
—*Charles H. Mayo, MD, 1926*

It is likely that you either have colon cancer now, will get it in the future, or have a close relative or friend with colon cancer. Colon cancer, which technically is called *colorectal cancer* because the colon and rectum are continuous, is very common (see Figure 9-11). Each year in the United States, about 145,000 new cases of colon cancer are diagnosed and nearly 60,000 people die of it, divided evenly between men and women. Colon cancer is lethal, ranking behind lung cancer in men and lung and breast cancers in women in causing death.

The mortality and complications of colon cancer seem to more than justify programs to detect or prevent it. Yet, awareness among the public and the medical profession of this deadly disease is low compared to such high-profile cancers as breast, prostate, and lung, perhaps due to lack of information or simply because it is not polite to talk about something to do with one's rectum and colon!

Colon cancer can be prevented. In this section we review the conceptually simple but sometimes uncomfortable diagnostic tests that are effective in identifying colon cancer at an early stage or colon polyps, which have the potential to become cancerous. Also, we discuss the evidence that certain common medications and dietary supplements, such as aspirin, other pain relievers, calcium, and vitamins, decrease the long-term risk of developing colon cancer. In other words, by having your stool checked for blood each year, getting a sigmoidoscopy or colonoscopy

(table 9-5)

RISK FACTORS FOR DEVELOPING COLON CANCER

NORMAL RISK	INCREASED RISK	VERY HIGH RISK
Living longer (age over 50 years)	Family history of colon adenomatous polyps or cancer	Adenomatous polyposis syndromes (familial adenomatous polyposis, Gardner's syndrome)
Diet: low fiber, high fat; carcinogens	Personal history of colon adenomatous polyps or cancer	Hereditary nonpolyposis colon cancer
	Genetic syndromes	
	Hamartomatous polyposis syndromes (Peutz-Jeghers syndrome, juvenile polyposis)	
	Inflammatory bowel disease (ulcerative colitis, Crohn's disease)	

when recommended, and taking low-dose aspirin or certain vitamins regularly, you will lower your risk of developing colon cancer.

WHO GETS COLON CANCER?

The concept of risk is not familiar to everyone. Risk refers to chance or probability. So to say that colonic polyps increase the risk of cancer does not mean that all polyps will become cancerous. In fact, most polyps are benign and remain so, but a small number degenerate into cancer. This means that a person with polyps is more likely to develop cancer than if he or she did not have them.

Table 9-5 identifies factors that are associated with normal risk and increased risk of developing colon cancer. The chance of developing colon cancer increases as we get older. A diet low in fiber and high in fat seems to add a little risk. Also, the diet may contain unknown carcinogens. Polyps in yourself or a family member confer an added risk. If you already have had colon cancer, you are at increased risk to develop another cancer, and cancer in a family member, particularly a first-degree relative (a parent, sibling, or child), puts you at increased risk. Certain unusual genetic syndromes (see Table 9-5) are associated with an increased probability of developing cancer, as are long-standing ulcerative colitis and Crohn's disease.

PERIODIC TESTING

Guidelines for screening for colon cancer have been published in recent years and have been endorsed by the American Cancer Society and many other professional societies. Here are some suggestions, based on official recommendations but modified slightly by my own experience.

People at normal risk: The following recommendations for people at *normal* risk; that is, you are over age 50 and have no symptoms or other risk factors.

Annual stool test for occult blood: If your annual stool test for *occult blood* (i.e., blood that is not obvious or is hidden in the stool) is positive, have a total colonoscopy or barium enema X-ray test. In preparing for the stool test, you will probably be asked by your physician to avoid aspirin, certain other arthritis medications, vitamin C, iron preparations, red meat, and some other foods that may interfere with the test for several days before obtaining stool.

Sigmoidoscopy every five years: You should have a *sigmoidoscopy* (examination of the rectum and colon through a flexible tube) every five years. If one or more polyps are found, have a colonoscopy, particularly if a polyp is over 1 cm in diameter or if a biopsy of a polyp shows cancer. This is because more polyps or cancer can reside beyond the reach of the sigmoidoscope. Removing colon polyps, which is usually a simple procedure through a colonoscope, reduces the expected development of cancer by over 90%.

People at increased risk: If you have had any of the following conditions, you would be considered to be at an increased risk for colon cancer and should follow the recommendations given.

Parent, child, or sibling with colon cancer or a polyp: If a parent, child, or sibling of yours has had any colon cancer or a polyp, you should have the same screening as normal-risk people (stool test for occult blood yearly and sigmoidoscopy every five years), but begin by age 40. Be particularly concerned if your relative had colon cancer before age 55 or a polyp before age 60.

Polyps: If you ever had any previous polyps, you should have a total colonoscopy. If new polyps are found, removed, and are benign, then have a colonoscopy every three years. If the three-year colonoscopy is normal, repeat the colonoscopy every five years. If cancer is identified in a polyp, or a polyp is too large to be removed through the colonoscope, or there are too many polyps, management will need to be individualized.

Surgery for colon cancer: If you ever had previous surgery for colon cancer and if no colonoscopy was performed before surgery, have a colonoscopy within six months after surgery to check for preexisting polyps or tumors. If your preoperative or postoperative colonoscopy is normal, repeat the colonoscopy after three years. If the three-year colonoscopy is normal, repeat every five years.

Genetic syndrome: If you have a family history of a genetic syndrome, in particular, *familial adenomatous polyposis* or *hereditary nonpolyposis colorectal cancer* (and it would be unlikely for you to reach advanced years and be unaware of having such a genetic condition), genetic counseling, expert medical consultation, and colonoscopy most likely would be indicated.

Ulcerative colitis or Crohn's disease: Ulcerative colitis or Crohn's disease is almost always identified in children or young adults. Nevertheless, they do occur in some older people. A specialist can recommend appropriate surveillance and treatment.

PREVENTING COLON CANCER BY ASPIRIN, VITAMINS, AND OTHER THINGS

Rather than wait for polyps or cancer to develop and then detect them by screening tests, would it not be better to prevent the problem in the first place? A number of agents, including aspirin, other *nonsteroidal anti-inflammatory drugs (NSAIDs)*, vitamins A, C, and E, calcium, beta-carotene, omega-3 fatty acids, and even postmenopausal replacement hormones, have been identified as possible therapies to prevent colon cancer, on the basis of both laboratory and clinical studies.

Among the most interesting observations have been the effects of NSAIDs on cancer risk and polyp regression. Several population studies have correlated use of aspirin, 2 tablets more than 10 to 16 times a month, with a decrease in risk of colon cancer or polyps. The NSAID SULINDAC causes regression in number and size of polyps in patients with familial adenomatous polyposis, although the polyps recur after the sulindac is stopped. High dietary intake of carotenes and vitamins A, C, and E has been linked to a reduced risk for development of colon cancer, perhaps because of their antioxidant properties.

When several of these agents have been compared in controlled clinical trials (that is, some people take the medication, some do not), the results have been equivocal or have shown no clear benefit in decreasing the prevalence of polyps and cancer. Perhaps longer periods of observation of a decade or more are needed.

What can we take from these observations? Although controlled clinical trials of these agents do not show a clear benefit, most of them are relatively safe and many, such as aspirin, calcium, and vitamins, already are being taken for other reasons. Thus, it makes sense to take one or more of these agents if they are tolerated well, are not contraindicated for some reason, and do not produce complications, such as bleeding associated with aspirin.

BOTTOM-LINE RECOMMENDATIONS

1. If you are at normal risk for colon cancer, get your fecal occult blood testing and sigmoidoscopy now!
2. If you are at increased risk, have a colonoscopy.
3. If already taking aspirin, calcium, or vitamins for other reasons, you might be reducing your risk of developing colon cancer. If you do not take these things now, I cannot recommend that you begin, on basis of scientific evidence, but it may not be a bad idea anyway.

GASTROINTESTINAL ENDOSCOPY

Endoscopy means "to look inside." This is accomplished in the digestive tract by highly sophisticated, flexible, fiberoptic endoscopes. Fiberoptic bundles pass through the shaft of these instruments to transmit light to the area being examined. Other fiberoptic bundles send the image back so

09

that it can be seen through the eyepiece or on a video screen. The display on a video screen allows several people to observe the examination, including the patient, if desired, and the procedure can be videotaped for clinical and educational purposes. In the handle of the endoscope are controls for maneuvering the tip and buttons to operate water irrigation, air insufflation, and suction. A small channel through the instrument allows the passage of biopsy forceps, tiny brushes for obtaining cell samples, snares for removing polyps, and devices to retrieve foreign bodies and control bleeding. Upper GI endoscopes and colonoscopes differ in detail and length and may be modified for specialized functions.

During routine upper GI endoscopy, the entire esophagus, stomach, and upper duodenum are examined (see Figure 9-12). The instrument can be used to obtain biopsies, take cell samples for examination under a microscope, and treat bleeding lesions by heat, laser, or injection of therapeutic substances. Endoscopic placement of gastric feeding tubes has largely replaced surgical methods.

A variation of upper GI endoscopy, called *endoscopic retrograde cholangiopancreatography (ERCP),* combines endoscopic and radiological techniques to visualize the bile duct and pancreatic duct systems (see the section "Gallstones," above). ERCP methods also have been used to cut the sphincter where the common bile duct enters the duodenum *(sphincter of Oddi)* to remove gallstones from the common duct and to place tubes in the common duct that unblock obstructing lesions.

Sigmoidoscopy examines the rectum, most or all of the sigmoid colon, and sometimes a portion of the descending colon, depending on the individual anatomy and tolerance of the patient. During colonoscopy, the entire colon from rectum through sigmoid colon, descending colon, transverse colon, ascending colon to cecum is examined, and polyps and other lesions can be biopsied or removed. A physician skilled in colonoscopy reaches the cecum about 90% of the time and often the *terminal ileum* (the last part of the small intestine) can be visualized.

PREPARATION FOR THE PROCEDURES

Patients should not have anything to eat or drink, except medications approved by the physician, for about 12 hours before elective upper GI endoscopy to ensure an empty stomach. In emergency situations, such as acute upper GI bleeding, food and blood clots are usually removed from the stomach by a tube that is inserted through the nose or mouth before endoscopy is attempted. Typically, before either elective or emergency endoscopy, a topical anesthetic is applied to the throat to numb the gag reflex and make it easier to swallow the endoscope. Most patients also like to have some intravenous sedation. Allergies or intolerances to the medications need to be recognized and appropriate adjustments made. Because patients are likely to feel sleepy and reactions may be impaired for several hours, most outpatients are advised to have someone take them home after the procedure.

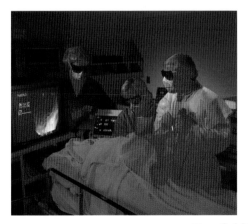

(figure 9-12*)*

Upper endoscopy allows the gastroenterologist to view directly the lining of the esophagus, stomach, and first part of the small intestine. Endoscopy has revolutionized the evaluation of gastrointestinal diseases. *(Courtesy of Sarasota Memorial Hospital).*

For sigmoidoscopy, tap water or commercial enemas are usually sufficient preparation, although enemas may be omitted if there is watery diarrhea, severe bleeding, or suspected colitis. Sedation is not typically required. Preparation for colonoscopy is more extensive. The evening before the procedure, the patient has a liquid meal, then either consumes about a gallon of a watery solution or drinks a cathartic that causes watery diarrhea. Although both methods are usually well tolerated, many people say that the preparation is worse than the procedure itself. This may be accounted for in part by the intravenous sedation that most people receive before colonoscopy. Also, some sedatives have an amnesic effect that diminishes the person's memory of the experience.

COMPLICATIONS

Endoscopy of the upper and lower GI tract is generally regarded as safe, but adverse effects do occur from time to time. Major complications, such

VIRTUAL COLONOSCOPY: WILL IT REPLACE CONVENTIONAL COLONOSCOPY?

Many of us prefer tests that can tell our doctors about our health without too much inconvenience and discomfort. Blood and urine tests don't bother most of us. Even a chest X-ray or electrocardiogram is not too troublesome. However, colonoscopy is a test most of us dread. Not only is the preparation unpleasant since it requires laxatives, but the test itself often requires sedation and a special trip to an outpatient department of a hospital or an endoscopy center. In addition, the examination is often quite expensive. Colonoscopy is recommended to those persons who may be at high risk for colon cancer, but increasingly more and more doctors are recommending it to others as the screening test of choice to detect colon cancer at an earlier, more treatable stage. Some cancers may be beyond the reach of a doctor's examining finger or the flexible sigmoidoscope (see Figure 9-11).

An alternative to conventional colonoscopy (in which a gastroenterologist looks directly into the colon with a fiberoptic scope) may be virtual colonoscopy in which CT scan images are taken. A computer then integrates the images so that a radiologist may reconstruct the colon into two and three dimensional images. At first, you might think this would be an ideal screening procedure. But like so many other diagnostic procedures, there are limitations. Laxatives still need to be taken before the procedure to adequately cleanse the colon. Also, a probe has to be inserted into the colon to introduce air. This may be uncomfortable. Since no sedation is given for virtual colonoscopy some people prefer conventional colonoscopy where they are "knocked out." Sedation does require that a relative or friend drive the patient home, whereas this is not necessary for virtual colonoscopy.

There are other limitations to virtual colonoscopy. One is the cost, although the expense may come down with more widespread use of the technology. Availability is another issue. Many hospitals are not acquiring the equipment until further studies confirm its advantage over conventional colonoscopy. Very small polyps may be missed with a CT scan, although a recent study suggested that virtual colonoscopy did nearly as well as conventional colonoscopy. Training and experience of the radiologists who review the CT images is important. Finally, the virtual colonoscopy can only help make the diagnosis of polyps or cancer. Biopsy or removal requires a conventional colonoscopy.

Despite the limitations, future studies may confirm that virtual colonoscopy is a great and cost-effective method for screening large segments of the population. However, because biopsy of tumors and excision of polyps cannot be done with this procedure, virtual colonoscopy will never supplant conventional colonoscopy.

as perforation, bleeding, serious cardiac irregularity, pulmonary aspiration (with upper GI endoscopy), are very uncommon. Mortality is reported as one in more than 10,000 procedures and usually occurs in patients with serious bleeding or other medical complications.

FOOD FOR FURTHER REFLECTION

There was a time when all the body's members
Rebell'd against the belly; thus accus'd it:
That only like a gulf it did remain
I' th' midst o' th' body, idle and unactive,
Still cupboarding the viand, never bearing
Like labour with the rest; where th' other instruments
Did see and hear, devise, instruct, walk, feel,
And, mutually participate, did minister
Unto the appetite and affection common
Of the whole body. The belly answered . . .
'True is it, my incorporate friends,' quoth he,
'That I receive the general food at first
Which you do live upon; and fit it is,
Because I am the storehouse and the shop
Of the whole body. But, if you do remember,
I send it through the rivers of your blood
Even to the court, the heart, to th' seat o' th' brain,
And, through the cranks and offices of man,
The strongest nerves and small inferior veins
From me receive that natural competency
Whereby they live.'
    —*William Shakespeare*
     Coriolanus, act 1, scene 1, line 99

■

WHAT YOU NEED TO KNOW

▶ Digestive disorders are extremely common. If simple heartburn or indigestion does not resolve with dietary changes and/or antacids, see your doctor for further evaluation.

▶ Many different things cause abdominal pain. The location, intensity, duration, and quality of the pain, as well as provoking and relieving factors, can help your doctor determine the cause.

▶ Intestinal gas is a disturbing problem for many people as they get older. Occasionally milk (lactose) intolerance may be the cause. A short period on a milk-free diet or use of Lactaid may be worthwhile. Certain fruits and vegetables may contribute to the problem. These include beans, peas, broccoli, turnips, onions, cabbage, Brussel sprouts, and cauliflower. Pectin-containing fruits (apples, pears) eaten raw can cause problems, as can apple, grape, and prune juices. Some individuals have tried simethicone (contained in many antacids) and activated charcoal, but clinical trials have not confirmed their efficacy. Air swallowing *(aerophagia)* can cause excessive burping, bloating, and abdominal discomfort. Careful chewing and not gulping food or drinks, especially carbonated beverages, may be helpful.

▶ A physician should evaluate constipation. It is a symptom, not a disease. It can be caused by a number of reasons, some of which are very serious. Do not take laxatives without consulting your doctor. They can cause some very serious bowel problems. Avoid practices such as colon lavage. Serious health consequences can result.

▶ Many things, including viruses, drugs, and alcohol, can cause liver disease. Alcohol consumption should be limited to an average of one or two beers, glasses of wine, or mixed drinks per day. Depending on other medical conditions, you may be encouraged to drink less or none at all. Be honest with your doctor, so that you can be advised on a safe amount. Acetaminophen should be limited to no more than 4 grams per day (eight extra strength tablets), but you may need to take less; check with your doctor. Some herbal products sold as health aids can cause serious liver injury. Do not take these products unless you have checked with your doctor.

▶ Almost 25 million people have gallstones in the United States. One in three persons over 80 has gallstones. In many cases, these stones produce no symptoms, and no treatment is required. When symptoms occur, surgery is usually required. In uncomplicated cases, removal of the gallbladder through small incisions in the abdominal wall with the guidance of fiberoptic scopes can be performed. If a stone is impacted in the cystic duct or common bile duct, traditional surgery is required, although occasionally these stones can be removed by ERCP.

▶ Cancer of the pancreas is the fourth leading cause of cancer death (behind lung, colorectal, and breast cancer). It occurs predominantly in older people and is very lethal. Early symptoms can be vague but include weight loss, poor appetite, upset stomach, stomach pain, and depression. Jaundice and back pain may eventually develop. Check with your doctor if you experience any of these symptoms.

▶ Every year in the United States 145,000 new cases of colon cancer are discovered and nearly 60,000 people die of it. It ranks only behind lung cancer in men and lung and breast cancer in women as the cause of cancer death. Follow the guidelines outlined in this chapter for screening. It can be a matter of life and death. Some studies have suggested that aspirin, calcium, and some vitamins may play a protective role. Check with your doctor.

FOR MORE INFORMATION

▶ National Institute of Diabetes, Digestive, and Kidney Diseases
Web: www.niddk.nih.gov

▶ MEDLINEplus
Web: www.nlm.nih.gov/medlineplus
A service of the U.S. Library of Medicine and the National Institutes of Health.

▶ Healthfinder
Web: www.healthfinder.gov
Searchable Health and Human Services Department site linked to government and not-for-profit agencies, and self-help and support groups selected for their reliability.

▶ American Gastroenterological Association
Web: www.gastro.org

▶ American Cancer Society
800-ACS-2345
Web: www.cancer.org

▶ American Liver Foundation
800-465-4837
Web: www.liverfoundation.org

09

The improvement of understanding is for two ends: first, our increase of knowledge; secondly to enable us to deliver that knowledge to others.

—*John Locke*

THE AUTHORS

10

RUTH L. WINTZ, MD, graduated from the University of Texas at Austin and the Baylor College of Medicine. She completed her internal medicine residency, chief resident year, and nephrology fellowship at the University of California Los Angeles. She is a clinical instructor at UCLA. Her professional interests include clinical nephrology, primary care, and medical teaching.

ALLEN R. NISSENSON, MD, FACP, is a professor of medicine and the director of the dialysis program at the University of California, Los Angeles. Dr. Nissenson was recruited to UCLA in 1977, where he has developed a comprehensive dialysis program with significant components including administration, patient care, teaching, and research. Dr. Nissenson has served as chair of the Southern California End-Stage Renal Disease (ESRD) Network and chair of the Council on Dialysis of the National Kidney Foundation. He has long been concerned with issues of health care delivery, and has consulted for the Rand Corporation on ESRD and Pacificare on the development of chronic disease management models for ESRD patients.

Dr. Nissenson served as a Robert Wood Johnson Health Policy Fellow of the Institute of Medicine in 1994–1995, serving in the office of Senator Paul Wellstone, and is a past president of the Renal Physicians Association. Dr. Nissenson is the editor of two dialysis textbooks and was the first editor-in-chief of *Advances in Renal Replacement Therapy,* an official journal of the National Kidney Foundation. He was appointed deputy editor of *Hemodialysis International,* the official journal of the International Society for Hemodialysis.

10 | THE KIDNEYS

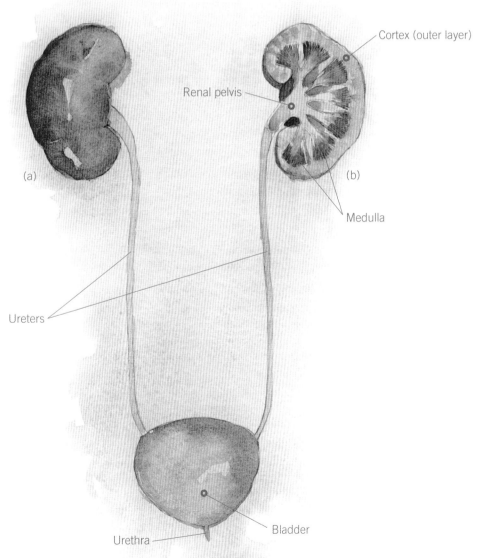

Cortex (outer layer)

Renal pelvis

(a)

(b)

Medulla

Ureters

Bladder

Urethra

(figure 10-1*)*
Anatomy of the kidneys. (a) Exterior view. (b) Interior view.

Why is kidney health important to older people? More and more seniors are living with kidney problems, some of which can progress and lead to the need for kidney dialysis treatment. In fact, about half the patients currently receiving hemodialysis are over the age of 65, while the average age of patients starting dialysis in the United States is 62 years, and this age continues to increase. The truth is that people are living longer, and as they age, their risk of diabetes, high blood pressure, and heart disease also increases. These diseases—diabetes, high blood pressure, and heart disease—are the major culprits leading to or complicating kidney disease in the Western world. Among all Americans 65 to 74 years old, in any particular year, one in 1,000 will need dialysis or a kidney transplant, making this age group the one at highest risk for kidney failure.

Fortunately, there are things you can do to lower your risk of kidney disease or to make sure that you remain as healthy and functional as possible despite having kidney disease. Good nutrition, exercise, and not smoking form a good foundation for avoiding diabetes and high blood pressure, or minimizing their adverse effects. If you have these problems despite a healthy lifestyle, regular visits to a physician to help you control them is essential. Even when your kidneys completely fail, there can be good quality of life on one of the forms of renal replacement therapy: hemodialysis, peritoneal dialysis, or kidney transplant. This chapter lays out the age-related changes of kidney health, describes the most common causes of kidney disease, recommends how you can maintain the health of your kidneys, and provides tips on how you can best consider the various choices of dialysis or transplant if necessary.

KIDNEY DISEASE

The primary function of the kidneys is to filter and clean the blood, removing toxins and wastes along with excess salt and water, excreting these in the urine (see Figure 10-2). Doctors estimate kidney function by measuring a creatinine level in the blood. Creatinine is a waste product from muscle. If the kidneys are not properly removing creatinine through the urine, creatinine will build up in the blood. People with kidney disease have elevated blood creatinine levels. In general, the higher the creatinine, the worse the kidney disease. The interpretation of the blood creatinine level, however, must be considered in the context of your age and state of nutrition.

Since creatinine comes from muscle, elderly people who have little muscle mass can have low serum creatinine values despite significant kidney disease. Doctors have mathematical formulas that are used to make adjustments for older age and small body size when determining the precise level of kidney function that is present for a particular blood creatinine value. Alternatively, some doctors will ask for a

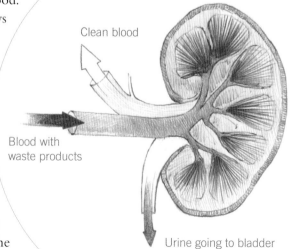

Clean blood

Blood with waste products

Urine going to bladder

(*figure* 10-2)

The movement of blood with waste products into the kidneys and "clean" blood out of the kidneys back into the circulation.

24-hour urine collection, along with the blood creatinine, to measure the creatinine in the urine and then use this information to estimate kidney function.

Another indicator of kidney problems is protein in the urine. Urine does not normally contain protein, but if the filtering function of the kidneys has been damaged, the protein may "leak" into the urine. The presence of protein in the urine may signify a serious kidney disease, such as diabetes, and requires evaluation by a doctor.

If you have either of these signs of kidney disease, an elevated creatinine or protein in the urine, you may benefit from referral to a kidney specialist, or nephrologist. Nephrologists focus on maintaining your kidney health and delaying the need for transplant or dialysis as long as possible. They also have special training to deal with the unique medical problems that frequently accompany kidney disease.

KIDNEY FUNCTION AND AGE

Scientific studies have shown that kidneys change with age. The kidneys tend to shrink in size, and on a microscopic level, some of the components which filter and clean the blood may become scarred and diminish in number. Alternatively, older individuals may lose kidney function due to kidney injuries from vascular (blood vessel) disease, infections, or side effects of certain medications. Studies have shown that on average humans lose between 0.5 and 1% of their kidney function each year after the age of 40. However, this is only an average value. On an individual basis, up to one-third of individuals do not lose any kidney function as they age or even have improved function, while the other two-thirds lose function even more rapidly. Thus older age implies an increased risk of kidney dysfunction, but most older individuals will not have significant kidney disease just because of increasing age. The average 80-year-old has about half the kidney function he or she had when 30 years old, but this is almost always asymptomatic and not in need of any medical treatment.

There are also age-related changes in the kidney's ability to conserve water and salt. For instance, during a heat wave, an older person is more likely to become dehydrated than a younger person since older kidneys will lose more water and salt in the urine. This is especially problematic since older individuals have a decreased sense of thirst. Older kidneys also cannot remove water as rapidly as younger kidneys. If you drink several liters of water in one sitting, older kidneys will require a longer period of time to eliminate that water in the urine. Likewise, it is more difficult for older kidneys to remove dietary salt from the body. This can lead to swelling and difficulty in breathing, a condition known as congestive heart failure (see Chapter 7).

Another impact of age on the kidneys is slower metabolism of medications. Older people are more sensitive to the effects of drugs since their liver and kidneys require more time to eliminate them from the body. The smaller muscle mass of older persons also increases their sensitivity to many drugs. Together these effects can cause the amounts of many ingested drugs to rise above safe levels. Doctors often need to lower drug dosages to adjust for age, weight, and kidney function.

ACUTE KIDNEY FAILURE

Sometimes kidney failure occurs rapidly and unpredictably, in contrast to the slow decline in kidney function usually seen in diabetes or high blood pressure. This sudden loss of kidney function is referred to as acute kidney failure. Older persons are more likely to suffer from acute kidney failure compared to younger individuals because older bodies are less adaptable to a variety of physical stresses. Thankfully, acute kidney problems often have a reversible cause and improve over days to weeks when appropriately treated. How much kidney function will return in an individual case, however, is often difficult to predict, and only time will tell. Older age does not worsen the prognosis of acute kidney failure, but severe medical conditions requiring a stay in an intensive care unit makes survival less likely if acute kidney failure occurs. The following section reviews the common causes of acute kidney dysfunction and their treatment.

DECREASED KIDNEY BLOOD FLOW

Dehydration and low blood pressure: Dehydration leads to decreased blood flow to the kidneys and can result in acute kidney failure or an increased creatinine value (see Figure 10-2). Dehydration can be caused by eating and drinking too little or losing fluids from vomiting, diarrhea, or diuretics ("water pills"). Fever can also increase the risk of dehydration. If the dehydration is not severe and prolonged, kidney function should improve promptly with rehydration by drinking or having an intravenous (IV) infusion. In comparison to younger persons, older individuals are particularly susceptible to dehydration since they have less thirst and more difficulty conserving salt and water from urinary loss. Very low blood pressure (systolic blood pressure less than 90 mm Hg) can also cause acute kidney failure because of decreased blood flow to the kidneys. This may occur during critical illness, such as sepsis or shock, hemorrhage, cardiac arrest, or surgery. In this case, the kidneys may be temporarily damaged and will require time to heal. Although dialysis may be necessary, this form of acute kidney failure is unlikely to be permanent unless dialysis is needed for six to eight weeks. Increasing urine production is usually the first sign of kidney recovery.

Heart failure: *Congestive heart failure* (see Chapter 7) is a circulatory disorder which decreases kidney blood flow and may result in acute kidney failure. Congestive heart failure may be due to a weakened heart muscle or an overly stiff heart muscle. As opposed to dehydration, however, patients with congestive heart failure usually have too much salt and fluid in the body, leading to fluid accumulation in the lungs and difficulty in breathing. There can also be foot and ankle swelling. The treatment for the kidneys in this case is to treat the heart condition, often with diuretics and other heart medicines. This will improve the heart's ability to pump blood to the kidneys and, generally, will reverse the acute kidney failure.

Liver disease: Individuals with cirrhosis of the liver may have kidney disease from decreased blood flow to the kidneys. Cirrhosis is associated with salt and water retention, leading to abdominal swelling (ascites). In this condition, as in heart failure, there is excessive fluid within the body, but it is not effectively delivered to the kidney. In the setting of advanced liver disease, the kidneys may fail, requiring dialysis. This serious development indicates that the liver will only last a few weeks to months and death is certain without a liver transplant. After a liver transplant, the kidney function usually recovers if the kidney failure has not been severe and prolonged. Infectious hepatitis may be associated with another kidney condition called *glomerulonephritis* (see the section "Glomerulonephritis," below).

DRUGS AND CONTRAST DYE

Certain medicines can be damaging to the kidneys. Powerful intravenous antibiotics called aminoglycosides, with names like GENTAMICIN and AMIKACIN, can cause acute kidney failure, usually after about a week of therapy. The treatment is to stop the drug; however, serious infections may require continued administration of these strong medicines despite the effects on kidney function. Rarely, other antibiotics and medications can cause an allergic reaction within the kidney and acute kidney failure.

Another class of medication that can cause acute kidney failure includes aspirin and nonsteroidal anti-inflammatory drugs. These are over-the-counter pain relievers which are commonly used for headache, muscle aches, or arthritis. NAPROXEN (NAPROSYN) and IBUPROFEN (MOTRIN, ADVIL) are examples of these drugs. Few people in the general public know that these medications decrease blood flow to the kidneys. Risk factors for acute kidney failure from nonsteroidal anti-inflammatory drugs include age over 60 years, dehydration, congestive heart failure, cirrhosis, and underlying kidney disease. It is important to avoid these medications if you have kidney problems. ACETAMINOPHEN (TYLENOL) is an alternative pain reliever which is much safer for the kidneys. Nonsteroidal anti-inflammatory drugs can also cause an allergic reaction within the kidney and acute kidney failure, as described above.

ACE inhibitors and angiotensin receptor blockers (ARBs) are cardiac and blood pressure medicines that are also used in chronic kidney disease. They have been shown to decrease protein in the urine and prolong the need for dialysis or transplant, both desirable effects. Because of additional effects on kidney blood vessels, however, these medications may cause modest increases in blood creatinine or even acute kidney failure. In general, doctors will accept a 20 to 30% increase in the creatinine value after these drugs are begun. If the creatinine rises more than this, the drug will need to be stopped and your doctor may order tests to look for kidney blood vessel narrowing (renal artery stenosis).

Intravenous contrast dye that is used for certain imaging tests, such as computed tomography (CT) scans, can cause acute kidney failure, particularly in individuals who already have some kidney disease and diabetics. This form of acute kidney failure is usually reversible with time, but can be permanent if there was significant kidney disease before the dye exposure. If contrast dye is necessary, being well hydrated before the test can help minimize the risk of kidney injury. There is also some evidence that a medicine called N-ACETYLCYSTEINE (MUCOMYST) may be preventative, and your doctor may prescribe this prior to the imaging study.

VASCULAR DISEASE

Atherosclerosis, or hardening of the arteries, increases with age. This involves cholesterol plaques forming inside the blood vessels, narrowing their diameter. This process is usually diffuse throughout the body. Individuals who have had a heart attack, therefore, are at risk for stroke and circulatory problems in their legs and feet. A cholesterol plaque can spontaneously break off and float into the kidney causing acute kidney failure. A plaque can also be dislodged during a coronary catheterization or vascular surgery procedure. The kidney failure usually occurs two to four weeks after the procedure and may be accompanied by flank pain and/or fever. Plaques can travel anywhere in the body, and may lead to blue toes or skin rash as well. There is no specific treatment, but blood thinners may make the condition worse. If the entire artery is blocked, rather than just being partially narrowed, however, blood thinners are necessary and appropriate. Kidney function recovers in 30 to 40% of these cases. Narrowing of one or both arteries going to the kidneys (renal artery stenosis) can lead to kidney failure as well as cause or aggravate high blood pressure (see the section, "Blood Pressure Control," below).

OBSTRUCTION

Since the major function of the kidneys is to make urine which removes wastes from the body, any obstruction to the flow of urine will impair this important function. Urine normally leaves the kidneys and travels down tubes called ureters to be stored in the bladder. When urination occurs, urine leaves the bladder through the urethra and exits the body. In men, the prostate gland surrounds the urethra. If the prostate gland is enlarged, this can impede the passage of urine and cause kidney failure. Likewise, female organs like the uterus or cervix can obstruct the bladder if they are enlarged from fibroids or cancer. Sometimes diabetic patients cannot empty their bladders completely due to nerve damage from diabetes. A kidney stone can also lodge in a ureter or urethra causing a blockage (see Figure 10-3).

The treatment for any of these conditions is to relieve the obstruction, thus permitting the passage of urine. For example, a catheter can be placed into the bladder to bypass an enlarged prostate. Doctors may sometimes place tubes through the abdominal wall to drain an obstructed ureter. Urologists can treat kidney stones with radio waves to break them up or can remove them surgically. The sooner an obstruction is relieved, the

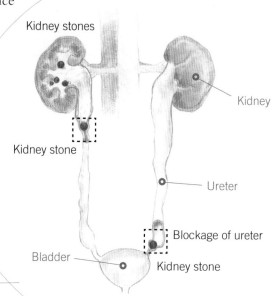

Kidney stones

Kidney

Kidney stone

Ureter

Blockage of ureter

Bladder

Kidney stone

(*figure* 10-3)

Blockage of the ureters by kidney stones resulting in kidney failure.

more likely kidney function is to improve completely. A long standing obstruction may cause irreversible kidney failure.

GLOMERULONEPHRITIS

In order to make urine, the kidney filters blood much like a kitchen colander filters water away from spaghetti. In glomerulonephritis, the filter becomes inflamed, leaking protein and blood cells into the urine. If severe, acute kidney failure may occur. Causes of glomerulonephritis include general inflammation of the body's blood vessels (vasculitis), autoimmune disease, infection, medications, and cancer. Some cases of glomerulonephritis have no known inciting cause. In order to determine treatment, your doctor may advise a kidney biopsy to diagnose what is going on in the kidney. Age does not increase the risk of kidney biopsy; therefore, older individuals should not be discouraged from undergoing biopsy on the basis of age alone. Depending on the cause and severity of glomerulonephritis, treatment with potent medications like steroids and chemotherapy drugs may be recommended and often can arrest or reverse the disease.

CHRONIC KIDNEY FAILURE

Diabetes is the number-one cause of chronic kidney failure in the United States. Diabetes has become an epidemic in the Western world. Obesity resulting from unhealthy diets and lack of exercise predisposes to adult-onset diabetes. The risk of diabetes increases with age, especially among minorities such as blacks, Latinos, and Native Americans. Fifteen to 30% of Americans over age 50 have adult-onset diabetes. The symptoms of diabetes occur when the sugar in the blood is very high and include thirst, hunger, frequent urination, weight loss, blurry vision, and yeast infections. However, many people with diabetes go for years without knowing it, due to the lack of symptoms until the blood sugar gets very out of control. Meanwhile, organs like the kidney and the heart are suffering damage from the high blood sugar (see Figure 10-4). Most diabetics have evidence of some kidney disease after a decade. Diabetic kidney disease can lead to protein in the urine and ultimately kidney failure, usually after 10 to 25 years of diabetes.

The good news is that although the risk of developing diabetes is largely genetic, a healthy lifestyle can help avoid its occurring or make its management less difficult. Maintaining a healthy weight, eating a healthy diet, and being physically active all help keep the blood sugar normal. If you have a family history of diabetes; are black, Latino, or Native American; are overweight; have high blood pressure, high cholesterol, or heart/vascular disease; or have any of the above symptoms, ask your doctor to check your fasting blood sugar for diabetes and your blood creatinine and urine protein to see if kidney disease has started.

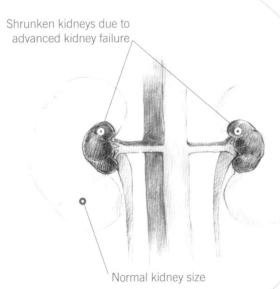

Shrunken kidneys due to advanced kidney failure

Normal kidney size

(*figure* 10-4)

Shrunken kidneys in severe kidney failure.

High blood pressure, also known as hypertension, is the second largest cause of kidney failure in the United States. Among persons age 65 to 74 years, 40% of whites and over 50% of blacks have high blood pressure. High blood pressure can damage many organs in the body: the brain (stroke), the heart (heart failure, heart attack), the eye (blindness), as well as the kidney. High blood pressure is known as "the silent killer" because a person usually feels no symptoms while the blood pressure is doing its damage. It usually takes years of uncontrolled high blood pressure to cause kidney failure; however, if the blood pressure is suddenly dangerously high (for example, over 200/115), the kidneys can be damaged immediately. Although high blood pressure is more likely in older persons, it is not just a natural part of aging. Studies have shown that medical treatment of high blood pressure in older people is of great benefit; it lowers the risk of stroke, heart attack, and death severalfold.

The only way to protect yourself from high blood pressure is to get your blood pressure checked. This can be done in the doctor's office or in many pharmacies. If your blood pressure is higher than 140/90 at times when you are rested, have not had caffeine, or have not smoked, you have high blood pressure and need a medical evaluation. The good news is that high blood pressure can be controlled, through lifestyle changes (physical activity and a diet low in salt, alcohol, and caffeine) and medication. Controlling high blood pressure is probably the most important thing you can do to protect against kidney disease.

Atherosclerosis can also cause kidney failure (see the section "Vascular Disease," above). Risk factors for atherosclerosis include diabetes, high blood pressure, high cholesterol, smoking, sex between males, and age over 50 and a family history of atherosclerosis in the heart (heart attack), brain (stroke), or legs (peripheral vascular disease). Other causes of chronic kidney failure, which progress slowly over time, include cancers of the blood called multiple myeloma and amyloidosis, chronic kidney infection, long-term use of medications such as LITHIUM, and glomerulonephritis (discussed in the section "Glomerulonephritis," above).

COMPLICATIONS OF KIDNEY DISEASE

ANEMIA

In addition to making urine, the kidneys also make hormones like erythropoietin and activated vitamin D. Erythropoietin is a protein produced in the kidneys which stimulates the body to make red blood cells. When kidney function is decreased to 50 or 60% of normal, anemia may occur due to erythropoietin deficiency. Your doctor may prescribe injections of this hormone every one to two weeks to treat the anemia. Anemia should be avoided if possible, since it causes fatigue, decreased quality of life, and increased stress on the heart.

Iron deficiency is also very common in patients with chronic kidney disease, and contributes to anemia. If your blood work shows iron deficiency, iron supplements can be taken. If iron levels do not improve on the oral supplements after several weeks, your doctor may prescribe an intravenous infusion of iron.

BONE DISEASE

Bone disease is a common complication of chronic kidney disease, in part because of abnormalities related to a deficiency of active vitamin D, a substance that is necessary for the maintenance of normal bone. Inactive vitamin D is ingested in the diet from foods like dairy products or made within the body during times of sunlight exposure. Vitamin D is then processed in the kidney to an "active," or effective, form. The activated vitamin D goes to the gut, to promote calcium and phosphorus absorption from foods and to the parathyroid glands where it decreases the output of parathyroid hormone (PTH). Parathyroid hormone pulls calcium out of bone, and can make the bones weak and brittle. In kidney disease, vitamin D cannot be activated by the kidneys, the level of calcium in the blood falls, and excessive PTH is produced leading to weak bones with the risk of fracture, deformity, and pain.

If you have chronic kidney disease, your doctor will likely check your calcium and PTH level and prescribe activated vitamin D if the PTH level is too high. The active form of vitamin D requires a prescription, since the over-the-counter vitamin D preparations contain inactive vitamin D that still requires a healthy kidney for its action. You will likely need regular blood tests to monitor your calcium, phosphorus, and PTH levels when on active vitamin D, but the inconvenience is worth the effort since it will help preserve the health of your bones.

PHOSPHORUS

When kidney function is decreased to about a third of normal, the mineral phosphorus may build up in the blood. Phosphorus is ingested through foods like dairy products, cola, beans, chocolate, nuts, and processed meats. High blood phosphorus levels may cause itching and hardening of the arteries. If your phosphorus level is high, a dietitian can review with you a detailed list of foods that should be avoided or eaten in moderation. In addition, your doctor may advise that you take medication with your meals called "phosphorus binders." When your meal is digested, some of the phosphorus will stick to the medication and not be absorbed into your body.

FLUID RETENTION

Since the kidneys are responsible for eliminating dietary salt and water, individuals with kidney disease may develop sodium and fluid retention. This can result in high blood pressure, foot or ankle swelling, or difficulty in breathing. The breathing problems are often more pronounced at night, with difficulty lying flat or nighttime awakening. It is very helpful to limit your sodium intake to 2 to 4 grams per day, by reading nutritional labels, and not adding salt to your food. Drinking less than 2 liters of fluid per day will also help. Your doctor may start you on a "water pill" to increase urination.

POTASSIUM

Just as the kidneys may inappropriately retain excess salt and water, they can also inappropriately retain too much dietary potassium. This can be a serious problem, as high potassium can cause dangerous heart rhythms and even cardiac arrest. If your potassium starts to exceed normal limits, you can avoid foods that are high in potassium, such as potatoes, bananas, melons, and orange juice. These foods are often consumed in significant quantities in the typical American diet. There are many other foods that are high in potassium as well. If your diet is more varied or you still have trouble controlling the potassium, a dietitian can give you a full list of foods and their potassium content. Certain medications, such as ACE inhibitors or SPIRONOLACTONE (ALDACTONE), may also contribute to high potassium. These medications have benefits for many kidney patients but require blood work monitoring to make sure that safe levels of potassium are maintained.

ACID RETENTION

A weakened kidney may not appropriately remove acid from the body. Acid is a normal by-product of protein metabolism, and is normally excreted in urine. Blood work can indicate that the acid level in the blood is high, which is a risk factor for osteoporosis and muscle wasting. Your doctor may prescribe bicarbonate tablets or sodium citrate solution to neutralize the extra acid.

CARDIOVASCULAR DISEASE

For reasons that are not completely clear, having kidney disease is a risk factor for having cardiovascular disease, such as heart attack, stroke, and poor circulation. In addition to treating the chronic kidney disease, when possible, you can improve your cardiovascular health by maintaining a healthy weight, eating a lowfat diet, participating in regular exercise, and avoiding tobacco. Your doctor may check your cholesterol and discuss the risks and benefits of preventative aspirin. Although anti-inflammatory medications can cause kidney problems, one aspirin daily is unlikely to have an adverse effect. If you develop symptoms of chest pressure, visual changes, numbness, weakness, or incoordination, it is always appropriate to seek medical attention immediately.

DELAYING KIDNEY FAILURE

Persons with kidney disease have the opportunity to make changes in their health that may delay or prevent the eventual need for transplant or dialysis. This section discusses what you can do to preserve your kidney function.

BLOOD PRESSURE CONTROL

It now appears that the most important factor in the progression of kidney disease is poorly controlled blood pressure. Studies have shown that strict blood pressure control can make a difference in the rate of kidney

Although almost two-thirds of her kidney function has been lost, Joan P. and I are very happy that her blood creatinine indicates that her kidney disease has not progressed in the past year. She is very motivated to protect her kidneys since I advised her that dialysis or possibly a kidney transplant might be necessary soon. She has a home blood pressure cuff to be sure she is meeting her goals of < 130/80 mmHg. She checks her blood sugars regularly, and aims to keep them between 80 and 120. She follows a special diet, watching her sugar, salt, and fat intake. She avoids eating bananas, potatoes, melons, or oranges since I told her that her potassium level is on the high side. She feels rewarded when her laboratory results show that her creatinine hasn't risen and the protein in her urine is low. I am pleased as well, but I have told Joan that eventually her kidneys may still fail completely, requiring dialysis or a transplant.

deterioration. If you have an elevated serum creatinine or more than 1 gram of protein in the urine per day, the current recommendations are to keep your blood pressure less than or equal to 125/75 mm Hg. Achieving this goal may require salt restriction, weight loss, regular exercise, and medication. A home blood pressure monitor can be very helpful to be sure you are meeting your blood pressure goals. You can bring your monitor to the doctor's office to check its accuracy.

BLOOD SUGAR CONTROL

In the United States, the largest cause of kidney disease is diabetes. High blood sugar causes abnormal changes in kidney blood vessels and kidney cells. If you are a diabetic, controlling your blood sugar will help delay kidney failure. Hemoglobin A1C is a blood test which monitors diabetic control over the past two to three months. The current recommendations are a hemoglobin A1C less than 7%. To achieve this goal, your medical team may prescribe carbohydrate restriction, exercise, weight loss, and medications.

DECREASING PROTEIN IN THE URINE

Protein in the urine often accompanies kidney disease. There is evidence that having excessive amounts of protein in the urine causes additional damage to the kidneys. Your doctor may prescribe medication in order to decrease the amount of protein appearing in the urine. Certain blood pressure medications, such as ACE inhibitors, angiotensin receptor blockers (ARBs), and DILTIAZEM can do this. Reduction to less than 1 gram per 24 hours is the current recommended goal.

Your doctor may prescribe a special diet due to your kidney disease. There is scientific evidence that eating a lot of protein increases the workload of the kidney and causes high blood pressure within the kidney. Also, if you have protein in the urine, theoretically eating more protein will lead to more protein being "spilled" into the urine. Although it has not been completely scientifically proved, many doctors will advise a moderate protein restriction (0.6 to 0.8 grams of protein intake per kilogram of patient's body weight) to delay kidney failure. A dietitian can advise you how to modify the protein in your diet to achieve your prescribed goal. However, this consideration has to allow for adequate nutrition as well. If you have a poor appetite, have very large protein losses in your urine, or are already underweight, this may not be a healthy option for you.

ACE INHIBITORS

In addition to decreasing protein in the urine and lowering blood pressure, ACE inhibitors have been shown to delay kidney failure. This is likely related to the effect of these medications to lower blood pressure in the kidney as well as other hormonal effects. These medications can have side effects and require blood work monitoring. Very rarely there can be severe allergic reactions. Occasionally, a dry cough develops which usually resolves in about two weeks after stopping the medicine. Blood potassium levels can increase, which at high levels can cause dangerous heart rhythms. In certain individuals, kidney failure seriously worsens and the medication needs to be stopped. In this circumstance, your doctor may order special tests to look for narrowing in the kidney arteries. A small, stable elevation in the serum creatinine, however, is not a serious consequence, and the medication is still beneficial. For these reasons, however, blood work to check the creatinine and potassium is necessary after starting or increasing the dose of ACE inhibitors. If you develop a cough while taking an ACE inhibitor, your doctor may substitute an angiotensin receptor blocker. This medication does not cause coughing, but can similarly slow the progression of kidney disease. Your doctor may choose to combine ACE inhibitors and angiotensin receptor blockers. The same blood work monitoring is necessary for angiotensin receptor blockers.

CHOLESTEROL

Studies suggest that high cholesterol can be damaging to the kidney. Cholesterol damages blood vessels, such as those of the heart, so it is not surprising that it can also affect the kidneys, which are largely made up of filtering blood vessels. Review your lipid panel with your doctor to see if you need a special diet or medication to optimize your cholesterol.

SMOKING CESSATION

Just as tobacco damages the blood vessels of the heart, brain, and extremities, it can also damage the blood vessels of the kidney. Delaying kidney failure is just one of the many health benefits of smoking cessation.

PREPARING FOR KIDNEY FAILURE

When remaining kidney function is only 10 to 15% of normal, the body will require assistance removing waste products and extra salt and water. The choices available are referred to as renal replacement therapy (RRT): hemodialysis, peritoneal dialysis, and kidney transplant. The term "renal replacement therapy" is important; although dialysis or transplant may prolong life by doing the work of the kidneys, it is unlikely that other medical conditions or disability will improve. Age alone, however, is not a reason to withhold renal replacement therapy.

If a renal replacement therapy is not begun, kidney failure causes several symptoms, referred to as uremia. This may include nausea, lethargy, and itching and may progress ultimately to malnutrition, coma, and death. A serious complication of uremia is pericarditis, in which the heart lining becomes inflamed and fluid may surround the heart. In addition, there is the risk of retained salt and water causing breathing difficulties.

The first step in preparing for renal replacement therapy is working with a nephrologist. Kidney doctors can estimate the time remaining until RRT is needed and help develop a time frame for preparation. Your doctor or another member of your health care team will discuss the RRT options and help you decide which one is right for you at that point in time. Choosing one form of RRT does not commit you to that option forever. People on dialysis can go off dialysis by receiving a kidney transplant. When transplanted kidneys eventually fail, those individuals must return to a form of dialysis. Hemodialysis patients can switch to peritoneal dialysis and vice versa. If the quality of life is very poor or there is a coexisting terminal illness, one may choose not to start dialysis and pursue comfort-oriented care only. If there is uncertainty regarding acceptability of dialysis, it can be initiated on a trial basis and abandoned if the results are unsatisfactory. Below is a detailed discussion of the RRT options and considerations.

HEMODIALYSIS

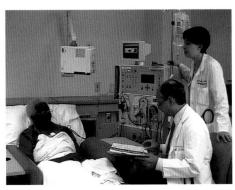

(figure 10-5)

Dr. Nissenson and Dr. Wintz with a patient undergoing hemodialysis.

Hemodialysis is the use of a machine to remove wastes and extra salt and fluid directly from the blood. Usually an individual travels to a dialysis center three days a week for a 3- to 4-hour hemodialysis treatment. While the individual reclines in a chair, a dialysis nurse or technician connects the machine tubing to the dialysis access, allowing the person's blood to circulate through a special filter which removes the toxins and extra fluid that would otherwise be removed by the kidneys (see Figure 10-5).

To get the patient's blood to flow through the filter, a form of vascular access is needed. There are three types of dialysis access: fistula, graft, and catheter. A fistula is the surgical connection of a patient's own artery and vein (see Figure 10-6). It is usually made in the forearm. This is an outpatient surgery and requires two to three months to "mature" and be ready to use for dialysis. In the dialysis center, a nurse or a technician places needles into the fistula under local anesthesia to connect the patient to the dialysis machine. Although this form of natural access requires months to be ready to use and necessitates the use of needles, this is usually the preferred dialysis access because it rarely clots or becomes infected. It also generates high blood flows through the dialysis filter, which leads to cleaner blood and better health.

A graft is similar to a fistula but uses a synthetic piece of tubing to connect the patient's artery and vein (see Figure 10-7). This outpatient surgery requires only two weeks to become ready for usage. Again, the dialysis nurse or technician will use needles and local anesthesia to connect the graft to the dialysis machine. Unfortunately, synthetic materials are more likely to clot and become infected than is the natural fistula. If a graft clots, dialysis cannot be done and the clot will need to be invasively removed under X-ray or by surgery. Infected grafts can sometimes be saved with antibiotics but often require surgical removal. If your veins are too fragile to be directly connected in a fistula, your surgeon may place a graft. This is a good reason to avoid IVs and blood draws in your nondominant arm as soon as you

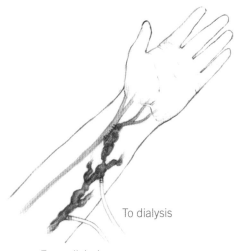

To dialysis

From dialysis

(figure 10-6)

Arteriovenous fistula (AV fistula) used for hemodialysis.

are diagnosed with kidney disease. It will protect the blood vessels in your arm for possible dialysis access. If you are right-handed, you should protect your left arm and vice versa. A graft also generates high blood flows for cleaner blood and better health.

A catheter is a plastic or rubber tube which is placed into a large blood vessel in the neck or chest during an outpatient surgery (see Figure 10-8). Because a catheter is synthetic material, it is also predisposed to clotting and infections. Clotted catheters may be fixed by placing blood thinners within the catheter or may require special procedures or surgery. Although no needles are used with a catheter, the blood flows are less than with fistulas or grafts, so the blood is not cleaned as effectively, but for small, elderly individuals, this may be adequate. Catheters also have the advantage of being ready for immediate use. This advantage is generally offset by the high rate of clotting or infection, which may lead to frequent hospitalizations or even be fatal.

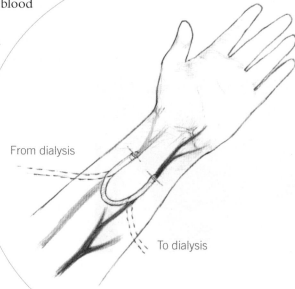

From dialysis

To dialysis

(figure 10-7)

Graft used for hemodialysis.

Hemodialysis has advantages and disadvantages. Although there is the inconvenience of coming to a dialysis unit for three to four hours three days during the week, the dialysis is done entirely by trained staff. Medications such as ERYTHROPOIETIN, vitamin D, and iron can be given intravenously by the dialysis staff. The visit is a chance for social interaction with staff and other dialysis patients. If your vision is poor, transportation to dialysis may be available. However, since the treatments are only three times a week, excessive salt and fluid intake can cause swelling and difficulty breathing between treatments. Dietary self-discipline is essential. Since fluid must be removed in a relatively short period of time, some people develop low blood pressure and dizziness during or after dialysis. Muscle cramps and nausea may also occur. These symptoms can usually be promptly reversed by dialysis staff returning fluid to the body. Although hemodialysis treatments are not uncomfortable, some individuals feel fatigued afterward.

Overall, most individuals feel improved once beginning hemodialysis. The removal of toxins and wastes can reverse prior feelings of nausea and fatigue. Aside from the time spent in dialysis treatments, many individuals continue to work and enjoy their previous lifestyles. Travel can be enjoyed with the help of your dialysis unit arranging continued treatments at your destination. Dietary restrictions, however, are necessary. Foods high in salt, potassium, and phosphorus (see the individual topics in "Complications of Kidney Disease," above) must be limited and fluid intake should not exceed 2 liters per day. If treatments are shortened to less than the time prescribed by your doctor, uremic symptoms of nausea, sleep disturbance, numbness, and swelling may recur. Inadequate dialysis treatments are damaging to the body and promote muscle wasting, prolonged bleeding, infection, and earlier mortality.

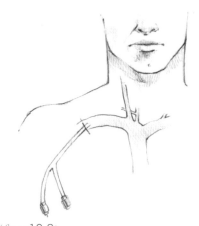

(figure 10-8)

Catheter used for hemodialysis.

PERITONEAL DIALYSIS

Peritoneal dialysis (PD) is a type of dialysis that you or your family can do at home under careful and sterile conditions (see Figure 10-9). The abdominal cavity is lined by a thin sack called the peritoneal membrane. A plastic catheter can be surgically placed through the abdominal wall into the abdominal cavity. After about two weeks of training, you or someone assisting you can connect the catheter to a bag of dialysis fluid. The fluid (about 2 liters) enters the abdominal cavity over about 15 minutes and surrounds the stomach and intestines. While the fluid is in the abdomen, wastes from the body cross the membrane and enter the fluid. After four to six hours the fluid is drained out and discarded, along with the impurities and excess salt and water, and fresh fluid is infused. Sugar from the fluid may also enter the body, causing elevated blood sugar in diabetics.

There are two types of PD: continuous ambulatory peritoneal dialysis (CAPD) and continuous cycling peritoneal dialysis (CCPD). In CAPD, dialysis fluid is changed in the abdomen usually four times a day. This is called an exchange. An exchange requires a private, clean environment for about 30 minutes in the morning, noon, evening, and bedtime. In CCPD, the abdominal catheter is connected at bedtime to a machine which infuses and drains dialysis fluid at intervals while you sleep. The advantage of CCPD is that only one sterile connection at bedtime and one sterile disconnection at awakening is required. If someone is assisting you in performing PD, this may be a good choice for you, since the person's presence would only be required at bedtime and in the morning, as opposed to periodically during the day as with CAPD.

The advantage of PD is that it can be done anywhere that clean supplies can be brought and used. Some people do exchanges in a private room at school or work (see Figure 10-9). PD supplies can travel with you or be shipped to your destination. There is no need to go to a dialysis center three times a week at a specified time. With this independence comes responsibility. PD patients are in charge of their own dialysis. They need to take their own weights and blood pressures and adjust their dialysis fluid accordingly, to remove more or less fluid. If they handle their catheter or solutions improperly, they risk a serious infection of the abdomen called peritonitis. For these reasons, PD requires motivation, mental capacity, good eyesight, good hand coordination, and a clean and supportive home environment. In addition, if you have had abdominal surgeries or abdominal hernias, you may not be able to tolerate 2 liters of fluid bloating your abdomen.

PD has some medical advantages and disadvantages as well. Since dialysis is done daily, there is little chance for extra salt, water, and potassium to build up in the body. This has benefits for blood pressure and heart disease, as well as allowing a more liberal diet than that allowed by hemodialysis. However, there is some evidence that older diabetics may not

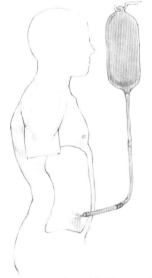

(figure 10-9)

Peritoneal dialysis.

do as well with PD. This may be due to the extra sugar in the dialysis fluid. The decision on type of renal replacement therapy, HD or PD, is a complex one that needs to be made after thorough discussion with your nephrologist and family and with consideration of the special circumstances of your health status and goals for the future.

KIDNEY TRANSPLANT

A kidney transplant is the surgical connection of a human kidney, donated from either a living person or a recently deceased organ donor, to your blood vessels and bladder (see Figure 10-10). The transplanted kidney will clean your blood and produce urine as your native kidneys once did. Since the transplanted kidney comes from someone else, your body's natural instinct is to attack the kidney as something "foreign." This is known as rejection. In order to prevent rejection and maintain your transplant, you need to take multiple medications to suppress your immune system and have regular, at first very frequent, clinic visits for blood work and checkups.

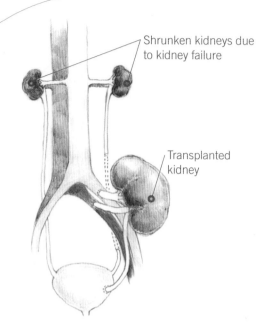

Shrunken kidneys due to kidney failure

Transplanted kidney

(*figure* 10-10)

Kidney transplant.

Is a kidney transplant for you? As with most things, there are risks and benefits to kidney transplantation. There is no age limit for kidney transplant. Each person's case must be individually reviewed by a team of health care workers to judge whether a transplant is right. There are known benefits of transplantation. For example, studies have shown that patients who receive transplants live longer than those who are maintained on dialysis. This holds true even for the elderly. Ten % of people currently waiting for a donated kidney are over the age of 65.

The risks of a kidney transplant, although uncommon, can be quite serious. The first risk is the operation, which lasts approximately three to four hours. Although not considered high-risk surgery, any surgery can strain the heart and may precipitate a heart attack. Before you undergo surgery, your doctor may advise a cardiac stress test to be sure your heart is in good condition. Other possible complications include stroke, bleeding, infections, open wounds, urine leaking from the urinary tract, and fluids collecting around the transplant. Some problems could require temporary placement of a catheter in the bladder or into the abdomen to drain urine or fluid.

In the long term, the risk of kidney transplant is largely related to the medications you will need to take to suppress the immune system and prevent rejection. The immune system has many functions, such as fighting infection and cancer cells. Older persons already have somewhat weakened immunity, and are at higher risk for infection than are younger transplant recipients. Infections in transplant recipients may be unusual or severe. There is also an increased risk of developing cancer, and skin cancer is particularly frequent. For this reason it is generally not safe to transplant anyone with an active infection or cancer, since these could become much worse and possibly life threatening. Transplant patients need to protect themselves from possible sources of infection and seek medical attention at any sign of illness. They also must have regular checkups and cancer screening.

Considering the large number of people who have kidney failure and are waiting for transplants, doctors are considering accepting kidneys from older donors. You may be offered a kidney from an older donor, with the idea in mind that the life span of even an older kidney will be long enough to keep you off dialysis for the remainder of your life. This is a decision between you and your doctors.

With current medical science and immunosuppressive medications, a transplanted kidney could last more than 20 years. How long each individual kidney transplant will last, however, is impossible to predict. Important factors include the recipient's immune system, adherence to medication regimens, blood pressure, blood sugar, and cholesterol. The condition of the donated kidney at time of transplant is also important; a younger kidney, which is free of changes of high blood pressure and scarring, may function longer. Last, the immune similarity between the donated kidney and the recipient, also known as *matching,* reduces the risk of rejection and transplant failure.

FINANCIAL COSTS

Dialysis and kidney transplant are both expensive. Currently, through Medicare, the federal government covers 80% of the costs of dialysis or transplant in the vast majority of cases. Medicaid or private insurance may cover the remainder of the cost. A social or financial worker can review your particular situation and advise regarding your benefits and costs.

END-OF-LIFE ISSUES

If one's quality of life is very poor, due to dementia, terminal cancer, or other advanced and disabling problems, it may not be very helpful to begin dialysis. These considerations must include the personal values of the individual with kidney failure and frank discussions with your doctor. If renal replacement therapy is not begun, one may die of kidney failure. This can be a comfortable death, involving a painless coma. Doctors or a hospice can still be involved to make sure that comfort is maintained. Another option is a trial of dialysis. If dialysis is begun and is not found to have a favorable impact on quality of life, it can always be stopped. About 50% of patients die within eight days of cessation of dialysis. Again, health care teams can still be involved after dialysis is discontinued, to minimize symptoms or discomfort and provide support to individuals and their families.

If an individual is too ill to make his or her own medical decisions, family members will usually work with the health care team to make decisions that they believe are in accordance with the patient's wishes and best interests. It is a good idea to discuss with your family your wishes about dialysis and other aggressive medical interventions in various circumstances, such as terminal illness or a chronically incapacitated state. An *advanced directive* is a legal document which can represent your wishes for your health care in circumstances in which you are unable to express them yourself (see Chapter 44). While you can fill out such a directive on your own, an attorney would be of much help, particularly if you have an overall planning strategy.

■

WHAT YOU NEED TO KNOW

■■ Half the people on dialysis in the United States are over 65 years of age. One in one thousand persons between 65 and 74 years old will need dialysis or kidney transplant each year, making this age group the one at highest risk for kidney failure.

■■ Good nutrition, exercise, and not smoking form a good foundation for avoiding diabetes and high blood pressure, which are the major causes of kidney failure.

■■ The best initial tests of kidney function require blood and urine samples, and your primary care physician can order them. If you have an elevated blood creatinine or protein in your urine, your doctor may ask you to see a kidney specialist (nephrologist).

■■ Although kidney function declines with age, this does not cause problems in most cases. However, ask your doctor before you take any medications, since many prescription arthritis drugs, as well as such OTC drugs as ibuprofen, can have adverse effects on your kidneys as you get older.

■■ There are medications that can help retard progression of kidney disease. Your doctor will decide if these are appropriate for you.

■■ When the kidneys perform at only 10 to 15% of their normal function, dialysis or kidney transplant is necessary to prevent complications including death. The decision to undergo these treatments can be made after a discussion with your family and your kidney specialist.

10

FOR MORE INFORMATION

■■ National Kidney and Urologic Diseases Information Clearinghouse
3 Information Way
Bethesda, MD 20892
E-mail: nkudic@info.niddk.nih.gov

■■ National Kidney Foundation
30 East 33rd Street, Suite 1100
New York, NY 10016
800-622-9010, 212-889-2210
Fax: 212-689-9261
E-mail: info@kidney.org

Dr. Allen R. Nissenson is supported, in part, by the Richard Rosenthal Dialysis Fund, and Dr. Ruth L. Wintz is supported by funds from Amgen.

> Prostate cancer is beginning to come out of the closet. Fifteen or twenty years ago, you couldn't even mention the word prostate in polite mixed company.
>
> —*Dr. William Fair, Time Magazine, 1996*

THE AUTHOR

11 Winston E Barzell

WINSTON BARZELL, MD, FACS, FRCS(C), received his medical degree from McGill University, Montreal, Canada. He completed a general surgical residency at the Montreal General Hospital and a urologic residency at the Royal Victoria Hospital, in Montreal, and the Hospital for Sick Children in Toronto. Afterward, he did a research fellowship in immunology for the Research Council of Canada, followed in 1974 by a fellowship in Urologic Oncology at Memorial Sloan Kettering Cancer Center (MSKCC), New York. In 1975 he joined the staff at MSKCC as an assistant attending surgeon and held the position of associate professor of surgery at Cornell University Medical College, New York. In 1978, he left New York City to go into private practice in Sarasota, Florida while retaining the position of consultant in Urology –Department of Surgery, MSKCC between 1978 and 1989. Dr. Barzell has written numerous scientific publications including two chapters in the authoritative Campbell's *Textbook of Urology.* He is a member of various medical societies including the Society of Urologic Oncology and the prestigious Society of Surgical Oncology and has served as Chief of Surgery at Doctors Hospital in 1986 and at Sarasota Memorial Hospital in 1988. He is a recipient of numerous awards and was included in *The Best Doctors in America* in 2002. Dr. Barzell, working with his partner, Dr. Whitmore, patented numerous inventions in the field of minimally invasive surgery. To market these inventions, they cofounded Barzell Whitmore Maroon Bells in 1996, a company now regarded as a world leader in brachytherapy equipment and accessories. Dr. Barzell served as President and CEO until its sale to Colorado Medtech, Civco subdivision, in the year 2002. He has recently helped developed accessories to facilitate a more general adoption of cryosurgery, and he has written articles describing a new prostate biopsy technique that allows for a more rational approach to the management of patients with prostate cancer. He has a fulltime private practice in Sarasota, with special interest and expertise in urologic oncology, prostate cancer, and BPH; and holds a consulting position in Civco's minimally invasive therapies division.

11 | THE PROSTATE

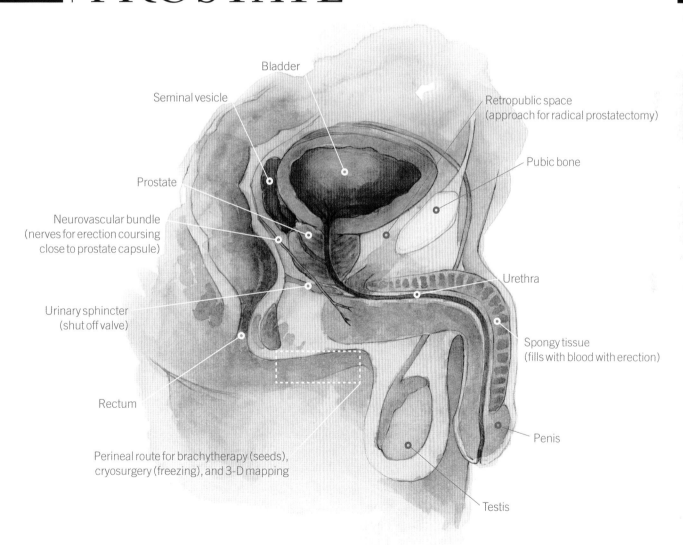

Bladder

Seminal vesicle

Retropublic space
(approach for radical prostatectomy)

Pubic bone

Prostate

Neurovascular bundle
(nerves for erection coursing
close to prostate capsule)

Urethra

Urinary sphincter
(shut off valve)

Spongy tissue
(fills with blood with erection)

Rectum

Penis

Perineal route for brachytherapy (seeds),
cryosurgery (freezing), and 3-D mapping

Testis

(figure 11-1)

A section through the male pelvis depicting the prostate and surrounding structures. The prostate is in a very strategic location. It encircles the urethra and neck of the bladder. The prostate is close to the rectum, and it sits on the urinary sphincter (valve). The ejaculatory ducts carry semen through the prostate, and the nerves responsible for erection travel along the prostate's capsule. Therefore, it is not surprising that prostate problems and their treatment can adversely affect urination, reproduction, ejaculation, erection, and rectal function.

After years of obscurity, the prostate gland has come out of hiding to occupy center stage. An aging population and newer screening techniques have swollen the ranks of those with prostate disease. Many high-profile individuals have brought media attention to this affliction. Rarely a month passes without hearing of some celebrity having his prostate "resected," "lasered," "heated," "radiated," "seeded," "frozen," "removed," or otherwise manipulated.

This chapter deals with benign prostatic hyperplasia (BPH) and prostate cancer. The other common condition of the prostate, known as **prostatitis** (inflammation or infection of the prostate), is covered in Chapter 22.

The **prostate** is a walnut-sized gland which produces prostatic fluid, a vital component of semen. Its main function, therefore, is in reproduction. Once the reproductive years have passed, the importance of this small, nonvital, and expendable organ relates to its strategic location at the intersection of the male urinary and reproductive systems (see Figure 11-1). Urine and semen exit the body by flowing through it. Furthermore, nerves essential for erections travel very close to its capsule. It is not surprising, therefore, that disturbances of the prostate can adversely affect urination, reproduction, ejaculation, and erections.

While all male mammals possess a prostate, abnormal growth, as seen with either a benign or malignant process, is limited to the prostate of humans and dogs. This may be due to shared dietary factors.

An understanding of normal prostate physiology helps in appreciating the rationale and basis for treating abnormalities of the prostate discussed in this chapter. The prostate has cells that secrete fluid, muscle cells that help propel the fluid, and a scaffolding, or matrix, which holds everything together. Prostate growth is stimulated by **testosterone,** the male hormone, and is restricted by its absence. Before testosterone can act on the prostate, it must first be converted to its active form known as dihydrotestosterone (DHT). In treating prostate disease, therefore, one may eliminate testosterone by surgical or chemical castration, block its conversion to the active component, **dihydrotestosterone (DHT)** (see Figure 11-13) with drugs such as Proscar and Avodart, or relax the smooth muscles that constrict the prostate and urinary passage with medications such as Flomax, Hytrin, Cardura, and Uroxatral. Each of these methods is discussed in this chapter.

BENIGN PROSTATIC HYPERPLASIA

Benign prostatic hyperplasia (BPH) is a very common disease affecting men beyond middle age. Approximately 50% of men within their lifetime will have symptoms as a result of BPH. Fortunately, however, only a minority will experience symptoms severe enough to require treatment.

Patients with an enlarged prostate often have symptoms of *prostatism,* which is now commonly referred to as **lower urinary tract symptoms (LUTS).** LUTS are mainly caused by two factors. The first is an increase in prostate volume (BPH) with resulting obstruction to urine flow, and the second factor is bladder muscle (**detrusor**) dysfunction. It should be noted that the process of aging as well as that of obstruction can

(*figure* 11-2)

BPH progression and bladder function: (a) normal prostate and bladder. (b) Early BPH: slight bladder wall thickening with the possibility of residual urine in the bladder after voiding. Patients have few if any symptoms. (c) Moderate BPH: significant bladder wall thickening with loss of reservoir function. Significant irritative voiding complaints and some obstructive complaints. (d) Advanced BPH: acute urinary retention and the bladder is overdistended with urine.

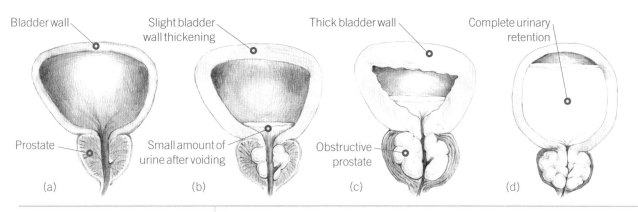

Bladder wall   Slight bladder wall thickening   Thick bladder wall   Complete urinary retention

Prostate   Small amount of urine after voiding   Obstructive prostate

(a)   (b)   (c)   (d)

independently induce bladder muscle dysfunction by causing the bladder to be stiff and less compliant with a resultant loss of storage (reservoir) function. Therefore, while BPH is the major contributor to LUTS, it is not the only cause of LUTS in aging men, and furthermore, prostate enlargement (BPH) may exist in the absence of LUTS, and LUTS can exist in the absence of significant prostate enlargement. The cause of BPH is unknown but the presence of the male hormone testosterone is required (*Castrati,* male eunuchs common in Italy in the 17th and 18th centuries, did not develop BPH.) The presence of estrogen (the female hormone) is also implicated (in males, a small amount of testosterone is converted to estrogen in the fat cells).

I find it helpful to mention the interplay of bladder function and the prostate (see Figure 11-2), in explaining BPH to my patients: Consider the bladder as fulfilling two functions. Its primary function is that of a pump to push urine out through the prostate (which acts as a resistance). Its secondary function is to act as a reservoir, storing urine so that a person can discharge this waste product when convenient. As the prostate enlarges, resistance to urine flow increases, resulting in compensatory enlargement and thickening of the bladder muscle. The bladder becomes a stronger pump, but in doing so, with thicker muscles, it begins to lose its normal reservoir function. The loss of storage results in the need for more frequent urination and a diminished ability to delay urination *(urgency)*. Since nature places a greater value on the pumping action of the bladder to excrete urine rather than on its reservoir function, which is mainly a matter of convenience, the first function to fail is that of the reservoir and the last function to fail is that of the pump. When the reservoir function fails, patients may complain to their physicians of *irritative* voiding problems, such as frequency, urgency, *urge incontinence* (loss of urine as soon as the urge to void is experienced; see also Chapter 14), and *nocturia* (getting up frequently at night to urinate). When the pump function fails, obstructive symptoms develop, such as hesitancy, diminished flow, interruption of flow, and, ultimately, urinary retention and *overflow incontinence* (loss of urine when the bladder is filled to capacity). The embarrassment from the irritative symptoms related to the loss of the reservoir function is an important determinant in men seeking medical advice.

It is important to emphasize that prostate size does not correlate with the degree of obstruction. A small prostate may be severely symptomatic, and a large gland may cause little if any difficulty. To understand this seeming paradox, compare the prostate to a doughnut wherein urine flows through the center. In this analogy, the critical diameter is the inside one. One can have a large prostate with a large inside diameter, permitting free urine flow and causing no LUTS. Or one can have a small prostate with a small inside diameter or hole that can cause many symptoms. Prostate volume increases slowly with age between the years of 40 to 59 and more rapidly between the years of 60 to 79. On average, the prostate increases approximately 20 to 25% in size per decade of life.

As noted above, many symptoms of BPH are not related to the obstruction itself but to changes in the bladder brought on by the obstructive prostate. These changes in the bladder are not always reversible. Indeed, one-third of men may still have voiding complaints after relief of their obstruction.

While BPH can significantly adversely affect an individual's quality of life, it is rarely fatal. However, when significant BPH is left untreated, several complications can arise. These include recurrent urinary tract infections, bleeding, formation of bladder stones, loss of bladder function, and kidney failure. **Acute urinary retention (AUR)** is a feared, painful condition (see Figure 11-2d), wherein the bladder musculature can no longer pump urine through the obstructing prostatic *urethra* (the tube leading from the bladder to the outside). The risk of developing AUR increases with prostate size, elevated postvoid residual, diminished flow, age, elevated international prostate symptom score, and high prostate-specific antigen values. The latter two measures are discussed in the following section.

EVALUATION

Evaluation is performed by the following methods.

Digital rectal exam: Digital rectal exam (DRE) is performed to exclude a prostate cancer, assess the size of the prostate, and evaluate the anal sphincter tone to rule out neurological conditions which can masquerade as prostate disease. (See Figure 11-3.)

International prostate symptom score: The international prostate symptom score (IPSS), also known as the American Urologic Association (AUA) symptom score, is derived from a questionnaire and provides a relatively objective way to assess the severity of LUTS (see Figure 11-4). The score helps physicians and patients assess the magnitude of the problem, its progression over time, and its response to treatment. Using

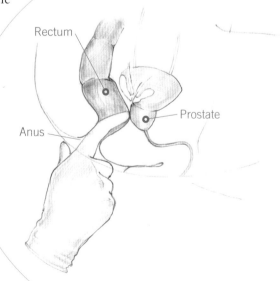

Rectum

Anus

Prostate

(figure 11-3)

Digital rectal examination: Physician inserts a gloved, lubricated finger into the rectum to assess size of the prostate, exclude a prostate nodule, and assess tone of the anal sphincter.

(figure 11-4)
International prostate symptom score (I-PSS). *(Courtesy of the International Scientific Committee.)*

	NOT AT ALL	LESS THAN 1 TIME IN 5	LESS THAN HALF THE TIME	ABOUT HALF THE TIME	MORE THAN HALF THE TIME	ALMOST ALWAYS
1. INCOMPLETE EMPTYING Over the past month or so, how often have you had a sensation of not emptying your bladder completely after you have finished urinating?	0	1	2	3	4	5
2. FREQUENCY Over the past month or so, how often have you had to urinate again less than two hours after you have finished urinating?	0	1	2	3	4	5
3. INTERMITTENCY Over the past month or so, how often have you found you stopped and started again several times when you urinated?	0	1	2	3	4	5
4. URGENCY Over the past month or so, how often have you found it difficult to postpone urination?	0	1	2	3	4	5
5. WEAK STREAM Over the past month or so, how often have you had a weak urinary stream?	0	1	2	3	4	5
6. STRAINING Over the past month or so, how often have you had to push or strain to begin urination?	0	1	2	3	4	5

	NONE	1 TIME	2 TIMES	3 TIMES	4 TIMES	5 OR MORE TIMES
7. NOCTURIA Over the last month, how many times did you most typically get up to urinate from the time you went to bed at night until the time you got up in the morning?	0	1	2	3	4	5

TOTAL I-PSS SCORE

MILD (symptom score less than or equal to 7)
MODERATE (symptom score range 8-19)
SEVERE (symptom score range 20-35)

the AUA symptom score, LUTS may be classified into three categories: mild (0 to 7), moderate (8 to 19), and severe (20 to 35).

Prostate-specific antigen determination: Prostate-specific antigen (PSA) determination measures the blood level of PSA, a protein released by prostate cells. I discuss the PSA blood test in more detail later in this chapter.

Uroflowmetry: Uroflowmetry is a noninvasive test that records urine flow rates.

Cystometrogram: If the cause of LUTS is not clearly related to BPH, a cystometrogram (CMG) pressure flow determination can help rule out neurogenic conditions that masquerade as prostate disease.

Imaging: Imaging studies, such as a renal ultrasound, an intravenous pyelogram (IVP), bladder scan, or a transrectal ultrasound, may be done to rule out obstructive changes in the kidneys and bladder and to assess prostate size.

Cystoscopy: Cystoscopy involves passing a cystoscope (usually flexible) through the urethra into the bladder and provides direct visualization of the prostate and bladder, thus permitting the visualization of the bladder interior to rule out concurrent unrelated abnormalities.

DECIDING TO TREAT BPH

Decisions regarding treatment are based on the severity of symptoms as judged by the IPSS, the "bother score" (the patient's assessment of how bothersome his symptoms are), the extent, if any, of urinary tract damage, and the patient's age and overall health status.

In general, no treatment is needed in those with few symptoms. Intervention is required when complications of BPH arise, such as recurrent infections, bleeding, bladder stones, acute urinary retention, and symptoms that significantly interfere with the patient's quality of life. The majority of patients fall between these two extremes, and for them treatment is purely elective and usually dictated by the patient's bother score.

The main treatment options for BPH include *watchful waiting* with or without lifestyle modification, medication, minimally invasive therapy, and surgery.

Since the progression of symptomatic BPH is not inevitable, watchful waiting is frequently used as the initial course of treatment. However, watchful waiting does not imply a total lack of intervention. In patients who elect this course but who have moderate symptoms, the following lifestyle modifications have proved on occasion to be helpful:

- Avoiding beverages containing caffeine
- Avoiding rapid intake of large amounts of fluid
- Avoiding beverages after 6 P.M.
- Limiting the use of alcohol
- Avoiding over-the-counter cold medications containing antihistamines and decongestants
- Avoiding certain antidepressants, such as AMITRIPTYLINE (ELAVIL) and IMIPRAMINE (TOFRANIL)

Patients with significant irritative complaints frequently improve with Kegel's exercises (to learn how to do Kegel exercises, see box in Chapter 14) and biofeedback. Approximately 40% of patients elect watchful waiting when first seen by their urologist.

TREATMENT

Medical Therapy: Ideal candidates for medical therapy have moderate to high symptom scores, a high bother score, and a willingness to take medication for prolonged periods of time, providing side effects are minimal. Therapy may consist of plant extracts, alpha-adrenergic blockers, and androgen suppression.

Plant extracts or phytotherapy: Phytotherapy includes extracts from the roots, seeds, bark, or fruit of various plants. They contain phytosterols,

(figure 11-5)

(a) BPH is associated with enlargement of the prostate, which may impede urine flow. (b) Alpha-adrenergic blockers relax the smooth muscle fibers within the prostate so that urine can flow more freely. (c) Alpha-reductase inhibitors can shrink an enlarged prostate but may not significantly improve urine flow. (d) Combining alpha-adrenergic blockers and alpha-reductase inhibitors may result in more improvement than either drug alone.

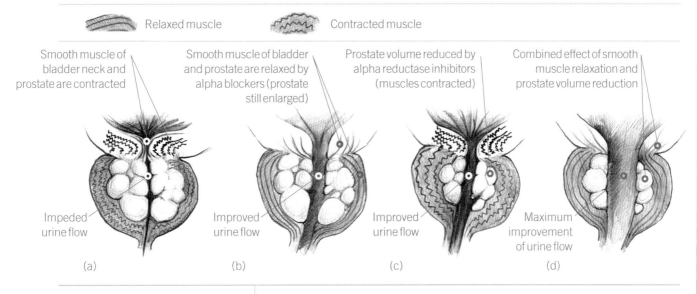

Relaxed muscle   Contracted muscle

Smooth muscle of bladder neck and prostate are contracted

Smooth muscle of bladder and prostate are relaxed by alpha blockers (prostate still enlarged)

Prostate volume reduced by alpha reductase inhibitors (muscles contracted)

Combined effect of smooth muscle relaxation and prostate volume reduction

Impeded urine flow

Improved urine flow

Improved urine flow

Maximum improvement of urine flow

(a)   (b)   (c)   (d)

plant oils, fatty acids, and phytoestrogens. The extracts and composition of the final product is different among different manufacturers and among different batches of the same manufacturer. Their purported mode of action is unknown. They may be anti-inflammatory, they may inhibit *alpha-reductase* (the enzyme that converts testosterone to dihydrotestosterone), or they may inhibit various growth factors.

Numerous plant extracts are reported to have beneficial effects in patients with BPH, but in general solid evidence is lacking. The only exception is *saw palmetto,* for which a recent trial suggested that men taking the plant extract were 75% more likely to report improvement than men taking a placebo. These results are similar to the improvement seen in patients taking PROSCAR (FINASTERIDE) or AVODART (DUTASTERIDE). Plant extracts are not classified as drugs; therefore, controlled studies are not clinically supervised by the Food and Drug Administration (FDA). The amount of saw palmetto contained in different batches can vary widely, and product-to-product consistency cannot be assured. Furthermore, the long-term safety of plant extracts has not been established. In summary, therefore, *phytotherapeutic* preparations are plant extracts with different components manufactured by different extraction procedures. While amelioration in symptom score has been noted in patients taking such extracts, it is rare to find evidence of objective improvement.

Medication: There are two different classes of drugs to consider: alpha-blockers and 5-alpha-reductase inhibitors.

Alpha-adrenergic blockers: Tension within the prostate on the urethra is partly related to contraction of smooth muscle fibers within the prostate (see Figure 11-5a). Alpha-adrenergic blockers, originally used to treat high blood pressure by reducing the muscular tension in blood vessel walls, were found to also relax muscle tissue within the prostate (see Figure 11-5b). The most common drugs used are TERAZOSIN (HYTRIN), given at the dose of 5 to 10 mg, DOXAZOSIN (CARDURA) 4 to 8 mg, and the so-called specific alpha$_{1a}$-inhibitor, TAMSULOSIN (FLOMAX), 0.4 to 0.8 mg per day. One usually titrates the dose to a desired threshold response or to the maximum tolerated dose. Higher doses may improve response but not without side effects, which commonly include dizziness, *orthostatic hypotension* (dizziness on standing due to a drop in blood pressure), weakness, insomnia, headaches, and nasal congestion. Retrograde ejaculation (ejaculating back into the bladder) is a frequent complaint, particularly with Flomax. A newer so-called uroselective alpha-blocker, ALFUZOSIN (UROXATRAL) has been released and is purported not to cause retrograde ejaculation. Because Flomax and Uroxatral are selective for the prostate, they do not usually require changes in their initial dose.

Numerous multicenter trials have unequivocally demonstrated the safety and efficacy of alpha-blockers in the treatment of BPH. Clinical response is rapid and dose-dependent. Hytrin or Cardura is usually taken at bedtime to decrease the likelihood of side effects. Flomax is taken a half-hour after breakfast to maintain a significant blood level through a 24-hour period, and UROXATRAL is taken once daily after the same meal.

Alpha-reductase inhibitors: Androgen suppression with alpha-reductase inhibitors causes regression of the epithelial elements of the prostate, thus reducing prostate volume (see Figure 11-5c). Maximum reduction in prostate size occurs at six months. FINASTERIDE (PROSCAR) and DUTASTERIDE (AVODART) inhibit the enzyme that converts testosterone to dihydrotestosterone (DHT), the active component in the prostate (see Figure 11-13). Proscar is best suited for men with large prostates with volumes of at least 40 cc or more. In a longitudinal study of more than 4000 men with prostates larger than 40 cc, Proscar significantly reduced the incidence of surgery and acute urinary retention. The main side effects of Proscar include erectile dysfunction in about 5% of patients, decrease in ejaculatory volume, occasional breast enlargement, and weakness. An important caveat is that these agents (finasteride and dutasteride) lower the PSA level by about 50%. In men taking these agents for more than six months, PSA values must therefore be adjusted to have a true comparison to pretreatment PSA levels.

Although Proscar may cause a 20 to 25% reduction in prostate volume, symptomatic improvement does not correlate well with the decreased size. Other reasons for using Proscar are for patients with recurrent bleeding due to friable prostatic tissue, and in certain circumstances, it is my personal bias to use it in those with very large prostates when contemplating a *transurethral resection of the prostate (TURP)*, by which prostate tissue is surgically resected through a cystoscope introduced into the urethra. In the latter instance, Proscar is used on a short-term basis preoperatively to decrease the amount of blood encountered in the prostate gland when surgery is performed.

Combination therapy: The results of the Medical Therapy of Prostatic Symptoms (MTOPS) trial were published in 2002. This five-year trial, involving more than 3000 men, concluded that combination therapy (finasteride plus an alpha-blocker) was more effective than using either drug alone (see Figure 11-5d).

The current approach to medical management of BPH is to opt for combination therapy if treatment with a single drug is not effective in significantly reducing symptoms. My own bias is to start with an alpha-blocker. Current agents are equally effective. One of the potential advantages of the so-called selective inhibitors Flomax or Uroxatral is that they may be given at full therapeutic dose immediately without having to increase the dose, which may be required with Hytrin and Cardura. However, Flomax and Uroxatral are more costly. Therefore, the side effect profile, the utility in a particular patient for a rapid onset of action, and possibly the cost determine which agents to use. If the patient's symptoms do not improve with an alpha-blocker, especially if he has a large prostate, then I add an alpha-reductase inhibitor such as Proscar or Avodart.

Minimally invasive therapy: In the past decade, a number of so-called nonsurgical procedures have been introduced with the label of "minimally invasive surgery." Their aim is to produce a subjective and objective improvement in urinary function comparable to the gold standard of transurethral resection of the prostate but with reduced hospitalization and anesthesia and with minimal morbidity. A number of the most popular are briefly discussed below. They all share one feature, namely the use of heat to destroy prostatic tissue. This is known as thermal ablation. It is not clear whether the tissue destroyed is smooth muscle, prostate epithelium, nerve tissue, or a combination.

Transurethral needle ablation: Transurethral needle ablation (TUNA) is a method used to deliver low-level radiofrequency waves through a catheter device, outfitted with adjustable needles, placed in selected prostate tissue areas (see Figure 11-6a). The delivered radiofrequency heats the prostate and produces tissue destruction. This procedure is associated with good patient tolerance and few complications but does require sedation or anesthesia. For the average patient, TUNA appears to be more effective than medical therapy but less effective than surgery in relieving symptoms.

(figure 11-6)

Examples of thermotherapy of BPH: (a) Transurethral needle ablation (TUNA), by which a radiofrequency antenna delivers heat to the prostate, and (b) a magnified view; (c) transurethral microwave therapy (TUMT), by which a microwave antenna inside the catheter applies heat to the prostate.

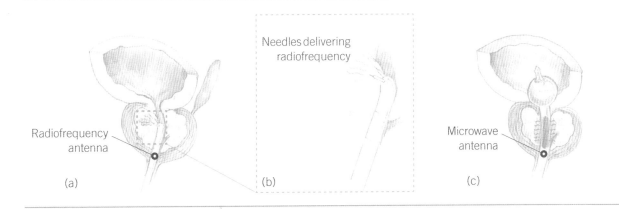

Radiofrequency antenna

(a)

Needles delivering radiofrequency

(b)

Microwave antenna

(c)

On average, there is a 10- to 12-point reduction in symptom score and a 3-point increase in urinary flow rates.

Complications include bleeding, irritative voiding symptoms, and urinary tract infection. It is important to note that ejaculatory function is usually preserved, and this treatment is ideally suited for patients in whom potential ejaculatory dysfunction is a major concern. Approximately 20 to 25% of the patients will require additional treatment within two years.

Transurethral microwave therapy: In *transurethral microwave therapy (TUMT),* heat is delivered to the prostate by microwave (see Figure 11-6b). An inserted urethral catheter incorporates a microwave antenna. Simultaneous cooling prevents damage to the sensitive urethral lining while permitting focused microwave energy to heat the obstructing prostate tissue. General anesthesia is not required. The heat injury causes clotting of the local blood vessels with destruction of the surrounding tissue, which later gets resorbed or sloughed. Four devices on the market include the Prostatron, the Targis, the CoreTherm system (high power, no cooling), and the Thermatrx (low energy, no cooling). For the average patient, TUMT appears to be more effective than medical therapy but less effective than surgery in relieving symptoms.

The TUMT is usually not well suited for small glands. The improvement in symptom score ranges between 10 and 12, and the improvement in flow rate ranges between 1.5 and 3. The durability of this minimally invasive treatment has not been well established since there appears to be a significant drop of symptom score improvement after four to five years.

Studies are underway to compare the effectiveness of TUNA, microwave, and maximal medical therapy.

Lasers: The word laser has universal appeal among patients. There are currently three categories of laser used in the treatment of BPH: *interstitial laser ablation, photoselective vaporization of the prostate,* and *holmium laser enucleation.*

In *interstitial laser ablation (indigo)* treatment, a laser fiber is introduced through the urethra into the prostate and produces a precisely controlled ellipsoid area of coagulation (see Figure 11-7a). The treatment is analogous to TUNA, but, in this case, laser energy is used to deliver the thermal, or heat, energy. The improvement in the IPSS and flow rates are similar to those seen with a TUNA. However, with the indigo treatment, retrograde ejaculation can occur in 40% of patients.

In my opinion, *photoselective vaporization of the prostate (PVP)* appears to be the most promising of the minimally invasive therapies (see Figure 11-7c). In this treatment, pulses of green light are absorbed selectively by the hemoglobin present in the blood and vascular prostatic glandular tissue. It therefore selectively vaporizes and removes the obstructing prostate tissue almost bloodlessly and provides immediate relief of symptoms associated with BPH. Most patients can have their urinary catheters removed within 24 hours. The improvement in IPSS and urinary flow rates are very comparable to those achieved with TURP. Indeed, there is an 80% improvement in IPSS and an approximately 200% improvement in voiding

(*figure* 11-7)

Laser therapy for BPH: (a) Interstitial laser therapy (e.g., indigo laser) and (b) magnified view; (c) side-firing laser therapy (e.g., PVP laser) and (d) magnified view.

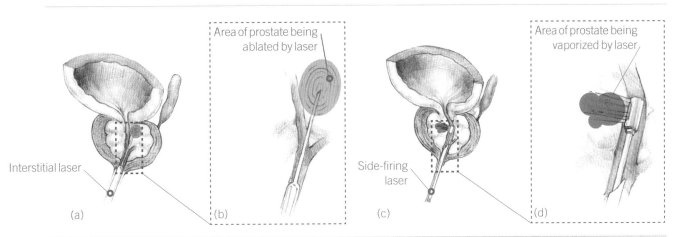

Area of prostate being ablated by laser

Interstitial laser

(a)

(b)

Area of prostate being vaporized by laser

Side-firing laser

(c)

(d)

flow rates. In one series of 84 patients, there was no reported incontinence or impotence, but in approximately 25% there was retrograde ejaculation.

At the time of this writing, while the PVP laser has not been widely used and therefore experience with it is limited, it appears to have the greatest promise in rivaling TURP.

In the very elegant *holmium laser enucleation (HoLEP)* procedure, perfected in New Zealand, a true *endoscopic enucleation* (removal of the prostate from its shell via an endoscope) that mimics open prostatectomy (removal of the prostate) has been developed. In a randomized trial of 60 patients comparing HoLEP to TURP, more tissue was removed at HoLEP than at TURP. Proponents of this technique argue that this procedure is equivalent or superior to a TURP for the relief of bladder outflow obstruction. While this treatment is very exciting, it is technically challenging to perform, with an anticipated steep learning curve that might limit its widespread adoption.

High-intensity focus ultrasound: Not yet FDA-approved, Sonoblate uses *high-intensity focused ultrasound (HIFU)* to heat the prostate by focusing the energy of high-intensity ultrasound on the prostate through a device inserted in the rectum. In a small number of patients using this Sonoblate, improvements in symptom score and flow rates were equivalent to TUMT. Complications include blood in the ejaculate and urine and transient urinary retention.

Stents: A urinary stent is a tubelike structure, similar to those used in coronary arteries. They are made of plastic, metal, or absorbable substance and are placed within the prostatic urethra to keep it open. This less attractive option is best for elderly men who are not candidates for other conservative measures.

SURGERY

Surgery for BPH accomplishes the removal of the obstructing inner portion of the prostate, also known as the *periurethral adenoma* or transition

(figure 11-8)

Transurethral resection of the prostate (TURP), the gold standard in BPH therapy: (a) Resectoscope loop engaging tissue at the bladder neck. (b) Magnified picture from (a) of the resectoscope loop. (c) The left lobe of the prostate (your right is patient's left) has been completely resected and about half the right lobe remains. (d) An empty prostate *fossa,* or bed, after all the BPH tissue has been thoroughly resected.

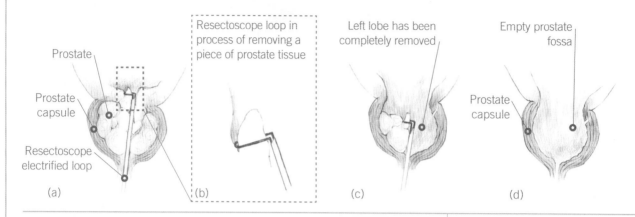

zone. This tissue is removed either at open surgery—a subtotal simple prostatectomy—or via the transurethral route, without incision, known as a transurethral resection of the prostate. The same tissue is removed with either technique, and both the anatomic and functional postoperative results are similar. An open surgical procedure is required for about 5 to 10% of patients, usually in those in whom the amount of prostate tissue to be removed is greater than 90 to 100 grams.

Transurethral prostatectomy: *Transurethral prostatectomy* or *transurethral resection of the prostate (TURP)* is considered benchmark or gold standard for BPH treatment: 90 to 95% of subtotal prostatectomies for BPH are performed by this technique. In 1986, approximately 350,000 to 400,000 Medicare patients underwent a TURP. Currently, on an annual basis, between 150,000 and 200,000 Medicare patients undergo a TURP. This change reflects the beneficial effects of medical treatment and other minimally invasive technologies discussed above.

It is estimated that the lifetime risk of requiring a TURP in a 40-year-old man is about 10%, whereas by age 60, the lifetime risk is about 30%. A TURP is best suited for men who have moderate to severe symptoms, a high bother score, and failed or not tolerated medical therapy.

A TURP involves removal of tissue from the inner portion of the prostate under direct vision by using an endoscopic instrument called a *resectoscope* without a skin incision (see Figure 11-8a). A wire loop attached to the end of the resectoscope is activated by electric current, permitting either cutting or coagulation of the tissue (see Figure 11-8b and c). Postoperatively, a catheter is usually left in place for two to three days. Using improved electrosurgical units and enhanced video, TURP is a very safe procedure. Most patients have a single overnight stay in hospital, and in some instances an outpatient procedure is possible. When appropriately performed and selected, more than 90% of the patients can expect marked improvement after surgery. The mortality of a TURP is exceedingly low, less than 0.2%. Complications include urinary tract infections, 5% with erectile dysfunction in 5% of patients, and a 90% incidence of retrograde ejaculation, a 2 to 5% risk of scar tissue forming postoperatively in the bladder neck or urethra, and a 2 to 5% incidence for requiring a repeat TURP.

Open simple subtotal prostatectomy: The *open simple subtotal prostatectomy* entails an incision in the lower abdominal region. The inner portion of the prostate gland is enucleated or shelled out by an open surgical technique. This open simple prostatectomy leaves the outer shell of the prostate intact and is not to be confused with the radical retropubic prostatectomy done for cancer and discussed in the section, "Radical Prostatectomy," below. The same tissue is removed during a TURP and open subtotal prostatectomy.

Transurethral vaporization of the prostate: Tissue is vaporized rather than resected and removed by a newer treatment called *transurethral vaporization of the prostate*. Its advantage is that it can be done in patients who must resume blood thinners soon after surgery. Its limitations are related to its side effect profile and the fact that tissue is not obtained for pathologic examination.

Transurethral incision of the prostate: In *transurethral incision of the prostate (TUIP)*, the prostate is transurethrally incised, and my own preference is to create a trough along this incision line. This treatment is very effective for men with smaller prostates, and for properly selected patients, the degree of improvement approaches that seen after a TURP. An advantage of TUIP is the resultant minimal adverse effects on sexual function, usually with preservation of normal ejaculation. In my opinion, TUIP is an extremely important option for the urologist. Patients who have smaller prostates and who undergo a TURP have a higher risk of developing bladder neck scarring (contracture), and in my opinion, a TUIP is ideally suited for this group of patients.

PROSTATE CANCER

When faced with a serious illness beyond our comprehension, [each of us] becomes childlike, afraid, and looking for someone to tell us what to do. It is an awesome responsibility for the surgeon to present the options to a patient with prostate cancer in such a way that he does not impose his prejudices which may or may not be based on the best objective information.
—*Dr. Thomas Stamey, Fortune, May 1996*

Prostate cancer is the most common male malignancy in the United States and the second leading cause of death. The American Cancer Society estimates that 220,000 new cases of prostate cancer will be diagnosed and nearly 30,000 men will die from the disease in 2003.

The introduction of PSA screening generated an apparent increase in the incidence of prostate cancer, which peaked in the mid-1990s at about 300,000 new cases per year but subsequently has steadily declined. This pattern would be expected with the introduction of a new screening test that uncovers a pool of patients whose prostate cancer would otherwise have gone undetected.

Prostate cancer is unique among cancers in that it can exist in two forms:

1. *Latent* (microscopic, dormant, occult, or incidental): found "incidentally" at autopsy in 30% of men over 50 and 70% of men over 80
2. *Clinical:* a clinically manifest form which affects up to one in six American men

Indeed, an American born in this decade has a 16% chance of developing clinical prostate cancer during his lifetime and a 3% chance of dying of the disease.

CAUSES OF PROSTATE CANCER

The underlying cause of prostate cancer is unknown. Implicated is a mixture of genetic and environmental factors. It is important to note that no association has been found between prostate cancer and benign conditions of the prostate, such as prostatitis or BPH.

Genetic influences are suggested by observations that race and family history influence the risk of prostate cancer. Prostate cancer is more prevalent in men of African-American origin. Men with first-degree relatives (brother or father) have a higher incidence of prostate cancer than men with unaffected relatives. For example, a man who has one first-degree relative with prostate cancer is twice as likely to develop prostate cancer as a man with no family history. If he has two first-degree relatives

WHAT'S NEW?

The Prostate Cancer Prevention Trial: In July 2003, results of the seven year Prostate Cancer Prevention Trial (PCPT) were published in *The New England Journal of Medicine*. This trial involved more than 18,000 men considered to be at low risk of developing prostate cancer (normal digital rectal exam, or DRE, and a PSA value of no more than 3). The men were randomly assigned to two groups. One group received finasteride (Proscar) 5 mg per day, and the other group received a placebo. Biopsies were done throughout the study on those men whose PSA or DRE became abnormal and on all the men at the end of the study. While the overall incidence of cancer detection was reduced by approximately 24% (from 24.4% in the placebo group to 18.4% in the finasteride group), high-grade cancer (Gleason 7 or greater) was detected with greater frequency in the finasteride group versus the placebo group (6.4% versus 5.1%).

In trying to interpret this data in a meaningful way to my patients, I excluded the patients who had a biopsy at the end of the study who had normal PSA values and DRE since this category of patients is not normally subjected to biopsy in everyday clinical practice. If we then consider only those patients who had a biopsy performed because they had an abnormal PSA or DRE, since this is precisely the population of patients in whom biopsies are currently recommended in the clinical setting, the results of the study show only a slight reduction in the incidence of cancer in the finasteride group (from 29.5% in the placebo group to 26.5% in the finasteride group) but a corresponding significant increase in the risk of high-grade cancer (from 7.7% in the placebo group to 11.5% in the finasteride group). These facts have led me not to recommend finasteride to my patients as a cancer-preventive agent. Furthermore, those patients who are taking finasteride in the treatment of BPH should be closely monitored for the potential development of high-grade prostate cancer.

DOCTOR'S DIARY

Gregory T. was a 52-year-old hard-driving executive. He was very athletic and health conscious, ate all the right foods, exercised regularly, never smoked, and hardly drank. He prided himself in having less than 10% body fat. His only risk factor involved his father succumbing to prostate cancer at age 74. While on a trip, Gregory T. developed a bout of acute prostatitis, and his PSA jumped transiently to 4.5. After appropriate antibiotic therapy, his PSA came down to 2.8, higher than his previous baseline obtained a year earlier of 1.8. A transrectal biopsy to everyone's surprise revealed multiple areas of Gleason 7 cancer, which at subsequent radical prostatectomy was found to be extensive but fortunately still organ-confined. He recovered uneventfully, retaining full urinary and sexual function.

This case illustrates several points: The fact that 20% of patients with prostate cancer have a normal PSA if 4.0 is used as the upper limit of normal. In high-risk individuals with a family history, any persistent elevation of the PSA otherwise unexplained is suspect.

with prostate cancer, the risk increases to five times. If he has three affected first-degree relatives, then the risk is 11 times that of men with no family history.

Population migration studies suggest that such *environmental factors* as diet and lifestyle play an important role in the development of prostate cancer. As previously mentioned, prostate cancer has two forms: a latent form that is common but causes no problem and a clinically manifest form that is fortunately less common. Latent cancer is believed to have a similar prevalence worldwide among all ethnic groups; however, the incidence of clinical cancer varies dramatically between countries and ethnic groups. It is lowest in China and Japan and highest in North America and Scandinavia. In summary, therefore, while the incidence of latent, incidental cancer has a similar worldwide prevalence, clinical cancer discovered on screening and examination varies among countries and ethnic groups. How do we explain this difference? The important question is: What triggers the transformation of latent cancer to clinical cancer in some patients? The clue to explaining this paradox comes from population migration studies, wherein Japanese and Chinese living in the United States have a greater incidence of developing and dying of prostate cancer than do their relatives in Japan and China. Indeed, when Chinese and Japanese persons migrate to North America, their incidence of prostate cancer increases with each successive generation until it approaches that of North Americans.

What is implicated in diet and lifestyle? Factors that appear to increase the risk of prostate cancer are diets high in fat, especially animal fat and red meat—the latter has the strongest positive association—a low amount of vegetables (especially cruciferous), and conditions that decrease our natural vitamin D, such as a lack of exposure to sunlight.

Protective factors include increased consumption of soy products containing soy isoflavones, such as genistein and diadezein, adequate selenium (200 micrograms per day), vitamin E, lycopene (in cooked tomatoes), and green tea and participation in relaxation and/or meditation.

In summary, it appears that both genetic and environmental factors have a causative role in prostate cancer. The complex interplay between genetics and environment in prostate cancer can be simplified by the statement that "genetics loads the gun, and environment, such as diet and lifestyle, pulls the trigger." Thus one could have a genetic predisposition to prostate cancer but not necessarily develop the disease if choosing the right diet and lifestyle.

SCREENING

When and whom to screen? It is recommended that men after the age of 50 have a yearly screening with a digital rectal exam (DRE) and a prostate-specific antigen determination. Those at high risk (e.g., African-American men or those with a family history of the disease) should be screened at the earlier age of 40.

Prostate cancer usually shows no early warning signs. The tumor most often appears in peripheral areas of the gland, away from the urethra, where it can grow silently for years. Indeed, prostate cancer in its early stages causes no symptoms. Waiting for symptoms from prostate cancer may be tantamount to waiting for advanced disease.

Once thought to be the gold standard, DRE has now been supplemented by the prostate-specific antigen determination.

Prostate-specific antigen determination: A few words about this seemingly controversial test are in order. The prostate-specific antigen (PSA) determination measures the blood level of PSA, a protein released by prostate cells. Since both normal and malignant cells secrete this substance, though in differing amounts, the test is not specific for cancer. It is, however, specific for prostatic cells. In general, the higher the level of PSA, the higher the risk of cancer. PSA levels under 4 nanograms per milliliter (4 ng/mL) are considered normal in men over age 50. Levels of 2.4 or lower are normal for ages 40 to 50. Numerous studies have shown that 25 to 30% of patients with PSA levels of 4 to 10 ng/mL eventually have prostate cancer, while the remaining 70 to 75% have nonmalignant conditions.

There are problems with the PSA test. First is its lack of specificity with false positives (i.e., patients with an elevated PSA but no cancer) and false negatives (patients with a normal PSA who have cancer). Second is its potential for detecting clinically insignificant cancer (discovering latent cancer that does not need to be treated). This lack of specificity with false-positive results can have significant consequences to the patient physically (discomfort and potential complications of biopsy), emotionally (concern about cancer diagnosis), and economically (expense of prostate biopsies, medication, and PSA testing).

This lack of specificity is analogous to a finicky alarm system that goes off without provocation. One can choose not to set up such an alarm system (not have a PSA screening) or deal with the fact that many of the responses to the system may be false. PSA is, therefore, a double-edged scalpel. I frequently tell my patients, "If you are destined to get prostate cancer, either by heredity or environment or both, then PSA is the greatest test developed, since your cancer will be diagnosed early. On the other hand, if you are not destined to be a prostate cancer patient, PSA testing may be most inappropriate because of the economic, physical, and emotional consequences of a false-positive test."

Notwithstanding the above, while recognizing the PSA test as imperfect, it is the best test we have. To make the PSA more specific, we use PSA derivatives, such as age-adjusted PSA, PSA density, PSA velocity, and free PSA. Under investigation are new tumor markers that hopefully will be as sensitive (in detecting cancer) as PSA but much more specific (correctly guessing if cancer is present) and protein pattern information (known as *proteomics)* that will increase PSA specificity. Currently, the most useful derivative clinically is the free PSA.

Free PSA: In the blood, PSA is present in two forms: bound and free. The standard PSA measurement includes both bound and free forms. With prostate cancer, there is less free PSA. By measuring the percentage of free PSA, one can estimate the risk of prostate cancer. The cutoff used in most labs is around 25%; the lower the percentage of free PSA, the higher the risk of cancer. The best way for patients to remember is that the higher your free PSA, the higher your chance of being "free" from prostate cancer.

To clarify certain misconceptions about the association of PSA and prostate cancer, and the utility of the PSA test, consider the following:

- Any disruption of prostate cells (forceful digital rectal exam, ejaculation, prostatitis, prostate biopsy, prostate massage, or urinary retention) can generate a transient increase in PSA level.
- More than 80 to 90% of cancers detected by PSA screening prove to be significant and warrant treatment, while the remainder belong to the latent group.
- Although the recognized upper limit of PSA is 4, in numerous studies, approximately 20% of men with a PSA between 2.5 and 4 had cancer on TRUS biopsy.
- The most common cause of PSA elevation to the 4 to 10 range is BPH, not cancer (70% of men with PSA between 4 and 10 ng/mL do not have prostate cancer).
- Once a cancer has been diagnosed, PSA becomes an invaluable tool in the staging (prediction of organ-confined disease versus spread outside the prostate), prognosis, and monitoring of the effectiveness of therapy.

Transrectal ultrasound: Like sonar on a boat, transrectal ultrasound (TRUS) creates pictures using reflected sound waves (see Figure 11-9). While it can sometimes "see" cancers that are not palpable on DRE, the main usefulness of TRUS is to assess the size of the gland, determine the

(figure 11-9)

(a) Transrectal ultrasound helps the urologist evaluate the prostate size and look for cancerous areas. (b) Information gathered from the ultrasound is converted to a video image that can be viewed by the physician.

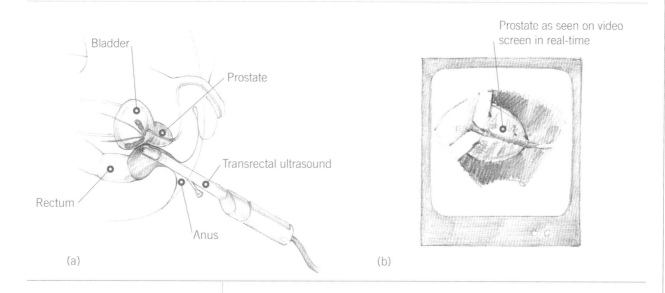

Bladder

Prostate

Transrectal ultrasound

Rectum

Anus

(a)

Prostate as seen on video screen in real-time

(b)

(figure 11-10)

(a) With ultrasound guidance, the urologist can biopsy areas of the prostate appearing cancerous. (b) The ultrasound image guides the urologist in "real time" to the area of the prostate to be biopsied.

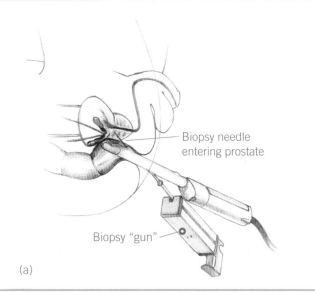

Biopsy needle
entering prostate

Biopsy "gun"

(a)

Urologist taking a needle biopsy of
a suspicious area with
real-time video guidance

(b)

PSA density, and to help guide the needle to make sure that all parts of the prostate are systematically biopsied.

Prostate biopsy: Usually the prostate biopsy is done with simultaneous ultrasound guidance (see Figure 11-10). This procedure may be performed in the urologist's office and takes about 15 to 20 minutes. Patients are given a mild oral sedative before the procedure, and local anesthetic is instilled with a fine needle to the tissues surrounding the prostate. In most cases this renders the procedure essentially painless. Patients may experience a vibration when the biopsy gun is fired and, at most, a sensation that a rubber band has been snapped. Current practice recommends obtaining 10 to 12 cores of tissue from different portions of the prostate for pathologic evaluation.

Transrectal-guided biopsies are appropriate for men with a life expectancy of more than 10 years and with an abnormal DRE and/or elevated PSA and/or significant PSA velocity or falling free PSA, or in other high-risk situations.

Confusion often arises if patients are told they have a negative biopsy but that one cannot exclude cancer with certainty. The best analogy I can give is that of trying to determine whether a watermelon has seeds without breaking the watermelon skin. If one inserts steel straws inside the watermelon and extracts several cores for examination, a seed found in one of the cores signifies the watermelon by definition has seeds (cancer). If none of the extracted cores has seeds, one cannot say with certainty whether this is a seedless watermelon or whether the straws missed the areas with seeds.

3D mapping: *Template-guided transperineal saturation biopsy* is a new approach, first reported by the Mayo Clinic. (The biopsy needle is introduced into the prostate via the *perineum,* the area between the genitals and rectum.) I have adapted and modified this strategy to help in the diagnosis and management of prostate cancer. In a selected group of patients with three prior negative sets of transrectal ultrasound needle biopsies, 35 to 40% were found to have cancer by the transperineal route. This system of biopsy allows a three-dimensional (3D) mapping of the extent and location of cancer and not only helps in fashioning appropriate treatment but also helps sort out which patients should be treated aggressively and which patients would benefit by expectant management. For example, in the current PSA "era," after a thorough pathological examination of radical prostatectomy specimens, we have learned that approximately 15% of patients undergoing radical prostatectomy (and by extrapolation radiation) may have insignificant cancers that could be managed conservatively with a "watchful waiting" approach. In an effort to spare this significant population of patients (estimated at between 10–25,000 annually in the U.S.) from needless surgery or radiation, a 3D mapping biopsy done on patients whose cancers meet certain pathological criteria, can help sort out those patients with extensive cancer who need treatment from those with minimal insignificant cancer who can be watched or geared towards less invasive therapy. (For a more detailed discussion, please refer to PAACT Newsletter, Volume 19, Number 3, September 2003. Newsletter web page: http://www.paactusa.org)

PATHOLOGY, STAGING, AND GRADING

Once a prostate biopsy has been taken, it is sent to the pathologist who determines whether the prostate cells are benign, atypical, show *prostate intraepithelial neoplasia,* or show prostate cancer. Before going any further, a few words about prostate intraepithelial neoplasia and atypia. Some believe that **prostate intraepithelial neoplasia (PIN)** is a precursor to prostate cancer, whereas others believe that it is simply a fellow traveler. Follow-up biopsies in patients with PIN ultimately reveal cancer in approximately 20 to 30% of patients. It should be noted that PIN by itself does not cause an elevation of the PSA.

Areas of *atypia* (cells that are not quite normal but not frankly malignant) are of concern and usually dictate the need for repeat biopsy in the same location where the original atypia was found. When atypia meets certain microscopic criteria, approximately 50% of patients will subsequently develop prostate cancer.

After determining that the cells are cancerous, the pathologist assigns a **Gleason score** to the prostate cancer. This is a very important characterization, which is calculated by adding the primary (predominant) microscopic pattern and secondary (second most prevalent) pattern, as revealed by the biopsy specimens. These patterns are assigned a grade of 1 to 5, where 1 is the least aggressive (most favorable) cancer and 5 is the most vicious, rapidly growing cancer. The grades for each of the two patterns are added for a total score somewhere between 2 and 10. For example, primary pattern Gleason 3 and secondary pattern Gleason 4 give you a Gleason score of 7.

(table 11-1)

STAGES AND TREATMENT OF PROSTATE CANCER

STAGE	SUBSTAGE			TREATMENT OPTIONS
PRIMARY TUMOR (T)				
T1: Microscopic cancer confined to prostate. Gland feels normal on DRE.	**T1a:** Microscopic cancer found in prostate tissue removed for benign conditions. Less than 5% of specimen involved.	T1a		Expectant management with repeat biopsy and frequent PSA determination.
	T1b: Same as T1a but more than 5% of specimen has cancer.	T1b		Expectant management, external radiation therapy or radical prostatectomy depending on the stage, grade, patient's age, and other factors discussed in the text. Brachytherapy and cryoablation are usually contraindicated in stages T1a and T1b.
	T1c: Prostate cancer found through a biopsy done because of an elevated PSA test. This is the most common presentation today in the PSA era.	T1c		Expectant management, external radiation therapy, brachytherapy, cryoablation, or radical prosta-tectomy depending on the stage, grade, patient's age, and other factors discussed in the text.
T2: Palpable cancer confined to prostate gland on DRE.	**T2a:** Tumor involves one lobe or less.	T2a		Same as T1c.
	T2b: Tumor involves more than one lobe.	T2b		Same as T1c.
T3: Palpable cancer beyond the prostate.	**T3a:** One-sided extension beyond the capsule.	T3a		Similar options: external beam therapy, hormonal therapy, cryoablation, and, in selected patients, radical surgery or combination external beam and brachytherapy.
	T3b: Extension beyond the capsule on both sides.	T3b		Same as T3a.

STAGE	SUBSTAGE		TREATMENT OPTIONS
PRIMARY TUMOR (T)			
	T3c: Cancer involves the seminal vesicles.	T3c 	External beam therapy, hormonal therapy, and in exceptional cases cryoablation.
T4: Cancer is fixed and has pushed well beyond the prostate into adjacent structures.		T4 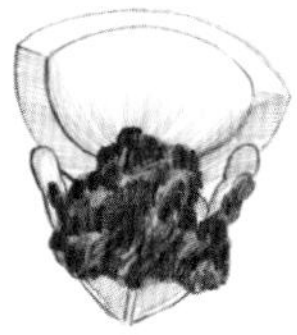	Hormonal therapy. If irradiation therapy is used, it is for easing discomfort but not curative.
REGIONAL NODES (N)			
N0: Nodes are negative.			No additional treatment.
N1: Cancer metastasis in regional node(s).		N1 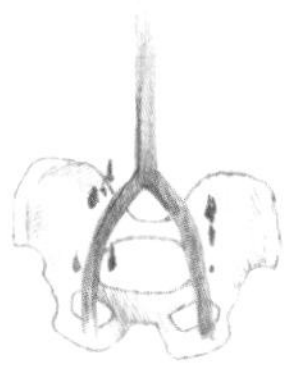	Observation, hormone therapy, and, in exceptional circumstances, external radiation therapy.
DISTANT METASTASIS (SPREAD) (M)			
M0: No clinical or radiologic evidence of metastasis.	**M0: (−PSA):** PSA is unmeasurable.		No additional treatment.
	M0: (+PSA): Measurable PSA after definitive treatment (such as radical prostatectomy, ERT, brachytherapy, or cryoablation) with no evidence of clinical metastasis.	M0 (+PSA) *Rising PSA but no clinical evidence of cancer* 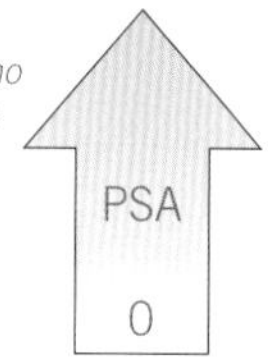 PSA 0	Expectant management, external radiation therapy or hormonal therapy, depending on the time of initial PSA rise and the PSA doubling time.
M1: Cancer metastasis beyond prostate into nonregional node(s), bone(s), and other site(s).	**M1a:** Metastasis to nonregional node(s).	M1a 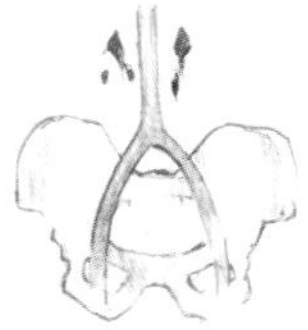	For all M1 categories: expectant management, hormone therapy or palliative external radiation therapy, chemotherapy, or investigational therapy.
	M1b: Metastasis to bone(s).	M1b	Same as M1a.
	M1c: Metastasis to other site(s).		

After determining the extent and location of the cancer, two systems of staging are used. The older Whitmore staging uses A, B, C, and D to describe the extent of the cancer. The more contemporary and universally accepted TNM system assigns a T number to a tumor based on its extent (T1 to T4), with a further division into substages a, b, and c (see Table 11-1). An N designation describes the state of the lymph nodes, where NX is unknown, N0 is negative nodes, and N+ is positive nodes; M indicates the absence or presence of metastasis (the spreading of cancer to other organs). In this setting MX describes the presence of metastasis as unknown, M0 indicates no evidence of metastases, and M+ designates the positive (presence) for metastasis. The TNM stage of the cancer characterizes its present extent and location, whereas the score or grade describes the tumor's potential aggressiveness.

The analogy I give patients is that if one is traveling by car (the malignant tumor) from New York City, where the cancer starts, to Los Angeles, where the cancer can cause serious harm or kill the patient, two important bits of information would be (1) Where is the car now? and (2) How fast is it going? In this analogy, the stage tells you where the cancer is (e.g., still in New York City = T1c), and the grade depicts the speed of the car (e.g., Gleason score 4 = 40 mph; Gleason score 10 = 100 mph). In identifying the parameters of PSA, stage, and Gleason score, probability tables (such as the popular Partin table) can then aid in estimating the likelihood of organ-confined disease, lymphatic involvement, and/or metastatic disease.

EVALUATION

Once prostate cancer has been diagnosed, a *bone scan* (radio isotope study) is performed to exclude the possibility that cancer has spread beyond the prostate into the bones. Some, however, do not advocate this study with a PSA less than 10 because of the very low positive yield.

If the cancer is statistically likely to be confined to the prostate gland based on the DRE, PSA, and biopsy results, computed tomography (CT) scanning, magnetic resonance imaging (MRI), and ProstaScint scans are not routinely ordered. Some studies have suggested the utility of doing endorectal MRI to determine whether to add external radiation therapy to **brachytherapy** (prostate seed implants) and/or whether the neurovascular bundles can be safely preserved during radical retropubic prostatectomy. The utility of these added imaging studies remains unclear at this time.

TREATMENT

To treat or not to treat?

Many patients with untreated prostate cancer survive years without problems, often succumbing to unrelated disorders. In theory, therefore, treatment for this group of patients has only potential for harm. On the other hand, 30,000 Americans will die of the disease this year, a rate second only to lung cancer, and treatment is urgently needed for this group of patients. These observations have led to the dilemma facing both patients and physicians, namely, who to treat and who to watch.

We know that about 80 to 85% of cancers detected by PSA screening are significant and ideally require treatment, especially in men with a life expectancy of more than 10 years. Conversely, 15 to 20% of cancers detected by PSA screening may be insignificant and not require treatment. Template-guided transperineal saturation biopsy (see the section "3D Mapping," above) helps screen out this latter population from the need of aggressive therapy. In general, men with a Gleason score of 7 or more should be treated, particularly if they have life expectancy of over 10 years.

Treatment options: Broadly speaking, there are seven modalities of treatment. These include expectant management (observation), hormonal therapy, external beam radiation therapy (IMRT, proton beam), brachytherapy (Pd 103, I-125, HDR), cryosurgery (cryoablation or freezing), radical prostatectomy (retropubic, perineal, laparoscopic), and cytotoxic chemotherapy or other investigational therapies.

It is important in considering treatment options for both patient and urologist to address the risk-benefit ratio of any particular strategy. Factors affecting that ratio include host (patient) characteristics, such as age, the absence or presence of other diseases, and the patient's emotional response in contemplating potential treatment side effects versus the psychological burden of managing with an untreated cancer. Another factor is the particular character of the cancer itself. Prognostic features include the PSA value, biopsy evaluation of the tumor, the Gleason score, and the tumor stage. These characteristics lead to the concept of risk categories, which include low, intermediate, and high. Patients in the low-risk group have T1c or T2a lesions, a PSA of less than 10, and Gleason scores of 6 or less. Those of intermediate risk are stage T2c, or PSA greater than 10 but less than 20, and a Gleason score of 7. Patients at high risk have more advanced disease, with a stage greater than T2c, or PSA over 20, or a Gleason score of 8 or 9.

11

Table 11-1 summarizes recommended treatments based on stage, grade, PSA, and patient status. For example, consider a T2 stage, which is a palpable cancer confined to the gland on DRE. This pathologic stage can be divided into substage T2a, which is tumor in only one side of the prostate, or T2b, indicating cancer on both sides. The best therapy for an older man with a low Gleason score, low PSA, and the presence of significant health issues may be either observation or hormonal therapy. Radical prostatectomy is usually reserved for otherwise healthy men less than 70 years of age who have at least a 10-year life expectancy. Less invasive procedures, such as cryoablation, brachytherapy, and/or external radiation therapy are offered to patients over 70 or patients having a life expectancy of less than 10 years or who prefer not to have an operation.

While Table 11-1 offers a general guideline for treatment, following are a few words about each specific treatment.

Watchful waiting: Watchful waiting is usually recommended for older patients who are not likely to live long enough to benefit from the treatment or for those whose tumor characteristics (low Gleason score, low volume disease) make it likely they have a small, possibly insignificant cancer. Watchful waiting does not, however, imply no treatment. Dietary and lifestyle modifications include limiting the amount of fat (especially animal fat), increasing vegetable intake, limiting dietary calcium to less than 1 gram per day, increasing the consumption of soy isoflavones, taking adequate selenium (200 micrograms per day), vitamin E, lycopene, green tea, and participating in relaxation and/or meditation.

Radical prostatectomy: The surgical approach radical prostatectomy offers the best long term results in properly selected patients. As such, it is the first recommendation for those men less than 70 years old, with more than a 10-year life expectancy and no other significant medical contraindications. A nerve-sparing radical prostatectomy should be performed in patients whose disease is likely to be confined to the prostate. Complications of the procedure include incontinence and impotence. In experienced hands, the risk of severe incontinence requiring an artificial sphincter should be less than 2%. The chance of mild (usually insignificant) incontinence, requiring the use of one or two small pads per day, is usually between 10 and 20%. My personal experience with over 1000 cases is that this is an extremely well tolerated and effective procedure in *appropriately* selected patients. After radical prostatectomy the PSA should become undetectable or unmeasurable, usually reported as less than 0.05, 0.1, or 0.2, depending on the laboratory.

Unfortunately, even in men whose cancers preoperatively appear confined (stages T1 and T2), about 30% will experience a biological recurrence (rising PSA after a treatment known as PSA failure). When PSA levels become clearly detectable after surgery, recurrent cancer is the likely cause. The tumor can recur locally (in or near the original operative site) or

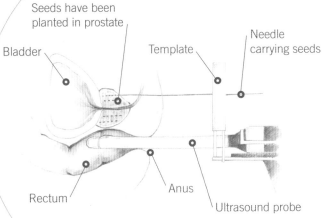

(figure 11-11)

Brachytherapy consists of implanting 60 to 120 radioactive seeds directly into the prostate to treat cancer.

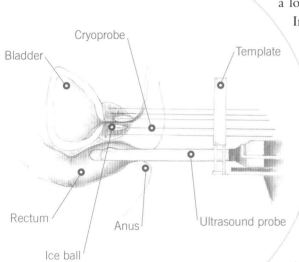

Bladder

Cryoprobe

Template

Rectum

Anus

Ultrasound probe

Ice ball

(figure 11-12)

Cryoablation of the prostate consists of freezing the prostate from –35° C to –40° C by placing probes, known as cryoprobes, under ultrasound guidance into the prostate.

distantly (outside the prostate, usually in neighboring lymph nodes or in bone), or both locally and distantly. As a rule of thumb, detectable PSA levels within one year after surgery indicate distant spread and a low likelihood that external radiation therapy will be helpful. Increased PSA values appearing several years postoperatively suggest local recurrence, and one can anticipate a reasonable response to "salvage" external radiation therapy aimed at the prostate "bed."

I find that patients have difficulty in understanding how cancer recurs at distant sites if the primary tumor, in this case the prostate, was removed and the preoperative evaluation suggested the absence of metastatic disease. In explanation, consider an area of 1 to 2 mm can represent roughly one million cancer cells, but one may require the volume of a small marble before conventional imaging studies can detect malignant tumor spread beyond the confines of the prostate. It follows, therefore, that areas containing several nests of microscopic cancer can remain undetected preoperatively, even with rigorous evaluation. The good news is that by the time the PSA first starts to rise after radical surgery, it may take six to eight years before the cancer can be detected with imaging tests. It may take another three to six years after that before the patient dies (thus 9 to 14 years after the PSA first starts to rise; in addition, it may take several years after surgery for the PSA to rise from these undetected nests of cancer cells).

SURGICAL ALTERNATIVES

In discussing surgical alternatives, note that radical prostatectomy can also be carried out via the perineal route (the area between the genitals and anus), and more recently some centers have approached this operation laparoscopically.

External radiation therapy is often reserved for older patients, usually 75 years, or younger patients with significant medical problems that pose an increased surgical risk. Recent advances in external radiation therapy are exciting, and it is hoped that by the time of publication of this book, *intensity-modulated radiation therapy (IMRT)* will be the new standard of care. With radiation therapy there is always the risk of "collateral" damage, whereby normal surrounding tissues may be damaged. IMRT is designed to minimize collateral damage while increasing the dose of radiation to the targeted prostate gland. Complications of external radiation therapy may involve bladder and bowel, and erectile dysfunction reportedly occurs in 40 to 60% of patients.

Brachytherapy was designed to decrease the risk of collateral damage to surrounding tissues while delivering a higher dose to the prostate (see Figure 11-11). This technique consists of implanting 60 to 120 radioactive seeds (tiny metal pellets containing I-125 or Pd 103) directly into the prostate. The location and number of seeds are designated by a computer program through a process known as *dosimetry*. This procedure

(figure 11-13)

Testosterone thermostat (regulation of testosterone production): Since many benign and malignant prostate cells require testosterone to grow, treatment may be aimed at blocking testosterone production.

(A) The hypothalamus is the "thermostat" that regulates the production of testosterone ⓣ. If production decreases, the hypothalamus releases a hormone called luteinizing hormone–releasing hormone (LHRH), which stimulates the pituitary gland to release luteinizing hormone (LH). ① LHRH release is blocked by LHRH superagonists (Lupron, Zoladex), LHRH agonists (Abarelix), and estrogen.

(B) The LH released from the pituitary circulates in the blood and stimulates the Leydig cells in the testes to produce testosterone.

(C) The Leydig cells produce testosterone in response to LH from the pituitary.

(D) The increase in testosterone production turns off the production of LHRH by the hypothalamus, thus producing a negative feedback loop. If testosterone production falls, LHRH production is stimulated.

(E) Testosterone from the testes stimulates the prostate cell.

(F) Testosterone is converted to dihydrotestosterone (DHT) by the enzyme 5-alpha-reductase. Both testosterone and DHT (also known as androgens) stimulate the prostate cell, whether benign or malignant, when they attach to the androgen receptor (AR) on the prostate cell. DHT, however, has more potent androgen effects. ② Proscar and Avodart block 5-alpha-reductase and inhibit production of DHT. ③ The effects of testosterone and DHT on the androgen receptor are blocked by Flutamide, Casodex, and Nilandron.

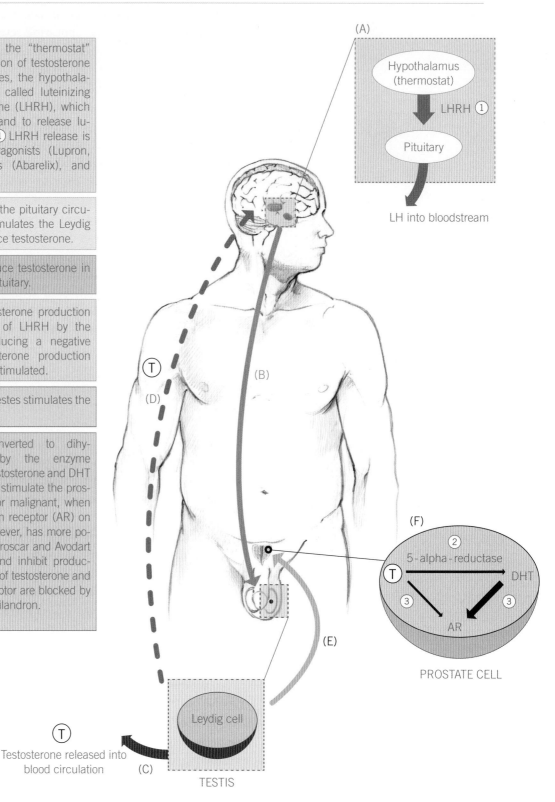

is performed on an outpatient basis with a quick return to normal activity. Brachytherapy is ideally suited for low-grade, low-stage cancers in patients with smaller prostates and few symptoms of BPH (LUTS). The results in carefully selected patients are equivalent to radical surgery at the 10-year mark. My personal experience with over 300 carefully selected patients undergoing this procedure is quite favorable.

Freezing the prostate is a newer modality that in my opinion holds promise for patients with higher-stage, higher-grade disease who may be incurable by other means. Cryoablation, or cryotherapy, consists of freezing the prostate from −35 to −40 degrees Celsius by placing probes (known as *cryoprobes),* under ultrasound guidance, through the perineum into the prostate (see Figure 11-12). Three- and five-year results are very encouraging. My personal limited and early experience with this procedure, done under the guidance and supervision of a world expert on cryosurgery with more than 45 carefully selected patients (high Gleason scores of 8 and 9, and high stage), has been extremely encouraging with unmeasurable PSA levels in over 90% of the patients at the 6- to 12-month mark.

Combination ERT and *brachytherapy* are used in patients at high risk, with a PSA greater than 10, a Gleason score greater than or equal to 7, or stage greater than T2a.

GENERAL REMARKS ON TREATMENT OPTIONS

Proper patient selection is crucial on recommending treatments, such as radical prostatectomy, brachytherapy, cryoablation, or IMRT, and can make the difference between treatment success with low complications and treatment failure with high complications. To quote my mentor, Dr. Willet F. Whitmore Jr., chief of Memorial Sloan-Kettering Cancer Center from 1946–1983, "Selection is the silent partner of the successful cancer surgeon." Additionally, it is my strong belief that urologists should be versed in all treatment modalities for prostate cancer so that they can fit an appropriate treatment to a particular patient rather than try to fit a patient into a particular treatment in which they have special expertise. In other words, it is important for the urologist to have in his armamentarium the entire set of tools for treating prostate cancer so as not to fall into the trap exemplified by the saying, "If your only tool is a hammer, you tend to treat everything like a nail."

HORMONAL THERAPY

The male hormone testosterone is necessary in maintaining normal prostatic function. Testosterone removal in most patients with prostate cancer produces regression of the malignancy, or at least a definitely retarded growth rate. In exceedingly rare anecdotal circumstances, eradication has been described.

While most prostate cancer cells are initially androgen-sensitive, requiring testosterone to grow, a small population of cells are androgen-independent; that is, they don't require testosterone for growth. Eventually these androgen-insensitive cells grow and may lead to hormone failure, wherein continued hormonal therapy is not efficacious. For this reason, hormonal therapy is not considered curative. It is, however, useful in many circumstances and is best reserved for those patients whose cancers have spread beyond the confines of the prostate (N+ M+). In patients with demonstrable metastatic cancer of the prostate, approximately 50% will survive three years and 25% will survive five years.

There is no general agreement on when to start hormonal therapy, that is, early versus delayed. Does one start early (as soon as the PSA starts to rise) or should treatment be delayed (until the cancer has progressed to the point that it is causing symptoms)? Cogent arguments exist in both camps. My personal bias, not based on strong scientific evidence, is to start hormonal therapy relatively early but to do so on an intermittent basis.

Hormone therapy is designed to interfere with the effects of testosterone by either blocking its release (castration) or preventing its action on cancer cells (antiandrogen).

Androgen withdrawal: Castration (androgen withdrawal) can be achieved surgically or medically. The surgical approach, in vogue for many years, is performed with much less frequency today. Medical castration is achieved with the administration of a variety of substances that interfere with the production of testosterone. To help understand how these work, consider that the body has its own built-in thermostat or feedback mechanism for controlling the testosterone level (see Figure 11-13). If an area in the brain senses low testosterone, the *hypothalamus* secretes luteinizing hormone–releasing hormone (LHRH), which stimulates the *pituitary gland* (in the brain) to secrete LH. This in turn drives the Leydig cells (in the testes) to produce more testosterone. This feedback mechanism or thermostat can be interfered with by blocking the release of LH with estrogens (female hormones), with an LHRH superagonist (for example, LUPRON, ZOLADEX), or with an LHRH antagonist (ABARELIX, recently FDA-approved). Superagonists cause an initial surge in testosterone, which occasionally result in worse symptoms, known as "flare," requiring the preuse of antiandrogens (see the following section, "Antiandrogens").

Antiandrogens: Antiandrogens prevent the action of testosterone on cancer cells. Testosterone must bind to receptors on the cell surface (known as *androgen receptors*) before it can act to promote cell growth. Drugs such as FLUTAMIDE (EULEXIN), the first to be used clinically, NILUTAMIDE (NILANDRON), and BICALUTAMIDE (CASODEX), the most popular in use today, bind to these receptors and prevent testosterone from entering the cell to stimulate cell growth. While these antiandrogens work well initially, cancer cells may adapt and ultimately sustain stimulation by the antiandrogen. Indeed, if the PSA starts to rise, it is time to stop them, and paradoxically in about 25 to 40% of patients the PSA might decrease. In this instance, the cancer cells have adapted so they are now stimulated by the antiandrogen. This phenomenon was first described with flutamide.

Neoadjuvant hormonal therapy, such as an LHRH superagonist, is used to shrink the prostate if it is too large for brachytherapy or cryosurgery

236

and to improve the effectiveness of external radiation therapy in high-risk patients.

There is significant risk of side effects with LHRH agonists due to testosterone withdrawal, such as loss of libido, impotence, increase in body fat, decrease in skeletal muscle mass, fatigue, and bone demineralization. With this in mind, some have suggested the use of intermittent androgen blockade, such as Zoladex or Lupron, until the PSA becomes unmeasurable. Patients are then carefully observed until the PSA rises to a preselected value before restarting the hormones. I routinely use intermittent androgen ablation but have no scientific basis for taking this approach. I think overall the patients feel better on this approach.

Herbs: PC Spes consists of a hormone preparation of eight Chinese herbs. It has produced significant response in patients who have failed hormonal therapy. Unfortunately, it was taken off the market when several batches were found to contain COUMADIN (a blood thinner), XANAX (an antianxiety drug), and an estrogen called *diethylstilbestrol (DES)*. It has recently been reintroduced on a limited basis in the so-called pure form. It is not under FDA control and caution must be exercised in its use.

■

WHAT YOU NEED TO KNOW

BPH

⫸ A large prostate does not constitute an indication for medical or surgical therapy.

⫸ Patients with a low symptom score of under 8 to 10 are best managed by watchful waiting unless they have a condition known as "silent" prostatism (advanced changes of urinary outflow obstruction but no symptoms experienced by the patient).

⫸ In the management of uncomplicated BPH, the patient should play a central role in determining *his* need for treatment, so that the patient and his physician can determine whether the benefits of a given treatment (improving symptoms) outweigh the risks (side effects, cost, and complications).

⫸ With the exception of advanced cases at first presentation, surgical therapy should only be entertained after failure of adequate medical therapy.

⫸ Combination therapy with an alpha-blocker, such as Hytrin, Cardura, Flomax, or Uroxatral, and an alpha-reductase inhibitor, such as Proscar or Avodart, appears to achieve better results than with either agent alone.

⫸ To entertain a minimally invasive procedure for BPH, it is incumbent on the patient to determine his urologist's personal experience with that modality of therapy, including the number of patients done to date and the urologist's personal experience with their outcome.

PROSTATE CANCER

⫸ PSA is not disease-specific. It is not a marker for cancer. It is prostate-specific. The most common cause of PSA elevation to the 4 to 10 range is BPH, not cancer (70% of men with a PSA between 4 and 10 ng/mL do not have prostate cancer).

⫸ Prostate cancer has an unpredictable natural history and occurs in a variety of forms, including a latent or dormant form that does not cause disease, a very slow-growing variety of clinical prostate cancer, and a rapidly dividing aggressive cancer that can metastasize. Therefore, a patient cannot extrapolate from the experience of his neighbor or friend in making his decision relative to therapeutic options. Prostate cancer is variable, and what held true for your neighbor, friend, or relative may not hold true for you.

⫸ Regardless of the stage or grade of your cancer, it is helpful to adopt as many of the diet and lifestyle modifications discussed in the text. In this way, the prostate cancer patient can immediately do something positive for himself. Even if these measures don't ultimately help in controlling the cancer, side benefits include loss of body fat, lowering of cholesterol, and decrease in the need for blood pressure medication—and, in diabetics, decrease in the requirement for medication.

⫸ Information on prostate cancer is readily available, and every patient should take the time to familiarize himself with the pros and cons of various treatment options available to him, on the basis of his tumor characteristics, age, and overall health status. Additionally, in considering any form of surgical procedure for prostate cancer (or BPH), whether surgery or minimally invasive therapy, it is incumbent on the patient to ask about his physician's personal experience with the procedure, including the number of patients who have undergone the procedure to date and their outcomes.

⫸ I try to point out that there is no single best treatment universally applicable to all patients. However, treatment can and should be individualized, so that each patient gets the treatment best suited for him. Treatment should be customized to honor each patient's own uniqueness.

FOR MORE INFORMATION

▶ **American Cancer Society**
5999 Clifton Road NE
Atlanta, GA 30329
800-ACS-2345
Web: www.cancer.org

▶ **American Foundation for Urologic Disease**
1128 N. Charles Street
Baltimore, MD 21201
800-242-2383
Web: www.afud.org

▶ **National Cancer Institute**
Cancer Information Service
31 Center Drive, MSC2580, Building 31
Suite 10A03
Bethesda, MD 20892
800-422-6237
Web: cis.nci.nih.gov
Latest, most accurate cancer information for patients, families, and the general public.

▶ **National Institutes of Health**
9000 Rockville Pike
Bethesda, MD 20892
Web: www.nih.gov

▶ **Man-to-Man Group**
American Cancer Society
344 E. Foothills Parkway, 2E
Fort Collins, CO 80525
970-226-0148
Web: www.acs.org
Education and support groups throughout the nation provide information about the diagnosis and treatment options for prostate cancer.

▶ **Us Too International**
5003 Fairview Avenue
Downers Grove, IL 60515
800-808-7866
Fax: 630-795-1602
Web: www.ustoo.org
Prostate cancer support group, offering education and emotional support through an international support network.

SUGGESTED READING

▶ **Prostate Cancer**
D. Bostwick. 1999.
Atlanta: American Cancer Society.

▶ **The Taste for Living: Mike Milken's Favorite Recipes for Fighting Cancer**
B. Ginsberg and M. Milken. 1998.
Prostate Cancer Foundation.

▶ **A Primer on Prostate Cancer (The Empowered Patient's Guide)**
Stephen B. Strum and Donna Pogliano. 2002.
Life Extension Media.

▶ **Prostate Brachytherapy Made Complicated, 2nd edition**
K . Wallner. 2001. Smartmedicine Press.

▶ **Guide to Surviving Prostate Cancer**
Patrick Walsh and Janet Farrow-Worthington. 2001.
Warner Books.
Excellent book: I strongly urge all my patients with prostate cancer to read it.

INTERNET

▶ Web: my.webmd.com
Society with a variety of information for prostate cancer patients.

▶ **American Urologic Association**
Web: www.auanet.org
Many services, including publications and guidelines.

▶ **CapCure**
Web: www.capcure.org
Largest private funder of prostate cancer research in the United States.

▶ Web: www.clinicaltrials.com
Comprehensive information for clinical trials conducted nationwide.

▶ Web: www.fda.gov
Government lists of proven drugs for prostate cancer; explains how drugs are approved.

▶ Web: www.nlm.nih.gov
Published information, current and archival.

Gladly I think of the days
When all my members were limber,
All except one.
Those days are certainly gone,
Now all my members are stiff,
All except one.

—*Goethe*

THE AUTHOR

12

JAYANT DEY, MD, is an endocrinologist with Endocrinology Consultants in Tupelo, Mississippi. He completed his residency in internal medicine at the State University of New York and Joslin Diabetes Center at Syracuse, New York. His fellowship in endocrinology was at the Alton Ochsner Medical Foundation in New Orleans, Louisiana. He is currently the medical director of the Diabetes Institute of North Mississippi and a clinical instructor for the University of Mississippi Family Practice Residency Program. Board-certified in internal medicine and endocrinology and metabolism, he has lectured extensively on topics in endocrinology and published an article for physicians on male sexual dysfunction in the Mayo Clinic Proceedings.

12 | MALE SEXUAL FUNCTION

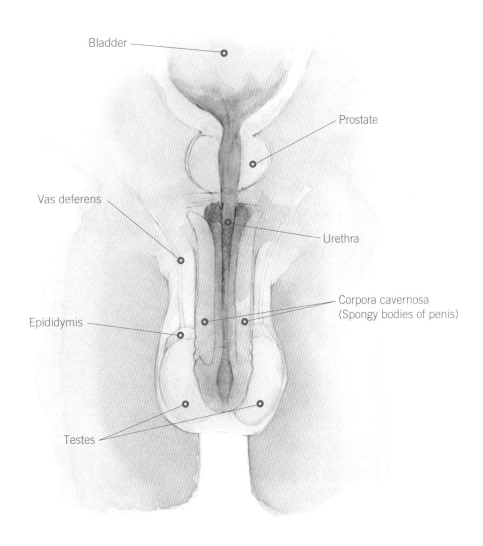

Bladder

Prostate

Vas deferens

Urethra

Epididymis

Corpora cavernosa
(Spongy bodies of penis)

Testes

(figure 12-1*)*

Male sexual system. The male sexual response is a complex interplay of psychological and physical factors. When a man is sexually aroused, the nervous system sends signals that cause blood vessels to the penis to dilate and the spongy bodies within the penis to fill with blood. This blocks the veins that take blood away from the penis, which becomes rigid in preparation for sexual intercourse. When orgasm occurs, seminal fluid, which is secreted by the prostate and seminal vesicles, is combined with sperm from the testes and epididymis. The muscles that line these channels contract, propelling the seminal fluid out through the urethra (ejaculation).

Sexual behavior is a universal and integral part of human existence. Sexual functioning is part of life with no clear beginning and much less clear an ending, extending well beyond the reproductive years. A vast majority of the senior population is interested in, and capable of, an active, satisfying sex life.

As we age, women do not ordinarily lose their physical capacity for orgasm (sexual climax) or men their potential for erection and ejaculation. There is, however, a gradual slowing of response, especially in men—a process currently considered part of "normal" aging but perhaps eventually treatable or even reversible. When problems with sexual performance occur, they should not be viewed as inevitable but rather as the result of disease, disability, medication side effect, or psychological causes and potentially curable with proper intervention.

MALE SEXUAL FUNCTION

EFFECT OF AGING

Older men often notice distinct changes in sexual functioning, although these vary greatly from man to man. It may take somewhat longer to attain an erection than when young. Sexual partners of elder men need to understand that the men may need more manual stimulation, like fondling of the sexual areas, to achieve an erection. The erection may not be quite as firm or as large as in earlier years. The ejaculation may also take longer to achieve, which can be an asset for the female partner because of the extra stimulation that can help her achieve an orgasm. The orgasm for the male is shorter than when younger. Some older men will notice that the volume of the ejaculate decreases slightly and the force of the ejaculate also decreases with age.

The older man also loses some of the focus on orgasm. The partner should not assume that he is not enjoying the intimate experience when the man does not ejaculate. On the contrary, older men can achieve a great deal of pleasure from sexual intimacy and yet not have an orgasm or ejaculate. Finally, the loss of erection following orgasm may be more rapid, followed by a longer "refractory period," or the time it takes to achieve another erection after ejaculation. It may take anywhere from 12 to 24 hours or longer before he can achieve another erection and/or is interested in intercourse again.

As we get older, our senses of taste, smell, and sight diminish and our capacity for strenuous activities and exertion decline. Naturally our sexual sensations and the ability to perform sexually will modestly decline. According to some researchers, if a man remains sexually active in his youth and middle years, he can continue to be active in his later years. However, if a man stops having sex in his 50s and 60s, the chance of becoming impotent is greater. If he and his partner are interested and are able to use special techniques that rely heavily on genital stimulation, then he will be able to stay sexually active well into his advanced years.

As shown in Table 12-1, being familiar with the normal physical changes that occur with aging could help older men overcome the

(table 12-1)

THE SEX AND AGING MYTH BUSTER

MYTH	REALITY
Impotence is a natural consequence of aging.	Not true
Sexual activity can be dangerous for the elderly.	Not if common sense is used
The sex drive or libido inevitably diminishes with advancing years for both men and women.	Not true
Emission of semen is debilitating.	Certainly not true
Sexual activity for older persons is immoral and suggests a "dirty mind."	Not so in the present American society
Sexual desires cease with menopause.	Not true
Sex is only for the young.	*Ha-ha-ha!*

anxiety of sexual inadequacy and also prompt them to seek professional help if needed. Evaluation and intervention by a health care provider may be needed and can be extremely effective in most cases of persistent impotence.

FEMALE PARTNERS

Women generally experience little serious loss of sexual capacity due to age alone. Those changes that do occur—mainly in regard to decrease in length, width, elasticity, and lubrication of the vagina—can usually be traced directly to lowered levels of the female hormone estrogen during and after menopause. The loss of lubrication can often result in painful intercourse, but fortunately this condition can be easily treated with lubricants, like KY jelly, or by using estrogen-containing vaginal creams.

Most healthy women can expect unimpaired sexual activity to the end of their lives if that was their pattern earlier. Studies indicate that the older woman has no physical limitation in her capacity to achieve and enjoy orgasm. However, at the time of orgasm the contractions are less and some women may find them painful. The relaxation phase after orgasm occurs more rapidly for the postmenopausal woman, but she is still capable of achieving multiple orgasms, as in her earlier years. (See Chapter 13, "Female Sexual Function.")

MALE SEXUAL DYSFUNCTION

MEDICAL ASPECTS

Impotence (the inability to maintain an erection adequate for sexual intercourse) has been a devastating problem since the beginning of recorded history. In the bible, the Lord inflicted impotence—described as living death—on Abimelech because he wanted to have sexual relations with Abraham's wife (Genesis 20:3). It is no surprise that impotence has been long regarded as a curse. In medieval times, it was thought to be caused by witches casting spells while acting as agents of the devil.

Misconceptions about what causes impotence have persisted into this century. As recently as the 1970s, experts including Masters and Johnson insisted that virtually all causes of impotence stemmed from psychological causes. It is now known that an erection is primarily caused by increased blood supply to the penis, triggered by neurological controls and facilitated in the presence of an appropriate hormonal milieu and psychological priming. Interference with any one or more of the above mechanisms causes difficulties with sexual functioning in men.

A crucial turning point occurred in 1975, when an expert committee of the World Health Organization (WHO) concluded, "problems in human sexuality are more important to the well-being and health of individuals in many cultures than has been recognized." This set the stage for the society's, as well as the medical community's, acceptance of impotence as a disorder that exacts an enormous toll on the affected man and his relationships. This also led to more interest in, and funding of, scientific studies into the causes and treatment of impotence. In 1993 the National Institutes of Health (NIH) Consensus Development Panel on Impotence recognized this as an "important public health problem" and proposed the less pejorative and more precise term *erectile dysfunction (ED)* to signify "the inability to attain and/or maintain penile erection sufficient for satisfactory sexual performance."

The extent of ED has been notoriously difficult to gauge. In the past, results of various "sex surveys" yielded significant underestimation of this problem. Not until the Massachusetts Male Aging Study was ED's prevalence assessed in a scientifically rigorous way in the United States. The results of the Massachusetts Male Aging Study, published in 1994, revealed that ED was far more common than previously estimated, a problem that to some degree affects more than half of all men aged 40 to 70. Within the study participants, ED became increasingly prevalent with age; by age 70, nearly 70% of men were affected. A small minority of these men sought medical advice regarding evaluation or treatment for ED.

ILLNESS OR DISABILITY AND SEXUAL POTENCY

Sexual expression among the elderly is a predictor of general health. The incidence of illness and disability increases with age. Although they can affect sexuality in later life, even the most serious diseases rarely warrant stopping sexual activity. Men with diabetes have a threefold higher risk of suffering from ED. Surgical removal of the prostate gland used to be a frequent cause of ED in the past. New surgical techniques that save

THE "BENT SPIKE" SYNDROME

Bending of the erect penis was first described by French surgeon François de la Peyronie in 1743. It is estimated that 1% of men have Peyronie's disease. The disease may occur at any age, but is mostly found in middle-aged men. A tough plaque forms in the erectile tissue of the penis, which causes it to bend when erect. This can make intercourse difficult or painful. It may also be associated with erectile dysfunction. Often the condition may resolve spontaneously within one or two years, but some individuals may try treatments with relatively innocuous supplements such as vitamin E and Potaba. In persistent cases, surgery may be recommended. Consultation with a urologist is necessary.

CONDITIONS ASSOCIATED WITH ERECTILE DYSFUNCTION

- Cigarette smoking
- Excessive alcohol consumption or other drug abuse
- Psychological problems (anxiety, depression, partner conflict, etc.)
- Diabetes
- High blood pressure
- Hormonal disorders (thyroid, testosterone, etc.)
- Blockages in blood supply to the penis
- Trauma to the spine or groin area
- Prostate cancer surgery
- Many medications (antidepressants, blood pressure medications, etc.)

the nerves going to the penis have significantly increased the chance of returning to the level of sexual activity prior to prostate surgery.

Cigarette smoking, especially when combined with other health problems, greatly increases a man's risk for ED. Excessive consumption of alcohol reduces potency in men and delays orgasm in women. A variety of medications including antidepressants, tranquilizers, and certain high blood pressure drugs can cause or worsen ED. Other drugs can lead to failure to ejaculate in men and reduced sexual desire in women. Such effects may be reversed if the medicine is stopped or changed. A doctor can often prescribe a drug with less sexual effect if he or she realizes that this is important to the patient.

Heart disease, especially if a heart attack has occurred, leads many older people to give up sex altogether for fear of causing another attack. Yet the risk of death during sexual intercourse is very low. Although a doctor's advice is needed, sex usually can and should be resumed an average of 12 to 16 weeks after a heart attack, depending on physical conditioning. An active sex life may in fact decrease the risk of a future heart attack.

Certain diseases like stroke or deforming arthritis may interfere with the physical aspects of sexual interaction. Proper instructions and rehabilitation by physical or occupational therapists can help make up for any weakness or paralysis that may have occurred. Exercise, rest, warm baths, and changes in position and timing of sexual activity (such as avoiding early morning hours of pain and stiffness) can be helpful in patients with muscle or joint inflammation.

SEEKING MEDICAL ADVICE

If you suffer from ED, then the family doctor or the primary care provider is the first health professional to see, many of whom now routinely treat this disorder. Depending on the individual clinical situation, the primary provider may refer you to a specialist. The following specialists play a role in the diagnosis and treatment of ED:

1. Urologists are surgical specialists who specialize in diseases of the genitals and urinary tract.

2. Endocrinologists are medical specialists who evaluate and treat persons suffering from hormonal and body chemistry imbalances and also chronic diseases like diabetes, high cholesterol, and high blood pressure.

3. Psychologists and psychiatrists are specialists who treat psychological causes of ED, such as depression, anxiety, and relationship problems.

ED is a sensitive subject for most people, and it is understandable that men feel somewhat reluctant to discuss it with their providers. Although not common, an increasing number of health care professionals are now cognizant of the high prevalence of this disorder and may initiate discussion on sexual subjects during appropriate encounters. The following list provides various tips that may help you communicate your concerns about evaluation and treatment for erectile dysfunction to your health providers.

- When you call to make an appointment, tell the receptionist or nurse that you'd like to see the provider about a possible sexual problem. If you are not comfortable giving this information over the phone, simply say you'd like to make an appointment for a checkup because you want to discuss some personal health concerns.

- When you talk to your provider, be as clear and to the point as you can. Use language that you are comfortable with. Make sure the provider understands exactly what you mean to say. For example, you may say, "I've been reading about erectile dysfunction and how common it is among men my age. I have some concerns about this issue that I want to discuss with you."

- Your spouse or sexual partner may want to accompany you to the clinic visit and is often the one to initiate discussion on this subject with the provider.

- Remember, you have as much right to ask for medical help for erectile dysfunction as you do for any other health condition. If your provider does not seem comfortable or interested in discussing erectile dysfunction, see another doctor or ask for a referral to a specialist.

Because ED has many different causes, a careful diagnostic workup is important to find the underlying problem and determine the best treatment options. This may take one or more visits. If possible, ask your partner to come with you to at least some of the appointments.

The evaluation starts with the medical history. Your doctor will ask you a series of questions to understand the specifics of your ED. Some questions about your sexual history and functioning may seem very personal, but this information is important to identify and enable successful treatment. You may write down some notes about your health and lifestyle as well as your specific concerns before your clinic appointment to help refresh your memory at the time of your visit.

Diagnosing and treating underlying, reversible causes of ED are important functions of your sexual health specialist. For example, if a

DOCTOR'S DIARY

Bill D., 58, had been a diabetic for 12 years. He had been married for 25 years to a wonderful wife, Jean, who was also a patient of mine. She told me that Bill had not been able to get an erection for the past year, but he was too embarrassed to tell me about it. I told her that diabetes is associated with erectile dysfunction and that effective treatments are available. She told me that he would never tell me about it and would be upset if he knew that she had told me. I reassured her that their sex life was important and that I could help.

At my next visit with Bill D., I asked, "Bill, are you having any new problems?"

He said no. That didn't surprise me. In the 20 years that I had been practicing medicine, I had seen many people hesitant to discuss their sexual lives. They get embarrassed, but I assure them that it is a common problem amenable to treatment. I said, "Bill, you know I see a lot of patients with diabetes, and many begin to experience problems with erections after a period of time. Sometimes the diabetes affects the blood vessels or nerve supply, and that can affect the ability to perform."

He looked down and said, "Doc, I didn't know what was happening. Jean understands, but I even started going to bed at a different time because I knew I would have trouble. Is there anything we can do about it?"

I told Bill that I wanted to do some simple tests as a part of the evaluation, but since he had a good heart exam recently, I prescribed Viagra. Bill had heard some negative reports in the press, but I told him that it is a safe medication and that it has helped millions of men. I told him that it may not work for every man, but it was worth a try. I told him it might take a half-hour to an hour to work, so give it some time. I scheduled a follow-up with Bill a month later.

"Doc, I can't thank you enough. The medicine works great. I had a good erection, even better than before! Jean is happy and so am I!"

It certainly is gratifying to me as a physician to see a medicine that has such a quick and favorable response. However, I caution my patients that it is not for everybody; however, the vast majority do great.

- Stop cigarette smoking.
- Avoid excessive alcohol intake.
- Stop illicit drug use (marijuana, cocaine, heroin).
- Stop or change medications interfering with sexual functioning under your doctor's supervision.
- Correct hormonal imbalances (thyroid, pituitary, sex hormones, etc.).
- Treat uncontrolled diabetes.
- Resolve untreated or undiagnosed depression, performance anxiety, or psychological conflicts.
- Surgically correct anatomical or blood flow abnormalities of the penis.

blood test shows that your testosterone (male hormone) level is too low, the doctor may prescribe testosterone replacement therapy. This therapy can be given as regular injections or in the form of a testosterone-containing skin patch or gel. If ED does not improve with hormone therapy, the erection problem may be due to another cause.

Some men have erection problems that are due mainly or entirely to stress, depression, anxiety, or other psychological problems. These men frequently benefit from psychotherapy or counseling. Sex therapy is a more structured type of counseling that usually includes specific exercises for the couple. Please understand that every person is different, and what works with one man may not work with another.

TREATMENT FOR ERECTILE DYSFUNCTION

Selecting a treatment for ED is a personal decision, and you should receive information from your physician regarding the various options available for your specific situation as well as their safety and efficacy. The ease of use and acceptability of the treatment option to you and your partner are important considerations. The cost of the treatment options and insurance coverage of part or all of the treatment choices should be addressed up front. We now discuss some of the specific treatment options for ED.

VIAGRA

With its relative ease of use, favorable safety profile, and remarkable efficacy in treatment of ED of different underlying causes, SILDENAFIL (VIAGRA) in 1998 revolutionized the treatment of ED and made it more acceptable for providers other than specialists to initiate treatment in their practices. The approval of Viagra by the Food and Drug Administration (FDA) also touched off an unprecedented media firestorm, which helped create more awareness among men silently suffering from this disorder and allowed them to seek medical help.

A normal erection requires an increased blood supply to spongelike erectile bodies in the penis, and ED frequently results from inadequate penile blood flow. Viagra blocks the effect of a certain enzyme whose action is to constrict the muscles around small blood vessels in the penis and choke off blood flow. Thus Viagra works by relaxing the erectile tissues of the penis that make room for blood to enter the penis. Like a sponge, these tissues fill with blood, causing them to press against the veins taking blood away from the penis. This traps the blood in the penis, making it firm enough for intercourse.

Viagra should be taken approximately 30 to 60 minutes before engaging in sexual intimacy to enable the drug to exert its optimum effect. The effectiveness of this drug usually lasts four to six hours though some men report the beneficial effects to last longer. For best results the drug should be taken at least a few hours away from fatty food or alcohol consumption to promote its absorption from the gut. A man must have sexual stimulation for this medication to work. Viagra does not apparently affect a man's libido, ejaculation, or orgasm. Viagra may be useful to men with various types of ED, including impotence caused by psychological problems, diabetes, or spinal cord injury. The tablets are available in various strengths, and the doctor may need to adjust and titrate to the most effective dose in individual patients.

Headaches, flushing, sour taste in stomach, and nasal congestion are common side effects. A very small percentage of men report a temporary visual disturbance mainly as increased perception of brightness and blue haze. *Nitrates and nitroglycerin are medications for the treatment of chest pain in patients with heart disease and should not be taken with Viagra.*

There appears to be a great fear in the lay population, and among some health care providers as well, regarding risks associated with Viagra. Men with ED who may safely benefit from this drug often refuse the drug either due to their own worries or the anxieties of their spouses. If appropriate precautions are taken to make sure that Viagra and nitrates are not taken closely together, the combination of which can cause severe low blood pressure, the simple use of Viagra should not cause death.

There is a misperception that men with any kind of heart ailment cannot take Viagra. The fact is that because sex makes the heart work harder, strenuous sexual activity is not advisable for men who have unstable heart conditions like congestive heart failure or continuing chest pain. This leaves room for many men who have been adequately treated for past heart disease to benefit from this drug. If the man is physically active without heart problems like chest pain or shortness of breath, he may be an excellent candidate for sildenafil. In men who are not exercising, an exercise stress test may be in order to assess their exercise tolerance. Clinical judgment should be used in prescribing Viagra to men with past heart diseases, but to refuse this therapy across the board is not warranted. The suggestions herein and in the product package insert can serve as a guide to the prescribing physician.

Elderly men may also benefit from Viagra. Sexual activity requires some exercise, and thus the physician should assess the fitness level of the senior man before prescribing any treatment for ED. It is recommended that smaller starting doses of Viagra be used in men over the age of 75.

Although very effective in a broad range of conditions causing ED, Viagra may not cure all men with ED. Among elderly patients trying this drug, about 30% fail to respond adequately. Other options may be considered in these men and also in those for whom Viagra is contraindicated.

OTHER MEDICATIONS

Other oral pills, such as TADALAFIL (CIALIS) and VARDENAFIL (LEVITRA), which work in similar fashion to Viagra, have recently been introduced in the market and may help drive the prices down and be useful in some men not responding to or are intolerant of Viagra.

Apomorphine is a compound that may help correct ED when placed under the tongue. It is not yet available for clinical use in the United States.

A host of alternative drugs have been advertised and marketed to unsuspecting consumers through the popular media and lately through the internet. Many of these are listed as "dietary supplements" and hence escape close scrutiny by regulatory agencies with regards to their safety and efficacy. Some of these over-the-counter compounds may contain potent hormonal derivatives like *androstenedione* or *dehydroepiandrosterone (DHEA)*. Unsupervised and prolonged use of these products may lead to prostate or heart disease. Additionally, many men with underlying health problems like thyroid disorders may have their diagnosis and treatment delayed by being lulled into complacency by misleading claims of cure for ED by the manufacturers and promoters of these "drugs."

VACUUM ERECTION DEVICES

Vacuum erection devices (VEDs) can be used by virtually any man with ED, regardless of his age or the underlying problem. VEDs come in a variety of models, but the basic unit is a clear plastic cylinder that fits over the penis (see Figure 12-2). A pump is connected to the cylinder that draws out air, creating a partial vacuum around the penis. This negative

(figure 12-2)

A vacuum erection device. *(Reproduced with permission of the American Foundation for Urological Disease.)*

pressure draws blood into the penis, keeping the blood "trapped," and causing an erection to form. Once an erection is achieved, an elastic ring is slipped around the base of the penis. The ring sustains the erection and can be left in place safely for up to 30 minutes.

Although VEDs are generally very safe, be aware that some side effects are possible. These include numbness of the penis, bruising and swelling of the penis, and slowed ejaculation. Also, an erection achieved with a VED may not feel as hard as a normal erection. A professional sex therapist should provide careful instructions on how to use the VED, to ensure that the user knows how to operate the device safely and effectively.

PENILE SELF-INJECTION THERAPY

Penile self-injection therapy involves injecting a small amount of medication into the spongy part of the penis before sexual activity. A commonly used medication is ALPROSTADIL (CAVERJECT and EDEX), which is identical to a naturally occurring substance that helps keep blood vessels open and increases blood flow resulting in an erection. Alprostadil is sometimes combined with one or more other drugs (PHENTOLAMINE and/or PAPAVERINE) to help restore a man's erections.

Although the thought of injecting the penis with a needle may sound scary and unpleasant, for most men the sensation is no worse than pinching an earlobe (see Figure 12-3). What's more, the technique is relatively easy to learn. Similar to Viagra, this therapy is effective in a broad spectrum of ED. In addition, most men who do not respond to Viagra will respond to injection therapy.

Self-injection therapy should be initiated under a doctor's supervision. Generally, men are advised to use the injections no more than two to three times per week. The most common side effect is over the site of the injection. A serious but rare side effect is a painful erection that lasts too long, a condition known as **priapism**. A man who experiences this side effect for longer than three hours should seek medical attention immediately, lest there could be irreversible damage to the penis.

TRANSURETHRAL THERAPY

ALPROSTADIL, the same compound used in injection therapy, is also available as a tiny pellet for transurethral therapy, which is the insertion of a pellet into the urethra through the tip of the penis (see Figure 12-4). Transurethral therapy is available by prescription, under the brand name MUSE. Although generally safe, this method is somewhat less effective than self-injection therapy. Proper

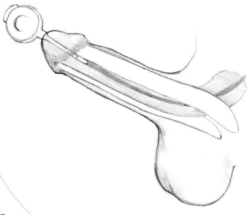

(figure 12-3)

Penile self-injection. *(Reproduced with permission of the American Foundation for Urological Disease.)*

(figure 12-4)

Transurethral pellet insertion. *(Reproduced with permission of the American Foundation for Urological Disease.)*

training with regards to insertion technique should be carried out in your doctor's office.

Possible side effects include pain or burning in the tip of the penis, prolonged erections, and low blood pressure. The partner may also experience mild vaginal irritation. This therapy should not be used if a man's partner is pregnant or planning to become pregnant, unless the man wears a condom.

SURGICAL TREATMENTS

Surgery to correct problems with blood vessels to the penis may be recommended in rare cases, particularly young men with groin injuries or in men with structural abnormalities like leakage through veins; however, penile implant surgery can be done in men of advanced age as long as they are medically stable.

For certain men for whom all other treatments have failed or are inappropriate, a surgically inserted penile implant may be a very effective last option (see Figure 12-5). An experienced implant surgeon who regularly performs this procedure should be sought. This form of treatment may be rarely associated with serious problems, including infection and mechanical breakdown.

Flexible rods implanted within the spongy part of the penis are one possibility. To achieve an erection, a man simply bends his penis upward into an erect position. Some men choose to go for an inflatable implant, in which case a pair of inflatable cylinders is attached to a fluid reservoir and a pump hidden inside the body. To achieve an erection, a man presses on the pump, which transfers fluid from the reservoir into the cylinders, creating rigidity.

CONCLUSION AND FUTURE DIRECTIONS

As medicine has made significant advances, more men are living longer. As a result, quality-of-life issues, such as male sexuality, become more important. The good news for many senior men and their partners is that ED can usually be treated safely and effectively. Thanks to medical advances, men no longer have to suffer in silence with ED and couples can regain the pleasure of sexual intimacy.

The keys to regaining long-term sexual function are trust and open communication, both with your partner and a knowledgeable health care provider. This teamwork is an ongoing process. If you have ED, it's important to see your treating specialist periodically. During these follow-up visits, you and your provider can discuss your progress and evaluate whether a change in your treatment is needed.

The future has never been brighter for the millions of couples who are confronting ED. As a result of the impact of Viagra, a host of new oral medications and other treatments for ED have been and are being

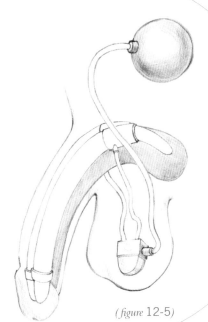

(figure 12-5)

Inflatable penile implant. *(Reproduced with permission of the American Foundation for Urological Disease.)*

developed. You may want to check with your health care provider from time to time to see if new treatments are available and to learn if any of these new options might be suitable for you. Enjoy!

■

WHAT YOU NEED TO KNOW

➤ A vast majority of the senior population are interested in and capable of an active, satisfying sex life.

➤ When problems with sexual performance occur, they should not be viewed as inevitable but rather as the result of disease, disability, medication side effect, or psychological causes and potentially curable with proper intervention.

➤ There are many possible causes for erectile dysfunction. Some are reversible, such as excess alcohol intake, cigarette smoking, certain medications, and hormone imbalances. Some causes may not be reversible, but most men can be helped with proper evaluation and treatment.

➤ If you suffer from erectile dysfunction, then the family doctor or the primary care provider is the first health professional to see, many of whom now routinely treat this disorder. Depending on the individual clinical situation, the primary provider may refer you to a specialist.

12

FOR MORE INFORMATION

➤ **National Kidney and Urologic Diseases Information Clearinghouse**
3 Information Way
Bethesda, MD 20892
E-mail: nkudic@info.niddk.nih.gov

➤ **American Urological Association**
1120 North Charles Street
Baltimore, MD 21201
410-727-1100
E-mail: aua@auanet.org
Web: www.auanet.org
AUA can refer you to a urologist in your area.

➤ **American Foundation for Urologic Disease**
1128 North Charles Street
Baltimore, MD 21201
410-468-1800
Fax: 410-468-1808
E-mail: admin@afud.org
Web: www.afud.org

➤ **American Association of Clinical Endocrinology**
1000 Riverside Avenue, Suite 205
Jacksonville, FL 32204
904-353-7878
E-mail: info@aace.com
Web: www.aace.com

➤ **American Association of Sex Educators, Counselors, and Therapists**
P.O. Box 238
Mount Vernon, IA 52314
Web: www.aasect.org
Check the website to find a certified sexuality educator, counselor, or therapist in your area.

➤ **Sexual Function Health Council**
American Foundation for Urologic Disease
1128 North Charles Street
Baltimore, MD 21201
800-433-4215, 410-468-1800
E-mail: impotence@afud.org
Web: www.impotence.org

The art of love . . . is largely the art of persistence.

—*Albert Ellis*

THE AUTHOR

13   *Deborah J. Lightner*

DEBORAH J. LIGHTNER, MD, is an associate professor and consultant in urologic surgery at the Mayo Clinic, joining the staff in 1995. She did her medical school training at Vanderbilt University, residency training at Yale, and fellowship training at the University of Minnesota. Her professional interests are in female pelvic floor medicine and reconstructive surgery and the development of new treatment strategies for urge and stress incontinence. In addition to becoming a surgeon at the Mayo Clinic, Dr. Lightner is president of the Society for Women in Urology, an organization within the American Urologic Association. She serves as secretary for the officers and councilors of the Mayo Staff.

FEMALE SEXUAL FUNCTION

13

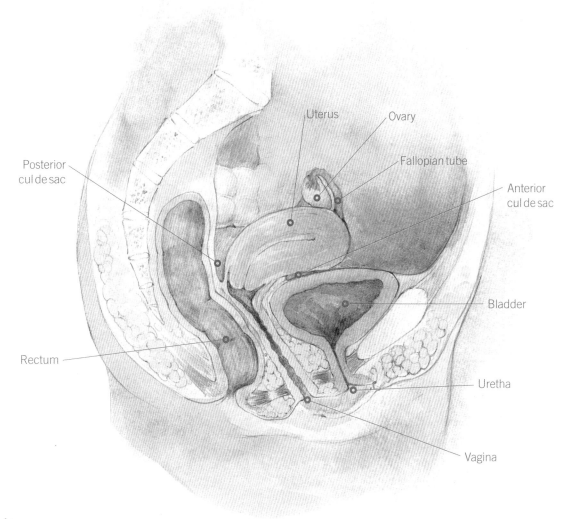

(figure 13-1)

Female sexual system. Many factors can affect sexual function as a woman ages. Partner issues are common. These might include erectile dysfunction, medical or psychological problems, or even absence of a partner. Physical changes at menopause may include inadequate vaginal lubrication, pain with intercourse, and diminished libido. Concomitant medical illness is increasingly recognized as a cause of female sexual dysfunction. Good overall health is the best protector of female sexual function.

THE CERTAINTY OF CHANGE

Most of us modify our physical expressiveness over time; the intimate life of young couples with children is vastly different from that of the empty nester, and it is natural for adjustments to occur as life changes. Modifications may result from lack of interest, privacy, available partners, reduced sexual responsiveness, or from physical disabilities. These changes do not mean that we are no longer desirable or desiring. We have grown to expect change and be flexible in our responses.

Sexuality is not something that is reserved for the younger woman. *Female sexual dysfunction (FSD)* is not an invariable part of growing older. Poor sexual function can result from illnesses and the medications we need to maintain health and from the psychosocial hardships life throws our way. This brief overview looks into what we know about women's sexuality as our life changes and, importantly, what we can do to maintain and improve our sexual health.

Sexual dysfunction in both men and women is age-related, progressive, and highly prevalent. Interestingly, while psychological factors and poor interpersonal relationships have been assumed to be the most likely reason for declining sexual function in women, medical diseases were thought to be the most likely cause of male sexual dysfunction. Yet the associated risk factors for sexual dysfunction in both genders are strikingly similar. Neurologic and vascular diseases, aneurysms, atherosclerosis, hypertension, smoking history, elevated serum cholesterol, and lipids are common risk factors for both genders. It is becoming increasingly recognized that women can suffer sexual dysfunction as a result of medical disease. It is increasingly obvious that if you wish to preserve your sexual function, you should look to maintain your overall health: good cardiac health and weight control, serum lipids and glucose in the normal range, and the avoidance of tobacco products.

This is not to negate the other factors that put people at risk for sexual dysfunction. One of the obvious risks includes the social isolation that can follow after the loss of a spouse. Many widows know the difficulty of having a satisfying personal life when partners are no longer available. We should recognize that our society has strong prejudices about the physical intimacy appropriate for an older woman. It's not deemed attractive or pleasing anymore; sexual charms are purported to belong to the young. Most of us never perceived our parents or our grandparents as having physical intimacy. There is little physical touching in the popular culture's portrayal of older women; images of older people touching are often farcical in their presentation. Positive images from literature, film, and television are remarkable in that they are so rare. Those few tender characterizations are strikingly childlike, and not erotic. These long-standing cultural attitudes strongly influence our expectation that we will be less sexual in our older years. The translation of these messages to our own lives means that we expect that as we age, we will be devoid of sexual thoughts and abstain from intimate physical activities. Many people give up their physical intimacy for these cultural expectations alone, a poor justification for eliminating that which can give such depth and meaning to our lives.

FAMILY JOURNAL

My wife Rosemary W., 62, was hospitalized for a heart attack. She underwent coronary angiography, which is a dye-study to visualize the coronary arteries, and was found to have a blockage of the right coronary artery. Her cardiologist performed a balloon angioplasty to open the blocked artery, and a stent was placed to prevent renarrowing of the artery. She was placed on some heart medicines and a medicine to lower her cholesterol.

For the next several weeks, I noticed that she did not seem to display much affection for me and spurned my sexual advances. Finally, after three or four weeks I asked her what was wrong. She admitted that she was very afraid the physical exertion required for sexual intercourse would be bad for her heart. I said that she should discuss this with her cardiologist. She learned from her doctor that her heart was in good shape and that she could resume a normal sexual life.

Education on what sexuality can be in our senior years is important in reducing both the self-imposed and the societal constraints on our capacity to be intimate. Despite the negative characterizations of our sexual potential, sexual expression is not lost as we age. A high proportion of women remains both interested and sexually active after menopause. Studies have correlated the cultural factors associated with maintenance of physical intimacy with age: negative societal attitudes toward physical intimacy in the older adult were strongly associated with sexual inactivity. This disapproving attitude is often seen in nursing homes and correlates very strongly with residents giving up physical intimacy. This repressive attitude affects even the long-married resident couples, even though there is no medical reason and no cultural rationale for the older female to give up on her sexuality.

Taking a different paradigm, menopause and beyond can be a liberating change as contraception is no longer a significant concern. The sexual liberation as contraception became widely available in the 1960s can still be ours as the risk of pregnancy naturally declines. Caution is advised, however, as menopause does not equate with infertility. Pregnancy is still a possibility, albeit remote, even if the last menstrual cycle has not occurred for a twelve-month period of time.

However, equally critical is the knowledge of and active protection against sexually transmitted diseases (STDs). Chlamydia and syphilis remain largely treatable, but herpes virus infections are highly infectious, widespread, and chronic. HIV infections, productive of the highly lethal disease AIDS, are transmittable with either heterosexual or homosexual intercourse; there is a small but distinct reservoir of this disease in the older adult population.

Latex condoms should always be used during male-female sexual activities. Condoms reduce the transmission of infected body fluids to one's partner. Knowing that many of the organisms and viruses causing sexually transmitted diseases can be asymptomatic (particularly early on in the infection), the routine use of condoms is the cornerstone of safe sex. Condoms should be used for anal, oral or vaginal sex regardless of sexual orientation. It is well established that lesbians are not immune to sexual transmitted diseases. So for all sexually active people, regardless of orientation, safe sex means reducing risk of STDs by not sharing bodily fluids vaginally, orally, or anally. While younger people are most at risk for STDs, given higher numbers of partners and the higher prevalence of STDs in the younger population, STDs can and do happen to sexually active older people.

FEMALE SEXUAL DYSFUNCTION

A study in the *Journal of Family Practice* covering almost 1500 women undergoing routine gynecologic care showed that over 90% of the questionnaire respondents (65% responded) reported one or more sexual concerns. Admittedly, women having gynecologic concerns and coming to physicians are a high-risk group for female sexual disfunction (FSD), but the breakdown of symptoms is very telling. The most frequently reported were lack of interest (over 85%), difficulty with **orgasm** (over 80%), inadequate lubrication (nearly 75%), or pain with intercourse (over 70%). More than 40% of these American women also reported a history of sexual coercion. Rape, violence against women, and emotional and physical abuse are common, and the risk of subsequent sexual dysfunction is very high.

As outlined in a *Journal of American Medical Association* article for women, there are two times during the life span at risk for sexual dysfunction. One is in the years we first become sexually active, marry and establish our families, but the other larger time of risk starts around the time of menopause, as we'll discuss this further.

FSD is not one simple diagnosis; it is a cluster of differing symptoms with unique findings on history and physical examination. FSD has recently been redefined, dividing the diagnostic classifications into four subcategories that can be easily understood and discussed by layperson and professional alike. Note that in each subcategory the disorder results in personal distress for the woman.

1. *Hypoactive sexual desire:* A persistent or recurrent lack of sexual thoughts or feelings.
2. *Sexual arousal disorder:* The persistent inability to obtain or maintain sexual excitement. This may present such symptoms as poor vaginal lubrication. A decrease in genital sensation and poor muscle relaxation of the vagina and pelvic sidewalls may also occur.
3. *Orgasmic disorder:* The long-term loss of orgasmic potential after sufficient sexual stimulation.
4. *Sexual pain disorder:* Chronic pain associated with sexual activity.

The most commonly reported problem is hypoactive sexual desire, which may result from common life problems: poor interpersonal relationships, poverty, anxiety, poor sleep, and fatigue. But many prescription and OTC medications figure in the short list of associated causes of low libido.

The second most commonly reported problem includes orgasmic disorders, which may occur with poor understanding of the female sexual response or may result from pelvic operations and certain neurological diseases.

Difficulty in arousal, including difficulty in vaginal lubrication, is very common in the postmenopausal female. Least frequent, but terribly distressing, is painful intercourse and the other sexual pain disorders.

Each of these four problems occurs independently of the others. For example, a woman with hypoactive sexual desire may be very responsive to sexual stimulation with a good arousal response and orgasms. Likewise, a patient with poor arousal may still be orgasmic with modifications in the type or duration of stimulation. The couple needs to be intimately involved with the solution to the problem; sexual therapists play a major role in improving the intimate life for older couples whether the cause is psychological, interpersonal, or medical. You should not despair if your evaluation for ongoing sexual dysfunction results in a referral for sexual

FAMILY JOURNAL

Aunt Catherine S., 58, discontinued her estrogen medication after publicity about the potential adverse effects of hormones. She didn't have any serious medical problems, but had a hysterectomy several years earlier. My aunt noticed some troublesome hot flashes initially and then significant sleep problems. Within a few months she noticed that intercourse with her husband was becoming uncomfortable, and on the most recent occasion, she had some vaginal bleeding.

She visited her gynecologist who diagnosed atrophic vaginitis, a thinning of the lining of the vagina that was causing her dryness and bleeding. He explained the benefits and risks of estrogen therapy, and my aunt decided to restart her medication. He advised her that they would continually reevaluate the need for this therapy based on her age, symptoms, and future medical studies. Within a few weeks, my aunt felt like her old self again. The hot flashes were gone, her sleep improved, and she no longer had any pain with intercourse.

counseling, as it is the most thoroughly evaluated and effective therapy regardless of the etiology of the sexual dysfunction. Specific medical treatments for female sexual dysfunction are not yet as advanced as for males, but the research in this area is rapidly expanding the promise of effective medical therapies for women.

Why is the aging woman at risk for sexual dysfunction? Beyond the societal restraints we've discussed, there are well-known physiologic changes that occur throughout one's life. Human sexual function, like other bodily functions, is possible only with normal physiology in both sexes. The primary systems necessary for sexual activity are the **vascular** and **autonomic nervous systems**: active smooth muscle relaxation occurs in the genital organs and blood vessels via a chemical called **nitric oxide**, with a simultaneous and passive decrease in venous blood outflow. These produce a similar erectile response in both **penile** and **clitoral** tissues. Vaginal lubrication requires a normal vascular supply, as vaginal lubrication is serumlike fluid derived actively from the adjacent blood supply. Orgasm requires an intact nervous system. Unfortunately, age and disease adversely affect many of these systems. For example, after menopause, there is a degree of foreshortening of the vagina as well as narrowing and thinning of the walls. Blood flow to the vaginal tissues often decreases, with a resultant reduction in vaginal secretions and lubrication with sexual excitation. While the vaginal dryness can be easily offset with the multiple water-miscible lubricants available in the over-the-counter market, the reduction in vaginal elasticity and plasticity may not be as well compensated; this may result in poor expansion of the vaginal tissue in response to excitation and occasionally to painful intercourse. Vascular disease, endocrine abnormalities, and certain medications are also associated with significant reductions in the ability of the vaginal tissues to respond to sexual stimulation with appropriate lubrication. Most of these diseases occur with more prevalence in the older adult, with a cumulative effect producing FSD.

Hysterectomy or other pelvic floor surgical procedures performed for **prolapse** do not invariably interfere with sexual function, and the repair of painful fibroids or high degrees of vaginal prolapse may enhance sexuality. Several studies of women undergoing hysterectomy suggest that there is no adverse affect of sexual functioning in most women. Occasionally these procedures may cause changes in the vaginal access or a significant reduction in the vaginal **introitus** size and vaginal capacity that results in sexual difficulties. Competent pelvic floor surgeons are aware of these risks, use operative methods to reduce the possibility of postoperative dysfunction, and are able to discuss them with their patients. Regrettably, pelvic operations and radiation therapy for pelvic cancers, such as rectal cancer and cervical cancer, are associated with a significant risk of sexual dysfunction as the nerves supplying the genital organs are often damaged after treatment for these life-threatening malignancies. There is little way around these side effects at the current time.

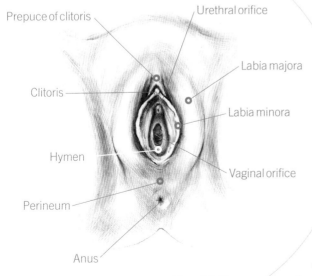

Prepuce of clitoris

Clitoris

Hymen

Perineum

Anus

Urethral orifice

Labia majora

Labia minora

Vaginal orifice

(figure 13-2)

Perineal anatomy (external genitalia).

Other medical conditions can indirectly affect the ability to be sexually active. Commonly, the fear of urinary or fecal incontinence will lead to avoidance of sexual activity. Patients with significant cardiac disease may fear another heart attack during sexual activity. While the chances of having a heart attack during sexual intercourse are very low, your cardiac physician can advise you on this risk. Arthritis, strokes and other physical limitations can make certain sexual positions uncomfortable and/or impossible. However, a sexual therapist and a caring partner can help overcome these limitations.

EVALUATION

The evaluation of a patient with FSD includes a complete history, the specifics of her sexual dysfunction, all medications, over-the-counter and street drugs, and her smoking history. The physical includes a limited general examination, a pelvic examination, and an evaluation of vaginal atrophy, dryness, and trigger spots. Select patients will have serum endocrine levels drawn; serum FSH, LH, estradiol, and testosterone levels are most commonly obtained. Other more specific hormone levels may be obtained as either clinically indicated or as a part of research evaluations. Often a questionnaire is helpful to determine the specific disorder, its severity, and responses to treatment. Sexual therapists should be consulted early, with the understanding of the patient that symptoms are often multifactorial and that a psychological evaluation is part of every evaluation and treatment plan.

Evaluations at specialized centers or as a part of research may include evaluations of blood flow to the genital skin and other organs, vaginal acid-base changes, measurements of the ability of the vaginal wall to expand, and of genital sensation. Currently, these are more helpful in monitoring the response to experimental protocols than in the routine evaluation and management of female sexual dysfunction. Normative data are being established for many of the tools, which may become screening and diagnostic devices.

TREATMENT

The mainstay of therapy is education, in order to streamline the possible treatment. A sexual therapist may be consulted; sexual function is a very complex interpersonal interaction. Sexual education and psychological evaluation should not be misread as implying that the symptom is psychiatric or interpersonal and without a more organic cause. Therapists are also helpful in overcoming physical disabilities.

All patients with sexual dysfunction should seek to optimize their vascular function. Given the negative effects of smoking on blood vessels and tissue oxygenation, no patient should continue to smoke if she wishes to regain or maintain her sexual function. Likewise alcohol, while removing short-term inhibitions, is associated with long-term loss of sexual function. If possible, certain prescription drugs may need to be tapered or changed; the list of medications with adverse side effects on sexual function includes antihypertensive medications, sedatives, hypnotics, and antidepressants. No prescription medications should be changed without consultation with your prescribing physician, as the morbidity and even mortality associated with untreated high blood pressure or heart disease certainly outweigh the loss of genital function. Over-the-counter medications, including antihistamines and cold preparations, can also cause poor sexual function, but since these drugs are used in the short term, they do not result in long-term sexual difficulties.

Sometimes disease processes themselves are reversible. For example, a patient at end-stage renal failure with FSD may respond to renal transplantation with a marked improvement in sexual function.

While hormone replacement therapy is common, the data on maintenance and/or improvement of sexual function with estrogen replacement for the postmenopausal female are still underdeveloped. Increases in libido, decreased pain during coitus, and improved clitoral sensitivity have been reported in early trials in select patient groups. Given that the data on the degree and durability of improved sexual function with hormonal agents are preliminary and the data showing that estrogen-progesterone replacement are not cardioprotective in women, you should discuss the risks versus the benefits of these therapies with your physician.

Note: Many charlatans and pseudoscientists sell over-the-counter drugs and dispense off-label prescriptions with no data to suggest that these medications are safe, let alone helpful. Formal research trials, performed in or sponsored by reputable academic institutions, have federal and medical institutional monitors, informed consent, and the scientific know-how to answer the urgent question of how we most effectively diagnose and treat female sexual dysfunction.

A perfect example of this practice is the widespread use of androgen replacement therapy in the menstruating female. There are no widely accepted data to suggest that this is either appropriate or efficacious. Androgen replacement may be dangerous.

Androgen levels in women decline substantially at the time of menopause and plateau thereafter. Could this be one of the causes of FSD at the time of menopause? Could androgen replacement be therapeutic? Low serum testosterone levels do not predict a therapeutic response to androgen replacement in women, and alterations in these levels only weakly correlate with changes in sexual arousal. While the use of exogenous androgens, such as the combination of esterified estrogen and methyltestosterone or dehydroepiandrosterone (DHEA), is widespread, early studies report efficacy only in patients with androgen deficiency and secondary female arousal disorders. But androgen replacement occurs at a cost: it may cause liver disease (particularly when given orally), or blood abnormalities (such as polycythemia). Androgen medications can adversely affect serum lipid profiles. Hence, patients on such therapy should have serum lipid and liver function levels checked every three months, and the medication be discontinued if it is either not effective or causing laboratory abnormalities. Androgen therapy is also associated with hair loss, acne, and female hirsutism. Hypoglycemia (low blood sugar levels) may occur in an insulin-dependent diabetic. Lastly, fluid overload leading to heart failure may also occur in people placed on androgens and who have compromised heart, kidney, or liver function; each of these diseases occurs more frequently in the elderly and may be undiagnosed until complications occur.

ALTERNATIVE TREATMENTS

With receptor-active medications such as SILDENAFIL (VIAGRA), clitoral smooth muscle responds similarly to penile smooth muscle. Could the medications used for male erectile dysfunction prove useful for women? Studies with a 50-mg dose of sildenafil appeared as safe as in men but with little efficacy in one early trial. Only 20% of postmenopausal women with FSD chose to continue sildenafil after the three-month trial, and 10% dropped out of the trial because of clitoral pain and hypersensitivity. L-arginine, another precursor of the smooth muscle receptor medication, has been used in men, but there are no reported trials yet in women. New trials of these medications in subpopulations of women with FSD are planned.

Classes of medications called alpha-antagonists are associated with decreased female sexual function. These include LABETALOL and CLONIDINE. Could the opposite, that is, adrenergic stimulants, such as EPHEDRINE and exercise, augment the physiologic responses in vaginal blood flow and improve arousal? Studies of medications like these are ongoing. They include PGE_1 (used topically) and PHENTOLAMINE (taken orally or as a vaginal suppository). APOMORPHINE, a short-acting dopamine agonist, has been used with some success in men, but use of this sublingual medication has not been reported in women. Parenthetically, YOHIMBINE has not been demonstrated to offer any therapeutic benefit beyond being a placebo but is widely sold as a "sex drug."

The FDA has approved the use of the *Eros-Clitoral Therapy Device* for women. This device applies a gentle vacuum over the clitoris causing increased cavernosal blood flow and engorgement, similar to vacuum erection devices (VEDs) used for assisted erections in men (see Chapter 12).

Patients suffering from depression and FSD secondary to their medications can ask their doctors for a dose reduction, drug holiday, different antidepressants, or adjunctive pharmacotherapy. Studies have also suggested that FSD is a more common side effect of most antidepressant medications than initial therapeutic trials have reported.

In summary, sexual function doesn't stop as we age, though it certainly changes. Good overall health is the most likely protector of sexual function. The prognosis for future effective therapies for FSD is excellent as women report the problem, researchers objectively evaluate the diagnostic and therapeutic options, and women push the culture to see ourselves as vital, physical, and capable of great intimacy throughout our adult lives.

■

WHAT YOU NEED TO KNOW

■ Female sexual dysfunction is not a normal part of growing older.

■ Most sexual dysfunction in women in midlife and beyond is a result of medical illnesses. However, sexual education and psychological counseling may be helpful in overcoming physical challenges.

■ Sexual expression is not lost with age.

■ Sexually transmitted disease can occur at any age. If there is any question whatsoever about a sexual partner having an STD, protection should be used.

■ Female sexual dysfunction is a common problem after menopause. The proper treatment requires that you overcome any hesitancy and discuss it with your doctor. Effective treatments are often available.

FOR MORE INFORMATION

■ Mayo Clinic
200 First Street SW
Rochester, MN 55905
507-284-2511
Fax: 507-284-0161
TDD: 507-284-9786
Web: www.mayoclinic.org

■ American Association of Sex Educators, Counselors, and Therapists
P.O. Box 238
Mount Vernon, IA 52314
Web: www.aasect.org
Check the website to find a certified sexuality educator, counselor, or therapist in your area.

One of the delights known to age and beyond the grasp of youth is that of
Not Going.

—*J. B. Priestly*

THE AUTHOR

14

RODNEY A. APPELL, MD, FACS, is professor of urology
and gynecology and chief of the Division of Voiding
Dysfunction and Female Urology, at Baylor College of
Medicine in Houston, Texas. He holds the F. Brantley
Scott Chair in Urology at St. Luke's Episcopal Hospital
in Houston. Dr. Appell received his medical degree from
Jefferson Medical College in Philadelphia and completed
a surgical residency at George Washington University
Medical Center in Washington, D.C., and urology residency at Yale University School of Medicine in New
Haven, Connecticut. Dr. Appell serves on the board of
directors and nominating committee of the National
Association for Continence and on both the guidelines
committee and the special women's issues in urology
committee of the American Urological Association. He
is on the editorial boards of many publications, including
the *Archives of Physical Medicine and Rehabilitation, International Urogynecology Journal, Journal of Urology, International
Journal of the Proctological and Perineal Diseases,* and *Urology.* For over 25 years, Dr. Appell has been invited as a
visiting professor or speaker at numerous national and
international society meetings, symposia, and conferences. He has received many grants to investigate urinary
incontinence, and he is the author or coauthor of over
150 journal articles, 15 books, and 40 book chapters. In
1990, Dr. Appell received the VideoUrology Times Award
for outstanding videotape segment; was selected in 1998
for the *Cleveland Magazine's* "Best Doctors in Northeast
Ohio"; and has consistently been included in *Best Doctors
in America.*

14 | URINARY INCONTINENCE

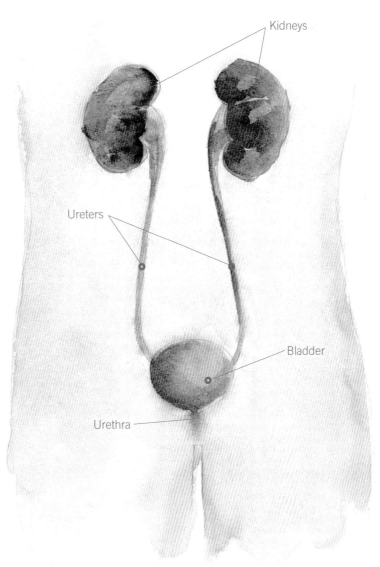

Kidneys

Ureters

Bladder

Urethra

(figure 14-1)

The urinary system: Urine flows from the kidney through the ureters to the bladders where it is stored until the bladder distends and sends signals to the brain to stimulate the need to urinate. These signals can be ignored initially, but eventually the urge to urinate becomes very powerful. Contraction of the bladder muscle allows urine to pass from the bladder through the urethra and then to the outside.

Urinary incontinence, the involuntary loss of urine, is a significant worldwide health problem affecting the quality of life of millions. It has been estimated that 15 to 30% of persons over 65 have at least one episode weekly. If only women were considered, the prevalence leaps to between 30 and 50%. Those living in nursing homes and long-term care (LTC) settings show a prevalence of greater than 50%. Many individuals are embarrassed by their incontinence and deny it if questioned. Therefore, most studies actually underestimate how common this problem really is. However, a key point to remember is that *while the prevalence of urinary incontinence increases with age, it is not a normal part of the aging process.* Incontinence may be a precipitating factor in the decision to place a loved one into a LTC setting, as the condition is commonly associated with dementia and immobility. Thus, urinary incontinence can and does have significant social and economic consequences. The social stigma leads to psychological changes of anxiety and depression. The lack of control of this bodily function leads to self-isolation on the one hand and loss of independence on the other. The result is an overall decline in the quality of life for the individual as well as a significant interference with activities of daily living. Clearly, other health problems such as impaired mobility and/or cognitive function, common in the elderly, can aggravate the problem. There can be significant physical consequences from incontinence also. Studies have indicated that incontinence increases the risk of falls by an astounding 26% and the risk of fractures of hips, arms, and legs is increased by 34%! Urge incontinence is a significant risk for falls and injuries, especially in the nursing home population. In this case, the fall is due to rushing to the bathroom. These persons are often frail or have poor balance. They may be on medications that can cause lightheadedness or fainting when they jump up quickly. A bedpan or portable commode next to the bed may reduce this risk.

The economic implications associated with urinary incontinence are significant, particularly in the LTC setting. Beyond the cost of containment management (diapers, pads, etc.) are the costs related to labor, laundry, waste disposal, and medical treatments of the consequences of the incontinence problem described above, such as the psychological problems and falls. Consequently, the annual direct cost of incontinence in the United States is estimated at over $11 billion in the community-dwelling elderly and over $5 billion in LTC facilities. (This does not take into account the significant costs associated with compliance with federal and state regulations, retention of nurses and nursing aides, the loss of productive employment of affected individuals, etc.)

TYPES OF URINARY INCONTINENCE

Urge Incontinence (UI) is the involuntary loss of urine preceded by a strong urge to void. This is one of the three symptoms that make up the *overactive bladder (OAB):* urgency, frequency of urination (including *nocturia,* which is frequent urination during the night hours), and urge incontinence. There are two types of overactive bladder: *OAB-dry* (the urgency and frequency

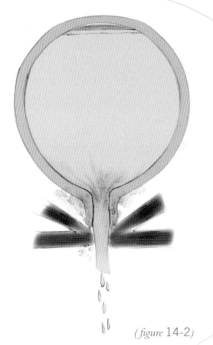

(figure 14-2)

Overflow incontinence occurs when the bladder cannot hold any more urine. It can be caused by damaged nerves to the bladder or by blockage of urine flow at the outlet to the bladder.

with no incontinence) and *OAB-wet* (the urgency and incontinence). The dynamics of OAB-wet are that the bladder contraction overwhelms the individual's *sphincter* (muscular tissue that helps prevent urine from flowing out of the bladder) and urine is lost involuntarily. Causes for this can include neurological disorders (such as multiple sclerosis, strokes, Parkinson's disease, and certain spinal cord injuries), infections and inflammation of the urinary tract, and bladder cancer. Occasionally urge incontinence may occur without a specific cause being identified.

Stress incontinence (SUI) is the involuntary loss of urine that occurs with coughing, sneezing, or bending over ("stress" in this context means physical stress maneuvers, not emotional stress). This is primarily a disorder of women but may occur in men as a complication to prostate surgery (see Chapter 11). In women it is secondary to weakening of the muscular support of the bladder or to incompetence of the sphincter or urethra (the short tube that leads from the bladder to the outside). Vaginal childbirth and pelvic surgery are the key risk factors to women.

Mixed incontinence (MI) describes the combined conditions of OAB and SUI. It is the most common form of incontinence in the LTC setting.

Overflow incontinence (OI) represents the condition by which the bladder, being filled to capacity, can hold no more, so urine leaks out (see Figure 14-2). Here the involuntary loss of urine can be due to an obstruction, such as an enlarged prostate, resulting in a constant dribbling of urine. The symptom may also be due to a bladder that cannot contract properly. This can happen with certain medications (such as cold medicines, sleeping pills, and sedatives) or with certain medical disorders (such as diabetes mellitus, lumbar disk disorders, or previous pelvic surgery). In either case, the bladder does not empty itself completely, and the lower urinary tract acts like a leaking faucet.

Functional incontinence (FI) is the involuntary loss of urine unrelated to urinary tract causes but results from chronic physical or cognitive impairment that prevents the individual from reaching the toilet. Impaired mobility due to severe arthritis or neurological diseases can cause this type of incontinence. Dementia caused by Alzheimer's disease or multiple strokes may prevent the individual from alerting caregivers about the need for going to the toilet.

DIAGNOSIS IN URINARY INCONTINENCE

In order to make an accurate diagnosis regarding the type of incontinence, the doctor must be told about the problem. This means overcoming any embarrassment about the issue. Remember that incontinence is common and you are not alone. Most causes can be effectively treated. If your doctor does not diagnose or treat incontinence, ask for a referral to a physician who does. Do not accept that incontinence is a normal part of aging.

The doctor who is evaluating the problem will try to determine if there are reversible causes. Therefore, a history is obtained regarding the symptoms, length of time of the problem, current medications, previous surgery, and other medical conditions, as this will often be helpful in determining the cause of the voiding problem. Your doctor may have you provide a *voiding diary,* as shown in Figure 14-3, in which you record how much fluid you take in and how often and how much you urinate. This diary should also include the time of each episode of incontinence and the number and time of bowel movements. The diary can help sort out problems that may cause or contribute to incontinence. For example, excessive urine volume *(polyuria)* may be caused by excessive caffeine or alcohol intake, poorly controlled diabetes mellitus, or fluid overload from congestive heart failure.

The physical will include an abdominal and rectal examination, as well as a pelvic examination in women. A urinalysis and assessment of how much urine is left in the bladder after voiding *(postvoid residual,* or *PVR)* will be determined by catheterization or ultrasound. Certain abnormalities may require the expertise of a urologist and/or gynecologist, including blood in the urine, recurrent urinary tract infections, elevated postvoid residual urine, weakening of the pelvic muscles in women, or lack of response to therapy. Specialty investigations may be necessary, such as urodynamics, *cystoscopy* (examining the bladder with a fiberoptic scope), or X-rays. Your doctor can explain the details of any required procedures.

MANAGING URINARY INCONTINENCE

Although total dryness may be unrealistic, maximizing quality of life by reducing the number of incontinent episodes, by improving activities of daily living, and by diminishing social isolation without adversely affecting the individual's mental status is an attainable goal. While identification of incontinence type and formulation of individualized patient treatment goals and strategies are important, managing other associated medical conditions is also crucial in effectively managing urinary incontinence, even if they are not completely correctable.

Management of urinary incontinence proceeds from the simpler to the more complex strategies on the basis of a stepped approach. However, treatment is individualized. For example, surgery may be the best option

(figure 14-3)
A sample voiding diary.

YOUR DAILY BLADDER DIARY

This diary will help you and your health care team. Bladder diaries help show the causes of bladder control trouble.

Your Name: _____ Date: _____

TIME	DRINKS		URINE		**ACCIDENTS** ACCIDENTAL LEAKS	DID YOU FEEL A STRONG URGE TO GO?	WHAT WERE YOU DOING AT THE TIME?
	What kind?	How much?	How many times?	How much? (cicle one)	How much? (cicle one)		Sneezing, exercising, having sex, lifting, ect.
Sample				sm med lg	sm med lg	yes no	
6-7 a.m.							
7-8 a.m.							
8-9 a.m.							
9-10 a.m.							
10-11 a.m.							
11-12 noon							
12-1 p.m.							
1-2 p.m.							
2-3 p.m.							
3-4 p.m.							
4-5 p.m.							
5-6 p.m.							
6-7 p.m.							

(Courtesy of National Institute of Diabetes and Digestive and Kidney Diseases, or NIDDK, National Institutes of Health.)

KEGEL EXERCISES

Kegel exercises, also called pelvic muscle-strengthening exercises and pelvic floor exercises, were developed by Dr. Arnold Kegel in 1948 as a method of controlling incontinence in women following childbirth. These exercises are now recommended for women with urinary stress incontinence, men who have urinary incontinence after prostate surgery, and people who have fecal (stool) incontinence. The Kegel exercises are designed to strengthen the muscles of the pelvic floor, thereby improving the urethral and rectal sphincter function. The success of the exercises depends on proper technique and adherence to a regular exercise program.

Some people have difficulty identifying and isolating the muscles of the pelvic floor. Care must be taken to learn to contract the correct muscles. Typically, most people contract the abdominal or thigh muscles, not even working the pelvic floor muscles. These incorrect contractions may result in worse pelvic floor tone and incontinence. Several techniques exist to help the incontinent person identify the correct muscles.

One approach is to sit on the toilet and start to urinate. Try to stop the flow of urine midstream by contracting your pelvic floor muscles. Repeat this action several times until you become familiar with the feel of contracting the correct group of muscles. Do not contract your abdominal, thigh, or buttock muscles while performing the exercise.

Another approach to help you identify the correct muscle group is to insert a finger into the vagina (in women) or rectum (in men). You should then try to tighten the muscles around your finger as if holding back urine. The abdominal and thigh muscles should remain relaxed.

Women may also strengthen these muscles by using a vaginal cone, which is a weighted device that is inserted into the vagina. The cones are commercially available. The women should then try to contract the pelvic floor muscles in an effort to hold the device the place.

For those people who are unsure whether they are performing the procedure correctly, biofeedback and electrical stimulation may be used to help you identify the correct muscle group. Biofeedback is a method of positive reinforcement. Electrodes are placed on your abdomen and along the anal area. Some therapists place a sensor in the vagina in women or anus in men, to monitor contraction of the pelvic floor muscles. A monitor will display a graph showing which muscles are contracting and which are at rest. The therapist can help you identify the correct muscles for performing Kegel exercises.

Electrical stimulation involves using low-voltage electric current to stimulate the correct group of muscles. The current may be delivered using an anal or vaginal probe. The electrical stimulation therapy may be done in the clinic or at home. Treatment sessions usually last 20 minutes and may be performed every one to four days. Some clinical studies have shown promising results in treating stress and urge incontinence with electrical stimulation.

Performing Pelvic Floor Exercises:

1. Begin by emptying your bladder.
2. Tighten the pelvic floor muscles and hold for a count of 10.
3. Relax the muscle completely for a count of 10.
4. Perform 10 exercises, three times a day (morning, afternoon, and night).

You can do these exercises any time and any place. Most people prefer to do the exercises while lying down or sitting in a chair. After four to six weeks you should notice some improvement. It may take as long a three months to see a drastic change.

A word of caution: Some people feel that they can speed up the progress by increasing the number of repetitions and the frequency of exercises. However, overexercising may cause muscle fatigue and increase your leakage of urine. You should not feel any discomfort in your abdomen or back while performing these exercises. If you do, you are probably performing the pelvic floor exercises incorrectly. Some people have a tendency to hold their breath or tighten their chest while trying to contract the pelvic floor muscles. Relax and concentrate on contracting just the pelvic floor muscles.

If properly performed, Kegel exercises have been shown to be 50 to 80% effective in curing or improving urinary stress incontinence.

Source: National Institutes of Health and the U.S. National Library of Medicine.

DOCTOR'S DIARY

Henry Powell, 78, has had diabetes for many years. He experiences numbness in his feet due to peripheral neuropathy (nerve damage) caused by the diabetes, and he has eye problems related to diabetic retinopathy. Recently he had developed continual dribbling of urine. He did not experience any urge to go to the bathroom; his urine simply continued dribbling out. He went to see his doctor who referred him to me for a urologist's opinion. I obtained a urinalysis, which was normal and I performed a Bladder Scan (ultrasound) in the office that showed a very large distended bladder, which did not empty properly even when he tried to void. I placed a catheter in the bladder to drain the urine and taught Henry how to perform intermittent self-catheterization. I advised him that the risk of infection was less with this technique than with a catheter continually in the bladder. I explained to Henry that diabetes could occasionally damage the nerves to the bladder so that it does not contract properly, but the problem could also be caused by obstruction from his prostate gland. Urodynamic studies and cystoscopy were indicated to separate these two possible causes of his problem, as the treatment is quite different depending on which one was causing his inability to empty the bladder. If the urinary volume gets excessive, it can cause serious problems to the function of the kidneys and may lead to kidney infection and kidney failure. The tests demonstrated that he had poor bladder contractions due to the effect of the diabetes on the nerves and muscles to his bladder. Prostate surgery would not be necessary, but I informed Henry that he would need to catheterize himself every 6-8 hours in order to properly drain the bladder.

THEN AND NOW

Urodynamics is the study of the filling and emptying of the bladder. In the 1800s water was infused into the patient's bladder via a catheter, and the volume of water that was instilled before leaking was observed.

Today, urodynamics employs sophisticated equipment to monitor bladder pressures with filling and emptying. Urine flow rates can be measured. Special X-ray studies can be done at the same time.

Urodynamics can be helpful in evaluating patients with urinary incontinence. It may also be helpful in determining if there is an obstruction, as with an enlarged prostate.

for a 55-year-old woman with stress urinary incontinence who is very active as an athlete and who has not had a favorable response to pelvic muscle exercises, whereas surgery may not be the best option for an 86-year-old man who has an enlarged prostate and who also has a past history of congestive heart failure and diabetes.

BEHAVIORAL MODIFICATION AND PELVIC MUSCLE REHABILITATION

The goals of behavior modification and pelvic muscle rehabilitation center around three general principles:

1. Maintain a regulated bladder volume by the control (not restriction) of fluids.
2. Increase the ability of the nervous system and pelvic muscles to inhibit bladder contractions in OAB patients.
3. Increase the strength of the pelvic muscles in SUI patients.

These goals are attained by pelvic muscle *(Kegel)* exercises with or without biofeedback. They require the cooperation of the patient and may not be feasible for the patient who is in a nursing home and who has Alzheimer's disease or has dementia from previous strokes. However, the exercises may be very helpful for cognitively aware people in assisted living facilities.

SURGERY

Surgery has been primarily used in the treatment of stress incontinence and remains the treatment of choice in the community-dwelling patient and rightly so, as the success rates remain in the 80 to 85% range and are durable. In the LTC setting or in the cognitively impaired patient, building up the urethral sphincter by injection under a local anesthetic has been demonstrated to be effective, although repeat injections are common with the currently available agents (collagen and carbon-coated zirconium beads). Up to two-thirds of patients can be rendered continent with a durability of two years, with rarely a complication. It is certainly warranted in those patients with poor sphincter function as a minimally invasive technique to improve their quality of life.

MEDICATIONS

Currently, there are no medications approved by the Food and Drug Administration for the treatment of SUI. Off-label use of certain drugs, such as pseudoephedrine, phenylpropanolamine, and imipramine, has not been supported by any randomly controlled trials. In addition, these drugs may have dangerous side effects, including rapid heartbeat, elevation of blood pressure, and headache. Phenylpropanolamine, which was an ingredient in many cold formulas, was pulled from the shelves of pharmacies throughout the United States due to studies showing a higher risk of strokes. Trials are in progress with some newer agents, but whether the benefit-risk ratio will make it helpful in the management of SUI or MI in the elderly has yet to be determined.

WHAT'S NEW?

The Interstim, manufactured by Medtronic, is used to treat the intractable overactive bladder by modulating the nerve reflexes in the bladder. The first phase is stimulation under local anesthesia to see whether the desired response is obtained before permanently implanting the device. This prevents needless surgery, but requires a cooperative, cognitively intact patient for the initial testing. Thus, its utility is reduced in many older persons who could benefit from it the most.

Showing great promise is the technique in which low doses of Botulinum A toxin are injected into the bladder. The procedure can be performed as an outpatient and under local anesthesia, with a durability up to nine months. It paralyzes small sections of the bladder only where injected, which is enough to reduce the overall activity of the bladder without paralyzing the entire bladder muscle. Thus, the patient still has the sensation of bladder filling and can urinate and empty the bladder adequately. There have been no significant complications reported. Durability has been the issue, but many patients would likely have the procedure twice a year if it could alleviate their urgency and incontinence. Studies on overall safety and efficacy have yet to be performed, so its use is anecdotal and off-label.

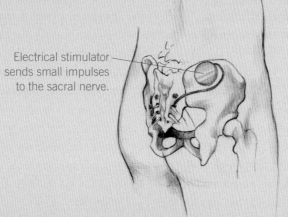

Electrical stimulator sends small impulses to the sacral nerve.

The Interstim device is a new method for managing an overactive bladder. *(Reproduced with permission of Medtronic.)*

14

The primary utility of drug treatment has been for OAB. Behavior management and drug therapy of UI are mutually supportive, since neither used alone will work for all patients. Estrogen treatment may be necessary in order for these medications to work effectively. Estrogen is available in pills, patches, or topical creams. It is important that a woman discuss the benefits and risks of estrogen with her physician since there may be contraindications to its use. Another key point is that older patients generally have multiple chronic illnesses and may be using several other medications. A wide variety of drugs prescribed for older patients can contribute to or worsen OAB symptoms. It is important to review the drug list in detail to see whether any medicine affecting the functioning of the lower urinary tract can be stopped or replaced. The physician will also need to consider the potential for interactions of the current medicines with bladder-relaxant drugs.

The two standard medications for OAB are OXYBUTYNIN extended release (DITROPAN-XR) and TOLTERODINE long acting (DETROL-LA). Both medications are FDA-approved for UI and OAB. Appropriately monitored, the adverse drug effects are manageable. Both preparations provide an improvement over the older immediate-release oxybutynin, which always provided satisfactory efficacy for OAB, but side effects (especially dry mouth) often resulted in discontinuation of treatment. There are similar adverse-effect profiles for both drugs, but reported side effects of sedation, confusion, or tiredness are low. Physicians will try one drug and, if there are side effects or it does not seem very effective, may try the other to see if it offers any therapeutic advantage.

Advanced drug-delivery systems include *transdermal* (skin patches), *intravaginal* (vaginal suppository), and *intravesical* (instilled in the bladder) oxybutynin therapy. The transdermal system received FDA approval after the clinical trials were completed. Since the drug bypasses the liver where it is normally metabolized, administration of smaller doses achieves the same effects as larger doses of oral oxybutynin, thus increasing patient tolerance. Possible disadvantages include local skin irritation and, in patients over the age of 75, lack of adequate skin moisture to allow drug penetration. This product contains an enhancing agent to force the oxybutynin through the skin and thus may be helpful in the geriatric population to enhance efficacy and compliance while reducing any side effects.

There are other oral preparations under study in the United States and abroad; however, it is disappointing that the studies are on classes of drugs already in use. Attempts at developing new drugs for OAB are rare at this point. Theoretically, among the drug groups that could be helpful but are not in clinical trials are calcium-channel blockers, potassium-channel openers, and other mechanisms to slow bladder activity.

SUMMARY

Coexisting medical conditions, functional status, and finances are a few of the numerous considerations affecting the diagnosis and management of urinary incontinence in older patients. Setting realistic goals for treatment and communicating them clearly to both patient and caregiver are crucial. The decision on whether to assess the problem and initiate therapy depends on two factors:

1. The patient's cognitive ability and motivation for therapy (this may relate to the individual's circumstances—whether living in the community, assisted living accommodations, or an LTC facility).
2. The patient's perception of symptom severity in relationship to the risks and costs he or she is willing to undertake.

If you or someone you love has urinary incontinence, the first step is discussing it with your physician.

■

WHAT YOU NEED TO KNOW

▶ Urinary incontinence is a common problem.

▶ Urinary incontinence is often treatable and sometimes curable.

▶ A doctor's evaluation begins with your disclosure of the problem. If the doctor doesn't ask, tell him or her.

▶ Request a referral to a urologist, gynecologist, or geriatrician if your doctor tells you that incontinence is a normal part of aging or if your doctor does not evaluate you.

▶ If a loved one is incontinent and cannot provide a history (due to Alzheimer's disease, strokes, etc.), go with the person to the doctor's office to help explain the problem. If your loved one resides in a nursing home or long-term care facility, arrange to meet the doctor there or call the doctor to discuss the situation. If necessary, request a referral to someone who does treat incontinence.

WHAT YOU NEED TO KNOW

▶ **National Association for Continence**
P.O. Box 8306
Spartanburg, SC 29305
800-BLADDER, 864-579-7900
E-mail: memberservices@nafc.org
Web: www.nafc.org

▶ **Simon Foundation for Continence**
P.O. Box 835
Wilmette, IL 60091
800-23-SIMON, 847-864-3913
E-mail: simoninfo@simonfoundation.org
Web: www.simonfoundation.org

▶ **American Foundation for Urologic Disease**
1128 North Charles Street
Baltimore, MD 21201
800-242-2383, 410-468-1800
E-mail: admin@afud.org
Web: www.afud.org

▶ **American Urogynecologic Association**
2025 M Street NW, Suite 800
Washington, DC 20036
202-367-1167
E-mail: augs@dc.sba.com
Web: www.augs.org

▶ **National Kidney and Urologic Diseases**
Information Clearinghouse
3 Information Way
Bethesda, MD 20892
800-891-5390 or 301-654-4415
E-mail: nkudic@info.niddk.nih.gov
Web: www.niddk.nih.gov

▶ **Society for Urologic Nurses and Associates**
P.O. Box 56
East Holly Avenue
Pitman, NJ 08071-0056
888-TAP-SUNA, 856-256-2335
Web: www.suna.org

The good physician knows his patients through and through, and his knowledge is bought dearly. Time, sympathy, and understanding must be lavishly dispensed, but the reward is to be found in that personal bond which forms the greatest satisfaction of the practice of medicine. One of the essential qualities of the clinician is interest in humanity, for the secret of the care of the patient is in caring for the patient.

—Dr. Frances Weld Peabody, 1927

THE AUTHOR

15 *Vincent Stenger MD*

VINCENT G. STENGER, MD, graduated from the Johns Hopkins University School of Medicine. He completed his residency at the University of Florida College of Medicine where he subsequently joined the faculty. He was appointed the first professor and chairman of the Department of Obstetrics and Gynecology at the Milton S. Hershey Medical Center of the Pennsylvania State University College of Medicine. After 20 years in research, teaching, and administration in academic medicine, he moved to Sarasota, Florida, where he practiced obstetrics and gynecology. In the last 10 years, he has limited his practice to gynecology and gynecologic oncology. He has had leadership roles as president of the Florida Obstetric and Gynecology Society, chairman and board member of the Florida Section of the American College of Obstetricians and Gynecologists, and past examiner for the American Board of Obstetrics and Gynecology. Dr. Stenger is a member of the medical staffs of Sarasota Memorial Hospital and Doctors Hospital in Sarasota.

15 | GYNECOLOGY

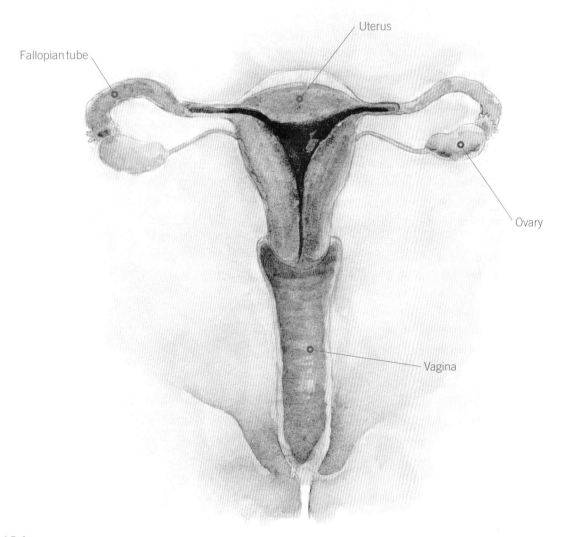

Uterus

Fallopian tube

Ovary

Vagina

(figure 15-1)

A woman's reproductive system consists of the vagina, the uterus or womb, and the ovaries. The ovaries produce eggs that move into the fallopian tube. If a sperm fertilizes the egg, it passes into the uterus and, after implanting on the wall of the uterus, eventually leads to the development and birth of a baby.

During the 1970s I had the privilege of serving as a consultant in a geriatric mental hospital in Pennsylvania that by law required annual pelvic exams and Pap smears for the female population. This provided me with a tremendous educational opportunity. That experience combined with 24 years of practice in a community in Florida with a very high percentage of retired seniors has given me the basis of practical knowledge in the care of the senior women. My current medical practice is composed mostly of women over 65 years of age.

There are changes that have occurred in recent years that need to be considered. Rapid advances in medical and scientific information have influenced medical practice. Much of this health information is easily accessible by the public. This allows you as a consumer of health care services to have a better understanding of the options available. It also enables you to have a more active role in decisions about your diagnostic and treatment programs. Whereas in the past physicians had a more "parental" role, in which recommended advice and treatment were seldom questioned, physicians and their patients are now willing to have the physician take the role of "health care consultant." Rather than make decisions for the patient, the physician acts as a guide to the patient in her own decision making.

Since both benign and malignant conditions are covered in this chapter, a few terms need to be defined. The *etiology* is the cause of a disease or condition. *Pathophysiology* is the process that causes the transition from a normal to an abnormal condition. *Diagnosis* is the determination by your physician of the nature of a disease or condition. This may require any or all of the following: the information given by the patient, the examination by the physician, laboratory tests, X-rays and other imaging studies, biopsies and pathology reports, and consultations with specialists. *Treatment* (therapy) is the regimen of medicines, surgery, and radiation therapy, or a combination of these, used to manage a disease or condition. *Outcome* is the result, short-term and long-term, of treatment.

The very broad area covered by this chapter requires brevity and conciseness. There are hundreds of medical books available in the area of gynecology, with each disease commanding its own chapter. As you read this, remember that I do not nor could I give you information on all treatment modalities or minor variations thereof. Because your doctor's particular treatment may vary somewhat from mine does not make his or hers wrong. Remember, most physicians try to practice the art and science of medicine. The humanistic and caring approach for many gynecologic problems may be as important as the medication given. You want to find a physician who takes a personal interest in you and with whom you have a relationship of trust and confidence.

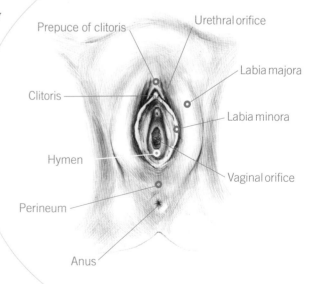

(figure 15-2)

The anatomy of the female external genital organs.

(figure 15-3)
Female pelvic organs. (Internal side view).

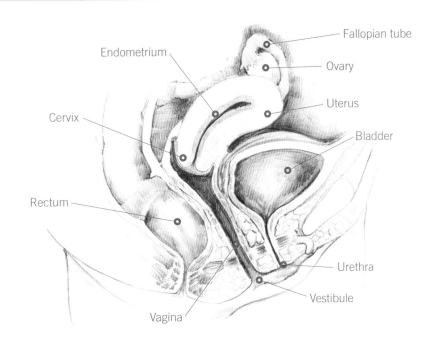

Endometrium

Fallopian tube

Ovary

Cervix

Uterus

Bladder

Rectum

Urethra

Vestibule

Vagina

FEMALE ANATOMY

To understand the physical changes and gynecological problems in the aging female, you need a basic understanding of female anatomy (see Figure 15-2). The vulva represents all the external female genitalia visible without using instruments. It is composed of the labia majora, which consists of large folds of protective skin and fatty tissue. The labia minora are the smaller and less prominent folds at the entrance to the vagina. These folds are generally considered to include the clitoris. The clitoris is an appendage in the upper folds of the labia minora analogous to the penis in the male. It is part of the organ complex involved in sexual stimulation. The mons pubis is the fat pad over the pelvic bone that protects the upper entrance to the vagina and the clitoris. The perineal body is the skin between the vagina and the rectum.

The internal female genitalia consists of the vagina, a 6- to 8-inch tube that is the sexual receptor organ of the female. The vestibule is the outer entrance to the vagina penetrated by the urethra. It ends at the hymenal membrane. The cervix is entrance to the uterus. Part of the cervix protrudes into the vagina (see Figure 15-3).

The uterus is the womb. It is composed of the *fundus,* or body, and the cervix. It is made up of smooth muscle and a lining called the endometrium. The endometrium responds to hormones and changes in a cyclic manner and sheds each month. The shedding of the endometrium is associated with bleeding and is responsible for menstruation. The fallopian tubes are 4- to 6-inch tubular organs that connect to the uterus on either side and receive and transport the fertilized egg from the ovary that eventually implants into the endometrium to become the embryo (early stage of development from conception to about the end of the second month of pregnancy) and fetus (the unborn child from the end of the second month until birth) of pregnancy. The sperm pass through the fallopian tubes to fertilize the egg at ovulation (release of the egg from the ovary).

The ovaries are 2.5- to 3-centimeter organs supported by ligaments on either side of the pelvis. They produce the eggs for conception. They also produce estrogen and progesterone in a cyclic manner as a response to hormones produced by the pituitary gland.

The development of the female breasts begins with the formation of *breast buds* at menarche (onset of menstruation). Eventual size depends on many factors. These include genetics, the hormone production of the ovaries, and the general nutritional environment. The female breast is an anatomic and physiologic structure designed to feed offspring by producing milk, called *lactation* (see Figures 15-4 and 15-5). The breast is made up of a glandular branching system lined with secretory cells that can be pictured as a branching tree with many trunks that empty into a central collecting area called the nipple. Around the nipple is the areola that may be pigmented secondary to pregnancy or oral contraceptives and contains secretory glands for lubrication. Smooth muscle cells around the areola may cause erection of the nipple when stimulated. The breast lobules are the milk-producing structures within the breast. There are 15 to 20 lobules within each breast. The major fillers in the breasts are fibrous supporting structures and fat deposits. They also go through cyclic changes related to the ovarian hormones. Lactation occurs as a result of hormone production by the pituitary gland.

A woman goes through stages of the life cycle that include the ability to reproduce offspring and the cessation of that ability. This is rather sharply delineated. Puberty occurs over a year or two but is delineated by menarche. Puberty coincides with maturation of the ovaries and the production of the eggs that will allow conception and pregnancy. Menopause, or the cessation of menstruation, typically occurs in women in the United States in the late 40s to mid-50s. This coincides with the period of ovarian failure and onset of infertility. In this chapter on the aging woman, we deal mostly with menopause and the postmenopausal states.

All organ systems start a procession of atrophy (wasting of tissues and cells) with aging. However, at the time of menopause, a woman's production of the hormones estrogen and progesterone decreases, and all tissues that are stimulated by

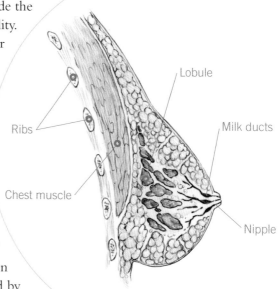

(figure 15-4)

Anatomy of the female breast.

(figure 15-5)

Inside structure of the breast.

these hormones change. The uterus, ovaries, vagina, vulva, base of the bladder, skin, muscles, breasts, brain, and so on, show significant changes throughout the years after menopause. I address these issues in more detail as we go through the benign and malignant diseases affecting the aging population.

VULVA AND VAGINA
BENIGN DISEASES

Vulvovaginitis is inflammation and/or infection of the vulva and/or vagina. It represents the most common gynecological disease in the female. The diagnosis requires an examination, frequently a culture, and a Pap smear if it has not been obtained within 1 year. Atrophic vulvovaginitis is thinning of the vulva and vaginal tissues that occurs commonly after menopause. The thinning (atrophy) of the tissues of the reproductive tract varies from person to person but can be severe enough to prevent satisfactory intercourse. It responds dramatically to low-dose estrogen vaginal cream. In those women where estrogen is not advisable or when it is refused, other vaginal lubricants may be prescribed.

Yeast (*Monilia,* also called *Candida)* is the most common organism involved in infection of the vulva and vagina. It can be treated with antifungal vaginal creams or oral antifungal drugs. In early cases or when the problem is chronic or recurring, use of vinegar or water douches may be helpful. These infections are most common in the aging patient who has taken prolonged antibiotic therapy. They are also more common in diabetics.

Bacterial vulvovaginitis can be caused by streptococci or a bacterium called *Hemophilus,* but is commonly mixed in type (more than one type of bacteria) and referred to under the general heading of *bacterial vaginosis.* They are diagnosed by culture and treated with a METRONIDAZOLE (FLAGYL) preparation or other appropriate antibiotics depending on the specific organism and sensitivities found on culture.

Polyps are growths that are most always benign but must be examined and excised if there is any bleeding or suspicious appearance. Premalignant diseases of the vulva and vagina include any abnormal growths, elevations, or pigmentation. They must be evaluated with a Pap smear and biopsy.

Condylomata acuminata, also called *venereal warts,* is less common in the aging patient but do occur. The responsible infecting agent is the human papilloma virus (HPV). Though mostly benign, they can be malignant or premalignant. They can be treated with topical medication or excision. One of the more common treatments when topical medication fails is laser evaporation of all the lesions. This is generally done under local anesthesia, but if the warts are extensive, general anesthesia may be required. Since their etiology is viral, they may recur.

MALIGNANT DISEASES OF THE VULVA AND VAGINA

Carcinoma in situ and dysplasia are considered cancer but preinvasive types that are treated by local therapy. This treatment cures over 95% of this disease. Wide local excision is both diagnostic and therapeutic for the majority of these lesions. A less disfiguring and highly effective method is laser evaporation of the lesions under local anesthesia. They must be biopsied to be certain they are not invasive cancer.

Invasive cancer of the vulva is a surgical disease with the extent of surgical excision depending on the size and type of cancer. **Basal cell cancer** is the most common skin cancer. It can affect the vulva, but can be excised and cured most of the time. Malignant **melanoma** must be treated with a more extensive excision including removal of local lymph nodes. The cure rate depends on the extent of the disease. Wide local excisions in early melanomas (stages I and II) cure a high percentage of these lesions. Large melanomas and/or those that deeply penetrate the skin recur frequently and are mostly fatal, especially stage III (lymph node positive) and stage IV (distant spread) disease. **Squamous cell cancer** is the most common vulvar cancer. If lesions are small, a wide local excision is done. If over one centimeter in size, a radical excision is indicated with regional lymph node removal. Even a fairly large lesion of this type has a very good prognosis if properly treated. Although the surgery removes all the vulva and the regional lymph nodes, the cure rate approaches 90% if regional nodes are negative, and 50% if no extension beyond the regional nodes is detected. Radiation therapy plays no role in the treatment of this disease. The tissues of the vulva don't tolerate this treatment. It may result in a major ulceration that many patients have said is worse than the disease. Most vulvar cancers grow slowly and can be detected early by yearly pelvic exams. With removal of suspicious growths, progression to advanced disease is less likely thus increasing the overall survival in this cancer.

Carcinoma of the vagina is relatively uncommon. Dysplasia or carcinoma in situ is best treated with laser evaporation after biopsy. If dysplasia persists or there is a recurrence, the use of intravaginal Efudex (5-fluorouracil) is quite successful but requires vigilant follow-up, as recurrence is common. Invasive cancer of the vagina is less satisfactorily

(figure 15-6)

Cervix (as seen by a doctor on pelvic examination): (a) normal; (b) cancerous.

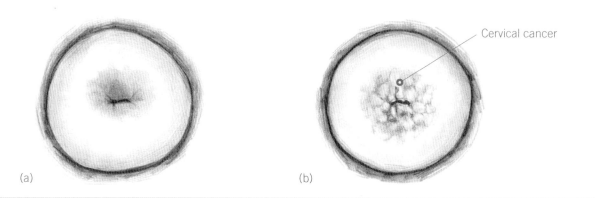

Cervical cancer

(a)   (b)

15

treated. Mostly it occurs in people who have had a previous hysterectomy (removal of the uterus) for cervical disease. Radiation therapy is generally the treatment of choice, but radical *vaginectomy* (removal of the entire vagina) is sometimes a preference. Prognosis is limited mainly because of deep pelvic spread.

CERVIX

The cervix will be dealt with as a separate organ even though it is a part of the uterus. This is primarily because it protrudes into the vagina and is always dealt with in medical books and the literature as a separate structure.

BENIGN DISEASES OF THE CERVIX

Cervicitis or inflammation of the cervix is a common disease that mainly starts at or around the time of the onset of menstruation. The reason for this is not clearly understood but certainly becomes common after starting to use tampons and having regular intercourse. Acute cervicitis occurs with bacteria such as streptococcus and gonorrhea. Chlamydia is frequently a silent partner in acute infections. These all produce leukorrhea (a profuse puslike discharge) and a foul odor. These should be diagnosed by culture and treated with the appropriate antibiotics. Chronic cervicitis is a very common long-term problem in many women. Unless there is some other abnormality, this condition is not always treated.

Cervical and endocervical polyps are growths that occur on the cervix or within the cervical canal. They are a common problem. If they become large or cause bleeding, or if they are associated with abnormal Pap smears, they are surgically removed.

MALIGNANT DISEASES OF THE CERVIX

Cervical dysplasia and carcinoma in situ are sometimes referred to as premalignant diseases of the cervix, when in fact it is a continuum from superficial to invasive cancer. Cellular changes occur that classify the gradation of the changes from *mild dysplasia* to *moderate dysplasia* to *severe dysplasia*. The etiology of cervical cancer is undoubtedly viral, although many factors serve as inducers as with all cancers (see Figure 15-6). The *human papilloma* virus has over 80 different types with at least three or four being associated with vulvar, vaginal, and cervical cancers. Years of research have failed to develop a vaccine against these viruses.

Squamous cell cancer of the cervix accounts for about 95% of all cervical malignancies. It starts at the junction of the outer and inner surface of the cervix, called the *squamocolumnar* junction. This is a transitional zone from squamous cells to the glandular-type cells within the cervical canal. Adenocarcinoma of the cervix comes from the glandular component of the cervix and accounts for the other 5%.

With the advent of regular pelvic examinations and Pap smears in the majority of the female population in the United States, early detection has allowed treatment in the preinvasive stage and reduced the late stages to a rarity. Two decades ago the most common cancer surgery in my practice was for cervical cancer. Today I see fewer than two per year, and they are mostly treated with radiation therapy. On the other hand I treat at least one patient per week for dysplasia of the cervix or vagina, always in the office setting with local or no anesthesia. The carbon dioxide laser and the loop electrosurgical excision procedure (LEEP) cure most of these early lesions. LEEP uses a thin wire loop electrode that emits a painless electrical current that excises the abnormal tissue. The cure rate with one treatment is 94%, with 6% needing a repeat treatment. When the residual disease is high in the cervical canal, we sometimes need to do a simple hysterectomy to eradicate residual disease. Although rare, a small percentage of patients (less than 1%) have a highly *anaplastic* (aggressive cancer) cell type that grows rapidly and may be advanced at the time first seen.

UTERUS

BENIGN UTERINE CONDITIONS

The most common complaint after vaginitis in the female is abnormal bleeding. This can be from cervicitis, vaginitis, or cancer of the cervix, although quite frequently it is from the endometrium. All "abnormal" bleeding must be investigated. Bleeding is considered abnormal in the premenopausal woman if it occurs between menstrual periods or if the menstrual blood flow is excessive. With the advent of menopause, there is a gradual lengthening in the interval between the periods and a gradual decrease in the volume of flow. Another pattern that fits in the normal menopause is the total cessation of all bleeding. After the menopause any bleeding is abnormal. Although some bleeding can occur when hormone replacement therapy (HRT) is used, all bleeding must be investigated even when a woman is on HRT. When using combined estrogen and progesterone therapy (as is always done when the uterus is still present), the incidence

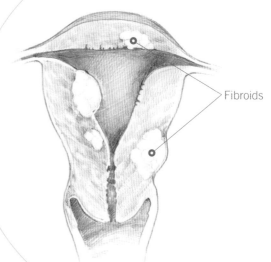

Fibroids

(figure 15-7)

Uterine fibroids are benign muscular tumors of the uterus.

284

of endometrial cancer is significantly reduced but not totally eliminated. The Pap smear is used but is not as reliable for endometrial problems. An endometrial biopsy (biopsy of the lining of the uterus) or dilatation and curettage (D&C) is mandated in most instances where the cervix and vaginal evaluation show no abnormality. Common causes of abnormal bleeding include polyps and fibroid tumors (benign muscular tumors) of the uterus (see Figure 15-7). With a negative endometrial biopsy, an ultrasound of the pelvis is done to evaluate the thickness of the endometrium and/or to see if polyps are present. Ovarian and uterine enlargement can be defined more precisely as well. A D&C, with a hysteroscopy (examination of the inside of the uterus with a special scope), will allow for the removal of polyps. Although most cervical polyps are benign, we occasionally see a polypoid malignancy that must be evaluated by the pathologist. Fibroids that distort the endometrial cavity enough to cause bleeding frequently require a hysterectomy to control the bleeding. Another common condition causing uterine enlargement at or around menopause is adenomyosis. This occurs when the normal endometrial lining grows into the wall of the uterus. It may also be associated with pain.

Endometrial hyperplasia is caused by continuous stimulation of the endometrium by estrogen without the normal cyclic changes produced by progesterone. This is a common cause of bleeding during the perimenopause (the time leading up to menopause). The production of progesterone requires ovulation, which gradually decreases as part of the changing state of aging ovarian function. The doctor can add cyclic progesterone for a few cycles to easily reverse this. When, however, the hyperplasia becomes atypical (i.e., the microscopic evaluation of the tissue shows a more abnormal pattern), the condition has generally been going on for some time, and the treatment with progesterone may not permanently reverse the process. We usually advise hysterectomy at that point.

MALIGNANT UTERINE CONDITIONS

Endometrial cancer is the most common pelvic cancer after menopause (see Figure 15-8). The most common cell type is adenocarcinoma, accounting for more than 90% of all the endometrial cancers. As with all cancers they are graded by the pathologists from the biopsy specimen and staged by the gynecologist by size and extent of the disease at discovery. Fortunately, bleeding eventually occurs in all endometrial cancers. It is the early bleeding that causes the patient to see her doctor that allows for a very high cure in this disease. Education about our bodies and the demise of the myth that cancer can't be cured have led to more and more people being cured of their cancers. The standard of treatment today for endometrial cancer involves surgery, which also helps determine

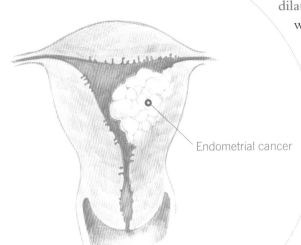

Endometrial cancer

(figure 15-8*)*

Endometrial cancer starts in the lining of the uterus.

the staging of the disease. Adjuvant therapy, be it with radiation or chemotherapy, will be necessary in only about 10 to 15%. These women have aggressive cancers or late detection of their disease.

OVARIES AND FALLOPIAN TUBES

BENIGN CONDITIONS

Pelvic masses detected at the time of a pelvic examination are most frequently found on routine checkups. Distinction between benign and malignant conditions cannot always be determined. The pelvic ultrasound is considered the best single test for determining the nature of a pelvic mass. Inflammatory masses due to infection involving the ovary and tubes are usually bilateral (on both sides of the pelvis) and cause pain and fever, especially in the acute stage. The treatment is antibiotic therapy, and the resolution of the problem should be dramatic. Only if the masses do not resolve or if there is a suspicion of abscess formation is surgery required. Since pregnancy can still occur in women in their 50s, we have to consider **ectopic pregnancy** (the fertilized egg implants in the fallopian tube rather than the uterus) when there is a unilateral (on one side of the pelvis) mass in the absence of normal periods. Multiple cystic masses can be seen with chronic infectious processes and may cause recurring pain. Chlamydia infection is frequently the causative agent.

Endometriosis (when the endometrium is in an abnormal place, such as in the ovaries and posterior pelvis) is a relatively common disease. In general it is detected before menopause. At times the disease goes undetected until the perimenopause. As with all pelvic masses, a *diagnostic laparoscopy* is performed when the cause is not certain. With this procedure we can generally view with a fiberoptic scope the entire pelvis, uterus, ovaries, tubes, appendix, and so on, to determine if and what further treatment is needed.

Benign ovarian tumors or cysts can become quite large. Until they are removed, we often cannot be certain if they are benign or malignant. A solid ovarian tumor should always be removed to determine its nature. A clear small cyst (less than three centimeters) is most always benign. A complex cystic mass can be either benign or malignant and generally must be removed. A large mass that persists in any postmenopausal female must be removed.

MALIGNANT OVARIAN AND TUBAL DISEASES

Cancer of the fallopian tubes is rare, and it is very difficult to detect until late in the disease process. They seem to be uniformly fatal. When found, it is treated like ovarian cancer.

Ovarian cancers on the other hand are seen frequently in the postmenopausal age group. Although they are seen in younger people, the majority occur starting around the age of 40. As women are living longer, we continue to see ovarian cancer develop in women well into their 80s. It will be interesting to see if this trend continues as women are living even longer into the 90s and 100s. The ovary may develop different types

(figure 15-9*)*
Ovarian cancer.

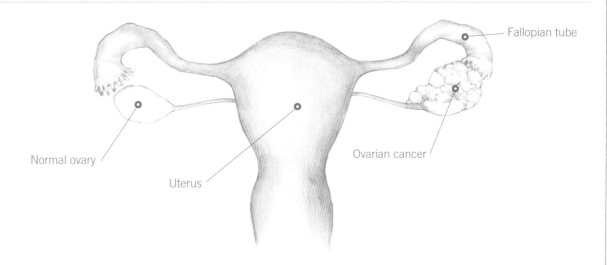

Fallopian tube

Normal ovary

Ovarian cancer

Uterus

of tumors (see Figure 15-9). Some are composed of cells that are usually seen only in the embryo. Others are composed of cells that usually are found in other tissues. The most fascinating and revealing is the *dermoid cyst*. This benign tumor has all the embryonic tissues present, including bone, teeth, hair, fat, glandular tissue, nerve cells, and so on. Depending on the rapidity of growth, it can appear as a huge abdominal mass in a child or a teenager, or be found accidentally in a 60- or 70-year-old woman who underwent a hysterectomy for other reasons.

The most common type of ovarian cancer is unfortunately discovered late and has had a bad prognosis. With the gradual improvement of drugs that kill cells and the refinement of methods of administration of those drugs, the prognosis is improving. I have more and more ovarian cancer survivors in my practice, some now over 20 years and considered cured.

Early detection remains the problem. There may be no symptoms whatever in the very early stages. Sometimes ovarian cancers can produce nonspecific symptoms, such as abdominal bloating, discomfort in the belly, and change in bowel habit. These symptoms may suggest a gastrointestinal problem. Physicians need to be alert that these types of symptoms may signal ovarian disease and consider it in the list of possible diagnoses. This is important since early detection of an ovarian cancer or a borderline malignancy provides the best chance for a cure.

You may have heard in the popular press or from a well-intentioned friend that you should have a CA-125 blood test to screen for ovarian cancer. The problem is that this test is negative in 50% of women with the earliest stage of ovarian cancer, and elevated levels may be found in a small percentage of normal women, as well as in those with certain benign conditions such as uterine fibroids, endometriosis, and pelvic infections. It may even rise with menstruation. Therefore, screening the general population of women with the CA-125 blood test is not recommended. You should have regular pelvic examinations by your physician who will discuss with you if further tests such as pelvic ultrasound and the CA-125 test are appropriate.

The treatment principles for ovarian cancer in the early stages are the same as those with advanced disease, that is, complete and total resection of the disease, aggressive chemotherapy, and close follow-up after therapy.

SELECTION OF A GYNECOLOGIC CANCER SPECIALIST

The gynecologic cancer specialist you select should have the following characteristics:

- Extensive training and experience in gynecologic oncology (cancer of the female genitalia or pelvic organs)
- Provides you with an objective presentation of the treatment program and advises you of the risks and benefits of that program
- Being honest and forthright
- Willing to be aggressive in the treatment of your cancer if that is consistent with your wishes
- Having a positive attitude and is willing to communicate with you regarding your treatment and prognosis
- Being caring and compassionate

If you do not feel that the above list describes your oncologist, select another.

The outcome data of the most malignant advanced ovarian cancers demonstrate that approximately 60% have short-term remission of the disease, 30% have moderate or long-term remission, and approximately 10% are cured.

As you reach a decision with your doctor as to what you will do with any serious malignant disease, you must weigh all your options, select the one best suited for you, and have no regrets, since the treatment you selected will be the best choice you could make at the time.

BREASTS

BENIGN BREAST CONDITIONS

Dense fibrocystic changes (cysts situated within ample surrounding connective tissue) are present in 99% of all breasts to some degree. This can limit the clinical evaluation, as well as the accuracy, of the imaging procedure in extremely dense breasts.

Breast lumps are frequently found by a woman on self-examination (see the box, "Are You Doing It Right?") or by the physician during physical examinations. They are often benign but require further evaluation. Ultrasound imaging is often recommended. If the lump can be felt by the doctor and is cystic, it can be *aspirated* (fluid drawn out with a needle and syringe) in the office. If the ultrasound indicates it is a cyst, but the doctor cannot feel it, it can be aspirated with ultrasound guidance. Solid masses if smooth are generally fibroadenomas (benign glandular tumors) and should be removed if they are growing or are large when detected.

BREAST SELF-EXAMINATION
Are You Doing It Right?

Breast self-examination (BSE) is one of three important steps the American Cancer Society recommends for the early detection of breast cancer. Recently public health experts have argued about whether large population studies prove that this method finds cancer early enough to save lives.

ACS still advises women to do this self-exam monthly and not to forget the other two critical parts of our guidelines for the early detection of breast cancer. They're explained below with www.cancer.org offering more information.

Women age 20 and older should examine their breasts monthly for lumps or other signs of cancer using a reliable method such as the one described below. Once you learn how to do a thorough breast self-exam, it takes only a minute or two each month.

Women should also get a clinical breast exam from a health professional every three years, and an annual mammogram after age 40 to help detect breast cancer early when it is more easily treated.

The best time for breast self-examination (BSE) is about a week after your period ends, when your breasts are not tender or swollen. If you are not having regular periods, do BSE on the same day every month.

- Lie down with a pillow under your right shoulder, and place your right arm behind your head.
- Use the finger pads of the three middle fingers on your left hand to feel for lumps in the right breast.
- Press firmly enough to know how your breast feels. A firm ridge in the lower curve of each breast is normal. If you're not sure how hard to press, talk with your doctor or nurse.
- Move around the breast in a circular, up and down line, or wedge pattern. Be sure to do it the same way every time, check the entire breast area, and remember how your breast feels from month to month.
- Repeat the exam on your left breast, using the finger pads of the right hand. (Move the pillow to under your left shoulder.)
- If you find any changes, see your doctor right away.
- Repeat the examination of both breasts while standing, with your one arm behind your head. The upright position makes it easier to check the upper and outer part of the breasts (toward your armpit). This is where about half of breast cancers are found. You may want to do the standing part of the BSE while you are in the shower. Some breast changes can be felt more easily when your skin is wet and soapy.
- For added safety, you can check your breasts for any dimpling of the skin, changes in the nipple, redness, or swelling while standing in front of a mirror right after your BSE each month.

Source: American Cancer Society.

15

Inflammatory masses such as mastitis (breast infection or inflammation) in the young are mostly benign and treated with antibiotics. If they occur in the aging patient, it could be an inflammatory cancer and should be carefully evaluated.

The treatment of breast cancer is discussed in Chapter 24. However, I would like to reinforce the guidelines for breast cancer screening, which were updated by the American Cancer Society in 2003 and which are presented in the box, "What Has Changed and Why."

WHAT HAS CHANGED AND WHY
Women at Average Risk

Mammography:

- Annually starting at age 40.
- No change from 1997 recommendation. There is a tremendous amount of additional, credible evidence of the benefit of mammography since 1997, especially regarding women in their 40s.
- Women can feel confident about the benefits associated with regular screening mammography. However, mammography also has limitations: it will miss some cancers, and it sometimes leads to follow up of findings that are not cancer, including biopsies.

Clinical breast examination (CBE):

- Every three years for women 20–39; annually for women 40 and older.
- CBE should be part of a woman's periodic health examination, about every three years for women in their 20s and 30s and annually for women 40 and older.
- CBE is a complement to regular mammography screening and an opportunity for women and their health care providers to discuss changes in their breasts, risk factors, and early detection testing.

Breast self-examination (BSE):

- Monthly starting at age 20.
- Women should report any breast change promptly to their health care provider. Beginning in their 20s, women should be told about the benefits and limitations of BSE. It is acceptable for women to choose not to do BSE or to do it occasionally.
- Research has shown that BSE plays a small role in detecting breast cancer compared with self-awareness. However, doing BSE is one way for women to know how their breasts normally feel and to notice any changes.

Older women and women with serious health problems:

- Additional research is needed.
- Continue annual mammography, regardless of age, as long as a woman does not have serious, chronic health problems. For women with serious health problems or short life expectancy, evaluate ongoing early detection testing.
- There is a need to balance the potential benefits of ongoing screening mammography in women with limited longevity against the limitations. The survival benefit of a current mammogram may not be seen for several years.

Women Known to Be at Increased Risk

- Women with a family history of breast cancer should discuss guidelines with their doctors.
- Women known to be at increased risk may benefit from earlier initiation of early detection testing and/or the addition of breast ultrasound or MRI.
- The evidence available is only sufficient to offer general guidance. This guidance will help women and their doctors make more informed decisions about screening.

Source: 1997 guidelines, updated May 2003, of the American Cancer Society.

OTHER GYNECOLOGIC PROBLEMS

A frequent question that menopausal women have is, "I'm having severe hot flashes, and I'm confused about my options. I want to feel better and do what's best, but I don't want to get cancer." There is no simple solution to the problem. Every woman faces it at menopause. Following are some options for you to consider.

The first option is to take no hormones, natural or otherwise, under any circumstances. This is one option but clearly doesn't solve your problem with hot flashes. If you don't take hormones, you may reduce your risk of getting hormone-related cancers, but the risk is not eliminated. If you avoid hormones, how will it affect the quality of your life?

Another option is to take the available estrogens, including those that have been studied in the Women's Health Initiative Multi-Center Study. In this case, you should get all the facts together and decide if the preparations studied should be used, or if they fit your objectives.

Major clinical studies have shown that there are certain hormones that clearly increase the risk for some cardiovascular diseases and breast cancer.

15

DID YOU KNOW?

The *Pap smear* derives its name from its inventor, Dr. George Nicolas Papanicolaou. He was born in Greece in 1883. He graduated from medical school in 1904, and began his career as the physician at a leper colony near his home town of Coumi. In 1907 he went to Germany for postgraduate study at the Zoological Institute in Munich, getting his PhD in 1910. He joined the Balkan Alliance in the war against Turkey where he met Greek-American soldiers who told him of the opportunities in the United States. He then traveled to New York City where he worked as a rug salesman, a violinist at a restaurant, and a clerk for a Greek language newspaper. He finally landed a research job in the anatomy department at Cornell Medical College. While studying sex chromosomes in guinea pigs, he started evaluating the cells from the vagina, thus the birth of cytology in medicine. After noting some grossly unusual cells, he began studying cells from known cervical cancer patients. He noticed there were differences between healthy and abnormal cells. This discovery led to his presentation in 1928 of a lecture entitled, "New Cancer Diagnosis." However, there was very little enthusiasm or acceptance of his work initially.

Dr. Papanicolaou and Herbert F. Traut, a gynecologist who appreciated the importance of the research, published "Diagnosis of Uterine Cancer by the Vaginal Smear," in 1943. It showed how lesions could be detected in their incipient, preinvasive phase, and was a turning point in management of cervical cancer, the most deadly form of cancer in women at the time. The Pap smear soon became widely accepted as a routine screening technique, and in two decades, cervical cancer went from first to third most deadly form of cancer. In the following years, Dr. Papanicolaou extended his technique to the respiratory, urinary, upper gastrointestinal tracts, and breast. His method has been used to screen for cancer in many organs and to predict cancer radiosensitivity and evaluate the efficacy of radiotherapy.

Dr. Papanicolaou received accolades and rewards from many societies here and abroad. He was honored by having his picture on stamps of many countries. On May 18, 1978, he was on the first-day issue of the U.S. 13-cent stamp. Although he made the short list for the 1960 Nobel Prize in medicine, he did not receive it. He clearly made the most outstanding contribution to the discovery of early cancer in women in the history of medicine to date.

Source: Adapted with permission of the American Society for Clinical Pathology.

I would caution you about continuing these. Although your individual risk may be quite small, the numbers become more significant when you extrapolate them to all the women who take hormone preparations. However, before stopping any of your medication, you should consult your physician. Your physician may suggest that you wean off the hormones slowly to minimize the risk of hot flashes. You may be one of those women who do not feel well when she is not on hormones. Perhaps you have other indications for the use of hormones, such as atrophic vaginitis or urinary incontinence. You might wish to use an estrogen cream. In those who need or wish to stay on hormones, I am shifting my patients to bio-identical estrogen and progesterone preparations. I'm doing this as a precaution until more studies shed light on the risks and benefits. Based on my 30 years of experience in use of hormone replacement therapies in an aging patient population, I have seen too many benefits to shun hormone replacement therapy (HRT) entirely. Each woman is unique and will need to decide what is best for herself after she has considered all the positives and negatives and the quality of her life.

■

WHAT YOU NEED TO KNOW

⯈ Understanding gynecological problems as you age requires a basic knowledge of your anatomy, as discussed in this chapter.

⯈ With the onset of menopause, the production of eggs by the ovaries cease and the levels of estrogen and progesterone decrease. These changes result in many different effects on your body. Your doctor can help you through this transition.

⯈ Benign and malignant diseases of your reproductive system are common. Most are treatable and curable with early detection. Discuss with your doctor the scheduling of regular examinations of your breasts and pelvis, as well as mammograms and Pap smears.

⯈ Learn how to do breast self-examination.

⯈ Report to your doctor any unusual vaginal discharge or bleeding.

15

FOR MORE INFORMATION

⯈ **American College of Obstetricians and Gynecologists**
409 12th Street, SW
P.O. Box 96920
Washington, DC 20090
Web: www.acog.org

⯈ **American Cancer Society**
1-800-ACS-2345
Web: www.cancer.org

⯈ **National Comprehensive Cancer Network**
888-909-6226
E-mail: patientinformation@nccn.org
Web: www.nccn.org

⯈ **National Cancer Institute**
NCI Public Inquiries Office, Suite 3036A
6116 Executive Boulevard, MSC8322
Bethesda, MD 20892
Web: www.nci.nih.gov

I don't deserve this award, but I have arthritis and I don't deserve that either.

—*Jack Benny*

THE AUTHOR

16 *Desmond O'Duffy*

J. DESMOND O'DUFFY, MD, completed his premedical and medical education at St. Macartan's College in Monaghan, Ireland, and the National University of Ireland in Dublin, Ireland. He did his internship at St. Vincent's Hospital in Dublin and St. Joseph's Hospital in Parkersburg, West Virginia. He subsequently completed a residency in internal medicine and a fellowship in rheumatology at the Cleveland Clinic. Prior to moving to Sarasota, Florida, in 1999, he was a professor of medicine at the Mayo Clinic in Rochester, Minnesota, where he had served on the faculty since 1969. He is certified by the American Board of Internal Medicine and has subspecialty certification in rheumatology. He received the Phillips Award of the American College of Physicians in 1971, the Distinguished Career Award from the Mayo Clinic in 1996, and the Master Award of the American College of Rheumatology in 1999. He has done extensive original research in rheumatology, and he has published numerous articles in leading medical journals.

BONES, MUSCLES, AND JOINTS I

16

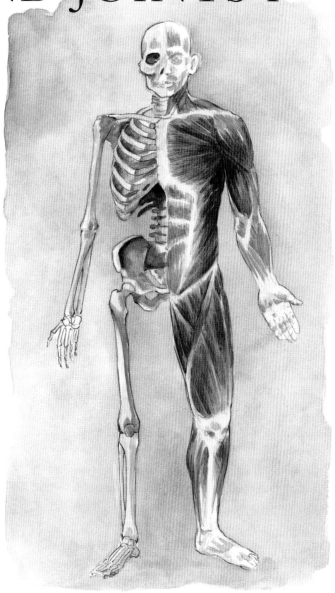

(figure 16-1)

The musculoskeletal system. Your muscles are responsible for the movement of your skeleton.

The moans and groans we associate with aging are often attributable to disorders that affect the muscles, bones, and joints. Rheumatology is the specialty within medicine that deals with disorders of the musculoskeletal system. Orthopedic surgery may be required for the surgical management of musculoskeletal problems. Necessarily, these two disciplines overlap and complement one another. For example, a patient with arthritis of the hip may get along well for years with simple medications and a cane prescribed by his primary care physician or rheumatologist. Eventually the hip arthritis may become so severe that pain or limited movement requires a hip replacement by the orthopedic surgeon. Problems that affect the muscles, bones, and joints as we get older are so common and affect so many people that three chapters are dedicated to them in this manual. This chapter focuses on the evaluation and nonsurgical treatment of musculoskeletal problems. Chapter 17 covers these issues from an orthopedic surgeon's perspective, and Chapter 18 covers the special problems of the back.

Musculoskeletal disorders not only affect muscle and bone but also other tissues of the body that help the muscles and bones work together, such as the ligaments, tendons, and bursae. *Ligaments* connect bones to each other. *Tendons* are the tough cords that connect muscles to bones. A *bursa* is a fluid-filled sac that allows tendons to glide more easily over bony prominences. The other supporting tissues that help your body parts work together are called *connective tissues.* In this chapter, I discuss the disorders that rheumatologists treat in older persons.

OSTEOARTHRITIS

Osteoarthritis, also called *degenerative joint disease,* is the most common joint disease. It usually affects the hands, feet, spine, and the hip and knee joints (see Figure 16-2). Although any individual can be affected, osteoarthritis is often genetically determined. Since you don't get to pick your parents, there is nothing you can do it about if you have a genetic predisposition. However, osteoarthritis can be triggered by joint injury and aggravated by obesity.

The smooth cartilage at the end of the bones becomes thinned and fissured. The nearby bone becomes thickened, and bony spurs called osteophytes develop. Besides water, which is the main "juice" in cartilage, there is a lattice of fibers and spongelike sugar proteins called *proteoglycans* that hold the water in place. The result is a low-friction, well-lubricated service that allows the bones to glide freely in motion. There is little inflammation involved. The changes associated with osteoarthritis take place over years and decades, eventually resulting in decreased joint surface, increased pain and tenderness, restricted joint motion, and instability of the joint.

If you have osteoarthritis of the hands, you usually maintain a good grip and function well indefinitely. The prominent bumps you see at the ends of the fingers of some people are called Heberden's nodes (see Figure 16-3). If the base of your thumb is involved, you might have discomfort

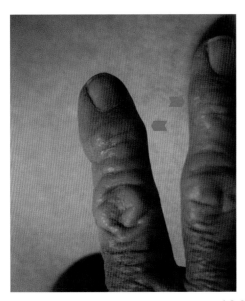

Osteophytes

Narrow joint space

Osteophytes

Cartilage on bone surface worn away

(figure 16-2)

Osteoarthritis is the most common joint disease. Note the narrowed joint space, the worn down cartilage, and the bony spurs called osteophytes.

(figure 16-3)

Caused by osteoarthritis, Heberden's nodes are bony bumps on the ends of the fingers (arrowheads).

when you shake hands or try to open jars. You may require a steroid injection, thumb splinting, or, rarely, surgery. Pain in your hand could also be due to *trigger finger,* which is not related to osteoarthritis. The point here is that if you have hand problems, you could have something other than osteoarthritis. You should let your doctor check you for sticking tendons and other forms of arthritis. Carpal tunnel syndrome (discussed in the section "Pinched Nerves," below) can also cause pain and numbness in the hands.

There are two drawbacks to osteoarthritis of the hand. One is that the response to arthritis drugs is disappointing. Second, there is less benefit from orthopedic surgery. By contrast, the prospects for joint replacement for osteoarthritis of the hip and knee, even in the late stages of the disease, are excellent.

There are no blood abnormalities for osteoarthritis, so there are no blood tests that you should request your doctor to do for this condition. Typical joint changes are shown in Figure 16-2: an uneven, narrowed joint space, increased bone density, osteophytes, and cysts (holes in the bone) under the cartilage. **Magnetic resonance imaging (MRI)** commonly shows cartilage tears in osteoarthritis. If the knee is the affected joint, arthroscopic knee surgery by an orthopedic surgeon can sometimes help. Patients are usually admitted and discharged on the same day. An instrument allows the surgeon to look into the knee and repair the damage.

Despite advertised claims to the contrary, there is no cure for osteoarthritis. However, there are things you can do to help yourself if you have osteoarthritis. If you are overweight, lose weight. Achieving your recommended body weight would be ideal, but every few pounds you lose have a major impact on reducing the stresses on your joints, especially the knees. Modest exercise can help, but you don't want to overstress the joint. Generally, if the exercise causes pain, it is probably not good for the joint. Although exercise can theoretically increase the wear and tear of the joints, it is usually more than offset by the strengthening of the muscles and bones that occur. Check with your doctor or physical therapist if you have any question about the advisability of a particular exercise. Walking is good not only for your bones but for your heart as well. Swimming and aquatic exercises have helped many people with arthritis. Other activities include bicycling (a stationary bike is preferable if you have limited joint motion or coordination problems!) and low-impact aerobics.

A cane can help relieve some of the stress on a painful hip, knee, or ankle joint (see Figure 16-4). Although it is often recommended to use the cane on the side opposite the arthritic joint, you might prefer it on the same side. You should use it on whatever side feels most comfortable. The length of the cane is important, and you can get help from your equipment supplier or from a physical therapist. Some people look on a cane as a sign of "old age" and infirmity. If you have arthritis, try not to worry about what people think and do what is going to help relieve your discomfort. Braces should only be used when advised by your physician to do so. They can cause problems to the skin or even more pain if they are not fitted properly.

A variety of medicines are available to treat arthritis, but remember that there is no cure for osteoarthritis. Some people can do quite well with ACETAMINOPHEN (TYLENOL) up to 4 grams a day. Glucosamine sulfate in a dose of 1500 milligrams per day has helped some people, but it may take as much as three months to show positive effects. Stomach problems do not seem to be a major problem with glucosamine, but diabetics should check with their doctors before using it. A division of the National Institutes of Health is conducting the GAIT trial that hopefully will help further clarify the role that glucosamine should play in the treatment of osteoarthritis. In the section "Drugs for Arthritis," I discuss the pros and cons of the various drugs used to treat arthritis.

Orthopedic surgery has a definite role in the management of arthritic joints if the response to medical therapy has not been adequate or if the patient is experiencing severe limitation due to arthritis (see Chapters 17 and 18). Joint replacement for arthritic hips and knees has helped many persons resume a reasonable quality of life. Advances in orthopedic surgery allow the replacement of arthritic shoulders, elbows, ankles, wrists, and finger joints.

RHEUMATOID ARTHRITIS

Rheumatoid arthritis (RA) is a chronic inflammation in the *synovial,* or lining membrane of joints, tendons, and bursae. The cause is unknown. We do know that inflammatory cells called *lymphocytes* and *macrophages* invade the lining membrane where they cause an inflammatory reaction. Activated white blood cells called *T lymphocytes* produce a protein called a *cytokine* that signals other cells to come to the inflamed area. The main cytokine in the joint inflammation is called *tumor necrosis factor-alpha (TNF-alpha),* and this cytokine has been the target for several novel treatments for rheumatoid arthritis (see section "Drugs for Arthritis," below).

The diagnosis of RA is generally based on the history given by the patient and the doctor's clinical examination. Morning stiffness for one or more hours is common. If three or more joints are painful and swollen simultaneously, RA is likely the cause. However, the arthritis may involve just one spot, such as the wrist and knuckles closest to the fist. If the same joints are painful and swollen on both sides of the body, RA is probably responsible. Rubbery nodules may develop near the elbows or on the forearms and other pressure areas. These nodules are less common in the lungs, heart, and other internal organs.

Although the history and physical examination are most important in the diagnosis of RA, laboratory and X-ray findings can support the diagnosis and help in monitoring the activity of the disease. Rheumatoid

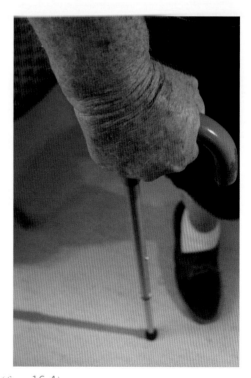

(*figure* 16-4)

A cane can help relieve stress on arthritic joints.

Katherine M., 54, began experiencing stiffness in her hands and weakness of her grip three years ago. Swelling and pain in other joints subsequently developed. At that time, she saw another rheumatologist who diagnosed rheumatoid arthritis. She was treated with prednisone and methotrexate tablets, and her pain, stiffness, and swelling subsided. After four months of treatment, the prednisone was tapered and then stopped. After her rheumatologist retired two years later, she decided on her own to stop the methotrexate and try "alternative therapy," which consisted of a variety of herbs, vitamins, and ibuprofen. Within six months, a severe flare of her arthritis occurred, and she came to see me.

Katherine M.'s knuckles, wrists, elbows, knees, ankles, and feet were swollen and tender. I drained the fluid from her knees and injected a steroid medication. I asked her to resume the prednisone and methotrexate. Within three months, she felt much better. I stopped her prednisone within the next few months. Both Katherine M. and I hoped to achieve maximum benefit from her medicines, and we started two other oral drugs. At her last office visit, I noticed no joint inflammation. Her knuckles were slightly bent, but she had no serious deformity of her other joints. Her bone density test was normal, so special osteoporosis drugs were not necessary. I suggested that she take calcium and vitamin D. I still see her every three months to monitor her progress on the three medicines she is taking. I remind her regularly that herbs and vitamins have no role in the treatment of rheumatoid arthritis.

factor is found in over 90% of patients with RA, but its helpfulness in diagnosis is limited by the fact that it can be negative early in the course and it may not turn positive for months or years. Some RA patients never develop a positive rheumatoid factor. The sedimentation rate and C-reactive protein levels are usually elevated if the disease is active. However, the number of tender and swollen joints, as well as the patient's symptoms, gives a good estimation of the activity of the disease.

Older treatments for rheumatoid arthritis, such as HYDROXYCHLOROQUINE (PLAQUENIL), SULFASALAZINE (AZULFIDINE), and gold injections, reduce inflammation by interfering with the action of lymphocytes. Accordingly, most of these agents work by reducing the patient's immune response. Thus the person's susceptibility to infection can be increased. This explains why patients who take these drugs should first be vaccinated against influenza and pneumococcal pneumonia. Since the newer drugs for RA are usually combined with METHOTREXATE, precautions are taken against reactivation of hidden tuberculosis (TB). Patients who have positive TB skin tests need to take drugs active against TB.

In the past decade, three major changes have improved the outcome of RA. First, treatment is initiated with drugs that actually modify the course of the disease as soon as the diagnosis is made. These drugs are called disease-modifying antirheumatoid drugs (DMARDs). This is best if done within the first three months. Second, combined therapy with two or even three DMARDs works better than reliance on one drug. Third, we have potent biologic agents to use if the DMARDS, whether singly or in combination, are ineffective.

Future advances in the treatment of RA will include ways to test patients who may have more aggressive disease so that a more intensive approach can be used in their treatment. Further research will help clarify the best combinations of drugs. Hopefully, you will also see a streamlining of the process of approval of these drugs, so that more options will be available. Competition might also drive costs down, so that these agents are more readily available to the people who need them.

GOUT AND PSEUDOGOUT

Gout describes a condition of the joints that is usually quite painful. Often the affected joints are swollen and warm to touch. The big toe is the joint most commonly involved, but other joints can be affected. Gout is often associated with elevated uric acid levels in the blood, but these levels can be normal in a significant percentage of patients at the time of an attack. Acute illness such as a heart attack, stroke, or infection can precipitate a gout attack. Alcohol use is often cited as a precipitating factor, but many patients with gout do not drink. Use of diuretics (or water pills), which is common in older persons to treat high blood pressure and a variety of other conditions, elevates uric acid levels in the blood and thus represents a major cause of gout attacks. Some blood diseases are associated with elevated uric acid levels and gout.

Typically, gout manifests itself as a swollen, red, and warm joint. In the elderly, several joints may be involved, and gout may be superimposed on joints affected by osteoarthritis. A joint infected with bacteria can look similar to a joint affected by gout, so aspirating (drawing fluid with a needle) the joint and examining the fluid for crystals can establish the diagnosis. Persons with long-standing gout may have collections of uric acid crystals called *tophi* that form firm bumps on tendons, around the joints, and on the external ear (see Figure 16-5). They can even develop in the kidneys. Large tophi are seldom seen these days due to the availability of drugs to reduce uric acid levels in the blood.

The treatment of acute gout consists of nonsteroidal anti-inflammatory drugs (NSAIDs), but caution needs to be exercised in older persons. The elderly have a higher incidence of decreased kidney function, and the use of NSAIDs can lead to kidney failure. Therefore, close monitoring of kidney blood tests is important. An alternative is COLCHICINE, but this, too, must be used with caution in those with kidney, liver, or heart disease. Oral colchicine may cause upset stomach and diarrhea, but this does not occur as frequently with the intravenous form. Injecting steroids into an inflamed joint can be very helpful. In those with contraindications to the use of NSAIDs and colchicine, a course of oral steroids may be worthwhile. Pain relievers might be required.

Once the acute gout attack subsides, attempts to lower the uric acid levels are made. Aggressive diets are not necessary. Losing weight and restricting alcohol intake are sensible. There are two classes of drugs for this purpose. One class enhances the excretion of uric acid by the kidney, and the other actually blocks the production of uric acid. The drug most commonly used from the first class is PROBENECID (BENEMID). Aspirin blocks the effects of probenecid; therefore, these two drugs should not be taken together. The drug used from the second class is ALLOPURINOL (ZYLOPRIM). Allopurinol should be used if the patient has tophi, impaired kidney function, or previous uric acid kidney stones or requires continued administration of diuretics, aspirin, or certain types of chemotherapy. Allopurinol can occasionally have serious side effects. The lowest dose

BAD HUMOR

In ancient times, disturbances of the body were attributed to problems in the bodily fluids, called humors. If a person was well, the fluids were in a state equilibrium or harmony. If ill, there was an excess of one of the humors. A cold was attributed to an excess of phlegm. A digestive illness was attributed to an excess of bile. Gout was thought to be caused by an undue concentration of humors in the feet.

Illustrations from years past of gout attacks depict demons gouging the big toe with pitchforks. Gout was also called the disease of kings, since it was associated with excesses of rich foods and alcohol: a bad humor causing a bad humor.

DOCTOR'S DIARY

Juanita C., 58, came to me because she was not satisfied with her current arthritis management. Her arthritis came on so explosively nine years ago that she went to an emergency room with severe pain and stiffness in her joints. She was started on NSAIDs and sent to a rheumatologist. She subsequently tried Plaquenil, Arava, and several other medications. She had taken methotrexate for nearly nine years and was on a maximum dose. No remission occurred.

I initiated Juanita C. on a newer drug called Remicade and continued the methotrexate. She had an excellent response, but due to a change in her employment, her insurance changed and the Remicade was not covered. Within four months of stopping the Remicade, her arthritis flared up. Her handgrip was weak, and she had twelve swollen and tender joints. After I discussed her case with the medical director of the insurance company, the company agreed to cover her treatments. Intravenous infusions of Remicade were given, and within two months she had only a single, slightly inflamed joint. Her grip strength was normal. I was able to reduce the dose of methotrexate but continued the Remicade.

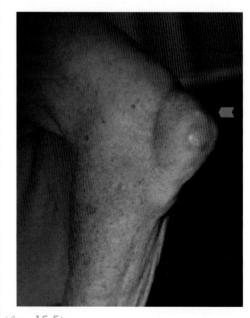

(figure 16-5)

A tophus is a collection of uric acid crystals. This photograph depicts a large tophus on the elbow (arrowhead).

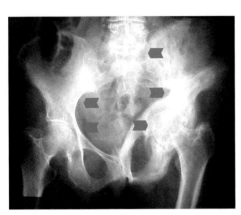

is used to keep the blood level of uric acid between 5 and 6. An anti-inflammatory drug or colchicine is continued for several weeks or months to prevent flare-ups of gout that can occur when uric acid–lowering drugs are used.

Pseudogout, or false gout, received its name in 1962 because joint swelling and inflammation similar to gout was described. However, instead of uric acid crystals being responsible, the crystals are calcium pyrophosphate. X-rays of joints involved with pseudogout typically show calcium deposits in the cartilage (chondrocalcinosis), but calcium deposits can also occur in tendons, bursae, and the lining of the joints. Occasionally, chondrocalcinosis is associated with other conditions, such as an underactive thyroid *(hypothyroidism),* overactive parathyroid glands *(hyperparathyroidism),* gout, excess body iron *(hemochromatosis),* and low magnesium levels. Many patients with chondrocalcinosis have no symptoms, and the diagnosis is based on X-ray findings. In these persons, no treatment is required. Pseudogout, on the other hand, is associated with pain and swelling of a joint, usually the knee although other joints may be affected. Not unlike gout, a hot, swollen, painful joint can mimic a joint infection. Aspirating the joint fluid and finding the calcium pyrophosphate crystals provide a definite diagnosis.

Pseudogout is treated with NSAIDs and steroid joint injections.

PAGET'S DISEASE

Paget's disease is due to a disturbance in bone breakdown and formation (see Figure 16-6). Approximately 3% of elderly persons are affected with Paget's disease, but the vast majority has no symptoms. Diagnosis is usually made after a blood test, called the *alkaline phosphatase,* is found to be elevated. X-rays or bone scans confirm the diagnosis. Occasionally, the radiologist makes the diagnosis after X-rays are done for other reasons. Some patients, however, might have pain in the bones. Since the skull can be involved, headaches might occur. Even hat size might increase. If the legs are involved, the patient may become bowlegged, due to weakness of the bones. Though gratefully rare, the most feared complication of Paget's disease is a cancer of the bone called *osteosarcoma.* Onset is usually heralded by a sudden increase in bone pain and a marked rise in the alkaline phosphatase.

Treatment of Paget's disease is not necessary if there are no symptoms. However, if pain is significant or if there is disease of the legs that can lead to deformity, treatment should be initiated. Significant skull involvement requires treatment, since deafness can result from pressure of the expanding bone on the hearing nerve. Marked elevation of the alkaline phosphatase or pressure against nerves necessitates treatment. In some cases, surgery is required to relieve pinched nerves or correct deformities. The drugs used to treat Paget's disease include ALENDRONATE (FOSAMAX) and RISEDRONATE (ACTONEL), which are more frequently used to treat osteoporosis. An intravenous drug called PAMIDRONATE (AREDIA) is also used.

(figure 16-6)

Paget's disease may manifest as dense bones on X-rays (arrowheads).

POLYMYALGIA RHEUMATICA

Polymyalgia rheumatica (PMR) is a condition characterized by aching and stiffness of the muscles predominantly of the shoulders, neck, and hips. The elbows, ankles, and feet are seldom involved. The words *polymyalgia rheumatica* are derived from Latin and Greek and mean "many rheumatic muscle aches." We now know that most of the discomfort arises from joint structures. Researchers using MRI, ultrasound, nuclear scans, and biopsies have located the inflammation in the synovial lining of joints, as well as the tendons and bursae around the joints. Some patients have tendon inflammation in the hands. PMR may cause carpal tunnel syndrome due to the median nerve getting squeezed by swollen tendon sheaths as it enters the hand through the carpal tunnel.

PMR should not be confused with fibromyalgia, a condition that usually has its onset in younger women between the ages of 20 and 50. Fibromyalgia is associated with multiple symmetric tender areas. Affected patients "hurt all over." These individuals often feel tired and lack energy. However, no consistent laboratory or imaging abnormalities are found.

Following are the diagnostic rules for polymyalgia rheumatica:

1. Over a month of pain in the shoulders, hips, and neck
2. Morning stiffness greater than one hour
3. Sedimentation rate greater than 40
4. Over 50 years of age
5. Good response to low-dose prednisone

The symptoms of PMR are rapidly abolished by low doses of PREDNISONE (DELTASONE, STERAPRED), an oral corticosteroid. This is gratifying for both the doctor and the patient, since there are few diseases that respond so dramatically in just a few days. However, the treatment does require a long course of corticosteroids, often as long as one or two years. Some patients require much longer courses of treatment, lasting four years or more. An attempt is continually made to taper and withdraw the steroids, but a flare-up of symptoms or increases in the sedimentation rate or C-reactive protein indicate that the disease has not gone into remission. This requires temporarily increasing the prednisone dose.

Prednisone side effects are common with use greater than a month and include easy bruising, thinning of the skin, and thinning of the bone (osteoporosis). Cataracts can form in some patients. To prevent bone loss, extra calcium and vitamin D are recommended. Due to the prolonged course of treatment, drugs that inhibit breakdown of bone, such as ALENDRONATE (FOSAMAX) or RISEDRONATE (ACTONEL), are recommended.

A small percentage of patients, perhaps 10 to 15%, develop inflammation of the temporal artery. This condition, called *temporal arteritis,* is associated with blindness due to inflammation of the main artery to the eye.

TEMPORAL ARTERITIS

Temporal arteritis is an inflammation in the arteries that branch off the main blood vessel (the aorta) that leads out of the heart (see Figure 16-7).

DOCTOR'S DIARY

Joan P., 70, suddenly noticed severe "all over stiffness and pain" six weeks before she came to see me in the office. The worst pain was in the neck, shoulders, and hips. The muscles of her arms, thighs, and low back were stiff and achy. She felt weak and tired. On a few nights, she woke up feeling sweaty. Her husband had to actually help her get dressed since she couldn't lift her arms enough to get them into her blouse. She had some tenderness in the muscles around the shoulders and hips.

I knew right away she had polymyalgia rheumatica. Her lab work showed a significant elevation of the sedimentation rate and C-reactive protein, giving further credence to the diagnosis. Rheumatoid factor was negative. I started her on 10 milligrams of prednisone daily. Within two to three days she was markedly better and was back to her normal level of function. Over the next two years, I gradually lowered the prednisone and monitored the sedimentation rate. She had some flare-up of her aching and stiffness when I dropped her prednisone dose below 3 mgs, and I had to increase the dose temporarily. Since long-term steroids can increase the risk of osteoporosis, I started her on supplemental calcium, vitamin D, and Actonel to preserve bone.

After about two years, her symptoms remained in remission after I withdrew her prednisone altogether, and the sedimentation rate remained normal.

Since other blood vessels of the head and neck are less commonly involved, the condition has also been called *cranial arteritis.* Occasionally the aorta and the arteries to the arms are affected. Seldom are the coronary arteries or brain arteries involved. To add to the confusion, this condition has also been labeled *giant cell arteritis* because of the kinds of cells that are seen in the wall of the blood vessel on biopsy.

The most feared complication of temporal arteritis is inflammation of the artery to the eye. Blood flow to the retina is compromised, causing sudden and irreversible loss of vision. Treatment is urgent as is getting a diagnosis! Usually this involves biopsy of the temporal artery. Since the inflammation in the blood vessel wall is often spotty, there may be "skip areas"—areas where the blood vessel looks normal under the microscope. Therefore, a sizable segment, usually 2 to 3 cm, of the temporal artery must be removed and serial sections of the artery examined. In fact, if the biopsied artery looks normal and the doctor is still very suspicious that the patient has temporal arteritis, a biopsy is taken from the temporal artery on the other side. The procedure is usually done as an outpatient, and the risks are generally few.

Temporal artery

(figure 16-7)

The temporal artery runs in front of your ear. Temporal arteritis is a potentially serious inflammation of the temporal artery.

CONNECTIVE TISSUE DISEASES

Connective tissue diseases (CTDs) represent several different conditions, each one associated with inflammation and cell damage yet without infection. The main body tissues involved include the skin, muscles, blood vessels, and the joint linings. The problems caused by these various diseases can overlap with one another. A person may have a few or many of the manifestations of the different CTDs. They all tend to be chronic and progressive. Interestingly, they are more common in women. For instance, system lupus and Sjögren's syndrome affect women 7 to 10 times more often than men.

The CTDs are caused by problems in the body's immune system. Often antibodies are formed to the body's own tissues. These are called **autoantibodies.** When the antibodies are directed against the cell's "control room" (the nucleus), they are called **antinuclear antibodies (ANA).** The level of antinuclear antibodies can be measured in a person's blood. Following is a list of the most common connective tissue disorders:

- Systemic lupus erythematosus
- Scleroderma
- Sjögren's syndrome
- Myositis (inflammation of muscles)
- Overlap syndrome (also known as undifferentiated CTDs)
- Systemic vasculitis (inflammation of blood vessels)

In this chapter, I discuss the three most common CTDs: systemic lupus erythematosus, scleroderma, and Sjögren's syndrome. For more information on the other disorders, contact the Arthritis Foundation (listed in "For More Information").

Systemic lupus erythematosus (SLE) is more common in women. Although more common in women during their reproductive years, it can occur in men and in older persons. In addition, many patients with SLE live well into their older years. SLE can affect many body systems. The following list contains the criteria used for diagnosis. At least four out of the eleven criteria need to be present for a diagnosis of SLE:

1. Facial rash: a red rash over the bridge of nose, cheeks, and chin (creases between the nose and mouth usually spared)
2. Discoid rash: red patches with scaling (may cause some scarring)
3. Photosensitivity: skin rash on exposure to sunlight
4. Oral or nasal ulcers
5. Arthritis
6. Serositis: inflammation of the lining around the lungs (pleura) or heart (pericarditis)
7. Nephritis: inflammation of the kidneys resulting in protein spilling into the urine
8. Neurological problems: Seizures or psychosis
9. Blood cell disorders: low blood count, low white cell count, low platelet count
10. Autoantibodies: anti-DNA, anti-Sm, antiphospholipid antibodies, positive LE prep, false positive test for syphilis
11. Antinuclear antibodies

Several special features add strength to the diagnosis. The red rash over the nose and cheeks is called a "butterfly rash," due to its resemblance to a butterfly. It is present in almost half of all patients at some time in their disease course. The joint pain can come and go quite quickly, sometimes in just a few hours. This is uncommon in other types of arthritis. About half of all SLE patients get kidney disease. Seizures and psychosis are less common problems. Although the joint disease associated with lupus does not usually destroy the joints, it can deform the hands.

SLE involves the expertise of a rheumatologist, but other specialists may be necessary, most commonly nephrologists, cardiologists, and psychiatrists. The rheumatologist determines the patient's treatment based on symptoms and laboratory tests. Although drug treatment is often required, I can give you some general advice if you are a lupus patient.

First, I can reassure you that the disease is not always deadly and that many patients have mild forms of the disease. However, your own doctor knows your condition best and is in the best position to advise you regarding the severity of your condition and its prognosis. You should know that the disease is not contagious and cannot be transmitted by casual or sexual contact. Your siblings or your children do not have a high risk of getting the disease. Since flare-ups of SLE happen more commonly when you are overtired, you should pace yourself and make sure you get

DOCTOR'S DIARY

When I first saw Marilyn S., 78, she looked frail and tired. She had not slept well because of sharp pains in her head during the previous few weeks. She had a fever almost daily, occasionally over 100°F. She had discomfort in her jaw when she ate, and as a result she had lost 10 pounds in the previous month. When her symptoms first started, she had gone to a walk-in clinic. She was given a prescription for antibiotics for a suspected dental infection. However, she got no relief.

She came to see me when she had "gray outs" in her vision in the left eye. I noticed that the left temporal artery, which runs in front of the ear, was tender and thickened and that the pulsations were diminished. I suspected an inflammatory disorder of the temporal artery called temporal arteritis. I ordered a sedimentation rate, which was strikingly elevated to 110 (normal is less than 30). The C-reactive protein was also increased to 15.6 (normal less than 0.9). I asked one of my surgical colleagues to perform a temporal artery biopsy, which confirmed "florid inflammation" of the temporal artery. The diagnosis of temporal arteritis was confirmed.

I initiated Marilyn S. on a high dose of prednisone, starting at 60 milligrams per day on the day I saw her. Once I suspected temporal arteritis, I did not to wait the two or three days for the surgical procedure and then the biopsy reports to get back to me. Since she already had some visual problems, I was concerned that the disease could cause blindness. Once visual loss occurs in temporal arteritis, it is usually irreversible. I also placed her on calcium, vitamin D, and Fosamax to protect her bones. Within two weeks, her sedimentation rate dropped to 25, and I started to gradually reduce her prednisone over the ensuing weeks and months. Within six months, I was able to stop the prednisone. Marilyn S. did have some side effects that included easy bruising, a 20-pound weight gain, and some mild hand tremors. Early in the course when she was taking high doses of prednisone, she had some sleeping problems. However, she was extremely grateful that she had no vision problems and that she felt much more energetic.

Ruth T., 52, was diagnosed with systemic lupus erythematosus (SLE) 20
years ago. Her first problems included a red facial rash about the nose
and cheeks, low blood count, joint
pains, and tiredness. She had a positive ANA, and a more specific blood
test for SLE was then requested.
This test, called anti-DNA antibodies, was also positive.

Three years ago when I saw her for
the first time, she had developed a
red rash of her face and arms as well
as enlarged lymph nodes in her neck.
Her urinalysis showed that she had
protein in her urine, and special
blood tests confirmed that her lupus
was very active. Ruth T. had no medical insurance and could not afford
to go into the hospital for a kidney biopsy to confirm the diagnosis.
Therefore, I decided to treat her
without a biopsy. I started her on
40 milligrams of prednisone per day
and 200 milligrams of Plaquenil per
day. She gradually improved, and all
her symptoms cleared up. The urine
also tested negative for protein.
I gradually reduced the prednisone
and continued Plaquenil.

She is off prednisone altogether.
Her blood pressure and cholesterol
have required medication, but she is
doing quite well. I see her every two
to three months to monitor any new
developments.

adequate rest. Sunscreen, at least SPF 15 or greater, is advised for everyone, but it is even more important if you get skin rashes with sun exposure. In some cases, you might be advised to avoid prolonged sun exposure all together.

Raynaud's phenomenon is not uncommon in lupus patients, but it can also occur in such other diseases as scleroderma. Most persons who have Raynaud's phenomenon do not have another disease associated with it. This phenomenon is due to spasm of the arteries to the fingers, so that the ends of the fingers turn white with cold exposure. When blood flow returns, the fingers can turn blue or red. Cold exposure needs to be avoided, not just for the hands but the whole body. Prevention is the best approach. You should use gloves or mittens when handling items from the refrigerator. When drinking cold beverages, use an insulated cup preferably with a handle or use a rubber sleeve so that your hands are not in direct contact with the cold surface. You should not smoke, since it causes constriction of the blood vessels. If the condition does not respond to preventive measures, medicines can be used. These are usually calcium channel blockers, such as NIFEDIPINE (PROCARDIA, ADALAT) or DILTIAZEM (CARDIZEM, DILACOR, CARTIA, TIAZAC).

Antiphospholipid antibody syndrome can cause blood clots and strokes. Although antiphospholipid antibodies can occur with SLE, these antibodies can also be found in otherwise healthy people and can be detected with a blood test. Strokes and blood clots associated with this condition require long-term use of anticoagulants ("blood thinners").

Drug-induced lupus produces a clinical syndrome that looks identical to SLE, but is caused by a drug that the patient is taking. It tends to happen in older men. Generally this can be determined with some blood tests. Removal of the responsible drug causes resolution of the symptoms.

Treatment of SLE often means prolonged courses of medications. A supportive family and physician are extremely important since the disease is characterized by flare-ups and remissions. NSAIDs and the newer cyclooxygenase-2 (COX-2) inhibitors are not usually that helpful. Although they benefit people with arthritis, there are potential problems with their use in SLE. Toxic effects on the kidneys are more common in SLE patients, possibly due to underlying kidney inflammation. Aseptic meningitis (noninfectious inflammation of the lining about the brain and spinal cord) is more common if NSAIDs are used in SLE patients.

The drugs used to treat the more severe problems associated with SLE affect the body's immune function. Corticosteroids are usually reserved for the serious problems associated with the disease, but they can be useful in milder cases if NSAIDs or PLAQUENIL are not tolerated well. Long-term use of steroids presents an increased risk of infection, "hardening" of the arteries, thinning of the bones, and ulcers. Therefore, continual attempts are made to wean down to the lowest dose that controls the symptoms. Table 16-1 lists the drugs commonly used in SLE and their effects.

Kidney lupus *(lupus nephritis)* can become severe enough that the kidneys are irreversibly damaged. This scenario can occur with delayed

(table 16-1)

DRUGS FOR THE TREATMENT OF SLE

DRUG	EFFECTS AND COMMENTS
Corticosteroids, such as prednisone	Controls most phases of lupus. The dosage varies from 5 to 60 mg, depending on the problem.
Hydroxychloroquine (Plaquenil)	An antimalarial drug that helps treat skin rashes and arthritis. Reduces flare-ups. Requires regular examinations by eye doctor due to small risk (less than 1%) of damage to the retina.
Azathioprine (Imuran)	Reduces immune function. Requires regular blood monitoring.
Cyclophosphamide (Cytoxan)	Reduces immune function. Used primarily for kidney lupus. Requires urine monitoring since there is a risk for bladder cancer.
Mycophenolate (CellCept)	Reduces immune function. Used for kidney lupus.

treatment or overwhelming inflammation. Noncompliance (not taking medicine properly) can also be a cause. If the kidneys can no longer remove the body's waste products adequately, **hemodialysis** is required (see Chapter 10). A kidney transplant might be considered, and the results compare favorably with those who are transplanted for nonlupus kidney diseases. Interestingly, SLE becomes less aggressive in patients having kidney failure but managed with either hemodialysis or transplant.

The Food and Drug Administration is studying novel approaches for the treatment of SLE. One such approach is the use of **stem cells,** which are the "parent" cells in the bone marrow from which red blood cells, white blood cells, and so on, originate. First, the patient is given a powerful drug that puts the lupus into remission. Then another drug is given to stimulate production of stem cells, which are subsequently harvested for future transfusion back into the patient. After that, chemotherapy is administered to wipe out the patient's current marrow cells and to suppress the immune system. This is followed by transfusing the stored stem cells back into the patient to repopulate the bone marrow. As you can imagine, the risks associated with this procedure are many. Long-term observation of the brave patients who volunteered for this experimental procedure are necessary before there is widespread acceptance. Although just a few patients have undergone this procedure, some have no obvious evidence of their disease. But researchers still can't be absolutely sure that the disease will not recur at some later time.

SCLERODERMA

Scleroderma means "hard skin." A structural support of the skin called **collagen** is overproduced, causing the skin to become firm and tight. Raynaud's phenomenon is common in patients with scleroderma. The finger ulcers are caused by a shutdown of the arteries to the fingers, mostly because of an overgrowth in the cells lining the blood vessels (endothelial cells). What causes the overstimulation of endothelial cells and collagen overproduction is not known. A relatively new theory is being studied based on the observation that the blood of patients with scleroderma has more "foreign" cells than normal. The foreign cells may come from the mother during fetal development. The reverse might also be true. Fetal cells cross the circulation of the placenta and take up residence in the mother. In these situations, the foreign cells attack the normal tissues, causing an inflammatory reaction that causes the manifestations of scleroderma.

Heartburn is common in scleroderma patients. Excess collagen is deposited in the lower esophagus, impeding the normal function of the muscular ring between the esophagus and stomach. This ring *(lower esophageal sphincter)* contracts to keep food in the stomach from refluxing into the esophagus. It relaxes when food is moving from the esophagus into the stomach. In scleroderma, acid and food go the wrong way and irritate the lining of the esophagus. Drugs that block gastric acid production are prescribed. Occasionally the acid irritation causes an esophageal stricture (narrowing of the esophagus) that requires a gastroenterologist to "stretch" the esophagus.

A less common, but more serious, type of this disease is called *systemic scleroderma,* or *progressive systemic sclerosis (PSS).* PSS causes more rapid and extensive hardening of the skin, scarring of the lungs and lining around the heart, arthritis, and kidney disease. Shortening of the tendons around joints might lead to diminished motion of the joint, called a contracture. Contractures around the hand and fingers may produce a "claw hand" that is disabling. Carpal tunnel syndrome may be the first problem that prompts the patient to see a doctor.

Treatment is aimed at control of such symptoms as heartburn and Raynaud's phenomenon. No drug exists that has been proved to modify the disease, but METHOTREXATE (RHEUMATREX) and CYCLOSPORINE (NEORAL, SANDIMMUNE) show promise in being helpful. New treatments that have emerged to help relieve the symptoms of pulmonary hypertension include BOSENTAN (TRACLEER) and EPROSTANOL. These drugs seem to reverse the constriction that occurs in the blood vessels of the lungs.

The sudden onset of high blood pressure in a person with scleroderma is usually due to the effects of scleroderma on the kidneys. Urgent treatment with medication is required to prevent kidney failure. The blood pressure medicines that work best are in a class called angiotensin-converting enzyme (ACE) inhibitors. If acute kidney failure occurs, dialysis should be started promptly. However, in about half the patients, the kidneys recover enough function that dialysis can be stopped. They are continued on ACE inhibitors to preserve their kidney function as much as possible.

SJÖGREN'S SYNDROME

Sjögren's syndrome (pronounced *Show-grin's)* is caused by inflammation in the glands that produce tears and saliva. Other areas of the body that might be involved include the joints, skin, nerves, and small blood vessels. This disease is related to a disturbance in the body's immune system. Usually the ANA and rheumatoid factor are positive. The condition is

16

DOCTOR'S DIARY

After becoming disabled, Melissa S., 54, moved from Michigan to Florida. Nine years ago she noticed that the tips of her fingers turned white, then blue. She was diagnosed with Raynaud's phenomenon, a condition associated with spasm of the small arteries to the fingers. Subsequently, the skin on her hands became tight, and ulcers of her fingertips developed. She tried drug treatments and then operations on the nerves responsible for the spasm in the blood vessels. Special X-ray tests (angiograms) showed blockage of the arteries to several fingers. Unfortunately, she continued to smoke cigarettes despite her doctor's admonition to quit.

I saw her in my office shortly after she moved to Florida. She had fewer problems with Raynaud's phenomenon since moving to the warmer climate. However, I noticed that the tips of several fingers had been amputated and that the skin of her hands was tight up to her wrists. She had raspberry-colored patches on her hands, face, and lips. She was taking methotrexate to loosen her skin and Prevacid for heartburn. She wanted to explore new treatments for her disease.

Melissa S. had a limited form of scleroderma. One of the more serious complications of limited scleroderma is pulmonary hypertension, which can cause shortness of breath and heart failure. Melissa S.'s prognosis was fairly good as most of her symptoms can be alleviated. She quit smoking, which had significant benefits not only for her scleroderma but for other health reasons as well.

lifelong, but it is generally not life-threatening. However, the symptoms can be quite troublesome. As with all connective tissue diseases, there is a slightly increased risk of developing lymphoma.

The following list has the criteria used for a diagnosis of Sjögren's syndrome (note that three of the following six items must be fulfilled):

1. Definite *eye dryness* that is not caused by medicine being taken
2. Definite *oral dryness* preferably if the salivary glands are swollen
3. Findings of the eye doctor include a positive **Schirmer's test** (a test for dry eyes) and a positive **Rose bengal stain** (a test for damage to the cornea)
4. Inner *lip biopsy positive* for immune cells
5. A positive test for reduced saliva flow in the salivary glands (seldom done)
6. Sjögren's antibodies in the blood

Some patients with other connective tissue diseases, such as rheumatoid arthritis or SLE, have dryness of the eyes and mouth as well. This is called *secondary Sjögren's syndrome.* Since other serious conditions can mimic Sjögren's syndrome, consultation with an ophthalmologist and laboratory tests are helpful in making the correct diagnosis. Many medications, including antidepressants, antihistamines, sedatives, and blood pressure modifiers, can cause dryness of the eyes and mouth. Overdiagnosis (diagnosing a disease that the patient does not have) of Sjögren's syndrome is common. Such objective findings as swollen salivary glands, diminished tear production, and Sjögren's antibodies in the blood have a higher weight than do symptoms alone in the diagnosis. The reduction in tears can lead to cornea and vision problems and the decrease in saliva to dental cavities. Thus the patient also needs to be monitored by an ophthalmologist and a dentist.

Other possible features of the disease include dry skin inflammation of the small blood vessels (vasculitis), dry cough, and, rarely, kidney problems. Women might experience vaginal dryness. Most patients with Sjögren's syndrome can lead a fairly normal life using simple treatments to keep the eyes and mouth moist. In some cases, the symptoms of fatigue and difficulty with eating and talking due to mouth dryness can be incapacitating. Psychological support is important, and support groups are available in most communities. You can check for local support groups by contacting the Arthritis Foundation, the Sjögren's Syndrome Foundation, or the National Sjögren's Syndrome Association (see "For More Information").

SOFT TISSUE PROBLEMS

The soft tissues refer to those structures outside of bones and joints. Since they are not hard like bones and joints, they are aptly named *soft tissues.* However, this does not mean that these structures are weak. Tendons, for example, are quite tough and strong since they are the attachments for muscles to bone. Inflammation and injury of these tissues are a common

(figure 16-8)

Trigger finger.

cause of pain and temporary disability. The common soft tissue pain syndromes include tendonitis, bursitis, costochondritis, pinched nerves, and frozen shoulder. (Frozen shoulder is discussed in Chapter 17.)

Tendonitis and bursitis are by far the most common. Costochondritis and pinched nerves occur frequently and can mimic other medical problems.

TENDONITIS

Tendonitis is an inflammation of a tendon, the tough fibrous tissue that attaches a muscle to bone. *Lateral epicondylitis* is commonly know as "tennis elbow," since it occurs frequently in tennis players. If the inside of the elbow is tender, "golfer's elbow" is diagnosed; however, this condition can occur in other persons if overuse occurs. Degenerative changes or tears in an overworked tendon cause tendonitis. Tennis elbow and golfer's elbow usually respond to a combination of rest, pain relievers, splinting, injections, and lifestyle changes. However, recurrence is typical. Surgery is seldom required. Tendonitis occurs at other sites as well, such as the wrists, shoulders, and knees.

An interesting phenomenon that can involve the hand is called *trigger finger* (see Figure 16-8). Affected persons find that without help from the other hand they cannot open a finger (or thumb) after it is flexed. The finger is locked in place, looking like it squeezed a trigger. This condition is associated with inflammation of the ring that fixes the flexor tendons of the hand in place. A steroid injection on the palmar surface of the hand at the base of the finger often corrects the problem. If it recurs, consultation with a hand surgeon is required.

BURSITIS

A *bursa* is a fluid-filled sac that helps cushion tendons in areas of friction, usually where tendons cross over a bony prominence. Bursitis, inflammation of the bursa, results after wear and tear due to overuse or injury. In some cases, calcium deposits can occur. The most common forms of bursitis in older adults include *subacromial bursitis* and *trochanteric bursitis*. Subacromial bursitis can cause a painful shoulder. Trochanteric bursitis causes pain and tenderness of the outer part of the hip. The *greater trochanter* (see Figure 16-9) is the large bony prominence of the hip where the large buttock muscles attach. This area is usually more exposed in women than in men, which accounts for the higher incidence of trochanteric bursitis in women. Often, individuals with trochanteric bursitis find that sleeping on the affected side is uncomfortable, or it may wake them from sleep when they roll over onto that side.

Pes anserinus bursitis and *olecranon bursitis* are less common but not infrequent. Three tendons come together on the inside aspect of the shin bone *(tibia)* just below the knee to

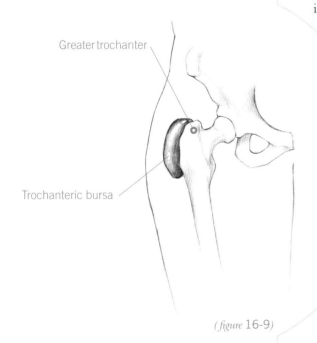

Greater trochanter

Trochanteric bursa

(figure 16-9)

Trochanteric bursitis is an inflammation of the fluid-filled sac over the hip.

form a structure that looks like a goose's foot (see Figure 16-10), thus the term *pes anserinus* (Latin for "goose foot"). Bursitis here causes pain just below the knee on the inner part of the leg. Olecranon bursitis causes a swollen saclike protrusion over the elbow (see Figure 16-11).

Bursitis is treated with rest the of the affected area, cold packs, NSAIDs, steroid injections, and, occasionally, physical therapy. In rare cases, bursitis can be caused by an infection. The bursa may feel warm to touch, and the skin over the area may be red. In this case, withdrawing fluid from the bursa for cultures and antibiotics is necessary. Examination of the fluid for crystals is also important since gout and pseudogout may sometimes cause bursitis.

COSTOCHONDRITIS

Costochondritis causes pain and tenderness of the cartilages that join the ribs with the breastbone (see Figure 16-12). It can cause difficulties in diagnosis. If it is localized to the left side, the pain can mimic the discomfort associated with a heart attack. The pain often gets worse with a deep breath, which can also be seen with a blood clot to the lung. However, there will be tenderness when the doctor palpates the cartilages in costochondritis. Tietze syndrome may be diagnosed if a swollen area develops over the cartilage. Since costochondritis cannot always be reliably distinguished from other more serious diseases, the doctor may recommend such tests as blood tests, an ECG, chest X-ray, rib X-rays, or lung scans.

Treatment for costochondritis includes drugs used for arthritis, cold packs, and local steroid injections. Eliminating activities, such as vigorous exercise, that may aggravate the condition is often advised. Ultrasound treatments provided by a physical therapist might offer some benefit.

PINCHED NERVES

Pain, numbness, tingling, and burning are common symptoms of a pinched (compressed) nerve. If the nerve injury progresses, weakness of the muscle supplied by the nerve can occur. The symptoms experienced by the patient depend on the nerve involved and the cause of the compression. Chapter 18 covers problems in the spine that can pinch nerves in the neck and back.

Carpal tunnel syndrome results when the main nerve to the hand *(median nerve)* is compressed by the main ligament of the wrist or by swollen tendons (see Figure 16-13). The condition occurs more commonly in women and may involve one or both hands. The symptoms might include pain or numbness, often worse at night. If weakness in the hand muscles develops, the person may be prone to dropping things. Carpal tunnel syndrome is associated with diabetes, rheumatoid arthritis, hypothyroidism, or previous wrist fracture. Ganglions are benign soft

(figure 16-10)

The pes anserinus (highlighted in yellow) is a group of three tendons that come together on the inner aspect of the shin bone to resemble a goose's foot.

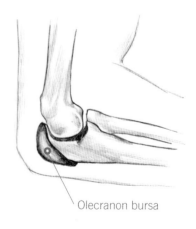

Olecranon bursa

(figure 16-11)

The olecranon bursa is located over the outside of the elbow.

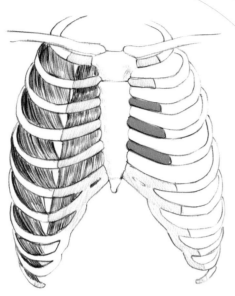

tissue tumors that arise from the lining of joints. If the wrist is involved, they may grow large enough to cause pressure on the median nerve and produce carpal tunnel syndrome.

When the doctor taps on the wrist with a rubber hammer *(Tinel's sign),* persons with carpal tunnel syndrome often experience tingling in the fingers supplied by the median nerve. Flexion of the wrist for a minute may produce or increase the numbness *(Phalen's sign).* More severe cases involve weakness and wasting of the hand muscles. The diagnosis can be confirmed with an electrical test of the nerve that shows slowing of the nerve impulses.

If the symptoms of carpal tunnel syndrome are mild, simply splinting the wrist at night may be adequate. If this is not effective or if the initial symptoms are more severe, a hand surgeon should be consulted. Treatment might involve steroid injections or surgery to remove the pressure within the carpal tunnel.

Tarsal tunnel syndrome is due to compression of the nerves to the foot where they travel along the inside part of the ankle. The patient experiences tingling, numbness, or burning of the sole of the foot (see Figure 16-14). Although a previous ankle fracture increases the risk for this condition, most cases do not have an obvious cause. This syndrome is not nearly as common as carpal tunnel syndrome.

(figure 16-12)

Costochondritis is inflammation of the cartilages (highlighted in red) that join the ribs to the breastbone.

DRUGS FOR ARTHRITIS

Every rheumatic disease requires a different treatment plan. For example, a person with osteoarthritis of the knee has pain due to friction of the bony surfaces rubbing against each other. The cartilage that allows the bone surfaces to glide painlessly over each other has been worn down and damaged. Since there is usually not a lot of inflammation involved, this person could get nearly as much pain relief from ACETAMINOPHEN (TYLENOL) as from anti-inflammatory drugs, such as IBUPROFEN or NAPROXEN. In addition, there can be a significant cost savings over the more expensive prescription arthritis drugs. On the other hand, rheumatoid arthritis is an inflammatory disease and requires anti-inflammatory drugs. Usually disease-modifying antirheumatic drugs (DMARDs) are necessary as well. Moreover, each patient's response to the drugs is different, so tailoring the medication regimen requires the skill of the rheumatologist. No one can reliably predict exactly how a person or disease will respond to treatment; therefore, some trial and error is involved.

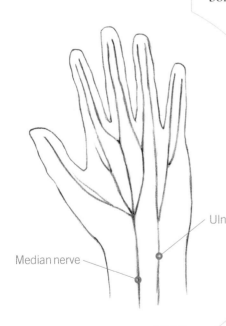

Ulnar nerve

Median nerve

(figure 16-13)

Carpal tunnel syndrome is caused by compression of the median nerve to the hand at the wrist.

NONSTEROIDAL ANTI-INFLAMMATORY DRUGS

Nonsteroidal anti-inflammatory drugs (NSAIDs) reduce inflammation by blocking the production of prostaglandins.

Prostaglandins are substances that generate inflammation within the joint. In recent years, a new class of NSAIDs, called *COX-2 inhibitors,* has been produced. They block an enzyme that allows prostaglandins to be made. It was hoped that this class of arthritis drugs would be safer for the stomach than the older drugs. Although the risk of stomach ulcers is reduced, there is still a small risk. In addition, they can cause salt and water retention like the older arthritis drugs. Therefore, they usually need to be avoided in patients with congestive heart failure and cirrhosis. Patients with hypertension need to be monitored since these drugs might increase the blood pressure. Adverse effects can occur in patients with compromised kidney function. Older persons generally will have their kidney function checked with a blood test shortly after starting these drugs and periodically thereafter. Table 16-2 lists commonly prescribed NSAIDs.

CORTICOSTEROIDS

Corticosteroids, commonly abbreviated as *steroids,* produce miraculous short-term benefits in the inflammatory diseases. However, their use is controversial. They cure no diseases, are habit-forming, and can have very undesirable consequences. PREDNISONE (DELTASONE) is the preferred oral cortisone drug. It is inexpensive and acts rapidly. The doses vary greatly, depending on the disease being treated. For example, very high doses might be required in critical conditions, such as kidney lupus or temporal arteritis. Relatively low doses on the order of 5 to 10 milligrams per day are used in the treatment of polymyalgia rheumatica. Low doses can be helpful in treatment of rheumatoid arthritis until the DMARDs "kick in," at which point the prednisone dosage can be tapered down and then stopped.

Corticosteroids reduce inflammation by several mechanisms. One is by reducing prostaglandin release, which otherwise triggers inflammation. Another is by blockage of another mediator of inflammation called *tumor*

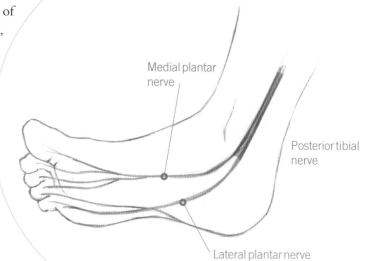

(figure 16-14)

Tarsal tunnel syndrome is cause by compression of the nerves (highlighted in blue) to the foot as they pass the ankle.

(table 16-2)

NONSTEROIDAL ANTI-INFLAMMATORY DRUGS

BRAND NAME	GENERIC NAME	ADULT DOSE PER DAY (MG)	INDICATIONS*	AVERAGE COST PER MONTH†
Celebrex	Celecoxib	200 once or twice	RA, OA	$91 or $178
Vioxx	Rofecoxib	12.5 or 25 once	RA, OA	$106 or $207
Bextra	Valdecoxib	10 or 20 once	OA	$103‡
Naprosyn, Aleve	Naproxen	500 twice	RA, OA	$22
Motrin, Advil, Nuprin	Ibuprofen	1200–2400 in divided doses	RA, OA	$16–25
Relafen	Nabumetone	750 twice	RA, OA	$91

*RA = rheumatoid arthritis; OA = osteoarthritis
†Listed costs quoted by Walgreen's pharmacy in Sarasota, Florida, in June 2004.
‡The cost is the same for 10- or 20-mg Bextra.

necrosis factor-alpha. Steroids also reduce the activity of cells important in our immune response called *T lymphocytes.* Every day you and I secrete from our adrenal glands our own natural steroid called cortisol. Cortisol acts as a "stress hormone" by going to sites of injury and reducing the inflammation.

Short-term use of steroids over a few days or two to three weeks carries little risk of adverse effects. Still the benefit versus the risk needs to be weighed in those with diabetes, since the blood sugar can rise significantly. Long-term use, for months to years, carries numerous potential risks, including diabetes, cataracts, ulcers, osteoporosis, weight gain, and mood changes. Moreover, with prolonged use, the adrenal glands shrink and turn off their own production of cortisol. This can cause serious adverse effects if steroids are withdrawn abruptly. This condition, called acute adrenal insufficiency, can be associated with extreme fatigue, weakness, low blood pressure, dizziness, loss of appetite, nausea, vomiting, abdominal pains, and joint pains. Acute adrenal insufficiency is considered a medical emergency. Therefore, when the decision is made to withdraw someone from steroids, it must be done very gradually. If a person on long-term steroids requires major surgery, a "steroid booster" is required before and after surgery since that person's adrenal glands cannot respond to the increased stress presented by an operation.

Corticosteroids can be given by injection. Injections allow delivery of the medication directly to the site of inflammation and for that reason are especially useful in the treatment of tendonitis and bursitis. Steroid injections can provide fairly quick pain relief for acute arthritis due to gout and pseudogout.

Patients receiving steroids on a long-term basis should be monitored for osteoporosis. Bone density measurements are helpful in assessing bone loss. Many physicians routinely prescribe calcium, vitamin D, and exercise. In addition, prophylactic use of such drugs as FOSAMAX or ACTONEL may be recommended.

DISEASE-MODIFYING ANTIRHEUMATIC DRUGS

Disease-modifying antirheumatic drugs (DMARDs) reduce pain, inflammation, and swelling in rheumatoid arthritis. They can also heal joint erosions seen on X-ray. DMARDs suppress the function of immune cells called *lymphocytes.* In the past, these drugs were usually tried one at a time. Now they are often used in combination since their effects appear to be additive.

The older DMARDs included gold salts, MINOCYCLINE, AZATHIOPRINE, and CYCLOSPORINE. Either due to toxicity or inadequate disease control, they are now seldom used. Four DMARDs still in favor are METHOTREXATE, HYDROXYCHLOROQUINE, SULFASALAZINE, and LEFLUNOMIDE (see Table 16-3). The benefits of these drugs may take 1 to 3 months to be seen, but these benefits are sustained for months or years of use. They all require monitoring by a physician.

(table 16-3*)*

DMARDS FOR RHEUMATOID ARTHRITIS

GENERIC NAME	BRAND NAME	DOSE	SIDE EFFECTS	MONITORING
Methotrexate	Rheumatrex	7.5–20 mg/wk	Nausea, oral sores, bone marrow, or liver toxicity	CBC, liver enzymes
Hydroxychloroquine	Plaquenil	200–400 mg/d	Rash, blurred vision	Eye exams
Sulfasalazine	Azulfidine	1000–2000 mg/d	Nausea, allergy	Occasional blood test
Leflunomide	Arava	10–20 mg/d	Diarrhea, weight loss, liver toxicity	CBC, liver enzymes

Methotrexate is the DMARD that is usually first tried in the treatment of rheumatoid arthritis. It is well tolerated, but side effects can occur. Patients are advised to take supplemental folic acid in a dosage range of 400 to 1000 micrograms daily to reduce toxic effects (many multivitamins contain 400 micrograms of folic acid per tablet). The starting dose for methotrexate is 7.5 to 10 milligrams per week. The dose may need to be increased to 15 to 20 milligrams per week. If the response is not excellent after two to three months, it is customary to add other drugs. Combinations of three or more DMARDs may be necessary to bring the disease under control. The goal is to reduce swelling and pain in the joint. It is no longer acceptable to wait for the joints to be badly damaged before getting aggressive about treatment! Much of the damage is done or at least mapped out in the first year of rheumatoid arthritis if the inflammation is not brought under control as quickly as possible. Therefore, aggressive treatment programs are being used, usually with methotrexate as the mainstay of treatment. Patients on methotrexate should avoid alcoholic beverages since severe liver problems may develop.

Sulfasalazine is a combination of an antibiotic with an anti-inflammatory drug. Sulfasalazine is inexpensive but effective by itself in only about one-half of rheumatoid arthritis patients. More commonly, it is used in combination with other DMARDs. Two or three months may be required to see its full effect. This drug should not be used in persons allergic to sulfa.

Hydroxychloroquine was invented over 50 years ago as a drug for malaria. Accidentally, it was found to help patients with discoid lupus and then patients with SLE and rheumatoid arthritis. Its full effect may take three to twelve months. Since the drug binds tightly to body tissues, it can be months before rheumatoid arthritis flares up after a patient stops the drug. Rarely, harmful effects on the retina have been reported after years of use. Annual examinations by an ophthalmologist are recommended as a precaution.

BIOLOGIC AGENTS

Biologic agents interfere with the chain of events that cause inflammation by interrupting the body's immune response. In most rheumatic diseases, the body's own defense system goes awry. Inflammation is produced because the body's immune cells attack its own tissues. There are many theories on the initial event trigger. Perhaps a virus or some other infectious agent alters the cells in some way, so that the immune system "thinks" they are foreign cells and tries to get rid of them. Genetics may play a role, since research has shown that people with certain gene types may be more susceptible to these problems. Thus the biologic agents promote *immune tolerance*. These drugs help turn off the system that causes immune cells to reject altered cells.

Biologic agents are often used with methotrexate. The response can vary from modest help to complete suppression of rheumatoid arthritis. On average, these drugs reduce the signs of the disease by over 50%. The main problems with biologic agents are the expense and the risk of infection. Since they reduce the vigilance of the body's defense system, they increase the risk of infections. Testing is done for undiscovered or inactive tuberculosis (TB) with skin testing and possibly chest X-ray. If testing is positive, these patients are given anti-TB medication as well to prevent an active TB infection.

The biologic agents have several advantages, not the least of which is their effectiveness. They cause less blood or liver toxicity than some of the other drugs for rheumatoid arthritis, which means fewer "needle sticks" and laboratory tests. Biologic agents help prevent erosions in the joints. Patients report a heightened sense of well-being when their disease is suppressed. Already there appears to be less need for orthopedic surgery for joint replacement than in years past. Thankfully, further innovations in biologic therapy are on the horizon. Numerous studies are in progress to figure out the best combinations of medicines to use in rheumatoid arthritis. In addition, the indications for biologic agents are expanding. Positive results are being reported in the treatment of other rheumatic diseases.

(table 16-4)
BIOLOGIC AGENTS

GENERIC NAME	BRAND NAME	DOSE	AVERAGE COST PER MONTH
Etanercept	Enbrel	25 mg twice a week*	$1300
Infliximab	Remicade	200–300 mg bimonthly†	$700–1400
Adalimumab	Humira	40 mg twice a month*	$300
Anakinra	Kineret	100 mg daily*	$2000

*Subcutaneous injection.
†Intravenously.

WHAT YOU NEED TO KNOW

■ Many of the aches and pains that we associate with aging are due to disorders of the muscles, bones, and soft tissues. Rheumatology is the medical specialty that concentrates on problems with the musculoskeletal system.

■ Osteoarthritis is not a curable disease, despite advertised claims to the contrary. However, medications, exercise, assistive devices, and surgery all play a role in management of osteoarthritis. Older persons should discuss the proper dosage of medications with their doctors. This includes over-the-counter medicines, since they may have adverse effects in persons with other medical problems.

■ Many advances have been made in the treatment of rheumatoid arthritis. Disease-modifying antirheumatic drugs are usually initiated early in the course of treatment in order to limit joint damage.

■ Gout and pseudogout are caused by deposition of crystals in the joints that leads to swelling and pain. NSAIDs and steroid joint injections help alleviate the symptoms. Medicines to lower uric acid levels can reduce the risk of recurrent attacks of gout.

■ Paget's disease is often diagnosed when a bone enzyme called alkaline phosphatase is found to be elevated in the blood. In most cases, there are no symptoms. However, occasionally it is associated with pain, deformity of the legs, and headaches. Osteosarcoma, a type of bone cancer, is a rare complication.

■ Polymyalgia rheumatica is a common disorder that causes aching and muscle stiffness of the neck, shoulders, and, sometimes, the hips. The sedimentation rate is usually markedly elevated, and the condition is very responsive to low doses of prednisone.

■ Temporal arteritis is a potentially serious condition that results from inflammation of the arteries that carry blood to the head and brain. The symptoms include headache, scalp tenderness, and, occasionally, discomfort when chewing. The most feared complication is blindness caused by inflammation of the artery to the eye. Urgent treatment with high doses of prednisone is required. Temporal arteritis can be superimposed on polymyalgia rheumatica in a small percentage of patients.

■ Connective tissue diseases, such as SLE, Sjögren's syndrome, and scleroderma often have their onset in younger women. However, men can be affected, and these diseases occasionally occur later in life. It is not unusual for older persons to be affected with these conditions.

■ Tendonitis, bursitis, and soft tissue injuries are among the most frequent reasons why people see a doctor. Simple measures, such as pain relievers, NSAIDs, and steroid injections, are usually effective. In some cases, physical therapy may be prescribed.

FOR MORE INFORMATION

■ National Institute of Arthritis and Musculoskeletal and Skin Diseases
Information Clearinghouse
National Institutes of Health
1 AMS Circle
Bethesda, MD 20892
877-22-NIAMS or 301-495-4484
TTY: 301-565-2966
Fax: 301-718-6366
E-mail: niamsinfo@mail.nih.gov
Include your mailing address and, if possible, a telephone number in your e-mail.

■ Arthritis Foundation
P.O. Box 7669
Atlanta, GA 30357
800-283-7800
Web: www.arthritis.org

MedlinePlus
A service of the U.S. National Library of Medicine
and the National Institutes of Health
Web: www.arthritis.org

SUGGESTED READING

Mayo Clinic on Arthritis
Hunder, G.G, ed., 2002.
Kensington Books.

16

> When somebody says to me, which they do every five years, "How does it feel to be over the hill," my response is, "I'm just heading up the mountain."
> —*Joan Baez*

THE AUTHORS

17

ROBERT SEEBACHER, MD, graduated from Williams College and the Georgetown University School of Medicine. He did a residency in general surgery for two years at Mount Sinai Hospital in New York City, and then he completed his training in orthopedic surgery at the Hospital for Special Surgery at New York Hospital–Cornell Medical Center, in New York City. He subsequently did a one-year fellowship in children's orthopedics at the Hospital for Sick Children, University of Toronto, in Ontario, Canada. Dr. Seebacher is a senior attending physician and director of the Joint Replacement Service at the Phelps Memorial Hospital Center in Sleepy Hollow, New York. He has served as the president of the Orthopedic Section of the Westchester County Medical Society. *New York Magazine* bestowed on him its Best Doctor Award in 2001.

SAMUEL HOISINGTON, MD, graduated from Harvard University and Albany Medical College. He completed his orthopedic training at Montefiore Medical Center–Albert Einstein College of Medicine. He spent an additional year doing a foot and ankle fellowship at Allegheny University Medical Center in Philadelphia.

Traveling to Vietnam and Bhutan, Dr. Hoisington and his wife Dr. Angela Damiano worked with Health Volunteers Overseas.

Dr. Hoisington practices orthopedic surgery in Westchester County, New York. He is an attending orthopedic surgeon at Phelps Memorial Hospital Center, Sleepy Hollow, New York; and serves as medical director at the Phelps Memorial Hospital Wound Healing Institute. He specializes in the reconstruction of the traumatized and posttraumatic foot and ankle, rheumatoid and psoriatic arthritis of the foot and ankle, diabetic foot problems, sports medicine of the foot and ankle, adult-acquired flatfoot, nerve entrapment, neuromas, and bunions.

17 | BONES, MUSCLES, AND JOINTS II

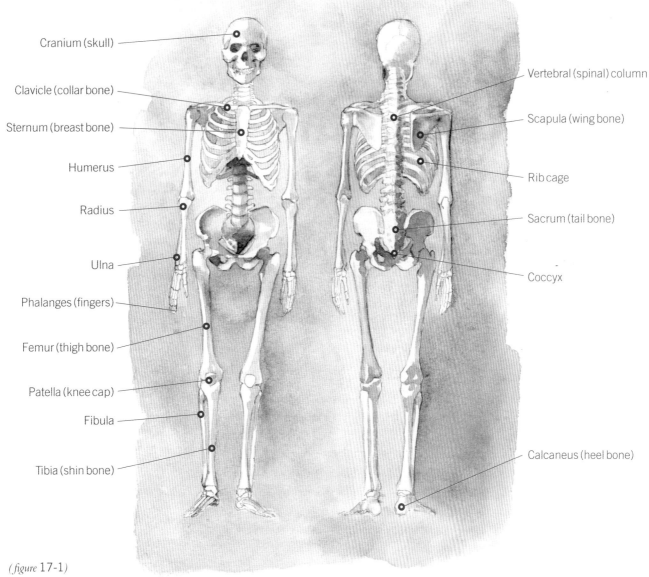

Cranium (skull)

Clavicle (collar bone)

Sternum (breast bone)

Humerus

Radius

Ulna

Phalanges (fingers)

Femur (thigh bone)

Patella (knee cap)

Fibula

Tibia (shin bone)

Vertebral (spinal) column

Scapula (wing bone)

Rib cage

Sacrum (tail bone)

Coccyx

Calcaneus (heel bone)

(figure 17-1)
The bones of your skeleton form the structural framework for your body.

The bones are the basis for your body's structural framework, or skeleton. Just as a house or a building needs firm supports, your body needs a framework to which muscles can attach. Your body's electric wires, the nerves, can then command the muscles of your head and limbs to move. The intricate interactions of your nerves, muscles, and bones allow you to conduct yourself in a purposeful fashion from one place to another as you eat, walk, dance, play golf or tennis, and lift a shopping bag or grandchild.

As the world has changed, so have we. Most of us will live much longer than our ancestors. We have learned to take better care of ourselves, and many of us are fortunate to live our lives free of the harsh stresses that can so easily wear down the body. A life span of 60 to 70 years was rare just a century ago; now it is the norm.

Aging brings with it the problems associated with long use. Your car will eventually have parts that need to be replaced. Your home will need repairs. Similarly, your bones, joints, and muscles will develop such problems as arthritis, fractures (broken bones), muscle tears, or tendon ruptures. However, you want to remain active until the end of your life. You may enjoy volunteer work at your local community hospital. Perhaps you enjoy tennis or golf. Maybe you like to travel. Or you may take pleasure in gardening or spending time with your grandchildren. Whatever your circumstances, you don't want problems with your body keeping you from participating in activities that you enjoy. This may require that you occasionally fix body parts. Orthopedic surgery is the specialty that focuses on the surgical management of bone, joint, and muscle problems. Orthopedic surgeons treat sprains, fractures, muscle tears, and back injuries. Joint replacement surgery for arthritis is also a common procedure done by orthopedic surgeons. Getting you back to an optimal level is the goal.

The main part of this chapter reviews the anatomy, function, and disorders of the bones, joints, and muscles. The chapter concludes with a discussion of the problems of the feet and ankle that affect so many older persons.

THE MUSCULOSKELETAL SYSTEM

BONE STRUCTURE

You might find it hard to believe that your bones are living tissue and that they are in a constant state of breakdown and formation. The bones have a rich blood supply that carries oxygen, nutrients, minerals, and water. The blood returning to the circulation from the bones carries with it waste products, carbon dioxide, and water.

The human body has 207 separate bones, which connected together make up the human skeleton (see Figure 17-1). The six major functions of your skeleton include lightweight support, movable articulation, points of attachment for muscles and ligaments, protection, a major reservoir of calcium, and contains blood-forming bone marrow.

Lightweight support: Bone is nearly rigid, and it is capable of withstanding tremendous loads because of its great strength. Compared to common building materials, bone is far stronger than wood and most closely resembles reinforced concrete. This is because bone is comprised of thin, flexible protein strands that run through a rigid, somewhat brittle, mass of calcium-containing bone crystals. Joined together in this fashion, the resulting composite is ever so slightly flexible and far stronger than either of its individual components. The long, thin hollow bones of your arms and legs are very much like the cylindrical columns once used in the great temples of Greece and Rome. On the other hand, the irregular-shaped bones that make up your pelvis, spine, wrists, and hindfeet consist of a dense outer shell of bone with reinforcing struts of bone within the interior. These bones can be stacked one upon the other producing columns or arches of great strength while remaining extremely lightweight.

Movable articulation: Bones assume complex shapes, often at their ends, which allow them to connect *(articulate)* one against the other. The shapes of the ends of the bones also allow the bones to provide and control movement in the joints. Your hip joint is an excellent example. Since the hip is a ball-and-socket joint, movement can occur in many different directions. Your ankle, on the other hand, moves up and down quite easily but not well side to side.

Points of attachment for muscles and ligaments: The amazing structure of the bones provides bumps and ridges that provide strategic attachment points for stabilizing ligaments and powerful muscles.

Protection: The curving ribs form an expandable cage around the heart and lungs; the vaulted plates of the skull, a rigid dome above the brain; the encircling pelvis, a safe cavity for numerous organs and a protected passageway for waste and progeny; and the intricate vertebrae (backbones), a labyrinth of canals through which pass the spinal cord and dozens of nerves.

Major reservoir for calcium: The element, calcium, has two functions in the human body. First, it is the major constituent of bone crystal. Second, calcium is essential for the contraction of all three types of muscle in your body. This includes the specialized muscle of the heart, the intestines, and the walls of the blood vessels, as well as the more familiar muscles which power your skeleton.

Contains blood-forming bone marrow: All bones, whether the tubular bones of your arms and legs, the flat bones of your skull and pelvis, or the cubelike bones of your wrists and ankles, contain interior spaces filled with bone marrow. Much but not all of the marrow in the body forms blood, including the red cells which carry oxygen, the white cells which help fight infection, and the platelets which help blood to clot.

With so many roles to play, it is not surprising that the metabolism of bone is highly complex and extremely active. Collectively speaking, all the bone in your body is subject to the two processes of bone breakdown and bone formation. In normal circumstances, these two processes are so rapid and precisely matched to one another that your entire skeleton is removed and replaced every two years! Specialized cells within the bone marrow are responsible for building up and breaking down bone. These cells, in turn, are regulated by several hormones that are discussed in Chapter 20.

In addition to the effects of hormones, bone-forming cells are stimulated to rapidly produce new bone by physical activity. The crystalline structure of bone is similar to flint. When stressed by the impact of a load, as would occur with walking, small electric currents are induced in the bone crystals. As a result, the cells that surround the involved bone increase their bone-forming activity.

Bone formation may not proceed normally unless calcium is available in the blood and delivered to the bone-forming cells. First, calcium needs to be eaten. Rich sources of calcium include milk and milk products, leafy green vegetables and broccoli, and sardines (with bones). Vitamin D facilitates the absorption of calcium from the intestines into the blood. Vitamin D is contained in meats, as well as most multivitamin supplements. In addition, vitamin D is made in the skin upon exposure to sunlight. The diet of most older persons contains insufficient vitamin D to absorb calcium properly. Persons from northern climates or those who spend much of the time indoors may not be exposed to sufficient sunlight to maintain adequate stores of vitamin D in the body. Therefore, most physicians recommend that their older patients take a multivitamin with vitamin D. Proper functioning of the liver and kidneys are required to convert vitamin D to its active form. If you have liver or kidney disease, your doctor may prescribe larger amounts or give you a prescription supplement.

A final point of importance about bone is its ability to heal. When bone is injured or broken, it is capable of healing itself completely without scarring. For this to occur properly, the bone ends must be held together in the proper position. With time, the injured bone will be remodeled and fully healed. Few other tissues in the body have this great capability to repair themselves.

ANATOMY AND FUNCTION OF JOINTS

Most, but not all, of the 207 bones of your body are connected in one way or another. Of the half-dozen different types of connections that exist, several are rigid, fixed, and immobile, like the teeth in their sockets in the jaw or the sutures where the plates that make up your skull are fused. Other groups of joints are partially mobile, sometimes bound by tough fibrous ligaments and separated by slightly springy "shock absorbers." Examples of these include the spinal column, where the backbones alternate with the discs, as well as the spongy, springy connection where the two halves of the pelvis connect at the pubis. Of greater interest are the highly flexible, muscle-powered synovial joints (see Figure 17-2). The synovium is the special lining of the joint that secretes a fluid that lubricates and nourishes the bone surfaces.

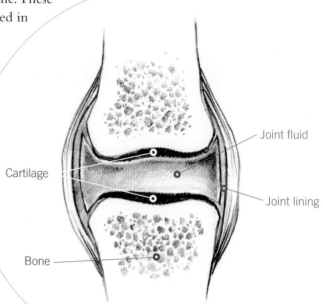

Cartilage

Joint fluid

Joint lining

Bone

(figure 17-2)

The bones that articulate at the synovial joint are coated with smooth cartilage and are bathed in a slippery joint fluid that allows them to move with little friction. The joint lining secretes the fluid that lubricates and nourishes the cartilage.

All synovial joints have several important common features. The end of the bones where contact occurs is covered by a thin (1.5- to 3-mm) layer of joint cartilage. This unique pearly white, glistening, extremely slippery, and spongy substance is familiar to anyone who has seen the end of a chicken bone. Cartilage consists of a microscopic fine layer of protein mesh that entraps live cells underneath it. These cells produce giant mucouslike molecules that attract the water secreted by the lining of the joint to flow in and out of the cartilage, thus lubricating the surface of the cartilage and producing its spongy or springy qualities. This is the basis for the nearly frictionless movements within your joints, which with a little luck remain active throughout your lifetime.

Another important feature that your joints share is a surrounding leathery, but flexible, membrane or capsule. This capsule is thickened or reinforced in crucial locations by denser bands of sinewy tissue known as *ligaments.* The ligaments bind and support the joints as well as control the direction in which the joints are capable of moving. Additionally, certain joints contain fibrous rubbery discs or lips at the margins of the joint that are partially interposed between the ends of the bones in order to cushion, support, and control the motion patterns of the joint.

The many synovial joints of your body can be further subdivided into some half-dozen different types based on their mechanical characteristics. Simple names such as the "ball and socket" of the hip and shoulder, the "hinge" of the elbow or ankle, or the "rolling curve on flat" of the knee and finger have immediate and intuitive appeal.

Each bone connected through a joint moves under the combined influences of the pull of the controlling muscles, the influence of gravity on the body weight, and any and all other external forces imposed. Some joints like the ball and socket of the hip and shoulder are free to move in a wide range of directions, as is the double-saddle joint that makes up the base of your thumb. Other joints are more restricted and have less freedom of motion. The built-in factors that restrict a joint stabilize it. Varying contributions from three structural factors produce the stability of any joint. These factors include the bone cartilage contours, the ligaments that surround the joint, and dynamic muscular control.

ANATOMY AND FUNCTION OF MUSCLE

Spanning the joints and connected to the adjacent bones, the muscles provide the dynamic influences that resist the pull of gravity in order to produce movement and perform work. This process requires energy, which means that muscle usage burns calories.

Basically, each muscle has three portions (see Figure 17-3). First, the muscle *origin* is a short fibrous area that attaches the top of the muscle to a bone. Second, the *muscle belly* is the longer red fleshy section that contains the contractile (tightening or shortening) region. Finally, the tendon is a long sinuous strap of noncontractile material that travels from the end of the muscle belly. Sometimes the tendon twists or turns and then inserts on another bone. Generally, the beginning (origin) of the muscle is separated

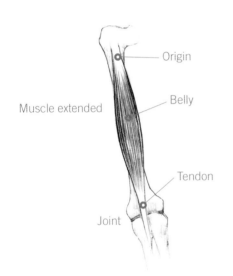

Muscle extended

Origin

Belly

Tendon

Joint

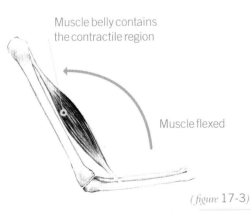

Muscle belly contains the contractile region

Muscle flexed

(figure 17-3)

The structure of muscle makes it ideally suited to move your joints.

from the end where the tendon inserts by at least one joint. Muscles have a rich blood supply of arteries that carry in oxygen and energy-rich substances and veins that remove from them carbon dioxide and waste products. Muscles also have a rich network of nerves. Some nerves stimulate the muscles to contract, and others carry information to the spinal cord and brain about the length of the muscles and their position.

When a muscle is stimulated to contract, it shortens by using oxygen and energy. Interestingly, in order for a contracted muscle to relengthen, it must again be stimulated and energy must be expended. It does not stretch out like a rubber band or release its load like an electromagnet disconnected from its current. This little known fact is not a trivial one. Restated, more energy and effort is required for your thigh muscles to descend a flight of stairs slowly than rapidly. The working action of your muscles, especially when lengthening, cushions and protects your joints, like the knee when descending a flight of stairs.

The belly of a muscle, the portion that lengthens and shortens actively, is composed of muscle cells. The cells are arranged parallel to each other. Although very small in cross section, they are very long, running the entire length of the muscle belly. Within each cell is the biochemical machinery that allows the muscle to shorten or lengthen by using oxygen to burn sugar. A muscle that is used repeatedly and hard tends to strengthen by enlarging. This enlargement process is called hypertrophy and results in an increased amount of the muscle's contractile apparatus. The actual number of muscle cells does not change. Conversely, if a muscle is not used often or not forced to work hard, weakening or thinning called atrophy is the consequence. Within each cell there is a loss of the amount of machinery used to produce contraction. The cells become thinner as does the entire muscle belly.

Any muscle at any given time has a maximum length to which it can extend and a minimum length to which it can contract. Under ordinary circumstances, after growth is completed, muscles tend to maintain given maximum and minimum lengths while used normally and regularly. If a muscle belly is injured directly, it heals by the formation of a fibrous, flexible, but noncontractile area of scarring. The outcome is a slight overall shortening of the muscle belly. Muscle bellies also shorten and thin out with disuse. Finally, a muscle undergoing special strengthening, as with weight training, also tends to shorten somewhat.

ANATOMY AND FUNCTION OF YOUR SKELETAL SYSTEM

The human skeleton is similar to that seen in all the *vertebrates* (animals with a spinal column), particularly other mammals but also birds, reptiles, and fish. Your skeleton is jointed and internal, but it is still capable of providing external protection in critical areas. Unlike the vast group of *arthropods,* which have no spine and include *crustaceans* (lobsters) and insects, whose skeletons are outside their bodies, affording them far greater protection, our soft parts are free to be in contact with the world around us, affording us far greater potential for sophisticated interaction and thus performance.

This internal position of our skeleton, besides offering us less protection, makes us pound for pound much weaker than an insect whose external skeleton affords far greater mechanical advantage for the attachments of the internally positioned muscles.

MUSCULOSKELETAL DISORDERS

The title of this book, *Optimal Aging Manual,* is succinct but deserves more than a moment's attention. The focus is clearly on health but recognizes that we cannot always avoid sickness. This mirrors widespread emerging trends among both health care recipients and providers to consider disease and illness while always recalling the desired state of normalcy and wellness. This positive approach offers much to patients and their caregivers. Thus the initial focus in this chapter was upon the normal structure and function of the adult musculoskeletal system, as well as its reparative and regenerative capabilities.

Besides health and wellness, this manual refines its scope of concern to the enlarging segment of the population referred to as seniors. Socially and politically it is always dangerous to define exactly who is on or out of that group. Sidestepping these built-in pitfalls and looking for some medical or scientific category or set of defining points is only slightly easier. Increasingly, the boundaries for groups such as retirees, grandparents, empty nesters, or persons with social security insurance are more and more blurred. We all know 50-year-olds who are out of shape, overweight, and have heart attacks. Yet we also know 80-year-olds who play tennis and golf, ski, and lift weights. Recognizing the inherent difficulties in identifying exactly whom this manual is meant for, the conditions and diseases more commonly associated with aging are considered here.

GRID OF THE FIVE Ds

For purposes of easier understanding, we divide disorders into sections depending on whether the bone, joints, or muscles are primarily involved. Diseases will be taken to include illness and injury related to any of the *five Ds:* 1) *defects* in metabolism; 2) *deficiencies* of vital substances; 3) *deviations* from normal healthy responses; 4) *disturbances* of normal function; and 5) *deterioration* of health related to age. The following grid of the five Ds provides a conceptual framework to help you understand the disorders which affect the bones, muscles, and joints.

FIVE Ds	BONES	JOINTS	MUSCLES
Defects in metabolism			
Deficiencies of vital substances			
Deviations from normal healthy responses			
Disturbances of normal function			
Deterioration related to age			

Separate consideration is made for bones, muscles, and joints, forming a grid of 15 subcategories based on understanding the form, function, and problem. This approach encourages you to develop a holistic pattern of thought which depends on common sense and understanding and virtually begs for proactive consideration and decision making.

DISEASES OF BONE

Defects in bone metabolism:Osteogenesis imperfecta, more popularly known as "brittle bones," is an inherited defect of bone formation. This

FIVE Ds	BONES	JOINTS	MUSCLES
Defects in metabolism	O		
Deficiencies of vital substances			
Deviations from normal healthy responses			
Disturbances of normal function			
Deterioration related to age			

condition is almost always diagnosed in childhood or early adult life; however, with proper care persons with milder forms of the disorder can reach their senior years.

Two types of anemia may be associated with inherited defects in bone growth and formation. Abnormalities in the structure of hemoglobin, the oxygen-carrying pigment of the red blood cell, are responsible for sickle cell anemia and thalassemia major (also called *Cooley's anemia*). In these conditions, abnormally shaped red blood cells clog the very small blood vessels called capillaries. Widespread damage results from oxygen deprivation of the tissues. The damage to the bone tissue results in sudden bone and joint aches. In addition, because the body's immunity is impaired, bone infections are more common. Improvements in medical care have allowed many affected persons to survive into their senior years, although they require highly specialized attention and care.

Deficiencies of vital bone substances: Strong bones in later adulthood depend on long-term exposure to sunlight, diets rich in calcium and

FIVE Ds	BONES	JOINTS	MUSCLES
Defects in metabolism			
Deficiencies of vital substances	O		
Deviations from normal healthy responses			
Disturbances of normal function			
Deterioration related to age			

vitamin D, and regular exercise. Individuals who lack any of these factors experience slow but steady reductions in their total bone volume which results in bone weakness, softness, or both. The condition of thin bones that are otherwise normally formed is known as **osteoporosis** (see also Chapter 19). Affected bones have thinner walls with larger central cavities. Soft bones, however, are caused specifically by a lack of calcium crystal but a normal amount of the reinforcing protein fibers known as *collagen*. This condition can be seen in young or growing individuals lacking vitamin D in their diets and is known as *nutritional rickets*. Older persons with fair skin, often accompanied by blue eyes, blond or red hair, freckles, and a northern European background, may be forced to avoid exposure of their skin to sunlight. When coupled with a poor dietary intake of vitamin D, chronic vitamin D deficiency may result in a condition associated with soft bones called **osteomalacia.**

Persons with osteoporosis or osteomalacia often have abnormal X-rays. Their bones may be less opaque, thin-walled, and sometimes slightly bowed or bulging. This can be seen in the upper thigh bone or the hip or even the hip socket. On the other hand, bones may be collapsed as may occur in the vertebrae in the bottom of the ribcage and low back. Normally, bones look white on an X-ray film, but because the bones are less dense in these conditions, their ability to block a passing beam of radiation is reduced. Therefore, the bones look darker than normal (see Figure 17-4). However, X-rays typically show these problems only if the problem is quite advanced. For that reason, **bone densitometry** has emerged as the preferred method for evaluating bone density, since it can detect problems very early when treatment can make a greater difference.

Deviations from normal bone responses: Deviations in normal processes, such as calcium metabolism and blood production, include the

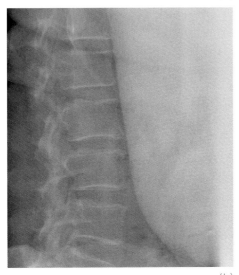

(a)

(b)

(figure 17-4)

X-ray appearance of a (a) normal and (b) osteoporotic spine. Note that normal bones look whiter on an X-ray than osteoporotic bones.

FIVE Ds	BONES	JOINTS	MUSCLES
Defects in metabolism			
Deficiencies of vital substances			
Deviations from normal healthy responses	○		
Disturbances of normal function			
Deterioration related to age			

formation of benign and malignant bone tumors. These can be localized to a single site in a single bone, be distributed throughout an entire bone, or involve many bones.

Primary tumors are those that originate in bone. A cancer that spreads to bone from other areas such as the lung or breast is called a **metastasis**. Warning signs of bone tumors include pain or swelling due to microscopic or obvious fractures of the bone.

Tumors may produce or remove bone, thus causing visible changes on X-ray. New bone formation either caused by a tumor or by the bone trying to repair itself can also be detected by a bone scan. Changes in the number of cells in a region of bone or changes in the blood supply to bone can best be detected by magnetic resonance imaging (MRI). Bone scans and MRI may detect problems before there are visible changes on an X-ray.

Disturbances of normal bone function: Disturbances of normal bone function include trauma or injury of bone and infections of bone. In both

FIVE Ds	BONES	JOINTS	MUSCLES
Defects in metabolism			
Deficiencies of vital substances			
Deviations from normal healthy responses			
Disturbances of normal function	○		
Deterioration related to age			

cases, problems are visited on the bone by outside forces or invading factors. Trauma to various parts of the skeleton is an all too familiar scourge in the lives of older persons. These range from severe injuries as would occur in motor vehicle accidents or from falling off a bicycle, to seemingly trivial and minor incidents, as would occur when picking up an 18-month-old toddler. Thus it becomes obvious that our attempts to classify causes and sources of wellness and illness in the musculoskeletal system to a neat grid or matrix are rendered imprecise because of overlapping categories. For example, osteoporotic bones or bones weakened by a tumor are more liable than normal bones to fracture from trauma (see the following section, "Disorders Eluding Precise Classification"). Your realization that no classification system of the causes and roots of illness can ever be exact will help you better comprehend the treatment options reviewed later in this chapter.

Disorders eluding precise classification: Some disorders elude attempts to classify them into a single category. For example, a woman

FIVE Ds	BONES	JOINTS	MUSCLES
Defects in metabolism			
Deficiencies of vital substances	○		
Deviations from normal healthy responses			
Disturbances of normal function	○		
Deterioration related to age	○		

with osteoporosis who falls and breaks her hip would have a grid that looks like the above. Osteoporosis is a disorder associated with aging, but it is also caused by a deficiency of a vital substance.

Although fractures tend to occur in recognizable patterns, locations, and frequencies, the variations are as numerous as the possible ways a China vase can smash after it falls on the floor. The most common fractures of elderly persons include those of the lower vertebrae, pelvic fractures, hip fractures, shoulder fractures, and fractures of the end of the forearm or wrist.

The word *fracture* encompasses a wide variety of breaks. A fracture may be a simple or single crack in the bone. A squashed vertebra is called a *compression fracture.* Or the bone may be broken into many pieces *(comminuted fracture).* Some fractures occur where the bone ends remain close to each other, while others are displaced. Some fractures result from an external blow that has also penetrated the skin. In other cases, the deformation of the bone that occurs leads to the jagged bone end popping through the skin *(compound* or *open fracture).*

Infections of bone are disturbances caused by external invading organisms. Osteomyelitis is the term to describe bacteria infecting bone (see Chapter 22). An enlarging and penetrating ulcer of a diabetic's foot typifies sudden and severe infections. Long-term slow infections of the bone may be related to old war injuries, particularly involving penetrating injuries of bones from bullets or shrapnel. Paget's disease *(osteitis deformans)* is another example of an infectious disturbance of bone that leads to disturbances of bone formation and breakdown. As a result, the bone weakens and deforms. The incidence of Paget's disease increases after age 55 and becomes even more common in persons in their 60s and 70s. Bone enters a phase of greatly accelerated deposition and removal in which there are vast and alarming differences in the microscopic architecture of the bone that lead to the bone being grossly deformed due to expansion and bending. Because the bone is weaker, both microscopic and large fractures are common that lead to further disturbances in bone shape due to improper healing. Paget's disease usually involves a single bone initially, but spreads throughout the entire bone over a period of years. However, eventually multiple bones are involved. When bone ends are affected, the involved joints often become arthritic. The distortion and overgrowths of bone that occur when the skull or vertebrae are affected may lead to entrapment of nerves as they pass through the bony "windows" and grooves resulting in nerve-related symptoms including pain, paralysis, and deafness. Even prior to fractures, arthritis, or nerve irritation caused by Paget's disease, the inflammatory process within the bone is painful in and of itself. The cause of Paget's disease, unknown for a century, has recently been linked to a latent infection with the measles virus. The measles virus may remain sequestered in the human body for many decades only to reemerge in later years in much the same way that the chicken pox virus may emerge in later years to produce shingles.

17

IMAGING TESTS FOR THE MUSCULOSKELETAL SYSTEM

X-ray: Doctors use various types of X-rays and scans to diagnose problems of the muscles and bones. X-rays of bone taken from the front and side are useful in showing details of the bone's quality and character. The amount of radiation is minimal, and the tests are obtained quickly and painlessly. Following is an X-ray of the upper arm bone called the humerus. Note that since bones are denser than muscles or soft tissue, they block the X-ray beam better and show up white on X-ray film.

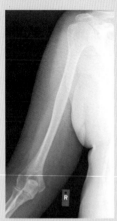 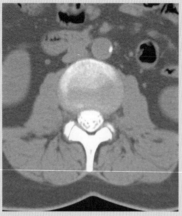

X-ray   CT scan

CT Scan: A CT scan allows serial X-rays to be obtained, each picture varying in the angle or depth of focus by a few degrees or millimeters. All the images are then compared with one another either directly by the visual inspection of the radiologist or orthopedic surgeon or with a computer-generated reconstructed series of images. Above is a CT scan of a backbone (vertebra). The scan takes "slices" at various levels of the bone.

The CT scan images show much greater detail than regular X-rays due to the fact that tissues of different densities transmit varying amounts of radiation to precisely positioned screens or film, which are subsequently analyzed.

Bone Scan: A bone scan or radionuclide imaging study of bone involves the injection of a minute amount of a radioactive element called technetium, which looks very much to the bone forming cells like calcium. The technetium is picked up anywhere in the body where bone is undergoing repair or growth. Actually, the majority of the technetium is rapidly excreted in the urine.

Each atom of technetium undergoes radioactive decay, releasing a small amount of radiation that passes harmlessly out of the body, leaving behind smaller atoms that are no longer radioactive or harmful in any way. The technetium that has been taken up by the areas of repairing bone emits special signals. A scanner that resembles a Geiger counter picks up those signals. The image that is generated points out the "hot spots" which represent areas of arthritis, healing fractures, bone infections, bone bruises, and areas of bone healing adjacent to bone tumors. The bladder also shows up as a hot spot due to concentration of the technetium in the urine. Note in the bone scan here of a person with lung cancer which has spread to the bones, the white spots which represent where the cancer has spread.

Bone scanning is highly sensitive, which means that it can identify that there are problems; however, it does not tell the doctor or you exactly what the problem is. In some cases, the clinical situation helps. For example, if a person with lung cancer has many sites of pain, a bone scan showing many hot spots is highly suggestive that the cancer has spread to the bones. However, if person with knee pain and swelling has a bone scan that shows a hot spot over the knee, you cannot reliably know whether that is due to arthritis, a joint infection, or an injury. Therefore, bone scanning is almost always used in conjunction with other tests, such as X-rays, CT scan, or MRI.

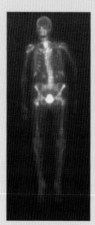 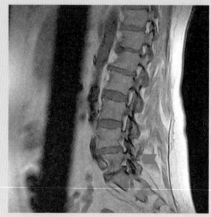

Bone scan   MRI

MRI: Unlike X-rays and tomograms, which differentiate between different areas of bone and tissue based on differences in density, an MRI is sensitive to the varying chemical qualities of different tissue types, particularly the fat or water content. Dense bone contains little fat or water and is fairly nondescript on an MRI image. Ordinarily, the spongy or porous bone—seen at the ends of the long bones such as the femur (thighbone) or the flat bones such as the ribs—contains bone marrow, much of which is fatty. Little water is found in this region unless there has been a bruise or fracture with bleeding. Bone tumors generally have a rich blood supply, which also brings water into the bone. Thus the MRI is far less sensitive to the details of bone shape, such as small spurs in the spine, which might be pressing on nerves, or bone fragments at a fracture site. Yet MRI is far more sensitive to the changes in the quality of bone related to infection, damage from tumors, or injury from lack of oxygen-carrying blood. An MRI is particularly good at "seeing" the contours of cartilage, which is a soft material that cannot be seen too well on regular X-rays. Thus an MRI can be especially helpful to the doctor in diagnosing a herniated disc (arrowhead) that squeezes out between vertebrae (backbones) and pinches a nerve.

Doctors also use an MRI to diagnose torn cartilages in the knee or to assess the severity of arthritis and cartilage wear in a joint.

Bone Density: The density of bones blocks the passage of X-rays to a sensitive piece of radiographic film. The thicker the bone, the less the radiation that passes through it and the more white or dense it appears on the X-ray film. This principle can be employed safely with less radiation exposure for the purpose of measuring the density of certain bones (usually the spine and hip) in the body. Regular X-rays may require as much as a 30% loss of bone mineral before a doctor can diagnose osteoporosis. Therefore, bone mineral density, or BMD is the preferred technique for the evaluation of osteoporosis. Scores are obtained that allow a doctor to reliably determine the severity of bone loss.

Even less severe degrees of bone weakness can be diagnosed at an early stage, so that treatment to prevent future problems can begin. Since there is so little radiation exposure, this test can be repeated periodically to monitor responses to calcium supplements, vitamin D, and medications.

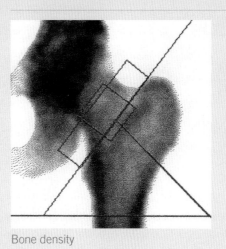

Bone density

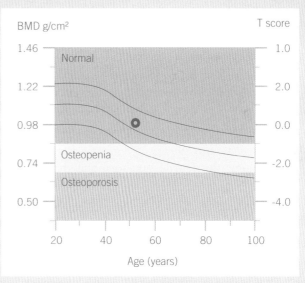

Osteoporosis is diagnosed with a T-score of -2.5 or lower. A T-score between -1 and -2.5 is considered low bone density, or osteopenia.

As I noted before, closer scrutiny of the 15-category grid shows the overlap of entities within particular categories and the seeming commonality of advanced or end-stage diseases. The similarities have long been recognized between chronic ongoing infection and malignant transformation to cancer at the sites of chronic bone and skin infections. This also applies to bone involved with Paget's disease for a long period of time. Skin cancer may develop along the *sinus tracts* or *fistulae* (abnormal channels) where chronic bone infections drain. Cancerous tumors called bone sarcomas may develop at the site of chronic infection from osteomyelitis or Paget's disease.

Deterioration of bone with age: When considering bone and its deterioration over time, the familiar processes of active bone deposition

FIVE Ds	BONES	JOINTS	MUSCLES
Defects in metabolism			
Deficiencies of vital substances			
Deviations from normal healthy responses			
Disturbances of normal function			
Deterioration related to age	○		

and remodeling should return to your mind. A well-known analogy for this process is that of a huge silo with an endless number of workers performing one or two functions simultaneously at opposite ends of the tank. At the top end, an endless supply of buckets of material (in this case, bone ingredients) are added to the reservoir whose contents represent the total bone volume of the individual's body. Simultaneously, and at an identical or nearly identical rate, a second group of workers remove bone on the bottom end of the tank. Thus the contents of the tank remain constant over time. How then and why does the total bone mass diminish with deterioration in overall bone strength with aging? Well, even a small change in the rate of the processes, either due to diminished formation or increased breakdown, leads to an overall loss in bone volume and strength within a very short time.

Estrogen (the female sex hormone) has a preserving or protective effect on bone by retarding its rate of removal. At the end of a woman's reproductive years, there is a drop in the levels of estrogen. This decrease is partial in most women but may be nearly complete in about 20% of women. The complete loss of estrogen leads to a sudden increase in bone resorption without a matching increase in bone formation. Ultimately, if left untreated, osteoporosis may ensue. Chapter 19 discusses osteoporosis and its treatment in detail.

DISEASES OF JOINTS

Although a complex subject, the final common pathway of all that goes wrong with the joints of the human body can be encompassed by the simple term *arthritis*. Familiar to everyone, arthritis encompasses many of the causes of irritation or sickness of one or more joints. Indeed, only a lucky few upon becoming a senior can claim to be entirely free of any arthritis. Before reviewing how the many routes that lead to arthritis can be assigned to the grid of the five Ds, I would like to digress for a moment. In keeping with this manual's purpose of focusing on wellness,

WHY DO BONE SPURS FORM?

Bone spurs are bony enlargements forming on the normally rounded margin of a joint. In effect, they broaden or widen the potential area of contact of the joint, but they lack the smooth covering of the joint cartilage. They form in attempt to repair or compensate for overload or instability or abnormal joint slippage related to muscle weakness and/or ligament damage. Their presence tends to stabilize the joint in which they develop, but in so doing, they also limit flexibility. Bone spurs may also irritate the adjacent soft tissues and nerves causing pain.

even though it is important to recognize that sickness occurs, I would like to discuss with you six critical prerequisites for healthy joint function.

Being principally mechanical in nature, the essential requirements for proper joint function sounds like an engineering checklist: (1) proper alignment, (2) congruous surfaces, (3) stability, (4) motor control, (5) sensibility, and (6) nutrition. Reading the following discussion can strengthen your understanding of not only the wellness but also the sickness of joints.

Proper alignment: Each joint must be correctly aligned within the limb or between the portions of the skeleton in which it is situated. If resting between bowed or curved thigh and leg bones related to rickets, Paget's disease, or crookedly healed bones from a previous fracture, the knee joint will ultimately become over worn on one side. Force concentrates on the inner or concave side of such a joint. Thus, bowed legs tend to produce arthritic wear on the inner side of the knee, whereas knock-knees become worn and painful on the outer side. A crooked spine curved either to the side (scoliosis) or forward (kyphosis) tends to form buttressing *bone spurs* on the inner side of the deforming curve. Although formed as a means of protection, the spurs eventually may press upon and irritate the adjacent nerves passing from the spinal cord within the spine into the limbs. The pressure on the nerves can cause pain and/or numbness in the affected arm or leg.

Congruous or matching surfaces: The well-known saying "to fit a square peg in a round hole" captures the essence of what goes wrong when the mirror surfaces of a joint no longer match one another. There are two particularly common causes for loss of joint congruity. First, fractures of the bone and joint surface cartilage displace and heal with a *step off* or irregularity. These, of course, can occur anywhere in the body related to the location of the trauma. Second, and most typically related to the bones of the knee, the ball of the hip, or sometimes the ball of the shoulder, joint congruity is lost when the bone that lies just beneath the joint surface collapses. The collapse follows ongoing pressure or usage of bone that has died due to an interruption of the blood flow to the bone. As time passes, the dead bone weakens and deforms, producing an incongruity of the joint surfaces. Curved surfaces tend to flatten, and flat surfaces tend to dent.

17

TYPE OF HIP FRACTURES

	FEMORAL NECK	INTERTROCHANTERIC
	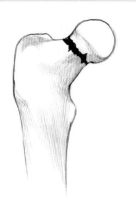	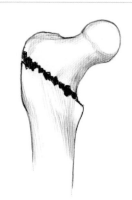
AGE GROUP USUALLY AFFECTED	60-70 years old	70-80 years old
DEGREE OF SEVERITY OF FRACTURE	Cracks at the top of the neck just beneath the ball. May be displaced, slightly tilted, or completely separated from the rest of the neck and femur below.	May range from simple undisplaced cracks to complete disruption of bone into as many as four fragments consisting of the shaft below, one or both tuberosities, and the combined ball and neck.
RATIONALE OF TREATMENTS	Cracks of the femoral neck sometimes don't go through the whole bone and are considered partial or relatively stable, as occurs when the ball is crushed down over the crack. If protected from being jostled, by doing little or no walking, these fractures tend to heal in a month or two. However, if the head gets displaced after a fracture, its blood supply is jeopardized resulting in gradual bone death *(necrosis)*. Yet displaced femoral head fractures can be left untreated in patients too sick to undergo surgery. These might include patients with advanced dementia or those with paralysis of the fractured hip following a stroke. These patients can be moved comfortably from a bed to a chair almost immediately and with time can bear limited amounts of weight on the limb when briefly standing or transferring to a bed or chair.	Without surgery, these fractures are too painful for the patient to be moved into a sitting position. In sicker older patients, the cost of lying in bed for six weeks while one of these fractures heals might include pressure sores with overwhelming infection, pneumonia, or blood clots. A painful death is a significant possibility unless surgical stabilization of the fracture fragments is employed to treat most of these fractures. Intertrochanteric fractures consisting of a single undisplaced or incomplete crack are often stable enough and become rapidly painless. Even when walking carefully, they will go on to heal within a month or two.
SURGICAL TREATMENTS	Undisplaced or incomplete femoral neck fractures are at risk for displacement. Once displaced, the ball often dies, and thus the treatment of even the undisplaced fracture requires surgery. The goal of surgery is to prevent the ball from displacing, which can be done simply by inserting a few long thin screws to hold everything together. These screws can often be inserted through simple stab wounds in the upper outer thigh, rather than requiring a larger incision. When the ball displaces in a senior citizen, the surgery almost always involves a replacement with a new identically sized metal ball attached to the end of a four- or five-inch stem placed solidly in the top of the thigh bone.	Displaced or fragmented pieces of bone are reattached to one another using a metallic device euphemistically called a "nail." It consists of a metal plate that is screwed to the top of the shaft of the femur and a larger screw is mounted at the top of the plate at exactly the right angle to reposition the fragments as close as possible to where they were originally.

	FEMORAL NECK	INTERTROCHANTERIC
SURGICAL TREATMENTS	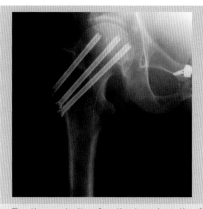	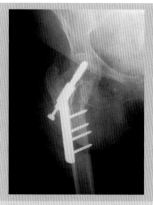
REHABILITATION	For the majority of patients, when the femoral head is replaced with a prosthesis, the outcome is usually good as far as restoration of painless function, length, motion, strength, and balance. In cases where the femoral head is only minimally displaced and thus capable of being pinned back with screws, restoration rates can again be anticipated in about 75% of cases.	The surgical goal is to stabilize the fragments sufficiently enough that weight-bearing and walking can be resumed immediately. This is not always possible, but at the very least the patient should be capable of being helped to a chair immediately after surgery to reduce the risk of pressure sores, pneumonia, and blood clots. The length of time to maximal recovery varies from two to eight months.
OUTCOMES	After surgical pinning, most undisplaced femoral neck fractures go on to full recovery in three months. A significant number (about 25%), however, go on to death of the femoral head and partial collapse leading to painful arthritis that requires hip replacement. When the femoral head is replaced immediately, full recovery occurs within three to four months.	The degree of recovery is most directly related to the severity of the fracture. The crucial factor is how severely comminuted (fragmented) the fracture is. The more simple fractures can be expected to heal in normal or near normal positions. The more severe fractures tend to heal with distortion, which may shorten and/or weaken the leg and hip. Contractures of the surrounding soft tissues may limit the motion of the hip and cause pain with hip movement. A small number of these fractures fail to heal. This may lead to collapse of the bone, which is often painful, and requires further, even more difficult, surgery.

Stability: All joints regardless of their shape and location have built-in stabilizing factors related to their shape and the surrounding ligaments and muscles. Any loss in stability, as would typically occur after ligament damage from an injury, results in abnormal movement of that joint. Usually the joint will be overly mobile with one side of it riding up over the edge of the other, bruising its bony margins, and stretching the remaining ligaments and the joint capsule. The damaged areas tend to calcify, leading to bone spurs. Each time the unstable joint slips abnormally, stretching and damaging the tissues on its margin, a sprain occurs. If the sprain is great enough, previously undamaged ligaments may tear, leading to bleeding into the joint. When the joint fills with blood under pressure, the remaining ligaments and joint capsule are further stretched, producing pain, stiffness, soreness, and, ultimately, weaker controlling muscles. As it becomes increasing unstable and as the muscles progressively weaken, the joint becomes more prone to further injury. Despite the body's corrective attempts of forming bone spurs to restabilize and block abnormal motion of the joint, instability often increases in the pattern just described. Doctors call this a vicious cycle.

BONES NEED BLOOD

The strength of bone is related to the combination of the arrangement of bone crystals around protein strands. Both these substances are inert, or not living material. However, they are both surrounded by and filled with living cells constantly engaged in the act of breaking down and building new bone. These cells are dependent on the blood flow to and within the bone. The blood delivers oxygen and nutrients to the bone. Blood also removes carbon dioxide and water from the bone. If the blood supply is interrupted, as might occur from an injury or a blood clot, the cells die while the structural portion of the bone remains intact and unchanged. This event may be heralded by the sudden onset of pain, which may last for a few days or weeks and then gradually remits. Living cells from adjacent unaffected bone gradually migrate into the area of dead bone and begin the process of repair.

During the reparative process, living cells first invade and form new blood channels in order to reestablish circulation. Next, special cells resorb the dead bone in preparation for the arrival of the bone-forming cells that replace the dead bone with new bone. At the point where the dead bone has been removed and before new bone replaces it, the bone is especially vulnerable, since there is a tremendous decrease in the strength of the entire region. If this region is directly underneath the surface of the joint, as is often the case, collapse and alteration of the joint surface might occur. If the area was somehow protected during the period of vulnerability and collapse did not occur, the circulation would eventually be reestablished, the dead bone replaced, and the strength of the bone restored.

The terms doctors use to describe the process of bone death due to interruption of blood flow include *avascular necrosis, bone necrosis,* and *osteonecrosis*.

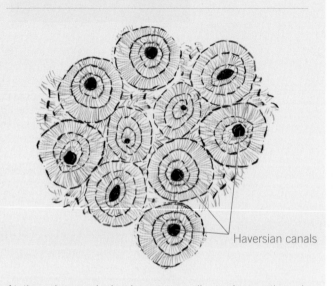

Haversian canals

At the microscopic level, many small canals run through bone. These Haversian canals carry small blood vessels that carry blood to the bone cells.

Motor or muscle control: The surrounding muscles that control a joint not only power it but also cushion and protect it. Any condition that weakens or paralyzes these muscles will gradually result in damage to the very same joint they control. A good example of this is seen in the limbs of polio victims. Similarly, overactive muscles, such as those rendered spastic following a stroke, can overstress the joint by grinding away the surfaces of the hip, knee, or shoulder.

Innervation or sensibility: The very same nerves that stimulate the muscles that surround and power a given joint also provide innervation to the membranes and ligaments that surround the joint. In this way, feedback is given to the brain as to where that joint is in relation to the rest of the body and how much pressure or stress is being placed on it. This sophisticated feedback system is critical for proper functioning of the joints. Without it, either damaged or rendered nonfunctional in some way, there would be rapid and catastrophic failure of the joint and surrounding bone. The destructive process that befalls numb or insensible joints is referred to as neuropathic arthropathy. Simply stated: disease of nerves leads to disease of joints. The most common cause of these severe problems in the

United States is diabetes, which typically involves the ankles and feet and sometimes the knees. A far less common cause, but one that was more frequent in the past, is the later or tertiary stage of syphilis. Interestingly, in other parts of the world leprosy is still a common cause of this type of joint destruction. Here, damage to the sensory nerves can be so severe that the fingers and toes become nothing more than shapeless blobs of skin at the ends of the hands and feet.

Balanced nutrition of the joint: The nutrition of the joint, considered broadly, is related to a number of factors that include the proper function of the inner membrane of the joint lining *(synovium),* which secretes lubricating fluid that is rich in oxygen and vital nutrients and also removes carbon dioxide and waste products. The actual living cells within the joint cartilage are dependent on this process in order to continue their role of secreting the complex mucous that lubricates and provides the sponginess of the joint surface. From an engineering perspective, this represents the most slippery interface known. The regular and repetitive movement of the joint is critical to these processes by forcing joint fluid to circulate around and through the entire joint. There are numerous conditions that disturb these complex nutritional mechanisms. One category of these disruptions is crystal-induced arthritis, such as gout and pseudogout, which are discussed in Chapter 16. Briefly, the crystals which form within the joint are intensely irritative to the joint surfaces due to mechanical abrasion (like grit or sand in a gearbox). The cells in the lining of the joint respond to the irritation and overproduce joint fluid, causing a joint effusion (swelling of the joint). The buildup of fluid and pressure in the joint results in stiffness and pain. If this occurs frequently, the capsule and ligaments will stretch producing instability. Other conditions (discussed in Chapter 16) that disturb the complex nutritional mechanisms include rheumatoid arthritis and systemic lupus erythematosus. Psoriasis may also be associated with a destructive arthritis, and some intestinal conditions, such as Crohn's disease and ulcerative colitis, may have arthritic manifestations. In all these situations, the joint is the battleground where the immune system fights against an unknown invader or at the behest of a poorly understood stimulus. Unless the process is interrupted locally or throughout the entire body, ongoing destruction of one or more joints is the rule. The affected joints swell, become stiff, unstable, and weak. This is another example of a vicious cycle or downward self-perpetuating spiral of progressive joint deterioration. A final example of the interruption of the normal nutritional state of the joint, either by itself or as part of some greater illness, is joint infection, which is discussed in Chapter 22.

This completes our discussion of disease of the joints based on the essential prerequisites for proper joint function. It is a good starting point for your study of joint diseases because it focuses on the specialized unique functions of joints and the processes that threaten to interrupt them. Consideration of the five Ds allows further enhancement of your understanding of the maladies that might affect the body's joints.

Defects of joint metabolism: Defects in joints might result from abnormalities of development (congenital abnormalities) or genetically

FIVE Ds	BONES	JOINTS	MUSCLES
Defects in metabolism		⊙	
Deficiencies of vital substances			
Deviations from normal healthy responses			
Disturbances of normal function			
Deterioration related to age			

inherited defects in biochemical or physiological processes that lead to a cascade of secondary events and effects that ultimately result in arthritis.

A large fetus in a smaller first-time mother approaching the end of pregnancy may become so cramped in the uterus that the legs are forced up against the body. The hips may be dislocated or become so limited in their ability to move as to retard the development of the socket. The socket at birth is too shallow or not deeply molded. After treatment, the individual may do well through childhood and even the early part of adulthood but may run into problems in midlife or beyond, due to the fact that shallow or dysplastic (abnormally developed) hips are prone to wear out earlier because reduced contact or coverage of the ball in the socket leads to concentration of forces over smaller areas of the joint surface.

Genetic, or inherited defects, in the quality of joint cartilage have long been suspected, but only partially proven, to set the stage for accelerated wear or reduced ability to undergo repair. In either case, inherited defects in the quality of the joint cartilage would be one possible path leading to osteoarthritis. A family history may reveal that parents or siblings have arthritis. However, it is well known that many other noninherited variables play an important role in osteoarthritis. Excessive weight is known to increase the risk of osteoarthritis in the hips and knees. Repetitive trauma can produce arthritis in many joints. For example, jackhammer operators are particularly prone to arthritis of the shoulder joints.

Deficiency of vital joint substances: Deficiencies of calcium or vitamin D cause osteoporosis and osteomalacia, which weaken bone and can lead

FIVE Ds	BONES	JOINTS	MUSCLES
Defects in metabolism			
Deficiencies of vital substances		⊙	
Deviations from normal healthy responses			
Disturbances of normal function			
Deterioration related to age			

to collapse of the bony surfaces of the joints in heavy individuals. In active persons, sudden trauma or heavy activity might damage weak bones. This leads to a gradual or sudden change in the joint surface or a loss of congruity, causing arthritic deterioration.

You have already learned the importance of regular exercise as a means of distributing and circulating joint fluid, which is vital for the nourishment and maintenance of the joint. Additionally, regular exercise maintains the strength of the supporting musculature of the joints and also causes the bone, which forms and supports the joint, to renew and strengthen itself. Thus deficiency of regular activity, or prolonged inactivity for any reason, would be expected to have adverse effects on any joints denied their normal usage.

Such deficiencies might occur temporarily during the course of severe illness accompanied by prolonged bed rest, as might be seen following a major head injury causing a coma state from which recovery ultimately occurred. More localized temporary deficiencies might occur following burns or fractures, in which immobilization of a limb in a cast was necessary to facilitate healing of the bone in proper position. Permanent deficiencies of proper usage might occur in limbs rendered flaccid by polio or stiff and spastic after a stroke.

In the absence of proper activity and exercise, the joint surfaces gradually enter a malnourished state and become thinner, less healthy, and less able to tolerate normal stresses. Additionally, the surrounding and supporting musculature becomes weakened, sometimes contracted, and less able to guide, move, and support the involved joint, all of which leads to a predilection for increasingly rapid arthritic deterioration.

Deviations from normal joint responses: Having already considered the disease of joints as far as the six critical prerequisites, you should be

FIVE Ds	BONES	JOINTS	MUSCLES
Defects in metabolism			
Deficiencies of vital substances			
Deviations from normal healthy responses		○	
Disturbances of normal function			
Deterioration related to age			

able to assign certain of the conditions, already discussed, to this category of deviations in normal joint responses when considering the entire grid of diseases of bones, joints, and muscles. Both gout and pseudogout, which lead to inflammation and wear, represent intrinsic deviations from normal joint behavior. Similarly, the inflammatory arthritic conditions, such as rheumatoid arthritis and lupus arthritis, are other good examples of disorders that damage joints and lead to deviations from normal function.

You may argue that gout is inherited genetically and that perhaps it should be more properly assigned to the category of defects in metabolism of joints, rather than to the category of deviations. Don't be disturbed if these questions arise! Their presence only indicates that you have become more astute and have a better understanding of the complexities of joint function and the abnormal conditions that can affect the joints. Classifications systems, such as the five Ds, are only useful in creating the framework for learning and understanding these abnormal states. Ultimately this system forms a critical basis for our various sections on treatment, below, which cover treatment options with a goal of interrupting vicious cycles and restoring normalcy, health, and wellness.

Disturbances of normal joint function: For the purposes of this chapter, the word *disturbance* is taken to mean an outside interruption or

FIVE Ds	BONES	JOINTS	MUSCLES
Defects in metabolism			
Deficiencies of vital substances			
Deviations from normal healthy responses			
Disturbances of normal function		⊙	
Deterioration related to age			

action against the healthy, normally functioning joint. Injury or trauma is considered such a disturbance. Trauma, whether gradually occurring and microscopic or sudden and severe, affects the bone and cartilage leading to gradual arthritic wear or to sudden acute failure of the joint. Similarly, obesity of long-standing duration is considered such a disturbance since excessive weight leads to a gradual accelerated wear of the joint surfaces, culminating in arthritis.

In these cases, as the joint surfaces wear away to a point at which the underlying bone is exposed, first on one side and then on both sides of the joint, an inflammatory process is initiated within the joint. Although initially caused by the mechanical process of bone on bone, it triggers a series of chemical reactions in the lining cells of the joint membrane (synovium) that cause oversecretion of fluid into the joint, known as an effusion. This undoubtedly sounds familiar to you since it is a replay of the events that lead to osteoarthritis, but it points out that different mechanisms can lead to similar results.

Other problems that can rightly be placed in this category, as well as the categories in which they have been placed previously, include joint infections and avascular necrosis. Since joint infections are explained in Chapter 22, we don't review them here. However, it is important that you understand avascular necrosis, so that you will be better prepared to appreciate the treatment options discussed later.

(figure 17-5)

Avascular necrosis: Poor blood flow causes death of bone followed by its softening. The overlying cartilage can be forced up and down.

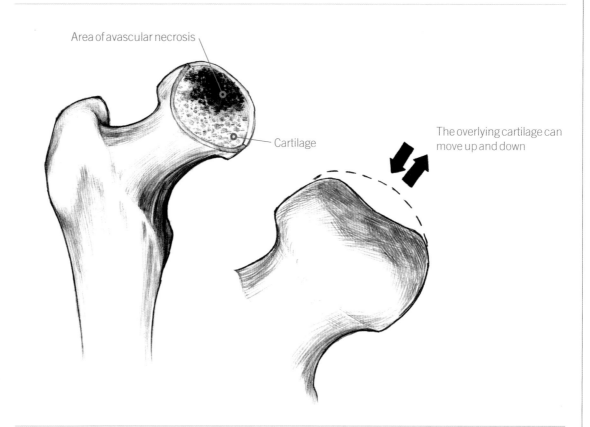

Area of avascular necrosis

Cartilage

The overlying cartilage can move up and down

Avascular necrosis means bone death secondary to lack of blood flow. The bone underlying the surface of the joint is then pressed down by the opposing or matching surface of the joint during normal usage (see Figure 17-5). The thin (3- to 5-mm) layer of joint cartilage over the collapsed area of bone is forced up and down like the surface of a ping-pong ball dented due to the pressure of your finger but springing back into normal position once the pressure is removed. Similarly, if the load is shifted away from the crushed area of bone as the joint's position changes, the cartilage springs back into its usual position. However, just as a ping-pong ball eventually cracks if you dent it over and over again, the joint cartilage over the collapsed bone cracks if it is repeatedly dented. The crack initially appears at the edge of the dented surface and then propagates in a semicircular fashion along the edge of that portion of the cartilage that overlies the collapsed bone. Joint fluid flows under this area of the joint cartilage forming what looks like a blister. As the crack travels further and further, a flap of joint cartilage develops that sometimes catches painfully against the opposite matching surface of the joint when motion occurs. Depending on the stage of this complex process, which can go on for months or years, patients experience a wide variety of symptoms, such as stiffness, soreness, swelling, pain, and locking or catching of the joint.

Deterioration of joint function with age: This final category for joint disease in the grid of the five Ds is a fitting ending for our discussion of

FIVE Ds	BONES	JOINTS	MUSCLES
Defects in metabolism			
Deficiencies of vital substances			
Deviations from normal healthy responses			
Disturbances of normal function			
Deterioration related to age		⊙	

the joints. By now, it is apparent to you that end-stage arthritis has many common features, such as pain, limitation of movement, loss of function, weakness, and swelling. However, there are many starting places from which severe arthritis can be reached. And undoubtedly you recognize that all the disorders that I discussed in the other categories ultimately lead to deterioration in joint function (see Figure 17-6).

Despite all that you have learned about what can go wrong, the joints of the human body are actually exquisitely constructed and have remarkable capabilities of mobility, strength, and repair. When considered as mechanical linkages, your joints demonstrate exceptional longevity of useful function. In the vast majority of cases, the deterioration associated with arthritis is a long, slow process characterized by upturns and downturns. The natural reparative processes of the body with regard to the joints, coupled with the very nature of the indomitable human spirit

(figure 17-6)
Severe arthritis is associated with loss of cartilage, narrowing of the joint space, bone spurs, and bone rubbing against bone.

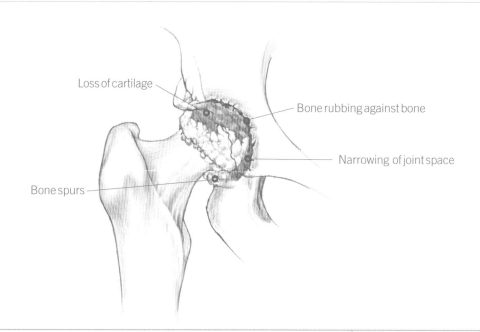

Loss of cartilage

Bone rubbing against bone

Narrowing of joint space

Bone spurs

of perseverance in the face of adversity, makes the study of arthritis one of the best examples of the body's ability to compensate.

The protective bone spurs that form to stabilize an injured joint do so often at the expense of mobility and fluidity, but they would allow an injured pioneer, hunter, or farmer to go on with life. These compromises result in shortening and weakening of supporting muscles as well as shifts in balance and posture and, considered cumulatively, make up the familiar picture of the aged body—stooped spine, an upward craned neck, bent knees and hips, and a slow unsteady gait, perhaps aided by a cane or supporting arm of a family member (see Figure 17-7).

DISEASES OF MUSCLE

The study of muscle disorders is important in your overall understanding of the skeletal system. To focus on the bones and joints alone would severely limit your understanding of anatomy and function, disease states, and the basis for treatments. Muscles function in widely different areas of the body, including the movement of the skeleton, the pumping of the heart, the movement of food and waste in the gastrointestinal system, and the constriction and relaxation of the arteries of the circulatory system. In this section, again using the grid for the five Ds, we focus on the disease states of the muscles that power the skeleton.

Defects in muscle metabolism: During the last decade, the newest and greatest increases in medical understanding of all human diseases have been

FIVE Ds	BONES	JOINTS	MUSCLES
Defects in metabolism			◉
Deficiencies of vital substances			
Deviations from normal healthy responses			
Disturbances of normal function			
Deterioration related to age			

concerned with inherited defects in metabolism, the first of the five Ds. At present, you need to be concerned with only a few known conditions of muscle metabolism, none of which is completely understood. Further scientific and medical advances will undoubtedly elucidate that many conditions currently considered as deviations in normal function or deteriorations related to age are, in fact, linked to inherited or genetically controlled patterns of metabolism. Thus your genetic makeup may make you more likely to develop problems that have traditionally been classified in the categories of deviation or deterioration. The best understanding of form, function, sickness, and wellness comes from a panoramic rather than a focused view.

Polymyalgia rheumatica is an inflammatory disease of muscles that affects individuals who are genetically predisposed (diagnosis and

(figure 17-7)

The typical appearance of a person with severe arthritis includes a stooped spine, an upward craned neck, bent knees and hips, slow unsteady gait, and holding a cane.

treatment of polymyalgia rheumatica are covered in Chapter 16). Several other muscle disorders have also been linked to genetics or heredity.

Polymyositis is an inflammatory disease of muscles that produces pain and weakness. Laboratory tests may show elevation of muscle enzymes, but other tests may be required, such as an **electromyogram (EMG),** which measures electrical activity in the muscle, and a muscle biopsy. When skin rashes occur with polymyositis, the diagnosis is **dermatomyositis.** When polymyositis or dermatomyositis is diagnosed, an investigation for cancer is usually launched, since the body's immune reaction to the cancer may trigger a reaction against the muscle cells as well.

Deficiencies of vital muscle substances: Now confined largely to the third world, diseases of muscle related to vitamin or protein malnutrition

FIVE Ds	BONES	JOINTS	MUSCLES
Defects in metabolism			
Deficiencies of vital substances			⊙
Deviations from normal healthy responses			
Disturbances of normal function			
Deterioration related to age			

are too rare to be discussed in this manual. Not uncommon, however, is the muscle weakness that develops with **hypothyroidism,** in which there is a deficiency of thyroid hormones. The thyroid gland situated in the front of the lower part of your neck uses iodine ingested in your diet to manufacture its hormones, which are then secreted into the bloodstream and carried to the entire body. Thyroid hormones exert vast and significant effects on the general activity level of muscles (including the heart) and nerves. Although deficiencies of thyroid hormones are often accompanied by a wide range of symptoms (see Chapter 20), significant muscle weakness may be an isolated problem and the complaint that brings the patient to the doctor.

Another important deficiency state to consider, although clearly extending beyond the subject of muscles alone, is alterations in wound healing related to malnutrition. The effect of mildly malnourished states, often seen in the frail and sick elderly, may not be enough to produce overt disease or dysfunction. However, problems may become apparent following injury or surgery. The normal healing response of skin, fat, muscle, and bone may be delayed as a consequence. A good example of this is the failure of a surgical wound to heal in a debilitated elderly patient following surgery to stabilize a fractured hip. Lacking the nutritional and metabolic wherewithal to form a healing or reparative clot, the surgical wound though sutured closed continues to ooze serum (a straw-colored body fluid that includes protein, white blood cells, and salt). These individuals are vulnerable to penetration of the open wound by bacteria on the skin. The body's normal defense mechanisms may also be weakened due to malnutrition, heightening the risk that an infection will develop. Similar trouble may be precipitated in malnourished persons by relatively minor wounds such as abrasions or scrapes.

Deviations in normal muscle function: An important deviation in normal muscle behavior occurs following injury or, more frequently,

FIVE Ds	BONES	JOINTS	MUSCLES
Defects in metabolism			
Deficiencies of vital substances			
Deviations from normal healthy responses			○
Disturbances of normal function			
Deterioration related to age			

surgery around the hip. Each of the many tissues in the body has specialized and distinct healing abilities following injury, surgery, or other forms of damage. I described the ability of bone to heal, oftentimes perfectly, earlier in this chapter. You are familiar with the healing abilities of skin. Small cuts and abrasions usually heal perfectly. Large cuts, abrasions, or burns heal with varying amounts of scar tissue, which has properties different from the original skin it replaces.

Compared to the other tissues of the body, muscle has good reparative qualities. When you exercise, the stress causes microscopic changes in the individual muscle fibers or cells. The production of the "machinery" inside the cells that causes muscle contraction is then stimulated. Exercise, including both contraction and stretching, causes muscle cells to thicken and strengthen (hypertrophy).

You should easily be able to envision how the same processes affect muscles subjected to larger amounts of trauma or major surgery. While damaged or exercised muscles have the ability to thicken, enlarge, and thus become stronger, large injuries that tear muscles in half or crush them heal by a more complex process. This process includes the formation of bridging scar tissue that is strong, fibrous, and flexible but that does not contract. Depending on the location and size of the injury, the remaining muscle cells that are not injured or still connected to their nerve supply retain their functional contractile capabilities. These muscle cells may enlarge in a compensatory fashion and overstrengthen, thus effectively making up for those muscle cells that have been rendered incapable of further function. The injured muscle is able to readjust with tremendous versatility and, as a result, can often maintain its strength, flexibility, and function and often regain its original shape and size.

For reasons that are not completely understood, but may conceivably someday be shown to be genetically determined, certain muscles, particularly around the hip and to a lesser extent the elbow and forearm, tend to heal abnormally. Rather than forming a thin pliable bridging scar following the initial period of inflammation and swelling, bone forms within the muscle where the injury occurred. This process is called myositis ossificans (also called *heterotopic ossification*). Neither flexible nor well suited to moving and sliding, the end result of myositis ossificans may include both restriction of movement and pain.

Disturbance of normal muscle function: Based on our previous discussions of the disturbances of bone and joints, you may correctly

FIVE Ds	BONES	JOINTS	MUSCLES
Defects in metabolism			
Deficiencies of vital substances			
Deviations from normal healthy responses			
Disturbances of normal function			○
Deterioration related to age			

surmise that much of this discussion concerning the disturbances of muscle involves a group of commonly seen injuries. These injuries are divided into those that occur gradually from repeated overstress and those that occur suddenly from a single sudden extreme injury. There are many situations where the two patterns are combined, as when a chronically overstressed muscle is suddenly and severely damaged by another injury. In such instances, the magnitude of the single injury may not need to be nearly as great as it would to damage or rupture a previously healthy muscle. Continually overstressed muscles are already predisposed to further injury by a single sudden event.

Please recall the three individual parts of each muscle: the origin arising from bone; the central, contractile, red fleshy section known as the belly; and the tendon, which is a cordlike structure where the muscle inserts on bone. Discrete injuries can occur in any of these distinct areas. Although the number of muscles in your body is far greater than the number of bones, a fairly small group of disorders that involve muscle origins, muscle bellies, and tendon insertions are seen again and again and deserve special mention.

Tennis elbow, which is discussed in Chapter 16, is a good example of an injury at a muscle origin. And playing tennis need not cause it. This problem can occur either suddenly following a single episode of overstressing the muscle origin on the outside of the elbow or gradually over time from repeated small stresses. Microscopically, the noncontractile fibrous origin of the muscle begins to tear away from the bony prominence

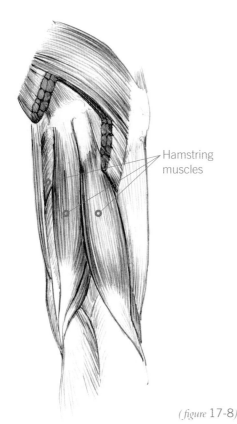

(figure 17-8)

The hamstring muscles are composed of three large muscles on the back of the thigh that allow the knee to bend or tilt your pelvis back or forward when standing up.

Hamstring muscles

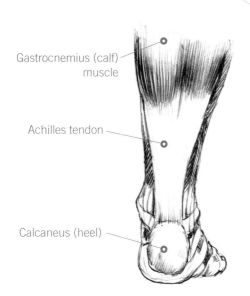

Gastrocnemius (calf) muscle

Achilles tendon

Calcaneus (heel)

(figure 17-9)

The Achilles tendon is a common site for injury and rupture. The calf muscles, which pull through the Achilles tendon, drive the foot down or put you up on your toes.

to which it is attached. Pain occurs both with use and rest. Picking up a pitcher of water or shaking hands may aggravate the pain. Although the healing response is immediate, ongoing usage of the muscles tears the healing tendon fibers or injures new ones, thus hindering the process.

A good general rule about the healing time for injured muscles and tendons is 6 weeks. This is considerably longer than it takes for your skin to heal following a cut or incision and is related to the relatively larger stresses which must be accommodated by the parts of a contracting muscle. In order for an injured muscle to heal without being redamaged by further activity, a six-week period of rest is necessary.

Injury to the muscle belly, the red fleshy contractile portion, is most commonly seen in the middle of the calf, but it also occurs with great frequency in the hamstring muscles on the inner back side of the midthigh (see Figure 17-8). Injuring a muscle belly usually occurs suddenly with a single episode of overstress, as might occur if someone suddenly broke into a run. The muscle fibers actually tear in half. The severity of the injury can be very small, but complete tears through the whole muscle occasionally occur. Most tears are partial, with a significant number of the muscle fibers still intact, thus holding the damaged fibers in place and preventing a wide separation through the area of the tear. Holding these fibers in place, along with rest, sets the stage for the healing response to occur.

Initially, a muscle tear is associated with pain and perhaps a visible or palpable indentation at the site of the tear. Fairly quickly, more diffuse pain and swelling follow. Within a few days, bruising is noted, first as a reddish-purple discoloration that may extend over a much larger area than the area of the torn muscle. The reason is that the bleeding is initially localized to the ends of the torn muscle fibers. This collection of blood is called a hematoma. However, gravity causes the blood to leak through noninjured tissues down the thigh or leg. Thus it would not be unusual for a calf muscle rupture to cause a purple discoloration as far down as the inner ankle and foot. A "hamstring pull" could produce similar involvement from the buttock to the knee. Although this can be alarming to a patient, generally the extent of the discoloration is of little consequence. Certain medications that affect the clotting of blood may enhance this tendency. These include, but are not limited to, aspirin, IBUPROFEN, CLOPIDOGREL (PLAVIX), CILOSTAZOL (PLETAL), DIPYRIDAMOLE (PERSANTINE), and WARFARIN (COUMADIN).

Among the traumatic disturbances of muscles are tendon ruptures. Many, if not all of these assorted traumatic disturbances of muscles, are strongly predisposed if the muscle involved has become excessively tight or contracted. In this situation, the contractile portion of the belly of the muscle is no longer able to relax and lengthen to the fullest extent that the joints it powers can otherwise naturally move. This is the mechanism for a common injury: the Achilles tendon (heel cord) rupture (see Figure 17-9).

If a person with a tight Achilles tendon, while stepping up on the edge of a curb, misses and suddenly lands on the ball of the foot rather than the entire flat foot, the foot is suddenly driven up hard. A tight tendon is not elastic enough to compensate and a tear in the tendon occurs.

Many conditions lead to tight or contracted muscles. Some persons have naturally tight muscles following the end of their growth, and this situation may remain during adulthood and late life. Other people can develop tight muscles as a result of repetitive exercising without accompanying stretching exercises. Muscle tightness may also follow the healing of a muscle injury. Finally, as we discuss in the next section, "Deterioration of Muscle with Age," muscle tightness might develop later in life as a consequence of aging and lack of full usage, particularly stretching.

Tendon injuries may be partial, as with a bulbous tender enlargement of the Achilles tendon, or complete. Complete tears lead to immediate loss of power of a joint in a certain direction. A complete tendon rupture may be associated with a sudden pulling or "pop," and a hole or indentation may be noted at the site of the rupture. The attached muscle might shift and bunch up since it is no longer attached to bone at one of its ends. Many older persons have experienced a biceps tendon rupture (see Figure 17-10). This is the big arm muscle that tenses in the front of your arm when you flex the elbow. When the tendon ruptures, the muscle bunches up into an irregular shape. Typically, the pain following a tendon rupture may be minimal or brief in duration. A small amount of swelling may follow, but since tendons do not have a lot of blood flow to them and are smaller than the muscle belly, they tend to bleed very little after a rupture.

Besides rupture of the Achilles and biceps tendons, a common and serious tendon rupture involves the quadriceps tendon, which is situated in the lower front of the thigh attaching to the top of kneecap (patella). A complete rupture of this tendon prevents the knee from extending against gravity, and walking becomes difficult or impossible and certainly dangerous (see Figure 17-11).

A final and fairly common type of tendon rupture is that which occurs if a tendon rubs against a bone spur formed because of arthritis or following a healed fracture of an adjacent bone. A healing wrist fracture called a Colles' fracture that is common with older age (see Figure 17-12) occasionally ruptures the tendon that straightens the thumb where it crosses over the end of the forearm bone at the wrist. Far more common are the tendon ruptures that occur when the flat tendons of the shoulder cuff are injured by an adjacent bone spur, as will be discussed in the next section.

(*figure* 17-10)

Biceps tendon rupture at its upper end in the shoulder usually does not cause significant disability in an older person. Notice how the biceps muscle (arrowhead) bunches up into an irregular shape.

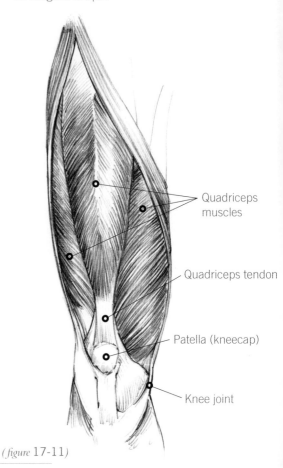

Quadriceps muscles

Quadriceps tendon

Patella (kneecap)

Knee joint

(*figure* 17-11)

The quadriceps is the large group of four connected muscles on the front of your thigh that together draw through the patella and straighten the knee. Rupturing this stout tendon just above the kneecap can be very disabling and make walking difficult.

(figure 17-12)

Fractures at the end of the forearm bones can occasionally cause rupture of the tendon that straightens the thumb.

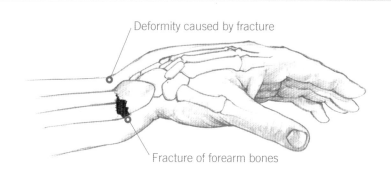

Deformity caused by fracture

Fracture of forearm bones

17

Deterioration of muscle with age: In the discussion of muscle disturbances related to both acute trauma and chronic overstress, I

FIVE Ds	BONES	JOINTS	MUSCLES
Defects in metabolism			
Deficiencies of vital substances			
Deviations from normal healthy responses			
Disturbances of normal function			
Deterioration related to age			●

mentioned that muscles could become predisposed to injury if they became short or tight, but briefly mentioned that deterioration with age might be caused by *contracture* (a short, tight muscle) from lack of use and accompanying loss of flexibility. Let's expand this discussion to include weakness of loss of muscle bulk (**atrophy**) not only from disuse but also from disorders that interfere with the nerve signals that stimulate the muscle to contract or relax (see Figure 17-13). Although many of these nerve disorders are discussed in Chapters 18 and 21, we briefly classify them here by using the five Ds:

- *Defects in nerve metabolism* that are inherited and give rise to a gradual deterioration of the motor and sensory nerves later in life. They can cause severe weakness, atrophy, and deformity of the feet and hands. A large group of these disorders has been identified and are grouped under the term hereditary sensorimotor neuropathies.
- *Deficiencies of vital nerve substances* that lead to deterioration in nerve function and consequently impaired balance, strength, and coordination. Ultimately, muscle atrophy occurs. Deficiencies of vitamin B12 and folic acid are two good examples.

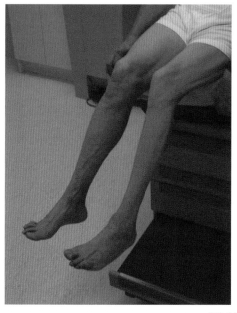

(figure 17-13)

Muscle atrophy can be caused by disuse, injury, or muscular or nervous system disease. In this case, childhood polio was responsible.

- *Deviations in normal nerve function* that may principally produce loss of sensation but may also cause weakness and muscle atrophy. Diabetes is the best and most common example. Less common, but not rare, are a group of inflammatory diseases of nerves related to dysfunction of the body's immune system.
- *Disturbances of nerve function* that lead to diminished sensation, power, and coordination and that may be accompanied by muscle atrophy. These disorders can be divided into two major subcategories. The first includes disorders caused by external compression applied to the nerve and rendering it nonfunctional. Causes might include local pressure from a bone spur, enlarging tumors, injury with hematoma pressing on the nerve, abscess or inflammatory process that surrounds the nerve, or a herniated or bulging disc in the spine. The second subcategory includes disorders caused by ingesting of toxins or medications that damage nerves. Excess alcohol is unfortunately a common cause. Some medications that are helpful in fighting cancer may nonetheless be toxic to nerves. In these serious situations, the benefit of continued treatment may justify the risk of injury to the nerves.
- *Deterioration in nerve function* with age that involves the central nerves of the brain and spinal cord, such as occurs with Alzheimer's disease or Parkinson's disease, as well as multiple sclerosis.

The purpose of the above brief list is to reinforce for you the important and complex interdependence of the nerves, muscles, and skeleton on one another and also to help you better understand how disorders of nerves and muscles can profoundly affect the skeletal system.

Deterioration of the tendinous portion of the muscles with age is very common. Recall that the tendon, unlike the fleshy contractile belly, has a relatively limited blood supply. Compared to the dynamic nutritional requirements of the muscle belly and bones, tendons are relatively inactive. Although capable of healing, they do so slowly, requiring at least 6 weeks and maybe even longer. Return of full strength takes a few months.

Some tendons are notoriously prone to deterioration with age, and they have a very limited capacity for healing spontaneously, even with protective treatment. The tendons of the rotator cuff hold the ball of the shoulder joint down in its socket (see Figure 17-14). The **rotator cuff** is a group of four ribbonlike tendons that surround the back, top, and front of the shoulder. These relatively soft tendons pass through tight passageways composed of firm and unyielding bone and ligaments, against which the soft tendons are prone to rub or impinge. The friction from rubbing against these firmer surfaces irritates the rotator cuff tendons and causes them to thicken with inflammation, which results in even more rubbing. Gradually, the rotator cuff tendons get abraded, degenerate, and tear. This process, which may occur

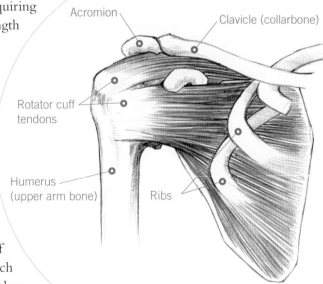

Acromion

Clavicle (collarbone)

Rotator cuff tendons

Humerus (upper arm bone)

Ribs

(figure 17-14)

The rotator cuff is composed of four flat tendons that allow the shoulder joint to turn properly.

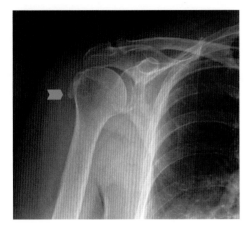

(*figure* 17-15)

X-ray showing calcium deposit (arrowhead) in the shoulder tendons.

over weeks to months or years, may produce pain at various times on the outside of the shoulder and sometimes part way down the arm. Overhead movement may aggravate the discomfort. Pain may even occur at rest, particularly when attempting to roll or sleep on that side. Increasing weakness of the shoulder, when raising and rotating the arm, occurs. The weakness is initially from lack of use from favoring the painful shoulder. Eventually, if one or more tendons tear or rupture, the weakness becomes much greater as the muscles become disconnected and completely lose their ability to assist in moving the arm through the shoulder joint.

You are now better prepared to understand the process that causes a calcium deposit in the shoulder. As discussed previously, some people are more prone to form bone spurs on the edges of their joints or calcium deposits in bruised muscles. Similarly, a pocket of liquid or chalky calcium can deposit within an irritated rotator cuff tendon. This process can occur suddenly, perhaps superimposed on the backdrop of chronic intermittent episodes of shoulder aches and pains. The area of calcification, generally about the size of a lima bean, can be thought of as a noninfected or sterile abscess. The shoulder becomes so painful and sensitive that most persons avoid moving the shoulder. Initially, the calcium deposit is a pastelike consistency and can be carefully withdrawn through a needle to halt the process. With the passage of days and weeks, the calcium crystallizes into a tiny nugget within the tendon which thickens slightly. With careful and gentle examination, the painful area of the rotator cuff can be appreciated just to the side below the top or point of the shoulder. Just like bone, calcium is denser than tendon, fat, or muscle, and therefore, this calcium deposit can be visualized on an X-ray (see Figure 17-15). The shoulder may be slightly stiffer, the surrounding muscles slightly weakened. In addition, the rotator cuff tendon has a tendency to rub further against the overlying arch of ligaments, thus setting the stage for even more shoulder problems.

A frozen shoulder typically occurs gradually from lack of use, which often may be related to a painful episode of rotator cuff tendonitis with or without a calcium deposit. The shoulder, formerly painful, becomes much less irritated but very stiff and no longer able to allow the arm to be raised overhead. The process that leads to a frozen shoulder is complex and involves runaway inflammation within the joint itself, perhaps triggered by pain in or near the shoulder. Diffuse and thin fibrous scarring develops in the internal membranes of the shoulder. The entire shoulder then becomes stiffened. The end result is a relatively painless stiff shoulder.

Posterior tibial tendon dysfunction and rupture is also common with aging. Seen far more frequently in women than in men, this problem begins in the sixth decade (above age 50), starting with pain triggered by walking or particularly by raising up on the toes. Swelling frequently develops behind and sometimes below the inner anklebone. Unless this process is interrupted by treatment, the tendon degenerates and goes on to rupture or becomes so degenerated and painful as to render its attached muscle nonfunctional. Gradually, as the arch of the foot drops, the foot becomes flattened and rolls out to the side in a deformed position that the patient typically notices (see Figure 17-16). Walking becomes painful, balance is impaired, and the ability to thrust onto the toes is lost. If treatment still does not occur, the joints of the foot gradually become arthritic.

TREATMENT OPTIONS

At this point, you have gained a fairly significant amount of knowledge about the structure and function of the musculoskeletal system, which will enhance your understanding and appreciation of this section on treatment. I have not attempted to produce an encyclopedia of diseases and treatments. There are at least three good reasons for this. First, the complexity and magnitude of the subject is so vast that even university training programs in orthopedics are hard-pressed to complete all the training of a prospective orthopedic surgeon in five years. Likewise, the American Board of Orthopaedic Surgeons has increasing difficulty in formulating a fair but comprehensive certifying examination for their candidates upon the completion of their training. Second, there are major differences of opinion between numerous experts about anatomy and function that blurs the borders between what is considered normal and abnormal; thus, many different treatment options may be suggested. Third, neither the description of form, function, wellness, and illness nor the myriad approaches to treatment are static but are constantly evolving, changing, and being reevaluated. It is not unusual for widely held ideas to be suddenly overturned and sometimes even completely reversed. Perhaps you will not be surprised that ideas or treatment concepts which were discarded years ago are resurrected for investigation and reevaluation by a fresh generation of doctors who are prompted to do so by a deeper understanding of the nature of structure, function, wellness, and illness.

By focusing on the six prerequisites for normal joint function (proper alignment of the joint within the skeleton; congruity or matching of the articulating surfaces of the joint; proper stability of the joint as maintained by its shape, ligaments, and supporting muscles; proper motor or muscular control of the joint; normal sensibility or nerve supply to the joint; and normal nutrition of the joint), you have been compelled to develop an understanding of the logic of the treatment process. In this chapter, we used the term "vicious cycle" to describe a downward spiral from wellness to illness which was triggered by a progression of causal factors. The word "cycle" invites you to think as to how such a trend could be interrupted and how wellness could be restored in such a situation.

We also need to consider two extremely important points that are unfortunately linked. The first concerns the art of decision making in orthopedics.

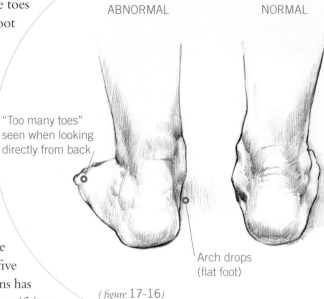

ABNORMAL   NORMAL

"Too many toes" seen when looking directly from back

Arch drops (flat foot)

(*figure* 17-16)

An example of posterior tibial dysfunction. Note the difference between the normal and affected foot.

DECISION MAKING IN ORTHOPEDICS

Three crucial steps need to be taken for making decisions about complex treatment programs for the imperfect musculoskeletal systems of elderly persons.

Step 1. Understanding the illness: The first step requires a precise understanding of the illness and how it affects the individual's quality of life. Thus, other aspects of that person's health need to be considered. Perhaps that person has other serious medical problems that will affect the response to a given treatment or to rehabilitation. For example, suppose an elderly gentleman with advanced Alzheimer's disease fell and broke his wrist. Prior to his fall, he was incapable of feeding himself. Such a person would not require a complex surgical procedure to restore precise function to his wrist. A simpler approach that allowed the bones to heal painlessly, perhaps with less restoration of precise function, might serve that man just as well. Similarly, a very ill person with a severely weakened heart is not going to be able to exercise vigorously regardless of the progression of arthritic involvement in the hips or knees. Therefore, total joint replacement surgery for this person is not a viable option, not only because the surgical procedure itself is too risky in someone with advanced heart disease but because the level of function even with an artificial hip or knee is not going to be much better. Likewise, it does no good to focus on a single arthritic joint in a limb, such as the hip or knee, if there are disabling problems in other parts of that limb, such as the foot or ankle. We can sum all this up by saying that a person needs to be considered as a whole, not just as a knee or a hip but as a unique and complex individual. This means taking into consideration that person's physical capabilities and afflictions, psychological status, social situation, and even their family and financial resources.

Step 2. Ideal plan versus practical plan: The second step in decision making is the formulation of what is needed for that particular individual as far as the ideal restoration of wellness and function and then, more importantly, the practical restoration of as much wellness and function as is reasonable. It is important to recognize the difference between an ideal plan and a practical plan. Sometimes a person's advanced age or deteriorating health necessitate that potential solutions be simplified, perhaps with the intention of restoring just enough function to give that person the needed boost to function independently. Although the results may be less than satisfying, at least that person can function well enough to enjoy daily living. Consider, for example, the following case.

MURIEL'S STORY

Muriel L., 74, was caring for her husband who had terminal cancer. She had severe arthritis in her right hip and moderate arthritis in her knee and back. The hip pain had progressed to the point where she could no longer walk without pain, leaving her with a severe limp. She had avoided surgery until now because she did not want to leave her husband. However, after realizing her inability to care for him at home, she decided upon consultation with her orthopedic

As you can see, this woman's social situation dictated the magnitude and timing of the entire process of her orthopedic care. For many months, she tried to get along in spite of her pain so that she could care for her husband. However, when the pain became unbearable and she realized that only by having the surgery would she be able to care for her husband at home, she made a decision to go ahead with the operation. Such issues are faced every day by doctors and patients alike. Complex treatment plans may be constructed with numerous contingencies, perhaps beginning with surgery on the most severely afflicted and disabling area of the body and using a combination of nonoperative treatments, such as drugs, injections, and physical therapy, to control the other problems. The treatment plan may require modification, depending on unanticipated events.

The risks of any treatment program must be considered for each step of this process and then for the global package. These risks can be divided into general risks and specific risks. General risks are those that apply to all patients who are going to have surgery, injections, medications, and anesthesia, as well as hospital- or home-based convalescence. Specific risks are those that apply to the particular person, which involves considering other medical problems, age, social and psychological circumstances, and so forth. When you have a discussion with your doctor about the risks of treatment, I would recommend that you be accompanied by a spouse, sibling, child, or friend. Sometimes this person, by being more objective, can help you delve into the potentially frightening yet still important nature of these deliberations. Part Three, "Legal and Financial Issues," emphasizes the importance of your designating someone who can make health care decisions for you if you are not able to do so. Communicate with this person before entering into a treatment program, especially if surgery is involved.

When discussing the benefits and risks of surgery or treatment with your doctor, it is advisable to be accompanied by your spouse, sibling, child, or friend.

Considerations of the risk naturally leads to the desire to explore alternative treatment plans, which may then appear in a better light. Common sense is useful, but don't discount the importance of emotions, general preferences, or intuition. For example, consider the process of deciding whether to have both severely arthritic knees replaced at once or done separately several months apart. Even though the experts don't totally agree, it is generally stated that for a reasonably healthy patient, either of these two choices is acceptable. In such a situation, it is reasonable to follow your own feelings.

Step 3. Progress checking: The third step in orthopedic decision making is important but often overlooked. Following each step or development in the course of a treatment program, particularly one with an unexpected or undesirable outcome, it is crucial to stop and ascertain the following:

1. Where are you in relationship to the planned path of care?
2. Should you return to the planned path of care, and if so, how?
3. Should a new or slightly different path of care be selected?

In a situation where reassessment of the patient's current position or outcome demonstrates that a new path of care must be selected, it is incumbent on the patient, family advisors, and the doctor to mutually restart the process of orthopedic decision making, again employing the first two steps, as previously described.

Often, the necessity of changing the plan of care is obvious based on common sense. In other situations, the process of reconsideration may involve stress, fear, frustration, disappointment, or anger. Nevertheless, it must be done. The process of orthopedic decision making is cyclical and ongoing and requires adjustment and modification. While the patient may not always be willing or fully able to participate in this process, the caregiver or at least one decision maker should always be able to do so.

Another aspect of the decision-making process relates to the role of the orthopedic surgeon. His or her role is more than being a surgeon but must also include being a teacher and counselor, so that the patient and family can be sufficiently informed to participate in the decision-making process.

PROFESSIONAL EXPERIENCE OF YOUR DOCTOR

The remarks in this section deal specifically with issues relating to the professional experience of your doctor and a few remarks to help you if considering new treatment approaches. You undoubtedly realize that there has been a rapid expansion in the understanding of musculoskeletal disorders and their treatment. This has invited, and almost necessitated, subspecialization on the part of the orthopedic surgeon. Clearly, no one can be a master of all trades today, and ideally, each practitioner selects an area of interest in which to focus. In effect, the doctor learns to do a few things well. This is not to say that a superspecialist is required for each and every problem but that patients are best served by orthopedic surgeons who have familiarity and experience and who have developed expertise by repetitive treatments of other patients with similar or overlapping problems. Choosing a doctor, however, should not be based on a numbers contest as far as who did the most cases. Some problems are so rare as to be encountered only once or twice in the career of the average orthopedic surgeon. In these situations, an informed patient should seek out a superspecialist who has more extensive experience with these rare problems. How do you know if your particular problem is common or rare? Ask your orthopedic surgeon and your primary physician. They will tell you, and then you can decide about obtaining other opinions.

More routine problems, the kind encountered every day in the practice of orthopedics, are still better handled by practitioners that have a special area of concentration. You might be surprised to learn that of the several thousand joint replacements performed annually in the United States, over half these operations are performed by orthopedic surgeons who do less than 10 joint replacements annually.

For considering new treatment approaches, remember several points. Clearly, it is only through new ideas and approaches that progress can be made, but you should be advised that some novel treatments are preliminary and are occasionally found at some later time to be ineffective or harmful. There are tremendous financial incentives to orthopedic investigators and manufacturers who devise and introduce successful new treatments. Unfortunately, in the face of modern media marketing, it may be extremely difficult for you to sort out the practical, useful, and safe from wishful thinking or hype. Anything sounding too good to be true probably is.

You should be cautious when it comes to new or novel techniques offered by a practitioner who is not known as a university-affiliated educator or researcher. However, this is not to suggest that every orthopedic problem belongs in the hands of such an individual. Some patients find the experience of visiting a superspecialty hospital, usually some distance from their homes, where high volumes of patients are treated by extremely capable and experienced surgeons, to be dehumanizing, frustrating, and unpleasant. Clearly, there are some problems of such complexity that the superspecialist and superspecialty hospital is mandatory. The more standard problems can be handled just as well by experienced practitioners with reputations of being caring, careful, and appropriately conservative about when to operate or not operate in a local community hospital.

Your decision in selecting an orthopedic surgeon should be based on a number of factors, such as a referral from your primary doctor, the recommendations of family and friends, the testimonials of other patients of that surgeon, and reputation. As you develop a relationship with your orthopedic surgeon, you will develop a sense of what he or she is like, which may further guide you in your decisions about initiation or continuation of treatment.

FOUR MAJOR CATEGORIES OF TREATMENT

I will now discuss the four major categories of treatment which may be used separately or in combination. I will provide examples to illustrate points, but you should keep in mind the earlier discussions of form, function, wellness, and illness, as well as the fact that complex treatments are often combinations of several elements taken from two or more of the broad categories of treatment options. These four categories are based on a certain humanistic perspective, as well as on commonsense and historical perspectives, beginning with the most simple and obvious and then going on to increasingly complex and invasive interventions. The four categories include (1) rest, support, and immobilization; (2) exercise, stretching, strengthening, and mobilization; (3) medications; and (4) surgery.

In considering the first category, namely rest, immobilization, and support, each of us can be guided by our own physical experiences following injuries. Perhaps you recall the sore back that followed a day of shoveling snow or weeding your garden. You can imagine from your knowledge of history the tribulations that the pioneers faced when an arm or leg was broken and badly deformed. In those days, "fracture setters" used wooden splints bound by strips of cloth. Certainly, many of the senior members of our society recall the horrors of the great polio epidemics that ravaged the country a half century ago. It was not uncommon to see individuals with metal leg braces to support weakened limbs. To support himself while standing, President Franklin Roosevelt required canes and braces for his paralyzed legs.

The image of the injured patient lying bandaged in bed and with arms and legs in traction devices has a fascination in our culture and is often depicted in movies and cartoons. After your earlier reading in this chapter, you have a better understanding of the processes of bone and soft tissue healing, and while this approach to treatment is one that we intrinsically grasp, it is essential to focus on the social and economic trends that have influenced the first category of treatment.

In our increasingly complex and fast-paced lives, rest, immobilization, and support are seen by many as an undesirable feature of most treatment programs. The tremendous expenses and the nature of reimbursement in our health care system, combined with the market forces that govern the behavior of orthopedic manufacturers, hospitals, and doctors, have led to the advancement of many techniques that involve surgery and have vastly reduced or completely eliminated the need for immobilization and support.

Interestingly, time and experience have shown that in many instances the end results with more aggressive intervention are far superior to immobilization and splinting. However, this is not always the case, and the astute health care consumer should always review treatment options and alternatives, comparing and contrasting them as far as their nature, rationale, benefits, risks, and convalescence before making a decision.

There are still many injuries, including some fractures, that are best treated with immobilization and support. Some of these injuries are quite frequent, such as simple fractures involving the ball of the *humerus* (part of the shoulder); many of the fractures that involve the elbow, wrist, hand, and fingers; undisplaced fractures of the kneecap; and the more simple fractures of the ankle and foot which fortunately are the majority.

New developments in bracing arthritic knees have allowed relatively thin individuals to control arthritic symptoms without undergoing surgery, although many people find these devices cumbersome and confining. Many useful adaptations of the principles of support have been employed in treating the problems of the aging foot in senior citizens, including degenerative tendon disorders and falling arches. These are discussed more fully in the part of this chapter beginning with the section "Foot and Ankle Disorders."

REST, SUPPORT, AND IMMOBILIZATION

I have attempted to give you a general education in orthopedic disorders and have stressed the importance of common sense. A good transition from this section on rest, support, and immobilization to the next section on exercise, stretching, strengthening, and mobilization can be summed up by the familiar maxim: Walk it off! Anyone who has twisted their ankle or knee has heard these three words. These words resound with several deeper layers of meaning that encompass the understanding that (1) minor injuries should not be babied, (2) too much immobilization leads to stiffness and atrophy, and (3) rest and immobilization can precipitate their own vicious cycle of weakness, stiffness, helplessness, and depression (as all who read *The Secret Garden* will poignantly recollect). You should remember that no single treatment category is ever used exclusively from start to finish for a given problem. With the process of healing, new treatment modalities must be used to optimize the return to wellness.

EXERCISE, STRETCHING, STRENGTHENING, AND MOBILIZATION

The next category, which includes exercise, stretching, strengthening, mobilization, and physical therapy, is broad, important, and embraces the concepts of development, conditioning, maintenance, and/or restoration of wellness and prevention of illness. In many instances, patients are instructed in specific regimens that involve exercising, including a warmup, strengthening and stretching, and a cool-down period, perhaps with the use of moist heat or ice. If you have ever awakened in the middle of the night with a cramp in your calf, you have learned the importance of massage and stretching as a very effective treatment.

In more complex situations, patients will be referred by a physician to licensed physical and occupational therapists, who are guided by specific orders as well as their own knowledge, certification, and experience in helping patients optimally recover function after injury or surgery. The controlled rehabilitation of a person following surgical repair of a torn rotator cuff or a knee or hip replacement under the combined supervision of a physician and a group of therapists represents a delicate balancing between gentle encouragement and what may seem like controlled mayhem, where the patient is pushed physically as far as stamina, endurance, and tolerance of pain. Obviously, everything possible is done to minimize discomfort by using a series of strategies that include:

1. Education about the reasons and goals for therapy
2. Modalities, such as heat, cold, or massage, or the use of various energy pulses of electricity or ultrasound, delivered precisely by the therapist
3. Use of various medications

Chapter 30 provides an extensive discussion of rehabilitation and various physical and occupational therapy techniques.

Physical therapy plays an important role in restoring function after orthopedic surgery.

The length of the rehabilitation process can range from only a few weeks for minor injuries to many months for more severe and complex injuries or surgical procedures. Since there are limitations on the amount of therapy covered by most insurance plans, including Medicare, most treatment programs end with patients being carefully instructed in a home program that they can continue on their own with ongoing supervision by their physician.

As we finish this section, it is useful to recall another aphorism often heard at health clubs and athletic contests: No pain, no gain! Usually intended as a motivational statement or a form of encouragement, it should be obvious to the increasingly knowledgeable reader that there are hidden pitfalls and risks for anyone who embraces a blind devotion to exercise. Exercise has risks, and the importance of your education from manuals, such as this one, websites, your primary care doctor, your orthopedist or rheumatologist, and your therapists cannot be overemphasized.

MEDICATIONS

The use of medicinal remedies taken by mouth, inserted in the rectum, or applied to the skin in the form of salves or poultices dates back thousands of years and has a rich and fascinating history in which folklore, tribal medicine, witchcraft, and herbalism intertwine with the various branches of modern medicine. Our ever-increasing understanding of the biochemistry of the body has given us the ability to reproduce or modify, often in vast quantities, substances that are usually quite scarce in nature but which have tremendous biomedical potency and potential.

The field of human pharmacology has become staggeringly complex, and it is critical that you as an informed consumer take an active role in protecting yourself against adverse reactions that may arise related to single medications or combinations of medicines. In Chapter 33, steps that you can take to minimize your risk for these complications are presented. I strongly suggest that when you visit a doctor for the first time you should provide an exact list of all the medications you are taking. Revisits to a doctor, after an interval during which medications were altered or changed, should also begin with the presentation of an updated list of medications to that physician. I recommend that you carry a current list of all your medications in your wallet or pocketbook, perhaps with a brief notation indicating why each of the medicines is taken. Additionally, you should give your list to your pharmacy or pharmaceutical supplier so that you can benefit from the pharmaceutical computer programs that double-check for potential adverse drug interactions or side effects.

The list of orally ingested medications or pills prescribed by orthopedic surgeons is fairly short. There are four basic categories of drugs used by orthopedic surgeons: analgesics, anti-inflammatories, antibiotics, and bone-forming and antiresorptive agents. Antibiotics, which are used to treat bone and joint infections, are reviewed in Chapter 22. Chapter 19 covers the bone-forming and antiresorptive drugs. However, I would like to make a few brief points about analgesics and anti-inflammatory drugs.

ANALGESICS

Also called *painkillers,* analgesics include nonnarcotic drugs and narcotics. ACETAMINOPHEN (TYLENOL) is a good example of a nonnarcotic analgesic. It is available without a prescription and is highly effective for mild to moderate pain. There are limitations as to how much can be taken in a day, generally no more than 4 grams. Anyone taking Tylenol repeatedly through the course of the day should avoid alcohol consumption, since the combination of acetaminophen and alcohol can lead to serious liver problems. In addition, it is important to check other medicines that you might be taking since many drugs contain acetaminophen as one of their ingredients. If you are taking one of these medicines, you need to make sure that the total daily dose of acetaminophen is less than 4 grams per day. If you have liver or kidney disease, you should talk with your doctor to determine whether you should take any products that contain acetaminophen.

Narcotic analgesics may be natural derivatives of opium or synthetic variations and include MORPHINE, CODEINE, HYDROCODONE, MEPERIDINE (DEMEROL), PROPOXYPHENE (DARVON, DARVOCET), HYDROMORPHONE (DILAUDID), and numerous others. Some can be taken by mouth as pills or liquid, whereas others are injected under the skin or into the muscles or given intravenously, depending on the requirements for rapid onset of action, duration of effect, and the anticipated length of usage. The potency of the available narcotic agents varies tremendously. Some are not much more effective than acetaminophen; others are a hundred or thousand times more potent pain relievers. Not infrequently, the milder narcotics are combined with acetaminophen to boost the pain-reliever effects.

All narcotics have certain effects that may be less desirable, such as drowsiness, constipation, loss of mental acuity or confusion, altered balance and coordination, and nausea. A common misconception is that these side effects represent a drug allergy. As a result, difficulties may arise when these individuals require more potent analgesics to manage their pain. The doctor should explain and the patient should understand that while some people are more sensitive to these preparations than others, these useful agents should not be abandoned. Often, simply reducing the dose or changing the way the drug is given can be effective. Problems such as constipation can be managed with stool softeners and nausea with prescription antinausea pills or suppositories.

Another common concern is addiction. While drug dependency is a real concern with prolonged use of these agents, it is by no means a reason to avoid their usage. A combination of an educated patient and a careful and knowledgeable physician should allow narcotic analgesics to be used as a powerful and useful tool in alleviating the patient's suffering. It is quite reasonable for an individual to use these medications fairly steadily for 3 to 6 weeks following major surgery and then wean down on the dose at the end of this period, perhaps finally changing to a milder drug that does not have the same risks. Other drugs, especially the nonsteroidal anti-inflammatory drugs (NSAIDs) may be used at the same time in order to potentiate the effects of the narcotic analgesics or to allow dosage reductions in the narcotics.

Chemists and pharmacologists have labored over the last 30 or 40 years to create the ideal analgesic, which has the potency of the narcotics but without the side effects, especially that of addiction. This desirable goal has been elusive despite the emergence of several agents that have been produced, marketed, and tried over the last quarter century. At present, ULTRACET is closest to this long-sought goal. A combination medication consisting of acetaminophen with a nonnarcotic agent called TRAMADOL, Ultracet is viewed increasingly as a satisfactory agent for long-term palliation of significant pain from arthritis with few side effects and very little potential for addiction. Naturally, the same precautions we mentioned previously regarding the use of acetaminophen apply to this drug as well, and there are certain medications that should not be taken concomitantly with Ultracet. Your doctor or pharmacist can alert you to those drugs that should be avoided with Ultracet.

ANTI-INFLAMMATORIES

The anti-inflammatory drugs can be divided into two classes. The first class are those based on the body's own natural hormone called cortisone. Cortisone is known as a corticosteroid, or *steroid* for short. Cortisone is a steroid hormone produced by the outer portion of the *adrenal glands,* which are situated above each kidney and are responsible for the production of another important and well-known hormone called *adrenaline.* When first isolated and administered as a treatment agent over a half century ago, cortisone was hailed as a miracle drug. Numerous devastating and previously untreatable conditions such as systemic lupus and rheumatoid arthritis were bridled for the first time. There was great excitement amongst patients and health care practitioners alike. As time passed, a large group of side effects and toxic reactions were noted to occur that included a general suppression of immunity, wasting of muscles, fluid retention, redistribution of body fat, osteoporosis, and a generalized fragility of the skin, tendons, and ligaments. Additionally, it was found that the use of these powerful agents were capable of inducing a sudden release of fat globules from the liver which showered through the bloodstream often clogging vital blood vessels to the bone resulting in bone death or *infarction.* Another term for bone death, which I discussed earlier in this chapter, is avascular necrosis.

Despite the undesirable side effects and the fact that orthopedic surgeons more than any other medical specialist are forced to confront and treat patients with such devastating complications of steroids such as tendon ruptures or collapse of bone around joints such as the shoulder, hip, and knee, the ongoing use of steroids remains essential in the treatment of many diseases including asthma, polymyalgia rheumatica, rheumatoid arthritis, lupus, and temporal arteritis. Although steroids are not often prescribed by the orthopedist, it is fitting that steroids be discussed in this section as orthopedic surgeons and their patients must often deal with their side effects. Many promising and recent developments in pharmacology may eventually relegate the use of steroids to a lower level of use, but for now they remain very necessary.

I would like to make a few comments about joint injections with steroids. It is indeed unfortunate that the expression "cortisone injection" is common in the parlance of physicians and the public. Fears of all the negative aspects of steroids are invoked. You should be aware that the preparation injected into the joints by orthopedic surgeons is not actually cortisone, but a chemically modified variant called METHYLPREDNISOLONE (DEPO-MEDROL). By virtue of its being insoluble in body fluids, methylprednisolone is virtually incapable of leaving the joint in which it was injected. As such, it will not interfere with the body's immunity, disturb the blood glucose control of diabetic patients, or cause the more serious effects associated with long-term use of oral steroids. The results of the injection of methylprednisolone into the joint include a potent reduction of inflammation, a reduction in swelling, followed by the restoration of movement, function, and relief of pain. Furthermore, it can be safely administered every three months with no known long-term side effects, either local or widespread. Under its useful umbrella, which unfortunately may only last a few weeks, patients may be able to strengthen the muscles around a joint previously too irritated to be exercised. In addition, it might allow some patients the opportunity to receive injections of a joint syrup that both lubricates and potentially nourishes the damaged joint cartilage.

The other class consists of the nonsteroidal anti-inflammatory drugs (NSAIDs) because they are not related in structure or effect to cortisone. The NSAIDs currently include two dozen or so medications manufactured by nearly as many different drug companies, each looking for the ideal product that will produce maximum positive benefits of reducing soft tissue and joint inflammation and the resulting pain and stiffness with a minimum of undesirable side effects. One of the earliest and best known of these agents, still in wide use today, is aspirin. Besides its abilities to suppress local inflammation in the tissues of the body, it also directly inhibits pain, suppresses or reduces fever, and "thins" the blood slightly by reducing the ability of platelets to stick to one another to form clots. Although rarely used as an anti-inflammatory agent today, aspirin in low doses remains a mainstay in the prevention of heart attacks and strokes. Over the years, there have been numerous new agents introduced to reduce inflammation and pain, as well as stiffness. Many of these drugs have properties similar to aspirin in thinning the blood and/or reducing fever. Acetaminophen (Tylenol) is not included in this class and it does not thin the blood or reduce inflammation, but may reduce fever and pain. Although some of the NSAIDs are proven to be more potent than aspirin, almost all of them share a very significant side effect of irritating the stomach, sometimes gradually and sometimes suddenly, to a point where ulcers or bleeding can occur. Obviously, given their ability to thin the blood, the potential for serious bleeding, even life-threatening, is enhanced when the stomach is irritated. Over the last decade or two, various strategies have been employed to counter this dangerous side effect. One common approach is to administer a medication that coats the stomach lining with a protective mucous. Another is to give a medicine that inhibits the formation of stomach acid, thereby reducing but not eliminating the potential of the NSAIDs to cause stomach irritation and bleeding. In fact, medications have been developed that include the NSAID and one of these protective medications within a single capsule or tablet. These efforts to lower the toxicity of the NSAIDs have been quite positive, but a more recent development has been the introduction of a whole new class of NSAIDs that deserves special attention.

The COX-2 inhibitors are a new class of NSAID that are effective and potent as anti-inflammatory agents, and they are also capable of relieving pain and have a much reduced tendency to irritate the stomach. Of course, this is highly desirable and is precisely why these drugs were developed and heavily marketed to physicians and the public alike. They have different side effects than the original class of NSAIDs, which may cause some undesirable interactions with other medications that a patient may be using. This has earned the COX-2 inhibitors some overly distorted "bad press."

Firstly, the COX-2 inhibitors have a direct effect on the kidney causing the retention of sodium and water that can lead to fluid buildup and/or high blood pressure. This is generally not a problem in a healthy individual, but is particularly undesirable in some patients, particularly those with diabetes, who take a popularly prescribed class of drugs called angiotensin-converting enzyme (ACE) inhibitors. These drugs are frequently prescribed for the control of hypertension because they have fewer side effects than some of the other classes of antihypertensive medications. Patients who receive an ACE inhibitor should not be routinely given a COX-2 anti-inflammatory drug without careful monitoring for blood pressure elevation and swelling during the first few days and weeks of therapy. This is especially true for diabetic patients receiving this combination of drugs.

Secondly, much confusion and a somewhat unfairly earned reputation have been caused by the fact that the COX-2 inhibitors do not inhibit the coagulation of blood as do many of the original NSAIDs. A fairly convoluted but legitimate logical argument has and can be made that individuals who take the original class of NSAIDs, by virtue of their blood being thinned, have some protection against heart attack. Conversely, since COX-2 inhibitors do not thin the blood, a patient receiving a COX-2 inhibitor has no cardiac protection. Thus, a person on the COX-2 inhibitor might be more prone to experience a heart attack than if he/she received one of the original NSAIDs where the blood was thinned and the heart protected. It can be further argued that if these agents are injudiciously administered to individuals who depend on ACE inhibitors to control their blood pressure and also have diabetes that the overall risk for developing a heart attack while using these drugs

17

is significantly increased. These facts were presented and highly publicized at a time several years ago when massive marketing by the pharmaceutical manufacturers was leading to a widespread abandonment of the original NSAIDs and was a useful counterbalance serving to emphasize that no perfect anti-inflammatory agent yet exists.

An informed consumer, a judicious physician, and a list of all currently used medications is the best answer. One further and somewhat confounding point about the potential of COX-2 inhibitors regarding their decreased potential to irritate the stomach is that this beneficial effect is completely lost if low-dose aspirin is being administered at the same time. Despite the complexities of this subject, most patients can successfully use a NSAID at least for a short period of time during which they are carefully monitored. When these medications are used for more lengthy periods, as in the chronic treatment of arthritis or other inflammatory conditions, a program of periodic medical monitoring is required. Tests that may be requested include a blood count, liver and kidney blood tests, and stool for occult (hidden) blood. The frequency of testing may be reduced at the discretion of the prescribing physician once the safety of the medication has been proven in a given patient. However, it should never be discontinued as long as the patient is taking an NSAID.

ANTIBIOTICS

The next category of medications is the antibiotics, which clearly are among the greatest advancements ever to occur in the history of medicine. Antibiotics and their use are extensively discussed in Chapter 22. In discussing joint infections, you should appreciate that the joint is a relatively sheltered space within the body. In many cases, antibiotics may not be able to adequately penetrate this space to kill an infecting organism. As a result, some type of invasive intervention might be required to restore the joint to a normal state. We will discuss this in more detail in the section on surgery, but we mention it here to inform you that joint infections cannot always be treated with antibiotics alone. Although truly wonder drugs, antibiotics depend on the circulation of blood to living tissue for their delivery to the site of an infection. The antibiotics are then able to act in concert with the body's natural defenses. Any large cavity, whether it be a joint or an abscess, involved with an infectious process is poorly penetrated by antibiotics. As a result, an invasive procedure is required to remove the infected contents of the joint or abscess. This might include the use of a needle or a drain inserted into the cavity or perhaps lancing through the skin and tissues overlying the infected area. This discussion serves to underscore the fact that the treatment of serious infection often consists of a combination of interventions, which might include antibiotics, immobilization, drainage, and/or surgery.

A peculiar or special situation that sometimes arises is the presence of an infection at a site where a metallic implant has been placed. This type of problem is not unique to orthopedics. For example, cardiologists may need to deal with infections around pacemakers. The presence of an inert or foreign object at the site of an infection creates special problems. A similar problem occurs if dead bone is in the area. In these instances, the body's natural healing responses, even when coupled with the addition of antibiotics, are rarely able to eradicate the infection. There are two reasons for this. First, antibiotics depend upon the circulation for delivery to the site of infection. Clearly, there is no circulation to a piece of dead bone or to a prosthetic implant. Second, many of the infecting bacteria commonly seen in humans produce and secrete a sugary thick layer of slime which coats prosthetic implants and into which the bacteria become imbedded. This slime is thick and insoluble enough to be impenetrable to the antibiotics that are given. The general maxim for an orthopedic surgeon is: an infection around a metallic implant or dead bone cannot be eradicated unless the implant or dead bone is surgically removed. Thus surgery is often required as part of the complex treatment regimens for infections of the musculoskeletal system.

There are certain situations, however, that require a different approach. Perhaps the patient is too old or too frail and sick to withstand surgical removal of an implant, such as an infected hip or knee prosthesis. An attempt may be made to control or suppress the infection with a combination of treatments that include less invasive intervention. Possibly, instead of removing the implant, just the removal of dead tissue and pus in conjunction with antibiotics may be adequate to suppress or control the infection. Obviously, this type of approach is a compromise, which almost never eradicates the infection but may be necessary in such extreme and special circumstances.

BONE-FORMING AND ANTIRESORPTIVE AGENTS

Another category of medications used in the treatment of diseases of the musculoskeletal system includes the bone-forming and antiresorptive agents used to treat osteoporosis. Although these drugs are in Chapter 19, I would like to give you some exciting information on the use of these drugs to slow down the rate of loosening and bone loss of and around a failing or failed hip prosthesis.

A great boon to the person with arthritis, the hip prosthesis is highly effective and increasingly perfected, but not completely so. Any patient who has undergone one of these operations should have annual X-rays reviewed by an orthopedic surgeon. The status of the prosthesis can be monitored so that any early deterioration that might alter or deleteriously influence its fixation and function can be detected. Often X-ray changes are not sudden or extreme but occur gradually over a period of months or years. The treating physician is often in the position of recognizing that more surgery may be required in the future to revise or reconstruct the prosthetic hip. Patients, who are feeling fine with no problems related to the hip prosthesis, are happy to postpone surgery especially given the magnitude of a revision. A complex waiting game then begins in which the status of the prosthesis and surrounding bone is carefully observed, and as long as the patient remains comfortable and satisfied, surgery is planned for some future time before too much damage occurs.

The actual biology of events and reactions in the tissue surrounding a failing prosthesis is well understood. A critical factor is loss of bone (osteolysis) due to a local inflammatory reaction around the stem of the prosthesis. The stem is the long tapered part that inserts in the thighbone (femur). In many instances, before the prosthesis is loosened, the area of osteolysis begins at the upper end of the prosthesis and gradually works down the length of the thighbone surrounding the implanted stem. As this progresses and further bone loss occurs, the fixation of the prosthesis in the upper end of the thighbone can be compromised, leading to loosening of the stem or fracture of the bone.

Recent research has shown that the process of osteolysis around a prosthetic hip stem can in some cases be retarded considerably by treatment with some of the drugs used to treat osteoporosis. The bisphosphonates are drugs that inhibit resorption of bone. Examples include ALENDRONATE (FOSAMAX) and RISEDRONATE (ACTONEL). In so doing, they ever so slightly tilt the balance between the competing processes of bone formation and bone breakdown toward formation of bone. When one of these drugs is taken, the bisphosphonate is taken up into the bone where it has the effect of perfecting the crystal structure. That is, the crystal structure becomes more regular than naturally occurs. The net effect is that the bone crystal is less soluble, or relatively resistant, to the process of bone breakdown or dissolution that typically occurs in osteoporosis and in the bone around a failing hip prosthesis.

A final and very important group of medications to consider are the biologics. Although a nebulous term, it is fitting for it encompasses within its boundaries a wide array of promising agents with potent reparative and rejuvenating capabilities insofar as the health and wellness of the musculoskeletal system is concerned. Although the use of biologics is only in its infancy, our limited discussion of a few simple agents provides a tantalizing glimpse of the myriad possibilities that exist for a future, in which genetically engineered molecules and cells are used to maintain or restore wellness. For now, doctors and their patients must be content with far more humble beginnings, two of which I discuss as to their usefulness in delaying the progression of osteoarthritis.

These therapeutic agents have the goal of delivering various-sized building blocks, or *precursors,* of the giant mucouslike molecules to the joint cavity. As you recall from our earlier discussion, these giant mucouslike molecules are trapped in a protein mesh which makes up the pearly white and slippery joint cartilage. In the very least, it is hoped that this will facilitate lubrication and reduce the wear and tear that contributes to the worsening of osteoarthritis. Even more optimistically, we hope that the incorporation of these building blocks by the living cartilage cells would help restore the thickness, sponginess, and self-lubrication of partially damaged joint surfaces. These supplements are known as oral *chondroprotective agents.*

Over the last 15 years, numerous preparations have been devised and widely used, including *glucosamine sulfate, chondroitin sulfate,* or both. Initially viewed with skepticism by traditional medical doctors, the oral chondroprotective agents have been increasingly recognized and accepted as beneficial. Since they do not require a prescription, they are considered a supplement and do not require the same rigorous scrutiny and testing that prescription medications require. The National Institutes of Health is conducting research on how and to what extent these agents exert their effects in osteoarthritis. Nevertheless, many individuals have been clearly helped by them, and it appears that they have few side effects and rarely interfere with other medical conditions. However, you should check with your primary care physician before taking any over-the-counter products to ensure that there will be no adverse reactions with other medications you are taking and no adverse effects on other medical conditions that you have.

Oral chondroprotective agents are most effective for osteoarthritis that is mild or moderate in degree. They do not reduce inflammation, but they can be safely taken in conjunction with the NSAIDs. This can contribute to the difficulty in determining whether these agents do any good. It may be hard to determine if other medication is causing the favorable response. On top of this, osteoarthritis typically has a natural waxing and waning course that may be partially dependent on exercise, overuse, rest, changes in the weather, and so forth. I usually recommend that my patients try them for a month or more when they will not be going through unusual physical stresses that could further irritate their joints. Finally, when purchasing these supplements in the pharmacy or health food shop, beware of preparations that contain additional ingredients beyond glucosamine and chondroitin. Small amounts of vitamin C may be added as a preservative and to facilitate intestinal absorption, and a low dose of manganese (4 mg or less) is sometimes added to potentiate the effects of these preparations. There are no hard data to substantiate the claims about these additives, but many people swear by the preparations that contain them. It is almost certainly safe to take them in this form. However, other additives include a number of various herbal preparations that are probably not advisable given the lack of control in their preparation, the lack of understanding of their action, and the lack of precise understanding of their side effects or of their potential interactions with other medications. Of particular concern is the addition of the *substance methylsulfonal methane (MSM),* a derivative of *dimethyl sulfoxide (DMSO).* DMSO has a known benefit and reliability in reducing joint aches when rubbed on the skin of racehorses. It became fashionable for human use about 20 years ago and clearly reduced pain when rubbed over sore knees, wrists, and ankles. However, many of the persons who used DMSO noticed a strong taste in their mouth within seconds after applying it to their skin, which only served a proof that it was entering the body through the skin and thus in no way resembled a locally acting liniment, such as the familiar oil of wintergreen. DMSO probably has significant long-term side effects even if used sparingly on the skin overlying an arthritic knee, although there is no hard proof. I would caution you similarly to avoid the use of MSM.

Before going on to the subject of injected chondroprotective agents, I would like to say a few words about liniments, or *rubefacients,* which countless people use to treat painful muscles and joints. Long employed successfully by healers dating back over the centuries, certain substances when smeared or rubbed onto the skin of a sore joint provide relief similar to what every child who has fallen and bruised a knee has learned when he or she reflexively rubs the skin over the injured area. It wasn't until the 1950s that neurobiologists provided an explanation for what everyone intuitively had known. Research suggested that a "gate" existed in the upper portions of the nervous system through which all incoming sensory stimuli had to pass before reaching the level of conscious recognition. If a barrage of sensory stimuli arrived simultaneously, this pain gate could be overwhelmed. This research suggested that in a situation of overcrowding at the pain gate, a certain proportion of the electrical impulses would be blocked from entering, and as a result, the overall perception of pain would be reduced. Thus the rubbing of the skin with the hands following the application of mild irritants such as oil of wintergreen or capsicum pepper (the active ingredient in Tabasco sauce and capsaicin cream) or even the application of a nylon or cloth wrap or sleeve is capable, by virtue of its stimulation of innumerable skin nerves, of blocking the pain sensations that arise from the underlying arthritic and irritated joint. Thus there is a sound basis for the use of liniments containing wintergreen and capsaicin. This may also explain some of the benefit of acupuncture. Supporting sleeves or wraps are likewise useful as long as they are not made so tight that they occlude the venous and lymphatic circulation and cause swelling, skin breakdown, or phlebitis.

Beginning in Europe roughly a decade ago and increasingly used now in the United States and Japan, injection of *hyaluronic acid* into arthritic knees has become increasingly recognized as a treatment to reduce arthritic pain and possibly to delay the progression of the arthritic process. The validity of these treatments, however, virtually defies being proved or disproved experimentally, at least for the time being. You can be reassured that hundreds of thousands of patients have safely and often beneficially undergone these treatments over the past 15 years. While there are no hard and fast rules, a few cautious and commonsense arguments are worth considering. Compared to glucosamine and chondroitin, injected hyaluronic acid can be a thousand times larger in terms of its molecular size. It is a delicate molecule and therefore is immediately degraded and rendered useless if there is any inflammation in the joint. The analogy of attempting to land a blimp on a battlefield is appropriate. The volatile contents of the blimp will cause it to immediately explode upon being hit by artillery fire. Thus it stands to reason that before attempting hyaluronic acid injections in an osteoarthritic knee, every attempt should be made to suppress the inflammatory reaction in the joint as much as possible. This is probably best achieved by the injection of a steroid. Oral anti-

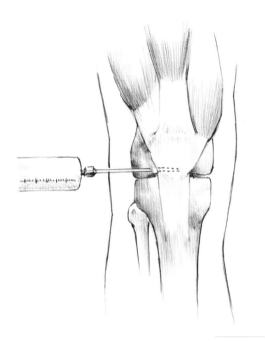

inflammatory medications can be also used for the same purpose. A simple test that can help the doctor determine if the knee is still significantly irritated is to have the patient flex the knee as much as possible, perhaps with the doctor's aid. If significant discomfort is still produced, the hyaluronic acid injection should not be given. Furthermore, hyaluronic acid injections have no value in other inflammatory arthritic processes, such as rheumatoid arthritis and pseudogout.

Hyaluronic acid injections are probably not best thought of as a single or individual treatment but as one component of a larger and more complex series of treatment steps, with the common goal being to slow down the rate of progression of osteoarthritis or reducing its symptoms without resorting to surgery. The first step, as previously noted, is reducing inflammation with oral or injected anti-inflammatory medications. Then hyaluronic acid is administered as a series of injections every week or so for the next three to five weeks, depending on the product or brand used. Finally, and probably as important as any of the other steps in the process, every patient should perform a comprehensive therapy program which focuses on strengthening the supporting musculature of the buttocks and thighs and stretching to relieve tightness of the hip flexors and hamstrings. The therapy will only be effective if the patient is pain-free and can fully participate to the extent required to meaningfully strengthen muscles (3 times a week for 4 weeks). This often requires analgesic medications. At the conclusion of this comprehensive therapy program, which often lasts two to three months, patients should expect a significant degree of improvement if their osteoarthritis was not very severe at the outset.

A question that arises is whether a second series of hyaluronic acid injections should be given in those who previously had a good response. The answer is still unknown, and may take years before a definitive answer is given. Many individuals do tolerate a program of repeated injections and do so willingly rather than undergo surgery. These treatments are costly, and Medicare and most private insurance companies require that a minimum period of six months must pass before the injections can be repeated. In Japan, the practice is to administer a single repeat injection of hyaluronic acid every three months to those who have completed the first complete series of injections.

This subject cannot be completed without a strong piece of sobering information. Osteoarthritis is an ancient malady. It even antedates human beings: it has been found in the bones of the feet of giant two-legged dinosaurs, such as *Tyrannosaurus rex*. This bit of trivia serves to elucidate an important point about osteoarthritis. It is not a condition limited to humans. However, better living conditions and medical advances have allowed the extension of our lives far beyond that of our ancestors who often confronted joint problems earlier in life. While the onset of osteoarthritis for the average person living in the 21st century can be delayed, it is still very much part of the human condition. Going back a hundred or two hundred years, there were few if any meaningful treatments for osteoarthritis. Where rest and time off were not options, we can envision that most afflicted individuals continued to live their lives as best they could. The human response to osteoarthritis is thus very much determined by the demands in one's life. This fact should never be underestimated nor should the will of the individual be discounted when considering the spectrum of human physical and emotional responses to this ancient affliction. Self-determination and the will to survive, in conjunction with the natural ups and downs in the course of osteoarthritis, are often responsible for seemingly miraculous improvements. This impairs our ability to measure the precise effects of short-term palliative treatments that have as their goal the slowing down or temporarily halting of osteoarthritic deterioration.

ORTHOPEDIC SURGERY

My goal in this section on surgical treatment is to acquaint you with the various types of operative treatments that orthopedic surgeons use in the management of musculoskeletal disorders. An erroneous but frequently held bias of physicians, surgeons, and patients is the notion that treatments in which surgery is avoided are conservative and that treatments that involve surgery are aggressive or radical. These ideas should be put aside, substituting a more informed understanding that begins with the nature of a disease process and how the various treatment options can be expected to influence that process. Different approaches need to be compared on the basis of their nature, rationale, benefits, risks, and convalescence. Next, the specific individual whose welfare is at stake must be considered, and the impact that the various treatment options may have on him or her must be weighed. Various outcomes are possible, and the astute surgeon will reflect on many things, including the disease or problem, the medical condition of the patient, that person's unique psychological and social circumstances, and so forth. Only then will the best approach become clear. The decision to operate may then be recognized to be prudent, sensible, humane, and far safer than avoiding surgery, which might then be construed as unrealistic, neglectful, irrational, or even outrageous. Examples abound. Consider the case of a healthy, active 78-year-old widow terrified at the prospect of a surgical repair of her broken hip. It would be absolutely ridiculous to subject her to six weeks of bed rest as a "reasonable" treatment alternative. With surgery, she could be walking and active within a matter of a few days. Six weeks of bed rest could cause all kinds of complications, including blood clots, bedsores, acceleration of osteoporosis, and severe deconditioning. Although surgery is by definition *invasive,* it is by far the safest and most expedient treatment for this patient. Nevertheless, if you or a loved one is confronted with these types of decisions, you want to gather as much information as you can, so that you can weigh the benefits and risks of each approach.

I have divided surgical approaches into six categories: (1) incision and debridement, (2) repair of tendon and bone, (3) surgical release, (4) realignment of bones, joints, digits, and limbs, (5) joint reconstruction, and (6) joint fusion. Before presenting these categories in detail, we would like to make a few comments about *open* versus *minimally invasive* procedures, as well as *combined procedures.* This discussion should be kept in mind when we explore the categories of surgery. The goals of surgery have always been palliative, restorative, or curative, and to whatever extent possible, an attempt is made to keep the size of the incision to a minimum. Technological advances in orthopedic equipment and the increasing knowledge and skills of orthopedic surgeons have prompted a move in the direction of less invasive surgical techniques for every category of surgery. The goal is reduced pain, shorter periods of hospitalization and disability, and less expense. Although desirable, I must stress that a smaller *skin incision,* as might be done for a laparoscopic procedure, does not mean that the actual surgical procedure performed in the body is less major than a similar or identical one performed through a larger skin incision as far as pain, disability, and the length of recovery. In many instances minimally invasive surgery becomes more difficult for the surgeon and more fraught with the peril of a technical mishap or an inadequate operation. *Combined procedures* are those that require elements from two or more of the six categories. For example, a person with severe rheumatoid arthritis may require debridement of a joint at the same time as a joint replacement.

INCISION AND DEBRIDEMENT

Incision is the cutting into the skin or deeper tissues. Debridement is the trimming and cleansing of dead or damaged tissue, such as that which occurs at the site of an infection or that which follows an injury with a blunt or sharp object. Tissues may also be removed because they are inflamed without necessarily being infected or because they are involved with cancer. Even benign tumors can press or rub against important adjacent structures.

The general goal of surgical debridement is shaped by a balance between two conflicting principles. The first is to remove all tissue that is either dead or damaged, or if left untouched, it will go on to grow more as in the case of tumors. Likewise, growths such as bone spurs that press or damage important adjacent structures like nerves should be removed. The second principle is to remove as little tissue as necessary but still achieve the goal of surgery. While a complete cure and perfect restoration are always desirable, they are not always possible. Often the disease process can only be arrested. In some infections, extensive surgery may need to be done at the expense of permanent damage to some muscles or joints, which may be left weakened, contracted, stiffened, or more prone to the development of arthritis. Tumors, whether benign or malignant, may not be always entirely removable either, because they are too inaccessible to approach surgically or because they have already spread to other sites. In these situations, the outcome after surgery may depend on additional therapies, such as drug or radiation treatments. If surgery is done to slow down or temporarily stop the disease process, the goal may not be cure but easing of the patient's suffering. Ultimately, the underlying disease process might worsen, requiring further treatment, possibly of a radical nature. In some cases, the patient and doctor recognize that further surgical attempts are futile, and that palliative care is all that can be done.

While performing debridement, the surgeon must be guided in part by the reparative and/or reconstructive steps to be subsequently taken, either during the very same or later procedures to optimally restore function and wellness. In the case of overhanging bone spurs in the shoulder, which are impinging against and damaging or tearing the flat conjoined tendons of the rotator cuff, the removal of the offending bone spurs must be followed by repair or reconstruction of the damaged but vital tendons if active shoulder motion is to be restored. Furthermore, although increasingly sidestepped by newer and less invasive techniques, if the approach to the rotator cuff and the involved bone spur involves detaching a portion of the large outermost and empowering deltoid muscle, surgery must include replacing and protecting the deltoid to allow healing and reattachment (see Figure 17-17).

For extensive surgery, such as the stripping or removal of the synovial lining of an inflamed joint, even when performed with an arthroscope through a series of small puncture wounds, the subsequent irritation and pain can be considerable. The pain may inhibit or interfere with efforts to mobilize or exercise that joint through its full range of motion. As a result, the raw surfaces might bind or adhere to one another in a process of scarring which would, if unchecked, lead to a loss of mobility. Other treatments may then be brought into play, including the use of pain medications and physical therapy.

In instances where muscles have been detached as part of the surgical approach or where the muscles have been repaired or reconstructed because of their rupture, a conflict may arise between the mutually exclusive requirements of resting the repaired or reconstructed muscle or tendon and the need to continue moving the limb and involved joints. Rest allows a muscle or tendon to heal itself. In situations where surgery has involved tacking, stapling, or suturing the muscle or tendon, rest enhances the attachment to bone. On the other hand, moving the limb and joints helps prevent abnormal scar tissue (adhesions) from forming, which can lead to permanent loss of movement and defeat the goals of surgery. In these instances, a special type of joint mobilization and controlled motion is used. Active motion occurs as a result of muscle action, which may be voluntary or involuntary. If this were to occur during the critical period of healing, a repaired or reconstructed muscle might tear again or detach itself since sutures, staples, tacks, and patches provide only limited strength and temporary control. Completion of the healing process requires four to six weeks to restore the strength and resilience necessary to withstand the full forces of muscle action. Passive motion describes the motion of a limb or joint where the power is supplied by external forces, such as gravity or

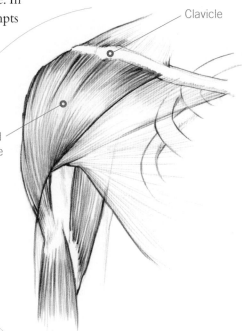

Clavicle

Deltoid muscle

(figure 17-17)

The deltoid muscle is the large muscle that gives the shoulder its shape, and raises the arm.

the hands of a physical therapist or some specifically designed and powered device which might include pulleys, ropes, or motor-powered-exercising splints. The muscles that would normally move the joint are allowed to rest and heal while held together by the reparative devices just mentioned. Passive motion prescribed by the orthopedic surgeon and performed by nurses, physical therapists, and technicians provides the solution to the conflicting requirements of protecting repairs of muscles and tendons while preventing the formation of scarring, adhesions, and contractures of involved joints during the crucial first six weeks following surgery.

Before moving on to the next category, a brief discussion of orthopedic surgery for tumors of the musculoskeletal system is warranted. There are three surgical approaches. In the first, an incision is made and a piece of tissue is removed for examination by a pathologist under the microscope. Known as *incisional biopsy,* it is seemingly the simplest of the three tumor operations, but it should never be underestimated. The very fact that a biopsy is being performed indicates that neither the examining hands of the surgeon nor the combined judgments of all those who reviewed the X-rays and scans have revealed the type of tumor present and whether it is benign or malignant. The possibility that the tumor is malignant is what makes the performance of the biopsy so critical. How that particular cancer behaves determines the best treatment approach. For the greater part of the last century the only cures for aggressive malignancies of the musculoskeletal system were amputation, frequently of an arm or a leg. Only in the last 40 years have the successful techniques of *en bloc resection* (removal of a tumor in its entirety along with some surrounding normal tissue), sometimes in combination with chemotherapy before surgery to reduce the size of the tumor, become a reality. After examination of the tumor specimen, the cancer can be graded and the initial chemotherapy may be continued or modified. In addition, prosthetic replacements that allow specialized bone and joint implants have given afflicted patients the use of a functional limb.

The second and most common surgical approach to musculoskeletal tumors is *excisional biopsy,* in which the tumor is excised and sent to the pathologist for microscopic examination. The vast majority of tumors are benign, and this can be predicted in most instances by preoperative examination and testing. The challenge for the surgeon is to avoid damaging adjacent critical structures while removing the entire tumor to prevent its recurrence and preserving the function of the limb after surgery. In cases where a benign tumor is located entirely within a bone and is scraped out *(curettage),* leaving a defect or weak spot, it may be necessary to fill the "hole" with a substitute material to restore the strength of the bone. Typically, the materials that might be chosen could include bone, bonelike biologic substitutes, or acrylic cement. The choice will be governed by the preferences of the surgeon and the nature of the requirements of the substitute as far as its immediate and long-term function, all of which is further influenced by the age of the patient.

We discuss bone grafting and bone substitutes in more detail in the next category on repair of tendon and bone.

The third surgical approach to musculoskeletal tumors is more radical, by which the entire tumor is removed along with a margin of surrounding normal tissue. This is intended to prevent the spread of the cancer, which is possible even if a single tumor cell remained. These operations have become tremendously sophisticated and complex, developed not unexpectedly by the mutual desires of patients and their surgeons to remove cancerous tumors and the local tissue where cancer cells may have already spread without amputating the limb. The amount of skin, muscle, and bone removed is dependent upon the location and type of tumor, as well as the way it responded before surgery to chemotherapy. Chemotherapy is sometimes administered as a first step to shrink a tumor prior to surgery. Although the removal of the entire tumor is of paramount importance if the patient is to survive, the reconstruction of the limb, including long segments of bone and joints, is an equally formidable task, and the surgeon must consider this when evaluating the patient for the tumor excision. In order for these operations to be both feasible and effective, they must be performed through critically positioned incisions that must encompass and excise the entire scar tissue remnants of the recently performed biopsy since it must be assumed that the scar is contaminated with living tumor cells. This means that *en bloc* resections must incorporate not only the tumor itself but also the initial biopsy scar. Because these operations are performed by orthopedic surgeons who have specialized in the removal of musculoskeletal tumors, it has become expected that these biopsies be done only by those surgeons who would not compromise what the musculoskeletal tumor surgeon may need to do to continue ideal surgical care for a patient with a biopsy proven malignancy. The other option is to refer the patient directly to the musculoskeletal tumor surgeon for the initial biopsy on any suspected cancerous tumors.

REPAIR OF TENDON AND BONE

In the minds of many, repairing tendon and bone epitomizes the essence of orthopedics. Operations to reposition and stabilize broken or shattered bones, repair torn muscles and tendons, and similarly damaged ligaments, through increasingly small incisions, with improved predictability and safety, and with vast reductions in the length of time of immobilization and postoperative disability, have been great boons to patients and their families. Many fractures including those that do not displace or shift position, as well as others that can be repositioned and held correctly in a splint or cast, can be expected to heal back together again. There is an increasing trend to stabilize fractures surgically. The orthopedic surgeon may use an array of plates, rods, screws, and anchors of every conceivable size and shape designed especially for the individual bones of the body. This hardware allows the surgeon not only to put bones back together, which are too badly shattered to be held correctly in position with a cast, but often to eliminate the need for any splinting or immobilization after surgery. This in turn reduces or eradicates the stiffness that follows the treatment of a fracture by using the more traditional techniques, which hold the limb immobile while healing occurs often over intervals as long as three months. Newer, minimally invasive techniques are being performed in which a smaller incision is used, and there is less deep exposure and stripping of soft tissues from bone fragments. As a result, there is not only less pain after surgery but also increasingly rapid healing of the bone fragments. This is a perfect example of an area for which surgical advancements have overturned the traditional notion of nonoperative treatment being conservative. As the risks of surgery are steadily reduced by an unending stream of new technology, operative treatment for many fractures is actually the safest, most reliable, and least painful option.

In cases where the bone is not just shattered *(comminuted)* but also crushed *(impacted),* defects or cavities in the bone often remain. Conventionally, these defects or cavities have been filled with bone harvested from local or distant sites from the very same patient who is being treated. Any tissue (e.g., bone, blood, tendon, or skin) removed and used elsewhere in the same patient is called an autologous graft. An autologous bone graft, containing the living cells of the *donor-recipient* has been widely used to facilitate bone-to-bone healing across fractures and gaps for nearly three-quarters of a century. This bone was often harvested from the knobby ends of the large bones around the knee or from the front and back rims of the pelvis where the bone is quite thick. If more bone was needed or if it was inconvenient, insufficient, or unsafe to harvest it from the patient, bone from cadavers (dead bodies) was used. Tissue taken from one person and transplanted into another is called an allograft. Stored or banked cadaver bone, when subjected to preservation techniques such as freezing, leads to the destruction of the living cells of the donor. However, the structural portion of bone composed of protein and hydroxyapatite crystal is preserved. Unfortunately, freezing alone doesn't kill all bacteria or viruses, so these types of grafts could actually cause an infection to be transmitted to the recipient.

A more recent option is the preparation of bone grafts by using a combination of gamma irradiation and freeze-drying, thus producing bone material that can be stored in a sterile state at room temperature. Concern over the transfer of bacteria or viruses residing within bone or tendon grafts to the person receiving the graft has led to stringent, federally regulated standards controlling the harvesting, preparation, storage, and use of human musculoskeletal allografts. While freeze-drying bone eradicates any or all infectious organisms, ligament and tendon grafts cannot be subjected to this process without sacrificing their mechanical usefulness for the intended purpose. Despite some of the limitations, frozen allografts for tissue transplantation are exceedingly safe and useful, particularly for the repair of damaged ligaments and tendons in a recipient who has insufficient, inadequate, or inferior material of his or her own.

Not surprisingly, a great deal of effort has been expended searching for sterile biological preparations to substitute bone or tendon. A wide

17

variety of sources have been explored, including microcrystalline powders and nuggets of coral as a bone-crystal substitute, as well as powders and gels containing bone protein harvested from the tendons of cows. These substances used singly or mixed together can be inserted as small pieces or paste, much like grout, into bone gaps with the dual intention of *bridging voids* and *inducing* new bone formation. These biological substitutes have the advantage of eliminating the side effects of harvesting tissue from the patient for autologous grafts and the eradication of the risk of infection related to allografts.

The repair of ruptured tendons, including the Achilles tendon in the heel, the rotator cuff in the shoulder, the extensor tendon of the thumb in the wrist, and the posterior tibial tendon in the foot, can sometimes be achieved by direct end-to-end suture (sewing the ends together), followed by a period of protection consisting of complete immobilization or controlled passive immobilization. In many instances, the end of the tendon ruptures or pulls off from the bone, in which case the tendon can be reattached to bone by suturing through drill holes, stapling, or attaching with fixation tacks. At other times, an adjacent tendon can be spliced into the gap, substituting and bypassing the damaged or missing section of its neighbor and allowing both tendons to continue to function. Alternatively, tendon or tendonlike tissue (fascia) can be borrowed from more distant sites in the body and transplanted into defects. In extreme situations, tendon and attached bone can be taken from cadavers and transplanted often with good results. Small patches of sterilized woven protein fibers manufactured from the tissues of pigs and cows are being employed for bridging small gaps and serving as temporary scaffolds for healing when repairing the flat tendons of the rotator cuff in the shoulder.

In conclusion, the surgical repair of broken bones and ruptured tendons and ligaments is currently at an unprecedented level for usage and success while reducing pain, risk, and debility for patients. This will continue to improve in future years.

SURGICAL RELEASE

Surgical release, which needs only a brief description, is nevertheless important. Releasing tight or contracted soft tissues, such as muscles and tendons, ligaments, joint capsules, or scar tissue, is often performed as one of several steps of an operation. Sometimes soft tissue releases comprise the entire operation.

Releasing can be performed to restore motion to a joint, to weaken or reduce the effects of an overly active *(spastic)* muscle on a limb or digit (finger or toe), or to remove tissue that abnormally compresses another structure, such as a nerve, muscle, or tendon. Ligaments and joint capsules can be released as part of the correction of angulated deformities of the joints, such as *bow-legged* or *knock-kneed deformities* during knee replacement.

You might wonder what happens to the tissues that have been released or surgically detached. Do they heal back? Are they left forever free of their former attachments? If they reattach, will they cause problems again? The answers to these questions are complex and best discussed on a case-by-case basis with the treating surgeon. Suffice it to say that in many instances it is expected that the released structures will reattach themselves in a corrected position. Released muscles will also heal back in some instances, able to perform their job again. In these circumstances, it is the job of the surgeon and the physical therapist, perhaps with the use of braces and splints in the postoperative period, to ensure that the reattached tissues perform as desired. In other situations, the intention is not for the tissues to reattach, in which case the limb may be deliberately weakened or destabilized as part of a greater plan. An example would be the release of an Achilles tendon in the heel to allow the contracted foot of a person who has suffered a stroke to be brought into a more neutral position. A light plastic splint can then be used to help restore the ability of that person to walk again.

REALIGNMENT OF BONES, JOINTS, DIGITS, AND LIMBS

Although crooked joints are mentioned in the previous section, it is sometimes necessary to change the alignment of a bone by cutting it. In effect, the surgeon creates a controlled fracture called an osteotomy. The surgeon may bevel the bone ends or shave away a small portion of the bone at the place where it is divided, realign the bone ends as desired, and use a metallic implant and/or cast or brace to hold the bone together until healing occurs. These operations serve in a variety of situations. They include the correction or straightening of bones that have been previously fractured and healed in a crooked fashion *(malunion)*. Another could be the lengthening of bone that has shortened following the malunion of a fracture or has always been shorter than it should have been for optimal function of its limb to result. Another circumstance might be to angle the bone around the joint and shift the forces away from an arthritic corner or side of a joint. Finally, as is discussed in the part of this chapter beginning with the section "Foot and Ankle Disorders," these operations can be used to change the contour of a foot for which bunions or severe arthritis causes pain and inability to wear shoes. These operations, known in common parlance as "breaking the bone," have been often supplanted by joint replacements, but they still have an important place in selected situations in orthopedics.

Issues to ponder before undergoing such a procedure include the effects of the desired outcome and how long a period of time those effects will remain useful to you. Furthermore, you should discuss the risks of complications and the surgeon's experience with the particular procedure, especially since its usage has become less frequent in the last 20 years. An osteotomy or realignment procedure should be compared and contrasted to alternate tenable surgical options, such as joint replacement. The performance of an osteotomy might subsequently affect the ability to undergo a joint replacement in the future should the need arise. Obtaining at least a second orthopedic opinion for these types of procedures is recommended.

JOINT RECONSTRUCTION

The term describing surgery for improving joint function is arthroplasty. Although now most often used to describe the replacement of an entire joint or some part of the joint with metallic, plastic, or ceramic parts, arthroplasty still encompasses a number of other operative options which deserve some mention here.

Joint replacement is now commonly and successfully done on the hip, knee, and shoulder. Less frequently, orthopedic surgeons are replacing joints in the ankles, fingers, and toes. Before the development of joint replacement, a variety of operative approaches were used to treat arthritic joints:

- The removal of bone spurs from joint margins
- Removal of loose fragments of bone and cartilage which often grow larger over time within a joint due to their being nourished by the nutrients and ample oxygen supply within the joint fluid
- Drilling holes into the joint surface to encourage bleeding and formation of a fibrous scar to substitute for the lost joint cartilage
- Trimming the damaged *menisci* (crescent-shaped cartilages within the knee joint that act as shock absorbers) and the surface of the joint
- Removing or stripping the inflamed joint lining (synovectomy)

Formerly, these procedures were possible only through fairly large incisions into the joint (arthrotomy), but now the standard is to perform these procedures by arthroscopy. Small puncture wounds are made for the surgeon to enter the joint, and the pain and stiffness following surgery are only a fraction of that which occurred following arthrotomy.

Arthroscopic joint debridement: After 20 years of widespread usage throughout the United States and the industrialized nations of the world, it is increasingly recognized that *arthroscopic joint debridement,* a term that encompasses any and all of the surgical steps I outlined in the previous list, has very little usefulness in persons over 60 years of age and has significant potential to even make the problems related to the arthritis worse. Simply stated, trimming the damaged shock-absorbing *menisci* in the knee and the partially damaged joint surfaces may only serve to throw the worn areas against each other to a greater extent. Often the knee is better off with its worn or partially damaged parts not tampered with, compared to what can happen with their meddlesome removal or trimming. The real benefits of arthroscopic debridement derive from washing large volumes of saline solution through the knee and perhaps injecting a small amount of steroid at the conclusion of the procedure, which work synergistically to reduce inflammation if only for a short time. However, this can be accomplished equally well by a steroid injection performed in the doctor's office and/or by an NSAID. With the suppression of inflammation, further judicious care involving physical therapy or even hyaluronic acid injections will result in most of the damaged, frayed, or fragmented tissues including the menisci and joint surfaces gradually rubbing themselves smooth,

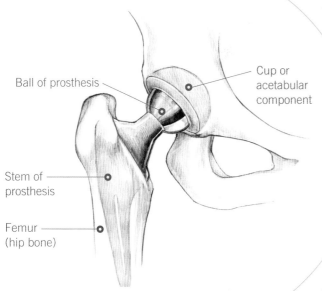

Ball of prosthesis

Cup or acetabular component

Stem of prosthesis

Femur (hip bone)

(figure 17-18)

The total hip replacement has two main components. The cup or acetabular component is inserted into the pelvic bone. The stem and attached ball is inserted into the thigh bone.

one against the other, in a natural way. True, this represents the ongoing process of arthritis, but that process can be influenced in a positive way and slowed down and to some extent controlled and well tolerated by properly educated and motivated patients.

The controversy regarding arthroscopic debridement was fueled by a widely publicized study several years ago. A group of elderly patients with mild to moderate arthritis of the knees were recruited to compare the effects of arthroscopic debridement to a cortisone injection alone. All the patients were taken to the operating room, given anesthesia, and then two small puncture wounds were placed in front of the knee as is routinely done for arthroscopy. They were then divided into two groups. The first group underwent arthroscopic debridement in the standard fashion plus a cortisone injection. The other group had no arthroscopy with just the cortisone inserted into the knee, and the two punctures then closed with sutures. After the surgery, neither the patients nor the doctors who cared for them knew who had arthroscopic debridement or just the skin punctures. All the patients were treated with physical therapy, oral anti-inflammatory drugs, and subsequent cortisone shots as needed over the next year. When the results were analyzed, it was found that there was no difference in how patients felt after six months regardless of whether they had arthroscopic debridement or just the cortisone injection.

Despite this persuasive evidence, the subject of the usefulness of arthroscopic debridement in elderly arthritic patients remains a hot controversy in orthopedics. Hundreds of thousands of patients continue to undergo this operation each year, as often advised by well-respected orthopedic surgeons. This demonstrates the fact that not everything in medicine is "black and white," and there is often disagreement about the best ways to manage some problems. Our next topic, prosthetic joint replacement, is one in which a number of disagreements exist. Our intent is to review the subject with you generally so that you can become acquainted with the basic principles of the subject. Although many different joints can now be replaced, our discussion will focus on the two most common procedures, total hip (see Figure 17-18) and total knee arthroplasty (see Figure 17-21).

Hip replacement: Total joint replacement began in England in the 1950s and became widespread in the United States by the late 1960s. Femoral head replacement for fractures was adopted widely 15 years earlier. Although the surgical procedure has undergone numerous modifications, surprisingly the operation has changed very little overall. After an incision is made, the hip joint is surgically opened, and the worn or destroyed ball called the femoral head is removed. The socket *(acetabulum)* is prepared by removing spurs both inside and around it, and a layer of bone is ground away from its inner surface until fresh raw and bleeding bone is uniformly exposed. An artificial half-shell or cup usually now made of metal is carefully squeezed into the prepared raw bone of the patient's former socket and fixed there. An inner layer of plastic, ceramic, or metal is locked into position within the outer metal shell and presents a precisely machined hemispherical opening into which the new prosthetic head will be inserted. The new head is attached to a stem, which is driven down and fixed inside the upper thighbone. The precise orientation, location, and position of the ball and cup as well as the action of the surrounding muscles in conjunction with the scar tissue that forms after the surgery will control the motion, strength, stability, and length of the limb. The goals of surgery are to permanently eliminate pain, preserve motion of the hip, and reestablish or match leg length.

Although highly successful and usually considered one of the greatest achievements of the last half century, the operation is by no means perfect. In some cases, the popularity of the operation and attempts to improve it and broaden its application have led to numerous and sometimes humbling failures. The public is easily influenced, sometimes even led or misled, in every conceivable direction by various interests, individuals, and organizations that may include spouses, friends, relatives, primary physicians, surgeons, hospitals, insurance companies, equipment manufacturers, sports and entertainment personalities, and the media. There are numerous motivations for any and all of the above groups that might range from love and friendship, genuine concern, sincere desire to help mankind, and pride regarding a new invention to egotism and a quest for fame, recognition, and financial gain.

How can you as a prospective patient or as a spouse, relative, or close friend help with the decision? How can you even hope to make a decision with all these things to consider? What are you supposed to believe? No one has all the right answers, if a right answer even exists. However, I will offer a group of informative points and general recommendations.

The factors that adversely affect the longevity of hip prostheses include young age, high activity levels either at work or in recreation, obesity, weakened bone, and previous hip surgeries. I have no intention of frightening or discouraging you if you are being considered for hip replacement surgery. Surgery must be selected carefully, perhaps with special modifications or some concessions. Sometimes surgery should be postponed until the situation makes it absolutely necessary. Other conditions known to adversely affect outcomes of hip joint replacements include deterioration of mental function, paralysis or spasticity of the muscles of the involved limb (especially those that power and control the hip joint), as well as any medical conditions that predispose to blood-borne infections.

Technical choices exist regarding the fixation of the stem in the thighbone. Broadly considered, there are two basic options. The first option is a *cemented stem,* that is, a stem that is fixed in the bone with acrylic cement. With the second option, the *press-fit stem* or *bony ingrown stem* is covered with ridges or porous surfaces and sometimes coated with chemically manufactured bone crystal. The stem is implanted into the bone cavity, and over the next few weeks to months, the bone grows into or against the stem, thus tightly gripping or fixing it within the shaft of the thighbone. Though numerous other variations exist, the two options of cemented versus bony ingrown stems have been carefully investigated, modified through better understanding, and therefore nearly perfected in recent years. Properly placed in the ideal patient, either type can be expected to last 20 years or more.

A few other generalizations about the kinds of stems can be made. Cemented stems are immediately and fully fixed into the bone. They can be inserted into relatively weakened or soft bone with enlarged interior dimensions and still be initially well fixed. Full weight bearing can be initiated immediately after their insertion. Following the insertion of a cemented stem, there is rarely any subsequent bone or thigh pain. However, the technique for perfectly and precisely cementing a stem is demanding, and it is difficult for the surgeon to perform the operation through a small incision. In addition, the overall strength of a cemented stem within the surrounding bone is not as great as that of a well-fixed bony ingrown stem as far as withstanding a single high or repetitive moderate load.

Press-fit stems, which vary considerably in their design and the precise ways in which they are attached and fixed, are considerably more expensive to manufacture and thus for hospitals to purchase. They are generally suited for persons with heavier, thicker bone, although there is a fairly broad range of latitude for their use in this regard. They are relatively simple for the surgeon to implant, and a smaller incision is possible. Their immediate fixation cannot always be ensured, and it is often necessary to protect against too much weight bearing by the use of a walker or crutches for a period of time following the surgery during which bony ingrowth is allowed to occur. Furthermore, even when properly inserted, there is an unpredictable incidence of achiness or even significant bone pain in the upper thigh that may last for a period of weeks, less frequently for months, and sometimes even indefinitely even though the stem is solidly and stably fixed in the bone. The overall strength of the fixation of a bony ingrown stem is greater than that of a cemented stem, and thus they are more suitable for young, vigorous, active, healthy, heavy, and/or large individuals.

A final point relates to the occasional situation in which a well-fixed and well-positioned cemented or bony ingrown stem must be removed even though it was properly implanted. This might be prompted by a serious infection surrounding the hip prosthesis even months or years after surgery. Immediate drainage of an abscess and removal of a bony ingrown stem can be a formidable problem compared to the easier removal of a cemented stem.

The insertion of the acetabular or cup component is standardized among most orthopedic surgeons. In addition to my previous comments about the insertion and fixation of the cup, the surgeon may elect to

17

insert one or more screws driven through preexisting holes that the cup device may optionally include. Orthopedic surgeons choose to use cups with holes or without them and/or screws as they see fit and depending on what they encounter in the course of the operation. The cup must be initially supported by screws or by a "cork-in-bottle" jam fit. Over the next few months the contacting bone must grow into the cup's porous outer surface to provide long-term support.

The inner lining or *bearing surface* of the artificial socket has been manufactured from polyethylene, a plasticlike material, for nearly 40 years. Although initially highly successful as far as its material properties were concerned, a number of problems have surfaced in recent years. After extremely detailed investigations and studies, a combination of numerous factors and variables were identified and manipulated to produce the best quality polyethylene liners that were capable of long use with the types of low wear seen during the early years of usage. However, the wear of polyethylene, whether due to manufacture, sterilization, storage, design, or overstress, can result in the shedding of minute plastic particles into the joint cavity which provokes a chronic intense, localized inflammatory response capable of destroying the adjacent supporting bone of the pelvis and upper thigh. Under ideal conditions, this problem would not occur, and as a result, investigators have been searching for better bearing surfaces for total hip replacements. Now, better combinations of metal balls and polyethylene socket liners are in use.

Titanium metal heads have been tried and found to wear poorly. Titanium is no longer used for this purpose, but it is still frequently used in the manufacture of the stem on top of which the metal ball of chrome-cobalt or stainless steel is mounted. Femoral heads and/or socket liners made of ceramic, made from aluminum and silicon (not unlike the familiar zircon) have been manufactured and tried with various design modifications and by a group of different manufacturers on a number of occasions in the last 25 years. Success has varied, again related to complex and numerous factors. Many of the early designs were abandoned due to brittleness and breakage. These substances do, however, have the advantage of superior wear with no particle degeneration and thus no destruction or dissolving of bone. A group of ceramic implants is currently being widely used in Europe, and the results of long-term success should be available in the next few years. Nevertheless, it is worth mentioning that recent years have witnessed massive product recalls of ceramic-bearing surfaces, again for reasons of brittleness and breakage. These devices are under investigation in the United States, but until further data on the most recent designs are forthcoming, they should still be considered with caution.

A final option for the bearing surfaces of prosthetic hips is actually one that was used over 30 years ago and has been resurrected. That is metal-on-metal joint surfaces. Exhibiting superior wear characteristics and great strength, these implants are extremely attractive for consideration in young, vigorous, active, or heavy individuals. Two of the chief metals used in their construction are chrome and cobalt, and their implantation does lead to marked increases in the blood levels of these two elements in the persons who receive them. The long-term effects of serum cobalt or chrome levels many hundred times higher than what is normally encountered are not known. However, given that this manual is oriented to persons in midlife and beyond, the use of metal-on-metal surfaces can be dismissed for now, since seniors can be safely and adequately treated with the proven and revised combination of a metal head with a polyethylene socket liner.

A final but exceedingly important subject for consideration in this section involves the increasingly promoted operations that involve smaller incisions, sometimes described as *minimally invasive* surgery. I would suggest that you view this subject with a certain amount of caution and perhaps even skepticism. I offer you several points to provide a better understanding of the pitfalls and fallacies regarding this subject.

During the last decade, hip replacements have been performed through one of two surgical approaches. One is the anterolateral approach, in which the hip joint is entered just in front of the upper thighbone, and the other is the posterior approach, in which the hip joint is entered from just behind the upper thighbone. Both approaches are extensively used in the United States, and each has its proponents as the superior technique for various technical reasons that include the ease of insertion of the prosthesis, the relative resistance of the reconstructed hip joint to dislocation after surgery, and the strength or weakness of the hip and leg. Most surgeons fall into one camp, choosing either the anterior or posterior approach (see Figure 17-19). This is usually based on their experiences in orthopedic training, and they rarely vary or change once they commit to a particular approach. Interestingly, surgeons in different parts of the country tend to prefer one approach over the other, although this is by no means clear-cut.

The anterolateral approach provides the surgeon with a better view of the surgical site. Thus the operation is relatively easier to accomplish, and it has the added benefit of being associated with a lower incidence of dislocations where the ball of the prosthesis pops out of the socket. If this happens, a trip to the emergency room is required, sedation is given, and a physician must manually replace the ball in the socket by pulling and twisting the leg.

The posterior approach is technically more difficult, and it is associated with an increased risk of damaging the sciatic nerve which rests just behind the socket. Visualization and particularly insertion of the cup are also more difficult. The posterior approach is associated with a risk of dislocation, which may only occur once but which can also occur repetitively and even require a second operation. If this were the entire story, the choice would seem a nonissue: the anterolateral approach is superior. Unfortunately, there is one other factor that serves as a counterbalance. The anterolateral approach very frequently produces permanent weakness of the major muscle that lifts the leg or hip sideways (recall the famous Jane Fonda exercise!) even when performed by expert surgeons. The result is a subtle but permanent limp and to a certain degree a lack of balance.

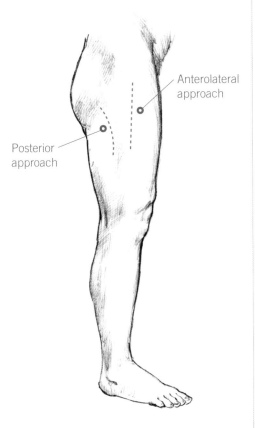

Anterolateral approach

Posterior approach

(figure 17-19)

In the anterolateral approach for total hip replacement, the surgeon makes the incision just in front of the upper thigh bone. In the posterior approach, the incision is made just behind the upper thigh bone.

Experts from either camp argue that perfected techniques should virtually eliminate the risk of a weak hip muscle after an anterolateral approach and the risk of dislocation after a posterior approach. Unfortunately, nothing definitive can be said at this time, but these facts are useful in understanding the subtleties that cause many orthopedic surgeons to be concerned about the dangers of performing hip replacement surgery through mini-incisions. Tremendous attention has been focused on this subject as the result of intense research and marketing efforts of several manufacturers and groups of surgeons. Often, seemingly miraculous claims are made about reducing or eliminating the pain from the operation and even going home on the same day as the surgery.

In many instances, small incision or mini-incision surgery is nothing more than a reduction in the size of the skin incision that can be accomplished by practice, patience, special equipment, and perhaps an additional surgical assistant. The same operation, either an anterolateral or posterior approach, is performed, and there is a similar amount of pain, bleeding, and virtually any of the other effects associated with a larger incision. Small incisions are easier to use in thin, small patients. A minimally invasive technique is much more difficult in persons who are heavy or robust. However, new modifications and surgical approaches are being developed that are significantly different and truly qualify as novel. They are far more time-consuming to perform. They can only be accomplished on small, thin patients, and only with uncemented stems (best suited for persons with thick nonosteoporotic bone). Because of the extremely limited surgical exposure, the ability of the surgeon to remove bone spurs and release contractures may be impaired. Since bone spurs and contractures are frequently present in advanced arthritis, failure to take care of these problems may result in compromised outcomes, especially with regard to the patient's mobility.

The public has been riveted by the promise of painless surgery and minimal hospitalization due to the strong promotional efforts and marketing of certain orthopedic equipment manufacturers and some orthopedic surgeons. This has caused a significant degree of anxiety among the other orthopedic equipment manufacturers and the remainder of orthopedic surgeons, all of whom are being pressured to adopt a new technique which may well prove, like so many past discarded ideas, to be disastrous either because it is less reproducible, too difficult to learn, ineffectively deals with the full scope of the problem, or creates a whole new set of complications and side effects in large numbers that were either unforeseen or just not preventable. I suggest that you exercise caution.

Knee replacement: Now, let's move on to total knee replacement. Although knee replacement is a more recent development than hip replacement, it has a higher degree of reliability and a considerably higher rate of usage than total hip replacement. Because the knee is situated between the two longest bones of the body (the femur and tibia) and because it is capable of only two basic movements (flexion and limited rotation), it is far more exposed and susceptible to injury than the highly

(figure 17-20)

Ostearthritis can lead to angular deformities of the knees: (a) bow-legged (varus) and (b) knock-kneed (valgus).

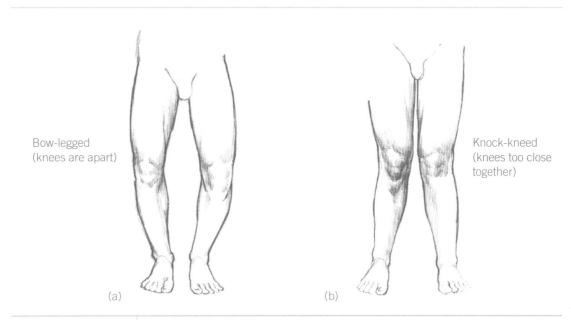

Bow-legged
(knees are apart)

Knock-kneed
(knees too close
together)

(a)

(b)

mobile, less constrained, and better protected hip joint. The knee is both exposed and vulnerable and, not surprisingly, wears out more often than the hip does, which explains, in part, why knee replacement is performed with greater frequency than hip replacement in the United States.

From an engineering perspective, simply stated, all the components of a prosthetic knee are *surface replacements.* This is easily appreciated when compared to the familiar practice of capping teeth. The ends of the bones that make up the joint surface are shaved or cut away, followed by the application of precisely fitted caps of metal and/or plastic, which are most often cemented into position. In this sense, the term "replacement" is probably confusing and would be better substituted by the term "resurfacing."

The tissues overlying the front of the knee are sliced open vertically and then peeled to the sides, allowing the bones to be extruded or popped out into view so that they can be shaved. Subsequently, the caps or components of the knee prosthesis are applied. The resurfaced bone ends are pushed back into position one against the other, and the tissues are allowed to fall back into their normal location around the "new knee." Thus the muscles, ligaments, and bones that support, power, and stabilize the knee joint remain in their normal location; only the joint surfaces are replaced.

Stoic individuals may be able to tolerate knee arthritis a very long time. As a result, the arthritis may progress to the point where these persons develop *flexion contractures* and angular deformities. A *varus* deformity is associated with a bow-legged appearance; a *valgus* deformity is associated with a knock-kneed appearance (see Figure 17-20). In order for the knee replacement to be successful and long-lasting, such deformities must be corrected in the surgical procedure. The new knee must be properly aligned within the leg, free to move in a normal fashion, but appropriately stabilized so that it does not sag or slip abnormally. Correction of deformity is surgically accomplished by the releasing of contracted ligaments, joint capsule, and even muscle. Sometimes, large flexion contractures may require additional resection (removal) of the bone ends for optimal correction. To whatever extent possible, the stability of the prosthetic knee should be dependent on the surgically achieved rebalancing of the soft tissues around the joint. Occasionally, if the preexisting deformity is unusually severe or if revising a failed knee replacement, sufficient stability can only be achieved by using specially designed prosthetic parts which hinge or interlock to some degree. Stability is derived from the interdigitation of the moving mechanical implants because the soft tissues are no longer capable of lending their support.

You may intuitively appreciate that knee replacements function best and last longest when their control and stability are provided in large part by the muscles and ligaments surrounding the joint. If this cannot be accomplished and stability has to be built into the prosthetic components (a more *constrained* design), further stresses are thrown on the junction where the prosthesis attaches to the bone and on the moving parts themselves. This increases the likelihood of an earlier failure of the replacement.

During the last 30 years, various design concepts have been designed and tried, producing a better understanding of how to achieve the ideal knee replacement. Here we have many parallels with hip replacement surgery. Again, factors that work against the long-term success of a knee replacement include young age, obesity, and high activity levels. Different designs have been devised to address these problems. A short discussion about these issues will help you if you are faced with making a decision about knee replacement.

Considered biomechanically, the knee is more complicated than the hip in structure and function. When knee replacements were first invented, it quickly became apparent that some compromise would be required. The notion of exactly recreating the complex features of the human knee had to be abandoned. This became even more obvious when attempting to replace the surfaces of knees that had become highly deformed or contracted from advanced arthritis. The replacement of very crooked knees led to the realization that the design of the prosthetic implants often had to substitute for certain critical ligaments that had to be sacrificed in order to straighten deformities and relieve contractures.

Two schools of thought emerged, each with supporting manufacturers and orthopedic surgeons. One school included those who attempted to retain and use an internal ligament of the knee called the *posterior cruciate ligament*. The other school sacrificed the posterior cruciate ligament and substituted a specific modification of the prosthetic design *(post-and-cam mechanism)*. The "cruciate retainers" claimed that their approach was more natural and would lead to knees that functioned better and lasted longer. The "cruciate sacrificers" countered that preserving the cruciate

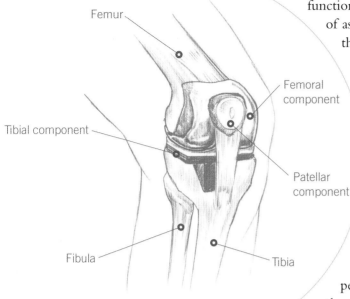

Femur

Femoral
component

Tibial component

Patellar
component

Fibula

Tibia

(figure 17-21)

Total knee replacement includes three
components: the femoral, the tibial, and
the patellar components.

ligament was too exacting a technique, was not applicable to knees with deformity, and, unless executed precisely and perfectly, would lead to poor function and accelerate failure of the knee replacement. Both groups of assertions were correct. The majority, but certainly not all, of the knee replacements performed today sacrifice and substitute for the posterior cruciate ligament. The *posterior-stabilized* prosthetic implants that substitute for this ligament are easier to implant, more reliable in the hands of the average orthopedic surgeon, and more adaptable to knees with advanced arthritis where deformities and contractures are common. Furthermore, cruciate-substituting implant designs have demonstrated great longevity, particularly in appropriately selected patients such as those who are not too young, active, or heavy. The majority of senior citizens are well served with this implant. However, exceptions may occur depending on a particular patient's needs and depending on a surgeon's experience and expertise. Older persons who are contemplating knee replacement should bear the above facts in mind and carefully consider and question the rationale for a cruciate-retaining prosthesis.

Three components comprise the usual total knee replacement (see Figure 17-21). The first is the *total condylar prosthesis* or *femoral component,* a metal cap that covers the knucklelike condyles at the lower end of the femur. The condylar prosthesis rolls and glides over the second part of the prosthesis (the *tibial component),* which is a gently dented polyethylene or plastic piece that is snap-fit or locked into the upper surface of a strong metal tray that is pegged into and rests on top of the *tibia.* The third part is a small-domed button, which is fixed to the undersurface of the kneecap and glides up and down in a groove between the condyles of the femoral component. Each of the three parts are fixed separately to a bone and move one against the other as the three bones move, controlled and supported by the muscles, tendons, and ligaments that surround the knee.

One other and important design variation must be mentioned that further complicates the surgical selection process for knee replacement in senior citizens. This early and very different modification involved the surface of the tibial component. Unlike the majority of knee replacements where the polyethylene surface is inserted or locked into the supporting metal tray, the designers created what is known as a *rotating platform.* The polyethylene surface has a small cone-shaped peg projecting from its underside that fits into a precisely matched indentation on the top of the otherwise smooth and polished metal tray which, in turn, is fixed to the top of the tibia. The polyethylene piece is free to rotate in different directions as the knee bends and straightens with activity. The total amount of rotation that occurs is only about 15 to 20 degrees, but parallels that seen with the normal knee. Although not widely embraced by the majority of joint replacement surgeons, this very different design approach was used for many years and in large numbers by a small but dedicated group of orthopedic surgeons who developed great expertise with the somewhat more exacting techniques required for the rotating platform. These surgeons were able to demonstrate high-level results particularly for long-term wear in young, active, and heavy patients. After 20 years, with the expiration of patent exclusivity, several major orthopedic appliance manufacturers designed and introduced their own versions of the rotating platform. These designs were marketed as being easier to use than the original proven version while still offering the same advantages in terms of longevity. The verdict on these newer versions is not yet available. Most orthopedic surgeons are not experienced in the technique of inserting the original design. The usual knee replacement prostheses can be expected to last 15 to 20 years in the average patient who is not too young, not too vigorous, and not too heavy. Therefore, any senior citizen considering knee replacement should think twice before accepting a rotating platform design for implantation.

Acrylic cement is the method most often used for the fixation of knee replacements. Although other techniques of fixation have been successfully employed, they offer no special advantage for senior patients. Uncemented fixation of the femoral component offers few, if any, advantages over cement fixation. Although the uncemented prosthetic femoral component is reliable, it is considerably more expensive to manufacture. It was hoped that uncemented fixation of the tibial component would be stronger and less prone to failure than cemented fixation was, but proved to be far less reliable. In young, active, or heavy patients, uncemented fixation offers little protection against the major cause of failure of knee replacement, which is related to the generation of wear particles of the polyethylene and the damage to bone that occurs regardless of how the components are fixed.

Knee surgeons as well as the engineers who design knee replacements subdivide the human knee joint into three compartments. The first compartment is between the inner *(medial)* condyle of the femur and the tibial plateau. The second is between the outer *(lateral)* femoral condyle and the tibial plateau. The third compartment is defined as the articulation between the kneecap and the groove or notch between the condyles of the femur. Osteoarthritis, or wear and tear arthritis, usually occurs focally in one or two of the compartments, sparing the remaining ones. As an example, in a bow-legged patient, the inner or medial compartment is worn. In contrast, in the knock-kneed patient, the outer or lateral compartment is worn. These patterns are respectively referred to as medial or lateral compartmental osteoarthritis. The compartment that involves the kneecap against the femur *(patellofemoral articulation)* may be involved separately or in conjunction with other parts of the joint.

For instances in which only the medial or lateral compartments are affected by osteoarthritis, bioengineers and orthopedic surgeons have devised and implanted unicompartmental replacements, where half-caps are fixed into position only replacing the damaged surfaces and leaving the other two unaffected compartments intact (see Figure 17-

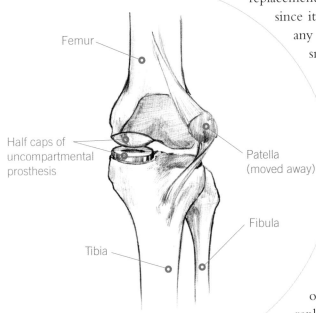

Femur

Half caps of
uncompartmental
prosthesis

Patella
(moved away)

Fibula

Tibia

(figure 17-22)

For a unicompartmental prosthesis, half-caps
are fixed into position on the side affected by
arthritis. The other compartments of the knee
are left untouched.

22). This operation requires less surgical manipulation than a total knee replacement. Intellectually, it appears to be a more focused operation, since it addresses only the diseased portions of the joint and spares any uninvolved areas. The prosthesis can be inserted through a smaller incision during a shorter operation, perhaps requiring less anesthesia. Postoperative bleeding and pain are usually less, often resulting in a more rapid and simple recovery. You might ask, "What's not to like?"

Unicompartmental replacements are not new and indeed go back 30 years to the very beginnings of prosthetic knee replacement. There have been three major surges of interest in this procedure. The first occurred in the late 1970s, the second was at the end of the 1980s, and the third is taking place at the present time. Twice in the past, unicompartmental knee replacements were tried for the reasons stated in the previous paragraph, and twice fell into disfavor due to unacceptably high rates of failure compared to other techniques, such as total knee replacement, osteotomy (in which bone was removed in order to shift forces to the area of the knee unaffected by arthritis), or no surgery at all.

The surgical technique for implanting a unicompartmental prosthesis was demanding, requiring precise positioning of the half-caps on the bone ends. This was difficult to achieve for two reasons. First, the surgeon had to estimate "by eye" that the half-cap was positioned properly in relationship to the other untouched condyle of the knee. This is in contrast to a total knee replacement in which both prosthetic condyles are perfectly matched one to the other by the implant itself. Second, the use of smaller incisions limited visualization of the uninvolved part of the knee. This operation does not allow for the correction of deformity or contractures. Indeed, if deformities or contractures are present, unicompartmental knee replacement will probably not be successful. Furthermore, experience from the two previous periods of popularity with this procedure has demonstrated that unicompartmental implants failed quickly in heavy patients.

The current resurgence in interest in unicompartmental knee replacement has not translated into widespread acceptance, but it has its devotees. Those orthopedic surgeons experienced in this procedure would point out that the new designs have been improved significantly over the two earlier sets of versions. In addition, instruments and techniques have been developed to improve accurate insertion and positioning of the implant through small incisions. Restrictions still apply concerning which patients are best served with a unicompartmental prosthesis. Some would argue that those persons who are heavy, who have contractures or deformities of their joints, or who have arthritis of the patella are probably best excluded. However, the tendency for surgeons who frequently perform this operation is to push back the edges of the envelope with regard to the application of this procedure.

At present, there is some positive data about long-term results with unicompartmental implants, and when performed by experienced surgeons the operation has been significantly improved. This raises two important questions. If inserted into the knee of a young and active person with arthritis limited to one compartment, will the unicompartmental knee replacement hold up as that person gets older and moves into the senior years? Happily, we already know that a unicompartmental knee replacement can be converted to a total knee replacement if either the unicompartmental prosthesis fails or the remainder of the knee develops arthritis. The second question is one which is more applicable for dealing with issues of senior wellness and relates to the insertion of a unicompartmental knee prosthesis in an older patient. If chosen, will it be as reliable a final solution as a complete knee replacement? Although there is no definite answer yet to this question, there is an important counterpoint. The average senior citizen with only moderate arthritis localized to one part of the knee, who desires to have relief of pain and restoration of activities such as walking, golfing, swimming, bicycling, and traveling (but not running!), can be successfully treated and restored with a nonoperative arthritis control program. This program may include drugs to suppress inflammation, hyaluronic acid injections, and physical therapy to maintain the strength of the buttocks and thighs. Nonoperative treatment does not work for every patient, nor can it be expected to work indefinitely even for those who initially found it beneficial for several years. Individuals who no longer derive benefit from nonoperative methods might then conceivably turn to unicompartmental knee replacement. However, in some instances their osteoarthritis may have progressed to the point that the only remaining option is total knee replacement. Thus, the selection of nonoperative treatment, albeit successful for a few years, may be an irrevocable decision, leaving the larger procedure of total knee replacement as the only viable option in the future. Would the knowledge of this fact lead most patients to select unicompartmental knee replacement at the outset? Even though the procedure is a smaller operation than total knee replacement, it is our human nature to avoid surgery if possible. Most senior citizens, after being fully apprised of the options including the benefits and risks, select nonoperative treatment over unicompartmental knee replacement with the hope that it will offer them significant relief for a few years. By doing this, they accept the possibility that they might require total knee replacement at some future date.

Over the next few years, further information will be forthcoming comparing and contrasting nonoperative treatment with unicompartmental knee replacement. In addition, studies will be available comparing unicompartmental knee replacement with total knee replacement. These studies will stratify the results decade by decade for patients of various shapes and sizes, for patients of varying states of health, and for patients desiring various levels of activity.

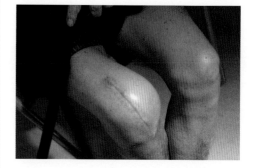

Knee surgery has helped many people who have been limited by knee arthritis.

Joint replacement surgery continues to be an exciting and evolving field as new surgical techniques are explored and new devices are invented. Although hip and knee replacements are the most frequent joint replacement operations, almost any joint in the body can be replaced. Best of all, many people's lives have been markedly improved as pain is relieved and function restored. Although complications can occur as in any type of surgery, physicians have learned methods to reduce risks. As a result, these orthopedic procedures are among the safest operations performed.

JOINT FUSION

The term for surgical fusion of a joint is *arthrodesis.* Much of our knowledge on this subject is derived from past experience with the victims of trauma or infection. Arthrodesis involves shaving off the joint cartilage until raw bone is exposed. The two denuded bone ends are then held one to the other in a useful position. After several months, these bones become solidly fused into a long single bone. The joint space becomes obliterated, no longer capable of movement, and the appendage or limb loses a moving segment but is rendered completely painless. Arthrodesis was used extensively in the first half of the twentieth century for polio infection and post-traumatic arthritis, but has been largely supplanted by newer treatments and techniques for repairing fractures of bones that form the joints, eradicating infections within joints, and replacing joints damaged by arthritis. Arthrodesis still has a useful role in certain situations.

Arthrodesis is by its very nature a tremendous compromise, as the mobility that is so essential to our welfare is impaired. However, mobility may sometimes be traded for restoration of stability, return of useful though partial function, and elimination of pain. The loss of movement of a single joint in a limb can be often overcome to a large degree through the compensatory movements of the remaining unhindered joints in the limb. The degree of possible compensation varies considerably, depending on which joint is fused.

The fusion of the small joint of a very painful toe is usually a welcome alternative to the walking disability that toe causes. All of us have had the experience that even a single painful toe can seriously diminish our ability to get around. Similarly, the deformity that occurs with arthritis in the ends of the fingers may make activities such as typing or playing the piano virtually impossible. Although there is currently no ideal solution to restoring alignment and painless mobility, the flexibility of the wrist, hand, and nonarthritic joints of the finger makes the surgical fusion of the joint at the end of the finger a useful restorative procedure for some individuals.

Fusion may be useful in other situations as well. Degenerative disc disease and arthritis in the back may require fusion of the bones and/or joints of the spine, most commonly the lower back but not infrequently the neck too. This topic is extensively discussed in Chapter 18. Other joints that are often fused for painful arthritis include the joints of the hindfoot, the ankle, and the wrist.

A final situation where fusion is sometimes but not always employed is in the management of an infected or failed knee replacement.

FOOT AND ANKLE DISORDERS

Think of the magic of that foot, comparatively small, upon which your whole weight rests. It's a miracle.
—Martha Graham

During the course of a normal day, your feet and ankles take an inordinate amount of stress and strain. Foot and ankle disorders can range from mild deformities causing minimal discomfort to severe debilitating deformities causing chronic pain. The common factor is that with every step there is a repetitive stress on the affected area.

The foot can be divided into the forefoot (front of the foot), midfoot (middle of the foot), and hindfoot (back of the foot). The foot and ankle are made up of multiple bones held together by supporting structures called *ligaments* which cross the joints and keep the bones in place. Muscles control the movement and attach to the bones via *tendons,* which serve to transmit the pull caused by muscle contraction (see Figures 17–23 and 17–24).

Also, please note the additional directions indicated on Figures 17-23 and 17-24. *Medial* indicates toward the midline, or inside, of the foot, while *lateral* refers to the outside of the foot toward the lesser toes. *Distal* indicates toward the tips of the toes, while *proximal* indicates toward the back of the foot or higher up on the leg toward the body. *Dorsal* refers to the top of the foot, and *plantar* refers to the bottom, or sole, of the foot.

(figure 17-23)

Top view of the foot showing (a) bones, (b) ligaments, and tendons.

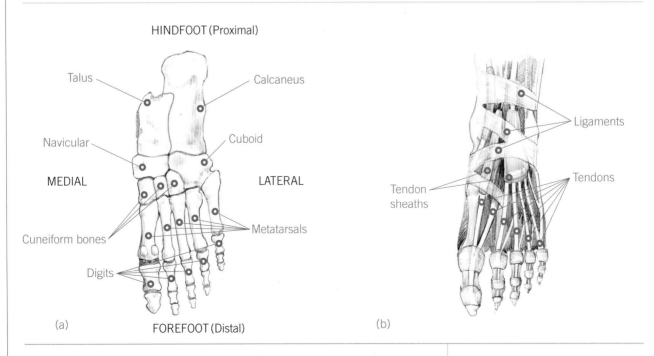

(figure 17-24)
Side view of the foot showing (a) bones, (b) ligaments, and tendons.

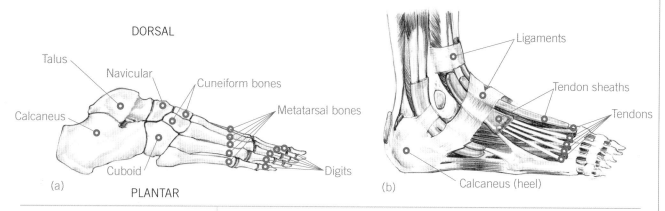

DORSAL

Talus

Navicular

Cuneiform bones

Calcaneus

Metatarsal bones

Cuboid

(a)

PLANTAR

Digits

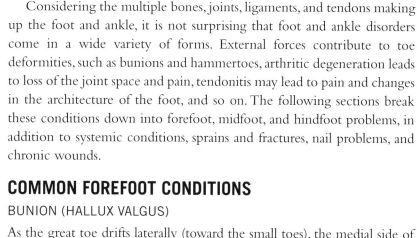

Ligaments

Tendon sheaths

Tendons

(b)

Calcaneus (heel)

17

Considering the multiple bones, joints, ligaments, and tendons making up the foot and ankle, it is not surprising that foot and ankle disorders come in a wide variety of forms. External forces contribute to toe deformities, such as bunions and hammertoes, arthritic degeneration leads to loss of the joint space and pain, tendonitis may lead to pain and changes in the architecture of the foot, and so on. The following sections break these conditions down into forefoot, midfoot, and hindfoot problems, in addition to systemic conditions, sprains and fractures, nail problems, and chronic wounds.

COMMON FOREFOOT CONDITIONS

BUNION (HALLUX VALGUS)

As the great toe drifts laterally (toward the small toes), the medial side of the first metatarsal head becomes prominent. This prominence, referred to as a bunion, is easily irritated by shoes, causing pain and inflammation (see Figure 17-25). Bunions are much more common in women. The most significant cause of a bunion deformity is wearing shoes, with narrow shoes and high heels driving the great toe laterally. These shoes not only cause the deformity with long-term wear but also contribute to a steady worsening of the deformity.

Conservative (or nonsurgical) treatment includes wider shoes, checking that your shoes do not have seams that run across the bunion, and having your shoes stretched. The best device for shoe stretching is the ball–and–ring device, which a local shoemaker may have. The ball is placed on the inside and the ring on the outside in the area of the bony prominence, thus the ball does the shoe stretching rather than your bone. Examples of shoes that come in multiple widths are Easy Spirit shoes and New Balance sneakers.

Orthotics (shoe inserts) can also help prevent progression of a bunion in those patients in whom the foot pronates (rolls to the outside). A podiatrist (a foot doctor) or an orthotist (a person who makes and fits orthopedic appliances) can make orthotics. By reducing pronation, the lateral deforming force on the great toe is reduced.

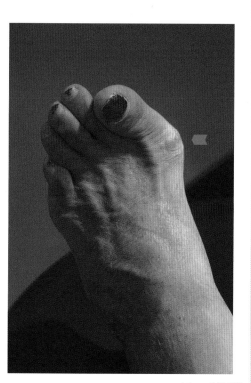

(figure 17-25)

A bunion is a bony prominence at the base of the big toe (arrowhead).

If relief cannot be achieved via conservative measures, then surgical treatment can be considered. Surgical correction, called a **bunionectomy**, is intended to relieve pain by correction of the deformity by narrowing the forefoot and realigning the toe. It is best not to have surgery for cosmetic purposes alone. It is important to understand that full recovery after bunion surgery can easily take four to six months or more.

Many procedures are available for bunion correction. Most involve an **osteotomy** (cutting the bone) of the first metatarsal and shifting the head of the metatarsal laterally, thus narrowing the foot (see Figure 17-26). This is combined with a soft tissue correction, with release of tight lateral structures about the joint and tightening of loose medial structures to hold the toe aligned and derotate the toe as necessary. The metatarsal osteotomy is often fixed with screws or pins. Determining the correct procedure will be up to your surgeon and his or her evaluation of your foot and radiographs.

Postoperative recuperation will depend on the type of surgery performed. For certain procedures you will be allowed to walk on the heel and lateral aspect of the foot in a wooden postop shoe, while for others you will need to be non-weight-bearing and use crutches or a walker for four to six weeks. Usually after a bunionectomy with metatarsal osteotomy, you will be allowed back into sneakers at approximately eight weeks after surgery. Physical therapy may be required. The risks of surgery should be discussed with your surgeon.

ARTHRITIS OF THE GREAT TOE

Arthritis of the first metatarsophalangeal joint of the great toe leads to stiffness, spurring, and, ultimately, joint destruction. Patients experience pain with activity. Shoes can cause irritation of the skin overlying the spur, contributing to pain and inflammation (see Figure 17-27).

Extrawide, extradeep shoes help relieve pressure over a large spur but do not address the underlying arthritis. Stiff shoes or orthotics may also be tried. These help reduce stress across the arthritic joint. Shoes with heels should be avoided, since these cause more stress at the dorsum (top) of an already stiff joint and contribute to impingement.

An injection of the arthritic first metatarsophalangeal joint with steroids and local anesthetic can be considered. This will help reduce inflammation and pain. Response to an injection is dependent on the severity of the arthritis. This does not eliminate the spur or cure the arthritis.

For patients that continue to have pain despite the above steps, surgery can be considered. The type of surgery depends on the severity of the arthritis. Patients with mild arthritis with dorsal spurring may benefit from a *cheilectomy*. This operation involves resection of the dorsal spur and the dorsal 20 to 30% of the first metatarsal head to eliminate

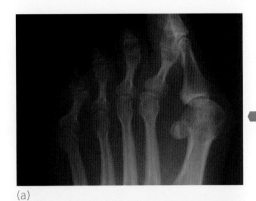

(a)

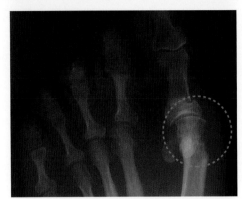

(b)

(*figure* 17-26)

X-rays of a bunion (a) before surgery and (b) after surgery. Note the bony prominence (arrowhead) at the base of the big toe. After the bone is cut away (circled), the toe is straightened.

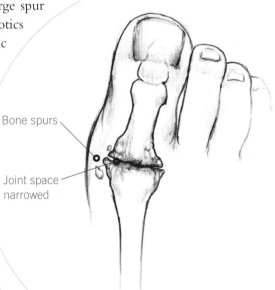

Bone spurs

Joint space narrowed

(*figure* 17-27)

Arthritis of the great toe leads to stiffness, bone spurs, and eventually destruction of the joint.

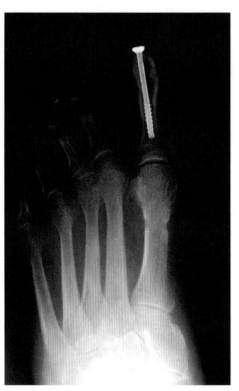

impingement and the arthritic portion of the first metatarsal head. This is not a good choice for patients with significant arthritis. This operation requires approximately three weeks in a postop wooden-soled shoe, and the patient may return to comfortable shoes or sneakers at approximately three weeks after surgery. Exercises to maintain the range of motion are very important in the postoperative period, and physical therapy may be considered.

For patients with moderate to severe arthritis with narrowing and loss of the joint space, the preferred option is a fusion of the joint (see Figure 17-28). This means removing the joint entirely and fusing it (growing the bones together). This eliminates all motion across the involved arthritic joint and, in doing so, reduces if not eliminates the pain. Following this surgery the patient will need to ambulate with crutches or a walker. The patient will need to minimize weight bearing to the surgical extremity for approximately six weeks after surgery, with protection of the foot through approximately eight weeks after surgery.

We are frequently asked about replacing the first metatarsophalangeal joint. Unfortunately, no joint replacement for this joint that has a long track record. Due to the stresses that occur across this joint during the course of a regular day, joint replacement has a high incidence of failure. In addition, reconstruction after a failed joint replacement is very difficult. Considering this, joint replacement of the first metatarsophalangeal joint is best avoided.

(figure 17-28)

An X-ray showing a surgical fusion (arthrodesis) of a severely arthritic great toe.

LESSER TOE DEFORMITIES: HAMMERTOES AND CLAW TOES

Hammertoes and *claw toes* refer to deformities in which the small joints of the toes are flexed (bent) and the larger joint joining the toe to the foot is extended, thus causing the toe to curl up. The flexion occurs at the proximal interphalangeal joint in the hammertoe and at both the proximal and distal interphalangeal joints in the claw toe (see Figure 17-29).

These deformities may be either fixed or flexible. In a fixed deformity, the interphalangeal joints are stiff and cannot be straightened out manually, while in a flexible deformity the joints are supple and can be straightened

(figure 17-29)

(a) Hammertoe and (b) claw toe.

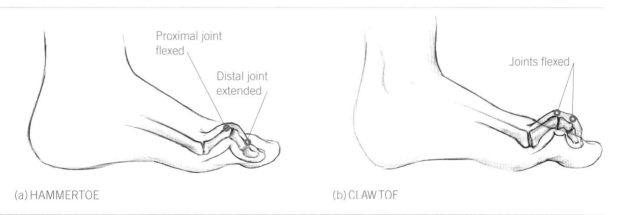

Proximal joint flexed

Distal joint extended

Joints flexed

(a) HAMMERTOE

(b) CLAW TOE

Step 1: Stand on a sheet of paper in your bare feet and have your assistant trace your feet. This must be done with you standing.

Step 2: Place the shoes in question over the tracings of your feet and trace them as well. Make sure they line up.

Evaluation: Your forefoot should be no more than 1/2-inch wider than your shoes, while 1/4-inch or less is better.

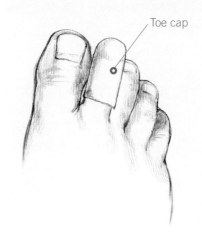

(figure 17-30)

Toe cap.

manually. Patients may start with a flexible deformity that progresses to a fixed deformity over time.

Pain is associated with pressure from a shoe over the interphalangeal joints (usually the proximal interphalangeal joint) and beneath the metatarsal heads. As extension of the metatarsophalangeal joint increases, the metatarsal fat pad shifts distally thus uncovering the metatarsal head making it prominent and often painful.

Wearing shoes usually contributes to these deformities. When multiple toes on both feet are involved, another medical condition should be considered such as peripheral neuropathy or spinal cord disorders among other possibilities.

Conservative treatment includes extradepth shoes to accommodate the deformed toes as well as assorted devices to improve alignment of the toes via splinting or strapping the toes. The stiffer, more rigid the toes, the less effective the splinting and strapping devices. Toe caps can also be used to cushion the prominent area of the interphalangeal joint. These often are lined with silicone and need to be cut to the appropriate length (see Figure 17-30). Metatarsal pads, orthotics, or metatarsal bars can be used to reduce pressure beneath the prominent metatarsal heads (see Figure 17-31).

If nonoperative treatment is unsatisfactory, surgical correction can be performed for painful deformities. For fixed deformities, straightening of the toe requires bony resection of the head of the proximal phalanx of the toe for decompression of the joint. Although this will provide a straight toe at the interphalangeal joint, the toe will still be extended at the metatarsophalangeal joint where it joins the foot. Often release of the metatarsophalangeal joint is required to release the tight structures at this joint and achieve full correction. This can be combined with a *plantar condylectomy* (removal of the bony prominence of the metatarsal head on the plantar side) to relieve the pressure in this area. Our preference is to pin the toe for a few weeks postoperatively to maintain alignment. The pin is removed in the office. Tape strapping and a postop wooden shoe are usually used for approximately six weeks after surgery until sufficient healing has occurred, thus making recurrence unlikely.

METATARSALGIA AND MORTON'S NEUROMA

Pain beneath the ball of the foot is usually related to either pressure beneath the metatarsal heads, known as metatarsalgia, or pressure

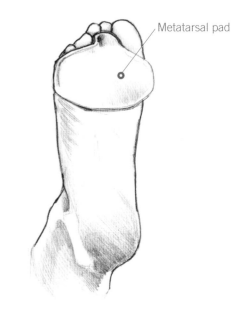

(figure 17-31)

A metatarsal pad appropriately positioned for pressure relief.

beneath a benign nerve tumor, known as a **Morton's neuroma**. Patients with metatarsalgia often describe pain beneath the metatarsal heads as "walking on marbles" or "pebbles." As a person ages, the plantar fat pad that cushions the metatarsal heads thins out. This leads to compression of the skin between the metatarsal heads and the ground contact leading to pain and callusing (see Figure 17-32).

Clawing and hammering of the lesser toes also lead to a distal shift of the metatarsal fat pad, uncovering the metatarsal heads and contributing to pressure on the skin. A bunion deformity of the great toe also contributes to metatarsalgia. Since the great toe no longer supports as much weight and becomes dysfunctional, pressure is transferred to the lesser metatarsal heads, especially the second, causing pressure-related pain.

Patients with a Morton's neuroma also complain of pain beneath the forefoot, often described as a burning or radiating pain and sometimes with complaints of numbness. The most common location for a neuroma is in the third web space between the third and fourth toes (see Figure 17-33).

Other causes of pain beneath the ball of the foot include stress fracture and arthritis of the lesser metatarsophalangeal joints among others but are less common. Differentiating between the causes of forefoot pain is not always easy. Pressure directly beneath the metatarsal heads with callusing is consistent with metatarsalgia. Pain with pressure between the metatarsal heads and with shooting or burning into the toes and numbness is consistent with a neuroma. Your doctor will also often notice a click when squeezing the forefoot in the presence of a neuroma.

Determining the exact cause of the pain is not absolutely necessary in order to treat it, but it does help. Pressure relief is the key to achieving pain relief for both metatarsalgia and Morton's neuroma. Metatarsal pads or supports are of significant benefit, as they transfer pressure away from the inflamed painful area and into the midfoot. They can be purchased at your local pharmacy. Cushioned shoes such as sneakers are also of significant benefit. Shoes with hard insoles should be avoided. Heels should also be avoided, since wearing heels puts more pressure on the painful area.

Custom-made orthotics are a higher-priced option but are certainly effective. These can be made by a podiatrist or an orthotist, and these problems are solved by cushioned material with a metatarsal support. Occasionally a well (scooped-out area) beneath the painful spot can also be used to improve pressure relief.

If callusing is present beneath the metatarsal heads, a podiatrist can shave the callus. Maintenance treatment with a pumice stone will also help.

For a painful neuroma, an injection of steroids and anesthetic into the web space may be of benefit by reducing localized inflammation.

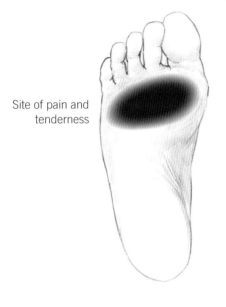

Site of pain and tenderness

(figure 17-32)

In metatarsalgia, the fat pad that cushions the ball of the foot thins out as we get older, leading to compression of the skin between the metatarsal heads and ground contact leading to pain and calluses.

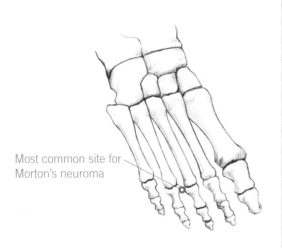

Most common site for Morton's neuroma

(figure 17-33)

The most common location of Morton's neuroma is in the web space between the third and fourth toes.

This injection is both therapeutic and diagnostic. Pain relief following an injection into the web space is consistent with a neuroma. No injection should be given to a patient with pain clearly beneath the metatarsal heads, since an injection beneath the metatarsal heads can lead to plantar fat pad atrophy and worsening of the pain.

If nonoperative treatment does not give relief, surgery may be considered. For pain specifically localized to one or at most two metatarsal heads, a plantar condylectomy can be performed, as described above in the section "Lesser Toe Deformities." The goal of a plantar condylectomy is to remove the plantar aspect of the metatarsal head and thereby reduce pressure beneath it. This is combined with the appropriate procedure to correct the toe deformity, if present. This operation does not work well for diffuse pain beneath the metatarsal heads but is best reserved for localized pain.

If it is determined that the forefoot pain is from a neuroma, surgical excision may be considered. It is important to understand that when the neuroma is resected, the nerve is removed as well. This leaves the adjacent borders of the toes numb. In addition to the standard surgical risks, there is also a risk that the neuroma may recur. The neuroma is approached through the dorsum of the foot. Our preference is to cut the nerve as proximal as possible to keep the nerve stump away from the ball of the foot. We also tie off the nerve stump and bury it in the adjacent muscle. The goal is not only to remove the neuroma but also to reduce the chance of it coming back.

BUNIONETTE DEFORMITY

A **bunionette** is associated with pain and deformity of the fifth toe, associated with prominence of the fifth metatarsal head laterally and drifting of the toe medially (see Figure 17-34). As in the bunion deformity of the great toe, women are more commonly affected and shoes are the

(*figure* 17-34)

Bunionette deformity is a bony prominence at the base of the small toe.

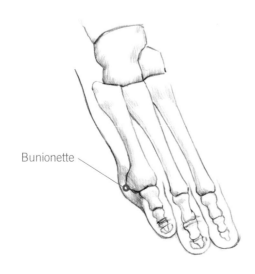

Bunionette

main cause. Underlying factors include the shape of the foot, metatarsal shaft, and metatarsal head.

The most important nonoperative step is purchasing wider, comfortable shoes. Shoe stretching using a ball-and-ring type device can also be helpful.

When nonoperative treatment fails to give sufficient relief, surgical options are available. The main choice is between simple resection of the prominent portion of the fifth metatarsal head laterally or cutting the metatarsal (osteotomy) and shifting the metatarsal head to narrow the foot.

The difference in recuperation and postop protocol is significant. After a simple resection, weight bearing on the full foot in a postop shoe is allowed and a person can usually return to comfortable, wide shoes in approximately three weeks. Following an osteotomy, a period of reduced weight bearing is required and patients will need to use either crutches or a walker for approximately six weeks while the osteotomy is healing. For either procedure, residual discomfort may take three months or more to resolve. This recuperation is longer for patients who have had an osteotomy, and there are also additional surgical risks of having an osteotomy, such as poor healing of the osteotomy. The decision regarding the type of surgery is dependent on the shape of the foot and severity of the deformity.

METATARSOPHALANGEAL SYNOVITIS

Synovitis refers to inflammation of the joint lining. When this occurs in the forefoot, it usually involves the second toe. The pain and swelling are usually present dorsally. The localized inflammation can lead to weakening of the supporting ligaments and drifting of the toe.

The goal of nonoperative treatment is to reduce stress on the inflamed joint. This can be accomplished by using a toe splint and or metatarsal pads. A steroid injection of the inflamed joint can also be considered. This helps to break the cycle of inflammation and can often lead to dramatic improvement. If a second injection is required, we usually like to hold off three to four months between injections.

Surgery is rarely required. The procedure involves *debridement* (cleaning out the debris within the joint) and *synovectomy* (removal of the lining around the joint). In a very few cases, residual deformity of the toe may benefit from realignment.

CORNS

Corns occur between the lesser toes and at the lateral aspect of the fifth toe. These may be very painful and are related to pressure on the skin either from adjacent bony prominences or from a bony prominence and tight shoe that leads to buildup and thickening of the skin (see Figure 17-35a).

Pressure relief will help decrease pain and reduce buildup and thickening of the skin in the area of the corn. Toe caps or spacers may

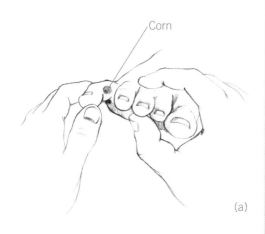

Corn

(a)

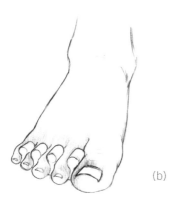

(b)

(figure 17-35)

(a) Corn between fourth and fifth toes.
(b) A toe spacer helps relieve pain and reduce thickening of the skin in the area of the corn.

be used (see Figure 17-35b). Wider, more supple shoes will also help significantly. Regular callus shaving by a podiatrist is also of benefit.

Surgical management involves resection of the underlying bony prominence to relieve pressure on the overlying skin, thereby reducing pain and leading to resolution of the corn.

WARTS

The *Papilloma virus* causes warts by causing a buildup and thickening of the skin. They are usually located on the sole of the foot. Warts may or may not be associated with pain and may occur in both weight-bearing and non-weight-bearing areas (see Figure 17-36). This is in contrast to calluses, which always occur beneath a bony prominence in a weight-bearing area. Shaving a wart also helps to differentiate a wart from a callus. A wart will demonstrate small bleeding areas as it is shaved, while shaving a callus exposes yellowish waxy tissue. Due to the risk of infection and bleeding, shaving should be done by your doctor, not by you!

Use of a salicylic acid patch to burn away the wart is often effective. You should be checked by your podiatrist or primary care physician first to make sure you are dealing with a wart and not a callus, since salicylic acid should not be used on a callus. The salicylic acid patch should be applied once or twice a day, and progress should be followed by your doctor. Shaving warts by a podiatrist is also of benefit, and this can be followed by use of the salicylic acid patch. In order to reduce pressure beneath a plantar wart, cushioned orthotics can be used with a well beneath the affected area.

Warts can be difficult to eradicate. For recalcitrant cases liquid nitrogen or electrocautery (burning with an electric needle) can be used. Another option is simply cutting away or *curetting* the wart (i.e., using a sharp scoop to remove the affected tissue). Laser treatment may also be used to burn away the wart. The greatest concern after ablation with the above measures is painful plantar scarring. Even with the above treatments, there is a risk of recurrence.

NAIL PROBLEMS

Fungus: Toenail infection with fungus, called onychomycosis, is very common. The moist environment inside shoes encourages fungal growth. As the infection progresses over months and years the nails become thickened and irregular (see Figure 17-37). Different types of fungal infections occur, but the most common leads to changes in the nail and nail bed distally, which ultimately leads to separation of the nail from the bed. Fungal involvement of the toenails is often associated with increasing age as well as with systemic conditions such as diabetes. Psoriatic arthritis can also cause toenail abnormalities that can be difficult to distinguish from a fungus infection. Special scrapings of the material under the nail or a culture of the nail may be required to make the proper diagnosis.

Debridement and trimming of the affected nails is required on a regular basis. There isn't any good way to eradicate fungal infection of the

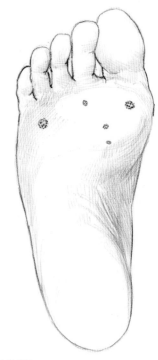

(figure 17-36)

Plantar warts are warts that grow on the sole of the foot.

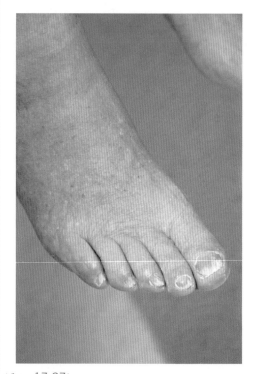

(figure 17-37)

Toenail fungus.

(*figure* 17-38)
(a) Ingrown nail with (b) strip removed.

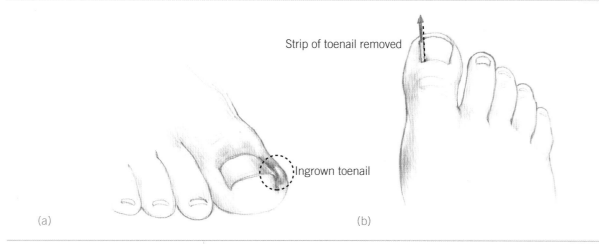

Strip of toenail removed

Ingrown toenail

(a)　　　　　　　　　　　　　　　　　　　(b)

nails. Treatment with local antifungal solutions or drops is rarely successful. For those who are determined to try to eradicate the fungal infection of the toenails, oral antifungal medications can be taken. Unfortunately, an extended course is required, and these oral antifungals may have significant side effects, specifically on liver function. Some of these drugs can adversely interact with other prescription medications. Considering this, we personally do not prescribe these medications but leave this decision to the discretion of the primary care physician, who can make the decision after weighing the potential benefits versus the risks. Despite treatment, recurrence of the infection may occur.

Ingrown nails: An infection may develop at the border of the nail due to impingement and cutting in of the nail into the soft tissues. This area becomes very painful, red, sometimes swollen, and may drain pus. The great toenail is the most commonly affected, although the lesser toenails may occasionally be involved.

Causative factors include inappropriate cutting of the nails and tight shoes. It is important to cut the nails straight across. By trimming a nail down into the corner, a spike may be left that cuts into the soft tissues, initiating the infection.

Once this problem develops, medical care should be sought as soon as possible. A localized infection can progress, and this needs to be prevented. This is especially true in patients with diabetes or peripheral vascular disease. We find that removing a strip of nail along the affected side and cleaning out the pus under local anesthesia in the office are the best steps to achieve quick resolution of the infection (see Figure 17-38). Following this, warm soaks may be performed twice daily, and the affected area dressed with a topical antibacterial cream or ointment. Your physician will likely have a preference. Our preference is MUPIROCIN (BACTROBAN), but such preparations as bacitracin or triple antibiotic ointment also work well. We also use a short course of oral antibiotics. An open-toed postop shoe is used initially following the procedure to reduce pressure in the affected area. Cutting away the toe box of an older shoe to relieve pressure also works.

For an ingrown nail that keeps returning despite shoe modification and appropriate cutting of the nail, surgical ablation of a portion of the nail can be considered. This is usually done in the operating room and requires complete excision of the nail matrix (from which the nail grows) on the problematic side.

COMMON CONDITIONS OF THE MIDFOOT

MIDFOOT ARTHRITIS AND COLLAPSE

Arthritis of the midfoot causes pain and spurring and ultimately joint destruction and collapse of the arch of the foot. Pain is worst with walking, standing, or activity. Spurring usually occurs over the top of the midfoot, and pressure from shoes in this area causes local irritation and pain. As midfoot arthritis progresses, the architecture of the foot changes, and arch collapse gradually occurs. Arch collapse is associated with instability across the midfoot, significant pain, and loss of push-off strength. With severe midfoot collapse, the midfoot bones may become prominent at the bottom of the midfoot, causing additional pressure and pain in this area.

In order to determine the best treatment for midfoot arthritis, understand that the pain associated with midfoot arthritis has two main causes. First, pain can be directly related to the arthritic joints and stress across these joints. Second, pain can come from pressure on arthritic spurs which develop as the arthritis progresses or from pressure on bony prominences associated with arch collapse. Pain is usually a combination of these two factors, but one factor may play a more important role in any one person. Understanding these issues helps guide treatment.

Pain related to stress across the arthritic joints can be treated nonsurgically with stiff-soled shoes or orthotics that help to reduce stress across the midfoot. This is usually the first step in an effort to achieve pain relief. An injection of the painful midfoot joints with steroids and local anesthetic can also help to relieve pain and inflammation. However, the midfoot joints can be difficult to inject, especially if they are severely arthritic with significant narrowing and large spurs. An injection would not be expected to help pain related to pressure on spurs or bony prominences. For those cases where pain is directly related to pressure over a spur, shoe modification may be of benefit. Shoes made of a supple material help, and make sure there is no pressure caused by seams. For localized pain related to a spur directly on the top of the midfoot, patients often have success by modifying their shoe-lacing technique. This is a simple step, but running the laces up the sides rather than crossing them directly over the spur can help. For pain related to a plantar bony prominence from midfoot collapse, soft, cushioned orthotics with a well beneath the prominence can be of benefit. These are often used with custom shoes.

Surgery can be considered if patients do not respond to conservative measures. For patients with pain related to the arthritis, a fusion of the arthritic joints is usually of benefit. This is a significant undertaking. The operation requires removal of all the arthritic bone and cartilage, realignment of the midfoot, and fixation with multiple screws. The goal is to have all the bones grow together into one solid block of bone. If there is no motion across an arthritic joint, pain relief can be expected. Occasionally extra bone (bone graft) is required. Following a midfoot fusion, patients are not allowed to bear weight on the affected foot and therefore require crutches or a walker for approximately six to eight weeks. Even when weight bearing is eventually allowed, the foot needs to be protected up until 2½ to 3 months after surgery. Full recuperation can easily take six months or more from the time of surgery. Physical therapy is often required. In a limited number of patients with pain directly related to a prominent spur, a spur resection can be performed. This will relieve pain related to pressure on the spur but not due to underlying arthritis. The main reason for choosing this option is that recuperation is comparatively quick. Again, this should only be done if the painful symptoms are those of pressure-related pain over a spur and not for more diffuse arthritic pain.

GANGLION CYSTS

A ganglion cyst is a fluid-filled sac that emanates from a joint or a tendon sheath. A ganglion cyst may be 1, 2, or 3 cm in diameter. Ganglion cysts become problematic when they are located over the top of the midfoot or the top and side of the mid- and hindfoot. In these locations they are easily irritated by shoes. Ganglion cysts can also occur about the ankle but are often less of a problem in this area. If you have a mass that you think may be a ganglion cyst, it is always worth having your physician check it out. Although much less common, tumors both benign and malignant may initially have a similar appearance.

Shoe modification is the simplest step to achieve some relief of discomfort from pressure against a ganglion cyst. Make sure that shoes are of a supple material, and there are no sharp borders or seams pushing on the cyst. For cysts that continue to be problematic, an aspiration can be performed by your physician. A needle is used to suck out the thick gelatinous fluid. The wall of the cyst can also be scratched with the tip of the needle in order to encourage the collapsed cyst to scar down and reduce the chance of recurrence. A steroid injection into the cyst cavity may also be of some benefit in reducing localized inflammation and recurrence. Unfortunately, despite the above steps there is a high incidence of recurrence (upward of 50%) following aspiration.

Surgical excision can be considered if the cyst recurs following aspiration. It is important to remove the entire cyst wall and tie off the base of the cyst. Even with surgical excision the ganglion cyst may recur, and the whole process begins again.

COMMON CONDITIONS OF THE HINDFOOT AND ANKLE
POSTERIOR TIBIAL TENDONITIS AND DYSFUNCTION (ADULT-ACQUIRED FLATFOOT)

The posterior tibial tendon runs along the inner aspect of the ankle behind the bony prominence called the *medial malleolus*. The tendon eventually inserts into the *navicular* bone. It performs a very important function, supporting the arch and hindfoot. If the posterior tibial tendon fails, the arch collapses, the hindfoot collapses, the foot rotates outward, and a flat foot develops (see Figure 17-16, on page 352).

Tendonitis refers to inflammation about the tendon. The spectrum of posterior tibial tendonitis runs from mild transient inflammation, to more severe inflammation associated with tendon degeneration, and to severe inflammation with a partial or complete tear of the tendon. Deformity related to dysfunction is progressive. Pain associated with posterior tibial tendonitis and dysfunction can take a number of forms. In the earlier stages of posterior tibial tendonitis patients experience pain and swelling along the course of the tendon. Patients often notice some fullness just behind the ankle. The pain can be quite severe and disabling. Pain is usually worse with activity, as well as standing and walking. As the condition deteriorates and deformity appears, the location of the pain may shift. As the foot rotates outward and the arch and hindfoot collapse, pain will appear over the head of the talus, which becomes prominent at the inside of the foot. Pain also occurs at the outside of the hindfoot related to overload in this area and impingement between the *calcaneus* (heel bone) and the *fibula* (small bone at the side of the ankle.) With a long-standing deformity, arthritis will develop, and the patient will be left with a severe deformity and arthritic pain. The pain associated with the tendon itself often has resolved by this stage.

Ambulation is affected by all stages of posterior tibial tendonitis and dysfunction. Push-off strength is reduced, and a limp is common. The altered gait and hindfoot deformity may contribute to knee pain, especially at the lateral side of the knee joint related to overload as the abnormal forces are transmitted up the leg. Flatfoot related to posterior tibial tendon dysfunction needs to be differentiated from flat foot related to midfoot arthritis as the location of the deformity affects the treatment. Differentiating between these two conditions can be accomplished by exam of the foot while standing along with X-rays, preferably done with the patient standing. Flatfoot associated with posterior tibial tendon dysfunction occurs with collapse through the hindfoot, while flatfoot associated with midfoot arthritis occurs with collapse through the midfoot.

Nonsurgical treatment of an acutely inflamed posterior tibial tendon is aimed at reducing stress on the tendon and thereby reducing inflammation. As an immediate treatment for an acute episode of pain of only a few weeks duration, a CamWalker (removable cast) can be used. For longer-term pain of one to two months or more, we prefer to send our patients for an orthosis to support the foot and reduce stress on the tendon. A simple off-the-shelf arch support may be used as a brief temporary measure while awaiting a custom orthosis. A shoe maker can also rapidly apply a medial heel wedge, again to reduce stress on the tendon. A wide variety of orthoses exist for posterior tibial tendon dysfunction. Simple plantar orthotics with medial posting can be used when the problem is mainly pain with or without a mild deformity. As the deformity increases, the importance of support extending up the foot or leg also increases. For these cases a hinged supramalleolar orthosis is our preference. These are also custom-molded and include not only a foot plate but also two struts extending up on either side of the ankle for improved support. Finally, a molded ankle foot orthosis (MAFO) can be considered for very severe cases (see Figure 17-39). This is a large brace which extends up the calf, and it gives the most support of the listed orthoses. Although it may significantly decrease pain, its height and the fact that it prevents ankle motion make it problematic for some patients. Occasionally patients will complain of knee, back, or hip pain related to use of the MAFO.

Nonsteroidal anti-inflammatory drugs (NSAIDs) may be used to decrease inflammation and pain associated with all stages of posterior tibial tendonitis, dysfunction, and the subsequent arthritis. Steroid injections of the tendon sheath should not be performed as they may lead to further weakening of the tendon. On the other hand, steroid injections of arthritic joints related to severe progressive posterior tibial tendon dysfunction and deformity might be of benefit.

Conservative measures often work, but in those cases of continued pain and progressive deformity surgery is an option. For simple tendonitis, cleaning out the tendon sheath may be considered. Unfortunately, there are few cases that fall into this category, as most of the mild cases resolve with conservative management. Those patients that require surgery usually fall into a more severe category and require a more significant procedure. There are two main options for surgical reconstruction. If the tendon is dysfunctional and hindfoot collapse is present but not severe, a tendon reconstruction using a flexor digitorum longus transfer can be considered, supported by a bony procedure. This maintains mobility of the hindfoot. If the patient has severe collapse, stiffness, and arthritis a *triple arthrodesis* (fusion of three joints) with possible bone graft is appropriate. In this second case all motion across the arthritic joints is eliminated. Both these procedures are considered major surgery. We often keep our patients in the hospital from two to five days following either procedure, with the longer stay required for the triple arthrodesis. Following either type of surgery the patient will need to ambulate with crutches or a walker. The patient is non-weight bearing for six to eight weeks postop with protection for three to four months postop depending on healing. A course of physical therapy is usually required. Full recuperation after either procedure takes six to eight months or more. The goal of either procedure cannot be a normal foot but a foot that is less painful and more functional.

ANKLE ARTHRITIS

Arthritis of the ankle causes pain with weight-bearing activities. Standing or walking may cause pain, and patients often complain of worse pain when walking on stairs. Pain is often localized to a horizontal band across the front of the ankle. Early ankle arthritis is associated with spurs at the front of the ankle joint. As the arthritic process progresses, cartilage wear progresses, the joint space is lost, and the ankle becomes stiff. Severe ankle

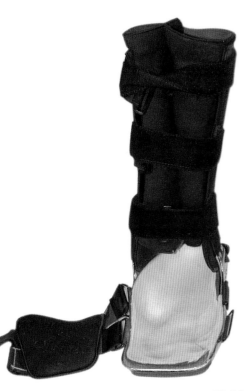

(figure 17-39)

The molded ankle foot orthosis (MAFO).

arthritis does not have to be associated with a significant deformity, but deformities may occur.

Nonsurgical treatment might include using a molded ankle foot orthosis to reduce stress across an arthritic ankle joint. This plastic brace extends from the sole of the foot to the calf. This significantly limits ankle motion and pain. The height of this brace may be troublesome to some, and occasionally, use of the brace may contribute to knee, back, or hip pain. Lesser braces or supports are of little value in truly reducing stress across the arthritic ankle joint, although we have had an occasional patient who has liked boots that come to the midcalf and thereby reduce stress on the ankle. Injections of the ankle joint with steroid often will help relieve pain and inflammation. Nonsteroidal anti-inflammatory drugs may also be of benefit.

Two surgical options exist for patients with severe ankle arthritis unresponsive to conservative treatment. A fusion of the ankle joint is the gold standard and has the most certain outcome. With an ankle fusion, the arthritic cartilage and bone are removed and the tibia and talus are grown together, thereby eliminating all motion across the ankle joint and reducing pain. Recently, ankle replacement has come into consideration. The main benefit of an ankle replacement over an ankle fusion is maintenance of motion across the ankle joint. Long-term concerns are present with either procedure. Following an ankle fusion stresses are transmitted to the adjoining joints of the midfoot and hindfoot. These joints may become arthritic over the course of five to ten years. If there is underlying arthritis of the adjacent joints, this progression may be more rapid. Following an ankle replacement, the main long-term concern is regarding loosening of the prosthesis and collapse. The decision between these two procedures should be carefully weighed. We still consider an ankle fusion to be the procedure of choice in many patients with severe ankle arthritis. Although knee replacement surgery has an excellent track record, the long-term outcome following ankle replacement surgery is less certain. Considering this, the average age for ankle replacement surgery is 60. Ankle replacement is best avoided in manual laborers and obese persons, as the additional stress across the prosthesis will increase the risk of failure. Ankle replacement should also be avoided in patients with a significant ankle or hindfoot deformity. On the other hand, an ankle fusion could be used in any of these cases. Either procedure requires three to five days in the hospital. Following either procedure crutches or a walker will initially be required for non-weight-bearing ambulation. Following a fusion, non-weight bearing is required for approximately two months with protection for three to four months postoperatively while the fusion heals. Following an ankle replacement, non-weight bearing is required for approximately six weeks although range-of-motion exercises may be started early on. Advancing weight bearing following total ankle replacement is dependent

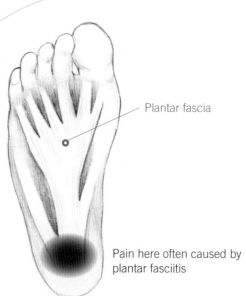

Plantar fascia

Pain here often caused by plantar fasciitis

(*figure* 17-40)

The plantar fascia is a fibrous band of tissue that runs from the heel along the bottom of the foot and inserts at the bases of the toes. Plantar fasciitis is a common cause of heel pain and is not necessarily associated with a heel spur.

(figure 17-41)
Plantar fascia stretches.

on bony ingrowth to the prosthesis. Physical therapy is required in either case. Full recuperation after either procedure may take six to eight months or more.

HEEL PAIN AND PLANTAR FASCIITIS

Plantar fasciitis is the most common cause of plantar heel pain. The plantar fascia is a fibrous band of tissue that runs from the plantar aspect of the heel along the bottom of the foot and inserts at the bases of the toes (see Figure 17-40). Pain often occurs first thing in the morning and then tends to improve as the plantar fascia stretches out. Pain also occurs after getting up from a seated position and becomes worse as the day progresses. Patients may be quite tight and lack the ability to turn up the foot or toes. Improving flexibility is the mainstay of treatment. A heel spur may or may not be visible on X-rays of the foot and is immaterial to the presence of plantar fasciitis. We always obtain X-rays of both heels, and it is often quite a surprise to our patients that heel spurs are present in both heels but only one heel is painful. Many patients with plantar fasciitis do not have heel spurs. We emphasize that the plantar fascia originates on the calcaneus (heel bone) below and behind the heel spur and that it is the plantar fascia and not the heel spur that causes the pain.

A regular stretching program is key to achieving pain relief. Stretching sessions should be performed three times a day, and each of the three exercises should be performed three times per session and held for 30 seconds (see Figure 17-41). Cushioned inserts for the heels are also of benefit. Gel heel pads cushion the impact of ambulation and also raise up the heels, reducing stress on the plantar fascia. These should be worn on both sides. Dorsiflexion night splints are quite helpful, especially in those patients with morning pain. The night splint holds the foot up at night and prevents the morning tightness that causes pain. The night splint may take some getting used to but does have a cumulative effect. With anywhere from a few days to a few weeks of use, patients often notice a significant reduction in pain when combined with stretches and cushioned heel inserts. NSAIDs can also be of benefit (see the section "NSAIDs and Tylenol," below). Some patients also require formal physical therapy. In addition to stretches, anti-inflammatory modalities can be used. Well-cushioned orthotics can also be of benefit. Occasionally injections of the plantar fascia with steroids may be used. We usually reserve this for difficult cases in which the plantar fasciitis does not respond to the above steps, since injection of the plantar fascia may lead to rupture with additional complications.

Surgical treatment of plantar fasciitis is reserved for only the most recalcitrant cases and is rarely if ever required. The plantar fascia performs an important function—supporting the arch—and this needs to be kept in mind. Complications of surgery may occur, including nerve laceration associated with endoscopic release and the late complication of arch collapse.

ACHILLES TENDONITIS AND TENDINOSIS

Inflammation along the Achilles tendon (tendonitis) often starts with mild pain and swelling but is often progressive (see Figure 17-42). In later stages degeneration and nodularity of the tendon develop (tendinosis). Pain can occur at the insertion of the Achilles on the heel bone (calcaneus) or higher up at the level of the ankle. There is often an initiating factor such as heavy activity or sports injury or strain, but this is not always the case. Some patients develop pain without any inciting factor. As the condition progresses, pain can occur even with minor activity or at rest. Achilles tendonitis is often associated with calf tightness and a loss of dorsiflexion.

The nonsurgical treatment protocol is very similar to that outlined above for plantar fasciitis. Most cases respond to nonoperative treatment. A regular stretching program is the mainstay of therapy. Heel inserts should be used to reduce stress on the Achilles tendon and should be worn on both sides. At times we have ordered shoes with bilateral heel lifts for men. Women often find that a shoe with a heel is more comfortable. NSAIDs can help especially in the acute inflammatory period. Orthotics can also be of benefit. We never inject steroids along the Achilles tendon since this increases the risk of rupture.

Surgery is occasionally required when a patient does not respond to the above steps. The tendon sheath can be cleaned up with removal of inflamed tissue for those cases in which inflammation surrounds the tendon. When the Achilles tendon is degenerative with nodularity and thickening, the tendon is opened and the degenerative tissue cut away. In these cases a reconstruction of the Achilles tendon with another tendon or a flap of the Achilles itself may be required. The type of procedure that is required can usually be determined by an MRI scan which will show the extent of degeneration within the tendon itself. The postoperative recuperation will depend on the type of surgery that is required, but can take four to six months or more.

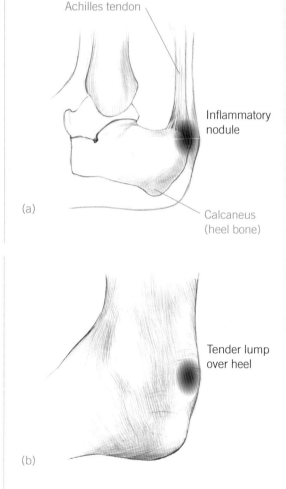

(a)

Achilles tendon

Inflammatory nodule

Calcaneus (heel bone)

(b)

Tender lump over heel

(*figure* 17-42)

(a) Achilles tendinosis is associated with inflammatory nodules and pain of the large tendon in back of the ankle. (b) A tender lump can be felt on the back of the heel.

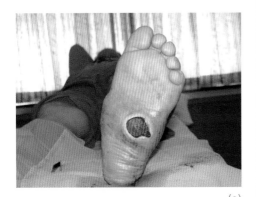

(a)

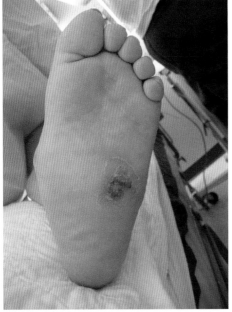

(b)

(*figure* 17-43)

(a) Diabetic foot wound; (b) healed wound.

ANKLE SPRAINS

A sprain is an injury to the ligaments around a joint when the joint is put through excessive motion. You may have twisted your ankle while running or hurt your ankle while skiing. Although most ankle sprains are associated with transient pain and swelling and can be treated initially with elevation, ice packs, anti-inflammatory drugs, and compression dressings, some ankle sprains can be quite serious and require a cast or surgery. A painful "pop" associated with sudden severe swelling and inability to walk after twisting an ankle may indicate a more severe type of sprain. X-rays may sometimes be ordered to make sure no bones are broken. Mild sprains usually heal without incident, but complications can occur following more severe sprains. Nerve injury can cause pain and numbness. Sometimes pain persists within the ankle joint and around the joint due to tearing or inflammation of the ligaments and tendons. Rarely, spasm of the blood vessels in the injured area can cause reflex sympathetic dystrophy (RSD), a condition that leads to wasting of the tissue and bone as well as persistent pain. Chronic deformity of the ankle and foot can be a result, and special therapy and pain medication are required.

ANKLE FRACTURES

The ankle joint plays an important role in our ability to walk and bear our weight. If a bone in the ankle is broken and the surfaces of the joint do not line up properly, serious long-term consequences, such as severe arthritis, can ensue. Most ankle fractures will require a cast, but if bones on both sides of the ankle are broken or if the fracture is associated with dislocation of the ankle, surgery will likely be necessary. Complications following an ankle fracture can include instability and deformity of the ankle, nerve injury, arthritis, and RSD.

MEDICAL CONDITIONS THAT AFFECT THE FOOT AND ANKLE

DIABETES MELLITUS

Diabetes can have a profound effect on the feet and ankles. Prevention is the best course of action, so we will reinforce the importance of meticulous management of your blood glucose if you are a diabetic. Some diabetic foot problems are caused by problems in the circulation to the legs and feet, but most are caused by damage to the nerves called peripheral neuropathy perhaps compounded by disease in the blood vessels. The peripheral nerve damage leads to loss of normal sensation to the feet. As a result, the affected person does not appreciate when the skin is breaking down. Repeated injury can lead to further breakdown, ultimately resulting in the formation of a diabetic foot ulcer (see Figure 17-43). Infection of the ulcer and often the bone can ensue, leading to serious consequences such as amputation of toes or feet. A significant number of these amputations could be avoided with scrupulous foot care.

Diabetic patients should examine their feet daily and sometimes two or three times a day if they are at risk and spend a lot of time on their feet. Since diabetic patients do not perspire normally, many have dry skin which is prone to cracking and ulceration. They should apply moisturizing cream or Vaseline to their feet on a daily basis. Well-fitted footwear is extremely important in those with peripheral neuropathy. Shoes should be appropriately and carefully sized and should be of a supple material. Patients who lack protective sensation also benefit from Plastizote inserts to relieve pressure against the skin (see Figures 17-44 and 17-45). The Plastizote compresses before the skin compresses, thus protecting the skin from developing ulcers. Many communities and hospitals now have wound care clinics or diabetic foot care clinics where an orthotist provides inserts that are customized for each patient.

Another complication that may affect diabetic patients is called a Charcot's joint (see Figure 17-46). Nerve damage causes the loss of normal sensation in the foot and ankle that leads to multiple fractures in the ankle, which in turn leads to progressive deformity and damage to the ankle joint. In the early stages of development of a Charcot's joint, a cast may be necessary and weigh bearing is avoided. In advanced stages, surgery may be required.

RHEUMATOID ARTHRITIS

Most patients with rheumatoid arthritis (RA) have foot problems. In nearly 20% of patients with rheumatoid arthritis, foot and ankle problems are what bring them to the doctor. The forefoot is the site most commonly affected. The fat pad that normally cushions the ball of the foot is pushed away. As a result, there is constant pressure over the heads of the metatarsal bones, causing pain in the forefoot. Large, painful calluses on the sole of the foot are common. Severe bunions and hammertoes are commonly seen. Special shoes with a wide toe box and extra depth may be helpful. Molded shoes, Plastizote shoes, and arch supports may be recommended. Pressure can be kept off the heads of the metatarsal bones with a *metatarsal bar* or a full-length cushion insert. In some cases, steroid injections may be required to treat acutely inflamed areas. In special cases, surgery is necessary. The most common procedure involves resection of the heads of the metatarsal bones and fusion of the big toe joint.

GOUT

Gout refers to severe inflammation of one or more joints caused by uric acid crystals. An acute gout attack can come on over a few hours and become progressively more painful. The joint at the base of the great toe is most commonly involved and can be red, swollen, warm, and extremely painful. Chapter 16 discusses the medical evaluation and management of gout. In most cases, the primary care physician will treat gout. Surgical treatment is seldom required except in advanced cases where lack of treatment has caused chronic joint destruction or large deposits (see Figure 17-47). With improvements in medical treatment, progression to this stage seldom occurs these days.

(figure 17-44)

Plastizote (arrowhead) is a soft material that can be inserted into the shoe to relieve pressure beneath an ulcer.

Wide toe box

Extra depth

(figure 17-45)

Extra wide and extra depth diabetic shoes are recommended to avoid pressure against toes.

(*figure* 17-46)

In Charcot's joint, diabetes may lead to loss of protective sensation in the foot resulting in small fractures and collapse of the midfoot.

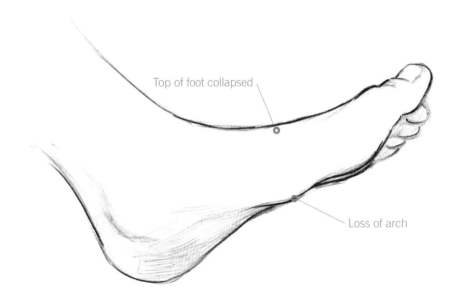

Top of foot collapsed

Loss of arch

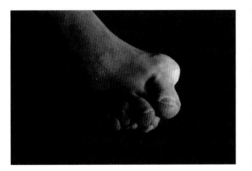

(*figure* 17-47)

This large bump of the base of the big toe is a tophus, a large deposit of uric acid due to many years of untreated gout. With modern medical treatment, a tophus is seldom seen anymore.

REVIEW OF TREATMENT OPTIONS

ORTHOTICS AND CUSTOM SHOES

Orthotics are appliances that help compensate for certain orthopedic problems. A custom orthotic is often a good option for many foot and ankle problems. These help to reorient the deformed foot and ankle and normalize stresses. When a problem is pressure-related, orthotics can be used to transfer pressure from one area to another, thereby reducing pressure beneath a bony prominence or painful neuroma. Orthotics may be full length or span a portion of the foot. There are many different materials that can be used. In patients with pressure-related pain, a soft, cushioned material is preferred. In diabetics for whom pressure relief and protection is key, a foam-cushioned orthotic is a necessity. Stiffer orthotics of leather, plastic, cork, or laminate may be used when the goal is to reorient the foot rather than simply relieve pressure. A podiatrist or orthotist can make orthotics. Extradepth, extrawidth shoes are of significant benefit to accommodate many foot deformities. Not only do extradepth shoes accommodate patients with hammertoe or claw toe deformities, but they also allow use of an orthotic. If one tries to use a thick, cushioned orthotic in a shoe with inadequate depth, the top of the foot and toes will be pushed up into the toe box, causing irritation and pain. In order to avoid problems like this, always bring your shoes with you when you are fitted for your orthotics. Show your shoes to your podiatrist or orthotist, so that you are all thinking along the same line.

STEROID INJECTIONS

A steroid injection into a joint can be of significant benefit in relieving pain and inflammation. Most patients will get some pain relief. The steroid usually takes a few days to take effect, and pain relief may last anywhere from a few weeks to a few months. The extent of pain relief is in part based on the severity of the underlying problem, and there are some patients that do not get any relief at all. We usually combine the steroid with a local anesthetic. The extent of the immediate relief from the local anesthetic is often a good indicator of pain relief from the steroid once it begins to act in a few days. It is important to note that when the local anesthetic wears off in a few hours after the injection, more pain may be experienced. This is in part related to joint distension, and for this reason we try to limit the volume that we inject in the joints of the foot and ankle. In order to understand this effect in the foot and ankle, consider the size of the joints involved. A small 1 cc injection in the joint of the great toe causes more distension than a few cc of fluid injected into the knee joint and therefore causes more distension-related pain. Ice, anti-inflammatory drugs, or Tylenol will often help with this temporary increase in pain. Many patients will be experiencing significant pain relief from the local anesthetic which masks the pain. We always tell our patients not to overdo their activity in the first few hours after an injection with steroid and local anesthetic just because it temporarily feels so much better.

There are risks from steroid injections. In addition to the standard risks of infection and allergy, the steroid may cause weakening of the ligamentous restraints of a joint and thinning of the overlying skin with loss of pigmentation. Although there are no hard and fast rules regarding the number of steroid injections that can be used, the general opinion is that it is best to limit the number and frequency of steroid injections. We also try to avoid injecting in and about tendons, since this may contribute to weakening and rupture.

NSAIDs AND TYLENOL

Nonsteroidal anti-inflammatory drugs work to reduce inflammation and pain as well as reduce fever. In the foot and ankle they are effectively used to treat arthritis and tendonitis along with other causes of pain and inflammation reviewed in this chapter. There are many NSAIDs. Over-the-counter anti-inflammatories, obtained without a prescription, include MOTRIN, ADVIL, and ALEVE. Note that Motrin and Advil are both the generic IBUPROFEN. Many prescription NSAIDs exist, including RELAFEN, DAYPRO, NAPROSYN, VOLTAREN, and INDOMETHACIN. The latest generation of prescription NSAIDs includes BEXTRA, VIOXX, MOBIC, and CELEBREX. Different people respond to different NSAIDs. It may take a few tries to find an anti-inflammatory which is right for you.

The main concern with use of NSAIDs is gastrointestinal side effects, such as gastritis or ulcer formation. With extended use, liver and kidney side effects are also a concern, and blood work is required. Other concerns include the effects of NSAIDs on blood pressure and fluid retention. Generally, these drugs are avoided in persons with congestive heart failure. Infrequently, patients may have an allergy to anti-inflammatory drugs. Side effects may be more severe in the older population. These issues should be discussed with your prescribing physician and/or your primary physician.

Taking NSAIDs with food can reduce the gastrointestinal side effects. When the gastrointestinal side effects are a greater concern, such as with a history of gastritis, ulcers, or reflux, consideration should be given to using Bextra, Vioxx, or Celebrex. These NSAIDs are much less likely to cause gastrointestinal side effects. In those patients who are unable to take NSAIDs, acetaminophen (Tylenol) can be used. Tylenol will help reduce pain, but does not reduce the underlying inflammation. The dose of acetaminophen should be limited to no more than 4 grams per day. The main risk of extended use of Tylenol is its effect on the liver, especially in heavy drinkers. Patients with underlying liver problems will be limited in their ability to use Tylenol. Periodic blood work may be done to check liver function.

SURGICAL CONSIDERATIONS AND RISKS

Surgical options can only be considered if the risks of surgery are clearly understood. As surgeons we know the risks that are involved with any procedure, even a minor one, and we feel it is important to convey this to you. The standard risks of surgery are usually described as the risk of anesthesia, risk of infection, and risk of nerve and blood vessel injury. Additional risks include the risk that the operation could fail or that the patient's pain may not be relieved by the operation or could even be worse. Risks of foot and ankle surgery are significantly increased in patients with peripheral vascular disease and/or diabetes. Smoking also significantly increases the risks of surgery. All these conditions may lead to delayed soft tissue and bony healing, as well as increased risk of infection. At times these conditions entirely prevent any surgical intervention. Patients on prednisone, commonly used to treat rheumatoid arthritis, are also at increased risk of poor wound healing. If there is a concern regarding possible peripheral vascular disease, vascular studies or a consultation with a vascular surgeon may be required before your procedure.

Patients with medical issues usually require a medical evaluation in preparation for surgery. No one likes to go into surgery, thinking the worst, and it is a common feeling among patients that "those bad things are not going to happen to me." The reason to do any operation is that the potential benefits outweigh the risks. It is important to discuss the planned operation with your surgeon in detail, so you understand just what will be done, the expected recuperation, and risks of surgery. Earlier we stated that during the course of a normal day the feet and ankles take an inordinate amount of stress and strain. Not only does this apply to the underlying problems of the foot and ankle, but also to

17

1. Which operation is being planned and why?
2. What are the risks of surgery?
3. What type of anesthesia is required?
4. How long do I have to stay in the hospital?
5. How long do I have to use crutches or a walker following surgery?
6. Am I allowed to put pressure on my foot after the operation?
7. Will I be in a cast, splint, or other protective device?
8. How long do I have to keep my foot elevated?
9. Do I need a wheelchair after the operation?
10. How long do I have to stay out of work and/or stay home following surgery? (Also check with your job regarding temporary disability if necessary.)
11. How long is the expected recuperation? (This is a very important question and you want a realistic answer, so you know what is in store for you.)
12. Will I require physical therapy?
13. When can I expect to be able to increase my activity or return to sports?
14. What are my nonsurgical options?

Many of these questions will likely be answered by your surgeon whether you ask them or not. Run through the list yourself, and if you do not know the answer, make sure you ask the question. A complete understanding of all the issues surrounding your surgery will improve your satisfaction with the entire process and improve your outcome.

the recuperation from any surgical procedure on the foot and ankle, no matter how small. Full recuperation following a simple spur resection or excision of a ganglion cyst may take two to three months or more. Recuperation following a bunionectomy may take four to six months or more. Recuperation following a hindfoot or ankle fusion may take eight to eight months or more. Even a year or more after a procedure a patient will sometimes say that the foot aches when the weather changes or when the outside environment is wet or cold. All this must be understood when committing to any procedure.

A majority of the procedures for the foot and ankle are designed to make the problem better but not to make the foot or ankle normal. Once a deformity has developed, achieving a completely normal foot or ankle through surgery is usually impossible. A good example is a hindfoot fusion, as discussed in the section "Posterior Tibial Tendonitis and Dysfunction," above. With this operation, the deformity is corrected, but now the hindfoot is stiff. This is clearly not a normal foot but one that is most likely less painful. The box "Questions to Ask Your Surgeon" covers the questions that may be of benefit to you in a general way and may be applied not only to foot and ankle procedures but to other procedures as well. When considering a procedure, we feel that is important to have a general understanding of the answers to all these questions, and that way you will be able to make a decision that is right for you.

■

17

WHAT YOU NEED TO KNOW

■ Your bones, muscles, and nerves play a vital and interactive role in your ability to perform purposeful movement. Your skeleton, the bony framework of your body, is designed to protect your internal organs. However, the movement of your bones allows you to walk, talk, work, and interact with other people in your environment. Your nerves and muscles provide the messages and motor power that your bones need to perform your daily functions.

■ Problems that arise with your muscles, bones, and nerves as you get older may be related to a predisposition that you inherited from your parents but, more often than not, are related to the problems that occur with long use. Wear and tear with age may take its toll on your musculoskeletal system. Proper nutrition, exercise, and maintenance of good body weight can help retard or reduce the severity of any problems.

■ Disorders of the bones, joints, and muscles can be classified into the grid of the five Ds. Although some problems may overlap into other categories, the grid serves as a useful method for understanding these disorders. The five Ds include defects in metabolism, deficiencies of vital substances, deviations from normal healthy responses, disturbances of normal function, and deterioration of health related to age.

■ The studies used to evaluate problems in the bones, joints, muscles, and nerves include X-ray, bone scan, CT scan, MRI scan, and bone densitometry. Each imaging study has benefits and limitations, as well as significantly different costs. Your doctor decides which study is most appropriate based on your symptoms and physical examination.

■ The four major categories of treatment for musculoskeletal disorders include rest and immobilization, exercise and strengthening, medications, and surgery. Each has advantages and disadvantages. The decision as to which treatment or combination of treatment is based on the unique circumstances of the patient as well as the benefits and risks of the various therapies.

■ The six categories of orthopedic surgery include incision and debridement, repair of tendons and bones, release of entrapped structures, realignment of crooked bones, joint reconstruction, and joint fusion. Depending on the situation, one or more of these surgical procedures may be applied in the treatment of a patient.

■ Joint replacement surgery is an exciting and evolving field as new surgical techniques are explored and new devices are invented. Although hip and knee replacements are the most frequent joint replacement operations, almost any joint in the body can be replaced. Many people's lives have been markedly improved as pain is relieved and function restored.

■ If confronted with the possibility of orthopedic surgery, learn as much as you can about the procedure and discuss the benefits, risks, and options with your orthopedic surgeon. You will need to see your primary care physician before surgery to make sure that you are medically fit for the operation.

■ Foot problems are very common as we get older. After the age of 65, nearly 75% of us will experience problems with our feet.

■ The foot can be affected by such medical conditions as osteoarthritis, rheumatoid arthritis, gout, and diabetes. Proper care of the feet may require the collaboration of your primary care doctor, a podiatrist, and, possibly, an orthopedic surgeon.

■ If you have diabetes, meticulous foot care is essential. Both you and your doctor should regularly inspect your feet.

■ Diseases of the skin, nerves, and blood vessels may affect the feet and ankles. When you have your physical examination, make sure you remove your shoes and socks so that your doctor can do a thorough examination of your feet.

FOR MORE INFORMATION

▶ Your Orthopedic Connection
Web: www.orthoinfo.aaos.org
A service of the American Academy of Orthopaedic Surgeons.

▶ Your Foot Connection
Web: www.orthoinfo.aaos.org
A service of the American Academy of Orthopaedic Surgeons.

▶ National Institute of Arthritis and Musculoskeletal and Skin Diseases
Information Clearinghouse
National Institutes of Health
One AMS Circle
Bethesda, MD 20892
877-22-NIAMS (toll free)
301-495-4484
TTY: 301-565-2966
Fax: 301-718-6366
E-mail: niamsinfo@mail.nih.gov
If sending e-mail, include your mailing address and telephone number.

▶ American Podiatric Medical Association
9312 Old Georgetown Road
Bethesda, MD 20814
800-366-8227; 301-571-9200
Fax: 301-530-2752
E-mail: askapma@apma.org
Web: www.apma.org

▶ NIDDK Clearinghouses Publications Catalog
5 Information Way
Bethesda, MD 20892
800-860-8747; 301-654-3810
Fax: 301-907-8906
E-mail: catalog@niddk.nih.gov
Has available the publication "Prevent Diabetes Problems: Keep Your Feet and Skin Healthy," in English (DM-205) or Spanish (DM-219).

I'm saving that rocker for the day when I feel as old as I really am.

—*Dwight D. Eisenhower*

THE AUTHOR

18 *Ashvin L. Patel*

ASHVIN PATEL, MD, is an orthopedic spine surgeon in Sarasota, Florida. He is a graduate of Tufts University in Massachusetts where he received both his undergraduate and medical education. He completed his surgical internship and orthopedic residency at Montefiore Hospital and the Albert Einstein School of Medicine in Bronx, New York. Dr. Patel did a spinal fellowship at the Lakewood Orthopedic Clinic in Colorado.

Dr. Patel has written numerous articles and chapters and lectured extensively on disorders of the spine. He enjoys teaching and has been a preceptor to medical, nursing, and physician assistant students. He is a faculty member of AO North America and the NOVA Southeastern University College of Allied Health and Nursing. Dr. Patel is a member of the North American Spine Society and the American Academy of Orthopedic Surgeons.

18 | THE SPINE

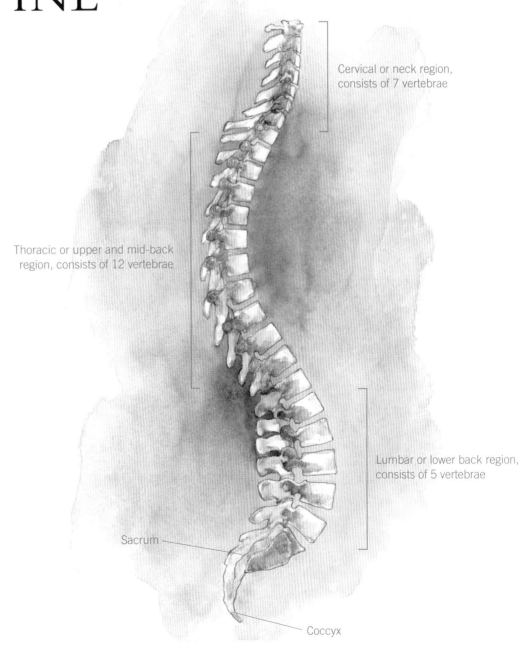

Cervical or neck region, consists of 7 vertebrae

Thoracic or upper and mid-back region, consists of 12 vertebrae

Lumbar or lower back region, consists of 5 vertebrae

Sacrum

Coccyx

(figure 18-1)
The spine (side view).

Disorders of the spine are extremely common as we age. Problems with the aging spine include spinal stenosis, disc herniation, spinal instability, fractures as a result of osteoporosis, and pain from spondylosis (a form of arthritis). In this chapter, I review the clinical presentation, diagnosis, and treatment of some of the more frequent disorders that affect seniors. My hope is that you will find this section both informative and practical.

Low back pain can be episodic or a chronic (long-term) problem. It ranks as one of the four most common reasons for a patient visit to a physician in the United States. It is estimated that between 50 and 80% of the adult population suffers from at least one memorable episode of low back pain per year. Low back pain can occur alone or in conjunction with lower-extremity pain, depending on the cause of the problem. When the pain is in the midline it is often referred to as *axial pain*. Pain that is experienced in the extremities is referred to as *radicular pain*. When the lower-extremity pain is in the sciatic nerve's distribution, it is called sciatica. The sciatic nerve runs in the posterior (back) part of the lower extremity, and thus sciatica refers to pain that radiates down the back or the side of the thigh and calf. The other major nerve in the lower extremity is the femoral nerve. It runs in the anterior (front) part of the lower extremity, thus causing symptoms in the front of the thigh, knee, or the inside part of the leg.

A brief introduction to spinal anatomy is helpful in understanding these disorders. The spine is made up of a series of connected bones called **vertebrae** (see Figure 18-1). These vertebrae interlock via (1) bony protrusions called *facets,* (2) muscles and ligaments, and (3) soft jellylike material, surrounded by a ring made of fibers and cartilage, called discs (see Figure 18-1). A spinal unit can be defined as two vertebrae joined together posteriorly by their facets, on each side, and anteriorly by a disc (see Figure 18-2). Abnormalities in one or more of these areas result in back or neck pain and/or extremity pain.

LOW BACK PAIN

There is significant controversy regarding the cause of low back pain. This is due in part because the spine is made up of many joints. Thus, it is difficult to determine exactly where along the spinal column lays the "pain generator" for an individual patient. This is compounded by the fact that an abnormality in one of the upper joints can cause pain in areas much farther down the spine. This is in contrast to sciatica or other lower-extremity pain, which is often seen along specific areas, depending on the individual nerve root that is compressed. Accordingly, lower-extremity pain is usually more *predictably* treated than low back pain.

Despite the above limitations, researchers feel that there are several potential sources of low back pain. These include the paraspinal muscles of the low back, the facet joints, the ligaments, and the discs. All these areas are innervated by nerve fibers that can potentially cause low back pain.

Persistent pain from a muscular origin is referred to as *myofascial pain syndrome*. Pain that occurs as a result of a facet joint abnormality is

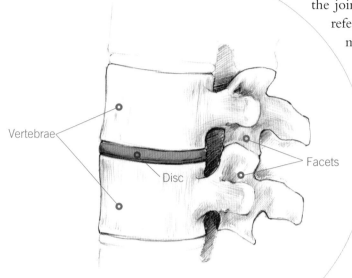

Vertebrae

Disc

Facets

(figure 18-2)

A spinal unit is composed of two vertebrae joined together posteriorly by their facets on each side and anteriorly by the disc.

referred to as *facet joint syndrome*. As previously mentioned, a *facet* is a bony projection from one vertebra that interlocks with another facet to form the joints of your spine. Pain that results from an abnormal disc is referred to as *discogenic* low back pain. Again, a *disc* is a jellylike soft material surrounded by a ring of tough fiber and cartilage that is present between two adjacent vertebrae. The disc and the facet joints allow motion in your spine. Unfortunately, like other joints in the body, they can be injured after trauma or become painful as a result of arthritis.

Fortunately, the majority of patients who suffer from low back pain get better *on their own*. They do not require long-term medications, physical therapy, or any invasive procedures. However, there is a subgroup whose pain does not improve with the above measures. It is these patients that require repeat visits to physicians and other caregivers. All sorts of treatments, scientifically proven and unproven, have become popular for these patients. Some nonsurgical treatments include magnetotherapy, acupuncture, chiropractic adjustments, anti–inflammatory medications, and an array of physical therapy modalities and methods. These "conservative" treatments may or may not relieve the low back pain.

Invasive procedures are generally reserved for a very small group of patients that do not get better with the passage of time or respond to the above measures. These patients have chronic daily pain that has been present for months and years. The treatment is based on what the physician believes is the pain generator for that particular patient. Diagnostic injections or tests are performed in an attempt to define the pain generator better. These may include facet injections, facet rhizotomies, and discograms. *Facet injections* involve injecting one or more joints in your spine with a combination of a local anesthetic (such as NOVOCAIN) and steroid solution. *Facet rhizotomy* (also known as *radiofrequency facet denervation)* refers to a procedure that disrupts the nerve that innervates the facet joint with the use of various techniques (such as heat, cold, or injection of chemical compounds). *Discogram* refers to the injection of an anesthetic and/or saline into the degenerated disc to determine whether the morphology of the disc is abnormal. More importantly, it is also used to see whether stimulating or injecting the disc reproduces the patient's typical back pain. Facet injections and rhizotomies are considered diagnostic and therapeutic tests, while discograms are considered only diagnostic tests that do not offer any pain relief.

Note: It should be emphasized that all three of the above procedures are extremely controversial and are not universally accepted for their diagnostic or therapeutic value.

Spinal surgery for low back pain (axial) without any associated lower–extremity pain (either from nerve root compression or spinal instability) is rarely performed by this author. It is generally considered as a last resort when the patient does not respond to other nonoperative methods and continues to suffer from severe pain. The patients for surgical intervention are picked very carefully and informed that the surgical results are not always predictable. In general, it has been my experience that patients who have single-level involvement do better than ones who have multilevel involvement. In addition, patients who have pain-free intervals, in between their episodes of severe pain, seem to do better than patients who have constant pain. Finally, the success rate of spinal surgery, for axial pain alone, tends to be lower with each subsequent operation. Thus, it is critical that the patient be fully aware of the difference between axial and radicular pain as it applies to success from surgical intervention.

The most common surgery performed for axial low back pain is a fusion (also called **arthrodesis**). Spinal fusion is the surgical procedure that deliberately unites two or more vertebrae to prevent motion between those vertebrae. The theory behind this operation is that by preventing motion across the pain generators (the facets, ligaments, and disc), the chronic pain will improve or resolve. Bone grafts, bone graft substitutes, screws, rods, hooks, plates, and cages may be used to achieve the fusion. There are many different types of fusions being performed, and it is not yet clear which one is superior. Thus, the type of surgery is yet another major controversy in the treatment of low back pain.

HERNIATED LUMBAR DISC

Lumbar refers to the lower five vertebral bodies of the spine. A disc is located between each vertebral body, functions as a "shock absorber," and aids in the mobility of the spine. A disc is primarily composed of water with a gel-like center called the nucleus pulposus and a fibrous outer layer called the annulus fibrosus (see Figure 18-3). Behind the discs and vertebral bodies lie the spinal canal and the nerves that travel within the canal. A *disc herniation* occurs when the central portion of the disc migrates backward towards the spinal canal and the nerves (see Figure 18-4). Other terms used to describe a herniated disc are *ruptured disc* and *slipped disc*. In most cases, the exact causes of a disc herniation are not clear. A weakened or torn outer area of the disc can result in the herniation of the gel-like nucleus. The most common reason for a herniated disc is thought to be from degenerative changes within the disc that are commonly associated with aging. Disc herniations are more common in smokers and those who perform repetitive vibratory activities such as truck driving and jack hammering.

Before I discuss the clinical presentation of a lumbar disc herniation, caution is recommended regarding interpretation of

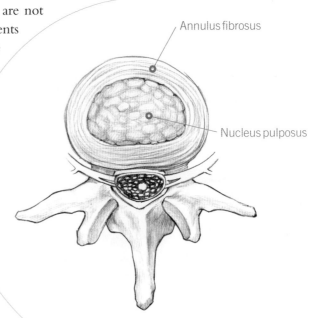

(figure 18-3*)*

A vertebral disc is composed of a tough outer coating called the annulus fibrosus and a gelatinous central material called the nucleus pulposus.

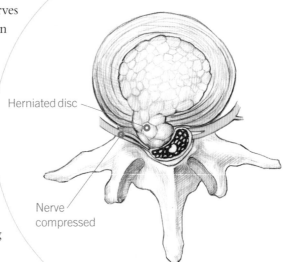

(figure 18-4*)*

A herniated disc occurs when the annulus fibrosus deteriorates and the central gel-like portion of the disc migrates backward toward the spinal canal and the nerves (highlighted in yellow).

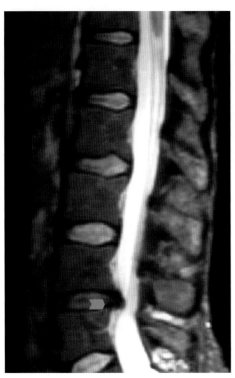

(figure 18-5)

MRI scan showing a herniated lumbar disc (arrowhead).

imaging studies in older patients. Several excellent studies have confirmed that up to 50% of asymptomatic patients, over the age of 60, have *abnormal* MRI scans, with approximately 35% having a disc herniation (see Figure 18-5). Thus both the physician and the patient must interpret the imaging studies in the context of the clinical symptoms.

Common complaints after a herniated lumbar disc include low back pain and spasms followed by radicular symptoms. Often, the low back pain improves rapidly as the lower-extremity complaints get worse. The symptoms may occur suddenly or gradually and depend upon the exact location and the severity of the herniation. Pain traveling from the low back and extending down through the buttock and into the leg is the most common feature. This is called radiculopathy. The pain may be a dull ache or a sharp stabbing sensation. Numbness and tingling may also be present. The distribution of the complaints can often lead the doctor to determine which nerve is pinched from the herniation. If one of the branches of the sciatic nerve is involved, then the symptoms will be more prominent in the posterior (toward the back) part of the leg. If a branch of the femoral nerve is involved, then the symptoms will be anterior (toward the front) part of the extremity. The symptoms are often made better or worse with certain positions and activities such as coughing or sneezing. Weakness of the affected muscle groups may be present and may make walking or climbing stairs difficult.

In general, a disc herniation only compresses one nerve root. However, in rare cases, if a patient herniates a particularly large fragment towards the midline, then multiple nerve roots can be involved. This can result in *cauda equina syndrome* (see Figure 18-6). The patient may develop progressive weakness and loss of sensation in lower extremities, saddle anesthesia (numbness in the area that would contact a saddle), and difficulty controlling urination and bowel movements. The diffuse symptoms are a

(figure 18-6)

A large disc herniation can compress multiple nerve roots and produce the cauda equina syndrome. *Cauda equina* is Latin for "tail of a horse," which the many nerves exiting from the lower spinal cord look like.

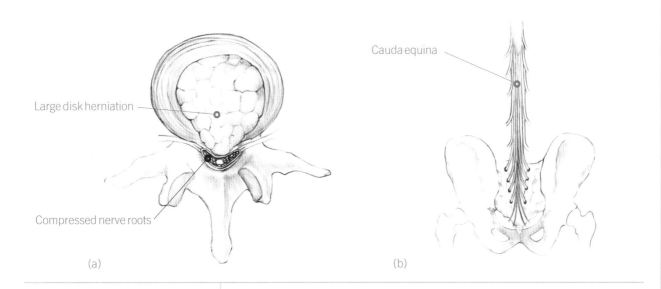

result of compression of multiple nerve roots, rather than compression of one nerve root. In general, patients who develop this syndrome require emergency surgery. The surgery, if done early enough, results in a good prognosis and recovery for most patients.

Initial treatment consists of rest, physical therapy, anti-inflammatories, and pain medications. Most patients improve with these measures. If the symptoms continue or worsen, then surgical removal of the disc herniation is recommended.

Surgery is performed if nonsurgical interventions fail to show significant improvement within four to six weeks. If the symptoms are severe or progressive weakness is present, surgery may be recommended sooner. As discussed, emergency surgery is performed if a disc herniation results in the cauda equina syndrome.

The goal of surgery is to remove the portion of the disc that is compressing the nerve root. The most common procedure is called a microdiscectomy, in which part of the herniated disc is removed. In order to see the disc clearly, it is often necessary to remove a small portion of the *lamina,* the bone that covers and protects the neural elements. Bone removal is usually minimal. During the surgery, an operating microscope is often used for better visualization of the nerves. The incision is small, and there is generally little bleeding. The success rate of lumbar disc surgery is greater than 90% in relieving the lower-extremity symptoms. However, the relief of low back pain is less predictable. Also, it is important to recognize that weakness due to a disc herniation does not consistently resolve after surgery. Pain is the most reliable complaint to resolve. The complication rate for a discectomy is low, and the patient usually goes home the same day or the day after the surgery. Most patients resume normal activities by six weeks.

HERNIATED CERVICAL AND THORACIC DISC

Cervical refers to the first seven vertebral bodies of the spine. Thoracic refers to the following 12 rib-bearing vertebral bodies of the spine. There are three points worth discussing regarding these herniations. First, these herniations, unlike the lumbar, involve the portion of the spine that includes the *spinal cord.* The spinal cord is a structure that begins in the brain and usually ends at the first lumbar vertebra (L1). Beyond L1, the nerves present in the spinal column are called the *cauda equina* (Latin for "tail of a horse"; note the resemblance of the nerves in the lower spine to a horse's tail) and behave similarly to the peripheral nerves seen in our arms and legs. Unlike the spinal cord, they are more resilient and can be manipulated during surgery without risking further damage. As a result of this anatomic difference, surgery for disc herniations that involve the cervical and thoracic spine are typically done from an anterior (front) approach. This is because most symptomatic herniations are in front of the neural elements. In the lumbar spine, the surgeon simply manipulates the neural elements out of harm's way and pulls the offending disc fragment out without any additional risk from the manipulation. This is not possible in the cervical and thoracic spine, which house the spinal cord. The spinal cord is not a peripheral nerve, and it is fixed by important ligaments and cannot safely be manipulated without causing further neurologic damage. Second, the thoracic spine is surrounded by the fairly rigid rib cage. Thus there is little motion in the thoracic spine, and hence there are fewer disc herniations in the thoracic spine. Remember, the less motion that is present, the less chance of developing spinal disorders. Third, most thoracic disc herniations occur in older patients and are usually asymptomatic.

As in the lumbar spine, a disc herniation in the cervical and thoracic spine can cause axial and radicular pain. The radicular pain is in the upper extremity for a cervical herniation and along the rib cage or the trunk of the body for thoracic herniation. However, as in the case of the cauda equina syndrome, a large herniation that is in the midline can cause more diffuse symptoms, resulting in *myelopathy* (discussed in the section "Cervical Myelopathy," below).

Because cervical pathology is far more common than thoracic, I limit my discussion to the clinical presentation and treatment of cervical radiculopathy. It is important to recognize that in the older population a cervical radiculopathy is often caused by a bone spur, called an osteophyte, or by a "hard disc" rather than a soft disc (nucleus pulposus). This is due to various changes that occur in the aging spine. For example, a disc may bulge and later become "calcified" (hardened). This is often called a disc-osteophyte complex, and the radiculopathy that results from this is called *cervical spondylitic radiculopathy*. The symptoms that occur are similar whether one suffers from a hard or a soft disc. If the disc-osteophyte complex is causing a myelopathy, then it is called *cervical spondylitic myelopathy*.

Pain traveling from the neck extending down through the shoulder blade and the arm is the most common feature. The pain may be a dull ache or a sharp stabbing sensation. Numbness and tingling may also be present. The symptoms are often made better or worse with certain positions. Typically, extension of the neck combined with a head turn on the side of the symptoms will make the symptoms worse. In contrast, placing the hand, of the involved extremity, on top of the head and holding the neck in a neutral position will often decrease the intensity of the radicular pain (see Figure 18-7). Weakness of the affected muscle groups may be present and may make using the arm more difficult.

Initial treatment consists of rest, physical therapy, anti-inflammatories, cervical traction, and pain medications. Most patients improve with these measures. Surgery is recommended if nonsurgical interventions fail to show significant improvement within four to six weeks. If the symptoms are severe or progressive weakness is present, surgery may be recommended sooner.

(figure 18-7)

Placing the hand of the involved extremity on top of the head and holding the neck in a neutral position will often decrease the intensity of pain caused by a pinched nerve in the neck.

(figure 18-8)

For an anterior cervical discectomy and fusion, an incision is made in the front of the neck. The disc and osteophytes are removed, which allows pressure to be taken off the nerve. (a) The disc space in between the vertebral bodies is filled with a shaped piece of bone graft. (b) Once the bone graft is placed, a small titanium plate is applied over the entire construct to stabilize it.

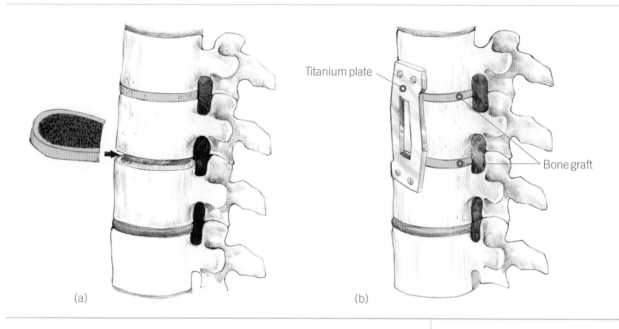

Titanium plate

Bone graft

(a)   (b)

The goal of surgery is to remove any disc or osteophyte that is compressing the nerve root. The most common procedure performed is called an *anterior cervical discectomy* and fusion (see Figure 18-8). An incision is made in the front of the neck. The disc and osteophytes are removed, which allows the pressure to be taken off the nerve. The disc space in between the vertebral bodies is filled with a shaped piece of *bone graft*. Once the bone graft is placed, a small titanium plate may be applied over the entire construct to further stabilize it. During the surgery, an operating microscope is often used for better visualization of the spinal cord and nerves. The incision is small and there is very little pain or bleeding. If multiple nerve roots are compressed, then a more extensive operation may be required.

The success rate of a single-level anterior cervical discectomy and fusion in relieving the extremity symptoms is greater than 90%. Most spine surgeons consider this operation as the most successful one they perform. Patients will often awaken from anesthesia and happily report that their extremity pain has resolved. It is important to recognize that weakness due to a disc herniation does not consistently resolve after surgery. Pain is the most reliable symptom to resolve. The complication rate for a cervical discectomy and fusion is low, and patients usually go home the day after the surgery. Unlike radicular pain, the relief of neck pain after this operation is not as predictable.

SPINAL STENOSIS

Spinal stenosis is a very common syndrome that often afflicts the older population. It is most simply defined as progressive compression of nerves

Narrowed spinal
canal

(figure 18-9)

Lumbar spinal stenosis occurs when degenerative changes in the bony structures of the
spine cause compression of the nerves due to
narrowing of the surrounding bony canal.

(figure 18-10)

Leaning forward on a grocery cart, which enlarges the spinal canal for those with lumbar
spinal stenosis, allows a person to walk further
with less discomfort and is known as the
"grocery-cart posture."

due to narrowing of the bony canal that surrounds these structures (see Figure 18-9). There are several contributing factors that lead to this problem. The most common cause is degeneration due to *lumbar spondylosis,* or arthritis in the lower back. The narrowing of the spinal canal that occurs as the result of this degeneration causes mechanical compression of the spinal nerves in the lower back. These nerves are responsible for providing sensation and strength in the lower extremities. In many individuals, the compression leads to no symptoms, while in others, a variety of clinical symptoms can occur. Interestingly, the severity of symptoms does not necessarily correlate with the magnitude of compression seen on spinal imaging studies.

Because spinal stenosis most commonly occurs as a result of the aging process, it is not surprising that the early symptoms are slow in onset. Spinal stenosis is a progressive and dynamic process. As a result, symptoms are not identical from individual to individual. Before our more universal awareness of the diagnosis of spinal stenosis, the bizarre or frequently atypical and varying symptoms and inconsistent signs (often with a lack of any neurological deficit) commonly prompted physicians to recommend psychiatric evaluation of their older patients. Now, however, the clinical manifestations of spinal stenosis are better understood, and much more precise diagnosis and treatment are available.

Although low back pain is commonly associated with spinal stenosis, the most typical reason the patient consults a physician is leg and buttock pain in one or both legs that is often made worse by standing and/or walking. The patient will typically describe such symptoms in the leg as pain, heaviness, soreness, cramping and weakness and may also report a feeling of tingling or numbness. The distribution of pain is usually in the buttock, back of the thigh, calf, and top of the foot. Symptoms in the front of the thigh are less common, but may also occur.

The majority of patients with spinal stenosis describe a history of progressively decreased walking distance over a period of months. Their walking is limited by the pain, heaviness, and cramping in the buttocks and legs. Neurogenic claudication is a term that is used to describe these complaints. Patients may sit or bend forward to obtain relief after walking a short distance. They will also lean forward when they walk because it reduces buttock and leg pain. That is because *spine flexion* (or leaning forward) "enlarges" the spinal canal and creates more space for the nerves. The classic revelation by patients is to volunteer that their symptoms are less aggravating in the grocery store: they are unknowingly leaning on the grocery cart in a flexed position, which enlarges the spinal canal (see Figure 18-10). Complaints of limited spine movement are common, particularly extension of the spine (or leaning backward).

Occasionally, the extension leads to "jolts of lightning" down the buttocks and legs. This is due to the additional compression of the nerves in the extended position. Treatment of this problem begins with obtaining the correct diagnosis. As mentioned, the symptoms are often vague and can be similar to symptoms from vascular disease, a hip problem, or other musculoskeletal problems.

Vascular claudication can be very similar to neurogenic claudication. There are several distinctions, however, that set them apart. First, unlike spinal stenosis, claudication from vascular disease generally resolves when the patient stops walking and stands still. This is mainly because the muscle demand for oxygen diminishes greatly in the lower extremities when the patient stops walking. Second, in a great majority of patients, claudication from spinal disorders diminishes significantly if the patient walks in a forward-flexed posture. Third, the patient with spinal stenosis may have tingling and numbness in the lower extremity as well as significant low back pain. Thus, a vascular study may be necessary if there is any doubt regarding the circulation in the lower extremities.

A hip joint problem, such as arthritis, may mimic spinal stenosis. Typically, the patient with a hip problem experiences pain that begins in the groin and radiates to the front of the thigh. Occasionally, however, the pain can be in the buttock and even radiate to the front of the knee from the groin. Pertinent physical exam findings with a hip problem include (1) limited rotation of the hip joint and (2) increased pain with flexion and internal rotation of the hip. If the diagnosis is not clear, an injection of a local anesthetic (such as NOVOCAIN) into the hip joint can be performed. A patient who suffers from a hip problem will experience immediate relief, from their specific type of pain, as a result of the anesthetic. This injection only takes minutes and is performed by a radiologist on an outpatient basis.

Once a diagnosis of spinal stenosis is accurately established, patient education is extremely important. Patients should be reassured that their pain is not dangerous and is the result of degenerative changes in the spine.

Anti-inflammatory medications and controlled physical activity are the safest and most effective initial treatments. A program of lumbar isometric flexion exercises followed by a gradual increase in activities may result in a return to more normal living. Patients who complain of persistent lower-extremity and low back pain after six weeks of conservative treatment may require more aggressive intervention. This may be in the form of an *epidural steroid injection,* in the spinal canal, and/or a nerve root block, to decrease inflammation surrounding the involved nerves. Some patients seem to respond very well to these injections, while others do not experience any significant lasting benefit. Unfortunately, there are no reliable predictors as to which patient will respond favorably to the epidural injection. In general, the injection is very safe and is similar to

WHAT'S NEW?

There is a true revolution that is occurring in the field of spinal surgery today. New techniques, as well as new products, are being used and reported at a faster pace than ever. Numerous scientific studies are in progress, under the supervision of the Food and Drug Administration, to determine the efficacy of the new techniques and products. I list three items that are new:

1. *The use of bone graft substitutes and bone growth factors in achieving spinal fusion.* One such factor is bone morphogenic protein, an extract of bone that induces spinal fusion.
2. *The use of minimally invasive techniques and instruments to perform spinal operations.* This includes the use of thoracoscopy and laparoscopy in which a small incision is made in the chest or abdomen, and the surgery is performed with the assistance of small video cameras.
3. *The use of artificial discs in the cervical and lumbar spine to preserve motion and to avoid a spinal fusion.*

It is clear that there is much that is not known regarding disorders of the spine. However, these newer techniques and instruments appear very promising in helping individuals who suffer from these common ailments.

the one given to women at childbirth for anesthesia. It is done as an outpatient procedure and only takes minutes to perform. If the first one is successful, the patient can have two more in the next six-month period for any recurrence of pain.

A significant percentage of patients may not respond to any of these treatments on a long-term basis. In these cases, surgical intervention is recommended if the symptoms are severe enough to adversely affect quality of life. A special test, such as magnetic resonance imaging (MRI) or a *myelogram* (X-rays taken after a dye is injected into the spinal canal), may be required to confirm the diagnosis and to prepare for the surgery. Fortunately, the success rate for spinal stenosis surgery is quite high. It is one of the most common reasons for spinal surgery. Most patients experience complete resolution of their lower-extremity symptoms. The low back pain is not as predictably relieved. The best candidate for spinal stenosis surgery is the one who suffers from lower-extremity pain, as the predominant complaint, rather than low back pain.

The surgical treatment involves either an isolated *laminectomy* or a laminectomy with a fusion (see Figure 18-11). A laminectomy is the removal of the back part of the vertebra (the lamina and part of the facet joint and supporting ligament) in order to create more space for the neural elements. In essence, you "unzip" the spine to make more room for the nerves. There is controversy, among spine surgeons, as to when a fusion should be added to the laminectomy in the treatment of spinal stenosis. The most common reason is a "slipped vertebra," or spondylolisthesis, in the presence of spinal stenosis. Spondylolisthesis is a forward slip of a vertebra in

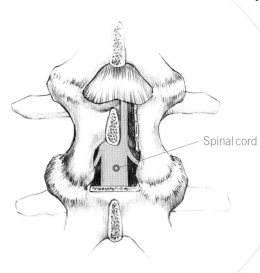

Spinal cord

(figure 18-11)

A laminectomy is the removal of the back part of the vertebrae in order to create more space for neural elements. The surgeon "unzips" the spine to make more room for the nerves.

relation to the one below it (see Figure 18-12). The presence of this slip indicates instability between the two vertebrae. Moreover, the slip often contributes to a tighter spinal canal. It is believed by most surgeons that a slip can progress further with the destabilizing effects of the laminectomy. Thus a fusion is often performed with the laminectomy to prevent further slippage of an already unstable segment (see Figure 18-13).

Another common reason to add a fusion is the presence of spinal stenosis in conjunction with a deformity, such as scoliosis (curvature of the spine). A laminectomy alone may not decompress the nerve adequately and may actually make the deformity worse. A fusion using spinal instrumentation can often correct the deformity and allow more space for the exiting nerve as it leaves the spinal canal. Similarly, if a disc space has collapsed enough as a result of the degenerative process, it can lead to nerve root compression in the foramen. The foramen is the space through which a nerve root leaves the spinal column in the low back to enter the abdomen. This is called *foraminal spinal stenosis* (see Figure 18-14). A fusion that restores the disc height is the procedure of choice for this particular type of stenosis. This is often accomplished by the placement of structural bone graft or metallic devices in between the two vertebrae, to "jack up" the disc space and make more room for the nerve root in the foramen (see Figure 18-15).

Yet another reason to include a fusion with a laminectomy is for a patient who develops recurrent spinal stenosis after a previous laminectomy. These patients often continue to have their lower extremity pain and/or develop new back pain unless they are both fused and decompressed during the second operation. A final reason is the patient who has lower-extremity symptoms from spinal stenosis but who also has significant low back pain. As mentioned, the lower-extremity symptoms usually resolve with the laminectomy. Unfortunately, the relief of low back pain after a laminectomy, in a patient with a tight spinal canal, is often unpredictable. Thus, a fusion may be added to the laminectomy to increase the success rate of back pain relief. The rationale for the relief of back pain is that there will no longer be any abnormal motion across the fused segment.

SPONDYLOLISTHESIS

Spondylolisthesis is a forward slip of a vertebra in relation to the one below it. There are two main kinds of spondylolisthesis: *isthmic* and *degenerative* (see Figure 18-16). In isthmic spondylolisthesis, a fracture in the posterior part of the vertebra leads to instability or a slip. In the case

LEARNING MEDICINE: THE HARD WAY

Galen was a Greek physician around 100-200 A.D. One of his first appointments was physician to the gladiators. Needless to say, he received valuable experience in anatomy and trauma. His early writings gave very accurate and detailed accounts of the workings of the muscles, nerves, and skeleton. He is considered the father of the specialty of sports medicine.

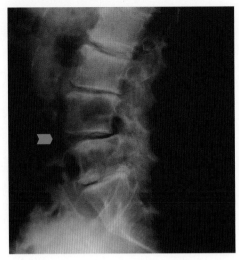

(figure 18-12)

Spondylolisthesis is a forward slip (arrowhead) of a vertebra in relation to the one below it.

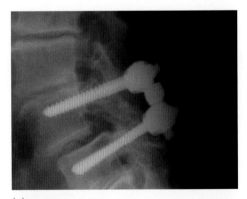

(a)

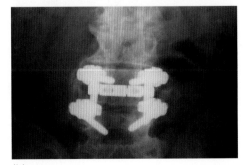

(b)

(figure 18-13)

Lumbar fusion for spondylolisthesis at the L4-5 level with spinal instrumentation. (a) Side view (b) front view.

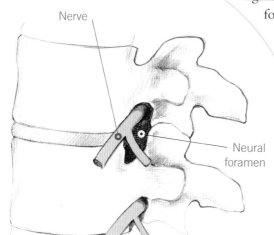

(figure 18-14)

The neural foramen is the opening by which a nerve from the spinal cord exits the spinal column.

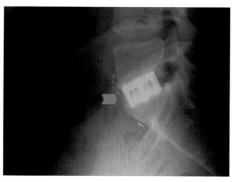

(figure 18-15)

A "jack" for the spine (arrowhead) is a metallic device that opens up the disc space to allow more room for the nerve as it exits the spinal canal (side view).

of degenerative spondylolisthesis, the failure is generally either where the facets join together to form the "joints" in the spine or in the surrounding ligaments. If the joints or ligaments become lax, the vertebrae can slip forward over the one below it.

Women are affected more frequently than men by degenerative spondylolisthesis. Diabetics are also more frequently affected. It is estimated that 10% of the female population has this condition. Oddly enough, there are people who have spondylolisthesis and are completely asymptomatic. If it does become symptomatic, the most common complaint seems to be low back pain. However, a radiculopathy (pain radiating down the thigh and/or leg) may also occur if the patient develops spinal stenosis. In general, both the low back pain and the radiculopathy improve with rest and are exacerbated by standing and walking. Activities such as bending and twisting can also make the symptoms worse.

Usually, nonoperative care is initiated unless the pain is unrelenting and/or the patient is developing progressive neurologic deficit. Nonoperative care may include anti–inflammatory medications, a short course of steroids by mouth, narcotics, and physical therapy. A series of epidural steroid injections may also be prescribed if there is significant lower-extremity pain. The epidurals seem to be more successful if the patients have a predominance of lower-extremity pain, rather than low back pain. In general, no more than three epidurals in any given six-month period are performed. Many patients seem to improve to their satisfaction with these nonoperative treatment methods.

Surgery is reserved for those patients who are not happy with their progress with the above measures. In addition, surgery is recommended for those few patients who develop a neurologic deficit or have a progression of their neurologic deficit. Several different types of surgeries are performed for degenerative spondylolisthesis. If there is symptomatic spinal stenosis associated with the slip, then a laminectomy and a fusion is performed. A fusion is often performed with the laminectomy to prevent further slippage of an already unstable level. It is believed by most surgeons that a slip can progress further from the destabilizing effects of the laminectomy. Once the fusion occurs, the vertebra can no longer slip and the nerves can no longer be pinched.

Lower-extremity pain is more successfully treated than low back pain. Most patients experience complete resolution of their lower-extremity symptoms. The relief of back pain is not as predictable. Patients who have not had chronic back pain generally do better than patients who have had low back trouble for years and years.

(figure 18-16*)*

The two main kinds of spondylolisthesis are degenerative and isthmic. (a) Degenerative spondylolisthesis is a failure where the facets join together to form the "joints" either in the spine or in the surrounding ligaments. If the joints or ligaments be-come lax, the vertebra can slip forward (arrowhead) over the one below it. (b) Isthmic spondylolisthesis is a fracture in the posterior part of the vertebra that leads to instability or a slip.

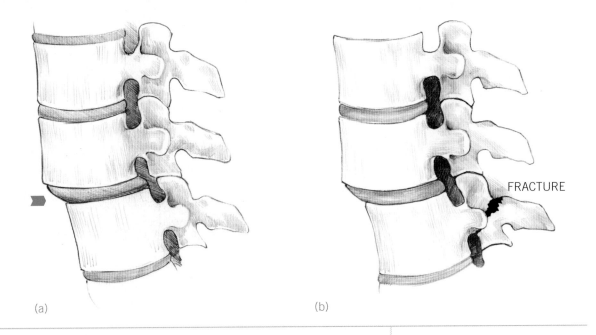

FRACTURE

(a)　　　　　　　　　(b)

ISTHMIC SPONDYLOLISTHESIS

Isthmic spondylolisthesis is a slip that is the result of spondylolysis. *Spondylolysis* is a crack or a fracture that occurs in the pars interarticularis of the vertebra as a result of repetitive extension forces (backward movement of the spine; see Figure 18-17). This type of spondylolisthesis is more common in athletes who play sports that require hyperextension of their lower spine (e.g., gymnasts, football linemen, weight lifters). In addition, unlike degenerative spondylolisthesis, isthmic spondylolisthesis starts when you are much younger. The symptoms, however, may be dormant until the patient reaches adulthood. It should also be pointed out that one could have the fracture in the pars (spondylolysis) without the spondylolisthesis. In fact, it is postulated that some children go on to unite the fracture of the pars and thus do not develop the spondylolisthesis.

Unlike degenerative spondylolisthesis, the isthmic slip can occasionally progress to a high degree. This is because the back part of the vertebrae is not connected, and there is no limit to how far it can slip. In degenerative spondylolisthesis, the facet joints may be "loose," but they will prevent the superior vertebrae from sliding more than 25% of the width of the body.

As with degenerative spondylolisthesis, the patient can be totally asymptomatic with isthmic spondylolisthesis. If symptoms do occur, they include low back pain, radicular pain, claudication, and hamstring tightness. Physical therapy, anti-inflammatories, and epidural or selective nerve root injection can all be tried to alleviate the symptoms.

Surgical indications and treatments are very similar to the ones for degenerative spondylolisthesis.

CERVICAL MYELOPATHY

Cervical myelopathy is the clinical syndrome that occurs as a result of narrowing of the spinal canal in the cervical spine. The narrowing of the spinal canal causes compression of the spinal cord. Often, affected individuals are born with a narrow spinal canal. There may be several contributing factors that lead to the problem. The most common cause is degeneration due to cervical spondylosis, a term used to describe arthritic changes in the cervical spine. Over time, these arthritic changes lead to narrowing and mechanical compression of the spinal cord. A large central disc herniation can also cause or contribute to the problem.

The spinal cord is responsible for sending signals to and receiving signals from the arms and legs. These signals within the spinal cord are responsible for pain, sensation, position sense, and motor strength in the arms and legs. In some individuals the compression of the spinal cord does not lead to symptoms. In others, spinal cord compression can cause a variety of complex symptoms. Interestingly, the severity of symptoms does not necessarily correlate with the magnitude of compression seen on spinal imaging studies. Patients with severe spinal cord compression can be completely without symptoms. Thus, the diagnosis is made by the presence of both the clinical syndrome and compression of the spinal cord on imaging studies such as an MRI, a CT, or a myelogram. It is one of the most commonly misdiagnosed syndromes as it often occurs in elderly patients who attribute their symptoms to "arthritis and old age" and do not seek medical attention. In addition, the early findings are often very subtle and protean such that the diagnosis is difficult to make even for a well-trained health care provider. Symptoms are not identical from patient to patient. Cervical myelopathy is generally a progressive process.

Neck pain is commonly associated with cervical myelopathy but is not always present. The most common reasons why patients consult a physician are numbness and tingling in the arms or hands, problems with function of the hands, and weakness in the arms or hands. Patients complain of difficulty with fine motor movements of their hands and fingers (combing hair, buttoning a shirt, or turning the ignition key in a car). Symptoms in the legs may include difficulty with walking (wide broad-based gait with frequent falls) or a sense of imbalance. Weakness in one or both legs may be present. If there are pinched nerves in the neck along with compression of the spinal cord, arm pain may be an associated feature. Another common symptom includes a sharp, stinging, shocklike sensation extending from the neck down the spine or into the arms by looking directly up or down. Burning, tingling, and spasticity (increased muscular tone) of the arms and legs with a change in bowel and bladder habits can also occur.

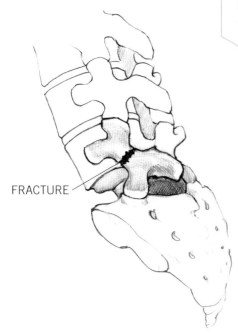

FRACTURE

(*figure* 18-17)

Spondylolysis is a crack or fracture that occurs in the pars interarticularis of the vertebra as a result of repetitive extension (backward movement of the spine) forces.

If any symptom and sign is present, then an X-ray and an MRI of the cervical spine are ordered. MRI is the best study to assess the size of the spinal canal, degree of compression, and overall condition of the spinal cord (see Figure 18-18). X-rays are best used to assess the bony structure around the spinal cord and to show the degree of arthritic changes in the cervical spine. Cervical alignment and stability are also best assessed with X-rays.

If the clinical syndrome of cervical myelopathy is present with compression of the spinal cord noted on the MRI, initial treatment will usually consist of physical therapy to address any painful symptoms in the neck or extremity weakness. Medications such as anti-inflammatories or pain medications may be prescribed to address any painful symptoms. Should the symptoms be mild or not progressive, monitoring the clinical course over time may be recommended. Should the symptoms be progressive or advanced or if weakness is noted in the arms or legs, surgery is usually recommended.

Surgery consists of removing the arthritic bone or the herniated disc that has narrowed the spinal canal and can be approached from the front of the spine or from the back, depending on several variables. A fusion procedure to stabilize the affected areas is usually performed at the same time. The type of surgery is dependent on the age and general condition of the patient, number of levels involved, location of the compression, and alignment of the cervical spine. The main objective of surgery is to stop the progression of myelopathy. Significant improvement in symptoms can occur, but it is often difficult to predict which patients will have noticeable clinical improvement once the compression is relieved from the spinal cord. *Note:* The success rate for halting the progression of myelopathy with surgery is quite high.

Briefly, I would like to discuss the syndrome of *thoracic myelopathy.* It is caused by essentially the same problem except that it occurs in the thoracic spine. Thus the upper extremities are spared because nerves that control these areas have already exited the spinal canal. However, if the thoracic cord is compressed, the lower extremities are not spared because the lumbar nerves have not yet exited the spinal canal. Thoracic myelopathy is often a hard problem to treat because the thoracic spine is within the rib cage. The compression of the thoracic cord is usually anterior, so the surgical approach is often anterior. Remember, unlike the lumbar spine, one cannot manipulate the neural elements in the cervical and thoracic spine without risking neurologic injury. Accordingly, a thoracotomy is often necessary to adequately decompress the thoracic cord. A *thoracotomy* is a procedure by which the surgeon removes part of one rib and enters the chest or the upper abdomen through an interval created by the rib excision. Obviously, this is a substantial operation with some risks involved, particularly for an older patient. *Note:* The thoracic cord does not often require decompression, and thoracic myelopathy is rather rare.

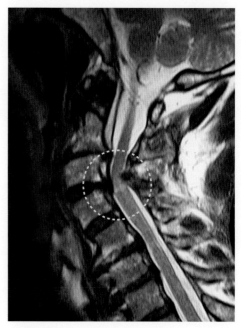

(figure 18-18*)*

The best study for the evaluation of cervical myelopathy is MRI. The spinal canal, degree of compression, and overall condition of the spinal cord can be assessed. Note the compressed area of the spinal cord (circled).

(figure 18-19)

Four types of vertebral compression fractures are recognized: (a) the top and bottom of the vertebra, (b) the top, (c) the bottom, and (d) the middle.

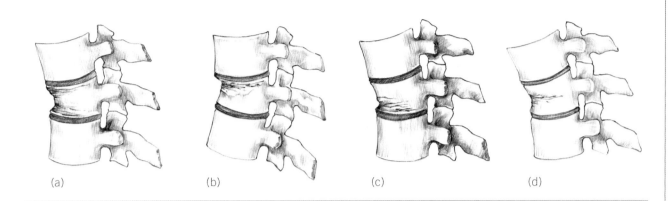

(a)   (b)   (c)   (d)

COMPRESSION FRACTURES

Compression fractures refer to fractures that result in a loss of height of the vertebrae in the spine. Such fractures develop more commonly in persons with osteoporosis (see Chapter 19). A compression fracture can occur in these individuals even with the most trivial trauma. Moreover, a compression fracture can occur even without any trauma. These fractures represent one of the greatest challenges confronted by any health care provider that treats the older population (see Figure 18-19).

The patient will typically have a sudden onset of pain near the area of the fracture. However, the pain can be at an area remote from the fracture site. The pain is usually worse with increase in activity, deep breathing, coughing, or sneezing. Multiple or recurrent compression fractures can cause a "dowager's hump" (hunchback) and decrease in the overall height of the patient. This may lead to chronic pain and even lung problems. Plain X-rays may be diagnostic. However, an MRI or a CT is often needed to determine the stability and or morphology of the fracture. A bone scan is often used to determine whether the fracture is old or new.

The type of treatment is dependent on the severity of the pain and the extent of the fracture and deformity. A stable fracture without much associated pain is treated with a short period of bed rest and some medications. A light brace is offered but is not always tolerated by the patient due to age as well as spinal deformity. If there is severe pain and the fracture is stable, a *vertebroplasty* or *kyphoplasty* is usually recommended. In unstable fractures and fractures associated with neurologic deficits and severe *kyphosis,* bracing and/or surgery may be recommended.

Two relatively new procedures are used to treat stable compression fractures. In **vertebroplasty**, methyl methacrylate (bone cement) is injected directly into the fractured vertebra through two small stab wounds in the

(figure 18-20)

X-ray appearance after kyphoplasty: (a) side view (b) front view.

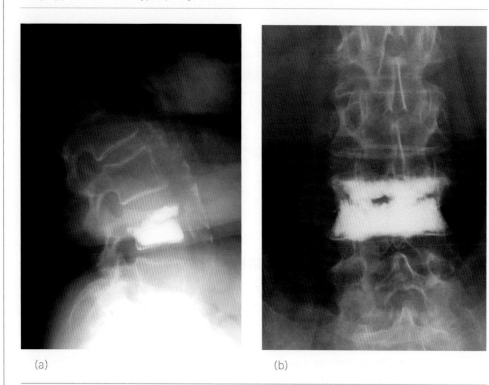

(a)   (b)

back. The cement hardens, giving the fractured vertebra more stability and causing a reduction in pain. A kyphoplasty is very similar to vertebroplasty. In **kyphoplasty**, a balloon is inflated and then deflated in the vertebra to create a void in the bone. This is followed by an injection of cement. It is controversial as to whether one procedure is better than the other. Central to the controversy is whether kyphoplasty corrects the deformity better than vertebroplasty and whether correction of the deformity has any effect on pain relief or prevention of future fractures at other levels. Vertebroplasty is done with a local anesthetic, while kyphoplasty is done with a general anesthetic (see Figure 18-20). Patients can go home the same day after either procedure.

Most patients seem to do very well with these procedures and have significant pain relief. It has been my experience that mild, stable, single-level fractures respond more favorably than other fractures. It should be emphasized, however, that if the underlying osteoporosis is not treated, the patient remains at risk for developing another fracture in the spine.

Prevention and treatment of osteoporosis is discussed in Chapter 19. Bone density testing can be used to diagnose and monitor osteoporosis.

WHAT YOU NEED TO KNOW

▶ The spine is an area of the body that is frequently injured or affected with ailments in seniors. There is still a great deal that is not known regarding disorders of the spine. However, because these disorders are so common, there is extensive research currently being done to increase our understanding and knowledge. Hopefully, this will translate into better patient care year by year.

▶ Pain over the back and spine is very common and usually improves on its own.

▶ Chronic low back and neck pain is harder to treat than radicular pain (pain in the arms or legs).

▶ Unless the pain associated with the disorder is severe and there is progressive neurologic deficit, non-operative care should be attempted before surgery.

▶ Surgery is more successful if it is being done to treat radicular pain rather than isolated low back pain.

▶ Osteoporosis should be treated aggressively as it results in a high incidence of spine fractures. There is significant mortality associated with elderly women who have compression fractures.

FOR MORE INFORMATION

▶ National Institute of Arthritis and Musculoskeletal and Skin Diseases Information Clearinghouse
National Institutes of Health
One AMS Circle
Bethesda, MD 20892
301-718-6366
TTY: 301-565-2966
Web: www.niams.nih.gov

▶ North American Spine Society
Web: www.spine.org

▶ Your Orthopedic Connection
American Academy of Orthopedic Surgeons
Web: www.aaos.org

Osteoporosis is a preventable and treatable disease and should not be considered an inevitable consequence of aging.

—*Robert Lindsay, MD*

THE AUTHOR

19

SILVINA LEVIS, MD, is an endocrinologist and associate professor and director of the Osteoporosis Center at the University of Miami and the Geriatric Research, Education, and Clinical Center (GRECC) at the Miami Veterans Affairs Medical Center. She has long and varied experience in the medical care of patients with osteoporosis. Dr. Levis has conducted many clinical trials with patients who suffer from this disease and has published articles on the topic. In her efforts to increase osteoporosis awareness and promote prevention and early detection of the disease, she organizes and participates in educational programs for both the medical community and the public. In 1998 Dr. Levis was appointed chair of the State of Florida Osteoporosis Advisory Committee, which counsels the Departments of Health and of Elderly Affairs in osteoporosis education and prevention programs. She is also cochair of the Florida Osteoporosis Coalition–Unifying Solutions (FOCUS) and a director of the Osteoporosis Center, University of Miami, and Miami Veterans Affairs Medical Center.

Dr. Levis graduated from the University of Buenos Aires School of Medicine in Buenos Aires, Argentina, where she also trained in internal medicine and endocrinology. She continued her training at the University of Miami School of Medicine and has been a faculty member since 1989.

19 | OSTEOPOROSIS

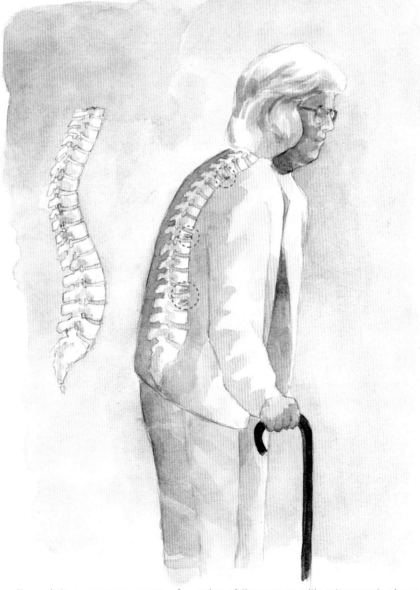

(*figure* 19-1)

Osteoporosis (brittle bone disease) is a common cause of height loss, back pain, and spinal deformity in post-menopausal women. However, osteoporosis is not rare in men. On the left, notice the normal spine anatomy. On the right, the spine of the woman with osteoporosis shows vertebral compression fractures (circled) and the hump of the upper back (dowager's hump).

Osteoporosis, or brittle bone disease, is one of the major health problems facing aging men and women. Until recently, this disease and its debilitating fractures were considered an inevitable part of the aging process for which little could be done in terms of either prevention or cure. New discoveries and treatments have given hope for managing the progression of osteoporosis and its symptoms.

The progressive loss of calcium from the bones all through adulthood leads to a thinning of the skeleton, fragile bones, and higher risk for fractures. Osteoporosis is often called the "silent disease," because no symptoms are present until a fracture occurs. Although bone loss occurs throughout the skeleton, osteoporotic fractures are most common in the spine, hip (see Figure 19-2), wrist, and ribs.

It is estimated that osteoporosis affects more than 28 million people nationwide and that these numbers will increase significantly as the baby boomer generation ages. Approximately 1.5 million osteoporotic fractures occur in the United States every year, including 500,000 vertebral (spine), 260,000 hip, and 250,000 wrist fractures. In 1997, the annual cost of caring for individuals with osteoporotic fractures in the United States was estimated at $13.8 billion. This calculation did not include the cost of diagnostic tests or medical treatment for prevention of the disease.

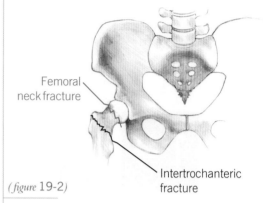

Femoral neck fracture

Intertrochanteric fracture

(figure 19-2)

Common sites for hip fractures due to osteoporosis.

CONSEQUENCES OF FRACTURES

Hip fractures are a life-changing event, as they generally result in hospitalization and numerous medical complications, some life threatening, such as blood clots, pneumonia, urinary infections, or skin ulcers. It is estimated that after a hip fracture, 50% of the individuals never recover their previous level of independence and 25% require long-term nursing home care. There is about 24% increased mortality in the first year following a hip fracture. Although more women sustain fractures than men do, mortality in men after a hip fracture is twice as likely as for women.

The vertebrae in the spine fracture by compressing (see Figure 19-3), resulting in a loss of height of the individual. Vertebral compression fractures are debilitating and associated with reduced quality of life. These fractures can happen suddenly, often after lifting an object, or as "silent fractures," occurring slowly over time. While a single vertebral fracture might cause only temporary discomfort, as additional vertebrae fracture, the normal curvature of the spine becomes more pronounced, known as "dowager's hump." This change in the shape of the back leads to chronic back pain, inability to dress and to perform the routine activities of daily living and, consequently, depression and loss of independence. For many women, their role in the household can change dramatically. It may be necessary to restrict some of their activities in the home, such as cleaning, lifting, and gardening.

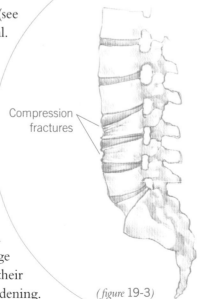

Compression fractures

(figure 19-3)

Osteoporosis with vertebral compression fractures. Note reduction of height of the vertebrae due to fractures.

(figure 19-4)

Bone remodeling. (a, b) Normally bone-resorbing cells called osteoclasts dig pits in the bone, and (c) bone-forming cells called osteoblasts fill them in with new bone. In osteoporosis, the bone-resorbing cells overcome the ability of the bone-forming cells to fill the pits.

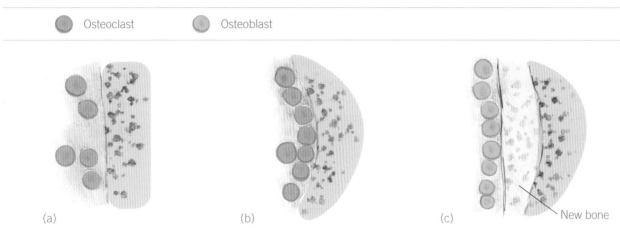

○ Osteoclast   ○ Osteoblast

(a)   (b)   (c)   New bone

19

Individuals with fractures often have chronic pain and are unable to stand or sit for prolonged periods of time. Pain limits their participation in their usual activities, such as shopping, entertaining, and traveling. Because of the changes in the shape of the back, clothes often do not fit properly, resulting in a deteriorating self-image and a spiraling depression. In severe cases, as the lungs and stomach become compressed by the pronounced curvature of the spine, the patient can have difficulty in breathing and decreased appetite.

People with wrist fractures require a cast for several weeks. They are inconvenienced for a few months until the fracture heals but usually have no long-term complications. Osteoporotic rib fractures frequently occur after coughing or sneezing. These fractures do not require a cast or surgery, but can create constant pain that worsens with deep breathing and arm movements.

Commonly, there is a considerable change in behavior after the first fracture. The usual reaction to a fracture is to try to prevent further fractures by restricting social interaction and overall activity and exercise, believing that these activities expose them to an increased risk for more fractures. However, this reaction only leads to further deconditioning, social withdrawal and isolation, hopelessness, and deepening depression.

BONE REMODELING

Our skeleton is constantly being renewed by a process called *bone remodeling* (see Figure 19-4). This is how bones grow and fractures are healed. At different sites in the skeleton, bone cells called osteoclasts remove small amounts of bone, forming a cavity or bone remodeling unit. Osteoblasts, or bone-forming cells, later deposit new bone, which is mineralized, or hardened, over the following few months. By this process, the entire skeleton is renewed every seven years.

As children grow, their bones increase in height and width. Although most children achieve their final height by age 18, their bones continue to become wider and denser until their mid-30s, when they reach *peak bone mass.* Young men grow bigger skeletons; by the time they achieve peak bone mass, they have about one-third larger bone mass than women of the same age. Sometime in their early or mid-40s both men and women begin to lose small amounts of bone mass every year, a process that will continue for the rest of their life. This slow, continuous loss of bone is attributed to an imbalance between bone resorption and bone formation. In addition, at the time of menopause women go through a short phase of rapid bone loss, when blood levels of **estrogens,** or female hormones, drop dramatically. Men who have low levels of **testosterone,** or male hormone, such as those receiving hormonal injections for the treatment of **prostate** cancer, are also at risk for rapid bone loss.

RISK FACTORS

Many factors contribute to the overall risk of developing osteoporosis, and no single risk factor can identify all individuals with this disease (see Figure 19-5). Some risk factors can be changed, but some cannot.

Age: As mentioned above, age-related bone loss begins at about age 40 and continues throughout life. Thus, the risk of osteoporosis increases with advancing age.

Gender: Women are at higher risk of developing osteoporosis not only because they reach adulthood with a smaller bone mass than men do but also because of the rapid bone loss that occurs at the time of menopause. Estrogens play a major role in maintaining skeletal health. The decline in ovarian function after menopause is associated with a sharp decline in estrogen blood levels and, consequently, a phase of rapid bone loss that can last 3 to 10 years.

Race: Caucasian and Asian men and women are at highest risk for developing osteoporosis; however, this disease also affects individuals of all races.

Heredity: Family history of osteoporosis and osteoporotic fractures is a strong risk factor. Having a parent with a hip fracture doubles an individual's risk of also having a hip fracture.

Diet: A sufficient amount of dietary calcium is needed in order to build and maintain a healthy skeleton.

Vitamin D: Vitamin D is necessary for calcium to be absorbed in the small bowel. Sources of vitamin D include diet and exposure to sunlight. When the skin is exposed to the sun, the ultraviolet rays induce a reaction resulting in the production of vitamin D. This process becomes less efficient with age and is prevented by clothing and sunscreen. Mild vitamin D deficiency is common in older individuals because of inadequate dietary intake, decreased exposure to sun (some are homebound), decreased ability of the skin to produce vitamin D, and inability to metabolize vitamin D into its most active form. Other factors that influence the production of vitamin D in the skin include geographic location, season, and time of day. Sunlight is weaker in northern latitudes, winter, and early morning or late afternoon, resulting in a lower production of vitamin D. Studies in the adult population of northern United States and Europe report up to 50% vitamin D deficiency in the winter.

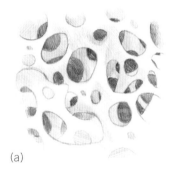

(a)

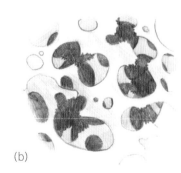

(b)

(*figure* 19-5)

(a) Normal versus (b) osteoporotic bone. The supporting structure of bone gets weaker, increasing the risk for fractures.

Exercise: Bones build up in response to weight-bearing and strength-training exercise. Prolonged periods of bed rest and immobilization are very detrimental to bone health, as it is associated with rapid bone loss.

Alcohol and caffeine: Through various mechanisms, excessive drinking of alcohol (more than one drink per day for women and more than two drinks per day for men) or of caffeinated beverages (more than three or four per day) can result in a lower bone mass.

Smoking: Bone mass is lower in both male and female smokers.

Corticosteroids: Corticosteroids are medications (cortisone, steroids) used to treat a variety of diseases, such as asthma, Crohn's disease, rheumatoid arthritis, lupus, and some cancers. Corticosteroids can be life-saving in many instances, but if used for a prolonged period of time, these medications can cause very rapid and severe bone loss. It is highly recommended that individuals on chronic treatment with corticosteroids get tested for osteoporosis.

Most hip fractures occur in individuals 65 years of age and older. Individuals in that age group have an increased risk of a hip fracture if (1) they have a parent who had a hip fracture, (2) they smoke, (3) weigh less than 57 kilograms, or (4) are unable to get up from a chair without using their arms.

DIAGNOSIS: BONE DENSITY TESTING

Bone densitometry by dual X-ray absorptiometry (DXA) is the gold standard technique to diagnose osteoporosis (see Figure 19-6). This procedure scans the skeletal sites where osteoporotic fractures commonly occur, the lower *(lumbar)* spine and/or the hip *(proximal femur)*. The test is painless, takes about 10 minutes, involves minimal radiation, and does not require injections. Many portable instruments can also test for osteoporosis in other parts of the skeleton, such as the wrist, finger, or heel, but a DXA is required to confirm the diagnosis before initiating treatment. Each patient's result is compared to the normal database already incorporated into the instrument's software. Bone density results are expressed as a T-score. Osteoporosis is diagnosed with a T-score of −2.5 or lower. A T-score between −2.5 and −1, is considered low bone density, or osteopenia. A normal result is reflected by a T-score of −1 or above.

Osteophytes, or osteoarthritis of the spine, are common after the age of 50 or 60 years. These abnormal arthritic bone formations in the spine mislead the instrument and result in falsely elevated spinal bone density measurements and a deceivingly "normal" result. Thus, in older adults, bone density tests of other areas of the skeleton, such as the hip or a part of the thighbone called the femoral neck, are the most reliable. Due to the rather slow process of bone loss and the precision of the instruments, repeat tests to determine the rate of bone loss or the effectiveness of a treatment are usually performed not more often than every two years.

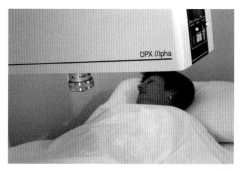

(figure 19-6)

Bone density testing.

PREVENTION AND TREATMENT

LIFESTYLE

Physical activity, adequate calcium and vitamin D intake, and a healthy lifestyle are the basic steps for maintaining bone health. Once bone density is low or the diagnosis of osteoporosis has been established, medical treatment is necessary to prevent further bone loss and decrease the risk of fractures.

Calcium: An adequate amount of calcium is necessary to build and maintain strong bones. Although many foods contain small amounts of calcium, the richest calcium-containing foods are dairy products and some juices and cereals that are fortified with calcium. A diet that does not include several daily servings of dairy or calcium-fortified products is unlikely to fulfill the daily calcium requirements. Calcium supplements might be necessary in elderly individuals who have decreased appetite or are unable to ingest dairy products. Calcium carbonate is considered the most cost-effective calcium supplement. Calcium citrate is recommended for individuals who have decreased acidity in their stomach, as is the case in many elderly individuals. While calcium carbonate tablets should be taken with or right after a meal, calcium citrate tablets should be taken in between meals. Calcium supplements that are manufactured are preferable to natural products. In the past, some of these natural products have been found to have contaminants, such as lead. Calcium tablets should not be taken with high-fiber meals or bulk laxatives as these can prevent calcium absorption. Common side effects to calcium tablets include bloating, flatulence, and constipation (see Chapter 9). These symptoms might be prevented by drinking plenty of fluids or by switching to a different preparation. Foods rich in calcium are less likely to cause side effects. Because the amount of calcium that can be absorbed in the bowel at one time is limited, it is highly recommended that the total calcium daily intake be divided into two or three doses in the day. It is recommended that men and women over the age of 50 years take at least 1200 mg per day, preferably 1500 mg.

Vitamin D: Vitamin D plays a major role in the absorption of calcium in the small bowel and in the mineralization of bone. Although vitamin D is mostly known for its role in preserving bone health, studies have demonstrated that it is also important for maintaining muscle strength. It has been reported that elderly individuals who are deficient in vitamin D have more falls than those who are not. Sources of vitamin D include some foods, vitamin supplements, and sunshine. Among the very few foods that contain vitamin D naturally are eggs, liver, and fatty fish. In the United States, milk and some cereals are fortified with vitamin D and can provide an easy way to obtain vitamin D through the diet. Vitamin D is also included in multivitamins and many calcium supplements. The recommended daily dose is 400 to 800 IU. In individuals who are vitamin D–deficient, these doses might not suffice the replenishment of their vitamin D levels.

Exercise: Although the type of exercise and the exercise frequency for optimal bone health are yet to be determined, extensive experience demonstrates that weight-bearing and strength-training exercises are the best for helping build up a strong skeleton and prevent bone loss. Weight-bearing exercises include walking, running, hiking, stair climbing, dancing, gymnastics, calisthenics, and so on. Strength-training exercises involve the lifting of weights, either free weights or weight machines. Training should progress slowly, preferably under supervision. In older or deconditioned individuals, a progressive walking program and physical therapy might be all that is recommended. Special exercises can be prescribed for individuals who want to minimize the curvature of the back that resulted from several vertebral fractures (kyphosis). These exercises are designed to strengthen the abdominal and spinal muscles and to stretch the muscle groups in the chest and hip. In addition to its skeleton-building effect, exercise can also prevent falls by improving muscle strength, gait, and balance. Once osteoporosis is diagnosed, exercise alone will not reverse the process. A drug regimen should be considered in addition to calcium supplements, vitamin D, and exercise.

PRESCRIPTION MEDICATIONS

Bisphosphonates: The group of drugs known as *bisphosphonates* affects mainly the skeleton by slowing down the process of bone loss. Although treatment will result in small changes in bone density, large studies have reported an average 50% reduction in fractures. Several oral and intravenous formulations are available, but only ALENDRONATE and RISEDRONATE are FDA-approved for the prevention and treatment of postmenopausal osteoporosis, male osteoporosis, and corticosteroid-induced osteoporosis. The tablets should be taken in the morning, fasting, with a full glass of tap water. It is important to remain in upright position (sitting, standing, or walking) and not lie down or bend over for 30 minutes after taking the medication. For better absorption, it is also important not to eat and only drink water for this same period of time. Alendronate (FOSAMAX) can be taken daily (10 mg) or once weekly (70 mg). Risedronate (ACTONEL) can also be taken daily (5 mg) or once weekly (35 mg).

Selective estrogen receptor modulators: Selective estrogen receptor modulators (SERMs), or designer estrogens, are drugs that have actions both like and unlike estrogen. TAMOXIFEN is commonly used in breast cancer, but RALOXIFENE (EVISTA) is the only FDA-approved SERM for prevention and treatment of postmenopausal osteoporosis. Studies show that treatment with raloxifene does not decrease the risk of hip fractures; it can produce worse hot flashes but, unlike estrogens, does not cause vaginal bleeding or breast tenderness.

Calcitonin: SALMON CALCITONIN (MIACALCIN) decreases vertebral fractures but does not reduce the risk of hip fractures. It is used as a nasal spray.

Parathyroid hormone: The medication parathyroid hormone, or TERIPARATIDE (FORTEO), is the only drug available that stimulates bone formation. It produces large increases in bone density, particularly in the spine, and reduces the risk of fractures. Administration is by a daily injection in the skin. Because of concerning side effects in animals, treatment is recommended for only two years.

Estrogen: Treatment with the female hormone estrogen reduces osteoporotic fractures by about 50%. However, information regarding the increased risk for heart disease, stroke, blood clots, and breast cancer in women after prolonged treatment with estrogen has led to a reconsideration of its use for the prevention or treatment of osteoporosis.

SURGICAL PROCEDURES

Surgery is the treatment of choice after a hip fracture. The type of procedure may vary, from a total hip replacement to the placement of such devices as pins, screws, and plates to fixate the fracture.

Vertebroplasty and kyphoplasty (see Figure 19-7) prevent further crushing or restore the height of a compressed vertebra. A special cement is introduced into the body of the vertebra through a catheter inserted in the back under radiological guidance. Often, this procedure results in decreased back pain.

PAIN MANAGEMENT

Pain management after a fracture can be challenging. Although in the first few days bed rest and a brace for the trunk might be needed to alleviate pain, early ambulation and restoration of mobility is often recommended. Different types of pain medication may be prescribed, with caution in using narcotics that may cause dizziness and falls. In some individuals, ice packs or a massage is helpful.

SAFETY: FALLS PREVENTION

Preventing falls is crucial in the elderly. Fall prevention measures involve the evaluation of the patient's medical conditions and drug regimens; a prescription for exercise to improve muscle strength, gait, and balance; and an assessment of their homes for environmental hazards, as listed in Table 19-1. Chapter 31 contains an extensive discussion of the evaluation of falls and their prevention.

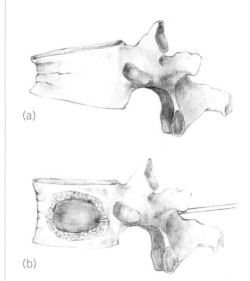

(a)

(b)

(figure 19-7)

(a) Vertebral compression fracture. (b) Kyphoplasty is a procedure in which a needle is inserted into a fractured vertebra and a balloon is inflated. A special cement that strengthens and stabilizes the bone is injected with the intention of relieving pain and restoring the height of the compressed vertebra.

(table 19-1)

COMMON ENVIRONMENTAL HAZARDS INCREASING THE RISK FOR FALLS

PERSONAL	HOME
High heels or nonslip-resistant shoes	Slippery floors
Inadequate eyeglasses	Throw rugs
Not using necessary walking aids	Clutter or cords on the floor
	Stairwells or steps in poor condition or poor lighting
	Low furniture (coffee tables)
	No night lights
	No grab bars in bathroom or tub

WHAT YOU NEED TO KNOW

▶ Risk factors for osteoporotic fractures in individuals age 65 and older are (1) a parent who had a hip fracture, (2) smoking, (3) body weight less than 57 kilograms, and (4) being unable to get up from a chair without using the arms.

▶ Osteoporosis is diagnosed with a bone density test. Results are expressed as a T-score. A T-score of −2.5 or lower is indicative of osteoporosis, and a T-score between −2.5 and −1 is considered low bone density, or osteopenia. A normal result is a T-score of −1 or above.

▶ It is recommended that men and women over the age of 50 years take at least 1200 mg to 1500 mg of calcium daily. Healthy adults should have a daily intake of 400 to 800 IU of vitamin D.

▶ Maintain an active lifestyle. Find a physical activity that you enjoy and is appropriate for your health status. Avoid long periods of bed rest and immobilization.

▶ Do not smoke; drink alcohol and caffeinated beverages in moderation.

▶ Osteoporosis is diagnosed by bone densitometry. Often, in individuals over the age of 60, hip or femoral neck results are most reliable.

▶ Treatment with prescription medication is advised for all persons with osteoporosis and for those with bone density values that are close to the osteoporotic range.

▶ Review all personal and environmental factors to prevent falls.

19

FOR MORE INFORMATION

▶ National Institutes of Health, Osteoporosis and Related Bone Diseases Resource Center
Web: www.osteo.org

▶ American Association of Clinical Endocrinologists
Web: www.aace.com

▶ National Osteoporosis Foundation
202-223-2226
Web: www.nof.org

▶ AgeNet Eldercare Network
800-732-6643
Offers a free booklet, "Healthy Bones for Life."

▶ Elder Floridians Foundation
P.O. Box 16183,
Tallahassee, FL 32317
850-205-2500
Offers a booklet, "Bones."

The want of energy is one of the main reasons why so few persons continue to improve in later years.

—*Benjamin Jowett, Introductions to Plato*

THE AUTHOR

20

Mark W. Shepherd MD

MARK SHEPHERD, MD, FACE, is the founder and medical director of Endocrinology Consultants in Tulepo, Mississippi. He completed his medical education at Emory University and an internal medicine–pediatrics residency at Vanderbilt. He subsequently did a fellowship in endocrinology at Willford Hall Medical Center in San Antonio, Texas, and a research fellowship in diabetes and lipid metabolism at the University of Texas Health Sciences Center. He is a former director of the Diabetes Care Center and the Metabolic Research Unit at the David Grant Medical Center in California. Certified by the American Board of Internal Medicine, he is a fellow of the American College of Endocrinology.

HORMONES, THE ENDOCRINE SYSTEM

20

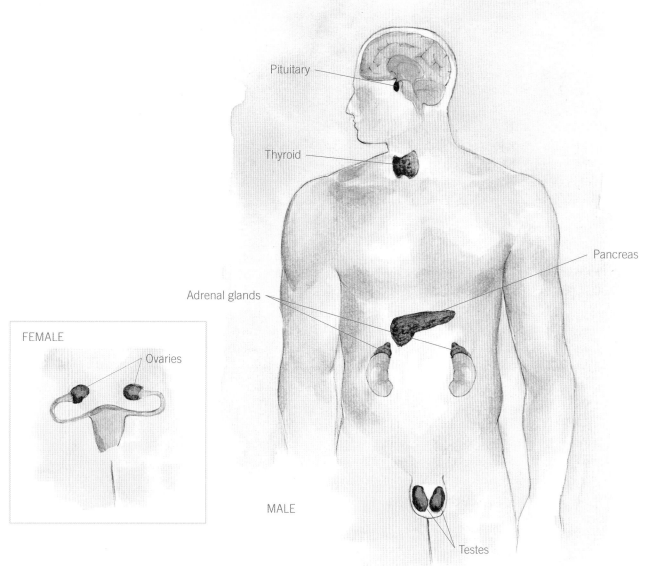

Pituitary

Thyroid

Pancreas

Adrenal glands

FEMALE

Ovaries

MALE

Testes

(figure 20-1)

The endocrine system is an intricate system of glands and hormones that regulates the delicate balance in your body.

In this chapter, I examine the contribution of your system of hormones, the endocrine system, to maintaining the delicate balance of the body's internal regulatory structure. This balance between too little and too much is called *homeostasis,* or the maintenance of a state of equilibrium within the body by coordinating the responses of various organ systems to changes in the environment. The word *endocrine* refers to "internal secretions," which are also known as *hormones.* A hormone is a substance produced by an organ in one part of the body that on being secreted into the bloodstream has effects on tissues nearby or elsewhere throughout the body. The endocrine system is a critical part of our internal communication system, coordinating and maintaining the optimum structure and function of the human body. Hormones exert their effect on target tissues through the action of receptors. Located on the surface or within a cell, a receptor is a "receiver" component. On being hit by a hormone, the *receptor* reacts by activating or deactivating the cell's internal machinery (see Figure 20-2).

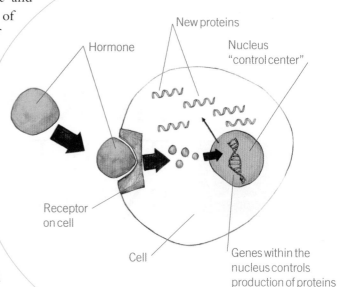

(figure 20-2*)*

How a hormone works: A hormone binds to a specific receptor on the cell wall. As a result, a series of second messengers transmit information to the cell's control center called the nucleus. The nucleus then activates or deactivates the cell's internal genetic machinery.

Diseases of the endocrine system can generally be classified according to whether a particular hormone is decreased (hormone deficiency) or increased (hormone excess). Syndromes of hormone deficiency or excess are detected by correlating certain signs and symptoms with characteristic findings on physical examination and subsequent confirmation by laboratory testing of blood, urine, or biopsy specimens. On occasion, specialized tests that stimulate or suppress hormone production are performed in an endocrinologist's office to diagnose an endocrine disorder.

Endocrinology, diabetes, and *metabolism* cover the subspecialty of internal medicine involving the diagnosis and treatment of disorders of the hormonal system. An endocrinologist is a physician who, after finishing medical school, has completed a three- or four-year residency in internal medicine followed by a two- or three-year fellowship in endocrinology, diabetes, and metabolism. As well treating the disorders shown in Table 20-1, endocrinologists are consulted by other physicians regarding those disorders.

The aging process generally has two effects on the endocrine system. The first is the tendency toward hormone deficiency, which may be slow and insidious, escaping detection for years since the symptoms are often missed or attributed to "old age." Patients may not be aware that general and nonspecific symptoms, such as fatigue, weakness, poor concentration, increased forgetfulness, depression, poor appetite, unexplained weight change, alterations in bowel function, sleep pattern, or physical mobility, can be secondary to a decline in endocrine function. The second effect of aging is to predispose the endocrine glands to tumor formation that on occasion can be cancerous (malignant). A palpable knot or swelling may be found in a gland, as would be the case for thyroid nodules. Or perhaps

(table 20-1)

DISORDERS TREATED BY ENDOCRINOLOGISTS

Diabetes mellitus	Osteoporosis, metabolic bone disease
Hypoglycemia	Recurrent kidney stones
Thyroid problems	High cholesterol or triglycerides
Adrenal disorders	Abnormal weight gain, obesity
Ovary, female reproduction	Abnormal weight loss, malnutrition
Testosterone, male reproduction	Inherited metabolic problems
Pituitary diseases	Refractory or difficult to control hypertension

unexplained pain or hormone deficiency or excess alerts the doctor to tumors of the internal organs, such as the pituitary gland, adrenal gland, or gonads. Fortunately, endocrine cancers are rare and usually not life threatening.

THE PITUITARY GLAND

The pituitary gland is a small, pea-sized gland situated at the base of the brain in a special pocket of bone known as the sella turcica (see Figure 20-3). It functions as the "master gland," directing and monitoring the function of the adrenal gland, thyroid gland, ovaries, and testes. The pituitary gland produces other hormones as well that have important functions throughout the body. It is connected to the hypothalamus, a specialized part of the brain which functions as a "relay station," transmitting signals from other parts of the brain to the pituitary gland through a small stalk which contains a special network of blood vessels and nerves. The pituitary gland is divided into two parts: (1) the anterior portion that

(figure 20-3)

The pituitary gland is a very small gland at the base of the brain and functions as the master gland for the rest of the endocrine system.

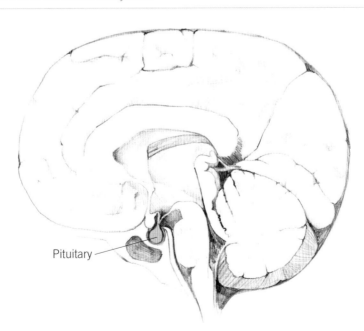

Pituitary

(*figure* 20-4)

Your body has an ingenious system for regulating production of your hormones. The brain stimulates the hypothalamus to secrete hormones that in turn stimulate the pituitary gland to produce its own hormones. The pituitary hormones stimulate such glands as the thyroid (shown in figure), adrenals, and testes to produce their own hormones which circulate in the blood and act at other sites in the body. The hypothalamus detects the levels of these hormones in the bloodstream and will turn the pituitary off or on depending on whether less or more is needed.

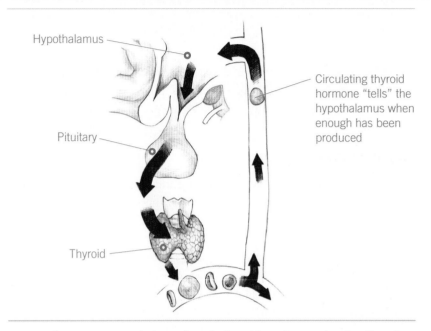

Hypothalamus

Pituitary

Thyroid

Circulating thyroid hormone "tells" the hypothalamus when enough has been produced

secretes hormones regulating adrenal, thyroid, and reproductive function, growth, and metabolism and (2) the posterior portion that regulates water balance.

In response to signals from the brain, the hypothalamus produces *releasing hormones,* which travel through the pituitary stalk and act on the front part of the pituitary gland. In response to these releasing hormones, the pituitary gland produces *stimulating hormones* that are released into the blood circulation to exert their effects on other endocrine organs. These target organs are responsible for the actual production and secretion of *hormones* (i.e., thyroid hormone, cortisol, estrogen, and testosterone) that, in turn, are released into the circulation to regulate body functions. When the hormones have been produced in adequate amounts, they turn off the stimulating signals from the hypothalamus and pituitary. As you can see in Figure 20–4, this is an ingenious system. The endocrine system is flexible and resilient. In fact the endocrine system is so "overengineered" that one can lose up to 90% of the function of most of the endocrine system and still maintain normal life!

The tiny pituitary gland makes eight different hormones. Prolactin stimulates normal breast milk production after birth. Excess amounts can impair estrogen production in women and testosterone production in men. Growth hormone (GH) regulates growth in childhood, but is also important for well-being in adults, including maintaining a healthy body composition, muscle mass, body fat distribution, and bone density. Adrenocorticotropic hormone (ACTH) stimulates production of

(*table* 20-2)

HORMONES FROM HYPOTHALAMUS AND PITUITARY AND THEIR TARGET ORGANS*

RELEASING HORMONE FROM HYPOTHALAMUS	PITUITARY HORMONE	TARGET ENDOCRINE GLAND	HORMONE RELEASED BY TARGET GLAND	FUNCTION OF HORMONE RELEASED BY TARGET GLAND
Corticotropin-releasing hormone (CRH)	Adrenocorticotropin (ACTH)	Adrenal	Cortisol	Metabolism, stress, circulation, water balance, inflammation
Thyrotropin-releasing hormone (TRH)	Thyroid-stimulating hormone (TSH)	Thyroid	Thyroxine (T4) Thyronine (T3)	Brain, heart, nervous system, circulation, metabolism, and others
Gonadotropin-releasing hormone (GnRH)	Luteinizing hormone (LH), Follicle-stimulating hormone (FSH)	Gonads	Estradiol (female) Testosterone (male)	Secondary sexual characteristics, reproduction, bone, muscle mass
Growth hormone–releasing hormone	Growth hormone (GH)	Liver	Insulin-like growth factor (IGF-I)	Growth, metabolism, bone density
Dopamine (inhibitory)	Prolactin	Mammary gland	None	Lactation

*All the hormones produced by the hypothalamus stimulate release of pituitary hormones, except dopamine, which inhibits release of prolactin. Prolactin is only released when dopamine from the hypothalamus is inhibited.

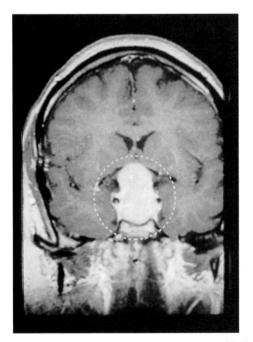

(*figure* 20-5)

MRI (frontal view) shows a pituitary tumor (circled).

cortisol from the adrenal glands, which is a vital "stress" hormone, helping maintain blood pressure and glucose levels. Thyroid-stimulating hormone (TSH) stimulates the thyroid gland, which helps to regulate metabolism, energy, growth, development, cardiac, and nervous system activity. Antidiuretic hormone (ADH), also known as *vasopressin,* is stored in the back part of the pituitary gland and regulates water balance. Luteinizing hormone (LH) stimulates estrogen in women and testosterone in men. Follicle-stimulating hormone (FSH) promotes sperm production in men and enables ovulation in women. Together, LH and FSH are known as *gonadotropins* and regulate overall human reproduction. Table 20-2 outlines the major anterior pituitary hormones along with the important body functions that they regulate.

PITUITARY TUMORS

Pituitary tumors, also known as *adenomas,* are the most frequent disorder of the pituitary gland (see Figure 20-5). They are fairly common, affecting up to 10% of all older adults. The tumors are usually silent and are not a form of cancer. Pituitary tumors can, however, interfere with the normal formation and release of pituitary hormones, leading to pituitary insufficiency, or *hypopituitarism.* In addition, some pituitary tumors can make too much of the hormone produced by the cells forming the tumor, leading to a state of hormone excess or *hypersecretion.* Pituitary tumors can cause three different types of problems:

1. *Hypersecretion (oversecretion).* Too much hormone is produced, leading to harmful effects throughout the body. Common examples are tumors that make too much prolactin (called *prolactinomas*) or growth hormone, a condition known as *acromegaly.* Less common forms of pituitary hormone excess involve ACTH and the adrenal glands

(Cushing's disease), TSH (TSH-secreting adenoma), and LH/FSH (gonadotroph adenomas). Sometimes, medications used to treat certain psychiatric conditions can lead to oversecretion of prolactin, also known as hyperprolactinemia.

2. *Hyposecretion (undersecretion).* Since the sella turcica, the location of the pituitary gland, is a small enclosed space, tumors (secretory or nonsecretory) can compress or damage the normal pituitary tissue, rendering it unable to make enough hormones to meet the body's needs. This can also result from surgery or radiation to the pituitary gland or nearby regions of the brain. Loss of pituitary function has been reported following major head trauma. The prolonged use of steroid medications, such as prednisone to treat inflammatory conditions, can suppress levels of ACTH and lead to cortisol deficiency which can take up to one year to resolve after the steroid medications are discontinued.

3. *Tumor mass effects.* As the tumor grows, it can press against normal pituitary tissue or other areas of the brain, causing headaches, visual problems, or undersecretion of hormones. It can expand upward and compress the optic nerve (the nerve to the eye) leading to decreased vision, particularly in the peripheral visual fields. This causes "tunnel vision," or difficulty making out objects that are not directly in front of you. If the tumor expands to the sides, it can interfere with blood flow to the brain or press on nerves that innervate the face, causing numbness, weakness, or pain in the facial area or elsewhere in the body.

PROLACTINOMA

A **prolactinoma** is a tumor that produces too much prolactin (or "milk" hormone). It is the most common pituitary tumor, accounting for up to 40% of all pituitary tumors. Excess prolactin reduces estrogen production in women and testosterone production in men. Symptoms in young women include decreased or loss of menstrual periods, infertility, and increased milk discharge from the breasts, a condition known as *galactorrhea*. Symptoms in older women and men can be nonspecific, making this a difficult tumor to diagnose. Other symptoms might include headaches, visual disturbances, reduced sex drive, mood changes, depression, osteoporosis from low estrogen or testosterone, and inability to get or maintain an erection in men. Prolactinomas are diagnosed by measuring an excess of prolactin in the bloodstream and finding a pituitary tumor on a brain **magnetic resonance imaging (MRI)** scan, a special procedure that uses signals induced by a changing magnetic field to produce a high-resolution image superior to X-rays.

Approximately 90% of prolactinomas can be treated successfully with medications that decrease prolactin levels in the blood, often shrinking the tumor as well. The most common medications are BROMOCRIPTINE (PARLODEL) and CABERGOLINE (DOSTINEX), which are taken as pills and usually well tolerated. The most common side effects are nausea and dizziness. On rare occasions, if medication is ineffective or not tolerated, or the tumor extremely large with impaired vision, surgery is the preferred option. Radiation therapy is almost never required for management of prolactinomas. Very small tumors with few or no symptoms may warrant a course of careful monitoring and observation.

ACROMEGALY

Acromegaly is caused by overproduction of growth hormone in adults, usually from a pituitary tumor. It is an insidious disorder producing few or subtle symptoms and often remaining undetected for years (or even decades). It can cause changes in appearance and adverse effects on many body systems, including the heart, bones, joints, gastrointestinal tract, and metabolism. Symptoms may include:

- Enlarged hands, feet, head, nose, and jaw, often detected as a progressive increase in hat, ring, and/or shoe size
- Thickening of the flesh on the palms and feet
- Course facial features
- Increased space between teeth
- Enlarged tongue
- Loud snoring and interrupted breathing while sleeping (sleep apnea)
- Deepening of the voice
- Oily skin, acne
- Excessive sweating
- Skin tags (small growths of skin over the neck, back, and trunk)
- Rapidly progressive osteoarthritis
- Carpal tunnel syndrome
- Multiple colon polyps
- Headache or peripheral vision loss
- Pituitary deficiency, such as fatigue, weakness, and reduced sex drive

The diagnosis is confirmed by testing the blood for growth hormone (GH) and *insulin-like growth factor (IGF-I)*. In borderline cases, a GH suppression test may be performed. Glucose is given orally, and the level of GH in the blood is then measured. Glucose normally suppresses GH secretion but will fail to do so in patients with acromegaly. An MRI usually shows a pituitary tumor that can be as large as an inch or sometimes even larger, depending on the severity and duration of symptoms.

A neurosurgeon will usually be consulted about removing the tumor through a procedure known as *transsphenoidal microsurgery,* by which an incision is made through the sinuses behind the nose and the tumor is removed without drilling a hole or cutting through the skull or brain. Removing the tumor relieves pressure caused by the tumor itself and lowers but rarely normalizes the GH level, especially if the tumor is large initially. Surgery alone is curative in only about 30% of cases. If the IGF-I or the GH suppression test remains abnormal after surgery, medication and/or radiation therapy will be required to normalize GH secretion and relieve symptoms.

In acromegaly, the use of medication has been shown in clinical studies to improve symptoms and prolong survival. The most commonly used medication is OCTREOTIDE (SANDOSTATIN), which can be given by a small injection under the skin three times daily until the goal dose is achieved, and then converted to a long-acting form of the medication given by a deep intramuscular injection every four weeks. Octreotide acts directly on the tumor cells to inhibit hormone production. It can be given indefinitely to patients in whom surgery was not curative or while waiting for radiation therapy to be effective. This might take several years. A newer medication known as PEGVISOMANT (SOMAVERT) is an impersonator of GH, in that it binds to the GH receptor in the liver and works by inhibiting IGF-I, which is the hormone directly responsible for the damage that occurs to the body from acromegaly. Pegvisomant is given by a daily injection under the skin and is usually given to patients who do not tolerate or respond completely to octreotide.

Many of the symptoms of acromegaly, such as sweating, hypertension, or glucose intolerance, disappear almost immediately with treatment. Others, such as swelling of the hands or feet and sleep apnea, may take longer to improve. Severe osteoarthritis or bone changes may not go away even with appropriate therapy, highlighting the importance of earlier diagnosis and treatment. It is important to note that patients with acromegaly are at increased risk for colon cancer and should undergo colonoscopy initially and at regular intervals.

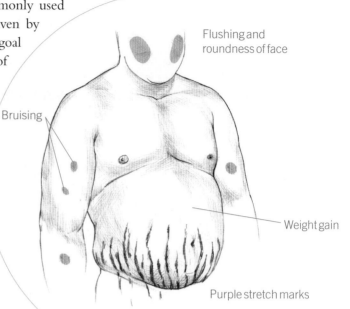

Flushing and roundness of face

Bruising

Weight gain

Purple stretch marks

(*figure* 20-6)

Some common symptoms of Cushings disease.

CUSHING'S DISEASE

Cushing's disease occurs when a pituitary tumor overproduces *ACTH,* which leads to excessive *cortisol* production by the adrenal glands (see Figure 20-6). This is an uncommon condition but affects as many as 4000 people annually in the United States. Symptoms may include:

- Rapid and unexplained weight gain, especially in the face, neck, and abdomen with thinner arms and legs
- Increased fat deposition above the collarbone and upper back ("buffalo hump")
- Increase flushing over the face
- Wide purplish stretch marks on the skin
- Easy bruising
- Poor healing
- Progressive muscle weakness
- Poor concentration and/ or increased forgetfulness
- Moodiness, change in personality, and/ or depression
- High blood pressure
- Fluid retention and/ or swelling

- High blood glucose levels
- Low blood potassium levels
- Unexplained or severe osteoporosis (decreased bone density with increased fracture risk)

The diagnosis is often difficult to make and requires a series of timed urine collections and blood samples to test for ACTH and cortisol production. Other conditions, including cortisol-producing tumors of the adrenal glands and tumors outside the pituitary gland, can also produce ACTH (known as *ectopic* ACTH-secreting tumors) and mimic Cushing's disease. A relatively new test known as *inferior petrosal sinus sampling (IPSS)* involves positioning small catheters in the veins that drain the pituitary to sample directly for ACTH. This can be very helpful to distinguish between the various diagnostic possibilities.

Treatment must be individualized but usually requires surgical removal of the tumor, which is curative about 90% of the time. Medication to block the adrenal gland is often used as an adjunct to surgery. Radiation therapy may be required to treat any remaining tumor mass. In extreme cases, the adrenal glands themselves may need to be removed to gain control over excess cortisol secretion. Other problems, such as hypertension, high glucose levels, and osteoporosis, may require separate therapy.

OTHER PITUITARY TUMORS

Extremely rare, *TSH-secreting tumors* cause the thyroid gland to overproduce thyroid hormone, a condition known as *hyperthyroidism* and discussed in the section "Too Much: Hyperthyroidism." A TSH-secreting adenoma increases the TSH level rather than decreasing it, as occurs in hyperthyroidism caused by primary disease of the thyroid gland itself. Surgery followed by radiation of any remaining tumor is the treatment of choice. Medications are less effective although some TSH-secreting tumors may respond to octreotide.

Nonsecreting pituitary tumors are usually derived from cells that originally made LH or FSH *(gonadotroph adenomas)* but do not produce any syndromes of hormone excess. They are often discovered incidentally when the brain is being imaged for some other reason. Such tumors may cause symptoms of pituitary insufficiency because of compression or destruction of normal pituitary tissue. Tumor mass effects include headache, visual field disturbances, or abnormal control of eye movements. Loss of normal pituitary function may cause fatigue, weakness, poor appetite, unexplained weight loss or gain, decreased sex drive, increased thirst and/or urination, joint pains, decreased mobility, low blood pressure, and light-headedness (especially when standing). Transsphenoidal microsurgery is employed, as well as radiation, for any remaining or recurring tumor. Some form of pituitary replacement therapy is often required. Small nonsecreting tumors that are not producing any mass effects or alterations in pituitary function may be safely monitored by periodic exams, hormone testing, and serial MRI scans.

MORE ON RADIATION THERAPY

Radiation uses high-energy X-rays to kill pituitary tumor cells and/ or to shrink tumors. It may be used if surgery and medication fail to control the tumor. The radiation comes from a source outside the body and thus is known as *external radiation therapy*. There are three primary types of external radiation therapy for pituitary tumors:

1. *Standard external beam radiotherapy* uses a radiation source that is nonselective and delivers radiation to all the cells in the path of the X-ray. This can cause injury to adjacent normal tissue. The collateral injury is usually minor and does not produce significant brain injury.
2. *Proton beam radiotherapy* directs protons to the pituitary gland and may produce less collateral damage.
3. *Gamma knife radiotherapy* directs standard external beam radiotherapy through different ports to focus more energy on the tumor and less on adjacent normal tissue. It is coupled with an imaging procedure, known as *stereotactic tumor localization,* to treat selected patients if surgery is not feasible, resection is incomplete, or the tumor reoccurs.

PITUITARY HORMONE REPLACEMENT THERAPY

Pituitary tumors, infiltration, injury, or transsphenoidal surgery can lead to complete loss of all or some pituitary hormones, conditions known as *panhypopituitarism* and *partial hypopituitarism,* respectively. Lifespan is shortened in patients with hypopituitarism. Appropriate hormone replacement therapy in these patients is critical for survival, symptom relief, and optimal function of body systems.

Hydrocortisone: HYDROCORTISONE (or its equivalent) is administered orally at an average dose of 15 to 30 mg/day given in one or two doses. Since cortisol is critical to the regulation of blood pressure and glucose levels during times of stress, the dose needs to be doubled for fever, nausea, or vomiting. For severe illness requiring hospitalization or surgery, intravenous hydrocortisone at higher doses may be required for a few days until the oral route can be reestablished. The dose is adjusted primarily on the basis of symptoms.

Desmopressin: DESMOPRESSIN (DDAVP) is given orally (0.1 to 0.3 mg twice daily), intranasally (10 to 20 mcg twice daily), or by subcutaneous injection (1 to 2 mcg twice daily) to maintain water balance and prevent excessive thirst and urination, a condition known as diabetes insipidus (vasopressin deficiency). Lack of vasopressin can also be life-threatening, especially during periods of altered consciousness as can occur during acute illness, trauma, or surgery when access to free water is interrupted or impaired. The dose is adjusted on the basis of symptoms and occasional testing of the blood sodium level.

Levothyroxine: LEVOTHYROXINE (L-THYROXINE), more commonly known as *thyroid hormone,* is given as a pill once daily. The dose can vary from 25 to 200 mcg daily. It can also be administered intravenously when oral intake is interrupted for prolonged periods. L-thyroxine is critical to survival and well-being but does not need to be adjusted during periods of acute stress. The dose is adjusted on the basis of symptoms, physical exam findings, and blood testing. TSH testing is the most reliable test for adjusting the dose of l-thyroxine in patients with primary disorders of the thyroid gland. TSH is *not* a reliable test in patients with pituitary disease since it is decreased or absent. The free thyroxine (T_4) level is generally maintained in the upper half of the normal range. The free triiodothyronine (T_3) test has been shown to be a more useful test although it is expensive and should be performed only in an endocrine specialty laboratory. Patients who require thyroid hormone replacement due to pituitary disease usually require higher doses for thyroid hormone replacement than those with primary thyroid gland disorders (approximately 2 versus 1.7 mcg per kilogram of body weight each day).

Estrogen and testosterone: Estrogen and testosterone may need to be replaced but are not critical for survival. They are discussed in the section, "The Gonads: Menopause and Andropause."

Somatropin: Growth hormone (GH) therapy has traditionally been used only in children to promote normal growth and achieve normal adult stature. However, GH is secreted throughout life and is critical for maintaining muscle mass and strength, decreasing excess body fat, maintaining normal bone density, maintaining healthy cholesterol levels, and preventing atherosclerosis which can cause heart attacks and strokes. Consequently, SOMATROPIN has been approved for use in adults with GH deficiency due to pituitary disease. The diagnosis is confirmed by measuring the GH response in the bloodstream to an intravenous stimulating agent, such as insulin or arginine. GH replacement in somatotropin-deficient adults has been shown in clinical studies to increase lean body mass; reduce body fat; increase strength, exercise tolerance, and stamina; improve physical mobility; increase bone density; improve cholesterol levels; slow the progression of atherosclerosis; and improve one's overall sense of well-being.

Somatropin is administered by a small injection under the skin every night at bedtime. The average dose ranges from 0.2 to 0.8 mg/day. The dose is adjusted on the basis of symptoms, physical exam findings, and monitoring IGF-I levels. Side effects may include headache, joint pains, hand or wrist pain, fluid retention, and high blood sugar levels. The benefits of GH replacement therapy have not been demonstrated in adults without pituitary disorders or documented GH deficiency. GH replacement has not been well studied in adults over the age of 70 with GH deficiency due to pituitary disease, but the few patients who have been studied generally demonstrate the same beneficial clinical response as younger patients show.

SYNDROME OF INAPPROPRIATE ANTIDIURETIC HORMONE

Certain conditions may stimulate abnormal secretion of ADH (vasopressin), which has an effect on the kidneys to promote retention of excess water. This can cause the blood sodium to fall to dangerously low levels, which can in turn lead to altered consciousness, seizures, coma, or death. Syndrome of inappropriate antidiuretic hormone (SIADH) is diagnosed by finding a low blood sodium concentration and a higher than expected urine sodium concentration in the absence of dehydration. Predisposing conditions include disorders of the brain, tumors, major surgery, lung diseases, and certain medications.

Treatment involves treating the underlying condition causing the SIADH and restricting water intake to only 1 or 2 liters per day to counteract the effect of increased water retention by the kidneys. In more severe cases, the oral administration of a little-used antibiotic known as DEMECLOCYCLINE (DECLOMYCIN) at a dose of 250 to 500 mg four times daily may also be useful. The recent discovery of the free water channel in the kidney, known as *aquaporin,* which is the target for vasopressin action, may lead to improved treatments for SIADH in the near future.

THYROID GLAND

The thyroid gland is a small, butterfly-shaped gland located at the base of the front part of the neck, just above the breastbone and just below the Adam's apple (see Figure 20-7). Thyroid hormone, also known as *thyroxine (T$_4$),* is an iodine-containing molecule secreted in response to the pituitary hormone, thyroid-stimulating hormone (TSH). Thyroxine circulates throughout the body, supporting a host of important body systems including:

- Brain and nervous system
- Heart and blood vessels
- Lungs
- Stomach and intestines
- Kidney
- Reproductive system
- Metabolism and the production of body heat
- Skin, hair, and nails

Disorders of the thyroid gland may produce severe symptoms that dramatically impair health and well-being, or they can be more subtle and insidious, causing few or mild symptoms that may progress more slowly over a period of many years. Thyroid disorders are more common in women and tend to cluster in certain families as well. Moreover, the presence of thyroid disease increases with age, such that as many as 15% of women may develop thyroid hormone deficiency after the age of 70. Thyroid disorders are typically classified as thyroid hormone deficiency, or *hypothyroidism* (too little); thyroid hormone excess, or *hyperthyroidism* (too much); and tumors, or *thyroid nodules* (thus the need for "a neck check").

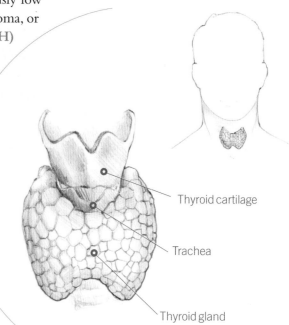

Thyroid cartilage

Trachea

Thyroid gland

(figure 20-7)

The thyroid gland is located at the base of your neck.

TIGHTENING OF THE GOITER BELT

In years past the area around the Great Lakes, Midwest, and inland mountains was referred to as the "goiter belt." A deficiency of iodine in the soil and diet caused an enlargement of the thyroid gland known as a goiter. In some cases, the thyroid swelled to a massive size. Iodine is a necessary precursor to the production of thyroid hormone by the thyroid gland. Goiters are rarely seen these days due to public health measures, such as the addition of iodine to the water supply and table salt.

TOO LITTLE: HYPOTHYROIDISM

Hypothyroidism occurs when the thyroid gland is unable to make enough thyroid hormone to keep the body running normally. This is the most common thyroid disease and can be caused by either an abnormal antibody that attacks and destroys the gland or a medical treatment for other thyroid conditions, such as surgical removal of the thyroid gland or radioactive iodine treatment to destroy thyroid tissue. Ninety-five % of all patients develop thyroid hormone deficiency due to a problem with the thyroid gland itself, known as *primary hypothyroidism*. Rarely, hypothyroidism can stem from decreased TSH production from the pituitary gland. This type of underactive thyroid condition is known as *secondary,* or *central hypothyroidism*.

Symptoms of hypothyroidism are numerous and often nonspecific. They may mimic many of the normal changes seen with aging and include:

- Unexplained weight gain
- Fatigue
- Increased sensitivity to cold
- Dry skin
- Course hair
- Brittle nails
- Puffiness around the eyes
- Slow heart rate
- Hoarseness
- Shortness of breath
- Constipation
- Heavy menstrual periods
- Inability to concentrate
- Increased forgetfulness
- Depression

Thyroid tests are ordered whenever a patient has signs or symptoms that could be due to thyroid disease. It is also recommended that all women over 65 years of age have a screening thyroid test. A simple and readily available blood assay for TSH is the most sensitive test for an underactive thyroid. The TSH level *increases* when there is not enough T_4 circulating in the blood stream. TSH is the best and most sensitive test since it may increase even when the circulating T_4 levels are still in the normal range, as occurs in early mild hypothyroidism. The *free T_4* level may also be ordered to help confirm the diagnosis and assess the severity of hypothyroidism. In central hypothyroidism due to pituitary disease, the TSH may be normal or decreased in the setting of a low blood concentration of free T_4.

Simple and straightforward treatment involves synthetic thyroid (T_4) hormone replacement using *levothyroxine (LT$_4$)*, which is identical to the T_4 made by the thyroid gland itself and given once daily as a pill. The goal of therapy is to restore the thyroid hormone levels to normal as determined by the TSH test and to alleviate symptoms related to hypothyroidism. Individual needs for LT_4 can vary widely and depend on a variety of factors, including age, concurrent illnesses, and concomitant medications. In rare cases, part of the overall dose of thyroid hormone may be administered as *liothyronine (LT$_4$)*, which is a more potent but shorter-acting form of thyroid hormone given in low doses together with LT_4. A small percentage (less than 5%) of hypothyroid patients experience better symptom relief on this combination, although this is somewhat controversial. Symptoms generally begin to improve within two weeks. Six to ten weeks are required for the TSH level to stabilize and several months may be required for full recovery. Most patients require lifelong treatment.

The LT_4 dose needs to be adjusted carefully under close medical supervision on the basis of evaluation of symptoms, physical examination, and periodic TSH testing. Testing is performed every 8 to 12 weeks until the TSH level falls to normal. After the optimal dose is identified, patients are seen twice yearly for a few years, then annually. Special situations may arise which require more frequent monitoring, such as the presence of advanced age, coronary heart disease, congestive heart failure, elective surgery, or pituitary disease. Situations that may require an increase in LT_4 include worsening of the underlying thyroid disease, weight gain, gastrointestinal conditions which may impair thyroid hormone absorption, high-fiber diet, calcium- or aluminum-containing medications, and iron-containing medications, including some multivitamins.

Normal aging or weight loss may necessitate a reduction in dose. The primary side effects of therapy are related to under- or overtreatment. This may occur in the presence of symptoms of hypo- or hyperthyroidism but often occurs in the absence of any symptoms whatsoever. Mild undertreatment may contribute to high blood pressure, elevated cholesterol, premature atherosclerosis, and subtle deficits in the ability to think, concentrate, or remember. Mild overtreatment can lead to abnormal heart rhythms, stroke, heart failure, and accelerated bone loss and osteoporosis. Silent, or *subclinical,* thyroid disease can only be detected by TSH testing.

Many patients believe that an underactive thyroid gland is a major cause of weight gain and responsible for most cases of obesity. The medical literature does not support this notion. Less than 2% of patients who experience clinically significant weight gain (greater than 10 to 15%

above baseline) have hypothyroidism, and those who do rarely lose more than 5 to 10 pounds after thyroid hormone replacement alone. The use of thyroid hormone for the purpose of inducing weight loss is dangerous and should not be permitted or pursued under any circumstances. Obesity is a chronic and complex metabolic disorder that requires long-term calorie restriction, increased physical activity, behavioral modification, and, occasionally, the closely supervised use of approved antiobesity agents in a multidisciplinary medical setting.

TOO MUCH: HYPERTHYROIDISM

Hyperthyroidism occurs when the body makes more thyroid hormone than is necessary, leading to a spillover of excess thyroxine and toxic effects on thyroid hormone-responsive tissues. In some but not all cases, hyperthyroidism is associated with a goiter, an enlarged thyroid gland (see Figure 20-8). Hyperthyroidism can be caused by:

- An abnormal antibody that stimulates glandular growth and overactivity (Graves disease)
- An abnormal antibody that causes inflammation (silent, painless, or postpartum thyroiditis)
- A viral infection of the thyroid gland (subacute thyroiditis)
- Tumors that secrete excess thyroxine (toxic uni- or multinodular goiter)
- Taking too much thyroid hormone (levothyroxine or liothyronine)

Hyperthyroidism usually affects women between the ages of 20 and 40 but can affect males and females at any age. **Graves disease** is the most common cause of hyperthyroidism overall but the risk of *toxic multinodular goiter* increases with age, making the later diagnosis more common in women after menopause. Hyperthyroidism is especially dangerous in the elderly since it can have adverse effects on the aging heart, including heart attack, heart failure, and abnormal heart rhythms, which can lead to stroke. Moreover, it can accelerate bone loss leading to an increased risk for osteoporosis and fractures of the spine and hip, particularly in older women already at risk for this condition. Symptoms are common and often alarming:

- Muscle weakness in the upper arms and thighs, making it difficult to climb stairs or lift heavy objects
- Anxiety, irritability, or increased nervousness
- Tremor of the hands, affecting handwriting or ability to hold objects steady
- Unexplained weight loss, often with a normal or increased appetite
- Rapid or irregular heart beat
- Increased sweating or poor tolerance to warm temperatures
- Fatigue
- Increased frequency of bowel movements
- Irritated eyes or difficulty seeing

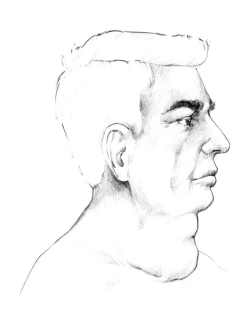

(figure 20-8)

A goiter is an enlarged thyroid gland that may cause the lower part of the neck to bulge out.

Less common symptoms include rash, increased itching, light menstrual periods (in women), or enlarged breast tissue in men. An unusual condition in older individuals is known as *apathetic hyperthyroidism:* a generalized failure to thrive that often mimics hypothyroidism except for the tendency to lose weight in the former condition.

Hyperthyroidism is suspected if an individual has typical symptoms and palpable abnormalities of the thyroid gland itself. The diagnosis is confirmed by testing the blood for concentrations of *TSH, free T₄,* and, occasionally, *total T₃.* In contrast to hypothyroidism, the TSH level is undetectable due to increased circulating levels of T_4 and T_3 which suppress TSH secretion by the pituitary gland. Other diagnostic studies are required to ascertain the actual cause of hyperthyroidism and may include a *radioactive iodine uptake study (RAIU), thyroid scan,* and/or *thyroid ultrasound* (see Figure 20-9).

Hyperthyroidism is treated with medication, surgery, or radioactive iodine (RAI) ablation. Several factors, including age, severity, and type of thyroid disease, will determine the best treatment for any given individual.

Beta-blockers oppose the effects of excess thyroid hormone on the nervous system, which is responsible for many of the symptoms of hyperthyroidism. Examples include PROPRANOLOL (INDERAL), ATENOLOL (TENORMIN), and METOPROLOL (LOPRESSOR, TOPROL): the -olol drugs. They are used to control symptoms and generally reduce tremor, anxiety, sleeplessness, palpitations, and heat intolerance. Beta-blockers are initiated at diagnosis and continued until the underlying thyroid condition itself is controlled or resolves.

Antithyroid drugs work by decreasing production of thyroid hormone by the gland itself and, to some extent, interfering with activation of thyroid hormone in the peripheral tissues. Also known as *thionamides,* examples include PROPYLTHIOURACIL (PTU) and METHIMAZOLE (TAPAZOLE). They are administered in pill form by mouth once or twice daily. Antithyroid drugs may be used temporarily prior to surgery or RAI therapy for Graves disease or toxic multinodular goiter, or for one to two years in some patients with Graves disease in an attempt to induce remission. Side effects include rash, hives, jaundice, fever, abdominal pain, nausea, and painful joints. A rare, but potentially life-threatening complication is *agranulocytosis,* by which the body stops producing white blood cells, which are important for fighting infection. It is necessary to check the blood count anytime someone taking antithyroid drugs develops fever in order to make sure there are enough white blood cells to fight any underlying infection. Side effects are generally more common in individuals over 60 years of age. This fact, coupled with the low long-term response to antithyroid medications in the elderly (less than 20 to 30%), make this form of therapy less than ideal for the long-term management of most patients in the over-60 age category. It is, however, preferred for short-term treatment prior to RAI ablation or surgery for severe symptoms or in the presence of concurrent heart disease. Patients taking medications for hyperthyroidism are seen every

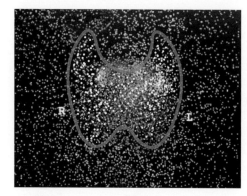

(figure 20-9)

The thyroid scan shows an increased uptake of iodine by the thyroid (outlined) in a patient with hyperthyroidism.

two to six weeks in the clinic for symptom review, physical examination, thyroid testing to monitor progress, and eliciting any possible treatment-related adverse side effects. Once the condition is controlled, the visits are scheduled at three-month intervals.

Radioactive iodine (RAI) ablation involves the oral administration of a unique form of iodine, known as *iodine-131*. Iodine-131 is absorbed into the bloodstream where it is concentrated in the thyroid gland and releases a special form of radiation into the thyroid tissue itself, causing it to melt away, usually painlessly, over a period of 6 to 12 weeks. It is generally a safe procedure with the total amount of radiation exposure approximately the same as many common X-ray procedures. Most individuals who receive this form of treatment will develop hypothyroidism, which is a much easier and safer condition to treat with thyroid hormone replacement in pill form. Risks of RAI ablation include:

- Temporary worsening of the underlying hyperthyroidism
- Need for retreatment (approximately 5 to 10% of cases)
- Worsening of eye symptoms in patients with Graves disease
- Thyroid hormone deficiency, or hypothyroidism (over 90% of cases)

Exposure to others, particularly young children and pregnant women, is discouraged for three to seven days following iodine-131 treatment and specific precautions will need to be taken to limit exposure to others. These guidelines are reviewed with the treating physician prior to actual administration of the iodine-131 capsule. It is important to have the thyroid levels monitored at six- to eight-week intervals following treatment to monitor for the development of hypothyroidism. Both the TSH *and* free T_4 tests are performed until the TSH level becomes detectable again, making it reliable for titrating the dose of levothyroxine needed to treat iodine-131–induced hypothyroidism.

Surgery to remove the thyroid gland is recommended far less often than RAI ablation or antithyroid drugs because of the risks, expense, and inconvenience of thyroid surgery. Thyroid surgery is recommended for the following conditions:

- A large goiter is present with compressive symptoms, such as severe choking, pain, or difficulty swallowing or breathing
- Antithyroid drugs are neither indicated nor tolerated
- Radioactive iodine ablation is neither feasible nor available

The specific risks of surgery include (1) damage to the nerves which control the voice box, causing *permanent hoarseness,* and (2) inadvertent damage to the parathyroid glands, which are important for regulating blood calcium levels. This can lead to dangerously low calcium levels, or *hypocalcemia,* which may cause weakness, muscle cramps, confusion, or seizures. For these reasons, an experienced thyroid surgeon who performs at least 10 to 15 cases per year should be consulted if a decision is made to perform an operation to remove the thyroid gland. The blood calcium levels should be monitored frequently for at least 24 hours following thyroid surgery to monitor for this complication.

Follow-up is similar for patients treated with medications or RAI ablation with regular appointments to monitor symptoms and perform blood tests for TSH and free T_4. Most patients will require thyroid hormone replacement.

THYROID NODULES

Thyroid nodules are tumors or growths different from the surrounding thyroid tissue. The nodules are very common, and perhaps as many as 50% of older women have at least one nodule although most are not aware of it. They may be detected incidentally by exam or during tests for unrelated conditions. Thyroid nodules are often discovered by noticing a lump in the neck region but may also cause discomfort, trouble swallowing, hoarseness, or difficulty breathing. They can be caused by inflammation, fluid-filled cysts, or abnormal growths of thyroid tissue that may or may not produce thyroid hormone. Thyroid nodules are usually benign, but up to 5% of nodules larger than 0.5 inch may represent early thyroid cancer. It is important to establish a correct diagnosis in order to successfully treat the 5% of thyroid nodule patients who have thyroid cancer and to avoid unnecessary surgery in the 95% of patients who do not. Fortunately, the vast majority of thyroid cancers are completely curable with surgical resection often followed by radioactive iodine ablation therapy. Among patients with thyroid nodules, the following factors increase the likelihood that a particular nodule is malignant:

- Age over 60
- Male gender
- Previous radiation to the head and neck, especially if it occurred at an early age
- Rapid growth of the nodule
- Pain
- Hoarseness
- Swollen lymph nodes elsewhere in the neck

Many different tests are available to assist in the evaluation of a thyroid nodule. Consultation with an endocrinologist who is a specialist in the evaluation and management of thyroid nodules can prove invaluable. He or she can discuss the pros and cons of each test and explain the results.

Thyroid function tests: Thyroid function tests, including TSH with or without free T_4, may indicate if the nodule is producing excess amounts of thyroid hormone or if there is thyroid hormone deficiency. Both of these are benign conditions whose management has previously been discussed.

Thyroid ultrasound: Thyroid ultrasound provides the best anatomic information regarding a tumor's size, differentiating whether a tumor is solid or fluid-filled, and identifying the presence of multiple tumors *(multinodular goiter).* It is also useful in improving the accuracy of thyroid fine-needle aspiration (discussed next). Ultrasound is probably the best test to follow nodules that do not require surgery initially.

Fine-needle aspiration: Fine-needle aspiration (FNA) is a relatively quick, painless outpatient procedure that involves placing a very small needle into the nodule and using a syringe to draw out groups of cells to examine under a microscope. It is often performed in conjunction with thyroid ultrasound, and a local anesthetic may be used as well. FNA is the single most accurate test apart from surgery to determine if a nodule is benign. Fifty to 60% of biopsies are *benign* and will not require surgery. They must, however, be followed closely by an experienced examiner, often in conjunction with period ultrasound evaluation. Five % of biopsies reveal the presence of *papillary cancer,* which is the most common form of thyroid cancer. These will require complete removal of the thyroid gland, which is usually curative. Ten % of biopsies are *suspicious,* and these are also known as *follicular neoplasms.* Many of these will require surgery, and a thyroid scan is often ordered to aid in making this decision. A biopsy may be *nondiagnostic* or *inadequate* in up to 20% of the cases. These may require surgery, repeat FNA, thyroid scanning, and/or very close follow-up, depending on the clinical judgment of the physician.

Thyroid scanning: Thyroid scanning, also called *scintigraphy,* involves the administration of a radioactive tracer, usually iodine-123, to see if the thyroid nodule concentrates iodine. It is usually reserved for patients who have a suspicious FNA or who are suspected of having hyperthyroidism due to an overactive nodule *(toxic adenoma)* or nodules *(toxic multinodular goiter).* A cold nodule does not take up the tracer normally and appears as a clear defect on the scan. Patients who have a suspicious FNA and cold nodule on scintigraphy will require surgery. If the thyroid scan is performed as the initial test, all cold nodules will require FNA to see which ones require surgery. A nodule is said to be *functioning* if it takes up the same amount of iodine as the surrounding thyroid tissue. A *hot* nodule concentrates more iodine than the surrounding normal cells do. Functioning or hot nodules are virtually never cancerous and can be observed over time without surgery as the initial treatment.

All malignant and suspicious nodules will require surgery to remove the entire thyroid gland by an experienced thyroid surgeon. This is usually curative. RAI ablation is an adjunct to reduce the risk for recurrence, treat metastatic disease that has spread beyond the gland itself, or make it easier to detect residual or recurrent disease. Nodules that do not require surgery will be watched closely every 6 to 12 months by examination with or without ultrasound. Sometimes thyroid hormone (LT_4) therapy is used in an attempt to shrink the nodule. This is known as LT_4 *suppression therapy.* Repeat FNA and sometimes surgery are required if a nodule that was initially benign or nondiagnostic gets bigger over time.

Thyroid neck check: The thyroid "neck check" is a very simple examination that you can do yourself at home to look for the presence of a thyroid nodule. All that is required is a glass of water, a hand-held mirror, and five easy steps:

1. Hold the mirror in your hand, and look at the area of your neck just below the Adam's apple and immediately above the collarbone. Your thyroid gland is located in this area of the neck.
2. While focusing on this area in the mirror, tip your head back slightly.
3. Take a drink of water and swallow.
4. As you swallow, look at your neck. Check for any bulges or protrusions in this area when you swallow. *Reminder:* Don't confuse the Adam's apple with the thyroid gland. The gland is located further down in the neck, closer to the collarbone. You may want to repeat this process several times to be sure.
5. If you do see any bulges or protrusions in this area, see your physician. You may have an enlarged thyroid gland (goiter) or a thyroid nodule. This should be checked to determine whether cancer is present or if treatment for thyroid disease is necessary.

PARATHYROID

A stable blood calcium level is required for normal heart, brain, nerve, muscle, and gastrointestinal function. For this reason, a highly specialized control system has developed to keep the blood calcium level "in line." As shown in Figure 20-10, the **parathyroid glands** comprise four pea-sized glands (adjacent to the thyroid gland) that monitor and regulate the blood calcium concentration through secretion of *parathyroid hormone (PTH)*. The parathyroid glands continually monitor the blood calcium level via a highly specialized protein on the cell surface known as the *calcium receptor.* When the blood concentration of calcium falls, the calcium receptor sends a signal to the parathyroid cell's secretory machinery to manufacture and secrete PTH into the bloodstream. PTH acts on several tissues to restore normal calcium balance.

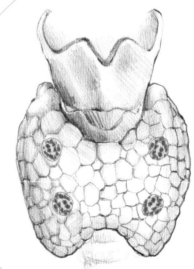

- PTH acts on a specialized bone cell, known as the osteoclast, to increase resorption of calcium from the bones. Our skeleton is a vast storage depot for calcium, housing up to 80% of the body's total calcium stores.
- PTH acts on the kidneys to increase calcium resorption from urine as it passes through the renal tubules (part of the kidney's filtering unit). PTH literally keeps the blood calcium from leaking out through the kidneys.
- PTH works on the kidneys to turn vitamin D into its active form, the hormone *calcitriol,* which mediates absorption of dietary calcium from the intestines. One cannot simply increase the blood calcium level by ingesting more dietary calcium in the form of milk or calcium

(figure 20-10)

The parathyroid glands are four pea-sized glands adjacent to the backside of the thyroid and are important in regulation of calcium balance.

supplements. Calcitriol, acting under orders from PTH, is responsible for this process.

Once the blood calcium concentration is restored to normal, the PTH concentration falls via a negative feedback circuit. If excess calcium is ingested or infused into the body, this results in a decrease in PTH which yields the expected decrease in blood calcium through decreased action on the PTH-sensitive tissues.

HYPOPARATHYROIDISM

Parathyroid hormone deficiency, or **hypoparathyroidism,** results from decreased PTH secretion or action. As a result the body cannot assimilate calcium normally. This can result in (1) low blood calcium, or *hypocalcemia,* and (2) inadequate bone mineralization, known as *osteomalacia* in adults and *rickets* in children. Symptoms of hypoparathyroidism include (in order of severity):

- Muscle weakness
- A tingling sensation in the hands and feet or around the mouth
- Aching in the long bones, most prominent in the collarbones, and the long bones of the arms and legs
- Muscle spasms or cramping of the hands and feet
- Lethargy or loss of consciousness
- Seizures

In adults, hypoparathyroidism results from inadvertent damage to the parathyroid glands or their blood supply during neck surgery for thyroid or parathyroid disease. This complication of neck surgery generally occurs about 1% of the time and is usually recognized within 24 to 48 hours after surgery. The diagnosis is confirmed by demonstrating a low serum concentration of calcium and a normal or low PTH level, as one would expect the PTH level to rise in this setting.

In rare cases, one may be born with a defective PTH receptor, which results in resistance to parathyroid hormone. These individuals have all the symptoms and signs of *hypo*parathyroidism. However, when the blood is tested, the calcium level is decreased as expected, but the PTH level is actually *increased* due to a compensatory response to the body's resistance to PTH. This condition is known as **pseudohypoparathyroidism.** Its treatment is identical to that for hypoparathyroidism.

A somewhat more frequent cause of clinical hypoparathyroidism occurs during the course of normal aging of the kidney. It is also seen frequently in diseases of the kidney that lead to decreased kidney function, or *chronic renal insufficiency.* The diseased or aging kidney loses the capacity to activate vitamin D, with a resultant decrease in calcitriol. This results in inadequate absorption of dietary calcium from the intestines. As in PTH resistance, the PTH concentration actually increases in response to the decrease in blood calcium. This is known as *secondary hyperparathyroidism,* due to the increase in PTH, but is best considered a form of hypoparathyroidism since the effect on the body is nearly identical to that of hypoparathyroidism, although usually not as severe.

Proper treatment of hypoparathyroidism, pseudohypoparathyroidism, and the secondary hyperparathyroidism of aging or renal insufficiency involve:

- Adequate dietary calcium intake, usually 1000 to 1500 mg of elemental calcium daily from diet and/or oral supplements such as calcium citrate, calcium phosphate, or calcium carbonate.
- *Calcitriol,* taken orally in doses of 0.25 to 0.5 mcg two or three times daily with meals. Newer analogues of calcitriol are often used in the secondary hyperparathyroidism of renal insufficiency, especially when treating bone disease if the blood calcium concentration is close to normal. Occasionally vitamin D alone in higher doses of 800 to 1200 units daily is sufficient to prevent or treat mild secondary hyperparathyroidism of aging.

It is extremely important to monitor the blood and urine calcium concentrations frequently in the course of treating hypoparathyroidism since mild overtreatment can result in excessive urine calcium excretion, which over time can lead to calcium accumulation in the kidney leading to kidney stones or nephrocalcinosis (calcification of the kidneys themselves), both of which can lead to permanent kidney damage.

HYPERPARATHYROIDISM

It is not uncommon for one (or more) of the parathyroid glands to develop a hormone-producing tumor, or adenoma, which results in excessive parathyroid hormone production beyond that needed to regulate the blood calcium concentration. This condition is known as *primary hyperparathyroidism.* The typical manifestation of the condition is an asymptomatic elevation of the blood calcium concentration, *hypercalcemia,* noted on a routine chemistry panel. Other presentations of primary hyperparathyroidism include:

- Symptomatic hypercalcemia, which can cause excessive urination, kidney stones, peptic ulcer disease, abdominal pain, nausea, vomiting, decreased appetite, constipation, unexplained weight loss, bone and/or joint pain, fatigue, depression, impaired concentration, increased forgetfulness, confusion, lethargy, or altered consciousness
- Premature or severe osteoporosis, or weakening of the bones, with increased fracture risk and incidence
- Hyperparathyroid bone disease, or *osteitis fibrosa cystica,* which shows up as one or more areas of bone pain and has a distinctive appearance on X-ray (see Figure 20-11)

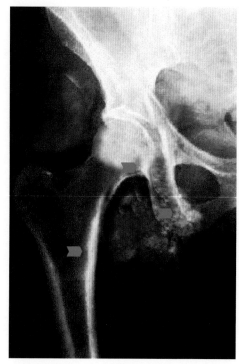

(figure 20-11)

Typical punched-out areas of bone (arrowheads) in a patient with osteitis fibrosa cystica caused by hyperparathyroidism.

The diagnosis is confirmed by demonstrating a persistent increase in the blood calcium concentration with an elevated or inappropriately normal serum PTH level and a normal or increased urine calcium level. It is important to exclude a rare condition known as *familial hypocalciuric hypercalcemia (FHH),* which usually combines asymptomatic hypercalcemia, normal or slightly increased PTH, and a low urine calcium concentration, as this is a benign condition that almost never requires treatment. When primary hyperparathyroidism is diagnosed in an asymptomatic individual from a routine blood test, a careful history and physical examination with appropriate assessment of bone and kidney health are necessary to ascertain any underlying damage to PTH sensitive tissues, since this affects the preferred treatment option.

Symptomatic disease, marked hypercalcemia, or demonstration of decreased bone mineral density (osteoporosis) or increased urine calcium almost always requires surgery to find and remove the diseased parathyroid gland (or glands). It is extremely important to secure an experienced parathyroid surgeon who performs at least 10 such operations yearly. There are several imaging procedures that assist the surgeon in identifying the exact location of the tumor. These are used with variable success since the tumors are often too small to see on traditional X-ray studies. With an experienced parathyroid surgeon in association with an endocrinologist to confirm the diagnosis, assist in making the correct treatment decision, and to provide adequate follow-up care, neck surgery for parathyroid disease is generally minimally invasive, safe, and effective in treating hyperparathyroidism.

The correct course of action regarding asymptomatic disease is somewhat more controversial. Younger, healthier patients (less than 50 years) should consider surgery as the disease usually progresses, albeit slowly, over time. Older patients (greater than 50 years) can generally be followed closely with periodic examinations, measurement of blood and urine calcium levels, and determination of bone density to monitor for disease progression. Surgery is usually reserved for those who develop worsening symptoms or interval disease progression as measured by increasing blood and/or urine calcium levels or decreasing bone mineral density, usually as assessed by *dual-energy X-ray absorptiometry (DEXA).*

ADRENAL GLAND

The adrenal glands are small, triangular-shaped glands that sit on top of the kidneys and produce three different classes of hormones (see Figure 20-12):

- *Glucocorticoids* (cortisol) help regulate blood sugar levels, metabolism, the immune system, blood pressure, and the body's overall response to stress.
- *Mineralocorticoids* (aldosterone) regulate sodium, potassium, blood volume, and blood pressure.

- *Androgens* (DHEA and androstenedione) affect body hair distribution in both men and women and may affect sex drive in women. Androgens are also secreted to a greater extent by the testes in men and to a lesser degree by the ovaries in women.

Cortisol and adrenal androgens are regulated by the pituitary gland and tend to be somewhat higher in the morning, falling throughout the day to lower levels during the evening hours. **Aldosterone** is regulated by the hormone *angiotensin II,* which is produced in response to renin, a hormone secreted by the kidneys when the body needs to conserve sodium. This series of interactions is often known as the *renin-angiotensin-aldosterone axis* and is critical for regulating blood pressure and overall vascular health. Like many other endocrine systems, it is capable of withstanding multiple assaults and is able to function normally on as little as 10% of its full capacity. Although glucocorticoid and mineralocorticoid levels remain normal throughout life, adrenal androgen levels decline gradually but steadily as one ages. The decline does not appear to cause any adverse affects, and studies of adrenal androgen replacement in the elderly have not shown consistently beneficial results.

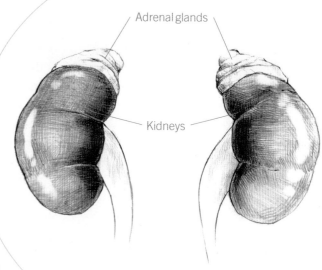

Adrenal glands

Kidneys

(*figure* 20-12)

The adrenal glands sit on top of your kidneys.

ADRENAL INSUFFICIENCY

Adrenal insufficiency occurs when the body is unable to produce an adequate amount of cortisol and/or aldosterone. *Primary* adrenal insufficiency, also known as **Addison's disease**, occurs if the adrenal gland itself is destroyed by inflammation (autoimmune adrenalitis), infection (most commonly tuberculosis), infiltration by abnormal cells (sometimes cancerous), bleeding, or surgery. Primary adrenal insufficiency is rare, affecting only 35 to 120 per million people. *Secondary* adrenal insufficiency occurs if the pituitary gland is not functioning properly and is unable to produce ACTH. Tertiary adrenal insufficiency is due to hypothalamic disease for which corticotropin-releasing hormone (CRH) is not secreted. Together, secondary and tertiary adrenal insufficiency are known as *central* adrenal insufficiency, since the problem occurs in the brain's central relay station for the endocrine system: the hypothalamus and pituitary gland. Central adrenal insufficiency can be caused by damage to the hypothalamus or pituitary gland by tumors, infection, infiltration, hemorrhage, surgery, trauma, stroke, or irradiation. The most common form of central adrenal insufficiency occurs if high doses of glucocorticoids, such as HYDROCORTISONE, PREDNISONE, or DEXAMETHASONE, are (1) used for prolonged periods, such as two to three weeks, and (2) then abruptly withdrawn. High doses feed back on the hypothalamic-pituitary-adrenal axis and lead to suppression of endogenously produced cortisol. The body may not be able to produce adrenal glucocorticoids for a period of several weeks to months.

Symptoms of primary adrenal insufficiency include fatigue, generalized weakness, unexplained weight loss, darkening of the skin, gastrointestinal symptoms (such as abdominal pain, nausea, and/or vomiting), low blood pressure (often with light-headedness when standing), muscle and joint pain, and increased salt craving.

Symptoms of central adrenal insufficiency include the above except that darkening of the skin, salt craving, and dehydration do not occur; gastrointestinal symptoms are much less common; and symptoms of low blood sugar (hypoglycemia) are more common and include sweating, tremor, palpitations, anxiety, and nausea. Symptoms of hypothalamic-pituitary disease or the recent withdrawal of high-dose glucocorticoid hormones (cortisone, prednisone, or dexamethasone) should also alert one to the possibility of central adrenal insufficiency.

Adrenal crisis is a sudden, overwhelming, and life-threatening episode of adrenal insufficiency, usually seen in conjunction with primary adrenal insufficiency and severe stress, such as infection, trauma, or emergency surgery. Warning signs are very low blood pressure and coma (shock), often preceded by fever, nausea, vomiting, and abdominal pain. This is a life-threatening emergency. Prevention and treatment are discussed below.

Treatment involves appropriate glucocorticoid replacement for primary and central adrenal insufficiency and mineralocorticoid replacement for primary disease. Low-dose androgen replacement has been shown to be effective in relieving symptoms related to decreased libido in some women with primary adrenal insufficiency.

- HYDROCORTISONE (or its equivalent) is administered orally at an average dose of 15 to 30 mg daily given in one or two doses. Since cortisol is critical to the regulation of blood pressure and glucose levels during times of stress, the dose needs to be doubled or tripled for fever, nausea, or vomiting. For severe illness requiring hospitalization or surgery, intravenous hydrocortisone at higher doses may be required for a few days until the oral route can be reestablished. The dose is adjusted primarily on the basis of symptoms. Overtreatment should be avoided since even mild glucocorticoid excess over time can contribute to weight gain, osteoporosis, immune suppression, diabetes, high blood pressure, vascular disease, and depression.
- FLUDROCORTISONE is administered orally at a dose of 0.5 to 2.0 mg daily, given as a single dose in the morning. The dose is adjusted on the basis of symptoms, blood pressure determination (lying and standing), and blood electrolyte and renin testing. Liberal salt intake is usually permitted for those with Addison's disease. In warmer climates or with increased sweat loss, higher intake of dietary sodium, fludrocortisone, or both may be required to maintain adequate salt and fluid balance.
- DEHYDROEPIANDROSTERONE (DHEA) is sometimes administered orally at a dose of 25 to 50 mg daily, given as a single morning dose to women with primary adrenal insufficiency. This may improve libido and overall sense of well-being in such individuals.

It is important for people with adrenal insufficiency to learn as much as they can about the condition and to share this information with family, friends, and other caregivers to recognize early warning signs and be prepared to act in case of emergency or suspected adrenal crisis. Patients with adrenal insufficiency in any form should wear a medical alert bracelet or pendant and carry an emergency medical information card.

Adrenal crisis is prevented by "stress dosing" of the glucocorticoid component of therapy for fever, nausea, or vomiting. The overall dose is usually doubled or tripled during the period of stress but reduced to maintenance levels once the illness has resolved. Hydrocortisone, for example, is increased to 20 mg three times daily during such episodes. The mineralocorticoid is usually not increased since the higher dose of glucocorticoid has a crossover effect on the renin-angiotensin-aldosterone system. An injectable glucocorticoid, such as METHYLPREDNISOLONE (SOLU-MEDROL) 125 mg or DEXAMETHASONE (DECADRON) 4 mg, should be kept on hand and given by intramuscular injection if vomiting precludes oral administration of glucocorticoid prior to seeking emergency medical attention. Emergency treatment of adrenal crisis involves the administration of intravenous fluids and higher doses of glucocorticoids. Intravenous glucocorticoids may also be necessary prior to elective surgery or invasive diagnostic or therapeutic procedures.

The prognosis for patients with primary adrenal insufficiency is good. Most people can lead an active life and have a normal life expectancy. The prognosis for central adrenal insufficiency depends on the underlying cause but is generally good for most people.

CUSHING'S SYNDROME

Cushing's syndrome is caused by an excess of cortisol production from the adrenal glands *(hypercortisolism)*. Cortisol is an important glucocorticoid hormone necessary for life, but excessive amounts have well-known adverse effects on the body. Cushing's syndrome is three times more common in women than men and can have several different causes depending on whether the problem is within the hypothalamic-pituitary-adrenal system or elsewhere in the body. One cause of Cushing's syndrome is *Cushing's disease,* caused by excess ACTH production from a pituitary tumor (see the section, "Pituitary Tumors," above). Excess ACTH from tumors elsewhere in the body, usually the lung, is known as ectopic ACTH syndrome. One of the most common causes of Cushing's syndrome is the use of glucocorticoids to treat inflammatory conditions, such as rheumatoid arthritis. These agents mimic the effects of excess cortisol in the body. Rarely, excess cortisol is produced by the adrenal gland itself, including benign or malignant tumors of the adrenal gland or adrenal gland overgrowth, also known as *adrenal nodular hyperplasia.* The symptoms of Cushing's syndrome result from the excess cortisol production, can be subtle and insidious in older individuals, and tend to progress over time:

- Weight gain, especially in the face, neck, trunk, and abdomen, resulting in a rounded facial appearance ("moon facies") and collections of fat on the upper back and/or base of the neck ("buffalo hump")
- Thinning and excess bruising of the skin, and wide, purplish streaks in areas of rapid weight gain, also known as stretch marks, or striae
- Infrequent or absent menstrual periods
- Increased facial and body hair, facial flushing, oily skin, and acne
- Muscle loss and weakness, making it difficult to get out of a chair or climb stairs
- Thinning of the bones (osteoporosis) and increased risk of fracture of the ribs, hip, and vertebra
- Elevated blood glucose levels, which can lead to diabetes
- Elevated blood pressure and premature heart and vascular disease
- More frequent infections and poor wound healing
- Depression, anxiety, and poor concentration or thinking ability

The diagnosis of Cushing's syndrome is confirmed by measuring the free cortisol concentration in a 24-hour urine specimen or measuring the serum cortisol level the morning after taking a low dose of dexamethasone (1 mg), which suppresses cortisol production in healthy people but not in those with Cushing's syndrome. Once excess cortisol production is confirmed, an ACTH level is drawn to determine whether the elevated cortisol is ACTH-dependent (pituitary or ectopic) or not (glucocorticoid ingestion or excess adrenal cortisol production). Appropriate imaging studies, including computerized tomography (CT) or magnetic resonance imaging (MRI) scans can identify tumors of the pituitary, lung, abdomen, or adrenal glands (see Figure 20-13).

Differentiating pituitary from ectopic ACTH excess can be challenging and may require one or more specialized tests, including the high-dose dexamethasone suppression test, octreotide scanning, and sampling the venous blood draining from the pituitary gland, a procedure known as *inferior petrosal sinus sampling (IPSS)*. These tests are performed under the direction of an experienced endocrinologist, who can coordinate and supervise the tests, properly interpret the results, and make appropriate treatment decisions. To make matters more complicated, Cushing's syndrome can be mimicked by excess stress, severe depression, and alcoholism that can lead to a false-positive result on screening tests for Cushing's syndrome. Finally, Cushing's syndrome can be cyclic in that it comes and goes over time, making detection and confirmation more difficult.

Treatment of Cushing's syndrome depends on accurately identifying the exact cause and can involve surgery to remove the ACTH- or cortisol-producing tumor, pituitary irradiation to treat tumors that are not successfully removed by surgery, medications to block or decrease adrenal cortisol production, or, in rare cases, surgical removal of the adrenal glands themselves.

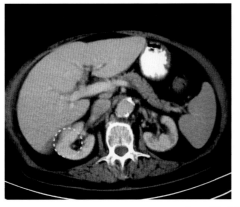

(figure 20-13)

CT scan shows an adrenal tumor (circled).

Today, almost all patients with Cushing's syndrome can be treated effectively and cured. Treatment may result in the immediate normalization of cortisol levels, and in fact, most patients are rendered temporarily cortisol-deficient until the body regains the ability to regulate cortisol production. Symptoms generally improve over a period of 2 to 12 months although hypertension, glucose intolerance, and psychiatric symptoms may persist but usually at a lesser severity. Close medical follow-up is essential.

THE PANCREAS AND INSULIN

DIABETES MELLITUS

Metabolism refers to how the body converts food into energy. The body has a very elaborate mechanism to accomplish this task that involves the hormone insulin. Insulin is secreted by the pancreas in response to a meal and regulates how the body uses carbohydrate, protein, and fat. Diabetes mellitus is a systemic disorder of metabolism due to a defect in insulin action on body tissues. This can result from an absolute or relative deficiency of insulin with or without resistance to the effects of insulin on body tissues (insulin resistance).

The primary manifestation of abnormal insulin action is elevated blood glucose, or hyperglycemia. Glucose is continuously being produced by the liver to ensure that the body's energy needs are adequately met between meals. When one ingests carbohydrate, the blood glucose concentration increases, causing the pancreas to secrete insulin. Insulin has two primary effects on blood glucose. First, it *decreases* glucose production by the liver, and second, it increases glucose use by body tissues, primarily skeletal muscle. People with type 1 diabetes mellitus have an inability to secrete any insulin due to the complete destruction of the pancreas, which results in hyperglycemia. People with type 2 diabetes gradually acquire four separate defects over time that contribute to hyperglycemia:

1. Decreased insulin secretion in response to a meal *(pancreas defect)*
2. Increased production of glucose by the liver *(liver defect)*
3. Decreased glucose use by skeletal muscle *(muscle defect)*
4. Increased release of free fatty acids from fat cells *(adipocyte defect)*

Insulin resistance (muscle and adipocyte) develops early in life, and the other two defects (pancreas and liver) develop later over time. Treatment to restore the blood glucose to a more normal level is directed at one or more of the defects.

Diabetes affects more than 20 million Americans. In fact, we are in the midst of an epidemic of diabetes in the United States. In some states diabetes affects as many as 1 in 10 people! Most of these (95%) have type 2 disease. Because diabetes is often without symptoms in its early stages, about half the patients with type 2 diabetes do not know that they have the disease. In addition, the symptoms may be so mild or nonspecific that they do not prompt the health care provider to screen for the disease. At the time diabetes is diagnosed, the average patient has had the disease for four to seven years and 20% of patients will already have complications, such as eye disease *(retinopathy)* or nerve damage *(neuropathy).*

Type 1 diabetes, formerly known as **insulin-dependent diabetes mellitus (IDDM),** is due to the complete destruction of the insulin-producing cells in the pancreas and usually occurs during childhood through early adulthood. However, up to 10% of adults who present after the age of 40 years may have type 1 disease. Without insulin therapy such individuals can die within days to weeks from a complication known as **diabetic ketoacidosis (DKA).** Thus it is known as an insulin-*dependent* disease because these people need insulin not only to control their blood glucose levels but also to stay alive. Type 1 diabetic patients comprise about 5% of all patients with diabetes.

Type 2 diabetes, formerly known as non-insulin-dependent or adult onset diabetes mellitus (NIDDM), is by far the most common form of the disease and accounts for about 95% of all patients with diabetes. These persons usually develop diabetes after the age of 40 years, often have a positive family history of type 2 diabetes in first-degree relatives, and approximately 90% are overweight to some extent. However, due to the dramatic increase in obesity among children and adolescents, as many as 50% of diabetic patients presenting at this age may actually have type 2 diabetes. These individuals do make some insulin but not enough to keep the blood glucose in the normal range. They can usually be treated with a combination of weight reduction, increased physical activity, and oral medications. Whereas they do not usually need insulin to avoid DKA, they may require insulin therapy to control blood glucose. It is therefore not uncommon to see patients who have insulin-*requiring,* non-insulin-*dependent* diabetes mellitus.

Gestational diabetes mellitus is first recognized during pregnancy (usually the third trimester) and almost universally resolves following delivery of the fetus. It can result in an increased risk of miscarriage or birth trauma. In addition, approximately 50 to 70% of women with gestational diabetes develop type 2 diabetes later in life. Diabetes can also occur in conjunction with certain rare congenital diseases, hormonal disorders, or medications.

Another form of diabetes is **impaired glucose tolerance (IGT),** a defect in glucose metabolism not severe enough to warrant treatment to restore the glucose to normal. It is, however, associated with insulin resistance, hyperlipidemia, hypertension, obesity, and heart disease. About 30 to 50% of people with IGT develop overt diabetes at some point in the future. This condition is now called *prediabetes.*

It should be emphasized that nowhere in the classification of diabetes are the words *borderline diabetes, mild diabetes,* or a *touch of sugar.* One cannot "sort of" have diabetes any more than one can be sort of pregnant. Either one is or isn't. It is better to think of diabetes that is "controlled" (which is good) or "poorly controlled" (which is obviously bad). *Remember:* control determines outcome. If it is necessary, one is better off taking multiple injections of insulin daily with excellent glucose control ("good" diabetes) than to continue to have severe hyperglycemia with or without oral medications ("bad" diabetes). It should be pointed out also that impaired glucose tolerance is a strong risk factor for cardiovascular disease and future diabetes. In this sense, IGT may be considered a prediabetic condition that warrants aggressive intervention with weight reduction, increased physical activity, and frequently medications to prevent heart disease, stroke, and the progression to overt diabetes mellitus.

Risk factors for diabetes: The occurrence of diabetes can be compared to a loaded gun. The bullets in the gun are like the genes that can lead to the development of diabetes. A loaded gun cannot fire itself, and the same is true for inheriting diabetes. You are not inexorably predestined to develop diabetes just because your mother or father had the disease. You do however have an increased *risk* for developing diabetes, and whether you actually do or not depends on how many environmental *triggers* you pull along the way. Certain triggers (or risk factors) for developing diabetes include obesity, increased age, lack of physical activity, a previous history of gestational diabetes or impaired glucose tolerance, certain medications, hypertension, hyperlipidemia, and certain ethnic groups including Native Americans, Mexican and Latin Americans, Asian Americans, and African Americans. Note that the risk for developing diabetes is stronger if the family history is positive in type 2 than in type 1 disease, suggesting that genetics plays a larger role in the development of type 2 diabetes.

The risk of diabetes increases markedly if the body weight exceeds 135% of the considered ideal. In addition, *central obesity*, or the tendency to accumulate fat around the abdomen (a waist greater than 40 inches in men or 35 inches in women), is strongly associated with diabetes, hypertension, and heart disease. The lack of regular, moderate physical activity is an additional risk factor for developing diabetes. Several studies, including the Diabetes Prevention Program have clearly demonstrated that modest weight reduction (5 to 10 pounds) and increased physical activity (150 minutes per week) can reduce the risk of developing diabetes by as much as 60%. This is indeed reassuring news as this amount of weight reduction and exercise can be accomplished by just about anyone who is serious about improving health and longevity.

Diagnosing diabetes: As mentioned, diabetes is an insidious disease and often escapes detection for several years. Diabetes can be diagnosed by any of three ways:

1. A random blood glucose measurement greater than 200 mg/dL, usually in conjunction with symptoms of hyperglycemia, such as increased thirst, frequent urination, increased hunger, unexplained weight loss, excessive fatigue, or blurred vision
2. Two separate blood glucose measurements greater than 125 mg/dL following an overnight fast
3. Two positive oral **glucose tolerance tests (GTT)**, defined as a blood glucose greater than 200 mg/dL two hours after consuming 75 grams of glucose by mouth

Seriousness: Not only is diabetes a common disorder, but it is a severe disorder as well. In the United States, diabetes is the fourth leading cause of death by disease and a major contributor to the leading cause of death, which is heart disease. It is the leading cause of acquired blindness. It is the number-one cause of kidney failure and the subsequent need for dialysis or kidney transplant. It is the leading cause of nontraumatic limb amputation. Diabetics are hospitalized three times more often than nondiabetics, and the cost of their care is 3.6 times higher than for those without the disease.

Diabetes costs the health care system over $100 billion yearly, which amounts to one in every seven health care dollars spent. During the five-year period from 1987 to 1992, the direct costs of treating diabetes in the United States increased 300%, and the amount continues to increase at an alarming rate as the epidemic continues. An unfortunate correlate is that approximately 70% of this amount was spent on the hospital treatment of diabetic complications that are largely, if not completely, preventable with good medical care and education. Another unfortunate fact is that the disease is more common in minorities and those over 70 years of age, two populations that are increasing at a more rapid rate than the rest of the U.S. population.

Complications: As mentioned, control determines outcome, and elevated blood glucose (hyperglycemia) is responsible for much of the damage that occurs due to diabetes. Following are three significant consequences of hyperglycemia:

1. *Neuropathy* (or nerve damage). Possible nerve damage includes numbness, pain, weakness, and sexual dysfunction, and it can contribute to foot infection, ulceration, and amputation.
2. *Retinopathy* (or eye disease). The retina is the membrane in the back of the eye that converts visual images into electrical signals, which are transmitted to the brain and interpreted. The retina can be silently damaged by hyperglycemia over a period of 5 to 20 years, resulting in decreased vision or even blindness.
3. *Nephropathy* (or kidney disease). Hyperglycemia can silently damage the kidney and its ability to filter waste products from the circulation. If this damage is complete, dialysis or kidney transplantation is required to sustain life. The development of nephropathy further exacerbates the risk for heart disease.

However, by far the most serious and life-threatening complication of diabetes is atherosclerosis (or blockage of the arteries). If occurring in the arteries to the heart, atherosclerosis can result in a myocardial infarction (or heart attack), the number-one killer of patients with diabetes. Atherosclerosis of the arteries that supply the brain leads to stroke. Atherosclerosis in the lower extremities contributes to pain with ambulation (claudication), impotence (in males), infection, and amputation. Atherosclerosis is related not only to hyperglycemia but also to other well-known risk factors that are more common in diabetes, such as insulin resistance, obesity, high blood pressure, physical inactivity, elevated blood lipids (cholesterol and triglycerides), and cigarette smoking. Eight out of every ten patients with diabetes will succumb to a heart attack or stroke unless steps are taken to reduce their risk.

Treatment: Good *diabetes* control means not only control of blood glucose but also attention to achieving an optimal body weight, improving control of blood pressure and lipids, and avoiding such destructive habits as tobacco abuse. It all begins with *disease monitoring,* which enables one to determine not only his or her level of control but how blood glucose is affected by changes in diet, exercise, stress, and medications. *Note:* You cannot determine how high your blood glucose is by how you feel; you must measure it yourself. The standard practice is to use the technique of *self-blood glucose monitoring (SBGM)* to measure glucose throughout the day at home, work, or play and to use those results to improve diabetes control. It is also important to have routine visits with your physician to measure your blood pressure and cholesterol levels, as well as to obtain a hemoglobin A_{1C} test, which measures your overall level of control for the previous three months.

Developing a sensible and balanced strategy for eating, or *meal plan,* is clearly the cornerstone for managing diabetes. It is recommended that every diabetic meet initially with a registered dietitian to initiate the process of improving the family's eating habits, and every three to six months thereafter to monitor the progress. It requires education, motivation, consistency, patience, and time to complete the process of the dietary makeover, but the results are critical to achieving successful diabetes management. The standard dietary recommendations for diabetes include:

- Normal caloric intake for optimal body weight (usually modest calorie restriction)
- Balanced distribution of calories between carbohydrate, fat, and protein
- Regularly and evenly spaced timing of meals and snacks
- Adequate intake of dietary fiber

Regular, moderate, aerobic exercise is the best form of treatment for diabetes for a number of reasons. It improves glucose use by working muscles independent of insulin and decreases overall insulin resistance.

Aerobic exercise can help improve insulin secretion and assists in weight loss and maintenance. Regular physical activity improves blood pressure, decreases lipid levels, and can reduce or eliminate the need for medications to control glucose, blood pressure, or high cholesterol. Moreover, exercise is a proven method for reducing stress and improving energy levels.

If diet and exercise alone are not sufficient to achieve ideal diabetes control, medications can be added to improve glycemic control. There are medications that stimulate insulin secretion, decrease glucose production by the liver, and improve overall sensitivity to insulin. Agents are also available that slow down the rate of absorption of carbohydrate from the intestine to minimize the rise in glucose that occurs following a meal. Studies have shown that the insulin sensitizer medications may have the additional benefits of combating vascular disease and slowing the progression of the diabetes over time. These medications, including METFORMIN (GLUCOPHAGE) and the *glitazones,* ROSIGLITAZONE (AVANDIA) AND PIOGLITAZONE (ACTOS), have also shown promise in early clinical studies to prevent diabetes in select high-risk individuals.

Insulin is a very successful form of therapy that is usually reserved for patients who have severe or life-threatening hyperglycemia or who fail to achieve their goals with diet, exercise, and oral medications. Since diabetes is a progressive disease, insulin replacement therapy is usually needed in some form at some point in the natural history of the disease. Insulin therapy is inherently more involved than other forms of therapy and does require additional decision-making skills on the part of the patient, but it remains one of the more successful forms of therapy and is not something to be avoided at all cost. It is wrong to have the primary goal of "not taking insulin." The ultimate objective is excellent glucose control and whatever is required for its achievement, including the use of insulin when necessary.

The early and aggressive treatment of related conditions—including hyperlipidemia, hypertension, and obesity—are critical to the successful treatment of diabetes and its complications. The results of several studies highlight the benefits of treating hyperlipidemia in diabetes with statin medications to prevent coronary heart disease, strokes, and premature death. The same results have been demonstrated with regard to the aggressive use of medications to normalize blood pressure and the prevention of coronary heart disease, stroke, kidney failure, and premature death. These medications include angiotensin-converting enzyme (ACE) inhibitors, angiotensin II receptor blockers, calcium channel blockers, thiazide diuretics, and beta-blockers. A comprehensive, multidisciplinary approach to weight management including diet, exercise, behavioral modification, and the use of approved antiobesity agents, such as SIBUTRAMINE (MERIDIA) and ORLISTAT (XENICAL), has been shown in clinical studies to improve overall diabetes control and also to prevent or delay diabetes in people with impaired glucose tolerance. Last, the use of antiplatelet agents such as aspirin and clopidogrel (Plavix) are important adjuncts for

20

preventing heart attacks and stroke in individuals with diabetes at risk for vascular disease.

Responsibility: Diabetes is one of the few disorders managed almost entirely by the patient who has the disease. If you are waiting for your doctor to treat your diabetes, you will die out of control and prematurely. The same holds true for those who refuse to admit that they have a problem or are waiting for a good day to get started. Those who step forward, assume responsibility for their own care, and take an active approach to diabetes management are the ones who succeed. They likewise provide inspiration for others to do the same. This is why it is critical to obtain the knowledge, training, skills, and tools needed to accomplish this task. Yes, if you have diabetes, you are a victim, and no, it is not fair, but that does not change the problem or its solution. One does not volunteer to get diabetes, but one does make an individual choice regarding the pursuit of intensive control versus premature death following a series of diabetes complications.

There is indeed hope on the horizon. Our understanding of diabetes is increasing at a rapid rate, as is our ability to treat it. Perhaps in our lifetime, a cure will be found. The Diabetes Control and Complications Trial (DCCT) in patients with type 1 diabetes and the Kumamoto and United Kingdom Prospective Diabetes Studies (UKPDS) in patients with type 2 disease have demonstrated that intensive blood glucose control prevents or slows the progression of diabetes complications. The FDA is reviewing several new drugs and classes of drugs for the treatment of type 2 diabetes. The insulin pump is being used increasingly to improve glucose control in both types of diabetes, and the implantable pump is undergoing human trials. New and improved forms of insulin, including inhaled insulin, have been approved or are undergoing human trials. New technology may enable patients to test their blood glucose without pricking their finger. Dramatic progress is being made with transplanting islet cells (which are the cells in the pancreas that make insulin) to cure type 1 diabetes and a closed-loop artificial pancreas to treat both type of diabetes.

One is of course not alone in the quest to improve diabetes control. A diabetes care team has the following members:

- The physician (often an endocrinologist or internist with a specific interest or focus on diabetes) confirms the diagnosis, prescribes a treatment plan, monitors progress and control, prescribes medications, and screens for diabetes complications.
- The *certified diabetes educator (CDE)* provides training in diabetes management skills and can help assess compliance, control, and decision making.
- The *registered dietitian (RD)* provides an initial dietary assessment and meal plan, techniques for weight management, guidelines for dining out, and monitors your progress. He or she can also provide instruction in advanced dietary techniques and special diets for those who need them.

- Your family is an indispensable member of the team and can literally make or break you, depending on their willingness and enthusiasm.
- Other branches of medicine are involved to a somewhat lesser extent and include physical therapy, optometry, ophthalmology, podiatry, pharmacy, and social services.

It is important to make a conscious decision to become a dedicated student of diabetes and to update your knowledge continually. Be patient and persistent. You will also need to become comfortable with a certain degree of variability and uncertainty. No one can have perfect control all of the time.

In conclusion, the entire approach to diabetes management can be summarized in these three words: assess, act, and reassess. Assess your degree of control. Decide what to do about it, and act on that decision. Then reassess the situation to see if you made the correct decision and learn from your mistakes and, preferably, those of others. Hard work, knowledge, organization, focus, faith, hope, and a sense of humor are all valuable assets to be cultivated in the pursuit of ideal diabetes control.

HYPOGLYCEMIA

Hypoglycemia means low blood glucose and is a clinical syndrome with multiple causes in which the low blood glucose concentrations may lead to some uncomfortable symptoms. The low blood glucose can activate the body's "fight-or-flight" response by triggering the release of epinephrine (or adrenaline) from the adrenal glands. The symptoms include anxiety, tremor, sweating, palpitations, nausea, hunger, and pallor.

20

(table 20-3)
CAUSES OF HYPOGLYCEMIA

FASTING	POSTPRANDIAL
Excessive insulin production by the pancreas or pancreatic tumor	Following surgery of the upper gastrointestinal tract
Hypopituitarism	Early type 2 diabetes
Adrenal insufficiency	Ingestion of unripe akee fruit
Malnutrition	Following gastric bypass surgery for severe obesity
Severe illness and/or infection	Surreptitious or inadvertent administration of insulin or insulin-stimulating medications
Severe heart failure	Following ingestion of large amounts alcohol and simple carbohydrates
Liver disease	Following pancreas transplant surgery
Kidney disease	"Functional hypoglycemia"
Surreptitious or inadvertent administration of insulin or insulin-stimulating medications	
Side effect of numerous medications (salicylates, alcohol, quinine, haloperidol, disopyramide, beta-blockers, pentamidine, trimethoprim-sulfamethoxazole)	
Cancer	
Prolonged, intense exercise	
Rare disorders of carbohydrate metabolism (usually diagnosed in childhood)	

Low blood glucose may affect the brain and nervous system, causing lethargy, confusion, bizarre behavior, seizures, or coma. The symptoms are usually episodic and often quite uncomfortable. Fortunately, the body has developed several mechanisms to guard against hypoglycemia so that although the symptoms may be dramatic, they are rarely dangerous or life-threatening.

There are numerous causes of hypoglycemia, and the disorder is best characterized by whether the symptoms tend to occur while fasting (8 to 14 hours after eating) or in the *postprandial* state (four to six hours after eating). Table 20-3 provides examples of the more common causes of hypoglycemia.

The diagnosis of hypoglycemia is confirmed by documenting (1) a low blood glucose concentration concurrent with (2) symptoms of hypoglycemia and (3) complete and prompt resolution of symptoms following treatment that restores the blood glucose level to normal (carbohydrate ingestion or the administration of intravenous dextrose or glucagon given subcutaneously, intramuscularly, or intravenously). It is critically important that all three criteria be met to avoid making an incorrect diagnosis which may lead to unnecessary invasive, dangerous, and/or expensive diagnostic tests or therapeutic interventions. The use of fingerstick capillary blood glucose testing, although useful for monitoring and treating diabetes, is totally inadequate and unreliable for diagnosing true hypoglycemia. It is quite common for certain healthy individuals to have episodic symptoms, such as weakness, dizziness, light-headedness, anxiety, palpitations, tremor, hunger, or extreme fatigue, which may improve after eating. This is rarely, if ever, associated with true verifiable hypoglycemia. It is not uncommon for such individuals to undergo an oral glucose tolerance test by a well-meaning physician, be mislabeled as "hypoglycemic," and be assigned to a "hypoglycemia diet." This is rarely necessary except for the conditions noted in Table 20-3. If there is any doubt regarding the diagnosis of possible hypoglycemia, an endocrinology consultation can prove most useful. Treatment is directed at correcting the underlying cause of the hypoglycemia.

THE GONADS: MENOPAUSE AND ANDROPAUSE

Menopause and the role of hormone replacement therapy are discussed in Chapter 15. The aging male may also have a syndrome related to hormone deficiency, which is called andropause. Andropause may have a more insidious onset and be more difficult to recognize than menopause.

Testosterone is produced in the testicles under the influence of the gonadotropins, FSH and LH, secreted by the pituitary gland. Testosterone has multiple effects on body tissues (including sexual function and virility), brain function (including mood and concentration), body composition (fat and muscle), bone mineral density, red blood cell mass, glucose and lipid metabolism, and muscle mass, strength, and stamina.

Testosterone deficiency, also know as hypogonadism, is a condition by which testosterone production is inadequate to meet the body's needs.

(table 20-4)

CAUSES OF HYPOGONADISM

PRIMARY	SECONDARY	COMBINED
Congenital (Klinefelter's syndrome)	Congenital (Kallman's syndrome)	Aging
Infection (mumps)	Pituitary tumor, trauma, or irradiation	Alcoholism
Trauma	Acute illness	Hemochromatosis
Toxins	Glucocorticoids	Chronic illness
Chemotherapy		Sickle cell anemia
Radiation		
Chronic illness		

Hypogonadism can be due to disease affecting the testicles (primary hypogonadism), the hypothalamus and pituitary (central hypogonadism), or both (combined hypogonadism). Table 20-4 lists some of the more common causes of hypogonadism. Hypogonadism in the aging male is often referred to as andropause to highlight its importance as a clinical entity. Not all men develop testosterone deficiency as they get older, and not all men with low testosterone have clinical symptoms or need treatment. Andropause is therefore the development of symptoms compatible with hypogonadism in conjunction with low serum-free testosterone in a male over the age of 50 years in the absence of any other condition known to impair testosterone production.

Like many other endocrine illnesses, the symptoms are often nonspecific and develop insidiously over time. They may include:

- Decreased libido
- Decreased energy and well-being
- Higher-pitched voice
- Decreased beard growth
- Decreased strength or endurance
- Decreased height or osteoporosis
- Anemia
- Decreased ability to think or concentrate
- Depression
- Moodiness or loss of equanimity
- Erectile dysfunction
- Decrease in work performance
- Increased weight or obesity
- Glucose intolerance

Andropause is distinct from menopause in women for whom the symptoms can be dramatic, develop over a period of months to years, and are associated with the cessation of menses. Many of the symptoms of andropause have been attributed to "normal aging." This misconception, coupled with the slow and subtle progression of symptoms over a more extended period of time, often leads to a missed or delayed diagnosis. It is very difficult to ascertain the actual prevalence of hypogonadism in the

(table 20-5)

ST. LOUIS QUESTIONNAIRE FOR ANDROGEN DEFICIENCY

☐ 1. Do you have a decrease in libido (sex drive)?

☐ 2. Do you have a lack of energy?

☐ 3. Do you have a decrease in strength or endurance?

☐ 4. Have you lost height?

☐ 5. Have you noticed a decreased enjoyment of life?

☐ 6. Are you sad and grumpy?

☐ 7. Are your erections less strong?

☐ 8. Have you noticed a recent deterioration in your ability to play sports?

☐ 9. Are you falling asleep after dinner?

☐ 10. Has there been a recent deterioration in your work performance?

aging male. Approximately 10% of males over 50 years old in one study had bioavailable (effective on body tissues) testosterone levels that were below the normal range. This can increase dramatically to 70% of men by age 70. Moreover, there are an estimated three to four million androgen-deficient men in the United States, and the majority remains undiagnosed or suboptimally treated.

The diagnosis of andropause is confounded by the presence of nonspecific symptoms that can overlap with depression, another common disorder in the aging male. Therefore, it is useful to screen for male hypogonadism with a screening tool, such as the 10-point St. Louis University Questionnaire for Androgen Deficiency in Aging Males (ADAM), which is shown in Table 20-5. A positive response to questions 1 or 7 or any other three questions warrants diagnostic testing.

Testosterone secretion is usually maximal during the morning hours and then decreases during the day. This *diurnal variation* is lost in the aging male. Thirty % of testosterone is tightly bound to a protein known as *sex hormone–binding globulin (SHBG)* and not available to the cells as an active hormone. Sixty-eight % is loosely bound to albumin in the bloodstream, and 2 % is unbound (free) in the circulation. Thus approximately 70% of the total serum testosterone is bioavailable, or able to have an effect on the body's tissues. Total serum testosterone levels decrease, SHBG increases, and free or bioavailable testosterone decreases sharply with age. This can make diagnosis difficult, since the total testosterone level may be in the normal range and up to 22% of symptomatic individuals may have low bioavailable testosterone levels and true hypogonadism. It is therefore recommended that a symptomatic male should have a bioavailable or free-testosterone level obtained in the morning. If low, a second blood sample is obtained one week later for confirmation along with LH, FSH, prolactin, PSA, and digital rectal exam of the prostate in anticipation of testosterone replacement therapy (TRT). Consideration should be given to pituitary imaging for markedly decreased testosterone in the setting of low or normal LH and FSH levels to exclude a possible pituitary tumor.

Treatment is directed at improving symptoms and restoring the testosterone level toward normal. Oral preparations (METHYLTESTOSTERONE, OXANDROLONE, and FLUOXYMESTERONE) are limited by their increased risk for liver toxicity and lack of long-term efficacy and safety data. Their use is clearly discouraged. Injectable testosterone preparations (TESTOSTERONE ENANTHATE, TESTOSTERONE CYPIONATE, and TESTOSTERONE PROPIONATE) were the mainstay of androgen replacement therapy for years and remain a viable treatment option for hypogonadal males. They are administered by intramuscular injection every one to four weeks, produce inconsistent testosterone levels, and can be associated with waxing and waning libido, sexual function, energy, and mood. Transdermal delivery (skin patches) systems have become the preferred treatment due to their ease of administration, mimicking of normal physiology, and safety profiles. They include ANDRODERM, TESTODERM, ANDROGEL, and TESTIM. They are administered on a daily basis and produce consistent testosterone concentrations in the bloodstream that approximate normal physiological levels. The patch preparations sometimes do not stick to the skin well, and they may have a tendency to cause skin irritation. Recently, testosterone tablets (STRIANT) have become available, which are applied to the gums every 12 hours. They release testosterone across the lining of the mouth and into the bloodstream. They are effective and well tolerated. Some individuals may have trouble initially with placement and retention of the tablets. Investigational approaches include injection of biodegradable microcapsules or aqueous TESTOSTERONE BUCICLATE (every 8 to 12 weeks), oral TESTOSTERONE UNDECANOATE (twice daily), implantable testosterone pellets (every four to six months), and selective androgen receptor modulators (SARMs) which are designer drugs that maximize the beneficial effects on sexual function and body composition with minimal effects on the prostate gland. Some contraindications to testosterone replacement include severe heart, liver, or kidney disease and prostate cancer.

■

WHAT YOU NEED TO KNOW

▶ Your body's system of hormones (the endocrine system) is responsible for maintaining the body's internal regulatory system.

▶ Diseases of the endocrine system are classified according to whether a particular hormone has decreased or increased. Symptoms and physical examination findings can suggest hormone deficiency or excess, but they require confirmation by laboratory testing of blood, urine, or biopsy specimens.

▶ The major effects of aging on the endocrine system include a tendency toward hormone deficiency and tumor formation. Hormone deficiency may be slow to develop and difficult to recognize early on. Symptoms may mimic those of "normal aging" and escape detection for years. You should inform your doctor if you are experiencing unusual tiredness, weakness, depression, poor appetite, sleep problems, or unexplained weight loss or weight gain. Even if you feel fine and attribute your slowing down to age, your doctor might suggest that you have periodic blood tests, such as a blood glucose to check for diabetes or a thyroid blood test to check for an underactive or overactive thyroid gland.

▶ Tumors of the endocrine glands are usually benign. They may cause a knot or swelling of the gland, such as a neck swelling with a thyroid nodule, or they may cause hormone deficiency or excess as would be the case for tumors of the internal organs, such as the pituitary, adrenal, or parathyroid glands.

▶ The pituitary gland is the master gland that directs the production of the other hormones of the body. It is a small pea-sized gland located at the base of the brain.

▶ Thyroid gland disorders are among the most common problems of the endocrine system. An underactive thyroid may cause tiredness, weight gain, brittle nails, constipation, and depression. An overactive thyroid gland may cause weight loss, anxiety, tremor, muscle weakness, and tiredness. Many of the symptoms of thyroid disease can mimic the effects of aging or other medical conditions. Alert your doctor if you are experiencing such symptoms.

▶ Hyperparathyroidism is being recognized more frequently since serum calcium measurements are included in routine blood chemistry tests. Most often, this condition is asymptomatic. Surgery is recommended if problems occur, such as ulcers, kidney stones, altered mental status, or depression, as well as premature or severe osteoporosis or bone disease.

▶ Diabetes mellitus affects up to 20 million Americans. Often there are no symptoms in the early stages of diabetes, and many people are walking around unaware that they have diabetes. Make it a point to have your blood glucose checked by a doctor.

▶ True hypoglycemia is relatively rare. Many persons who have anxiety or other problems have been labeled "hypoglycemic" and placed on diets. These diets are almost never necessary. If you have any doubt regarding a diagnosis of hypoglycemia, seek an endocrinology consultation.

▶ Andropause is related to testosterone deficiency in the aging male. Symptoms include decreased sex drive, decreased energy and strength, decreased ability to think and concentrate, moodiness or depression, and height loss. The decision to use testosterone replacement therapy should be discussed by you and your doctor. Treatment for severe heart, liver or kidney disease and prostate cancer are contraindications to testosterone therapy.

FOR MORE INFORMATION

⯈ National Institutes of Health

9000 Rockville Pike

Bethesda, MD 20892

301-496-4000

Web: www.nih.gov

⯈ American Diabetes Association

1701 North Beauregard Street

Alexandria, VA 22311

1-800-342-2383

Web: www.diabetes.org

⯈ American Thyroid Association

6066 Leesburg Pike, Suite 650

Falls Church, VA 22041

1-800- 849-7643

Web: www.thyroid.org

Activity of the nervous system improves the capacity for activity, just as exercising a muscle makes it stronger.

—*Dr. Ralph Gerard, neurobiologist*

THE AUTHOR

21   *Maurice Hanson, MD*

MAURICE HANSON, MD, graduated from medical school at the University of Utah. He completed his medical residency at Parkland Hospital in Dallas, Texas, and his neurology residency at Case Western Reserve University. Dr. Hanson has been with the Cleveland Clinic since 1973 and with its southern branch in Florida since 1988. He is the author or coauthor of about 75 articles and book chapters. His interests include movement disorders and clinical neurophysiology.

21 | THE NERVOUS SYSTEM

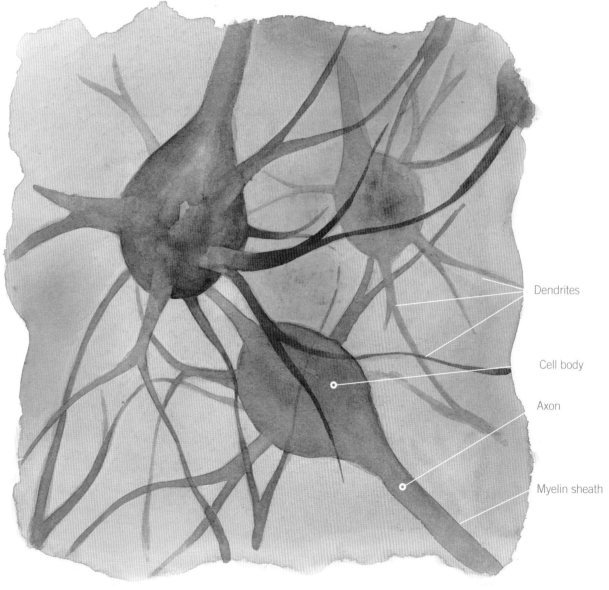

Dendrites

Cell body

Axon

Myelin sheath

(figure 21-1*)*

The nerve cell is called a neuron. The dendrites receive messages from other nerve cells, and the single axon sends messages to other nerve cells or to muscles. The myelin sheath functions in the same way as insulation around an electric cord.

Your nervous system is "mission control" for your body. Everything you do starts with an impulse in your nervous system. Your thoughts originate in your brain and allow you direct your muscles and bones to move so that you can eat, walk, and exercise. Even activities that are on automatic pilot, such as your breathing, digestion, and circulation, are under the control of your nervous system.

Although we find that many of the changes our bodies go through as we get older are unwelcome, none are more devastating to our families or to us than diseases of the nervous system. Even normal changes that occur in the nervous system can be upsetting. You may be shocked to learn that you lose 50,000 to 100,000 brain cells per day! However, you should be comforted that you have over 10 billion to start with.

Nevertheless, most of us find that as we get older, it is more difficult to learn new information. You may find that you have more difficulty remembering people's names. Perhaps you have to keep lists to avoid forgetting something you were expected to do. Has someone commented that you are absent minded? Maybe you find that your gait is slower and unsteadier. Sometimes it may be difficult to distinguish what is considered normal aging of the nervous system from what is abnormal. In most cases, your physician will be able to help you figure this out. In some cases, he or she may ask for a consultation from a neurologist, a specialist in disorders of the nervous system. In this chapter, I discuss some of the problems that affect the nervous system as we get older. Memory disorders, including Alzheimer's disease, are reviewed in Chapter 26. Stroke is discussed in Chapter 8, and the rehabilitation following stroke is discussed in Chapter 30.

TREMOR

BERNICE S., 69 YEARS OLD

I started shaking four years ago after the death of my husband. At first I thought it was related to stress, but after two years it got much worse. I could not write well or drink from a cup. I got embarrassed when I was with other people. I went to my doctor, and I was relieved when he told me that I did not have Parkinson's disease but a condition called essential tremor. He tried some medicines that initially helped, but after two years nothing seemed to work. Finally, after weighing the pros and cons, I agreed to a procedure called deep brain stimulation in which a neurosurgeon implanted a small wire into the area of the brain that controls the tremor. Although the tremor is not completely gone, it is much better. I feel much more comfortable in social situations. Since the tremor does not bother me when I am sleeping, I can even turn the stimulator off at night.

Tremor is an involuntary trembling movement. All of us have a very fine tremor that in most cases is imperceptible. However, you may have experienced more severe tremor if you drank too much coffee or got very nervous. The most common tremor affecting older adults is essential tremor, which is characterized by rhythmic movements about a joint or joints. Each movement back and forth is called a *cycle,* and essential tremor has a frequency of 4 to 8 cycles per second. It is absent at rest and occurs with action and maintenance of posture. Essential tremor is highly variable in severity but predictably worsens with increasing age. It involves principally the hands and arms (see Figure 21-2), but can affect the head and voice, and rarely the legs. Essential tremor occurs with goal-directed activities, such as eating, holding the paper, writing, drinking, and fine movements of the hands. While it is called "benign" essential tremor, this may be a misnomer as the tremor may be sufficiently severe to interfere with function; hence it may not be so benign. It does however lack the disabling features of Parkinson's, such as slowness of movement and rigid muscles. Essential tremor is often hereditary (other family member affected) and is known to be sensitive to alcohol in the sense that alcohol dampens the tremor. There has always been concern about the excessive use of alcohol in patients with essential tremor, but all the studies have shown that the incidence of alcohol addiction is no greater in patients with essential tremor than in the general population. A doctor will likely order a thyroid blood test since an overactive thyroid gland can also cause a tremor.

(figure 21-2)

Hand tremor has a variety of causes. An evaluation by a doctor can determine the cause and the treatment.

21

Treatment depends on the extent of the disability. Your doctor's reassurance that you do not have Parkinson's disease is essential. Essential tremor has often been misdiagnosed as such. If you have a tremor that is mild or moderate and not interfering with your activities of daily living, you need to do nothing but see your doctor periodically. If sufficiently symptomatic, two drugs are effective in about half the patients with a 50% reduction in severity of the tremor: PROPRANOLOL (INDERAL) and PRIMIDONE (MYSOLINE). If your symptoms are disabling only in special situations, such as social gatherings or public speaking, you can consider the use of propranolol about 20 to 30 minutes before the event. You may not be able to use propranolol if you have asthma or heart rhythm disturbances associated with slow heart rates.

Modest amounts of alcohol can be used to suppress tremor but, obviously, cannot be recommended if you are driving or going on stage! Neither police officers nor the courts will accept the medicinal value of alcohol if you are stopped for driving under the influence. And your stage performance may make you look more like a clown than a celebrity. In addition, tremor may be worse after the effects of alcohol wear off.

For the severe tremors that are resistant to medications, deep brain stimulation is an alternative. In this procedure, a neurosurgeon implants a small wire into the area of the brain that controls the tremor. The wire runs through a small hole in the skull and travels under the skin to a small device implanted under the collarbone that sends electrical impulses to the brain. As described in the case above, it can have a very favorable

(table 21-1)
OTHER TYPES OF TREMORS

TREMOR	DESCRIPTION
Action	Occurs at the end of a movement. Doctors test for this by asking you to touch your finger to your nose and touch your finger to the doctor's finger. Most are due to a problem with the motor control system of the brain known as the cerebellum. Very difficult to treat.
Dystonic (torticollis or wry neck)	Usually a head tremor with pulling to one side. Best treated with Botox injection.
Iatrogenic	Induced by a substance, such as caffeine, or by a medication, such as metoclopramide (Reglan), lithium (Eskalith, Lithobid), valproic acid (Depakote), chlorpromazine (Thorazine), steroids, albuterol (Ventolin, Proventil), and metaproterenol (Alupent).
Medical condition	An overactive thyroid gland (hyperthyroidism) or kidney failure, for example.
Primary orthostatic (or shaky leg)	Rapid tremor present when standing and very disabling. Responds to both pramipexole (Mirapex) and clonazepam.
Psychogenic	Mimics other types of tremor and usually responds to psychological therapy.

effect on a person's quality of life. It was initially developed to treat the tremor associated with Parkinson's disease, but now its applications have expanded to include essential tremor. Research is ongoing with regard to other neurological conditions.

The second most common tremor is *Parkinson's tremor.* The tremor is much less frequent than essential tremor is, usually asymmetric (on one side), and a rest tremor when the body part is completely relaxed. It is enhanced by attention and external discomfort. Seventy-five % of Parkinson's disease patients whose tremor is a major part of their disease *(tremor dominant)* often have telltale signs of additional problems, including a loss of normal facial expression, decrease in voice volume and pitch, drooling, slow movement, which is called bradykinesia, rigidity of muscles resulting in stiffness, and gait disorders, including stooped postures.

Treatment is similar to that for Parkinson's disease in general, which is discussed in the following section. A disorder known as monosymptomatic rest tremor, in which a rest tremor occurs, has no other evidence of Parkinson's disease and may not progress. Other types of tremor are summarized in Table 21-1.

PARKINSON'S DISEASE

Involuntary tremulous motion, with lessened muscle power, in parts not in action and even when supported; with the propensity to bend the trunk forwards, and to pass from walking to a running pace. The senses and intellects being uninjured.
—James Parkinson, 1817

Parkinson's disease is the most common degenerative neurological disease after Alzheimer's disease. Approximately 100 to 120 persons out of 100,000 have Parkinson's disease. The number of newly acquired cases averages 12 to 20 per 100,000 per year in the United States and United Kingdom. These figures have remained stable over the past 50 years. Parkinson's disease rarely begins before the age of 50 and tends to increase in frequency until the age of 90. Men are slightly more affected than women. Worldwide, it is more prevalent in North American Caucasians. It is intermediate in frequency in Asians, and the lowest frequency is in African blacks.

The most important risk for Parkinson's disease is advancing age. Family history plays some role, as does life experience including trauma, stress, environmental metal exposure, a rural life, exposure to herbicides, and growing up on a farm. Interestingly, in some studies risk has been reduced with alcohol and tobacco use. However, one can hardly recommend the use of these substances to prevent Parkinson's disease. The potential adverse effects far outweigh the benefits in most cases. In addition, studies suggest that it is quite possible that persons predisposed to develop Parkinson's disease shy away from these behaviors.

On a historical note, James Parkinson first described the disease in 1817. The famous French neurologist Charcot is credited with the introduction of the first beneficial treatment, belladonna, in the late 19th century. In 1957, researchers in Sweden discovered the neurochemical basis for Parkinson's disease when dopamine (a chemical in the brain that helps the nerve cells to communicate with each other) deficiency was found in brain tissue, especially the basal ganglia. In the 1960s, the first trials were begun using levodopa, a dopamine precursor, and by 1967 it had become an established practice. In the early 1970s, it was discovered that LEVODOPA combined with CARBIDOPA prevented breakdown of levodopa and dopamine in the body before it reached the brain. This significantly enhanced its effectiveness, and the current practice is to use the combination of carbidopa and levodopa (SINEMET).

DIAGNOSIS OF PARKINSON'S DISEASE

DOCTORS DIARY

I saw Eleanor S., 60, in the office because of a tremor in her left hand that had progressed over the past year to involve both hands. She observed that it was also harder for her to climb out of bed, get out of a car, and arise from a chair. Her previously legible handwriting had become cramped and small. Her steps had become shorter, and she felt as if she was toppling forward. Relatives commented on her soft voice and sad face, even though she was not depressed. I also noticed that she had a stooped posture and a decrease in her arm swing while walking. When I informed Eleanor S. that she had Parkinson's disease, she was surprised that I did not order tests. I reassured her that Parkinson's disease was still a diagnosis made by a physician after a good medical history and examination. It did not require blood tests or brain scans.

The diagnosis of Parkinson's disease is straightforward and requires no more than a clinical examination. Eleanor S., our case patient, displayed all the cardinal features that we require to diagnose Parkinson's disease:

- A tremor, which characteristically occurs at rest while the limb is relaxed, usually beginning in the hand and arm

- Slowness of voluntary movements (called bradykinesia) and the resistance of muscle relaxation, rigidity
- Tightness and resistance of movement in the joints is a common feature
- Tendency to fall forward, due to the loss of postural stability

Taken together, the diagnosis is unmistakable. Most of the time, the tremor dominates the picture, but about one-quarter of the patients will experience other features in the absence of the tremor, especially slow movement. Other common symptoms of Parkinson's disease are drooling of saliva; a change in handwriting; oiliness and flakiness of the skin, especially of the forehead; soft and strained voice; and the lack of facial expression (see Figure 21-3).

A few medical conditions can mimic Parkinson's disease. Some unusual degenerative diseases may be misdiagnosed in the early phases, conditions that we refer to as *atypical Parkinson's disease*. The most common of these is a disorder called progressive supranuclear palsy. In patients with odd or unexpected features, neuroimaging usually with magnetic resonance imaging (MRI) of the head is used, but this is relatively infrequent. A consultation with a neurologist may be helpful if the diagnosis is in doubt or assistance is needed in treatment.

The cause of Parkinson's disease, as with most degenerative neurological disorders, is not known although an interaction of genetic predisposition with an environmental agent is suspected. There are rare families for which Parkinson's disease is clearly genetic and the gene location has been isolated. The more common genetic influences are an increased frequency of Parkinson's disease in close relatives of a patient with Parkinson's.

Environmental factors, including repetitive head trauma, chemicals (herbicides and insecticides), and metals (such as manganese), have been long suspected of playing a role in Parkinson's disease. A chemical known to produce Parkinson's disease is methylphenyltetrahydropyridine (MPTP), which will cause the same brain disorders in experimental animals and is used as a model for Parkinson's. Some environmental substances and industrial chemicals are suspected to have an MPTP-type property. Some illicit drugs have been shown to contain MPTP. A popular theory holds that the breakdown of the body's normal metabolism of neurochemicals creates free radicals, which are not degraded normally. This has led to the promotion of free-radical scavengers, such as vitamin E and SELEGILINE (ELDEPRYL), to fight the free radicals. To date, the evidence that they are helpful is tenuous.

TREATMENT OF PARKINSON'S DISEASE

Parkinson's disease is the only degenerative disease of the nervous system for which there is an effective therapy that has favorably affected the course, improved the quality of life, and decreased mortality. It is also a classical example of how good science led to a highly beneficial outcome. The effective management of Parkinson's disease is a complex task, requiring

(figure 21-3)

Parkinson's disease may cause a stooped posture, diminished arm sway while walking, and blank facial expression.

the collaboration of physician, patient, and family, as demonstrated in the following story of Joseph R.

JOSEPH R., 68 YEARS OLD

I was diagnosed with Parkinson's disease at age 62 when I complained of shaking in my right hand. A neurologist confirmed the diagnosis and observed that I dragged my right foot. I was not hampered by the symptoms, so I took no treatment and continued to work in my accounting practice until two years later when I retired. At that point, I began Eldepryl on advice of the neurologist. I responded well and was quite functional until two years later when the tremor involved both hands. Artane was added but discontinued after my memory had become affected. At that point, I found it more difficult getting out of bed and walking. Sinemet was begun. After a gradual increase in the dose to three times daily, my symptoms improved significantly, and I did well for three years. Then I noted that the beneficial effect lasted only three hours. Despite increasing the dose frequency, I began experiencing effects of sudden loss of benefit often preceded by peculiar involuntary movements of the head, face, and arms, which were worsened by increasing the dose. Eldepryl was stopped, and Requip was added, which made the fluctuations less evident. After one year, I began experiencing disturbing visual hallucinations. Requip was stopped, Comtan was added, but the abnormal movements and hallucinations worsened. My neurologist stopped everything except Sinemet, and Symmetrel twice daily was added. Currently, I take the Sinemet every three hours and the Symmetrel twice daily. I am doing as well as can be expected. I remain active and walk daily. I remain independent, and I am grateful for this. I understand further challenges lie ahead and my doctors are beginning to mention surgery.

Joseph R.'s account encapsulates the typical course and modern-day treatment of Parkinson's disease. It also emphasizes several principles. In the early phases, there is no compelling reason to begin any treatment until the patient's quality of life is affected. To date, there is no evidence that any treatment alters the natural course of Parkinson's disease. Treatment at this point involves careful education of the patient regarding the disease (with a realistic account of its course), a structured exercise program, proper diet, and good general health principals.

Active treatment (medication) should be tailored to the symptoms, age of the patient, and the severity. There are medications that have been around for some time and are considered to have a modest but definite benefit: SELEGILINE (ELDEPRYL), AMANTADINE (SYMMETREL), and TRIHEXYPHENIDYL (ARTANE). If the patient is young (less than 65) with predominant tremor, trihexyphenidyl is often of great benefit but has little effect on the slowness of movement. With mild to moderate disease in the earlier phase, medications called *dopamine agonists* are moderately effective and can delay the need for levodopa by one to three years. These drugs bypass the degenerating nerve cells in the brain and directly stimulate the dopamine receptor areas in the part of the brain called the *corpus striatum*.

(table 21-2*)*

CONDITIONS ASSOCIATED WITH PARKINSON'S DISEASE

CONDITION	TREATMENT
Constipation	Prevention is the key. High-fiber diet and stool softeners.
Dementia	Simplify the drug regimen. Drugs for Alzheimer's disease may be helpful (see Chapter 26).
Depression	SSRI antidepressant (see Chapter 25).
Drooling	Propantheline (Pro-Banthine); botulinum toxin (Botox).
Low blood pressure	Fludrocortisone (Florinef); midodrine (ProAmatine).
Pain	Identify the cause and treat with analgesics.
Psychosis or hallucinations	Simplifying the regimen and keeping levodopa-carbidopa as the bedrock. Adding a medicine such as clozapine (Clozaril) or quetiapine (Seroquel) is also an option.
Urinary frequency	Tolterodine (Detrol) can be helpful.

In the majority of individuals, levodopa is eventually required, and it is used early in the older patient with significant impairment. It may be used alone or in combination with another agent such as ENTACAPONE (COMTAN) or one of the dopamine agonists. Entacapone is an agent which blocks an enzyme that metabolizes levodopa and prolongs its duration. When levodopa is first begun, the benefit is often notable and prolonged. For the next three to five years, the patient remains quite stable.

Nearly all patients will experience a wearing off or on-off effect, abnormal body movements *(dyskinesias),* hallucinations, and other unpleasant side effects, which are managed by changing the dose and frequency of carbidopa-levodopa or by adding other medications, such as the dopamine agonists, amantadine, or entacapone. Generally, the problems become more difficult to control, heralding a new phase of the disease when the symptoms become even more severe.

Other problems sometimes arise requiring considerable experience and judgment of the physician. These conditions and their treatment are summarized in Table 21-2.

Some persons benefit from surgery. In selected patients, especially those with abnormal body movements and on-off fluctuations who have normal mental function, surgery is a consideration. Several surgical procedures have been explored. Transplantation of fetal brain tissue has met with controversy, but these cells may produce dopamine in the brain of the recipient. This is not a practical option for most persons, as it is usually reserved for clinical trials in major medical centers. Thalamotomy (destruction of a part of the brain called the *thalamus)* is of limited usefulness.

Pallidotomy involves surgical destruction of an area in the brain called the *globus pallidus.* It can only be done on one side, but it is effective. Deep brain stimulation, which I discussed earlier in the section "Tremor," is becoming the surgical procedure of choice for Parkinson's disease that has not responded adequately to medication. Deep brain stimulation has fewer complications than the other procedures, and it can be done on one or both sides of the brain.

In summary, Parkinson's disease remains a challenge for the patients and the doctor alike, but the positive developments, which include newer and better medicines and surgical techniques, are remarkable, and in a relatively short period of time, the outlook for this disease has become increasingly bright. Persons with Parkinson's disease and their families can expect that these treatment approaches will help improve their quality of life.

BRAIN TUMORS

Brain tumors can be benign or malignant. Benign tumors do not invade the surrounding brain and do not spread to other sites (see Figure 21-4). Meningiomas are tumors of the lining around the brain *(meninges)*, and neurofibromas are tumors of the cells that form the protective coating around the fibers of nerve cells. Malignant tumors include those called gliomas that originate in the brain and those that have spread to the brain from other sites *(metastatic cancer)*. Metastatic cancers to the brain often originate in the lung and breast, but other sites may be responsible. The clinical manifestations of benign and malignant brain tumors depend on the area of the brain involved, how much swelling there is around the tumor(s), and how many there are. The principal complaints are those of diminished mental capacity, headaches, and gait instability. Another common presentation is a seizure. Any adult who has a seizure for the first time needs an imaging study of the brain, such as a *computed tomography (CT)* or, better yet, magnetic resonance imaging (MRI), to exclude a brain tumor.

The treatment of tumors depends entirely on the type of tumor as well as its location. Benign tumors can be observed without surgery unless they start producing symptoms. Cancerous brain tumors are first identified by a brain biopsy. Treatment may require surgical removal of the cancer as well as chemotherapy and radiation. The general health of the patient is important. If the patient is frail and the prognosis is poor, no treatment other than comfort measures and hospice care may be appropriate. However, if the patient is in reasonable health, a single metastasis is treated by brain surgery *(craniotomy)* and the removal of the metastasis. If there are multiple metastases or the location does not allow for safe removal, whole head radiation and chemotherapy are the treatments of choice.

TRAUMA

The consequence of a head injury in an older person may not immediately be obvious, as the following story related by the patient's daughter demonstrates.

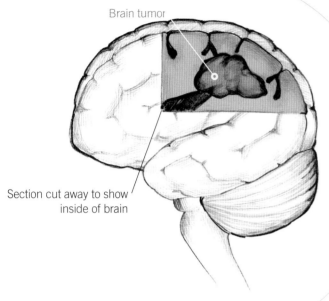

Brain tumor

Section cut away to show inside of brain

(figure 21-4)

Brain tumors can be benign or malignant. The adverse effects of brain tumors are related to the area of brain involved, the degree of swelling around a tumor, and the number of tumors.

MARTHA Q., 50 YEARS OLD

My mother, Rosemary W., 78, began acting differently for a few weeks. She was forgetting names and where she put things. She started having headaches, which she seldom had before. One morning when I went to see her at the retirement center where she lives, I got very alarmed when she didn't recognize me. My first thought was that she had developed Alzheimer's disease. I called her doctor who arranged to see her right away. He asked me to come in as well. The doctor was surprised that she didn't recognize him either, and he noticed that her walking was unsteady. He asked me a lot of questions. When he asked me if she had any recent falls, I recalled that a few months earlier that she had taken a tumble when she tried to jump out of bed to go to the bathroom. She tripped and fell. She had a "goose egg" on her forehead for a week or so, but it didn't seem that she hurt herself. She told us she was okay and not to worry.

The doctor told me that it was unusual for Alzheimer's disease to cause this degree of confusion so suddenly. He suspected she had a subdural hematoma, and this was confirmed with a CT scan. A neurosurgeon drilled a hole in her skull and removed the clot. Mom had an amazing recovery. Within a week she recognized me and the doctor. She still had some memory difficulties and required rehabilitation to improve her walking, but she had improvements every day.

Head injuries in the elderly have similarities with head trauma in younger individuals. In both, the severity of the head trauma is judged by the occurrence of loss of consciousness and the duration of amnesia after the injury. In older adults, men and women are equally represented. In younger persons males are more commonly affected, probably because of contact sports and other activities that pose more risk.

Falls are the most common cause for head injuries in an older person and account for 75% of the cases. In addition to loss of consciousness and amnesia after the injury, evidence of abnormalities, such as swelling, bleeding, and bruising on MRI or CT scans of the brain, help determine the severity of the brain injury.

Older persons often have significant injury to the brain, such as subdural hematoma (a collection of blood between the brain and skull; see Figure 21-5), after relatively minor trauma. A significant delay may occur before symptoms become more obvious and the diagnosis is suspected. More obvious injuries, such as a hip fracture, may distract attention away from any subtle neurological abnormalities.

Common symptoms of significant head trauma include disturbance of executive functions, such as initiation of action, planning, organization, problem solving, and reasoning. Difficulty in concentration, memory loss, and language disorders may be prominent.

The evaluation of any person with a head injury and neurological problems needs an imaging study, usually an MRI or CT scan to exclude hematomas, brain contusions, and so forth. However, not every head injury requires these tests. If the person has no abnormal symptoms and the neurological examination is normal, close observation may be sufficient. Skull X-rays have not been shown to be very useful in the evaluation of head trauma.

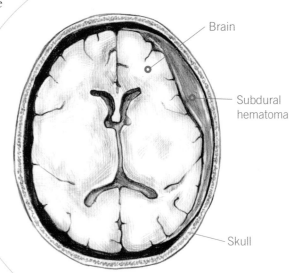

Brain

Subdural hematoma

Skull

(figure 21-5)

Subdural hematoma is a collection of blood between the brain and the skull. It is usually caused by a head injury, such as a fall.

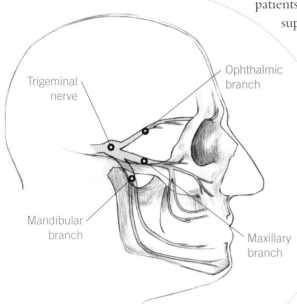

(figure 21-6)

Tic douloureux usually causes pain in the mandibular or maxillary distribution of the trigeminal nerve.

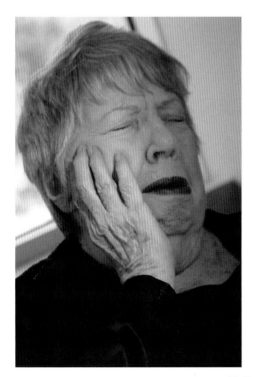

(figure 21-7)

Tic douloureux or trigeminal neuralgia usually causes severe, sharp stabbing pain.

Older age leads to increased long-term disability in head injury patients. They are more likely to require increased family involvement and support. They are more likely to require nursing home placement after hospitalization. Progression of cognitive impairment after a head injury suggests that the patient probably had some cognitive impairment even prior to the injury that was uncovered by the head trauma. Particularly if has been severe and repeated, head trauma is a risk factor for the development of dementia.

The treatment depends on the nature of the cognitive dysfunction. Problems with arousal may respond to psychostimulants, such as small doses of METHYLPHENIDATE (RITALIN). Memory impairment may respond to cognitive rehabilitation and drugs commonly used for Alzheimer's disease, such as donepezil (ARICEPT), RIVASTIGMINE (EXELON), and GALANTAMINE (REMINYL). Executive dysfunction may respond to AMANTADINE although care must be taken in prescribing this drug as it can result in confusion.

In our case patient, Rosemary W. was experiencing problems that suggested a more severe brain injury: fluctuating headaches, change in her mental status, and walking difficulties. The diagnosis of subdural hematoma was confirmed with CT scan, and the treatment was the surgical removal of the clot. Recovery was slow, but ultimately she was able to return to independent function.

Not all subdural hematomas need to be evacuated. Many of them will resolve on their own, particularly the small ones. Periodic scanning is often all that is necessary, along with clinical surveillance.

TIC DOULOUREUX

DOCTORS DIARY

Roberta B., 68, came to see me after her dentist reassured her that her toothache was not due to a problem in the teeth or gums. She recalled that 10 years ago she had a similar toothache and suffered for about two months before it cleared up. She described a severe sharp, stabbing pain, which she felt in her right lower jaw, that traveled to the right ear. Brushing her teeth often triggered the pain. She compared it to being stabbed by an ice pick. I advised her that her symptoms were classic for tic douloureux, another name for trigeminal neuralgia. I prescribed carbamazepine 200 mg twice daily, which promptly arrested the pain. Roberta B. was ecstatic. However, I advised her that this condition might resolve this time but flare up in the future.

Trigeminal neuralgia, or tic douloureux, is a relatively common cause of facial pain in the elderly (see Figures 21-6 and 21-7). It is characterized by brief stabbing pains, usually in the *mandibular division* or *maxillary division* of the trigeminal nerve. It almost never starts in the upper or ophthalmic division. It is always on the same side. There is a predictable trigger to the pain, such as chewing, talking, touching the face, or even a light breeze. There is a distinct absence of other neurologic problems, such as facial numbness, weakness, or visual disturbances.

About 10% of the cases are due to some structural problem, such as a tumor. Ninety % are idiopathic (cause unknown). It is believed that most cases are due to compression of the trigeminal nerve by a loop of a normal artery that presses on the nerve at its junction with the brain. Over time the pain tends to be more frequent and intense as was the situation with our case patient, Roberta B.

The most effective treatment over the years has been CARBAMAZEPINE (TEGRETOL), a drug initially developed to treat seizures. Its effect is dramatic. A newer antiseizure drug, OXCARBAZEPINE (TRILEPTAL), has proved as effective as carbamazepine but with fewer side effects. Monitoring of blood counts is not required. Carbamazepine requires checking blood counts and liver chemistries periodically. BACLOFEN and LAMOTRIGINE (LAMICTAL) are also used as backup agents.

In patients who fail medical treatment, a variety of surgical procedures have been tried. The most effective, but most invasive, is microvascular decompression, in which a neurosurgeon places a Teflon implant between the trigeminal nerve and the blood vessel that is compressing the nerve.

Roberta B., our case patient, was treated with Tegretol XR 200 mg twice a day for six months with complete response. The medication was gradually withdrawn, and she did well for another six months without reoccurrence and then it returned. The treatment was repeated, and she again was free of the pain.

Another common neuralgia involving the trigeminal nerve is postherpetic neuralgia, which occurs in the wake of shingles (herpes zoster). However, this condition often involves the upper division (ophthalmic division) of the fifth nerve, which includes the eye and the forehead, as opposed to trigeminal neuralgia, for which the upper portion is spared. Pain in the head precedes the rash or blisters by three to five days. The rash is initially red and then becomes a blister or blisters followed by crust and healing. Ten to 15% of patients have pain of variable severity that persists longer than three months after the onset and may be quite severe and agonizing. This is the group that constitutes postherpetic neuralgia. Treatment is pain relief, including such drugs as gabapentin, tricyclic antidepressants, carbamazepine, and analgesics. The prognosis is worse in terms of severity and medication responsiveness in older patients.

PERIPHERAL NEUROPATHY

Peripheral neuropathy (PN) is a malady having an incidence of about 40 out of 100,000. The frequency and severity definitely increase with age, and it is one of the commonest causes of chronic pain. These neuropathies are divided into those which involve the core of the nerve called axonal neuropathies and those which involve the lining of the nerve or the insulating material (myelin) called the demyelinating neuropathies.

Guillain–Barré syndrome is an example of the latter, in which profound weakness and numbness develops in the legs and then progresses to involve the arms. In a small percentage of patients, even the breathing muscles can become paralyzed, requiring a mechanical ventilator to support breathing. Typically, this syndrome is seen in younger persons. In older persons, demyelinating neuropathies might take the form of a progressive, chronic disorder of sensation, muscular strength, and gait instability. They have characteristic findings on the physical examination. Special tests called electromyogram (EMG) and nerve conduction studies help confirm the diagnosis. They evaluate muscle and nerve activity with special small needles that are connected to a machine that records the electrical activity. Treatment consists of medicines that suppress the immune system such as corticosteroids and intravenous immunoglobulin. In some cases, plasma exchange is performed, which removes toxic substances from the blood that are thought to play a role in these diseases.

Axonal disorders are more common than demyelinating neuropathies. The cause can be identified about 50% of the time. Some of the more common disorders responsible include diabetes, vitamin deficiencies, malnutrition, exposure to drugs or environmental toxins that injure nerves, alcohol excess, kidney failure, immune system disorders, and some cancers. Multiple myeloma (a type of bone marrow cancer) and some related diseases may cause peripheral neuropathy. In the other 50% the cause cannot be found. These are the most common peripheral neuropathies of the older adult and are known as cryptogenic peripheral neuropathies. Often they are quite painful but are not otherwise disabling.

The evaluation of these neuropathies includes EMG and nerve conduction studies, a blood count, chemical analysis, blood glucose testing, thyroid function tests, B_{12} levels, serum protein electrophoresis, and an antinuclear factor.

Treatment depends on the cause if it can be discovered. Otherwise the main effort is control of the pain. We use the same agents that we use in facial neuralgias, including gabapentin, tricyclic antidepressants, oxcarbazepine, carbamazepine, and analgesics.

MYASTHENIA GRAVIS

Myasthenia gravis occasionally starts in older persons and is the interruption of the normal chemical communication between nerves and muscles. Normally when released from a nerve cell, acetylcholine crosses a short channel and binds to a receptor on the muscle membrane. This then triggers the events leading to contraction of the muscle. In myasthenia gravis, an antibody develops to the muscle receptor for acetylcholine. The typical symptoms that this produces in the older adult are most often double vision that may get better and worse, difficulty swallowing and speaking, and easy tiring of the muscles. All these symptoms tend to improve at rest and worsen with activity and use of the muscles.

The diagnosis is made by EMG and nerve conduction studies, analysis of chemicals in the blood known as acetylcholine receptor antibodies,

DIZZINESS

Dizziness is a frequent complaint of young and older persons alike, and it can have different meanings for the different people who experience it. In some cases, patients describe a feeling of lightheadedness or feeling faint. Some may feel unsteady on their feet. Others describe a sense of motion in which either they or their surroundings seem to move or spin around *(vertigo)*. Many cases of vertigo are related to a disturbance in the middle ear and can be effectively treated with some simple body positioning procedures in a doctor's office. Medication may be required in other cases. However, some cases of vertigo can be caused by serious disturbances in the brain including strokes, aneuryms, or tumors. Usually, other neurological problems in addition to vertigo suggest a diagnosis other than a middle ear problem. Special tests such as MRI or CT scans may be required.

Heart disease, especially certain rhythm disturbances, can cause lightheadedness and even fainting. Many medications such as those used to treat high blood pressure, congestive heart failure, and fluid retention may cause dizziness, especially when standing up quickly or for a prolonged period of time. Other neurological diseases that affect the spinal cord or peripheral nervous system can cause unsteadiness.

As you can see, dizziness is a very imprecise symptom, and all cases require an evaluation by a physician to determine the exact cause. Most cases will have a simple explanation and can be easily treated, but it is important that you do not take this for granted. Talk to your doctor to pinpoint the source.

and a Tensilon test. TENSILON (EDROPHONIUM) is injected into a vein, and if the symptoms resolve or improve, it is good evidence that the patient has myasthenia gravis.

The treatment in the older person differs from that in younger people. In the younger individual, a thymectomy (removal of the thymus gland under the breastbone) is performed, which tends to lead to a more favorable course and sometimes a complete remission. In the older individual, the treatment of choice is to begin with a medicine called MESTINON (PYRIDOSTIGMINE), which increases the ability of the acetylcholine to interact with the muscle receptor. Other effective therapies are plasma exchange in patients who are acutely weak and whose breathing is impaired, corticosteroids and other immunosuppressive drugs such as IMURAN (AZATHIOPRINE), and, finally, intravenous immunoglobulin. These treatments are aimed at overcoming the immune system problem responsible for the disease. The present therapies have made the prognosis of myasthenia more favorable than it was in the past.

■

WHAT YOU NEED TO KNOW

▶ Tremor is a common problem. The type of tremor needs to be defined so that effective treatment can be prescribed.

▶ A physician makes the diagnosis of Parkinson's disease after reviewing symptoms and physical findings. Brain scans and blood tests are not helpful in making the diagnosis.

▶ Treatment of Parkinson's disease is tailored to the patient's limitations. No medicine may be required in the very early stages. Levodopa-carbidopa (Sinemet) is the most effective treatment, but its effectiveness may diminish with time. Other medicines are available that may be useful. Surgery is an alternative if medicines fail and is largely focused on deep brain stimulation.

▶ Relatively minor head injuries can lead to serious consequences in older persons. Symptoms may not be readily apparent. Clinical observation can help detect any neurological change that might require special tests and treatment.

▶ Tic douloureux is a severe, sharp stabbing pain that usually occurs in the jaw and radiates toward the ear. It may mimic a bad toothache.

▶ Peripheral neuropathies are common. They may be due to diabetes, vitamin B_{12} deficiency, alcohol excess, and a host of other causes. Proper treatment requires identifying the cause, but no cause can be identified in as many as half the persons affected. In these cases, treatment is aimed at controlling pain and protecting the affected areas.

▶ Dizziness is a very imprecise symptom, and all cases require an evaluation by a physician to determine the cause. Most cases will have a simple explanation and can be easily treated, but it is important that you do not take this for granted. Talk to your doctor.

FOR MORE INFORMATION

▶ **National Institutes of Health**
9000 Rockville Pike
Bethesda, MD 20892
800-352-9424
Web: www.nih.gov

▶ **NIH Neurological Institute**
P.O. Box 5801
Bethesda, MD 20824
800-352-9424, 301-496-5751
TTY: 301-468-5981
Web: www.ninds.nih.gov

▶ **National Parkinsons Foundation**
1501 NW 9th Avenue
Miami, FL 33136
800-327-4545, 305-243-5595
E-mail: mailbox@parkinson.org
Web: www.parkinson.org

Despite significant progress, infectious diseases remain the world's leading cause of death, and the third leading cause of death in the United States. . . . In addition to their human toll, the financial and psychological burdens of infectious diseases on families and communities are enormous.

—Anthony S. Fauci, MD, Director, National Institute of Allergy and Infectious Disease

THE AUTHOR

22   *Jack L LeFrock M.D.*

JACK LEFROCK, MD, FACP, is a graduate of Lafayette College and the University of Amsterdam School of Medicine. He did his residency in internal medicine at New York Hospital, Sloan-Kettering Memorial Hospital, and North Shore Hospital. He completed his fellowship in infectious diseases at Tufts New England Medical Center. He was professor of medicine and chief of Infectious Diseases at Hahnemann University School of Medicine in Philadelphia before moving to Sarasota, Florida. He repeatedly received the teacher of the year and clinician of the year awards, and he was voted into the Leon Smith Infectious Disease Hall of Fame. He has published over 250 journal articles and book chapters and has delivered over 200 scientific presentations. He has won the Golden Quill Award five times for his journal articles.

22 | INFECTIONS

The Petri dish is a shallow plastic dish that contains special nutritive material to culture bacteria. It is important in helping identify the cause of an infection and the appropriate antibiotic for fighting the infection.

Aging of the immune system (the body's defense system) is thought to play a role in the increased susceptibility to infections in the older person. It may also account for the unusual presentations of many life-threatening infections. For example, a young person with pneumonia may have a high fever, severe cough, and shortness of breath. However, an elderly person may simply act confused. There may be no fever or cough. Symptoms of infection include weakness, loss of appetite, weight loss, falling, urinary incontinence (involuntary loss of urine), or an increased rate of breathing. Therefore, it is imperative that the elderly and their families recognize that a significant change in symptoms may be a warning of a serious medical condition that warrants evaluation by a health professional.

Other important factors include the older person's medical conditions and place of residence. There may be a difference in the type of infections to which they are exposed depending on whether they live in their own homes, in an assisted living residence, or in a nursing home. Diabetes, chronic lung disease, Alzheimer's disease, and underlying cancer are a few of the conditions that predispose an individual to infection. Many elderly are frail and therefore at greater risk due to poor nutrition, immobility, urinary incontinence, and dementia. Pressure sores, indwelling urinary catheters, and feeding tubes may further increase their risks.

Infectious diseases are the leading cause of hospitalization in the elderly. Pneumonia, urinary tract infection, skin and soft tissue infection, sinusitis, gallbladder and intestinal infections, tuberculosis, and shingles are common conditions in the older age group. Less common, but not unusual, include *endocarditis* (infection of the heart valves), *osteomyelitis* (infection of the bone and joints), and such nervous system infections as *meningitis* (infection of the lining of the brain), *brain abscess* (a localized collection of pus and destroyed tissue), and *encephalitis* (infection of the brain).

The elderly are at least three times more likely to die or have complications from their disease than are younger persons with the same disease. Other reasons include delays in diagnosis and therapy (occasionally due to unusual presentations of the disease), poor tolerance to invasive diagnostic and therapeutic procedures, delayed or poor response to antibiotics, higher incidence of adverse drug reactions including antibiotics, and the frequent presence of other underlying conditions which already compromise that person's defenses.

FEVER AND INFECTION

You may find it interesting that the range of normal temperatures and clear criteria for what constitutes a fever have not been clearly established for the elderly. To add to the confusion, the body temperature may vary with the time of the measurement, the method by which it is measured (mercury thermometer versus an electronic thermometer), and even in the same body when it is recorded at different sites. For example, the rectal temperature may be as much as one degree higher than the oral temperature is. The temperature taken from the ear or from under the arm

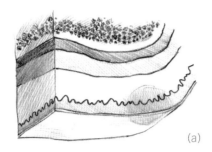

(a)

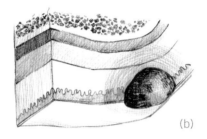

(b)

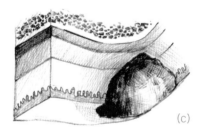

(c)

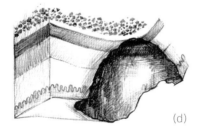

(d)

(figure 22-1)

Stages of development of a pressure sore. (a) In stage 1, the skin is reddened due to leakage of blood from small blood vessels. (b) In stage 2, the ulcer is a shallow crater or blister. (c) Stage 3 ulcers involve the whole thickness of the skin. (d) In stage 4, the sore causes destruction of underlying structures such as muscle and bone.

may differ from the other sites. Occasionally the temperature measurement may be spuriously low due to the individual wearing dentures or recently drinking a cold beverage.

In spite of these problems, the oral temperature remains the most frequent method for measuring and monitoring body temperature in people of all ages. Many investigators have noticed that the elderly have a lower normal temperature than do young adults. For that reason, an oral temperature greater than 99°F should be considered elevated. The astute physician realizes, however, that 20 to 30% of elderly individuals with serious infections may have an absent or blunted fever response. If a fever is present, that individual is more likely than is a younger adult to have a serious viral or bacterial infection.

Sometimes it may be difficult to diagnose the exact cause of a fever in an elderly person. The blood and urine tests may not show an infection. The chest X-ray may be normal. When a fever up to 101°F occurs repeatedly for at least three weeks and a cause is not identified, that person is said to have a *fever of unknown origin (FUO)*. More extensive testing may be required, such as CT or MRI scans, and even occasionally invasive testing, such as tissue biopsies or bone marrow tests. Approximately 90% of the time a specific diagnosis can be established. Very often the FUO is due to an unusual presentation of a common disease (pneumonia may not always show up on a regular X-ray and may require a CT for correct diagnosis). In other cases, it may be due to an infection with a "bug," such as tuberculosis (TB), that is less common yet still not rare. Certain diseases that are not infections and that are more common as we age may cause fever. These include *temporal arteritis* (an inflammation of the blood vessels about the scalp), *polymyalgia rheumatica* (aching and stiffness of the muscles of the shoulders and hips that may be associated with temporal arteritis), and *lymphoma* (cancer of the lymph tissue). Thus, fever in an elderly person, especially if persistent, may not necessarily be due to an infection and therefore requires evaluation.

SKIN INFECTIONS

Skin infections that occur commonly in the young, such as *cellulitis* (infections of the skin) and boils (skin abscess), also occur commonly in the elderly. However, skin infections associated with circulatory disease and diabetes occur more often in the elderly. There is also a higher incidence of pressure sores, postoperative wound infections, and *shingles (herpes zoster)*.

PRESSURE SORE

A **pressure sore** is a breakdown in the skin over a bony prominence such as the hip. Continued pressure against the skin stops the blood flow to that area. As a result, the skin cells die and a sore develops (see Figure 22-1). This occurs more commonly in the frail elderly who may be bedridden. The most common sites are over the *sacrum* (tailbone) and hip, but the heel and ankles are commonly involved. Pressure sores can develop anywhere

(table 22-1)

ANTIVIRAL DRUGS FOR SHINGLES

MEDICATION	DOSE	FREQUENCY	DURATION	AVERAGE COST
acyclovir (Zovirax)	800 mg	5 times daily	1 week	$30
famciclovir (Famvir)	500 mg	3 times daily	1 week	$150–175
valacyclovir (Valtrex)	1000 mg	3 times daily	1 week	$150–175

that pressure is unrelieved for a length of time. The best treatment is prevention, and there are few conditions that require even a frail person to be in bed continually. Activity should be encouraged. Sitting in a chair is significantly less risky for the development of pressure sores than is staying in bed. If bed rest is required, the person should be turned regularly.

In those patients with pressure sores who manifest clinical signs of infection (fever, chills, confusion, or drop in blood pressure) without an obvious cause, it must be assumed that the primary source of infection is the pressure sore, even if it does not look infected. Bacteria may be active deep beneath the wound surface. These sores are often complicated by infection of the surrounding skin and nearby bone. Not infrequently, bacteria from these wounds get into the bloodstream and cause an overwhelming generalized infection *(sepsis)*.

SHINGLES

Many older individuals fear herpes zoster, more commonly known as shingles. However, new treatments are available to reduce the impact of this once dreaded condition. The disease is caused by reactivation of the varicella virus, the same virus that causes chicken pox. Therefore, an individual can only get shingles if he or she had chicken pox in childhood. The virus becomes dormant in nerve cells near the spinal cord, and as the individual ages and presumably as immune function declines, the virus reactivates by spreading down a sensory nerve, and the characteristic rash develops (redness and blisters). Often the initial symptom is pain on one side of the body in the distribution of a *dermatome* (the skin area supplied by a sensory nerve). One to three dermatomes are usually involved. Since the pain often precedes the development of a rash, the symptoms can occasionally mimic those of a heart attack, a kidney stone, a gallbladder attack, or even a herniated disk.

Shingles is usually treated with antiviral drugs (see Table 22-1), which are best started within two or three days of the development of the rash. The pain and rash often are self-limited and resolve within a few weeks.

Shingles can occasionally be associated with protracted and disabling pain in elderly individuals, a condition called postherpetic neuralgia. Some physicians prescribe PREDNISONE in the early stages to try to reduce the risk of this condition, but it may not always be successful. Although postherpetic neuralgia is not life threatening, it can be associated with depression, sleep disturbances, loss of appetite, and weight loss. Physicians will often prescribe pain relievers, topical creams, anticonvulsants, and antidepressants for postherpetic neuralgia. Each of these has advantages and disadvantages, and the physician can prescribe a treatment program on the basis of that person's circumstances. Recent studies suggest that GABAPENTIN (NEURONTIN) may be quite effective and well tolerated. Often it is started at a low dose of 100 mg three times a day and gradually increased up to 1800 to 3600 mg a day if necessary. A topical cream, available over the counter, called *capsaicin,* may be effective, but it should not be applied until the skin is healed. It requires applications three to four times a day, and it may require several weeks to be effective. Other analgesics may be required in the meantime. A patch containing a topical numbing agent called LIDOCAINE (LIDODERM) is available and can be applied directly to the painful area. The patch can be cut to size, and it is applied for up to 12 hours. The average cost of 30 patches is about $125. Occasionally a local nerve block may be tried. The "Jaipur block" involves the local injection of two numbing agents (XYLOCAINE 2%, BUPIVACAINE 0.5%) and a steroid (DEXAMETHASONE 4 mg/cc).

Shingles can also involve the *trigeminal nerve,* which supplies the area around the eye. It is important that an *ophthalmologist* (a physician specialist in eye diseases) be involved in the care of those with eye involvement to minimize the risk of blindness. Rarely, shingles may involve the auditory (hearing) nerve and cause hearing loss, and the *facial nerve* causing transient paralysis. It may even involve the area around the mouth and make eating difficult.

LUNG INFECTIONS

Pneumonia and influenza combined are the sixth leading cause of death in the United States. About 90% of these deaths occur in adults 65 years and older. In fact, more than 60% of people 65 years and older are admitted to hospitals because of pneumonia. Some of the factors contributing to our diminished defenses against respiratory infections as we age include:

- Decreased activity of the ciliated cells (**Cilia** are hairlike projections of the respiratory cells and help clear pollutants and infection from the lung passages.)
- Diminished glottic closure, which can result in bacteria and food particles from the mouth traveling down the breathing passages into the lungs (The **glottis** is the structure in your throat that covers your windpipe when you swallow.)
- Loss of elastic tissue around the small air sacs of the lung, resulting in possible collapse of the air sacs and infection
- A decrease in strength of the respiratory muscles
- Diminished cough reflex

An older person may have other medical problems that affect the risk and the outcome of pneumonia, for example, diabetes, cancer, chronic obstructive pulmonary disease (COPD), asthma, liver or kidney disease, or recent surgery.

The surfaces of the skin and the mouth may become colonized with certain bacteria that can cause serious infections in the older individual residing in a nursing home or hospital. Doctors call these **nosocomial infections** to distinguish them from infections that people acquire in their home or community. The distinction is very important since nosocomial infections are often resistant to the typical antibiotics used to treat infections, and they may require more expensive and powerful antibiotics. These infections are generally caused by *Staphylococcus aureus* or by such Gram-negative bacteria as *Pseudomonas* and *Klebsiella*. (The *Gram stain* is used to visualize bacteria under the microscope. The type of bacteria can be determined by the reaction to the stain. Gram-positive bacteria pick up the stain, and Gram-negative bacteria don't.)

Older persons with pneumonia often pose significant challenges to the physician. They typically have fewer symptoms than do younger patients, and older persons often have *cerebral* (brain) symptoms. These may include subtle changes in their normal function or frank confusion. The body temperature may actually be low. In fact, a famous physician of the past, William Osler, stated that the combination of a low body temperature and brain symptoms was almost always related to "senile pneumonia."

Other subtle signs of pneumonia might include an increase in breathing rate or heart rate. Some of the classical physical findings that physicians have been taught to use may not be present in the elderly, and even the chest X-ray has to be interpreted with caution since other diseases can affect the appearance of the lungs. The elderly often produce little or no *sputum* (the yellow to green phlegm that is often caused by pneumonia), so that treatment may have to be initiated without the benefit of sputum cultures.

Streptococcus pneumonia (the cause of **pneumococcal pneumonia**) is the most frequent cause of pneumonia in older persons who live at home. It is also the most common type of pneumonia in younger persons. Viral pneumonia is relatively infrequent, with the possible exception of the *respiratory syncytial virus*. This virus has occasionally been implicated in outbreaks of respiratory illness in nursing homes. Protection with the **pneumococcal vaccine (Pneumovax)** is recommended for all people over 65 years of age and for younger individuals with such risk factors as diabetes, asthma, or COPD. (See the section "Recommended Immunizations," below.)

Aspiration pneumonia is more common in the elderly and is usually related to material from the mouth going down the breathing passages to the lungs. Normally small amounts of this material pass this way but are cleared by the defenses of the respiratory system. In older persons, the coughing and gag reflexes are not as vigorous and the other defenses not as strong. Bacteria from the mouth travel along with saliva and food particles, eventually causing an infection in the lungs. In more severe

Abscess cavity

Pus

(*figure* 22-2)

Lung abscess.

cases, this infection can cause severe destruction of lung tissue. The body's attempt to control the infection results in a walled cavity called a lung abscess, as shown in Figure 22-2.

INFLUENZA

Influenza is a viral illness and a major cause of death and illness in older adults. Persons over 65 account for 80 to 90% of the deaths from influenza. The symptoms of influenza are similar to those experienced by younger adults except that the fever may be absent in the elderly. Influenza is different from the common cold in that body aches are usually more severe, especially in the back and legs, and there is often a rather severe headache. Older patients have a greater risk of complications, such as pneumonia, and they may develop weakness that persists for many weeks.

Several office-based tests have become available to help doctors detect influenza in nasal secretions. However, if the patient has typical symptoms and influenza is prevalent in the community, a doctor will often prescribe antiviral medication without resorting to the extra time and expense required for these tests.

It has been often said that an ounce of prevention is worth a pound of cure. That is more than true in the prevention of influenza. The flu vaccine can significantly reduce your risk of acquiring influenza. The discussion of the flu vaccine is in the section "Recommended Immunizations," below.

Four medications are available for the treatment of influenza, as shown in Table 22-2.

TUBERCULOSIS

Most older persons with tuberculosis (TB) were actually infected with the TB "bug" when they were younger. Most were never aware of it, and the infection did not produce the symptoms that we usually associate with tuberculosis. Some of the factors, which are associated with "reactivation" of TB and the development of serious disease in the elderly, include diminution in the person's immune responses, poor nutrition, diabetes, chronic renal failure, residence in a nursing home, use of steroids, and chemotherapy. Such symptoms as cough, blood in the sputum, and night sweats may occur less frequently in the elderly. More commonly, older individuals will have chronic tiredness, difficulty with memory and cognitive functions, loss of appetite, low-grade fever, and difficulty performing their daily living activities. These problems can

FAMILY JOURNAL

My mother Martha N., 85, was in a nursing home since her stroke earlier this year. She had been progressing quite well with her physical therapy until one day she decided she didn't feel up to it. The following day when I visited, she didn't want to get out of bed. By that evening she was confused and not making any sense when she talked. I told her nurse who checked her temperature. It was 97, but the nurse told me that a normal temperature did not exclude an infection. I didn't know that. The nurse contacted the doctor to let him know about the change in Mom's status.

Mom was taken to the hospital where her chest X-ray confirmed pneumonia in her right lung. She was hospitalized and placed on intravenous antibiotics. After a few more days of confusion, she turned the corner and began taking fluids. Her intravenous antibiotics were discontinued, and she was placed on an oral antibiotic. She perked up, and her confusion cleared. She was able to resume her physical therapy and was transferred back to the nursing home a week later.

(table 22-2)

DRUGS FOR INFLUENZA

MEDICATION	DOSE	FREQUENCY	DURATION	AVERAGE COST
amantadine (Symmetrel)	100 mg	2 times daily	24–48 hours after symptoms disappear	$10–15
rimantadine (Flumadine)	100 mg	2 times daily*	7 days	$35
zanamivir (Relenza)	2 inhalations	every 12 hours	5 days	$60
oseltamivir (Tamiflu)	75 mg	2 times daily	5 days	$80

*100 mg once daily in renal/liver dysfunction or frail elderly.

occur with other medical conditions, but when these kinds of symptoms persist for weeks to months, the physician should consider the possibility of tuberculosis.

Tuberculosis should always be a consideration in the elderly with unexplained fever. It may also cause abnormalities of the blood count such as anemia and either an elevated or reduced white blood cell count. It can involve the lymph nodes and cause a slowly enlarging neck mass. This has been described more commonly in elderly women. If it is not recognized and treated, infected material may actually drain from the lymph node through the skin. Involvement of the spine may cause back pain and even fractures of the bones in the back. TB can cause arthritis that may be difficult to diagnose since osteoarthritis and rheumatoid arthritis are much more common problems. Infection can also involve the kidneys, adrenal glands, intestines, nervous system, and even the lining sac around the heart *(tuberculous pericarditis)*.

Diagnosis of tuberculosis may involve a chest X-ray, sputum stains and cultures, as well as skin testing. Skin testing is done by injection of small amounts of a purified protein derivative (PPD) from the TB bacteria under the skin of the forearm. A two-step technique is recommended for the elderly on admission to nursing homes. The first test is done at the time of admission and then repeated within one to two weeks. Only if the second test is negative is the PPD regarded as negative. Patients with serious illness, including TB, may sometimes not react to the PPD since the immune system is not working properly. This condition is called anergy. As a result, a few skin tests may be done on the other forearm; such tests include substances to which most people would react. If a reaction occurs, it is presumed that the immune system is functioning properly, and the negative PPD is reliable. If the reactions to the "control panel" are all negative, it means that the immune system is not functioning properly, and the negative PPD does not rule out the possibility of TB. Therefore, other tests would be required.

Therapy for tuberculosis in the elderly is challenging because of the higher incidence of drug reactions. Treatment often requires the use of more than one drug. In those individuals who have a positive skin test and no other evidence of disease, preventive therapy is not recommended without other risk factors for reactivation of TB, since the drug used for prophylaxis is more likely to cause liver injury in the elderly. However, if they have been known to have a negative skin test in the recent past and have converted to a positive test, treatment with ISONIAZID (INH), 300 mg daily for 6 to 12 months, is recommended. "Recent converters" have a higher risk of progression to active disease within the next year. Liver blood tests are monitored while on isoniazid.

URINARY TRACT INFECTIONS

Urinary tract infections (UTIs) are the most common cause of bloodstream invasion by bacteria in older adults. The frequency of these infections increase with age, from approximately 1% in younger

(figure 22-3)

Comparison of (a) male and (b) female urethra (highlighted in red). The male urethra is significantly longer.

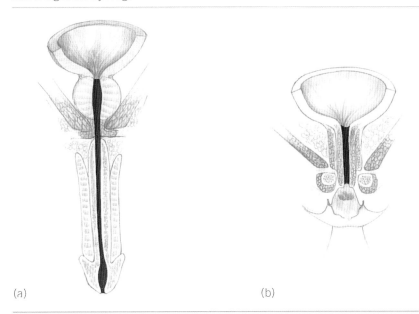

(a)   (b)

women to 20% in women over 70 years old. UTIs are rarely seen in men under the age of 50 and occur in approximately 4% of men over age 70. Anatomical factors may partly account for this since a woman's urethra is shorter than the male's, as shown in Figure 22-3. This may allow bacteria from the skin around the genitals to more easily travel to the bladder and cause infection. In addition, as women age, the lack of estrogen causes the lining of the vagina and urethra to atrophy (thin out) and allows bacteria to adhere more easily to these surfaces. There is a higher incidence of incomplete bladder emptying in elderly women that increases the risk of recurrent UTIs.

Among nursing home residents of both sexes, the incidence of bacteria in the urine has been reported to be as high as 50%. However, it is often best not to treat these individuals unless there are symptoms such as fever, burning on urination, urinary frequency and urgency, and so forth. Treating a person with bacteria in the urine in the absence of symptoms can lead to development of more resistant bacteria and the use of more powerful and expensive antibiotics. Many individuals have a *colonization* (or a large number of bacteria) in their bladder without necessarily having an infection. In such situations antibiotic use can result in more severe problems.

The development of a UTI in a hospitalized patient may cause significant illness and even death. Often these hospital–acquired infections are related to more aggressive bacteria that are resistant to common antibiotics. Risk factors predisposing to such infections include use of urinary catheters, neurological diseases that impair normal emptying of the bladder, prostate enlargement in males, and atrophy of the vaginal

(table 22-3)

DRUGS FOR URINARY TRACT INFECTIONS

INFECTION	ANTIBIOTIC	TREATMENT TIME
Cystitis	Trimethoprim/ sulfamethoxazole*	3 days
Complicated cystitis†	Fluoroquinolone	7–14 days
Pyelonephritis	Fluoroquinolone	14 days

*If bacteria resistant to sulfa, use fluoroquinolone.
†For example, nursing home or hospitalized patients; catheter-associated.

and urogenital tissues in females. Often urinary catheters are temporarily required to monitor accurately urinary output in an individual who may not be able to void into a measuring device, or it may help prevent irritation of the skin from urine in the incontinent person being treated for a pressure sore. The important principle is that these catheters should be used for the shortest period possible; they should never be prescribed simply for the convenience of the staff of the hospital or nursing home.

Urinary tract infections may also cause subtle symptoms in the elderly, such as a decline in appetite, confusion, or urinary incontinence. The symptoms that we typically associate with a bladder infection, such as frequency and burning on urination, may not be present in the older person. Moreover, when present, the symptoms may actually have other causes, such as *atrophic vaginitis* (thinning of the vaginal lining due to estrogen deficiency). A urinalysis and culture are required to make the diagnosis with certainty.

If an older person with a UTI has symptoms persisting beyond one week of treatment, the physician needs to consider the possibility of kidney involvement. This is important, since there can be a high risk of progression to bloodstream invasion and sepsis. Antibiotics may be required for a longer period of time and in higher doses than those used for a simple bladder infection. Generally, those persons with more serious types of infection or recurrent infections require evaluation by a urologist to determine whether there are problems within the urinary tract, such as a blockage, a kidney stone, or some anatomical abnormality.

Table 22-3 summarizes some of the common antibiotic treatments of urinary tract infections in the older person.

PROSTATITIS

Prostatitis is a major health problem for men over 50 years old and causes an estimated one million visits to physicians' offices each year. It can cause as much disability as other serious medical conditions such as a heart attack or Crohn's disease. While many men respond well to treatment, the overall cure rate is low. Relapses are common. It is a disease that frustrates those affected as well as their physicians. (See Chapter 11 for illustrations of the location and anatomy of the prostate.)

Prostatitis actually refers to several disorders, ranging from acute bacterial infection of the prostate to chronic pain syndromes. The prostatitis syndromes are the third most important disorder of the prostate after *benign prostatic hyperplasia (BPH)* and *prostate cancer* (see Chapter 11). Prostatitis literally means an inflammation of the prostate gland; however, in actual practice there may or not be any inflammation. The reason this seems confusing is that prostatitis is quite poorly understood by physicians due to several factors: limited access to the prostate gland, uncertainty regarding the causes of prostatitis, lack of distinguishing clinical features, lack of uniform diagnostic criteria, and a protracted course of treatment. A renowned urologist, Dr. Stamey, termed prostatitis "a waste basket of clinical ignorance."

Prostatitis is important to consider if evaluating a man for prostate cancer, since many of the same features can be present including an enlarged and hard gland, elevated *prostate specific antigen (PSA)* levels, and an abnormal ultrasound image. The proper diagnosis can still be difficult in the elderly male since tenderness to palpation of the prostate may not occur even if an infection is present. Diagnosis may rest upon examining the prostatic secretions after massage of the prostate or possibly even a biopsy.

Approximately 5 to 10% of prostatitis is related to a bacterial cause. The other 90 to 95% is attributed to nonbacterial prostatitis and prostatodynia (painful prostate of unknown cause). Prostatitis will affect 35 to 50% of men at some time in their life.

Treatment depends on the cause. Since many cases are not due to infection, routine use of antibiotics is not warranted. In the elderly, the physician also needs to be concerned about the cost and side effects of such treatment, as well as the potential emergence of antibiotic resistance. A *nonsteroidal anti-inflammatory drug (NSAID)* may be prescribed in some cases to relieve pain, hasten the clearing of the inflammation, and liquefy the prostatic secretions. If the diagnostic evaluation does indeed confirm a bacterial infection, antibiotics are chosen that have been demonstrated to adequately penetrate the prostatic tissue. Prolonged courses of therapy of six to eight weeks may be required. Other measures that have been suggested to offer some benefit include intermittent prostatic massage, warm sitz baths (immersion of the buttocks and pelvic area), and more frequent ejaculation.

HEART INFECTIONS

The medical term for a heart valve infection is infective endocarditis. Although endocarditis can occur in younger people, it is more common in older persons. More than half of all cases occur in persons over 60 years of age. The reasons for this include the greater prevalence of persons over 60 who have had surgical implantation of an artificial heart valve; the greater use of such devices as pacemakers, dialysis shunts, and intravenous catheters; and the longer survival of people who have had underlying diseases of their heart valves. Moreover, rheumatic heart disease and acquired diseases of the heart valves, such as aortic stenosis, are more common in older persons.

The mortality of infective endocarditis is higher in the elderly than in younger patients. The range in various studies has been 44 to 72% in older persons versus 14 to 33% in younger persons. Like other infectious diseases in the elderly, infective endocarditis can cause vague symptoms, such as fatigue, loss of appetite, and weight loss. The murmur (a whooshing noise heard with a stethoscope due to turbulent blood flow) usually produced in younger persons due to the destruction of the valve may be difficult to distinguish in the older person from preexisting murmurs caused by valves that have become stiff due to age-related changes. There may also be changes in the chest cavity and the lungs with aging that make it more difficult for a physician to hear these murmurs. These problems can lead to delays in diagnosis, which causes delays in treatment.

Most patients suspected of having endocarditis are hospitalized for evaluation. Multiple blood cultures are usually required since the bacteria responsible may only intermittently "seed" into the bloodstream. One set of blood cultures may miss this if they are taken at a time that seeding is not taking place. Echocardiography is an ultrasound examination of the heart and may demonstrate clumps of bacteria and debris on heart valves called vegetations. These infections require prolonged courses and high doses of intravenous antibiotics. If significant damage has been done to the valve or the infection is not being eradicated, surgery may be required to remove the diseased valve.

Infective endocarditis can involve a person's own heart valve ("native valve") or an artificial valve (see Figure 22-4). Native valve endocarditis is more common in men. Organisms that are commonly found coincidentally in the mouth or gastrointestinal tract can infect a structurally abnormal valve and cause endocarditis. This is why your doctor will recommend that you take antibiotics prior to dental, urological, or gastrointestinal procedures if you have mitral valve prolapse, aortic or mitral stenosis, an artificial heart valve, or other heart valve abnormality.

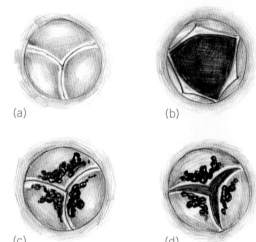

(a)　　　　(b)

(c)　　　　(d)

(*figure* 22-4)

Normal heart valve (a) closed (b) open. Endocarditis vegetations are clumps of debris and bacteria on the valve. (c) They may cause leaking of blood through the valve when closed or (d) restrict the motion of the valve leaflets when open.

NERVOUS SYSTEM INFECTIONS

A lining called the meninges covers the brain. Bacterial meningitis remains a highly lethal disease in older adults, with mortality rates averaging over 20% despite modern antibiotic therapy. The elderly may not manifest the classical signs of meningitis, which include fever, neck stiffness, and headache. Many persons over the age of 60 have other underlying diseases that can be confused with those of meningitis. Older individuals often have arthritis of the neck or poor mobility of the neck. A previous stroke or Parkinson's disease could make interpretation of physical findings difficult. A change in mental status can occur from a seizure, a new stroke, medications, or even infections in other areas of the body.

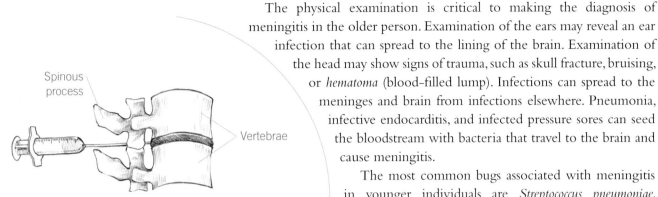

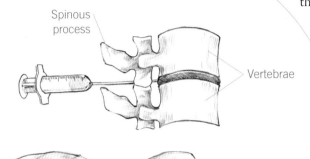

Spinous process

Vertebrae

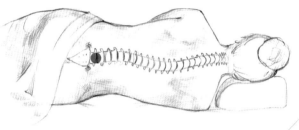

(figure 22-5)

Spinal tap. The needle for lumbar puncture is usually introduced into one of the spaces between the spinal processes of the lower back vertebrae (highlighted in blue).

The physical examination is critical to making the diagnosis of meningitis in the older person. Examination of the ears may reveal an ear infection that can spread to the lining of the brain. Examination of the head may show signs of trauma, such as skull fracture, bruising, or *hematoma* (blood-filled lump). Infections can spread to the meninges and brain from infections elsewhere. Pneumonia, infective endocarditis, and infected pressure sores can seed the bloodstream with bacteria that travel to the brain and cause meningitis.

The most common bugs associated with meningitis in younger individuals are *Streptococcus pneumoniae, Hemophilus influenzae,* and *Neisseria meningitides.* However, in older persons *Neisseria* and *Hemophilus* are unusual causes of meningitis. More commonly seen are *Streptococcus pneumoniae, Mycobacterium tuberculosis* (also the cause of TB in the lungs), and Gram-negative bacteria. A particularly frequent cause of meningitis in the elderly is *Listeria monocytogenes.*

The key to diagnosis is the lumbar puncture (spinal tap; see Figure 22-5) and laboratory examination of the cerebrospinal fluid (CSF). A CT or MRI scan is usually done first to exclude other problems that could make a lumbar puncture hazardous, such as brain tumor, brain abscess, stroke, brain hemorrhage, or subdural hematoma. The fluid is examined immediately for cells, protein and glucose levels, and bacteria. Culture results generally require at least 24 to 48 hours.

Once meningitis is suspected on the basis of the physician's evaluation, treatment must be initiated immediately. It is considered an emergency. Since culture results may not be available for one to two days, antibiotic coverage is selected on the choice of the most likely bacteria. After the culture results are known, testing is done for "sensitivity." The antibiotics to which a bug is sensitive are those that will kill it. The doctor can then fine-tune the antibiotics so only the necessary ones are continued. Treatment usually requires 7 to 14 days. Gram-negative bacilli require three to four weeks of therapy.

BONE AND JOINT INFECTIONS

Osteomyelitis is an infection of the bone. Older adults have a higher predisposition to osteomyelitis either because of underlying diseases, such as diabetes and peripheral vascular disease, or because of surgical procedures, such as open-heart surgery or prosthetic (artificial) joint replacement.

Although young people may also get osteomyelitis, the sites of involvement are often different in the elderly. Infection of the *sternum* (breastbone) may complicate open-heart surgery. Infection in pressure sores may spread to neighboring bone or invade the bloodstream by which bacteria can travel to other sites including bones far away from the sore. Diabetes is often associated with circulatory problems in the legs that can lead to breakdown of skin. Diabetic foot ulcers frequently become associated with infection in the bones of the foot. Infections can occasionally develop after joint replacement surgery or, rarely, after steroid injections.

Preexisting joint disease is considered a major risk factor for septic arthritis (joint infection or *infectious arthritis*). These joint diseases include osteoarthritis, rheumatoid arthritis, gout, pseudogout, and *traumatic arthritis* (arthritis due to a previous injury, such as a fracture). Some individuals receive such medications as steroids and drugs that suppress the immune system and further increase the risk. Joint infections are usually the result of an infection that has spread though the bloodstream but can occasionally be due to spread from a nearby site. The most common joints to become infected are the knee, followed by the hip, foot, wrist, and shoulder.

The bugs responsible for joint infections in the elderly are different from those in younger individuals. *Neisseria gonorrhoeae*, the agent responsible for *gonorrhea*, is the most common cause of infectious arthritis in the young. In older persons, *Staphylococcus aureus, Streptococcus pneumoniae*, and other *Streptococcus species* are responsible for about 70% of cases of septic arthritis. Other types of bacteria, which may include the TB bug, cause the other 30%, and a few cases may be caused by yeast.

Like many diseases in the elderly, diagnosis of infectious arthritis can sometimes be difficult. Fever may not be present. Most individuals already have joint problems; therefore, an increase in pain can often be attributed to a flare-up of the underlying disease. Thus proper diagnosis may be delayed. If there is clinical suspicion or if there is a question about whether an infection is present, the suspect joint must be aspirated with a needle and syringe. This procedure is called arthrocentesis (see Figure 22-6). The fluid is examined for white cells, bacteria, and crystals. It is also cultured. Some joints may be technically difficult to aspirate, such as the hips, *sacroiliac joints*, and shoulder. Radiologists, rheumatologists, or orthopedic surgeons may be consulted to perform these procedures with the guidance of special imaging equipment. Blood cultures should be routinely obtained in all patients with suspected infectious arthritis.

The principles of treating septic arthritis in older persons are the same as in the young: antibiotics, joint drainage (removal of the infected fluid by aspiration), early immobilization of the joint, and, afterward, physical therapy. If three joint aspirations have been performed and the fluid continues to accumulate rapidly or if the fluid is too thick to aspirate, surgical drainage by an orthopedic surgeon should be strongly considered. Surgical drainage may also be required for joints that are not easily accessible to aspiration with a needle and syringe.

Not unexpectedly, the mortality from infectious arthritis is higher in the elderly. Clinical studies have reported death rates as

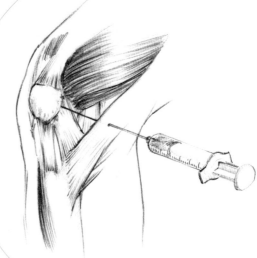

(figure 22-6)

Arthrocentesis of knee joint.

high as 20 to 30%. Those who survive may have limitation of joint motion and more severe arthritic pain in the involved joint.

PROSTHETIC JOINT INFECTIONS

Replacement of damaged joints with prosthetic elements has become commonplace and represents a significant improvement in the treatment of joint diseases. However, infection of prosthetic joints in older persons is a serious disease. It is often difficult to manage and may lead to poor outcomes.

Prosthetic joint infections that occur immediately after and up to one month postoperatively are called *early prosthetic joint infections. Late prosthetic joint infections* are those that occur more than one month after surgery. It is postulated that the majority of early infections are a result of seeding of the joint by bacteria around the time of the surgery. However, occasionally bloodstream invasion from other sites can lead to infection of the artificial joint. Most cases of late prosthetic joint infections are related to the latter mechanism—infection from the bloodstream. Those individuals at greater risk include the very elderly, those with rheumatoid arthritis, diabetics, and those with disorders of immunity, such as cancer and AIDS, or who may be on drugs that suppress the immune system.

Pain is the most common symptom of a prosthetic joint infection, and it is usually present even at rest. Pain that occurs with activity or activity-related pain of gradual onset suggests the possibility of loosening of the prosthesis. Persistent pain since the time of the operation should alert the physician to the possibility of a deep infection. Fever or chills may or may not be present. Drainage from the surgical wound that lingers several weeks after surgery also strongly suggests the possibility of infection. Distinguishing between the pain associated with the surgery itself and an infected joint can challenge even the most seasoned physician. Clues to an infection if present include warmness of the joint compared to that on the other side, redness of the overlying skin, progressive stiffness and pain, and a sinus tract (a hole in the skin which drains pus from the joint). *Joint effusions* (fluid within the joint) can occur commonly after surgery even without infection. An infected hip prosthesis can be especially difficult to diagnose since there may be few symptoms and the examination is often unremarkable. Persistent pain for months after surgery for an artificial hip should heighten the index of suspicion.

The most reliable diagnostic tests for prosthetic joint infections are aspiration of the joint and examination of the joint fluid for white cells and bacteria. The joint fluid is also cultured. Some promising new techniques using molecular genetics are being developed that may be more helpful in the diagnosis of these infections.

The treatment of prosthetic joint infections includes a prolonged course of antibiotics, drainage of the involved joint, and early immobilization. Despite these measures, more than 70% of older people with this problem will require removal of the prosthesis, surgical *debridement* (removal of dead and infected tissue), partial resection of bone, or a combination of these.

DOCTOR'S DIARY

Deborah M., 83, lived in a nursing home. She had arthritis pain for which she took acetaminophen now and then. Otherwise she was doing well until last week when she had a dull headache. On the following day, she felt nauseous and vomited two or three times. The nursing staff found that she was difficult to arouse the following morning and contacted me. I said that she be brought to the emergency room.

Her chest X-ray and urinalysis were normal, but her white blood cell count was elevated to 23,000 (normal being from 5000 to 10,000). I could not find any skin sores or other obvious source of infection. I was concerned about a stroke, and I ordered a CT scan of the brain, which was negative. Having excluded other more obvious sources of infection, such as pneumonia, urinary tract infection, and infected pressure sores, I performed a spinal tap. The laboratory results on the spinal fluid showed a high white cell count and protein level. I made a diagnosis of meningitis and started her on two intravenous antibiotics. The spinal fluid cultures confirmed an infection with a bacterium called Listeria monocytogenes. Within two days Deborah started to become more alert and within a few days she was nearly back to normal.

Many people with prosthetic joints ask their physicians if it is necessary to take antibiotics prior to dental work. Those individuals with pins, screws, and plates do not require antibiotics. Nor is antibiotic prophylaxis required for most persons with total joint replacements (check with your orthopedic doctor). This opinion agrees with that of the Council of Dental Therapeutics, the American Academy of Oral Medicine, and the British Society for Antimicrobial Therapy.

GASTROINTESTINAL INFECTIONS

The most common gastrointestinal infections in the elderly include infectious diarrhea (due to Norwalk virus, *Clostridium difficile*, and *Cryptosporidiosis), diverticulitis, cholecystitis* (gallbladder infection), abdominal abscess, and appendicitis. Cholecystitis and diverticulitis are discussed in Chapter 9.

Changes in the gastrointestinal tract that contribute to the increased risk for these infections include diminished production of stomach acid, thinning of the stomach lining, diminished motility in the intestines, and a decrease in the blood flow to the intestines. The disability and mortality caused by these infections are much higher in the elderly than in younger people.

Diarrhea due to outbreaks of the Norwalk virus and *rotavirus* are more common in nursing homes in the winter months. The Norwalk virus drew national attention as the agent implicated in illness among numerous passengers on cruise ships. It is highly contagious. *Cryptosporidiosis* is also frequently associated with diarrhea in AIDS patients. Within the last few years, a diarrhea outbreak occurred because of contaminated raspberries from South America.

Clostridium difficile is increasingly being reported as a cause of diarrhea in the elderly. It is associated with *pseudomembranous colitis,* an inflammation of the lining of the colon. Certain antibiotics may be associated with a higher risk of this type of colitis, but almost any antibiotic has been implicated. Some looseness of stool is common with antibiotics, but if severe diarrhea occurs, stop your antibiotic and let your doctor know. It may also be transmitted from person to person. As a result, outbreaks in nursing homes and hospitals have been reported.

Appendicitis in the elderly can be particularly difficult to diagnose. The usual pattern seen in younger individuals with pain around the belly button eventually localizing to the right lower abdomen is rarely seen in the elderly. For this reason, symptoms may be initially mistaken for gastrointestinal infections, diverticulitis, cholecystitis, or a bowel obstruction. Other symptoms that may be seen include upset stomach and vomiting, loss of appetite, constipation or diarrhea, or urinary complaints. Fever may not be present. Most persons will have some right lower abdominal tenderness. The white blood cell count is usually elevated, but may be normal in up to 20%. Abdominal X-rays usually are not helpful, but abdominal ultrasound and CT scan may help with the diagnosis. Early surgical consultation is important since delays in diagnosis in the elderly have resulted in a high rate of perforation and abdominal abscess.

An abscess is a sequestered collection of pus and debris. The body attempts to control the infection by walling it off. However, the infection continues to smolder, and the abscess may grow larger and involve other tissues. If the abscess bursts, an overwhelming life-threatening infection might occur. An abscess can complicate any intraabdominal infection. Therefore, you may hear of someone having a diverticular abscess, a liver abscess, a kidney abscess, or a pancreatic abscess. Imaging studies such as CT and MRI are very useful in confirming the diagnosis. Antibiotics may help fight the infection, but surgical drainage is necessary for cure. As you might expect, these infections are very serious in the older patient and result in high complication and death rates.

BACTEREMIA AND SEPSIS

Bacteremia means bacteria in the bloodstream. In many cases, such as dental cleaning, bacteria normally gain access to your bloodstream but are rapidly killed by your body's immune system. However, older persons are more prone to a serious problem called sepsis (bloodstream infection) if bacteremia occurs. Factors contributing to this heightened susceptibility include a decrease in the body's immune functions, coexisting medical illnesses, and perhaps a suboptimal response to vaccines.

Although fever and shaking chills are considered the hallmark for sepsis in younger individuals, these responses may be blunted in the elderly. The older person may become confused, agitated, lethargic, or even difficult to wake up. Weakness and falls are not uncommon in these patients.

The urinary tract is the number-one source of bacteremia in the elderly, followed by the *biliary tract* (gallbladder and bile ducts) and infections elsewhere within the abdomen. Pneumonia accounts for 10% of all cases of bacteremia. Pressure sores and other skin infections can cause up to another 10%. Urinary catheters, prosthetic joints, and even intravenous catheters have to be considered as possible contributors to bloodstream infections.

Cultures of blood and other body fluids (such as urine, sputum, or drainage from sores) may be required to identify the causative organism. However, if the individual has recently been started on antibiotics, it may be difficult to identify the responsible bug. Therapy is initiated on the basis of the suspected source and organisms. In severe cases, blood pressure may drop to dangerous levels—a condition called septic shock. This is a medical emergency and requires close monitoring in an intensive care unit. Special monitoring devices may be required. Medicines and intravenous fluids are used to try to keep the blood pressure up, but even with the best care, kidney failure and other serious complications often ensue. Mortality has been reported as high as 35%; however, the mortality in patients over 70 years old is greater than 50%.

AIDS

The virus that causes acquired immune deficiency syndrome (AIDS) is called human immunodeficiency virus (HIV). Although it is generally regarded as a young person's disease and more common among the homosexual population, the number of new HIV cases is rising the fastest in heterosexuals over age 55. This group now accounts for 10% or more of all patients with AIDS. This increase is related primarily to sexual transmission and intravenous drug use.

According to the Centers for Disease Control, the reason for this increased prevalence among the 55 and over group is that they are one-sixth as likely as younger adults are to use condoms during sex and one-fifth as likely to be tested for HIV. In addition, more people are living longer with AIDS due to the advent of better medicines to treat and keep it in remission.

One of the biggest barriers to diagnosing HIV infection in the elderly is that physicians don't often suspect or test for HIV in older persons. This can result in delayed diagnosis and treatment or even premature death. Early signs that may be overlooked or attributed to aging include recurrent *thrush* (an oral yeast infection), *seborrheic dermatitis, shingles,* and recurrent *herpes simplex* infections. These problems often do occur in persons without AIDS, but if you have a sexual history that puts you at risk for AIDS, let your doctor know so that you can be tested. Most states require informed consent before an HIV test is administered. In addition, the results are given to you in a confidential manner.

Elderly individuals are often further along in the course when first recognized with AIDS. Therefore, they may have had weight loss, fatigue, and diminished mental and physical capabilities. These symptoms can be seen with many other diseases, including cancer, thyroid disease, depression, and so forth. A workup will include testing for these possibilities.

Treatment may be more difficult in older persons. The disease may progress quicker, and older persons often have other conditions that compound the problems associated with the disease. Older individuals are more vulnerable to drug side effects and drug interactions that may lead to reduced compliance with their therapy.

AIDS in the elderly has been called the "new great imitator," because the presentation of HIV-associated conditions mimics so many disorders that confront older people, such as cancer, Alzheimer's disease, or thyroid dysfunction. Physicians and the public need to recognize that high-risk sexual behaviors can lead to AIDS and that a sexual history is an important aspect of the individual's examination. Physicians and their patients need to overcome hesitancy about discussing these important issues.

RECOMMENDED IMMUNIZATIONS

The most effective means of preventing disease and death from infectious diseases is immunization, the administration of a vaccine to prevent or reduce the risk of infection. This is especially true for those in high-risk

NURSE'S NOTES

Greg D., 63, had lost about 20 pounds in the previous six months. He had developed a flaky rash on his face that his doctor diagnosed as seborrheic dermatitis. He was treated with Nizoral cream with good results. He subsequently developed an oral yeast infection that his doctor treated with an oral nystatin rinse. It cleared but then came back again. Greg's doctor became concerned with the recurrent infections as well as his weight loss and tiredness.

When his doctor asked Greg about his sex life, he became offended and told the doctor, "It is none of your business."

The doctor calmly explained to Greg that AIDS was rising rapidly among older persons and that his sexual history was important. Greg was embarrassed but acknowledged that he had several sexual relationships since his wife died five years ago. One year ago, he went to a convention and had sex with a prostitute.

Greg's laboratory tests confirmed that he was positive for HIV. After counseling, he adjusted to the diagnosis and initiated drug treatment at our AIDS clinic for the disease. Although he had some side effects from the drugs early on, he began feeling better, and his energy level, appetite, and weight improved.

22

categories due to age (older than 65), lifestyle, chronic diseases. or problems with their immunity. In the United States, somewhere between 50,000 and 90,000 adults die each year from influenza, hepatitis B infection, and pneumococcal disease (usually pneumonia). In contrast, approximately 300 to 500 children die annually of diseases that are preventable by vaccines. Despite this, adult immunization rates remain disappointingly low.

Immunization is the act of artificially inducing immunity (providing protection) to a disease. Immunization can be active or passive. Active immunization consists of the administration of a vaccine or toxoid that stimulates your body's immune system to produce antibodies or cells that protect against the infectious agent. A vaccine is a suspension of weakened live or killed microorganisms. A *toxoid* is a modified bacterial toxin that has been rendered nontoxic but still retains the ability to stimulate your body to form antitoxin. Passive immunization consists of providing temporary protection through the administration of antibodies not produced by your own body, such as an individual receiving a gamma globulin shot after being exposed to hepatitis A.

Vaccine reactions are relatively rare. The benefit in most cases far outweighs the risks. Occasionally, local redness and swelling can develop at the injection site. A history of severe allergic reactions to eggs is a contraindication to the influenza vaccine.

TETANUS AND DIPHTHERIA

Elderly persons who did not serve in the U.S. military during World War II are unlikely to have been vaccinated during childhood and may be unprotected. Blood tests done in surveys suggest that more than 48% of those over 75 years old have less than protective levels of antibody to diphtheria.

We recommend that if you have not had a primary series of tetanus and diphtheria toxoids or if your vaccination history is uncertain, you should have three doses of adult tetanus and *diphtheria toxoid (Td)*. The adult vaccine has a smaller dose of diphtheria toxoid than does the children's vaccine and causes fewer side effects in adults. The first two doses should be given four weeks apart and the third dose 6 to 12 months after the second dose. Adults who have completed the primary vaccination series should receive a booster dose of Td vaccine every 10 years. Ask your doctor for it if it has been more than 10 years!

CHICKEN POX

Approximately 10% of adults in the United States are susceptible to chicken pox *(varicella)*. Adults who contract chicken pox are more at risk than are children for lung and nervous system complications. Adults make up 10% of all encephalitis cases and 20% of all varicella-related deaths.

If you cannot remember or have not been told that you had chicken pox as a child, you may be susceptible. A blood test can be done as a cost-effective way to determine whether vaccination is indicated. The vaccine is administered to adults as two doses spaced four to eight weeks apart. The vaccine is safe.

HEPATITIS

Hepatitis A vaccine: Hepatitis A is one of the most common causes of acute viral hepatitis. There are 75,000 to 125,000 cases per year and 100 deaths. The hepatitis A vaccines licensed in the United States are *Havrix* and *VA QTA*. The recommended dose of either vaccine is 1 cc intramuscularly with a booster dose six months later for *VA QTA* and six to 12 months later for *Havrix*. These vaccines are exceptionally safe, and they should be administered to older persons with chronic liver disease (cirrhosis, alcoholism) or clotting disorders or who are drug users, engage in homosexual male activity, or travel outside the United States (except northern and western Europe, new Zealand, Australia, Canada, and Japan).

Hepatitis B vaccine: Hepatitis B causes significant disability and mortality. Currently in the United States, 1.25 million have chronic hepatitis B virus (HBV) infection. Approximately 4000 to 5000 of these die yearly from liver failure, 250 from fulminant hepatitis, and 800 from liver cancer. This is hard to believe considering the fact that we have had a safe and effective vaccine against the virus since 1982. In spite of this, the incidence of hepatitis rose 37% from 1979 to 1989. Hepatitis B vaccine is 85 to 95% effective in healthy young adults, 70% effective in persons 50 to 59 years old, and 50% effective in those over 60 years of age. This decline in efficacy with aging is related to the change in the body's immune system. Other conditions that decrease the antibody response include kidney failure, diabetes, chronic liver diseases, AIDS, smoking, and obesity.

The hepatitis B vaccines are safe. However, if you have had a serious allergic reaction to yeast, you should not receive the vaccine. Three shots are required: the first two doses should be given a month apart and the third dose five months after the second shot. You should receive the vaccine if any of the following applies to you:

- Multiple sexual partners
- A male engaged in homosexual activity
- Receive blood products
- On hemodialysis
- Chronic liver disease
- Inject drugs
- Are in sexual contact with a hepatitis B carrier

PNEUMOCOCCAL VACCINE

Diseases caused by *Streptococcus pneumonia* (also called the *pneumococcus)* include 50,000 cases of bloodstream infection, 500,000 cases of pneumonia, and 3000 cases of meningitis each year in the United States. This infection causes 25 to 35% of the cases of community-acquired pneumonia that require hospitalization. The rate of bloodstream invasion with this bug is highest in persons over 65 years of age. Even with appropriate treatment, the fatality rate is 30 to 40% in elderly patients. The risk of more aggressive disease is higher in African Americans. Risks are also increased in smokers and those with chronic illnesses.

The pneumococcal vaccine *(Pneumovax)* significantly reduces the risk of pneumonia and bloodstream infections with *Streptococcus pneumonia.* It is important to recognize that many other infectious organisms can cause pneumonia; therefore, the vaccine does not protect you against all forms of pneumonia. However, it is the most common cause identified in the community setting. In spite of this, only 14% of persons 65 or older and only 5 to 7% of those from 18 to 64 who have conditions that predispose them to this infection have received the pneumococcal vaccine.

The vaccine is recommended for all persons 65 years and older. Medicare provides partial reimbursement for the cost of the vaccine and its administration. The American College of Physicians recommends that persons aged 65 and older who were initially vaccinated before age 65 should receive one revaccination, provided at least five years have elapsed since the initial vaccination. I feel that professional organizations need to rethink the recommendations for use of the vaccine in adults: We should lower the age to 50 years for the initial dose when the responsiveness to the vaccine is more uniform and revaccinate at age 60.

INFLUENZA VACCINE

In each of 10 recent influenza *(flu)* epidemics in the United States, the estimated related deaths totaled over 20,000. During some epidemics of influenza A, approximately 172,000 hospitalizations were attributable solely to influenza and pneumonia. The cost of a severe influenza epidemic has been estimated to be $12 billion. The attack rate and mortality for influenza is higher in older persons, often because they have other chronic medical conditions. More than 90% of the deaths due to influenza occur in persons 65 years or older.

It is recommended that all persons 50 years and older receive annual influenza vaccination. It is hoped that the reduction in age from 65 to 50 years old for immunization will result in a decrease in time lost from work, with its associated costs, fewer hospitalizations, and reduced number of office visits to physicians. The vaccine significantly reduces the risk of acquiring influenza. It does not eliminate it. However, it may also reduce the severity of the illness in those vaccinated individuals who "catch" the flu. The vaccine may reduce the risk of influenza up to 70% in older persons who live at home. Persons under 50 who have a medical disease that places them at risk should also be vaccinated.

The influenza season in the United States usually starts in December and peaks in January and February. Some outbreaks have occurred in the early spring. Protective antibodies may take up to two weeks to develop after vaccination, and immunity may last up to six months. This duration of immunity can be substantially reduced in the elderly. Therefore, the best time to receive the vaccine is probably early November. Since the protection by the vaccine is relatively short and influenza virus strains responsible for the flu can change from year to year, annual vaccination is recommended. As previously noted, severe egg allergy is a contraindication to the vaccine. Having some activity against the flu virus, several antiviral drugs are available for those who cannot take the vaccine.

Many people say they do not want to get the flu vaccine because they are afraid it will give them the flu. *Note*: You *cannot* get the flu from the flu vaccine. The vaccine does not contain live influenza virus. There is a small risk of minor reactions to the vaccine, such as local soreness, low-grade temperature, and muscle aches that some people have misinterpreted as the flu; however, the incidence of severe reactions is rare. The benefit far outweighs the risk. Many more people die each year from influenza and its complications than have vaccine reactions. If you are undergoing chemotherapy, you should ask your doctor for the appropriate time to get the vaccine since chemotherapy may blunt the immune response to the vaccine, thus diminishing your protection.

■

WHAT YOU NEED TO KNOW

▓▶ Infectious diseases are the leading cause of hospitalization of the elderly.

▓▶ Aging of the immune system (the body's defense system) is thought to play a major role in the susceptibility to infections in the older person.

▓▶ Infections in older persons may produce unusual symptoms. These can lead to delays in seeking treatment as well delays in the diagnosis and treatment of infections.

▓▶ Vaccines can substantially reduce the risk of some common diseases. The benefits outweigh the risks in most cases.

WHAT YOU NEED TO KNOW

▓ National Institute of Allergy and Infectious Disease
Building 31, Room 7A-50
31 Center Drive MSC 2520
Bethesda, MD 20892
Web: www.niaid.nih.gov

All the soarings of my mind begin in my blood.

—*Rainer Maria Rilke*

THE AUTHOR

23

JOHN GARTON, MD, graduated from the University of Colorado and the Georgetown University School of Medicine. He did an internship and residency in internal medicine, as well as a fellowship in hematology, at the Mayo Clinic in Rochester, Minnesota. He is board-certified in internal medicine and hematology. Dr. Garton was an assistant professor of medicine and head of the Department of Hematology at the Mayo Clinic until 1994 when he moved to Sarasota, Florida. He has written two book chapters, and he has been an author or coauthor of a number of journal articles on hematology. He has done special research in multiple myeloma and Waldenström's macroglobulinemia.

23 | THE BLOOD SYSTEM

(figure 23-1*)*
Red blood cells move through your circulation carrying oxygen to your organs and tissues.

You have heard the expression, "Blood is thicker than water." What is definitely true is that blood is more complicated than water. While this statement may seem obvious at this point in history, before the development of the microscope (see Figure 23-2) in the 17th century, blood was thought to be made up of different "humors," or substances, that separated when blood clotted. After the microscope's invention, the complicated nature of the blood system gradually became evident. It was not until the 1920s when the modern era of blood studies began in earnest. In the 21st century, hematologists (physicians who specialize in blood disorders) use a great number of modern scientific methods, including immunology, biochemistry, nuclear medicine, molecular genetics, and physical chemistry. Great advances have been made in diagnosis and treatment of blood disorders. Thankfully, most of the problems seen in doctors' offices do not require many of these technical study methods in order to determine proper treatment programs.

NORMAL CIRCULATING BLOOD

The study of blood is quite complex, but by looking at the normal contents of the blood circulating in your blood vessels, we can separate the different elements and make the study easier and interesting. Blood can be separated into two basic components, formed elements, or cells, and plasma. The cellular elements are red blood cells, white blood cells, and platelets. Plasma contains the liquid aspect of blood, but from the hematologist's standpoint, it also has clotting factors and substances important to the body's defense mechanism called the immune system.

Red blood cells (RBCs) are produced in your bone marrow and are released into the circulation after they mature. A mature red blood cell has no ability to reproduce itself as it did in the bone marrow. Circulating red cells look like flat discs and are basically envelopes containing proteins and enzymes. These proteins include hemoglobin, the oxygen carrying protein. Due to the presence of iron in hemoglobin, blood appears red when oxygen is present. Normal adults tend to maintain a very stable level of red blood cells from adolescence to older age. As you will see, many processes affect red blood cells in amount and appearance.

Red cells can be studied in a number of ways. We can determine the number of red cells in a specific quantity of blood, the amount of hemoglobin in a red cell, the size of an average red cell, and several other measurements all from a single sample of blood and all from one laboratory instrument. The results of these studies give much useful information as to the health of your red blood cell system.

The second cellular component of circulating blood is the white blood cell (WBCs), also called a leukocyte. Although we call these white cells, there are several types of cells that are considered white cells and have quite different functions in your body. These cells include neutrophils, lymphocytes, eosinophils, and basophils. In general terms, *neutrophils* react against bacterial infections, *lymphocytes* against viral diseases, *eosinophils* react in allergic disease, and *basophils* help in parasitic infections. By

(*figure* 23-2)

The microscope is an essential instrument in the evaluation of blood diseases.

measuring the number and different kinds of white cells in the blood, we can help determine if an infection is present and help diagnose the type of infection that might be present. The same lab instrument that measures the red blood cells also performs these measurements. Therefore, only one blood sample is required for both measures.

The third and last cellular component of your circulating blood is the platelet. The platelet is the smallest of the three cell types and, like the red cell, is normally unable to reproduce once it leaves the bone marrow and begins to circulate. The platelet is the body's first line of defense against bleeding. When you cut yourself, platelets are attracted to the injured blood vessel and begin clumping to each other and to some of the surrounding cells and tissues. A platelet "plug" forms and begins the complex process of clotting. Platelets are counted and sized by the same lab instrument we have mentioned previously.

We have briefly introduced to you the cellular parts of circulating blood, but there remains the liquid portion, or plasma, which normally is about half the total blood volume. You may have noticed if you have had blood drawn that the tube of your blood is put in a special machine called a *centrifuge.* The blood sample is spun at a high speed. When the machine is turned off and the tube is removed, there are usually two layers. One layer is red; this contains your red cells, white cells, and platelets. The straw-colored layer is the plasma, the liquid component of your blood. Plasma contains many chemicals, proteins, and enzymes. Those contents of particular interest to blood specialists are the coagulation factors and immunoglobulins. Coagulation factors allow your blood to clot. Immunoglobulins can be helpful when they fight infection since antibodies are immunoglobulins. However, immunoglobulins might play a harmful role in some diseases, such as rheumatoid arthritis and systemic lupus erythematosus. To a certain extent, the coagulation and immune systems and their factors tend to be quite complex and require a series of events to occur to reach their desired result. Therefore, the tests to measure these factors in the circulating blood are more specialized, complex, and expensive than those to measure the cellular components. Thankfully, the need to use all the available studies occurs relatively infrequently.

Your blood coagulation system is made up of proteins, the majority being produced in the liver. There are over 18 separate proteins, which may play a role in clotting of blood. Most of these proteins circulate in the blood in inactive form. When bleeding occurs, a series of complicated steps develop, almost like the humorous Rube Goldberg machines of the comics, for which each step has to occur before the next and in a precise pathway, to achieve the desired result, a clot. The coagulation system can also stop clotting before it goes too far and can then begin the work of dissolving the clot it just produced. I discuss some of the more common diseases involving the coagulation system later in this chapter.

The immunoglobulins mentioned previously are the circulating part of the immune system. These molecules are made by lymphocytes or *plasma cells,* found in the bone marrow, lymph nodes, or spleen. Immunoglobulins are the first line of defense against foreign invaders in our bodies. The immune system has the capacity to produce millions of different proteins that may or may not ever be required to fight an infection or foreign cell. The ability to recognize something as foreign to the body requires both the protein and lymphocytes of different types to interact in very specific fashions. Almost like the coagulation sequence, several steps are required before the desired result of recognizing and removing foreign material can occur. The amount of immunoglobulins can be measured in the blood plasma, and only rarely is it necessary to try to identify specific types of immunoglobulins or antibodies. The process that provides such marked variability, but causes very specific responses, is remarkable and more complex than we have space to describe in this chapter. Simply stated, your genes and chromosomes do it!

BONE MARROW, RETICULOENDOTHELIAL, AND LYMPHATIC SYSTEMS

I have briefly introduced you to the circulating, or moving, portion of your blood. However, there are important parts of the blood system involving production of cells, production of proteins, and supporting tissues for these functions, which do not circulate. In adults, the bone marrow is the site of essentially all blood cell production. The reticuloendothelial system is the supporting system for much of the immune defense of the body. The lymphatic system is a partially separate circulation for moving fluids and material to areas in the body where more specific functions may occur. Following is an overview of each of these topics, so their interactions in various diseases may be more easily understood.

The bone marrow is that apparently fatty, middle part of the bones of the body. Although in infants and children bone marrow is found in most bones of the body, the marrow tends to be more centrally located in the pelvic, vertebral (spinal), skull, and breast bones in older adults. The bone marrow is a very complex organ. There is a highly defined system of arteries and veins that supply not only high levels of nutrients and oxygen to the blood-forming tissue but also a means of moving the new cells rapidly to the rest of the body. There are complex cavities, or *sinuses,* within the marrow lined by cells which apparently help regulate the production of the red and white cells and platelets. Holes in the walls of the sinuses then help determine when the mature cells are released to the general circulation. There are multiple hormones, enzymes, and other proteins produced in the body which impact on the production site in the marrow. The bone marrow can be sampled by using a hollow needle that is inserted (Ouch!) into a marrow-containing bone, such as the breastbone or iliac crest. The sample can be stained, strained, separated, and even grown to help diagnose diseases or follow treatment progress. Bone marrow can be transplanted to others to try and cure previously incurable disease or can be harvested and returned to the same individual after aggressive chemotherapy.

The reticuloendothelial system (RES) is somewhat difficult to define, because it is quite widespread throughout the body and has several components. One definition includes those cells and tissues that take up certain stains that can be seen under the microscope. These cells originate in the bone marrow and are called tissue macrophages. **Macrophages** are responsible for clearing bacteria, viruses, and cellular debris. The macrophages can be found in the tissue portion of the RES. The tissue portions include lymph nodes, the spleen, and parts of the liver. It has been estimated that there are 200 billion cells that make up the RES and are distributed throughout the body. As noted, the RES is responsible for clearing particles, especially foreign cells which may cause infection or other disease. It also transports material to areas where antibody production and attack are more effective. The RES may also store certain material like silica or carbon that may invade the body through the lungs. Biopsy of lymph nodes may be necessary to diagnose infections like tuberculosis, lymph cancers (lymphoma), or cancer that originated from another site.

The lymphatic system is closely related to both the bone marrow and the RES. The lymphatic system includes tiny vessels which connect the lymph nodes and bring lymph fluid (basically tissue water) back to the general circulation, as well as a complicated cellular defense system. The cellular system is made up of various types of lymphocytes, plasma cells, and macrophages. These cells are located in special tissues called *lymphoid organs.* These include lymph nodes, spleen, thymus, tonsils, adenoids, and lymph patches in the intestines. The architecture of the tissues is complex with a mix of vessels, supporting cells, and regions of immature and maturing immune cell components. The lymphoid organs have the proper environment to allow lymphocyte production and development. These organs are in the optimum location to identify foreign invaders such as bacteria, viruses, and cancer cells, so that the immune system can be stimulated to mount an attack with defending cells and antibodies. Lymph node biopsy and special tissue stains can be helpful in diagnosis and therapy of a variety of diseases.

ANEMIA

Anemia is the deficiency of an adequate amount of oxygen-carrying hemoglobin in the bloodstream to allow normal functioning of the body's organs. **Hemoglobin** is the protein in the red blood cells that transports oxygen from the lungs to the tissues where the oxygen is released. Oxygen is necessary to the functioning of the cells. Anemia is the most common blood disorder and can be mild or severe.

Inherited forms of anemia, such as sickle cell disease, are usually recognized at an early age. Anemia that develops in adults may be due to a primary problem in the bone marrow where the red blood cells are made, or anemia may be associated with other disease states, such as cancer or kidney disease. You should understand that anemia is never a diagnosis of its own. Anemia is always caused by some other problem. Therefore, the presence of anemia requires an investigation to discover the cause.

The normal level of hemoglobin for older adults is generally the same as for younger adults. Although there are bone marrow changes that occur with aging, most healthy older persons maintain their blood hemoglobin within the generally accepted range for the normal population. However, there are a significant number of elderly persons who have mild anemia, and some hematologists argue that the majority of these persons show no serious underlying cause. Possibly these individuals are demonstrating a decrease in bone marrow function due to less demand by their body for oxygen. Resistance to changing the normal values for adults over 70 years old stems from the fear of missing a treatable disease, such as colon cancer. Since the work-up for anemia can be very extensive and possibly invasive, the physician needs to weigh the benefits and risks of testing in the person being evaluated. In a man over 70, a hemoglobin level that is 1 to 2 grams below the traditional normal range may be normal, but the conscientious physician will generally watch for any further drop that might suggest a more serious underlying problem.

Many people who are found on a general physical examination to be anemic have no symptoms. The problem is discovered when they have their blood checked. Other persons with anemia might experience tiredness, weakness, rapid heartbeat, chest pain, shortness of breath, dizziness, or headaches. The type and severity of symptoms are determined by the severity of the anemia, the speed with which it developed, and the underlying health of the patient. Every physician has had the experience of finding a very anemic person who looked great. The anemia undoubtedly developed very slowly, and the body accustomed itself to the low blood count. In other cases, such as severe bleeding, the same low blood count produces life-threatening symptoms since that patient's body has had no chance to adapt to the low blood count. These individuals require emergency treatment with intravenous fluids, oxygen, and blood transfusions.

The **complete blood count (CBC)** is typically the test that confirms the presence of abnormally low hemoglobin (normal values in men are about 14 to 18 grams per deciliter (g/dL) and in women about 12 to 16 g/dL). Another value that is reported is the *hematocrit,* which is the percentage of a volume of blood that is due to the red blood cells (normal in men is about 42 to 54 and in women 37 to 47). The test may have been ordered as part of a physical examination in someone with no symptoms, or the doctor may suspect that the patient is anemic based on symptoms or physical examination. Further studies to evaluate the anemia include an examination of the peripheral blood smear (see Figure 23-3). Examining the red blood cells under the microscope can give many hints to the cause of the anemia. The size, shape, and color of the cells may suggest the diagnosis. For example, small, pale red blood cells point to iron deficiency. Large cells suggest the possibility of B_{12} or folic acid deficiency. The machines that are used to report the CBC also give the size of the RBC, as well as the average hemoglobin content of the cells. This can help direct the physician's work-up of the anemia. Anemias are then classified as *microcytic* (small cells), *normocytic* (normal-sized cells), and *macrocytic* (large cells).

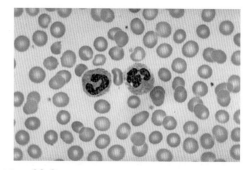

(figure 23-3)

Normal peripheral blood smear. The larger cells are white blood cells. The small purple dots are platelets *(Courtesy of Edward C. Klatt, MD, Florida State University College of Medicine).*

MICROCYTIC ANEMIA

Iron deficiency anemia (see Figure 23-4) is the most typical of the microcytic anemias and the most common form of anemia in the world. Iron is necessary for the production of hemoglobin. Younger women commonly have iron deficiency anemia due to blood and iron loss from menstrual bleeding. Thus it can be promptly corrected with iron supplements. In older persons, iron deficiency is still the most common type of anemia, but its causes are different. They include decreased iron intake in the diet, lack of normal absorption of iron in the intestines, or iron loss from often undetected gastrointestinal bleeding. In fact, once the diagnosis of iron deficiency anemia is made in an older person, a rigorous search for the cause is usually initiated even before giving supplements to replenish the low iron. Although the most feared cause is cancer of the colon or stomach, benign sources of the bleeding are often discovered, such as stomach ulcers, inflammation in the esophagus perhaps in association with a hiatal hernia, colon polyps, or colitis.

A fairly common feature of iron deficiency anemia is known as pica, the compulsive intake of a food or nonfood item related to iron deficiency. Types of foods have included celery, potato chips, carrots, and pretzels. The eating of ice, clay, or even cardboard has been reported. Once the iron deficiency is treated, the symptom resolves, but can recur if the anemia returns. This is an interesting example of one type of symptom that is rather specific for iron deficiency and can make history taking quite intriguing.

Many physicians prefer that you do not take over-the-counter iron supplements or vitamins with iron routinely, since such products could mask a loss of blood possibly from a serious source. Your doctor will check your CBC periodically, and if you develop an iron deficiency anemia, he or she can find the cause and treat it appropriately. Replacement iron can then be given. Finding an iron supplement that does not cause side effects, such as upset stomach, constipation, or diarrhea, can be difficult. However, many forms of iron are now available, so that the majority of persons can be effectively treated with minimal or no side effects. Do not be alarmed if your stool turns as black as tar. This is expected. Adequate treatment can be monitored simply by checking the CBC or iron levels. The anemia will often be corrected within a month or two, but the iron supplements need to be taken for three to six months to replenish the bone marrow iron stores.

Sideroblastic anemia is a less common form of microcytic anemia. Like iron deficiency, sideroblastic anemia may have several causes. The red blood cells look pale under the microscope. In this type of anemia there is actually an increased amount of iron in the body, but the red cells do not use the available iron efficiently. Thus the hemoglobin in the red blood cells is deficient. Certain drugs, such as those that treat tuberculosis, and excess alcohol can cause sideroblastic anemia. Pyridoxine (vitamin B_6) deficiency can also be a cause. The anemia may respond to the removal of the offending drugs, stopping alcohol intake, or receiving vitamin B_6 replacement. However, commonly no specific cause can be identified. If

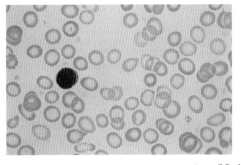

(figure 23-4)

For iron deficiency anemia the blood smear shows small, pale red blood cells. *(Courtesy of Curtis Hanson, MD, Mayo Clinic).*

significant symptoms are present, chronic transfusion therapy may become necessary. Iron supplements or vitamins with iron should be avoided in sideroblastic anemia.

MACROCYTIC ANEMIA

Let us turn to look at the large red cell anemia, or *macrocytic anemia*. This type of anemia is important because it can relate directly to your lifestyle. The causes of macrocytic anemia are related to diet, dietary or vitamin supplements, alcohol usage, living arrangements, and knowing how past medical problems can affect our future health. Importantly, macrocytic anemia is more likely to occur in the older population. The general symptoms of anemia still apply to this type of anemia, but additional signs or symptoms may be present. Liver disease and **myxedema** (very low thyroid activity) can cause macrocytic anemia and have their own specific symptoms. We are interested in two specific deficiencies, B_{12} and folic acid. Because B_{12} and folic acid have important functions in other body systems, the problems in those systems may actually be more prominent than those due to what may be a rather modest decrease in hemoglobin. The neurological and psychiatric areas are most often affected.

Both B_{12} and folic acid are necessary in the production of **deoxyribonucleic acid (DNA)**, the basic genetic material of your cells. Lack of either of these vitamins will result in abnormal maturing of red blood cells, white cells, and platelets. The function of the nerve tissue will also be affected. About half the patients with B_{12} deficiency will show neurological problems. These symptoms may include numbness in the hands and feet, muscle weakness in the extremities, and occasionally spastic or jerky movements of the hands and legs. The doctor may find that the ability to detect the vibrations of a tuning fork is lost (see Figure 23-5). The ability to detect light touching of the skin over the feet and legs may be impaired. Mental changes of irritability, memory loss, depression, dementia, and confusion can be present. People who drink excess alcohol and also lack folic acid due to their poor diets can develop peripheral nerve problems. In addition, insomnia, memory loss, and irritability can occur on folic acid–deficient diets.

I have mentioned diet frequently, but what specifically do I mean? Folic acid is found in plentiful amounts in fruit, fruit juices, and fresh vegetables. Folic acid is not present in alcohol. Therefore, people who drink large amounts of alcohol and have diets lacking in fruits and vegetables can develop folic acid deficiency. Most multivitamins include adequate folic acid. Vitamin B_{12} is not found in plants but in meat. Strict vegetarians may develop B_{12} deficiency. Vitamin B_{12} deficiency might also occur in older people who avoid meat due to difficulty swallowing or have loss of taste for meat. Living alone can lead to disinterest in cooking meat that can result eventually in B_{12} deficiency. Because of the liver's great ability to store B_{12}, even with a total lack of B_{12} in the diet, the more serious symptoms of B_{12} deficiency may take two years to develop.

Both B_{12} and folic acid can be directly measured in the blood. If a deficiency is found, further studies can help pinpoint the cause and direct

(*figure* 23-5)

A doctor uses a tuning fork to test vibration sense in the legs. Patients with nerve damage from B_{12} deficiency may not be able to detect the vibrations.

the treatment. For the most part, folic acid deficiency is diet-related and relatively straightforward to address with diet and supplemental vitamins. Causes of B_{12} deficiency include pernicious anemia, prior surgery on the stomach or small intestine, regional ileitis (Crohn's disease), and overgrowth of bacteria in the intestines. By performing an *intrinsic factor antibody test,* the doctor can determine if pernicious anemia is the diagnosis. A radioactive tracer study, called the Schilling test, can determine if B_{12} deficiency is due to a problem in the intestines that prevents absorption of B_{12} or if the deficiency is caused by pernicious anemia.

Measuring the B_{12} levels before beginning folic acid therapy is important. Treating a person who has neurological symptoms, due to B_{12} deficiency, with folic acid can cause the symptoms to worsen if B_{12} is not given in appropriate fashion. Vitamin B_{12} can be given orally to overcome loss due to diet, Crohn's disease, or bacterial overgrowth. However, B_{12} by injection or by nasal spray must be given to people with pernicious anemia or surgical causes, as oral absorption will not occur in these people. Luckily, the blood problems respond quickly and almost always completely to B_{12} or folic acid treatment. Unfortunately, if the neurological symptoms are long-standing or severe, complete recovery may not be possible. Therefore, it is important to evaluate B_{12} and folic acid levels as early as possible in people with neurological symptoms even if anemia is not significant or even identified.

NORMOCYTIC ANEMIA

The final, relatively common form of anemia in the older population is the *anemia of chronic disease.* This anemia usually has normal-sized, or normocytic, red blood cells. The anemia usually is found in people with chronic inflammatory disease, such as rheumatoid arthritis, long-standing infections, cancer, or liver and kidney disease. The low blood count is usually moderate, but occasionally, especially in chronic kidney failure, severe enough to consider transfusion or other therapy. Measuring levels of iron, B_{12}, folic acid, and ferritin (the storage form of iron, rather than the circulating iron) are frequently helpful but not specific in making the diagnosis. A bone marrow test may be necessary to ensure the problem is not due to a defect in the way blood cells are made. The bone marrow will usually appear fairly normal except for possibly an increase in iron stores. In the past, transfusion therapy was all that was available for people with this type of anemia. In the past 10 years, the use of erythropoietin therapy has been effective in many patients. Erythropoietin is a normal hormone produced by the kidney that stimulates red blood cell production in the marrow. Erythropoietin can now be produced in bacteria, harvested, and given as replacement therapy, frequently with good results, although it will not be effective if other deficiencies are present at the same time. Erythropoietin is also quite expensive and may not be indicated in all instances of the anemia of chronic disease. It is marketed under the brand names EPOGEN and PROCRIT.

LEUKEMIAS

Leukemia is the proliferation of abnormal white blood cells in the bone marrow, as well as in other tissues and organs. This usually causes an increase in the white blood cells in the circulating blood that can be detected on a CBC. However, sometimes the white blood cell count can actually be depressed due to infiltration of the bone marrow with abnormal cells that do not get released into the circulation. Since the production of red blood cells might also be affected, anemia may coexist with leukemia.

While the diagnosis of leukemia is always frightening, we have to be aware that there are several types of leukemia and many subtypes that have quite different signs, symptoms, and therapy. The nomenclature for the different types of leukemias can be confusing. The four basic types are acute and chronic lymphocytic, acute nonlymphocytic, and chronic myelocytic leukemia. While information about all the leukemias is interesting, we discuss the two types seen most frequently in seniors.

The most common leukemia seen in people over 50 years of age is chronic lymphocytic leukemia (CLL). CLL makes up less than 1% of all cancers for all age groups, but its incidence increases after age 50. No area of the country has a higher incidence than another, and no causative factors have been identified. Nearly 25% of diagnoses of CLL are in people with no symptoms. The symptoms that do bring a person to the doctor are fatigue, enlarged lymph nodes, or infection. Most patients with symptoms will have several enlarged lymph nodes, about half will have an enlarged spleen, and some may have a mildly enlarged liver. The enlarged lymph nodes and spleen are usually painless. The specific diagnosis is reached by checking the peripheral blood for an increase in mature lymphocytes (see Figure 23-6) and obtaining a bone marrow examination that shows at least 30% involvement by the same lymphocytes. While in the past some nonmalignant diseases could be mistaken for CLL, we now have very specific lymphocyte studies that are easily performed on peripheral blood and can make the diagnosis rapidly and with very little chance of error.

Once the diagnosis is made, the patient and physician will determine the proper timing of treatment. If no symptoms are present, watchful waiting is the best course, as many people with CLL will actually not die of complications of this type of leukemia. If symptoms are present or if anemia or decreased platelets are noted, then treatment may help prevent complications. As one might expect, the more disease that is present at the time of diagnosis, the more likely that treatment will be necessary. CLL is one of those situations of good news and bad news. The good news is that there are several types of treatment that can help control the disease. The bad news is we cannot yet cure CLL despite some very new and exciting therapies. These new therapies include antibodies against the lymphocytes, which can be given with little side effect. The chemotherapy for CLL is still effective and generally well tolerated. The most common severe problems in CLL are infection and bleeding.

DOCTOR'S DIARY

Gloria T., a 72-year-old retired schoolteacher, was referred to me for evaluation of an abnormal white blood cell count. She had felt perfectly well and had continued to travel extensively with her retired colleagues. She had seen her personal physician for her annual physical exam, and a complete blood count had shown an increase in white blood cells. Further questioning showed that she had no symptoms of infection, had never had an abnormal blood test in the past, had no family history of leukemia or cancer, and was not on medication. She seemed to be in great health. Her physical exam was normal.

Laboratory tests were normal except for a white blood cell count of 25,000 (normal is 4000 to 10,000) with 80% mature lymphocytes. Special studies showed these to be B lymphocytes.

I made a diagnosis of chronic lymphocytic leukemia. I requested that she send me a postcard from her next trip and check in with her home doctor in six months. I scheduled an appointment for her to see me in a year unless any new symptoms developed. She returned yearly for the next six years. The only change noted, other than requiring a new passport, was a slowly increasing lymphocyte count. She never required therapy for her leukemia.

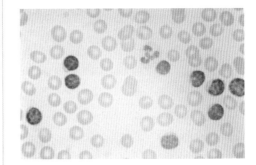

(*figure* 23-6)

Notice the large number of lymphocytes for chronic lymphocytic leukemia (purple cells). (*Courtesy of the Mayo Clinic*).

Acute leukemia is often thought of as a disease of children, but the type of acute leukemia seen in older adults is not the same as is seen typically in children. In fact, adults over the age of 50 make up 70% of all the cases of acute nonlymphocytic leukemia (ANLL). Unlike CLL, ANLL does not have a slow onset that allows an observation period. ANLL is an aggressive malignancy of immature white blood cells called myeloblasts. The myeloblasts overproduce in the bone marrow, do not go on to normal maturation, and eventually crowd out the normal elements of the marrow (see Figure 23-7). This crowding out can result in dangerously low levels of red blood cells, normal white cells, and platelets. We can guess that people with ANLL are therefore anemic, susceptible to infections, and prone to bleeding. In fact, these are the typical problems that lead people with ANLL to see a doctor. Older patients may also complain of fatigue, weight loss, and generalized weakness.

The diagnosis is made from studying the complete blood count, examining the peripheral blood smear under the microscope, and performing a bone marrow exam. The bone marrow is examined with special stains and chromosome analysis to help determine the subtype of ANLL present. There are several different subtypes of ANLL. One subtype, which you may have heard about, is *acute myelogenous leukemia (AML)*. The classification schemes are complex and based on different factors, such as the appearance of the cells and immunologic or genetic features. The subtyping of acute leukemia will provide better choices of the drugs to be used in therapy.

Unfortunately, the therapy for ANLL has to be quite aggressive to obtain a *complete remission*. A complete remission means that after therapy there is no evidence of abnormal myeloblasts in the bone marrow and blood counts are near normal levels. The aim of all the drug combinations is to kill the myeloblasts and allow normal marrow elements to regrow. The problem of therapy occurs after the drugs are given. Due to the effect of the drugs on the body's defense system, the patient has a very high chance of severe infection or bleeding. In the past, older patients were not thought to be good candidates for this type of aggressive therapy, but as supportive measures have improved, the survival rates for older individuals has essentially equaled that of young adults. At present, there is about a 65% chance of a complete remission, which may last nearly two years. Without therapy or without obtaining a complete remission, the survival of a person with ANLL is only about six months.

Many factors have to be considered by the patient, the family, and the physicians when approaching the treatment of ANLL. Among these factors are the underlying physical status of the patient, social support available, and spiritual considerations of the patient. At times, it may be necessary to obtain an opinion regarding therapy at a cancer specialty institution before going ahead with a decision to treat or observe. As a final word about ANLL, bone marrow transplantation is performed for this disease but rarely in patients over the age of 50.

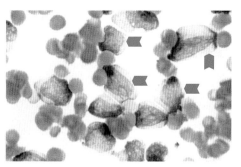

(*figure* 23-7)

Note the large immature lymphocytes (arrowheads) for acute nonlymphocytic leukemia. (*Courtesy of the Mayo Clinic*).

OTHER BONE MARROW DISORDERS

There are two further groups of primary bone marrow diseases similar to leukemia but with quite different natural histories. Theses two groups are the myeloproliferative diseases and the *myelodysplastic* disorders. As one can see, the words are similar as are some of the features of each group. Each category affects at least one of the cell lines in the bone marrow and therefore may cause symptoms related to red blood cells, white cells, or platelets. Luckily, all the diseases in these two groups are fairly uncommon.

The four diseases which make up the myeloproliferative group are *agnogenic myeloid metaplasia (AMM),* polycythemia vera (PV), chronic myelogenous leukemia (CML), and *primary thrombocythemia (PT).* Simply listing them is a mouthful. Interestingly, CML and PT tend to occur in the young adult age groups, whereas AMM and PV occur most frequently in people over 60 years of age. Each disease appears to correlate with the excessive growth (or proliferation) of one the bone marrow's cell lines.

In AMM, macrophages, a white cell, grow in large amounts and may relate to the fact that the bone marrow becomes fibrous (or scarred) in appearance. Anemia, abnormal white cell counts, and massive increase in spleen size are the common findings in AMM. The spleen can grow to nearly fill the abdomen as the disease progresses (see Figure 23-8). Treatments have included surgical removal of the spleen, low-level radiation therapy, and mild chemotherapy agents. Most patients with AMM experience fatigue, abdominal discomfort, bleeding problems, liver disease, and, often, severe infections. New treatments aimed at preventing the apparent scarring of the bone marrow are being evaluated.

PV is the unregulated increase in red blood cells. PV is often diagnosed at a routine examination when the CBC shows an elevation of the

WHAT'S NEW?

Molecular genetics and molecular biology have combined to produce an innovative treatment for chronic myelogenous leukemia (CML). Although CML is not too common in older individuals, the breakthrough in understanding the chromosomal or genetic changes which cause CML and the subsequent development of specifically engineered drugs to treat the disease may be a model for many other cancers or diseases that affect older persons.

In very general terms, the gene abnormality causing CML has been shown to cause a specific enzyme to be overproduced, and this eventually results in the prevention of the normal pattern of cell death which white blood cells follow. By developing a specific drug, imatinib (Gleevec), which blocked the enzyme activity, researchers were able to bring back to the white blood cells the normal pattern of maturing and eventual cell death. While this has resulted in new treatment programs, cure of CML has not been assured; however, new drugs and combinations of effective therapy are being studied. Eventually, the actual cause of the genetic abnormality may be identified and even more directed treatment would be available to patients. We all hope that this type of investigation leading to specific therapy for many illnesses will become quite common in the next decades.

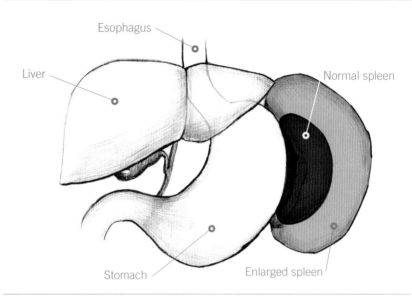

(figure 23-8)

An enlarged spleen occurs in a variety of blood diseases and can be detected on a physical examination.

Esophagus

Liver

Normal spleen

Stomach

Enlarged spleen

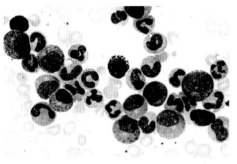

(figure 23-9)

Cells found normally in the bone marrow appear in increased numbers in the peripheral blood for chronic myelogenous leukemia. *(Courtesy of Curtis Hanson, MD, Mayo Clinic).*

hematocrit. The symptoms of PV are headache, dizziness, visual changes, loss of ability to concentrate, and occasionally an unusual feeling of heat and pain in the feet. Blood clots and bleeding problems can occur. Due to the increase in blood volume, the blood acts as if it were quite thick, which may cause the symptoms noted. The most common treatment remains phlebotomy, or blood removal. Thankfully, leeches are not necessary for this procedure! This treatment alone can be effective for years, as PV tends to progress rather slowly. Other therapies are aimed at slowing the production of the red blood cells in the bone marrow and can be helpful as well.

While CML and PT can occur in older patients, they are much less common than AMM and PV. Suffice it to say that CML is a proliferation of white cells (see Figure 23-9) and PT is related to a marked increase in platelet production. All these diseases are uncommon enough to warrant obtaining specialty evaluation if suspected.

The second relatively rare group of bone marrow diseases is the myelodysplastic syndromes. These syndromes tend to occur only in the older population unless patients were exposed at an earlier age to certain types of chemotherapy, especially a group of drugs known as *alkylating agents*. The five syndromes making up this group are *refractory anemia (RA)*, *refractory anemia with ringed sideroblasts (RARS)*, *refractory anemia with excess blasts (RAEB)*, *chronic myelomonocytic leukemia (CMML)*, and *refractory anemia with excess blasts in transformation (RAEB-T)*. Simply reading the names of the syndromes certainly suggests that anemia is a major finding in these disorders. In fact, anemia, with its typical symptoms, is the most common finding leading to evaluation and diagnosis. The five syndromes are probably interrelated and may be varying forms of each other rather than distinct disease entities. The order in which I have listed them also corresponds to their severity, in that the survival of people with RA is nearly 15 times longer than seen in RAEB-T. While RA and RARS have a small incidence of progression to ANLL, nearly all patients with the other three syndromes will go onto a form of ANLL with very poor response to even aggressive therapy. Bone marrow examination with special studies is almost always required in the diagnostic evaluation for this group. The treatment tends to be supportive with blood transfusions and antibiotics as needed. Attempts at using aggressive therapy in patients have tended to be unsuccessful. Bone marrow transplantation has been used with some benefit in the rare younger patient with these problems. Again, luckily, the incidence of this group of syndromes is very low.

MULTIPLE MYELOMA

Multiple myeloma is a malignancy caused by the unregulated proliferation of plasma cells in the bone marrow (see Figure 23-10). As we noted earlier, plasma cells produce proteins called *gamma globulins,* or *immunoglobulins,* which are a normal part of the immune response. If plasma cells become malignant, they reproduce and begin to crowd out normal aspects of the bone marrow. Anemia and infections are common complications of myeloma. Due to the production of other molecules, plasma cell diseases also cause the bone itself to be destroyed, resulting in weakening of the bone and possible bone pain and fractures. Almost all cases of myeloma occur in patients over the age of 55, with a slight but continued increase in frequency with age. Myeloma accounts for 1% of all new cancer cases in the United States and 13% of blood-related cancers. There is no known cause for myeloma.

Signs of multiple myeloma include anemia, abnormal bone X-rays, abnormal protein in the blood and/or urine, and, commonly, kidney dysfunction. The presence of the proteins is a fairly reliable tumor marker to follow disease progress or therapeutic response, but as you can imagine, not all cases follow the pattern of lower protein, better response. Bone marrow studies can include sophisticated measures of growth patterns of plasma cells that have been used to help follow and guide therapy.

Unlike most cancers which nearly always require intervention at the time of diagnosis, multiple myeloma has been found to have a rather unusual natural history. The finding of the abnormal gamma globulin *(monoclonal gammopathy)* is key to suspecting the diagnosis, but often after evaluation, it can be monitored at appropriate intervals before any therapy is indicated. People with monoclonal gammopathy of undetermined significance (MGUS) have been followed for as long as 20 years. It has been shown that only 20% of these individuals will develop diseases like multiple myeloma and require therapy. Therapy for myeloma has traditionally been oral drugs, but a number of cooperative cancer groups around the world have been studying more aggressive programs to try and increase the response rate and survival time for patients. Bone marrow transplant, interferon, and thalidomide are being studied for possible benefit in myeloma. New medications are also being given to try and prevent or reverse the damage to bones that results in severe bone pain, which is one of the most difficult symptoms in patients with myeloma.

Another condition associated with abnormal proliferation of plasma cells in the bone marrow is Waldenström's macroglobulinemia. In this

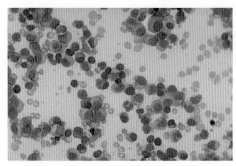

(figure 23-10)

Excess numbers of plasma cells (blue and purple) proliferate in the bone marrow in multiple myeloma. *(Courtesy of Edward C. Klatt, MD, Florida State Univeristy College of Medicine).*

condition, there is an increase of a large antibody *(immunoglobulin M)* that can make the blood thicker and more viscous. As a result, dizziness, visual disturbances, fatigue, and bleeding from the nose and mouth may occur *(hyperviscosity syndrome)*. These persons may have more problems with exposure to cold. Peripheral neuropathy and kidney dysfunction are other complications.

HODGKIN'S AND NON-HODGKIN'S LYMPHOMA

The final area of blood system malignancies that I review is the malignant lymphomas. Lymphomas involve the RES, lymph system, and, frequently, the bone marrow, thereby involving all the components of the blood system. There are many types of lymphomas. The typing of lymphomas is important because of significant differences in aggressiveness of the disease, as well as therapy needed. At the present time, some form of tissue, typically a lymph node biopsy specimen, is required to make the proper diagnosis. Microscopic analysis is the primary method of analysis, but new techniques including *flow cytometry* and chromosome studies are helping define more precise categories of lymphoma. All the diagnostic techniques are important due to the variety of lymphomas that exist and the importance of initiating the best possible treatment. I cover the basics of the variety of lymphomas, but much more information is available from physicians and specialists.

The two major categories of lymphomas are Hodgkin's disease (HD) and non-Hodgkin's lymphoma (NHL). HD occurs most commonly in two age distributions, one in young adults and the second beginning at age 50 and increasing slowly thereafter. Men are affected more commonly than are women in all age groups, which is also true in NHL. The incidence of NHL rises steadily with age, with higher occurrences after the age of 40. There are four basic subgroups in HD, which correlate fairly well with severity of disease, response to treatment, and survival. Each subgroup has a distinct microscopic appearance, which is the basis for the typing. NHL has been much more complex in attempts to classify subgroups. There have been at least five major attempts at subgrouping, each with some positive aspects, but each has had drawbacks as well. There are at least 10 and perhaps as many as 20 different categories in each of these classification schemes. The overriding criterion has been how they relate to clinical (real-life) approaches to management and survival. Pathologists, immunologists, and molecular biologists are continuing to identify features that may further change the classification systems.

The symptoms and signs of HD and NHL tend to be similar and correlate to some extent with the severity of disease. The most common early sign of lymphoma is the presence of an enlarged lymph node. The enlarged node can occur anywhere in the lymph system (see Figure 23-11) but often in the neck, armpit, or groin. There are many other causes of enlarged nodes, with infection being prominent on the list. Other findings could include multiple enlarged nodes, fever, fatigue, weight loss, anemia, and night sweats. In older individuals, and especially those with more aggressive types of lymphoma, lymph node enlargement may not be as prominent a finding as the other symptoms listed. The work-up of

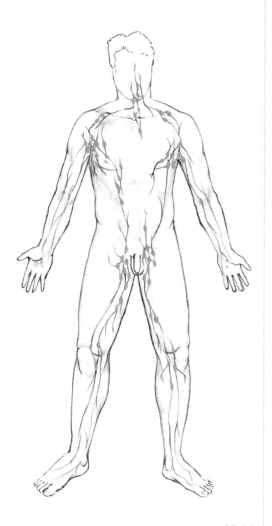

(figure 23-11*)*

The lymphatic system is an extensive drainage system that plays an important role in your body's defense system. An enlarged lymph node is often the first sign of lymphoma and can occur in any of the body's lymph nodes but more commonly starts with an enlarged node in the neck.

a patient with malignant lymphoma may require a number of specialized studies beyond an initial lymph node biopsy. These studies include CAT scans, bone marrow biopsies, MRI scans, and specialized blood tests. The purpose of these studies is to determine the extent and location of the lymphoma. These results help determine the best therapeutic approach to the patient.

HD was first described in 1832, but effective therapy using radiation was not truly begun until the 1950s. Over the past 50 years there have been significant advances in the treatment of both HD and NHL. As I have noted, the approach to treatment is truly dependent on making the proper diagnosis. Today, the treating hematologist is hopeful to be able to offer a curative form of therapy to a large number of people with lymphoma. The treatment programs may include a period of watchful waiting as in CLL or may require immediate aggressive chemotherapy. At the present time, many cancer centers are undertaking research programs to identify the treatments that have the best results with fewest side effects; however, local specialists have a wide range of effective therapies available.

Treatments often include multiple drugs, which may be given through the vein and by mouth, as well as possible radiation therapy. Newer therapy programs include a form of bone marrow transplant or use of antibodies that recognize and attack lymphoma cells. Because of the variation present in many of the treatment programs, it is not really feasible to give you a list of therapies, drugs, or protocols available. In fact, many of the abbreviations of the therapies look like alphabet soup, even to the specialists. The most significant impression I want to leave with you is that the initial diagnosis needs to be as accurate as possible, which may require consultation from specialized pathology centers around the country. Your specialists will decide with you whether further studies or consultations are necessary.

THE BLEEDING PATIENT

As previously discussed, the blood system has two separate compartments that respond when you are bleeding. The platelets are part of the cellular compartment, and the coagulation or clotting sequence is part of the blood plasma. As you have seen in all previous topics in this chapter, all normal systems have abnormal or pathologic counterparts. The coagulation system is no different. Certain diseases, such as hemophilia, are hereditary and usually diagnosed when the individual is young. In this section, I review problems that are more typically acquired in the later stages of life.

The medical history and patient's symptoms are of great importance in the initial evaluation of a bleeding patient. A family history of a bleeding disorder may be less important in the older age groups, but some patients with chronic low-grade bleeding problems may actually have a mild form of hemophilia called von Willebrand's disease. It is important to note that nearly 90% of inherited bleeding disorders occur in males and are usually evident in childhood. Patients with platelet problems often have gum bleeding, nosebleeds, multiple red pinpoint lesions *(petechiae),* and superficial bleeding under the skin *(purpura).* They also complain of prolonged bleeding from minor scratches. In contrast, even minor injury may cause patients with coagulation defects to develop large blood collections in the tissues called hematomas. They may also have multiple large bruises without trauma. Rarely, bleeding into joints occurs. Occasionally they may have prolonged bleeding from cuts and rarely bleeding from the rectum.

Typically, bleeding problems related to platelet disorders arise from having too few platelets, called thrombocytopenia, or from abnormal functioning of the platelets in the circulation. There are multiple causes for reduced platelet numbers, but these disorders can be conveniently divided into those caused by a decrease in platelet production in the bone marrow or by an increase in platelet destruction. By far, the most common cause is a drug or chemical exposure. Therefore, determining possible exposure to medications, chemotherapy, or toxic agents is a very important part of the evaluation of decreased platelets. One disease which causes marked platelet destruction by immune processes is idiopathic thrombocytopenic purpura (ITP). However, ITP is almost never found in patients over 60 years of age. Obviously, if an agent is suspected as the cause for low platelets, it needs to be stopped or removed from the patient's environment if possible. Some of the drugs which cause platelets to function abnormally include anti-inflammatory agents, antibiotics, antidepressants, and a variety of miscellaneous drugs. The classic drug which inhibits normal platelet functioning is aspirin. This action can be beneficial, and aspirin is recommended for many individuals to prevent strokes and heart attacks. However, aspirin can cause significant problems if surgery is necessary or with major trauma. Luckily, by stopping the drugs in question, platelet function reverts to normal over time. Primary bone marrow diseases, such as RAEB, may also cause platelet dysfunction and, as we noted earlier, do not have easy approaches to therapy. Laboratory studies used to screen for platelet-related problems include the platelet count, examination of the platelets on the peripheral blood smear, and occasionally the bleeding time. The *bleeding time* is a measure of the time for bleeding to stop from a small cut usually made on the forearm or earlobe. Depending on these results, further studies of platelet function may be necessary, but usually require referral to a specialized coagulation laboratory.

Despite the marked complexity of the coagulation system, bleeding problems in an otherwise normal adult are quite uncommon. The most frequent difficulties occur in people with significant preexisting diseases, acute or sudden severe illnesses, postoperative complications, or drug reactions. The most common cause of coagulation factor abnormalities is liver disease. Since clotting factors are made by liver cells, patients with marked liver abnormalities from cirrhosis, hepatitis, or drug causes are not able to manufacture adequate amounts of normal coagulation factors, or the factors may have abnormal functioning. Patients with liver disease may require treatment with transfused fresh frozen plasma, which contains active factors, prior to surgery or with trauma.

There are some rare instances of people developing antibodies in their bloodstream that interact with specific coagulation factors and inhibit the function of that factor. These instances are unusual and most often develop in individuals with chronic immune disorders. The patient may experience severe bleeding, and the treatment can be quite complex and expensive. In patients with life-threatening infection, a problem called **disseminated intravascular coagulation (DIC)** may occur. DIC results in bleeding that can also be life-threatening and is most effectively treated by reversing the underlying acute problem. Obviously this is more easily said than done. Finally, a variety of drugs may interact with the coagulation system and result in abnormalities. At times, the abnormalities may be of no concern and simply cause a change in a coagulation lab test, but as one can imagine, there are times when bleeding can occur. Chemotherapy agents are the most common drugs that can occasionally initiate significant bleeding. Most of these situations can now be anticipated and avoided or diminished in severity by pretreatment interventions.

Our final area of interest in coagulation relates to the use of drugs that prevent clotting. HEPARIN and WARFARIN (COUMADIN) are two drugs that interfere with the normal clotting sequence. Heparin is given through the veins or as an injection under the skin and acts by inhibiting a factor called *antithrombin III (ATIII)*. Heparin is active only while it is present in the system and is rapidly cleared by the body which means doses have to be given frequently for adequate results. Heparin is used most often in acute clotting problems or to prevent clots from developing in postoperative patients. The proper dose of heparin can be determined with lab monitoring, but bleeding can occur if other drugs are present, if excess heparin is present, or if trauma occurs. The action of heparin can be rapidly reversed by another drug if absolutely necessary. A relatively new class of drugs include the low molecular weight heparins, such as ENOXAPARIN (LOVENOX) and DALTEPARIN (FRAGMIN). They can be given by injections under the skin, and have replaced the use of intravenous heparin in many situations where an anticoagulant is necessary. These drugs do not require the frequent blood monitoring that intravenous heparin requires. As a result, many persons with blood clots in the leg veins can be treated at home, sparing the inconvenience and expense of a prolonged stay in the hospital.

Coumadin is a commonly prescribed oral medication, especially in individuals with histories of blood clots or heart disease. Coumadin works by impairing the production of the coagulation factors in the liver. Coumadin works on those factors which need vitamin K to be manufactured. The level of Coumadin is monitored regularly by checking the prothrombin time and then adjusting the daily oral dose of Coumadin accordingly. Unfortunately, bleeding problems due to Coumadin are fairly common, but can be avoided for the most part. The problems with Coumadin arise because a wide variety of drugs can either inhibit or promote the anticoagulation action of Coumadin. Whenever a patient is on Coumadin, the person responsible for monitoring the dosage needs to be informed of any change in the patient's medication regimen.

BLOOD TYPING

History books date the first transfusions of blood to the 17th century when physicians in England and France initially experimented with dogs and subsequently tried transfusions from animals to humans. Adverse reactions resulted in the prohibition of transfusions in England and France. Little progress was made in transfusion until 1900 when Karl Landsteiner, an Austrian physician and researcher, showed that blood from some, but not all, groups of individuals clumped when transfused. His research resulted in the recognition of blood types: A, B, AB, and O. All blood from donors and recipients is typed according to blood group to reduce the risk of severe reactions when blood is transfused. His discovery was recognized with the Nobel Prize in Physiology or Medicine in 1930.

Many nutritional supplements and alternative medications can increase or decrease the action of Coumadin; therefore, they should not be taken unless your doctor is aware and permits them. Serious bleeding has been reported in a few patients taking Coumadin and ginkgo biloba together. Even diets that contain foods rich in vitamin K may cause problems in decreasing the effectiveness of the Coumadin. As a result, you should maintain your normal balanced diet while taking Coumadin. A sudden increase in consumption of green leafy vegetables could decrease the effectiveness of Coumadin, but it is all right to consume salads and spinach as long as you don't drastically change the amount. Unfortunately, Coumadin can cause significant bleeding if taken in excess. Some patients have had bleeding problems by taking too much Coumadin by mistake, so being very cautious of the labeling and dosage is very important. Giving vitamin K can help correct the problem. In an emergency, the administration of fresh frozen plasma provides the clotting factors that can reverse bleeding from Coumadin excess. Clearly, you can see that close follow-up is recommended if you are on Coumadin. In some cases, your doctor may recommend that you attend a specialized clinic where your blood can be tested immediately with a simple finger prick, and your Coumadin dose adjusted immediately if necessary. Despite these precautions, you should not be overly afraid to take Coumadin if your doctor prescribes it. The benefits usually far outweigh the risks. If you need to take Coumadin for a prolonged period of time, it is a good idea to get a medical alert bracelet or necklace so that emergency personnel are aware in the event that you are injured and unable to provide your medical information.

TRANSFUSION THERAPY

For some of us, the thought of receiving a blood transfusion is a frightening prospect. For others, the thought of giving blood for transfusion causes light-headedness. The first human blood transfusion occurred in 1667. There has been a dramatic increase in the knowledge and techniques of transfusion therapy over the following three centuries. In 2003, advances in anticoagulants, cell preservation, component transfusion, immunologic matching, and safety are impressive and ongoing. If you have given blood at any time, you are aware of screening measures for donors to protect the blood supply. The screening questions number nearly 60 and are concerned with personal health, travel history, and high-risk behavior.

Following the nearly risk-free donation, the donated blood is subjected to a sophisticated series of lab exams designed to exclude blood which may be a risk to pass on a blood-related disease. These tests screen for AIDS, HTLV I/II, hepatitis B and C, syphilis, and West Nile virus. Blood banks are very aggressive in deleting certain donors who may have questionable results on any of these tests.

At present, over 50% of all transfusions are given to patients over 69 years old. Although both the blood transfused and the recipient are matched as closely as possible, an occasional reaction can occur. These reactions take various forms. Allergic reactions may be mild and cause a rash or hives that can be managed readily with temporarily stopping the transfusion and giving antihistamines. Usually, the transfusion can be restarted when the symptoms have resolved. More severe allergic reactions may require EPINEPHRINE *(adrenaline)* and steroids. The transfusion should not be restarted. If the need for transfusion still exists, "washed" red cells are given. The washing process removes substances in the plasma that cause the allergic reaction.

Hemolytic reactions are caused by breakdown of red blood cells due to transfusion of incompatible blood. As you know, the blood that a person gets has to be compatible with his or her own blood type. Clerical error is the most common reason for these types of reactions, but thankfully, meticulous attention to detail in the labeling and administration of blood products has reduced such errors. Hemolytic reactions may cause anxiety, pain at the IV site, fever, shaking chills, back and chest pain, and shortness of breath. The transfusion is stopped immediately, and intravenous fluids and special medicines to maintain the blood pressure, as well as improve the urine flow, are given.

Febrile reactions are an increase of temperature of two or more degrees caused by sensitivity to the white cells of the donor. Since it may be difficult to distinguish a febrile reaction from the early stage of a hemolytic reaction, the transfusion is stopped and blood is tested. If there is no evidence of a hemolytic reaction, simple fever reducers, such as acetaminophen, are given. Special blood filters can reduce the risk of subsequent febrile reactions.

Occasionally the volume of fluid given with a transfusion can cause problems for those who have a weak heart or too much fluid already in the body due to conditions such as cirrhosis or kidney failure. Transfusion in these persons may provoke shortness of breath, headache, and chest discomfort. The treatment involves administering diuretics and slowing down the rate of the transfusion.

Although this list of reactions sounds intimidating, the chance of a significant reaction are as low as one in 35,000 transfusions. Despite the low incidence of severe problems, physicians are happy to avoid the use of transfusions if possible. Most of the problems of transfusion can be avoided by using one's own blood for elective procedures. This process is known as autologous donation and is quite effective if the condition of the patient and time allows.

WHAT'S NEW?

In the not so distant future, there may be an alternative to warfarin (Coumadin) for the treatment of blood clots that will not require regular blood tests. XIMELAGRATAN (EXANTRA) is an oral medication taken twice daily that has shown comparable or greater efficacy to warfarin in the treatment of blood clots and in the prevention of stroke in patients with atrial fibrillation. In addition, the bleeding risks were no greater than that reported with a placebo.

WHAT YOU NEED TO KNOW

▶ Blood can be separated into two basic components: formed elements or cells and plasma. The cellular elements are red blood cells, white blood cells, and platelets. Plasma contains the liquid aspect of blood, but from the hematologist's standpoint, it also has clotting factors and substances important to the body's defense system called the immune system.

▶ Anemia (low hemoglobin and hematocrit) is never a diagnosis by itself. Anemia is always caused by something else, such as iron deficiency, vitamin B_{12} deficiency, kidney disease, or microscopic blood loss. Laboratory investigation and, occasionally, special studies are required to determine the cause of the anemia.

▶ A diagnosis of leukemia is always frightening; however, you should be aware that there are several types of leukemia and many subtypes that have quite different signs, symptoms, and therapy. The four basic types of leukemia are acute and chronic lymphocytic, acute nonlymphocytic, and chronic myelocytic. The most common type in older adults is chronic lymphocytic leukemia and generally has a rather favorable prognosis.

▶ There are many different types of lymphoma, and prognosis depends on the type of the disease as well as the nature of the treatment. A hematologist or oncologist (some physicians specialize in both areas) will work with the patient and family to help decide the best course of treatment.

▶ Transfusions have saved the lives of many people. Although the risks of transfusion are relatively low, certain reactions can occur. The screening of donors has reduced the risk of transfusion-associated infections.

23

WHAT YOU NEED TO KNOW

▶ **National Institutes of Health**
9000 Rockville Pike
Bethesda, MD 20892
Web: www.nih.gov

▶ **National Cancer Institute**
NCI Public Inquiries Office
6116 Executive Boulevard, MSC8322, Suite 3036A
Bethesda, MD 20892
800-422-6237
TTY: 800-332-8615
Web: www.nci.nih.gov

▶ **National Heart, lung, and Blood Institute**
NHLBI Health Information Center
P.O. Box 30105
Bethesda, MD 20824
301-592-8573
TTY: 240-629-3255
Fax: 301-592-8563

E-mail: nhlbiinfo@rover.nhlbi.nih.gov
Web: www.nhlbi.nih.gov
If requesting health information, please include your postal address, since many resources are available only as printed publications.

▶ **The Mayo Clinic**
200 First Street, SW
Rochester, MN 55905
507-284-2511
Web: www.mayoclinic.com

Cancer is a particularly insidious disease. Because the cells in your own body are turning against you, it feels like a betrayal from within.

—Rudy Guiliani, Leadership

THE AUTHOR

24

SARAH HOFFE, MD, is a graduate of Brown University in Providence, Rhode Island. She received her medical degree from the University of Vermont College of Medicine in Burlington. After her internship at the Mayo Clinic in Jacksonville, Florida, she completed a radiation oncology residency at Duke University Medical Center in Durham, North Carolina, and at Memorial Sloan-Kettering Cancer Center in New York City. She subsequently did fellowship training in thoracic radiotherapy at MD Anderson Cancer Center in Houston, Texas. She continued to pursue a special interest in the treatment of lung cancer when she joined the staff of the Mayo Clinic in Jacksonville. As a senior associate consultant at Mayo, she served as the radiation oncologist on the bone marrow transplant team, and she devoted a significant part of her practice to the care of lymphoma patients. She was involved in the Mayo-sponsored hematology-oncology review course and lectured on the role of radiotherapy in lung cancer management. Dr. Hoffe is board-certified in radiation oncology by the American Board of Radiology, and she is a member of the American Society for Therapeutic Radiology and Oncology.

24 | CANCER

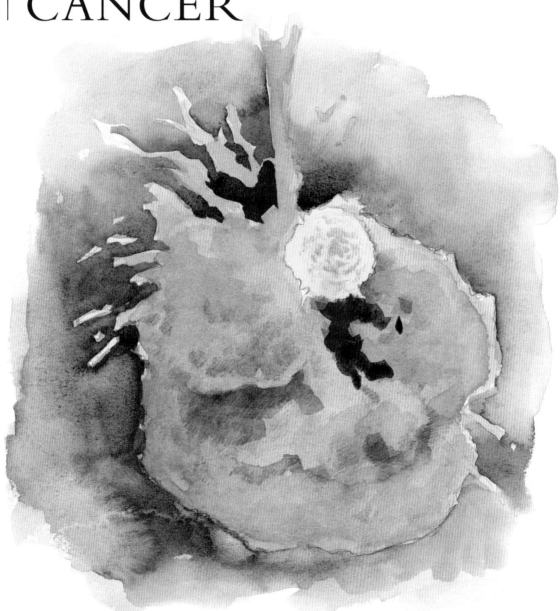

(figure 24-1)
Activated *killer cell* destroying a cancer cell. As we get older, the vigilance of the body's natural defenses breaks down, thus increasing our risk for developing cancer.

The exact pathways that cause a normal cell to become capable of immortal proliferation with the ability to spread throughout the body continue to be the subject of intense national and international research. What investigators do know is that a normal cell goes through a journey before becoming malignant.

There are both acquired and genetic factors that can change the internal composition of any cell in the human body. Some of these that can be acquired include chemical carcinogens (cancer producers) like tobacco smoke, ultraviolet carcinogens like sunlight, and viral carcinogens like human papilloma viruses. If a normal cell is altered in this way, it has been *initiated*. An initiated cell is not, by itself, a tumor cell. Yet by having its DNA damaged, it becomes more susceptible to the action of a diverse group of chemicals called *promoters* that can induce a tumor to form. Promoters are believed to act by altering the expression of genetic information in the cells.

At the cellular level, the genetic flow of information controlling normal growth and development is very precisely regulated. If the normal cell is initiated and then promoted, it is "hijacked" by these processes. The damaged cell can then become immortal by the activation of growth-promoting genes called oncogenes or the inactivation of genes called suppressor genes that inhibit cancer. The end result is a new cell that forms a new growth, or neoplasm. The neoplasm can be benign or malignant. Unlike benign growths, malignant cell populations have the capacity to spread to distant parts of the body; this process is called metastasis.

Each time a neoplasm is "born," it must find a way to survive inside its host. The new cellular population is a virtual parasite, competing with the normal tissues for blood supply, energy supply, and nutrients. Under the microscope, pathologists can identify how aggressive the cell appears by evaluating its pattern. For example, in prostate cancer a numerical score (Gleason score) is given to the tumor. A higher score indicates a more aggressive tumor. A score of 9 would indicate a tumor that would be expected to behave more aggressively than a tumor with a score of 4.

In the twenty-first century, much attention is being devoted to the study of these complex cellular interactions. The root problem is that the cell cannot turn itself off, almost as if the cell were receiving a constant satellite feed 24 hours a day. If the cell were cut off from that incessant signaling, then the growth could be terminated. There has already been progress on this front in the leukemia trenches. A drug called GLEEVEC works by affecting the molecular cause of chronic myelogenous leukemia (CML). With CML, there is a continuous signal inducing the body to produce abnormal white blood cells. Gleevec works by interfering with the abnormal protein that tells the body to send out the signal. There are active clinical trials incorporating these novel molecular therapies for many other types of tumors.

In addition, there is increasing interest on the complex tumor-host interactions. For a variety of reasons, most carcinomas occur in patients

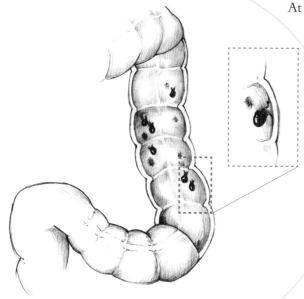

55 years of age and older. The incidence in the older population may be related, in part, to a perceived decrease in the host defense complex. At the extreme, consider the increased frequency of malignancy in transplant recipients who are immunosuppressed. If researchers can find effective ways to boost the immune function of the host, then perhaps the body can perfect its ability to recognize the altered cell population and destroy it with its armies of cells. These cells are called *natural killer (NK) cells, macrophages,* and *cytotoxic T cells* (see Figure 24-1). Many institutions are working on tumor vaccines for just this purpose.

CANCER DETECTION

Cancer treatment works best if the tumor is identified at its earliest stage. Many cancers are clinically silent when they start so it is important for your doctor to go looking for them. The process of evaluating asymptomatic individuals who are at risk for the development of cancer by testing is called *screening.* Screening guidelines are published by the American Cancer Society and the National Comprehensive Cancer Network and constantly updated as new information becomes available. Cancer is the second leading cause of death in the United States (after heart disease) with over 500,000 Americans dying every year.

The National Comprehensive Cancer Network (NCCN) recommends for men a yearly digital rectal exam to identify any nodules in the prostate or rectum. A prostate specific antigen (PSA) blood test is recommended at age 50 for men who have at least a 10-year life expectancy. It should be offered to younger men if there is a higher risk, such as a father or brother being diagnosed at a young age. For African Americans, PSA screening should begin at age 45. It is believed that early detection of men with prostate cancer is saving lives each year.

For women, a breast self-exam should be done monthly, starting at the age of 20 (see Chapter 15). A physician exam should be obtained every three years from ages 20 to 39. Mammograms should be done starting at age 40 if there is no family history and repeated every year. If there is a family history of breast cancer in a sister or mother, then the first mammogram should be done earlier. It is felt that with early detection and improved treatment, more breast cancer deaths are avoided and more women have the choice to preserve their breasts.

With cancers of the colon and rectum, the majority are diagnosed in patients older than 50. These cancers are known to develop slowly over many years. Prior to the development of a frank invasive malignancy, there are precancerous changes that occur. These are described as polyps, which are often benign and can be eradicated before they can become promoted into a malignant cell population (see Figure 24-2). Since these new growths do not cause symptoms at first, screening has a very important role.

(figure 24-2)

The colon polyps known as adenomatous polyps are associated with a higher risk of developing into cancer. Polyps may be pedunculated (on a stalk) or sessile (flat).

The four methods of early detection include the fecal occult blood test, flexible sigmoidoscopy, colonoscopy, and double-contrast barium enema. (See Chapter 9 for colon cancer screening recommendations.)

Lung cancer is a malignancy also frequently diagnosed in the older population. Unfortunately, there is at this time no agreed-upon screening test. Years ago Mayo Clinic researchers conducted a trial to evaluate whether more lung cancers could be diagnosed earlier and lives saved if smokers were given a chest X-ray every year. The study did not show what the researchers had hoped. Newer studies are evaluating whether spiral CT scans of a smoker's chest, as shown in Figure 24-3, can identify tumors at an earlier stage than that identified by a chest X-ray. A study in Europe suggests that screening with chest CT may be the answer. The National Lung Screening Trial in the United States is attempting to confirm whether this is indeed the case. In addition, there is significant interest in trying to determine if some of the molecular changes associated with cancer could be identified in the sputum (phlegm produced by coughing). The hope certainly is that if lung cancer, which grows silently until it typically reaches a larger size, could be detected early enough, then a substantial number of the projected 150,000 annual deaths could be avoided.

To detect skin cancer early, a monthly skin self-exam is advised. The habit should become routine after a bath or shower using a full length and hand mirror to detect anything new. By using the mnemonic abcd (see Chapter 1), worrisome lesions can be detected early. In general, a physician should evaluate any abnormality on the skin that is changing in size, shape, or color. A doctor should be looking at a patient's skin every three years between ages 20 and 40 and then annually after 40.

Many other cancers, such as those of the esophagus, pancreas, or brain, have no early detection tests to screen the general population. In uterine cancer, the Pap test is effective to diagnose tumors of the lower part of the uterus called the cervix (see Figure 24-4) but is not able to detect most cancers of the *endometrium* (the lining) of the uterus. However, most endometrial cancers present early warning symptoms: abnormal bleeding or discharge.

In addition to following recommended screening guidelines, patients need to report new symptoms. A person who smoked 20 years ago and who notices a new hoarseness of his voice should be evaluated. Although that person could just have laryngitis, there is the possibility of larynx and lung cancer as well. A primary care physician should evaluate someone who experiences an unintentional weight loss and symptoms of fatigue. The public health key to saving more cancer lives is detecting malignancy early!

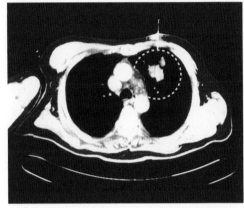

(figure 24-3)

CT scans of the lungs are being studied as a screening test to see if lung cancer (circled) can be detected at an earlier and more treatable stage.

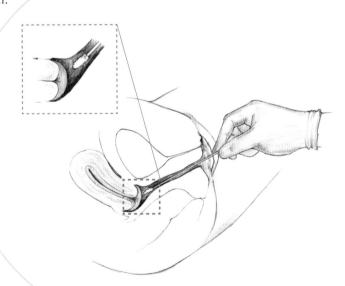

(figure 24-4)

A Pap smear requires a gentle brushing of the lower part of the uterus called the cervix. The cells are examined by a pathologist to determine if cancer or precancerous cells are present.

CANCER DIAGNOSIS AND STAGING

If the primary care physician tells you that an abnormality has been detected, the next step is establishing the diagnosis. This requires obtaining a sample of tissue so that the pathologist can review the material under the microscope to determine if the abnormality is benign or malignant. How this tissue is obtained depends on the part of the body affected and the physician's suspicions.

For example, if a physician tells a 60-year-old man that his PSA is abnormally high, the next step is typically a referral to a urologist. A urologist may run additional tests, such as the PSA density test, and consider a transrectal biopsy of the prostate gland. Once the biopsy is obtained, the pathologist then evaluates the tissue to determine if the sample is diagnostic of prostate cancer. If this is the case, a Gleason score will be assigned to the malignant sample. If a woman has a new lump in her breast, her primary care physician will order a mammogram be done to evaluate the area. A surgeon will likely then be called in to perform a biopsy of the lump. If the lump is benign, then nothing further is required. If, however, the lump is malignant, then a discussion of treatment options from mastectomy to lumpectomy and radiotherapy to the breast is pursued.

After the cell of origin is established, cancers are staged via the TNM classification system. The T indicates the size of the primary cancer in the site where it started. The T stage generally ranges from a T1 lesion, which is the smallest, to a T4 lesion, which is the most advanced. The criteria, which differentiate the different T stages, are specific for each cancer site. The N stage indicates whether lymph nodes are involved. The M stage indicates if the cancer has spread to other areas, such as the liver or bones. The combination of the TNM stages yields an overall stage, which ranges from stage 1 to stage 4. For example, if a woman is found to have a 1-cm invasive breast cancer that has not spread to lymph nodes and not spread outside the breast, then she is classified as having a T1N0M0, or stage I, breast cancer.

In order to stage a cancer properly, the physician must not only know the cell of origin but also actively investigate with laboratory studies and X-rays other potential sites of spread. The physician must have knowledge of which imaging studies are appropriate for each stage of disease. For example, if a patient coughs up blood and is found to have a 4-cm right lung cancer, which has spread to the lymph nodes in the middle of the chest, then other studies including a brain scan and a scan of the upper abdomen to evaluate the liver and adrenal glands will be pursued. A CT scan provides images of the patient's anatomy and is useful to determine whether structures either don't belong or are enlarged. For example, in the case of the patient coughing up blood, if a CT scan of the abdomen is done and there are multiple tumors in the liver, the concern would be that the lung cancer has metastasized to the liver. A biopsy of one of the lesions in the liver could be done to know with certainty whether this was the case. For staging cancer, positron emission tomogram (PET) scanning has been very helpful. A PET scan works by the injection of a specially prepared glucose solution that is taken up in metabolically active regions. Cancer cells are "hungry" and will incorporate the glucose into their cells. An X-ray is then taken to determine the location of these abnormal cell accumulations to see whether the cancer has spread to other sites. A PET scan in the same patient would likely show "hot," or positive, areas in the liver consistent with actively growing cancer cell colonies. PET scans are approved for the staging of melanomas and lymphomas, as well as cancers of the lung, breast, esophagus, head and neck, colon, and rectum. As more research accumulates on the usefulness of PET imaging, other sites could be added as well.

CANCER TREATMENT OPTIONS

The most important consideration before a person can begin to understand treatment options is to understand the specifics of his or her individual case. People are often influenced by what their relatives or neighbors faced and generalize this to their situation. Treatment options vary according to the condition of the patient, the aggressiveness of the cells seen in the biopsy specimen, and the stage of the cancer at the time of diagnosis. This information is best discussed with the patient by a multidisciplinary cancer team that includes the primary care physician, the surgeon, a medical oncologist, and a radiation oncologist. For example, the operation a neighbor had after being diagnosed with lung cancer has no bearing on the person whose cancer has already spread to the brain and liver.

It is critical that, before determining which treatment option to pursue, the patient have a solid understanding of the disease. What stage is the cancer? What is the appearance of the cells under the microscope (the grade of the tumor)? What do other blood tests indicate about the prognosis? Is the cancer potentially curable? If not curable, is it treatable? What effect would treatment have on quality of life? What is the prognosis with treatment? These are all-important questions that the patient must confront in order to make an informed decision with a team of physicians.

The other key consideration before determining an option is to fully recognize the condition of the patient's own body. If the patient is elderly with a limited life expectancy from medical causes, such as a serious heart condition, then the issue is whether the person would die from heart disease before effects of the cancer were felt. Physicians face these issues every day in the treatment of prostate cancer since the question is whether the cancer is growing slowly enough that it would not be expected to progress during the patient's lifetime. Estimating prognosis in prostate cancer is a function of the clinical stage, the Gleason score, and the PSA. If a 92-year-old with a serious heart condition has a favorable cancer (clinical stage T1, Gleason 6, PSA 5), then a course of watchful waiting would be very reasonable. A 62-year-old, on the other hand, with the identical treatment parameters, would be treated differently since his longer life expectancy would favor consideration of active curative treatment.

Second opinions are often useful ways for people to explore treatment options more fully and to understand the cancer facing them. Cancer treatment options range from the standard of care to the experimental. Modern medicine is evidence-based, which means the recommendation a physician makes to a patient is based on clinical studies. There are different levels of evidence that guide decision making. For example, some of the best studies in cancer have been done in women with breast cancer by the National Surgical Adjuvant Breast Program (NSABP). Years ago, women diagnosed with breast cancer underwent mastectomy routinely. In 1976, the NSABP enrolled over 1500 women in a trial (NSABP B-06) that evaluated the question of mastectomy (removal of the breast) versus lumpectomy (removal of the breast lump without removing the breast) versus lumpectomy *and* radiotherapy (see Figure 24-5). This trial has reported 20 years of follow-up in these patients and has not shown any survival advantage in those women treated with mastectomy. This forms the basis for the recommendation that in appropriately selected patients (women with a tumor less than 4 or 5 cm, in one quadrant of the breast, without connective tissue disorders, and with enough breast tissue for adequate cosmetic appearance after a lumpectomy), it is a woman's choice whether she wishes to keep her breast and undergo radiation following lumpectomy or whether she wishes to undergo a mastectomy. In essence, then, the standard-of-care option reflects the preponderance of medical evidence. In the experimental option, investigators enlist patients in clinical trials. The patients understand that they are part of a research study and that their treatment has not yet been proved to be effective. Major cancer centers tend to have more choices in experimental options, and some patients seek second opinions to find out whether they are eligible for any studies.

With the advent of the internet, many patients have access to unprecedented cancer information. Organizations such as the American Cancer Society and the National Cooperative Cancer Network have useful websites. Other patients find support groups online and learn through the experience of others. The individual patient should have as much information as possible in order to feel comfortable with the chosen treatment option.

TREATMENT MODALITIES

The two main types of cancer treatment options include local therapy and systemic therapy. The goal of *local therapy* is to eradicate the tumor in the area where it started, whereas *systemic therapy* takes aim at cells that may have migrated elsewhere throughout the body. In modern oncology (study of cancer), combinations of treatment are often recommended, with some patients benefiting from surgery, radiation, chemotherapy, and/or hormonal therapy. There are even molecular and gene therapies, which are being incorporated into treatment regimens.

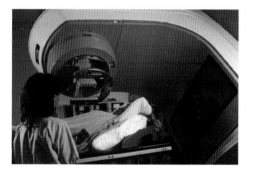

(figure 24-5)

Radiation for breast cancer.

Surgery continues to have a critical role in many cancers. The guiding principle is that a cancer surgery must be done. For the individual cancer, the surgeon must know which tissue is at risk. In general, this involves removal of the primary cancer as well as the neighboring lymph nodes. The surgeon must feel comfortable that the tumor has been removed with an adequate margin of normal tissue included (see Figure 24-6).

In breast cancer, surgery, radiation, chemotherapy, and hormonal therapy are often recommended in combination. After the diagnosis is known, the woman must decide whether she wishes to proceed with a lumpectomy and keep her breast or undergo mastectomy. In either case, the surgeon removes the visible tumor and also removes sample lymph nodes. If possible, a sentinel lymph node evaluation is performed to lower the risk of chronic arm swelling. A special dye is injected around the tumor site in the breast to locate the lymph node drainage position. The lymph nodes in this area are then removed and sent for evaluation. If this cannot be done, a more complete sampling of the lymph nodes, called an axillary dissection, is carried out. With the lymph nodes sampled, the pathologist can determine whether malignant breast cells have traveled to the lymph nodes. The medical oncologist uses this information to decide if the woman would benefit from chemotherapy. In this example, the patient first must undergo definitive surgery. If she chooses lumpectomy, then the physician team sees her after her surgery and estimates her risk of disease recurrence. Factors influencing this decision include the size of her tumor; if she had lymph node involvement and how many; if her tumor had a high grade under the microscope; if the tumor has estrogen and progesterone receptors; if the tumor overexpresses a protein called her-2-neu; and if the tumor shows evidence of lymphatic channel invasion. If the patient is felt to be at increased risk of recurrence based on her individual profile from her own tissue removed, then the medical oncologist must decide whether the patient should receive chemotherapy, antiestrogen therapy, or both. To complete the woman's treatment, she should undergo radiation to the breast, since that remains the standard of care. In this example, the medical oncologist recommends adjuvant therapy, since it is therapy being delivered to decrease the risk of a patient developing the disease again. If the patient above had presented with a 7-cm tumor, she may have been offered neoadjuvant chemotherapy to reduce the size of the cancer and allow a chance at breast preservation.

A medical oncologist prescribes chemotherapy, which can either be injected intravenously or taken orally. In either case, the effect is on the body's rapidly dividing cells. Depending on the agent used, the patient could experience hair loss, nausea, diarrhea, lowered blood counts, and so forth. The side effects depend on which drugs are delivered. In current

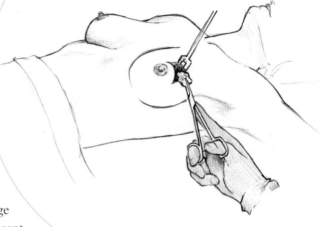

(figure 24-6)

Breast biopsy.

practice, there have been numerous advances in medications that the patient can take to prevent and minimize side effects. Chemotherapy can be given alone, either before local treatment or after local treatment. Chemotherapy can also be given concurrently with radiation therapy. In this setting, the effects of chemotherapy and radiation are synergistic.

Hormonal therapy is prescribed in both prostate and breast cancer. In prostate cancer, the effect of an injection to block testosterone is that the cells do not get the signal telling them to divide. The cancer is thus arrested until it can find a way to grow independently of the testosterone signal. In breast cancer, if the malignant cells express a receptor for estrogen, then the patient can take an antiestrogen pill for 5 years that will block the receptor and lower the risk of disease recurrence. The best-studied antiestrogen is the oral pill NOLVADEX (TAMOXIFEN). The NSABP has extensively studied this agent and discovered that it not only decreases the risk of breast cancer recurrence but also can help prevent a new cancer from developing. In addition, newer antiestrogens, such as ARIMIDEX, are becoming more commonly prescribed as clinical studies accumulate to document their effectiveness.

Molecular therapies have been designed to interfere with the cell's ability to communicate and receive signals. HERCEPTIN is an antibody effective in metastatic breast cancer that works by targeting a malignant cell that is overexpressing the her-2-neu protein. IRESSA is a selective inhibitor of a receptor (the *epidermal growth factor receptor,* or *EGFR)* on the cell's surface that acts inside the cell to block the growth pathways. It is being studied in many tumor sites and is showing promise. Other strategies being investigated by researchers include cutting off the tumor's blood supply, known as antiangiogenesis. Examples of two proteins being tested for their potential ability to deny tumors their source of nutrition are endostatin and angiostatin.

Gene therapies are also being developed. In the beginning of this chapter we discussed the concept of how a damaged cell can become immortal by the activation of growth promoting oncogenes or the inactivation of cancer suppressor genes. Researchers, such as those at the WM Keck Center for Cancer Gene Therapy at MD Anderson Cancer Center, are exploiting these pathways to see if redesigned genes can be transferred to the patient to reverse the process. For example, in some lung cancers, there is the loss of a tumor suppressor gene. There are ongoing trials to see whether normal function can be restored if a corrected copy of the gene is administered to the patient.

Radiation is a form of local cancer therapy that can be delivered internally, externally, or in combination. Radiation works by damaging the cell's "command center" so that it can no longer reproduce eternally. Internal radiation can be delivered at multiple sites, including the prostate, lung, bile duct, and cervix. Mechanisms of delivery range from implanting permanent radioactive seeds to inserting catheters, inside which temporary radioactive sources can dwell. Such mechanisms are examples of brachytherapy, which means the delivery of radiation to a short distance (see Figure 24-7). In men with prostate cancer, the object is to deliver a high uniform dose to the prostate and minimize the dose to surrounding normal tissue. Permanent seeds implanted directly into the prostate tissue accomplish this goal. A seed implant can be done as a definitive treatment or as a boost, depending on the patient's risk profile. The radioactive seeds decay over time and deliver the majority of the dose within a few months after the insertion. Temporary implants can also be done for men with prostate cancer. This involves the placement of catheters into the prostate and the insertion of radioactive sources inside the catheters for a short time. This is called *HDR brachytherapy,* since the treatment is delivered with a high dose rate allowing just a few minutes to complete. The source is then removed and the procedure can be repeated. Thirty years ago all temporary implants were delivered using *low dose rate (LDR)* technique. In these cases, the patient would have the implant in place for hours. Women with cervix cancer, for example, would undergo placement of a radioactive source into the vagina. The patient would stay in isolation in a hospital room for several days until it was time for the implant to be removed.

Alternatively, radiation can be delivered externally. This involves the patient coming to the radiation facility in repetitive fashion over many weeks. Typically, the patient comes in five days a week for anywhere from two to nine weeks, depending on the tumor site. The patient lies on the treatment table of a linear accelerator which generates high energy X-rays that penetrate through the patient's skin and concentrate in the tumor area. The treatment does not hurt and takes normally less than 15 minutes a day to deliver. There are side effects, which are cumulative and which depend on the site of the body being irradiated. For example, the only way a patient's hair would fall out from radiation would be if the radiation were being aimed at the head. Radiation can be delivered once a day or more often. If the treatment is delivered more than once a day, this is called *altered fractionation*. There are some tumors where studies have shown a benefit to increased daily fractionation, such as in small cell lung cancer and in some head and neck cancers.

The specialty of radiation oncology has benefited from the explosion of advances in computer technology achieved over the last decade. With improved treatment techniques, higher doses can be delivered to the tumor while keeping the doses to the adjacent normal tissues within acceptable limits. This has proved particularly successful in prostate cancer. With the advent of three-dimensional (3D) computer-planning techniques in the 1990s, the prostate, rectal, and bladder volumes could all be precisely delineated. With this computerized vision, physicians became able to use multiple beams to maximize the dose to the prostate gland and decrease the dose to the rectum and bladder. Studies validated this approach, showing increased biochemical (meaning PSA) control of the disease and low rates of long-term complications.

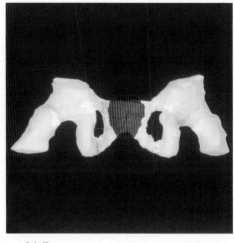

(figure 24-7)

Brachytherapy for prostate cancer. Radiation is delivered over a short distance by seeds implanted in the prostate.

Technology has evolved beyond 3D conformal techniques to include *intensity modulated radiation therapy (IMRT)*. IMRT spares normal tissue better while increasing the escalation of the therapeutic dose to the target tissue. Memorial Sloan-Kettering Cancer Center (MSKCC), in New York City, is one of the institutions pioneering new strategies. Investigators from MSKCC have compared their prostate cancer patients treated with 3D conformal radiation and IMRT and found that the incidence of late rectal bleeding dropped from 14 to 2% with implementation of IMRT. IMRT is being used in a number of other sites, such as breast, brain, and head and neck. Researchers from the University of California at San Francisco have reported improved tumor control and improved long-term salivary function by using IMRT for nasopharynx cancer.

Other new radiation treatment delivery systems include *stereotactic radiosurgery* and the *gamma knife*. With these two modalities, a patient with a brain metastasis, for instance, can receive a single fraction of radiation delivered to the tumor with minimal dose delivered to the adjacent normal brain tissue (see Figure 24-8). The treatment requires placing the patient in a device, which is fixed to the head so that precise treatment down to a few millimeters can be delivered. The goal of radiation treatment delivery is to minimize patient motion. In precise delivery to brain tumors, having the patient's head immobilized is critical. In other cancer sites, there is organ motion, which has to be accounted for. Another new advance is the BAT ultrasound system that allows men with prostate cancer to have their daily treatment field verified to account for the constant variations in bladder and rectal filling during the minutes of treatment.

Organ preservation is one of the dominant themes of cancer treatment in the twenty-first century. Focus has shifted toward identifying which treatments will destroy the tumor but leave the function of the underlying tissue intact. Chemotherapy and radiation therapy are often used concurrently in this regard. In sites such as the tongue base and bladder, combined programs can lead to the patient retaining satisfactory function of the organ.

QUALITY-OF-LIFE ISSUES

With constant advances allowing physicians to design more effective treatment regimens, there has been significant interest in studying the side effects of each regimen and its cost to the patient. Successful cancer treatment has been measured in survival. For years, physicians have focused on 5-year survival, median survival, relapse-free survival, and many other permutations. Yet with increasingly toxic regimens, much interest has been redirected toward *quality-adjusted survival*.

Lung cancer provides the clearest illustration of these principles. Since there is no screening test for lung cancer, many patients have advanced disease when they are first diagnosed. They quite often have cancer not only in the lung but also in the lymph node regions in the center of the chest. Most of the time, these patients are not candidates for surgery, and they are recommended to undergo chemotherapy and radiation

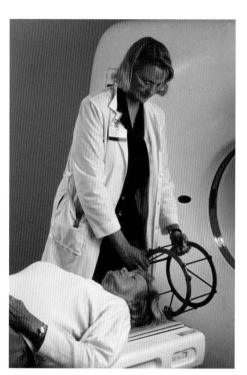

(figure 24-8)

Dr. Hoffe preparing a patient for a brain radiation treatment.

therapy. Radiation in the chest is complicated by the presence of the esophagus, which becomes irritated during therapy. Studies have shown that chemotherapy and radiation therapy in combination yield the highest chances for survival, yet most studies show only a 20% 5-year survival rate. A recent national trial showed that the average survival improved from 14.5 months if the chemotherapy preceded the radiation to 17 months if the radiation and chemotherapy were delivered concurrently. The question that researchers have been noting for the last few years, however, is at what price is that extra 2.5 months? In other words, if the time spent by the patient dealing with the added toxicity was subtracted from the improved average survival, then the survival would not actually be different. Quality-adjusted survival is one parameter that national investigators are focusing on to ensure that the toxicity of a better treatment is accounted for. Thus, the goal catapults to not only extending the patient's life but also achieving reasonable quality.

Treatment strategies are now focusing on how to better protect normal tissue. One approach during radiation delivery is to administer AMIFOSTINE, which is a radioprotector to normal tissue. Studies have shown a statistically significant lessening of severe dry mouth in head and neck cancer patients who received this medication during daily irradiation. IMRT is also being used to protect normal tissue differentially, so that the patient can tolerate the course of therapy better while the tumor is still receiving full dose.

COMPLEMENTARY MEDICINE

Many patients are interested in exploring alternative therapies after being diagnosed with cancer. Currently, many cancer institutions have embraced this interest and expanded it with extensive programs. At Memorial Sloan-Kettering Cancer Center, for example, there is a center of integrative medicine where a patient can receive counseling on herbal mixtures, can investigate therapeutic massage, and can focus on integrating a mind–body approach to dealing with the disease.

When patients receive chemotherapy or radiation therapy, it is important that their own physician knows which herbs they wish to take. Some herbal medicines can interact with traditional treatment, while others may be effective to improve the patient's well-being. Answers to questions about specific herbs can often be found on the internet (see "For More Information," below).

■

WHAT YOU NEED TO KNOW

▶ Cancer is the second leading cause of death in the United States after heart disease.

▶ If diagnosed with cancer, it is important that you understand the type and stage of the cancer.

▶ Find out your chances for a cure or, if incurable, the chances of treatment.

▶ Find out your treatment options, with benefits versus risks, including the projected outcome in terms of quality of life.

▶ Learn all you can about your cancer. By understanding the disease itself, you can then begin the process of dealing with it, knowing that in the twenty-first century, the resources for battle are many.

FOR MORE INFORMATION

▶ **American Cancer Society**
800-ACS-2345
Web: www.cancer.org

▶ **National Comprehensive Cancer Network**
888-909-6226
E-mail: patientinformation@nccn.org
Web: www.nccn.org

▶ **Memorial Sloan-Kettering Cancer Center**
1275 York Avenue
New York, NY 10021
212-639-2000
Web: www.mskcc.org
Web: www.mskcc.org/aboutherbs
The latter site includes information on specific herbs.

▶ **Mayo Clinic**
200 First Street SW
Rochester, MN 55905
507-284-2511
Fax: 507-284-0161
TDD: 507-284-9786
Appointment office: 507-284-2111
Web: www.mayoclinic.org/cancercenter-rst

▶ **National Cancer Institute**
NCI Public Inquiries Office
Suite 3036A
6116 Executive Boulevard, MSC8322
Bethesda, MD 20892
Web: www.nci.nih.gov

▶ **Dana-Farber Cancer Center**
Dana-Farber Cancer Institute
44 Binney Street
Boston, MA 02115
866-408-3324
Web: www.dana-farber.net

▶ **Moffitt Cancer Center**
Web: www.moffitt.usf.edu

▶ **Clinical Cancer Center at Stanford**
703 Welch Road, H-1
Palo Alto, CA 94304
Clinical trials office: 650-498-7061
Fax: 650-724-4042
E-mail: cancercenter@med.stanford.edu
Web: cancercenter.Stanford.edu

▶ **MD Anderson Cancer Center**
The University of Texas MD Anderson Cancer Center
515 Holcombe Boulevard
Houston, TX 77030
800-392-1611
713-792-6161
Web: www.mdanderson.org

To know how to grow old is the master-work of wisdom, and one of the most difficult chapters in the great art of living.

—*Henri Frederic Amiel*

SPECIAL HEALTH ISSUES

Aging optimally involves more than just the health of our bodies. History has demonstrated that many persons have lived fulfilling lives despite serious health challenges. Lance Armstrong amazed the world when he won the Tour de France after battling advanced testicular cancer. Franklin Roosevelt ascended to the presidency of the United States despite leg paralysis from childhood polio. Such stories are an inspiration to all of us. Yet there are unsung heroes in hospitals, nursing homes, and rehabilitation centers throughout the world. These are people determined to live fulfilling lives despite serious adversity.

In Part Two, the experts of *Optimal Aging Manual* discuss challenges and solutions that affect your psychosocial, spiritual, and physical health as you get older. Sir William Osler, a famous physician of the early 20th century, stated, "Patients should have rest, food, fresh air, and exercise—the quadrangle of health." The roles of nutrition, exercise, and sleep are addressed, but we also explore the problems that occur due to deficiencies or excesses in these areas. Obesity is an epidemic in the United States and is directly related to high blood pressure, diabetes, arthritis, lipid disorders, and heart disease. Exercise may help not only to control your weight but also to keep you mentally sharp, reduce your risk for falls, and prevent many diseases. Poor sleep can affect your mood and concentration and can make you more prone to motor vehicle accidents and falls. Sleep is not a time of inactivity but a dynamic state that al-

lows us to "recharge our batteries." Occasionally, such serious problems as sleep apnea may disrupt your sleep without your being aware of it. This can lead to daytime tiredness, difficulty with concentration, and accidents.

Our authors discuss the emotional issues encountered with aging. These include happy issues that you actually look forward to, such as retirement, but other issues may be very difficult, such as the need to go to a nursing home or assisted living facility. Some issues may be very sad; the death of a spouse or a child. Maybe your parent or spouse has Alzheimer's disease and you are feeling the stress associated with being a caregiver. Perhaps you yourself have wrestled with depression or anxiety. We hope the insights provided in this book will encourage you to seek the help you need if you have not already reached out for it. If you are talking to a psychiatrist or counselor, we hope that what you learn will help you cope a little better.

The process of dying and death are never comfortable topics. Yet we all will face the death of loved ones, as well as our own. Thankfully, compassionate people and organizations exist to help us face death with dignity and with the knowledge that pain and the other problems associated with dying can be effectively managed.

Many people say they fear disability more than death. They do not wish to be dependent on other people or a burden to their family. Progress in re-

habilitation medicine has allowed many victims of stroke, heart attacks, hip fractures, and amputation to return to independent living. In cases where the disability is more severe and permanent, rehabilitation may provide education and tools so that only a minor amount of assistance is required.

Do religion and health mix? You bet they do. Most studies suggest a positive effect of spirituality on health, but this is certainly not always the case. If your spiritual life is important to you, it plays a role in your overall health. Doctors and nurses are learning more about these issues from respected researchers, and you should feel free to include a discussion of your spiritual beliefs and concerns with your physician.

Do you feel intimidated when you go into the doctor's office? Do you have trouble communicating effectively with your physician? After all, you and your doctor have the same goals: making the best medical choices for you. You will learn techniques to help you get the most out of your office visit. You will also learn the pros and cons of alternative therapies and the importance of discussing them with your physician.

Over 90% of people over 65 years of age take one or more medicines. In Part Two, we explore how your body, as it ages, metabolizes your medicines. Although medicines are intended for good purposes, adverse side effects and drug interactions do occur. You will learn the importance of bringing a list of

your medicines or, better yet, the actual pill bottles with you to your doctor visits.

Your senior years are a time in your life when you want to travel and see new places and people from other cultures. You want to enjoy yourself on such trips, so certain precautions are advisable to protect you from annoying problems, such as seasickness and traveler's diarrhea, or very serious illnesses, such as malaria.

Aging may bring some unwanted changes in your body. You might not like those bags under your eyes, the extra chin, or the sagging breasts. Is plastic surgery an option? Age itself does not preclude cosmetic surgery. Naturally, you and your doctor need to weigh the benefits and risks.

The importance of staying fully involved with life cannot be overly stressed. Good nutrition, exercise, and proper rest are essential to maintaining a healthy body. Nevertheless, you are a social being, and how successfully you age can be measured by your relationships with your family, friends, and community. You will undoubtedly face challenges in your older years, and our hope is that this part of *Optimal Aging Manual* will provide the tools to assist you in writing your own chapter in the great art of living. Let's conclude this introduction with the following letter from Lorraine Rife, 83, of North Port, Florida, who is a great real-life example of someone who has overcome some of life's adversaries and who has been the author of her life's manuscript:

Dear Doctor O'Neil,

After the death of my husband, I moved to the country for some peace and quiet. Since I was 75 years old, I decided it was time to do all the things I wanted to do. The three most important things that were on my mind were: (1) Learn to play the piano. So I took music lessons, and I am still taking them today. (2) Become acquainted with the quilters in my area and start teaching quilting again, which I did. (3) Take good care of this poor old aging body that God has given me to live in all these years! So I signed up for Tai Chi, kickboxing, and karate.

Karate! Tang Soo Do, to be specific, means a great deal to me. I learned to breathe properly, drink about a gallon of water a day, keep on moving, and never give up!! I learned to appreciate and respect my body. I learned I always need a goal in life to make it worth living at this age. I still have two goals to accomplish, so I haven't given up yet!

After signing up for karate, it wasn't long before I was invited to attend the state tournaments in Jacksonville, Florida, to compete with others in my class. Well, the first one did it—I won a six-foot trophy. I was in "hog heaven"!!

During the next four years, I won seven first place trophies, one second place, one third place, and two state championships. My accomplishments have been recognized in numerous newspapers, and the Elder Hostel paper recognized me and three elderly men who were also doing something about the aging process.

After four and a half years of steady exercise and study, I was thrilled to earn my Black Belt in karate at the age of 79½. Tang Soo Do has ten belts, with three stripes for each belt. Sometimes if you worked hard, you could earn one stripe in a month. Thus, it would take you at least four months to earn one belt. I used to tease my instructors and say, "I am going to be a Black Belt by the time I am 80." Well, I made my goal!

I am thrilled to say that I have inspired other older people to get out and exercise, because they felt that they could do it if I could! I feel great today, and I want to thank you for your care all these years and the considerate things you have done for me. I love you for it!

Best wishes on your new book, and I'll expect a signed copy!

Lorraine Rife

LORRAINE RIFE

Retired!

> The Constitution only gives people the right to pursue happiness. You have to catch it yourself.
>
> —*Benjamin Franklin*

THE AUTHORS

25

SUSAN MAIXNER, MD, is a clinical assistant professor of psychiatry at the University of Michigan Health System. She completed her fellowship in geriatric psychiatry in 1999 at the University of Michigan. Prior to this, she completed her residency in general psychiatry at the University of Michigan and graduated from Medical School at the University of Nebraska Medical Center in 1993. Dr. Maixner is the director of the Geriatric Psychiatry Clinic at the University of Michigan Health System. Dr. Maixner's interests are behavioral disturbances in dementia and education issues in geriatric psychiatry. She is a member of the American Association for Geriatric Psychiatry's (AAGP) Teaching and Training committee, is a former Geriatric Caucus cochair of the American Association of Directors of Psychiatry Residency Training (AADPRT), and is the assistant training director for the University of Michigan Health System's fellowship in geriatric psychiatry.

KARYN S. SCHOEM, MSW, received her education at Brown University and Smith College School for Social Work. She has worked in community mental health, family service, outpatient geriatric medicine, and private psychotherapy practice settings. She is an adjunct lecturer, University of Michigan School of Social Work; on the faculty, Geriatric Psychiatry Core Curriculum, University of Michigan Medical School; a staff social worker, Turner Geriatric Clinic, University of Michigan Health System; and she maintains a private practice in geriatric psychotherapy and caregiver consultation. Ms. Schoem has presented papers nationally, including "Motivating Older Adults into Substance Abuse Treatment," for the American Society on Aging, and "Giving Voice to the Unexpressed: Creativity in Care Management," for the Gerontological Society of America. She is codirector of a program recognized by the Substance Abuse and Mental Health Administration as a "promising prevention program for older adults" and won a Best Practice in Mental Health and Substance Abuse award from the National Council on Aging. Her most meaningful professional achievement was being nominated by her colleagues in the Department of Geriatric Psychiatry for the honor of Social Worker of the Year, 2003.

25 | MENTAL HEALTH

For years, mental illnesses have incorrectly been considered to be a personal failure or a constitutional weakness. Research has shown these are biological illnesses, just like hypertension or diabetes.

ADAPTING TO CHANGE

RITA AND JOHN'S STORIES

Rita R., 78, has had macular degeneration, a loss of central vision, for five years. Several months ago, she had to give up driving, a real blow, since she had been a school bus driver most of her life and prided herself on her safety record. Afterward she moped around, not wanting to bother her family or friends to drive her places but feeling lonely at home. Finally, disgusted with herself, she called the transportation department and got a special cab card so that she could get around town. She joined a low-vision support group and discovered new gadgets to compensate her vision loss. She made some new friends in the group too.

John S., 69, loved his work. He had been an accountant with a prestigious firm for 35 years and was well respected in his town. The only thing that bothered him was his chronic back pain. He tried various therapies and equipment to make his back feel better, but the only thing that helped was taking rests periodically throughout the day. Since it gave his life meaning and structure, John S. refused to think about changing his work habits for many months. He pressed on in pain and feared doing a poor job until he read about an opportunity in the local senior news. An agency was looking for volunteers with financial and accounting experience to help older adults with tax and insurance questions. John S. and his wife reviewed their own financial plans and decided that they could manage without John continuing to earn an income. He signed up for the volunteer job, picked his own hours to accommodate his back problem, and said that he finds great satisfaction in helping others.

Rita R. and John S. were able to cope with frustrating and limiting changes by finding new ways to meet their needs for independence, satisfying work and interesting relationships. They struggled before giving up their old ways. At first they felt angry and resentful about the challenges they faced but, finally, were able to make their lives fulfilling again.

As we age, we still need a measure of independence, opportunities for decision making, a sense of purpose, positive relationships, a feeling of dignity and respect, a sense of safety, and hope for the future. In our older age, new challenges can threaten getting our needs met. We may need to use several different strategies to cope with change. Physical changes may require that we use equipment to get around or that we change our pace. Relationship changes may force us to look for new friendships or adjust to living alone. Work changes may make us reevaluate our skills and interests. Housing and financial changes may require us to sort out which of our possessions and activities are the most meaningful and which we can live without.

All these changes involve stress. Rita L. found herself praying to find the right answers. She remembered how she'd been devastated by the loss of an infant years ago and told herself that if she was able to get through that, she could certainly get through the loss of driving. To remind himself of his accomplishments, John S. hung his awards, diplomas, and certificates in his study at home. On his way out to his volunteer job, he would glance at this wall and feel inspired to do a good job in his new role.

BAT'S STORY

Bat L. became a widower at 87. His wife had been the social organizer for the couple, and he felt he could not take up this

25

role at his age. His children pushed him to join a group at the local senior center. Bat L. did it—not because he wanted to but because he wanted the children to stop pestering him and worrying about him. He never really liked it but he kept going. The people fretted about their illnesses and other petty issues. He did say, though, that it got him up and moving, got him into a sociable mood, and forced him to get some errands done while he was out. He supposed it helped him "keep in touch with the world." Bat L. was able to see some good points in going to a social group even though it wasn't really his "thing." For him, this was a successful adaptation to a change that disrupted his entire world.

Those of us who can look at situations from several points of view and who can see ourselves as having a range of strengths have an easier time adjusting to the changes of late life. On the other hand, those of us who see things in black and white, right and wrong, and who have a set idea of who we are and can be, have a harder time coping with change.

HELEN'S STORY

Helen H., 62, lived down the street from the bakery where she worked for 39 years. She and her partner, Alice C., had lived together for most of that time. When Alice had a massive stroke, Helen H. became her primary caregiver as well as the primary breadwinner for the family. After the visiting nurse service ended, Helen H. would come home at lunch time to care for her partner. She would spend every evening and weekend caring for her as well. Over the course of the year, Helen H. began to experience outbursts of anger at Alice. She felt guilty about her "short fuse" and vowed to be a better caregiver. She finally confided in her boss who suggested that she take a break from her routine. Helen H. was horrified at the suggestion. How could she leave her partner at home? How could she have a good time without feeling guilty? How could she let someone else care for Alice? Later that month Helen H. came down with a bad flu. She became dehydrated and was forced to spend a couple of days in the hospital. During that time, friends from the bakery took turns staying with Alice. They enjoyed visiting her, and she enjoyed their company. One young man took her around the block in her wheelchair, the first time she'd been out in months. When Helen H. came home, she was able to see that there might be other ways to meet both their needs. She wished she had taken her boss's advice long before getting sick.

(figure 25-1)

Caregivers must learn to take care of their own emotional and physical needs, as well as those of the person cared for. Networks of friends and family are crucial to caregivers. Formal respite and support services are also a big help. Caregiver support groups can provide emotional support by sharing experiences with other caregivers.

THEN AND NOW

The ways in which our ancestors managed the care of the mentally ill may look to us today more like tortures than treatments. In addition to confinement in insane asylums and straight jackets, other horrid practices included tranquilizing chairs and cold water immersion. *A Beautiful Mind* portrayed insulin-shock treatment for schizophrenia that fortunately has been abandoned since clinical study confirmed it does not work. Insulin was injected until the blood glucose fell so low that a seizure was induced. Frontal lobotomy is a surgical procedure in which a device that looks like an ice-pick was used to sever the nerve connections to the frontal lobe of the brain in order to make a disturbed person more docile.

Fortunately, psychiatry and the treatment of mental illness have come along way since the days when a mentally disturbed person was considered a witch or possessed by demons. Medical and psychological research has given us remarkable new insights into the workings of the human brain that have resulted in effective treatments for millions of people. This has helped many persons become happy and productive persons in society.

A major challenge to mental health in late life is the experience of caregiving. While there are premarital courses to teach couples how to adjust to being partners and parenting classes to teach parenting skills, none of us is formally taught how to be a caregiver to an older adult. How do we attend to our own needs while fulfilling the expectation that we provide care to someone else? In the above case, Helen H. was able to learn all the practical care routines that Alice C. required. She learned how to use a catheter. She learned how to fix food so that Alice C. wouldn't choke. The harder part, she found, was understanding the depression that Alice C. developed several weeks after the stroke. It seemed that Alice C. wasn't trying to get well. It seemed that she cut herself off from the intimate conversations they used to have. This was extremely difficult for Helen H. to accept. She could feel her anger rising up when Alice C. would call her to pick up something she had dropped on the floor.

Networks of friends and family are crucial to caregivers. Formal respite and support services are also a big help. Alice C. had read about a caregiver support group and suggested that her partner attend one (see Figure 25-1). Helen H. was surprised to find that she was so eager to blow off steam in front of total strangers. Several other participants gave good tips on finding reliable respite care, wheelchair van transportation, and accessible restaurants. This group eventually became Helen H.'s lifeline. At their suggestion, she went to the community's senior citizen center where her feelings of loneliness were dispelled by meeting new friends (see Figure 25-2).

All the stories above are examples of how people cope with changes that occur in later life. While there were some struggles involved, all the people were able to redesign their lives or their sense of themselves in order to move forward. The next section illustrates how various mental illnesses can prevent people from working through these kinds of changes. It also addresses how people can get help in moving forward again.

MENTAL ILLNESS

For years, mental illnesses have incorrectly been considered to be a personal failure or a constitutional weakness. Research has shown these are biological illnesses, just as hypertension or diabetes. These illnesses have physical symptoms, such as weight loss, constipation, insomnia, and shortness of breath. With advanced brain imaging techniques, we now can "see" differences in brain function as a psychiatric illness responds to medications and therapy. These illnesses are more disabling than most physical illnesses are: depression is second only to coronary artery disease in lost productivity, yet many people go undiagnosed, untreated, or undertreated. With proper treatment, most mental illnesses do get better, functioning improves, and relationships improve.

This chapter provides an overview of several common psychiatric disorders. A case example opens each section, and a discussion of the illnesses and treatment follows. A discussion of therapy and medications in more detail completes the chapter. We hope to provide information to help you understand the available treatments and seek help if necessary.

(*figure* 25-2)

Social interaction can help dispel feelings of loneliness and isolation by allowing older persons to meet new friends and enjoy recreational activities. Many senior citizen centers have sprouted up throughout the nation to meet the needs of the aging population.

MAJOR DEPRESSION

JOSEPHINE'S STORY

Josephine N. has been withdrawn for four months and stopped playing cards with friends, did not plant a garden, and refused to go to family parties. She can't explain why she doesn't feel right. Her clothes have become baggy, and her daughter nags her to eat. She finds it difficult to make decisions—even deciding which clothes to wear has become so overwhelming that she sometimes stays in her pajamas. She dreads nighttime, because she has not been able to fall asleep. This is the time she churns problems over and over in her mind, and they snowball and seem like they will never be conquered. It's an effort to get washed and dressed for the day. Her daughter notices that Josephine N. paces, wrings her hands, and rarely smiles. Josephine N. does not feel depressed. She feels like she's a burden to her family and wishes she could die in her sleep.

Five years ago she had similar symptoms and became dehydrated because of her fear that if she drank water, her subsequent urinating would clog the toilet. At that time, too, she was convinced there was no hope for her, and she attempted to take her own life. She was treated at that time for depression and within a few months had resumed playing cards, gardening, driving her car, and volunteering at the hospital.

Josephine N. has many of the features of major depression. Many older adults with depression, like Josephine N., deny feeling depressed, sad, or blue. A person does *not* need to feel depressed to have a major depressive episode.

Anxiety is a prominent symptom in many older adults with major depression. Approximately 50% of those who complain of anxiety actually have major depression. Detecting depression is very important so that the proper treatment can be prescribed. Many people will have some symptoms of depression, but not as many as Josephine N. These people can also be helped.

Occasionally, a depression can become so severe that it is called a psychotic depression.

A psychotic depression may occur when a person has fixed false beliefs (delusions) that can't be reasoned with, such as Josephine N.'s.

SHOCK TREATMENTS: ARE THEY SAFE?

The image of electroconvulsive therapy (ECT) or shock treatment that many of us have is the punishment given to Jack Nicholson as McMurphy in the 1975 movie, *One Flew Over the Cuckoo's Nest.* However, ECT is still used effectively in the management of major depression. Its role is definitely more limited with the advent of newer and safer medications for the treatment of depression. However, these medications may take weeks or months to exert their effects, and in some cases, an individual may not be able to take these drugs due to side effects. In very severe cases of depression where suicide is being contemplated, ECT can be life saving.

A small electric current is administered across the scalp to induce a seizure in the brain. Anesthesia is given beforehand to relax the muscles, so there is not much body movement. Some people have no side effects. Others may have some short-term memory impairment, confusion, or headache. These symptoms usually resolve with time. Over eighty percent of patients with depression who receive ECT have a favorable result making it the most expedient and effective treatment for severe depression. However, the benefit and risks always need to be evaluated by the patient, and an informed consent document will be required. If ECT has been recommended to you or a loved one, a second opinion from another psychiatrist may be helpful.

MAJOR DEPRESSION

A major depression is

> An ongoing sad or empty mood for two weeks or more
>
>   or
>
> A loss of interest in most activities for two weeks or more

Plus several of the following symptoms

- Sleep changes (trouble sleeping or sleeping too much)
- Appetite changes (down or up)
- Inability to enjoy life (including sex)
- Trouble with memory, concentration, or decision making
- Low energy; feeling fatigued
- Feeling restless, anxious, pacing, or wringing hands
- Feeling sluggish; lying around all day
- Crying more than usual
- Feeling guilty, hopeless, helpless, like a burden
- Thoughts of life isn't worth living; hoping to die in sleep
- Thoughts of committing suicide

You do not have to feel sad to have major depression!

prior depression with concern about the toilet plugging up. Some people may believe they have done terrible things, and God will punish their family. Other people may have hallucinations: seeing or hearing things that are not really there. Older adults may be more prone to psychotic depression.

LIKELIHOOD OF MAJOR DEPRESSION

Women have up to a 20% chance of having a major depressive disorder at some point in their lives, and men have a 10% chance. Some reports have shown lower rates of depression for older adults, but this is contested. There appears to be a genetic predisposition to depression in some people, especially those who have an early onset of their depression.

Depression's typical age of onset is before age 40, but there is also a late-onset depression. Fifty % of depressed patients over 60 years old report their first episode in late life.

People who are at increased risk of depression include those with physical illness as well as their caregivers. Those residing in nursing homes have a higher rate of depression, as do those with chronic pain. People with a current or past history of chemical dependency are also at risk. A prior history of depression is a very strong risk factor, as shown in the following table:

NUMBER OF DEPRESSED EPISODES	PROBABILITY OF ANOTHER EPISODE
One	50%
Two	70%
Three or more	90%

CAUSES OF MAJOR DEPRESSION

A change in brain metabolism can cause depression. Often, in first-episode depression, there is some stress that predisposes to depression, such as a move, retirement, death, family crisis, or financial stress. Some illness may alter the brain metabolism and predispose someone to depression. The brain *neurotransmitters* (chemicals that allow nerve cells to communicate with each other) most commonly implicated in depression are norepinephrine, serotonin, and dopamine. Research demonstrates that people who have experienced an early or ongoing stressor (such as being abused or witnessing abuse, losing a parent at a young age, or other traumatic incident) have long-standing elevations in the body's stress hormones (cortisol and others). These elevations increase susceptibility for depression and anxiety.

Depression is often a prominent feature of treatable medical conditions, such as high or low thyroid levels. Some medications have depression as a side effect.

DEPRESSION AND OTHER ILLNESSES

Often, depression is not recognized if other illnesses occur. The signs of depression are incorrectly thought to be a progression of the other disease or a reaction that would be expected. Because of lack of recognition by doctors, families, and patients, treatment of depression is neglected, leading to greater disability and poorer outcomes.

Heart disease and stroke: Thirty-three % of those who had a heart attack will become depressed in one year (versus 5% of those without heart attacks), and 17% of depressed patients die within six months of a heart attack (versus only 3% of those who are not depressed after a heart attack). Up to a third of those who have suffered a stroke may have depression. Depressed people do worse in rehabilitation, and have more residual disability.

Diabetes: Diabetes doubles the risk for depression, especially when people have more diabetes-related complications, and people who are depressed are at a greater risk of developing diabetes. Depressed patients do worse physically and mentally, and blood sugars are less well controlled if the depression is not treated (with medications or talk therapy).

Parkinson's disease: Up to 50% of patients who have Parkinson's disease may have a concurrent depression, and depression or anxiety may occur a few years before the diagnosis of Parkinson's is made. Treatment of depression improves functioning.

CANCER

Although 25% of people with cancer are depressed, only 2% of people with depression and cancer are treated for depression.

GRIEF AND DEPRESSION

Grief after a loss is a normal reaction. People grieve to varying degrees, depending on the type of loss they experience. People may grieve when

(figure 25-3)

Depression is not an unusual after a heart attack or bypass surgery.

they relocate, retire, lose a pet, lose physical or mental abilities, and, of course, lose family or friends. People report feeling shock, anger, guilt, fear, and sadness in the weeks and months following a loss. Over time, the feelings of grief become more bearable, and the grieving person is able to refocus on the pleasures of life as well as the experience of loss. Many support and education groups exist to help people of all ages integrate the experience of loss into their lives. Hospice organizations offer such groups for the general public. (Chapter 40 has an extensive discussion on bereavement.)

In acute bereavement after a death or loss, many depressive symptoms are common and gradually improve. Grief is not the same as depression. However, clues to major depression in bereavement include extreme weight loss, social isolation, ongoing severe sleeping problems, preoccupation with death, wanting to die, or thinking of suicide. These symptoms are not normal in bereavement and need immediate treatment for depression.

SUICIDE

Ten % of all people who experience major depression, bipolar illness, or schizophrenia will commit suicide. Older adults have the highest completed suicide rate of all ages. Most people who have committed suicide had an untreated or undertreated depression.

Caucasian men living alone with chronic medical problems and recent losses have the very highest rate of suicide. Persons who have alcohol, street drug, or prescription drug problems have a higher risk as well.

If you or someone close to you has suicidal thoughts, a doctor must be told immediately. Talking about suicide with a health care provider will allow a person to get treatment. Discussing suicide does not strengthen this idea; rather, it allows a person to get help.

Depression is a treatable illness. Suicide is a permanent solution to a temporary problem, but a severely depressed person may not be able to see this. It is recommended that all guns and ammunition should be removed from the house if someone is suicidal.

TREATING DEPRESSION

If suffering from depression, talk to your family doctor. Most primary care clinicians are up to date on depression treatment. We recommend a psychiatrist become involved if a depression does not respond to treatment, is severe, or has a psychosis associated with it. Also, as noted above, your doctor may want to order blood work to make sure there are no medical problems occurring that look like depression. Also, be sure to tell your doctor about all medications you are taking (prescription, over the counter, and vitamin or herbal supplements), to look for side effects and drug interactions.

There are two ways to treat depression: *somatic treatments* (medications and electroconvulsive therapy) and *talk therapy* (counseling, including cognitive–behavior therapy and interpersonal therapy). Details about

(figure 25-4)

If you think you suffer from depression, talk to your family doctor. A psychiatrist may be recommended if you are not responding to treatment or if your depression is severe.

specific medications and therapies are in the section, "Treatments for Psychiatric Illness," below.

Talking therapies have demonstrated efficacy in mild to moderate depression. In moderate to severe depression, medications should be considered. Usually, a combination of talking therapy and medications is superior. Electroconvulsive therapy (ECT) is a form of treatment in which a seizure is induced after the patient has been medicated. These treatments are still used and considered safe with proper monitoring. They are especially useful in a depression with severe agitation or psychosis or if a person cannot tolerate medications.

Medications typically used are the antidepressant agents. The selective serotonin reuptake inhibitors (SSRIs) and the "other antidepressants" (BUPROPION, MIRTAZAPINE, VENLAFAXINE) are first-line. Seventy % of people will respond to the first antidepressant chosen. The response time is longer in older adults: treatment response may show at four to six weeks but not be complete until 10 to 12 weeks. Sometimes, medications from other classes (mood stabilizers, antipsychotics, antianxiety, and stimulants) may be used with antidepressants to help control other symptoms or augment the antidepressant response.

Medications should be taken for a minimum of six to nine months after a person has returned to a normal mood. Persons who stop medications before this time are subject to a relapse of depression, which may then last longer, become more severe, and become much more resistant to treatment.

The same medication dose leading to a response should be continued for the entire course of treatment. Maintenance antidepressant medications have been shown to prevent recurrences of depression. Lifetime antidepressant maintenance medications should be considered for the following conditions:

- Two or more previous episodes of depression
- Severe disability (being nonfunctional or bed-bound) from depression
- A very slow response to treatment
- A psychotic depression

BIPOLAR ILLNESS

ARNOLD'S STORY

Although not a spendthrift during his 40 years of marriage, Arnold K. has had occasional spells of one- or two-month periods of "ants in his pants." Requiring only a couple of hours of sleep, he thought himself the next Thomas Edison and started many projects without bringing any of them to completion. During such periods he would buy a new sporty car, a new hunting dog, and many other items. Arnold K. would forget to eat meals while talking rapidly. His family and friends asked him what kind of dope he was on, but he said that he felt great and nothing was wrong. However, he was easily irritated with the children and still is on rocky ground with two of them. He would often get quite drunk during these spells although he was otherwise not a heavy drinker. His marriage almost ended 30 years ago after he had an affair during one spell. Often, after these spells, he would become very withdrawn for a few months. His wife Cindy K. had to cancel two cruises Arnold had arranged, when high, because he no longer wanted to go.

He was hospitalized once about 25 years ago after threatening the police officer who stopped him for reckless driving. Arnold K. stopped the medication as soon as he got out of the hospital, because he said he felt fine and nothing was wrong.

After Cindy K. threatened to leave him for his running through their retirement savings during one of his highs, Arnold began seeing a psychiatrist and went on medication. A year later, he still claimed to feel fine and was only getting treatment because of Cindy's threat to leave otherwise.

Formerly known as "manic depression," bipolar illness is characterized by having at least one *manic episode* and may also have recurrent major depression spells.

Arnold K. demonstrates many characteristics of bipolar disorder: the manic symptoms, noted above, and also having major depression episodes. People in a manic state often do not recognize they are having problems, making treatment difficult.

LIKELIHOOD AND CAUSES OF BIPOLAR DISORDER

About 1% of the population has the full-blown bipolar type I. More people may have bipolar type II, which has less disruptive manic symptoms. Men and women are equally affected. Like depression, it is thought that

MANIC EPISODE

A manic episode involves

- A week or more of an abnormally elevated or irritable mood, interfering with normal functioning or relationships

Plus several of the following

- Increased self-esteem and/or grandiosity
- Sleeping less but feeling rested
- Talking rapidly and much more
- Racing thoughts
- Distractibility; inability to focus
- Increased activity (more sociability, sex, work, and/or writing)
- Agitation
- Spending money excessively; running up debts
- Promiscuity
- Poor investments
- Psychotic symptoms (see the section, "Schizophrenia")

dysregulation of neurotransmitters plays a role in bipolar illness. There are genetic predispositions too.

Bipolar illness usually declares itself before age 40. New cases starting above age 60 need a thorough evaluation. Substance abuse is quite common in people with bipolar disorder.

TREATING BIPOLAR DISORDER

Most people have a recurrent course of bipolar illness, with repeated manic and depressed spells if untreated. Medications are central to the treatment of bipolar illness. Ongoing medication treatment has been shown to prevent or reduce the severity of recurrences. Preventing recurrences is important, because of the grave personal and social consequences of manic episodes. Regular sleep cycles are important: Sleep deprivation can trigger manic episodes. Therapy can be helpful too, to help recognize early signs of a depressed or manic phase and also to help sort out the repercussions of previous episodes.

Mood stabilizers provide the foundation of medication treatment for bipolar disorder. Mood stabilizers treat both the manic and depressed phases of bipolar disorder. LITHIUM (LITHOBID, ESKALITH) is the best researched with the most evidence for acute treatment and prevention of future cycles. VALPROIC ACID (DEPAKOTE, DEPAKENE) also has Food and Drug Administration (FDA) approval. CARBAMAZEPINE (TEGRETOL) has been used for a number of years. Antidepressants, and occasionally antipsychotics, and other medications may be added. Your doctor must be told of any prior manic episodes if an antidepressant is given for a depressed episode. If no mood stabilizer is present, an antidepressant can cause someone with bipolar disorder to become manic.

ANXIETY DISORDERS

HARRY'S STORY

Harry A. has been complaining to his wife about feeling keyed up and on edge for most of the past year. He worries about their finances (which are fine), he worries about his health (which is also fine); he worries about traveling; and he worries about his backyard (which is beautiful). He feels fatigued; his arms and legs move like lead. He is easily distractible. And Harry A. feels like this throughout the day.

Five years ago, he had "anxiety attacks." A doctor told him they were panic attacks: Harry A. felt an impending doom coming over him and was afraid of fainting, having a heart attack, going crazy, or losing control of his bowels and bladder. He became short of breath, felt his chest going tight while his fingertips and mouth went numb, had butterflies in his stomach, felt light-headed, and proceeded to shake. These intense spells lasted 5 to 10 minutes. He was afraid of having additional episodes and had his wife drive him to work. His doctor checked his thyroid, found the level of thyroid hormone was too high, and treated it. The panic attacks went away.

Anxiety is an unpleasant, vague feeling which signals an impending danger. An anxiety disorder is characterized by excessive worry that is out

(table 25-1*)*

ANXIETY DISORDERS

DISORDER	CHARACTERISTICS
Panic disorder	Has panic attacks: Intense, sudden onset of an impending feeling of doom, losing control, or going crazy; physical symptoms including palpitations, butterflies in stomach, nausea, numbness in fingers or toes, throat constriction, shortness of breath, sweating, and tremors. Symptoms last about 10 minutes, and the person fears having another attack and changes lifestyle to avoid this.
Agoraphobia	Fear of going out, often in response to panic attacks. May also be due to fear of crime or falls.
Generalized anxiety disorder (GAD)	Excessive anxiety and worry; causes impairment in functioning. People may feel restless, on edge, fatigued, tense, or irritable and have trouble concentrating or sleeping.
Posttraumatic stress disorder (PTSD)	After experiencing or witnessing a traumatic incident, person may feel numb, detached, or dazed and can't remember details of the event, which feels unreal. May have nightmares, daydreams, intrusive thoughts of the event. Avoids situations that recall memories. Has trouble sleeping; is irritable, on guard, and restless. Impaired daily functioning; may be distant in relationships.
Simple phobia	Fear of heights, blood work, dogs, cats, spiders, snakes, flying, etc.
Social phobia	Fear of being in a social situation in which one could be scrutinized by others (e.g., public speaking or performance anxiety). Some people experience extreme anxiety in daily situations: Not going to a meeting or answering the phone, because of fearing what the other person thinks of them.
Obsessive-compulsive disorder (OCD)	*Obsessions:* Unwanted thoughts, impulses, or images that pop into a persons mind, and cause distress. People know these are just thoughts but the thoughts cause great anxiety. Examples include fearing infection or fearing sexual thoughts. *Compulsions:* Repetitive behavior or mental acts to reduce distress. Examples include washing hands so often that the hands bleed or praying the same prayer eight times and then counting to eight times.

of proportion to an event and interferes with daily activities. Some anxiety is beneficial; it helps us focus and protects us from danger. However, if anxiety is set off without a real danger, people cannot function. Anxiety is a very physical experience, involving the heart, lungs, stomach, bowels, bladder, and skin. Many people do not recognize anxiety and look for other causes. Table 25–1 shows several different anxiety disorders.

Harry A. has generalized anxiety disorder. He worries excessively about many subjects and finds it too difficult to focus because of the anxiety. He had panic attacks in years past, but this was due to a high thyroid level. As often is the case with anxiety and depression in older adults, medical problems can present with psychiatric symptoms.

LIKELIHOOD AND CAUSES OF ANXIETY DISORDERS

Anxiety disorders are the most common mental illness, with about one out of five people having the disorder at a single point in time and one out of three having an anxiety disorder in his or her lifetime.

There is a genetic predisposition to anxiety disorders: The most striking figure is almost 50% of people with panic disorder have a family member with panic disorder. Substance abuse is more common in people with anxiety disorders.

Anxiety disorders usually begin in young adulthood, and will flare up periodically through the years. It is unusual to have an anxiety disorder start in later years, but it may. A thorough physical exam and blood work need to be done before declaring a new anxiety disorder in an older adult. A major depressive episode often masquerades as anxiety in later life too.

It is thought that abnormal regulation of brain neurotransmitters predispose a person to an anxiety disorder. The neurotransmitters include serotonin, norepinephrine, and gamma-aminobutyric acid (GABA). Some people with physical anxiety disorders may have a sensitive autonomic nervous system which requires only a little stimulus to produce anxiety symptoms.

TREATING ANXIETY DISORDERS

Cognitive-behavior therapy is the primary treatment for anxiety disorders and gives a person the tools for long-term management without medication (see the section, "Treatments for Psychiatric Illness," below).

Medications are commonly used too. Antidepressants, especially the SSRIs, have been shown to help anxiety disorders, as well as panic, generalized anxiety disorder, obsessive-compulsive disorder, posttraumatic

(figure 25-5)

Anxiety can be associated with many different symptoms, such as tension headaches, rapid breathing, a racing heart, stomach distress, and shaky hands. Treatment can reduce or eliminate these symptoms.

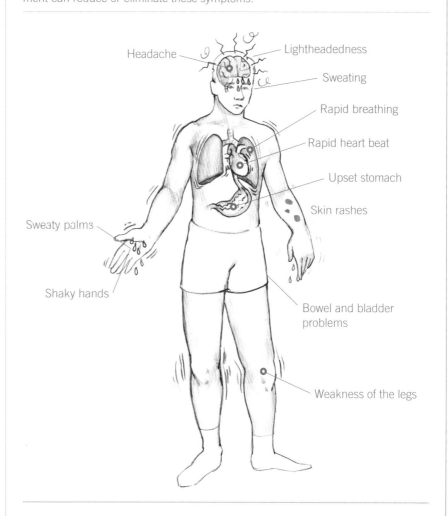

Headache — Lightheadedness

Sweating

Rapid breathing

Rapid heart beat

Upset stomach

Skin rashes

Sweaty palms

Shaky hands

Bowel and bladder problems

Weakness of the legs

stress disorder, and social phobia. VENLAFAXINE (EFFEXOR) might be tried for generalized anxiety disorder. For many people, the antidepressant category of medications is helpful because many people have a concurrent depression. The antidepressants are not addictive but do not offer quick relief; it may take 8 to 12 weeks to see a full response.

Anxiety medications are helpful, too, especially in the short term. The benzodiazepines—tranquilizers such as DIAZEPAM (VALIUM) and ALPRAZOLAM (XANAX)—offer relief in about 30 minutes, but the anxiety symptoms usually return after the medication wears off. The benzodiazepines have the potential for addiction, which is a downfall. Also, older adults metabolize medications more slowly, causing more side effects with the benzodiazepines, including falls, gait imbalance, sleepiness, and clouded thinking.

Some are safer than other in older adults (see the section, "Treatments for Psychiatric Illness," below).

BUSPIRONE (BUSPAR) is a nonaddictive anxiety medication, which is most helpful for generalized anxiety. It has few side effects and works well in some people but has little effect in others. One may have to take buspirone a few weeks to see its effects.

SCHIZOPHRENIA

JANE'S STORY

Jane S. has seen her family only briefly and intermittently during the past 40 years. However, after Jane S. had fallen and was hospitalized for a broken hip, the hospital social worker got in touch with Jane S.'s family, who visited and asked how they could help Jane S.

Since her mid-20s, Jane S. has been suspicious of her family and thought they were plotting against her to steal her clothes, money, and ideas. They often heard her talking to herself, carrying on a conversation with an invisible person who Jane S. would yell at to be quiet. She talked about god, angels, and devils while walking around town. She referred to herself as the "next prophet." She was never able to hold a job or maintain a relationship because she was too suspicious of everyone around her. She lived in homeless shelters or on the street. On several occasions, her family barely recognized her but offered financial support.

Schizophrenia is a devastating illness in which a person cannot distinguish reality from fantasy. People with schizophrenia have psychotic symptoms (see Table 25-2), trouble maintaining close relationships, trouble functioning at work, and difficulty taking care of themselves, as demonstrated by Jane S. Often, too, people may have trouble communicating due to disorganized speech. People may have activity disturbances to the extremes: being in constant motion or nearly frozen. People suffering from schizophrenia usually have little facial expression and have difficulty motivating themselves. In contrast to patients with nonpsychotic depression or anxiety disorders who recognize something is wrong and seek help, most people with schizophrenia lack the insight that they are ill, making treatment challenging. Very few people with schizophrenia are violent, contrary to what is portrayed on television.

Several types of psychotic symptoms are listed in Table 25-2. Other illnesses like major depression, bipolar illness, substance abuse, and dementia can have psychotic symptoms, but in schizophrenia the symptoms are the prominent feature. It is important to get a complete evaluation if psychotic symptoms are present to rule out any medical conditions.

Many people in the past had been diagnosed as "schizophrenic" when actually they had psychotic symptoms associated with a major depression or bipolar disorder.

LIKELIHOOD AND CAUSES OF SCHIZOPHRENIA

About 1% of the population has schizophrenia, and men and women are equally affected. Usually the age of onset in men is before age 25, and in women before age 35. Less than 10% of schizophrenia occurs at ages above 60. Symptoms tend to have exacerbations and remissions, but may not entirely clear, even with treatment. The negative symptoms (flat facial expression, reduced speech, and motivation troubles) respond less to medications than do the positive symptoms (hallucinations and delusions). If schizophrenia develops late in life, a thorough medical, neurological, and psychiatric workup must be done. People with late-onset schizophrenia tend to be female, married, and have been fairly socially connected.

There are several theories on the causes of schizophrenia. Research has shown that *neurons* (nerve cells) in certain areas of the brain did not migrate in a uniform fashion during brain development in people with schizophrenia. For unknown reasons, more people with schizophrenia are born in the late winter and early spring, with associated theories on potential viral mechanisms (not proven). There appears to be some genetic predisposition as well, with about a 10 times greater risk for developing schizophrenia if a sibling or parent is also affected. Neurotransmitter

(table 25-2)
PSYCHOTIC SYMPTOMS*

SYMPTOM	CHARACTERISTICS
Hallucination	Experiencing a nonexistent sensation involving
Auditory	Hearing
Visual	Sight
Tactile	Touch
Olfactory	Aroma
Gustatory	Taste
Delusion	Fixed false beliefs. Paranoid themes, such as someone is out to harm or steal, are very common. Other themes include self-importance; believing one is dead or the body is doing unusual things; sex; or religion.
Illusion	Misperception of something actually there, such as a picture on the wall is a person.
Idea of reference	Assumes that others, the radio, and/or the television are talking about the person. Usually has paranoid themes.

*Not limited to schizophrenia.

abnormalities have been researched as well, looking at the dopamine, gamma-aminobutyric acid (GABA), and glutamate systems.

TREATING SCHIZOPHRENIA

Treatment for schizophrenia includes medications, community services, and therapy (see the section, "Treatments for Psychiatric Illness," below). Community services are an important part of treatment, to ensure that the patient has adequate food, shelter, and medical care. Therapy may be helpful, though not widely used in the United States. It appears the United Kingdom has demonstrated some benefit in symptoms with a modified cognitive-behavior therapy.

Medications used to treat schizophrenia have dramatically changed in the past decade, with fewer short- and long-term side effects but still working on the dopamine neurotransmitter system. The core medications used to treat schizophrenia are the antipsychotics. It is recommended that a person with a new onset psychosis be prescribed an "atypical" antipsychotic. They seem to be better tolerated, have fewer acute side effects, and fewer long-term side effects of medication-induced movement disorders. For people with a long-standing illness doing well on an older "typical" antipsychotic, it is not necessary to change them to a newer drug unless there are problems with the old medication.

Other medications are often used in conjunction with the antipsychotics for schizophrenia: mood stabilizers, antidepressant, and antianxiety drugs.

DEMENTIA WITH BEHAVIORAL DISTURBANCE

MELISSA'S STORY

Melissa G., who is 85 years old and was diagnosed with Alzheimer's disease five years ago, keeps asking her daughter (with whom she lives), "When will my mother be home?" Her daughter responds, "Granny died 40 years ago. Will you quit asking about her?" Melissa G. begins crying and refuses to eat the rest of her dinner. Her daughter is frustrated.

Although dementia is discussed specifically in Chapter 26, here we present the psychiatric perspective on diagnosing and managing dementia.

Dementia of the Alzheimer's type can have a concurrent major depression associated with it up to 40% of the time. Treating the depression can improve daily functioning, thinking, anxiety, appetite, and sleep. Psychotic symptoms are quite common in the middle stages of Alzheimer's disease. Common symptoms are delusions that someone is in the basement, "I need to go home," the caregiver or spouse has been replaced by an impostor, that people break in and rearrange or steal things, or that family members who have long been dead are alive again. People may also have hallucinations: hearing or seeing nonexistent people. Unfortunately, the caregiver is usually the target of suspicion, making care both difficult and frustrating. Wandering, repeated questions, and verbal outbursts also occur.

(*figure* 25-6)

Alzheimer's disease is associated with behavioral problems that require medical treatment. The family physician or internist can treat these problems, but a psychiatrist may be consulted if the symptoms are severe or not responding to the initial treatment.

(figure 25-7)

Pets have a very helpful role, allowing a person to overcome loneliness. They may actually provide a calming influence to persons with Alzheimer's disease. Many nursing homes have involved their residents in pet therapy. A pet can sometimes connect with a person if human relationships have failed.

In frontal-temporal dementias (like Pick's disease), a personality change often precedes memory problems. Common behaviors include becoming uninhibited: being more irritable, saying inappropriate things, getting angry easily, increased sex drive, and increased appetite for sweets. This can be very frustrating and embarrassing for family members.

In Lewy body dementia, people often have visual hallucinations—seeing imaginary people—before memory problems are evident. People have symptoms similar to Parkinson's too (shuffling gait, tremor, or little expression) and have memory fluctuations.

Environmental and behavioral treatments are preferred in people with dementia, but medications are used to improve quality of life for the patient. Medications are prescribed to target the symptoms and include use of antidepressants (for depression, anxiety, impulse control problems, agitation, sleep, and appetite), mood stabilizers (for impulsivity, anger, and agitation), antipsychotics (for psychotic symptoms, agitation, impulsivity, and anger), and, occasionally, anxiety medications. Benzodiazepines are usually not recommended due to their mind-clouding side effect. The medicines used to treat Alzheimer's disease, the cholinesterase inhibitors, are showing promise for such behavioral symptoms as anxiety, agitation, and wandering.

Environmental and caregiver behavior recommendations include keeping a calm environment, providing orientation cues, not testing the person's memory, having pets around (if the person likes animals), and playing music the person enjoys.

Challenging a delusion is not recommended in a patient with dementia. It usually causes more distress for the person and makes them less cooperative.

Melissa G. experiences the news of her mother's death as the first time she's been told, and it is very distressing to her. Saying something reassuring or changing the topic works better for both the patient and caregiver. For example:

Her daughter could have replied, "I understand you are feeling worried about your mother. I've been assured everything is okay. How about we eat dessert now and then watch our game show on TV?"

This reply accomplishes four aims: recognizing, naming, and reflecting the underlying feeling (worry); reassurance (everything is okay); redirection (finishing the meal); and distraction (watching TV).

PERSONALITY DISORDERS

In general, personality is established by young adulthood. Personality differences show up in the ways people make and keep relationships, how they view the world, and how they behave. These styles continue into healthy older adulthood. For instance, people who have always been optimistic and trusting tend to stay that way as they age. People who have been suspicious or solitary tend to stay that way too.

ETHEL'S STORY

Ethel O. is a divorced woman with one son, two daughters, and two grandchildren. Her children are frustrated because she puts "guilt trips" on them frequently if they choose to spend time with their own children rather than with her. It seems Ethel O. is becoming helpless and dependent and requesting her children come and do errands for her, especially if they have events with their children. When the children express frustration with her "selfishness," Ethel O. says, "You'll be sorry when I'm gone!" and stomps out of the room. They hear her mutter, " I might as well be dead; they don't care about me anyway."

While her children were growing up, Ethel O. attempted suicide several times: once cutting her wrists and another time overdosing on sleeping pills mixed with alcohol. Her moods would swing rapidly, often several times a day. She could be very nice and loving and would then switch and say hurtful things. For her, everything is right or wrong, she either loves you or hates you, and you are either good or bad. She has never been able to find the middle ground. She had a volatile off-on relationship with their father and with several other men. Ethel O. has dropped hints she was abused as a child and that her mother was depressed and spent much time in bed. Now, Ethel O. complains of being depressed, empty, and lonely her entire life. The children offer to take her to get help; however, she declines, because she went to see a therapist for one session, declared it made her feel worse, and refused to go back. Her primary care doctor has prescribed medications, but she only takes them intermittently. With regard to her physical health, it seems she asks for help and then refuses it. She seems to sabotage relationships. If someone makes her upset, she shuts them off or alienates them, rather than discussing how she has been hurt.

People who have extreme maladaptive personality traits and long-standing difficulties in most relationships may be diagnosed with a **personality disorder**. Personality disorders, like personality styles, develop by early adulthood and persist into older adulthood. Sometimes these disorders become less extreme as a person ages. Sometimes people become "more" of what they were as younger adults, particularly if they have a medical illness or other stressors. People with personality disorders have difficulty seeing their own behavior and how it affects others. Because of their extreme personality characteristics, adapting to the changes of aging can be very difficult. Without a range of coping strategies, they can be very susceptible to depression and anxiety. Taking care of an older person with a personality disorder can be challenging. As in the case of Ethel O., her children felt guilty and frustrated with her unpredictable demands. In this kind of case, some caregivers opt to manage their loved one's care from a distance, employing others to provide the "hands-on" care. This allows the family to make sure that care is provided while avoiding hurtful interactions.

There are several different types of personality disorders. Ethel O. had developed a *borderline personality disorder* earlier in life. Her extremes of hot and cold behavior and difficulty maintaining stable relationships are typical of this kind of disorder. (She has mood swings but does not have bipolar disorder. Bipolar disorder mood swings occur over weeks or months, not several times a day.) Other types of personality disorders are listed in Table 25-3.

LIKELIHOOD AND CAUSES OF PERSONALITY DISORDER

Personality disorders are relatively rare. In the general population between 1 and 3% of people are estimated to have a personality disorder. Both men and women are susceptible to personality disorders. Depression and anxiety disorders commonly coexist with personality disorders, as does substance abuse.

One theory about how people develop a personality disorder includes aspects of both nature and nurture. A person may be born with a great sensitivity to reactions from the people and environment around him or her. If the environment is extremely inconsistent or abusive, the young person may have great difficulty developing a balanced sense of self and, instead, develop extreme personality traits in an attempt to make sense of a chaotic or unpredictable world.

People develop personality disorders by early adulthood. It is thought that these disorders do not begin in later life. However, when older people develop illnesses, they may demonstrate changes in behavior and thinking which resemble characteristics of a personality disorder. If people develop

(table 25-3)
PERSONALITY DISORDERS

DISORDER	CHARACTERISTICS
Paranoid	Suspicious of others without any basis; unforgiving; feels that others are attacking his or her character; does not confide in others; reads hidden negative meanings into comments others make
Schizoid	Does not enjoy close relationships; chooses solitary activity; does not care about praise or criticism; is emotionally detached
Schizotypal	Superstitious; has odd beliefs; lacks close friends; is anxious in social situations
Antisocial	Repeated acts of unlawful behavior; lying, impulsive, irritable and aggressive; irresponsible
Borderline	Impulsive; unstable and intense relationships; reacts strongly; feelings of emptiness; inappropriate anger
Histrionic	Likes to be center of attention; sexually seductive; shallow expression of emotions; dramatic; easily influenced
Narcissistic	Grandiose sense of self-importance; believes themselves to be special; lacks empathy; is envious and/or arrogant; requires admiration
Avoidant	Avoids activities that require interaction with people; fears being ridiculed; preoccupied with being criticized or rejected
Dependent	Has difficulty making everyday decisions; doesn't disagree for fear of loss of support; feels uncomfortable alone
Obsessive-compulsive	Perfectionistic; inflexible about rules; miserly; stubborn; preoccupied with details

dementia, depression, or a substance abuse problem, for instance, they may become suspicious, self-absorbed, or unreasonable when previously they might have been trusting and giving. These changes result from illness and are not considered a new personality disorder.

TREATING PERSONALITY DISORDERS

Some psychotherapies, such as dialectical-behavior therapy, have been developed specifically for the treatment of personality disorders (see the section, "Treatments for Psychiatric Illness," below). Cognitive-behavior therapy and interpersonal therapy have also been used with some benefit.

There are no medicines for personality disorders per se. Antidepressants are often used in treating personality disorders for concurrent depression, anxiety, and impulsivity. Mood stabilizers and, occasionally, antipsychotics may be used too. Sometimes anxiety medications are used, but, again, the risk of addiction to benzodiazepines must be considered.

TREATMENTS FOR PSYCHIATRIC ILLNESS

Medications normalize the chemical imbalances in the brain of a person with a mental disorder. Medication treatments currently affect the serotonin, norepinephrine, dopamine, gamma-aminobutyric acid (GABA), and acetylcholine balances in the brain.

In general, medications work as well for older adults as they do for younger people. However, because of changes in physiology and metabolism, older adults may be more susceptible to initial side effects if medications are started at doses used in younger people.

"Start low, go slow, but don't stop" is the recommended strategy. Most psychiatric medications should be started at a quarter to half the usual starting dose for younger adults. The medications can be increased over a few weeks to usual adult dosages. If there is an incomplete response, older adults tolerate dosage increases, as do younger patients.

Different categories of medication are discussed below, after a brief discussion of the medication classes.

ANTIDEPRESSANTS

Table 25-4 presents an overall view of medication classes.

Selective serotonin reuptake inhibitors: Selective serotonin reuptake inhibitors (SSRIs) are first-line medications for depression and anxiety disorders (panic disorder, generalized anxiety disorder, obsessive-compulsive disorder, social phobia, and posttraumatic stress disorder). They only need to be taken once a day, have relatively few side effects, and are well tolerated. The most common side effects include some nausea, transient anxiety, occasionally diarrhea, and vivid dreams. About half the people may have sexual side effects: decreased libido, difficulty achieving an orgasm, and trouble achieving or maintaining an erection. All the medications work equally well. Sometimes if one is not tolerated, a switch to a different SSRI may help. FLUOXETINE is the only one available as a generic. The rest are $60 or more per month.

(*table* 25-4)

ANTIDEPRESSANT MEDICATION (WITH TRADE NAMES IN PARENTHESES)

TYPE	NAME
Selective serotonin reuptake inhibitors (SSRI)	Citalopram (Celexa)
	Escitalopram (Lexapro)
	Fluoxetine (Prozac, Prozac weekly, Sarafem)
	Fluvoxamine (Luvox)
	Paroxetine (Paxil, Paxil CR)
	Sertraline (Zoloft)
Tricyclic antidepressants (TCA)*	Nortriptyline (Pamelor)
	Desipramine (Norpramin)
Other agents	Bupropion (Wellbutrin, Wellbutrin SR, Zyban)
	Mirtazapine (Remeron, Remeron SolTab)
	Nefazodone (Serzone)
	Venlafaxine (Effexor, Effexor XR)
	Trazodone (Desyrel)
Monoamine oxidase inhibitor (MAOI)	Phenelzine (Nardil)
	Isocarboxazid (Marplan)
	Tranylcypromine (Parnate)

*Recommended for older adults but avoid amitriptyline

Tricyclic antidepressants: Tricyclic antidepressants (TCAs) were the first medications developed to treat depression, and work by normalizing the norepinephrine neurotransmitter system. They work very well, but have side effects that may limit getting to an effective dose. Most have a generic form, making them some of the most affordable antidepressants. They are sometimes used to treat chronic pain. The most troublesome side effects are the "anticholinergic effects," which can cause clouded thinking, sedation, constipation, urinary retention, dry mouth, and increased risk of falls.

The tricyclics that we recommend for use in older adults are the ones with the fewest anticholinergic side effects: NORTRIPTYLINE (PAMELOR) and DESIPRAMINE (NORPRAMIN). There are many other tricyclics available that have a much higher risk of side effects, like DOXEPIN (SINEQUAN), IMIPRAMINE (TOFRANIL), and MAPROTILINE (LUDIOMIL). CLOMIPRAMINE (ANAFRANIL) is helpful for obsessive-compulsive disorder, but has many more potential side effects than the SSRIs. AMITRIPTYLINE (ELAVIL) should be avoided in older adults because it has the most anticholinergic side effects, putting people at a markedly increased risk for confusion, falls, and constipation.

Other antidepressants: Many antidepressants have been designed with mechanisms of action different from the tricyclics or SSRIs.

BUPROPION (WELLBUTRIN) tends to be more stimulating than most antidepressants. It usually needs to be taken twice a day. We recommend taking the last dose in the afternoon, because it may interfere with sleep if taken too late at night. There may be initial heightened anxiety when this medication is started, which should wear off in a few days. It does not have sexual side effects. People with a history of seizures or eating disorders (like anorexia or bulimia) should not take this medication because

25

of a heightened risk of seizures. A generic is available for the regular release variety.

MIRTAZAPINE (REMERON) significantly helps with sleep and appetite. It also appears to help decrease anxiety associated with depression. The risk of weight gain may be beneficial for some but not for others. It does not have sexual side effects and is available as an orally dissolving tablet (SolTab) preparation.

NEFAZODONE (SERZONE) is also helpful for anxious depression. It also helps to improve sleep. It does not have sexual side effects. Periodic blood tests need to be done due to a few cases of liver failure. It has some drug interactions.

VENLAFAXINE (EFFEXOR) helps with depression and also has an indication for generalized anxiety disorder. It works on both the serotonin and norepinephrine systems, and is well tolerated. The XR version is taken once a day, and the regular release needs to be taken at least twice a day. Blood pressure needs to be monitored, because at higher dosages a risk of increased blood pressure exists.

TRAZODONE (DESYREL) is rarely used for its antidepressant qualities because it is very sedating. At low doses, it is a very safe and useful sleeping medication, often used in conjunction with some other antidepressants. It is sometimes used to treat agitation in dementia patients as well. A potentially serious side effect in men can be a painful, prolonged erection of the penis. This is quite rare, but if it happens, emergency medical attention must be obtained.

Monoamine oxidase inhibitors (MAOIs) are very good medications but rarely used today. They seem to work well in refractory depression, anxious depression, or some anxiety disorders. They increase dopamine, norepinephrine, and serotonin by irreversibly blocking the enzyme that normally degrades these neurotransmitters. These medications require a tyramine-restricted diet (no red wines, fermented foods, aged foods like most cheeses, or smoked or cured meats), or else a person may develop extremely high blood pressure, which can be fatal. This reaction can also occur when many over-the-counter medications are used, like cold medications, decongestants, or antihistamines. Certain pain medications like Demerol can also cause a hypertensive crisis and death. People may develop sudden drops in their blood pressure, making them feel dizzy or fall.

ANTIANXIETY MEDICATIONS

Although SSRIs are now used for anxiety, there are other medications used primarily for anxiety.

Benzodiazepines: The benzodiazepine class of medications has been used for many years to treat anxiety. They work rather quickly too. However, they do have the potential to become addictive and have significant side effects of memory problems, balance problems, sedation, and falls. It is recommended that these medications be used short term in older adults. They can be very helpful when treatment for anxiety or an anxious depression is initiated; then the benzodiazepine is gradually tapered off. There are some people who do well on small, regular doses of these medications.

There are many types of benzodiazepines. We recommend two for use in older adults: LORAZEPAM (ATIVAN), and OXAZEPAM (SERAX). These are recommended because the liver metabolizes them completely and relatively quickly, so there are fewer drug by-products in the bloodstream to cause the side effects listed above.

ALPRAZOLAM (XANAX) is a very popular medication but less recommended for older adults. It is metabolized relatively quickly, but has several active drug by-products that can cause side effects. Also, rebound anxiety is often seen when the medication wears off, causing the person to want more. CHLORDIAZEPOXIDE (LIBRIUM), CLORAZEPATE (TRANXENE), and FLURAZEPAM (DALMANE) all are metabolized very slowly, and have many by-products. They are not recommended for use in older adults.

Benzodiazepines cannot be stopped cold turkey. They cause a physical dependence, and there can be significant withdrawal symptoms, including seizures. They must be tapered gradually under a doctor's supervision.

Other antianxiety medications: BUSPIRONE (BUSPAR) is a nonaddictive anxiety medication that works well in some people with generalized anxiety. It is less effective for panic attacks. It occasionally is used to help boost antidepressant response. It does not work quickly, though, taking a few weeks to reduce symptoms.

MOOD STABILIZERS

Mood stabilizers are used primarily in the treatment of bipolar disorder, as well as to treat both depression and manic symptoms and to keep the mood more stable. They may also be used to boost antidepressant treatment, as an additional medication in schizophrenia, and, sometimes, to treat behavioral symptoms of dementia.

Mood stabilizers, listed in order of evidence of efficacy, follow:

- Lithium (Lithobid, Eskalith)
- Valproic acid (Depakote, Depakene)
- Carbamazepine (Tegretol)
- Olanzapine (Zyprexa)
- Lamotrigine (Lamictal)
- Topiramate (Topamax)
- Gabapentin (Neurontin)

Lithium has been used the longest to treat bipolar disorder, and has the most evidence that it prevents future manic and depressed episodes. It is well tolerated in most people, including older adults. The most common side effects are tremor and frequent urination. Occasionally, people may experience an upset stomach. It is very affordable.

Lithium must be used with caution in people with kidney problems. Kidney function should be periodically monitored in all who take lithium. Thyroid levels should also be monitored once or twice a year, because people on lithium are more likely to have decreased thyroid production.

Lithium levels need to be monitored since the difference between the therapeutic and toxic blood levels is quite small. The recommended lithium level for older adults is lower than for younger persons due to changes in metabolism.

Lithium levels can become toxic quite easily. Dehydration, taking certain blood pressure medications like HYDROCHLOROTHIAZIDE (DYAZIDE) and ACE inhibitors, taking nonsteroidal anti-inflammatory drugs like IBUPROFEN (MOTRIN), or starting a cyclooxygenase-2 (COX-2) inhibitor arthritis medicine like CELECOXIB (CELEBREX) or ROFECOXIB (VIOXX) can quickly increase lithium levels into the toxic range. It is important to talk to your pharmacist or doctor before taking any medication, even over-the-counter ones. Symptoms of lithium toxicity include nausea, vomiting, diarrhea, dizziness, confusion, severe tremor, unsteady gait, and blurred vision. If you think you may have lithium toxicity, this must be evaluated urgently, because kidney failure and heart rhythm problems may occur, as well as death in severe cases.

Aspirin and ACETAMINOPHEN (TYLENOL) are safe to use with lithium.

VALPROIC ACID (DEPAKOTE or DEPAKENE) has been approved for use in bipolar disorder. It is also well tolerated in most people. Side effects include some nausea, diarrhea, tremor, some sedation, weight gain, or occasional hair loss. Blood levels need to be monitored to prevent toxicity, with the medication titrated to effect, or 50 to 100 mg/mL, and the blood drawn 12 hours after the last dose. Liver function blood tests and blood counts should also be monitored. If a person is on WARFARIN (COUMADIN), the anticoagulation (PT/INR) needs to be monitored more frequently until the dose is stabilized. Discussing any new medications with your doctor or pharmacist is recommended because of potential drug interactions with valproic acid.

OLANZAPINE (ZYPREXA) has been approved for the treatment of acute mania. Time will tell if it helps prevent future episodes. It does not require blood levels, and has few drug-drug interactions. The most common side effects are weight gain and sedation.

LAMOTRIGINE (LAMICTAL) and TOPIRAMATE (TOPAMAX) have shown promise in younger adults. Rarely, lamotrigine can have a severe rash associated with it. Topiramate often dulls thinking. GABAPENTIN (NEURONTIN) has less evidence to support its use in bipolar disorder but is relatively safe.

ANTIPSYCHOTIC MEDICATIONS

Antipsychotic medications help reduce psychotic symptoms in schizophrenia, depression, and bipolar illness. Also, they can help reduce agitation and impulsivity in other illnesses such as dementia. In schizophrenia, antipsychotic medications are used for long-term treatment. For depression, antipsychotic medications will be used for a few months and then gradually tapered off as the depression improves.

There are two main categories of antipsychotics: *typical (older)* and *atypical (newer)*. The typical class tends to have more side effects;

(*table* 25-5)

ANTIDEPRESSANT MEDICATION (WITH TRADE NAMES IN PARENTHESES)

ATYPICAL ANTIPSYCHOTICS	TYPICAL ANTIPSYCHOTICS RECOMMENDED*	TYPICAL ANTIPSYCHOTICS NOT RECOMMENDED†
Clozapine (Clozaril)	Fluphenazine (Prolixin)	Chlorpromazine (Thorazine)
Olanzapine (Zyprexa)	Haloperidol (Haldol)	
Quetiapine (Seroquel)	Perphenazine (Trilafon)	Thioridazine (Mellaril)
Risperidone (Risperdal)	Thiothixene (Navane)	
Ziprasidone (Geodon)	Trifluoperazine (Stelazine)	

*Used less often for older adults now that atypical antipsychotics have been developed.
†Not recommended for older adults.

the atypical class can have these same effects but usually not to the same degree.

The main side effects can be sedation, weight gain, and *extrapyramidal side effects (EPS)*. EPS can include an inner sense of restlessness, tremors, decreased facial expression, or shuffling steps. EPS are quite prominent with FLUPHENAZINE (PROLIXIN), HALOPERIDOL (HALDOL), and THIOTHIXENE (NAVANE), and much less common with the atypicals. A side effect called *tardive dyskinesia (TD)* may develop with long-term exposure to antipsychotics, but the risk may be lower with the atypicals. Tardive dyskinesia can cause irreversible abnormal movements: lip smacking, tongue movements, chewing movements, irregular arm or leg movements, grunting, or pelvic thrusting. Risk factors for tardive dyskinesia are length of exposure to antipsychotics, older age, and being a woman. Table 25-5 has an overview.

Atypical antipsychotics: CLOZAPINE (CLOZARIL) is the classic atypical antipsychotic. It has very low EPS but causes quite a bit of sedation and weight gain. It often can help treat psychosis when all other atypical and typical antipsychotics have failed. It can also help people with Parkinson's disease tolerate higher dosages of medication by decreasing hallucinations without worsening movements. Clozapine, however, may have a side effect of decreasing white blood cell (infection–fighting cell) counts. For this reason, blood tests must be done weekly for six months and then every two weeks thereafter. Clozapine is the only antipsychotic medication that requires regular blood work.

OLANZAPINE (ZYPREXA) is well tolerated, and has some sedation and weight gain as well. It has low EPS, which however occurs more frequently in older adults. It also treats the manic phase of bipolar illness. One formulation dissolves in the mouth.

QUETIAPINE (SEROQUEL) has sedation as a main side effect. It has very low EPS, and can be useful in Parkinson's disease.

RISPERIDONE (RISPERDAL) is less sedating than the medications listed above. It has the greatest potential of EPS of any of the atypical antipsychotics but is still much better than the older typical antipsychotics. Risperidone also has a liquid formulation, and an orally dissolving tablet is being developed.

ZIPRASIDONE (GEODON) is the least sedating, has low EPS, and has the least potential for weight gain of the atypical antipsychotics. It does require monitoring of the heart for rhythm problems.

Typical antipsychotics: Typical antipsychotics are very good medications and effectively treat psychotic symptoms. They are affordable. Especially in older adults, though, they have a high incidence of EPS, and a higher risk of TD than do the atypicals.

FLUPHENAZINE (PROLIXIN) and HALOPERIDOL (HALDOL) come in "depot" form, which is a long-acting injection that lasts two to three weeks. There are no atypical depot antipsychotics, though they are under development.

The older typical medications like CHLORPROMAZINE (THORAZINE) and THIORIDAZINE (MELLARIL) are not recommended for use in the elderly because of excessive sedation, confusion, and risk of falls.

ACETYLCHOLINESTERASE INHIBITORS

The acetylcholinesterase (ACE) inhibitors are indicated for use in Alzheimer's dementia. They also appear helpful in Lewy body dementia, and studies are being undertaken in vascular dementias and other dementia types. These medications do not stop the progression of the dementia but tend to stabilize mental functioning while the person is taking them. Once the medication is stopped, cognition drops to the point it would have been without the medication. If medication is restarted, mental function does not return to previous levels.

It can be hard to monitor response to these medications, because many people don't "improve" but stay at about the same or decline less rapidly. These medications may delay placement in a facility for six months to one year. They also may help behavior, mood, and anxiety in people with dementia.

They all may have side effects of nausea, diarrhea, vomiting, and low appetite and/or weight loss. Overall, they are well tolerated but costly.

DONEPEZIL (ARICEPT) is taken once a day. GALANTAMINE (REMINYL) is taken twice a day as is RIVASTIGMINE (EXELON). TACRINE (COGNEX) is the oldest medication in this category and is given four times a day; it has many side effects and is poorly tolerated. It also requires blood tests every two weeks to monitor for liver damage. For these reasons, tacrine is not recommended anymore.

STIMULANTS

Stimulants are sometimes used to help attention and concentration, especially in medically ill people or people with a stroke or brain injury. METHYLPHENIDATE (RITALIN or CONCERTA) is a common medication used in this class. Side effects can include agitation, anxiety, decreased appetite, and insomnia if taken too close to bedtime.

SLEEPING MEDICATIONS

Sleep is a problem for many older adults. The best way to help sleep is to improve sleep hygiene. Alcohol should be completely avoided, and caffeinated beverages should be avoided in the afternoon and evening. The majority of fluid should be consumed before supper, to avoid trips to the bathroom at night. The bed should only be used for sleeping and not for watching television or reading. However, some people may sleep better with medications, especially in the early stages of a mental illness.

Sleeping pills, like TEMAZEPAM (RESTORIL) and TRIAZOLAM (HALCION) are not recommended because of the addiction potential, risk of falls, and confusion. The newer medications ZOLPIDEM (AMBIEN) and ZALEPLON (SONATA) may also show the risk of addiction. The above medications are recommended for short-term use only, if at all. DIPHENHYDRAMINE (BENADRYL) is not recommended for use in the elderly, because it may cause confusion. TRAZODONE (DESYREL) seems to be the best-tolerated sleep medication in older adults (see the section, "Antidepressants," above, for a discussion of side effects).

OTHER SOMATIC TREATMENTS

Previously called "shock treatment," *electroconvulsive therapy (ECT)* has been used since 1938 for treatment of depression, bipolar illness, and, occasionally, schizophrenia and mood disorders in early dementia. Present ECT methods are much different from those portrayed in movies or used in the 1950s and 1960s. ECT employs a light anesthetic and a muscle relaxant, with an anesthesiologist present.

ECT uses electricity to induce a seizure in the brain, which resets the neurotransmitter balance. The elderly represent a large percentage of patients receiving ECT. There is no age limit. Data suggest that this treatment is very efficacious, with an 80 to 90% response rate in the elderly. ECT is also safe in this age group; one study showed that ECT caused fewer side effects than medications did in the elderly. Close monitoring of medical problems with other doctors may be necessary.

ECT is given three times a week, and the average number of treatments for a full response is 6 to 12. It is used when a patient has not responded to medications, cannot tolerate medications, or cannot wait the several weeks for medications to work.

The elderly may be more prone to acute confusion, and reducing the frequency of ECT from three to two times a week is helpful in this case. There may be some memory loss for the time around the treatments. Other side effects may include headache and muscle aches. A book by Max Fink, *Electroshock: Restoring the Mind,* is a good reference on ECT.

Other treatments achieve antidepressant response by brain stimulation, though less globally than ECT. *Rapid transcranial magnetic stimulation (RTMS)* is under investigation for depression treatment. One study suggests it may be less effective in the elderly. *Vagus nerve stimulation (VNS)* is also under investigation as a treatment for refractory depression.

NONTESTED MEDICATIONS

Herbal and natural preparations are real medications with real chemical actions and potentially life-threatening side effects. They are not regulated by the Food and Drug Administration, and the claims for such preparations are not tested. They are not cheap either.

The amount of active drug may vary from batch to batch and from brand to brand. The "inert ingredients" may be harmful.

They are not necessarily safe, and several agents have been recalled. They can have significant drug interactions with prescribed medications. St. John's Wort—marketed for depression—can have drug interactions with commonly prescribed medications like warfarin (Coumadin) and digoxin (Lanoxin). It is important to tell your doctor about all medications you are taking: prescription, vitamins, over-the-counter, and natural or herbal preparations.

PSYCHOTHERAPY

In an attempt to cope with change, people may get stuck in certain negative patterns of thinking, feeling, or behavior. If this happens, psychotherapy, or "talk therapy," can help. Research suggests that psychotherapy is an effective way to treat mental illness. Research also shows that psychotherapy has benefits for physical health as well. Psychotherapists use various techniques to help people find their own solutions to problems. They build on people's innate strengths and life experiences to find realistic ways to treat mental illness. The relationship that a person builds with a psychotherapist is confidential and should be of a trusting, open nature. Psychotherapy has the best results if the patient and therapist work as a team, the patient attends regularly and the patient works on assignments between sessions. Psychotherapy is not easy. It requires motivation to make changes in one's own thinking and behavior and a willingness to confront uncomfortable feelings.

Psychotherapy sessions generally take place in the therapist's office. Individual, couple, family, or group sessions are the most typical. Psychotherapy sessions can range from one-half hour to two hours long, depending on the individuals involved. Sessions are often held weekly. Toward the end, therapy sessions may occur less frequently. Psychotherapy can be as brief as a dozen sessions or as long as several years. Length of treatment depends on the type of treatment, the severity of the problem, and whether insurance or private payment is involved.

It is important to find a professional who has had training in psychotherapy. This can be a psychiatric social worker, psychologist, psychiatric nurse, marriage and family therapist, psychiatrist, or psychoanalyst. People can find reputable therapists through their primary care provider and through friends and family. There are also referral networks through professional associations listed in this chapter's "For More Information." It is important to interview a potential therapist and ask questions about the person's training, treatment approach, and fees. Contact your insurance carrier to find out whether your coverage includes mental or behavioral health services.

Types of psychotherapy: There are many different types of *psychotherapy* that have shown benefits for older adults. People tend to think of psychotherapy as psychoanalysis, which involves the patient lying on a couch and associating freely. The focus is on early childhood experiences.

Psychodynamic psychotherapy emphasizes unconscious conflicts that cause problems in a person's life. In both psychoanalysis and psychodynamic psychotherapy, the patient gains insight into thoughts, feelings, and behavior to make positive changes.

Behavior therapy is often used to help people overcome fears and worries about particular situations. Patients are gradually exposed to the situations they fear so that they become desensitized to the situations. Patients and therapists work together to plan exposure events and rewards for successful behavior. Patients learn new ways to reduce and tolerate anxiety so that they can function more effectively in their daily lives.

Cognitive-behavior therapy combines both cognitive and behavioral approaches to make changes in here-and-now situations. People learn how thoughts affect their moods. They learn to identify inaccurate thoughts that lead to negative moods and to change their thoughts to reflect reality more accurately. People also learn how to change their behaviors in problematic situations in order to produce more positive outcomes. Homework assignments are a key part of this treatment.

Interpersonal psychotherapy addresses current relationships with family, friends, or coworkers. Patients learn to identify conflicts or make changes in their interpersonal roles, focus on complicated grief, or learn more effective communication skills. As in cognitive-behavior therapy, patients try new behaviors between sessions.

Dialectical-behavior therapy helps patients integrate extremes of thinking, feeling, and behavior. Patients learn four core concepts of mindfulness, emotion regulation, distress tolerance, and interpersonal effectiveness. Again, homework assignments help patients practice new strategies for getting their needs met in the real world.

Some psychotherapists use integrated psychotherapy to combine several of the above techniques to fit the individual needs of their patients.

CONCLUSION

Mental illnesses are real illnesses, and there are many available treatments. We have highlighted common mental illnesses and have provided an overview of treatment options: both medications and talk therapy. We hope you will feel more comfortable talking to your physician about your own concerns or discussing a family member's treatment.

■

25

WHAT YOU NEED TO KNOW

➤ Later life brings many changes. You may retire or experience a change in your work environment. People you love may get sick or disabled. You may become a caregiver for an older parent or a disabled spouse. You may experience the death of friends or your spouse. Coping with these changes may require some struggle. You may need to redesign your life or your sense of self in order to move forward. This may require the support of family, friends, health professionals, and spiritual advisors.

➤ Mental illnesses can prevent people from working through the challenges that life presents. For many years, mental illnesses have incorrectly been considered to be a personal failure or a constitutional weakness. Research has shown these are but another biological illness or other biological illnesses, such as hypertension or diabetes. Mental illnesses have physical symptoms such as weight loss, constipation, insomnia, and shortness of breath. Appropriate evaluation by a health professional can lead to effective treatment.

➤ Depression is very common and can cause intense suffering. In older persons, it may often go undiagnosed. You do *not* have to feel sad to be depressed. You may have lost interest in activities that you previously enjoyed. Changes in appetite, insomnia, sexual dysfunction, poor energy level, and memory problems are some of the symptoms that may indicate depression.

➤ People who are at increased risk of depression include those with physical illness as well as their caregivers. Those residing in nursing homes have a higher rate of depression, as do those with chronic pain. People with a current or past history of chemical dependency also are at risk. A past history of depression is a very strong risk factor.

➤ If you or someone close to you has suicidal thoughts, a doctor must be told immediately. Talking about suicide with the health care provider allows a person to get treatment. Discussing suicide does not strengthen this idea; rather it allows a person to get help.

➤ Anxiety disorders are the most common mental illness, with about 20% of the people having an anxiety disorder at a single point in time and 33% of all people having an anxiety disorder in their lifetime. Effective and safe treatments are available.

➤ Other mental illnesses discussed in this chapter are less common but not rare: bipolar disorder, schizophrenia, dementia with behavioral disturbance, and personality disorders.

➤ Mental illness may require medications, psychotherapy, and other treatments. Often, a primary care physician may initiate treatment. In other situations, the services of a psychiatrist or psychologist is necessary.

➤ Older adults may require a reduction in the dosage of medications normally used for younger adults due to changes in drug metabolism with aging. Alternative medications and herbs are not regulated by the FDA and should be avoided in the treatment of mental illness. Seek the services of a professional who you can trust and who will work with you to select the most appropriate treatment.

FOR MORE INFORMATION

➤ Alzheimer's Association
919 N. Michigan Avenue, Suite 1100
Chicago, IL 60611
800-272-3900
Web: www.alz.org

➤ American Association for Geriatric Psychiatry
7910 Woodmont Avenue, Suite 1050
Bethesda, MD 20814
301-654-7850
Web: www.aagponline.org

◐ **American Association of Retired Persons**
Program Division
601 E Street, NW
Washington, DC 20049
800-424-3410
Web: www.aarp.org

◐ **American Geriatrics Society**
The Empire State Building
350 Fifth Avenue, Suite 801
New York, NY 10118
212-308-1414
Web: www.americangeriatrics.org

◐ **National Alliance for the Mentally Ill**
Colonial Place Three
2107 Wilson Boulevard, Suite 300
Arlington, VA 22201-3042
800-950-NAMI
Web: www.nami.org

◐ **National Association of Area Agencies
on Aging**
927 15th Street, NW, 6th Floor
Washington, DC 20005
202-296-8130
Web: www.n4a.org

◐ **National Association of Professional
Geriatric Care Managers**
1604 N. Country Club Road
Tucson, AZ 85716-3102
520-881-8008
Web: www.caremanager.org

◐ **National Depressive and Manic-
Depressive Association**
730 N. Franklin, Suite 501
Chicago, IL 60610
800-82-NDMDA
Web: www.ndmda.org

◐ **National Hospice Foundation**
1700 Diagonal Road, Suite 625
Alexandria, VA 22314
703-516-4928
E-mail: info@nhpco.org

◐ **National Institute of Mental Health–
Public Inquiries**
6001 Executive Boulevard
Room 8184, MSC 9663
Bethesda, MD 20892-9663
800-421-4211
Web: www.nimh.gov

◐ **National Mental Health Association**
1021 Prince Street
Alexandria, VA 22314-2971
800-969-NMHA
Web: www.nmha.org

◐ **NeedyMeds**
Web: www.needymeds.com
Information on pharmacy assistance for
low-income people.

25

They may forget what you said, but they will never forget how you made them feel.

—*Carl W. Buechner*

THE AUTHORS

26

BRUCE E. ROBINSON MD, MPH is chief of geriatrics at Sarasota Memorial, director of the Sarasota Memorial Hospital Memory Disorder Clinic, and medical director of three Sarasota nursing homes. His master of public health is from the University of South Florida, where he holds the rank of professor of medicine and teaches medical direction in long-term care. He completed his internal medicine training at the University of South Florida and his geriatrics training at Harvard and the United Kingdom. He is board-certified in internal medicine and geriatric medicine. He has more than 40 publications, and serves on the editorial boards of two national journals. Dr. Robinson is a fellow of the American College of Physicians, the Gerontological Society of America, and the American Geriatrics Society. He is listed in the national edition of *Best Doctors in America*.

KATHLEEN HOUSEWEART, MBA has over 18 years experience in the field of geriatrics and has worked with area agencies on aging in Massachusetts, Virginia, and Florida. Her experience includes in-home assessment and care planning for frail seniors, training and education for professional and family caregivers, and program planning and development. She received her degree in sociology from Holy Cross College in Worcester, Massachusetts, and a master of business administration at Saint Leo University. At this time, Kathleen serves as manager of Geriatrics Services and coordinator of the Memory Disorder Clinic at Sarasota Memorial Hospital in Florida. Active in her local community and in a number of organizations, she provides advocacy for older adults and caregivers.

26 | MEMORY

(figure 26-1*)*

Memory may begin to slip in middle age and decline further with old age. However, memory loss that interferes with daily activities such as shopping, cooking, and driving should prompt a medical evaluation.

MEMORY AND AGING

Some changes in the way your mind works are a normal part of aging. Pure, raw memory power, for example, for a list of words or items, begins to slip in middle age (see Figure 26-1). However, memory for things in a context, such as the details of a story, does not fall off substantially. As you age, you may need to repeat facts or link them with something you already know well, in order to recall them later. Keeping written notes may become necessary to help you remember. Memory slips even more in late life, especially after age 75. The process of remembering takes more time. Even so, your memory is still easily jogged.

Changes like these are not signs of Alzheimer's disease. These normal changes are mild and do not get worse over short periods of time. The person usually recognizes small memory lapses as such, and they do not interfere with the ability to perform daily activities like shopping, cooking, and driving. If a person cannot perform daily activities, it's time to begin seeking medical aid.

SEEKING MEDICAL AID

If you or someone you love has a memory problem, there are three good reasons to go to your doctor.

1. Sometimes, you can be cured. Perhaps one person in ten with memory impairment has a reversible condition—such as a vitamin deficiency or a drug side effect—which if treated will completely cure the memory problem.
2. Often, you can be helped. The two most common causes of memory loss are Alzheimer's disease and small strokes. Both can be helped by medicines that boost memory and slow the progress of the disease.
3. Always, you can learn ways of living with the problem better, ways that benefit both you and your family. Important decisions about living arrangements and finances, as well as a review of your wishes regarding your future care, are best made when all involved have their wits and can discuss everything clearly. Waiting too long to plan can leave you or your family with terrible burdens should decisions be needed.

10 WARNING SIGNS

Alzheimer's disease is the leading cause of dementia, a set of symptoms that includes loss of memory, judgment, and reasoning and changes in mood and behavior. People sometimes fail to recognize that these symptoms are warnings. They may mistakenly assume that such behavior is a normal part of aging—it isn't. Symptoms may develop gradually and go unnoticed for a long time.

To help you notice the warning signs of Alzheimer's disease, the Alzheimer's Association has developed a checklist of common symptoms (some of which apply to other forms of dementia as well). Review the list. If you notice several symptoms, the person with the symptoms should see or be taken to a doctor for a complete examination.

FAMILY JOURNAL

Anne S. is worried about her mother. After the death of her father two years ago, she had to take over the checkbook and bill paying as her mother had ignored the bills for several months. Last week she noticed that her mother had six nearly full gallons of milk in the refrigerator, most of them sour. The house was noticeably dirty, as were her mother's clothes. The bottle of blood pressure pills in the cabinet was two months old but completely full. Her sister, who was in another state, said, "Mom sounds fine when I talk to her on the phone."

1. Memory loss that affects day-to-day function: It's normal to occasionally forget appointments, colleagues' names, or a friend's phone number and remember them later. A person with Alzheimer's disease may forget facts more often and not remember them later, especially facts that have happened more recently. Memories of incidents from long ago often remain after the ability to learn new information is lost.

2. Difficulty performing familiar tasks: Busy people can be so distracted from time to time that they may leave the potatoes au gratin on the stove and only remember to serve them at the end of the meal. A person with Alzheimer's disease may be unable to prepare any part of a meal or forget having eaten it.

3. Problems with language: Everyone has trouble finding the right word sometimes, but a person with Alzheimer's disease may forget simple words or substitute the wrong words, making his or her sentences difficult to understand.

4. Disorientation of time and place: It's normal to forget the day of the week or your destination—for a moment. But people with Alzheimer's disease can become lost on their own street, not knowing how they got there or how to get home.

5. Poor or decreased judgment: People may put off going to a doctor if they have an infection but eventually seek medical attention. People with Alzheimer's disease may not recognize the need for a doctor at all. Or they may dress inappropriately, wearing two shirts or heavy clothing on a hot day.

6. Problems with abstract thinking: From time to time, people may find balancing a checkbook difficult. Someone with Alzheimer's disease could forget completely what the numbers are and what needs to be done with them.

7. Misplacing items: Anyone can misplace a wallet or keys. A person with Alzheimer's disease may put things in inappropriate places: an iron in the freezer or a wristwatch in the sugar bowl.

8. Changes in mood or behavior: Everyone becomes sad or moody from time to time. Someone with Alzheimer's disease can exhibit rapid mood swings—from calm to tears to anger—for no apparent reason.

9. Changes in personality: People's personalities change somewhat with age. But a person with Alzheimer's disease can change dramatically, becoming extremely confused, suspicious, or withdrawn. Changes may also include apathy, fearfulness, or acting inappropriately.

10. Loss of initiative: It's normal to tire of housework, business activities, or social obligations, but most people regain their initiative. A person with Alzheimer's disease may become very passive and require cues and prompting to become involved.

The 10 warning signs are useful as described for persons with significant dementia due to Alzheimer's disease or other related disorders. However, more people are coming forward with milder changes in brain function that do not actually meet the scientific criteria for Alzheimer's or dementia.

- Listen carefully and take time to remember.
- Think about what you want to remember.
- Repeat the memory out loud.
- Link new incidents to past memories.
- Practice using the new information.
- If it's important, write it down.

Many of these people are diagnosed with mild cognitive impairment, which means the changes are somewhat more than expected for normal aging but don't yet meet the criteria for dementia. After a few years, over half these people progress to Alzheimer's disease (and nearly half do not!). Medical science now appreciates that the brain cell destruction that leads to Alzheimer's goes on for years before the level of impairment called *dementia* is reached. There are also other conditions, such as tiny strokes, that can cause minor memory impairment.

MEDICAL ISSUES

THE BRAIN

The first observations of Alzheimer's disease were descriptions of the behaviors and progression of the disease. Alzheimer's disease is uncommon before age 65, but the prevalence doubles every five years between 65 and 85 years of age: 1 to 2% at 65, 2 to 4% at 70, 4 to 8% at 75, 8 to 16% at 80, and 16 to 32% at 85, nearly half of those over 90. Alzheimer's was actually an uncommon disease until advances in medicine kept humans alive into the age range at which the disease is common.

The brain changes seen through the microscope were first described by Dr. Alzheimer, hence the name of the disease. The changes include brain cell death and formation of neuritic plaques and neurofibrillary tangles, the residual brain changes from the destruction of brain cells (see Figure 26-2).

In the past decade great advances have occurred in the understanding of the biology of Alzheimer's disease; for example, a person with Alzheimer's will lose the critical chemical, acetylcholine, which causes movement of a nerve impulse from one cell of the brain to the next. Thousands of impulse movements are required for every thought, movement, or sensation. New treatments for Alzheimer's boost acetylcholine levels in the brain by blocking the breakdown of the chemical.

Chemical changes are also just symptoms of the cell death in the disease. The cell death continues despite the treatments now available. Progress in understanding the cause has followed many directions. One of the most promising leads involves a brain protein called *amyloid*. Amyloid has long been

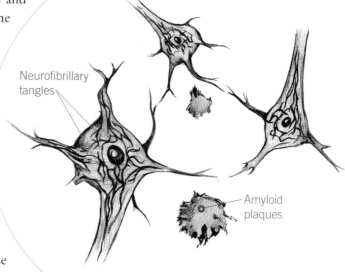

Neurofibrillary tangles

Amyloid plaques

(*figure* 26-2)

Amyloid plaques and neurofibrillary tangles.

recognized as a component of the plaques found in Alzheimer's affected brains. It is toxic to brain cells. Specific mutations in the structure of amyloid in which one single building block is exchanged for another can cause the onset of Alzheimer's disease in young people. A vaccine against amyloid protects against Alzheimer's disease in mice genetically engineered with the human early-Alzheimer's genetic mutation. These mice are engineered to get Alzheimer's changes in behavior and brain tissue at 12 months of age and have been instrumental in Alzheimer research. Many scientists are actively pursuing the amyloid hypothesis in the search for the cure of Alzheimer's.

The genetics of Alzheimer's disease is another layer of understanding. Alzheimer's risk is partially genetic: first-degree relatives (parent or sibling) of an Alzheimer's affected person have about a 50% higher risk of acquiring the disease than those without an affected relative. However, since Alzheimer's risk doubles every five years, this means the risk at a given age, with an affected relative, is that of someone two or three years older without an affected relative. The most exciting genetic discovery is the actual mutation in the genetic code that leads to early Alzheimer's. This mutation is transmitted to half the children of an affected person. While these mutations are thought to cause only a tiny fraction of the cases of Alzheimer's disease, these cases have dramatically increased our understanding of the mechanism of brain injury in Alzheimer's.

MEMORY LOSS EVALUATION

The evaluation of the memory problem should focus on two questions: whether a memory disorder is present and whether the cause of a memory disorder can be determined.

Is an important memory disorder present? The evaluation tests the functioning of the mind in a number of areas. Simple memory screens will give a ballpark answer to brain function. The Folstein Mini-Mental State Examination is an example of a memory screen. Normal performance will vary, particularly with lower scores from those who are very old or those with less education. Highly educated older people often pass the screens despite significant dementia. Many physicians who work with memory loss have other ways to screen memory and thinking at the bedside. If the problem with memory loss causes significant loss of personal function and the memory test results are very abnormal, the doctor can diagnose dementia with this information alone (see Figure 26-3).

When simple screening tests aren't convincing, more extensive testing of individual brain functions is performed, usually by neuropsychologists. Neuropsychological testing examines memory, language skills, intelligence, visual spatial abilities, planning, and organization by measurements that are adjusted for age and education. The testing generally takes hours but is the best way (called the "gold standard") for deciding which brain functions are impaired and by how much.

(a)

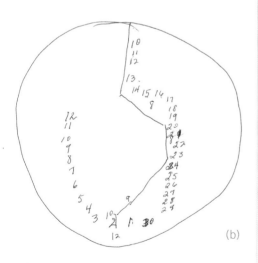

(b)

(figure 26-3)

Clock-drawing test. The patient is asked to draw the face of a clock, then put the hands so the clock reads ten past eleven. (a) Normal (b) Alzheimer's patient.

Delirium is sudden confusion due to another medical or mental condition, with problems of alertness in addition to those of thinking. Persons with delirium are confused and often either agitated, sleepy, or both. Delirium may cause abnormal thinking, such as believing someone is trying to hurt you or having hallucinations (seeing something nonexistent). The severity of the problem varies enormously in delirium, with the person near normal at one moment and very disturbed the next.

Delirium is usually caused by a medical condition. Anything that makes an older person sick can cause delirium. Both prescription and over-the-counter drugs can cause delirium. Alcohol is a drug that with excessive use causes delirium. The first thing to check when delirium develops is the medications that the person is taking.

Unfortunately, people with dementia are much more likely to become delirious if they get sick, so some older persons can have both dementia and delirium if ill. Delirium usually comes on quickly. People with dementia will have a sudden loss of mental function (abnormal thinking and changes in alertness) if they also develop delirium.

Delirium usually improves rapidly if the cause is found and corrected. Medical evaluation of a person showing signs of delirium is critical.

Other common physical causes of chronic memory loss that can be fixed include vitamin B_{12} deficiency, thyroid disease, and high blood calcium. Evaluation for memory loss should generally include a vitamin B_{12} level and thyroid tests, with other tests as indicated by the findings of the history and examination.

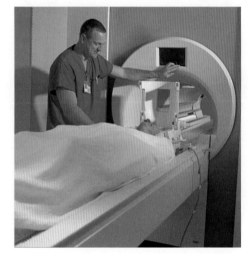

Medication side effects are common causes of problems with memory and thinking. More prescription drugs can cause memory problems than those that can't. During an evaluation for memory loss, be sure that the doctor looks at the medicine list carefully and ask whether any drug could be causing a thinking problem.

Depression is overall the most common cause of memory complaints that go away after treatment. A person with depression will often complain bitterly of problems with memory and thinking. This is different from usual Alzheimer's, for which the person denies any trouble. Depression usually comes on over weeks or months, while Alzheimer's usually comes on very gradually over many months or years. Part of a good examination for treatable causes of memory loss is a depression evaluation.

Rarely, a structural brain disorder, such as a subdural hematoma (blood clot on the brain), a brain tumor, or hydrocephalus causes memory loss and confusion. Most persons with these problems have specific symptoms of such disorders, but a few do not. For this reason, current evaluation guidelines recommend one brain imaging study in persons with significant memory loss.

Two similar technologies are used for imaging the brain. Computed tomography (CT) scanning is an X-ray method that generates a series of images showing slices of the entire brain. CT scans allow doctors to detect strokes, tumors, and other uncommon causes of memory loss. A CT scan of the brain takes 5 to 10 minutes.

(*figure* 26-4)

Patient having a brain MRI. (*Courtesy of Sarasota Memorial Hospital.*)

Magnetic resonance imaging (MRI) is another method for imaging the brain that is more expensive than a CT scan, but it may give more precise images of the brain and be especially helpful in identifying the amount of *vascular* (blood vessels) disease regions (see Figure 26-4). The other disadvantages of MRI are that it takes longer to perform than a CT scan, and it may not be appropriate if you have *claustrophobia* (fear of enclosed places) or a pacemaker. Medicare covers most of the cost of both types of imaging, as well as most X-rays.

What is the cause of the memory problem? Over a hundred different diseases can cause serious memory loss. However, a few of them account for over 90% of all dementia cases. Alzheimer's disease and other degenerative variants *(dementia with Lewy bodies* or *frontotemporal dementia)* make up about 40% of cases. *Vascular* or *multi-infarct dementia* account for 30 to 40% of the cases, if you count those that have both vascular brain damage and Alzheimer's elements. *Parkinson's dementia complex* and *alcoholic dementia* account for about 5% each.

Determining the cause of dementia is best done by comparing the clinical pattern of the person's illness to the patterns understood for that type of dementia. The pattern includes the history, the findings on neurological examination, the types of problems in brain function, and the brain imaging results.

The most common disease causing dementia, Alzheimer's disease, has the following pattern. The onset is generally around age 65. At onset, Alzheimer's patients will look and act perfectly normal. Their social graces and polite conversation are intact. The thinking and responses of an Alzheimer's patient are quick for what they know. They will often be able to give good reasons for why they can't answer specific questions, as their reasoning still works. The problems become apparent, particularly in the middle stages of the disease, if they are challenged in areas of weakness, such as discussed in the section, "10 Warning Signs," above. Their decline is slow and gradual.

The neurological examination in Alzheimer's disease is normal until very late. Brain imaging studies, particularly the MRI, most often show atrophy (shrinkage) that is particularly apparent in the temporal lobes and hippocampus.

A clinical diagnosis of Alzheimer's disease by a skilled evaluation team will be confirmed around 90% of the time, with the person having Alzheimer's in the brain after death. A number of other tests have been described for Alzheimer's disease. Special brain imaging studies (with names like SPECT and PET) are not as good as a skilled clinical diagnosis. Blood testing for genetic markers does not reliably predict who will get Alzheimer's disease, and in clinical practice, such tests are not used in making the diagnosis of Alzheimer's disease. Tests for special proteins in spinal fluid and urine also lack added value. Any of these tests could be considered for very specific situations, but none is recommended for routine evaluation.

26

Dementia with Lewy bodies (DLB) is recognized as being second only to Alzheimer's disease in causing degenerative dementia. The central clinical feature of dementia with Lewy bodies is a progressive, often rapid decline in brain function. Early in the disease this may not affect memory as much as other mental abilities. Problems with paying attention, organizing, and spatial skills may be affected first.

Dementia with Lewy bodies is also unusual in that considerable variation in alertness and attention can occur throughout the day. Early in their disease, persons with dementia with Lewy bodies often have hallucinations and delusions (beliefs which aren't true) and may describe them very clearly and in much detail. Dementia with Lewy bodies also affects muscular activity, with most patients experiencing stiffness and tremors like those found in Parkinson's disease. Falls and fainting are also common. Depression is more often seen in dementia with Lewy bodies than in Alzheimer's disease. A disturbance in the dream phase of sleep also occurs.

Dementia with Lewy bodies is important to identify when present, because persons affected have unusual sensitivity to the tranquilizers most often used for hallucinations (neuroleptics) and have severe adverse reactions if given these drugs. It is also felt that persons with dementia with Lewy bodies respond unusually well to the medications used in treatment of Alzheimer's disease. The speed of deterioration of dementia with Lewy bodies varies, but is generally faster than in Alzheimer's disease.

Frontotemporal dementia is a description of a pattern of mental decline which can be particularly hard and heartbreaking. It is most often degenerative, with the same brain changes as Alzheimer's, but occasionally is caused by another disease called Pick's disease. In frontotemporal dementia the early changes in brain function cause changes in personality and a loss of inhibitions. These people can become very easily angered, show increased interest in sex, and become emotionally unrecognizable to those they love. All of this can occur before the memory problems are notable. Neuropsychological testing can often identify specific losses in executive functions (planning and organization) and other brain functions of the frontal lobes. Brain imaging studies may show atrophy that affects the frontal lobes out of proportion to other areas of the brain.

The vascular dementia pattern includes an abrupt onset (with a stroke) and a stepwise decline, as multiple strokes take away more and more functioning brain tissue. The vascular process that leads to brain cell death is often affecting other body areas: history of heart attacks and blood vessel disease in the neck or legs is common. Risk factors for atherosclerosis (hardening of the arteries), such as high blood pressure, smoking, diabetes and high cholesterol, are often present in a person with vascular dementia.

Vascular dementia has several forms. The easiest form to identify is if definite strokes with paralysis have occurred at the same time with changes in brain function. However, some people have multiple tiny strokes or even just a couple of critically placed strokes that do not cause any symptoms apart from the gradual loss of memory and other brain functions. The pattern of brain function loss is somewhat different, with vascular dementia causing memory loss that benefits from hints or cues, suggesting that information is getting in but isn't reliably getting out. These patterns of vascular dementia often require an MRI to distinguish them from Alzheimer's with any certainty.

Parkinson's dementia is diagnosed by the history of Parkinson's disease, usually for years or decades before the dementia problem is identified. Alcoholic dementia is identified by a history of heavy alcohol use, usually for decades, followed by dementia.

In some situations, dementia can best be described as a disease of bits, whereby several different mechanisms, each having the potential for causing the loss of functioning brain cells, come together to cause dementia. All people have substantial "reserves," or brain functions not used in daily activities. Brain trauma, boxing, alcohol use, and small strokes that kill brain cells may cause no problems at the time they occur. However, after age advances and particularly after Alzheimer's begins, the further losses begin to interfere with daily function. Dementia is diagnosed on the basis of the interaction of multiple causes.

Specialists can help with evaluating and managing memory problems. After completing the medical evaluation, the doctor decides whether other professionals are necessary to evaluate or manage a person's memory problem. Neurologists are medical doctors who specialize in diseases of the brain and nervous system. They have broad experience in these diseases and understand the unusual causes of memory loss. They are the experts in the differential diagnosis of memory loss, that is, determining which specific cause is most likely. Neurologists are particularly valuable if the symptoms are atypical. Psychiatrists are medical doctors who specialize in disorders of mental function and emotion. Those with special training or interest in older persons are experts in the management of the mental complications of memory disorders. Depression, behavior problems, and severe confusion often interfere with an affected person's best functioning level. They can also affect the family. Depression is also a common cause of memory problems. *Neuropsychologists* are experts in the measurement of mental function. They can evaluate a person's pattern of mental changes, which can be useful in determining the cause, particularly in mild or unusual cases.

TREATMENT FOR DEMENTIA

A common question regarding treatment of memory loss is whether "mental exercise" can slow or prevent the losses that occur in Alzheimer's disease. It is true that losses in specific mental function can sometimes be overcome with compensating strategies that rely on different, intact areas of brain function. Finding these strategies can involve some trial and error. A professional who measures brain function (such as a neuropsychologist) may be able to suggest such strategies. However, finding these compensating strategies is not always possible. It is also true that keeping mentally active is important for good mental health. As dementia progresses, previously stimulating and enjoyable activities become difficult and frustrating. Pushing a person to do that which they cannot do helps no one. Looking for substitute activities that provide stimulation and pleasure should be tried.

A number of medical treatments have shown promise in improving function or slowing the decline in Alzheimer's type dementia. Cholinesterase inhibitors, which boost the amount of acetylcholine in the brain to improve nerve function, are the only prescription medications for Alzheimer's approved by the Food and Drug Administration (FDA). (Limited information suggests the drugs may also work for people with vascular dementia.) The four cholinesterase inhibitors are TACRINE (COGNEX), DONEPEZIL (ARICEPT), RIVASTIGMINE (EXELON), and GALANTAMINE (REMINYL). Tacrine is no longer in common use due to its side effects. These drugs cause a small improvement in mental function overall. However, some people do much better, whereas some aren't helped at all. The cholinesterase inhibitors treat the symptoms of loss of brain function but are not thought to affect the speed of the deterioration in Alzheimer's disease. The benefits of the drugs are usually seen at the maximum-recommended dose and disappear as soon as they are stopped.

The most common side effects are stomach upset and diarrhea, which do not affect everyone who takes these drugs. To avoid such side effects in a patient, the medication is started at a low dose and gradually increased to the highest recommended dose. These medications are expensive, generally costing more than $100 a month.

Vitamin E is an antioxidant that has been shown to improve mental function in people with Alzheimer's disease. In clinical trials, a dosage of 1000 units twice daily was found to be effective in slowing the progression of dementia due to Alzheimer's disease. Vitamin E is thought to work by slowing damage to the nerve cells. There is little evidence of side effects. However, always discuss new treatments with your physician before you start any. It is not a cure and the overall effect is small. Another drug, SELEGILINE, tested in the same clinical trial as vitamin E, also showed a small benefit. Selegiline is much more expensive, with more adverse effects than with vitamin E, and is therefore generally not recommended.

A plant derivative from the tree of the same name, ginkgo biloba has been shown in limited studies to cause small improvements in the mental function of people with Alzheimer's disease. It is relatively safe, although occasional headache or gastrointestinal symptoms are common side effects. It may promote bleeding in combination with other drugs, like aspirin or WARFARIN (COUMADIN), which diminish the clotting of blood. There have been reports of serious bleeding, including brain hemorrhage, in a few individuals who were taking ginkgo biloba and warfarin. Do not take this combination unless you have discussed it with your doctor.

Many other medicines, such as the nonsteroidal anti-inflammatory drugs (NSAIDs), antioxidants, and other anti-inflammatory drugs, have been supported by less well-designed studies. While science has been unable to state definitively that such drugs do not work, at present there is insufficient evidence to argue that the benefits of these drugs outweigh their risks. As active research in Alzheimer's treatment is expanding every day, many other new leads are being followed in hopes of future treatments that will improve function and slow progression if not simply cure the disease. Be aware, though, that the high level of interest in Alzheimer's generates news about potentially effective treatments years before they are either known to work or available for patients. Many drugs initially considered capable of preventing or curing Alzheimer's are now in the ash heap of treatments proved not to work.

Preventing small strokes is an important issue in people with dementia. Small strokes can accumulate as the cause of dementia and can contribute to the behavior problems of persons with Alzheimer's disease. Control of blood pressure, cholesterol, and blood thinners, such as aspirin, are the treatments most often recommended in stroke prevention. Those with memory loss should pay close attention to the management of these health problems.

CARING FOR SOMEONE WITH DEMENTIA

INITIAL ISSUES

No two persons with dementia are alike. As brain function deteriorates, the abilities affected vary from person to person. Communication and completing daily activities can become challenging as dementia advances. For a caregiver, understanding the symptoms of dementia helps in preparing for future difficulties while reducing stress.

The term *dementia* covers several areas of brain functions. Memory loss is only one symptom associated with dementia. Other possible impairments include at least one of the following areas: aphasia (language), agnosia (visual–spatial skills), apraxia (movement), and executive functions (organization and planning). Each area of brain functions affects communication, behavior, and independence.

The most common type of memory trouble occurs if the person is unable to make new memories. This means that a demented patient has trouble learning new tasks and remembering recent events (see Figure 26-5 and Otto Graham's story on page 617). In essence, the tenth time you instruct the person the correct procedure to use the microwave oven, it is just as if you are telling the person for the first time. Old memories, like the name of the street the person grew up on or name of the third-grade teacher, are available, but new memories, like appointments or whether medicine was taken, cannot be made. Trouble in this area often requires supervision with medication management, meal preparation, bill paying, and escorts to medical appointments.

Language difficulty begins with word-finding problems, but can progress to an inability to communicate needs or understand instructions. The demented person attempts to compensate for language difficulties by using all clues available in communication; therefore, the caregiver should provide those clues. Speak clearly and directly to the person. Use language that is easily understood, not slang or metaphors. Persons with dementia often understand words very literally. Use positive facial expressions and tone of voice. Use gestures, and repeat instructions if necessary. Difficulty with communication could become worse under stress. Even those having only mild trouble with communication may have trouble talking to the 911 operator and articulating the problem in an emergency. Wearing personal identification, such as an ID bracelet or ID card, at all times is an important safety recommendation.

Visual-spatial problems occur if the visual messages are jumbled in the brain or if the person has trouble identifying objects or organizing what the eyes see. A person may have 20/20 vision but have trouble reading or recognizing items that should be familiar. This problem is often confused with language difficulty. Persons who can't identify objects often have trouble following directions. If you can't identify objects in space, you may be unable to respond to simple requests like passing the salt or picking up a toothbrush. Safety while driving becomes a particular concern if this symptom is present and organizing visual information is required to make good decisions on the road. For instance, drivers who cannot immediately identify and recognize a red octagon (STOP sign) while driving could get into serious trouble on the road.

Movement problems generally occur in the later stages of dementing illness. The brain is unable to direct the body to make smooth movements, and even simple overlearned tasks, like walking and dressing, become difficult. At this point the person may require assistance for urinating or defecating at a toilet or to get out of a chair, though there may be nothing physically wrong with the person's body. It is important that the environment be kept safe and walking areas free from obstacles. Throw rugs, electric or phone cords, glass tabletops, and sharp-edged furniture should be removed from the living area. Furniture should be sturdy, as it may be used for leaning or support. Persons with spatial difficulties can benefit from modeling, with the caregiver walking in front of the otherwise steady person who copies the caregiver's movements. Keeping the person safe and preventing falls should be the chief concern at this stage.

Among the earliest signs of dementia are the problems with executive function. These include difficulty with organization and planning, managing complex tasks, and judgment. The person may have trouble preparing a holiday meal for the family, packing for a trip, or navigating from a map. These early symptoms are often hidden by giving up such tasks. However, as these problems become worse, previously routine tasks become difficult. Often, as judgment becomes impaired, changes in mood and personality are also seen. Behavior can also change, as the person may become less inhibited.

Even if problems with executive function occur at the earliest stages, it is difficult to gauge a person's decisions. While it is important to allow competent adults autonomy, identifying these problems early gives a family an opportunity to begin making plans. Candid discussions should begin as early as possible about how the impaired person would like care to be provided or how decisions should be made, if there is ever a need. Remember that persons with dementia often cannot see their own

FAMILY JOURNAL

Living with her daughter, Irene N., 84, was in the later stages of Alzheimer's disease. Her daughter was distressed by accusations made by Irene N. that she was stealing her things. This usually involved some personal item that Irene N. had misplaced.

Irene N. was also refusing to change clothes and bathe, saying that she "just took a bath yesterday," despite the obvious aroma from her urinary incontinence. Her daughter pushed hard for a bath. When she tried to help her mother take off her sweater, Irene N. slapped her arm, leaving a bruise.

impairment. Well-intentioned families are often too quick to take over critical decision making from someone with early dementia. The best planning should include the person affected. This is more likely to reduce fear and resistance. Chapter 44 provides legal information on planning for disability.

In other cases, families ignore or are not aware of the extent of the problem until a crisis occurs. This is often the case with out-of-town caregivers. It is important to deal with the particular crisis first (e.g., paying overdue bills or cleaning unkempt homes) and then to move quickly to make up for lost time. Schedule a thorough evaluation, and seek help in assessing the home situation for safety. Make arrangements for supervision if necessary. Investigate options for alternative living arrangements, such as assisted living or retirement communities. A local office of the Alzheimer's Association or Area Agency on Aging can provide information on the types of services available in a particular area of the country.

Becoming a caregiver is not always a choice. It is a role that most people do not anticipate and no one can be completely prepared for. Getting good information regarding the diagnosis, obtaining education about symptoms, and investigating services and resources available can make the process of becoming a caregiver less stressful and more successful.

BEHAVIOR PROBLEMS IN ADVANCED DEMENTIA

Behavior problems often occur in the later stages of a dementing illness, and can be extremely frustrating and stressful for caregivers. These behaviors vary from minor annoyances, like repeating questions, to severe agitation and violent outbursts. The patient's and caregiver's safety must be the first concern should challenging behaviors occur. Medications can help in severe situations, particularly if the demented person is fearful, anxious, or depressed. However, medications always come with side effects. Caregiver education regarding behavior management can reduce the need for such medication.

It is important to understand that difficult behaviors are generally not an intentional attempt by someone with dementia to make a caregiver's life more difficult. Persons with advanced dementia do not have the ability to form that kind of intent. However, most behaviors do have a cause, and finding the cause can often prevent any behavior problems.

Looking for the causes of behavior problems takes some skill. Having knowledge about the person's history, personality, and habits can be helpful. Generally, the causes of behavior problems are broken into two categories: internal and external. *Internal causes* can include illness, as described above, pain or discomfort, constipation or need to use the toilet, hunger, or fatigue. Look for signs of discomfort or a toilet need. Is the person fidgeting or showing signs of being in a pain, such as holding or protecting a particular part of the body? Do these behaviors occur at a specific time, like right before or after a meal? Is the person showing signs of being too hot (taking off clothing) or too cold? Any one of these issues could lead to agitation and behavior problems.

External causes are usually related to environment or activity. Persons with dementia often have a distorted view of the world. They can overreact to situations that we take in stride. Look at the environment. Is the room well lit? Is there a safe path for the person to walk and get things they need? Also, consider the schedule of activities. Is there enough activity and structure to the day? Is there too much activity, such as a large number of guests or loud activities? Is the person lonely or bored? Is the person being rushed to accomplish something, like getting ready for an appointment? Is the person being asked to accomplish a task that they are not able to do? Another external cause to difficult behavior can in fact be the caregiver. Persons with dementia can often sense anger and anxiety. What is the mood of the caregiver? Has the caregiver unwittingly instigated the negative behavior?

In general, do not contradict or argue with someone with dementia. If the person believes something to be true that is not and the belief doesn't interfere with care or cause safety concerns, why correct the person? If you can work around the delusion through distraction or redirection, a confrontation might be averted. Trying to be logical or trying to bring the demented person into your world is much less successful than going to the person's world. Overall, it is best to avoid conflict when possible.

If you are a caregiver for someone who exhibits difficult behaviors, stay positive and stay calm. Issues like repeating questions, using foul language, or making suspicious accusations can be extremely frustrating, but they usually are a phase that will eventually pass, and new behaviors emerge. The best course of action is to reassure the person that everything is okay and that they will be cared for. Redirect or distract the person with other activities that interest them. Food often works, and knowing the person's previous interests helps in this regard. Restructure the environment if possible. Remove the person from overwhelming situations, such as large family gatherings. Allow enough time to get necessary activities like bathing and grooming to be completed without rushing. Be creative. What works today might not work tomorrow, so you must be willing to reevaluate and plan new strategies. Most of all, keep your sense of humor.

Prescription medications have a limited role in dealing with difficult behaviors. If depression contributes to the behavior problem, antidepressants can be very helpful. The antianxiety drugs, or minor tranquilizers, can help with sleep and agitation but sometimes achieve the opposite effect of increasing agitation. The antipsychotic medications have the best evidence of effectiveness in dealing with the serious agitation and abnormal thoughts that occur in later stages of dementia. If delusions (abnormal or untrue beliefs) or hallucinations (hearing or seeing something nonexistent) are present, antipsychotic medications are likely to help. However, the antipsychotic medications can cause changes in body movements or abnormal movements (called tardive dyskinesia) that can interfere with personal function and may be permanent. For this reason, these drugs should only be used for a serious behavior problem in the smallest doses and for the shortest time required for managing the symptoms.

(*figure* 26-5)

Otto Graham, 2003.

A CHAMPION FOREVER: OTTO GRAHAM 1921-2003

Otto Graham is best remembered as the famous quarterback who led the Cleveland Browns to four AAFC championships and three NFL titles. He was voted Most Valuable Player (MVP) in the NFL in 1953 and 1955, and was All-Pro five times. His uniform, number 14, was retired by the Browns, and he was inducted into the Pro Football Hall of Fame in 1965.

Otto Graham has also had a major impact on millions of people off the gridiron. After he underwent a colon resection for cancer, he had to learn to live with a colostomy. Rather than get depressed and withdrawn, Otto went on the road. He gave speeches on behalf of the American Cancer Society and encouraged and supported others who were trying to adjust to living with a colostomy. He promoted screening strategies that help doctors identify and treat cancer at earlier, more treatable stages.

Probably Otto's biggest life challenge was when his wife Beverly noticed that he was becoming more forgetful and occasionally confused.

BEVERLY'S STORY

Something was different about Otto. When he began asking the same questions over and over, I wondered if his confusion meant a change in the dosage of his heart medicine was in order. Months later, Otto became confused at the airport and was chided by a clerk who said, "How could you lead the Cleveland Browns for ten years and yet not be able to figure out how to return a rental car."

During Otto's next appointment with Dr. O'Neil, I asked about Alzheimer's disease and dementia. The tests proved to be relatively simple, but clearly indicated some confusion and memory loss. I was devastated. Otto's brother had just died of Lou Gehrig's disease (ALS), and I had said there was only one disease I feared more—Alzheimer's.

Having been married 56 years at the time, I knew Otto better than anyone and was ready to be by his side for whatever lay ahead. Our daughter, Sandy, who lives nearby, gave me Tuesdays off and a few hours Sunday morning so I could go to church. Otto was fine with Tuesdays but would rather have gone to church than to be left at home.

Otto's biggest disappointment was when Dr. O'Neil and I agreed that he shouldn't drive a car anymore. He showed more anger and frustration over this than any other change in his routine because he then had to face reality. Once accepted, Otto's selfless sense of humor returned.

Beverly Graham

Alzheimer's disease has no respect for who you are and what you have accomplished. Presidents, famous actors and actresses, professors, and, yes, even star athletes have been afflicted. Even after his diagnosis, Otto continued to be a tough competitor. He appreciated that even though there is no cure yet for the disease, medications have become available that may help. Although he cherished his independence, he accepted the instructions and guidance of his physicians, his wife, and children, when it became clear that he could no longer safely operate a motor vehicle.

Otto Graham died on December 17, 2003 at the age of 82 from a dissection of the aorta. Both on and off the field, Otto Graham has inspired countless numbers of people. He truly was a champion of champions.

WHAT YOU NEED TO KNOW

▶ Memory changes do occur with normal aging. However, there are good reasons to see a doctor if you or someone you know has memory loss: to find out whether the loss is reversible; to obtain medications to slow the loss; and to learn coping skills.

▶ Alzheimer's disease is the leading cause of dementia. The 10 early warnings are given in the section "10 Warning Signs." The warnings screen for loss of memory, judgment, and reasoning, as well as changes in mood and behavior. Your doctor can help you or your loved one determine whether a problem is present or developing.

▶ Other disorders can mimic Alzheimer's disease. A medical evaluation can determine possible causes and treatments.

FOR MORE INFORMATION

▶ **Alzheimer's Association**
919 North Michigan Avenue, Suite 1000
Chicago, IL 60611
**800-272-3900 (24-hour hotline),
312-335-8700**
Fax: 312-335-1110
TTY: 312-335-8882
E-mail: info@alz.org
Web: www.alz.org
The association is a voluntary organization that serves Alzheimer's disease patients, their families, and their physicians by supporting medical research through programs and providing support (e.g., adult day care, respite care, telephone help lines) to patients and caregivers. It publishes information for health professionals and patients, both in print and online. An extensive bibliographic database organized by clinical topics and accessible on the internet is useful to the practitioner. Brochures and pamphlets may be purchased in bulk quantities. The national office has links to more than 200 local Alzheimer's Association chapters.

▶ **Alzheimer's Disease Education and Referral Center (ADEAR)**
P.O. Box 8250
Silver Spring, MD 20907
800-438-4380 or 301-495-3311
Fax (301) 495-3334
E-mail: adear@alzheimers.org
Web: www.alzheimers.org
A service of the National Institute on Aging, ADEAR provides a wide range of information and publications on Alzheimer's disease for health professionals, including an annual report of research (which can be ordered by telephone) and an online bibliographic database. ADEAR also provides patients and caregivers with information, publications, and referral services to national and state services and programs.

▶ **American Academy of Neurology (AAN)**
1080 Montreal Avenue
St. Paul, MN 551116
651-695-1940
Fax: 651-695-2791
Web: www.aan.com
The AAN offers fact sheets and resource lists on Alzheimer's disease, as well as information on current research and continuing education courses for physicians on dementia care.

▶ **American Geriatrics Society (AGS)**
Empire State Building
350 5th Avenue, Suite 801
New York, NY 10018
212-308-1414 or 800-247-4779
Fax: 212-832-8646
Web: info.www.americangeriatrics.org
The AGS is a nationwide, not-for-profit association of geriatrics health care professionals dedicated to improving the health, independence, and quality of life of all older people. It supports this mission through activities in professional education on the clinical care of older people, research, public information and education, and public policy efforts and by collaboration with other organizations.

▶ Eldercare Locator
800-677-1116
Established in 1991 as a public service of the U.S. Administration on Aging, the Eldercare Locator lists information and referral services provided by state area agencies on aging. Individuals who telephone receive information on more than 4800 state and local information and referral service providers identified by every zip code in the United States.

SUGGESTED READING

▶ The Loss of Self: A Family Resource for the Care of Alzheimer's Disease and Related Disorders.
D. Cohen and C. Eisdorfer. 1994. Revised edition.
New York: New American Library.

▶ The 36-Hour Day: A Family Guide to Caring for Persons with Alzheimer's Disease, Related Dementing Illnesses, and Memory Loss in Later Life.
N. L. Mace and P. V. Rabins. 1991. Revised edition.
Baltimore: John Hopkins
University Press.

Addiction is not a mysterious chemical process; it is the logical outgrowth of the way a drug makes a person feel. . . . A person repeatedly seeks artificial infusions of a sensation, whether it be one of somnolence or vitality, that is not supplied by the organic balance of his life as a whole.

—*Stanton Peele, Love and Addiction*

THE AUTHOR

27 *Melinda S. Lantz*

MELINDA S. LANTZ, MD is a board-certified, fellowship-trained geriatric psychiatrist with additional certification in addiction psychiatry. She has served as director of psychiatry for the Jewish Home and Hospital since 1993 and is assistant professor of geriatrics at the Mount Sinai School of Medicine. Her work includes care of elderly nursing home patients, teaching, research, and administration of mental health services to older adults. Dr. Lantz has been the principal investigator of several clinical trials, including the development of new psychotropic medications and the integration of complementary and alternative medicine in the nursing home. She has been active in promoting behavioral alternatives to the use of psychotropic medication and teaches a course for medical students, residents, and fellows, "Behavioral Therapy with the Older Adult." She is the series editor for the monthly column "The Psychiatry Consultant" in the journal *Clinical Geriatrics,* which is sponsored by the American Association of Geriatric Psychiatry.

27 | ALCOHOL ABUSE

Many adults, young and old, enjoy alcoholic beverages. But when does drinking become a problem? Is there a safe amount? You have probably heard that there are even health benefits. We will explore these issues in this section, but we also look for clues that might suggest that you or a loved one is a "problem-drinker."

Alcohol in moderation (one to two drinks per day for women and two to three drinks per day for men) has been reported to have positive health benefits, such as reduction in the risk of coronary artery disease, the most common cause of death in the United States. Some reports have even suggested a benefit in diabetics and in cancer prevention. However, other studies have challenged or contradicted these findings. So what are you to do?

Remember that most clinical studies are done on younger populations or on groups in which elderly persons may not be well represented. In addition, it would be difficult to put a group together that reliably matches the general population of older persons. As you know, many older adults take several medications that may adversely interact with alcohol. As you grow older, your metabolism changes and so does the way you react to alcohol. Therefore, there can be no one-size-fits-all recommendation. Suffice it to say that it is difficult to recommend alcoholic beverages for their medicinal effects on older adults. More complications have arisen from heavy use of alcohol than any possible positive effects. These complications include falls, adverse drug interactions, traffic accidents, liver disease, ulcers and gastrointestinal bleeding, memory loss, depression, and the list can go on and on. Am I suggesting you become a teetotaler? It depends. If you take multiple prescription drugs, especially WARFARIN (COUMADIN), tranquilizers, or antidepressants, it is probably a good idea. If you are prone to falls or have a neurological condition that affects your balance, I would recommend abstinence. If you have ulcers, liver, or pancreatic disease, drinking is a bad idea. It won't help if you are depressed or have sleep problems, and will likely make things worse.

The best advice I can give is to check with your doctor, and be honest (see Figure 27-1). Measure how much you actually drink. If you drink whiskey, vodka, or other hard liquor, measure the amount with a shot glass. If you drink beer or wine, measure how many ounces. Do this over the course of a typical week, and then bring the total to your doctor. He or she knows your unique situation. Your doctor will tell you whether this is a safe amount or whether you should cut down your consumption.

Alcohol abuse and dependence in older adults is less common than in younger persons, but presents a greater challenge because older persons tend to deny that they have a problem. In addition, it may be more difficult for the family and physician of the older alcoholic to recognize impairments in functioning due to alcohol use until they reach a severe stage. The lifetime prevalence for alcoholism in those over age 65 is approximately 14% for men and 1.5% for women. Alcohol abuse is a significant factor in hospitalizations of older adults, due to the medical problems that develop because of excessive drinking.

(figure 27-1)

Honestly discuss your alcohol use with your doctor.

Older adults with drinking problems do not typically seek help voluntarily. They may have developed alcohol-related illnesses, such as anemia, peptic ulcer, diabetes, hypertension, liver disease, peripheral nerve damage, and mental status changes. The emotional impact of alcoholism on the family is often tremendous. Family members who are concerned about their loved one's drinking are vital sources of information to the primary care physician. This is extremely helpful in order to recognize the alcohol problem and encourage referral for treatment.

There are some warning signs that suggest that alcohol abuse might be a problem. Obviously, these difficulties occur more often than not in persons who are not problem drinkers, but should alert you to the possibility. They include unexplained falls, neglect of personal hygiene, mood problems such as depression and anxiety, and sleep or memory problems. Alcohol use that results in impairment in functioning, threatens health, or places the adult at risk for harm is considered problematic and often meets criteria for abuse or dependence.

To determine whether someone is having a drinking problem, physicians use a tool called the *CAGE questionnaire,* which is shown in Figure 27-2.

The National Institute on Alcohol Abuse and Alcoholism has identified a potential problem of alcohol use in the older adult as drinking more than one alcoholic beverage per day or seven drinks in a week on a regular basis. This is due to the significantly higher blood alcohol levels that accumulate in the elderly. Just as the handling of many drugs is altered in the body of an older person requiring smaller doses of the medication, alcohol is metabolized differently as we get older. A young adult will achieve a blood alcohol level of approximately 0.03% after one drink of 1.5 ounces of distilled liquor, 5 ounces of wine, or 12 ounces of beer, while in a 75-year-old the level may rise as high as 0.08% (the legal limit for intoxication in many states). Older drinkers often develop complications from alcohol use with much lower levels of consumption. Many elderly suffer from chronic medical conditions, such as congestive heart failure, hypertension, and diabetes, or use medications, such as nonsteroidal anti-inflammatory drugs, tranquilizers, and other psychoactive medications, that place them at high risk for adverse events if combined with alcohol.

The risk factors associated with the development of alcoholism in late life include prior history of alcohol abuse, a family history of alcoholism, the

DOCTOR'S DIARY

Sam G., 73, was accompanied to my office by his two daughters. They had confronted their father about his increased drinking of beer and brandy over the past year since the death of his wife. He lives alone, and had kept himself isolated since his wife died. Sam G. appeared disheveled, and his breath smelled of alcohol. He admitted to drinking "a few beers at night," but he did not feel he had a problem. His daughters had found his apartment in disarray, with little food and many bottles of beer and brandy. I suggested an inpatient alcohol detoxification program to which he agreed after a great deal of coaxing from his daughters. Sam G. had a difficult withdrawal period and thought of suicide. After five days I transferred him to an inpatient psychiatry unit where he was treated for major depression. I discharged him from the hospital three weeks later on an antidepressant, and I referred him to an outpatient substance abuse program and encouraged him to attend Alcoholics Anonymous meetings.

(figure 27-2)

THE CAGE QUESTIONNAIRE

To find out whether you have a drinking problem, check each of the following questions that applies to you.

C: Have you ever tried to cut down your intake of alcoholic beverages?

A: Have you been annoyed by criticism of your drinking?

G: Have you ever felt guilty regarding your drinking?

E: Have you felt the need for an eye opener in the morning?

If your total includes two or more checks, there could be a problem, and you should discuss it with your doctor.

development of new medical problems, loss of a spouse, recent retirement, and social isolation. In the United States older men are three times more likely than women are to suffer from alcohol abuse or dependence. Recognition of alcohol problems in older women, however, is believed to be low, with limited treatment and resources available. Women alcoholics are more likely to be married to an alcoholic, be victims of domestic violence, and suffer from psychiatric disorders, including depression and anxiety.

Older adults with alcohol problems fall into two types. One group includes chronic alcoholics who started drinking when they were young and have continued drinking throughout life, often punctuated by periods of more or less drinking. The other group includes the problem drinkers who begin a pattern of destructive drinking in later life in response to the stresses of aging, including retirement, loss of a spouse, or the need to cope with increasing medical frailty. The approach to treatment in both groups is essentially the same, but a history of any prior interventions is important to obtain.

Elderly alcoholics are at an extremely high risk for suicide. In part, this is due to depression, isolation, and the erratic and violent behavior that often accompanies alcohol intoxication. All patients with alcohol problems should be assessed for depression and suicidal ideation. If a person's suicide risk appears high, emergency inpatient treatment is necessary.

Treatment of the older alcoholic requires a comprehensive approach. Older adults are far more likely to require inpatient treatment in order to to avoid complications associated with sudden withdrawal from alcohol. This to is especially important if there are other medical or psychiatric conditions that require monitoring during the withdrawal period. Outpatient counseling and education may be sufficient for a medically stable patient who is identified early and has strong social supports. Medications used as a disincentive to drinking, such as DISULFIRAM (ANTABUSE) or NALTREXONE (REVIA), may be prescribed for some highly motivated patients, but their tolerability and efficacy in older persons is questionable. Linkage to outpatient services, which should include social support, ongoing alcoholism counseling, and 12-step programs including Alcoholics Anonymous or alternatives, such as SMART or Women for Sobriety are vital for maintaining sobriety. Family education and referral to Al-Anon and other groups is extremely helpful in allowing the family to focus on their own needs and coping skills. Alcoholism is a chronic disorder, and therefore requires ongoing support just like many other diseases that affect older adults. Relapses may occur, but success can be achieved with the support of the family, friends, physician, and organizations as the follow-up report by his family on our case patient shows (see Family Journal).

FAMILY JOURNAL

My sister and I were so happy when our Dad, Sam G., agreed to be admitted to an alcohol treatment program. He really didn't think he had a problem, but said he would do it because he loved us. It became clear shortly after he was admitted that Dad was extremely depressed since Mom died last year. Drinking helped numb his pain and get him to sleep. However, he found out in treatment how destructive his alcoholism had become. It actually made his depression worse. We wish we could say that Dad recovered completely and his depression cleared up. He did not feel he needed any help staying sober, but he started drinking again a few weeks later. We were able to get him back to his psychiatrist who reinforced the need for Dad to go to AA meetings. My sister and I joined Al-Anon. Dad has been alcohol-free now for two months, and we hope that he is on his way to permanent recovery.

WHAT YOU NEED TO KNOW

▶ Alcohol may be safe in small or moderate amounts, but age-related body changes might cause problems with alcohol use.

▶ Many prescription drugs and over-the-counter medications can adversely interact with alcohol.

▶ Alcohol may be harmful if you have many medical conditions. Check with your doctor to see if any of your medical conditions make alcohol use inadvisable.

▶ Treatment programs are available to help an alcoholic recover. It may require hospitalization in an alcohol treatment unit to manage withdrawal symptoms. Support groups, such as Alcoholics Anonymous, Rational Recovery, and SMART, have helped many alcoholics recover.

▶ Family members can receive help through programs, such as Al-Anon and Alateen, and community service agencies that offer substance abuse counseling. A family member may get help even if the alcoholic is not ready to stop drinking.

27

FOR MORE INFORMATION

▶ **National Institutes of Health**
9000 Rockville Pike
Bethesda, MD 20892
Web: www.nih.gov

▶ **Alcoholics Anonymous**
Grand Central Station
P.O. Box 495
New York, NY 10163
Web: www.alcoholics-anonymous.org

▶ **Al-Anon/Alateen**
1600 Corporate Landing Parkway
Virgina Beach, VA 23454
Web: www.al-anon-alateen.org

▶ **Women for Sobriety**
P.O. Box 618
Quakertown, PA 18951
215-536-8026
Fax: 215-538-9026
Web: www.womenforsobriety.org

▶ **SMART Recovery**
7537 Mentor Avenue, Suite 306
Mentor, OH 44060
440-951-5357
Fax: 440-951-5358
E-mail: srmail1@aol.com

▶ **Rational Recovery**
Box 800
Lotus, CA 95651
530-621-2667
Web: www.rational.org

You don't have to cook fancy or complicated masterpieces—just good food from fresh ingredients.

—*Julia Child*

THE AUTHOR

28

Linda Bobroff

LINDA BENJAMIN BOBROFF, PH.D, RD, LD/N, is a professor in the Department of Family, Youth, and Community Sciences at the University of Florida, as well as a Cooperative Extension Nutrition specialist. Dr. Bobroff earned her MS and PhD in nutrition from Rutgers University. She is a registered and State of Florida–licensed dietitian. She has been on the faculty of the University of Florida since 1985.

Dr. Bobroff's Extension education programs address significant nutrition and health concerns, including heart health, cancer risk, and weight management, and life-cycle nutrition, including maternal and infant nutrition and nutrition in aging. She develops educational curricula and prepares Extension publications that are used statewide. Dr. Bobroff has received over $400,000 in grant funds in support of Extension programs.

Dr. Bobroff served on the board of directors of the Society for Nutrition Education from 2000 to 2003 and was president of the Gainesville District Dietetic Association and the north central district of the Florida Association of Family and Consumer Sciences.

In 2001, Dr. Bobroff received the Florida Extension Association of Family and Consumer Sciences' Outstanding Specialist Award, and in 2002, she was honored by the Florida Dietetic Association with its highest award: Distinguished Dietitian.

28 | NUTRITION AND DIET

Lifestyle choices, including food, physical activity, and smoking, influence the health risks one faces in life. Although choices made early in life can affect health in later years, it is never too late to change a lifestyle to promote successful aging.

A significant lifestyle indicator for short- and long-term health risks is diet—the food that a person eats on a regular basis. Diet affects all aspects of health. A healthy diet provides essential nutrients in amounts that support all body functions. In addition, a healthy diet (along with regular physical activity) contributes to a healthy body weight. Finally, a healthy diet reduces the risk of having a chronic disease, such as heart disease, cancer, stroke, diabetes, or osteoporosis, which are the major causes of disability and death in the United States. By making proper food choices, seniors can reduce their risk of disease and promote overall good health, which will increase their chance of remaining active and independent throughout their lives.

National surveys indicate that 60 to 70% of older people in the United States have diets that need improvement and 12% have poor diets. Diets were rated on the type and variety of foods eaten, as well as how much fat, saturated fat, cholesterol, and sodium were included. The lowest scores were found in people with low income, indicating that poor people are at higher risk for health problems. Clearly, there is room for improvement in the eating patterns of older people, just as there is with younger people.

This chapter begins with an overview of physiological (normal body processes) changes that occur as people age and shows how these changes influence nutrient needs. Practical strategies for obtaining the key nutrients needed for good health and gauging your nutritional risk are covered next. The chapter ends with an exploration of dietary guidelines to promote health and reduce risk of disease.

PHYSIOLOGICAL CHANGES

During aging, changes in body composition taste, and smell, gastrointestinal tract, and liver, kidney, and immune system function affect nutritional needs. By learning to adjust food intake to meet nutritional needs, we promote positive nutrition and health.

Remember that physiological changes occur in individuals at different rates. Not everyone ages in the same way. How we age depends on genetic makeup and lifestyle. Lifestyle choices, even at an older age, can influence how bodies age, within limits set by genes.

HEALTHY DIET

- Supports positive nutritional status
- Promotes a healthy immune system
- Helps with weight management
- Decreases risk of infection, illness, falls, and chronic diseases
- Supports successful aging

DECREASED ENERGY REQUIREMENT

A person's estimated energy requirement begins to decline after age 19! For men or women the decrease is 10 or 7 calories per year, respectively, for each year over 19. For example, a 19-year-old man has an estimated energy requirement of 2550 to 3545 calories per day. At age 65, his requirement would be 2090 to 3085 calories. A 19-year-old woman's estimated energy requirement is 1910 to 2670 calories per day, which would decrease to 1590 to 2350 by age 65.

Note: Estimated energy requirements do not reflect the caloric needs of all older persons.

BODY COMPOSITION

Lean body mass: Lean body mass includes muscle, bone, organs, water, and connective tissue. As we age, our lean body mass decreases, affecting overall strength and increasing risk of bone fractures (see the box, "Decreased Energy Requirement with Age"). The decrease in lean body mass reduces the amount of energy required to keep the body functioning, and so the amount of energy (kilocalories) needed in the diet also decreases. If seniors do not reduce the quantity of food eaten (or increase their physical activity), body weight will increase. For most people this is undesirable, since being overweight increases the risk of diabetes, heart disease, and some forms of cancer.

For seniors, strength training (using weights or machines) can reduce muscle loss and even build muscle mass. Older persons who minimize muscle loss with strength training have higher energy needs and can therefore eat a more varied (and satisfying) diet. It is never too late to begin strength training, but sedentary people should first check with a health care provider before starting a vigorous physical activity program.

Body water: Another change with aging is a reduction in the body's water content. The body of an infant is about 75% water and the body of an 80-year-old about 50%. Coupled with an older person's decreased thirst, the change in body water is related to a high risk of dehydration. Dehydration is more common in persons with cognitive impairments, such as Alzheimer's disease, uncontrolled diabetes, diarrhea, or fever. Also, persons who use diuretics or abuse laxatives are at high risk for dehydration.

Recommendations for fluid intake vary, and some older people struggle to drink lots of water. To stay well hydrated, a person should have the goal of replacing 1 to 1.5 ml of water per calorie expended. The higher recommendation would be about 10 cups of water daily for a person who expends 1600 calories per day. Not all of this water has to come from fluid intake. About 1 cup of water is produced in the body by

HELPFUL HINT

To maintain body weight as you age, reduce your portion sizes and be physically active. Eat foods that are rich in nutrients to make every calorie count.

(figure 28-1)

Many older persons do not drink enough fluids. A reasonable goal is seven to eight 8-oz cups of water and other beverages.

normal metabolism, and 1 to 2 cups may be obtained from foods eaten. The remaining 7 to 8 cups should come from water and other beverages.

TASTE AND SMELL

Older persons often have a decreased ability to taste and smell foods. This change may be due to the aging process itself or to the effects of disease and/or medications. Many medications commonly taken by older persons, such as lipid-lowering drugs, antihypertensives, antidepressants, and cardiac medications, alter taste.

Whatever the cause, changes in taste and smell can profoundly affect appetite and eating, with reduced consumption resulting in nutritional deficiencies and increased health risks. To increase the enjoyment of foods, people with taste and/or smell deficits can select foods that are highly flavored with herbs and spices. It is best to avoid the temptation to oversalt foods since salt can increase the risk for high blood pressure.

GASTROINTESTINAL TRACT

Changes in the gastrointestinal (GI) tract, from the mouth to the anus, can affect appetite, food intake, and nutrient requirements. A healthy diet and staying physically active can help keep the GI tract healthy.

Mouth: Decreased saliva production, often caused by medication, makes eating and swallowing difficult and increases risk of gum disease and tooth loss, which can further affect eating. Drinking adequate fluids is especially important for anyone with reduced levels of saliva.

Stomach: Older persons have decreased production of pepsin (an enzyme) and hydrochloric acid. These changes affect the digestion of protein, vitamin B_{12}, folate, iron, calcium, and zinc. Eating a well-balanced diet provides adequate protein and most vitamins and minerals. However, getting adequate vitamin B_{12} can be a challenge due to the change in stomach acidity, and older persons should be sure to obtain this vitamin from fortified foods or a supplement.

Small intestines: A decrease in the enzyme *lactase*, needed to digest milk sugar *(lactose)*, can cause GI discomfort if milk is consumed.

FYI

Changes in eyesight can affect eating, by decreasing your ability to shop, read food labels or recipes, and cook. If you are having difficulty with these activities due to poor eyesight, seek help from family, friends, acquaintances, or government and volunteer agencies. Also, see an eye doctor annually for diagnosis and treatment of conditions or diseases of the eyes.

Lactose intolerance is fairly common among African Americans but can be experienced by people in any ethnic group. Some people with lactose intolerance can comfortably consume small amounts of milk if consumed with other foods, and most can enjoy yogurt and cheese, which are low in lactose. Also, varieties of lactose-reduced milk are available. Keep in mind that people who avoid milk and milk products put themselves at risk for osteoporosis, a major cause of falls and fractures.

Persons who avoid milk and milk products can eat alternate food sources of calcium. Green leafy vegetables, tofu processed with calcium, canned fish with mashed bones, and calcium-fortified foods provide calcium in the diet (see the box, "Calcium from Plant Sources").

Our intestines tend to slow down with age. Decreased *intestinal motility* (movement) can cause a sense of fullness and limit food intake. Also, as the gut contents move slowly through the large intestines, more water than normal is reabsorbed into the body, which causes the gut contents to harden, resulting in constipation. Chronic constipation is a common complaint among older people. The following suggestions can reduce your risk for constipation:

- Drink enough fluids, especially those without caffeine or alcohol.
- Eat foods rich in fiber, especially insoluble fiber found in whole grains and fresh fruits and vegetables.
- Be physically active every day.

SKIN AND KIDNEYS

Due to age-related changes, the skin and kidneys affect the nutritional status of an older person, particularly in regard to vitamin D. The requirement for vitamin D increases with age because the skin's ability to

STOMACH ACID AND VITAMIN B_{12} ABSORPTION

Stomach acid separates naturally occurring vitamin B_{12} from its protein carrier, so that the vitamin can be absorbed. If stomach acid decreases, vitamin B_{12} cannot be separated from the protein and absorption of the vitamin decreases. Over time, this can result in a vitamin B_{12} deficiency. Synthetic vitamin B_{12} is not attached to a protein and does not need acid to be absorbed. Synthetic vitamin B_{12} is found in fortified foods and supplements, and it is recommended that seniors get their vitamin B_{12} from these sources.

CALCIUM FROM PLANT SOURCES

Green leafy vegetables contain calcium, but a substance called oxalic acid, found in some vegetables, binds to calcium and keeps it from being absorbed into the body. Spinach and rhubarb contain enough oxalic acid to make them poor calcium sources (although they are good sources of other nutrients).

synthesize vitamin D decreases with age. Even when exposed to the sun's ultraviolet light, an older person's skin does not form as much vitamin D as the skin of a younger person. As we age, we can't depend upon skin synthesis for our vitamin D requirement; we need to get vitamin D from food sources or supplements. Since vitamin D is not widely available in foods other than fortified foods, seniors should consider taking a vitamin and mineral supplement to obtain this critical nutrient.

Neither the vitamin D that is manufactured in the skin when exposed to sunlight nor the vitamin D in vitamins or the diet is the active form required by the body. It has to be (1) modified by the liver and (2) converted by the kidneys to its active form, calcitriol. As our kidneys age, the ability to form calcitriol decreases, which contributes to the change in vitamin D requirements. The reduction in calcitriol affects calcium status since calcitriol enhances calcium absorption. Seniors need to be sure to get adequate calcium since the amount they absorb is less than in younger adults.

The kidneys also become less efficient in concentrating urine as we get older, and water losses may be excessive, increasing risk of dehydration. This is another reason for older persons to focus on staying hydrated by drinking fluids and eating a well-balanced diet.

IMMUNE FUNCTION

The immune function starts to decline before we reach our older years, and the effects of these changes begin to appear by age 65. Older persons are at higher risk for infections due to changes in the skin and stomach, which are two major barriers against invasion by bacteria and other microorganisms. Seniors may suffer severe reactions to colds, flu, and food-borne illnesses due to a weakened immune system.

Adequate amounts of protein, vitamins C and E, beta-carotene, and zinc are needed to help keep the immune system functioning well. A well-balanced diet includes plenty of fruits and vegetables (for vitamin C

HELPFUL HINT

A multivitamin and mineral supplement provides nutrients that may be marginal in the diets of older persons or that are required in larger amounts as people age. These include vitamins B_{12}, B_6, and D and calcium. Avoid individual supplements as they can cause problems with nutrient interactions. Also, most vitamins and minerals are harmful in large doses. This includes not only the fat-soluble vitamins (A, D, E, and K) but also water-soluble vitamins and minerals.

and beta-carotene), as well as foods from all the food groups (for the other nutrients), as nutrient deficiencies contribute to a poorly functioning immune system.

NUTRITIONAL TECHNIQUES

NUTRITIONAL RISK

How do you know if you are at high risk for poor nutritional health and related health problems? Experts in nutrition for the older population developed an activity to identify persons who are at high risk and who could benefit from nutritional counseling with, for example, a registered dietitian (RD). To check your nutritional risk, complete the activity in Figure 28-2.

You can ask a health professional to help you with an indicated problem, as circled in Figure 28-2. For example, if you have tooth or mouth problems, go to your dentist. If you take multiple medications, check with your pharmacist to be sure that they are not causing interactions that affect appetite or induce another nutrition-related problem.

If your total nutritional score from Figure 28-2 is "good," check it again in six months. If at moderate risk, you can improve your eating habits through the tips you learned from this chapter. Also, you can inquire at your Area Agency on Aging, local senior center, county extension service, or health department for information, educational programs, and/or

(figure 28-2)

Determine your nutritional health. *(Adapted with permission from the Nutrition Screening Initiative.)*

Circle the number next to each item that applies to you:

I have an illness or condition that made me change the kind and/or amount of food I eat. **2**

I eat fewer than two meals per day. **3**

I eat few fruits or vegetables or milk products. **2**

I have three or more drinks of beer, liquor, or wine almost every day. **2**

I have tooth or mouth problems that make it hard for me to eat. **2**

I don't always have enough money to buy the food I need. **4**

I eat alone most of the time. **1**

I take three or more different prescribed or over-the-counter drugs a day. **1**

Without wanting to, I lost or gained 10 or more pounds in the past six months. **2**

I am not always physically able to shop, cook, and/or eat by myself. **2**

INTERPRETATION OF TOTAL NUTRITIONAL SCORE   TOTAL NUTRITIONAL SCORE

Good **0—2**
Moderate risk **3—5**
High risk **6+**

DIETARY GUIDELINES FOR AMERICANS

AIM FOR FITNESS

- Aim for a healthy weight.
- Be physically active each day.

BUILD A HEALTHY BASE

- Let the Pyramid guide your food choices.
- Choose a variety of grains daily, especially whole grains.
- Choose a variety of fruits and vegetables daily.

CHOOSE SENSIBILY

- Choose a diet that is low in saturated fat and cholesterol and moderate in total fat.
- Choose beverages and foods to moderate your intake of sugars.
- Choose and prepare foods with less salt.
- If you drink alcoholic beverages, do so in moderation.

---

services. Recheck your nutritional score in three months. If your score is 6 or higher, you are at high nutritional risk and should take Figure 28-2 to your doctor or other health care professional and discuss the items you circled.

DIETARY GUIDELINES

Every five years since 1980, the U.S. Department of Agriculture (USDA) and U.S. Department of Health and Human Services have published a set of dietary guidelines, "Nutrition and Your Health: Dietary Guidelines for Americans." The guidelines apply to everyone from the age of 2 to over 100.

The fifth version of the guidelines has a three-part theme—aim for fitness, build a healthy base, and choose sensibly (ABC)—to help you select a diet that meets your nutritional needs, promotes a healthy weight, and reduces long-term health risks. The guidelines can be applied to many different cultural and ethnic food patterns.

Two of the key dietary guidelines are to "let the pyramid guide your food choices" and "be physically active each day."

FOOD PYRAMID

Although the USDA has not published a pyramid specifically for older adults, the University of Florida designed the Elder Nutrition and Food Safety (ENAFS) pyramid, as shown in Figure 28-3, as an educational tool for programs with persons 60 years of age and older. The ENAFS pyramid made use of research from the USDA Human Nutrition Research Center on Nutrition and Aging at Tufts University.

Letting the pyramid guide your food choices can help ensure that you eat flexibly enough to meet your dietary needs. Choosing from each of the five food groups every day helps build a varied and sound diet. The food groups also allow variations for cultural or ethnic food ways; for example, the bread, cereal, rice, and pasta group includes tortillas, rice, matzoh, pita bread, and other grain products. Even vegetarians (particularly those who

(figure 28-3)

DAILY FOOD GUIDE PYRAMID FOR ELDERS
Elder Nutrition and Food Safety Daily Food Guide Pyramid for Elders. *(Adapted with permission from the University of Florida.)*

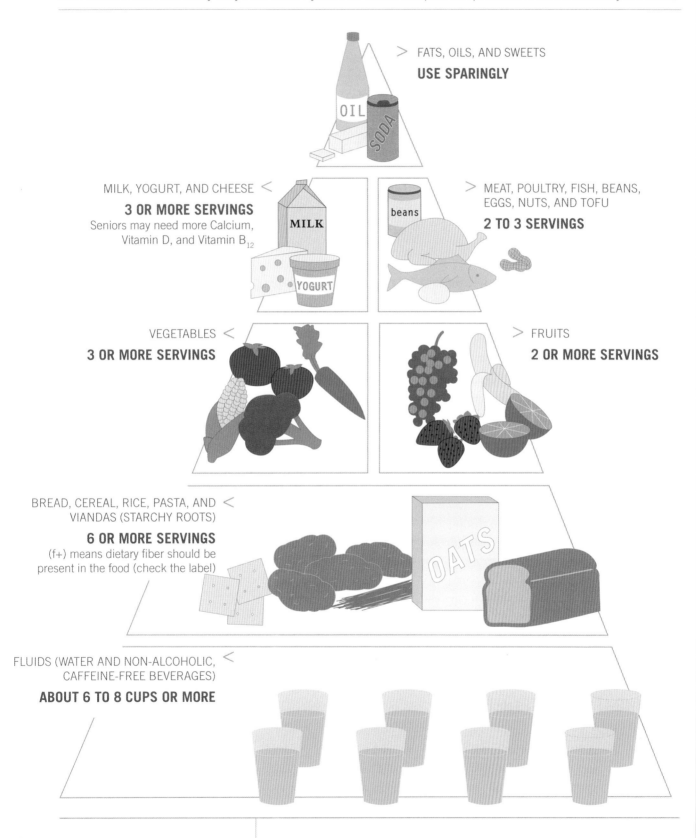

include milk products in their diets) can select a variety of foods from each of the food groups to meet their special needs.

The ENAFS pyramid represents the lower calorie needs of most older persons. The base of the pyramid includes fluids, since drinking adequate fluids is a concern. Included in the graphics are canned and frozen foods, which can be healthful options for older persons. For example, if tooth problems prevent consumption of fresh fruits, canned fruits or soft fresh fruits, like bananas, kiwis, or mangos, are good alternatives. Canned beans are easy to prepare and are an inexpensive protein source that also provides fiber and other nutrients. Frozen vegetables are convenient and nutritionally sound choices when truly fresh vegetables are not readily available. Note that it can be quite a challenge for older persons to obtain from their meals adequate calcium, vitamin D, and vitamin B_{12} unless they include, on a regular basis, *fortified foods,* which have extra amounts of these nutrients.

BEING PHYSICALLY ACTIVE

Older people benefit from weight-bearing exercises (walking, dancing, or bicycling), strength training, stretching, and leisure activities (gardening and cleaning house). Staying physically active has numerous benefits, many of which are related to nutrition and diet:

- Helps maintain muscle mass and strength
- Helps maintain bone mass
- Reduces risk of falls
- Promotes a healthy appetite
- Reduces stress
- Helps weight management
- Promotes heart health

Stay as physically active as you can throughout your life. Be sure to check with your physician if you plan to begin a strenuous exercise program, especially if you have been sedentary for a long time.

All the dietary guidelines are important for good health, and you are encouraged to use them for your own personal eating plan. They can help you meet your nutritional needs and reduce your risk for the chronic diseases that are common in older persons. *Note:* The section "For More Information" has addresses by which you can obtain your own copy of "Dietary Guidelines for Americans," by either mail or the web.

PUTTING IT ALL TOGETHER

KEY NUTRIENTS

Adequate protein is important to minimize loss of muscle mass with aging. People who eat foods from all the food groups in adequate amounts typically get more than enough protein. The recommended dietary allowance (RDA) for protein in older adults is the same as for young adults: 0.8 grams of protein per kilogram of body weight. For example, for a man or woman weighing 60 kg, the RDA is 48 grams of protein.

Note: This amount of protein will meet or exceed the protein needs of about 98% of adults of this weight. This is what recommended dietary allowance means!

Folate, vitamin B$_{12}$, and vitamin B$_6$ are water-soluble, and all are important for a variety of body functions. They are needed for proper use of the energy nutrients: protein, fat, and carbohydrates. These vitamins also help keep blood levels of the amino acid homocysteine low. High blood homocysteine has been linked to an increased risk of heart disease, the leading cause of death among men and women in the United States. A well-balanced diet can supply all of the folate and vitamin B$_6$ needed. It is recommended that older persons get their vitamin B$_{12}$ from fortified foods or a vitamin supplement since naturally occurring vitamin B$_{12}$ is not well absorbed.

Adequate intake of calcium and vitamin D over a lifetime helps prevent bone loss and fractures. Older persons should eat a diet rich in these nutrients and, if necessary, use supplements to increase their consumption. The requirement for vitamin D increases with age, and persons who do not drink milk may need to take a supplement. Some calcium supplements and most multivitamin preparations contain vitamin D.

(figure 28-5)
SAMPLE MENU

BREAKFAST
¾ cup 1% low-fat milk
1 cup bran flakes cereal
1 small banana
¾ cup orange juice with calcium
8 ounces decaffeinated coffee
3 tablespoons 1% low-fat milk

SNACK
8 dried apricots
1 cup club soda

LUNCH
3 ounces turkey breast
2 slices whole wheat bread
½ small tomato, sliced
2 leaves romaine lettuce
mustard
1½ cups water

SNACK
1 medium apple

DINNER
1 cup cooked mashed pinto beans (no salt added)
3 tablespoons salsa
3 tablespoons grated sharp Cheddar cheese
1 whole wheat tortilla
1½ cups water
¾ cup steamed cut green beans

SNACK
½ cup low-fat frozen yogurt

(figure 28-4)

Your physician may recommend the services of a dietitian or nutritionist to plan healthy menus.

Fiber can help prevent constipation and also can play a role in blood cholesterol control. It is easy to get adequate fiber by eating a diet rich in whole grain foods, legumes, fruits, and vegetables. Animal foods do not contain fiber. When increasing the amount of fiber in the diet, it is important to drink extra fluids to avoid GI distress. Also, it is helpful to increase dietary fiber slowly over a period of several weeks to give the body time to adjust to the change.

MENU PLANNING

Let's look at two menus at different calorie levels and see how they meet the needs for the key nutrients protein; vitamins B_6, B_{12}, and D; folate; calcium; and dietary fiber. A well-balanced diet that meets the needs for these nutrients probably will supply other required nutrients as well. Figure 28-5 shows the first menu.

This menu provides 1400 calories (70% of the estimated requirement for women and 55% for men).

76 grams protein	(21% of calories)
240 grams carbohydrate	(65% of calories)
23 grams fat	(14% of calories)
39 grams dietary fiber	(Over 25 grams for women and 38 grams for men are recommended.)
105 milligrams cholesterol	(Below 300 milligrams is recommended.)
1930 milligrams sodium	(Below 2200 milligrams is recommend.)
1100 milligrams calcium	(92% of AI)
2.1 milligrams vitamin B6	(140% of RDA for women and 122% for men)
2.9 micrograms vitamin B12	(122% of RDA)
311 micrograms folate	(78% of RDA)

The menu shown in Figure 28-5 provides over 75% of the recommended intake of all other vitamins and minerals except:

4.0 micrograms vitamin D	(26% of AI)
2.8 milligrams vitamin E	(19% of RDA)

This menu is very low in calories and fat. Adding a teaspoon of margarine on the green beans and having an extra quarter of a cup of frozen yogurt would add fat and calories, as well as additional calcium and vitamin E. Adding another serving of milk would increase vitamin D. A low-potency multivitamin supplement could be used to increase vitamin D and E.

With a few changes, the menu in Figure 28-5 can be expanded to provide about 2100 calories and additional nutrients. Add an extra one-half cup of cereal and one-quarter cup of milk at breakfast, a cup of vanilla yogurt with the morning snack, and a spinach salad for dinner. (Spinach salad includes 1 cup chopped spinach leaves, 3 tablespoons grated carrots, 2 tablespoons mandarin oranges, 2 tablespoons walnuts, 2 teaspoons balsamic vinegar, and 2 tablespoons olive oil.) The nutrient values then become the following:

96 grams protein	(18% of calories)
310 grams carbohydrate	(56% of calories)
64 grams fat	(26% of calories)
45 grams dietary fiber	(Over 25 grams for women and 38 grams for men are recommended.)
120 milligrams cholesterol	(Below 300 milligrams is recommended.)
1835 milligrams sodium	(Below 2200 milligrams is recommended.)
1650 milligrams calcium	(138% of AI)
3.0 milligrams vitamin B6	(200% of RDA for women and 175% for men)
5.2 micrograms vitamin B12	(217% of RDA)
773 micrograms folate	(193% of RDA)

This menu provides over 75% of the RDA of all other vitamins and minerals except:

5.3 micrograms vitamin D	(35% of RDA)
9.25 milligrams vitamin E	(62% of RDA)

Adding the spinach salad brought the folate level up to almost twice the RDA and increased fat to a more desirable level that is still below 30% of calories. Adding the yogurt added calcium and vitamin B_{12}, but the small amount of milk in this menu keeps the vitamin D level low (yogurt is not fortified with vitamin D). Keep in mind that the recommended intake for vitamin D increases with age, and these percentages compare the nutrient with the AI for women age 71 or older. As with the first menu, a low-potency multivitamin supplement could be used to increase vitamin D and E.

RESOURCES FOR OLDER ADULTS

The Older Americans Act Nutrition Program (OAANP) is a federally funded and community-based program that provides food and nutrition services for persons age 60 and older. At a variety of community sites, the OAANP provides congregate meals, nutrition education and counseling, and other services. Home-delivered meals, often called "meals-on-wheels," are provided to homebound older persons.

Older persons can find local programs by calling their regional Area Agency on Aging or local aging, elder, and/or senior services agencies. County Cooperative Extension offices, listed under county government in the blue pages of telephone books, are good sources of information about local services. Cooperative Extension provides a variety of educational programs, including nutrition education, for consumers of all ages.

Older persons in difficult financial straits may be eligible for Food Stamps. For a variety of reasons, only about one-third of eligible persons age 60 and older actually participate in this program—the lowest rate of all demographic groups. For assistance in applying for Food Stamps, older persons can contact their Area Agency on Aging or local aging, elder, and/or senior services agency.

■

WHAT YOU NEED TO KNOW

▶ Physiological changes due to aging cause nutritional challenges for older people.

▶ For most people, older age means lower calorie needs while their need for most nutrients remains the same; careful planning must be done to avoid gaining too much weight while fulfilling all your dietary requirements. The "Dietary Guidelines for Americans" and the food guide pyramid are useful tools in building a healthy diet.

▶ Staying active and making wise food choices can help older persons obtain all the nutrients they need to stay healthy while reducing long-term health risks.

When calorie needs are low and food choices limited, a multivitamin supplement can ensure adequate consumption of required nutrients, such as vitamins D, E, and B_{12}.

▶ A variety of nutrition and health resources are available to assist older persons of all backgrounds and resources in meeting their nutritional needs.

28

FOR MORE INFORMATION

▶ **Food and Nutrition Information Center**
Agricultural Research Service, USDA
National Agricultural Library, Room 105
10301 Baltimore Avenue
Beltsville, MD 20705
301-504-5719
Fax: 301-504-6409
TTY: 301-504-6856
E-mail: fnic@nal.usda.gov
Web: www.nal.usda.gov/fnic

▶ **Nutrition.gov**
Web: www.nutrition.gov
Easy access to all online federal government information on nutrition. This is your one-stop resource for obtaining government information on nutrition, healthy eating, physical activity, and food safety.

▶ **Center for Nutrition Policy and Promotion**
www.cnpp.usda.gov
"Dietary Guidelines for Americans" and other USDA publications can be downloaded.

▶ **U.S. Government Printing Office**
Superintendent of Documents
Mail Stop: SSOP
Washington, DC 20402
"Dietary Guidelines for Americans" (ISBN 0-16-050376-0) is available for purchase by mail.

We spend $117 billion a year on obesity-related diseases and 300,000 Americans die.

—Tommy Thompson, Health and Human Services Secretary

THE AUTHOR

29   *Monica L. Mathys*

MONICA MATHYS, PharmD, is an assistant professor of pharmacy practice at Midwestern University College of Pharmacy in Glendale, Arizona. In addition to her teaching responsibilities with the university, Dr. Mathys also provides clinical services and tutors pharmacy students at Bryans Extended Care Center in Phoenix, Arizona.

Before accepting her position at Midwestern University, Dr. Mathys was a member of the Pharmacy Practice faculty at Southwestern Oklahoma State University.

Dr. Mathys earned her doctor of pharmacy from the University of Arkansas for Medical Sciences and completed a geriatric specialty residency at Central Arkansas Veterans Healthcare System in Little Rock, Arkansas.

29 | OBESITY

Obesity (excessively overweight) is a common disease affecting all age groups and most racial and ethnic groups. The number of obese American adults has increased by 50% over the last 40 years. In the period from 1991 to 2001, obese American adults increased from being 12 to 20.9% of the population. The percentage of overweight and obese individuals increases with advancing age until the age of 60; then the numbers begin to decline. However, statistics show that 37% of Americans over the age of 70 years are considered overweight and 15% are obese.

BODY MASS INDEX

The most common measurement used by researchers and health care professionals to determine whether a person is overweight is body mass index (BMI):

$$\frac{\text{WEIGHT IN KILOGRAMS}}{(\text{HEIGHT IN METERS})2} = BMI$$

If you don't know your weight in kilograms and your height in meters, Table 29-1 shows you how to obtain your BMI from pounds and inches, as well as the weight ranges considered normal, overweight, and obese. The National Institutes of Health (NIH) defines a person as overweight with a BMI between 25 and 29.9 and as obese with a BMI over 30. BMI provides a more precise measurement than just using body weight alone. However, it is not a direct measurement of body fat and will tend to be less accurate for adults with very high or very low muscle weight.

CAUSES OF OBESITY

In simple terms, obesity occurs when calories consumed exceed calories expended. However, the exact cause of a person's caloric imbalance may be harder to determine.

Genetics appears to play a role in obesity. Those who have obese parents are four to five times more likely to develop obesity themselves compared to those who do not have obese parents. Obviously, genetics cannot be the only cause of obesity since the United States has had such an increase in prevalence over the last few decades. America has turned into a fast-paced society, which provides little time for healthy meals. Americans often settle for snack and fast foods, which usually contain many calories and few nutrients. (See Figure 29-1.) Also, advances in technology have caused a significant decrease in physical activity. People drive instead of walk or take elevators and escalators instead of the stairs. Television, the internet, and video games are also responsible for decreased physical activity.

Most people notice, as they get older, that it becomes harder to maintain their normal weight. The reason for this is because as people age, the amount of body muscle begins to decrease. A decrease in muscle results

(figure 29-1)

Our fast-paced society leaves little time to prepare nutritious meals. Fast foods contain many calories but few nutrients.

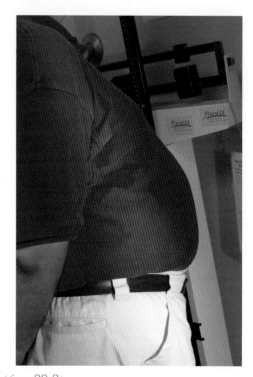
(figure 29-2)

Overweight persons have a higher chance of developing diabetes, high blood pressure, arthritis, and other medical conditions.

(table 29-1)

BODY MASS INDEX

Find your height in the first column. Using that row, find your weight on the right. Travel down the weight column to learn your BMI.

HEIGHT, INCHES	BODY WEIGHT, POUNDS NORMAL						OVERWEIGHT					OBESE					
58	91	96	100	105	110	115	119	124	129	134	138	143	148	153	158	162	167
59	94	99	104	109	114	119	124	128	133	138	143	148	153	158	163	168	173
60	97	102	107	112	118	123	128	133	138	143	148	153	158	153	158	174	179
61	100	106	111	116	122	127	132	137	143	148	153	158	164	169	174	180	185
62	104	109	115	120	126	131	136	142	147	153	158	164	169	175	180	186	191
63	107	113	118	124	130	135	141	146	152	158	163	169	175	180	186	191	197
64	110	116	122	128	134	140	145	151	157	163	169	174	180	186	192	197	204
65	114	120	126	132	138	144	150	156	162	168	174	180	186	192	198	204	210
66	118	124	130	136	142	148	155	161	167	173	179	186	192	198	204	210	216
67	121	127	134	140	146	153	159	166	172	178	185	191	198	204	211	217	223
68	125	131	138	144	151	158	164	171	177	184	190	197	203	210	216	223	230
69	128	135	142	149	155	162	169	176	182	189	196	203	209	216	223	230	236
70	132	139	146	153	160	167	174	181	188	195	202	209	216	222	229	236	243
71	136	143	150	157	165	172	179	186	193	200	208	215	222	229	236	243	250
72	140	147	154	162	169	177	184	191	199	206	213	221	228	235	242	250	258
73	144	151	159	166	174	182	189	197	204	212	219	227	235	242	250	257	265
74	148	155	163	171	179	186	194	202	210	218	225	233	241	249	256	264	272
75	152	160	168	176	184	192	200	208	216	224	232	240	248	256	264	272	279
76	156	164	172	180	189	197	205	213	221	230	238	246	254	263	271	279	287
BMI	19	20	21	22	23	24	25	26	27	28	29	30	31	32	33	34	35

Source: Adapted from Clinical Guidelines on the Identification, Evaluation, and Treatment of Overweight and Obesity in Adults, National Institutes of Health—National Heart, Lung, and Blood Institute, June 1998.

in decreased metabolism (the rate your body burns calories) and physical activity. If metabolism and physical activity decrease, then consumed calories should also decrease to prevent weight gain. However, this is not the case for most people. Most tend to eat the same amount of calories even though they are not expending the same amount as when they were younger.

As people age, their bodies do not break down fat as easily as when they were younger. Also, fat tends to distribute in the abdominal area of the body. This redistribution of fat may be caused by a decrease in testosterone, estrogen, or growth hormone levels.

HEALTH AND OBESITY

Scientific studies have shown that obese and overweight adults have a higher chance of developing diabetes, high blood pressure, high cholesterol, heart disease, stroke, gallbladder disease, arthritis, and certain forms of cancer (see Figure 29-2). Mobility and daily function also decrease in overweight individuals. Complications and death rate have been shown to increase as BMI increases. Therefore, obese individuals (with a BMI over 30) have a higher risk status than those who are overweight (with a BMI over 25 but under 30). Conversely, weight loss improves blood sugar levels, blood pressure, and cholesterol levels, which then decreases the risk of diabetes, heart disease, stroke, and early death. Arthritic pain due to excessive weight will decrease as weight is lost, resulting in increased mobility and function.

One limitation of most obesity studies is they only involve adults under 65 years of age. Therefore, many researchers and health care specialists question whether the results of these studies apply to the aged population. Does weight loss reduce risk factors in older adults? Does weight loss prolong the lives of older adults?

The few studies involving older adults did show that overweight and obese individuals ranging from the age of 65 to 75 had reductions in complications when weight was lost. However, data are limited regarding people over 75. Also, the question of whether weight loss increases survival for people over the age of 65 remains unanswered at this time. Although you might expect that overweight persons over 65 would have a higher death rate due to complications from their obesity, this has not been actually confirmed in clinical studies. Hopefully, further research on these issues will help you and your doctor decide which weight is best for you and what needs to be done to reduce your risk of complications and improve your life expectancy.

TREATING OBESITY

To determine whether you should lose weight, complete the activity in Figure 29-3, which presents guidelines published by the National Institutes of Health.

WEIGHT LOSS GOALS

The three main aims for treating obesity include (1) preventing further weight gain, (2) gradually losing weight, and (3) keeping the lower weight. Those who are overweight or obese should first try to prevent further weight gain. If eating and behavior habits can be changed to avoid gaining more weight, then this is essentially a good step toward losing weight.

The next step should be to visit a health care professional (physician, nurse, or dietitian) and develop a safe and effective weight loss regimen. Scientific studies have shown that a modest weight loss of 10% results in a reduction of cardiac risk factors and other obesity complications. Therefore, individuals should first shoot for a weight loss goal of 10%. This goal is more realistic then trying to reach an ideal body weight. If the goal is easy to reach, people are more likely to stick with their regimen. Once the 10% goal is reached and the individual wishes to lose more weight, a new goal can be set.

Weight loss should occur slowly (no more than one-half to one pound per week), especially for older adults who are more at risk for muscle loss, bone loss, and complications from malnutrition. Losing weight too quickly usually results in weight regain, whereas weight lost slowly is more likely to be maintained.

(figure 29-3)

CHECKLIST

Should you lose weight? *(Adapted from guidelines published by the National Institutes of Health.)*

THE SCALE

If you have a BMI of 30 or more, stop here and start a weight reduction program.
  or
If you have a BMI under 30 but over 25, go straight to "Risk Factors," below.
  or
If your waist is over 35 inches (women) or over 40 inches (men), go straight to "Risk Factors," below.
  or
If you have met none of the above criteria, congratulations! You're doing fine.

RISK FACTORS

Place a check in the box of each cardiovascular risk factor that applies to you:

☐ Age: over 45 (men) or 55 (women)

☐ Diabetes

☐ Heart disease: occluded coronary arteries, previous heart attack, heart failure, or abnormal heart rhythm

☐ Other vascular diseases: stroke; decreased circulation in the arms, hands, legs, and feet; occluded carotid arteries (arteries leading to the brain)

☐ Sleep apnea

☐ High blood pressure (or taking medication for high blood pressure)

☐ Abnormal cholesterol levels: high LDL (bad cholesterol) and/or low HDL (good cholesterol)

☐ High blood sugars

☐ Cigarette smoking

☐ Family history of heart disease: father or brother who had a heart attack or died suddenly before the age of 55; mother or sister who had a heart attack or died suddenly before the age of 65

RESULTS

Count the number of checks you've made. If your total is two or more, start a weight reduction program.

The third aim is maintaining the lost weight. Obesity is a long-term disease; therefore, obese people must realize that the diet, exercise, and behavior changes they have made should be continued. They should also visit their health care provider periodically to have their weight and nutrition status monitored and to enjoy a little encouragement.

DIET

The most essential part of a weight loss regimen is a reduced calorie diet. Weight loss can occur with just increased exercise, but the loss occurs quicker if combined with a low-calorie diet (LCD). Older adults are highly encouraged to seek advice from a health care professional before lowering their daily calories. Most health care professionals agree that decreasing a person's diet by 300 to 500 calories per day is a safe beginning. This 300-

29

OBESITY

(table 29-2)

RECOMMENDED DAILY NUTRIENTS FOR OLDER ADULTS

NUTRIENT	RECOMMENDED INTAKE
Total fat	No more than 30% of total daily calories
Protein*	15 to 20% of total daily calories*
Carbohydrates	50 to 55% of total daily calories
Cholesterol	No more than 300 mg per day
Sodium	No more than 2400 mg per day
Calcium†	1200 to 1500 mg per day†
Fiber	20 to 30 grams per day

*Some references suggest that older adults should consume more protein per day (20%), compared to younger adults (15%), to help maintain muscle.
†Taking a calcium tablet two or three times a day may be necessary.
Source: Clinical Guidelines on the Identification, Evaluation, and Treatment of Overweight and Obesity in Adults, National Institutes of Health—National Heart, Lung, and Blood Institute, June 1998.

to 500-calorie deficit will result in a one-half to one pound weight loss per week. Very low calorie diets (800 or less calories per day) should be avoided. Very low calorie diets (VLCD) could result in excessive muscle loss and malnutrition. Also, VLCD haven't been shown to cause any more weight loss over a long period of time compared to LCD.

The three main components of a diet include fat, protein, and carbohydrates. Older adults should consume adequate amounts of protein (15 to 20% of total daily calories) to prevent muscle loss. Fat intake should be less than 30% of total daily calories, which leaves 50 to 55% of daily calories for carbohydrates. Table 29-2 summarizes the recommended daily nutrients for older adults who wish to start a low-calorie diet. Table 29-3 shows the breakdown of calories and grams in a 1200 per day calorie diet.

Those choosing to start a low-calorie diet should take one multivitamin with minerals per day to ensure that all daily requirements are met. Calcium intake should also be monitored. It is recommended that older adults receive 1200 to 1500 mg of calcium per day. Many may need to take a calcium tablet two to three times a day in order to meet this requirement. Individuals should limit their consumption of alcohol, which is high in calories and has no nutritional value, and drink adequate amounts of water per day (six to eight glasses). Once started on the diet, individuals should continue visiting a health care provider routinely (about twice a month) for nutritional counseling while ensuring they are not losing weight too quickly.

EXERCISE

Exercise is an important element not only of a weight loss program but also for everyone. Exercise helps to burn calories and decreases waist size and cardiovascular risk factors, such as high blood pressure, high blood sugars, and abnormal cholesterol levels. People who exercise regularly are less likely to be placed in nursing homes, have a higher number of active years, and are more likely to maintain muscle and strong bones.

(figure 29-4)

One of the first steps in losing weight is to visit a health care professional (physician, nurse, or dietitian) and develop a safe and effective weight loss regimen.

(figure 29-5)

Exercise is an important part of your weight loss program.

(table 29-3)

DIET OF 1200 CALORIES PER DAY

NUTRIENT	CALORIES PER DAY	GRAMS PER DAY
Fat (no more than 30% per day)	360	40
Protein (20% per day)	240	60
Carbohydrates (50% per day)	600	150
TOTAL	1200	250

(figure 29-6)

Weight training can help you lose fat and build muscle.

Before beginning an exercise program, a sedentary older adult should visit a physician to ascertain suitability. An exercise regimen should consist of stretching exercises, strength training, and cardiovascular training. Stretching exercises should be performed 10 to 20 minutes before and after each workout. These exercises will help prevent muscle injury during the strength and cardiovascular portion of the regimen. Strength training can be accomplished by using light hand weights to increase upper-body strength. For those who have access to exercise equipment, leg weights can be used to increase lower-body strength. Such cardiovascular exercises as walking and cycling will also suffice for those who do not have access to equipment. Strength training should be performed three times per week. Start with a low number of repetitions (2 sets of 10 repetitions) and increase every two weeks to reach a goal of 30 repetitions.

You have often heard about cardiovascular exercises called *aerobic exercises*. These exercises require the repetitive movement of large muscle groups in your legs and arms and include walking, running, swimming, bicycling, rowing, cross-country skiing, and so forth. They are not intended to build muscle mass in the way that weight training does. The work that these muscles perform for aerobics requires oxygen. That oxygen is delivered to your muscles by the red blood cells. In order to get to the muscles, the red blood cells have to be pumped by the heart through your blood vessels. The heart usually responds to the increased oxygen requirement by beating faster and with a more vigorous contraction. This is why you notice your heart thumping in your chest when you run fast or exercise vigorously.

You can improve the condition of your heart and blood vessels with regular aerobic exercise. This may require as little as 20 minutes at a time three days a week. The goal of your aerobic training is to reach a target heart rate and maintain it during your exercise times. Your heart rate per minute is determined by checking your pulse at the wrist for 15 seconds and multiplying by four. (If you don't know how to check your pulse, ask your doctor, a nurse, or a physical trainer.) The following formulas are helpful guides:

For men, multiply your age by 0.8 and then subtract from 214.
For women, multiply your age by 0.7 and subtract from 211.

However, as you get older, certain medical conditions and medicines may blunt your heart rate response to exercise. In this case, talk with your doctor or trainer. Another measure, such as the Borg scale (discussed in Chapter 36), may be used. Just like strength exercises, cardiovascular

(table 29-4)

SAMPLE EXERCISE REGIMEN FOR OLDER ADULTS*

WEEK	LIGHT HAND WEIGHT LIFTING†	WALKING
1 and 2	2 sets of 10 repetitions	20 minutes 3 times per week
3 and 4	2 sets of 13 repetitions	30 minutes 3 times per week
5 and 6	2 sets of 16 repetitions	40 minutes 3 times per week
7 and 8	2 sets of 20 repetitions	50 minutes 3 times per week
9 and 10	2 sets of 23 repetitions	60 minutes 3 times per week
11 and 12	2 sets of 25 repetitions	60 minutes 4 times per week
13 and 14	3 sets of 25 repetitions	60 minutes 5 times per week
15 and 16	3 sets of 28 repetitions	60 minutes 6 times per week

*Stretching exercises should be done before and after each workout.
†Three times a week.

exercises should be started gradually and increased in frequency and duration, as shown in Table 29-4.

WEIGHT LOSS MEDICATION

Weight loss medications, such as FASTIN, MERIDIA, and XENICAL, have caused additional weight loss if a person also exercises and has a low-calorie diet. However, these medications have not been adequately studied in older adults and are not usually recommended. Also, they cause many unwanted side effects and interact with other medications. Therefore, such medications should only be used under the regular supervision of a physician. A physician will weigh the benefits versus the risk of these medications. For example, the use of Xenical may be justified in a very overweight diabetic, whose blood sugar is not being controlled with oral medications, and the decision is either profound weight loss or administration of insulin with a needle.

Herbal preparations may have unpredictable side effects and should not be used. The Food and Drug Administration does not regulate these products. They may contain ephedra or decongestants that may cause serious adverse effects in older persons or those with other medical conditions.

WEIGHT LOSS SURGERY

Weight loss surgery is only recommended for those who have failed more conservative measures and who have severe obesity (BMI over 40) or have a serious medical condition, such as diabetes, hypertension, or sleep apnea, in addition to being obese (BMI over 35). The surgical procedures for weight loss may involve stapling of part of the stomach to make the person feel full with smaller food intake or bypassing of part of the stomach and small intestine. Procedures that have been popular in the past, such as jaw wiring and special stomach "balloons," are seldom performed these days. Liposuction is done for cosmetic reasons but is not a procedure for obesity. Careful patient selection is required, and the surgery is best performed in medical centers with extensive experience in these procedures. Since metabolic disturbances can occur following the surgery, lifelong medical follow-up is required.

WHAT YOU NEED TO KNOW

▶ For Americans over 70 years, 37% are considered overweight and 15% obese. NIH defines overweight as having a BMI over 25 but under 30 and obese as having a BMI of 30 or more.

▶ An obese person should lose weight. An overweight person who has either a large waist size or cardiovascular risk factors should lose weight.

▶ Treating obesity means (1) preventing weight gain, (2) gradual weight loss, and (3) keeping the lower weight. A health care professional (physician, nurse, or dietitian) can develop a weight loss regimen. A modest weight loss of 10% can reduce cardiac risk factors and other obesity complications.

▶ A low-calorie diet is central to weight loss. Weight loss can occur with increased exercise, but the loss is quicker if exercise is combined with a low-calorie diet. Before lowering daily calories, seek advice from a health care professional.

▶ Exercise is important for everyone, whether trying to lose weight or not.

▶ Do not use weight loss medications except under the supervision of a physician.

▶ Weight loss surgery has not been adequately studied in older adults.

FOR MORE INFORMATION

▶ **Weight-Control Information Network**
One Win Way
Bethesda, MD 20892
877-946-4627, 202-828-1025
Fax: 202-828-1028
E-mail: win@info.niddk.nih.gov
Web: www.niddk.nih.gov/health/nutrit/nutrit.htm

▶ **National Institutes of Health**
9000 Rockville Pike
Bethesda, MD 20892
Web:www.nhlbi.nih.gov/guidelines/obesity/ob_home.htm

▶ **Weight Watchers**
Web: www.weightwatchers.com
Low-fat recipes and weight loss advice.

▶ **American Heart Association**
National Center
7272 Greenville Ave.
Dallas, TX 75231
800-242-8721
Web: www.americanheart.org

> Keep your face to the sunshine and you cannot see the shadows.
>
> —*Helen Keller*

THE AUTHORS

30

Masayoshi Itoh, M.D.

MASAYOSHI ITOH, MD, MPH, is a clinical professor of rehabilitation medicine at New York University and senior management consultant at Coler-Goldwater Specialty Hospital and Nursing Facility. He graduated from the Medical College at Tokyo University, and he completed his residency training in physical medicine and rehabilitation at New York University. He received a master of public health from Columbia University. He has served as an expert for the World Health Organization, a consultant to the Pan American Health Organization, and a technical expert to the Vocational Rehabilitation Administration of the Department of Health, Education, and Welfare. He was the chairman of the Expert Commission on Rehabilitation for the Dominican Republic, and he was a consultant for the control of the poliomyelitis epidemic in the Dominican Republic from 1971 to 1972. He has written 41 scientific papers, articles, and book chapters.

Mathew Lee, M.D.

MATHEW H. M. LEE, MD, MPH, is Howard A. Rusk Professor and chairman of the Department of Rehabilitation Medicine and director of the Rusk Institute of Rehabilitation Medicine at New York University Medical Center. His major interests cover chronic disease, geriatric rehabilitation, the epidemiology of disability, and chronic pain. He has written numerous books and articles and has lectured in 30 countries.

He has served as president of the New York Society of Physical Medicine and Rehabilitation, chairman of the Ad Hoc Committee on Geriatrics of the American Academy of Physical Medicine and Rehabilitation, president for the American Society of Legal and Industrial Medicine and was a founding member of the American Academy of Acupuncture and the American College of Acupuncture.

Using acupuncture and thermography, Dr. Lee has been active in the investigation and treatment of oral facial pain and has coedited the book *Dentistry for the Special Patient: The Aged, Chronically, Ill and Handicapped.* He is clinical professor of oral and maxillofacial surgery in the College of Dentistry, New York University.

Dr. Lee is also committed to the use of music in the rehabilitation process: he is an adjunct professor of music, School of Education, Health and Nursing Arts Professions, New York University, and has edited the book *Rehabilitation, Music, and Human Well-Being.*

30 | REHABILITATION

Today, you and I hear the word *rehabilitation* frequently. It has become almost a household word. We talk about the rehabilitation of alcoholics, drug addicts, and prisoners. *Rehab* is the abbreviated term often used in everyday speech. If a baseball player injures his shoulder during a game, a television commentator may say, "He will most likely require surgery and then go to rehab." In fact, the actual definition of rehabilitation has changed over the years. Back in 1954, *Webster's New World Dictionary* did not even mention restoration of health or recovery from injury in the definition of rehabilitation. However, by 1981 *Webster's Third New International Dictionary* listed the following as one of the definitions of *rehabilitation:* "Physical restoration of a sick or disabled person by therapeutic measures and reeducation to participation in the activities of normal life."

The origins of the medical specialty of physical medicine and rehabilitation date back to World War II when Dr. Howard A. Rusk developed a program for injured airmen in an Air Force hospital. The program was designed not only to take care of their physical needs but also to meet their emotional, social, economic, and vocational needs. This program was so successful that all veteran administration hospitals later adopted this approach. Dr. Rusk coined the word *rehabilitation* for this program. After the war, Dr. Rusk applied this rehabilitation program to the disabled civilian population. The word *disabled* refers to a condition in which a person is unable to perform certain activities that he or she could normally do. The success of this program was attributed to treating a disabled individual as a whole person, thus meeting physical, social, emotional, financial, and vocational needs.

Although physicians may specialize in rehabilitation, physical therapists carry out most of the hands-on physical therapy in the United States (Physicians who specialize in physical medicine and rehabilitation are called **physiatrists.** Note the difference from **psychiatrists,** specialists in mental disorders). Almost all large hospitals now have a rehabilitation department or unit, most of which are directed by a physiatrist. Specialty rehabilitation hospitals may serve persons with brain injury, spinal cord injury, strokes, amputations, and so forth. Independent rehabilitation centers have also sprung up throughout the country. These rehabilitation programs have benefited many thousands of disabled people, young and old.

The World Health Organization (WHO) has defined health as a "state of complete physical, mental and social well-being and not merely the absence of disease or infirmity." Dr. Rusk defined *rehabilitation* as "the ultimate restoration of a disabled person to his maximum capacity—physical, emotional and vocational." The goal of rehabilitation is to restore health as defined by the WHO although there might be some residual physical disability.

REHABILITATION BASICS
RECEIVING REHABILITATION TREATMENT

If you should become disabled, you might not have the benefit of a formal rehabilitation program in an acute care hospital or a rehabilitation center.

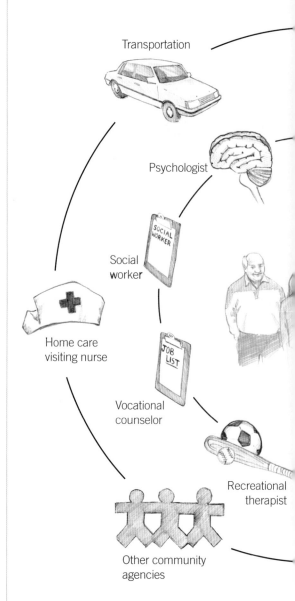

(figure 30-1)

The inner two circles represent the traditional rehabilitation team. The conditions in the outer circle influence the outcome of rehabilitation and the return of the person to the community.

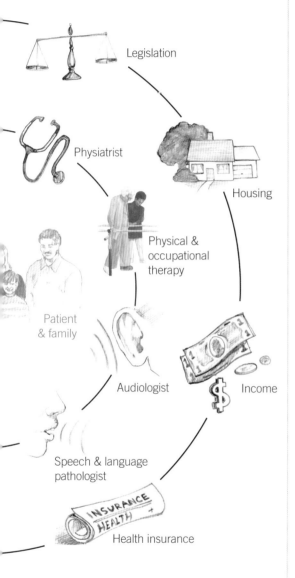

Legislation

Physiatrist

Housing

Physical &
occupational
therapy

Patient
& family

Audiologist

Income

Speech & language
pathologist

Health insurance

In some parts of the country, rehabilitation services may not be readily available to you or you may have to travel too far from your home. Even if rehabilitation services are available, you or your family may decide not to use them for various reasons. (The word *family* in this chapter refers not only to your spouse and blood relatives but may include people who are very close to you, such as friends or a guardian.) Thus, you may go directly home from the hospital. The staff of the acute care hospital can suggest an outpatient facility where rehabilitation services are provided.

Outpatient rehabilitation clinic: You may receive treatment at an outpatient rehabilitation clinic if the disability is relatively mild and you can travel to the clinic. The scope of services provided in a clinic may differ depending on the setup of the clinic. If the clinic is affiliated with the rehabilitation department of a hospital or major rehabilitation center, services can be comprehensive. Self-standing rehabilitation clinics usually offer limited services, such as physical and occupational therapy.

Nursing facility: All nursing facilities and nursing homes, today, must be able to provide needed rehabilitation services to their residents. There are hospital-based nursing facilities and self-standing facilities. Usually an acute hospital that has a nursing facility section also has a rehabilitation unit in the hospital. These facilities provide a wider variety of rehabilitation services than self-standing nursing facilities do. However, the pace of your rehabilitation treatment in the nursing facility is slower than that of the rehabilitation unit of the hospital. This slow pace may be advantageous if you are very elderly. A self-standing nursing facility usually provides a limited scope of rehabilitation services. If a state agency recognizes a nursing facility that provides subacute care, this facility most likely provides rehabilitation services.

Home care and visiting nurse service: If you are living at home and cannot travel to a rehabilitation clinic, you may seek rehabilitation care through home care or visiting nurse organizations. They usually cannot provide daily treatment. In order to make optimal use of their services, your family members must carry out therapy as the visiting therapist teaches them.

In the remainder of this chapter, we discuss the process of formal rehabilitation practiced in a rehabilitation department or center.

REHABILITATION TEAM

In many medical specialties, doctors and nurses provide most of your direct care. However, restoring your total health if you are disabled is a very involved and complicated task. In order to undertake this task successfully, a hospital-based rehabilitation department or an independent rehabilitation center requires a host of specialists that form an interdisciplinary team. The team consists of you, your family, a physiatrist, rehabilitation nurse, physical therapist, occupational therapist, speech pathologist, audiologist (specialist in hearing), social worker, psychologist, vocational counselor, and recreational therapist (see Figure 30-1).

The most important members of this team are you and your family. In other medical specialties, you may play a more passive role as a recipient of care. In the rehabilitation program, you and your family, not the rehabilitation professionals on the team, determine the goals of treatment with help of professionals. These specialists work in harmony and complement each other to assist you in reaching your goals. This does not necessarily mean that you will require all the various specialists on the team. The services required depend on the circumstances of your disability (see Figure 30-1). In many instances, your family is as important as the rehabilitation specialists in assisting you in setting your goals.

REHABILITATION GOALS

There are two types of goals: short term and long term. The short-term goal is the functional level that you hope to reach within a period of a week or 10 days. The long-term goal is the condition you hope to achieve in one or two months or even longer, such as years from now. This condition includes physical, educational, social, economic, and vocational aspects. The long-term goal is your final destination.

Both goals must be very realistic. If you set your goal too low, it is too easy to reach. As a result, you may not try hard enough and the progress becomes slow. If the goal is set too high, you may not be able to reach it. This may cause you to get discouraged and lose interest in the rehabilitation process. This is why rehabilitation professionals must guide you in realistic goal setting.

REHABILITATION SPECIALISTS

Physiatrist: The *physiatrist* is the doctor responsible for maintaining your general health, controlling pain if any, and developing a treatment plan for restoration of your physical function as well as other functions needed for your well-being. The physiatrist is the captain of the team and coordinates the treatment activities of all rehabilitation specialists.

Rehabilitation nurse: A rehabilitation nurse is a registered nurse who has been trained in the rehabilitation process and the care of disabled patients. The nurse is responsible for your daily physical care and encouraging you to practice daily self-care activities as taught by the physical and occupational therapists. Often, a physical or occupational therapist will let you demonstrate what you can do on the nursing floor. In this way, the nurse is able to follow up on your progress. Daily practice on the nursing floor is very important in order for you to master newly learned skills.

Physical therapist: The physical therapist (PT) is responsible for increasing or maintaining your joint mobility, strengthening weak muscles, and maintaining the muscle strength of normal muscles. Sometimes, it is necessary to train normal muscles to be stronger in order to compensate for the weak muscles. The PT teaches you how to get in and out of bed, to walk, and to climb stairs. If the muscles cannot regain strength and help is needed to compensate for the lost muscle function, the PT fits you with a mechanical aid (brace) and selects a cane or crutch for safe walking.

A physiatrist is a physician who specializes in physical medicine and rehabilitation. The physiatrist is the captain of the rehabilitation team.

A PT is also responsible for training you, if you should lose a leg (lower-extremity amputee), to walk with a prosthesis (artificial leg). Physical therapy may require the use of many different modalities, such as heat, water, cold, electric, and electromagnetic, in order to make you comfortable and speed up progress.

Heat therapy takes many forms. The simplest heat therapy is a special hot pack. A paraffin bath is another type of heat therapy. You dip your hand in a bath with melted paraffin mixed with mineral oil, or a therapist applies paraffin with a brush to the area to be treated and wraps it with a towel. This treatment lasts about one half hour. This treatment is often used for arthritic hands.

One form of hydrotherapy (water therapy) is a whirlpool treatment. You place your hand, leg, or sometimes the trunk in a tank with agitated warm water similar to a Jacuzzi whirlpool. This therapy enhances joint movement or heals skin ulcers. Cryotherapy (cold therapy) uses a special ice pack. Cold can reduce muscle spasm and often is effective for acute lower back pain and inflammation.

Low-voltage electric current (electrical stimulation) is applied to muscles to make them contract. This helps prevent paralyzed muscles from wasting while not being used. This treatment can help you after a stroke until such time that your muscles recover. While a hot pack or paraffin bath can give heat to a localized area on the surface of the body, electromagnetic waves, such as shortwave or microwave diathermy, give deep penetrating heat when it is needed.

Ultrasound treatment uses sound waves. At a certain frequency of vibration, it has destructive capability. This property is effective in breaking down calcium deposits around tendons. This may be helpful in treatment of tendonitis of the shoulder joint. It has also been used successfully in some individuals who have pain in the stump after an amputation.

Occupational therapist: The occupational therapist (OT) is responsible for improving the activities of your hands and fingers. Many different objects and equipment are used to improve arm, hand, and finger functions. The OT works with you on activities of daily living (ADL), such as eating, grooming, dressing, personal hygiene, bathing, and toileting. By observing how you negotiate these tasks, the OT will fit you with various gadgets that make it easier to perform these tasks. These gadgets are explained in detail throughout the remainder of this chapter.

In everyday life, we use both hands to do certain tasks without thinking. For example, tying a shoelace needs two hands. If you can use only one hand, this is an impossible task. There are two ways to solve this problem. There is a special way you can be taught to thread a shoelace so you can tie it with one hand. The other way is to use a pair of shoes with a Velcro or touch closure. The OT teaches such one-hand activities if necessary. If you lose an arm (upper-extremity amputee), the OT teaches you how to use a prosthesis (artificial arm).

If you cannot walk, you may need a wheelchair to move from one place to another. Although at first glance it may be difficult to recognize

30

the differences, there are many different types of wheelchairs. Each chair and its accessories are designed to meet a person's specific needs. Some are hand-driven, and others are motorized. Some motorized chairs look like traditional wheelchairs, and others look like scooters. The OT decides the type of wheelchair you need and trains you to use it efficiently.

Speech pathologist: The speech pathologist is responsible for evaluating and treating speech problems. This is a common disability after stroke and brain injury. Inability to communicate is a very frustrating experience. You may have difficulty using the muscles of your mouth and your tongue. In this case, the speech pathologist teaches you how to use them.

Speech therapy uses different equipment to help you learn how to pronounce words. If you can understand spoken words or sentences but cannot speak or reply, you may be taught to use a specialized computer that types output on a tape or displays a message on a video screen. To communicate very basic needs, you may learn how to use a letter board or picture board. You point to letters or to a picture to express your desires. The speech pathologist decides which type of communication device is best suited for your needs.

If you have difficulty in swallowing, the speech pathologist and an otolaryngologist (medical doctor specializing in ear, nose, and throat diseases) may evaluate you with a special X-ray study. According to the findings of this examination, the speech pathologist recommends the types and the consistency of food that you can eat safely. Without appropriate precautions, you could choke or develop pneumonia.

Audiologist: Hearing difficulty is common as we get older. If you have a hearing loss, you may have difficulty understanding instructions given by a PT, OT, nurse, or other rehabilitation specialists. The audiologist (hearing specialist) examines you using specialized equipment to determine the severity and type of hearing loss. If a hearing aid can help, the audiologist fits you with an appropriate hearing aid.

Social worker: The social worker interviews you and your family to assess your lifestyle, occupational history, family situation including extended family, and financial circumstances. If there is any conflict that may hinder your rehabilitation, the social worker tries to mediate. The social worker discusses and evaluates your thinking about your disability. The social worker, then, assists you and possibly your family in reaching a workable solution.

It may also be the social worker's responsibility to assist you with financial arrangements on leaving the hospital. The social worker helps prepare the family for your return to the community. This may involve purchasing equipment, minor remodeling of the home, transportation to your home, and arranging for a visiting nurse, home care, or clinic appointment.

Psychologist: The psychologist interviews you to assess your mental and emotional state. Depression is one of the most common psychological conditions among disabled people. Depression is a natural reaction for a newly disabled person. However, if symptoms of depression continue for several weeks, you most likely need counseling, psychotherapy, or even medication. Depression interferes with the progress of your rehabilitation program, and is sometimes very dangerous. It is important to communicate your feelings honestly to your psychologist. If you have thoughts that your life is not worth living or that you want to end your life, your psychologist can help you. Effective treatments are available.

Vocational counselor: The vocational counselor takes your educational and occupational history. According to the extent of your disability, the counselor may have to talk to your employer if you are still working. If it is feasible, the counselor may suggest that you plan for a job-retraining program. If you agree, the vocational counselor makes the necessary arrangements with outside agencies to carry out the plan.

Recreation therapist: Many people do not have hobbies or other activities to fill their leisure time. This can lead to isolation and boredom. This may be even a more significant problem for you if you are disabled because you may not be able to go out of the house easily. The recreation therapist explores leisure activities with you that make life easier and more pleasurable.

REHABILITATION PROGRAMS

Adult Rehabilitation: In most adult rehabilitation, the long-term goal is to resume your previous job. The job may include outside employment or self-employment. For example, if you are a spouse who was responsible for housekeeping and caring for your children before becoming disabled, your goal is to resume those activities. You may also need family, financial, and vocational services. You may need vocational retraining to meet your financial obligations.

Geriatric Rehabilitation: The long-term goal of geriatric rehabilitation (rehabilitation of the elderly) is rather limited compared with the rehabilitation of children or younger adults. The goal is to able to take care of your daily needs and resume some of the activities that you were involved in before the onset of your disability. You may not have a job, but you probably were capable of being independent. However, it is important to understand that no matter how effective the rehabilitation program, it cannot be expected to restore you to 100% of the life you had before the disability. Aging itself make us less resilient to injury and disease. There will probably be no need for education or job retraining. You may need counseling in leisure activities. This is true regardless of where you will be after the formal rehabilitation program ends. Table 30-1 summarizes the goals of various rehabilitation programs.

You may think from your reading that geriatric rehabilitation is simpler and easier than pediatric or adult rehabilitation. However, geriatric rehabilitation has special problems related to aging. As an older person, you may have other physical conditions in addition to your recent physical disability, such as high blood pressure, diabetes, poor blood circulation, poor vision, hearing loss, or memory dysfunction. These underlying

(table 30-1)

GOALS OF VARIOUS REHABILITATION PROGRAMS

GOALS REHABILITATION TYPE	GERIATRIC	ADULT
Maximum goal	Taking care of self	Resuming work
Physical restoration	Yes	Yes
School education	No	No
Vocational training	No	No
Job retraining	No	Yes
Leisure education	Yes	Maybe yes

conditions, present even before you became disabled, are obstacles to the geriatric rehabilitation process.

You may fatigue easily and not be able to perform strenuous exercises. This may impair your progress. Therapists may have to teach you a new trick to compensate for a lost function, but you may not be able to repeat it tomorrow due to difficulties with recent memory and your ability to recall. Consequently, the therapist has to reinforce the trick over and over again until it becomes a habit. You may have good days and bad days. On a good day, you make good progress. However, on a bad day, you may regress to where you were several days earlier. This is a very frustrating experience for both you and your therapist. It requires the patience of both of you to continue striving toward your goal.

To many people, getting old is not a happy thought. They do not view their older years as a natural progression in their lives. They become depressed because their self-image is tied to their image of their body and their appearance. Becoming disabled deepens this depression. These persons must have something to look forward to as they go through the rehabilitation program. It can be a small thing, such as wanting to go home, to be with their spouse, to see their grandchildren, or to eat home-cooked food. As long as they have a strong desire to reach a goal, they can strive toward that goal. If a person was very physically active before becoming disabled, that person will most likely fight to be as independent as possible. Counseling may be necessary to help some individuals deal with their self-image.

Some older people have learned to do things a certain way. They tend to be inflexible. Most nurses and therapists are young and may be in the age bracket of the patient's children or grandchildren. They have to tell the patient what to do, how to do it, and what not to do. How these professionals give their instructions is very important. The wrong tone of voice or choice of words can cause the patient to feel insulted and resentful. Such feelings make the person uncooperative, hostile, or withdrawn. Rehabilitation professionals must detect these warning signs as soon as possible and must change their approach.

Length of stay in geriatric rehabilitation: Your stay in a geriatric rehabilitation unit may extend anywhere from a few weeks to a few months. Medicare and many health maintenance organizations impose a restriction on the length of stay as an in-patient in the rehabilitation unit of the hospital. This may require that you go home before completion of the program. Some private insurance plans provide financial support beyond these limitations. If financially feasible, you can stay in the program and pay for the program privately. If you are eligible for both Medicare and Medicaid, the coverage period may be longer.

However, returning home before the completion of the program is not necessarily harmful. You are in a familiar environment and can maintain relations with your family. You can continue the rehabilitation program in an outpatient clinic or through home care services. To allow you to attend a clinic, your family can provide transportation. If not, there are agencies that provide this type of transportation for a disabled person. Your family can get such information from a social worker.

FAMILY OF ELDERLY PATIENT

Now we would like to "speak" directly to your family: During the entire process of rehabilitation, you are the most important persons next to your loved one who is disabled. This is especially true in geriatric rehabilitation. You need to be involved in setting rehabilitation goals, and your presence in the rehabilitation program and post-rehabilitation care is vitally important. Your physical presence, understanding, and encouragement are the best medicine to cure depression, despair, and loneliness. It is desirable but not necessary to make a daily visit. On recognizing that you care, your loved one's emotional outlook improves and steady progress is made.

Please maintain close contact with the rehabilitation professionals and understand the problems, if there are any. In some instances, you may have to act as an interpreter, so that your loved one understands the intentions, concerns, and instructions of the rehabilitation professionals. You may have to explain to your loved one why he or she has to do a certain activity in a certain way. Your loved one may hesitate to speak to or ask questions of the professional staff. In this case, you can be the best spokesperson for him or her.

When your loved one is about ready to go home, you need to be involved in all the arrangements. You can make him or her feel welcome back into the home. Your help with these preparations prior to discharge can go a long way in making your loved one feel as comfortable as possible.

Patient and family education: Your entire rehabilitation process is a learning experience. You may have to learn again how to use your fingers, hands, arms, legs, and body and how to balance your body when you want to stand up. Therapists teach you techniques to avoid injuries. You will learn how to place and use various types of apparatus and how to use gadgets to perform the normal activities of daily living. Rehabilitation specialists teach you how to maintain your general health. Your family has to learn how to help after you return home, but if the family does everything, it does not empower you. You want to maintain your dignity and a certain level of independence. Too much helping from your family may be harmful. Rehabilitation specialists will teach your family how to assist you. This may involve daily living activities such as dressing, bathing, toileting, as well as walking and understanding speech in some cases.

If you strongly desire to drive a car, the physiatrist must determine whether you are physically and mentally competent to drive. If you are capable of operating a car, a special instructor or occupational therapist must decide if any special equipment is necessary. After training, you have to pass the test given by the department of motor vehicles of the state in which you reside. Some rehabilitation centers have disabled driver training programs. Some offer driver evaluation programs to determine if you are capable of driving. It is important to comply with the recommendations of your rehabilitation professionals if they tell you that you should not drive. Most persons are very reluctant to give up the car keys, but you have a responsibility to your community, your family, and yourself.

Homecoming: Before homecoming, your family will make all necessary preparations. Such arrangements may include making the home accessible with special ramps and the purchase of such special equipment as a hospital bed, elevated toilet seat, grab bars for the toilet and bathtub or shower stall, skid-proof rubber mat for the bathtub or shower stall, and a shower chair. It may be necessary to rearrange furniture so that you can move easily. Some rehabilitation services dispatch an occupational therapist for a home visit to determine your needs.

Your family will learn how to get supplies and medications. The dates and times of home care nursing visits and clinic or doctor visits must be recorded. All these arrangements and details must be taken care of before you go home. The OT and social worker will be helpful in this process.

RESIDENCE

Most elderly disabled people live at home after rehabilitation. Some of those who are not severely disabled and can afford the expense may go to an assisted living facility. However, some may have to stay in a nursing facility after rehabilitation. The reasons for the nursing facility placement include any combination of the following:

1. No caregiver is available, or the patient or family cannot afford to employ a caregiver. Medicare or Medicaid may provide limited coverage for the caregiver, but it is not a long-term solution. In order to cover such cost, the patient or family must have special private long-term care insurance.

2. Suitable housing is not available. For example, in an urban area, an apartment may be too small for a wheelchair. On the other hand, the apartment may be large enough but is a walk-up. If unable to climb stairs or if wheelchair-bound, the patient cannot get out and must spend the rest of his or her life in this apartment. In this case, if the patient insists upon returning to the apartment, the family or caregiver must notify the local fire and police department for the patient's safety.

3. The patient is severely disabled and needs continuous, skilled nursing care.

You and your family will decide together the best and safest living arrangements. Occasionally, some disabled persons go first to a nursing home or assisted living facility but eventually go home when some of the conditions mentioned above become favorable for their return and/or they regain some function and can stay at home with less care.

STROKE REHABILITATION

Few medical conditions cause more fear than does a stroke. You may have heard someone say that they would rather die than have a stroke. You may not realize that strokes are the third leading cause of death in the United States and the leading cause of disability. Some people may have strokes that cause only minor impairments, and you may not be able to tell that they even had a stroke. However, you are familiar with other people who have severe disability due to a stroke. They may have hemiplegia. *(Hemi* means one-half, and *plegia* means paralysis.) A hemiplegic person has paralysis of one side of the body, either the right or left. This is because the right side of the brain controls the left side of the body, and the left side of the brain controls the right side of the body. Thus, a person who has right hemiplegia has had damage to the left side of brain. A stroke is a neurological condition caused by a cerebral infarction or a cerebral hemorrhage. A cerebral infarction refers to the damage to brain cells (neurons) caused by a blockage of a blood vessel in the brain. The blood carries *oxygen* and nutrients to the brain, and if the blood flow is interrupted, brain cells die. Sometimes these blockages can be caused by *atherosclerosis,* and sometimes they can be caused by clots that have traveled from the neck arteries or the heart to the brain. A cerebral hemorrhage occurs when a blood vessel ruptures and blood leaks into the brain. A transient ischemic attack (TIA) produces the symptoms of a stroke but clears up within a day. However, these individuals have a higher risk of a stroke and may need medication or even surgery. Although "minor" strokes and TIAs are common, in this chapter we discus your rehabilitation if you should have a stroke associated with a more severe disability.

After a stroke, two very different recovery processes take place. A natural recovery occurs in different degrees depending upon the cause, location, and size of the damage to the brain. In general, if the damage to the brain is less severe, you will most likely have a better and quicker recovery. About 90% of this recovery occurs within three months after the onset of a stroke. The remaining 10% of recovery takes a much longer period. Generally, recovery from a stroke caused by a hemorrhage takes a much longer period than a stroke caused by blood clots. Rehabilitation can play a significant role in your recovery and the improvement of your body functions. The prognosis for recovery from a massive hemorrhage in the brain is usually poor.

REHABILITATION OUTCOMES

The outcome of your rehabilitation depends on many factors. Physical factors include your general physical condition, the mobility of your joints, the strength of your muscles on both sides of your body, and your physical function before the stroke. Psychological factors include your ability to think and reason (cognitive function), your ability to learn and follow instructions, your desire for improving your condition, and your ability to deal with reality (coping skills). The social factors are your family support and a reasonable prospect for returning to the community.

The rehabilitation specialists on your team assess these factors through testing and interviewing. Specialists explain their findings, and you and your family then set short- and long-term goals with the help of your rehabilitation specialists. As we mentioned in the previous section, your goals must be realistic. In addition, your team members will be honest with you and will not give unrealistic hope to you or your family.

REHABILITATION PROCESS

The rehabilitation process must start while you are still in the acute phase of the stroke. The shoulder joint on the paralyzed (or affected) side needs to be supported using one or two pillows to prevent your upper arm slipping out of the shoulder joint due to weakness of muscles surrounding the joint. Your nurse will turn you frequently to prevent development of a bedsore (also called a decubitus ulcer or pressure ulcer), particularly of the buttocks and the back of the heel of the affected side. If your medical condition allows, your nurse will instruct you to move your arm and leg on the unaffected side. You usually cannot move the joints of your affected side because of muscle weakness. A nurse or physical therapist will move them gently at least four times daily. This movement of your joints is necessary to prevent them from becoming stiff and deformed. This is the very early stage of rehabilitation. However, these preventive measures are essential throughout the acute phase, as well as the entire course of your rehabilitation.

The acute stage of a stroke caused by blood clots usually last for 48 hours. If symptoms subside during the acute stage and you are conscious and can sit up safely, you must wear a well-fit sling on the affected arm to prevent paralyzed muscles around the shoulder joint from being stretched out by the weight of your arm.

During the acute phase, you may be lying on your back for an extended period. If you try to get out of the bed without proper preparation, you might feel dizzy or faint. If you can tolerate a sitting position in your bed without any dizziness or fainting, your nurse or physical therapist will instruct you to sit on the edge of the bed with your feet dangling. At this point, you may not be able to balance your body, so your caregivers have to be on guard to support you. If you feel fine and can maintain your balance, your nurse or therapist will assist you in getting into a chair or wheelchair. The chair must be steady. A folding chair must be avoided, since you will depend on the sturdy legs of the chair to pivot properly into the chair. By holding the arm of the chair, you can support and transfer yourself into the chair slowly.

The physical therapist now has to work on your legs. The muscle power of your good leg must become stronger so that it can support your body weight. The muscles of your paralyzed side need to get stronger as soon as possible. Different types of exercises help strengthen muscles. The physical therapist will spend a great deal of time trying to maintain the joint mobility of your extremities. With the close supervision of your therapist, you will repeat the method for moving from a bed to chair *(transfer activity)*. *Patience* is your key word. This can be very frustrating at first. After a while, you will be able to get in and out of the bed independently or with minimum help. You will feel a great sense of accomplishment on mastering the transfer activity.

A stroke causes weakness of the muscles that pull up your foot. As a result, you cannot bend your ankle and lift the foot off the floor *(foot drop)*. This condition eventually causes a shortening of the tendon at the back of your heel *(Achilles tendon)*. This condition can eventually cause a deformity of your ankle joint, which can make it very difficult to walk. Only a surgical procedure can correct such a condition. In order to prevent this, your therapist will apply a splint to the back of your ankle joint to hold the ankle at a 90-degree angle.

If you are hemiplegic, not only are your muscles weak but also your brain forgets how to contract your muscles and you are unaware of the sensation of muscle contraction. The physical therapist uses many different techniques to help your brain recall or relearn how to contract your muscles.

In some cases, the muscles of your arm, hand, and fingers are strong enough to perform certain tasks but the movements may be very clumsy. Again, many different exercises are useful to control movement for performing a task. Meanwhile, you will learn how to turn in bed, change position, and sit up without help.

The occupational therapist observes you and your performance of various tasks for activities of daily living, such as eating, grooming, dressing, bathing, and toileting. These observations help the therapist determine your abilities and difficulties. Accordingly, the therapist teaches you a different way to perform tasks that may be difficult at first. If absolutely necessary, the therapist will give you a gadget (self-help device) to make it easier for you to perform the task. However, it is important not to use too many gadgets since it may cause confusion.

At some point, your paralyzed muscles may slowly become *spastic* (contracted). Spastic muscles make performing the activities of daily living more difficult. Spasm of muscles is uncomfortable. Spastic muscles are difficult to control and may cause a deformed joint. Any type of heat relaxes spastic muscles for a short while. Some medications may alleviate spasticity, but they cannot eliminate it. In some cases, BOTOX has been tried to relieve muscle spasticity.

30

WALKING

If you are hemiplegic, you will not be able to walk normally. Before walking, you must be able to stand up. For safety and convenience, there are parallel bars in the physical therapy gym (see Figure 30-2). With the help of a therapist, you pull yourself up with your good arm and leg to the standing position in the parallel bars. The good leg supports all your body weight. This is easier said than done. At first, you will struggle to reach this position. However, repeating this exercise will soon make it easier for you to stand up.

The next step is to balance your body. The therapist will instruct you to shift your weight from side to side. There is no difficulty shifting weight to your good side. However, when you shift your weight to the weak side, you will bend your body forward slightly in order to lock the weak knee. When you learn how to lock your knee, balancing your body becomes very easy.

Once you are able to stand up and balance, walking exercise starts. You hold the parallel bar with your good hand. Your tendency will be to make a long step with your weak leg and a short step with your good leg. There is a reason for this. When your good leg is supporting your weight, you feel confident moving the weak leg as far front as you can. Now the weight is on your weak leg, which cannot support your weight for a long time. Thus, the good leg has to make a short step in order not to fall.

You need to learn to do the opposite. Take a shorter step with your weak leg and a longer step with your good leg. It is all right if you have to drag your weak foot. If you drag your foot, the therapist will try to strengthen the muscles in your hip and thigh. When these muscles become stronger, you will be able to lift your foot from the floor.

If a foot drop persists, the therapist will apply a short leg brace (see Figure 30-3). A short leg brace is made of plastic and holds the ankle joint at a 90-degree angle. With stronger hip and thigh muscles and a short leg brace, you can clear the floor and walk easier. This brace fits inside your shoe. If you have a heavy build or are overweight, a metal brace attached to the shoe may be necessary.

Some patients may not be able to lock the knee when standing on the weak leg. If the patient puts weight on the weak leg, the knee buckles. A special type of brace is available to stabilize the weak knee.

Once you can walk between the parallel bars safely, the next challenge is to walk outside the parallel bars. You will need a cane. There are different types of canes (see Figure 30-4). Many elderly patients prefer to use a tripod (three-pronged) or quadruped (four-pronged) cane because such canes are very stable. Your therapist will select the most suitable cane for you. Your therapist holds onto your belt while you start to walk slowly. The therapist reminds you constantly to take a short step with the weak leg and a long step with the good leg. Repeated practice gives you confidence, and soon you will be able to walk without the therapist holding your belt.

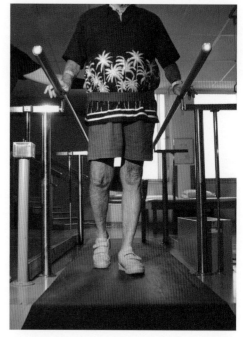

(*figure* 30-2)

The height of the parallel bars is adjustable according to the height of a patient.

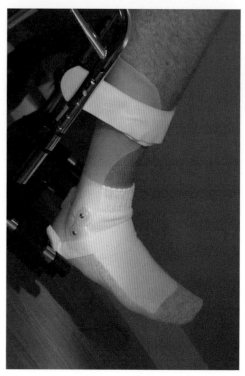

(*figure* 30-3)

A short leg brace (rigid ankle foot orthosis) prevents the foot from dropping. Foot drop can cause falls.

When you return home, you will realize there are steps everywhere: steps to the front entrance, steps to the upstairs, and even a step at the curb of the sidewalk. While in the rehabilitation unit, you must learn how to go up and down steps. The golden rule is that "good is up and bad is down." When you go up the step, the "good leg" goes up first, and the "bad leg" (weak leg) follows to the step on which your good leg is. If there is a banister on the good side, you must hold onto it. If a handrail is on the weak side, the body should be very close to the rail while you go up. When you come down the steps, the bad leg goes first and the good leg follows.

CONDITIONS ASSOCIATED WITH STROKE

Although paralysis and weakness are common manifestations of a stroke, many other conditions are associated with strokes. The following topics cover these conditions, which can make life difficult or trying. With luck, you may not suffer from any of them; however, please realize that they are not uncommon problems, so you should not feel embarrassed. Your physician and family will do their best to help minimize any discomfort.

Loss of Bowel and Bladder Control: You may lose control of your bowel and bladder immediately after a stroke, thus causing you to wet or soil the bed and your garments. The name of this condition is incontinence. In many cases, you regain your bowel and bladder control within a few days or a few weeks. Occasionally, you continue to have incontinence. The incontinence may affect the bladder, bowel, or both.

If you have bowel incontinence, your caregiver will be taught to find out the time of day you normally move your bowels. Once this period is determined, your caregiver can give you a bedpan or take you to the toilet in a timely manner and wait for defecation.

If you are a man with bladder incontinence, you can use a condom type of catheter on your penis, and the urine goes into a urinary bag. If you are a female, management is more difficult. External drainage systems do not work very well. You can have a flexible rubber tube with a balloon on the tip *(Foley or indwelling catheter)* inserted into your bladder. However, catheter use is associated with a higher risk of infection. Bladder training and voiding on a regular schedule may be helpful in avoiding catheters.

Incontinence of the bowel and/or the bladder make it difficult for a bedsore to heal. Meticulous attention by your nurses or caregivers is important in order to prevent pressure sores. Frequent position changes and special creams or ointments may be necessary.

Hemianopsia: Hemianopsia is blindness that affects the right or left half of your vision. For example, if the door of your bedroom is on the side of the hemianopsia, you will not see a person coming in. If that person speaks to you, you may be startled because you did not see the person coming into your room. In this case, changing the position of your bed in the room will allow you to see a person coming through the door. Another problem may be bumping into the door frame while passing through the doorway. The reason is the same. You did not see one side of

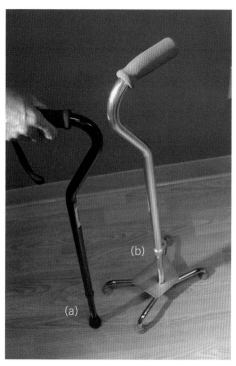

(figure 30-4)

(a) A regular cane and a (b) quadruped cane (quad cane). The length is adjustable. A quadruped cane is self-standing and very stable.

the doorway. Hemianopsia may cause you to bump into furniture or other objects in the room. No matter how good your condition is, you should not drive a car since your peripheral vision is impaired. You may not see a passing car or a person walking in a crosswalk. You must learn to turn your head or move your eyes to scan the environment for safety.

Psychological problems: You may experience memory problems, difficulty with thinking and logical reasoning, poor concentration, and difficulty with paying attention. You may fatigue easily. Some stroke victims may not recognize they had a stroke. Others may neglect the side of the hemiplegia. In this case, the person does not look at the paralyzed side of the body or even dress that side. They may not eat the food on the side of their plate that corresponds with the paralyzed side.

The patient does not realize that they have these problems. It is not easy for a caregiver to deal with this. If the caregiver is the member of the patient's family, it is emotionally difficult to observe the patient's behavior. The caregiver must be taught to understand that these are problems their loved one has no control over. No matter what the patient may say, the caregiver should not take it personally and must respond calmly. If correction is necessary, the caregiver should explain clearly and, if necessary, repeat until the patient understands. Under no circumstance, should the caregiver use "baby talk." The patient understands baby talk and will feel very insulted. Scolding the patient does not have any positive effect and may make the patient hostile, withdrawn, or depressed. If the patient shows signs of depression, the family should seek a physician's advice.

Swallowing difficulty: Although infrequent, you may have some difficulty after a stroke in swallowing, a condition known as dysphagia. In this case, you may cough after swallowing food or liquid. If you are a patient in a rehabilitation unit, the nurse or speech pathologist will most likely detect this difficulty. If you went home directly from the hospital without the benefit of a rehabilitation program and you or your family notices such problems, immediately contact your family physician. Unless you eat the right foods, you may choke or, even worse, develop bronchitis or pneumonia. As described in an earlier section, "Speech Pathologist," after proper tests, the speech pathologist will recommend the type of food and its consistency that you can eat safely. There is a substance available that can be mixed in water so that you can drink water without choking.

Speech disorders: Difficulty in speech is another relatively common condition among stroke victims. There are two types of speech problems related to a stroke: aphasia and dysarthria.

Aphasia: If you have aphasia, you may not be able to understand what is said to you *(receptive aphasia)* or you may not be able to express yourself properly *(expressive aphasia)*. The so-called speech center is located in the left side of the brain in 95% of right-handed persons and in 60% of left-handed persons. This is why aphasia occurs more often among people with right hemiplegia (damage to the left side of the brain).

If you have receptive aphasia, you cannot understand spoken words or sentences. This condition is as if someone speaks to you in a language you do not know. You can hear the voice but cannot understand the meaning. You do not understand spoken or written language. You may respond to certain words or sentences that have no relationship to the subject matter of the conversation.

If you have expressive aphasia, you understand spoken or written words. However, you are unable express yourself appropriately. You may nod your head appropriately or point to an object or make a facial expression. An experienced caregiver will learn to recognize what you are trying to communicate.

If you have global aphasia, you have features of both receptive and expressive aphasia. You cannot understand or find words and make minimum speech. People often erroneously think a person with global aphasia has lost his or her mind. A person with global aphasia is unable to communicate in spoken or written language.

Recovery from aphasia, if it occurs, is most noticeable during the first three months after a stroke but may take 1 to 2 years. If you are aphasic and speak two or more languages, it is most likely that you will regain your native language. The speech pathologist will try to find out the best way of communication for you. Speech is one mode of communication. The speech pathologist uses many different techniques to improve your ability to communicate. You and your caregivers may be able to communicate by pointing to images in photographs or by using letter or picture boards. If you have expressive aphasia, you may be able to use a computer-assisted device that prints messages. Unfortunately, those persons with severe aphasia will most likely not be able to communicate.

If you are a family member or friend of a person who has had a stroke, we would like to share a few pointers with you. You must be patient. When you speak to your loved one or friend, you must use simple sentences and speak slowly. You can use gestures and point to objects or pictures to help him or her understand. If he or she is speaking slowly, do not interrupt. Let him or her finish sentences. It is important for you to establish a means of communication if he or she is unable to call for help. You need to treat him or her as an adult with all the respect adults deserve. Under no circumstance should you use baby talk or make fun of the loved one.

Dysarthria: Dysarthria is an inability to pronounce words correctly. The causes of dysarthria are many. The basic problem, due to damage in the brain, is the weak or poor control of the muscles involved with speech. There are many different types of dysarthria. This condition is very common for the elderly, even for those who have not had a stroke. If you have dysarthria, you probably have a weak voice that makes your speech hard for someone else to understand. A speech pathologist will encourage you to make the correct pronunciation of words and will help you improve the pace of your speech and breathing. If you experience difficulties with your normal speech pattern, you can learn to modify your speech in order to communicate more effectively. If your dysarthria

30

is severe, you may want to use a letter or picture board or a specialized computer for communication. Your family and caregivers should take the same approaches outlined in the earlier section, "Aphasia."

PREVENTION

Strokes have many different causes. A person who suffers a stroke due to breakage of a weakened, bulging artery (aneurysm) is not likely to have another stroke if he or she survives the initial episode. However, others who have strokes related to blood clots or hemorrhage may face a higher chance of suffering another stroke than do other persons the same age. It is estimated that 20% of stroke survivors will have another stroke within five years.

If you have had a stroke or TIA, you should be under the care of a doctor to reduce your risk of recurrence. Although the risk cannot be eliminated, it can be reduced. It will likely require taking medication. You will be advised to avoid very strenuous physical activities, exhaustion, and emotional upset. You should eat a well-balanced diet, with adequate fiber to prevent constipation. During the summer months, you should keep yourself cool and take plenty of fluids. During the winter season, you should stay in a warm environment. These little things help prevent another stroke. Your family must be vigilant to protect you from extreme conditions.

If you have had a stroke and can walk, you have a greater chance of falling than other persons in your age bracket have. This may be due to poor balance, becoming careless, or depending on your paralyzed side as if it were normal. It is important that you keep your home as safe as possible (see Chapter 31). It is a known fact that a hemiplegic person who falls has a much higher risk of a hip fracture. The outcome for these persons is often poor. (See the section, "Hip Fracture," below.) Often they become bedridden or wheelchair-bound. Special attention by you and your family to your surroundings can reduce these risks. Do not be ashamed to accept whatever physical help you need from your family while you are walking.

CARDIOVASCULAR REHABILITATION

Your heart works continuously throughout your lifetime. As you get older, aging effects and disease can take their toll on your heart. Heart disease is a very common problem among middle-aged and older adults. Deleterious habits such as smoking and excessive alcohol intake may make matters worse.

The New York Heart Association (NYHA) has developed a classification to estimate prognosis and guide medical treatments of those with heart disease (see Table 7-2, in Chapter 7). Interestingly, many individuals who suffer a heart attack (myocardial infarction) never have any of these symptoms prior to actually having the heart attack. Treatment for heart disease may involve diet, such lifestyle changes as quitting smoking and reducing alcohol consumption, avoiding stress, and taking medications. Physical rehabilitation and exercise are important parts of the overall treatment program.

GOALS

If you have had a heart attack or heart surgery, your doctor will very likely refer you to a cardiac rehabilitation program. A heart attack causes damage to the heart muscle. The goal of rehabilitation following a heart attack is to resume your previous physical activity, perhaps with some modifications. The goal following heart surgery may be harder to establish. Since coronary artery bypass grafting (CABG) is performed to restore blood flow to your heart muscle, improvement in your heart's function may occur, and eventually you may be able to do more than you did before the surgery. For example, you might move from NYHA class III or IV to NYHA class II or even I.

Research studies have helped determine how much energy each physical activity requires. The heart pumps out more or less blood according to the energy needed. Thus, in the process of cardiac rehabilitation, you start with an activity that needs less energy and progress to activities that demand more energy.

REHABILITATION AFTER A HEART ATTACK

As soon as your acute symptoms (chest pain, shortness of breath, etc.) subside, you will be advised to sit up. If there is no ill effect, you will be allowed to sit by the edge of the bed. If you were healthy and engaged in normal daily activities until the onset of your heart attack, you should not have muscle weakness or joint mobility limitations. This will make the rehabilitation program progress quickly. If you already had some physical limitations, your progress may be slower than described here.

You will gradually engage in other activities as long as there are no heart-related problems, such as fatigue, palpitations, shortness of breath, or chest pain. With the assistance and supervision of a therapist or nurse, you will sit in a chair and stand up. If you can tolerate these activities, it is then time to try daily activities, such as dressing, grooming, and toileting. Now, you are ready for walking. You will often start your walking exercise with the parallel bars. The parallel bars provide some support and enhance your safety.

Once you can walk safely, under the supervision of a therapist, you will be permitted to go the toilet, the bathtub, or shower. The last activity is climbing stairs, since this is rather strenuous. Under the strict supervision of a therapist, you will climb steps slowly and one step at a time.

During the succession of increasingly physically demanding activities, the therapist or nurse monitors your pulse and blood pressure. If the pulse rate is too high or the blood pressure drops, you have to slow down that particular activity. Many rehabilitation units use heart monitors to observe the response of the heart during and after an activity. This is to protect you from stressing your heart too severely.

With careful monitoring of the responses of your heart in each activity, you can progress rather rapidly. Ten days to two weeks after the onset of the heart attack, you should be able to resume most of your normal activities. The important point is *moderation*. You have to avoid very strenuous activities and emotional stress in order to reduce the risk of the recurrence of a heart attack. You will need to continue seeing your physician regularly.

REHABILITATION AFTER HEART SURGERY

If you require heart surgery and are in very good physical condition before your surgery, you will usually progress rapidly through your cardiac rehabilitation program. However, if you, like many others, have had to limit your physical activities for a long period of time, your rehabilitation will take longer and be more complex. Physical inactivity causes weak and wasted muscles. Your emotional state may be very fragile since you have been disabled for so long. But cheer up! It's a good sign that you had the surgery. It is a sign of your desire to get well and your doctor's belief that heart surgery will help you. This desire is very important for achieving a better outcome from rehabilitation.

One of the goals of surgery is to improve the function of your heart. Hopefully, except for the discomfort associated with your incisions, you will feel better immediately after surgery. The therapist will instruct you to perform various exercises to strengthen your muscles, increase your joint movement, and boost your physical endurance. These exercises should not cause any symptoms of a weak heart, such as fatigue, shortness of breath, palpitations, or chest pain. These exercises will be slowly increased in intensity depending on your tolerance.

Once you reach a good physical condition, you will follow the same program as the person who has had a heart attack. If your activities were very limited before heart surgery, you may be satisfied with gaining the ability to perform ordinary daily chores. However, if you were actively engaged in more strenuous activities before your heart operation, your goal may be to resume these activities. Your doctor and you will decide which goals are most appropriate.

AFTER REHABILITATION

Almost all patients successfully complete the rehabilitation program and achieve their goals. They are independent in their self-care and all the activities of daily living. They can walk around, and some can climb stairs in the rehabilitation unit. After rest for a few days, those who have had a heart attack eventually resume their previous activities.

However, the situation after returning home can be very different. On returning home, some people lose or do not use skills that they learned during the rehabilitation program. There may be several reasons for this setback. In the rehabilitation unit, there is always a therapist or nurse with them. They encourage and assure them that they can do it. At home, there are no such psychological crutches. They become unsure of themselves.

Some are afraid that they may have another heart attack or injure themselves by doing activities. In effect, they become psychologically disabled—a "cardiac cripple."

Those who have had heart surgery may recall how and what they did before surgery. If they were inactive before, they tend to return to these old habits. Families may overprotect rehabilitated patients by doing things the patient should do without help. Families may also be afraid that their loved one may have a relapse. As a result, they will do things that their loved one can really do himself or herself.

The most important ingredient to prevent this from happening is the education of the patient and the family. The rehabilitation specialist must tell the patient what he or she should do. The specialist should give a very detailed schedule of home activities to be done every day during waking hours and should also tell the patient what not to do. Most elderly persons can be encouraged to resume sexual activity, but they need to stop and rest as necessary to avoid overexertion. Certain sexual positions may be less physically stressful, such as side to side or the partner on top. If you should have problems in this area, discuss them with your doctor (see Chapters 12 and 13).

The family must know what the patient can do and encourage the patient to continue these activities. The family also must know which activities the patient should not do and the type of assistance the patient may need. Rehabilitation specialists suggest that the family avoid spoiling the patient. This can be a delicate balance.

REHABILITATION AFTER HIP FRACTURE

Hip fracture is one of the most common injuries among the elderly, particularly women. The outcome of a hip fracture used to be very poor. Long periods of bed rest often resulted in bedsores and pneumonia. However, the outcome today is much brighter due to improvement in surgical techniques and the rehabilitation programs. The rehabilitation program following a hip fracture depends on the type of surgery used to treat the fracture.

REHABILITATION AFTER SURGERY

If you have had a hip fracture, your rehabilitation must start as soon after surgery as possible. If you stay in bed, your muscles tend to become weak and wasted and your joints become stiff. In order to prevent this from happening, strengthening your muscle power and maintaining the mobility of the joints of the unaffected leg and your arms are the first steps of rehabilitation. Following the instruction of a nurse or physical therapist, you will bend and stretch your hip, knee, ankle, shoulders, and elbows as often as possible. Lifting weights or other methods can increase your muscle power.

At the beginning, your affected leg has to rest in a fully extended position. You should not bend the knee. The caregivers should not place a pillow under the knee because this may lead to development of stiff joints in the hip and knee. With your leg in a straight position, your caregiver instructs you to contract your leg muscles without moving the joint (isometric exercise) as often as possible. This exercise prevents muscles from wasting and maintains muscle power.

After a day of these exercises, you gradually start to move the affected leg in bed, and you can sit up on the edge of the bed with your feet dangling. If there are no ill effects, such as dizziness or feeling faint, you can move from the bed to a chair by using only your good leg. The chair must be steady and should not be too low.

There are two types of surgery for repairing a hip fracture. One is to remove the head of thighbone (femur) and replace it with a metallic head (prosthetic hip replacement). The other is to secure the fractured fragments with a metallic nail or pin, plate, and screws. These two different surgical procedures make the speed of the rehabilitation process different.

If you have a prosthetic hip replacement and there are no complications, you can put full weight on the affected leg two days after the surgery. You stand up in the parallel bars with your good leg and slowly shift the weight to the fractured leg. These standing and balancing exercises are important to prevent falls. They are continued for a few days. Meanwhile, you should continue the strengthening exercises of your good leg and your arms. Once you can put full weight on the affected leg safely and can balance without discomfort, you can start walking in four to eight days. The walking exercise starts in the parallel bars. You can walk outside the parallel bars when your balance is improved and your gait is steady. You can start climbing stairs in about 11 days. You will need to follow the principle of "good is up and bad is down," described earlier in the section, "Walking." For going up the steps, your good leg (unaffected leg) goes up the step first and the fractured leg follows. In going down the step, your fractured leg goes down first and your good leg follows.

If you had a nail or pin, plate, and screws used, you will follow the same rehabilitation regime as those who had a prosthetic hip replacement— except that the program takes much longer. This is because weight bearing on the affected leg is delayed for two to three weeks after the surgery. There is a difference of opinion regarding when a person can safely put the body weight on the affected leg. Some doctors think it is about 10 to 12 weeks after surgery. Some feel that if you feel comfortable putting weight on your leg, you should be encouraged to do so. Your doctor is the best judge of this based on your own special circumstances.

You may need or want to have a cane. If you can walk safely and a cane gives you a sense of security, it is quite acceptable. Using two canes does not decrease the pressure over the fractured leg. At home, you should continue exercising to strengthen your muscle power. You should not sit on a chair or stool for a long period, particularly a low chair or stool. Some sofas, beds, or toilet seats may be too low. If you have no alternative, you can have someone place wood blocks under the legs of a sofa or bed. An extra cushion on a sofa may serve the same purpose. For the toilet, it is necessary to use a raised toilet seat. You must use the arms of the chair or sofa for support on standing up. Unless there is suitable furniture within reach of the toilet, a guardrail may be required for you to stand up. The following sections discuss such arrangements.

While sitting on a chair, you must avoid crossing your legs. Also, you must avoid activities involving pushing, pulling, or lifting of heavy objects, as well as stooping, reaching, or jumping. It is desirable to invite a therapist to your home before leaving the hospital to determine if any modification of your home environment is necessary.

REHABILITATION WITHOUT SURGERY

The outcome of a hip fracture without surgery is generally poor, and nonsurgical treatment is usually not recommended. However, surgery may be inadvisable if you have other serious medical problems or you did not walk before the fracture.

The nonsurgical treatment of hip fracture is to immobilize the hip and leg for a period of six to eight weeks. Methods may include a plaster of paris cast from the toes to the waist, a splint, or traction. This prolonged immobility can cause many problems, including development of a bedsore, wasting and weakening of muscles, stiffness of joints, and general weakness. Treatment aimed at preventing these unwelcome complications is often not effective. One of the most serous complications is pneumonia. Pneumonia in a person who is immobilized is very difficult to treat, and the outcome is generally extremely poor even with help of powerful antibiotics.

Rehabilitation after nonsurgical treatment is prolonged and difficult. Correction of the unfavorable conditions described above must take place. As soon as possible, you must turn your body side to side and sit up. Your general condition will need to improve. You have to strengthen your muscles and increase the mobility of your joints. However, even if these interventions are successful, it still takes a long time before you are able to take care of your daily needs.

HIP FRACTURE IN A HEMIPLEGIC PERSON

A hip fracture in a person with hemiplegia is not rare. (See section, "Stroke Rehabilitation," above.) The outcome of this fracture depends on many factors: Before the fracture, could the person walk independently and safely? What is the learning ability of this person? Which side of the hip is involved: the side of the hemiplegia or the good side? Is the general physical condition good enough for surgery? If the fracture occurred on the hemiplegic side, the outcome is promising if the person's general condition is good and the person is mentally alert and capable of learning. Prosthetic hip replacement is the preferred surgical treatment. The patient undergoes the rehabilitation process as described in the section, "Rehabilitation after Surgery," above.

If the fracture is on the patient's hemiplegic side, success depends on how well the patient can put the body weight on the hemiplegic leg. If the person can bear the weight on the hemiplegic leg, the outcome is promising. If a patient can stand up and make one or two steps, it is remarkable. Although this seems to be such a little gain, it makes a great difference in the patient's quality of life. For mobility, the person can use a wheelchair. However, if the person cannot stand up, at least two family members or caregivers must lift the person to and from the bed and wheelchair or chair. This also applies in transferring from a wheelchair to the toilet seat. From the bed to a wheelchair, a hydraulic lifter (see Figure 30-5) can be useful, but usually there is no space for the lifter in a bathroom. If a lifter is used, a nurse or physical therapist must teach the caregiver how to operate it. Once the caregiver learns, the caregiver alone should be able to move the patient from bed to a wheelchair.

A commode chair may be necessary if the person does not wish to use a bedpan. Again, two persons have to lift the individual to the commode chair or use a lifter. This is a very humiliating experience for the person. When two helpers are not available, the person has to stay in bed. In many cases, the patient becomes wheelchair-bound because many factors weigh against a successful recovery.

AMPUTEE REHABILITATION

An amputee is a person who has lost a limb or part of a limb. Amputation of an arm is much less common than of a leg in the general population. Most arm amputations are the result of an accident, usually a job-related accident. However, in the older population, amputations are more often related to such underlying diseases as diabetes or poor circulation. It is much more common for an elderly amputee to lose a leg rather than an arm. Diabetes may result in loss of normal sensation or poor circulation in the legs. This can result in leg ulcers, and infection that can ultimately require amputation to prevent more serious consequences. In addition, an elderly person who has lost one leg has a higher likelihood of losing the other leg since the underlying factors responsible for the loss of the first leg are still likely to exist and affect the remaining leg.

The loss of a limb is very traumatic for any person but particularly the elderly. In addition to the functional limitations caused by an amputation, the psychological impact can be significant. If you should require an amputation, you should remember that most persons still enjoy a relatively normal life although extensive rehabilitation is necessary. You should ask your rehabilitation specialists to explain what you can expect from the rehabilitation program. The involvement of your family in this process is important.

The level of amputation of the leg depends on the diseased area of the leg. It can be at the level of the toes to a complete removal of the leg at the hip joint (hip disarticulation) or the removal of one-half of the pelvis (hemipelvectomy). Happily, hip disarticulation and hemipelvectomy are not common surgical procedures. In general, a longer remaining leg results in a better functional outcome. For example, if you only require the amputation of a toe, you will be able to walk almost normally as soon as the wound heals. One the other hand, if you require the removal of

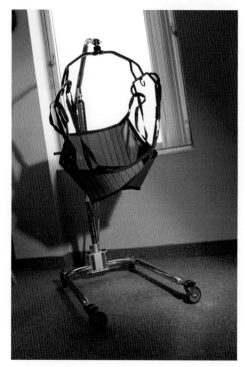

(*figure* 30-5)

The lifter may be mechanical or hydraulic. It occupies a rather large space and may not be suitable for a small room with a bed.

the entire leg, you will require a very special prosthesis (artificial limb). However, it may be difficult for you to walk with this type of prosthesis because it requires very good muscle power, good control of the muscles, good balance, and a large amount of energy.

Most elderly people who require an amputation will need a *below-the-knee (BK)* or *above-the-knee (AK)* procedure. The reason for this is that most amputations are due to poor circulation or infection that causes problems of the toes and feet. If the level of the amputation is within the diseased area, the surgical wound will not heal and another amputation higher up will be required for the wound to heal normally.

REHABILITATION OUTCOME

Walking with a BK prosthesis requires that you expend 10 to 40% more energy than you normally would. Walking with an AK prosthesis requires 60 to 100% more energy. This is why you will be instructed to walk slowly when you are taught to walk with your prosthesis in order to conserve energy. Assuming you have no heart problems or other significant medical conditions, you should be able to walk nicely with a BK prosthesis with or without a cane.

If you had an AK amputation, you may not have enough energy to carry the weight of the prosthesis or you may have trouble acquiring the skills necessary to control an artificial knee joint. There is a specially designed knee joint for elderly AK amputees. However, this knee joint adds more weight to the prosthesis. Many older AK amputees use the AK prosthesis for activities of daily living (ADL) only and use a wheelchair for moving around.

If you require amputation of both legs (double amputee), it will be more difficult to walk with two prostheses. It depends on how well you walked with your prosthesis after the first amputation. If the first amputation was a BK, and you walked well, and the second amputation is another BK, the chance of your walking again is better. You will use two prostheses. You may even be able to walk without a pair of crutches or canes.

If you lost both legs above the knee or one above the knee and the other below the knee, you will most likely be unable to walk because it requires a lot of energy. You still may use a pair of prostheses for activities of daily living and cosmetic purposes. Regardless of the level of amputation, walking distance is generally limited to a few steps and a wheelchair is necessary for outdoor use.

Prostheses have been developed that use electronics and computers to assist in their movement. Although at this time they are prohibitively expensive for most older persons, hopefully the price will come down or insurance companies will cover the costs.

REHABILITATION PROCESS

In order to minimize swelling of the surgical site, immediately after surgery, a caregiver usually places a pillow under the stump. This pillow should not stay in place more than 24 hours after surgery. Placement of a pillow under the stump for a prolonged period results in the development of limitation of joint movement. This usually results in the inability to extend the hip and knee joint fully (flexion contracture). If your physical condition allows, you should lie down on your stomach as long as possible. A BK or an AK amputee should not sit on a chair or wheelchair for a prolonged period. If you had an AK amputation, you must try to keep the stump as close to the good leg as possible. This positioning of the stump is to prevent limitations of joint mobility.

Stump conditioning: The amputated stump naturally shrinks as time passes. However, it takes a relatively long time. Stump conditioning is done to minimize swelling, to speed up the shrinkage, and to shape the stump to fit snugly into the socket of the prosthesis. There are two methods to condition the stump: the *elastic stump shrinker* and elastic bandages. The elastic stump shrinker looks like a sock and is easy to apply. Many patients can wear the elastic stump shrinker by themselves. The elastic bandages are the preferred method because the caregiver can control the amount and location of the pressure to the stump. A shortcoming of the elastic bandages is that the caregiver must be skillful in bandage application and must reapply the bandages whenever they are loose. You must wear either the elastic stump shrinker or elastic bandage 24 hours a day.

Prosthesis: You can start walking with a temporary prosthesis (pylon) within one to two weeks after surgery. The socket of the pylon can be made of plaster of paris and must fit to the stump snugly. There are many other types of temporary prostheses with adjustable sockets. The early walking exercise with a pylon helps you stay active and prevent flexion contractures. It also accelerates the shrinkage of the stump. You will start walking exercises in the parallel bars. Eventually, you will be able to walk outside the parallel bars with crutches or canes until a permanent prosthesis becomes available.

The permanent prosthesis must be lightweight and meet your needs and safety requirements. If you receive the permanent prosthesis before the completion of the shrinkage of stump, the socket soon becomes too loose. In this case, readjustment of the socket is necessary. An ill-fitted socket will cause pressure sores on the stump, and you cannot walk normally. In order to avoid the need for readjustment of the socket, making the permanent prosthesis should wait for a few weeks.

For an elderly BK amputee, the best prosthesis is the *patella tendon–bearing (PTB)* prosthesis (Figure 30-6). The patella tendon is located between your patella (kneecap) and tibia (shinbone). This is the area that your doctor strikes with the little rubber hammer to evoke the knee-jerk reflex. The socket of the prosthesis that has contact with this part of the stump supports your body weight. The PTB prosthesis is a relatively simple and lightweight and made of synthetic materials. If you need more support than the standard PTB prosthesis provides, you most likely will be unable to use a prosthesis. An elderly AK amputee can use a *suction suspension AK prosthesis.* The color of the prosthesis can match the color of the remaining leg. This is particularly important for women who wear a skirt or knee-length dress.

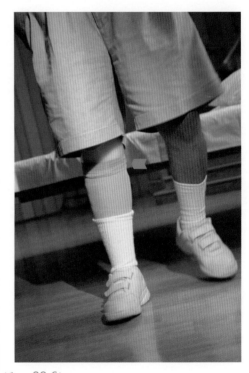

(*figure* 30-6)

A below-the-knee patella tendon–bearing prosthesis (arrowhead).

Before placing the stump into the socket of a PTB prosthesis, you put on stump socks. Stump socks are made of thin seamless cotton. They prevent friction between the skin and socket and absorb sweat from the stump. If you are an AK amputee using a suction suspension AK prosthesis, you do not wear stump socks while using the prosthesis. For going up and down steps, you use the technique of "good is up and bad is down" (see the earlier section, "Walking"). "Good" in this instance refers to your remaining leg, and "bad" refers to the leg with the prosthesis. When not wearing your prosthesis, you need to use crutches. If your arms are not strong or your body balance is not good enough, a walker (see Figure 30-7) is useful. You cannot use a walker on steps.

Stump care: At the end of a day or when no more walking is necessary, you remove your prosthesis, wash the stump with a mild soap and warm water, and dry the stump with a towel. Inspect the stump with the help of a mirror to make sure there is no wound. If redness of the skin stays for a long period, the socket may need adjustment. After this inspection, put talcum powder on the entire surface of the stump.

Your prosthesis is for walking only. Never sleep with your prosthesis on, because it causes a skin rash. If a skin rash on the stump occurs, you cannot wear the prosthesis until your skin heals. In addition, you should not swim with your prosthesis. It will weaken the parts of the prosthesis.

The caregiver should wash the stump socks with a mild soap after use every day. Every morning you must use a freshly washed and dried stump sock. Dirty socks can cause skin infection.

Prosthesis care: Your prosthesis must be kept dry all the time. If walking in the rain is unavoidable or you accidentally step into a puddle, take the shoe on the prosthesis off and dry the prosthesis thoroughly with a dry, soft cloth as soon as possible. The foot of the prosthesis is difficult to dry. Let it dry naturally. Dry your shoes as well. Never use any kind of heat to dry the prosthesis or shoes. Clean the socket of a PTB prosthesis with wet cloths and dry. Dust the inside of the prosthesis with a small amount of talcum powder.

For a suction suspension socket of an AK prosthesis, at the end of the day, after removing the prosthesis, clean the inside with moist cloths and dry it. Do not use talcum powder.

Keep all parts of your prosthesis as clean as possible. If any dirt is on the prosthesis, clean it with a slightly damp cloth and then dry it with a dry cloth.

When your prosthesis is not in use, place it on the floor on its side. Do not keep the prosthesis in the upright or standing position, since the prosthesis can fall over and be damaged.

Painful stump: After surgery, pain is common. This can be controlled with pain relievers. The pain should subside within a few days. However, you may experience mild to severe pain when you wear a pylon or prosthesis. The many causes of such pain: swelling of the stump, ill-fitted socket, too small a socket, or gain or loss of weight. The ill-fitted socket may cause a pressure sore, which is painful. After eliminating such causes, if you still have pain, your doctor will examine the stump. Ultrasound therapy is effective for some conditions, and surgery of the bone may be necessary for others.

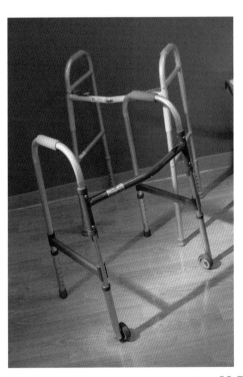

(figure 30-7)

If the walker doesn't include casters, the person has to lift the walker to advance it. Some walkers have a basket to hold items, and others have a seat for resting.

Phantom limb: Phantom limb is the sensation that you still have a whole leg after surgery. Most amputees feel the phantom limb for a different duration. You may experience a tingling sensation in a part of the missing leg. At the beginning, you may feel as if you have your whole leg. As time passes, the length of the limb will feel shorter. When you feel only the foot, the phantom limb sensation will soon disappear. This sensation itself is harmless, and there is no discomfort. However, during the night, you need to be careful early on since you may actually "forget" that you have had an amputation; consequently, on waking up to go to the bathroom, you may stand up and step on the amputated leg, resulting in a fall.

The phantom limb does not need treatment. Active use of your prosthesis may shorten the period that you experience the phantom limb. In the early stage after amputation, you must remind yourself not to attempt to stand up on the amputated leg since you may still feel that you have a normal leg.

Phantom limb pain: Phantom limb pain is very different from a painful stump. In the case of the painful stump, you feel pain in the stump. In the case of phantom limb pain, you feel pain as if it is in the lost part of your leg. This condition occurs if you experienced a great deal of pain before surgery or there was not sufficient pain management during and immediately after surgery. There are many physical therapy techniques to reduce or eliminate the pain. Sometimes medication is helpful.

Wheelchair: You need a wheelchair even if you can walk with a prosthesis. The reason for this is that walking with your prosthesis for a long distance is not desirable. You also need a wheelchair after removing the prosthesis in the evening. Although medical equipment stores or many drug stores sell wheelchairs, the purchase of a wheelchair for amputees must be carefully undertaken. A regular wheelchair is balanced for a person with two legs. A double amputee does not have the weight of two legs, which puts the chair out of balance. It tends to topple backward.

There is a special wheelchair called an *amputee wheelchair*. Construction of this wheelchair takes into account the loss of the weight of the legs. Usually, an occupational therapist at the rehabilitation unit suggests the type of wheelchair that an amputee can safely use.

You depend on your wheelchair for your mobility. Therefore, the wheelchair must be in good working condition. Upholstery such as the seat, backrest, and armrests must be cleaned with a mild detergent and dried thoroughly. Periodical cleaning of the wheels is desirable.

AFTERCARE

After successfully completing your prosthetic rehabilitation program, you should return to the rehabilitation clinic every three to six months for a follow-up. The follow-up consists of checking the condition of the stump and prosthesis and its components, as well as the fitting of the socket and examination of the remaining leg. Checking the remaining leg is especially important for those who lost a leg due to poor blood circulation or infection related to diabetes mellitus.

The stump continues to shrink as you use your prosthesis. At some point, you may have to use two stump socks. If several layers of socks allow a good fitting, realigning the socket is necessary. However, if you use your prosthesis daily, parts of the prosthesis may wear out. Usually, within two years, you will need a new prosthesis.

LIVING IN YOUR COMMUNITY

The older population is increasing in size every year. This is due to improvements in health care, nutrition, the environment, and many other factors. Some say this is a sign of an affluent society. However, it is necessary that we examine how the elderly live in our highly developed society.

An elderly person may face such problems as a fixed income, unavailability of affordable and accessible housing, and insufficient health insurance coverage. Our society has failed to address problems related to longer life expectancy. Living in a youth-oriented society, many elderly people are just trying to survive, but their existence may be lonely and frustrating. They deserve a better quality of life.

In addition to these social and economic disadvantages, many older people have age-related problems. The aging process begins at birth. Following your birth and infancy, you go through childhood, young adulthood, and adulthood. You become taller, heavier, and stronger. You learn to speak. You learn to walk and run. Your physical performance reaches its peak in your 20s. You go to school and learn to read and write. Your mental, emotional, and intellectual capacity reaches its peak in your late 20s and 30s. We often call these processes "growing up" or "maturing." In fact, these changes are aging processes.

In your 40s, you begin to notice graying or thinning of your hair and wrinkles on your face. You or others in your age group may have high blood pressure or experience dizziness. This is also part of the aging process. While the aging process in your early period of life is constructive and useful, this process in your later life is destructive and unwelcome.

Effects of the aging process differ from one individual to the other. In fact, the aging process does not affect every organ of your body in the same way. In addition, aging may cause different manifestations in different people. We all know people whose brain has aged faster than other parts of their body (Alzheimer's disease) and others for which their heart has aged faster (coronary artery disease and congestive heart failure). The aging process progresses slowly but continuously. Present scientific knowledge has elucidated some of the mechanisms responsible for aging, but we still cannot stop this process.

As your own aging marches on, you may notice that you tire more easily. As your reach your elderly years, you possess the experience and skill to perform your daily living activities, but you may find that performing them is more difficult. When you remember how easily things were done in your younger years, you may feel frustrated. Some people curtail their physical activities because they have less stamina. It is important that you resist this temptation, since the old adage holds true—"If you don't use it, you lose it." You may not be able to perform many activities as efficiently as before or as fast and vigorously, but regular exercise of your mental and physical "muscles" can help you keep functioning at a high level. This is what this book is all about—*optimal aging.* Even if you do things at a slower pace, you need to keep as physically and mentally active as possible in order to age optimally.

If you do have some medical or physical limitations, you can stop certain recreational activities that require a large amount of energy. However, you cannot stop performing the activities of daily living. Otherwise, you will need family or friends to help you. Most likely, you will want to maintain a certain level of independence. This may require the use of self-help devices. These assistive devices are gadgets, materials, or equipment to help you perform various activities. Some of them may be for daily activities and others for vocational or recreational activities. The main purpose of self-help devices is to take the place of a particular body function that was lost or diminished due to trauma or disease. Self-help devices or assistive devices were originally developed for physically disabled people. They are often custom-made. The use of self-help devices for the elderly is a new approach, and it does not mean that elderly people are disabled. However, elderly people often have many age-related conditions that affect their ability to perform some of their daily living activities. A specific assistive device can be chosen based on the activity with which the individual needs help. A self-help device is designed for one particular purpose. It is not meant to be interchangeable with other functions. The examples of assistive devices shown in this chapter are commercially available. These devices do not necessarily need to be purchased at surgical supply stores. Many mail-order catalogues sell the various devices mentioned here. Many items described here are not intended to be self-help devices. They are available to the public for convenience. If you require such a device, you and/or your family should look for a gadget that can help you from day to day. Selection of a self-help device may require some imagination and creativity.

Although a self-help device serves one particular function, it may be beneficial in other ways. For example, a reacher is used to pick up an object (see Figure 30-8), and using a reacher to pick up an object on the floor eliminates bending or crouching. A change in body position from crouching to standing up can cause some people to get dizzy. Bending may also stress the lower back, and crouching may hurt the knee joints. Using a reacher to pick up an object from a high shelf eliminates the need for a stepladder. Stepping on a stepladder increases the risk of a fall. The only caution in using a reacher is not to pick up heavy objects. Picking up a heavy object with a reacher is dangerous because you may drop the object or hurt your wrist or hand. Similarly, a person can use a long-handled dustpan in a standing position without the need to bend over.

ENERGY SAVING

When you become elderly, your circulatory system is less efficient and you tend to tire more easily. In some cases, you need to avoid unnecessary

(figure 30-8*)*

There are a variety of reacher designs depending on the objects to be picked up.

physical activities. Even standing in one position for preparation of dinner can prove time-consuming. Standing for a long period requires more energy than sitting on a chair does. Therefore, cooking from a chair is more desirable. Since the countertop is too high for a regular chair, a high chair, such as an "admiral's chair" or bar stool, is ideal for this activity. A bar stool should have a backrest to support the trunk. Instead of letting your feet dangle, you can rest them on the foot railing.

In order to prepare the dinner table, you have to carry many items, such as plates, eating and serving utensils, and food from the kitchen to the dining table. Using a rolling cart will save many trips. A folding cart can save space when the cart is not in use.

Many electric or gas ranges have the oven under the range top. In order to work with the oven, a person must bend, crouch, or kneel. It then requires more energy to stand up afterward, and the standing can result in dizziness. In order to avoid these body positions, use a portable electric broiler that is often combined with a toaster.

Reducing the number of trips required for carrying objects and avoiding bending, crouching, or kneeling is important to conserve energy and avoid dizziness or falls. For example, when gardening, you could make several trips between the backyard and the tool shed or garage to get small garden tools. Instead, by carrying a tote bag with all the necessary tools in it, you can save many trips. If you work with plants, you can eliminate bending, crouching, or kneeling by sitting on a milk stool or milk crate. A low stool has actually been designed and manufactured specifically for garden work. Long-handled pullers and pruners are useful to avoid undesirable body positions and the necessity for climbing ladders.

There are activities that are essential for daily living. However, you need to be mindful to conserve energy. You may need to avoid certain body positions that require extra energy. You should plan and organize your activities ahead of time and use the available self-help devices or gadgets intelligently.

FALL PREVENTION

In advanced age, your physical condition may be characterized by a decline in muscle strength, joint mobility, memory, and vision. Clumsy body movement is also quite common. In addition, you may lose minerals from your bones (osteoporosis), which causes bones to become brittle and easy to fracture (see Chapter 19). Often a fall will result in a fracture. The healing of a fracture among elderly people is slow. The section "Rehabilitation After Hip Fracture" described the difficulties with the rehabilitation of an elderly person with hip fracture. Therefore, fall prevention is extremely important for elderly people. See Chapter 31 regarding the causes and prevention of falls.

CLUMSY BODY MOVEMENT

If you are not steady in the standing position in a shower stall, a shower chair is useful. A shower chair is commercially available, but you have

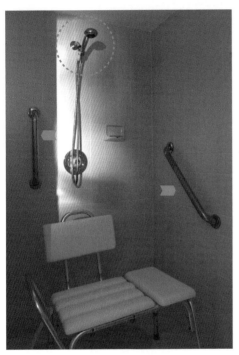

(*figure* 30-9)

A grab bar may come as a straight bar on the wall, as shown (arrowheads). A curved bar is also commercially available. A handheld shower head is shown in the center (circle).

other alternatives. A rustproof metal or plastic chair that can fit in a shower stall or bathtub serves the same purpose. You may find a handheld showerhead and grab bars useful (see Figures 30-9 and 30-10). If there is no soap holder in the shower stall, a shower caddy can be purchased. The caddy can store soap as well as brushes and a small shampoo bottle.

You may find the toilet seat too low, which makes it difficult for you to stand up. In this case, try a raised toilet seat (see Figure 30-11). You may prefer to use guardrails or both a raised toilet seat and guardrails.

If you shave but have clumsy body motion or shaky hands, you should not use a safety razor because it may cut your skin. An electric shaver is safer. However, you should not use an electric shaver in or near the bathtub, because it may cause an electric shock if coming into contact with the water. (This holds true for hairdryers and other electrical devices.)

When you are working in the kitchen, be careful to avoid burns. A gas range without an automatic pilot light needs matches in order to light the stove. Regular matches require that your fingers get very close to the gas burner and increasing the risk for burned fingers. It is safer to use long fireplace matches. You should always use padded mitts or pot holders whenever you handle pots and pans on the stove or in the oven.

After you mop the floor, the mop head needs rinsing. You have to bend over to put the mop over the bucket and squeeze the mop head. However, there is a mop with an attachment that eliminates the need to bend over the pail and wring the mop because you operate this mop while standing. A mop pail with caddy is a pail or bucket with casters. It is easy to move from one place to the other. There are new products using disposable towels as mop heads. Some come with a reservoir for cleaning fluid. These new products are designed to be more suitable for older people.

An ironing board with an electric outlet helps prevent tripping over the electric cord. A reacher is useful to pick up clothes from the hamper without bending over the hamper. If your hands are unsteady, you may drop dishes to the floor and break them. Plastic dishes are a good option. Many plastic cooking utensils are lighter in weight than metal ones and easier to handle. If you have difficulty getting up from a chair, you may want to use a "cushion-lifting chair" that assists you in standing up.

LIMITED JOINT MOVEMENT

You may have limited flexibility in your joints. Such limitations have many causes, including arthritis and shortening of the **tendons** (the attachments of muscle to bone). With limited finger joint movement, holding small objects is difficult. For example, even a zipper pull may be too small to grasp effectively. By attaching a ring or short looped chain, such as a key chain, to the pull, you can hook a finger to the ring and pull the zipper up or down (see Figure 30-12). A large safety pin or paperclip may serve the same purpose. Limited joint movement makes reaching difficult. A long-handled shoehorn or an extension handle attached to your reacher are good ideas. As we previously mentioned, many housekeeping utensils, such as reachers and garden tools, come with long handles. If you are a woman, you may find it difficult to put on your stockings. Figure 30-13

(figure 30-10)

Mail order catalogues show various types of bathtub grab bars. (Courtesy of Sammons Preston, AbilityOne Corporation.)

(figure 30-11)

Many different types of raised toilet seats are available.

(figure 30-12)

A zipper pull is attached to an appropriate ring size.

(figure 30-13*)*

There are many different types of sock, stocking, or pantyhose put-on devices.

(figure 30-14*)*

Lever-type doorknobs are made of rubber and slip onto a regular doorknob. Some styles include illumination at night. *(Courtesy of Life With Ease)*.

(figure 30-15*)*

Various types of jar openers can be attached to the wall or to the bottom of a cabinet or can be handheld.

shows a stocking or socks put-on device. A raised toilet seat and guardrails are helpful for those who have limited joint movement in the hips and knees.

It may take some ingenuity on your part to function optimally from day to day. For example, storing items too high or too low is a poor practice. Place them in areas of easy reach. Such a habit will eliminate climbing up a stepladder or bending over. Having a lazy Susan at an appropriate height makes reaching easy.

HANDS

Unsteady hands: If you have shaky hands or diminished grip strength due to arthritis or neurological disease, levers can help with difficult tasks such as turning a doorknob (see Figure 30-14). If you find buttoning shirts difficult, snap-on buttons are a good alternative. Sometimes Velcro closures are useful. There are even gadgets to help you with buttoning.

If you have difficulty opening a jar top, various jar openers are available (see Figure 30-15). Similarly, an electric can opener is helpful. If you have a weak grasp, you should avoid using glass bowls due to the risk of breakage. A plastic or metal bowl should be used for mixing. If the bowl moves around while mixing, a small rubber or plastic sheet under the bowl can stabilize it. There is a knit coaster that slips onto the bottom of a bowl and which serves the same purpose. Holding playing cards may not be easy for you. If so, try using a plastic or wooden cardholder, as shown in Figure 30-16.

Numb fingers: Many older persons have numb fingers, which result from a number of different causes. This condition may cause you to drop things or even burn your fingers without knowing it. Using plastic cooking utensils, cups, and plates can prevent breakage. Pots and pans should have non–heat-conducting handles. You should use insulated rubber gloves for dishwashing. If hot water runs for a long period, the metal faucet handle can become very hot. Use a pot holder or mitten gloves to prevent burning your fingers.

LOW VISION

Low vision is a common condition among elderly people. The room in which you are reading should have enough light. Various magnifying glasses are available. Some are designed specifically for reading a book or newspaper. Some magnifying glasses come with illuminating mechanisms. Avoid using inexpensive magnifying glasses made of plastic, which can distort images. A magnifying makeup mirror usually has two sides. One side is a regular mirror, and the other side is a concave mirror that works as a magnifying mirror.

Several large publishers have special editions for people who have low vision. For example, the New York Times publishes a weekly edition of a large-print newspaper. There are also large-print dictionaries (as shown in Figure 30-17) and many other books, not to mention the Reader's Digest. To find them, you can ask a sales agent at your local bookstore. On a computer, you can use your search function and enter "large print books."

The results will give you a number of books in large print in various categories. Some people prefer "talking books," which allow a person to listen to a book being read. A regular telephone set has small letters or if your hand movement is awkward, dialing may be difficult. Shown in Figure 30-18, a large-letter telephone is easier whether you have low vision or trouble with hand coordination.

Needle threaders are useful for sewing no matter your age. Sewing centers or thrift shops sell these threaders. Many items have large lettering. Again, look for such items on a website selling "large print items."

DIFFICULTY HEARING

If you have difficulty hearing, a hearing aid may be very helpful (see Chapter 3). However, for a variety of reasons, many elderly people do not like wearing a hearing aid. If this is the case, you should ask your family and friends to face you and speak slowly and slightly louder, so that you can understand what they are saying. Even if you are not adept at lip-reading, it will be easier for you to guess what is being said. If you have difficulty hearing the telephone ringing, a device is available that lights up whenever the phone rings. You can also purchase an amplifier for the telephone receiver.

SHORT-TERM RECALL

A common problem associated with aging is trouble with short-term recall. You may find it quite easy to recall events from weeks, months, or years ago, but you may have more difficulty recalling things you did in recent days, hours, or minutes. For example, some older people may forget that they put on water to boil to make tea. If they forget to turn the stove or gas flame off, there is a risk for fire. Use of a timer that rings or a teakettle that whistles can avert this kind of situation. In order to remind yourself of an often-used oven temperature, paste a colored tape on the dial of the oven, which will eliminate the need to remember the temperature.

CONCLUSION

Please remember that there is no shame to admit that you cannot do certain activities. If your family or friends do too many things for you, however, you will lose your independence in your activities of daily living. That is not helpful. Instead, you should work with your family members and friends to find out what kind of help you really need and what you can do by yourself. In this chapter, we have discussed many items that can assist you, but many other devices are available. You can buy numerous inexpensive items that are very useful, and although there are also specialty items, the majority can be found in discount stores and mail-order outlets.

The most important principle is that you maintain your independence in daily activities of living as long as possible. A little imagination and creativity will help you continue to enjoy the quality of your life.

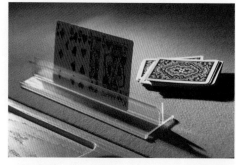

(figure 30-16)

Cards are inserted into a groove in a playing card holder, which can be made from either wood or plastic.

(figure 30-17)

Normal versus large-print magazine. (Courtesy of Reader's Digest).

(figure 30-18)

Large-letter telephone set.

WHAT YOU NEED TO KNOW

⚫ Rehabilitation is a medical specialty. Rehabilitation after a stroke, heart attack, amputation, orthopedic surgery, and so forth usually requires a multidisciplinary team. You and your family are the most important members of this team.

⚫ You will set goals for your rehabilitation in consultation with the rehabilitation team.

⚫ Rehabilitation can be provided in a variety of settings, including a hospital rehabilitation department, an outpatient clinic, a specialty rehabilitation hospital, a nursing or assisted living facility, or at home. You and your doctors decide the best environment for your therapy.

⚫ You may require special devices. Your therapist will guide you in the selection of appropriate self-help devices.

⚫ A positive attitude and a willingness to improve are vitally important for rehabilitation. The following quote may help give you some encouragement:

People are like stained-glass windows.
They sparkle and shine when the sun is out,
but when the darkness sets in,
their true beauty is revealed
only if there is a light from within.
—Elizabeth Kübler-Ross

30

FOR MORE INFORMATION

⚫ American Academy of Physical Medicine and Rehabilitation
One IBM Plaza, Suite 2500
Chicago, IL 60611
312-464-9700
Fax: 312-464-0227
E-mail: info@aapmr.org
Web: www.aapmr.org

⚫ National Institute of Neurological Disorders and Stroke
P.O. Box 5801
Bethesda, MD 20824
800-352-9424
E-mail: braininfo@ninds.nih.gov
Web: www.ninds.nih.gov
NINDS is part of the National Institutes of Health.

Falls are a serious public health problem among older adults. More than a third of adults aged 65 years or older fall each year.

—*National Center for Injury Prevention and Control*

THE AUTHORS

31

ADRIANA BIDA, MD, is a specialist in internal medicine with interest in geriatrics working as an attending physician at York Central Hospital, Richmond Hill, Canada. She graduated from the Institute of Medicine and Pharmacy in Iasi, Romania, where she also completed an internal medicine residency. She then did a cardiology fellowship at the Institute of Cardiology Fundeni in Bucharest, Romania. After immigrating with her family to Canada in 1995, she completed a residency in internal medicine at Brookdale University Hospital and Medical Center in New York and Norwalk Hospital in Connecticut. She completed a fellowship in geriatric medicine at the Medical College of Wisconsin, in Milwaukee, and at Baycrest Centre for Geriatric Care, in Toronto, Canada. She is certified by the American Board of Internal Medicine and the Royal College of Physicians and Surgeons (Canada). She received the John A. Hartford Foundation/American Federation of Aging Research Award to support the presentation "The Underuse of Therapy in Secondary Prevention of Hip Fracture among Elderly Veterans" at the 2002 Annual Scientific Meeting of the American Geriatrics Society in Washington, DC.

EDMUND DUTHIE, MD, is chief of geriatrics at the Medical College of Wisconsin. He graduated from the University of Notre Dame and the Georgetown University School of Medicine. He completed his residency in internal medicine at the Medical College of Wisconsin and his fellowship in geriatric medicine at the Jewish Institute for Geriatric Care at the State University of New York at Stonybrook. He received the 1993 Milo D. Leavitt Memorial Award from the American Geriatrics Society for his contributions in geriatric medical education. He received the Medical College of Wisconsin Distinguished Service Award in 2001 for making significant and distinguished contributions to the college, and he was recognized with the Medical College of Wisconsin Teaching Scholars Award for outstanding teaching contributions to the college. He has written numerous journal articles and is a coauthor of the textbook *Practice of Geriatrics*.

31 | FALLS

Falls and balance problems are among the most common and serious impairments facing older people. Falls are the leading cause not only for injury-related visits to emergency rooms in the United States but also for accidental deaths among people aged 75 years and older. In the United States, 75% of deaths due to falls occur in the 13% of the population aged 65 and over. Falls are also responsible for appreciable disability due to fractures, impaired mobility, and fear of falling. Falls are often a major reason for admission to long-term care facilities. But falls can be prevented, and gait and balance impairments corrected. Increasing awareness among elderly people and their caregivers about the magnitude of these problems could contribute to earlier diagnosis and intervention.

BASICS ABOUT FALLS

A *fall* is an event which results in a person coming to rest inadvertently on the ground or other level not due to loss of consciousness, stroke, seizure, or sustaining a violent blow.

The incidence and severity of falls and gait and balance impairment increase after age 60 and depend on the living setting and the age group. In community settings, the annual incidence of falls is 35 to 40% for the 65-year-old age group. With advancing age, the risk of falling rises. The incidence can be as much as three times higher for nursing home or hospital patients. Also, injury from falls increases from 5% for community settings to 10 to 25% for nursing home and hospital settings. Gait and balance problems vary with age, affecting 20 to 40% of persons age 65 and older and 40 to 50% of those age 85 and older.

Falls and mobility problems are associated with a much higher risk for death and disability (see Table 31-1). They are also responsible for premature nursing home admissions. There are a number of key points you should keep in mind regarding falls. As you get older, there is a higher likelihood that you will have other medical conditions that increase your

(table 31-1)
CONSEQUENCES OF FALLS

INJURY AND DEATH	SIGNIFICANT DISABILITY	ACTIVITY RESTRICTIONS*
Trauma is the fifth leading cause of death in patients over 65.	Doubles the time of a hospital stay	Fear of falling
		Loss of self-confidence
Falls are responsible for 70% of accidental deaths in persons age 75 and older.	Leading precipitating cause of nursing home admission	Self-imposed functional limitations
		Post-fall anxiety syndrome
5% of falls in community living elderly result in fracture or hospitalization.		
10 to 25% of falls of nursing home residents result in fracture, laceration, or hospitalization.		

Falling is the largest single cause of restricted-activity days among older adults.

(table 31-2)

INTRINSIC FACTORS RELATED TO FALL RISK

RESULT	MEDICAL FACTOR
AGE-RELATED FACTORS	
Unstable posture	Progressive degeneration of the nervous system structures that help maintain posture and mobility
Decrease in blood pressure	Decreased regulation capacity of blood pressure on standing
OTHER MEDICAL CONDITIONS	
Impairment of normal brain function	Dementia
Nerve or muscle abnormalities	Parkinson's disease, stroke, myelopathy (spinal cord disease), cerebellar degeneration, peripheral neuropathy
Vision problems	Cataracts, glaucoma, age-related macular degeneration
Inner ear problems	Positional vertigo
Sensation abnormalities	Peripheral neuropathy, vitamin B_{12} deficiency, diabetes
Musculoskeletal abnormalities	Arthritis, foot disorders, muscle weakness
Body system disorders	Postural hypotension, metabolic disease (thyroid), cardiopulmonary disease, acute illness (e.g., serious infection)

risk for falling. In addition, the reflexes that protect you against injury decline as you get older. The combination of a high incidence of falls and a susceptibility to injury can make a relatively mild fall very dangerous. Among older people, the injury severity is not as closely related to the mechanism of the fall. For example, same-level falls of younger people do not cause such severe injuries and mortality. Falls account for 6% of all medical expenditures for persons 65 years and older. In 1994, the cost of falls was estimated at $20 billion, and by 2020 it is expected to increase to $32 billion.

RISK FACTORS FOR FALLING

Risk factors are classified as intrinsic or extrinsic. *Intrinsic* factors include age-related changes and associated medical conditions that affect the individual's normal posture and mobility (see Table 31-2). Extrinsic factors (i.e., situational or environmental factors) include anything in the person's environment which increases the risks of falling. These can demand greater postural and mobility control than an individual possesses (see Table 31-3). Some medications are known to be associated with a higher risk of falls.

The risk for falling is usually related to more than one reason. Personal factors (e.g., age-related changes and other medical conditions) can render an individual less able to face the demands of environmental factors. Falls are strong indicators of frailty and can represent the presence of underlying treatable conditions. Furthermore, the risk of falling increases as the number of risk factors increases. The increase in risk factors from

(table 31-3)

EXTRINSIC FACTORS RELATED TO FALL RISK

MECHANISM	MEDICATION CLASS
MEDICATION INCREASING RISK OF FALLS	
Reduces alertness or retards the normal processing of the brain	Analgesic (narcotic), psychotropic, tricyclic antidepressant, benzodiazepine (tranquilizer), sedative, hypnotic (sleeping pill)
Impairs the brain circulation or affects balance	Antihypertensive, antiarrhythmic, diuretic, aminoglycoside, high-dose loop diuretic
Causes extrapyramidal syndromes (Parkinson-like features)	Phenothiazine
SITUATIONAL ENVIRONMENTAL FACTORS	
Slippery or uneven walking surface, loose carpets, poor lighting, stairs, rising from low chairs, changing position, risk-taking behavior	

zero to three or more increases the risk of falling from 8 to 100% in a 12-month observation period in one study. Note, too, that the use of four or more medications is predictive of increased risk of falling. Risk factors having the highest predictive value for falling are listed in Table 31–4.

EVALUATION BY THE DOCTOR

You should talk to your doctor if you fall. Falls should be distinguished from faints since fainting has an entirely different set of causes. After falling, discuss the circumstances so that the role of intrinsic (patient) and extrinsic (environmental) factors can be judged. Drug and alcohol use are important considerations. Injuries, of course, should be addressed, but they should not distract the physician from determining the cause for the fall.

(figure 31-1)

Hip protectors can reduce the risk of a broken hip from a fall. They are available with specially designed underwear in many surgical supply stores.

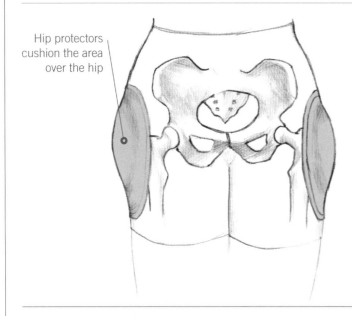

Hip protectors cushion the area over the hip

(table 31-4)

RISK FACTORS AND THEIR CONTRIBUTION TO INCREASED RISK OF FALLS

RISK	FACTOR MULTIPLIER*
Muscle weakness	4.4
History of falling	3.0
Gait deficit	2.9
Balance deficit	2.9
Use of assistive device	2.6
Visual deficit	2.5
Arthritis	2.4
Impaired activities of daily living	2.3
Depression	2.2
Cognitive impairment	1.8
Age over 80 years	1.7

Normal risk = 1. For muscle weakness, the risk is 4.4 times normal.

In the clinical setting it makes sense to assess the risk of falling for any individual elderly patient. This would be true whether or not a fall has occurred. Your doctor will want to know if you use assistive devices or if you need help performing daily living activities such as toileting, dressing, eating, and bathing. An assessment of the leg strength would include asking you to arise from a chair (without using your arms), take several steps, turn around, and sit back down. Arm mobility can be evaluated by asking you to raise your arms straight up in the air and bring your hands behind your neck and then behind your back.

If initial screening is positive, the next step is a fall evaluation. This requires a very detailed history of the circumstances of a fall if one occurred. Evaluating the medications you are taking, any acute or chronic medical conditions, and your mobility level is essential. The physical examination focuses on your gait and balance, musculoskeletal system, heart, nervous system, and vision. An assessment of your home environment by an occupational therapist is very worthwhile.

The evaluation might detect multiple contributors to the fall, including gait and balance abnormalities. Specific treatment for each contribution should be considered. This assessment and intervention approach has produced many important benefits, such as improved survival and function, reduced health care utilization and costs, and greater patient satisfaction.

INTERVENTIONS AND TREATMENT

Interventions can be classified as multifactorial and single strategies; however, the most effective strategies are multifactorial interventions. For a single intervention, exercise and environmental modification are effective.

MULTIFACTORIAL INTERVENTIONS

Multifactorial interventions are categorized according to the living setting: community or institutional (e.g., nursing homes and assisted living residences). The following are multifactorial interventions for community-dwelling adults:

- Gait training and advice on the appropriate use of assistive devices
- Review and modification of medication
- Exercise program, with balance training as one of the components
- Modification of environmental hazards
- Treatment of cardiovascular disorders: postural drop in blood pressure when arising and carotid sinus syndrome (sensitivity of the carotid artery to pressure leading to dizziness)

In an institutional setting the following multifactorial interventions should be considered:

- Staff education
- Gait training and advice on the appropriate use of assistive devices
- Review and modification of medication, especially psychotropic medication

Assistive devices: Assistive devices (bed alarms, canes, walkers, and hip protectors) are important measures of multifactorial intervention programs in community and institutional settings (see Figure 31-1). Assistive devices to reduce the risk of falls are discussed in Chapters 30 and 42.

Medication reduction: Reduction in medication numbers and dosages is a benefit in multifactorial intervention. This intervention is primarily important for older persons taking four or more medications and those taking psychotropic medications (e.g., sedatives, antidepressants, or antipsychotics).

Exercise: Exercise is known to decrease the risk of falls as a single intervention and also as part of multifactorial intervention for community-dwelling older persons. Long-term exercise and/or balance training should be offered to older people who have recurrent falls. The optimal type, duration, and intensity of exercise for fall prevention continues to be studied. Tai Chi is a promising balance exercise (see Figure 31-2).

Cardiovascular interventions: Cardiovascular interventions in decreasing falls are not that clear. There are studies that report an association between cardiovascular disorders and falls, particularly orthostatic hypotension (drop in blood pressure on standing), carotid sinus syndrome (sensitivity of the neck arteries to pressure, such as a tight collar), and vasovagal syndrome (fainting due to drop in heart rate, blood pressure, or both, usually triggered by emotional stress, trauma, or prolonged standing). Pacemaker therapy for the treatment of falls cannot be recommended until the results of ongoing trials become available.

(figure 31-2)

Tai Chi has been shown to reduce the risk of falls, and classes are offered in many communities.

SINGLE INTERVENTION

Exercise and environmental modification are the only interventions proved to be beneficial as a single intervention. Environmental modification through home safety assessment was found to be beneficial as part of multifactorial intervention. Also, it was effective as a single intervention in a subgroup of older people after hospital discharge.

OTHER INTERVENTIONS

Visual problems should be corrected if possible. Fall-related hip fractures have been shown to be more common in patients with visual impairment. Footwear modification has improved balance and sway, but there have been no reports that it reduced the risk of falling. Mobility was found to be better with walking shoes than being barefoot and with low-heeled rather than high-heeled shoes. In men, foot position awareness and stability were best with midsole hardness and low midsole thickness. Restraints can contribute to serious injuries. There is no experimental evidence showing that the use of restraints reduces the incidence of falls.

PREVENTING FALLS

Table 31-5 lists risk factors that can be corrected or modified with your help. For each risk factor, a specific intervention is suggested.

31

(table 31-5)

FALL DETECTION AND INTERVENTION

MODIFIABLE RISK FACTORS	INTERVENTION
Muscle weakness (difficulty rising from a sitting position without using hands)	Tell doctor about weakness. Exercise regularly to keep strong bones and muscles.
Gait and balance deficit (need to walk slowly or with a wide base of support to maintain balance)	Tell doctor if feeling off balance. Have regular exercise and good foot care. Limit alcohol intake. Discuss adaptive equipment use with doctor.
Postural hypotension	Tell doctor if you have dizziness on changing from lying or sitting to standing. Take time before standing up from a lying or sitting position. Drink enough liquids to keep yourself well hydrated. Review with doctor whether any medications influence blood pressure control.
Environmental hazards (slippery floors, loose rugs)	Provide good lighting in the home. Fasten rugs to the floor. Remove electric cords from floor walking areas. Install handrails in the bathroom for bath, shower, and toilet. Install stair rails on both sides for support. Ensure kitchen items are within reach. Wear shoes with firm, nonskid, nonfriction soles. Avoid wearing loose-fitting slippers. Consider a home evaluation by an occupational therapist.
Medications (e.g., some blood pressure medications, sedatives, antidepressants)	Inform doctor of all medications you are taking (including prescriptions, over the counter, and herbal). Report dizzy spells. Work with doctor on keeping medicine to a minimum. Find alternatives to sedative-hypnotic drugs used to promote sleep.
Visual deficit	Visit eye doctor.

WHAT'S NEW?

Could something as simple as a vitamin supplement reduce the risk of falls? As incredible as it may seem, recent studies have suggested that extra vitamin D may do just that. In recent years studies have shown reductions in falls by as much as 20-50% with vitamin D in doses of 800 units a day. This is higher than the 400 units found in many vitamin supplements. Although vitamin D levels can be increased by exposure to sunlight, many people avoid the sun due to concerns about skin cancer and wrinkling of the skin. Persons who live in nursing homes, especially in northern climates may have little if any sun exposure.

Clinical research has proven that the risk of fractures is decreased when vitamin D is given because it strengthens bones especially when given with calcium. However, an analysis of several studies was reported in *The Journal of the American Medical Association* in April, 2004. The bottom line is that the incidence of falls in older persons was reduced by over 20% in those who took at least 800 units of vitamin D daily. In these cases, the actual numbers of falls was reduced presumably because it improved muscle strength. It appears that vitamin D supplementation may not only make the bones sturdier, but the muscles stronger. The benefit was shown not only for the elderly residing in nursing homes, but for ambulatory older persons in the community as well.

Although some foods, such as cereals and milk, may be fortified with vitamin D, it may not be adequate. Generally, a vitamin D supplement in addition to your multivitamin will be required. But remember that megadoses (very large doses) of vitamin D can be harmful. As always, check with your doctor who knows you and your own unique circumstances.

WHAT YOU NEED TO KNOW

▶ Falls are a major health concern of older people. Falls are common, underreported, undertreated, associated with increased risk for death and disability, and decreased quality of life.

▶ Reducing falls and their consequences is a team effort, in which patients and their health care providers play an almost equal role. The increased awareness of older people about the signals for an increased risk of falling combined with screening and evaluation for falls, gait, and balance impairments from professionals should allow early diagnosis and intervention.

▶ Implementation of the interventions in Table 31-5 can reduce the risk of disability and death and improve your quality of life.

31

FOR MORE INFORMATION

▶ National Institute on Aging Information Center
P.O. Box 8057
Gaithersburg, MD 20898
800-222-2225
TTY: 800-222-4225
Web: www.nia.nih.gov

▶ U.S. Consumer Product Safety Commission
Washington, DC 20207
800-638-2772
TTY: 800-638-8270
Web: www.cpsc.gov
Free booklet available: "Home Safety Checklist for Older Consumers."

▶ National Center for Injury Prevention and Control
Mail Stop K65
4770 Buford Highway NE
Atlanta, GA 30341
770-488-1506
Fax: 770-488-1667
E-mail: ohcinfo@cdc.gov
Web: www.cdc.gov/ncipc/factsheets/falls.htm
Web: www.cdc.gov/ncipc/duip/spotlite/falls.htm

He has but half lived who has not been to the House of Pain.

—*Ralph Waldo Emerson*

THE AUTHOR

32

MARCOS FE-BORNSTEIN, MD, graduated from medical school at the Universidad Nacional Autonoma in his native Mexico City. He trained as a psychiatrist at Louisiana State University and Tulane University, in New Orleans, and became a psychoanalyst at the New Orleans Psychoanalytic Institute. Doctor Fe-Bornstein has been involved in the treatment of psychiatric conditions in the medically ill and in chronic pain since 1990. He has made professional presentations on the topic of chronic pain and has published in medical journals.

Doctor Fe-Bornstein holds three board certifications and is a clinical associate professor of psychiatry at Tulane University. He was director of the Behavioral Medicine Clinic at Tulane Health Sciences Center in New Orleans until 2002. He is a member of the American Academy of Pain Medicine and the Academy of Psychosomatic Medicine. Doctor Fe-Bornstein practices in Manhattan and Westchester, New York.

32 | PAIN

(figure 32-1*)*

Pain is a very common problem. As many as 50% of community-dwelling older persons and 80% of nursing home residents suffer from chronic pain.

We live in an awesome time. Technological gadgets that make our lives easy surround us. We also live longer. Life expectancy in the Unites States has been steadily increasing. Take a look at the statistics: those born in the year 1901 could expect to live an average of 49 years. By the end of the 20th century life expectancy soared to 77 years. What is the advantage of living longer? For some, it means more time to pursue pleasurable activities after retirement. For others, it is quite the opposite: more time to suffer from disease. Such is the quandary of aging in the new millennium. If you are an average American age 65 at the time you read this book, you are expected to live another 18 years and 11 years if you are 75. Hopefully, you have reached retirement age in good health and are ready to enjoy more of your family and hobbies. But what if you are one of the millions of seniors with a painful condition?

It is a sad reality that living longer does not necessarily mean living healthier. In fact, as we go up in age, so do our chances of getting sick. Several conditions that usually appear later in life, like arthritis, shingles, and nerve degeneration, are associated with pain. One survey found that as many as 50% of older outpatients and 80% of nursing home patients suffer from chronic pain (see Figure 32-1). However, many of these patients are not receiving adequate treatment. There are several reasons that contribute to this problem.

First, pain is frequently misunderstood. Many patients and even some physicians believe that any pain can be treated with the same approach, that is, a medication to relieve the pain. In fact, there are different types of pain, and what works for you may not work for someone else. This is confirmed by the experiences of hundreds of patients and their doctors and by recent research which reveals that the nervous system works differently in various types of pain.

Second, pain is often treated as an isolated physical symptom, without taking into account personal and social dimensions that are closely connected with the experience of pain. Effective pain management considers physical, emotional, and environmental factors as equally important.

Third, pain is a problem that may strain the relationship between patient and doctor. Pain is difficult to treat, and if it does not go away, it frustrates patients and doctors. Someone not getting relief becomes angry and disappointed and finds it increasingly difficult to cooperate with treatment. Physicians also experience frustration at the lack of progress, which may result in loss of interest or giving up. In such situations it is very difficult for patient and doctor to work together, which is necessary for successful treatment of pain.

Finally, in the current managed care environment there are several obstacles to obtain adequate treatment for pain. In their haste to "control costs," insurers may deny payment for comprehensive pain management as it is done by groups of professionals and force the patient to be treated by only one doctor. Rational pain management involves several medical disciplines. By not covering pain management, insurers actually prolong the suffering and disability, which in the long term is more expensive for the individual, the family, and society.

UNIQUENESS OF PAIN

Emerson's words remind us that the experience of pain is universal. If someone says, "My knee hurts," there is a very good chance that you will know how that person feels even if your knee has never given you any problems. The reason is that you have experienced physical pain at some time in your life. You also know where the knee is and perhaps will reach down and touch it to make sure it is fine. You may then imagine what you would do to relieve the pain: apply some balm or local heat, take aspirin, and rest. You might want to tell your friend what to do, aware that pain means suffering. If your friend tells you that, in fact, all your recommendations have been tried and the pain has gone on for months, then you will find it more difficult to relate.

The fact is that there are different types of pain. Acute pain usually results from traumatic injuries (e.g., breaking a leg), infections, and inflammation (e.g., a toothache or appendicitis), metabolic changes (e.g., soreness after exercise), surgery, and others. Acute pain persists for relatively short periods of time and eventually disappears by itself or with an intervention, such as extracting a bad tooth or using medication. *Chronic pain* is different, inasmuch as it is the pain that continues after the original injury has been treated. Chronic pain can be there even without physical findings. It can go on for months or years or for the remainder of the person's life. Another type of pain shares features of acute and chronic pain, and that is recurrent pain, which alternates with periods of no pain, or lesser pain, as may be the case with migraines.

If confronted with pain afflicting us or someone we know, we tend to think of it as acute pain. It is often difficult to comprehend that a pain extending for weeks, months, or years is quite different from acute pain. In this chapter, when referring to pain, I am talking primarily about chronic and recurrent pain, which are the most common types in older adults.

One of the first things I do to treat chronic pain patients is to help them understand that acute and chronic pains are two different conditions. Patients usually don't know this because regardless of the type of pain, it hurts the same, the difference being that pain does not go away if it is chronic. Scientific research is discovering differences in nervous system functioning in each type of pain, and this new knowledge is helping to develop better therapies. Many of the strategies to treat chronic pain apply to recurrent pain. However, few treatments for acute pain are effective for chronic or recurrent pain.

CAUSES OF PAIN

Another source of much confusion for the pain patient is its cause. Most people want to find out the reasons why things happen, especially when it comes down to personal health matters. We have learned to think that if we find the cause, we can solve the problem, which is true in many situations. A simple example would be a water leak in our living room. We look for the source of the leak and then fix a broken pipe or a roof tile, either by ourselves or with the help of a professional. The same problem-solving approach works well in the case of acute pain: The aching tooth is treated by the dentist. However, if we try to use this method in chronic pain, we are bound to fail. The reason is that once pain becomes chronic, there are many possible contributors to the pain.

Let's assume that a man experiences pain in the lower back after an injury at work. Let's also assume that such pain continues despite adequate treatment, such as medication, physical rehabilitation, and surgery. This person is not happy that the pain did not go away. He becomes quite frustrated when doctors say that there are no more physical problems to correct. In addition to the pain, the person is now sad and angry. He stays at home. His income under worker's compensation is a fraction of his regular salary, but he does not return to work out of fear of more pain. His wife is also unhappy, which affects the children. It is easy to see how emotional and family problems unfold after the original injury.

A basic understanding in modern pain management is that all these problems develop simultaneously. That is, physical pain is not the direct cause of the mental and social problems even if it looks that way. What's more, appropriate pain management addresses all the problems simultaneously. In the scenario presented above, it would be a mistake to think that doing something to the back can relieve the pain and all the other problems. It simply does not work that way. Our approach needs to consider that in addition to the back (i.e., the physical problem) there are psychological and social issues that are as important as the back. This methodology is often referred to as the *biopsychosocial* model to indicate the coexistence of biological (i.e., physical), psychological, and social factors in disease. The model is not exclusive to the field of pain but is particularly suited to the assessment and treatment of pain. If you or a loved one suffers from chronic pain, you need to grasp this concept. You also need to find a physician, or a team of professionals, who understands the multiple factors influencing chronic pain.

Sometimes it is difficult to understand how the biopsychosocial model works in clinical practice unless one has experienced it firsthand. As shown in the following case, many patients tell me that they did not believe in this approach until they saw results:

MITCHELL'S STORY

Mitchell A. was an elderly man who lived with his wife in the countryside. He had been disabled for years because of a back injury. He came to see me because the pain was intolerable, and he was depressed and did not want to live any longer. For years he had taken muscle relaxants and opiate painkillers but was still in pain. The medication was making him drowsy, and he felt tired most of the time. He would stay at home all day, in bed, without doing anything, sleeping on and off. He had stopped activities like visiting with friends and family and going fishing.

At the time of our first visit he could not report a single pleasurable activity and was convinced that he could no longer enjoy anything. He was also convinced that receiving treatment meant having full relief from the pain and refused to entertain the possibility that he could function without painkillers. In fact, the medication and the sedation, which came with it, were also threatening his life because of a chronic heart and lung condition, and it was necessary to admit him to the hospital to take him slowly off the prescription drugs.

He complained bitterly as the medication was lowered. But when feeling more awake and energetic, he found the motivation to remain in treatment. While in the hospital we had ample time to talk about his day-to-day life and his feelings. We had family meetings to address the problems that his disability was causing. He participated in physical therapy. We came up with ways to deal with problems other than taking pills. At the time of discharge from the hospital, he looked like a different person. He said he was still in pain, but it was not any worse than when he took all those medications. More importantly, he felt physically stronger, could stay awake all day and interact with others, and felt a renewed desire to live. Several weeks after discharge he called me and said that he had been fishing for the first time in years.

Mitchell A. believed, erroneously, that the cause of all his suffering was the back pain and if that were taken care of, everything would be fine. Thinking that way, he refused to give up his "treatment" with painkillers, even though it didn't work. Once he learned that there was more to the pain problem than the back, he was able to try other options.

PSYCHOLOGICAL COMPONENT

When I evaluate patients and explain how pain has to do with emotions as well as physical problems, I usually get this angry response: "Are you saying it is all in my head?" It is not hard to see how someone with chronic pain may feel insulted under the circumstances. By the time they consult me, most patients have been suffering daily for months or years, have had numerous unsuccessful treatments, and have been dismissed by other doctors. My usual response goes like this: "If I were in your place, I would feel depressed and angry too." And I really mean it. It is the expected human response. It is impossible not to have some sort of reaction after so much suffering. Even those who say they are not sad or angry have an emotional reaction; it is a matter of looking closely into it.

Emotional reactions are part of the chronic pain experience, and depression is quite common. We have seen how it is a mistake to attribute all the changes that occur in chronic pain to one single cause. To think that the depression will go away if the pain is cured is a recipe for failure. There are many other things that contribute to the mood changes. One such thing is how the person deals with the pain. This is also referred to as the person's *coping,* and it has to do with personality characteristics and social support. Some people are able to cope better with pain, whereas others seem to fall apart.

32

What determines coping? It can depend on one's expectations. In the case of Mitchell A., his expectation was to get rid of the pain through the use of medication. Mitchell A.'s expectations were incorrect because they were not realistic. Once in the hospital, we were able to work on changing expectations. Instead of pursuing a pain-free state, the goal was changed to the pursuit of a better quality of life, which was realistic and within grasp. Mitchell A. understood that he could live with some pain and enjoy life and that this option was better than having no pain but being asleep all the time. He also found out that being active helped as an antidote to pain. That is, the pain was still there, but he did not think about it all the time. His attitude changed from pessimism to optimism.

Chronic pain patients often develop erroneous beliefs that interfere with getting well. A common belief is that pain is an indication of a very serious illness leading to disability. Armed with such beliefs, patients actually do less and excuse themselves from many activities. The person's expectation may very well be that any productive or enjoyable activity is not possible because of the pain. Negative expectation is unrealistic. Sometimes these beliefs are so strong that people simply cannot be helped. I remember Martha X., a woman in her 60s with a chronic pain problem and minimal physical findings. She was convinced that she was totally disabled and would spend her days sitting or lying around the house doing nothing. Her life seemed quite depressing. She was also convinced that the only treatment for her was medication and refused to participate in anything we offered at our program. She soon dropped out complaining that we were making unrealistic demands. Her negative expectation was that she would hurt more if she were more active and that she could only get relief from rest and medication. She believed she was totally disabled and remained so.

Positive expectations can work in the exact opposite way. The main ingredients of a positive expectation are acceptance and realism. One has to come to grips with the permanence of a chronic medical condition that produces pain, and one has to set goals consistent with the reality of the condition. Being realistic also means being able to explore alternative activities that can be performed within the limitations that the pain imposes (see Figure 32-2). I once saw Harold B., a 60-year-old former executive who had to take medical retirement for a bad back problem. Having been an active man all his life, he quickly decided that he could not spend his days doing nothing. He took up a hobby that required him to use his hands to manufacture crafts. He got so good at it that he began selling craft work at country fairs. Harold B. did not let the pain get the best of him. He did not believe that he was either too sick or too old to do something productive. He developed a skill late in life that gave him pleasure and profit and kept him occupied.

False positive expectations, on the other hand, are quite common. These are the unrealistic wishes that everything will be all right once the pain goes away and usually only when the pain goes away. Patients with false positive expectations have not accepted the reality of their situation and

(*figure* 32-2)

Fostering new skills or hobbies can help you adapt to the limitations of chronic pain.

cannot adapt well to the pain. Is there such thing as adapting to pain? Yes, as long as the pain is bearable. One of the main goals of pain management is to reduce the pain to tolerable levels while helping the patient cope with it better.

Our beliefs and expectations are part of our mind. They determine many of our feelings and behaviors. It is not difficult to see how someone with chronic pain and negative expectations will feel discouraged and even depressed. This person will also have a poor self-esteem. To make things worse, there will also be a feeling of loss of control, which initially has to do with the physical symptom of pain but eventually spreads to other areas of the person's mind and life. It is not surprising to see such people give up. The perception that things are not under control is often a problem in the relationship with physicians. Many pain patients do not see themselves as participants in treatment decisions and actually resent doctors' recommendations. Such was the case of Bruce C., who was so openly angry with the medical establishment that during our first interview I felt compelled to leave the room. I didn't realize at the time (but did soon thereafter!) that this bear of a man was accustomed to being in charge of every aspect of his life but felt completely devoid of control now that he was unable to work and suffered from chronic pain. He felt at the mercy of insurance companies, lawyers, and health professionals. As we worked together, he realized that there were things he certainly did not control but others that he could, beginning with his mind. We worked on changing his attitudes, and this helped him regain control of several areas of his life.

We call individuals who adjust well to chronic pain "good adjusters." They share several characteristics like acceptance, realistic appraisal of the situation, taking control of their life, performing activities within their limitations, and finding alternatives to occupy their time such as hobbies. This group of patients tends to participate in all that pain management programs have to offer. "Poor adjusters" have few or none of the characteristics enumerated above. However, positive behaviors and expectations can be developed so that poor adjusters actually become good adjusters.

FAMILY LIFE

Another aspect is the roles that close relatives or significant others play in the pain conundrum. Anyone living with a person with chronic pain knows how difficult it is. Relatives often suffer the consequences of the pain condition. Unknowingly, a relative may contribute to the perpetuation of pain and disability. The wife of one patient took on all responsibilities, so that he was actually excused from doing anything. While her intentions were good, the result was reinforcing the idea that her husband was totally disabled. In fact, once in treatment her husband felt he could manage several tasks, thus relieving his wife from the burden. It is not unusual to see how a chronic pain patient behaves in ways that make others respond as if the patient were totally disabled. When this happens, the patient role is reaffirmed, and the person ends up doing less and less. Just as the patient may have negative beliefs and expectations, so does the family.

Other cases are more extreme. I once saw a middle-aged man, Carl D., who had been injured at work while operating heavy machinery. He complained of excruciating back pain, and his anxiety verged on agitation. In spite of the pain team's treatment, he continued to feel bad. He had lived in a semi-rural area with the same woman for several years, but they were not married. This relationship ended by her leaving him, and after this event he actually experienced less distress and was finally able to fully participate in our program.

This is an unusual case, of course, but it helps to illustrate how intangible issues like the dynamics of a relationship can actually influence the patient's perception of pain and the display of pain behavior. However, it would be a mistake to think that the bad relationship caused the pain. It is more accurate to say that as the pain developed, so did problems in the relationship and they fed on each other. Carl D. found relief in terminating the relationship, which I hardly advocate. It would have been more appropriate to examine the couple's problems and have them seek professional counseling.

PAIN MANAGEMENT

The first step in treatment is recognition of the problem. Pain that lasts several weeks or longer should be brought to the attention of a doctor. If your family physician determines that your pain is chronic, consult a specialist.

All chronic pain should be thoroughly evaluated by a multidisciplinary team. Typically, the first encounter is with the pain doctor who obtains a pertinent history and performs a physical examination. Some laboratory tests or diagnostic procedures may be ordered. The doctor or a physical therapist may perform an evaluation of physical function (see Figure 32-3). Do not be surprised or offended if the doctor refers you for a psychiatric evaluation or for psychological testing. These are usual components of a comprehensive pain evaluation and can yield valuable information.

Reporting pain to a doctor is difficult, since pain cannot be measured like body temperature or blood pressure. An easy and effective way to report pain is by placing it in a scale from 0 to 10, where 0 is absence of pain and 10 is unbearable pain. Some doctors will ask you to fill out a questionnaire or mark the location of your pain on a drawing of the human body. These tools are very valuable in helping a doctor determine the nature of your complaint. In addition, the pain team needs to know how the pain affects your life, that is, whether you stopped doing anything because of the pain.

Treatment of chronic pain is more than just treating pain. Understanding that brings us to the second important message I tell patients: "The goal of treatment is not to eliminate pain but to improve your quality of life," which includes bad and good news. The bad news is that some pain will

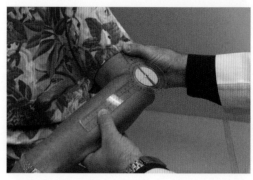

(*figure* 32-3)

Assessment of your physical function is an important early step in the evaluation of chronic pain.

persist. The complete elimination of pain would be an ideal goal, but for many, that goal is unattainable. Instead, the patient will be better off by adjusting expectations and considering the very possible fact that some pain will persist. Given the available methods for relieving pain, treatment efforts should concentrate in reducing the pain to tolerable levels while avoiding side effects. The good news, on the other hand, is that you will be able to do things that you thought you couldn't do anymore or learn new activities to replace the ones that are impossible. After the message sinks in, almost all patients welcome the prospect of less pain and higher functioning.

The general idea here is simple yet powerful: treat the patient, not the pain. Too many unsuccessful treatments are based on the premise of eliminating pain. All too often, this is unrealistic. The fact that the pain may be permanent has more to do with how the brain processes information about pain and less to do with the body part where the pain is felt. Moreover, quite a few cases have no physical findings to explain the pain. It is important to stress that this does not mean that the pain is "psychological" or that the patient has a mental problem. It has more to do with functions in the brain that generate the perception of pain, and the pain is real. It is only now that medical science is beginning to unravel the mysteries of pain.

Two important concepts help attain the goals of treatment. First, every individual is different. Second, treatment should include all aspects of a person—physical, psychological, and social—and all these areas have to be addressed simultaneously. In essence, the same treatment is not going to work in every patient, because therapy has to be tailored to the patient's needs and situation. Patient A requires a different approach from B or C even if their problems are similar. Focusing only on the pain while neglecting psychological and social issues has been a dismal failure; it is the inclusion of other treatment modalities that helped.

Professionals, particularly those with certification in pain management, are quite familiar with the concepts presented in this chapter. They recognize that in order to better treat a patient, it is necessary to include several specialists in a team. This is commonly referred to as the multidisciplinary approach to pain management. A given team includes physicians, such as anesthesiologists, neurologists, psychiatrists, and surgeons; psychologists and psychometricians; nurses, occupational and physical therapists, dietitians, and others. It is best to think of the team as a group of specialists assembled to meet the needs of individual patients. This means that two different patients treated at the same location may actually have two different teams working on their problem. The following cases illustrate this:

MELISSA'S STORY

Melissa Y. suffered from a rare neurological condition that, although not life threatening, produced excruciating pain for several years. By age 62, she was tired and burned out. She was in pain in spite of medications appropriately prescribed to treat her condition. It was clear that she was clinically depressed. She was also misinformed about her options for treatment and was somewhat surprised when I referred her to three other specialists: an anesthesiologist specializing in pain medication, a neurosurgeon, and a psychologist. The results of the multidisciplinary evaluation were that she did not need surgery but would benefit from stronger pain medication. The psychological testing showed that she was coping with the pain by expecting others to do things for her. With medical treatment and psychotherapy her depression lifted, the intensity of the pain decreased considerably, and she learned to be more assertive in getting her needs met. As a result, the quality of her life improved significantly.

Max E. was seen as a referral from a neurosurgeon, a member of the pain team. He had back surgery to correct an injury from an accident but was still in pain. He took so much medication that he could not remember events from one day to the next. His relatives were resigned to his disability and did not encourage him to participate anymore in family events. Psychological testing revealed that he saw himself as hopeless, helpless, and completely disabled. He was clinically depressed. Treatment consisted in adjusting the medications that worked, discontinuing the ones that did not work, and adding antidepressants and psychotherapy. He was also asked to attend a pain support group. His spouse and children were seen by another member of the team. After several months, a small device called a dorsal column stimulator was implanted to relieve the pain. With decreased pain but a clear mind, he resumed participation in family activities and spent time performing home improvement projects within his abilities.

These cases show how teamwork is essential in the treatment of chronic pain. By working together, different team members addressed specific problems simultaneously, and improvement followed. I want to stress that no single intervention, by itself, changed the course of illness; patients slowly improved as the physical, psychological, and social health areas were addressed.

I am often asked which treatment works best for a certain type of pain, or for depression in chronic pain, and so on. The answer, as it should be clear by now, is that the best treatment is the one that works for you. Someone else with similar symptoms may need a very different approach. I also remind you that success in treatment is defined by improvement in overall functioning and quality of life rather than by pain elimination. In reality, patients who achieve these goals also experience significant diminution of pain. In short, while we consider pain elimination unrealistic, we do think that pain diminution to tolerable levels is possible and that global improvement will follow. However, do not fall into the trap of thinking that to get rid of the pain is the first step in treatment. A better approach is to follow the pain team's recommendations even if the intensity of the pain does not seem to change right away. A well-planned approach will eventually lead to less pain and a better life, so be patient.

Once enrolled in treatment, you may be offered a number of options, such as medication adjustment, physical therapy, pain counseling, psychotherapy, biofeedback, pain support groups, and surgical procedures.

Your close ones may be asked to participate in one or more of the steps of treatment; for example, a spouse may help with medication administration or relatives can encourage adaptive coping. In addition to office visits to physicians and other professionals, you may be given a program of activities to follow at home.

In the following paragraphs I describe pain treatment strategies to give you a basic understanding of what to discuss if you see a pain professional. Not all treatment modalities will be useful for all pain patients; therapy has to be tailored to each individual; and to know what will work for you, it is best to consult professionals. Each treatment method has advantages and disadvantages, and as we get older, strategies have to be modified to maximize the benefits and minimize side effects.

Medications can be useful in the treatment of chronic pain but should always be used in conjunction with the other approaches. You and your physician need to decide which medications are the most likely to help while producing the fewest side effects. Several drugs for chronic pain are not known as painkillers and are normally used for other disorders, such as depression, seizures, and high blood pressure. One factor that these drugs have in common is the ability to affect a certain part of the nervous system which may add to the relief of pain. Taking medications for conditions other than their intended use is known as *off-label indications,* which means that the drug has only been approved by the Food and Drug Administration (FDA) for the treatment of one or two medical problems (like seizures, for example) but not others (like pain). However, pain practitioners have used these medications for years, attempting to diminish the pain in a variety of patients. We now know that, for certain types of pain, drugs used in off-label indications can be as effective as or more effective than painkillers in alleviating the symptoms.

Some of the most commonly used drugs for chronic pain are the analgesics or painkillers, which were originally developed to treat acute pain and may be severely limited in treating chronic pain. However, certain problems do warrant their use. One group of analgesics is the nonopiates, such as aspirin, acetaminophen (Tylenol), ibuprofen (Advil, Motrin), and newer drugs called COX-2 inhibitors, such as CELECOXIB (CELEBREX) and ROFECOXIB (VIOXX). It is highly advisable to take nonopiates for chronic pain only while under a doctor's care, because ongoing use can have complications. Another group is the opiates, which are related to morphine and can be taken by mouth or injection. Opiates are powerful painkillers and very valuable in some cases of chronic pain if used judiciously. They are extremely useful in the treatment of cancer pain. Opiates can cause physical and psychological addiction but, if used appropriately, will not cause addiction in the chronic pain patient.

Antidepressants are another group of drugs used in chronic pain. It has been known for several years that some of the antidepressants, particularly the older ones, are quite effective in relieving pain even if the person is not depressed. One problem is that the older medications have strong side effects. Newer antidepressants have few side effects but are not as good in treating pain with one or two exceptions. Older people are very sensitive to the side effects of the older antidepressants, such as AMITRIPTYLINE (ELAVIL). NORTRIPTYLINE (PAMELOR) has fewer adverse effects than amitriptyline but usually still more than newer drugs such as VENLAFAXINE (EFFEXOR). Generally the newer drugs should be tried first.

Medications commonly used for seizures can help treat certain pains. The main problem is that these medications work on only a few types of pain and usually have intolerable side effects at effective doses. Antidepressants and seizure medications are particularly useful in treating problems, such as peripheral neuropathy and other pain conditions in which the nerve fibers are involved, which includes many problems resulting from back injuries and the like. Some antidepressants may be useful in treating other problems, such as fibromyalgia.

Certain chronic pains can be helped with the use of medications normally employed in the treatment of high blood pressure. One important consideration in the senior population is that they may cause a sudden drop of blood pressure when standing up, and this may lead to fainting and falling, which in turn may lead to further major complications such as hip fractures.

Surgery should be considered when appropriate and when the benefits of the procedure outweigh the risks. For example, someone with a bulging disc in the spine producing chronic pain may benefit from surgery if the procedure has not been tried before. However, patients with multiple back surgeries may not experience the same degree of improvement. Another surgical procedure that helps certain patients is the implantation of a device known as *dorsal column stimulator (DCS)*, which is not too different in shape and function from a cardiac pacemaker, and it is usually inserted under the skin with wires that are placed on selected locations in the spinal cord. The DCS works by emitting electric impulses that tell the nervous system to curb the pain. There are still other devices that can be implanted like a DCS but actually deliver medication directly to the nervous system. These pumps are filled with drugs such as painkillers or muscle relaxants. A major limitation of these procedures is that only a minority of chronic pain patients may benefit from them. Any potential candidate for a DCS or a pump needs to be carefully evaluated and screened. Finally, any surgical intervention for chronic pain relief needs to be discussed at length with the surgeon, and if necessary, get a second opinion.

In addition to medication and surgical procedures, there are many other strategies, such as physical therapy (PT). A common experience is that the pain is more intense during the first few days after starting physical therapy. This is not because the problem that causes the chronic pain is actually getting worse but because the exercised muscles hurt after months or years of inactivity. The muscles are out of shape and need to regain their strength. Physical therapy may be accompanied by exercises at

(*figure* 32-4)

Biofeedback is used to help control the emotions that may affect your pain.

home, such as taking daily walks or riding stationary bicycles. Some older people may not be able to fully participate in all exercises, and the physical therapist will devise a tailored-made program to account for any physical changes from the aging process.

Biofeedback allows an individual to learn the connection between emotions and physical changes, including pain (see Figure 32-4). A psychologist normally does biofeedback, which involves measuring devices that tell a patient how the body is reacting. For example, the patient's arm may be monitored for blood pressure, which the patient can see on a computer screen. The patient will also see how the blood pressure changes when the mind relaxes.

Psychotherapy helps determine the connection between emotions and pain, helps a person achieve better coping skills, and helps with anxiety and depression which, if present, may increase the perception of pain. One difference between biofeedback and psychotherapy is that the latter does not require the elaborate setting of biofeedback to measure physiological variables. Another difference is that the person in psychotherapy may find that it is useful to talk about personal problems, which is not a major goal of biofeedback.

Counseling is different from psychotherapy in that it is a more informal approach to learning about pain. Counseling does not require talking about emotions, for example. It concentrates on helping the person understand the physical condition and the available options. Family counseling involves significant others as well.

Participating in a support group may be one of the most important additions to any pain management regimen. Pain support groups are usually community-based and run by their members. These groups are not intended to provide psychotherapy. Rather they are open forums for all pain sufferers to share their experiences and get help or help others with advice. Almost every patient of mine has had a positive experience in support groups, and the most consistent benefit reported is that they finally found people who actually understand them. Indeed, the chronic pain experience can be quite isolating, and one powerful neutralizer is the awareness that others have similar experiences, so the support group participant feels that he or she is not the only one dealing with chronic pain.

CANCER PAIN

Pain that occurs in cancer, especially in the later stages, requires a different approach. This pain is often referred to as *malignant pain* and is distinguished from other types of pain unrelated to cancer *(chronic nonmalignant pain)*. Cancer patients may not be expected to survive beyond a certain period of time. Cancer pain can be quite severe, especially if the tumor has spread. It is desirable to eliminate as much pain as possible and to make the person comfortable. In order to do this, large amounts of medications may be used with only secondary considerations to potential side effects. Whereas the goals of treatment in nonmalignant pain are to

(figure 32-5)

Palliative care for patients with advanced cancer is designed to reduce pain and suffering for the expected survival time.

improve the general level of functioning within tolerable pain levels, the goals in cancer pain are to treat the pain and decrease the suffering for the expected survival time, which may be as brief as weeks or months. This type of pain management is referred to as *palliative care* (see Figure 32-5), which encompasses a number of interventions designed to help a sick individual during the last days of life. Palliative care requires active interventions from other health professionals, such as physicians, nurses, and home attendants. Unlike chronic pain management, palliative care requires very little participation from the patient, and it usually takes place in a hospital, nursing care facility, or hospice. Health personnel actively coordinate palliative care that is given at home. Individuals with chronic nonmalignant pain should not expect the type of treatment provided to cancer patients.

■

WHAT YOU NEED TO KNOW

▶ Chronic pain in the elderly is very common and often undertreated.

▶ Chronic pain is different from acute pain and requires a different approach for evaluation and treatment.

▶ The biopsychosocial model of pain management is a combination of physical, emotional, and environmental factors. A rational approach to pain addresses all three components simultaneously.

▶ Pain is best treated by a multidisciplinary team of professionals. In the treatment of chronic pain, discontinue treatments that do not work and try alternative strategies.

▶ The goal of treatment should be to improve quality of life, not pain elimination. You should be able to conduct activities with tolerable levels of pain.

FOR MORE INFORMATION

▸ American Academy of Pain Medicine
4700 W. Lake Avenue
Glenview, IL 60025
Web: www.painmed.org
Website includes locator to find a pain specialist by geographic area.

▸ American Pain Society
4700 W. Lake Avenue
Glenview, IL 60025
Web: www.ampainsoc.org

▸ American Pain Foundation
1-888-615-PAIN
Web: www.painfoundation.org
Consumer-oriented organization that has a user-friendly website.

One of the first duties of the physician is to educate the masses not to take medicine.

—Sir William Osler

THE AUTHOR

33 *Monica L. Mathys*

MONICA MATHYS, PharmD, is an assistant professor of pharmacy practice at Midwestern University College of Pharmacy in Glendale, Arizona. In addition to her teaching responsibilities with the university, Dr. Mathys also provides clinical services and tutors pharmacy students at Bryans Extended Care Center in Phoenix, Arizona.

Before accepting her position at Midwestern University, Dr. Mathys was a member of the Pharmacy Practice faculty at Southwestern Oklahoma State University.

Dr. Mathys earned her doctor of pharmacy from the University of Arkansas for Medical Sciences and completed a geriatric specialty residency at Central Arkansas Veterans Healthcare System in Little Rock, Arkansas.

33 | DRUG THERAPY

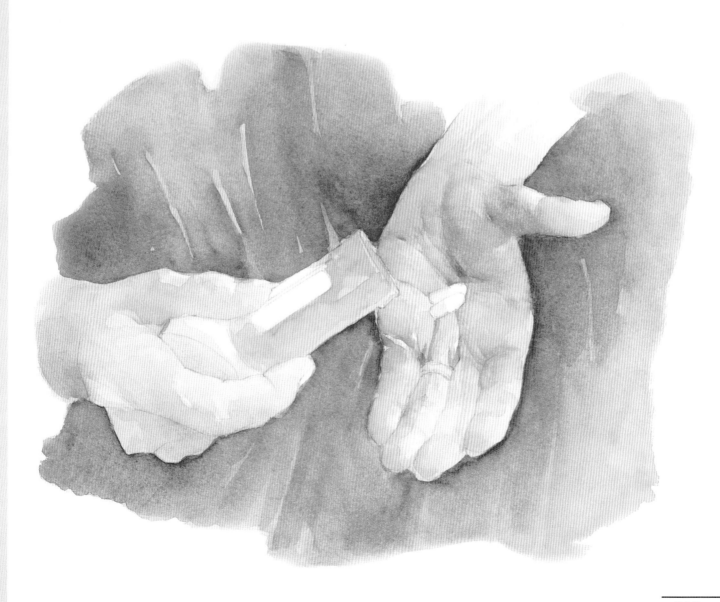

An eminent physician of his day, William Osler appreciated the benefits as well as the risks of medicine. One survey reported that 90% of people 65 years or older use at least one medication daily. Forty % claim to use five or more and 12% use 10 or more medications. These figures do not include nursing home residents who in most cases use quite a few medicines. Because older adults tend to use more medications than younger adults do, side effects and decreased compliance are more common in the older population. Since William Osler's time, remarkable advances have been made in understanding medicine and disease. However, you and your doctor should continually reevaluate your medicines and decide whether any should be discontinued.

The normal physical changes of aging influence drug therapy. Many times, older adults require smaller doses of medications due to decreased kidney function, decreased liver function, or alterations in how a drug distributes in the bodily tissues. The physical changes result in certain medications being totally inappropriate for older patients.

This chapter describes how drug therapy changes while you age. Other topics include adverse drug reactions and how they can be prevented, inappropriate medications or medications needing close monitoring, and ways to increase medication compliance.

PHYSICAL CHANGES OF AGING

There are four main components to describing the human body's influence on drug therapy:

1. Absorption of the drug from the stomach into circulation
2. Dispersion of the drug into body tissues
3. Breakdown, or metabolism, of the drug by the liver
4. Exit, or excretion, of the drug out of the body by the kidneys

The decrease of stomach acid production in 40% of people as they age may decrease the absorption of medicines needing an acidic environment to be activated, such as calcium carbonate and iron tablets. Other changes that may interfere with absorption are decreased blood flow to the stomach and slower movement of substances through the digestive tract. However, overall drug absorption is not affected significantly by aging. It

FOOD AND DRUGS

Your doctor and/or pharmacist may advise you to take some of your medicine with food or on an empty stomach. Certain foods should be avoided with some medications. For example, grapefruit juice enhances the absorption of some cholesterol-lowering drugs. Alcohol should be avoided entirely with some medicines.

Some medicines should be taken at different times from other medicines or supplements. Calcium tablets can interfere with absorption of thyroid drugs, so they should not be taken together. Absorption of alendronate (Fosamax) may be impaired by food, calcium, and fruit juice; it needs to be taken on an empty stomach with only water 30 minutes before breakfast.

If confused about the timing of your medications, ask your pharmacist or doctor to make a medication schedule.

(*table* 33-1)

AGE-RELATED CHANGES AFFECTING DRUG THERAPY

FUNCTION	CHANGE
Absorption	
Blood flow to the stomach	Decreases
Secretion of stomach acid	Decreases
Movement of food/drugs through the digestive system	Decreases
Overall absorption	Stays the same
Distribution (Dispersion)	
Body fat	Increases
Body muscle	Decreases
Body water	Decreases
Protein binding	Decreases
Metabolism (Breakdown)	
Liver size	Decreases
Liver function	Decreases
Excretion (Exit)	
Kidney function	Decreases

DOCTOR'S DIARY

I was asked to assume the care of Mrs. Bertha N., 83, when her family brought her back to Texas after she had lived several years in California. She recently suffered a stroke and was making poor progress with her physical therapy. When I first examined her at the nursing home, she seemed very distant and depressed. She spoke very slowly and seemed to have trouble finding words. She needed much assistance to move her from the bed to a chair. Although her stroke had affected her left side, she was able to move her left arm and leg. I reviewed her records from the hospital in California. I learned that she had been quite confused and agitated in the hospital there and was placed on lorazepam (a tranquilizer) and temazepam (a sleeping medication). In addition, she was taking 13 other medicines.

After reviewing her list, I felt that I could wean her off the tranquilizers and stop the sleeping medicine. Although she had some difficulty sleeping the first few nights, her nurse was able to provide reassurance that her sleeping pattern would eventually normalize. Within the next two weeks, she became progressively more alert and animated. Her physical therapist noted that she was able to cooperate more fully with her therapy. I had a meeting with her family, and we felt that if she continued to make progress, she would be able to go home within a few weeks.

may take longer for a drug to be absorbed when compared to younger adults, but the total amount absorbed does not appear to change.

Once absorbed from the digestive tract, the drug is dispersed into bodily tissues. Fat-soluble (fat-loving) drugs distribute into fat tissues, and water-soluble (water-loving) drugs distribute into muscle tissues. As you age, your percentage of body fat increases (18 to 36% for males and 33 to 45% for females), and your percentage of body water and lean muscle decrease by 10 and 20%, respectively. These changes result in lower doses for the aged population for the following reasons: Older adults have more dispersion of fat-soluble drugs because they have more fat tissue. However, these medications can stay trapped in the body longer and accumulate if doses are not adjusted. Water-soluble medications do not distribute as well since older adults have decreased muscle mass and body water. Therefore, less of the drug moves out of circulation, and blood concentrations become higher, causing side effects or toxicity. Again, lower doses are preferred.

Liver function is reduced as you age. Therefore, *metabolism* (breakdown) of medications decreases, which results in higher blood concentrations of a drug. The excretion of drugs out of the body also decreases as kidney function decreases. This also leads to higher blood concentrations of medications. Once again, older adults need lower dosages of medications than younger adults need. (See Table 33-1.)

PREVENTING ADVERSE DRUG REACTIONS

Adverse drug reactions (ADRs) are unwanted effects of medications. Older adults suffer from adverse drug reactions two to three times more than do adults younger than the age of 30. Adverse drug reactions can result from *polypharmacy* (the use of multiple medications), multiple diseases, *noncompliance* (not taking medications correctly), physical changes due to aging, *drug interactions* (when two or more medications change the actions of each other), using more than one pharmacy to fill medications, using more than one physician, and use of nonprescription or herbal medications without informing the pharmacist or physician.

POLYPHARMACY

The use of multiple medications is called **polypharmacy**. The number of routine medicines older people use increases due to the fact that more goes wrong with the body, as it gets older. Polypharmacy is a risk factor for adverse drug reactions. Taking more medications makes it harder for a person to remember when to take the medicines and to take them correctly. Multiple medications also increase the risk of drug interactions.

Although older persons require many medications, there are times when they may be able to decrease the amount of drugs they have to take.

(table 33-2)

INAPPROPRIATE DRUGS FOR OLDER ADULTS

DRUG	USES	REASON
Amitriptyline (Elavil)	Depression, nerve pain, insomnia	More side effects than other medications for depression (e.g., blurred vision, dizziness, constipation, sleepiness, dry mouth, confusion, hallucinations).
Barbiturates (phenobarbital)	Seizures, insomnia, anxiety	More side effects and addiction than other medications for sleep and anxiety. Side effects include severe drowsiness, decreased breathing rate, and physical dependence.
Chlorpropamide (Diabinese)	Diabetes type II	Trapped in the body longer and increases the risk of low blood sugar more than other diabetic drugs.
Disopyramide (Norpace)	Heart arrhythmias	Decreases the contraction of the heart more than other antiarrhythmics.
Doxepin (Sinequan)	Depression, nerve pain, insomnia, decreased appetite	Causes more side effects than other medications for depression (e.g. blurred vision, dizziness, constipation, sleepiness, dry mouth, confusion, hallucinations).
Long-acting tranquilizers or sleep medications (Valium, Librium, Dalmane)	Anxiety, insomnia	Trapped in the body longer, causing daytime sleepiness. Have been associated with increased dizziness and falls/fractures in older patients.
Meperidine (Demerol)	Pain	Cannot clear meperidine from the body as efficiently. Accumulations in the body can cause seizures and severe decreases in respiratory rate.
Meprobamate (Equanil)	Anxiety, insomnia	Highly addictive and causes drowsiness more than other medications used for anxiety.
Methyldopa (Aldomet)	High blood pressure	Causes slow heart rate and depression more than other drugs used to treat high blood pressure
Pentazocine (Talwin)	Pain	Causes more confusion and hallucinations than other pain medications.
Propoxyphene (Darvocet)	Pain	Not as effective for pain management as other pain medications. More side effects, such as confusion and hallucinations.
Ticlopidine (Ticlid)	Heart attacks and strokes	More side effects than aspirin and clopidogrel (Plavix).

Source: M. H. Beers. 1997. "Explicit Criteria for Determining Inappropriate Medication Use by the Elderly," Archives of Internal Medicine, Vol. 157.

(table 33-3)

MEDICATIONS REQUIRING CLOSE MONITORING IN OLDER ADULTS

DRUG	BRAND NAMES	EFFECTS
Antibiotics	*	Many antibiotics are cleared from the body by the kidneys. Due to decreased kidney function, lower doses may be prescribed.
Antidepressants	Prozac, Zoloft, Effexor, Remeron	More sensitive to such side effects as dizziness, drowsiness, loss of appetite, stomach irritation. Lower doses may be prescribed.
Antipsychotics	Risperdal, Zyprexa, Seroquel, Haldol	May be more sensitive to such side effects as dizziness, drowsiness. Lower doses may be prescribed.
Antispasm drugs for bladder and stomach	Ditropan, Detrol, Levsin	Can cause troublesome side effects: dry mouth, constipation, blurred vision, confusion, hallucinations, dizziness.
Diabetes medications	DiaBeta, Glynase, Glucotrol, Micronase	At risk for low blood sugar. Blood sugar should be monitored.
Digoxin	Lanoxin	Can be controlled with the smaller dose of digoxin (0.125mg/day). Heart rate, kidney function, potassium levels, and digoxin levels should be monitored.
High blood pressure medications	*	More likely to experience a drop in blood pressure when standing (orthostatic hypotension). More sensitive to the effects of blood pressure medications. Can cause depression.
NSAIDs	Motrin, Aleve, Indocin	More at risk for stomach bleeding.
Pain medications (narcotics)	Morphine, Dilaudid, Lortab, Percocet	Side effects should be monitored closely: constipation, nausea and vomiting, decreased breathing rate, drowsiness, confusion.
Tranquilizers and sleeping pills	Ativan, Xanax, Ambien, Restoril	Lower doses may be prescribed due to decreased liver function. Tranquilizer needs should be assessed periodically.
Warfarin	Coumadin	More sensitive to warfarin. Those at high risk for falls should discuss appropriateness with physician. Blood clotting time should be monitored at least once a month. Continue to observe for signs of bleeding (bleeding gums, bloody nose, dark stools, coughing, or vomiting blood).

* There are too many medications in these classes to list. Consult with your doctor or pharmacist.

Often, a person is taking more than one drug that has the same action. This is known as duplication of therapy. Some older patients take medications that are inappropriate for their age. (See Tables 33-2 and 33-3.) If this is the case, then a physician should discontinue such drugs. Many times one drug can be used to treat two different diseases, which also decreases the total number of medications.

Everyone should keep an updated list of his or her medications. Comprising prescription, nonprescription, and herbal medications, this list should include drug strength, how to take the drug, and what the drug is used for (see Figure 33-1). The physician and pharmacist should review this drug list periodically. Anyone having trouble making a drug list can bring in all his or her medications to the health care provider who can

(table 33-4)

DISEASE-DRUG INTERACTIONS

DISEASE OR CONDITION	MEDICATIONS	EFFECTS ON OLDER ADULTS
Benign prostate hyperplasia	Antihistamines (Benadryl), Detrol, Ditropan, tricyclic antidepressants (Elavil)	Can cause urinary retention.
Constipation	Antihistamines (Benadryl), narcotics (morphine), tricyclic antidepressants (Elavil)	Can cause or worsen constipation.
Peripheral vascular disease	Decongestants, stimulants (Ritalin)	Can cause constriction of the arteries and veins.
Dementia	Antihistamines (Benadryl) Ditropan, Detrol, Parkinson's medications, tricyclic antidepressants (Elavil, Doxepin)	Can worsen dementia by causing an imbalance between acetylcholine and dopamine in the brain.
Depression	Clonidine, muscle relaxants, narcotics (morphine), tranquilizers (Valium, Librium)	Can cause or worsen depression.
Diabetes	Niacin, prednisone	Can increase blood sugar.
Dizziness and falls	Antihistamines (Benadryl), blood pressure medications, tricyclic antidepressants (Elavil), warfarin (Coumadin)	Patients who fall frequently may be at increased risk for bleeding if taking warfarin. Blood pressure medications can cause dizziness or orthostatic hypotension, resulting in falls. Antihistamines and tricyclic antidepressants cause dizziness.
Gastritis, stomach ulcer, or reflux	Aspirin, Coumadin, Fosamax or Actonel, NSAIDs, potassium tablets, prednisone	NSAIDs, aspirin, and prednisone can cause stomach and intestinal ulcers. Fosamax, Actonel, and potassium tablets irritate the esophagus and stomach if not taken correctly. Coumadin can increase a patient's risk of stomach bleeding for those already at risk for ulcers.
Heart arrhythmias	Tricyclic antidepressants (Elavil, Doxepin, Pamelor)	Increased risk of arrhythmias in patients who are already at risk (e.g., heart failure patients, heart attack patients).
Heart failure	Metformin (Glucophage; severe heart failure only), NSAIDs (Motrin), prednisone, verapamil (Calan), diltiazem (Tiazac and Cardizem)	Prednisone and NSAIDs can increase sodium and water retention. Verapamil and diltiazem can decrease the force of contraction of the heart. Patients with severe heart failure are more at risk for a side effect called lactic acidosis if taking metformin.
High blood pressure	Decongestants, Effexor, medications for orthostatic hypotension (Florinef, ProAmatine), NSAIDs (Motrin), Stimulants (Ritalin)	Can increase blood pressure.
Insomnia	Albuterol, decongestants, Parkinson's medications, some antidepressants, theophylline (Theo-Dur)	Can cause or worsen insomnia.
Kidney failure	NSAIDs (Motrin), some antibiotics (gentamicin, vancomycin, Bactrim)	NSAIDs can decrease kidney circulation. The antibiotics can cause kidney toxicity.
Lung disease (asthma or COPD)	Long-acting tranquilizers (Valium, Librium), narcotics (morphine, hydrocodone, oxycodone), metformin (Glucophage)	Tranquilizers and narcotics can decrease respiratory rate. Patients with lung disease are more at risk for a side effect called lactic acidosis if taking metformin.
Parkinson's disease	Older antipsychotics (Mellaril, Haldol, Stelazine), Reglan	These medications block the action of dopamine in the brain, causing Parkinson's symptoms to be worse.
Seizures	Reglan, tricyclic antidepressants (Elavil), Wellbutrin or Zyban	Can increase the risk of seizures in patients predisposed to seizures.

(figure 33-1)

MEDICATIONS LIST: JULIE BROWN, AGE 74 JUNE 16, 2004

A medication list can help you and your doctor keep track of your medications. This is very important especially if you see other medical specialists. This list can be handwritten (legibly!) and should be reviewed at each office visit. This list should include each drug, dosage, frequency of administration, and the purpose. You should also list any vitamins, herbal supplements, or over the counter medications.

DRUG	TIME TAKEN
Furosemide 40 mg (fluid)	Before breakfast
Coreg 6.25 mg (heart)	Before breakfast and dinner
Lisinopril 20 mg (high blood pressure)	Before breakfast
Synthroid 0.1 mg (underactive thyroid)	½ hour before breakfast
Micro K 10 meq (potassium)	With breakfast
Multivitamin	With breakfast
Calcium 500 mg (bones)	With lunch and dinner.
Vitamin D 400 units (bones)	With breakfast
Aspirin 81 mg (heart)	After breakfast
Tylenol ES (arthritis)	2 tablets up to 4x daily as needed
Fosamax 70 mg (bones)	Weekly with glass of water. ½ hour before any other food, drink, or medicine. Avoid lying down for 30 minutes.

help write the list. Ask your physician periodically (every six months) if you need to continue all your current medications. Some drugs can be discontinued once a disease is treated.

MULTIPLE DISEASES

As you age, you are more likely to develop multiple diseases, resulting in polypharmacy. However, the diseases themselves can influence drug activity. For example, those persons with liver or kidney failure are more likely to develop drug toxicities if dosages are not adjusted. Also, some people may be taking a medication to treat one disease, but the drug might make another condition worse. For instance, Motrin or Aleve, which are used to treat arthritis pain, can increase blood pressure; therefore, these medications should be used cautiously in patients with high blood pressure. Table 33-4 lists a number of diseases and drugs that can make a disease worse.

Again, good communication must exist between you and your health care professionals. Make sure your physician and pharmacist are aware of all your medical conditions and allergies. A good practice is to have your medication list reviewed periodically by your physician and pharmacist.

NONCOMPLIANCE

Noncompliance is the failure to follow the doctor's directions. It ranges from 25 to 59% in the older population, mostly due to polypharmacy. Omission of a dose, wrong timing of a dose, inadequate knowledge of a drug, and taking a medication not prescribed are all examples of noncompliance. Aids such as pillboxes and cue cards help you remember to take your medication (see Figure 33-2). However, the best way to increase compliance is to decrease the number of medications you have to take on a daily basis. This may not be a possibility for everyone, but you should refer to your updated medication list and ask your physician to make your regimen as simple as possible. This may mean using combination products in which two medicines are included in one tablet. If high drug costs are causing you to skip doses, tell your physician and pharmacist. Cheaper and/or generic medications or possible funding from drug companies may be available.

HOME ECONOMICS: FOOD OR MEDICINE?

In response to concerns by older persons about their drug costs, many pharmaceutical companies have developed programs to discount their medications to people below certain income levels. Some companies have free programs for truly indigent individuals. If you are having a hard time paying for your medicines, tell your doctor. If you are on medicines manufactured by participating companies, he or she can give you an application.

See Appendix B for more more information on drug prices and programs.

DRUG INTERACTIONS

Drug interaction is defined as two or more medications changing the actions of each other. Many drugs increase or decrease liver metabolism of other medications. If drug A increases the metabolism of drug B, then drug B will be broken down quicker in the body, resulting in low blood concentrations of drug B. If drug C decreases the metabolism of drug B, then drug B will be broken down slower, resulting in higher blood concentrations.

A drug interaction can occur if a drug alters the dispersion, or distribution, of another medication. Also, two medications taken together can cause a significant side effect if they have similar actions on the body (e.g., morphine taken with a sleeping pill causes severe drowsiness).

Decreasing the number of medications to be taken daily can prevent drug interactions. Most importantly, you should make sure your physician and pharmacist know every medication you are taking (i.e., prescription, nonprescription, and herbal). Read your medication labels to make sure you are not taking the same medicine under different brand names (see Figure 33-3). Health care professionals can review medication lists to determine if any potential drug interactions exist. If so, therapy can be changed in advance to prevent any unnecessary effects.

MULTIPLE PHARMACIES AND PHYSICIANS

Having prescriptions filled at more than one pharmacy and having more than one physician increases the risk of patients experiencing an

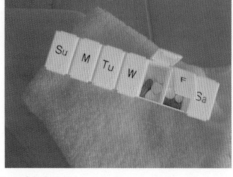

(figure 33-2)

Pillbox.

(table 33-5)

DOS AND DONT'S OF DRUG THERAPY

DO	DON'T
Do take your medication as directed.	*Don't* crush a tablet or capsule without asking your physician or pharmacist.
Do read the prescription label every time before taking.	*Don't* break a tablet that is not scored.
Do store medication correctly.	*Don't* stop taking your medication without the permission of your physician.
Do tell your physician and pharmacist about drug side effects you have had in the past.	*Don't* take more or less than the prescribed amount of any drug.
Do keep an updated drug list, including all prescription, nonprescription, and herbal medications.	*Don't* mix alcohol with your medications without the permission of your physician.
Do review your drug list with your physician and pharmacist at every visit.	*Don't* take drugs prescribed for another person or give yours to someone else.
Do make sure you can read and understand the prescription label once the drug is filled.	*Don't* keep medication past the expiration date.*
Do call your physician right away if you have any problems with your medications.	

*See the box entitled "Expiration Date" on page 724 for more details.

(figure 33-3)

AVOIDING MEDICATION MIX-UPS

(a) Your medication label is important. Unless you doctor writes "Medically Necessary" or "Dispense as Written" on the prescription, the pharmacist will usually fill the prescription with a generic drug to save you money. Thus the name of the drug may well be different than the name the doctor wrote on your prescription. In this case, the generic drug diltiazem ER has been substituted for the brand name drug Cardizem CD (circled).

GENERIC NAME
➤

➤
BRAND NAME

> **ABC PHARMACY (262) 574-6754**
> **33 Main St.**
> **Mayberry, TN 25674**
>
> **Rx: 751920** 6-18-04
>
> **For: John Smith**
>
> **Take one capsule daily. Swallow whole. Do not crush or chew.**
>
> (Diltiazem ER 180 mg) #60
>
> (Gen Eq: Cardizem CD 180 mg caps)
>
> **Dr. Jones, William M.** **Orig: 6-18-04**
> **Refills: 1 by 6/18/05** **Discard after: 6/18/05** **RPh: MP**

(b) Confusion can also occur because the same medication can also look different depending on the manufacturer. Here are pill pictures for extended release diltiazem, a drug commonly used to treat high blood pressure and some heart rhythm disorders. Bringing your medicines to your visits to the doctor can help eliminate confusion.

The generic is the actual name of the drug, which may have several brand names. For example, diltiazem sustained-release is a generic name. It is marketed under the brand names Cardizem CD, Cartia XT, Dilacor-XR, and Tiazac. Read all your labels to avoid taking multiples of the same medicine under different brand names.

Cardizem CD Cartia XT

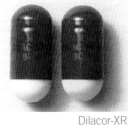 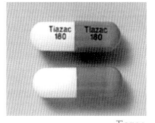

Dilacor-XR Tiazac

(Pill photos. Reprinted with permission. © First DataBank Inc. All rights reserved.)

adverse drug reaction. Pharmacists recommend patients to have all their medications filled at one pharmacy if possible. Pharmacies have software that aids in tracking drug–drug interactions, drug–disease interactions, and allergies. If different prescriptions are taken to different pharmacies, then each pharmacist will not have a complete list of a patient's medications. Therefore, a thorough review of the patient's medications cannot be done. Patients should also keep in mind that different stores within the same pharmacy chain are not always electronically connected. See Table 33-5 for a list of good and bad medication practices.

Limiting yourself to one physician is more difficult than limiting your pharmacies. Older persons may not only have a primary care physician but may have specialists as well. Patients with multiple physicians should make sure each physician has an updated list of all their medications, conditions, and allergies. Remember that your primary care physician and the specialists involved in your care should be a team, with your primary care doctor, usually an internist or family practice physician, the "captain." You should not take any medication until your primary doctor is informed. This can help prevent undesirable drug interactions or adverse

EXPIRATION DATE

The general consensus among most pharmacists and physicians is that most drugs are still effective past the expiration date. In fact, in the 1980s, the FDA evaluated a number of drugs that the U.S. military had stockpiled and were approaching expiration dates. This program, called the Shelf-Life Extension Program, demonstrated that many drugs are still useful well past their expiration dates. However, these drugs were maintained in optimal environments where they were not exposed to extremes of temperature, humidity, and light. It may not be possible to duplicate the same conditions in normal warehouses and pharmacies.

So what does this mean? Should you take the drug if the expiration date is past? Most likely, it will not do harm. Aspirin, for example, has been shown to be effective in stability testing for at least four to five years even though expiration dates are often two to three years after being packaged. Ciprofloxacin (Cipro) has an expiration date approximately three years after packaging, but stability tests have shown it to be effective for almost 10 years. But it is important to realize that some drugs, such as outdated tetracycline, have been associated with serious adverse effects. Outdated nitroglycerin may not help you if you are experiencing angina or having a heart attack. Many physicians encourage their patients to open their nitroglycerin bottle before they are having problems, so they are not fumbling around trying to get it open if they are having problems. Since nitroglycerin tablets deteriorate quite quickly once the bottle is open, many physicians and pharmacists suggest a fresh bottle every six months.

At the annual meeting of the American Medical Association in 2000, the Council on Scientific Affairs asked the FDA, the U.S. Pharmacopeia, and the pharmaceutical industry to evaluate drug expiration dates. Hopefully, this will prompt further study on the stability of drugs, and expiration dates will be determined by scientific testing. In the meantime, check with your doctor or pharmacist before taking any medicine beyond its expiration.

drug effects on other medical conditions that you have. Your primary doctor is charged with watching out for you as a whole person.

NONPRESCRIPTION MEDICATIONS AND HERBALS

Taking over-the-counter and herbal medications might seem harmless, but many of these drugs can interact with prescription medications. It is important that your pharmacist and physician know all the medications you are taking, including nonprescription, vitamins, and herbals. Also, discuss with your health care professionals what can be taken for headache, cold symptoms, stomach upset, and so on, before the need arises. Herbal products are often mistaken as harmless because they are considered "natural." However, a number of herbal medications can cause interactions with prescription medications and diseases.

WHAT YOU NEED TO KNOW

▶ Medications increase quality of life and life expectancy. If taking more than one medication per day, older adults are at risk for adverse drug reactions. However, good communication between you and your health care professionals minimizes drug problems. Any unwanted effects from medications should be communicated to a health care professional immediately.

▶ Over 90% of people over 65 take at least one medicine daily. Medicines have benefits as well as risks.

▶ Changes occur in your body as you get older that influence the blood levels of medicines. Doses commonly used when you were younger may need to be modified.

▶ Certain foods and other medicines alter the way a drug acts in your body. Your doctor or pharmacist may suggest that you take your medicines with food or on an empty stomach. They may suggest that you avoid certain foods, vitamins, or herbal supplements.

▶ Alcohol acts like a drug and affects how you respond to medication. Ask your doctor or pharmacist if it is safe to drink alcoholic beverages while taking your medication.

▶ Bring your medicine in a bag or container on your doctor visits, so the drugs can be reviewed and a medication list can be made.

▶ Always carry an updated medication list, and present this list at every physician and pharmacy visit.

▶ Periodically review with your doctor all your medications to see if any can be pruned.

▶ Sometimes the best medicine is no medicine. Don't pressure your physician to prescribe antibiotics for colds, which are viral infections that don't respond to antibiotics. The emergence of superbugs has been attributed to the overuse of antibiotics.

FOR MORE INFORMATION

▶ **Agency for Healthcare Research and Quality (AHRQ)**
540 Gaither Road
Rockville, MD 20850
301-427-1364
E-mail: info@ahrq.gov
Free brochure "Your Medicine: Play It Safe," available by phone (800–358-9295) or e-mail (ahrqpubs@ahrq.gov).

▶ **National Council on Patient Information and Education (NCPIE)**
4915 Saint Elmo Avenue, Suite 505
Bethesda, MD 20814
301-656-8565
Fax: 301-656-4464
Web: www.talkaboutrx.org and www.bemedwise.org
Offers information about safe medicine use.

INTERNET

▶ www.healthtouch.com
Includes health and drug information. Also provides information on vitamins and herbs.

▶ www.medlineplus.gov.
Learn about specific medicines.

▶ www.safemedication.com
Includes drug information, pharmacist's question and answer, and information regarding vaccines and medication use.

▶ my.webmd.com
Includes drug and herbal information, latest news from the FDA, and information regarding medication use.

> The secret of staying young is to live honestly, eat slowly, and lie about your age.
>
> —*Lucille Ball*

THE AUTHOR

34

BRAUN H. GRAHAM, MD, FACS, is a graduate of Indiana University and the Indiana University School of Medicine. He completed his residency in general surgery and plastic surgery at the University of Florida in Gainesville. He is a fellow of the American College of Surgeons, and he is certified by the American Board of Plastic Surgery. He is a clinical assistant professor of surgery at University of Florida. He is one of the founding members of the Harry Buncke Microsurgical Society. Dr. Graham is listed in *America's Best Doctors*. He resides in Sarasota, Florida, and he is president of Sarasota Plastic Surgery.

34 COSMETIC SURGERY

Not only does the normal aging process affect the major organ systems in the body, but it has a dramatic effect on the external facial and body features as well. Beginning in the late 30s and early 40s, most individuals become aware of changes in the texture, thickness, and elasticity of their skin. As the years progress, you may notice changes that you find undesirable and wish to have corrected. Although plastic surgery can be safely performed in most individuals, the decision to have surgery is a serious one.

FACE AND SKIN

One of the most obvious facial changes occurs in the upper eyelids. This is manifested by excess skin that hides the natural crease in the upper lid and by development of bulging of the fat that creates a "tired look." In the lower eyelid the excess skin and wrinkles can be associated with puffy bags caused by fat protruding behind the skin and muscle layer of the lid. In some individuals, the lower eyelid skin develops deposits of dark pigment forming dark circles under the eye. Often this noticeable eyelid aging can be a trait that runs in families and causes some individuals to seek cosmetic eyelid surgery even in their 20s or 30s. By the time one reaches 60 or 70 years of age, there can be such skin excess in the upper eyelids that this can cause significant obstruction of vision, especially when gazing upward. The surgical procedure for removing redundant skin, soft tissue, and fat in the eyelids is called **blepharoplasty** (see Figure 34-1). This is typically a procedure that is performed as an outpatient under

(figure 34-1)

Blepharoplasty is a procedure to remove skin, soft tissue, and fat from the eyelids. (a) As people age, the eyelid skin stretches, muscles weaken, and (b) fat accumulates around the eyes, causing bags above and below. (c) Before surgery, the surgeon marks the incision sites and follows the natural lines and creases of the upper and lower eyelids. (d) The surgeon closes the incisions with fine sutures, which will leave nearly invisible scars. (e) Underlying fat, along with excess skin and muscle, can be removed during the operation. *(Adapted with permission of the American Society of Plastic Surgeons.)*

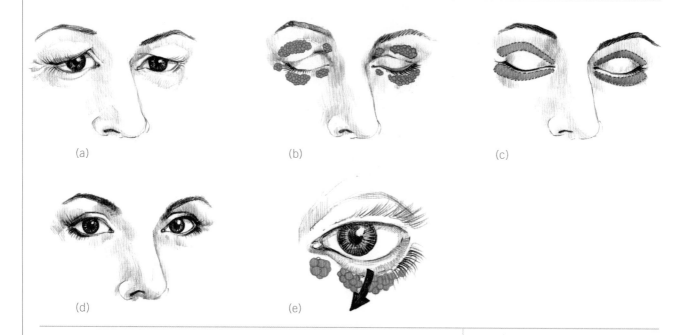

(a)

(b)

(c)

(d)

(e)

(figure 34-2)

Facelift: (a) Incisions usually begin above the hairline at the temples, follow the natural line in front of the ear, curve behind the earlobe into the crease behind the ear, and into or along the lower scalp. (b) Facial, neck tissue, and muscle may be separated; fat may be trimmed or suctioned and underlying muscle may be tightened. (c) After deep tissues are tightened, the excess skin is pulled up and back, trimmed, and sutured into place. Most of the scars will be hidden within your hair and in the normal creases of your skin. *(Adapted with permission of the American Society of Plastic Surgeons.)*

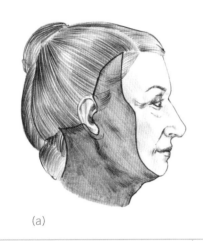

(a)

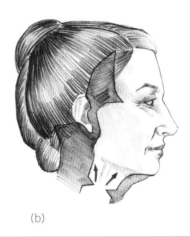

(b)

(c)

34

local anesthesia with sedation, meaning the surgery does not require the patient to be completely under general anesthesia. The postoperative recovery is complete within one to two weeks and there is minimal discomfort associated with the procedure. Most patients do not require pain medicine in the postoperative period, and their only restriction is to avoid heavy lifting for the first several days. Incision healing is rapid with the stitches usually being removed within 1 week of the surgical procedure. Over 225,000 cosmetic eyelid procedures were performed in the United States in 2002, as reported by the American Society for Aesthetic Plastic Surgery. This organization is composed of approximately 2000 board-certified plastic surgeons that specialize in cosmetic plastic surgery.

The typical features of normal facial aging include thinning of the fat layer under the facial skin associated with downward movement of the facial soft tissues. The gravitational descent of the skin leads to the accumulation of skin under the chin and neck, unaffectionately known as the "turkey neck" or "gobbler." Additional changes include downward movement of the cheek fat to create the bulges below the jaw line (jowls) and descent of facial fat off the cheekbone prominences to cause a deepening of the lines running from the nose to the corner of the mouth. In the neck, there can be excessive deposits of fat, particularly if there has been that middle-aged weight gain of 10 to 20 pounds that is often seen in menopausal patients. In individuals with thin necks there are often two noticeable vertical bands that occur in the front of the neck. These bands are caused by the separation of the muscle layer in the front of the neck. These gradual facial changes result in a tired or sad look. For many, looking in the mirror and seeing a face that does not reflect the way they feel inside causes them to seek a plastic surgeon. The facelift is a surgical procedure designed to remove excessive fat deposits in the neck,

(figure 34-3*)*

(a) A 62-year-old woman was displeased with the fat bulges in her lower eyelids that caused her eyes to look sad and tired, with the prominence of the jowls below her jaw line, and with the deepening facial line between her nose and jowl. (b) Note the improvement and natural appearance after her facelift combined with upper and lower blepharoplasty surgery.

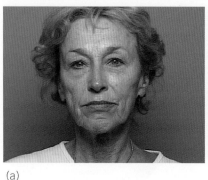 

(a)   (b)

reposition the loose muscle layer in the neck and face, and remove the redundant, stretched skin excesses in the cheek and neck. The procedure utilizes inconspicuous incisions hidden in the skin crease under the chin and around the normal skin creases around the ear (see Figure 34-2). This surgical procedure is performed as an outpatient under general anesthesia or local anesthesia with sedation. Patients are typically 45 to 50 years old when they first consider having a facelift. We have performed this operative procedure on patients as old as 85 years of age. Figure 34-3 shows before and after photographs of a 62-year-old woman who came to our office and complained of "looking tired all the time." The usual recovery time is two to three weeks, and postoperative discomfort is minimal. Surgeons certified by the American Board of Plastic Surgery in 2002 performed 125,000 facelifts.

In addition to the downward movement of facial soft tissue and skin with aging, here, in southwest Florida, we are constantly exposed to damaging ultraviolet rays from the sun. Years of ultraviolet damage

(figure 34-4*)*

(a) A 74-year-old woman, with severe sun damage and facial wrinkling that persisted despite a previous facelift, showed (b) significant improvement after laser resurfacing.

(a)   (b)

leads to accelerated skin aging with irregular skin pigmentation, loss of elasticity, and severe wrinkling. Although facelifts and eyelid surgery can remove loose skin, it cannot add elasticity back to the deeper skin layer to remove deep wrinkles. In the past decade, significant improvement in the appearance of sun-damaged skin and wrinkling has been made with the use of skin resurfacing lasers. Figure 34-4 shows the improvement in the sun damage and wrinkles as a result of full face laser resurfacing. The facial skin is treated with laser energy to vaporize the outer skin cells by creating a controlled, partial-thickness burn wound. New skin cells grow from the thousands of facial pores, ultimately resurfacing the face with new skin cells. In addition, to the superficial improvement, new collagen is deposited in the deeper levels of the dermis, which is responsible for the improvement in the facial wrinkles. Laser skin resurfacing is performed as an outpatient procedure under general anesthesia or local anesthesia with sedation. Because laser resurfacing involves healing from a burn-type wound, patients are typically required to be homebound for the first 7 to 10 days after the procedure until skin healing is complete enough to wear makeup. Skin redness is common for the first six to eight weeks and sometimes for several months after laser resurfacing. Newer dressings and healing ointments have dramatically reduced the discomfort associated with laser resurfacing. Patients are cautioned to protect their skin from the sun with sun block until all skin redness is resolved. In the United States 73,000 laser resurfacing procedures were performed in 2002.

BODY-CONTOURING PROCEDURES

The most frequently performed body-contouring procedure in the United States today is liposuction. This procedure is optimally performed in younger adults with good skin elasticity. It involves removal of deep fat deposits below the skin through small incisions. Small-diameter, blunt-

(figure 34-5)

Breast lift: (a) Over time, a woman's breasts begin to sag and the areolas become larger. (b) Incisions outline the area to be removed and the new position of the nipple. (c) Skin formerly located above the nipple is brought down and together to re-shape the breast. Sutures close the incisions, giving the breast its new contour. (d) After surgery, the breasts are higher and firmer, with sutures usually located around the areola, below it, and in the creases under the breast. *(Adapted with permission of the American Society of Plastic Surgeons.)*

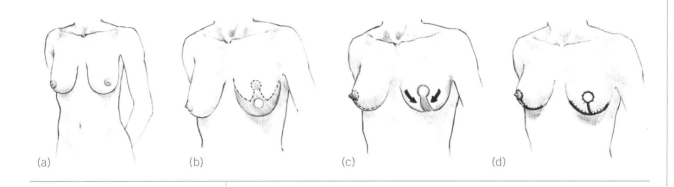

(a)   (b)   (c)   (d)

(figure 34-6)

(a) A 60-year-old woman, with complaints of neck pain, shoulder pain, and chest wall discomfort due to the heavy weight of her breasts, had (b) a breast reduction and lift procedure.

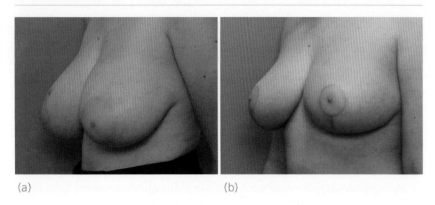

(a) (b)

tipped cannulas are passed through the incisions to gain access to the fat deposits. The other end of the cannula is connected to a suction source. The suction applied removes fat without causing damage to more solid structures, such as blood vessels and nerves. Liposuction, however, is not a substitute for weight loss in individuals that are obese.

Because of issues with diminished skin elasticity in middle-aged and older patients, skin removal is necessary in both cosmetic abdominal and breast surgical procedures. The changes associated with the aging breast include descent of the lower portion of the breast along with stretching of the skin bringing the nipple to a level below the lower breast crease. The breast can be lifted by removal of loose skin on the lower portion of the breast and tightening the skin to cause a pushup effect on the breast tissue. The breast lift, or *mastopexy,* can also be done with removal of breast tissue if the patient desires a reduction in breast size as well as improvement in the breast position. According to American Society for Aesthetic Plastic Surgery statistics, 125,000 breast reduction procedures and 62,000 breast lift procedures were performed in 2002. Figure 34-5 demonstrates the pattern of skin removal typically required to elevate the breast. After skin removal with or without breast tissue removal, the skin closure results in incisions placed on the lower portions of the breast where they cannot be seen when wearing bathing suits or low-cut clothing. Figure 34-6 demonstrates the change in breast size and position after a breast reduction and lift procedure.

Another common body-contouring procedure is known as the "tummy tuck," or *abdominoplasty.* With continued aging and a history of multiple pregnancies, many women develop a lower abdominal protrusion due to the separation of the midline abdominal muscles. In addition, these women also have a roll of excess skin and fat between the belly button and the pubic region. The surgical correction involves removal of the skin and underlying fat between the belly button and the pubic area. Next, the loose abdominal wall muscles are reinforced with a running suture

(figure 34-7)

Tummy tuck: (a) The surgeon draws underlying muscle and tissue together and stitches them, thereby narrowing the waistline and strengthening the abdominal wall. (b) Abdominal skin is drawn down and excess is removed. With complete abdominoplasty, a new opening is cut for the navel. Both incisions are stitched closed. (c) After surgery, the patient has a flatter, trimmer abdomen. Scars are permanent but will fade with time. *(Adapted with permission of the American Society of Plastic Surgeons.)*

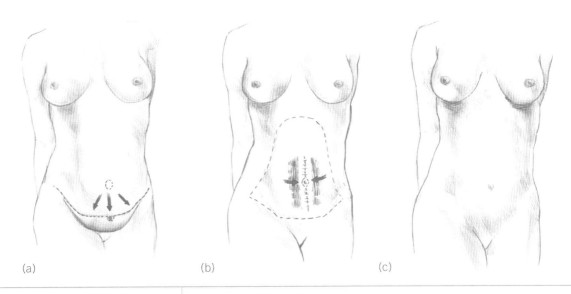

(a)　　　　　　　　　(b)　　　　　　　　　(c)

extending from the lower rib cage to the pubic region in the midline. The remaining abdominal skin is pulled downward like a window shade to tighten the abdominal skin. The resultant scar is hidden in the "bikini" line. Figure 34-7 shows a depiction of the tummy tuck procedure. In the United States 83,000 of these procedures were performed last year. Figure 34-8 shows pre- and postoperative photographs of an abdominoplasty procedure.

The number of cosmetic surgical procedures has increased from about 1 million in 1997 to over 1.6 million in 2002 (over 60% increase). The number of procedures in the 35- to 50-year-old age group has increased to 648,000, and the number in the 51- to 64-year-old group has increased to

(figure 34-8)

(a) Before and (b) after an abdominoplasty.

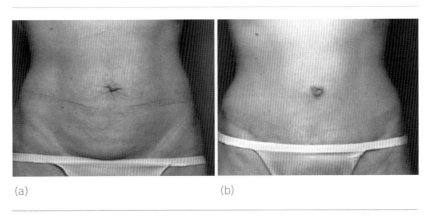

(a)　　　　　　　　　(b)

332,000. This does not include the over 4 million noninvasive procedures, such as Botox, collagen injections, microdermabrasion, and laser hair removal. With the intense media coverage that cosmetic procedures are getting, it is important for the consumer to be aware that many medical practitioners are advertising as being experienced in performing procedures for which they have minimal training or experience. Be certain your surgeon is certified by a board recognized by the American Board of Medical Specialties. Ask your primary care physician or internist to recommend a plastic surgeon should you desire a consultation regarding cosmetic surgery. Check to see that your surgeon has privileges to perform cosmetic surgical procedures at your local hospital and not just in his or her office setting. Above all, be certain you discuss with your surgeon the planned treatment options, expected postoperative course, and potential complications of any cosmetic surgical procedure. These procedures are safe in healthy individuals who have realistic expectations concerning their postoperative outcome.

■

WHAT YOU NEED TO KNOW

▶ Aging affects the major organ systems in the body but has a dramatic effect on the external facial features and body features as well.

▶ Age alone does not limit plastic surgery; however, coexisting medical conditions may make such surgery inadvisable. The benefits and risks should be discussed with your plastic surgeon and your primary care physician.

▶ Ask your primary care physician to recommend a plastic surgeon should you desire a consultation regarding cosmetic surgery.

▶ Be certain your surgeon is certified by a board recognized by the American Board of Medical Specialties. Check to see that your surgeon has privileges to perform cosmetic surgical procedures at your local hospital and not just in his or her office setting.

▶ Discuss with your surgeon your treatment options for any cosmetic procedure, including expected postoperative course and potential complications. These procedures are safe in middle-aged and older persons who have no serious underlying heart, lung, or kidney problems. The surgery can be safely performed in most persons with high blood pressure and diabetes if they are well-controlled.

34

FOR MORE INFORMATION

▷ **American Society of Plastic Surgeons**
Plastic Surgery Educational Foundation
444 E. Algonquin Road
Arlington Heights, IL 60005
Referrals: 888-475-2784
847-228-9900
E-mail: media@plasticsurgery.org
Web: www.plasticsurgery.org
Members of the American Society of Plastic Surgery are certified by the American Board of Plastic Surgery, a recognized member of the American Board of Medical Specialties.

▷ **American Society for Aesthetic Plastic Surgery**
Web: www.surgery.org

▷ **Sarasota Plastic Surgery Center**
Web: www.sarasotaplasticsurgery.com

▷ **American Board of Medical Specialties**
Web: www.abms.org

Perhaps travel cannot prevent bigotry, but by demonstrating that all peoples cry, laugh, eat, worry, and die, it can introduce the idea that if we try and understand each other, we may even become friends.

—*Maya Angelou*

THE AUTHOR

35

KEVIN W. O'NEIL, MD, FACP, graduated from Boston College magna cum laude and the Georgetown University School of Medicine. He did his internship at the Washington Hospital Center and his internal medicine residency at the University of Massachusetts Medical Center. He was an assistant professor in the Department of Internal Medicine at the University of Massachusetts Medical Center until moving to Sarasota, Florida, in 1984. He is currently an assistant professor of medicine at the University of South Florida College of Medicine. He is board-certified in internal medicine and holds a Certificate of Added Qualifications in Geriatric Medicine. He is a fellow of the American College of Physicians and a member of the American Geriatrics Society. He practices with the First Physicians Group in Sarasota and is on the staff at Sarasota Memorial Hospital and Doctors Hospital.

35 | TRAVEL

Do you remember the first time you got behind the wheel of a car to learn how to drive? Do you remember the sense of excitement? Do you remember the feeling of independence as you dreamed of the places you could visit—without mom and dad!

Do you recall the first time you went on a trip in a jetliner—the power you felt as the jet's engines hurtled you down the runway and into space? Did you contemplate how small the world really is if you can be anywhere in the world within a matter of hours?

Travel and exploration have been a fascination since the time of our earliest ancestors. Our natural curiosity impels us to visit new places and study other cultures. This is healthy because it stimulates us and helps us understand that all people are part of the human race. By understanding each other better, perhaps we can learn to appreciate our differences and yet help one another make the world a better place.

Although the benefits of travel are clear, there are certainly health risks as well. This chapter explores our various means of travel and the associated health risks as they relate to those of you in midlife and older. I focus primarily on preventive practices that will help you avoid serious medical problems. Although I discuss some common conditions that can occur while traveling, it is beyond the scope of this chapter to go into all the diseases that can occur from domestic and foreign travel. However, at the end of the chapter, I provide some websites where you can discover more information.

(*figure* 35-1)

Aging may be assumed with physical changes that can affect driving ability.

DRIVING

In my years of medical practice, one of the more difficult responsibilities I have had is telling anyone to give up the car keys. That sense of independence that you and I had when we first had access to a car does not go away when we get older. However, some changes occur that may make it unsafe for us to drive. It is important to realize that we have a responsibility to our community, our family, and ourselves to accept the judgment of professionals if they deem it necessary to take away the car keys. Everyone's life would be radically altered if you were involved in a serious accident. You need only imagine the effect on your family if you were killed or seriously disabled in an accident. What would be the impact on your life if you accidentally injured or killed a pedestrian? Although we don't like to dwell on such possibilities, we need to realize the serious responsibilities that we have when we get behind the wheel of a car.

As you get older, physical changes may affect your driving ability (see Figure 35-1). Many such changes are discussed in other chapters in this book. For example, aging of the eye may be associated with cataracts, macular degeneration, and glaucoma. Hearing loss may make it difficult for you to appreciate sirens. Arthritis and Parkinson's disease may affect your ability to turn the wheel or look around. Damage to peripheral nerves from diabetes can impair the sensations in your feet and affect your ability to feel the gas or brake pedals. Some physical changes can be treated and improved, so that you can continue to drive. For example, cataracts can be surgically removed, glasses may restore normal or near-normal vision, and hearing aids can compensate for many forms of hearing loss.

Mental changes can also affect our driving abilities. Our ability to concentrate on more than one item at a time may be impaired. You may have more difficulty with short-term memory (ability to recall recent information), which makes it more difficult to follow directions. More serious memory problems occur with dementia, such as Alzheimer's disease, which the affected person often does not recognize. Such individuals do not realize they have a problem, and they are often extremely reluctant to give up the car keys. Psychological difficulties, such as anxiety and depression, can adversely affect the quality of sleep, making falling asleep at the wheel a significant risk.

You may require medications as you get older. Many medicines have effects on your driving performance. Antianxiety drugs, sleeping pills, and some antidepressants cause drowsiness. Similar problems can occur with antihistamines and pain relievers. Drug metabolism is altered when you get older. Thus, the effects of drugs on your body and mind may be heightened. If you experience these types of side effects, make sure you alert your doctor so he or she can make changes in your drug therapy.

Remember, also, that alcohol metabolism is altered as you get older. Half of all traffic fatalities are related to alcohol use. Even though the legal limit for drunk drivers in most states is a blood alcohol level of 0.10, alcohol can have a more significant effect on the nervous system of an older adult even at lower blood alcohol levels. In addition, combining alcohol with prescription medication augments the effects of each. The best policy is not to drink and drive. If you cannot resist that drink, appoint a designated driver. Or take a cab.

There isn't any easy answer to the question, "When should you stop driving?" Age itself is not a limitation. In fact, as a group, older drivers who are much less likely to drink and drive or speed have far fewer accidents than teen drivers have. However, the risk of being involved and dying in an automobile accident rises significantly after age 70 and precipitously after age 80. As a result, many states require that elderly drivers pass road tests. Others are looking at the useful-field-of-view test, which evaluates your ability to process information in your visual field, screen out distractions, and respond correctly. With aging, your visual field contracts, and the smaller the field, the more likely an accident.

Many communities and hospitals offer driver training and driver evaluation. You are ready for an evaluation if any of the following has occurred:

- Has anyone remarked that your driving skills are not what they use to be?
- Have you had some accidents lately, even minor ones?
- Do you notice other drivers getting upset with you?
- Do other drivers honk or yell at you?

However, if advised that it is not safe for you to drive—either temporarily or permanently—you should give up the keys. Possible circumstances for temporarily stopping driving include having a recent seizure, major surgery, a heart attack or stroke, or surgery for a pacemaker or implantable cardioverter defibrillator (ICD). Your physician decides when and if it is safe for you to resume driving. Some states set specific durations before driving can be resumed, such as following a seizure. If the medical problem involves cognitive problems, such as Alzheimer's disease, you may have to stop driving permanently.

If not allowed to drive, you learn to depend on your family, friends, and public transport. Although such dependence can be annoying, it is important to realize that it is for public safety as well as your own.

AIR TRAVEL

Although one of the safest ways to travel, flying has its own health risks. Some of the problems I describe here are minor, whereas others are quite serious and life-threatening. Proper planning can go a long way toward ensuring your well-being.

Barotitis is the troubling sensation in your ears if there is a sudden change in altitude. Normally, at sea level, pressure between your middle ear and the surrounding atmosphere is equal. However, as you ascend rapidly in an airliner, the atmospheric pressure surrounding you decreases. As a result, air flows out of the middle ear through a small tube, called the eustachian tube, that connects your middle ear with the back of your

(figure 35-2)

Air travel is usually very safe, but you should be familiar with some of the risks.

SAFE DRIVING

- Use your seat belt, even if you have air bags. The National Highway Traffic Safety Administration has reported that seat belts reduce the risk of serious injury and death from an accident by 50%. They also reduce the risk of injury if an airbag is deployed.
- Don't use a cell phone while driving. Studies have shown a significant increase in accident risk if a person talks on a cell phone while driving.
- Make sure any children or pets are secured in the rear seat. This will help avoid distractions. Very young children should be in an infant carrier or a child safety seat. Pets should be in carriers that can be belted in.
- Don't drink and drive.
- Let someone else drive if you are tired, anxious, or depressed. Preoccupation diminishes your ability to drive safely.
- Drive with your headlights on, and make sure the headlights are clean. Studies have shown that these simple measures make it easier for other drivers to see you.
- Avoid driving situations if they pose problems for you (such as nighttime, bad weather, traffic congestion, or highways).
- Be particularly cautious at intersections. Studies have confirmed that older drivers have a higher incidence of accidents at intersections and especially with left-hand turns.
- Make sure your vehicle is maintained at regular intervals.
- Make sure you do not drive for more than a few hours without stopping to refresh yourself. If taking a long-distance trip, share the driving responsibilities. Getting out of the car and walking around periodically reduce the risk of blood clots in your legs and lungs.

throat (see Chapter 3). This allows the middle ear pressure to equalize with the surrounding air pressure. Usually discomfort is not associated with barotitis, but if you find it annoying, you might try chewing gum, sucking on some hard candy, drinking water, or chewing on some fruit. Swallowing helps relieve barotitis. These problems can be compounded in smaller aircraft. Earplugs in addition to chewing and swallowing might be helpful.

If descending, the opposite occurs: atmospheric pressure increases. Since the air pressure is now higher than the middle ear pressure (now that your middle ear has acclimatized to the higher altitude), air moves into your middle ear via the eustachian tube. You probably have experienced a fullness and blockage in your ears with the descent of an airliner. (This also explains why you sometimes hear children crying during ascent or descent.) Barotitis can be compounded by a cold or ear infection since the air does not move freely. You can relieve the problem by gently blowing air through your nose while pinching your nostrils and holding your mouth closed. This forces air into the middle ear and equalizes the pressure between the surrounding atmosphere and your middle ear.

If you have a cold, ear infection, or allergies, it may be best not to fly. However, if flying is unavoidable, you could use a nasal decongestant, such as OXYMETAZOLINE (AFRIN) about 30 to 60 minutes before flying and 30 minutes before landing. Avoid the long-acting preparations. If you have no contraindications, PSEUDOEPHEDRINE (SUDAFED) may be used. If you have heart disease or other serious medical problems, check with your doctor.

If susceptible to motion sickness, try sitting in an aisle seat near the wings where there is less motion of the aircraft. Some people find that looking at something outside the plane, such as the horizon, diminishes motion sickness. You will find a paper bag in the pocket of the seat in front of you if your stomach gets upset and you need to vomit. It is best to avoid TRANSDERMAL SCOPOLAMINE patches, if you are very elderly, since they have been associated with dry mouth, drowsiness, mental confusion, and constipation. Safer alternatives include MECLIZINE (BONINE, ANTIVERT) and DIMENHYDRINATE (DRAMAMINE), but they, too, may have undesirable side effects.

Changes in atmospheric pressure may cause gas in your gastrointestinal tract to expand. This can be very uncomfortable but generally can be avoided by restricting for the day of and the day before flying the following:

- Carbonated beverages and beer
- Legumes, such as peas and beans
- Pectin-containing fruits, such as apples and pears

It is also prudent to avoid air travel if you have had recent major abdominal or chest surgery. Ask your doctor when it would be safe to resume flying. If you have a colostomy, use a larger bag to allow more room for the extra intestinal gas.

Air flight exposes you to the risk of a drop in your blood oxygen concentration. Most persons who have stable conditions will not require oxygen while flying. However, if you have severe chronic obstructive pulmonary disease (COPD) or congestive heart failure (CHF), your doctor may need to prescribe oxygen for you. It is important that you make these arrangements with the airline well before flying. The humidity of the air within the cabin of an airliner is low. This can present problems for those with chronic bronchitis and thick respiratory secretions. Make sure you drink plenty of fluids, and use your inhalers if they have been prescribed.

If you have a pacemaker or ICD, carry a note from your doctor since you may encounter problems with the metal detectors at airports. The same holds true if you have other metallic implants, such as an artificial hip or knee. A *medical alert* necklace or bracelet helps identify your medical conditions, your medicines, your allergies, and emergency contacts. In emergency situations, medical alert jewelry allows medical personnel to treat you properly. You can buy alerts through your pharmacy or call 800-363-5985.

If you are diabetic and on insulin, you may need to adjust your insulin regimen if you are crossing six or more time zones. Frequent blood glucose monitoring will be required. Make sure you notify the airport security screeners that you are carrying diabetic supplies. The American Diabetes Association has excellent information for diabetic travelers (see "For More Information").

If you are taking a long overseas or domestic flight, take precautions against blood clots. Blood clots (venous thrombosis) can produce pain and swelling of the legs but often produce no symptoms at all. The most feared complication is pulmonary embolism, which can cause chest pain, shortness of breath, and sudden death. Blood clots pose a significant risk for those who have been sitting on an airliner for a long time. Getting up and walking around frequently can be helpful. Stretching excercises and drinking adequate amounts of fluids (other than alcohol!) are advisable. Use of support stockings and use of aspirin or other "blood thinners" is not routinely recommended, but your doctor may suggest these if you have other medical conditions that increase your chances of developing a blood clot. Even low-dose aspirin may increase the risk of ulcers and stomach bleeding. Compression stockings should be avoided in those persons with significant peripheral arterial disease. So check with your doctor before you travel to find out the measures that are most appropriate for you.

Jet lag is an uncomfortable feeling of fatigue, disorientation, and fuzziness that may persist for days after arriving at your destination. It usually occurs after crossing three or more time zones. MELATONIN has been touted as helpful, but I do not recommend this, because no one knows how effective it is or how long it should be used. In addition, Melatonin has the potential for significant side effects, including headache, drowsiness, and stomach cramps. Some studies have suggested that Melatonin may make jet lag worse. In addition, considering the potential

CONQUERING JET LAG

- Eat well-balanced meals and avoid excessive alcohol or caffeine.
- Drink plenty of liquids while flying.
- Try to adjust to the new time schedule by going to bed a little later for a few days before a westward trip and a few hours earlier before an eastward trip.

- Get regular exercise on your trip, but avoid strenuous exercise before going to bed.
- Sleep medication may be helpful, but discuss this with your doctor. Such medications can also cause side effects and may need to be avoided depending on your medical condition and your medicine.

for drug interactions and that you most likely take one or more medicines, Melatonin is best avoided.

You and I have frequently heard that airliners breed infection due to air recirculation. A report in the July 2002 *Journal of the American Medical Association* dispelled the notion that air recirculation increases the risk for upper respiratory infections. The likely cause is that infections generally spread more easily if people in a confined space are exposed to others with communicable diseases. It is wise to follow simple precautions, such as washing your hands after personal contact. While impractical and unnecessary for all airline passengers to wear masks, it is a considerate measure to use one if you have a cold or other respiratory infection. If you already have serious underlying lung or heart disease, consider a mask as a preventive measure. (Infections are covered in detail in the section, "Preventing Infections," below.)

Fear of flying is common, and if you are afraid, simply telling you that it is the safest way to travel is not reassuring enough. The fear can range from mild uneasiness to outright panic. Trying to focus on something other than your fear and where you are can help. Some people read a book, meditate, or focus on scenery outside. Others have tried hypnosis or other relaxation techniques, such as abdominal breathing, in which you keep your chest still and breath by pushing out with your abdominal muscles. If you have intense fear or panic attacks, ask your doctor to prescribe a medicine for you.

Remember to take a copy of your medication list and a list of your medical conditions along. I like to provide my patients with a copy of their most recent physical examination, which summarizes their medical condition, past medical and surgical history, and medications. The summary makes it easier for a physician in a different place to get a handle on the problems that my patient has had. It can save valuable time, especially in emergency situations. If you have a heart condition, carry a copy of your most recent electrocardiogram (ECG). If you have a pacemaker or ICD, carry the manufacturer's card listing the type and model number.

If you are going to a foreign country, remember that Medicare may not provide coverage for illness there. Check with your Medicare carrier before your trip. If you have other coverage, make sure it has coverage for services in another country. If not, you need to purchase temporary coverage. A good organization to become familiar with, especially if you travel to foreign countries, is the International Association for Medical Assistance to Travelers, a nonprofit organization established to advise people about health risks associated with travel (see "For More Information"). It can also give you information about doctors who are competent and speak English in the area in which you are traveling. It can tell you the immunizations you will need for your trip, or you can get this information from your local health department or the Centers for Disease Control.

Developed by the World Health Organization (WHO), the *yellow card* (a very useful item to possess) lists your immunizations and is recognized throughout the world. You can obtain a yellow card (also called the *international certificate of vaccination*) from your local health department, or it may be purchased for $1 from the Government Printing Office (see "For More Information").

CRUISES

Outbreaks of norovirus (formerly called *Norwalk virus*) on cruise ships have publicized the risks of infection in confined areas. Instead of shaking hands, travelers on ships are using the "forearm tap," by which the greeting parties touch each other's elbow. The forearm tap was suggested by the cruise lines to heighten awareness of the role of personal hygiene in preventing the spread of infection. The norovirus causes nausea, vomiting, stomach cramps, and diarrhea. Usually the infection is not serious, but if you are elderly and have other medical conditions, it may pose a significant risk. Frequently washing your hands with soap and warm water is the best single means of preventing gastrointestinal infections. Other measures you can take while visiting foreign countries are cited below in the section "Preventing Infections."

Seasickness is less common these days on modern ocean liners due to built-in stabilizers that minimize the rocking motion that you experience. However, it still can be a problem if rough seas are encountered or if you are on a small boat. Seasickness is treated in a similar manner as motion sickness, described in the section "Air Travel." Try to concentrate on other thoughts. Stay above the decks so that you can focus on something other than the swaying of the ship. The fresh air may help. Look forward toward the horizon, but do not fixate your gaze. Try to find an area on the ship, probably toward the middle which has less motion. Drink fluids to avoid dehydration. Laying on a deck chair may help. Eat lightly. If necessary, ask your doctor for medicine; however, such medications may be associated with drowsiness and other side effects. Some studies have suggested that ginger is helpful, but other studies have suggested no benefit. Ginger can cause heartburn.

ALTITUDE

If contemplating a trip to a higher altitude, some of the precautions I mentioned for airplane flight are also appropriate, especially if you have heart or lung disease. Check with your doctor if there is any question. Altitude sickness can occur at elevations above 6000 feet (see Figure 35-4). In addition, the risk of altitude sickness depends on the rate of ascent.

(figure 35-3)

Some precautions can help avoid problems on that long-awaited cruise.

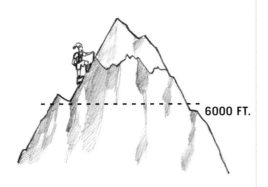

(figure 35-4)

Altitude sickness can occur at elevations over 6000 ft. The rate of ascent influences the risk of altitude sickness.

(figure 35-5)

Particular caution is necessary as you get older to avoid heat exhaustion and heat stroke. Drink more fluids if you are active

Interestingly, age and physical conditioning are not as important. In fact, altitude sickness may be more common in younger people because they tend to ascend more rapidly.

Medications that help prevent altitude sickness include ACETAZOLAMIDE (DIAMOX) and NIFEDIPINE (PROCARDIA, ADALAT). However, the most important measure you can take is ascending slowly. Another useful motto is, "Climb high. Sleep low." Returning to a lower altitude than you ascended to in order to sleep helps with acclimating to the higher altitudes. Restricting salt intake and consuming more complex carbohydrates (e.g., pasta, rice, and cereal) is recommended. Drink plenty of fluids but avoid alcoholic beverages.

If you develop symptoms of altitude sickness, such as headache, nausea, vomiting, weakness, sleep disturbance, or shortness of breath, seek medical attention. Medications and oxygen may be prescribed. Serious conditions such as high-altitude *pulmonary edema* (fluid in the lungs) or *cerebral edema* (brain swelling) require hospitalization.

HEAT AND COLD

Proper planning involves preparation for the temperatures to which you will be exposed. As you get older, your body's normal regulatory mechanisms for maintaining your body temperature become impaired. For example, in hot weather, you may not be able to reduce your body temperature by sweating as effectively as when you were younger. This can make you more prone to heat exhaustion or heat stroke. Heat exhaustion may cause light-headedness, fatigue, confusion, and even collapse, but responds to fluids and lying down. Occasionally intravenous fluids are required. *Heat stroke* is a medical emergency, by which the body temperature rises to dangerously high levels and leads to confusion, seizures, and even death if not treated aggressively. It is important to avoid overexertion in very hot weather. Try to get out early in the morning or late in the evening when the heat is less intense. Stay in an air-conditioned environment if it is hot and humid, as the humidity increases your risk. Drink plenty of fluids. If you are active (playing tennis or golf, for example), drink more than you feel you need (see Figure 35-5). If you notice that your urine looks dark or you are not urinating for several hours, you are not drinking enough. Push the fluids!

Pack your sunscreen (SPF 15 or greater). Certain medications are associated with photosensitivity, which means that you can break out in rash on sun-exposed areas. These medications include thiazide diuretics, sulfa drugs, nonsteroidal anti-inflammatory drugs, and amiodarone. Occasionally, the medications you take along to treat travel-related illnesses cause photosensitivity reactions, including the *quinolone antibiotics* (such as CIPROFLOXACIN) and TETRACYCLINE.

If you travel to a cold environment, pack warm clothing. If you are going to be skiing or engaged in outdoor activities, layer your clothing so that you can remove layers as you become more heated. Remember to wear a hat since a lot of heat is lost from the head. Mild cold injuries such as cold fingers and toes will respond to gentle rewarming. Frostbite is a serious condition associated with permanent damage to the body's tissues and requires medical attention. In some cases, surgical removal of the dead tissue is required.

More serious cold injuries are not uncommon in the very elderly. Most of us shiver if we get cold, which prompts us to put on more clothing. However, if you get very old, you may not have the same ability to regulate your body temperature, which can lead to a life-threatening condition, called hypothermia, by which the body temperature drops to very low levels. The result can be serious damage to the internal organs and even death. Unfortunately, most persons with hypothermia do not recognize the problem. They need to be identified by friends or family or medical personnel who notice mental confusion, drowsiness, or slurred speech. Certain medications and alcohol can increase the risk for hypothermia. The outcome for treatment of hypothermia in older persons is poor, so prevention is most important.

PREVENTING INFECTIONS

It is beyond the scope of this chapter to discuss all the infectious diseases that can be acquired during travel to foreign countries. These diseases should not prevent you from traveling as long as you have taken proper precautions. The focus here is on prevention. If you do get sick while traveling, you need to know where to get help. Factoring in the possibility of infection is important when you plan your itinerary. As noted in "For More Information," the International Association for Medical Assistance to Travelers is very helpful.

The first step is making sure you have received all the appropriate immunizations depending on the regions to which you are traveling. In addition, make sure you are up to date with your standard immunizations. The diphtheria-tetanus booster is recommended every 10 years after the primary series. Get your flu shot if you are traveling during the influenza season. If you are 65 or over, make sure you have had the *pneumococcal vaccine* (PNEUMOVAX).

If you travel to undeveloped countries, make sure your food is cooked and served hot. Avoid raw seafood, meat, and so forth. Food can be contaminated by the food handlers, so avoid raw fruit and vegetables unless you peel and cut it up yourself. Avoid buying food from street vendors. Avoid tap water and ice cubes. Boiled water, tea, and coffee are safer. Beverages in bottles and cans are generally safe, but wipe off the top of the can before drinking.

A common occurrence, traveler's diarrhea can be very serious for an older person who has other medical problems. The greatest risk for traveler's diarrhea is in going to South America, Africa, or Asia. Restoring fluid and electrolytes quickly is important. This can be done with bottled juices, decaffeinated soda, or water. Packets containing a powder of glucose and electrolytes that can be reconstituted are available worldwide. Salted crackers can be used. Avoid milk, cream, and dairy products if you have a gastrointestinal illness as transient lactose intolerance occurs. It is a good idea to let your doctor know that you will be visiting an undeveloped country, so that he or she can prescribe medication in the event you get traveler's diarrhea. Two recommended regimens are (1) CIPROFLOXACIN (CIPRO) 500 mg twice daily for three days and LOPERAMIDE (IMODIUM) 4 mg at the onset and then 2 mg with each loose bowel movement or (2) ciprofloxacin, 750 mg once and loperamide 4 mg at the onset, and 2 mg with each loose stool. If you are going to an area that has bacteria resistant to ciprofloxacin, such as Thailand, AZITHROMYCIN (ZITHROMAX) is an alternative. Taking antibiotics in anticipation of traveler's diarrhea is not recommended except in a high-risk situation.

Malaria presents a significant risk for the elderly. The chances of contracting malaria have increased as more older people visit places where malaria is common, and the death rate for malaria has increased. Therefore, caution is necessary if you decide to visit these places. Your doctor will prescribe medication for you, so it is important to let him or her know at least four or six weeks prior to your departure. Some malaria drugs are not recommended if you have certain heart conditions or one on certain heart medications. Your doctor will decide the appropriate regimen for you. Remember to bring insect repellant in your travel kit. Products with DEET are safe for the elderly.

Sexually transmitted disease (STD) is discussed in Chapter 22, but travelers should recognize that these diseases are worldwide.

TRAVEL KIT

A travel kit contains supplies for your trip, and you can make up your own kit or purchase one. Remember that security measures for airline travel do not allow such items as knives or scissors in your carry-on. If you keep your medical supplies in your luggage, be sure to bring enough prescription medications in your carry-on to last for a few days, so that you will still have your medications should your luggage be lost. If you have many medical problems, ask your doctor for a copy of your last complete medical examination to bring with you. If you have a problem on your trip, this will be very helpful to the doctor who is treating you. It can also save valuable time in an emergency. If you have a heart problem, bring a copy of your most recent electrocardiogram and the reports on any special tests, such as echocardiograms and stress tests. If you have kidney problems, copies of your laboratory work should be brought.

The contents of your travel kit will depend on the area to which you are going. Remember that common items available in the United States may not be readily obtained in other countries. If you are going to remote areas or to third-world countries, you may require special supplies for such injuries as lacerations, burns, and bites. Your physician may have some suggestions for your travel kit. You may be required to bring a letter from your doctor if you are carrying syringes, needles, narcotics, and so forth. But it is also helpful to keep in mind that not everyone speaks or reads English. I was painfully reminded of this when I went on a fishing trip with some friends to Venezuela. We were going to a very remote area in the interior, so I thought we should have some suture material in case one of us sustained a laceration. I was detained for several hours in the Caracas airport by two soldiers shouldering submachine guns and wondering why I was bringing in needles, syringes, and suture supplies. My medical license meant nothing to them. Gratefully, a Venezuelan who spoke English told the soldiers that I was a doctor, and the mess was cleared up. The moral of this story is that if you are going to bring these types of materials to a foreign country, it is probably a good idea to make sure you have your reasons translated into the language of the country to which you are going. Otherwise, your vacation may get off to a very uncomfortable start.

For additional guidance in putting together your travel kit, visit the following websites:

- www.mdtravelhealth.com
- www.travmed.com

WHAT YOU NEED TO KNOW

▶ Driving has major responsibilities. Recognize that as you get older, physical and mental changes affect your ability to drive. Follow the guidelines we cover in this chapter for safe driving. Learn to recognize the clues that indicate it is no longer safe for you to be driving.

▶ Travel is associated with health risks. The best way to reduce these risks is proper planning well in advance of your trip.

▶ Discuss the trip with your doctor who can provide medical information as well as medications. He or she may refer you to the local health department for immunizations or to a local travel clinic.

▶ Bring a travel kit.

35

FOR MORE INFORMATION

Centers for Disease Control
Travelers Health Information Hotline
Centers for Disease Control and Prevention
1600 Clifton Road
Atlanta, GA 30333
877-FYI-TRIP
Fax: 888-232-3299
Any information available by fax is also posted on the World Health Organization website.

World Health Organization
Web: www.who.int/en

International Association for Medical Assistance to Travelers
417 Center Street
Lewiston, NY 14092
716-754-4883
Web: www.iamat.org
Advises people on health risks associated with foreign travel; has information on doctors who are competent and speak English and on recommended immunizations.

American Diabetes Association
1701 North Beauregard Street
Alexandria, VA 22311
800-342-2383
E-mail: AskADA@diabetes.org

National Automobile Dealers Association
8400 Westpark Drive
McLean, VA 22102
703-821-7000
Web: www.nada.org

Superintendent of Documents
U.S. Government Printing Office
Washington, DC 20402
1-202-512-1800
To obtain a yellow card, which lists your immunizations and is recognized throughout the world. It costs $1, and the stock number is 017-001-00483-9.

Finish each day before you begin the next, and interpose a solid wall of sleep between the two. This you cannot do without temperance.

—*Ralph Waldo Emerson*

THE AUTHOR

36 ~~*Kevin W. O'Neil*~~

KEVIN W. O'NEIL, MD, FACP, graduated from Boston College magna cum laude and the Georgetown University School of Medicine. He did his internship at the Washington Hospital Center and his internal medicine residency at the University of Massachusetts Medical Center. He was an assistant professor in the Department of Internal Medicine at the University of Massachusetts Medical Center until moving to Sarasota, Florida, in 1984. He is currently an assistant professor of medicine at the University of South Florida College of Medicine. He is board-certified in internal medicine and holds a Certificate of Added Qualifications in Geriatric Medicine. He is a fellow of the American College of Physicians and a member of the American Geriatrics Society. He practices with the First Physicians Group in Sarasota and is on the staff at Sarasota Memorial Hospital and Doctors Hospital.

36 | SLEEP AND EXERCISE

■ SLEEP

Almost everyone has had a sleep problem, whether it is getting to sleep or staying asleep. Typical sleep complaints include such stressful times as financial worries, job anxieties, quarrels with your spouse or children, or nervousness about your teenager who has borrowed your car to go out with friends.

Sleep problems are more common as we get older. Over half the elderly experience disrupted sleep. This can be attributed to medical problems, such as pain from arthritis, a heart condition causing shortness of breath when you lie down, and heartburn, which is frequently worse at night. You may have to get up to go to the bathroom one or more times. During the menopause, many women experience interrupted sleep due to hot flashes. Such nervous system disorders as Parkinson's disease and Alzheimer's disease are often accompanied by sleep disturbances.

No matter the cause, sleep problems pose a significant concern for doctors and their patients. Poor sleep can result in irritability, problems with concentration, and driving accidents. Falls and hip fractures are another consequence of disrupted sleep.

In brief, you want a good night's sleep, and I'm here to tell you how to find that.

NORMAL SLEEP

Have you ever heard someone say, "I hate losing a third of my life in bed"? Sleep is not a waste of time, because a lot is happening during your slumber that is important for proper functioning. Sleep is divided into two general stages: rapid eye movement (REM) and non-rapid eye movement (NREM) sleep. REM sleep correlates with dreaming, and your muscles, except for the eye muscles, are relaxed. NREM sleep is divided into four stages:

1. Transitional phase between being awake and falling asleep
2. First real period of being asleep
3. Deeper sleep
4. Deepest sleep

You can be awakened quite readily during stages 1 and 2 but not so readily during stages 3 and 4. NREM sleep is usually followed by REM sleep. Normally, you have four to five cycles of NREM and REM sleep at night. The average amount of sleep for most adults is around 7 to 8 hours; however, normal variability would include your feeling rested after only 6 hours or requiring 9 hours of sleep.

Several changes occur during aging. The time spent in stage 1 sleep increases, while stage 4 sleep decreases. More time in a lighter stage of sleep results in more frequent awakenings since minor intrusions, such as the sound of a siren, a jet airplane, or a passing truck, can readily arouse you. Arthritis or other pain can get your attention more easily.

If you have retired and enjoy late mornings, your additional time in bed does not mean your total amount of sleep has increased. Some people do not get a good night's sleep but nap during the day, which affects sleep quality at night. If you have to get up early in the morning and disrupt your sleep, or if you did not get enough sleep, you build a "sleep debt." The debt has to be repaid; if not, you will experience problems with daytime sleepiness, your concentration, and your mood.

SLEEP DISORDERS

Everyone experiences transient sleep problems. However, if your sleep difficulty is persisting or you are excessively tired during the day, you need further evaluation. A variety of symptoms suggest that you could have a sleep disorder. Remember that a symptom is a manifestation of a problem and not the actual cause. Discuss your symptoms with your doctor who can then determine the cause and recommend a cure. Following are the names and descriptions of common sleep disorders.

- *Insomnia.* Do you have the perception of not getting to sleep or not getting enough sleep? Do you wake up frequently at night? In the morning, do you feel that you did not have enough rest?
- *Excessive snoring.* Does your spouse complain about your snoring or wake you up to move you onto your side? Do you and your spouse sleep in separate bedrooms because of your snoring? If your spouse snores, does your spouse ever seem to stop breathing or to be struggling to breathe? Do you use nose strips at night to prevent snoring?
- *Jumpy legs.* Do you wake up because your legs are jerking? Do your legs feel restless so that you have to get up and walk around? Do you have uncomfortable crawling sensations under the skin of your legs?
- *Daytime tiredness.* Do you feel tired all the time? Do you nap frequently during the day? Do you fall asleep while reading the newspaper or watching the television? Have you fallen asleep in the middle of conversations? Have you fallen asleep while driving? Do you ever have "sleep attacks" by which you suddenly fall asleep without any warning?
- *Sleep interruptions.* Do you stay awake because of pain, heartburn, or shortness of breath? Do minor noises wake you from sleep? Does your bed partner wake you from sleep because of snoring, jumpy legs, or getting up? Do you frequently get up to go to the bathroom?
- *Trouble concentrating.* Do you find it difficult to focus? Is it hard to remember what you have read? Are you more irritable due to tiredness?

SLEEP DISORDER EVALUATION

The first step if you or your spouse suspects a sleep disorder is to inform your doctor. He or she will usually obtain a medical history and perform a physical examination. More than likely, he or she will obtain blood tests to exclude common disorders, such as hypothyroidism (an underactive

(*figure* 36-1)

36

Sample sleep diary. Fill out for seven days. *(Courtesy of the National Sleep Foundation).*

COMPLETE IN MORNING	DAY 1
I went to bed last night at:	PM/AM
I got out of bed this morning at:	PM/AM
Last night, I fell asleep in:	Minutes
I woke up during the night:	Times
When I woke up for the day, I felt:	○ Refreshed ○ Somewhat refreshed ○ Fatigued
Last night I slept a total of:	Hours
My sleep was disturbed by: *(List any mental, emotional, physical or environmental factors; e.g. stress, snoring, physical discomfort, temperature).*	

COMPLETE AT END OF DAY	
I consumed caffeinated drinks in the:	○ Morning ○ Afternoon ○ Within several hours before going to bed ○ Not applicable
I exercised at least 20 minutes in the:	○ Morning ○ Afternoon ○ Within several hours before going to bed ○ Not applicable
Approximately 2-3 hours before going to bed I consumed:	○ Alcohol ○ A heavy meal ○ Not applicable
Medication(s) I took during the day:	
About 1 hour before going to sleep, I did the following activity:	

thyroid), **hyperthyroidism** (an overactive thyroid), and diabetes, which may impact your sleep. Bring a sleep diary, such as the sample shown in Figure 36-1. (A blank sleep diary can be obtained from the National Sleep Foundation, listed in "For More Information.") Your bed partner may be able to provide details of your sleep history that even you didn't know. In many cases, your primary care doctor will develop a treatment plan after the cause is determined. In some cases, your doctor may refer you to a sleep specialist for a special test called a **polysomnogram**. This is a test done in a specialized sleep laboratory in which your breathing, heart rhythm, and brain wave activity are monitored while you sleep (see Figure 36-2).

SLEEP DISORDER CAUSES AND TREATMENTS

Although more than sixty sleep disorders have been described, the following are those disorders that more commonly affect the elderly.

Sleep apnea: Apnea means absence of breathing. *Sleep apnea* describes those individuals who have periods during sleep when they transiently stop breathing. There are three types. **Central sleep apnea** is due to a problem in how the brain regulates breathing. This is usually due to a neurological disease, such as a stroke, or it may be related to heart or kidney failure. A potentially serious and actually quite common cause of daytime tiredness, headache, and high blood pressure is **obstructive sleep apnea**. This condition is more common in older persons and in those

(*figure* 36-2)

A sleep laboratory can assist your doctor in diagnosing a sleep problem.

who are overweight or drink too much alcohol (see Chapter 6). Their spouse often complains about their snoring. They may have no clue about the problem. Mixed apnea is a combination of central and obstructive sleep apnea.

Central sleep apnea is managed by identifying and treating the underlying problem. For example, congestive heart failure may require use of oxygen, water pills, digitalis, and other medications. Kidney failure may require dialysis. In some cases, antidepressants, such as PROTRIPTYLINE (VIVACTIL), have been tried, but the results have been inconsistent. Other treatments have included ACETAZOLAMIDE (DIAMOX), THEOPHYLLINE (used occasionally by persons with asthma and COPD), and PROGESTERONE. If breathing is severely impaired, usually as a result from brain injury or stroke, a mechanical ventilator is the only option; generally, the prognosis for these patients is poor.

For managing obstructive sleep apnea, see Chapter 6.

Periodic limb movement disorder: Periodic limb movement disorder (PLMS, also called *nocturnal myoclonus)* describes abnormal movements usually in the legs while you are sleeping. This condition is often associated with jerking of the legs that may wake you from sleep. This is different from *nocturnal leg cramps,* those painful spasms of the calf and foot muscles at night.

PLMS may respond to medicines used for Parkinson's disease, such as LEVODOPA/CARBIDOPA (SINEMET). Other options include sedative medication, such as CLONAZEPAM (KLONOPIN), or pain relievers; however, these can have undesirable side effects and require close monitoring by a physician.

Restless leg syndrome: Restless leg syndrome (RLS) is the very uncomfortable sensation of something crawling or creeping under your skin. You might feel that your legs are jumpy or restless. There is an irresistible urge to move the legs. It usually occurs at night when relaxing and often forces you to get up and move around or massage your legs.

Treatment involves good sleep hygiene (see the box "Ten Tips for a Good Night's Sleep"); avoidance of alcohol and caffeine; and eating a well-balanced diet. Limit those activities that you notice tend to aggravate the condition. Your doctor should check you for iron deficiency and recommend iron supplements if necessary. In some cases, other medications are tried, including levodopa carbidopa, sedatives, pain relievers, or antiseizure drugs, such as GABAPENTIN (NEURONTIN). As always, you have to weigh the benefit versus the risk of taking medication.

Nocturnal leg cramps: Nocturnal leg cramps are sudden painful spasms of the calf and occasionally the foot muscles that jolt you out of a sound sleep (see Figure 36-3). Often they respond to massaging the muscles. They can be frequent and have adverse effects on the quality of your sleep. No one really knows what causes them, but your doctor will check to make sure there is no underlying medical problem. A simple stretching exercise before you go to bed can help reduce or eliminate them. Stand at an arm's length from a wall with your palms against the

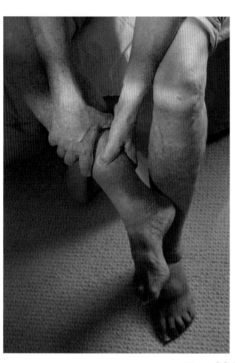

(figure 36-3)

Painful nighttime leg cramps disrupt sleep.

wall. Keeping your feet flat and your back straight, move toward the wall by letting your elbows bend. You will feel the stretching in the calf muscles in back of your legs. Hold this position for about a half a minute and then straighten up. Repeat the exercise a few times.

Occasionally drug treatment is required. QUININE is the most commonly used medication, but caution is required. At one time it was readily available over the counter, but the FDA had it removed due to sporadic cases of aplastic anemia, a potentially fatal condition caused by failure of the bone marrow to make blood cells. One alternative is to drink tonic water, which contains a small amount of quinine. If you take quinine by prescription, you should have periodic blood tests. Other people have tried vitamin E, antihistamines, muscle relaxants, and calcium-channel blockers. You and your doctor can decide which treatment is best for you if you do not respond to simple exercises.

Malfunctioning body clock: You have a natural sleep-wake cycle. Your body clock says that between midnight and 7 A.M. and between 1 and 4 P.M. you will be more tired. If not getting enough sleep, you will be more likely to fall asleep during these times, which is when motor vehicle accidents are more likely to occur in sleep-deprived people.

Jet lag can also influence your sleep (see Chapter 35). Some of the other conditions that can disrupt your natural sleep-wake cycle include the following:

Shift work: If you have a late-night shift, you are awake when other people are asleep. Most shift workers do not get as much sleep in a 24-hour period as those who work in the daytime. Trying to sleep during the daytime is difficult because of daytime activities and noise around the house, such as televisions, radios, and telephones. Treatment may require that you work a predictable schedule rather than keeping the night shift. Alternatively, you can try increasing the time devoted to sleep or taking a nap to make sure your total amount of sleep is adequate. Reducing distractions while you sleep is important. Keeping your bedroom dark and quiet, unplugging the telephone, or using an answering machine are helpful measures. Increasing the brightness of the light where you work may be tried. Occasionally prescription medication is required, but this should be done only intermittently. It is not wise to take medicine from someone else or to order sleeping pills from internet sites.

Delayed or advanced sleep phase syndromes: If you have delayed or advanced sleep phase syndromes, your body clock has adjusted to a different time setting. For example, you may not be able to get to sleep until the early hours of the morning, but then you sleep until 11 A.M. or later. In advanced sleep phase syndrome, you go to sleep at an early hour, say 7 or 8 P.M., but are up at 3 or 4 in the morning. Treatment for this may require that you plan your time to go to sleep slightly earlier or later, depending on which problem you have. In delayed sleep phase syndrome, if you have been going to bed at 3 A.M., you would go to bed the first few nights at 2:30 A.M. and then gradually earlier every few nights until you adjust to the new time schedule. This may take several weeks. In advanced sleep phase syndrome, gradually going to bed later and increasing your exposure to bright light should be tried.

Mental stress: Dwelling on stressful events or situations in your life, resulting in anxiety and depression, can make it difficult to sleep properly. Depression can also cause you to wake up in the early morning hours, and then you have difficulty getting back to sleep. It is important to understand that you do not have to feel sad to be depressed. You may simply have lost interest in doing things you enjoyed previously or feel that your zest for life isn't what it used to be. You may dread waking up in the morning or merely look on the day ahead as "just another day" of drudgery. (See Chapter 25 for information about anxiety and depression.)

Treatment for mental stress requires reassurance or counseling. Discuss your problem with your doctor. Occasionally, short-term use of sleep medicines is necessary, but often the problem will respond to treatment of the anxiety and/or depression. Do not resort to using over-the-counter sleep aids, which generally are antihistamines. Although causing drowsiness, antihistamines also cause mental confusion, dry mouth, constipation, and even the inability to urinate. If you have angle closure glaucoma, antihistamines can precipitate an acute glaucoma crisis (an abrupt rise of the pressure within the eye). Alcohol may initially relax you and make you feel drowsy, but it can disrupt the quality of your sleep. In addition, alcohol makes depression worse.

Narcolepsy: Narcolepsy usually has its onset in your younger years. However, not much attention was paid to sleep disorders by physicians in years past. Therefore, there are older persons who have managed to live with this condition untreated for years. Public campaigns in recent years have helped heighten awareness about sleep disorders, and more of these people are seeking medical attention. If you experience any of the following, you should be evaluated by your doctor:

- Uncontrollable "sleep attacks" during the day.
- Transient loss of muscle tone (cataplexy), which may be triggered by emotions such as joy, fear, or anger. Although it can involve the whole body, muscles around the face, arms, and knees are involved more often. Thus, falls can occur.
- Sleep paralysis just before falling asleep or after waking up. You cannot move or speak despite being awake. This is very frightening.
- Hypnagogic hallucination. These hallucinations have been compared to dreaming while awake, in that you see, hear, or feel things while you are conscious.

There is no cure for narcolepsy. Treatment may involve use of such stimulants as METHYLPHENIDATE (RITALIN) or AMPHETAMINE and DEXTROAMPHETAMINE (ADDERALL). Addiction is usually not a problem with these drugs in narcolepsy, but monitoring is required since they may cause high blood pressure, excitability, and other adverse effects. Alternatively, MODAFINIL (PROVIGIL) helps reduce daytime sleepiness.

PROTRIPTYLINE (VIVACTIL) is an antidepressant that is useful in managing various manifestations of narcolepsy, such as cataplexy, sleep paralysis, and hypnagogic hallucinations. If dry mouth and constipation are troublesome, try NORTRIPTYLINE (PAMELOR) instead.

All narcoleptics should try nondrug measures as well. Such measures include regular exercise, light meals, brief naps, keeping active, and avoiding tranquilizers. Caffeinated beverages can be used if not restricted by other medical conditions.

Medication: Some medicines have adverse effects on sleep. For example, beta-blockers used to treat high blood pressure and heart conditions sometimes cause nightmares. Included in various over-the-counter pain relievers, caffeine can make it difficult for you to get to sleep, and you may tend to wake up more frequently. Cold remedies that contain pseudoephedrine (Sudafed) may stimulate you and keep you awake. If diuretics force you to get up at night to go to the bathroom, take them earlier in the day. Some asthma medicines have stimulatory effects and make it difficult to get to sleep.

If you are experiencing sleep problems, let your doctor review your medicines to see if any of them are contributing to the problem. If you noticed that the difficulty started with initiation of a new medicine, tell your doctor, but do not stop any medicine unless you have discussed it with your physician.

Environment: Good sleep requires a restful environment. Therefore, noisy environments are not conducive to a restful night. In addition, very hot or cold temperatures may impair the quality of your sleep. Even a poor-quality mattress can be disruptive. If living at home, you can make changes to correct these problems. However, you won't have the same choice in a hospital or a nursing home. Most facilities are now taking measures to minimize the sleep interruptions. However, problems still occur. You may have difficulty sleeping in a hospital because you are in an unfamiliar place and bed. Other patients on the floor may require medical attention. Alarms, beepers, and overhead paging systems don't help the situation. The room temperature may not be to your liking. Your roommate might be a "night owl" who wants to keep the television on. In nursing homes, similar difficulties are encountered. In addition, nursing homes often have set routines, which may not be in harmony with your normal sleep-wake cycle. Perhaps a resident has Alzheimer's disease or another mental illness that leads to disruptive behavior.

Sleeping medication is used much less often in these situations. Initial focus should be on modifying the factors that have caused the problem in the first place. You may need to take an active role. If your medical condition is stable, it may not be necessary to wake you up at night to take your vital signs. If your roommate has different sleep habits, you can request a change to another room. Medications may be necessary in some cases. These should be used for short periods of time with care to avoid sleeping medicines that stay in the body for a long time.

From the previous discussion, you have learned that it is best if you are having sleep problems, especially insomnia, to avoid caffeine, alcohol,

36

and smoking before you go to bed. They may stimulate you or affect the quality of your sleep. In addition, exercising just before you retire might energize you and make it more difficult to get to sleep. Although many people read or watch television in bed before going to sleep, you should avoid these activities if you have insomnia. Part of your "training" for proper sleep is to restrict the use of the bed to sleep and sex. Such measures as a comfortable mattress and a quiet environment make sense, but most studies suggest that none of these things really solves the problem for someone who truly has insomnia.

For those of you who have trouble falling asleep and staying asleep despite these simple measures, clinical studies have shown that *sleep restriction* and *stimulus control* therapies offer the best nondrug approaches to sleep. In the sleep restriction approach, the total time in bed is limited to 7 or 8 hours, no matter how much time you are actually asleep. If you only sleep 4 hours, you still get out of bed after 7 or 8 hours, no matter how tired you might be. In addition, you have to fight the urge to nap during the day. This allows you to build up a sleep debt that eventually will help you overcome your insomnia. Once you are sleeping through the night, you can gradually increase your time in bed.

Stimulus control therapy includes the simple measures we discussed, such as limiting your use of caffeine, alcohol, and smoking just before retiring. You limit the use of the bed to sex and sleep, but you are required to go to bed only when tired. In addition, once in bed, if you have trouble falling asleep, you have to get up and engage in some unexciting activity, such as light reading. You also have to get out of bed if you awake in the middle of the night and don't get back to sleep within 15 minutes. The purpose here is to remove the association of insomnia and your bed. You are required to wake up at the same time each morning, no matter how tired you are, and you are not allowed to nap during the day.

As you might imagine, these techniques are not easy, and it is best that during the daytime you not operate a motor vehicle or engage in other activities that require mental alertness while you are attempting them. If you have tried one or both of these techniques for two weeks and are still experiencing insomnia, discuss it with your physician. A short course of drug treatment may be helpful.

MEDICATION FOR SLEEP

Physicians are usually reluctant to prescribe medications on a continual basis for sleep. The main reason is that you might develop a physical or psychological dependency, which can be difficult to break. Treatment will be aimed at the underlying cause for your sleep disorder, as reviewed above. However, there are situations in which short-term use of sleeping pills is helpful, such as an acute life stress (death of a spouse or loss of a job), if the sleep deprivation augments the stress. The important principle is to limit the medications for no more than two or three weeks. Occasional use for sporadic episodes of insomnia is reasonable. If you require sleeping pills for longer periods of time, you should try not to use the pills more than two or three times a week.

Since drug metabolism alters as you get older (see Chapter 33), a sleeping pill should be chosen that is less likely to accumulate in your body. Otherwise, the medication may affect your mental and physical activities during the daytime. Table 36-1 includes medicines that have been used for sleep and comments about benefits and risks.

If you have a loved one with Alzheimer's disease or other types of dementia, agitation and excitability at night can be a problem. You may hear this called **sundowning,** a term for behavioral problems (wandering, yelling, and/or fighting) which can disrupt your household or, if your loved one resides in a nursing home or assisted living facility, the routine of the nursing staff and other residents. There are ways other than medications to manage this type of problem-behavior. Establishing a consistent daily routine and minimizing stimulating activities in the mid- and late afternoon are helpful. Allow some quiet time later in the afternoon when your loved one can be alone. All of us need time by ourselves now and then. Keep the physical space relatively simple. Too much clutter can aggravate the confusion. Make sure there isn't any physical reason for discomfort, such as arthritis pain, constipation, hunger, or fatigue. The doctor can help manage discomfort by prescribing arthritis medications, stool softeners, and so forth. A midafternoon snack or nap may be warranted. If he or she is incontinent, find out whether the undergarments or diaper is dry or requires changing. If these measures are unsuccessful, the doctor may use medications.

EXERCISE

It is exercise alone that supports the spirits, and keeps the mind in vigor.
—Cicero.

No other activity has such a great effect on so many aspects of aging and health as exercise. Starting a lifetime program of exercise helps prevent

(*table* 36-1)
SLEEP MEDICATIONS AND OLDER PERSONS

MEDICINE	COMMENTS
Chlordiazepoxide (Librium) Diazepam (Valium)	Tranquilizer; can accumulate in your body with repeated use and cause daytime performance problems. Should be avoided.
Estazolam (ProSom) Temazepam (Restoril)	Less likely to cause daytime sedation.
Flurazepam (Dalmane)	Remains in the body too long and may affect daytime performance. Should be avoided.
Lorazepam (Ativan)	A short-acting tranquilizer; useful in short-term for sleep.
Trazodone (Desyrel)	Antidepressant; beneficial for depressed persons with sleep problems. In low doses, may be helpful to some persons with chronic insomnia. In men, a painful erection requiring emergency treatment is a rare side effect.
Triazolam (Halcion)	Short duration of action but likely to result in rebound insomnia when discontinued.
Zaleplon (Sonata) Zolpidem (Ambien)	Short-acting sleep medicine; less likely to cause rebound insomnia or memory problems.

many diseases, including hypertension, diabetes, osteoporosis, and heart disease. Exercise can even help preserve our mental functioning and reduce the risk of falls and injury in later life. Even if exercise has not been an important part of your life up until now, it is never too late to start and reap the benefits it provides.

After you have been evaluated properly to ensure that the exercise will not provoke any more serious problems, ask your doctor to get you started. If you have a medical problem, such as diabetes, exercising helps to lose weight and improve your blood sugar. If you have arthritis, swimming and "aqua-aerobics" can improve the flexibility of your joints and cause less pain than walking does. If you are very old and have heart and lung problems, you might find any exercise exhausting. In that case and for similar circumstances, you start by being evaluated by your doctor who can recommend an exercise therapist, a physical trainer, a physical therapist, or a fitness facility.

An evaluation by your physician is important before initiating an exercise program for a variety of reasons. Heart disease is the number-one killer of Americans. The chances of having coronary artery disease with minimal or no symptoms increase as you get older. You might attribute limited exercise tolerance and shortness of breath with exercise to poor conditioning when, in fact, these symptoms may signal a severe underlying heart disease that puts you at risk for a heart attack. You do not need to have chest pain to have heart disease! Some persons may feel a squeezing or tightness in the chest. Your doctor may want you to have an exercise test (also called a *stress test)* to see if there are any changes on your electrocardiogram that suggest that you are at risk for a heart attack. If you have lung disease, your blood oxygen may drop with exercise. For this reason, your doctor may want you in a supervised pulmonary rehabilitation program so that your blood oxygen can be monitored with a finger-clip device. Oxygen can be administered if it drops below a certain level. If you have arthritis, he or she may caution you to avoid activities that overstress an arthritic joint.

(figure 36-4)

Walking is a great exercise.

Although the cautions discussed above are important when exercising in your older years, it is generally accepted by everyone that exercise is good for you. Research studies have shown that exercise can retard the decline in physiological functions that occur with aging. If you do not exercise, your exercise capacity will decrease, which means that you become more inactive. This, in turn, leads to weight gain, immobility, and other illnesses, such as hypertension and diabetes. Exercise has shown benefits in the treatment of many medical conditions, including osteoporosis, diabetes, and sleep disorders. Clinical studies in recent years have yielded exciting results: regular aerobic exercise may preserve brain and nervous system function as we age.

Exercise programs involve endurance, flexibility, strengthening, and balance. Endurance exercise consists of those activities that increase your aerobic fitness, such as walking, swimming, running, rowing, and bicycling (see Figure 36-4). They require repetitive movement of the large muscles of the arms and legs and increase the heart rate in order to supply blood and oxygen to the muscles. Some people use their maximum-predicted heart rate as a guide to how hard they should exercise. However, many medicines affect the ability of the heart rate to increase with exercise, including beta-blockers and calcium channel antagonists. The Borg scale is a useful alternative in which your activity level is determined by how hard you feel you are working. This scale is fully explained in an excellent publication, *Exercise: A Guide from the National Institute on Aging.* I highly recommend *Exercise,* which is free. Ordering information is in the section "For More Information," under NIA Information Center.

Flexibility or stretching exercises enhance the mobility of your joints and allow you to move around more freely. Be careful if you have had joint replacement surgery or if you have osteoporosis. Balance exercises are designed to reduce your risk of falling, which can result in bone fractures or head injuries, and improve the strength of the leg muscles. Studies have also shown the benefits of Tai Chi, an ancient Chinese discipline. Many hospitals and YMCAs now offer balance training and Tai Chi.

Strength training involves weights to build muscle mass (see Figure 36-5). If you are a man between 40 and 50 years of age and are not doing strength training, you are likely to lose 10 pounds of muscle and gain 10 pounds of fat. If you are a woman in this age range and not doing strength training, you are likely to lose 10 pounds of muscle and gain 15 pounds of fat. The good news is that strength training is beneficial into very advanced age. Muscle mass can be built and strength improved even for persons in their 80s or 90s, so you are never too old to start! Just make sure you have discussed it with your doctor, in case you have a condition that limits strength training.

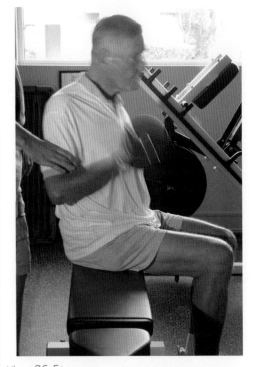

(figure 36-5)

Strength training builds muscle mass that benefits both men and women.

WHAT YOU NEED TO KNOW

))) Sleep is an active time during which you recharge yourself. Proper functioning of your body and mind requires sleep. Poor sleep can cause irritability, problems with concentration, and accidents.

))) Many older persons experience sleep problems. Treatment depends on the cause of the problem. Talk to your doctor who can evaluate your problem or refer you to a sleep specialist.

))) Avoid over-the-counter sleep aids, which have adverse effects on older persons.

))) Discuss any chronic problem about sleeping with your doctor, who may prescribe sleep medication for transient sleeping difficulties. Try to avoid long-term use, but if longer periods of medication are required, take it no more than two or three times a week.

))) Exercise has many benefits that enhance your optimal aging. It is never too late to start. If you have been inactive, discuss your exercise program with your doctor first.

36

FOR MORE INFORMATION

National Sleep Foundation
1522 K Street NW Suite 500
Washington, DC 20005
Fax: 202-347-3472
E-mail: nsf@sleepfoundation.org
Web: www.sleepfoundation.org

National Institute on Aging
National Institutes of Health
Building 31, Room 5C27
Bethesda, MD 20892
800-222-2225
TTY: 800-222-4225
Web: www.nih.gov/nia

National Heart, Lung, and Blood Institute
National Institutes of Health
Building 31, Room 4A21
Bethesda, MD 20892
800-575-9355
Web: www.nhlbi.nih.gov

American Sleep Apnea Association
1424 K Street, NW, suite 302
Washington, DC 20005
202-293-3650
Fax: 202-293-3656
E-mail: asaa@sleepapnea.org
Web: www.sleepapnea.org

Better Sleep Council
Web: www.bettersleep.org
A nonprofit organization supported by the mattress industry, the Better Sleep Council educates the public about sleep and its effects on quality of life.

Narcolepsy Network
10921 Reed Hartman Highway, Suite 119
Cincinnati, OH 45242
513-891-3522
Web: www.narcolepsynetwork.org

Restless Legs Syndrome Foundation
819 Second Street SW
Rochester, Minnesota 559002
507-287-6465
E-mail: rlsfoundation@rls.org
Web: www.rls.org

NIA Information Center
P.O. Box 8057
Gaithersburg, MD 20898
800-222-2225
TTY: 800-222-4225
E-mail: niaic@jbs1.com
Free publication available, *Exercise: A Guide from the National Institute on Aging,* which can be ordered by e-mail, mail, or telephone. The exercises are demonstrated by Margaret Richard, star of Body Electric, in an excellent video (which includes a companion booklet), available for a small fee.

I feel that our attitude as a profession should not be hostile, and we must scan gently our brother man and sister woman who may be carried away in the winds of new doctrine [alternative medicine].

—Sir William Osler, The Faith That Heals

THE AUTHOR

37

KEVIN W. O'NEIL, MD, FACP, graduated from Boston College magna cum laude and the Georgetown University School of Medicine. He did his internship at the Washington Hospital Center and his internal medicine residency at the University of Massachusetts Medical Center. He was an assistant professor in the Department of Internal Medicine at the University of Massachusetts Medical Center until moving to Sarasota, Florida, in 1984. He is currently an assistant professor of medicine at the University of South Florida College of Medicine. He is board-certified in internal medicine and holds a Certificate of Added Qualifications in Geriatric Medicine. He is a fellow of the American College of Physicians and a member of the American Geriatrics Society. He practices with the First Physicians Group in Sarasota and is on the staff at Sarasota Memorial Hospital and Doctors Hospital.

37 | ALTERNATIVE MEDICINE

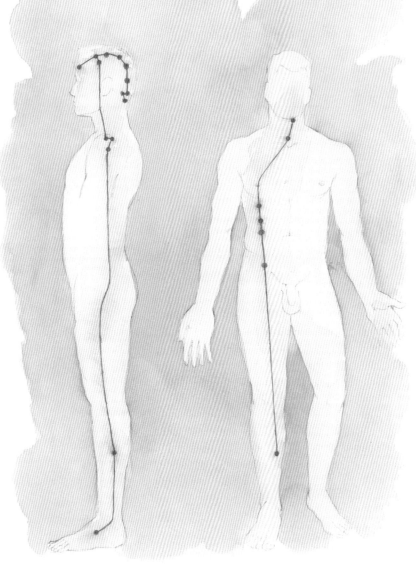

(figure 37-1)

Acupuncture involves the insertion of very thin needles into various body points that are believed to be connected to pathways called meridians.

In the past, most physicians equated alternative medicine with quackery. Although traditional medical practice has always combined the art of medicine with the science of medicine, medical doctors base most of their decisions regarding which diagnostic tests to order and which treatments to prescribe on scientific and clinical research. Studies published in reputable medical journals by respected researchers help guide doctors in their care of patients. Although some tests and treatments used in medical practice are potentially dangerous, the physician might order these tests and treatments if the benefits outweigh the risks. The guiding principle is to do what is best for you, the patient.

Therefore, physicians are by nature skeptical about treatments touted to be effective based on anecdotes or on opinions not backed by sound scientific or clinical research. However, in recent years, more and more physicians have been willing to explore alternative forms of therapy, especially in areas for which traditional medical treatments have failed or the results have not been satisfying. In addition, a significant number of people want to avoid prescription drugs and prefer to try natural remedies, such as herbs, vitamins and minerals, and physical modalities.

Billions of dollars are spent each year on alternative therapies. However, it is important to remember that these treatments might not always be effective and can occasionally be harmful. If you are in the baby-boomer generation or older, you probably remember the laetrile fiasco—millions of people jumped on a bandwagon based on anecdotes and health claims supported by poor research to legalize the use of laetrile in the treatment of advanced cancer. However, in the early 1980s the National Cancer Institute conducted a clinical study that proved the worthlessness of laetrile. As long as we have diseases that can't be cured, some people will promote unorthodox therapies with their motive being monetary gain. Among the especially vulnerable are those with cancer or other terminal diseases. Hopefully, this chapter will help protect you against unorthodox treatments while opening your mind to the potential benefits of new therapies.

How do you know which treatments are safe and which are effective? The National Institutes of Health has formed the National Center for Complementary and Alternative Medicine (NCCAM). NCCAM provides information to doctors and the public about alternative treatments that work and those that don't. Their findings are based on good scientific and clinical research, not on opinion or hearsay. In the following pages, I summarize the basic information that you should have in order to make an informed decision on whether to use certain alternative therapies. It is beyond the scope of this chapter to evaluate each herb, supplement, or alternative health practice. In "For More Information" at the end of the chapter, I list websites and organizations having comprehensive coverage. The topics that I discuss with you in this chapter are those that most of my patients ask about. These include herbs and supplements, chiropractic, acupuncture (see Figure 37-1), and cancer treatments. Although some older persons pursue yoga, aromatherapy, and hypnosis, I seldom see this in my geriatric practice, so I would suggest that you consult one of the resources in "For More Information" to learn more about these modalities.

It is estimated that as many as 40% of the American people use some type of alternative treatment. It is especially disturbing that most do not disclose this information to their doctors. The reason most often cited for this is that since these methods are considered safe, many people do not think it is important. If there is any one message that I can get across to you in this chapter, it is to let your doctor know *everything* you are taking. Bring all your medicines, including any vitamins or herbal supplements, with you to each office visit. That way your doctor can review them and make sure that you are not taking anything that will interact with your prescription medications. In addition, if you are having some health difficulties, he or she can determine if any of your medicines or supplements are causing or contributing to the problem. Some excellent resources are available to assist your doctor. No person can remember every single potential drug-drug or drug-herb interaction if you consider the thousands of medicines, herbs, and possible combinations. Computer applications enable your doctor to enter all your drugs and supplements and check for potentially dangerous interactions.

HERBS

Many people think that any "natural" product is safe. This is far from the truth. *Ephedra* has been promoted as an aid to weight loss or to enhance athletic performance. It was originally derived from a leaf, but can be synthesized in a laboratory. However, ephedra has been linked to serious heart arrhythmias, hypertension, and sudden death.

Many people take herbs or other supplements because a friend told them about it or they read a compelling advertisement. It is important to remember that you are different from anyone else, and the way you react to something may be totally different from someone else. In addition, many of these products can interact with prescription medications.

A significant number of complications following surgery have been linked to the failure of patients to tell an anesthesiologist that they were taking herbal supplements. Some supplements have been responsible for

WHAT'S NEW?

As *Optimal Aging Manual* was going to press, the Food and Drug Administration (FDA) announced that it plans to prohibit the sales of supplements containing ephedra. This is the first time in history that the FDA has barred the sale of a dietary supplement. Many deaths have been linked to ephedra. This serves to underscore the fact that many herbal supplements have not been regulated by the FDA. The most prudent course is to check with your doctor before taking any of these supplements to make sure they will not adversely interact with your prescription medication or have deleterious effects on your other medical conditions.

bleeding complications, as well as postoperative high blood pressure and heart rhythm disturbances. Garlic and ginkgo biloba, for example, may increase the risk of bleeding by altering the way that clotting occurs. If a patient is taking WARFARIN (COUMADIN) after surgery to reduce the risk of blood clots, these herbs can adversely interact with the drug and cause very serious bleeding.

From this discussion, you may wonder if it is ever safe to take a supplement. I strongly suggest that you ask your doctor. He or she is most familiar with your medical history and your medications. You need to be especially careful if you are very advanced in age and have multiple medical problems. You should also be aware that the Food and Drug Administration (FDA) does not regulate herbal products in the same way as prescription medications. As a result, manufacturers of herbal products are not held to the same standard of quality, efficacy, and safety.

Clinical research has shown some promise with some of these products. For example, *glucosamine* and *chondroitin sulfate* may help persons with arthritis. The NIH is conducting a study called the GAIT trial to determine whether the efficacy of glucosamine and chondroitin, alone or in combination, is more effective than a placebo is in controlling knee pain from osteoarthritis. Why is a placebo-controlled trial important? A placebo is a "dummy" pill, which does nothing. Our minds are susceptible to suggestion. If you think something is going to help, it likely will. If you think something is going to give you side effects, it probably will. Therefore, when studying whether a drug is effective, it is important to have a group that gets the active drug and a group that gets a placebo. That way researchers can determine if the drug really helped or caused side effects, based on the comparison to a placebo group.

Many menopausal women use *black cohosh* to treat hot flashes. Initial studies have suggested as much as a 70% reduction in hot flashes. Although there were some initial concerns that black cohosh could act similarly to estrogen and cause an increase in breast and uterine cancers, this does not seem to be the case. The NIH is conducting a study comparing the effects of black cohosh to placebo.

Saw palmetto is used by many men to relieve the symptoms caused by an enlarged prostate gland (saw palmetto is discussed in Chapter 11). Numerous reports from men who take the supplement, as well as some clinical studies, have suggested that saw palmetto is beneficial, and it is generally well tolerated. The NCCAM is conducting the STEP (Saw palmetto in the Treatment of Enlarged Prostates) study to determine whether saw palmetto is useful based on objective tests and symptom improvement.

St. John's wort is commonly used to treat depression, and it might be helpful in mild to moderate depression. However, it can interact with many prescription drugs. St. John's wort can decrease the efficacy of WARFARIN in blood clotting, and it can significantly decrease the blood levels of DIGOXIN (LANOXIN). This may reduce the efficacy of digoxin. Therefore, do not use St. John's wort unless you have discussed it with your doctor.

DOCTOR'S DIARY

My golf partner Nick M., 68, was experiencing more and more pain in his knees. He loved to golf and walk, and he was getting frustrated that he could only go a few blocks from his house on his morning walk before he had to turn around and go home. He also gave up walking the golf course. He hated resorting to a golf cart. He had used over-the-counter arthritis medicines in years past but had to stop them after he developed an ulcer. He tried some of the newer prescription arthritis drugs, but they, too, disagreed with his stomach. I told him there was some evidence that glucosamine might be helpful. He started taking 1500 mg a day, and after about three months he noticed marked improvement. Although realizing that he will eventually need knee surgery, he is happy that he can get along for now without it.

Wendy B. brought her mother Helena, who had severe nausea and vomiting, to the emergency room. Helena had a history of heart problems and was on digoxin. My first thought was that she was having a heart attack. I noticed that her heartbeat was very irregular. Her blood tests showed that her potassium level was very low and the level of digoxin was very high. I started medication immediately to reduce the digoxin level and intravenous fluids to replenish the potassium and fluid losses. I was perplexed since I had just checked her blood within the last month and everything was fine. I asked Wendy if Helena had taken anything else. Wendy first said no but then exclaimed, "Oh, Doc, she was depressed, and I was giving her St. John's wort. I stopped it a few weeks ago because she was doing better. That wouldn't do anything, would it?" She couldn't believe it when I told her that St. John's wort can cause reduction of digoxin levels and that the toxic levels we were seeing now were due to stopping the St. John's wort.

(*figure* 37-2)

A chiropractor performing spinal manipulation.

Ginkgo biloba has been used for memory loss. Some studies have even suggested a benefit in the treatment of Alzheimer's disease. Side effects are few, and it is usually well tolerated. However, it should not be taken if you are on warfarin since ginkgo biloba can significantly increase the risk of bleeding. There have been a few case reports of serious brain hemorrhage with this combination. It might also aggravate bleeding problems with aspirin and other antiplatelet drugs. In combination with thiazide diuretics, which are often used to treat high blood pressure, ginkgo biloba can aggravate hypertension. The mechanism for this is not known. The risk of a seizure is increased if ginkgo biloba is combined with BUPROPION (WELLBUTRIN).

Vitamin and mineral deficiencies are not uncommon in the elderly, and supplements are important in certain situations. Vitamins are necessary for the proper functioning of your body, and, except for vitamin D (which can be made in the skin with adequate sunlight exposure), they have to be taken in the diet. Chapter 27 covers the food sources for these vitamins and when a supplement may be warranted. Therefore, vitamins are not considered an alternative health practice unless *megadoses* (very high amounts) are ingested. It is important to remember that megadoses of vitamins can cause problems, some of which are very serious. Your doctor is in the best position to advise you if and when you should take a vitamin or herbal supplement. He or she may recommend that you see a nutritionist or dietitian if your medical problems indicate that you have special dietary needs or if you require extra vitamins or minerals.

CHIROPRACTIC

Chiropractic was founded in 1895 by Daniel David Palmer, an Iowa businessman. The principle of chiropractic is that misalignments in the spine contribute to various medical problems (see Figure 37-2). Chiropractors train for four years after at least two years of undergraduate study and receive a doctor of chiropractic (DC) degree. An osteopath, who receives a DO degree, is often confused with a chiropractor, but their training is very similar to traditional medical doctors, perhaps with more emphasis on the musculoskeletal system, and often they pursue specialty training in the same fields as medical doctors.

For many years, traditional medical practitioners had nothing to do with chiropractors. In fact, the American Medical Association (AMA), forbid its members to associate with chiropractors. This all changed after a series of lawsuits beginning in 1976 and ending in 1990. The AMA no longer restricts such associations or referrals.

Most studies that have been done on chiropractic support its benefit with regard to acute low back pain. The benefits are less clear with chronic back pain. Over the years, I have seen many of my patients benefit from the treatments given to them by chiropractors for acute low back pain. However, I would encourage you, as would most chiropractors, to consult with your medical doctor if you have persistent pain or pain that is getting worse. You may require tests and referral to a neurologist, neurosurgeon, or orthopedic surgeon.

NCCAM is conducting a clinical study to compare the efficacy of chiropractic treatment to medications in the treatment of neck pain. Chiropractic has also shown some benefits for migraine sufferers, in not only reducing pain but also the frequency of attacks. Chiropractic is not recommended for other medical conditions, such as high blood pressure, asthma, or cancer.

ACUPUNCTURE

Acupuncture has been practiced in China for thousands of years but has become very popular in western civilizations in recent years. Acupuncture is performed by many doctors and dentists, as well as acupuncture therapists. Acupuncture is the insertion of very thin, solid steel needles into various body points (see Figure 37-3) that are believed to be connected to pathways called *meridians*. Qi (pronounced "chee") is the body's energy force that flows along these meridians and regulates physical, mental, and emotional balance.

Various theories have been proposed to explain why acupuncture works. These include alteration of the brain's chemicals, release of electromagnetic signals, and discharge of endorphins into the central nervous system. Endorphins can be compared to your body's natural "morphine-like" substance. They seem to play an important role in the relief of pain. Acupuncture may also have an effect on the body's immune system, which would help with healing.

Acupuncture has been shown to be effective in the relief of pain after surgery. The need for potent pain relievers may be reduced significantly. Acupuncture has also shown encouraging results in the treatment of dental pain, chemotherapy-induced nausea, and a variety of musculoskeletal conditions, including fibromyalgia, tennis elbow, and acute sprains. NCCAM is conducting clinical studies to study the effects of acupuncture on such medical conditions as high blood pressure and congestive heart failure.

Acupuncture is usually quite safe. The FDA requires that acupuncture needles only be used once. The risk of infection is small, and injury to underlying body organs seldom occurs. However, if you feel that you might benefit from acupuncture, ask your doctor for a referral to a qualified acupuncture therapist. Most states have certifying and licensing requirements, but it is always best to get a referral to someone who is noted for his or her expertise. You should also check with your insurance company to see whether your treatments would be covered.

CANCER TREATMENTS

Tremendous strides have been made in the treatment of cancer in recent years. However, some forms of cancer are still incurable. Some individuals become desperate to try anything that might arrest or cure their disease. As a result "cancer clinics" have sprung up in various parts of the world where there is minimal or no government regulation. Unorthodox therapies are tried that are based not on science but financial reward. Some treatments

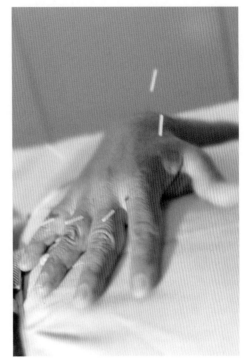

(*figure* 37-3)

Acupuncture is the insertion of small steel needles into specific body points, usually to reduce pain.

MAGNETS FOR PAIN?

You may have seen some professional athletes and even a few friends promote the benefits of magnets in the control of arthritis and pain. What is fact and what is fiction? You may want to consider the following points from before making a purchase:

- The vast majority of magnets marketed to consumers to treat pain are of a type called static (or permanent) magnets, because the resulting magnetic fields are unchanging. The other magnets used for health purposes are called electromagnets, because they generate magnetic fields only when electrical current flows through them. Currently, electromagnets are used primarily under the supervision of a health care provider or in clinical trials.

- Scientific research so far does not firmly support a conclusion that magnets of any type can relieve pain. However, some people do experience some relief. Various theories have been proposed as to why, but none has been scientifically proven.

- Clinical trials in this area have produced conflicting results. Many concerns exist regarding the quality and rigor of the studies conducted to date, leading to a call for additional, higher quality, and larger studies.

- The U.S. Food and Drug Administration (FDA) has not approved the marketing of magnets with claims of benefits to health (such as "relieves arthritis pain"). The FDA and the Federal Trade Commission (FTC) have taken action against many manufacturers, distributors, and Web sites that make claims not supported scientifically about the health benefits of magnets.

- It is important that people inform their health care providers about any therapy they are currently using or considering, including magnets. This is to help ensure a safe and coordinated course of care.

Source: National Center for Complementary and Alternative Medicine

have no more benefit than a placebo, and some are downright harmful. Persons with advanced and/or incurable cancers are especially vulnerable to deception. You might say, "So what? What else do they have to lose?" The answer is plenty.

Bogus treatments often cost tens of thousands of dollars, imposing major hardships on the victim's family. Some cancer patients have sold their remaining assets to afford these treatments. In addition, the medical complications are not insignificant. Several years ago, one of my patients with pancreatic cancer went to a South American cancer clinic and was injected with "purified" filtrates of his own stool in order to stimulate his body's immune system to fight the cancer. He became very ill, and after he returned to the United States, he had a florid infection of his arm related to the bacteria contained in the stool. We were not able to contain the infection with antibiotics, and he died. Although he had a terminal disease, his life was cut shorter than it needed to be by a very dangerous therapy.

Am I saying that alternative therapies for cancer should never be tried? Hardly. However, if you or a loved one is interested in pursuing such treatments, do it as part of a research protocol in which the potential benefits can be weighed against the risks and there is preliminary evidence to suggest a benefit. Your oncologist (cancer specialist) may be aware of clinical trials in your local area. NCCAM is conducting such trials with shark cartilage, enzyme supplements, and herbal therapies. You can investigate clinical trials that are being conducted by the government, as well as private organizations, at www.clinicaltrials.gov. These research projects require human volunteers. The information learned may help others in the future as well.

■

WHAT YOU NEED TO KNOW

▶ Many people use alternative medical treatments. Although many treatments are safe, some have serious adverse effects. If you desire to try an alternative treatment, discuss it with your doctor.

▶ There are hundreds of herbs and supplements. Some are safe and might be helpful in the treatment of certain medical conditions. Others can be very dangerous. If you are already on prescription medications, check with your doctor to make sure there are no adverse drug interactions.

▶ Chiropractic can be helpful in the treatment of acute low back pain. If your pain is persisting or getting worse, discuss it with your medical doctor. Chiropractic may help some persons with neck pain or migraines.

▶ Acupuncture has been used to treat surgical pain, dental pain, pain from a variety of musculoskeletal conditions, and chemotherapy-induced nausea. Future studies may show benefits in other medical conditions as well.

▶ You need to be careful when it comes to alternative therapy for cancer. Discuss this with your oncologist before pursuing alternative approaches.

37

FOR MORE INFORMATION

▶ National Center for Complementary and Alternative Medicine
National Institutes of Health
Bethesda, MD 20892
E-mail: info@nccam.nih.gov
Web: nccam.nih.gov

▶ MedlinePlus
A service of the U.S. National Library of Medicine and the National Institutes of Health
www.medlineplus.gov

▶ HerbMed
A service of the Alternative Medicine Foundation. An electronic interactive herbal database that provides impartial information based on sound clinical and scientific research.
www.herbmed.org

SUGGESTED READING:

▶ Alternative Medicine: What Works
Fugh-Berman, Adriane. 1997
Baltimore: Williams and Wilkins.

He is the best physician who is the most ingenious inspirer of hope.

—*Samuel Taylor Coleridge*

THE AUTHOR

38   *David R. Stutz ms.*

DAVID R. STUTZ, MD, FACP, is a graduate of the University of Michigan and the University of Michigan Medical School, where he received his BS and MD degrees with distinction. After completing his training in internal medicine at the University of Michigan Affiliated Hospitals, he spent two years in the U.S. Air Force and one year as an assistant professor of medicine at the University of Wisconsin Medical School. He is board-certified in internal medicine, with added qualifications in geriatric medicine, and he is a fellow of the American College of Physicians. He has practiced internal medicine and geriatrics for over 25 years in Sarasota, Florida, and has served as chief of staff at Sarasota Memorial Hospital. Dr. Stutz is the author of two books published by Consumer Reports Books: *The Savvy Patient* (with Bernard Feder, PhD) and *The Forty-Plus Guide to Fitness.*

38 | YOU AND YOUR DOCTOR

Americans over the age of 65 visit a doctor an average of six times each year, according to the National Center for Health Statistics. People see doctors for all kinds of reasons.★ You may be upset about a spot on your arm and want to find out whether it's something to worry about. You need the doctor's professional advice about immunizations and travel precautions. Sometimes, you need the doctor to sign a permission form for hospital volunteer work or to fill out the physician's section on a travel insurance refund claim.

Most of the time, however, you will see a doctor for the diagnosis and treatment of a medical problem. This chapter provides specific steps for you to take when you interact with your doctor. Following these steps will enable you to communicate more effectively and maintain better control over your own health and well-being.

WHO'S IN CHARGE?

You and the doctor should have the same goal: making and implementing the medical choices that are best for you. However, there may be a difference of opinion over what's best for you and how to achieve it. Communicating effectively narrows that gap.

RUSSELL'S STORY

Russell R. wears glasses, and he noticed that the TV was a little fuzzy when he sat more than eight or nine feet away. He is able to read just fine, and he has no problems driving at night. After his eyes are examined, the ophthalmologist says, "Your vision has changed. You have a cataract that's ready to come out, and you will see much better after that's done. It's a fairly minor surgery and you won't be put to sleep. We can do it next Friday, and you can schedule it on the way out." Before Russell R. can think of what to say, the ophthalmologist turns around and walks out.

Almost every medical decision involves two kinds of issues. Some questions are medical and technical: What is the problem, what's the probability of success with various treatments, what problems can occur with specific tests and treatments, and what are the odds of specific outcomes happening? These questions fall into the realm of the expert, the doctor, who is almost certain to know more about the medical aspects of your problem than you do.

Other questions deal with comfort, quality and length of life, risks, and expense: How much pain, hassle, disability, and dollar cost are you willing to accept in order to feel and function better? The answers to these questions reflect choices that are based on your own personal preferences and values. Doctors may have strong opinions about what they would want if they were in your shoes, and it's okay to ask their opinion. But if you do ask, remember that it is their personal opinion and value judgment, and it reflects what they would want if they were in your situation.

In Russell R.'s situation, the doctor measured the visual acuity and examined Russell R.'s eyes. Using her medical expertise and experience,

(figure 38-1)

Your doctor may have a brochure that explains the operations of the office.

★ *By the word doctor, I mean allopathic or osteopathic physicians (MDs and DOs). You can easily apply the information in this chapter to your interactions with additional health care providers, including dentists (DDSs or DMDs), chiropractors (DCs), nurse practitioners (RNs), physician assistants (PAs), and others who are licensed by your state's laws to practice "healing arts."*

the doctor told Russell R. that the cataract surgery was a "minor" procedure and that it would improve Russell R.'s eyesight. This is in the doctor's realm as an ophthalmologist. However, it is up to Russell R. to decide if he even wants his cataracts removed. From his perspective, he can see fine, and he can even drive at night without difficulty. He just wants his glasses made a little stronger so he can watch television more easily. It is in Russell R.'s realm to weigh the alternatives and to choose which course he prefers to follow.

COMMUNICATION

When you make an appointment to see a doctor for the first time, find out about the standard procedures for communicating with the doctor and the office staff. Often the most difficult step in communicating with a doctor is just making the connection. Try to avoid using your time with the doctor to find out everything you need to know about protocols for the office. The nurse, receptionist, or office manager can answer many of these questions. There may be a brochure that explains how the office operates (see Figure 38-1).

CONTACTING THE DOCTOR

Ask the receptionist, assistant, or nurse the following questions:

- What's the procedure for reaching the doctor if there's a question?
- Is there a specific time when the doctor or nurse returns calls?
- Does the doctor respond to fax or e-mail messages?

CONTACTING YOU

If you're expecting a call from the doctor's office:

- Keep the phone line open. Avoid frustrating the doctor with busy signals.
- Make sure you have the capability to record messages if you are away from the phone.
- Have a personal identifier on your own answering machine or voicemail message, because it's inappropriate (and in some cases illegal) for a doctor to leave private medical information without knowing who will be receiving it.

AFTER HOURS

Most physicians make arrangements to share after-hours and weekend coverage with other doctors. Occasionally, calls are forwarded to a nurse practitioner or physician assistant. Whoever responds to your call after hours may not know you. More important, he or she may not be familiar with your medical problems.

Note: For easy reference, have a list of your medical problems and your medications by the phone when the doctor calls back (See Figure 38-2).

(figure 38-2)

Have a list of your medications and your pharmacy telephone number available when the doctor calls.

EMERGENCIES

Emergencies occur at all times of day, during regular office hours and after the office has closed.

- If you have a serious or life-threatening emergency during office hours, make it clear to the person who answers the phone that you have an emergency so that you can get a prompt response.
- Clarify the procedure to follow if there is an emergency outside regular office hours. Should you contact the on-call physician first or dial 911?

INITIAL DOCTOR VISIT

When you see a physician for the first time, the doctor wants to find out about your medical history, as well as your current medications and problems. Prepare a concise and comprehensive medical record, and make several copies. Keep at least one copy at home, and give one to the doctor. Do it ahead of time, and then present it in list (not narrative) form. Even if the doctor doesn't need all the particulars at the time of your visit, the information will be there for future reference. Include the following information:

- *Major illnesses or injury*. List any major illness (heart attack, stroke, infection) and any injury for which you had to stay overnight in a hospital. Note the date and year and whether the problem is still being treated or has been resolved.
- *Medications (prescription and over-the-counter)*. Make a list of all the prescription medications you take on a regularly scheduled basis, or sporadically, along with the dosage strength, how many times each day you take it, the reason for taking it (if you know), and how long you have been on it. List all over-the-counter medications, supplements, and vitamins as well.
- *Surgeries*. List each surgery or operation for which you had a general anesthetic (were put to sleep). Include the year you had it, where you had it, and the reason that it was performed. Also indicate whether the operation was successful in your opinion.
- *Allergies*. List each medication that you had to stop because it caused a rash, made your lips swell, or caused you to choke.
- *Medications you cannot take*. List each medication that you had to stop for any other reason and why you had to stop it.
- *Personal habits*. If you smoke, list how many cigarettes (or cigars or pipes) you smoke each day and how old you were when you started. Indicate how many alcoholic drinks you have each day and in what form. If you no longer smoke or drink alcoholic beverages, indicate your previous level of usage, and when and why you stopped.
- *Diet*. Indicate if you've been told to follow a special diet.
- *Level of activity*. Describe any exercise or activity you do on a regular basis.

- *Family history.* Note the age of your parents or how old your parents were when they died and the cause of death. Indicate whether brothers or sisters have died, and if so, when and for what reason.
- *Personal information and contacts.* List the names, locations (city and state), and phone numbers of relatives (e.g., children) or close friends you would contact if you had a serious or life-threatening illness.
- *Advance directives.* Indicate whether you have an advance directive or living will regarding end-of-life issues. Note the person whom you designated to make medical decisions for you if you are unable to make them for yourself. Bring in the document so the doctor can make a copy to put in your record.

THE MEDICAL AGENDA

YOUR COMMUNICATIONS FRAMEWORK

Think of a visit with your doctor as you would a business or organization meeting, with the doctor sitting as chairperson. The meeting follows an agenda. In this case, however, the agenda is not printed out for everyone to see. Most of the time, the doctor creates the agenda during the first seconds and minutes of your visit. The doctor bases the agenda on his or her initial impressions, and at the top of the list are those things that appear to have the greatest medical importance.

But sometimes what the doctor feels is important and what receives all of the time and attention is not the reason why you're there. With a little thought and planning, you can have a satisfying and successful visit, instead of one that leaves you disappointed and frustrated. Here's a common scenario:

GAIL'S STORY

Gail C. takes medication to treat her high blood pressure and control her urinary incontinence. She is looking forward to a previously scheduled routine follow-up visit because she has pain in her abdomen, and this worries her. Since she already had the appointment scheduled, she assumes this would be a good opportunity to talk about her new problem. The doctor comes into the exam room, and before Gail C. can say anything, he opens her chart. "Are you taking the same medications for your blood pressure? I see it's up a little bit today. Let's recheck that." He proceeds to examine her and asks about her urination and whether she has any dry mouth with the medication. "Things appear to be under control. Make an appointment to follow up with me in four months." Then he turns and walks toward the door.

She says, "Doctor, I've also had some pain in my stomach, and by the way, I need a prescription refill for my blood pressure."

The doctor has his hand on the door, looks at his watch, and turns around with an annoyed look on his face, because there are two other patients waiting to see him.

Most doctors automatically pace themselves to have enough time to cover their own agenda. Gail C.'s abdominal pain was not put on it until the doctor was ready to see the next patient.

HOW TO PLACE YOUR CONCERNS AT THE TOP OF THE AGENDA

Most of us have experienced something similar to Gail C.'s situation. Remember, the first seconds and minutes of your encounter are the most important for you, because this is the most effective time to present your agenda items, especially if you have a new problem to discuss (see Figure 38-3). If you do not assert yourself, the doctor will run the meeting without your input. If you wait too long, there may not be enough time to explore what really concerns you, if you get an opportunity to discuss it at all.

A study by researchers at Michigan State University examined how experienced doctors approach their patients' problems. Doctors rarely listen to your whole story, mull it over, and then come up with a diagnosis and treatment plan. They tend to generate their hypotheses early, sometimes within moments from when you start talking. Then they interrupt to ask more questions, and the first interruption comes an average of only 18 seconds after you start to talk!

The bottom line is that unless you express your concerns from the outset and state them in clear manner, you may not have a good opportunity to explain what really bothers you. Here's the same scenario with a more satisfactory outcome:

> The doctor comes into the exam room, and before Gail C. can say anything, he opens her chart. "Are you taking the same medications for your blood pressure? I see it's up a little bit today. Let's recheck that."
>
> Before Gail C. holds out her arm, she replies, "Excuse me, doctor. I know I'm here for a blood pressure check, but what really concerns me is a pain I've been having in my stomach. Let me tell you about it."

The doctor may say, "Okay, tell me about the pain," or he may say, "Let me check your blood pressure first." In either event, Gail C. succeeded in placing her concern at or near the top of the doctor's agenda. If he still does not address it, Gail C. can assert herself and return to her agenda by asking, "But what about the stomach pain?"

YOUR PERSONAL AGENDA

MARTIN'S STORY

> Martin N. has diabetes (which requires insulin injections), angina (heart pains due to blockages in the arteries feeding the heart muscle), and high blood pressure. He complains of tingling in his feet due to diabetic nerve damage, pain in the chest if he walks too fast, some dizziness if he gets up quickly, and swelling in his ankles after standing more than 15 minutes. These are all potentially threatening problems, but thanks to the four prescription medications he takes regularly, his symptoms have been stable for the last 18 months. His real concern is that he might have prostate cancer like his older brother.
>
> "Mr. N., how are you feeling today?"

(*figure* 38-3)

The first few seconds of your visit to the doctor is the time to present your agenda items. Limit these to two or, at most, three items in order to maintain your doctor's focus.

38

(figure 38-4)

You may find using a tape recorder during your office visit very useful for later reference.

Martin N. replies, "Doctor, I've been urinating more at night, and it's harder to get it started. My blood sugar's been up and down, and I had some angina yesterday carrying out the garbage. My feet are burning, and they're really swollen by bedtime. Oh, did I tell you my brother found out he has prostate cancer?"

With all the other potentially alarming symptoms and serious underlying problems, the likelihood that the doctor will choose to focus on Martin N.'s urinary symptoms is small. Your agenda items should include the things that concern you the most and the questions you want to ask. It is not a chronicle of your symptoms and complaints. Rather it is a plan for what you want to accomplish.

Clarify in your mind what you're concerned about, and if there is more than one issue, rank them in the order of their importance to you. Limit your agenda to no more than two or, at most, three major items in order to maintain the doctor's focus. Here's a more effective way for Martin N. to present his agenda:

"Doctor, I've been urinating more at night, and it's harder to get it started. My brother found out he has prostate cancer, and I'm afraid that I might have it too. That's my real concern. Everything else is about the same."

The doctor may ask questions about the other potentially more serious medical problems, but Martin N. has focused the doctor's attention squarely on his major concern: that he might have prostate cancer.

Note: Write out your agenda items in advance.

The combination of being in a medical setting and how you are feeling affects your ability to communicate your concerns accurately and objectively. *Note:* Be honest with yourself and with the doctor about what is bothering you, and be as specific as you can.

Even if you're embarrassed by the problem (e.g., urinary incontinence, problems with erections, excessive flatulence), try to be straightforward and open, because the doctor cannot guess what you're thinking.

COMMUNICATION OBSTACLES

Hearing impairment: If you miss even a small portion of what the doctor says, it may be hazardous to your health. Hearing impairment is a common problem that is made worse if someone is too embarrassed or too reluctant to ask the doctor to repeat or rephrase what is said.

- Wear your hearing aid if you have one.
- Ask a spouse, relative, or friend to be with you during the conversation.
- Ask the doctor to write down crucial information or instructions for you, or take a pocket recorder with you and tape what the doctor tells you for later reference (see Figure 38-4).

Doctor's use of medicalese: Doctors use a language that is filled with medical terms and technical jargon. It is so second nature that many physicians do not realize they are using terms the patient does not understand, and if the patient is apprehensive or hard of hearing, it makes matters worse.

Note: If the doctor uses a term that is not familiar, just say, "Excuse me, I don't understand. What does that mean?" You may be surprised to find that many doctors enjoy teaching and explaining things to you.

Time: Doctors have busy schedules, and time is a scarce commodity in the office.

- Prepare your agenda items in advance. Be concise and well organized.
- Make another appointment if you need more time. If necessary, schedule an extended visit.

Cognitive impairment: Diminished memory and impaired reasoning can be more problematic in their earlier stages, because they may not be recognized by the doctor or acknowledged by the patient. *Note:* If you think a spouse, family member, or friend may be cognitively impaired, ask them if they will let you sit in with them when they talk to the doctor.

Failure to ask questions: It's normal to have concerns about diagnoses and treatments, and you may have specific issues with having a test, taking a medication, or undergoing surgery. When you see a doctor, your silence may represent the fact that you are confused or uncertain or that you just don't agree. However, if you do not assert yourself by asking questions, doctors assume that you understand what they are saying and that you agree with what they are advising.

MEDICAL ISSUES
SURGERY AND INVASIVE TREATMENT PROCEDURES

If a medication doesn't work or if it causes side effects or disagrees with you, you can always stop it, and it will be out of your system after a period of time. It's different with a surgical procedure or with an invasive procedure (instead of going through an incision in the skin, a tube, scope, or special needle is put into your body). Having a surgical procedure is like driving on a one-way street. With rare exceptions, you can't easily reverse your direction. You live with results, whether they're better or worse than you hoped and expected. Before you undergo surgery or invasive treatment procedure, here are questions to consider asking:

- What is the goal of the surgery or procedure? How will it make me better?
- Could the surgery or procedure make me worse than I am now?
- What are the common risks of this surgery or procedure?
- What will happen if I delay the surgery or procedure or don't do it at all?
- Who should perform the surgery or procedure and where should it be done?

- What can I expect to feel afterward, and when will I feel better?
- What is the surgeon's training and personal success with the procedure?

MEDICAL TESTS

Medical tests can range from something simple, such as drawing blood for the lab, to more involved and potentially risky procedures, such as a colonoscopy performed under general anesthesia. Medical tests are not always as precise and specific as people think, and sometimes test results lead to more testing. If the doctor advises further testing and you're concerned about risks and costs, you may want to ask:

- What exactly will this test tell us?
- Will the results of the test pin down the diagnosis?
- Will the results of the test tell me what to expect in the future?
- Will the results of this test change my treatment in any way?
- What will we do if the test is positive?
- What will we do if the test is negative or normal?
- What will happen if we wait to do the test or if we don't do it at all?

MEDICATIONS

Most people over the age of 65 take some prescription medication to treat acute or chronic conditions (e.g., arthritis or asthma) and to reduce the risk of future problems (e.g., cholesterol-lowering drugs). Before you start taking any prescription medication, here are questions you may want to ask:

- What is the purpose of this medication (for treatment, to lower risk, etc.)?
- How will we know the medication is working and how soon should I see it?
- How long will I be taking the medication?
- Is there a generic form available?
- What time of day and how often should I take it?
- Is there any special way to take it—with food or on an empty stomach?
- Can I expect any interactions with my other pills? Can I take them all together?
- What side effects should I look for and when should I call you?
- When should we follow up?

CONSULTATIONS

Your doctor may refer you to a consultant or you may choose to see a specialist on your own for a variety of reasons. Unless the reasons for the referral and your expectations of consultation are clear and focused, communications problems can occur. Here are questions to ask your doctor about seeing a specialist:

38

- What is the purpose of the consultation? What question are we asking?
- Will you set up the appointment and send records over?
- Will the consultant communicate with me directly?
- Will I follow up with the specialist, or will I come back to you?

Here are questions to ask the consultant:

- When and how will you communicate with my primary care doctor?
- Will I follow up with you directly, or will it be with my primary care doctor?

EMERGENCY ROOM AND HOSPITAL

The emergency room, hospital, surgery center, and nursing home settings can be strange and often hostile environments. Things can happen to you without your prior knowledge or preparation, but essentially nothing is done without a doctor's specific order. In any of those settings you may not even see your usual doctor. You may be assigned to a "hospitalist" who works solely in the hospital or to a new attending physician (doctor in charge of your case), and you may also be under the care of interns and residents.

No matter where you see the doctor, intrusions on your privacy will make things worse. Federal legislation mandates that your conversations and your medical record be kept private. If you're in an emergency room or a semiprivate hospital room, other people can overhear your conversation. *Note:* If only a curtain surrounds you, ask that the door be closed and that visitors wait outside while you talk with the doctor.

Your illness (or surgery) and the medications you receive can affect your alertness and concentration. *Note:* Before you go to the hospital, try to enlist an advocate (a spouse, child, or friend) who can act on your behalf and communicate for you if necessary.

You or your advocate should consider asking the following questions to the admitting doctor, the admissions personnel, or the nurse on the floor:

- Who is the attending physician? (Who has ultimate responsibility for your care?)
- Who will write the daily orders? (Which doctor will the nurses contact first?)
- Who will be making the decisions about tests and treatments?
- To whom should we direct any questions?

If a new doctor or consultant comes in to see you, ask:

- What's the reason my doctor asked you to see me?

Most tests or procedures are done in the morning, and generally they are done while you're fasting (not eating for at least six hours prior). At nighttime or first thing in the morning, ask the nurse:

- Which medications are ordered for me, and why are they ordered?
- What is the dosage, and which times are they ordered to be given?
- Which tests or procedures will I be having and when?
- Are there any special instructions about eating or drinking beforehand?
- Will I receive my usual morning medications, and if not, does the doctor know?

Ask the nurse to give you a list of your medications so you can be aware of what you should be taking. It should be easy for the nurse to make a copy of the pharmacy list in the chart.

CHOICES ABOUT END-OF-LIFE CARE

This is an area for which the choices are clearly in the patient's realm. If you have specific preferences about resuscitation, tube feeding, or breathing support machines, state them as clearly as you can in writing. A discussion of end-of-life choices is beyond the scope of this chapter, but if you have a living will and a durable power of attorney for medical decisions, make sure your doctor has a copy. That's the best way to communicate what you want.

WHAT YOU NEED TO KNOW

➤ The doctor creates the agenda for the encounter during the first seconds and minutes of the visit. If you have issues that you want to address, put them on the agenda right at the start, or they may not be addressed at all.

➤ The doctor cannot read your mind. Organize your thoughts prior to the visit, and be honest about what is bothering you. Limit your agenda to no more than two or, at most, three major issues.

➤ You and your doctor may look at things differently. Be aware of what is in your realm and what is in the doctor's realm.

➤ If you don't ask questions, doctors interpret your silence as your understanding what they've said and that you agree with them. Assert yourself, and don't be afraid to ask questions.

FOR MORE INFORMATION

➤ **American Association of Retired Persons (AARP)**
www.aarp.org
Click on Health and Wellness. Then click on Checkups and Prevention. Then click on How to Talk To Your Doctor.

➤ **MedicineNet.com**
www.medicinenet.com/pdf/howtohelpyourdoctor.pdf

➤ **Agency for Healthcare Research and Quality**
Rockville, MD
Quick Tips—When Talking with Your Doctor
AHRQ Publication No. 01-0040a, May 2002.
www.ahrq.gov/consumer/quicktips/doctalk

➤ **Cancer Care, Inc.**
"Doctor, Can We Talk?" Tips for Communicating with Your Doctor, Nurse, or Health Care Team if You Have Cancer
www.cancercare.org/EducationalPrograms/Educational Programs.cfm?ID=3478&c=381

➤ **NIA Information Center**
P.O. Box 8057
Gaithersburg, MD 20898
E-mail: niaic@jbs1.com
Web: www.nia.nih.gov/health/pubs/talking
Free pamphlet, "Talking to Your Doctor: A Guide for Older People," available by either download or mail.

SUGGESTED READING:

▶ American Medical Association Guide to
Talking to Your Doctor
New York: Wiley, 2001.

Paperback book, 256 pages $14.95. Also available in
e-book format.

> Whatever house I may visit, I will come for the benefit of the sick.
>
> *—Oath of Hippocrates, circa 400 B.C.*

THE AUTHOR

39 *[signature: Kevin W. O'Neil]*

KEVIN W. O'NEIL, MD, FACP, graduated from Boston College magna cum laude and the Georgetown University School of Medicine. He did his internship at the Washington Hospital Center and his internal medicine residency at the University of Massachusetts Medical Center. He was an assistant professor in the Department of Internal Medicine at the University of Massachusetts Medical Center until moving to Sarasota, Florida, in 1984. He is currently an assistant professor of medicine at the University of South Florida College of Medicine. He is board-certified in internal medicine and holds a Certificate of Added Qualifications in Geriatric Medicine. He is a fellow of the American College of Physicians and a member of the American Geriatrics Society. He practices with the First Physicians Group in Sarasota and is on the staff at Sarasota Memorial Hospital and Doctors Hospital.

39 | END-OF-LIFE CARE

Death is one of life's certainties. Although advances in medical science have increased the average human life span, death comes to every person. For some of us, death might come quickly in the form of a heart attack or motor vehicle accident. For others, death may come more slowly after a stroke or a protracted fight against cancer. Although death is not a pleasant topic to ponder, it is important to consider its impact on you and your family.

In this chapter, I discuss end-of-life care. But first, examine your own attitude regarding your death and your health care if you have an illness for which death is imminent. For example, if you have a weak heart and your quality of life is poor, do you want cardiopulmonary resuscitation if your heart stops? If you have a severe stroke and cannot swallow, do you want a feeding tube placed? You and your doctor should realize that you as a person are part of a family and a community. Your family should be involved in your decision making, and your community should play a role in your care. Programs and services have been implemented on a local, regional, and national level that can help relieve some of the anxieties and stress associated with a terminal illness.

We do not like to think of our own death, but we know it is going to happen. So why not prepare for it? Amazingly, most persons have not executed advanced care directives (living will and health care power of attorney) in spite of the fact that the Patient Self-Determination Act of 1991 requires that providers under the Medicare program inform their patients of their right to do so. Also, it is advisable to sign a patient authorization document naming the family and friends who should receive health care information about you upon their asking, including when you are not disabled. Dealing with these issues before a crisis makes the process less stressful for you and your family. In Part Three, experts in health care law write about the importance of preparing a will, a living will, and appointing a health care surrogate. They also cover long-term care insurance and estate planning. By considering these subjects now and preparing well ahead of your death or disability, you ensure that your desires are known. You can avoid conflicts among your family members and avoid financial disaster. If your spiritual life is important to you, discuss it with your doctor and clergyman or clergywoman. Doctors are learning more and more about the impact of spirituality and religion on health (see Chapter 31). Your spiritual advisor can help you at a time when your body is no longer doing what you want.

This chapter deals with the medical and psychosocial challenges that you might face if you have a terminal illness. Pain is cited as our most common fear, but other problems can be distressing, including skin sores, gastrointestinal problems, breathing problems, and psychological disturbances.

CHALLENGES

When I was in medical school in the 1970s, there were no courses on the care of the terminally ill. In fact, when I worked as an orderly at a terminal

COPING WITH DEATH

In London Dr. Cicely Saunders founded the first hospice in 1967. By organizing teams of professional caregivers, Saunders allowed terminally ill patients and their families to deal with death in a more positive way. The first hospice in the United States was established in New Haven, Connecticut, in 1974, and today there are over 3100 hospice programs throughout the United States. Hospice care may be provided in a hospital or a "hospice house," but most commonly it is provided in the patient's own home or a nursing home.

cancer hospital during the summer before I started medical school, the staff was forbidden to use the word cancer in conversation. Inadvertently, I let the *C* word slip out once by accident, and I got my first (but not the last!) chewing out by a rather large and intimidating nurse. The truth about their illness and prognosis was routinely held from patients. Thankfully, this has changed. It is now accepted that a patient and his or her family are best served by knowing the truth about the illness. Not only does this allow a patient to understand why he or she is not getting better, but also it allows the patient time to find some meaning and reconciliation with regard to death. Instead of the family avoiding talking about death, the door is opened for sharing between family and patient about fears, hopes, and desires. You may wonder how a dying person can have any hope. Hope can take many forms—the hope of seeing a grandson graduate from high school, the hope of seeing another sunrise, the hope of reuniting with loved ones who have previously died, or the hope of seeing God.

Much of what I learned about the process of dying is from a book written by Elisabeth Kübler-Ross called *On Death and Dying*. In this book, Kübler-Ross, who is a psychiatrist, describes her observations of the stages that a person goes through as death approaches. It certainly helped me understand the emotional and psychological issues that a dying person faces, and I recommend the book to you. However, the medical care of a dying person requires that the physician be attentive to all the physical challenges that arise. You might think that the physician's care of a dying person cannot be that complicated. In fact, the medical care of the terminally ill person can test the knowledge and personal resources of the most astute and gifted physician.

Physicians are generally trained to heal and cure. We look at death as the enemy, and sometimes we feel that a patient's death is a personal failure. Treating a dying person can arouse feelings and emotions that are uncomfortable. Some physicians may avoid dealing with the dying person altogether, but this is unfortunate since this is a time in a person's life when the compassion and comfort provided by the physician can mean the most. Thankfully, more medical schools are now teaching students to get in tune with their feelings regarding death, recognizing that the death of a patient is not a personal failure but a part of life. The psychological support that the physician can give to the patient and family at this time is profound. By sharing these thoughts with you, I hope you can see that your physician is a human being subject to the same fears and anxieties that you have. Most physicians are caring and compassionate and will want to help you and your loved ones at this important time in your life (see Figure 39-1).

Your physician might choose to use the resources of specialists in palliative care (that is, care provided for comfort, not cure). Hospice is a well-known form of terminal care in which services are provided by a team, which may include physicians, nurses, physical and occupational therapists, home health aides, and volunteers. Hospice can assist the physician in the management of the patient's pain but also help the patient and family deal with emotional and spiritual issues.

Probably the most important aspect of your care in this stage of life is good communication. You may wish to make an appointment with your primary care physician, for which there may be a fee, to receive and review all the reports from practitioners treating you. Specialists are usually focused on their own area of expertise. Your primary care physician, like a quarterback for a football team, will oversee the whole situation and coordinate the efforts of the individual members of the team. This will provide a professional who can speak to you and your family about the overall view of your situation.

Unfortunately, there may be numerous barriers to good communication that cause serious anxiety for you, as well as disruption of the care that you would like and deserve. Understanding these issues can help overcome them. An important issue for you to understand is that America's health system is seriously fragmented. The care provided in acute care hospitals is typically oriented to cure, not palliation. Although some hospitals do have beds that may be rented out for hospice patients, this varies from community to community. There are tremendous pressures on physicians and hospitals to discharge patients as soon as a medical condition is stabilized. However, this often leaves insufficient time for physicians to communicate effectively with families and their patients about the goals and strategies of palliative care.

If you are transferred from a hospital to a skilled nursing facility or to home, you have an entirely different group of caregivers. This may cause slipups in communication. Most physicians share night-call duties with other physicians. If you have a problem, the on-call physician may have little knowledge of your condition.

Payment for services can cause a lot of anxiety. Understand that Medicare and Medicaid are distinctly different programs. Medicare will cover services in the hospital and skilled nursing facility, but may not cover services in a home or nursing facility that are considered "custodial," such as assistance with bathing, eating, dressing, and grooming. Some states have "waiver programs," which cover some of these items in the home for people who qualify for Medicaid. Many terminally ill patients do not require what is called "skilled care," which is covered for a limited number of days by Medicare—intravenous antibiotic therapy, injections, wound care, and so forth. However, in order to qualify for hospice services under Medicare, the physician has to certify that the patient has a life expectancy

(figure 39-1)

End of life care requires compassion, as well as technical expertise on the part of doctors, nurses, and caregivers.

of six months or less. You can imagine the anxiety this can create for the patient and the family. It also places a burden on physicians since none of us has the ability to predict with certainty the time course of a patient's illness. Physical therapy is covered under Medicare, as long as the patient is improving. Although the terminally ill patient is not improving, the progression of their physical decline can be slowed down with physical therapy. Unfortunately, Medicare will not cover this.

You may have previously executed a living will and power of attorney, but it is not unusual for these documents to get misplaced or lost in the move from one place to another. It is wise to keep such documents in a three-ring binder or portfolio to enhance the chances of finding them. Also, you can place the documents with your primary physician and request that they are kept in your chart. If you have need of the documents, a request can be made to fax them to the place of need. Commercial companies such as DocuBank provide a service by storing your documents and faxing them upon a demand (see "For More Information").

Many people do not understand the difference between a living will and a *do not resuscitate (DNR)* order, as the following case illustrates:

VERONICA'S STORY

Veronica C., age 91, lived in an assisted living facility and participated in many of its activities. Her son and daughter lived nearby and visited her regularly. Veronica C. had two previous heart attacks that had weakened her heart muscle. One evening she awoke with severe chest pain. She rang her call button and a staff nurse came immediately to her room. The nurse noticed that Veronica C. was sweaty and clammy. She looked very pale and frightened and obviously was very uncomfortable with the chest pain. The nurse called 911 and gave Veronica C. some nitroglycerin and oxygen by nasal prongs. Suddenly, Veronica C.'s blood pressure dropped and her heart stopped. Her nurse started cardiopulmonary resuscitation (CPR). The paramedics arrived and inserted a breathing tube into Veronica C.'s mouth and gave her electric shocks. This brought her heart rhythm back, but she did not wake up. The paramedics transported Veronica C. to the emergency room at the hospital. Her heart stopped again just as the ambulance arrived in the emergency room. Again a heart rhythm was restored with electric shocks. When Veronica C.'s son and daughter arrived in the emergency room, they expressed disbelief that CPR was started in the first place—on a 91-year-old woman! They exclaimed, "She has a living will. She told us she never wanted to be brought back or hooked up to machines."

Veronica C. and her son and daughter did not understand that a living will states that you do not want your life prolonged if you have a terminal disease or if you have little chance of a decent quality of life after treatment for an illness. Veronica C. had been functioning quite well, and although she had a heart attack and serious arrhythmia, there was a chance that she could have been successfully resuscitated and maybe even had a few more months or years of decent quality of life. Yes, it is true that most older persons do not recover or they have serious complications after CPR. But there is a chance. Remember your doctor and health system are oriented to curing and healing, even if the odds are against it. If you want something different, you need to make your wishes clear. A living will is not a do not resuscitate (DNR) order. Physicians and hospitals in all states recognize a DNR. Veronica C. did expire in the emergency room when her heart stopped again. The emergency room physician understood the wishes of Veronica C. and her family and advised the staff that no more electric shocks would be given. However, if Veronica C. had a DNR order, her son and daughter would have been spared a lot of anguish. It would have also spared her the several hours of emergency treatment procedures she went through.

Some states have a specific statute permitting you to sign a DNR, which is effective outside a hospital or other medical care facility. Signing such an order is a very serious step. If you sign such an order, it is wise to wear a bracelet or other jewelry engraved to notify emergency personnel of your wishes. Some state statutes specify the words for the jewelry.

Unfortunately, the majority of older persons have not executed advanced care directives or signed permissions for family to obtain medical information about them. This creates tremendous stress for the family when decisions need to be made, especially if the patient is unable to make these decisions. You should give someone you trust the ability to make health care decisions for you if you are unable to make these decisions yourself (health care durable power of attorney). You should also sign a patient authorization allowing named people to obtain medical information about you.

You now see some of the challenges that face you and your family with end-of-life care. However, you can be part of the solution. This requires that you take an active role. You should talk with your family, physician, attorney, and spiritual counselor about your wishes for your care if you are terminally ill. Naturally, you should have preparations in place if you die suddenly. Make sure you have copies of important documents in the event that they should get lost when you transfer from one place to another.

I suggest that you become familiar with *Last Acts Partnership,* formerly Partnership for Caring (see "For More Information"). Last Acts Partnership is a national nonprofit organization that can provide you and your loved ones with information to help you receive excellent care near the end of your life. You can download free copies of advanced directives appropriate for the state in which you reside. You do not need an attorney to execute these documents. In addition, Last Acts Partnership has a 24-hour-per-day, 7-day-per-week hotline that can put you in touch with an expert during a crisis or provide answers to questions you might have about end-of-life care (800-989-9455). Last Acts Partnership has been the national program office for Last Acts, a program funded by the Robert Wood Johnson Foundation to improve the quality of care for persons nearing the end of life.

PAIN

Pain is cited as the most common fear associated with death, even more common than death itself. However, pain management methods have evolved over the years and allow the vast majority of patients to achieve reasonable relief of pain (see Chapter 39). The perception of pain differs for each one of us. Pain may be experienced more intensely if you are overtired, stressed, or depressed.

The management of pain might involve behavioral and/or drug treatments. Behavioral methods include hypnosis, meditation, and biofeedback. Distraction therapy aims to take your mind off your pain and onto something else. You probably have had the experience of getting so caught up in a task that you didn't know you were injured. Soldiers may not realize that they have been wounded in battle until the battle is over. Football and hockey players often don't feel the aches and pains from their injuries until the game is over. For chronic pain, you can use art, music, or hobbies to help keep your mind off the pain.

Drug treatment is often required for those with pain due to cancer or other terminal illnesses. However, a correctable cause for the pain should be sought. For example, cancer in the bones may be better treated with local radiation therapy than with drugs. In some cases, surgery may be necessary to prevent fractures of the bone due to cancer. Prolonged disability might be averted, and quality of life enhanced.

When pain medications are needed for terminally ill persons, the goal is to control the pain even if it causes some drowsiness or sedation. This might require administration of the medicine on a regular schedule in order to reduce the risk of recurrence of pain between doses. Physicians should avoid ordering *PRN* (as-needed) analgesics in treating chronic pain, especially in hospitals, nursing homes, or assisted living facilities. A significant period of time can pass between the patient experiencing the pain and notifying the nursing staff, the nursing staff responding to the order, and the medicine being delivered. For people who have breakthrough pain between doses of their regular pain medicine, extra as-needed doses can be prescribed.

Narcotic medications, such as MORPHINE (MS CONTIN, ROXANOL, AVINZA) or METHADONE (DOLOPHINE), are often required for the management of chronic pain. Physicians are misguided if they avoid using narcotics for fear that their chronic pain patient will become addicted. The doctor must become knowledgeable in the use of narcotics, but often experience with a few drugs for moderate to severe pain is all that is necessary. Oral medications are preferable whenever possible, and long-acting preparations have made them easier to administer. For those who cannot take medicines by mouth, skin patches and rectal suppositories are available for delivering analgesics. Injections under the skin are another alternative and are less painful than injections into muscle.

Nonsteroidal anti-inflammatory drugs, such as IBUPROFEN (MOTRIN IB, ADVIL) and NAPROXEN (ALEVE, NAPROSYN), can be helpful by themselves in controlling mild to moderate pain, but they may also enhance the pain-relieving effects of narcotic analgesics. However, adverse effects such as stomach irritation can occur. More expensive prescription drugs, such as CELECOXIB (CELEBREX) or ROFECOXIB (VIOXX), are less likely to cause stomach problems. Patients with weak hearts and serious kidney diseases generally need to avoid these medications.

A pinched or irritated nerve can cause pain. Often this does not respond to the usual analgesics. Medicines that treat seizures or depression are preferred. In some cases, special procedures performed by anesthesiologists or neurosurgeons are required. A nerve block is an injection of anesthetics that interrupt the pain impulses from being sent to the brain. In rare cases, intractable pain requires surgical disruption of nerve fibers in the spinal cord that carry the pain signals to the brain.

I hope this discussion provides some reassurance that even the most severe pain can be controlled by expert management. You have the right to request effective pain relievers. There is no ethical reason for a physician to withhold pain medication from a terminally ill patient even if the medication expedites the process of death. The aim in this case is the person's comfort, not death. This is different from euthanasia, by which a person's life is deliberately ended. Physician-assisted suicide is different from euthanasia in that the physician provides the prescription or information that the patient needs to commit suicide. Oregon is the only state in which physician-assisted suicide is legal.

TREATMENT OF COMMON PROBLEMS

The remainder of this chapter is dedicated to the treatment of common problems associated with the care of the dying person. In the hospital or nursing facility, the nursing staff in consultation with the physician typically provides the care. However, more and more frequently, families wish to provide terminal care for their loved ones in the home. In these situations, a spouse or a son or daughter, with or without the support of home health associations, home health aides, or hospice organizations, provides the care. The role can be very stressful but can also be very emotionally satisfying as you care for someone you love at a very difficult time in his or her life. If you are a caregiver, I would heartily encourage you to learn all you can about being a caregiver. You should use the resources (home health organizations, hospice, etc.) available in your community to help you. Experienced nurses and aides can help you and your loved one tremendously. You will learn from them not only the skills necessary to provide excellent care but also that it is important to care for yourself. You can't take care of anyone else if you get sick yourself. I have provided some resources for caregivers in "For More Information."

SKIN PROBLEMS

Terminally ill patients may spend much or all of the time in bed. Pressure ulcers (also called bedsores, pressure sores, or decubitus ulcers) are a frequent complication. Once a pressure ulcer develops, the likelihood

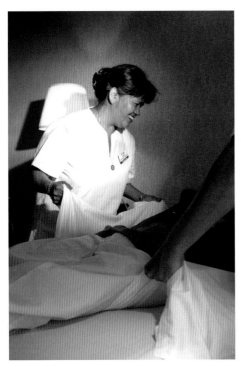

(figure 39-2)

A draw sheet, which requires two people, is helpful if the patient cannot cooperate with repositioning.

of its healing is low. This is because the body's mechanisms for healing itself are impaired. Prevention can be difficult since this requires frequent repositioning of the patient in order to keep pressure off the skin over bony parts, such as the hip, back, and heels. Foam padding of these areas might be helpful. Heel protectors are commercially available. If an area of the skin gets red, massage it and be very careful to keep pressure off it. This may require keeping the patient on his or her side. Folded pillows or rolled blankets can be used to keep the patient on the side. A pillow can be used between the ankles and knees while on the side. For those who are totally bedridden, foam mattresses ("egg crate"), air mattresses, or waterbeds have been used to prevent pressure ulcers.

The skin of frail and seriously ill persons is often fragile. The junction between the superficial skin layer (epidermis) and the deeper layer (dermis) flattens out during aging (see Chapter 1). Therefore, the skin can shear more easily. It is very important not to drag the patient across the sheets. Large segments of skin can be injured. A draw sheet can be helpful if the patient cannot cooperate with repositioning; however, this requires two people. A *draw sheet* is a folded sheet placed crosswise across the bed (see Figure 39-2). Often a rubber sheet is placed underneath, so that the soiled draw sheet can be removed without changing all the bed linens.

Dry skin is common due to dehydration and malnutrition. Treatment is explained in Chapter 1. Itching can be caused by dryness of the skin, but other causes should be considered. Allergic reactions to drugs or sensitivity to detergents and soaps are not uncommon. Removal of any suspected cause should be tried, but if that doesn't work, request a medicine to reduce itching.

STOMACH AND BOWEL PROBLEMS

A common problem for terminally ill patients is loss of appetite. Among the many possible reasons are alteration in smell, taste, ill-fitting dentures, and mouth sores. An attempt should be made to identify a correctable cause. For example, poor immune function can frequently cause a yeast infection of the mouth. This can be treated with a prescription oral rinse or lozenges. Weight loss can make dentures fit poorly, but this can be corrected by the dentist.

You should attempt to make meals look attractive by varying color and texture. You might also try flavor enhancers. Very large amounts of food on a plate can look overwhelming to a frail older person. Smaller portions tastefully presented are a better alternative. You can offer "seconds" if your loved one desires more food. Liquid nutritional supplements are available that provide meals in a can. They are fortified with vitamins, minerals, and nutrients. Liquid supplements can be used to provide extra calories and nutrients when the intake of regular food is not adequate, but they can also be used when solid food cannot be taken safely. Occasionally, steroids are given in an attempt to stimulate appetite and weight gain.

When should a feeding tube be considered? The extremely debilitated person might not be able to swallow at all. Some persons after a stroke cannot swallow. Your decision will depend on the circumstances. No one can force you or your loved one to have a feeding tube. Most people do not want a feeding tube if they are terminally ill and the quality of their life is not going to improve. However, there may be situations where a person's life expectancy might be several more months or even a year or two if his or her nutrition is maintained. A stroke might cause temporary swallowing problems, and the feeding tube will allow nutrition to be maintained in the hope that swallowing will improve. Many persons have dramatic improvements after a stroke. The decision to place or forgo a feeding tube should be made carefully after you have discussed and weighed the benefits and the risks with the physician (see Figure 39-3). If you decide a feeding tube is warranted, it does not mean that the feeding tube cannot be removed at a later time if your loved one's condition deteriorates.

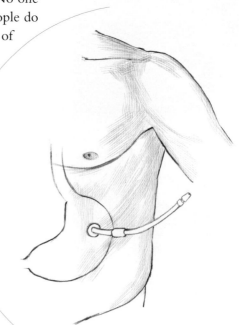

(figure 39-3)

A feeding tube is a flexible plastic tube that allows nutrition to be delivered directly to the stomach.

Constipation is frequently associated with use of such pain relievers as codeine and morphine. Dehydration and immobility can contribute to the problem, as can inadequate fiber in the diet. Certain preventive measures are helpful. Your doctor can guide you on the program that is best for your loved one. Psyllium products, such as Metamucil or Hydrocil, or stool softeners, such as Colace, should be given. If constipation is still a problem, stimulant laxatives such as Peri-Colace or Senokot are useful. Milk of magnesia and Dulcolax are available over the counter if constipation is still a problem. Mineral oil can be useful if the patient is alert and has no swallowing problems; however, it can cause a serious reaction in the lungs if it goes down the "wrong way." Therefore, avoid mineral oil if your loved one is very debilitated or has swallowing problems. MiraLax and lactulose are prescription laxatives that can be tried if other methods have failed. If a bowel movement has not occurred after three or four days or if the belly is getting distended, a rectal examination is necessary. A very hard stool can get stuck in the rectum (fecal impaction) and require enemas or manual removal by a professional. Bowel obstruction is a serious problem, since it may require surgery to correct. Naturally, this is a serious decision in a person who is terminally ill. If life expectancy is no more than a few days or weeks, administering medicines for pain and nausea may be preferable.

Diarrhea has numerous possible causes. Liquid nutritional supplements can cause loose stools. Diarrhea is also a common side effect of medicines. You might find it strange, but a fecal impaction can cause diarrhea. The water from the colon and intestines flows around the hard stool and causes watery bowel movements. As you can imagine, administering antidiarrhea drugs can make the problem worse. Proper evaluation includes a rectal examination. If the problem is not related to an impaction or to an infection, loperamide (Imodium) can be used for temporary relief. Drugs or supplements that cause diarrhea need to be stopped or their dosages modified.

The evaluation of persistent nausea and vomiting requires the physician and nurses involved in your loved one's care. You need to report these symptoms if they occur. You should not treat them with over-the-counter medicines without discussing it with the doctor or nurse. There are effective prescription medicines for relieving these symptoms.

URINARY PROBLEMS

Urinary leakage (incontinence) can be a frustrating problem for a caregiver and an embarrassment for your loved one. Generally, urinary catheters are avoided due to the high risk of urinary tract infection. Carrying around a drainage bag is also inconvenient. However, a catheter might be necessary if skin breakdown is occurring and the skin is constantly irritated by urine. If your loved one can move and reposition fairly well, a bedside commode makes it easier to void when necessary. Some incontinent episodes occur because he or she cannot get to the bathroom quickly enough. A bedpan for a woman or a urinal for a man is one alternative. Adult diapers or incontinent pads are frequently necessary. If the skin is irritated, you should talk with the doctor or nurse about use of creams or ointments that act as moisture barriers.

BREATHING PROBLEMS

Nothing is more terrifying than not being able to breathe. Breathing problems can be caused by heart failure, a blood clot in the lungs, pneumonia, COPD, and cancer. The decision to treat depends on the severity of your loved one's underlying condition. The goal here is comfort, not cure. Oxygen may be beneficial with all these conditions. In some case, diuretics or anticoagulants are necessary. If the patient has a life expectancy of more than a few months with a reasonable quality of life, antibiotics can be used to treat pneumonia. However, they can be withheld if the prognosis is very poor. Fluid can accumulate under the lungs with congestive heart failure or when cancer involves the chest. Removal of the fluid with a needle and syringe by the physician can help relieve shortness of breath.

When breathing problems occur in those who are near death, morphine and sedatives can provide comfort until death occurs. If there is congestion in the airways, helpful drugs are ATROPINE or SCOPOLAMINE. Sometimes events occur when death is near that could be very distressing to your family. If you discuss your wishes with the doctor ahead of time, *palliative sedation* can be used. The drug most frequently used is MIDAZOLAM (VERSED). This drug is typically used for sedation prior to surgery and other medical procedures, such as colonoscopy.

ANXIETY AND DEPRESSION

Confronting our own death or the death of a loved one stirs many emotions. The love and support of family and friends, the physician, the clergy, and others involved in the care of the dying person can make a huge difference in how that person deals with and accepts his or her condition. However, anxiety and/or depression may require medical therapy, which can be prescribed by the primary care physician. In some cases, a psychiatrist or the palliative care physician will be consulted. Chapter 25 discusses the treatment of anxiety and depression.

■

WHAT YOU NEED TO KNOW

▶ Death is one of life's certainties. Preparing for death and terminal illness ahead of time can prevent a crisis later. Talk with your family and prepare an advanced directive.

▶ The American health system is seriously fragmented. A number of organizations are working to help correct these problems so that compassionate care for dying persons can be provided. We should not see people dying in misery because of a broken health system. However, you need to take an active role. Discuss your wishes for your care at the end of life with your family, your doctor, and your clergyman or clergywoman. If you have an attorney, he or she will help you draft the documents you need. If you don't have or can't afford an attorney,

contact *Last Acts Partnership* for free documents (see "For More Information").

▶ Hospice is a form of terminal care in which services are provided by a team, which may include physicians, nurses, physical and occupational therapists, home health aides, and volunteers. Hospice not only assists the physician in the management of the patient's pain, but also helps the patient and family deal with emotional and spiritual issues.

▶ Most of the symptoms associated with a terminal illness can be effectively controlled with good palliative care. The focus in care of the dying patient is comfort rather than cure.

FOR MORE INFORMATION

▶ **Last Acts Partnership**
1620 "Eye" Street NW, Suite 202
Washington, DC 20006
202-296-8071
800-989-9455
Fax: 202-296-8352
Web: www.lastactspartnership.org

▶ **Hospice Foundation of America**
2001 S Street NW 300
Washington, DC 20009
800-854-3402
Fax: 202-638-5312
Web: www.hospicefoundation.org

▶ **National Hospice & Palliative Care Organization**
1700 Diagonal Road, Suite 625
Alexandria, VA 22314
703-837-1500
Fax: 703-837-1233
Web: www.nhpco.org

▶ **U.S. Administration on Aging**
Washington, DC 20201
202-619-0724
Web: www.aoa.dhhs.gov

▶ **Advance Choice**
DocuBank
109 Forrest Avenue, Courtyard, Suite 100
Narberth, PA 19072
800-362-8226
Web: www.docubank.com

SUGGESTED READING

▶ On Death and Dying.
Elisabeth Kübler-Ross. 1969.
New York: Simon & Schuster.

To everything there is a season, and a time to every purpose under the heaven. . . . A time to be born, and a time to die: . . . a time to weep, and a time to laugh: a time to mourn and a time to dance.

—*Ecclesiastes 3*

THE AUTHOR

40   *Christine Cauffield*

CHRISTINE A. CAUFFIELD, PSYD, is president and CEO of Coastal Behavioral Healthcare, a nonprofit corporation that serves the citizens of six counties in southwest Florida. She has served as an international consultant in Berlin during the reunification of Germany, presented at the United Nations on substance abuse issues, and assisted the Red Cross in the aftermath of the crash of Flight 587 in Queens, New York. She is a member of numerous boards, including Florida Council for Community Mental Health, Florida Alcohol and Drug Abuse Association, and Florida Juvenile Justice Association. As a licensed clinical psychologist, she is active in the American Psychological Association and Florida Psychological Association. Dr. Cauffield received her doctoral degree in clinical psychology from Florida Institute of Technology and, specializing in geriatric neuropsychology, completed her internship and postdoctoral residency at Harvard Medical School. Dr. Cauffield has also received recognition as an honored professional in the Nationwide Register's *Who's Who in Executives and Business* and is the author of numerous journal articles. Her clinical expertise includes substance abuse, trauma recovery, grief and loss issues, and brain diseases and disorders of the elderly.

40 | BEREAVEMENT AND CAREGIVING

Everyone at some point in life experiences a traumatic loss, whether it be the death of a loved one, a loss of position, loss of friends, or ill health or disability. As individuals we each grieve differently: some in healthy ways, while others lack the support and/or coping skills necessary to navigate the loss.

Bereavement is a normal reaction to a major loss and can precipitate experiences that impact on many levels, including emotional, cognitive, physical, behavioral, and spiritual. Over eight million Americans will suffer a significant personal loss in the next 12 months, and older people typically experience many losses in the last two decades of life.

Emotional effects include sadness, guilt, anxiety, fear, helplessness, vulnerability, intense rumination regarding the loss, and physical ailments. Additionally, the current loss often brings up memories of prior loss and trauma. These memories can further increase the individual's distress.

During times of grief the cognitive effects people describe include feeling disoriented, unable to make decisions, decreased concentration, confusion, and memory loss. These symptoms are normal reactions to the increased level of stress that accompanies loss.

The physical effects can include sleep disturbance, loss of energy, reduced appetite, and altered immunity. Bereaved older individuals often rate their health as poor, experience increased rates of hospitalization, and are eight times more at risk for death.

Behavioral effects which occur during grief include an increase in alcohol intake and/or overuse of prescription or nonprescription medications. Individuals may become irritable, moody, and display marked changes in their usual behavior.

If the bereaved embraces spiritual beliefs, a time of grief can bring about lapses in spiritual practice and faith. Thoughts such as "Why did God let this happen?" and questions about the meaning of life may arise. If a person has previously relied on the comfort of faith, these feelings of disconnection contribute to a sense of loss and despair. It's important to know that these feelings are normal, often temporary, and generally lead to redefining spiritual values. Spiritual health is often overlooked but is an important component to consider in the grief and loss process.

When most people think of grief, they typically associate it with the death of a human being. For many, particularly the elderly, pets are considered part of the family. The loss of a beloved pet may be grieved as deeply as the loss of a person. There are many other losses that we experience in life which cause grief. These losses also deserve

WHAT IS GRIEF?

Grief is a period of time when an individual:

- Experiences the loss
- Responds to his or her grief
- Heals
- Moves on with his or her life

LEVELS OF GRIEF

- Emotional
- Cognitive
- Physical
- Behavioral
- Spiritual

to be recognized as significant. Often, anticipated joyful events, such as retirement, result in grief and loss for the retiree. Issues to be grieved in this case include loss of identity, loss of stature, loss of daily routine, and camaraderie with colleagues.

BOB'S STORY

Bob had worked his way to become CEO of a manufacturing company in a medium-sized Ohio town. He was often asked to participate on boards of local charities and was given a great deal of respect in his hometown. He was a deacon in his church, president of the local Kiwanis club, and an influential member of the local Republican committee.

After 35 years with the company Bob decided to retire and move to Palm Beach. After the move Bob realized that he had become a small fish in a big pond. He missed the challenge of running a company and the status he enjoyed in his hometown. His attempts to become involved in Palm Beach did little to resolve his feelings of loss and lack of self-worth. Those feelings lead to anger, bouts of depression, and excessive use of alcohol. Bob was unable to deal with the loss of the person that he defined as himself.

Bob always saw himself as the person in charge, with great influence in his community. He did not prepare for the numerous changes that occurred when he retired, including the loss of friends and neighbors when he relocated. With encouragement from his son, Bob sought professional help from a licensed therapist. He began to allow his emotions to flow, facilitating the healing process. He became involved and socially connected in his new community, embracing a new identity.

Bob experienced the various stages of grief which include shock, denial, bargaining, anger, sadness, and guilt. He learned that grief is not a linear process. He often felt as if he were on an emotional roller coaster with his feelings changing from day to day, hour to hour, even minute to minute. Bob had a successful outcome because he sought professional help and was able to restructure his self-image to accommodate his new role as a retired executive.

Unfortunately, many older adults resist seeking professional mental health services. This generation typically embraces a philosophy of pulling yourself up by your bootstraps, which includes "not airing dirty laundry." Many were taught that it is a sign of weakness to seek help; however, research has shown that older adults who seek professional help have very high success rates for improved emotional health. An improvement in emotional health can, in turn, lead to a reduction in physical symptoms and an increase in immune functioning.

MYTHS ABOUT GRIEF

There are some common myths in our society regarding grief. Belief in these myths tends to interfere with the healthy progression of the grief process. Following are three of the most common myths about grief.

Inevitability of distress or depression: Although some of the symptoms of bereavement are similar to symptoms of depression (feelings of sadness, insomnia, poor appetite, and weight loss), depression is not an inevitable outcome of grief. People who experience sustained mood disturbance for over six months or who discuss suicide should seek professional counseling. Bereavement which is typical or uncomplicated can be treated through professional group and/or individual psychotherapy.

Absence of positive emotions while grieving: Laughter is healing. Experiencing humor while grieving is natural, as feelings of happiness and joy are just as much a part of being human as other emotions, including sadness and fear. Many people report feeling guilty or abnormal because they believe that having positive emotions during a time of grief is wrong. However, different cultural reactions to grief, such as an Irish wake, emphasize celebration as an important and acceptable form of grieving. It is necessary to recognize that different cultures may express grief in a variety of ways.

Time limit on grieving: Societal norms often interfere with the grieving process. Our Western culture discourages open displays of emotion. Our culture expects quick fixes and immediate relief from unpleasant experiences. Grieving is a process that does not proceed in a linear fashion but takes its own course with each individual. Suppressing grief is unhealthy, and people should be given permission to express their grief openly. Grieving does not have time limits, and many factors contribute to the intensity and length of the process.

LOSS OF A LOVED ONE

JANETTE'S STORY

Janette had been a homemaker almost her entire life and doted on her two grown children, a son and a daughter. Janette's husband had died several years ago, and she was satisfied with her role as an attentive mom and grandma. She would spend hours baking for her children and their families and would often take her grandchildren to the playground or shopping. She was a frequent and welcome visitor in the homes of her children, and they in hers. One day Janette received a phone call informing her that her son Rob had been critically injured in a traffic accident and was in the local hospital. She was informed that her son's injuries would, in all likelihood, be fatal. She immediately called her priest and told him that if Rob's life were spared, she would make the church the beneficiary of 50% of her estate. Janette spent the next three days at her son's side until he died from massive head injuries. Janette felt that God had betrayed her. She believed she had to be the strong one to support Rob's wife and children and her daughter in their time of sorrow. She would not allow tears to fall, even in private, and maintained her stoic calm through the funeral. As time went on, Rob's widow and Janette's daughter noticed that she was spending less and less time with them and the grandchildren and she was uncharacteristically short with the grandchildren. She often went days at a time without phoning. If they did have contact with her, she constantly spoke of her husband's death years before and focused on blaming medical staff at the hospital for his death. She also told them that her son Rob appeared at her bedside nightly.

There are few things that we anticipate with more dread than the death of a loved one. The loss of a spouse, child, parent, close relative, or friend results in the levels of grief discussed earlier in this chapter. The initial reaction, particularly to a sudden, unexpected loss, is typically shock. *Shock* is described as a feeling of disorientation and physical weakness, sometimes including a feeling of being sick, numb, and stunned. This and other stages may occur simultaneously because grief must be understood as a series of overlapping clusters of reactions or phases of time. Individuals differ in their speed of moving through the process and differ in the ways that they experience grief. In the above case, Janette's grief was delayed because she believed she had to sacrifice her own emotional well-being in order to provide a facade of strength for her family. Her unwillingness to express her emotions was not only unhealthy for her but also caused confusion and increased anxiety and stress for her family.

Denial is another stage in the grieving process. Initially unable to accept or cope with their loss, grieving people often deny to themselves that their loved one is dead. They sometimes express this verbally to others and may make statements like, "I know he (or she) is going to walk through that door any minute now." Denial is a defense mechanism that actually serves to buffer the shock, delay the reality, until one can better cope with it, or serves as a time period that helps the bereaved better prepare to deal with the loss. It is a necessary part of the process of grieving and sustains until one can gather the resources needed to navigate through the pain. Janette's account of Rob's nightly appearances at her bedside is not an

STAGES OF GRIEF

- Shock
- Denial
- Bargaining
- Anger
- Sadness or guilt
- Acceptance

unusual occurrence during the grief process. Many people report feeling the presence of their deceased loved one through dreams, apparitions, or other sensory manifestations.

Bargaining is an attempt to feel a sense of control and to alter the circumstances. This stage typically involves the offer of a personal sacrifice in exchange for a reversal of the loss. Such offers include promises to change personal behavior or bargaining with God. Jannette believed that she could make a deal with God to prevent the inevitable death of her son. After realizing that her attempt to bargain was futile, she felt that God had abandoned her. Her temporary loss of faith further increased her feelings of isolation and despair.

When the grieving persons realize that bargaining attempts are futile, anger is often expressed. People may be angry at their loved one for leaving them, at God for taking their loved one, or at themselves over things they perceive as unfinished business. A common phenomena is *survivor guilt*. Bereaved individuals may express extreme feelings of guilt, wondering why they were spared and their loved one was not. The feeling of anger during grief is normal, and its expression should be encouraged. Unexpressed anger often becomes displaced and directed toward others in an unhealthy manner. Janette's anger at God resulted in displaced anger at her daughter, daughter-in-law, and grandchildren. It is important for friends and loved ones to understand the grief process and anticipate that the bereaved will experience many emotions.

Sadness is one of the most frequently reported emotions associated with the grief process. Feelings of helplessness, crying spells, increased isolation, and decreased interest in pleasurable activities are common. Further feelings of disconnection occur when well-meaning friends try to sugarcoat the bereaved person's mood with such statements as, "He's better off where he is now," or "You'll meet someone else soon." These comments usually reflect the friend's own discomfort with feelings of sadness. A common fear about crying is that "if I start crying, I'll never stop." This is physiologically impossible, and suppressing tears does not allow one to move forward with healing. In the previous case Jannette did not allow herself to cry or express sadness. Her upbringing dictated that any display of sadness was considered a sign of weakness. Unresolved loss issues regarding her husband's death further complicated her ability to cope with her son's death.

Guilt often accompanies sadness, and recalling past interactions with the deceased is common. "If only I had said" and "If only I didn't" are thoughts that occur as the bereaved person relives past memories of the deceased.

Important mitigating factors that contribute to the grief process require examination. Often the nature of the relationship with the deceased has an impact on the grief process. If the relationship was ambivalent, with unresolved issues, or highly dependent in nature, the course of healing may be prolonged. Additionally, the availability of social support plays a paramount role in one's ability to navigate through loss. The stronger the social support network, the better the road to recovery for the bereaved. If the bereaved person has other stressful circumstances, such as economic hardship, health issues, or family conflict, the healing process could be impeded. Certainly, multiple losses experienced in a short period of time compound the trauma. Persons with preexisting emotional problems are at greater risk for depression, anxiety, and suicidal thoughts and being unable to cope with daily living. In these instances, it is advisable to seek professional help in order to reestablish emotional stability.

Acceptance is a goal that is thought by some to be the signal that the grief process is complete. For many, this is achieved in phases. One theorist describes the phases as follows:

- Initial awareness
- Holding on
- Letting go
- Awareness of grief
- Gaining perspective
- Resolving loss
- Reforming loss
- Transforming self

Navigating through the grief process is truly a journey. Many find comfort in searching for meaning in the loss. Increased self-awareness is often a positive growth experience. Acceptance should not be equated with forgetting. Some people report feeling that they are somehow betraying their deceased one's memory if they "move on." Acceptance allows one to mourn the loss and begin the process of rebuilding. To remain stuck in anger, guilt, or sadness robs the ability to fully experience the present.

CHANGING ROLES: THE SANDWICH GENERATION

Many baby boomers are caring for their aging parents, with little preparation for the challenge that role reversal has on emotional health. Witnessing a parent's declining health can begin the grief process, even if death is not imminent. Often critical decisions that were once the province of the parents are relegated to the adult children. This change in roles can be very difficult for both the parents and the adult children, as neither is willing to let go of their traditional role.

ANN'S STORY

Bob and Ann had been married 20 years, had two sons, ages 16 and 13, and lived near Ann's parents. Their sons were active in Boy Scouts and Little League, requiring a great deal of time commitment from their parents, who both held full-time jobs. Ann had relied on her parents help with baby-sitting, carpooling, and emotional support through the years. Ann's mother and father, John and Louise, were both in their 70s. Her father was recovering from a severe stroke, and her mother had always depended on her husband to make the decisions in the family and take care of everything around the house. Since her husband's stroke, Louise called Ann and Bob every day, asking them to make decisions for her and to take care of her yard, the plumbing problem in the guest bath, and to transport John and her to his physical therapy and doctor appointments. Louise often reminded Ann that she and John had done so much for her and her family and it was her obligation to help her parents now. Both Bob and Ann became resentful of the demands made by Louise and felt that they had no time for themselves or their sons. Ann felt increasingly guilty that she wasn't doing enough for her parents yet had little time for her husband and sons. She often thought that her only relief from this situation would be the death of her parents. These thoughts further exacerbated her guilt. The stress of the situation was creating serious marital problems for Bob and Ann, while Louise showed no gratitude for their efforts to help her and John, continually reminding Ann of her obligation to her parents.

Ann felt torn in many directions. The demands of her parents, husband, and sons, coupled with her career responsibilities, appeared overwhelming to her. It was painful to see her father, a former college football player and distinguished college professor, incontinent and paralyzed, with severe speech difficulties. She was sad and angry that he and her mother were no longer available for emotional support. She resented her mother's constant demands, with no apparent consideration for Ann's needs. As Ann's feelings of depression increased, so did her feelings of incompetence. She felt like a failure in every aspect of her life, despite her attempts to satisfy the needs of everyone else.

Ann's situation is an example of the stress that caregivers experience. Her thoughts that relief from this situation would only come from the death of her parents caused her increased guilt and anxiety. Ann's forbidden thoughts and feelings are actually common and normal.

CAREGIVING

The term *caregiver* refers to anyone who provides assistance to someone else who is in some degree incapacitated and needs help: a husband who has suffered a stroke; a wife with Parkinson's disease; a mother-in-law with cancer; a grandfather with Alzheimer's disease; a son with traumatic brain injury from a car accident; a child with muscular dystrophy; or a friend with AIDS.

Informal caregiver and *family caregiver* are terms that refer to unpaid individuals, such as family members, friends, and neighbors, who provide care. These individuals can be primary or secondary caregivers, full time or part time, and can live with the person being cared for or live separately. Formal caregivers are volunteers or paid care providers associated with a service system.

Ann's current life situation is becoming more common as the average lifespan has increased from 77.5 years in 1940 to 82.5 years in 2000. In 2002 approximately 12% of Americans were over the age of 65. Adults 65 and over are the fastest-growing segment of the population. The Center for Disease Control projects that by 2030 the number of older American's aged 65 and over will double to 70 million, or 20% of the U.S. population.

Almost 25% of Americans are caregivers to persons over 50 years of age.

Twenty-three % of Americans, or 22.4 million households, are involved in caregiving to persons aged 50 or over (see Figure 40-1). Of those caregiving for someone age 50 and above, the average age of family caregivers is estimated at 46. More than one-quarter (26.6%) of the adult population has provided care for a chronically ill, disabled, or aged family member or friend during the past year. Approximately 75% of those providing care to older family members and friends are female. The person most likely to be providing care to an older person is a daughter. Caregivers of people age 50 or over spend an average of 18 hours per week providing care. This figure increases to 20 hours per week among those providing care for individuals age 65 or over, and caregivers spend an average of 4.5 years providing care. Among caregivers an estimated 46 to 59% are clinically depressed. Approximately 49% of females and 31% of males experience depression as a result of caregiving. Caregivers use prescription drugs for depression, anxiety, and insomnia two to three times more than the general population does. Researchers have found that a person providing care for someone with dementia is twice as likely to suffer from depression as a person providing care for someone without dementia. If responsible for a person with dementia, caregivers who use adult day services experience less stress and have better psychological well-being than caregivers who don't use the service. A study of elderly spousal caregivers (age 66 to 96) found that caregivers who experience mental or emotional strain have a 63% higher risk of dying than noncaregivers have.

The average age of caregivers is 60 with a range of ages 19 to 98. Seventy-eight % lived with the patient, and 53% under the age of 65 were employed. Of those working, 18% quit their jobs to give care, and another 42% reduced their work hours.

Family caregiving differs across cultures and ethnic groups. A study of baby boomers by the National Family Caregivers Association found that 19% of Caucasians, 28% of African Americans, 34% of Hispanic Americans, and 42% of Asian Americans were caring for older relatives. This confirmed that a much higher percentage of Asian Americans provide care for older relatives than do white, non-Hispanic Americans.

LOSS OF HEALTH OR PHYSICAL ABILITIES

Aging can bring significant physical decline. Diminished energy, failing eyesight or other senses, sexual dysfunction, and decreased mobility are examples of losses that trigger the grieving process.

RALPH'S STORY

Priding himself in being very athletic and in excellent physical condition, Ralph, 67, played tennis, golf, and handball and worked out three times a week in the gym. Ralph married Becky, his second wife, four years ago. They enjoyed an active social life and had great sex.

Playing tennis one morning, Ralph suddenly complained of chest pain radiating to his left arm, shortness of breath, and nausea. His tennis partner recognized that Ralph was having a heart attack and dialed 911. Transported to the local hospital, Ralph underwent emergency quadruple bypass surgery.

In the months following his surgery Ralph underwent physical therapy and was distressed that he no longer had his customary strength or energy. He felt that he would never again be the man he once was, he was afraid that his heart attack signaled impending death, and he feared that Becky would love him less because of his diminished physical abilities. As time went on, he became depressed, with no interest in the activities he once enjoyed. He was unable to perform sexually, which further contributed to his sense of worthlessness and his fear that Becky would leave him.

Many males associate sexual functioning with their sense of manhood. Healthy sexual functioning represents youth, fertility, intimacy, and connectedness. Sexual dysfunction can result in serious emotional turmoil for both genders; however, research indicates that impotency impacts a male's self-worth in a more profound way. Ralph had felt very much in control as a male, being athletic, strong, and sexually active with his younger wife. After these self-defining strengths were stripped away, Ralph felt that a huge part of him had died. His grief reactions of shock, fear, anger, and sadness, although painful, were a necessary part of his healing process. It was critical for Ralph to receive professional emotional support as he coped with his physical rehabilitation and recovery. Becky attended the counseling sessions as well, to enable her to understand Ralph's feelings. The counselor encouraged Becky to express her pain regarding Ralph's health crisis. They learned new ways to express sexual intimacy as Ralph's recovery progressed.

GRIEF AND DEPRESSION

People often wonder whether grief and depression are the same. Nearly five million of the nearly 32 million Americans age 65 and older suffer from some type of depression. Depression is *not* a normal part of aging, nor is it a natural outcome of grief. Clinical depression has specific symptoms which can be easily recognized and diagnosed by a licensed clinician. It is important to understand that depression is an illness and can be successfully treated. The first step in dealing with what you believe may be depression is to make the effort to find out whether you are clinically depressed.

Figure 40-1 shows a brief questionnaire, the *geriatric depression scale,* an instrument often used to help determine if depression is indicated. After taking the quiz, score your answers per Figure 40-2. If your score indicates a possible depression, seek a therapist to determine if, in fact, you are suffering from depression.

(figure 40-1*)*

MOOD SCALE (SHORT FORM)

The geriatric depression scale. Choose the best answer for how you have felt over the past week:

YES NO   1. Are you basically satisfied with your life?

YES NO   2. Have you dropped many of your activities and interests?

YES NO   3. Do you feel that your life is empty?

YES NO   4. Do you often get bored?

YES NO   5. Are you in good spirits most of the time?

YES NO   6. Are you afraid that something bad is going to happen to you?

YES NO   7. Do you feel happy most of the time?

YES NO   8. Do you often feel helpless?

YES NO   9. Do you prefer to stay at home, rather than going out and doing new things?

YES NO   10. Do you feel you have more problems with memory than most?

YES NO   11. Do you think it is wonderful to be alive now?

YES NO   12. Do you feel pretty worthless the way you are now?

YES NO   13. Do you feel full of energy?

YES NO   14. Do you feel that your situation is hopeless?

YES NO   15. Do you think that most people are better off than you are?

(figure 40-2*)*

Scoring the geriatric depression scale. Score 1 point for each answer that matches the corresponding answer on the mood scale. A score of 5 or more points suggests depression and warrants an interview with a mental health professional.

	YOUR ANSWER	POINTS			YOUR ANSWER	POINTS
1. NO				10. YES		
2. YES				11. NO		
3. YES				12. YES		
4. YES				13. NO		
5. NO				14. YES		
6. YES				15 YES		
7. NO						
8. YES					TOTAL	
9. YES						

The importance of recognizing and dealing effectively with depression cannot be emphasized too strongly. Although a stigma is often attached to dealing with mental health problems, particularly for those over the age of 50, it must be understood that depression is a disease of the brain and is treatable, just as diabetes is treatable. Educate yourself about depression, whether you yourself or a family member appears to be depressed.

Depression has a variety of causes, each of which has an appropriate treatment. Some depression is believed to originate from dwelling on thoughts or from some traumatic experiences early in life. Depression also is believed to have an organic, or physical, cause. A chemical imbalance in the nerve receptors of the brain can malfunction and inhibit the flow of dopamine, serotonin, and norepinephrine. Some people may be more genetically predisposed to depression than others are. Regardless of the cause, treatment for depression is readily available and can allow the depressed person to resume a normal life. Untreated depression can lead to unfortunate behavior, such as overuse or abuse of prescription or nonprescription medication, abuse of alcohol, self-injury, or suicide. Typically, treatment of depression involves talk therapy with a licensed mental health professional and may include the use of prescription antidepressants.

Family members and friends are an invaluable asset in the treatment of a person with depression. They should educate themselves about the symptoms and causes of depression and the available treatment options. Encouragement, compassionate listening, and expressed understanding help provide the support necessary for the person to recover from depression. Remember that ordinary and easily accomplished tasks for most people, such as paying bills or choosing a restaurant, may feel overwhelming to someone suffering from depression. Dealing with people suffering from depression can be frustrating because they often set unattainably high standards for themselves or others and then react with anger when those standards are not met. Depressives tend to criticize themselves as being stupid, fat, lazy, or unworthy. Part of the understanding necessary for family and friends is knowing the pain of depression can be as strong and debilitating as the pain from a physical illness. Family and friends must continue to express understanding, listen sympathetically, and encourage a belief in whatever it is that offers the depressed person hope for the future.

JAN'S STORY

Jan retired as a schoolteacher in a northern New Jersey city. She was never married and, apart from a sister who lived in Pennsylvania, had no close family. She was well known to the neighbors in her apartment building but had no close friends. During her 33-year teaching career she had devoted herself to her job and had few interests other than her students and her nightly double martini at home before dinner.

After her retirement Jan attempted various activities. She visited museums in New York and took walks in a park near her apartment. Those activities soon became boring, and she became more reclusive. Other than weekly telephone conversations with her sister and an occasional visit, Jan had little meaningful human contact. Two years after retiring, she went to her doctor

SUICIDE WARNING SIGNS

- Talking of suicide, death, and/or no reason to live
- Preoccupied with death or dying
- Withdrawn from friends
- Socially isolated
- Experienced recent severe loss or anticipate a severe loss (relationship)
- Displayed drastic changes in behavior
- Little or no interest in work and hobbies
- Suddenly and unexpectedly made out a will and make final preparations
- Giving away possessions
- Taking unnecessary risks
- Losing interest in personal appearance
- Increased use of alcohol or drugs
- Expressing a sense of hopelessness
- Faced with a humiliating situation or failure
- History of violence or hostility
- Unwilling to seek help from family, friends, or professionals

and complained of sleeplessness, loss of appetite, restlessness, mood swings, lack of interest in anything outside her home, and the feeling that her life was over. Her doctor prescribed Valium for her. Although the Valium made her feel better, she found that by taking it in the morning and then having several martinis in the evening she was able to sleep. However, she never felt rested in the morning. She believed that the Valium and alcohol helped her forget her loneliness. As time went on, her consumption of prescription drugs and alcohol increased. In 1995 police were called to Jan's apartment after neighbors reported not seeing her for several days. Entering the apartment, the police discovered Jan's body on the couch, noted that she died several days earlier, and found prescription drugs and several empty bottles of gin. The medical examiner ruled Jan's death "accidental," a result of combining prescription drugs and alcohol.

The story of Jan is an all too common one in America. Jan failed to recognize her depression and, consequently, did not take advantage of any treatment options. She began overmedicating herself with both DIAZEPAM (VALIUM) and alcohol, increasing the downward spiral of depression combined with substance abuse. Unfortunately, her primary care physician also did not take seriously the depth of her depression and recommend other therapies in addition to medication. Primary care physicians miss diagnosing depression in half their older adult patients.

Alcohol and prescription drug misuse is estimated to a effect up to 17% of older adults in the United States. The primary substances of concern for drug misuse are alcohol, nicotine, caffeine, over-the-counter medications, and prescription drugs. It is estimated that 85% of older Americans take at least one prescription drug daily, 76% use more than one prescription drug, and 70% use over-the-counter drugs daily. Of hospitalized adults over the age of 40, 21% have a diagnosis of alcoholism resulting in related hospital costs as high as $60 billion per year. Alcohol is a depressant. In a study conducted by the Agency for Health Care Policy and Research, 16% of older adults surveyed displayed one or more tendencies toward depression. Adding alcohol to this equation results in a potentially deadly duo. Depression and dependence on alcohol or drugs increase the risk of suicide.

SUICIDE

Annually, suicide claims the lives of over 30,000 Americans, and attempted suicide results in some 500,000 hospitalizations. Suicide is the ninth leading cause of death in the United States, with suicide rates exceeding homicide rates by about 50%. The leading cause of suicide is depression, a brain disorder, which tends to affect people more as they age. It is estimated that 66% of people who completed suicide were depressed at the time of their act. Men commit suicide four times as often as women, and men who are divorced, separated, or live alone are at greater risk of suicide than men who are married and/or are socially active. Older persons tend to be more socially isolated, often because of health problems. People who have had multiple episodes of depression are at greater risk of suicide than those who have suffered only one episode. Suicide rates increase with age and are highest among Americans age 65 and older. Additionally, 70% of older adult suicide victims have visited their primary care physician in the month prior to committing suicide.

According to the American Association of Suicidology, people who are depressed and exhibit the following symptoms are at particular risk of suicide:

- Extreme hopelessness
- Lack of interest in activities that were previously pleasurable
- Heightened anxiety or panic attacks
- Insomnia
- Talk about suicide or a prior history of attempts or acts
- Irritability or agitation

Family members or friends of suicidal people are often afraid to confront the person about the possibility that the person is considering suicide. It's okay to ask about suicide, and if the answer is yes, ask about the suicide plan: how and when does the person intend to kill himself or herself. A helper should never call a person's bluff or talk about the people who will be hurt by the suicide; doing so causes greater guilt and anxiety. A supportive person should use statements like, "I can tell that you are in a great deal of pain" and "I will do everything that I can to help you." Getting a suicidal person to a mental health professional is urgent at this point and can be done either voluntarily or involuntarily. Most states have laws which permit the involuntary admission of a suicidal person to a mental health unit through a judge's order, certain licensed clinicians, or by a law enforcement officer. Ignoring the warning signs of suicide can easily lead to a tragic and avoidable loss.

HOW TO GRIEVE

You have suffered a serious loss in your life. A family member or close friend has died, or you are grieving the loss of your health or physical abilities, and you begin wondering if you will have feelings of grief for the rest of your life. Grief is a process, and there may be many, and possibly mixed, feelings that occur while you think about your loss. Remember, there are healthy ways of grieving and of reconciling yourself to the fact that your life has changed and will never be the same again.

Earlier in this chapter we discussed the six stages of grief: shock, denial, bargaining, anger, sadness or guilt, and acceptance. In order to move through all those stages, it's important to know how to grieve in a healthy manner. First, you must accept the fact that grieving is a normal and necessary part of getting through your loss. Often people who should be openly grieving "suck it up," holding all their thoughts and emotions inside themselves so that they appear strong and beyond tears or words of sadness. We sometimes hear people comment at viewings or funerals, "I can't believe how strong she [or he] is." This perceived strength works against an emotional healing. Accept the fact that you have suffered a traumatic loss in your life and that it is absolutely okay to experience and show grief.

Talking about your grief helps the healing process. Find supportive family members or friends who are willing to listen to you. Expressing thoughts and feelings openly reduce the emotional pain of your loss and should not be thought of as being weak or out of control. Caring people understand your feelings and help you carry the tremendous emotional burden associated with grieving.

Allow yourself to feel the emotions. Fear, guilt, sadness, confusion, relief, and anger are part of grief. Such emotions may be felt separately or simultaneously. They are a normal and healthy part of grieving. Allowing yourself to feel them, no matter how painful, allows you to move toward acceptance, especially if you share these feelings with supportive friends, family members, or a health care professional.

Understand that you have physical and emotional limits, and respect those limits. If tired, let yourself rest. Don't think that you have to keep going even if you feel physically and emotionally exhausted. Also, make time for periods of normalcy. Do some of your routine activities, such as washing the dishes, working in the garden, or enjoying a hobby. Routine activities allow periods of a seemingly normal life in what is an otherwise emotionally and physically draining time. Allow some humor into your life too. Laughing is a wonderful emotional relief, as is crying, and allows the release of natural hormones in your body, which make you feel better. Laughing is not disrespectful; it is natural and healing.

One of the most important things that you can do for yourself is to reach out to caring people who will help support you through your grief. Friends, other family members, or established support groups are vital to reaching acceptance in the grief process because they provide the sympathetic ear or the loving touch that is so necessary for healing. Social isolation during grief leads to depression and unhealthy behaviors, such as the use of alcohol or drugs to dull the pain, and causes the emotional pain of grief to be prolonged.

Suffering a sudden, traumatic loss, such as the suicide of a loved one, accidental death, or homicide, complicates the grief process. In addition to the other emotions and thoughts involved in grieving, survivors of a traumatic loss often struggle to make sense out of a senseless loss. Here the survivor must deal not only with family and friends through the grief process but also with the media, law enforcement, and the judicial system. Legal and financial affairs compound the fear, anxiety, and confusion that already exists as a part of grieving. Such additional burdens and stressors prolongs and complicates the grief process.

The question of how long to grieve is unique to each individual, but the emotions associated with grief should not remain the primary focus of life. Healthy grieving leads to a diminishing of the pain associated with grief over a reasonable period of time and to an acceptance of the loss. Memories of your loved one who is no longer in your life bring a mixture of emotions, which include sadness. If good memories exist, they can play a strong role in emotional recovery. Anniversary reactions in which grief unexpectedly reappears are a common part of the grief process. Birthdays, holidays, and other special dates trigger many of the emotions associated with the original grief, and the anniversary reaction may occur periodically for many years. Healthy grieving provides the opportunity to return to a normal, healthy, and happy life.

HELPING OTHERS GRIEVE

Being in the presence of someone experiencing grief is often an uncomfortable situation. It raises emotions we may not want to feel, as well as questions, such as, "What do I say? What should I do?" Helping someone through the grief process is an unselfish labor of love and requires understanding, a compassionate ear, and a willingness to be personally involved.

HEALTHY GRIEVING

- Show your grief, don't hold it inside.
- Talk about your thoughts and emotions.
- Allow yourself to feel emotions.
- Know and respect your physical and emotional limits.
- Create a support group for yourself.
- Laughter and crying are both okay.
- Create periods of routine in your day.
- Don't socially isolate yourself.
- Cherish your memories.

HELPING OTHERS GRIEVE

- Listen with a sympathetic ear.
- Allow the person to express their emotions.
- Be careful with your use of words.
- Don't say anything to diminish the loss.
- Be a supporter in practical ways as well as emotional ones.
- Understand that everyone grieves in his or her own way and in his or her own time.
- Recognize that anniversary reactions are common.

Be willing to listen without being judgmental. Everyone grieves in his or her own way and in his or her own time. Expect the grieving person to experience and show a variety of emotions: fear, anger, guilt, and sadness. Allow the person to feel and express these emotions without being critical, and do not discourage the person from expressing feelings. Healthy grieving is all about openly feeling and expressing emotions.

In attempting to be sympathetic, some mourners are unintentionally hurtful. Clichés, such as "I know how you feel," "She's in a better place now . . . no more pain," or "There'll be better times ahead for you," are not helpful to the grieving person and should be avoided. A more appropriate comment is, "When you want to talk, I'm here to listen. I'll stay in close touch with you."

Help the person who is grieving by being a friend who is on hand and takes the time to cook, clean, do laundry or just answer the telephone. This time of helpfulness provides an opportunity to be a compassionate listener.

MARGARET'S STORY

Arnold, Margaret's husband of 53 years, died from a sudden heart attack. Theirs had been a happy and productive marriage, and the loss of her life partner was devastating to Margaret. Eighteen months after her husband's death, Margaret was having lunch with two longtime friends when she suddenly started crying. One of her friends, trying to be helpful, said, "Margaret, it's time to get over Arnold's death and move on." Margaret felt guilty about still being sad and vowed not to show her lingering grief in front of her friends in the future.

In this case Margaret's friend was being less than helpful and, in fact, hurt Margaret by diminishing the importance of Arnold's death and Margaret's accompanying grief. Her friend's words gave Margaret the impression that expressing grief was inappropriate, and as a result, Margaret's ability to grieve in a healthy manner was cut short.

The appropriate response to Margaret, from a compassionate listener, would have been to encourage Margaret to talk about Arnold and her feelings. A supportive friend would have encouraged Margaret to cry and to show whatever emotions she was feeling. Margaret's resolve not to show her grief again in front of her friends may result in Margaret sustaining unresolved grief. Grief has no timeline.

WHAT YOU NEED TO KNOW

⟫ The journey through grief is truly an individual experience, having a wide range of emotions. Although it may seem like the pain will never end, those who are grieving and those who are providing support should recognize that with the proper support and understanding, the feelings associated with grief can and will diminish. The following key points serve as a compass for the process of grief and loss.

⟫ It is important to accept that grief is a necessary process following a loss.

⟫ Grief is a period of time when an individual experiences the loss, responds to his or her grief, heals, and moves on with his or her life.

⟫ Humans may experience grief on a number of different levels, including emotional, cognitive, physical, behavioral, and spiritual.

⟫ Distress or depression is *not* inevitable during grief.

⟫ Positive emotions, such as laughter, are appropriate and aid healing.

⟫ There is no time limit on grieving.

⟫ The six stages of grief are (1) shock, (2) denial, (3) bargaining, (4) anger, (5) sadness or guilt, and (6) acceptance.

⟫ Grief can result from a loss of health or physical abilities as well as from the loss of a loved one.

⟫ Recognizing depression or suicidal symptoms and then getting or encouraging appropriate treatment is vital to a healthy lifestyle.

⟫ The primary cause of suicide is depression.

⟫ Suicide rates increase with age and are highest among Americans age 65 and older.

⟫ Healthy grieving involves showing grief, talking about thoughts and emotions, allowing yourself to feel the emotions, knowing and respecting your physical and emotional limitations, creating your own support group, allowing yourself to laugh as well as cry, creating periods of routine in your daily activities, and cherishing memories.

⟫ Helping others grieve requires listening with a sympathetic ear, allowing the person to express emotions, being careful with your words, not saying anything that diminishes the loss, being a supporter in practical as well as emotional ways, understanding that everyone grieves in his or her own way and his or her own time, and recognizing that anniversary reactions are part of the grieving process.

FOR MORE INFORMATION

⟫ AARP
601 E Street NW
Washington, DC 20049
800-424-3410
Web: www.aarp.org

⟫ Alzheimer's Association
919 N. Michigan Avenue
Suite 1100
Chicago, IL 60611
800-272-3900
Web: www.alz.org

⟫ American Association of Suicidology
4201 Connecticut Avenue. NW, Suite 408
Washington, DC 20008
202-237-2280
Web: www.suicidology.com

⟫ American Psychiatric Association
1000 Wilson Boulvard, Suite 1825
Arlington, Va. 22209-3901
703-907-7300
Web: www.psych.org

⬛ American Psychological Association

750 First Sreet NE

Washington, DC 20002-4242

800-374-2721

Web: www.apa.org

⬛ Family Caregiver Alliance

690 Market Street, Suite 600

San Francisco, CA 94104

800-445-8106

Web: www.caregiver.org

⬛ Hospice Foundation of America

2001 S Street NW, Suite 300

Washington, DC 20009

800-854-3402

Web: www.hospicefoundation.org

⬛ National Association of Social Workers

750 First St. NE, Suite 700

Washington, DC 20002

800-638-8799

Web: www.naswdc.org

⬛ National Family Caregivers Association

10400 Connecticut Avenue, Suite 500

Kensington, MD 20895

800-896-3650

E-mail: info@nfcacares.org

⬛ National Hospice and Palliative Care Organization

1700 Diagonal Road, Suite 625

Alexandria, VA 22314

703-837-1500

Web: www.caregiver.org

Web: www.nhpco.org

⬛ Partnership for Caring

1620 I St. NW, Suite 202

Washington, DC 20006

800-989-9455

Web: www.partnershipforcaring.org

⬛ The Center for Loss and Life Transition

3735 Broken Bow Road

Fort Collins, CO 80526

970-226-6050

Web: www.centerforloss.com

SUGGESTED READING

⬛ The Complete Elder Care Planner New York:

Joy Loverde. 1997.

Warner Books.

⬛ The 36-Hour Day

Nancy Mace and Peter Rabbins. 1999.

Baltimore: Johns Hopkins University Press.

⬛ Caregiving: The Spiritual Journey of Love, Loss and Renewal

Beth Witrogen McLeod. 1999.

New York: Wiley.

⬛ The Comfort of Home: An Illustrated Step-by-Step Guide for Caregivers

Maria Meyer and Paula Derr. 1998.

Portland, OR: CareTrust Publications.

⬛ How to Care for Aging Parents

Virginia Morris. 1996.

New York: Workman Publishing.

Aging is a moral and spiritual frontier because its unknowns, terrors, and mysteries cannot be successfully crossed without humility and self-knowledge, without love and compassion, without acceptance of physical decline and mortality, and a sense of the sacred.

—*Thomas R. Cole, The Journey of Life*

THE AUTHOR

41

SUSAN H. MCFADDEN, PHD, is professor and chair of the Psychology Department at the University of Wisconsin–Oshkosh. Her main interests are in the area of adult development and aging and the psychology of religion. She has combined these interests in a number of research projects and scholarly articles that address religiousness and spirituality in the context of aging people.

Dr. McFadden is active in a number of national organizations, including the Gerontological Society of America and the American Society on Aging, for which she is a founding member of the Forum on Religion, Spirituality, and Aging. She is an associate director of the Center on Aging, Religion, and Spirituality (CARS), located in St. Paul, Minnesota. She teaches a course there every summer on spiritual development in later life. With her colleagues at CARS, she coedited the two volumes of *Aging, Spirituality, and Religion: A Handbook.*

41 | SPIRITUALITY AND HEALTH

In a 1910 medical book called *Old Age Deferred: The Causes of Old Age and Its Postponement by Hygienic and Therapeutic Measures,* the author, Dr. Arnold Lorand, included a chapter entitled "Hygiene of the Mind— Religious Belief as a Means of Prolonging Life." This chapter focused on observations by Lorand and his colleagues that religious people seemed better equipped to meet life's challenges and thus lived longer, healthier lives. His observations on religion appeared among chapters detailing how diet, exercise, marriage, and treatment of anxiety and depression can contribute to health and longevity. Today, we know from many research studies that these are some of the most important factors contributing to late life physical and mental well-being.

Since the 1980s, research on the effects of religious beliefs and behaviors on various measures of health has been rapidly accumulating. Overall, the emerging picture has shown positive health outcomes for older people who have a deep and authentic faith that is supported by private religious activities like prayer and public religious activities like worship attendance. The term *religious epidemiology* entered the gerontological vocabulary about 20 years ago, thanks largely to the efforts of Jeff Levin who documented over 200 research studies on religion, health, and aging conducted prior to 1989 and who also conducted many important studies himself.

Today, interest in the contribution of religiosity and spiritual awareness to older adults' health and well-being continues to grow. Increasingly, social workers, doctors, nurses, and other professionals who work with older people are recognizing the importance of a holistic approach to care that includes the spiritual aspect of human experience. Thus, in addition to gathering information about an individual's medical and psychosocial history, professional caregivers are also beginning to inquire about the person's *spiritual history* in order to understand religious coping resources as well as points of conflict that could have negative effects on health.

APPROACHES TO RELIGION AND SPIRITUALITY

When Lorand wrote his book in the early 20th century, he was concerned only with religious beliefs, primarily those related to what he called a "Superior Being." The notion that spirituality might be separate from religion has only emerged in recent years and would have seemed quite odd to Lorand. Today, we find that many people split spirituality from religion by the rather simplistic view that spirituality is good because its focus is on individual experience, while religion is bad because of repressive institutions and outdated beliefs. One hears people say, "I'm very spiritual, but I'm not at all religious." This is especially true of persons born after World War II and is an example of how attitudes of young and middle-aged persons about religion and spirituality may differ from those held by older adults.

Approaches to spirituality that exclude the sacred emerged in the 1960s from the human potential movement in psychology, which emphasized such qualities of the human spirit as awe, hopefulness, love, and insight into the interconnectedness of life. The humanistic model of spirituality has produced considerable debate among scholars because of the lack of reference to a transcendent realm. Nevertheless, several studies of how Americans conceptualize spirituality have found that most people do view it as related to the sacred beyond the self and they describe it using language rooted in religious beliefs about God, religious institutions, and creeds. Gerontologists (specialists in the study of aging) tend to view it as the expression of the human need for meaning beyond material existence. People seek meaning in experiences of connectedness—connectedness within themselves, with other persons, and with the world around them. The meaning of these experiences of connectedness—or integration—is grounded in a transcendent experience of connectedness with the sacred. However, because the motivation to seek this kind of experience of meaning is so hard to measure, most of the research on older adults' health has focused on religion.

Most gerontological researchers think of religion as a multidimensional phenomenon embraced by groups of people who share beliefs about transcendence and behaviors that lead to human fulfillment. Kenneth Pargament, a well-known psychologist who studies religious coping, defines *religion* as the search for significance (or meaning) in ways related to the sacred. Religions give people "maps" for undertaking this search in the form of language, stories, symbols, rituals, and social institutions. Religions also define what it means to be fulfilled as a human believer in relation to the divine. Finally, religions not only show people how to relate to transcendence but also develop faith traditions handed down through generations that enable believers to feel connected with other believers through time and space.

Over the years, researchers have developed many ways of measuring religious beliefs, practices, and attitudes. Other measures examine forms and levels of religious orientation, usually categorized as *intrinsic,* with religiosity as an end in itself and the believer's central motivator, or as *extrinsic,* with religiosity as a means to an end (e.g., worldly power, status, or wealth). There are also scales to measure religious commitment and religious experience, religious coping, concepts of God, religious fundamentalism, views of the afterlife, and forgiveness. Two highly regarded psychologists of religion—Peter Hill and Ralph Hood—edited a book published in 1999 called *Measures of Religiosity* that contained 126 different ways of measuring constructs related to religious faith.

In general, most studies of religion and health in older adults use measures of public religious activities (such as worship and religious education), private activities (like prayer, devotions, and meditation), and subjective religiosity (the importance of religion in a person's life). Although most research employs scales that quantify differences among persons, some researchers are conducting qualitative studies using interviews and focus groups. For example, Neal Krause and his colleagues at the University of Michigan used eight focus groups in which older people talked about the nature and meaning of prayer in their lives. Participants in the groups talked about their beliefs in prayers being answered, the timing of such prayers, the ways they felt prayers were answered, and their comparison of group and individual prayers. This approach allowed the investigators to learn much more about prayer than is usually revealed in paper-and-pencil measures.

Another interesting insight about older adults' religiosity has emerged from studies by Janet Ramsey and Rosemary Blieszner investigating *spiritual resiliency,* which is the ability of religious persons to bounce back from difficulties because of the strength, support, and meaning in the faith community, the ways they can share their deepest feelings with God and other believers, and the relationships they develop with other persons and with God. Although Ramsey and Blieszner did not specifically address health factors, their work pertains to health inasmuch as resiliency is an important indicator of how people respond to infectious agents and chronic stress.

RESEARCH ON RELIGION, SPIRITUALITY, AND HEALTH

Probably the most comprehensive source of information about research on religion, spirituality, and mental and physical health is the *Handbook of Religion and Health,* by Harold Koenig, Michael McCullough, and David Larson, published in 2001. Although not specifically focused on older adults, the *Handbook of Religion and Health* has a section on religion and mental health, on religious and physical disorders, and on religion's positive and negative effects on health and the use of health services. As documented in the book, researchers usually find that religion is associated with greater well-being, more hope and optimism, greater purpose and meaning, and better feelings about the self. Religious people adapt better to bereavement and show less depression than do nonreligious people. If depressed, religiously active people experience less severe and shorter depressions. Religious people also show less anxiety and fear.

Note that not all studies find positive outcomes. In some, the outcomes are mixed, and in others, religion is associated with poorer mental health. In addition, these studies employ different measures and research designs, making it difficult to compare them. Overall, however, most studies find a positive relationship between religion (especially intrinsic religiosity) and mental health. One of the strongest predictors of this relationship is the frequency of worship attendance.

Worship attendance is associated with better physical health, although because people who are very ill cannot attend services, attendance might be a proxy for health. However, longitudinal research by Ellen Idler and her colleagues has shown that religiously active people do live longer and that they attend regularly until close to the time of their death. In their

summary of findings on various illnesses, Koenig, McCullough, and Larson noted less heart disease and hypertension among highly religious persons. A few studies have also shown better immune system functioning among the more religious. The protective effects of religion have been found among persons of different age, ethnicity, race, and religious affiliation.

Studies on religiosity have their critics. Earlier research used one-dimensional measures of religiosity and cross-sectional designs that did not allow for conclusions to be validly drawn about whether high levels of religious participation or stronger religious beliefs actually *caused* the better health outcomes. More recent studies have used more sophisticated designs and measures, often following people for a period of years, and continued to find positive associations between religion and health. However, some interesting work is starting to emerge suggesting that under some circumstances more religious people may have poorer health outcomes. For example, Pargament and his colleagues have shown that when interactions with congregations are negative, more religious people experience greater depression than less religious people do. In another study, Pargament, Koenig, and others found that medically ill, older people had a greater risk of dying if they struggled with doubt about God's love or believed they were being punished for their misdeeds. Thus, it is important to recognize that some ways of being religious may increase people's physical suffering and psychological distress.

RESEARCH RESULTS

As research findings have accumulated on the mostly positive effects of religious observance and belief on mental and physical health, researchers have attempted to identify the mechanisms responsible for such outcomes. However, the word *mechanism* signifies a materialistic view of the body that is not congruent with the perspective of many world religions toward the relation of body and spirit. Thus, we find that attempts to explain scientific observations stimulate thinking outside the domain of a strictly scientific world view.

Most researchers conclude that there are multiple reasons for their findings about health and religion. For example, many religions extol healthy living through dietary regulations and controls on the use of alcohol and other addictive substances. Religious faith may also encourage a more optimistic, hopeful outlook on life's challenges that helps one recover from illness. Another major influence on health comes from the social support people experience within faith communities. Linda Chatters and her colleagues have conducted many studies of the African-American community that have shown how social networks in

RALPH'S STORY

Ralph is a 78 year old widower who used to be an active member of his congregation until a new pastor arrived and preached a couple of sermons with political views Ralph opposed. Ralph had also argued with the congregation's governing board about decisions they made concerning renovating the sanctuary. Thus, over the period of a few decisions, Ralph stopped attending dervices and rarely saw people associated with the congregation. Ralph recently underwen coronary bypass surgery. Because he's still listed on the rolls of the congregation, the pastor visited him in the hospital. Ralph responded in a surly way and indicated that he did not appreciate the visit. Ralph's daughter and son-in-law are concerned about him because he seems depressed and lonely. They asked the hospital chaplain to visit Ralph, but he treated her like he did the pastor. Ralph is beginning to feel that life is not worth living. He remembers that he used to believe in a loving God, but now he thinks perhaps God is punishing him by keeping him alive.

black churches enable members to cope with adversity and chronic illness. Through the support of its congregation, the ministry of clergy, and the kinds of emotional uplift experienced in worship, the church itself offers multiple, interwoven resources for people's coping. Religious groups not only provide support to older people experiencing various physical and mental difficulties but also provide support for caregivers. Research on caregiving shows that religious coping can be a buffer against stress-induced illnesses that often afflict caregivers.

Can religious life be reduced to the social resources it provides to the faithful or to the psychological uplifts that result from public and private religious observances? This question is currently being debated, and to address it, people need to revisit theological and philosophical reflections on the relation of body, mind, and spirit. Some persons would go further and reduce even that most profound of religious experiences—the mystical sense of unification with the divine—to changes in neurotransmitter levels and subsequent activation of certain parts of the brain. Clearly, the mounting evidence about how religious people differ from nonreligious people in rates and severity of physical and mental illnesses calls for thoughtful people to engage with these challenging intellectual problems by creating dialogues among theologians, philosophers, and scientists.

The available evidence on the mostly positive relation between religion and health should not lead to simplistic conclusions, such as religion being a shield against human suffering. An article in the *Journal of the American Medical Association* illustrates this. Harold Koenig interviewed an 83-year-old woman who experienced multiple severe medical problems producing horrendous, constant pain that could not be ameliorated medically. This very religious woman prayed constantly. Should we conclude that her prayers "didn't work"? Her own testimony affirmed that her prayer enabled her not to dwell on the pain. She said that by giving God her "heart and soul," she did not have to worry about anything, including her daily suffering. Although being so ill, she attended her church regularly, participated in a prayer group, and visited others in need. The meaning and purpose in her life transcended her suffering.

Religious faith gives people a broader context for comprehending suffering and loss. Religions point people toward transcendence and fulfillment that lies beyond physical existence. Some religions proclaim that there is one God above all who loves and values each human being regardless of his or her status or state of health. Through the lens of religion, the concept of healing can take on a much broader meaning than what most research studies measure. Among Jews and Christians, for example, healing means the restoration of a relationship with God. The woman described by Koenig had not had her chronic pain healed by being eliminated; rather, she felt healed in terms of her connection with her God. It gave her a sense of wholeness within and between herself and other persons. She experienced spiritual health while her physical health declined.

Older adults' illnesses force us to reexamine our understandings of healing and curing. Some people may be fortunate enough to find the treatment that truly does produce a cure, but if they remain bitter and despairing, or alienated from family and friends, they may continue to feel that they are not healed. On the other hand, no cure may be possible, but healing, in terms of the restoration of relationships, can occur. For example, the dreadful deterioration produced by Alzheimer's disease cannot be cured. Nevertheless, up to the end of life with this illness, people can experience the healing love of family and caregivers, the reinforcement of being a person through compassionate care, and the affirmation by religious persons that even in the midst of this cruel disease, God's love endures.

IMPLICATIONS FOR MEDICAL PROFESSIONALS, CLERGY, AND ADULTS

Some people have suggested that research showing positive benefits of religious belief, prayer, religious coping, and attendance at religious services means that medical personnel should *encourage* their patients to pursue religion. However, this raises profound ethical questions, primarily if patients feel coerced to embrace a particular religious perspective. A more conservative—and ethical—position holds that research points toward the importance of a holistic approach to medical care. Doctors, nurses, and others obviously need to identify medical conditions. They also need to know the psychological and social conditions in their patients' lives that can either support or interfere with medical interventions. The research reviewed in this chapter suggests that knowledge about the patient's spiritual history is important. Many standard medical interviews include questions about whether religious beliefs provide comfort and affect medical decision making, membership in a supportive religious community, and spiritual needs to be addressed. Doctors and nurses may not be equipped to meet these needs, but they should be sensitive to their importance and knowledgeable about other community resources that could help patients meet such needs.

Clergy need to be educated about older adults and the role religion can play in physical and mental health. Unfortunately, often burdened by the overwhelming demands of keeping a religious institution vital, clergy may erroneously conclude that attention is best directed toward youth and young families. Seminaries today are appallingly negligent about offering courses on aging despite the demographic profiles of most religious denominations. Clergy and lay ministry teams need to work with medical professionals to support older adults' religious coping and to ensure that their spiritual needs are met. The research on the deleterious effects of religious struggles with doubt and the feeling of abandonment by God indicates the critical need for clergy to talk seriously with older people about their spiritual resources for coping with late-life challenges and to encourage them to engage in end-of-life planning, including directives for terminal care.

Finally, older people themselves need to speak up about their spiritual needs. They need to inform their doctors and nurses when their religious beliefs lead them to conclude that life-prolonging interventions should be discontinued. They should let their medical professionals know about how their spirituality informs their decisions about health care and adherence to medical regimens. Older people also should speak to their clergy about such issues. Too often, elders think that their concerns are of little importance and that they dare not "bother" their clergy with their problems. As a result, clergy and other religious professionals may be unaware of how much an older person needs meaningful spiritual support. If older people have questions or doubts about a long-held religious faith, they should find persons with whom they feel comfortable discussing these issues. If they carry a burden of guilt and the belief that their actions are unforgivable, they need to talk about their feelings with a priest, chaplain, or spiritual director. Some older people may even be trained to be spiritual directors themselves. Or they may develop into being "spiritual elders," a role that social gerontologist Robert Atchley claims is increasingly needed in our society today. Spiritual elders can convey to younger people a different perspective on the meaning of healing, sources of well-being, and pathways to encounters with the sacred.

Researchers today are finding that one of the most important aspects of religious life is the encouragement to forgive and to accept forgiveness. Gratitude for the blessings of life has also been noted as predicting better health outcomes. Older people have much to teach about the support they find in various faith traditions for expressions of forgiveness and gratitude. The next few decades will undoubtedly bring more studies showing the contribution of forgiveness and gratitude to late-life health and well-being. An already robust area of research will continue to grow as more components of religious life are identified and examined. The research will be best conducted as a collaboration among medical professionals, behavioral and social scientists, religious leaders, theologians, and older adults.

■

WHAT YOU NEED TO KNOW

▶ Researchers have identified several dimensions of religiosity that contribute to the physical and mental well-being of older adults, including social support from clergy and fellow congregational members, worship attendance, private prayer and meditation, religious coping, and beliefs about God.

▶ The many ways of defining and measuring religion, spirituality, and health has complicated research on religiosity.

▶ Religious older people may experience healing through the restoration of relationships with persons and with God, even though cure of their illnesses may elude them.

▶ Medical professionals, clergy, and older adults need to discuss contributions of religious beliefs and experiences to health as well as the possibility of negative effects of religious conflicts.

41

FOR MORE INFORMATION

▶ Aging, Religion, and Spirituality: A Handbook, vol. 2
M. A. Kimble and S. H. McFadden, eds. 2003.
Minneapolis: Fortress.

▶ Handbook of Religion and Health
H. G. Koenig, M. E. McCullough, D. B. Larson 2001.
New York: Oxford University Press.

▶ Keeping the Faith in Late Life
S. A. Eisenhandler. 2003.
New York: Springer.

▶ Measures of Religiosity
P. C. Hood and R. W. Hood (eds), 1999.
Birmingham: Religious Education Press.

▶ Mental Health and Spirituality in Later Life
E. MacKinlay, ed. 2003.
New York: Haworth Press.

Sure I am for helping the elderly. I'm going to be old myself some day.

—Lillian Carter, age 80 plus

THE AUTHOR

42

KATHLEEN HOUSEWEART, MBA, has over 18 years experience in the field of geriatrics and has worked with area agencies on aging in Massachusetts, Virginia, and Florida. Her experience includes in-home assessment and care planning for frail seniors, training and education for professional and family caregivers, and program planning and development. She received her degree in sociology from Holy Cross College in Worcester, Massachusetts, and completed her master of business administration at Saint Leo University. At this time, Kathleen serves as manager of Geriatrics Services and coordinator of the Memory Disorder Clinic at Sarasota Memorial Hospital in Florida. Active in her local community and in a number of organizations, she provides advocacy for older adults and caregivers.

42 | LONG-TERM CARE

In a perfect world, most of us would choose to stay in our own home for the rest of our lives. For most families this is an achievable goal. However, it takes preparation and planning, which should begin many years *before* you encounter the health problems and disabilities that occur as you age. It's not unusual, in hindsight, to regret a move away from family or the purchase of that three-story dream home when unexpected health problems limit your mobility. So planning for long-term care should begin in your middle years, when things are going well and you begin to look forward to retirement. Remember, the worst time to start planning for long-term needs (and the most common) is in the emergency room.

BEING DISABLED AND LIVING AT HOME

HOME

The majority of us choose the home we wish to retire in well before being faced with health problems, changes in financial status, limitations on our driving, and changes in social support systems. That lovely home, possibly located in a warm climate far away from the bustle of city life, seems perfect unless you lose your ability to drive or find that the closest medical facility is miles away. The beautiful three-story colonial seems perfect, until you realize that the only bathroom is upstairs and the doorways are too narrow for medical equipment to pass through. Common luxuries, such as the deep whirlpool bath, may be a lovely respite after work, but it may be difficult to climb in and out of if your mobility becomes limited. When planning to purchase your retirement home, it is important to include options for meeting your daily needs if you become disabled. When making choices on where to locate that home, keep in mind access to medical care, proximity to shopping, pharmacy, social activities, and family support. Sometimes it may be possible to remain safely at home—just not in the home where you currently reside. Be willing to adjust your retirement plans to protect your independence.

HOME ENVIRONMENT

The best way to stay in your own home is to prevent avoidable accidents and mishaps that occur when simple rules of safety are ignored. No matter where you live, there are ways to improve your safety and mobility. Look around your house. Make sure that the home is well lit and that well-traveled areas are free of clutter. Check for fall hazards, such as throw rugs, electrical or phone cords, or excessive furniture. Install night-lights, especially in areas traveled at night, such as the bathroom or the hallway to the kitchen. Make sure that the furniture that is closest to walkways is sturdy and able to support your weight in an emergency. (See Chapter 30 for information about assistive devices and Chapter 31 for information on falling.)

Be aware of the daily activities that may become difficult as you age, such as bathing or dressing. Recognizing these difficulties offers opportunities to reduce risks. It is not surprising that many household accidents for older adults occur in the bathroom. Adaptive safety devices

FAMILY JOURNAL

My mother and father are nearly 80 years old and live in a three-bedroom, two-story home close to where I live. My Dad has chronic lung disease that is progressing. Mom is diabetic, and her vision is failing. Keeping up with the household chores is becoming more difficult, and getting around our small community is restricted due to Dad's illness and Mom's decision to give up driving. I am concerned about their safety and have been trying to help them as much as I can, but it is becoming very difficult. I have a full-time job and three children to support. My wife is getting tense because I am spending more and more time with my parents and less and less time with the kids. I have been reluctant to do it, but I either have to get some help or suggest that Mom and Dad go into an assisted living community.

I have finally contacted Eldercare Locator, a service of the U.S. Administration on Aging, and found the names and telephone numbers of geriatric care managers in our community who can help me.

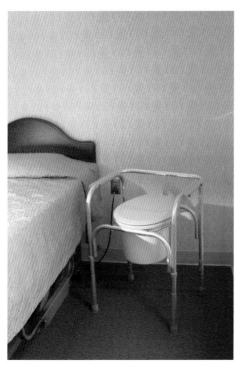

(figure 42-1)

A bedside commode reduces the risk of falls at night.

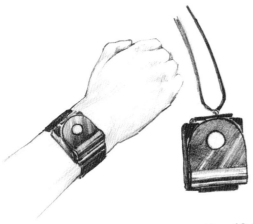

(figure 42-2)

An emergency alert response service is crucial if an injury makes it difficult to get to a telephone. A simple touch of a button sends a signal for help.

are now available that can improve safety in that area of the home. It is best to evaluate the bathroom area and how it is being used to make things as safe as possible.

Confirm that the bathroom floor, tub, and shower have nonslip surfaces, which are easily installed and available at most home improvement stores. Avoid throw rugs; however, if you must have them, make sure they are rubber-backed to adhere to the floor. Consider a raised toilet seat, possibly one with handles to assist in sitting and rising. These are often portable and can be easily removed when guests visit.

Grab bars, either temporary or professionally installed, provide assistance in the tub or near the commode. Be sure that anything that will need to support your weight is designed for that purpose and installed properly.

A tub seat could eliminate the need to climb all the way into the bathtub. Some tub seats are designed to extend over the edge of a standard tub, so that you can slide from outside to inside the tub. These should be set at the *appropriate* height to offer maximum benefit.

A bedside commode in the bedroom can prevent nighttime falls by reducing the need to travel to the bathroom (see Figure 42-1). These are usually very portable and require no installation.

Any assistive device should be installed properly, set at the proper height, and sturdy enough to support your weight. An improperly installed device can be just as dangerous as not having any support at all. A local home health agency or durable medical equipment (DME) provider can assess your safety needs and recommend appropriate equipment. Larger pharmacies often have showrooms to display various types of equipment and can recommend contractors to provide proper installation. In general, if you are having trouble with a specific activity, discuss it with your doctor. New devices are available all the time. Many equipment providers are glad to send you their latest catalog, so that you can see their latest products. Remember that if you are having trouble, someone else has probably already developed a solution, so don't be afraid to ask.

Emergency alert response services (EARS), such as the Lifeline program, provide a connection to a person or automated response system that can be alerted in case of emergency (see Figure 42-2). In some areas of the country these services are operated by a local hospital system or emergency medical services, but in most cases they are provided by private agencies. The systems use the phone to connect the older adult to help if needed. Often a button is hung on a necklace or pinned to the person's clothes. If an emergency, such as a fall, occurs, the person can alert the system simply by pushing the button. More sophisticated systems can contact persons at a prearranged time and alert caregivers if there is no response. These systems can be helpful, but they often only alert relatives after an accident occurs, and they are not helpful for confused patients who cannot understand how to use them properly.

In some areas of the country "granny cams" have become available and allow caregivers to observe what is going on in the home. The videocamera is set up in a specific area of the home, and the caregiver accesses the video from a website. Again, these can be helpful, but most caregivers are not available to monitor home activities throughout the day. However, in the near future, innovative devices will make it easier for working families to monitor the activities of their elderly loved ones.

OUTSIDE ASSISTANCE

Sometimes, no matter how well you plan or how safe your home environment, outside assistance is the only way to remain at home safely. If you find someone in need of assistance, follow the advice of previous chapters and seek a thorough medical evaluation to identify the cause of the symptoms. Many medical conditions can cause people to become temporarily unable to take care of themselves, and proper medical attention can resolve the problem. However, even as that evaluation is being completed, an investigation of local resources should begin.

Each state provides services designed to help seniors remain in their own home. These services are supported by federal, state, and local funds and usually target the most frail and those at risk for nursing home placement. The federal *Older Americans Act* provides funds, administered by state units on aging and local area agencies on aging, to all areas of the country. Even if your family does not qualify for publicly supported services, these agencies are a good first contact in discovering the resources available in a specific area of the country. Private services are available in most areas of the country, but vary among localities.

DEVELOPING A PLAN

Developing a plan to keep someone safely at home requires a subjective eye. Family members can tend to overestimate or underestimate a loved one's abilities. A professional assessment is often required to get a good idea about functional abilities and safety. Many areas have geriatric care managers who provide in-home assessments for a fee. Some agencies provide a free assessment to determine eligibility for specific services. Whether you call in a professional or evaluate the conditions on your own, be thorough and honest. This is not a time for false pride or polite ignorance of the real needs. A good plan of care can avoid unnecessary injury and expense. This may allow a person to stay in his or her own home safely, avoiding unnecessary nursing home placement.

A thorough assessment addresses home safety, as discussed in the section, "Home Environment," and evaluates abilities related to daily activities, such as walking, eating, transferring from a bed or chair, ability to toilet (including cleaning oneself), medication management, bathing, and dressing. In addition there should be an assessment of the instrumental activities of daily living, such as shopping, transportation, bill paying and financial management, meal preparation (including planning nutritious meals), household chores, laundry, and home maintenance. The assessment should look closely at how things are getting done (if they are getting done at all) and whether the current situation is safe.

Once gaps or problems are identified, specific plans should be made to obtain assistance with the tasks that are not being completed appropriately. Care plans should be creative and include all available resources. Bring in the whole "team," and provide everybody an opportunity to participate. Look for informal support, such as family members, neighbors, church members, and friends to assist when available. Those asked to assist should be given specific instructions on what is expected. Next, investigate the types of in-home services available, such as home delivered meals (Meals on Wheels), companion or homemaker services, and home health aides.

Keep track of plans in writing. A care plan can be very simple (see Table 42-1), noting how all needs are being addressed and who has responsibility for specific items. A good care plan will alert caregivers when changes or additions need to be made. Be specific about each person's role in the care plan. The idea is to address all the needs with a specific plan and appoint a responsible party, so that if something is not getting done, it will be easy to find out why and make adjustments. Care plans should be continually reassessed and updated, as needs change. The plan should be supplemented with contact information for each service provider and even list backup plans in case of emergencies.

IN-HOME SERVICES

In-home care can be provided by a friend or family member, an individual hired privately, or a licensed agency. Friends or family are often a good first option, but as care needs increase, these people often burn out, and a more specific plan should be investigated. Informal supports are not always available to provide assistance. In those cases where family and friends cannot provide the care, hiring assistants should be considered.

Keep in mind that while most of us would prefer to be cared for in our own home, depending on the amount and type of care needed, in-home care can become the most expensive care option. Hiring privately (finding someone you pay directly for care) can be less expensive than using an agency; however, be sure to check references and realize that you will have to deal with any employment issues that arise, such as worker illness, lateness, or unreliability. Also, discuss using private in-home assistance with your insurance agent to find out whether you have any coverage if the worker were injured.

Most areas have home health, companion, or homemaking agencies that provide in-home services. If hiring through an agency, make sure that its contract includes that (1) the employee has been screened, trained, and

(table 42-1)

SAMPLE CARE PLAN

NEED	ASSISTANCE	SUPPORT OR SERVICE
Laundry	Sally (daughter)	Visit Saturday A.M., to complete in home.
Shopping	Jim (son)	Visit Wednesday to take mom.
Banking	Tom	Visit first Monday of month to write checks.
House cleaning	MNO Home Care	Every Tuesday & Thursday, 10 to noon.

that backups are available if the worker cannot arrive as scheduled and (2) the agency handles employee's income and related matters, such as employee tax withholding, Social Security deductions, and vacation pay. As stated above, no matter who provides the care, specific instructions regarding what is expected should be prepared, and someone should be available to oversee that services are being appropriately provided.

If the care plan is specific and service needs are limited, short visits by companion services or home health aides are affordable to families as an alternative to moving with family or to a care facility. However, if the need for supervision or support becomes a 24-hour-per-day requirement, the cost can be overwhelming. Talk to your doctor about an in-home assessment by a Medicare-approved home health agency, which can determine if short-term needs are covered by Medicare. However, Medicare does not cover custodial or maintenance care, like bathing or dressing, unless it is accompanied by a need for skilled services, like nursing or physical therapy. Even then, service must be "short term and intermittent" to meet the criteria for Medicare payment. In some states Medicaid has limited assistance for in-home care if specific eligibility criteria are met.

Adult day care is becoming available across the country and offers socialization in a structured supervised setting during the daytime. Meals and snacks, as well as transportation to and from home, are usually included. The day care operates during weekdays, and can be a valuable resource for family caregivers who work or who need relief from caregiving responsibilities. Care is provided during the day at the day care center while family members provide care in the evening hours and on weekends, thus reducing the need for placement in a nursing home or assisted living facility.

There are many innovative services available in different parts of the country to assist older adults to remain in their home. Find out what is available in your area by contacting local service providers, which are often listed under "Nursing" or "Elder Care" in the Yellow Pages. Financial assistance for some of these services is available through local agencies listed at the end of the chapter.

LEAVING HOME AND/OR MOVING PARENTS

YOUR HOME

The decision to move from your home is never easy but sometimes necessary for safety reasons. As with other types of care planning, early planning is the best way to be prepared if a move is necessary. In evaluating your options, learn what is available in your community before a need arises. Most facilities offer free tours, community events, open houses, and written information about their services.

Often, the first response families have is to bring an older relative to live with children. Many families add rooms to their homes or make expensive renovations to accommodate such moves. Unfortunately, though these plans are made with good intentions, they are made without

NURSE'S NOTES

Dr. B. asked our home health agency to evaluate Robert P., 83, at home. On his last office visit, Dr. B. noticed that Robert P. had lost weight and looked unkempt. He lost his wife from cancer a few years back, but had eventually adjusted well. However, Dr. B. noticed in recent months that Robert P. was more forgetful and suspected that he was developing Alzheimer's disease. Dr. B. asked us to do a home assessment. What we found was shocking. There was almost no food in the refrigerator. Newspapers were strewn all over the floor. Unopened mail was piling up on his kitchen table. We notified Dr. B., and he contacted Mr. P.'s two children. They immediately flew in and made temporary arrangements with an assisted living facility in our community. One of the children was going to modify her house so that Mr. P. could live with her.

a clear understanding of the ongoing needs of the aging parent. It is not unusual for the construction of new living quarters to be completed and the family to find that the parent is too disabled to move in. In other cases, renovations are not completed in time, and a crisis requires a quick, unplanned move to another level of care.

Even if the home and place is ready, safe, and appropriate, bringing a relative to live with you should be discussed with all parties involved. First, what does the parent want? Many older adults do not want to live with younger relatives. Mom may not get along with her daughter-in-law or want to listen to grandson's music, for example. Second, if the older adult needs to make this type of move, there is obviously a need for care. That care may be limited to meal preparation, shopping, and cleaning or may include hands-on care with bathing, dressing, and so forth. In some cases 24-hour supervision is required for someone who is confused or at risk for falls. Is everyone involved aware of the needs?

Whatever the need, a plan should be developed *before* the move takes place, so that caregivers know and agree to their responsibilities in the care plan (see the section, "Developing a Plan," above). Finally, evaluate the budget. Review the expected expenses to make sure the plan is really affordable. Some families share the responsibilities by having the parent spend part of the year in one home and part of the year in another. While this can work in some situations, it is not always appropriate if the older adult is confused or memory-impaired.

ASSISTED LIVING FACILITY

If a move to a family home is not an option, there are alternatives in the community. Alternative living facilities can provide care that might avoid nursing home placement. Their names vary across the country but include adult foster care, residential care facilities, homes for adults, board and care homes, adult care facilities, and assisted living facilities. These facilities usually offer private or semiprivate apartments or rooms with a common dining area for meals.

The services provided by assisted living facilities vary, as do the fees. Generally, the resident signs a monthly lease agreement. Some facilities require entrance fees, which may be open to negotiation. Depending on the licensing requirements of your state, the facility can provide various levels of care, including meals, laundry cleaning, medication management, transportation, bathing and dressing assistance, and limited nursing services. There are usually added charges, depending on the amount of care. The benefit of these facilities is that they offer many of the custodial care services needed by older adults in an atmosphere that is more homelike than a medical facility or nursing home.

Assisted living facilities vary in size and specialty, with some being very large and having many levels of care and activities. For Alzheimer's care, specialized assisted living residences have trained staff, secured exits, and activities, as well as being equipped with an alarm system to notify the staff if someone tries to wander from the premises.

42

Another type of assisted living facility, the adult family care home, can be very small, often having less than five residents. Some older persons prefer a smaller facility due to the very special attention they get from their caretakers.

Choosing a facility has a lot to do with lifestyle and personal preference. Remember, if you are looking for a home for an aging parent or relative, choose what would make *them* happy. Caregivers often get caught in the trap of choosing the "newest" or "prettiest," without considering the needs of the aging parent.

NURSING HOME

Nursing facilities or nursing homes are often not a choice but a reaction to a crisis. Many people enter a nursing facility to receive rehabilitation for injuries or illnesses but are unable to return home. Remember Medicare does not pay for long-term nursing home placement. A nursing facility is designed to provide medical care or custodial care for those who are unable to ambulate or provide for their most basic needs. As with assisted living care, nursing homes vary in size and specialty. Some areas of the country have greater choices available to them. Medicaid can help pay for nursing home care if specific criteria are met. Admissions directors can help with the application process if necessary.

You are probably aware that the quality of care in nursing homes varies considerably. The website of the U.S. Department of Health and Human Services has a section called "Nursing Home Compare," which evaluates the performance of every Medicare- and Medicaid-certified nursing facility in the country (see "For More Information"). In addition, its website also has a checklist, which you can download, to assist you in making a nursing home selection.

RETIREMENT COMMUNITY

A retirement community is generally a campus with several levels of care, including independent living, assisted living, and nursing home care. Some include limited in-home assistance. Such communities are often buy-ins, by which a substantial initial investment entitles the resident entrance into any type of care available on the campus. The investment should be made cautiously. Be sure to check out each level of care available, not just the level of care that is currently needed. If a very large investment is required, be sure to understand which portion (if any) would be returned in the event of an unexpected death. Assure yourself that the facility is well managed and will be around when expensive care is needed. In brief, these communities can alleviate family fears by having a level of service for every need.

WHAT YOU NEED TO KNOW

▶ Early planning is the best. Start planning for your long-term needs well before you retire or require assistance.

▶ Most accidents are avoidable. Make sure your home does not have any hazards.

▶ Safety equipment can help prevent unnecessary injury.

▶ Care planning should include the "whole team," including informal and formal services.

▶ Sometimes care outside the home is the only safe alternative.

FOR MORE INFORMATION

▶ **Eldercare Locator**
800-677-1116
Established in 1991 as a public service of the U.S. Administration on Aging, the Eldercare Locator lists information and referral services provided by state area agencies on aging. Individuals who telephone receive information on more than 4800 state and local information and referral service providers identified by every zip code in the United States.

▶ **Family Caregiver Alliance**
415-434-3388
Web: www.caregiver.org
Has information and resources for family caregivers.

▶ **National Alliance for Caregiving**
Web: www.caregiving.org
Provides support to family caregivers and professionals. Increases public awareness of issues facing family caregiving.

▶ **National Association of Area Agencies on Aging**
202-296-8130
Web: www.n4a.org
Helps older Americans stay with maximum dignity and independence in their own home and community. Provides information on resources, training, and technical assistance to providers and publishes a national directory of area agencies on aging.

▶ **U.S. Department of Health and Human Services**
Center for Medicare and Medicaid Services
800-633-4227
TDD/TYY: 877-486-2048
Web: www.medicare.gov
Administers the Medicare and Medicaid programs and has information and publications on Medicare coverage. (Medicaid programs are administered separately in each state, and information for your state can be obtained from the national office.) Available by telephone is publication number 02174, Guide to Choosing a Nursing Home.

A society can be judged by the way it treats its most frail and vulnerable members.

—*Anonymous*

THE AUTHOR

43 *Kathleen Houseweart*

KATHLEEN HOUSEWEART, MBA, has over 18 years experience in the field of geriatrics and has worked with area agencies on aging in Massachusetts, Virginia, and Florida. Her experience includes in-home assessment and care planning for frail seniors, training and education for professional and family caregivers, and program planning and development. She received her degree in sociology from Holy Cross College in Worcester, Massachusetts, and completed her master of business administration at Saint Leo University. At this time, Kathleen serves as manager of Geriatrics Services and coordinator of the Memory Disorder Clinic at Sarasota Memorial Hospital in Florida. Active in her local community and in a number of organizations, she provides advocacy for older adults and caregivers.

43 | ELDER ABUSE

Elder abuse is often used as an umbrella term to include abuse, neglect, and exploitation of older adults by family members, caregivers, or anyone in a position of trust. The term also includes self-neglect in situations where seniors are not able to take adequate care of their own needs. In general, the mistreatment of elders can take the form of physical harm, neglect, financial or legal malfeasance, or psychological abuse. The true incidence of elder abuse is not known in this country, because many cases are never reported. However, experts believe that between one and two million elderly persons suffer from abuse in the United States each year. The greatest percentage of elder abuse involves neglect, though reports of physical and psychological abuse as well as exploitation are rising each year. As the older population grows, the number of cases is expected to increase dramatically.

THE PEOPLE

THE ABUSER

According to the National Center on Elder Abuse, adult children are the most frequent abusers. However family members, friends, paid or unpaid caregivers, and anyone in a relationship of trust or authority with the victim can commit elder abuse. There is no "typical" abuser. It is not more, or less, common in one socioeconomic class or ethnic or racial group. Elder abuse and neglect can happen anywhere and in the best of families.

The abuser may be financially dependent on the victim and use physical violence, threats, or intimidation to obtain support. Abusers are typically related to the victim and may suffer from mental illness or have substance abuse problems. Abusers often blame the victim, who is described as being demanding or ungrateful. In many cases the abuser is experiencing excessive stress, possibly from caregiving responsibilities and does not know where to get help.

THE VICTIM

The victim can be any older or frail adult. Statistics suggest that victims are more often female, which is likely related to the fact that women live longer than men. However, the gender gap is narrowing, and male victims are becoming more common. Victims typically live with the abuser or are dependent on them for care. In additions to physical frailty, victims are often impaired cognitively. A victim with memory loss makes a poor witness when abuse is discovered.

Victims often exhibit common behaviors that provide hints if abuse is occurring. Family members should be alert for such behavior and investigate situations that "do not seem right." Victims can become depressed or appear anxious or agitated. They might exhibit fear in the presence of the abuser or whisper in his or her presence. The abuser may prevent the victim from seeing friends or visitors (see Figure 43-1). The victim may become isolated, as a result of the abuser attempting to conceal his or her actions. In other situations the victims become withdrawn and resigned to their situation. If a family member commits abuse, the victim is often embarrassed and may even hide evidence of abuse or make excuses for the perpetrator.

UNDERSTANDING ELDER ABUSE

Elder abuse, neglect, and exploitation are defined by statute in most states. While specific legal definitions vary, they have many common aspects.

ABUSE

Abuse includes both physical and emotional abuse involving punishment or intimidation to force someone to do something against his or her will. Usually physical mistreatment is easy to recognize. A black eye, bruises, or broken bones may be obvious signs of abuse, but physical signs can also be hidden. Remember: Not all injuries are signs of abuse. Bruising, for example, can result from taking certain medications.

Emotional abuse is more insidious and difficult to identify (see Figure 43-2). It includes name-calling, insults, threats, or intimidation. In addition to implied violence, a threat can involve statements of withholding care or having someone placed in a nursing home. Threats can be very frightening to someone who is totally dependent on another person. Many frail older adults do not realize that unless they have been determined to be incapacitated, they cannot be "put" anywhere.

Physical and emotional abuse is hurtful and illegal. However, abuse is not always committed by bad caregivers with evil intent. Caregivers are under tremendous stress. Anyone who has ever provided care for another person understands the stress associated with 24-hour caregiving responsibilities. Even good caregivers can become frustrated when trying to bath a combative loved one or overwhelmed by the demands of a difficult relative. Good people who become stressed caregivers may let their frustrations lead to unintentional abuse. Even so, this abuse cannot be tolerated. Caregivers need support and respite and should be allowed (and encouraged) to ask for it.

Many areas of the country have respite programs that provide relief for stressed caregivers. The Older Americans Act included additional funding to provide services to caregivers. Respite, education, and other innovative supportive services are available in many parts of the country. Caregiver support groups also provide peer support and education to caregivers in the community. Good support groups offer caregivers a place to talk about their stress and learn techniques to make caregiving less difficult.

NEGLECT

Neglect occurs either because the individual has lost the ability to care for himself or herself (self-neglect) or because the caregiver has intentionally or unintentionally put the individual at risk. Many older adults in need of care require more than the basics of meal preparation and supervision. If an older adult needs to be lifted, bathed, or dressed and the caregiver is physically unable to perform the task, the elder may be neglected. Sometimes caregivers don't have the information or technical knowledge

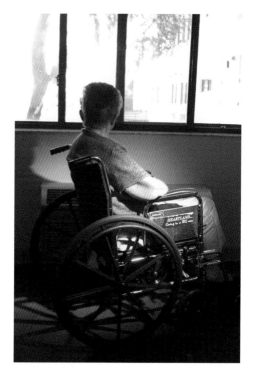

(figure 43-1)

Victims of abuse may be prohibited from seeing friends or having visitors.

(figure 43-2)

Emotional abuse can be more difficult to identify than physical abuse, but the impact is no less severe.

43

to provide adequate care and can unintentionally harm someone by giving medication incorrectly or developing unsafe care plans. One example is the caregiver who limits liquids to reduce the need to change an adult diaper and dehydrates the person.

The caregivers may be physically or emotionally unable to provide the care that is necessary to keep the elder safe. Caregivers are often family members who are themselves aging and dealing with health problems and stress from caregiving responsibilities. It is important to realize that even unintentional bad care can cause harm. Neglect is often first identified by weight loss, soiled clothing, or a foul-smelling living environment. Other signs include dirty or neglected fingernails and toenails or an unshaven or disheveled appearance. Serious neglect can lead to serious medical conditions such as bedsores and infection.

EXPLOITATION

Exploitation includes depriving someone of his or her property or use of the property by deception, force, or intimidation. Exploitation is almost always a willful act. Examples include writing checks without authorization, overcharging for goods or services, stealing money or property, or being paid for goods or services that are not provided. Exploitation may happen once or occur over an extended period. Look for unexplained withdrawals from bank accounts, the addition of names to accounts, or unnecessary purchases that are benefiting someone else. Exploitation is illegal; however, some family members justify taking an elder's money by saying, "It's going to by mine anyway. I might as well use it now." Exploitation within families is often the most complicated type of case to investigate.

Families are supposed to care for one another, aren't they? It is not unusual for an adult child to move in with mom or dad to provide care (though I would not advise it without careful consideration). In most cases, this is done with good intentions, by mutual agreement, to allow aging parents to remain in their own home. However, if the caregiver has no income and obtains all of his or her support from the aging parent, exploitation might ensue. Such arrangements can become further complicated as care needs change or if family members have disagreements.

Another form of exploitation can occur when younger family members expect grandparents to provide expensive gifts and financial support even when they no longer have the means to do so. This can be a significant problem if the older adult has cognitive difficulties or poor judgment caused by dementing illness or other medical problems. Children, teenagers, and adults are not always aware that their requests can take advantage of an older adult.

HANDLING ELDER ABUSE

Family members should not only look for physical signs of abuse but also listen to explanations regarding unusual injuries. If something

DOCTOR'S DIARY

Charles G., 84, can be a very difficult man. He does not like to take his medicines, and he refuses any tests that I recommend. His daughter has been caring for him at home, but she seems exasperated when she comes into the office with him. She tells me that he is a slob, and she doesn't like having him around when there is company. One day, my secretary was stunned when she saw Charles's daughter slap him several times as she tried to get him out of the car to come into the office. When I saw him alone in the exam room, I noticed he had a split lip and a red cheek. When I asked him what happened, he said he had fallen out of bed. I asked him if his daughter hit him, and tears came to his eyes. I confronted his daughter. Although she was contrite, I was obligated to notify our state agency for elder abuse. I made arrangements through our hospital social worker to have Charles admitted to an assisted living facility until an investigation was completed.

43

looks suspicious, ask for an explanation. If a story seems implausible, ask questions. Attempts should always be made to speak with the older adult separately from the alleged abuser. Contradictory explanations for injuries, bank account inaccuracies, or missing property could be signals that an elder is at risk and should be investigated further.

REPORTING ELDER ABUSE, NEGLECT, OR EXPLOITATION

At this time all 50 states and the District of Columbia have provisions in their laws that protect the elderly and disabled from abuse, neglect, and exploitation. These laws define penalties and methods of reporting. Most states have designated agencies responsible for investigating elder abuse and protecting those at risk.

Many states designate *mandated reporters,* who are people required by law to report incidents of elders at risk. Mandated reporters include physicians, nurses, social workers, nursing home workers, and others who provide care to older adults as part of their job description. In some states the definition of mandated reporter is very liberal and includes virtually anyone who works with older adults. Still most elder abuse goes unreported.

It is important to understand that each state has an elder abuse hotline that accepts anonymous referrals. It is also standard practice to protect the identity of anyone who suspects and reports elder abuse. Reporters are not required to prove anything, just report situations that may put an elder at risk. A listing of the phone numbers to call in each state is available through the National Center on Elder Abuse, listed in "For More Information."

NURSING HOMES OR OTHER FACILITIES

There are strict laws in most states that require training and adequate staffing for facilities providing care to older adults. Most facilities are inspected regularly to ensure that they meet state and federal standards of care. However, each state has different regulations regarding the requirements for the various levels of care. Some states provide no regulations for smaller facilities. Some facilities are inspected less than once per year.

If you see that someone is receiving inadequate care in a facility, talk to the administration or owner. Be specific and timely about your complaint. Don't wait for something to change; address problems as they occur. Most nursing homes provide good care and want to address issues regarding patient safety. However, if a complaint can't be resolved, assistance is available through the state ombudsman office. Each state has an ombudsman office, where trained volunteers or staff members work as advocates for residents of nursing homes, assisted living facilities, and board and care homes. They are trained to work with families and facilities to resolve complaints. Under the Older Americans Act, each state is required to have an ombudsman program. The contact information for each state office is available from the National Citizens' Coalition for Nursing Home Reform, listed in "For Your Information." If the situation is serious enough that it puts any resident of the nursing home at immediate risk due to poor care, it should be reported to the elder abuse hotline in the state where the elder resides. (A list of the phone numbers to call in each state is available through the National Center on Elder Abuse, listed in "For More Information.")

■

WHAT YOU NEED TO KNOW

))) Elder abuse, neglect, and exploitation can happen in any family, in any neighborhood, to any vulnerable adult.

))) Laws in each state protect the aged and disabled from abuse, and each state has an agency designated to investigate abuse.

))) Abuse can happen in a home environment or in a facility providing care. In either case it is illegal and should be investigated.

))) People working with the elderly are required by most states to report suspected cases of abuse, neglect, or exploitation.

FOR MORE INFORMATION

)) National Center on Elder Abuse
1201 155th Street NW, Suite 350
Washington, D.C. 20002-2842
202-898-2586
Fax 202-898-2583
www.elderabusecenter.org

The National Center on Elder Abuse (NCEA) is a national resource for elder rights, law enforcement and legal professionals, public policy leaders, researchers, and the public. The center's mission is to promote understanding, knowledge sharing, and action on elder abuse, neglect, and exploitation.

The NCEA is administered under the auspices of the National Association of State Units on Aging.

)) AARP
601 E Street NW
Washington, DC 20049
800-424-3410
Web: www.aarp.org

)) Alzheimer's Association
312-335-8700
800-272-3900 (24-hour hotline)
Web: www.alz.org

The association is a voluntary organization that serves Alzheimer's disease patients, their families, and their physicians by supporting medical research through programs and providing support services (e.g., adult day care, respite care, telephone help lines) to patients and caregivers. It has information for health professionals and patients, both in print and online. Local chapters often have support services including support groups.

)) National Citizens' Coalition for
Nursing Home Reform
1424 16th Street NW, Suite 202
Washington, DC 20036
202-332-2275
Fax: 202-332-2949
Web: www.nursinghomeaction.org

Each state has funding for an ombudsman office—though each state uses the funding differently. The coalition has contact information for all the states.

Failures don't plan to fail; they fail to plan.

—*Harvey Mackay, syndicated columnist*

LEGAL AND FINANCIAL ISSUES

III

A person's physical, psychological, and emotional health is paramount. Yet the reality is that as we age, we need money on which to live, we do not want to be a burden on our family, and, ultimately, we want to make sure that the people or causes that we care about receive our worldly goods. Part Three involves the legal and financial issues of growing older.

If we look at most people from an economic point of view, they spend their early years learning and growing in maturity. The transition from those years is to a period of accumulation, whether it be an accumulation of family, of possessions, of wealth, or any combination of the three. The final phase sees us thinking about using that which we have accumulated to support us as we turn our attention to retirement or other endeavors. With the leisure to rest on our laurels, we begin to recognize our mortality, and we give thought as to how we will finally finish our journey.

As a long-time estate planning attorney, I have learned the importance of planning for the future. Of course, none of us knows what the future holds, and there certainly is no certainty in life. There is, though, always the opportunity to create a roadmap for the future, planning for the worst and hoping for the best.

A myriad of legal and financial issues confront us at all times. Somehow, they are magnified as we grow older. Perhaps it is the sense that we are running out of time, or maybe it is just the culmination of experience and maturity, but there comes a time that we must confront how we are going to live, manage our assets as we age, and pass those assets on after we have died.

The sooner these issues are dealt with, the easier they are to manage. Ask any lawyer, financial planner, or insurance professional whether it is easier to plan for a 50-year-old or an 80-year-old, and the resounding answer will be the 50-year-old. Time is on the side of those who plan early and use seasoned professionals to help them.

Even a late start is better than not starting at all. While it is easier to plan for younger people, a great deal of planning can be done for those who have gotten a late start. Those who do no planning usually end up leaving a mess if they become disabled or they die. One of the unfortunate consequences of doing nothing is that the legacy left behind is more likely than not a morass of financial and legal entanglements, which magnifies the grief of others. Planning is just as much for those who survive as it is for the person who becomes disabled or dies.

It is not the purpose of the 10 chapters in Part Three to make you or your family experts in legal and financial planning. They are not written to offer legal, financial, or accounting advice. On the contrary, the purpose of this part is to create a framework to allow you to begin the planning process for yourself and those you care about if you have not started or to make the planning even better for those who have. The material will allow you and your family to work

more effectively with lawyers, financial professionals, accountants, and other advisors.

Chapter 44 is an overview intended to give the reader a sense of how to start preparing for retirement, disability, and death. Being organized and knowing what to expect are fundamental to making a person's life easier as he or she ages. This chapter also addresses the basics of disability and death planning in a legal sense.

Chapter 45 hits head on one of the most difficult issues that face adult children who look toward the future. Approaching a parent about planning can be emotionally charged, both for the child and the parent. Susan Bradley, in a straightforward and sensitive manner, shows how these discussions can take place with a great deal of caring.

Another very sensitive issue, and one that is often foremost in the minds of older people, is being able to stay in their home even if they face health problems. There is so much written about the technical aspects of having to go to a nursing home or another type of institution that the opportunities of home care are often ignored. In Chapter 46, John Schaub shares his personal and professional experiences in allowing older people to stay at home.

Chapters 47 and 48 take the mystery out of insurance. Mike Kilbourn, one of America's experts in life insurance, takes an incredibly technical subject and reduces it to fundamental points. Carlos Whaley then explains the nature and use of long-term care insur-

ance. Highly underrated but one of the most effective tools, long-term care insurance can ensure care for a person while avoiding financial burden.

Almost all of us have some sort of retirement plan, even if it is Social Security. Congress, over the last 50 years, has created numerous retirement plans, all of which are subject to complex rules. In Chapter 49, Scot Overdorf, one of the most knowledgeable estate planning and retirement attorneys in the profession, summarizes the many plans available and how they can be best used upon retirement.

Another confusing financial tool is an annuity. Almost the opposite of life insurance, annuities are a way of enhancing retirement income. Dick Duff, a prolific author and lecturer about annuities, separates the myth from the reality in Chapter 50.

One of the most important aspects of preserving and protecting assets so that older people have the income to last a lifetime is investing for retirement. David Partheymuller, an expert in investing, shows how a responsible and effective investment policy can be built to minimize risk and maximize performance. Using Chapter 51 as the foundation, almost anyone can develop, in conjunction with a good financial advisor, a portfolio to successfully navigate the retirement years.

The final two chapters of Part Three broach the topics of long-term care and Medicaid and the legal aspects of death and disability. Chapter 52 was written by Ira Wiesner, a national expert in elder law. Ira discusses Medicaid coverage, the rules that must

be followed to qualify, and the legal issues related to long-term care. For those who qualify for Medicaid and for those who are facing the possibility of long-term care, the information contained in Chapter 52 is invaluable.

Finally, in Chapter 53, David Kerr, a highly regarded estate planning attorney, takes on the legal aspects of disability and death. There are difficult problems that arise if a person becomes mentally disabled. If not planned for and understood, a family can be devastated by the consequences. Upon death, certain actions must be taken to ensure that the decedent's wishes are honored and to ensure that the legal and financial details are finalized. David, who has many years of experience in helping families in times of need, thoroughly covers virtually every aspect of disability and death.

As in Parts One and Two of *Optimal Aging Manual,* each of the chapters in Part Three has a summary of important points, called "What You Need to Know," followed by "For More Information." These two resources, respectively, help a reader understand the key issues in each chapter and how to get more detailed information.

A number of legal and financial terms are used in Part Three. Each one is defined in the legal and financial glossary at the end of the book. Whenever a term which is included in the glossary first appears in a chapter, it is in bold blue type. This is to alert the reader that that term is in the glossary.

Remember, the chapters in Part Three are general discussions of legal and financial issues of growing older. They were not written so that a reader could do his or her own legal work or financial planning. The chapters become your basis of general understanding, so that when you and your family work with legal and financial professionals, you will be able to communicate your desires effectively. These chapters can also be used to review and corroborate your advisor's recommendations. For up-to-date information, please go to our website, www.optimalaging.com.

It is my hope, and those of the authors, that the material in these chapters will allow you, and the others you hold dear, to be more comfortable and better prepared. *Optimal Aging Manual* is not only the title of a book; it is the reflection of a lifestyle that can be attained and maintained through your knowledge, your action, and your professional advisors.

RENNO L. PETERSON
MARCH 26, 2004

It takes as much energy to wish as it does to plan.

—*Eleanor Roosevelt*

THE AUTHORS

44

ROBERT A. ESPERTI & RENNO L. PETERSON are two of the foremost estate planning attorneys in the United States. They are coauthors of 28 books for professionals and the public on estate and wealth planning. As educators, they have been very active in teaching attorneys, accountants, and financial professionals better and more efficient methods to plan for their clients and create relationships with other professionals. Bob and Renno are founders of the National Network of Estate Planning Attorneys, the Esperti Peterson Institute, the Academy of Multidisciplinary Practice, and the Estate and Wealth Strategies Institute at Michigan State University and its affiliated outreach program, Institute for Stewardship and Philanthropy. Bob lives in Jackson Hole, Wyoming, with his wife Liz, and Renno lives in Sarasota, Florida, with his wife Karen. They both have two sons.

44 | ESTATE PLANNING

An estate plan is not merely writing a "last will and testament." It is not merely possessing a living will or a revocable living trust. Estate planning is a thoughtful, deliberate process to ensure that you and the ones you love, as well as your property, are insulated as much as is legally possible from the uncertainties of a complex society.

As we get older, and perhaps wiser, estate planning takes on more meaning. Our thoughts turn more to preserving and protecting what we have, rather than taking big risks in order to have more. We think more of our own mortality and the joy of helping those we care about have better lives.

This view of estate planning may be very different from the way you have looked at estate planning in the past. If it is, good. You have the opportunity to begin that process now. If you have viewed estate planning from our perspective, then you are ahead of the game. You can use the following information as a standard by which you can review your existing planning.

In this chapter, our aim is to motivate you and your family to take the time to create an estate plan that will protect all of you. We do not want to make you an expert, and we certainly do not want you to decide to get some software and do your own plan. What we would like for you to do is consider the options you have and then seek good advisors who will help you.

The advisors you find should not only be conversant with the legal aspects of estate planning but also able to work with other advisors who will coordinate your legal work with your financial and insurance planning. That is why Part Three of this book addresses not only the most important legal issues of planning but also the financial. The two cannot be separated. We hope to arm you with sufficient information so that you and your advisors can marry the legal and financial into a plan that fits you.

THE CONSEQUENCES OF FAILING TO PLAN

There are three phases of a person's life that require planning. The first is when we are alive and well. The second is if we become disabled. The third is when we die.

Estate planning when one is alive and well seems to be nonsensical. Yet if estate planning means protecting assets, values, and lifestyle, then it seems reasonable to start immediately. There are a number of methods to protect assets from unreasonable lawsuits and creditors. There are many ways to invest in retirement plans, insurance, and other vehicles to address the future.

According to a survey by AARP released in April 2000, for Americans who are 50 or older, 60% have a will, 45% have a durable power of attorney, and 23% have a living trust. Only 17% have all three of these planning tools, whereas 36% do not have any. As people get older, their likelihood of having a will increases. For example, 85% of those age 80 or older have a will. These statistics have not changed much since 1991, when AARP conducted a similar study.

The financial chapters of *Optimal Aging* help you with planning while you are alive and well. Take heed of the advice, because the longer you wait, the more dire the consequences. There is an old adage that says an ounce of prevention is worth a pound of cure. That is an absolute truth in estate planning.

DISABILITY WITHOUT PLANNING

For most of us, the odds of our becoming mentally incapacitated increase as we age. The consequences of mental incapacity to us and our families are potentially devastating. Mental incapacity raises very difficult issues.

If you become mentally incapacitated, you have to be cared for, personally and financially. You will not be able to function without a caregiver helping you in your everyday life. In addition, you will not be able to sign your name to checks or legal documents.

Without planning, the mechanism for appointing your day-to-day caregiver, called a guardian, and appointing someone to take care of your property and finances, called a conservator, is a court-controlled process. The name of this process varies from state to state, but it is typically called a *guardianship procedure.* It is a public process that allows testimony to decide if a person is mentally incompetent. The judge appoints your guardian, who acts just like a parent, and your conservator, who controls your money and property. The guardian and the conservator may be the same person, but they do not have to be. The guardian is usually a person—an accountant, or a financial professional—but the court can appoint an institution to act as the conservator.

You have no control over who is appointed. Judges do the best they can in appointing loved ones and responsible banks or individuals, but the process is far from foolproof. It can be humiliating and expensive and can leave a person without enough safeguards. Without any instructions from you, because you did not bother to plan, the guardian and conservator make decisions based on their views, not necessarily yours. It does not matter what you would have done in a similar situation; the guardian and the conservator do what they want to do, based on their best judgment.

This whole process can, and should, be avoided with planning. It takes time, effort, and money to put the planning in place, but planning is an investment in your future and the future of those you care about.

DYING WITHOUT PLANNING

Planning for death is not an attractive topic, at least on its face. As we all know (but may not accept), unlike disability, the odds of dying are 100%. The event is inevitable; only the timing is up in the air. Also inevitable is that if we truly care about those who survive us or about causes that we want to support after we are gone, we must plan. Without planning, the grief of survivors is only increased because, in addition to the psychological and emotional issues, they have to deal with the financial and other realities that we all leave behind.

There is a certain comfort and relief to be gained by having our planning in place. It alleviates a great burden from us, knowing that those whom we love are to be taken care of after we have passed away. Since none of us really knows when we are going to die, it is critical that we address the issues of death while we are alive and well. If we do not, then the consequences can be serious.

The good news (and, of course, we mean this facetiously) is that if you die without planning, a plan has already been set up for you. Without proper planning a great deal of property passes by operation of law. That means certain assets are destined to pass to someone just because of how the property is owned or how a beneficiary designation is filled out.

As to property that is directly owned in a person's own name at his or her death, if there is no will or trust that controls that property, it will pass under the laws of intestacy. *Intestacy* means a person has died without a will or some other mechanism that transfers property at death. Laws of intestacy exist in every state and control the property held in that state.

Intestacy is a statutory method of determining a person's heirs. Those heirs, once determined, are put in a hierarchal list of family members. The hierarchy determines how much of your estate each person will get. Your intent or wishes do not matter. The property passes as the statute mandates.

The bad news (and we mean this very seriously) is that without planning your property may very well go to unintended heirs. By failing to plan, you lose control of those assets that you have spent your whole life accumulating. Proper planning is your insurance policy that your wishes will be met after you have died.

TRADITIONAL PLANNING AND WHY YOU SHOULD AVOID IT

Many people think that if they have a will, they have an estate plan. They feel that they have met their obligation for planning and nothing else is necessary. This notion is not true in our experience. Let's examine what happens when planning is accomplished with the traditional will approach.

WILLS

One of the most common terms that is associated with estate planning is a *will*. A will is a formal set of instructions that control property at death. Wills allow the will maker to appoint a personal representative who is responsible for carrying out the maker's instructions.

A number of terms associated with wills are sometimes still seen, although they are disappearing. An *executor* (or executrix, if female) is the name for the personal representative. A *testator* (testatrix, if female) is the maker of a will.

We do not favor wills as the foundation of good planning. Frankly, wills have relatively few useful functions, but there are a few. Having a will is better than no planning at all, so having one, absent any other planning, is a good thing. Also, the initial cost of a will is small, so getting one is inexpensive. However, as we shall see, the long-term cost may be quite high. Before deciding on a will, you need to assess the long-range costs, as well as the initial cost.

Wills have a number of disadvantages. Here is a list of what we do not like about using wills as the primary part of planning:

1. *Wills are only effective on death; they take their lives from the death of their makers.* Wills cannot solve the many lifetime problems of proper estate planning. Unlike a revocable living trust, for example, a will does not help when its maker becomes disabled. Wills have one purpose, and that is to control property at death.

2. *Wills do not control all property.* Wills do not control joint tenancy property or beneficiary designation property. There are also other kinds of property that a will may not control. In fairness, other documents used in estate planning, such as a revocable living trust, do not control all property either. However, in our experience, it is far more likely that the planning associated with a will won't control property; those people who plan using a revocable living trust are far more likely to have addressed the control issue.

3. *Wills guarantee probate.* No matter where we go and whom we teach, there is always confusion among people about probate. In the next section, "Probate," we discuss it in more detail. Probate is not always necessary or advisable. However, one thing is for sure. A will guarantees probate, because the instructions in a will are subject to control by the probate statutes and potentially the courts in every state. A probate for a smaller estate can be avoided, and for many estates probate is not difficult. But the mere exposure to probate is usually not a good idea, especially if alternatives are available.

4. *Wills are public.* Because wills guarantee probate and probate is a public process, wills are public. Some wills are more public than others, but the probate process requires certain degrees of exposure that most people are not comfortable with.

5. *Wills are not good when the maker owns property in more than one state.* For individuals who own property in more than one state, wills do not work very well. If a person owns property in one state, one probate is necessary. If that person owns property in other states, then each state requires an ancillary probate proceeding.

6. *Wills offer an easy way for unhappy heirs to sue.* Wills require probate. Probate is a forum that actually invites unhappy heirs and others to file their claims. So if you have a will that controls some or all of your property at your death and if you have disappointed someone, that someone could contest the will quite easily. The disappointed someone may not win, but the will certainly offers an opportunity to take a shot.

7. *Wills are complex and require precise drafting and signing procedures.* Wills are only valid if very strict drafting rules are followed. If they are not, then

the will is likely to be invalid. This is one of the reasons that people should not use a software program or a form to do their own legal work. In our experience, it is highly unlikely that one of these wills could be entirely successful. At best, since wills and probate go together like salt and pepper, a will contest in the probate court is probable.

As you can see, we are not fans of using wills as the foundational document for estate planning. While we will concede that wills may be appropriate for very small estates with simple assets, we still feel strongly that if it is possible, one should use a revocable living trust for planning. When we explore revocable living trusts later on, you shall see that a will is still part of revocable living trust planning—but only a small part.

PROBATE

Probate is an administrative process to make sure that when a person dies, his or her bills are paid and his or her assets are distributed to the proper heirs. We are telling you what probate is supposed to do for the sake of simplicity. In reality, probate can—and often is—far more complicated than the administrative function that it is supposed to be.

When a person dies owning property in his or her name, it is impossible for that person to come back from the grave, pay bills, and transfer the title to assets to heirs. Those tasks are part of the administrative function of probate. It does not matter whether you have a will or any other planning. The first rule of probate is that if you own property in your name at death, probate will likely be necessary.

If you do die with a will, then a secondary function of probate is to prove the validity of your will. The word *probate* is Latin for "to prove." As we mentioned above, wills are subject to complex legal rules. Probate provides a process that allows a will to be contested if any of the rules may have been broken. In fact, probate is a ready-made forum that invites

PUBLIC VERSUS PRIVATE

Wills are public documents, because a will requires a probate. The probate process is public in that the will and other information has to be filed with a court. Court records are open to public scrutiny. Because probate is public, the media, unhappy heirs, or just the curious can find out what every will says.

A good example is the will of Jackie Kennedy Onassis. Immediately after Jackie died, her will appeared on the internet and in newspapers. It revealed both the size and beneficiaries of her estate. Maybe she intended all this publicity, but it is doubtful. She was a private person in life, so why would she want to open up her personal and financial affairs at her death?

Trusts are private documents, because they do not have to go through probate. There is no public disclosure of the beneficiaries receiving a person's property or how they received it. There is no disclosure of financial information.

Bing Crosby did almost all his estate planning in a living trust. So when the newspapers attempted to find out what he owned and whom he left it to, they were stymied. Bing did leave a simple will that included his burial instructions. Nothing was disclosed in that will about how he left his property, so to this day Bing's planning has remained private.

unhappy heirs to air their complaints in a court-supervised environment. It is not difficult for heirs, or others, to present their claims.

In the thousands of client meetings that we have participated in, we find that a great number of people are shocked to learn that wills go through probate. They are under the false impression that wills avoid probate. On the contrary, wills guarantee probate.

There is a lot of confusion about probate. Some professionals say that probate is no big deal and does not cost much. Others take the opposite view, saying that probate is a big deal and costs a lot. So who is right? In reality, both sides can be right and both sides wrong. It all depends on a number of factors, including:

- The types of assets you own
- The state law that controls the will and the probate
- Whether you have been married before and whether there are children from more than one marriage
- Your choice of lifestyle (for example, homosexual or heterosexual)
- The extent of your creditors
- The value of your assets
- How you organized your affairs before you died
- The attorney who handles the probate
- The personal representative (or executor) that is appointed in your will or by the probate court

Other factors can affect probate, but you can see that probate encompasses many issues. The more issues you have, the more complex, expensive, and time-consuming the probate.

There is a lot of misinformation about the cost of probate. We have spent our careers trying to convey to the public and professionals the costs of probate. We have done studies and surveys. Here is what we have found.

First, do not let any professionals confuse you about costs. Some attorneys say probate only costs a few hundred dollars. If they say that, they are saying the filing fees only cost a few hundred dollars. Ask these same attorneys about their fees, in addition to the filing fees, and the answer becomes far different.

Second, we have found that if a probate is required, the cost runs about 3% of the value of the assets and is not uncommon that it runs to 6% or higher. This range of fees is true in every state, even if the state has so-called statutory fees. Statutory fees, which are mandated by some state statutes, have a maximum fee that can be charged, unless the attorney can prove extraordinary fees for extraordinary work. Extraordinary fees are the norm, not the exception.

Probate fees are larger for smaller estates, as a percentage, than are probate fees for larger estates. Thus probate is worse for families with lesser amounts of money. The primary reason for this discrepancy is that there is a certain amount of work that is required in probate, no matter the size of the estate. However, virtually all probate work is not done by attorneys but is done by paralegals and other staff. Probate work is mostly a matter of filling in forms and filing them. It is not difficult, for the most part, and it is not complex. Even if the attorney does not do the work, it is common for the attorney to charge at his or her rates, rather than the rates of the people doing the actual work.

Every state also has what is called a simplified or unsupervised probate procedure. In our experience, these procedures do not substantially reduce the cost of probate. Our experience is that the fee stays in that 3 to 6% range. However, a complex probate can be really expensive. They become complex if litigation or very complex assets are involved.

REAL COST OF PROBATE

A number of years ago, we commissioned a survey of probate fees in four states to corroborate various other studies concerning probate fees. We chose Iowa, New York, Oregon, and Texas. Iowa had a statutory fee allowing a maximum of 2% for the executor and 2% for the attorney. The rate could be increased for extra work. We chose the other three states because they had different types of probate statutes. Here is what we found:

STATE	AVERAGE EXECUTOR FEES	AVERAGE ATTORNEY FEES	AVERAGE COMBINED FEES
Iowa	2%	2.6%	4.6%
New York	3.1%	5.66%	8.76%
Oregon	2.29%	5.06%	7.35%
Texas	2.1%	5.21%	7.31%

These percentages may seem high, and you or your attorney may have a different experience, but these percentages were taken based on a statistical analysis of random files from the probate offices of each state.

THE REAL COST OF PROBATE BY STATE

STATE	GROSS ESTATE	NET ESTATE	PROBATE COST	% GROSS ESTATE	% NET ESTATE
Iowa	$ 100,000	$ 75,000	$ 4,600	4.60 %	6.10 %
	$ 250,000	$ 180,000	$ 11,500	4.60 %	6.30 %
	$ 600,000	$ 400,000	$ 27,600	4.60 %	6.90 %
New York	$ 100,000	$ 75,000	$ 8,760	8.76 %	11.68 %
	$ 250,000	$ 180,000	$ 21,900	8.76 %	12.17 %
	$ 600,000	$ 400,000	$ 52,560	8.76 %	13.14 %
Oregon	$ 100,000	$ 75,000	$ 7,310	7.31 %	9.70 %
	$ 250,000	$ 180,000	$ 18,275	7.31 %	10.15 %
	$ 600,000	$ 400,000	$ 43,860	7.31 %	10.97 %
Texas	$ 100,000	$ 75,000	$ 4,600	4.60 %	6.10 %
	$ 250,000	$ 180,000	$ 11,500	4.60 %	6.30 %
	$ 600,000	$ 400,000	$ 27,600	4.60 %	6.90 %

One of the worst parts of these fees is that the percentages are based on the gross estate. That means that the total value of the estate was used *before* any debts or expenses were taken into consideration. For example, if a person died with an estate of $500,000, but had debts of $150,000 (a mortgage on a house, for example), and the executor's and attorney's fees were 6% of the estate, the cost would have been $30,000. As a percentage of the net estate, in our example $350,000, the true percentage taken would have been about 8.6%.

All in all, probate should be avoided. It is a waste of time and money for most families. There are exceptions when probate is necessary or unavoidable, but these exceptions can be minimized with good planning.

Probate may be required in an estate for which not all creditors are known and the family wants closure so creditors will not crop up in future years. Probate allows creditors to lose their claims against a deceased person. Usually, all that is required is a good faith attempt to contact all known or reasonably known creditors of the deceased person. Publishing a notice in a newspaper is also required. Creditors who do not respond to either method of notice are barred, after a period of time (usually about six months) from ever asserting a claim.

Probate may be required if the deceased person has a lawsuit that is pending at death or that arises after death. For example, if the deceased person was killed in a car accident and another person or company is at fault, any lawsuit must be initiated by the personal representative of the probate estate.

Probate may also be required if a deceased person does not leave enough assets to a spouse or if the deceased person forgot to leave money to an heir. Spouses in all states have some sort of right to the assets of their husband or wife, unless there is some kind of premarital contract preventing such a claim. Probate allows those rights to be asserted. And, in some rare occasions, a child is inadvertently left out of a will or trust. Probate allows those mistakes to be corrected.

HISTORICALLY SPEAKING

In 1540, King Henry VIII encouraged the English Parliament to pass the Statute of Wills. For the first time under feudal law, people could pass real property by a will. Incidentally, the Statute of Wills included an easy way for the king to collect inheritance taxes, so this statute was a gift with strings attached. It was not until the mid-1660s that all property in England could pass by will, allowing even more property to be subject to tax. Most state laws governing wills are based on King Henry VIII's law, because variations of the Statute of Wills were imported by the 13 original colonies.

Trusts are much older than wills. The first living trusts were used beginning in the thirteenth and fourteenth centuries to avoid *primogeniture,* the requirement that all property must pass to the oldest son. Many nobles had oldest sons who were, shall we say, not fit to inherit all of dad's property. So in order to control how their property passed at death, some nobles hired—you guessed it—lawyers, who invented a way that the gentry could pass property without the interference of primogeniture. These early trusts had another benefit. They circumvented taxes imposed on death. As you can imagine, these trusts were quite popular!

We prefer trusts over wills, because even today the statutes governing wills are restrictive. However, both planning methods have a long and venerable history.

We ardently believe that probate should be avoided if at all possible. Even if it can be minimized, that is better than a probate on all assets. Proper planning can avoid probate. We discuss the planning we believe should be in place in the next section.

THE ESTATE PLANNING PROCESS

Here, in a nutshell, is the estate planning process: Determine what you own and how you own it, gather the legal documents that affect your planning, gather all your insurance documents, assess your risk factors, decide what you want to happen if you become disabled, decide what you want to do with your property when you die, seek competent advisors, and implement and follow up.

If you follow this process, you will pay less in legal and other fees for your plan, you will understand the meaning of your planning, and you will sleep better at night. In the remainder of this chapter, we explain each step of the process, making your estate planning journey much more rewarding and maybe a little joyful! We then give you some recommendations as to the optimum foundational plan.

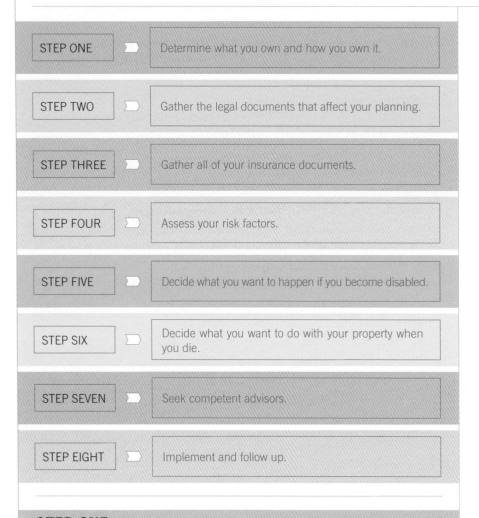

STEP ONE	Determine what you own and how you own it.
STEP TWO	Gather the legal documents that affect your planning.
STEP THREE	Gather all of your insurance documents.
STEP FOUR	Assess your risk factors.
STEP FIVE	Decide what you want to happen if you become disabled.
STEP SIX	Decide what you want to do with your property when you die.
STEP SEVEN	Seek competent advisors.
STEP EIGHT	Implement and follow up.

STEP ONE

DETERMINE WHAT YOU OWN AND HOW YOU OWN IT

Finding out what you own and how you own it is the most important and fundamental aspect of planning. Start by making a list of everything you own. If you have a financial statement, that is a good beginning, but even financial statements do not necessarily list everything a person owns.

Make sure that your list is complete. By complete, we mean list every asset that is of importance to you either financially or emotionally. You do not need to list all your clothes (unless they are financially or emotionally important) nor all of your other miscellaneous possessions that have nominal value.

You should put a value on each asset, but the value does not have to be exact. A good estimate works just fine. If you do not have a clue as to value, do not worry about it. In the process, you will find out whether an accurate valuation is necessary. Just keep in mind that having a complete list of what you own is more important, at this stage, than what each item is worth.

Do not forget to list life insurance policies that you own, even if they are on another's life. List all annuities, bank accounts, investment accounts, and individual investments. Include any notes that are owed to you and any businesses or other assets that you own. Valuable memberships in clubs should be listed. If you have purchased a burial plot or a prepaid monument for your grave, those should be listed. Try to include everything that you can think of.

After you have a complete list, you must then determine how each asset is owned. The technical word for ownership is title. Every asset has some sort of title that names the owner. For example, the deed to real property shows in whose name the property is titled. The same is true for the title to your car or boat or motorcycle. The signature card at your bank, credit union, or brokerage house shows who owns the account. If you own bonds or stocks, the certificate is your title of ownership. Your life insurance policy shows who owns it. If someone owes you money, then the promissory note is your title.

While most types of property have a document that shows title, some types do not. Furniture, artwork, collectibles, and other property seemingly do not have title. But they really do. When you buy any of these items, your receipt is your title. If you do not keep those receipts, then they are presumed to be owned in the manner in which you purchased them. So if you pay for furniture from a joint account, the property is presumed to be owned jointly. If you purchase it from an account solely in your name, then you are presumed to own it.

As you look through the documents that show title to your property, you may see a number of different variations of ownership. If you are confused as to how you own any property, that is all right. Simply gather together the documents that seem to show title and move on. A final determination of title can be done at a later time during the estate planning process.

Most property is held in a few different ways. The common types of ownership are fee simple, joint tenancy with right of survivorship, tenancy by the entirety, tenancy in common, beneficiary designation property, and community property.

FEE SIMPLE PROPERTY

Fee simple is a legal term which means that an individual owns property outright. With fee simple property, the owner has the right to sell the property, give it away, or leave it at death. If you own property titled in your name alone, it is fee simple property.

JOINT TENANCY PROPERTY

The proper name for joint tenancy property is joint tenancy with right of survivorship. This simple-sounding form of ownership is really quite complex. In joint tenancy, each owner, and there can be two or more, has a 100% right to the property while each owner is living. If the property is sold or given away, generally, all the joint owners must agree. If a transfer is made to a third party of a joint tenant's interest to property, the joint tenancy is "severed" (ended) as to that joint tenant: The new owner is a tenant in common as to the other owners. (See the box entitled "Disjointed Ownership.")

If a joint tenancy owner dies, he or she loses all right to the property. It passes by operation of law to the surviving owner or owners. When all the owners have died, except the last survivor, he or she is the owner of the property in fee simple. If all joint tenancy owners die at once, then state law determines how ownership is untangled.

The most important feature of joint tenancy is that a joint owner does not control where the property passes when he or she dies. *It must pass to the surviving owner or owners.* A will or a trust cannot change the outcome. Joint tenancy is not controlled by any document; it passes as a matter of law. Thus the owners have lost the right to control where their shares of property pass at death.

There is another aspect of joint tenancy that is important. Under virtually every state law, if one joint tenant has financial problems, his or her creditors can force the sale, or even take all, of joint tenancy property. Anyone worried about the creditworthiness of others should not hold any type property as joint tenants with them.

DISJOINTED OWNERSHIP

Ted, Sue, and Bob own land as joint tenants with right of survivorship. Ted decides to sell his share of the property to Peter and does so. Then Bob dies. What is the result? Ted's sale to Peter legally ends the joint tenancy relationship between Ted, Sue, and Bob. Sue and Bob continue to be joint tenants with right of survivorship as to the two-thirds of the property that they own. By law, Peter's one-third ownership is converted into tenancy in common with Sue's and Bob's two-thirds. Talk about confusing! So when Bob dies, Bob's ownership passes to Sue, because Sue and Bob were joint tenants with right of survivorship and Sue survived. Bob's death does not affect Peter, so Peter and Sue are tenants in common, with Peter owning one-third of the property and Sue owning two-thirds. Sue and Peter can sell their respective shares, give them away, or leave them at death. The joint tenancy between Sue and Bob died with the death of Bob.

TENANCY BY THE ENTIRETY

A number of states have a method of holding title to property called tenancy by the entirety. This form of ownership is almost identical to joint tenancy with right of survivorship. The major difference is that tenancy by the entirety is exclusively for married couples. It is restrictive in that neither spouse can transfer the property without the consent of the other. Unlike traditional joint tenancy with right of survivorship, tenancy by the entirety is great for creditor protection. If one spouse has creditor problems, his or her creditors cannot take or sell tenancy by the entirety property. When planning to protect assets, tenancy by the entirety can be extremely useful.

TENANCY IN COMMON

Tenancy in common is almost like owning property in a partnership. All the owners own an equal share of the whole property. If property is titled in two names as tenants in common, they are presumed to each own 50%; if three, then 33⅓%, and so on. However, if the title to the property allocates ownership differently, then whatever percentage ownership is shown on the title is how the property is divided for ownership purposes.

Absent a side agreement or a statute, there is no right of survivorship with tenancy in common property. A person who owns 50% can sell his or her 50%, give it away, or leave it on death. A creditor can take a tenant in common's share of the property, but does not have the right to the whole property, as do creditors of joint tenants.

BENEFICIARY DESIGNATION PROPERTY

A type of property that has a confusing aspect of title is called *third-party beneficiary property,* or beneficiary designation property. Examples of this type of property include an IRA, a 401(k) plan, a qualified retirement plan, and the death proceeds of life insurance. For these types of assets, how the property is titled is not always as important as who the beneficiary is. The beneficiary of these assets has the contractual right to the property held in these assets. Thus the beneficiary designation of a life insurance policy controls who receives the assets at the death of the insured. Interestingly, life insurance has an owner while the insured is living who has the right to the policy. However, at death, the proceeds pass to the beneficiary, who then owns the proceeds.

As the creator or owner of these assets, you can decide who receives them after you die. A surprising number of people do not coordinate their will or trust planning with their beneficiary designations. That can be a very big mistake.

Neither a will nor a trust controls beneficiary designation property. The beneficiary designation for the property controls it. So you must be sure that you re view your beneficiary designations to ensure that those assets are going to the people or charities that you want.

Chapter 47 on life insurance and Chapter 49 on retirement plans discuss beneficiary designation issues in more depth. Please read those chapters for more information.

COMMUNITY PROPERTY

Ten states have a type of ownership called *community property:* Alaska, Arizona, California, Idaho, Louisiana, Nevada, New Mexico, Texas, Washington, and Wisconsin. Each state has its own quirks as to the rules, but community property is generally defined as property acquired in a marriage. It does not matter which spouse's name is on the title to the property; there is a presumption that property acquired in a marriage is owned equally (much like tenancy by the entirety) by both spouses. Each spouse can leave his or her half of community property to whomever he or she desires. Each spouse can give his or her interest in community property away or sell it, but should get the consent of the other spouse prior to doing so. If not, the transfer may not be valid, but this aspect of community property varies from state to state.

Community property issues can get complex if two people have separate property prior to getting married. If the married couple treats their separate property as if it is the property of both, then it may be converted into community property. Also, even if the marriage partners keep their individual property separate, appreciation in value or income from the property may become community property.

STEP TWO
GATHER LEGAL DOCUMENTS THAT AFFECT YOUR PLANNING

As you list your assets and find the title to them, you will run into documents that affect this property. Make copies of deeds, certificates of title, account statements, and all other evidences of title. Organize them so that they are readily identifiable.

There are other documents that are important in estate planning. If you are subject to a divorce decree or separation agreement, that agreement is critical. If you have a pre- or postmarital agreement with your spouse, it, too, is critical. In fact, any agreement in force that affects your ownership of property, your right to use property, or your ability to dispose of property is important. If you have already made a will or a trust, include it with your other documents. Organize them as best you can.

You may find that some documents are confusing. That is very common. As part of your organization process, buy a pad of Post-it notes, which stick to paper, and flag your areas of confusion. Write your questions or comments on these notes. Use manilla folders to separate and organize your documents. For example, put all real property in one folder and all investments in another. Later, good organization will save you a great deal of time, and maybe, from even more confusion.

STEP THREE
GATHER ALL YOUR INSURANCE DOCUMENTS

Since estate planning is very much about protecting what you have, list *all* the insurance you own. Insurance comes in many forms, but all policies are relevant. Here is a list of the types of insurance that you may own or benefit from. If you are employed or have retired from a company, remember to include any benefits that you have from your place of employment. All these valuable assets need to be assessed.

- Life insurance, including any mortgage or other insurance on your life
- Disability insurance
- Long-term care insurance
- Casualty insurance, including any special riders
- Health insurance, including supplemental policies

Make sure that you find the policies and any correspondence relating to the policies. Make a list of the policies, including the company issuing the policy, the type of policy, and the insured. If the policy has a beneficiary designation, make sure that you have a copy. A way to keep this information organized is to buy manila folders and Post-it notes. Put each policy into a manilla folder, and use the Post-it notes to make comments. This method eliminates losing an extra piece of paper that has important information on it.

STEP FOUR

ASSESS YOUR RISK FACTORS

A great deal of estate planning is based on risk factors. For example, a person who is 23 with few assets and no dependents has few estate planning risk factors. The odds of our 23-year-old dying are low, as is his or her likelihood of becoming disabled. Knowing no one depends on him or her and knowing that there are many years to make up for mistakes, our 23-year-old can indulge in financial risks.

Contrast that with a widow who is in her late 70s. The risk factors are pretty much the opposite of the 23-year-old. In between the two extremes are varying levels of risk.

Here are some factors to look for when assessing your risk:

- Age
- Health
- Family history of health
- Degree of material wealth
- Types of property, for example, very liquid or illiquid
- Marriage status
- Status of parents, if living
- Status of children and grandchildren, including their health and wealth
- Employed or retired
- Engage in a risky business or hobby, such as a pilot or a race car driver
- Location of home or homes
- Travel a great deal or stay at home

There are more factors, but you understand the idea. All these factors influence the need and extent of your estate planning.

44

As you assess your risk, you will begin to see a picture of your needs. You may find that you have illiquid assets, you need to care for your children and grandchildren because they are not doing too well, or you may not have enough of some kinds of insurance. Assessing your risks objectively can motivate your planning, knowing that you need help. If your risk factors are low, your sense of urgency may not be as high. The important thing is to know.

STEP FIVE
DECIDE WHAT YOU WANT TO HAPPEN IF YOU BECOME DISABLED

As we stated earlier, for most of us, the odds of becoming disabled in any year are much greater than the odds of dying. Yet, in our experience, planning for disability is emphasized and practiced far less than planning for death. We think that a primary reason for the lack of disability planning is that, in many ways, disability planning offers more challenges than does planning for death, so people are reluctant to take action. It is because of those challenges that disability planning is so important.

DISABILITY DEFINED

In a broad sense, the term *disability* can mean any type of physical, emotional, or mental dysfunction. In the planning sense, disability is technically known as incapacity. *Incapacity* is a legal term that is generally defined as the inability, for any reason, of a person to care for his or her personal or financial affairs. Because the term disability is used more commonly than incapacity, we refer to legal incapacity as disability.

The consequences of *disability* without having any safeguards in place were discussed earlier in the section "Disability Without Planning."

QUESTIONS YOU SHOULD ADDRESS

Count yourself lucky if you have never experienced the tragedy of having a family member or friend who is in critical condition in a hospital or who, because of age or illness, has become mentally incompetent. It is a very difficult, emotionally draining experience. It is even worse if the person who is disabled has left no instructions with loved ones about how he or she wants to be cared for. Even that may not be so bad, but many of us do not even talk about the issues with our spouse or children or friends.

By not leaving instructions, you make it harder not only for you but also for those who have to make life and death decisions about your care. All of us should confront certain issues prior to having them happen. We should then let others know how we want to be treated if, for some reason, we cannot express our wishes because of illness or accident.

Here are a series of questions that you should ask—and answer—yourself to prepare yourself to discuss as part of putting your estate plan in place:

- If I am unable to make health care decisions because of illness or accident, who would I name to make those decisions on my behalf?

- If I am terminally ill or in a permanent vegetative state with no chance of recovery, should I be allowed to die naturally or do I want artificial care until I am cured or die?
- If I am ill or injured and there is a choice between having to be in a nursing home or getting home care, which would I choose?
- If I can no longer manage my property and financial affairs, who would I choose to act in my stead?
- If I am mentally incompetent, should my property and income be used just for me or should it be used for the benefit of myself and my spouse, or for the benefit of myself, my spouse, and children?

You may find that you have other issues to consider, especially if you have special health needs or members of your family have special needs. The point of this exercise is to really think about the consequences of becoming mentally incompetent. Giving this some thought will help prepare you to complete your estate plan.

STEP SIX

DECIDE WHAT YOU WANT TO DO WITH YOUR PROPERTY WHEN YOU DIE

Most of us have a better idea about what we want to happen to our property after we die than we do about our property should we become mentally disabled. Having a better idea does not mean that we have given the topic as much time or thought as we should.

A colleague of ours uses an interesting approach when talking about what happens after someone dies. He asks his clients to pretend that after dying they are in heaven and looking down on earth. He then asks the clients to relate what should have happened so that they, the clients, feel their death planning has met their needs.

We would ask you to go through the same exercise. Do you see a smooth transition? Has your family avoided a great deal of red tape and administration? Have they avoided litigation over your will or revocable living trust? Did any creditors pop out of the woodwork that you knew about but failed to tell anyone about? Did you organize your affairs so that the burden of straightening out your messes did not fall into your spouse's or children's lap? Did your loved ones and your charitable causes receive everything you wanted them to have? Did you adequately plan for a significant other or life partner?

As you ask yourself what you would like to happen after your death, think about the people or institutions you would choose to handle your affairs. Think about the types of property you own and how your heirs or other loved ones would use such property. Maybe some property should be sold; maybe some should be held on to. Think about all the issues that could arise if you died tomorrow.

No two estate plans are the same, at least in our experience, and we have either done or participated in thousands of them. Every person and every family is unique. The danger of having not thought about what will happen after you die is that if and when you decide to plan, it is all too easy to allow your advisors to impose boilerplate planning on you. Unless you insist on a tailored estate plan, you will get an off-the-shelf plan that probably won't fit your particular situation.

Write down your perfect scenario for what you want to happen to your property after you die. Then let your advisors tailor a plan to meet your specific needs.

STEP SEVEN
SEEK COMPETENT ADVISORS

Once you have listed all your property and how you own it, gathered your important papers and insurance documents, assessed your risk factors, and answered questions about your disability and death, you are ready to meet your advisors and get an estate plan going. How do you find those advisors? That is a struggle that many of us face.

To accomplish good estate planning, you need, at a minimum, an attorney who specializes in or spends a lot time doing estate planning. Any attorney will not do, and a part-time estate planning attorney is not as good as a full-time one. You should consider including a life insurance agent and a property and casualty insurance agent. If you have an accountant who does more than your income tax return, your accountant should be involved. If you have retirement accounts or investment accounts, a financial advisor should be one of your advisors.

Yes, cost is a consideration. You may feel that if you load up with advisors, the cost will be too high. It will not be, if you are prepared and you find the right advisors. Even if the cost is a little more than you anticipated, you will find that you have made a good investment in your future and the future of those you love. A good estate plan is one of the best insurance policies you can have. The peace of mind and comfort that you and your family will far exceed the dollars you invest. And, as with all other things of value, you get what you pay for.

Since an attorney is essential, that is where you should begin. If you already know an estate planning attorney, that's great! Otherwise, ask your friends and family if they have any recommendations. If you know an attorney who doesn't handle estate planning or you know other advisors, ask for their recommendations. Do not call the local bar association. You will only get the next name on a list of attorneys who have submitted their names. Word of mouth is the best way to find good advisors.

Once you have some candidates, interview them. Any attorney worth his or her salt will not charge you for an initial meeting. If one tries to, move on, unless you have a recommendation that totally intrigues you.

Ask the attorney to tell you about himself or herself. Spend a lot of time asking about the attorney's practice, such as what he specializes in and what she spends most of her time on. Do not be intimidated. You are hiring a very important advisor, and you should be sure that you are comfortable with that attorney.

Go through the same process with each advisor. Build a great group of advisors who want to look after you. Make sure that each advisor understands that he or she must coordinate with the other advisors and that their single task is working on a plan for you and your family.

You and your advisors should then set up a method for you to get their recommendation, as a group, of the plan that best fits you. That means that you have to share all the information you have gathered in the first seven steps of the process. You should then spend time with your advisors going through the information, allowing them to ask questions and clarify your materials. Expand on your feelings and desires. Your advisors cannot know too much about your hopes and dreams. The better they understand what you want, the better your plan will be.

Make sure that your advisors communicate with you on a regular basis and that you set up appointments. Do not allow the process to lose momentum. Get a recommended plan and its cost. Meet with your advisors, and ask them all the questions you want until you understand the plan. Refine it, if it needs refining. Then ask your attorney to draft the plan.

STEP EIGHT
IMPLEMENT AND FOLLOW UP

Your estate plan is no good unless you implement it fully and follow up to make sure it is always up to date. We are not sure whether an unfinished plan is better than no plan. We are sure that neither is a good alternative. Get it done, and keep on your advisors until it is.

Then make sure that your advisors and you have an agreement that you will update them on major changes in your life if they will update you on major changes in the law or other factors that affect your planning. Meet with your advisors at least every other year, or more often if you have changes in your family situation, changes in your finances, or just changes in your thinking.

Make sure your advisors do not mind—or charge—if you call from time to time with questions. Of course, you should not abuse this privilege, but you should have access to your advisors for questions. Ask them to bill you if your questions are becoming a substitute for a meeting. Remember, you want to be on the "A" list of your advisors as a good-paying, interested client. You do not want to be on the bottom of the list as a painful client who does not pay for advice.

In our experience, almost all advisors are in the service business because they want to serve people. By their nature, they are helpful. But they, too, must make a living, so treat them with respect by offering to pay them for their services.

ELEMENTS OF A GOOD ESTATE PLAN

For virtually all people who have assets and loved ones whom they care about, a solid estate plan should consist of the following documents: a revocable living trust, a pour-over will, a limited durable power of attorney, a living will, and a health care power of attorney.

44

ESTATE PLANNING

REVOCABLE LIVING TRUST

For many years, there has been a healthy debate among attorneys as to whether a person should have a will or a revocable living trust. In our view, which we have advocated for over 30 years and is now the prevailing view, good estate planning is based on a revocable living trust.

A will is only good when its maker dies; a will takes its life from its maker's death. It has no value for disability planning, and it guarantees probate. Earlier, in the section "Wills," we discussed the disadvantages of wills, so suffice it to say here that if you are committed to proper estate planning, a revocable living trust makes more sense as the foundation of estate planning.

In essence, a revocable living trust is a set of instructions as to how you would like your property and financial affairs to be managed while you are alive and well, if you become disabled, and when you die. Your instructions are in the form of a legally binding agreement that should be prepared by a lawyer.

A revocable living trust requires a maker, a trustee, and beneficiaries. The trust maker is the person who establishes the trust and the instructions contained in it. Sometimes, a trust maker is called a *grantor, trustor,* or *settlor.* The trustee is the person who follows the trust's instructions. The beneficiaries are the people or charities for whose benefit the revocable living trust has been created.

The trust maker (who also is almost always the trustee) is the primary beneficiary of the revocable living trust. The trust maker can name a spouse or others as secondary beneficiaries.

A trust can have more than one trust maker. It is not uncommon for a husband and a wife to create a joint revocable living trust. A joint trust is essentially two separate trusts in one document, containing instructions

SMOKE SIGNALS

Trusts are extremely versatile. The only restraint on a trust's instructions is that those instructions cannot be illegal or contrary to public policy. One of our favorite cases that demonstrates the possibilities of a trust occurred over 50 years ago.

A man who loved cigars was married to a woman who did not like the habit. She made him go outside, no matter the weather or time of day, to smoke his cigars. From the facts recited in the case, it is clear that he was not happy about this condition on something from which he derived great pleasure.

When the man died, the terms of his trust stated that he wanted to leave his wife a very generous amount, paid over her lifetime. The only stipulation was that to collect, she had to smoke a cigar each time she got a distribution. Saying that she shouldn't have to comply with this severe restriction, she sued the trustee.

At the time this case was decided, there was no public policy against smoking. It was quite acceptable. The judge, obviously sympathetic to the husband's feelings, ruled that if this man's wife wanted the money, she had to smoke the cigars. There was nothing wrong with a person's decision to put restrictions on how he or she left property to others.

We do not want to encourage draconian trust instructions, but the case gives you a taste of the power of a trust.

for each trust maker. Joint revocable living trusts should only be prepared by highly trained attorneys. They can create gift and estate tax problems if not drafted correctly, and they can create some confusion as to assets if not properly funded. See the section "Funding a Revocable Living Trust," below, for an explanation of funding.

The instructions in the revocable living trust should clearly spell out that the trust is primarily for the benefit of the trust maker or makers. It should contain extensive language about the rights of these primary beneficiaries and how their assets are to be used for their benefit.

The revocable living trust also names successor trustees, who take over if a trustee resigns, becomes disabled, or dies. Successor trustees are important elements of revocable trust planning and should be spelled out in detail.

A revocable living trust allows the trust maker, as the trustee and the primary beneficiary, to have full control over the revocable living trust and the assets contained in it. If there are two trust makers, then each one has full control over that part of the joint trust that is relevant to him or her.

To be most effective, a trust maker should transfer all of his or her assets into the trust. By transferring the assets into the revocable living trust, the trust maker can avoid probate on his or her death and can reduce or avoid the need for a guardianship or a conservatorship should a trust maker become disabled.

Not only can a trust maker reduce or avoid a guardianship or a conservatorship, he or she can also make sure that these assets are used the way a trust maker would like them used. There is no need for a court-appointed guardian or conservator to determine how the assets should be used, nor will a court have to approve how they are used. A trust maker's instructions dictate how and for what purpose the assets are used, ensuring that the trust maker's intent is followed.

A good revocable living trust also contains its own definition of disability. The reason for this provision is to avoid controversy as to when the successor trustee should take over the operation of the trust for the benefit of the trust maker and any other beneficiaries named in the trust. Here is a definition of disability that is typically found in a revocable living trust:

> Disability, for the purpose of this revocable living trust, shall occur when the trust maker, in the written opinion of his or her primary care physician, can no longer manage his or her financial affairs.

You can see that this definition only covers the trust maker's inability to manage his or her financial affairs. It does not address the inability of a trust maker to take care of his or her personal affairs. The reason for using a financial standard is that a revocable living trust is primarily directed to help a person manage property of all kinds. Generally, if a person cannot manage his or her financial affairs, it is very likely that he or she is having difficulty personally. The converse does not necessarily hold true; it is quite common for a person who has severe health problems to be mentally sharp. If a person is mentally capable of handling financial affairs, there is no need to bring a successor trustee. But if the person would like to have another person or financial institution take over his or her financial affairs, he or she can resign, allowing the successor trustee to step in.

We have found that the financial definition of disability in a revocable living trust works in a vast majority of situations. However, a revocable living trust needs backups, which is why other documents are absolutely essential in disability planning. We discuss those in detail below.

POUR-OVER WILL

Every good estate plan should contain a pour-over will. For many years, we have referred to a pour-over will as a legal pooper-scooper, because its function is to clean up if a revocable living trust has not been properly funded.

If all your assets are held in your revocable living trust at your death, then your assets can avoid the probate process. If somehow all your assets are not in your revocable living trust, then your pour-over will has instructions that those assets are to go into your revocable living trust. The pour-over will ensures that all your assets will be controlled by the instructions in your revocable living trust.

There are secondary purposes to pour-over wills. One is to limit the claims of creditors. If there is a concern that you may have unknown creditors after you die, it is wise to open a probate to limit the time in which creditors can file a claim against your estate. A pour-over will is a convenient method of doing so. In addition, if your death triggers litigation, say over a wrongful death claim or you were in personal litigation when you died, then a pour-over will allows the litigation to continue, with a minimum amount of administration. Your trust would be in existence but separate from the will. Remember, a will only affects property not in your trust.

You must choose a personal representative for your will. The personal representative, sometimes called an executor, should be the same as the trustee or trustees of your revocable living trust. By being consistent, there is less confusion, and any coordination that is necessary between your probate estate and your trust estate is minimized.

DURABLE POWER OF ATTORNEY

One of the fundamental backups to a revocable living trust is a durable power of attorney. A durable power of attorney (DPA) allows a person to appoint an agent, called an *attorney-in-fact,* to handle his or her financial affairs, just like an ordinary power of attorney. Unlike an ordinary power of attorney, a DPA does not end if the person granting the power of attorney becomes disabled.

Powers of attorney have long been part of the law in the United States. In a general power of attorney, a person, called a *principal,* grants another person or institution (a bank or trust company, for example) the power to act in his or her place. As such, a general power of attorney states that the attorney-in-fact can do everything the principal can do. Thus the attorney-in-fact can sign checks, borrow money, make investments, and generally have complete and absolute authority over the principal's finances without his or her consent. A general power of attorney is the ultimate power grant.

A general power of attorney terminates when a person is adjudicated as being mentally incompetent. Of course, this is the time when a power of attorney is most needed. A DPA overcomes this obstacle by allowing the power of attorney to remain in effect even if the principal is disabled. Continuity is thus preserved. To be a DPA, a power of attorney must contain specific language stating that the general power of attorney is durable, that is, in effect after the principal's disability.

Our recommendation is that, for most purposes, a DPA should not be a general power of attorney that grants the attorney-in-fact blanket authority. The DPA should be restricted to allowing the attorney-in-fact to transfer the principal's assets to the principal's revocable living trust. Remember, a revocable living trust has instructions as to how a person's property is to be used if he or she becomes disabled. Doesn't it make more sense to have your property managed the way you want, rather than how someone else would?

Of course, if the disabled person has already put all of his or her assets in the revocable living trust, then the DPA is not needed. However, if the disabled person has not, then the attorney-in-fact can finish the process. Having the assets in the revocable living trust removes the need for a court-supervised conservatorship.

Some professionals, instead of relying on a revocable living trust, include instructions in a DPA that allow the principal to define how he or she wants the attorney-in-fact to use the principal's property. DPAs that try to include extensive instructions are difficult to deal with. Frankly, many institutions, such as banks and brokerage firms, do not accept detailed DPAs. They do accept, however, a trustee of a revocable living trust. So it makes far more sense to use a DPA that is restricted to funding the principal's revocable living trust.

There may be some nondisability reasons to use general powers of attorney. But take care to whom you grant authority in a general power of attorney. If possible, restrict the activities in the power of attorney, so that it is clear what your attorney-in-fact can and cannot do. If you are using a power of attorney for disability planning, combine a restricted DPA with a revocable living trust. It will save you time, money, and worry.

LIVING WILL

A durable power of attorney addresses a disabled person's financial affairs. A living will addresses a person's health care. Simply stated, a living will is a medical directive that allows a person to express his or her wishes about health care if that person cannot express them because of accident, illness, or otherwise, and that person is terminally ill.

44

When most people think of a living will, they picture a situation in which they are connected to numerous machines in a hospital that are keeping them alive. A living will would state something like:

> If my death becomes imminent, I am in a permanent vegetative state, or I have a terminal illness or incurable condition, my dying shall not be artificially prolonged, as provided by the guidelines contained in this, my living will.

The living will then goes into detail about those issues that are important to that particular person. The living will addresses whether life prolonging measures are to be withheld and under what circumstances. The living will may state that painkillers and other procedures that keep the person comfortable, but are not life-prolonging, can be used.

It is difficult to appreciate how important the wording in a living will actually is until you have been in a hospital with a dying relative or friend and are faced with the reality of death. The experience is heart-wrenching, especially if no one knows the dying person's desires. A living will allows a person to express his or her wishes, and those expressions should be accurate and complete.

Most, but not all, states have statutes that regulate living wills. The few states without living will statutes have, by court cases, established guidelines that must be followed to validate a living will. It is extremely important that you consult a lawyer and your physician about your living will. To attempt to do your own living will by using a form, without professional counseling and information, is a mistake. Tragically, it may be more harmful to your surviving family and friends than it is to you; they would be left with the consequences of your failure to act.

HEALTH CARE POWER OF ATTORNEY

It is possible that you become ill or have an injury that prevents you from making your own health care decisions, but you are not terminal. For example, let's say that you are in a car accident and need surgery. A hospital requires your consent. But if unconscious, you cannot give consent. Or you may have a seizure or another health event that renders you incapable of making a health care decision.

A health care power of attorney appoints someone to make those decisions for you. Sometimes, a health care power of attorney is combined with a living will, and sometimes it is a stand-alone document. We prefer a separate document because combining documents can create time delays and confusion while someone has to find the relevant passages among a litany of legal phrases.

Your health care power should not only name a primary person to make decisions but also have at least one backup if your primary person is unavailable.

THE COST OF AN ESTATE PLAN

One of the most common questions asked about estate planning is, how much does it cost? It is a good question, but it is much like going to a

car dealership and asking how much a car costs. The answer is, of course, that it depends on what you want. Let's go over some general principles. Generally speaking, wills are less expensive than revocable living trusts, at least for most people. Wills are less expensive to create because the time spent on them is minimal; keeping the cost down while meeting the social responsibility of planning fulfill the objectives of most wills.

Revocable living trusts are usually more expensive to create. They tend to be more complex, and people who create them are likely to spend more time as they spend a little more money. Spending the time helps the maker and the maker's advisors create a much better product.

Wills are inexpensive because they are usually short and filled with legal boilerplate. Once done, they can be filed away. Unfortunately, those who make wills are not able to see if they work. A will is only tested after the maker dies. We have had more than one client come in and complain about planning. "I've had a will for 10 years," some of them say, "and I haven't had a problem." We tell them to count their blessings, because the only reason they have not discovered any problem is because they are still on the face of this earth.

Revocable living trusts cost more up front because they are initiated now, not on death. They help organize assets, take care of disability, and are fully able to continue a person's affairs after he or she has died.

Some people fall into the trap of spending as little as possible on a revocable living trust; they think that because they have a trust, all their planning problems have been cured. This is incorrect. A lot of terrible revocable living trusts were sold as commodities. They are filled with boilerplate and likely will not work very well when tested by disability or death. They usually do not avoid probate because they do not own the assets of the maker. *Note:* You get what you pay for, and treating a revocable living trust as a bare necessity may be as bad as or worse than having a will.

If you have people you love, take the time and pay the money to do the job right. Few things are more sad than seeing a family lose a loved one and then spend years cleaning up the mess that arose from poor planning. A fond and loving memory of a great man or woman fades very quickly when the survivors suffer the time, expense, and agony of probate, sorting out assets and debts, and making sense out of chaos.

The same thing happens if people take on their own planning. They buy software or forms, fill them in, and expect miracles. The miracles rarely occur. It is far more likely that the do-it-yourself plan will cost more in the long run than the most expensive revocable living trust. The do-it-yourself plans can cost more than having done nothing at all. At least if you retain a lawyer to do planning that turns out bad, your heirs can sue the attorney for malpractice. They certainly can't sue you, but we bet they may want to if you leave them a mess!

Thus far we have yet to give you the costs of an estate plan. And we cannot, because the costs vary from community to community and state to state. They vary on the complexity of a person's personal affairs and the complexity of a person's assets. We have seen estate plans that cost as little as a few hundred dollars to those that cost over a half a million dollars.

Your best bet is to find an attorney and other advisors whom you like and trust. Ask them how they charge. You should be able to get a set fee or a range of fees before you begin. If an advisor declines giving you a fee or fee range, don't do business with that advisor. Get your fee understanding in writing before you begin.

If you have any doubt about the reasonableness of a fee quote, tell the advisor. Ask other people what they have paid. And make sure that you understand what you are getting for the fee charged. The price you pay is not nearly as important as the value you receive. Good advisors make their fees, as well as their services, very clear. You will feel confident with their advice. Even then, check their fees out, and only proceed when you are satisfied that the price is reasonable for the value you will receive.

FUNDING A REVOCABLE LIVING TRUST

A revocable living trust controls property that it owns or that comes to it from a beneficiary designation or other means. To avoid probate, the trick is to have your revocable living trust, rather than you, own the property.

"Oh, sure," you may be thinking, "there is no chance that I am going to give up control of my property by letting some trust own it." This is an understandable but incorrect view.

One of the great characteristics of a revocable living trust is that you, the maker, control the trust while you are alive and well. Anything you put into your trust, you can take out. Don't like the people you named as a beneficiary or trustee? You can change them any time you want. Don't like your trust for some reason? You can revoke it. The point is, you have full control of your revocable living trust and the property in it. So anything you put into the trust—called *funding your trust*—you can take out.

For income tax purposes, your trust is treated as if it were you. All income and expenses are shown on your Form 1040. In fact, the federal identification number of a revocable living trust of which you are a trustee is your Social Security number.

While virtually every asset you own can be held in a revocable living trust, there are some exceptions. For the most part, if an asset cannot be titled in the name of your trust, such as an IRA or other beneficiary designation property, you can name your trust as the beneficiary.

GEORGE WASHINGTON LIVING TRUST

Trusts are not separate entities that can own property directly. When property is transferred to a trust, the property is titled in the name of the trustees rather than the trust. For example, if George Washington created a revocable living trust, he would have probably titled it as follows: "George Washington and Martha Washington, Trustees of the George Washington Living Trust, dated July 4, 1776." To be effective, the title should state the trustees, the name of the trust, and its date.

One last word of advice: Do not try to fund your trust without professional help. Get complete instructions from an attorney who knows how to fund a trust. You can do a lot of the work, as long as the attorney reviews it. For real estate, absolutely use a lawyer. Deeds can be complicated. One mistake can make real property unsellable for a long time, so do not try to prepare deeds on your own.

Funding a trust while you are alive can take some time and is not always easy. There are still some banks and other institutions that make it difficult to change the title of accounts to a revocable living trust. If you become frustrated, remember this: Funding a trust is a lot like probating an estate. If you think it is tough doing it while you are alive and well, think how really hard it would be if your spouse, children, or personal representative had to do it after you are gone. It's no wonder probate can cost so much!

TRUSTEES

One of the greatest concerns of our clients is whom they should name as the successor trustee of their revocable living trusts. As we discussed earlier, most often the trust maker is the initial trustee of a revocable living trust. Naming successor trustees is not easy and should be given serious thought. Over the years, we have learned a great deal about this issue, so we will try to make it as simple as we can.

At the outset, you should understand what a trustee does. A trustee is a fiduciary. That means that a trustee has a very high duty to protect the beneficiaries of a trust. The duty is so high that if a trustee violates his or her fiduciary duty, the trustee may very well be personally liable for any damages incurred.

The standard to which a trustee is held varies from state to state. The longtime standard is called the reasonable person standard, and requires a trustee to act in the same manner as a reasonably prudent person would who is serving in the same capacity, in similar circumstances. If a court, in hindsight, finds that the standard was violated, then a trustee will be liable for the consequences of his or her action.

The reasonable person standard is being replaced in most states by a higher standard, called the prudent investor rule. Under the prudent investor rule, a trustee must, in effect, act in the same manner as a professional trustee would have acted under similar circumstances. It is more of a prudent expert rule, which essentially means that a trustee is more than likely to be held responsible for any mistake. As you can see, trustees have a great deal of responsibility and a great deal of liability.

Long ago we reached the conclusion that trustees come in three groups: (1) individual trustees, (2) professional advisor trustees, and (3) institutional trustees. Each group has advantages and disadvantages, which we summarize in Table 44-1.

(table 44-1)

CHARACTERISTICS OF TRUSTEES

GOOD CHARACTERISTICS	BAD CHARACTERISTICS
INDIVIDUAL TRUSTEES (FAMILY, FRIENDS)	
Family knowledge	Not always objective
Caring	No experience as a trustee
Hard working	No investment expertise
Common sense	Uncollectible for mistakes
	May be indecisive
PROFESSIONAL ADVISORS (ATTORNEY, ACCOUNTANT, FINANCIAL PLANNER)	
Professional knowledge	May have conflicts of interest
Honest	May embezzle
Hard working	No investment expertise
	May be uncollectible for mistakes
	May not devote enough time
	May die or become disabled
INSTITUTIONS (BANK TRUST DEPARTMENT, TRUST COMPANY)	
Professional knowledge	No family knowledge
Experienced	Turnover among staff
Collectible for mistakes	Sometimes slow making decisions
Objective	Conservative
Will always be there	Worried about its liability
Subject to regulation	

As you can see, there is no such thing as a perfect trustee. Our recommendation to most of our clients is to create teams of trustees. For example, a bank or trust company may be teamed with a family member or a professional advisor. Depending on a client's family and financial circumstances, different combinations work best.

As you meet with your professional advisors, you must pick the best combination of trustees that you can, keeping in mind that your choice may not be 100% foolproof. If you have a well-written trust and good advisors, it is highly likely that your choice of trustees will be the best you could hope for.

THE FEDERAL ESTATE AND GIFT TAX

It is not our purpose in this chapter to go into the many methods of planning for federal estate and gift tax. We could devote the whole book to just those subjects (and we have) and still leave a great deal out.

Planning for federal estate and gift tax is extremely important if you have an estate of $1 million or more or if you and your spouse have a combined estate of over $2 million. If your estate is a little shy of these numbers, plan for federal estate and gift tax anyway. You never know what will happen to the size of your estate over time.

We picked these size estates because of the 2001 legislation that attempted the repeal of the federal estate tax in the year 2010. Prior to the 2001 legislation, single people with estates of $1 million and married couples with estates of $2 million needed tax planning. In the year 2011, the federal estate and gift tax law reverts to what it was prior to 2001.

Do not be deceived by the political hype that the so-called death tax will go away. The federal estate tax has been around since the Revolutionary War. It has come and gone, but it has always reappeared.

You can bet, however, that whatever revenue is lost with the repeal of estate tax, it will be made up with other taxes. In fact, the states are now imposing their own versions of the federal estate tax in an attempt to bolster their revenues. At the minimum, state death taxes should be planned for.

It is impossible to predict the laws Congress will pass. It is impossible to predict the future. To attempt to base tax planning on what may happen is pure folly.

The biggest mistake anyone can make, and this is especially true for older people, is to avoid planning, hoping against hope that the laws will be more favorable tomorrow or the next day.

Our strong advice to you, if you have an estate in the $1 million range ($2 million if you are married), is to make sure that you have basic federal estate tax planning that preserves as much of your estate as possible free of federal estate tax.

If your estate is greater than these ranges, then you may want to do more sophisticated planning, reducing your taxes even further and perhaps giving some of your assets to children, grandchildren, and charitable causes. If you make gifts or plan your estate, remember one adage that we have learned over the years. It is better to die with a taxable estate, having lived well, than to die without paying taxes but to have planned so well you had to decrease your standard of living. As you plan with your attorney and financial advisors, always make sure that you and your spouse, if you are married, have enough assets and insurance to take care of your needs, even if that means paying some tax. Do not let the tax tail wag the planning dog.

PLANNING IS ABOUT PEOPLE

Estate planning is all about people, not things. When you plan for your disability, you are planning for yourself and the people who depend on you. Your money and your property are merely a means to take care of yourself and your loved ones. Death planning is the same, except you are out of the picture. No matter whether you leave your money and property to loved ones, friends, or charity, how you leave it is the most important. Even if you leave your money and property to a pet, it is still how you do it that makes the plan work.

When you do not plan, the consequences fall on those who you leave behind, those who have to care for you and make difficult medical decisions if you are disabled, and those who still live on after you are gone.

As a close friend and colleague says all the time, procrastination is the biggest enemy of planning. Wishing is not planning. Take all the energy and time that you spend in wishing, and create a plan to meet your needs and the needs of those people or causes you leave behind.

WHAT YOU NEED TO KNOW

▶ Consider the consequences of not planning, and then commit to plan.

▶ Understand the difference between will planning and trust planning.

▶ Organize and prepare before you plan to save time and money.

▶ Seek competent advisors.

▶ Implement your plan and follow it up.

▶ Change your plan as your life changes.

▶ Do not let taxes control your decisions.

▶ Planning is about people, not things.

FOR MORE INFORMATION

SeniorMag: Elder Law and Resources
Web: www.seniormag.com/legal
Information about the legal aspects of aging. It includes a directory of attorneys who provide services in this area.

National Academy of Elder Law Attorneys
Web: www.naela.com
Although mainly for lawyers who belong to this outstanding organization, it has public information and a list of elder law attorneys.

United Seniors Association
Web: www.unitedseniors.org
Addresses all the important issues facing Americans who are over 50. It is a great resource to find the latest on planning and has links to many other websites for related information.

SUGGESTED READING

Protect Your Estate
Robert A. Esperti and Renno L. Peterson. 2000.
New York: McGraw-Hill.
The fundamental primer on the full array of estate planning tools. It includes a detailed discussion on wills, probate, property ownership, community property, revocable and irrevocable trusts, charitable planning, and much more. Easy to understand, it gives the reader a thorough survey of planning.

The Living Trust Workbook
Robert A. Esperti, Renno L. Peterson, and David K. Cahoone. 1995.
New York: Penguin Books.
A comprehensive guide to creating, implementing, and maintaining a revocable living trust. There are numerous sample forms for transferring almost any type of asset into a living trust.

All My Children Wear Fur Coats: How to Leave a Legacy for Your Pet
Peggy R. Hoyt. 2002.
Oviedo, FL: Legacy Planning Partners.
Ordering and more information at
www.legacyforyourpet.com. This book and website
are invaluable for those who want to care for a pet if
they are disabled or after they die.

The Elder Law Handbook: A Legal and Financial Survival Guide for Caregivers and Seniors
Peter J. Straus and Nancy M. Lederman. 1996.
New York: Checkmark Books.
A detailed explanation of virtually all issues facing the
elderly, from planning and paying for health care to
retirement and to end-of-life issues. Although out of print,
used copies are available, including a large-print edition.

If the building of a bridge does not enrich the awareness of those who work on it, then the bridge ought not be built.

—Frantz Fanon

THE AUTHOR

45 *Susan Bradley*

SUSAN K. BRADLEY, CFP, is a nationally recognized wealth coach, writer, and leader within the financial planning industry. With 20 years experience as a financial planner she understands how important it is for families to make the connection between their wealth and their values, goals, and beliefs. Since 1995, with the inception of Money Camp for Kids, Susan has continued to write about and develop unique educational programs for young adults, women, families, financial advisors, and sudden money recipients.

Susan is the author of *Sudden Money: Managing a Financial Windfall,* the first financial planning guide for the receipt of new money from inheritance, divorce, windfall, and/or the sale of a business. After her book she went on to form the Sudden Money Institute, which is taking a leadership role in education and orientation programs for new wealth recipients and their advisors.

In 2004 Susan began offering wealth coaching services to women in transition as part of the Women, Meaning, and Money project. Starting July 2004 the Women, Meaning, and Money workshops will be the subject of a PBS series to be aired nationally.

45 | HOW TO TALK TO YOUR PARENTS ABOUT THEIR MONEY, HEALTH, AND ESTATE PLANNING

Given the choice between (1) initiating a heart-to-heart conversation with their parents on the intensely touchy topics of their parents' money, health, and estate planning and (2) poking a sharp stick in their eye, many adult children would seriously consider the second option. Why is that? Why are these subjects so difficult for so many of us? And how can we make the process more comfortable for all parties?

Let's start by acknowledging that there is nothing simple about discussing three of the most private and sensitive areas of life—money, health, and estate planning—with your parents. Every family has its own culture containing unspoken rules, beliefs, and taboos regarding matters family members consider personal and private and these three topics are at the top of the list, along with sex. Worse, these subjects seem to get more complicated as our parents age. Members of our parents' generation are conditioned to never discuss these topics outside of a professional relationship. It may seem strange, but it is very common for our parents' doctor, financial planner, and attorney to know more about their health, finances, and estate planning decisions than their own children do.

Most families are more comfortable avoiding these topics and hoping that everything "just works out." Unfortunately, this approach rarely works out, and the consequences of denial and avoidance can be devastating—to you and to your parents. The popular premise is that your parents' personal finances, health, and estate planning decisions are none of your business . . . until they become your business. The difficulty is that once it is your business, you need to know what to do and you won't know what to do without some preparation.

The real question is not whether you have a need to know; it is at what point should the discussions begin, what should be discussed, and what do you do if the going gets rough?

WHEN TO START THE CONVERSATIONS

The best time for starting the conversations is to start early, before a crisis or life event triggers a sudden *need to know*. The time to start building the ark is before it rains. Start early, and start small, taking on the topics in manageable pieces. You shouldn't expect to accomplish everything in a single conversation. It may take months, or years, to develop a comfortable safe place to openly discuss these issues.

It starts with a recognition of the evolving nature of the roles and responsibilities of you and your parents. You're the adult child, and your parents are still your parents, but there may be some shifting of responsibilities at this point in your respective lives. You may be taking on some advice-giving and caregiving functions with your parents on the receiving end. Balance, between your responsibilities as an adult child and their need to be your parents with their own lives to live and end

THE PREMISE

Your parents' personal finances, health, and estate planning decisions are none of your business . . . until they become your business.

on their own terms, is your goal. Make it clear to them that you're not trying to take over their lives or their independence—you're trying to enhance it. Balance is usually achieved by managing the tension between two opposites, which begins by recognizing this is new territory that may initially feel awkward and uncomfortable for all of you.

Solutions are found through a communication bridge between you and your parents that allows you each to remain in your natural role but facilitates an easy flow of information and support on an as-needed-basis. A family does not automatically have such a bridge; each family must build its own. Communication bridges, like transportation bridges, take time to build; they both require thoughtful engineering, teamwork, and, once completed, regular maintenance.

Keep in mind there are two sides to wealth management and health care: objective and subjective. Both are equally important and equally difficult to fully understand in our own lives and perhaps more challenging when we are the outside party trying to help our parents manage their lives. The objective side, containing the facts and numbers, is quantifiable and easier to understand. The subjective side, made up of feelings, beliefs, values, taboos, and perhaps some old wounds still carried as personal baggage for years, is a powerful force that influences numerous life decisions. The same two aspects are true for health care; we have the medical facts and legal requirements on one side and the human experience of being cared for on the other. In the box "Timing Is Everything," Karen and Tucker saw both sides in their parents' reaction to their initial concern. Their bringing up this matter opened the door for future conversations on formerly sensitive topics.

As you contemplate initiating your own family dialogue, remember that you're not alone. There are experienced guides, professional advisors, to help you in both the technical and psychological areas. Guides have valuable wisdom to pass on from their extensive work with families that have come to this stage before you. The best use of professional advisors—doctors, attorneys, financial planners, and family therapists—is to have them actively participate rather than simply lead. Most of the time, it is best to allow your parents to form relationships with advisors of their choice and for them to be the primary participants. Your role may be not to act as your parents' advisor but to initiate the discussions, encourage them to find appropriate advisors, and explore ways to desensitize these topics so you can continue to have honest, useful discussions as the needs and desires arise.

In many families, talking about money, security, changes in living arrangements, and estate planning is silently discouraged. Children are afraid to appear controlling or greedy, while parents fear losing their autonomy and becoming dependent on their children—neither wants

GOOD ADVICE

- Start early
- Start small

- Encourage your parents to make their decisions and then take the steps necessary to implement the decisions.
- Let them know their safety and well-being are important to you and you are prepared to assume whatever responsibility they choose to delegate to you.
- Reassure them that you're not trying to take over or usurp control.
- Strive to create a comfortable and inclusive space for your family to discuss sensitive subjects.
- Be prepared to increase your involvement.

to confront mortality and loss. We are all accustomed to ignoring the enormous white elephant in the middle of the room until it becomes unavoidable. If an event necessitates immediate action, the suddenness of the situation compounds the emotions, confusion, and possible disagreements between siblings.

Though this might appear to be threatening new territory for you to enter, it may be equally unsettling for your parents in the beginning. The challenges are to remain respectful of your parents' privacy in an inherently revealing discussion. Remember: It is their life being discussed, not yours. Once there is enough trust between you for intimate discussions to take place, the discomfort may be replaced with a new closeness. Many families have healed old wounds, realized how much they cared for each other, and renewed their sense of family. The voyage may be rough at times, but the trip is well worth the effort.

WHAT YOU WANT TO TALK ABOUT

There are several good practical reasons why you should talk to your parents about their health, money, and their estate:

- Learning your parents' wishes and concerns
- Understanding their fears or what they do not want to have happen
- Knowing what is expected of you
- Knowing how to act on their behalf in an emergency or illness
- Learning in advance if you will need to help them financially
- Discovering small ways you can help that allow them to remain independent
- Understanding their confidence and capability levels so you can better judge whether they are declining or need extra help
- Decreasing tension between siblings
- Completing the natural cycle of the parent-child relationship

When we talk about the natural cycle of the parent-child relationship, we're talking about moving through the four life stages of families. This concept will help us see this relationship more clearly. As shown in Table 45-1, a garden metaphor can describe and differentiate the various stages.

Families naturally progress through four stages. The *foundation* stage was created when your parents married and started having children. They created a home life for nurturing, protecting, and educating their children. Family values were instilled. This is when relationships are formed and a sense of family identity is forged. Many beliefs about what is private and what is discussed openly come from these early years. There may be some unhealed wounds either between you and your sibling or with your parents that can be traced back to this time period. Whatever seeds are sown during this stage—positive or negative—will continue to come up again in the later stages of life.

As the family grows strong in the *transformation* stage, children grow up, begin careers, marry, and start their own families. The adult children use their own history as the basis for forming their new relationships and try new ideas of their own. This is a time of leaving the nest and testing the strength of their own wings. Mom and dad still exert some influence over the family, but their guidance now comes from a distance. They're looking forward to retirement and the joys of grandchildren.

In the *maturation* stage, everyone is in full bloom. Your parents retire, your children go off to college, and your career is on solid ground. The family may spread out to different parts of the country or even the world. This may necessitate new reasons to get together as a group, and new traditions are born. It's fulfilling to watch your parents establish a retirement lifestyle they can both enjoy and afford. If your parents are healthy and active, there might be a sense of great comfort and satisfaction. But this is also the stage at which we see the first subtle signs of aging. Your parents may still enjoy good health, but among their peer group, there is increasing illness and death. You and your siblings become concerned about the "what ifs" regarding your parents' continued health and well-being.

The *transition* stage may sneak up on you. The challenge of aging can take you by surprise even though it is a natural part of life. One decade everyone seems self-sufficient; then the next decade uncertainty creeps

(table 45-1)
THE FOUR LIFE STAGES OF FAMILIES

STAGE	CHARACTERISTICS	EMOTIONS & RELATIONSHIPS
Foundation, or planting seeds	Parents marry; children born; home; family identity formed.	Sibling relationships formed; parents nurture and protect; family values instilled.
Transformation, or growing strong	Children become adults, begin careers, marry, start their own families; parents prepare for retirement.	Family made up of independent units; parents' role to support, with advice and guidance secondary.
Maturation, or full bloom	Children have stable careers and family; parents retire; grandchildren enter college; family may live in different states; family develops new gathering and celebration traditions.	First signs of aging; illness and death among friends and relatives; children become concerned with "what ifs" while hoping for continued health and independence of parents.
Transition, or harvest time	Children retire; grandchildren become adults; parents' confidence and capabilities wane.	Loss of first parent; concern for surviving parent; increased need for children's involvement.

in and with it, a certain sense of a dreaded *something* lurking around the corner. That something could be the mental or physical decline, or death, of a parent. It could involve money issues, competency, health care, or living facilities. At the same time that you're looking forward to your own retirement, you find yourself more deeply involved in your parents' life than you're ready for or comfortable with. It may be your turn to protect and provide care.

This is all part of the natural progression of life. We're born, we grow, we thrive, we decline, we die. And then the cycle repeats itself. Each generation is first taken care of by its parents and then takes care of its parents at the end of their lives. As obvious as this is, sometimes we forget. Sometimes we think we're different from everybody else, that our situation is unique. It's not. It is unique to us, because it's the first time we're going through it. But whatever the situation is, someone else has already gone through it. And we can learn from that experience.

HOW TO BEGIN

Find a low-stress environment when there is time to have a discussion that can naturally continue. It's probably best to avoid large family gatherings with several things going on at once. Those affairs have their own set of issues, and introducing sensitive topics at that time is inappropriate. This is a special conversation that deserves full attention.

As we said before, start early. And *early* is defined as *now,* regardless of where you are in the family life cycle. The most logical time to begin is in the maturation stage when both you and your parents are self-sufficient and before the needs arise. This is a time when your parents' friends and relatives start to pass away, making the topics of illness and dying less remote. It's easy to use these experiences as a jumping-off point to begin a conversation with your parents:

- Have you and Dad thought about the kind of funeral you'd like?
- What would you want me to do if you had a stroke like Mr. Smith?

Many experts suggest that the conversation might be easier to begin if you start by telling your parents what your wishes are, given the same situations:

- After seeing what happened to the Andersons when George died suddenly, I've decided to get more life insurance.
- Jane and I recently updated our durable powers of attorney for health care and finance so we don't leave the family in the same kind of mess that the Martins did.

Other people's experiences—both good and bad—can be used as models for what you do or don't want to happen in your life. Ask your parents for their suggestions and advice; this puts both of you back in familiar roles where you should feel comfortable. This kind of conversation becomes a natural bridge to asking about their wishes and decisions.

FAMILY FEUD

Charlotte was between jobs when her father was diagnosed with inoperable brain cancer. She had recently returned to the West Coast after working in the southeast for five years. She seized the opportunity to once again be close to her divorced father and became his primary caregiver. The 11 months together before he died were generally happy times until the very end when he became quite ill. He named Charlotte the executor of his estate, which was to go to each of his three children equally, although the other two who lived close by had rarely visited him, even after his diagnosis.

Her siblings were suspicious of Charlotte's motives and challenged every decision she made while settling the modest estate. Consequently, the estate took a long time to settle, and the extra costs for lawyers, forensic accountants, and appraisers reduced the estate by 60%. Two years later when their mother died, the two siblings settled her small estate between themselves without consulting Charlotte, and have not spoken to her since.

You don't need to know all the details about your parents' life, but you do need to cover the basics to make sure there are no surprises. Here are some *good* questions to ask:

- What would you want me to do in case of an emergency? I'd like to be prepared to contact the right people, find the necessary paperwork, and, most of all, know what you would want done if you can't make your own decisions.
- How would you like me to help out if you weren't able to take care of everything by yourself?
- Is there anything I should know in case something happens to you? What would you expect from me, and how should I become prepared for this responsibility?
- What should we do to avoid the kind of trouble your *[friend or relative]* went through with their family?
- What do you think they should have done in advance, and should we start thinking about this topic even though it feels premature?

These questions may sound difficult to discuss now, when the time for decisions is still in the future. However, they are even harder to discuss when someone is really sick, emotions are high, and decisions need to be made quickly. Don't put off the conversation because it feels awkward or you're afraid of saying the wrong thing. If you blow it in the beginning, keep trying. The best way to start is simply to start.

WHO SHOULD PARTICIPATE?

If you're an only child, this could be a small intimate conversation with just you and your parents. However, if you have siblings, you'll probably need a bigger table. Your siblings should be invited to be part of these family discussions—your parents are their parents too. Observers of broken families frequently recommend that even estranged children should be invited into the family decision-making process regarding their parents' well-being. Leaving someone out may be convenient at the moment but can lead to irrevocable divisions in the future.

In the box "Family Feud," Charlotte thought she was doing the right thing by taking care of dad, but her siblings didn't see it that way. Had

TALKING

- How to start talking to your parents about their money and health: Very carefully, with respect and sensitivity. This is a family meeting, not a business meeting
- When to start: The earlier the better. You may find it becomes easier and more relaxed as you both get more comfortable and learn more about each other.

- Where to have conversation: Find a low-stress environment that feels safe and relaxed. This is probably not a family reunion, unless agreed upon beforehand by all involved.
- Who to include: Everyone who needs to be should be invited to partake.

Charlotte tried to involve them in his caregiving from the start, she might have prevented the flare-up that occurred at his death.

Families come with history—a history of roles and relationships, both past and present, of unresolved feelings, unspoken grudges, and jealousies. Because of the possible presence of strong undercurrents, it's a good idea to start early enough so that everyone has time to work out these issues without compromising the parents' well-being. Sometimes not all the old problems can be neatly resolved; the best you can do then is to acknowledge the inequities and move on, focusing on your parents' needs. Family members need to remember that the meeting is not a one-time event but a series of periodic gatherings. Holding regular meetings puts less pressure on family members to get everything resolved at one meeting and allows more time for processing information and decision making.

Take away the family taboos about money and minimize the potential for unfortunate surprises by opening up the discussion, and keeping it alive as an honest and safe place for everyone involved. Taboos exist because we allow them to exist; you can choose to dissolve them and let fresh thinking flow in like fresh air into a closed stale room. Begin now wherever the family is; if all is well with no crisis on the horizon, then you have the luxury of finding a comfortable starting point and acquiring the art and skill of communication over time. If you have a tough situation with difficult decisions to make, then you have the challenge of learning by doing. You will need to walk the fine line of being respectful and inclusive, while being focused on what needs to be done.

It can be very beneficial to enlist other people in these conversations as needed. You can get help facilitating family discussions from social workers, family therapists, wealth counselors, clergy, and other trusted family advisors. Check online or at your local library for other resources, ideas, and support.

Sometimes your parents may feel it is only necessary to talk with the person or people they have appointed as their personal representatives. Depending on the family situation, it's a good idea to involve all your siblings in a discussion but save the details for those who need to know more.

LEARN FROM OTHER FAMILIES

It is highly likely that other families close to you have faced the challenges of caring for a parent, settling a difficult estate, or feeling unprepared to help out financially. You can learn from their experiences: Ask them for advice, or, better yet, ask them what they wish they had done differently.

When you witness difficulties another family has experienced, speak with your parents about how your family would be prepared in a similar situation. Think of this as an opportunity to ask questions and have a fire drill, testing your own preparedness.

DECIDE WHAT NEEDS TO BE KNOWN

Unless your parents are incapacitated and you are in charge of their well-being, you don't need to know all the details about their money, life, or

LESSONS LEARNED

David's father was terminally ill when the family began talking about the estate planning decisions he already had in place. His father was a hard-working attorney who never felt it necessary to include his children in his affairs. Prior to going back to the hospital for what would be the last time, he held the first-ever family meeting and ran it like a business meeting. He told his two children and three grandchildren that they would all receive an equal share of his estate. This news did not sit well with David's divorced sister who did not have children; she had expected the estate would be split two ways, not five. Her father explained his concern that she might remarry and his money could end up going to someone he had never met—case closed.

David was not comfortable either; in addition to wanting to maintain a close relationship with his sister, David did not think it was a good idea to give his children such large sums of money at this point in their life. The family had no experience talking about their feelings and expectations, and their father was in no mood to change his style or mind.

The family of David's wife learned a wonderful lesson from this experience. They, too, had never had this kind of family meeting and had not given much thought to the possible consequences of avoiding the subject. Their discussion began with talking about the decisions of David's father and eventually circled back to talking about their own family. Fortunately, everyone was healthy, and they had plenty of time to think, do some research, have numerous conversations, and eventually reached some good decisions.

894

health. Many parents will talk about what should be done if they become ill, unable to manage their affairs and their estate planning decisions, without ever revealing how much money they have, where it is invested, or the amount of their income. It is important for you to know if they have enough income and that their money is being professionally managed by someone they know well and trust. Other facts you need to know are:

- What types of insurance coverage do they have? Do they have adequate medical coverage and a plan for long-term care? Is it the best they can afford?
- Is their income stable and sufficient? How much do they get from various sources (e.g., Social Security, pensions, and investment income)? Do they anticipate needing financial support from you, and if so, how much?
- Are their estate documents (including up-to-date wills or trusts and beneficiary information) current? Documents should be reviewed in case of divorce, death of a spouse, birth or adoption of children, marriage, or remarriage. Even if the situation is stable, review the documents periodically because laws change constantly and their plans may be out of date.
- Have they prepared health and financial powers of attorney? Have the appointees been informed?
- Do they have any special concerns you should know about? Sometimes asking a simple question like that will produce a response you didn't expect—people like to be asked.

If you have reason to feel your parents need some help managing their daily life, you need to know much more about their routines and their finances. In this case, your action list would include the following:

- Organize their income and expense information.
- Set up a meeting for them with their estate planning attorney while they are still capable of making their own decisions.
- Set up a system to collect mail and pay bills.
- Arrange for appropriate periodic check-ins with family members, neighbors, or a community service organization.
- Locate community resources.
- Create an information pipeline for all those involved.
- Review needs and resources periodically.

You may begin with simply understanding their ideas of what you should do if they need your help, where to find the necessary information, and names of advisors. Many attorneys and financial advisors provide family document organizers containing:

- Names and contact information for all advisors
- A list of all legal documents with dates of execution, name of attorney,

and where the documents are held, including safe-deposit boxes and the location of the keys *(Note:* For a safe-deposit box, copies of the papers should be kept outside the box so survivors know the contents of the box.)

- A list of insurance policies with policy numbers, date of issue, agent information, and amount of coverage
- A list of all your parents' accounts, passwords, and financial institutions

You need to know whether you have been given the responsibility to make financial or health care decisions for your parents if they become incapacitated. If so, you need to know more about their financial obligations and attitudes toward health care:

- Are their final wishes clearly spelled out, and do you know where the necessary documents can be found when you need them, in case of illness or death?
- Who do they want to make health care decisions if they cannot?
- Who is appointed to make financial decisions if they are not able?
- Do they have any special requests?

There are no guarantees about what your family will experience, but regardless of what happens, it pays to be prepared. You may never be called on to do anything more than provide a sense of security that someone is prepared if a need arises. And that will make you all feel better.

■

WHAT YOU NEED TO KNOW

➤ Most families need to build communication bridges. The more sensitive the topic, the stronger the bridge must be.

➤ Start early with the small issues, and learn how each members of the family thinks and communicates around money, health, and estate planning topics.

➤ Find out what needs to be done or learned; no one is born with the knowledge modern families need to make healthy decisions.

➤ Your role is to initiate and facilitate. Encourage your parents to make their own informed decisions; let them know their well-being is what counts.

➤ Pay attention to both the subjective and the objective sides of the issue. Understanding how people feel may be as important as knowing the facts.

➤ Determine the starting point, what needs to be discussed, and what you feel you need to know.

➤ Use other family's events, funerals, nursing home admission, and lack of estate planning to open the discussion.

➤ Plan a family meeting carefully with respect of everyone's time and sensitivity of family hot spots and taboos. The goal is to create an honest safe space for everyone involved.

➤ Start with easy topics: A small success will build confidence and give everyone a sense of achievement and a willingness to have another meeting.

FOR MORE INFORMATION

▷ Consultants: Richard Wagner, JD, CFP
WorthLiving LLC
19 University Boulevard #712
Denver, CO 80206
303-329-8309
dick@worthliving.com
Web: www.worthliving.com

▷ Fredda Hertz Brown, PhD
The Metropolitan Group LLC
300 Knickerbocker Road
Cresskill, NJ 07626
201-569-0100
E-mail: fhbrown@relative -solutions.com
Web: www.Relative-Solutions.com

▷ Susan Bradley, CFP
Sudden Money Institute
141 Green Point Circle
Palm Beach Gardens, FL 33418
888-838-9446
E-mail: susan@suddenmoney.com
Web: www.suddenmoney.com
Web: www.womenmeaningandmoney.com

▷ John Levy
842 Autumn Lane
Mill Valley, CA 94941
415-383-3951
E-mail: levy842al@aol.com

▷ Gayle Knight Colman, CFP
Colman-Knight Advisory Group
18 Audubon Lane
Carlisle, MA 01741
978-371-2015
Fax: 978-369-1504
E-mail: gaylecolman@prodigy.net

▷ Courtney Pullen
4099 Field Drive
Wheat Ridge, CO 80033
303-420-2908
Fax: 303-420-5912
E-mail: pullenconsulting@earthlink.net

Rona Bartelstone, LCSW, BCD, CMC
Rona Bartelstone Associates, Inc.
Care Management Home Health
2699 Stirling Road, Suite C-304
Ft. Lauderdale, FL 33312
800-678-7224

SUGGESTED READING

Sudden Money: Managing a Financial Windfall
Susan Bradley, CFP with Mary Martin, PhD. 2000.
Hoboken, NJ: John Wiley and Sons.

Wealth in Families
Charles W. Collier. 2001
Cambridge, MA : Harvard College.

Estate Planning for the Healthy,
Wealthy Family
Stanley D. Neeleman, Carla B. Garrity,
and Mitchell A. Barris. 2004
New York: Allworth Press.

Mid pleasures and palaces though we may roam,
Be it ever so humble, there's no place like home.

—*John Howard Payne, 1791–1852*

THE AUTHOR

46 *John Schaub*

JOHN SCHAUB is a graduate of the College of Business of the University of Florida. He has more than 32 years experience in the housing industry and 17 years experience in nonprofit housing, serving seven years on the board of Habitat for Humanity International. He is the publisher of the nationally distributed newsletter "Strategies and Solutions" and the author of 13 courses on real estate investing, financing, and taxation and the book *Buying Right*. He was an active realtor for 10 years and the vice president of the Florida Association of Realtors, president of the Florida Real Estate Exchangors. He is listed in the Hall of Fame of Who's Who in Creative Real Estate, and was featured in *Forbes and Personal Finance Magazine*. He serves on several nonprofit boards and is an instrument-rated pilot.

46 | STAYING IN YOUR HOME

As the son of parents living independently in their mid-80s, I have learned the value of my parents staying in their own home. It's a value that is hard to measure quantitatively. I can't say with authority that it helps you to live longer, but I can say that it allows you to live better.

If you live in a home that is appreciating in value, the increase in value may go a long way to paying for any services that you may require to stay in your home. Later, in the section "Financing Alternatives for Staying in Your Own Home," I suggest how to use this equity without moving out of your home.

Being forced to move out of your home can be a disaster. I have witnessed a friend being moved out of her home of 40 years to an apartment across the country, closer to her family. The move took her away from lifelong friends, church connections, physicians, and a familiar environment where she felt safe. Her new home, while physically more than adequate, was in a location far from any friends or familiar places. The result was that my friend became isolated and withdrawn.

If you are in a similar situation, be sure to communicate well and often with your remote relatives. Assure them that you are safe and that you want to stay in your home as long as possible. Take action if you know that you will need help living on your own. In this chapter I discuss a number of solutions which I have implemented for friends, family members, and others and which may allow you to stay in your home longer.

LIVING AT HOME

WITH PART- OR FULL-TIME CARE

Hazel, my secretary for 32 years, continued working with my company until her 85th birthday. She was a remarkable employee. Her daily routine of driving to work, going to the bank and post office, and working in an active office helped her stay mentally alert and physically fit.

While many of her peers spent their days watching TV, she actively participated in exciting for-profit and nonprofit work. If asked why she did not retire (which she could have comfortably afforded), she would say that she enjoyed the friendships at the office and the daily communication with the customers.

Hazel was able to live in her home her entire life, and enjoyed good health until shortly before her death. After her health declined, she employed at first part-time and eventually full-time nursing care in her home. Her caregiver would cook, clean, help her bathe and dress, and ensure that she took her medicine, as well as drive her to shops, church, and doctor appointments.

CHOOSING WHICH HOME WHILE YOU ARE STILL IN CHARGE

My parents are in their late 80s and living in their home, aided by a 40-hour-a-week caregiver. They are both able to care for themselves and do not require a high level of nursing care. However, neither drive, so the caregiver can chauffeur them to appointments and other activities. Most important, she is a daily contact who can immediately inform the children if additional care is needed.

About eight years ago Mom and Dad made a great decision that has helped them both stay in their home. They sold the family home of 40-plus years, an older, two-story model which demanded much attention, and moved to a newer one-story villa *in the same neighborhood*. My dad no longer worries about keeping the house in good shape and spends his time playing golf and fishing. Mom's friends are still close by, so she sees them often and they play bridge.

The decision to move was theirs, and this timely decision was important to their ability to continue to live in their own home. If you live in a home that will be a challenge to maintain or to move about in as you grow older, consider moving soon, while you are fully capable of making that decision independently.

Adult children may apply considerable pressure to move you into a safer place, if in their opinion your current home is unsafe because of its age, location (maybe just not close to them), or layout. By choosing the place yourself and initiating the move before you have to, you can live where you want.

LIVING NEXT DOOR TO A FAMILY MEMBER

My dad's brother has been diagnosed with Alzheimer's and is in his late 70s. He stayed in his home as long as it was safe and then moved next door to one of his nieces. Being next-door neighbors allows both to live with a degree of privacy. However, she can keep a watchful eye out for him. He feels safer knowing that family is just a few yards away. It gives him the courage to live semi-independently.

As nursing care becomes necessary, she can supervise from a short distance to ensure the quality of care is adequate and can be available in the event a big decision needs to be made.

His niece has the legal power to make medical decisions for my uncle. In addition, she helps manage his finances with input from another family member. While he is able, my uncle is involved in the decision making.

TAKING YOUR HOME PROFITS TAX-FREE AND RENTING NEAR A FAMILY MEMBER

It is not necessary to buy a property next door to a family member in order to benefit from living nearby. In many cases, renting a home or an apartment may be an even better solution to living near a family member. Typically, your housing needs change as your kids leave the nest. You may want less house and yard to maintain. You may want to relocate closer to shopping and medical care.

Should you sell your residence, renting your next home may be a better alternative than buying. If you own a home, you have a lot of cash tied up in a non-income-producing asset. Not only does it not produce income, but home ownership consumes a good part of your income to pay increasing taxes, insurance, and maintenance.

While most homes appreciate in value, you may not benefit from that appreciation during your lifetime. Your home may be a great investment for your heirs, but you could have both more cash flow today and access to the cash you sold your home for if you choose renting over buying another property.

You may be able to rent a home for a small fraction of what it would cost you to own it. This is especially true with properties that are more expensive. I rent one home to a retired schoolteacher in his 80s. He moved to be closer to his daughter and her family and to free himself from the responsibility of home ownership.

He pays me $1000 a month in rent, a fair rent in today's market, and I pay all the expenses: taxes $3400, insurance $400, and average annual maintenance $1200. After expenses, I net about $7000 on a house worth about $200,000. If he bought the same house for $200,000, he would give up the interest that he can earn on his money (or pay interest to a lender if he financed it) and then be responsible for the $5000 in annual expenses.

By investing his $200,000 in tax-free municipal bonds yielding 4%, he can generate $8000 in income, which he can use to pay the rent. If interest rates increase to 6%, the bonds will produce enough to pay the entire rent, and he will still have access to his principal if he needs it.

The tax law has changed regarding how the profits from your home are taxed when you sell. In 1997 Congress repealed the old rollover replacement rule that allowed you to reinvest in another home without paying any tax. The new law allows a married taxpayer to exempt $500,000 in profit, or a single taxpayer to exempt $250,000 in profit, from the sale of a personal residence (Internal Revenue Code section 121).

Should you own a home with a significant profit and have to move to another home, then this exemption allows you to take out your equity and profit up to the limits without paying tax. Please note that a profit more than these limits is taxable as a capital gain. Consult your tax advisor for up-to-the-minute advice before making a decision.

SHARING YOUR HOME WITH A COMPANION

When my grandmother reached an age at which she no longer felt comfortable living alone, she spread the word in her church that she would be willing to share her home with another woman, in return for some help with cleaning and cooking. A younger, single woman responded to the call and, for many years, shared my grandmother's home. My grandmother both enjoyed the company and benefited in many ways by having a younger, physically stronger woman in her home. Her companion shared the daily chores, helped with minor maintenance, and added an element of safety. She was an excellent companion.

Having a roommate allowed my grandmother to continue living in her home all her life, and I know that was a great comfort to her as well as the rest of our family.

FINANCING ALTERNATIVES FOR STAYING IN YOUR OWN HOME

Once you have decided to stay in your home, consider the following question: "Should I pay off my existing loan or borrow more against my home?" The answer to this question will vary based on your attitude toward debt and what you intend to do with your home as part of your estate plan.

PAYING OFF YOUR DEBT

When you are paying a higher interest rate on your home loan than you are earning on your savings, it appears that the right thing to do is to pay off or pay down the loan. However, before you do, consider your need for future liquidity. If you pay down $10,000 on your home loan and then need it back, a lender will require a new loan application and charge many dollars in up-front loan fees to give you your money back. When you make a prepayment or pay off your loan, do it with money that you are sure you will not need.

Prepaying part of a loan is typically a bad strategy as you get no immediate benefit. For example, if you prepay $10,000 on a $50,000 loan that has $500 monthly payments, your payment is still $500 a month. You will save the interest on the $10,000 you have paid, but if cash flow today is important to you, you will have more of it if you do not prepay your loan. The other reason not to prepay is the same reason I stated above. If you need your $10,000 back, you have to apply for a new loan and then pay bank closing costs.

Paying off other smaller debts, such as car loans or credit card debt which is at a higher interest, can be a good use of cash on hand. Refinancing your home to lower your interest rate and your monthly payment is a great strategy when interest rates dip.

BORROWING AGAINST YOUR HOME

The good news about owning a home is that it is your bank's favorite collateral. The reason is simple: People usually pay off their home loans. Because the default rate is low, the interest rates are much lower than the rates for credit card loans or car loans. Sometimes when cars are not selling well, car dealers offer cheap interest rates to move their inventory. Do not confuse these rates with the rates you would pay if you borrow cash. If you are confused, try to borrow some cash from a car dealer and see the rate you are charged.

There are several ways to borrow against your home. Most require you to make payments on your loan, so they are not attractive if you need more income.

For smaller, short-term needs, home equity loans are available at attractive rates and with low closing costs. Another good feature of these loans is that as you make payments of principal, your payments are reduced. For example, if you paid $3000 of a $5000 home equity loan, your next monthly payment should drop by 60%. Should you decide to borrow using this type of loan, confirm this feature with your lender.

A LOAN YOU DO NOT HAVE TO REPAY

Perhaps you have heard of a concept called a *reverse mortgage*. A reverse mortgage is the reverse of a conventional loan. Instead of making payments to the bank, the bank makes payments to you. It is a way to spend the equity in your home. It can be used to increase your monthly cash flow.

You give your lender a first loan against your home, and it agrees to fund the loan by writing you a check each month for a specified amount. You are not required to make payments, and interest is charged to your loan and added to the amount you owe on a monthly basis. It is possible to borrow a lump sum in the beginning and then receive smaller monthly payments. This may be necessary if you already have a small loan balance on your home, which needs to be paid off when the reverse mortgage is made.

There are some disadvantages. First, the up-front cost and interest rates are high. Because they can be financed into the loan, the closing costs are not a burden; however, if you pay $4000 in up-front closing costs but borrow only $20,000 over the life of the loan, the closing costs are a whopping 20%.

You would think that because of the almost nonexistent risk to the lender with this type of loan (it may begin making you payments of $500 a month on your $150,000 home) that it would give you a really low interest rate. If you use a reverse loan, visit several lenders to get the best rate that you can. Unfortunately, the rates seem to be higher than they need to be.

Another potential problem is that having a reverse mortgage on your home would probably prevent you from borrowing an additional amount on a second mortgage if you need it. A lender would be unlikely to make a loan behind a first that is growing in size each month. You would be forced to refinance the entire loan and pay the closing costs again.

A PRIVATE ALTERNATIVE TO INSTITUTIONAL REVERSE MORTGAGES

The concept of a reverse mortgage is a great one. However, one disadvantage is the high fees that lenders charge. If you have a relative or friend who is looking for a very safe investment, they may be a potential lender for you.

Consider the scenario in which your son or daughter would agree to lend you a certain amount each month, say $500, to be secured by a loan on your home. The amount they lend you would accumulate and earn interest, but the rate of interest could be lower and the up-front fees significantly less.

You could agree on any payment schedule that worked for both of you. For example, it may be easier to receive an annual payment of $6000 than twelve monthly payments of $500. If you need the money to pay your property taxes, a once-a-year payment would work well.

If the problem you are trying to solve requires just one payment, perhaps a major repair or remodeling of your home, a single payment could be made, and then that amount plus accrued interest could be repaid upon sale of your home or from your estate.

VACATION HOMES AND INVESTMENT PROPERTIES

At some point in your life you may want to reduce or eliminate your

responsibility for property that you own in addition to your home. A vacation home or family farm are examples of property that you would like to keep in your family.

If you have heirs who want the property, one solution that relieves you of the responsibility for maintenance and the day-to-day problems that come with property ownership is to lease the property to your heirs. The lease must be at a fair market value rate, and it can call for the lessee to take full responsibility for maintaining the property (even paying taxes and insurance). It may be simpler for them to pay you enough in rent to cover the taxes and insurance, which you would then pay yourself. By leasing rather than selling, the property remains in your name, and should you need additional funds, you could sell or borrow against the property.

The idea of leasing to reduce your involvement can also be applied to your investment property. If you have heirs interested in making money with investment property and willing and able to manage the property, you can lease one or more properties to them, and then they would sublet to the tenants and pocket any profits. Your lease could again require them to do all of the maintenance and pay all expenses. You could even give an heir an option to buy one or more of your properties. This may have the benefit of transferring any future appreciation of the asset to the heir. Check with your estate planning attorney to see if this strategy is right for you.

SELLING AND FINANCING THE PROPERTY THAT YOU SELL

If you have property that you no longer wish to manage and that you have no interest in passing to future generations, then consider selling and financing the property to generate income. Your income from financing a property may be four times or more the amount of income that you can get from a bank account or CD.

There are several advantages to you as a seller of using this idea. First, you can typically command a retail price for your property when you sell it. Because of your willingness to finance the property, buyers will pay more. A side benefit, is that your property should sell faster than a property that is for sale for all cash.

If you do not know how to sell and finance a property, look for a real estate attorney with experience in selling and financing his or her own property. The attorney will be able to prepare the documents you need and help you make the transaction. A real estate broker experienced in this area may also be able to guide you and help you complete the transaction.

The down payment should be large enough to protect you in the event that the buyer does not fulfill his or her obligations. When you sell and finance a property, you will be protected by a mortgage or deed of trust on the property. The cost of regaining possession and title to the property should be covered by the down payment.

I suggest that you finance a property for no longer than five years. At that time, you can agree to renew or renegotiate if interest rates have changed dramatically. The amount of the monthly payment during the five years is negotiable. It can be interest only or a larger amount that would return part of your capital to you each month.

Many buyers would rather have the owner hold the financing than go to a bank for a loan. One reason, of course, is that they may not have good enough credit or earn enough income to qualify for a bank loan. You can sell quicker if you accept a lower down payment.

Other buyers are wise enough to know that if they borrow from a seller, they avoid a lot of the closing costs that a bank charges. They may have the ability to borrow from a bank, but are looking for a better deal than a bank would give them.

I have sold and financed many homes. Often, without my help, the buyers would not have been able to afford to buy the house. Use common sense, and only sell to people who have enough income to pay for the home. If you're prepared to take a small chance on good people, you will be well rewarded.

PASSING IT ON TO THE NEXT GENERATION

Several of my good friends are estate planning attorneys. They tell me that many of their clients feel that they have a responsibility to leave a large portion of their estate to the next generation. In order to accomplish this, they often sacrifice certain luxuries or even necessities of life.

Your heirs want you to take good care of yourself first. This includes good health care, a safe and comfortable place to live, good food, safe cars or other transportation, and travel or social and sporting activities.

While it is a natural inclination for many to become financially more conservative as they age, there is no need in most cases to cut back on your lifestyle. In fact, living a full and active life may be a better investment for your heirs than sitting home to save them money. The active person is more likely to remain healthy longer, avoiding the most expensive activity you can imagine: checking into a hospital.

A local woman reported to be quite wealthy died several years ago after a flurry of activity in her later years: taking family members on extravagant vacations to exotic places, holding numerous parties for her friends, and making generous gifts to her family members, friends, and local charities. When she died, the local paper reported that she had spent nearly her entire estate. The paper reported it in such a way as to imply that she had squandered her heirs' estate. I see it as *great timing!*

WHAT YOU NEED TO KNOW

▶ Staying in your own home is good for you, both physically and financially.

▶ If you live in a home that is appreciating in value, the increase in value can go a long way to paying for any services that you may require to stay in your home.

▶ If you have adult children, they may apply considerable pressure to move you out of your home into what they see as a safer place.

▶ By choosing the place yourself and initiating the move before you have to, you can choose where you live.

▶ There are ways to access the equity in your home, without selling it.

46

FOR MORE INFORMATION

▷ Senior Citizen Homeowner Reverse Mortgage Tax-Free Income: Pros and Cons
Robert Bruss, Burlington, CA: Bruss.
Order by web (www.bobbruss.com), phone (800-736-1736), or mail (Robert Bruss, 251 Park Road, Burlington, CA 94010) for $4.

▷ Building Wealth One House at a Time
John Schaub

> You cannot predict the future, but you can plan the events that shape it.
>
> —*Ron Groenke, The Money Tree*

THE AUTHOR

47 *E.M.Kilbourn*

E. MICHAEL KILBOURN, CLU, CHFC, AEP, MSFS, president of Kilbourn Associates, Naples, Florida, is a family wealth transfer specialist who has lectured and written extensively on investment, estate, and financial planning topics during his 25-year career. He is founder and chairman of the Wealth Protection Network, a national network of estate planning professionals.

A decorated veteran who served in Vietnam, Mike has earned four masters, including a master of business administration (cum laude) from Western Michigan University and master of science in financial services from the American College. He is a fellow of the Esperti Peterson Institute and an adjunct professor of the Academy of Multidisciplinary Practice. Mike has earned 14 professional designations, including chartered financial consultant (ChFC), chartered life underwriter (CLU), and accredited estate planner (AEP).

He is the author of *Disinherit the IRS: Don't Die Until You've Read This Book* (Career Press, 2003) and a contributing author of *Ways and Means* (Esperti Peterson Institute, 1999), *21st Century Wealth* (Quantum Press, 2000), and *Giving* (Quantum Press, 2002).

Mike established his estate and wealth strategies practice in the early 1990s after an 18-year career in commercial real estate, syndication, and real estate securities. Since beginning his practice, he has earned the insurance industry's prestigious "Top of the Table" award virtually every year. His memberships include the Estate Planning Council of Naples, the Financial Planning Association, the Society of Financial Service Professionals, the Association of Insurance and Financial Advisors, and the National Association of Philanthropic Planners.

47 | LIFE INSURANCE

Life insurance is a bit of misnomer. Although life insurance has been around a long time, it is really "death" insurance. In fact, around the time of the Civil War, when the industry really got off the ground in this country, it was called *death* insurance. And it didn't sell very well. Then someone at one of the major insurance companies decided to call it *life* insurance, which turned out to be one of the greatest marketing strategies ever done. It not only sounds better, but after you examine what you can do with it, including all the lifetime benefits that have developed over the last 50 years, *life* insurance is, indeed, the more appropriate name.

To understand the value of life insurance in the wealth planning process, you first should understand life insurance and that's not an easy task. Most people—even financial professionals—are confused by life insurance. So it is not unusual to find yourself mystified by its complexity, structure, and pricing. In fact, you may feel very uncomfortable with the entire subject of life insurance. But it's too important to the financial fabric of your family and business to be ignored. Life insurance is a vitally important strategy in sound estate planning.

Many financial professionals make their living trying to explain how insurance actually works. But the jargon and vocabulary often create confusion. What most buyers want to know is quite simple: "What is the best policy for me? How much insurance should I buy and what will it cost?"

When those questions go unanswered, buyers often make a purchase that ends up not providing the expected benefit, or they make no purchase at all. This chapter is designed to clear up some basic confusion and provide a simple vocabulary to help you communicate your questions. It also covers the various types, typical uses, and how to buy life insurance. In addition, this chapter helps you understand how you might sell one or more existing life insurance policies through a process known as *life settlement*.

BASICS OF LIFE INSURANCE

Before explaining the key to understanding life insurance, let's examine the definition of life insurance along with a few fundamental terms.

Life insurance is a legal contract referred to as a policy. The contract guarantees to pay a certain sum of money (i.e., the death benefit) to a specified person or entity (i.e., the beneficiary) when the insured dies. The policy remains in effect as long as the cost of it (i.e., the premium) has been paid according to the contractual provisions.

You can own a policy personally or have some other person or entity, such as a trust, own it instead. The owner controls the policy and has the legal right to name the beneficiary, change the beneficiary, cancel the policy, and/or withdraw or borrow from the policy's cash value at any time. The owner is responsible for any tax consequences relating to the premium, cash value, and death benefit.

USES OF LIFE INSURANCE

Most people don't think of it this way, but life insurance is risk sharing among a group of people with the common goal of providing money to beneficiaries when an insured party dies. It is a little bit like a lottery in that money is pooled to provide a benefit (death benefit), which, in the case of life insurance, goes to the beneficiaries of those who die while their contract is in force. It is most often bought because a purchaser loves someone or something, but life insurance can be used for many purposes:

- Providing financial security for loved ones
- Paying estate taxes
- Paying a debt, such as a mortgage
- Purchasing an interest in a business
- Diversifying an investment portfolio
- Providing for retirement
- Offsetting gifts to charity
- Making up for a bad investment
- Protecting future generations
- Recovering the cost of a corporate obligation
- Replacing wealth
- Equalizing inheritance
- Protecting a business
- Giving to charity
- Replacing lost income

Life insurance is often the *only* way to effectively provide for many of the above needs. In most cases, it is the least expensive way. Life insurance is so versatile that it can provide benefits during life as well as after death. For example, as discussed below, in certain types of life insurance there is an accumulation of cash inside the policy from premium payments paid in excess of mortality charges and expenses. The policy owner can access this accumulation during the insured's lifetime via withdrawals and/or policy loans. These withdrawals and loans are often tax-free and can be used for lifetime needs, such as retirement income, college educations, and emergencies.

HOW TO DETERMINE NEED

As you may be starting to realize, life insurance is a diverse financial product capable of satisfying many needs. Your decision on whether to purchase a life insurance policy rests heavily upon the financial concern you are attempting to address. The most obvious use for life insurance is to provide for loved ones in the event of your untimely death, but as listed above, there are many more reasons why you may need or want to purchase insurance. For example, if you are 55 and worried about having enough funds to retire on, life insurance may provide the perfect addition to your retirement plan. This is because the cash value that accumulates inside an insurance policy, due to interest buildup or market growth (as in the case of "variable" life insurance—see the section "Variable Life," below) does so without tax. Thus, a policy can be designed to allow additional cash deposits, within certain limits, above what is needed to sustain the death benefit. This extra cash not only grows tax-free but can also be accessed—on a tax-deferred basis—through policy *withdrawals* and/or loans. And if the policy is held until your death, the *withdrawals* and/or loans are *tax-free*, not just deferred. While policy loans would typically reduce the ultimate death proceeds, insurance companies usually charge little or no net interest on these loans. Thus, for retirement planning or other purposes, the insurance policy acts like a tax-free savings plan.

Deciding on how much insurance to purchase requires some relatively simple math, working backward from your goal. For example, if a 55-year-old bread winner wanted to make sure that his or her family had enough assets to live comfortably in the event of his or her death, the steps are simple. The first step is adding up the family's liquid and nonliquid assets and determining how much income those assets generate. Assuming there is a shortfall of income from existing assets, the next step is determining the amount of insurance proceeds (cash) needed to be invested to provide the difference, using some assumed rate of earning, such as 5%. It is also prudent to factor a level of inflation into your calculations. As we discuss below, some policies allow an increasing death benefit, which is one way to cover the effects of inflation. Additional consideration should be given to the potential for estate taxes, which can be handled with extra death benefit and through proper estate planning.

(figure 47-1)

CHECKLIST
Checklist to analyze insurance needs.

DETERMINE FUTURE NEED

- [ ] Family income
- [ ] Estate tax exposure
- [ ] Supplemental retirement income
- [ ] Special needs

ADJUST AMOUNT DETERMINED FOR

- [ ] Inflation
- [ ] Growth
- [ ] Taxes (as applicable)
- [ ] Contingencies

DETERMINE WHO SHOULD OWN THE POLICY

- [ ] Insured (one or more)
- [ ] Beneficiary (one or more)
- [ ] Trust (recommended)

In addition to family protection and estate planning, it may also be possible to design a plan that provides supplemental retirement income. This could be accomplished by determining the amount of additional retirement income you desire beginning on your planned retirement date. This information can be added to the list of assumptions made in calculating the amount of the premium needed to cover both the income and the *increased* death benefit (don't forget withdrawals and loans could affect the total death benefit). The combination of your specific goals and other assumptions that ultimately determine the premium, such as health factors and the mortality table (discussed in the following section) will assist you in making an informed decision regarding insurance. Figure 47-1 is a checklist to help your analysis.

MORTALITY TABLE

Life insurance is based on the mathematical principle of probability. People die according to a predictable pattern. This pattern is reflected in a mortality table that is based on accumulated historical data. Insurance companies don't know who in a group will die in a given year—they just know how many. This predictable pattern allows the death benefit to be mathematically converted into a *present value amount*. A company needs this amount in order to make the contractual payment at death.

The present value amount is usually financed with annual payments (the annual premium) and is based on a specified rate of interest. By providing coverage to hundreds of thousands of people, insurance companies can offer coverage to each insured for a small amount of money each year. This is because each insured pays a proportionate share of the death benefits paid out, usually in a lump sum, to the beneficiaries of each insured on death. Life insurance is not a *gamble;* it is based on mathematics and on probability, and it is available to anyone who can qualify as being "insurable." Being classified insurable requires a physical as well as an economic evaluation of the insured, and there must be an *insurable relationship* between the insured and beneficiary. For example, a wife has an insurable interest in her husband but not necessarily in her employer. However, because of her status as an employee, her employer may have an insurable interest in her.

With this background, let's look at how life insurance works.

UNDERSTANDING LIFE INSURANCE

Life insurance is based on the statistical odds of one person among a group of insureds dying. Life insurance is simply a group of people sharing the same risk and funding the dollars needed when a member of the group dies, which gives rise to the analogy of a lottery winner—only, in this case, eventually, everyone wins. The first ones to die are paid by the last to die. So let's consider a group of 1000 men who are each 45 years old. Insurance company mortality tables assume they are all in good health today but project none will be alive by age 100. The mortality chart shown in Table 47-1 predicts the chances of a person's death in any given year between ages 45 and 100.

(table 47-1)

AGE-45 MORTALITY TABLE

CHANCE AGE	NO. DEATH, %	NO. LIVING	DEATHS	CHANCE AGE	NO. DEATH, %	NO. LIVING	DEATHS
45	0.11	1000	1	73	3.59	810	30
46	0.12	999	1	74	4.26	776	35
47	0.13	997	1	75	5.01	737	39
48	0.14	996	1	76	5.89	693	43
49	0.15	995	1	77	6.93	645	48
50	0.16	993	2	78	7.81	595	50
51	0.17	991	2	79	10.22	534	61
52	0.19	990	2	80	11.10	475	59
53	0.21	987	2	81	12.36	416	59
54	0.23	985	2	82	13.41	360	56
55	0.25	983	3	83	14.55	308	52
56	0.28	980	3	84	15.78	259	49
57	0.32	977	3	85	17.09	215	44
58	0.35	973	3	86	18.51	175	40
59	0.39	970	4	87	20.03	140	35
60	0.44	965	4	88	21.66	110	30
61	0.49	961	5	89	23.40	84	26
62	0.54	955	5	90	25.26	63	21
63	0.60	950	6	91	27.24	46	17
64	0.66	943	6	92	29.34	32	13
65	0.73	937	7	93	31.57	22	10
66	0.82	929	8	94	33.92	15	7
67	0.94	920	9	95	36.40	9	5
68	1.03	911	9	96	39.00	6	4
69	1.14	900	10	97	41.72	3	2
70	1.68	885	15	98	44.55	2	1
71	2.25	865	20	99	49.00	1	1
72	2.88	840	25	100	56.00	0	1

Source: Adapted with permission from "The Box," by G. Baker and J. Oberholtzer.

Let's assume the money paid in premiums earns no interest. If all participants die according to statistical probability and each member contributes the appropriate amount, there are enough funds to pay each participant's beneficiaries his or her share of the account. Those who die early benefit most on the basis of the ratio of their contribution to the proceeds. Those who die later still receive proceeds, but they have paid more compared to those who died earlier.

Even if interest earnings are factored in, the last to die has to pay more into the fund than the first. However, the compound interest earnings help offset the need for them to place the full value of their expected benefits into the pot.

Staying with the group of 1000 healthy 45-year-old males, let's follow the most likely events if they each want $1 million of life insurance coverage and examine how the cost is determined.

DETERMINING THE COST

The cost of life insurance is determined by the relative probability of death at various ages. Thus, the cost rises as the probability of death rises. If the people in the group of 1000 healthy 45-year-old males die as predicted by the mortality table, one of them will die in the first year. The cost of this death to the group is $1 million. Spreading this cost over the group of 1000 people results in a cost of $1000 per person ($1,000,000/1000), a relatively modest premium for $1 million of coverage.

However, at 50 years of age, 2 of the original 1000 will die. This equates to a cost of 2 deaths times $1 million of insurance divided by approximately 1000 people, or $2000 per person. At age 60, the cost is $4145 per person, at age 70, the cost is $16,949 per person, and so on.

If you graph the outcome of this analysis, you get a curve, known as the *mortality curve,* shown in Figure 47-2. Notice the flat part of the curve in the beginning. Obviously, the coverage is very inexpensive to own during the early years when the number of deaths in the group is low. The real increase in the cost of insurance coverage comes in the later years.

BUILDING A MORTALITY TABLE

So how does an insurance company develop information about a group of people in order to build a mortality table? Every insurance company has created its own database of experience based on its current book of insurance in force. In addition, the insurance industry has calculated nationwide statistical measurements of mortality probabilities.

Each company's table is based on death claims over an extended period of time. The national statistics are developed without the benefit of any physical examinations, whereas all the various companies' tables assume quality underwriting. This means that company underwriters have

(figure 47-2)

Annual cost of insurance for age 45 *(Adapted with permission from "The Box," by G. Baker and J. Oberholtzer).*

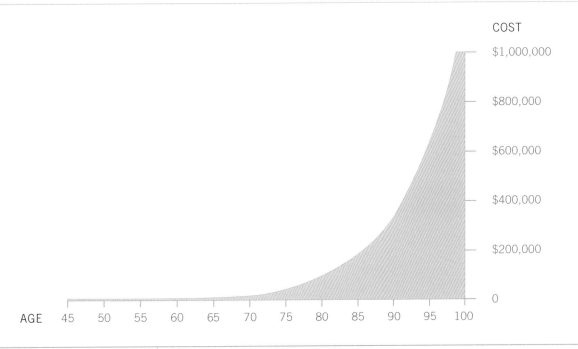

received full disclosure of any medical history so that they can make an accurate assessment of the insured's health. If, from the outset, a company can either eliminate or charge extra for people who are in poor health, it stands to reason that the mortality table will be more reflective of the actual statistical probability of death for that particular company's insureds. Thus, there is a significant difference between the cost of insurance based on statistics developed from the population at large and insurance based on a select group of people who are all in excellent health and have a lifestyle that suggests they will maintain their health over time. The more accurately an insurance company can determine the number of deaths in its group of insureds, the more likely it can competitively price its products. Again, the price, or premium, is based on the number of death claims each year, which is different for each company.

To determine pricing, insurance companies must have an accurate assessment of the number of deaths per year for a specific group, so they select the mortality table most appropriate to the risk they are willing to insure. If individual medical information is not readily available, the company uses the mortality table that best reflects that higher risk. For example, there are group rates, typically offered through employers, that require no medical underwriting. The mortality table and associated premium cost of such groups would reflect the higher mortality risk, which may be greater than the population at large.

Without dwelling on the relative merits of the various tables used to price insurance, it is important to understand that each table measures the cost of dying for different groups of people. Figure 47-3 shows the differences among five commonly used tables for determining premiums.

(figure 47-3)

Premiums for $1 million of life insurance from various sources *(Adapted with permission from "The Box," by G. Baker and J. Oberholtzer).*

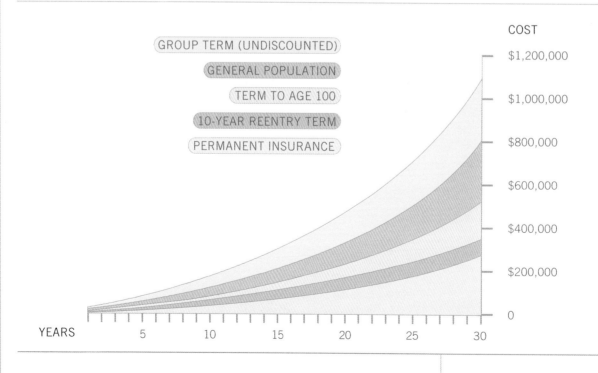

(*table* 47-2)

LIFE EXPECTANCY

AGE	AGE AT LIFE EXPECTANCY	AGE	AGE AT LIFE EXPECTANCY	AGE	AGE AT LIFE EXPECTANCY
45	80.58	64	81.05	83	87.60
46	80.59	65	81.11	84	88.34
47	80.60	66	81.18	85	89.09
48	80.61	67	81.25	86	89.86
49	80.62	68	81.33	87	90.66
50	80.63	69	81.42	88	91.47
51	80.65	70	81.55	89	92.28
52	80.67	71	81.72	90	93.09
53	80.60	72	81.93	91	93.93
54	80.70	73	82.20	92	94.79
55	80.72	74	82.51	93	95.67
56	80.75	75	82.86	94	96.56
57	80.77	76	83.26	95	97.44
58	80.80	77	83.72	96	98.30
59	80.83	78	84.21	97	99.17
60	80.87	79	84.84	98	100.00
61	80.91	80	85.49	99	100.90
62	80.95	81	86.17	100	
63	81.00	82	86.87		

Source: Adapted with permission from "The Box," by G. Baker and J. Oberholtzer.

47

LIFE EXPECTANCY AND COST

To determine the cost of insurance, you could simply total all the premiums you pay over time, but to which age would you choose for such a measurement—age 60? 70? 90? Any specific age would be arbitrary because you don't know the date of your death. Life expectancy is probably the most meaningful point at which to determine the total cost, but most people don't understand the true meaning of life expectancy.

When the newspapers announce that the life expectancy of a male in the United States is 71.2 years, the figure sends shivers down most spines. Fortunately, life expectancy is not the age at which a person is *expected* to die. Instead, *life expectancy (LE)* is the predicted age at which *half* the people in the measured group will be dead—it is the *median* age of death for the group. But LE is different for each given age group at any point in time.

So when the papers say the LE is 71.2 for males and 75.4 for females, they mean for people being born at the time of the statistic. And as you age, your LE readjusts upward. For example, the LE for a 45-year-old, as shown in Table 47-2, which lists life expectancies for various ages of males and females in the general population, is 80.58. That means that 50% of all 45-year-olds in the group will be dead by age 80.58. It also means that 50% of the group will still be alive. Thus, you have a 50% chance of living longer than the LE. An 80-year-old male has an LE of 85. Even a 95-year-old has an LE.

When you start adding up the annual premiums, which increase each year to cover increasing mortality costs, you realize the longer you live, the higher the total cost. Thus, if you are healthy and you live a long life, possibly past life expectancy, the total cost, determined by adding up the premiums, could be prohibitive and eventually lead you to terminate your policy. On the other hand, if you were terminally ill, you are more likely to keep your insurance coverage, even if the premium was high. This situation, for which healthy insureds drop their insurance and the sick insureds maintain coverage, is known as *adverse selection* and can cause economic disaster for insurance companies. Using the lottery analogy, if the lottery payout was a specified, predetermined amount but very few people bought lottery tickets to produce the funds to pay the winner, it would very likely put the lottery out of business. This would have the same result for insurance companies and, in the early 19th century, was the cause of many failures.

To avoid adverse selection and allow policy owners to pay a *level* premium so they could more easily budget for the cost of premiums and make sure they have affordable coverage that is permanent and lasts throughout their lifetime, the companies developed various types of cash value–building policies. The idea behind the design of cash value—building, permanent insurance policies—is to make life insurance affordable and predictable by leveling the premiums and allowing cash value to build up so that, when combined with compounding interest, it will cover the expenses and increasing cost of mortality. Depending on the *type* of cash value–building policy, the premium payments can be made in a lump sum, over a specified period of years, or spread out over a lifetime. The amount paid in plus the interest that accrues must equal or exceed the cost of insurance (the mortality cost) plus expenses. Figure 47-4 shows premium payments that are level for the life of the insured. This level premium exceeds the mortality cost in the early years and allows extra funds to build up, with interest, to cover the shortfall that would occur in the later years when the mortality cost rises above the level premium. Regardless of how the premium is determined, the mortality costs represented by the mortality curve are a major part of every type of life insurance.

TYPES OF LIFE INSURANCE

There are five basic types of policies: *whole life, universal life, variable life, indexed life,* and *term life.* With the exception of term life, these are all considered to be cash value—building, permanent policies. Each has a distinct purpose, and the decision regarding which will work best for you depends on your personal situation and goals.

WHOLE LIFE

Whole life insurance, sometimes called *ordinary life, straight life,* or *permanent insurance,* is a traditional form of insurance policy that is designed to help consumers handle the high cost of insurance in later years, when

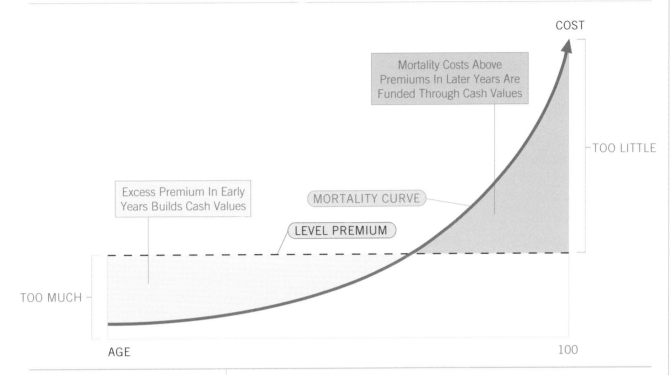

(figure 47-4)

Annual cost of insurance for age 45 *(Adapted with permission from "The Box," by G. Baker and J. Oberholtzer).*

premiums would otherwise become prohibitively expensive to match the increasing risk of death. By averaging premium costs and amortizing them over the projected lifetime of the policy, whole life guarantees a continued death benefit for the insured's entire life. The *fixed* annual premiums are usually level for the life of the insured and are based on the insured's age and health at the time the policy is issued.

As whole life insurance premiums are paid, cash value builds up in the early years in excess of the actual insurance costs. This excess is invested, and a return on the invested portion is added back into your policy in the form of dividends. The dividends increase with interest and can provide some flexibility by building up to a level that allows you to limit the premium payment period of the policy, but they are *not* guaranteed. Alternatively, some policies allow you to apply any excess buildup of cash value to the purchase of more insurance. Such additions are known as *paid-up additions.* Paid-up additions have a certain amount of cash value. Thus, it is possible to cash in these additions at some future date and apply them toward premium payments on the base policy.

Whole life policies generally fall into two classes: *participating* (dividend-paying) products, which are generally sold by mutual companies (companies that are owned by their policy owners rather than stockholders), and *fixed-premium accumulation products,* which are sold by both stock and mutual companies. In both, the interest and mortality costs reflect company experience. Participating products pay dividends based on the past experience of the company relative to each policy, returning gains in interest and mortality experience. The accumulation type insurance products contain interest credits and improvements in mortality costs based on the company's estimate of expected experience and, thus, are prospectively determined for the coming year.

Some types of whole life policies are tied more closely to market interest fluctuations, and policy performance may vary depending on rates. Such policies are known as *interest-sensitive* whole life.

The guaranteed death benefit and fixed premiums make whole life policies attractive to some but less attractive to others. To some people, whole life means less to worry about. They know in advance what they will have to pay in premiums and exactly what their death benefit will be. To others, this does not provide enough flexibility. If their situation changes, they will likely be unable to increase or decrease their whole life policy's premiums or death benefit without surrendering their policy and purchasing a new one.

UNIVERSAL LIFE

Universal life insurance was developed to overcome the primary disadvantages of whole life insurance. It is another type of cash value–building policy that provides flexibility by giving the policy owner (i.e., you, your spouse, your children, or your trustee) the ability to set and vary premium levels, payment schedules, and death benefits, within certain limits. This increased flexibility makes it easier to adapt universal life policies to your changing needs and financial conditions. Like whole life, a portion of each premium goes to the insurance company to pay for the mortality or "pure" cost of insurance. The amount of premium paid into the universal life contract that exceeds the mortality cost or pure cost of insurance plus company expenses is credited back to the policy owner with interest. The interest is declared ("fixed") by the insurance company on a periodic basis and depends on the earnings of the company's general account, which frequently contains a high percentage of investment-grade bonds.

Most universal life policies have a guaranteed level of mortality charge and interest. Any earned interest above the guaranteed minimum will vary with the performance of the insurance company's investment portfolio. Universal life expenses are often lower than those charged under whole life policies. This provides affordable, low-cost coverage. Unlike whole life policies, universal life policies are transparent: the annual policy report allows the policy owner to see the interest credited, along with all the mortality and expense charges, on a monthly basis. This enables the policy owner to make adjustments to meet his or her needs and objectives.

The advantage of flexibility in universal life allows you to purchase more coverage for the same level of premium dollars paid for whole life. However, it also introduces a certain level of risk, as the mortality charge and/or interest can vary from the assumptions made in computing the premium. So the premium is not fixed, as with whole life; it is calculated based on assumptions. This issue of risk is the most misunderstood element in the purchase of universal life insurance. If the policy assumptions are not realized (i.e., interest rates go down and/or mortality charges go up because of an increase in the rate of deaths), the policy may not perform as planned unless more or higher premiums are paid into the policy. Virtually all universal life policies come with a "floor" guarantee (minimum guaranteed interest and maximum guaranteed mortality charge), but the policy owner is responsible for fluctuations from the guarantees that would materially alter the policy's performance.

Universal life allows you to vary the frequency and amount of premiums and even skip planned premiums as long as there is sufficient cash value to cover current charges. You can also purchase a policy with an increasing death benefit, or you can elect to increase the amount of insurance (subject to continued insurability) to meet changes in your situation. Also, within certain limits, you can make lump-sum deposits or lump-sum withdrawals much as you can with a bank account. In addition, you can borrow, often at very low rates of interest, from the policy's cash value. However, these withdrawals and/or loans could affect the face amount of insurance.

Secondary guarantees: To serve the ever-changing needs of policy owners and to help eliminate the risk of fluctuations in interest and mortality costs, life insurance companies have, in recent years, designed special options ("riders") for universal life policies to provide better guarantees. The options, known as *secondary, extended,* or *enhanced guarantees* (because they are on top of the regular limited guarantees), add an additional layer of protection to universal life policies and, essentially, guarantee the face amount of insurance without the need for additional premiums, regardless of the level of interest rates or the size of mortality charges and expenses. The period covered by these added guarantees varies depending on each company's product and, in many cases, can be selected by the policy owner. For example, if the insured was convinced he or she would never live beyond age 95, the policy owner could select a premium level that carried a guarantee to that age. Most products with secondary guarantees offer coverage to age 100, while some cover to age 110, 115, or, simply, for life. These guaranteed policies continue to retain the flexibility inherent in all universal life policies, such as the ability to adjust premiums, coverage period, and death benefit amounts.

Some life insurance products that contain a secondary guarantee also offer a "makeup" provision, which allows a policy owner to pay a *lower* premium that would keep the policy in force under current assumptions of interest and mortality—backed up by the normal, limited guarantee. This provision allows the owner to take a wait-and-see approach to pay the higher premium required to yield a longer or lifetime guarantee. If interest rates and/or mortality charges changed to the degree that the life of the policy was in doubt, the owner could make up the difference between premiums paid and the specified secondary guarantee premium, usually with interest, but in some policies without interest. This type of flexibility allows the owner to optimize investment dollars while giving peace of mind that, at some known level of premium, coverage is assured—no matter what.

If you want the flexibility to be able to change your premium, the coverage period, or death benefit, a universal life policy may be ideal. One drawback, however, is the inability to control where the cash value within these policies is invested. And that may be important to those who are not relying on insurance products with secondary guarantees and want to optimize their insurance dollar.

VARIABLE LIFE

A form of universal life, variable life insurance offers all the flexibility that universal life provides but with a unique difference: cash values are invested in a separate account, instead of the insurance company's general account, at the *policy owner's direction*. The separate account is made up of a variety of pooled investment divisions that are similar to mutual funds. The policy owner chooses among the various funds offered by the insurer, so investments can be concentrated in common stocks, bonds, and other assets that are more volatile but may provide higher long-term results than does an insurer's general account. This enables the policy owner to participate more directly in gains and losses realized by the markets. Good performance in the separate account may build extra cash value and make it possible to reduce premium payments, increase the death benefit, withdraw previously paid premiums, or some combination of these options.

Unlike whole life or universal life, most variable life products do not provide a guarantee with respect to either a minimum rate of return or principal. The company guarantees only that the actual investment fund performance, both net investment income and capital gains and losses, will pass directly through to policy cash values after a reduction is taken for investment expenses and fund operating costs. Since assets under the variable insurance contract are segregated and held in a separate account, they are protected against any insolvency by the sponsoring insurance company and are not affected by the investment performance of the company's general account. It is for this reason that variable policies are *registered securities,* and anyone selling them must hold the appropriate securities license and make sure the policy owner-investor is properly informed of the risks.

In recent years, some insurance companies have added a minimal level of guaranteed death benefit to their variable life policies at a specified premium, regardless of market performance. These guarantees are usually more limited in their coverage period and death benefit amount than are regular universal life policies credited with interest (fixed interest) based on the earnings in the insurance company's general investment account.

Variable life insurance policies provide maximum flexibility and some very attractive benefits; however, expenses are significantly higher than those for whole life and regular fixed-interest universal life policies, and there is no downside rate-of-return guarantee. It is important to do a careful analysis before purchasing this type of policy.

INDEXED LIFE

Indexed life insurance, sometimes known as equity-based life, is another form of the previously discussed universal life. Actually, all universal life insurance plans are, in essence, indexed. The vast majority are indexed to the general account earnings of the insurance company selling the product. The insurance company collects your premium, deducts some expense charges and some cost-of-insurance (mortality) charges, and then puts the rest of the money into its general premium investment account. This account is then invested by the company's investment department, usually into several different types of investments. The majority most often goes into government and high-grade corporate bonds. Some goes into mortgages or directly into real estate, and a small portion may even go into common stock or other more speculative instruments. The variety of overall investment vehicles and the percentages put into each vary by company, competitive pressure, state regulations, the economy, and so on, but in the end most insurance companies' overall portfolios resemble one another. Safety, as well as total return, is important to all.

Of the total earnings on this account, the company will keep some as an investment profit—usually 1 to 1.5%. The balance will be deposited in the policyholder's cash value account. Therefore, it is not unreasonable or inaccurate to say that a policy's rate of return on cash value accumulation is indexed to the company's general portfolio earnings.

The real difference between equity-indexed products and the regular fixed-interest universal life plans that have been around for the past 25 to 30 years or so is that in indexed plans the policy earnings are tied *not* to the insurance company's general account portfolio but to the performance of some known and published stock index. The most commonly used index to date is the Standard & Poor's (S&P) 500 stock index, although the Russell 2000, the Wilshire 5000, and even the Dow Jones indexes are possible alternatives.

The main requirement is that it be an index of an equity investment that has a market position upon which *call options* (which give the option holder the ability to call, or buy, a specific security, such as a stock, at a certain price) may be written. This is because an issuing company must be able to *hedge* itself against having to pay a rate of return that it can't cover from its general account earnings. The perfect way for a company to do this is to purchase a call option. And this is why indexed life policies are not registered products like individual stocks, bonds, or mutual funds. In these policies it is not the insured who is buying or investing in the option; it is the insurance company. The company is doing so to protect itself in regard to its promise to pay a rate of return based on the index it has selected. Though it wouldn't be a very good idea, the company could, in fact, pay on the basis of some index but never actually invest in such a vehicle. In time, this would prove to be business suicide, but theoretically the company could index the policy cash values to anything it chose and then just take its chances that it could cover its promises from internal corporate returns. Of course, this is just theory—it never would be done that way. And thus the company buys an option on a specific index.

The obvious benefit to insureds is that they enjoy the possibility of higher rates of return than those normally offered by fixed-interest investments but have the counterbalancing security of knowing that, unlike variable universal life policies, the indexed version cannot lose its principal investment by going negative. It may go down from hoped-for rates of return, but there is always the safety of the original investment plus prior years' gains and some modest guaranteed interest earnings, typically, 2 to 3%. Because of this, indexed life has been described by some as being the "perfect compromise"—more potential for upside gains than a fixed-interest product without the same measure of downside risk as a variable product. Perhaps "flying with a parachute" is an apt analogy since we are talking about life insurance, itself something that's supposed to be a hedge against the risk of loss.

Keep in mind that all equity-indexed plans are not identical. While they all have similarities, there are also some important differences (e.g., in option types, option durations, guarantee rates, option gains, bailout provisions, and other unique riders). Before buying, you should review and understand the policy features, as is the case with any policy, whether fixed, indexed, or variable offered from company to company.

Although there are a few variations on the theme, indexed life policies basically operate as follows: Just as in the case of regular, fixed-interest universal life policies, the company receives the premiums, deducts a month's worth of cost-of-insurance and expense charges, and invests the balance in its general portfolio account. At this point, the process begins to differ from regular universal life: rather than leave all the excess in the general account, the company deducts some and uses it to purchase a one-year call option on the specific index being used. (An example is shown in Table 47-3. The example is an oversimplification. Companies don't buy an option per life contract issued; they buy options only when there is a large-enough block of business to make the transaction financially feasible.)

Depending on the current price of options, the net dollar amount available allows the company to purchase some amount of call option. How much option the net amount of money will buy determines what percentage of the index's performance will be credited to your policy. This percentage amount is known as the *participation rate*. The rate fluctuates

---

(table 47-3)

EXAMPLE OF INDEXED LIFE INSURANCE POLICY

$10,000	Annual premium received
-500	A month's worth of mortality & expense charges taken out
$9,500	Invested in the general account
$665	The general portfolio account amount earned at 7%
-66	Kept by the company as investment profit
599	Netted for the client policy
-237	Set aside (2.5%, a typical minimum interest guaranteed by contract)
$362	Available for purchasing a call option on the chosen index

from year to year in response to movement in both the portfolio earnings rate of the company and the price of call options on the options or futures exchange markets. Therefore, participation rates as low as 25% and as high as 80% are possible over the life of the contract. Ironically, some years in which the participation rate is low may produce higher policy earning than those in years in which the participation rate is very high. This is because percentages are meaningful only as they are applied to a whole number. For example, 25% of a 40% rise in the S&P 500 index earns 10%, yet 80% of a modest 7% rise in the S&P would earn only 5.6%.

The fundamental factor in choosing between fixed, indexed, and variable universal life plans is where one is on the risk spectrum. Fixed-interest products have the lowest risk but also the lowest earnings potential and the highest cost. Equity-indexed plans have a much higher earnings potential, and although they have minimal risk because of the guaranteed minimum-interest rate, the guaranteed rate is lower than that on fixed universal life plans. Variable universal life has the greatest rate-of-return potential but with little or no downside guarantees; therefore, it presents the greatest risk of principal loss. Indexed universal life products are increasing in popularity because of their broad and central position in the life insurance risk-reward universe—gain potential driven by equity growth on the upside, a downside guarantee that principal is protected, and a modest guaranteed interest rate is earned even in down-market years.

TERM LIFE

One of the most basic forms of insurance is term life insurance. Many people have purchased it because it offers substantial benefits at low cost. However, as its name suggests, term life insurance is beneficial only for a specific period of time, or term. For example, a term insurance policy with a decreasing face amount may be ideal for protecting a young family while there is a mortgage on their home.

The cost of term insurance is determined by the pure cost of insurance, which is tied to the mortality rate of the insured's age group. Cash values are minimal or nonexistent. The premiums, which may start out low, increase each year in accordance with the mortality table and become extremely costly as the years go by. Some term policies have level premiums for periods of 5, 10, 15, 20, and even 30 years (depending on age), but at the end of the period the premium typically skyrockets to make up for the difference between the premiums paid and the deferred portion of the increasing mortality costs. The premium increases can be so dramatic that they are often unacceptable, and the term policy is frequently dropped or converted to another type of permanent policy. Many term policies allow the policy owner to convert to a permanent policy up to certain ages, but usually not beyond age 65 or 70. Thus, term life insurance is not prudent for someone who plans to keep insurance coverage in force for the rest of his or her life, which is usually the case in estate planning. If you follow the numbers through the years, it will be clear that no amount of initial savings can offset the long-term cost of term life insurance compared with cash value–building permanent insurance and the benefits of guaranteed coverage for your entire life.

CHOOSING THE BEST POLICY

Table 47-4 summarizes the key features of the five types of life insurance discussed above. As the table demonstrates, it would be incorrect to conclude that any one of the five types is best for everyone. Each type of insurance provides significant and distinct benefits. Thus, the best policy is the one that fits your personal situation and risk tolerance. The policy that makes the most sense in your particular situation will become evident after proper analysis. In some cases, try considering more than one type of policy from one or more insurance companies to give you a diversified portfolio with the most flexibility.

Your choices regarding insurance products don't stop with the five types. You also need to decide on single-life versus multiple-life coverage and on various options or riders.

MULTIPLE-LIFE POLICIES

Most policies are written on a single life, but there are situations in which a policy can and should cover more than one life. A policy covering two

(table 47-4)

TYPES OF LIFE INSURANCE

TYPE OF POLICY	KEY FEATURES
TEMPORARY INSURANCE	
Term	Guaranteed death benefit at a guaranteed premium for the lifetime of the insured. Guaranteed cash value, but dividends and interest are not guaranteed. Premiums due for full contract period, which ranges from 20 years to life.
PERMANENT INSURANCE	
Whole life (also called straight or ordinary life)	Flexible premiums and flexible death benefits. Interest-sensitive policy, generally with some guaranteed rate of interest and guaranteed mortality charge. Insured shares the risk above guaranteed amounts. Some policies come with secondary guarantees, which guarantee the death benefit at a certain level of premium for extended periods, including the insured's lifetime.
Universal life	Flexible premiums. Cash value and, in some cases, death benefit fluctuate with the performance of an index of stocks. Can provide a hedge against inflation. Typically has a minimum rate guarantee below the guarantee rate on the insurance company's regular universal life policies. Medium level of risk.
Indexed life or equity-indexed life (a form of universal life)	Flexible premiums. Cash value and, in some cases, death benefit fluctuate with the performance of an investment portfolio (stock funds, bond funds, etc.). Protects against inflation. Limited guarantees. Policy owner can direct fund within separate investment subaccounts. Higher level of risk and costs.
Variable life (a form of universal life)	Simple and economical until later years when the cost of mortality increases substantially. Often best for short-term needs. No cash value and policy renews each year without evidence of insurability. Increasing premium but may be level for periods ranging from 5 to 30 years, depending on age and health. May have a feature that allows conversion to permanent insurance without evidence of insurability.

lives is known as a *survivor* or second-to-die life insurance policy and is typically used to insure a husband and wife—to provide liquidity at the second death to cover taxes and other expenses. A second-to-die policy could also be used in business situations. For example, two brothers, Bob and Ted, own several large industrial buildings which they want to pass to family members at the second death without debt. Thus, they purchased a second-to-die policy to make sure there is enough liquidity at the second of their two deaths to pay off the mortgages with money left over to pay any taxes attributable to the real estate. For potential taxes due at the first of their two deaths, Bob and Ted added a *first-to-die* rider (see the following section, "Options and Riders") which pays a specified amount at the first death. Multiple-life policies can cover many lives and is frequently used by corporations to purchase stock from deceased shareholders as part of a buy-sell agreement. For a corporate owner, the policy is typically set up on a first-to-die basis, with the death benefit paid at the first death, but can include renewal provisions for the remaining insureds. For example, the Mead Corporation purchased life insurance on its five principal owners under one multiple-life policy to be able to purchase the stock of each shareholder from their respective heirs upon death. The policy was designed to be renewable and to pay a death benefit at the death of each of the five major shareholders.

OPTIONS AND RIDERS

Most insurance companies offer options, or riders, that affect the premium to their policies. Some of the more common options follow:

- *Automatic premium loan* is an option under some fixed-premium whole life policies. Whenever a premium is not received, a policy loan is automatically created for the amount necessary to pay the premium. If the remaining net cash value is no longer sufficient to cover a premium due, the policy lapses with no (or minimal) net cash value unless premium payments from the policy owner are resumed.
- *Conversion privilege* on a term policy allows the policy owner to convert a term policy into a cash value–building permanent policy, such as universal life, without evidence of insurability. Because this conversion can be exercised without underwriting, it can be a very valuable option to an individual who is no longer as healthy and, therefore, no longer in as favorable a risk class as when the term policy was first issued. This option usually expires at a certain age, such as 65 or 70.
- *Dividend accumulation* is an option on a whole life policy by which the policy's total cash value is increased by the sum of the dividends paid each year with interest. No extra death benefit, above the accumulated dividend value itself, is associated with this benefit. The dividends paid are a reduction of the policy owner's basis in the policy, and the interest credited each year is taxable income.
- *Dividend options* allow the owner of a participating policy to take dividends in cash, apply them automatically to reduce current

premiums due, let them accumulate at interest, or purchase additional insurance called *paid-up additions*.

- With either whole life or universal life policies, a *first-to-die* rider pays a specified amount on the first death for second-to-die or survivor insurance.

- Usually offered in connection with a universal life policy, an *increasing* or *decreasing* death benefit allows the coverage to adjust upward or downward according to a specific schedule. For example, the face amount might increase by either a certain percentage each year or by the amount of the premium paid. In some cases it may be possible for your heirs to end up collecting the face amount plus all premiums paid to the date of your death.

- A *makeup* provision on a universal life policy allows a policy owner to postpone paying a higher level of premium that would provide additional guarantees. If the owner at some time in the future deems it necessary or desirable, he or she can make up the difference, in some policies without interest, between the guaranteed premium and the actual premium paid.

- *Paid-up additions* (PUAs) are a dividend option that uses dividends on a whole life policy to purchase small amounts of guaranteed single-premium life insurance that is fully paid to age 100. This option does not reduce the policy owner's basis in the policy and does not result in taxable income—until the policy is surrendered. PUAs can be surrendered for their cash value and be applied to offset any premiums due.

- *Term riders* give a whole life or universal life policy owner the ability to purchase a higher total death benefit for a small initial increase in annual premiums. Some term riders also permit the scheduling of future changes in the total death benefit.

- *Waiver of premium* is available on most whole life and some universal life insurance policies to keep a policy in force during the total disability of the insured. If a totally disabled insured has a waiver of premium, premiums are not charged, but the policy values will continue to accumulate as if those premiums had been paid. Normal mortality charges and expense loads continue to be deducted.

HOW TO BUY LIFE INSURANCE

Besides selecting the type of insurance and options you want, important considerations include how to find appropriate financial advice and how to evaluate specific insurance companies. In addition, you should understand how your age and health enter into the calculation of your premium and how the companies vary in their assessment of those factors in making insurance offers.

This process can be daunting, even for sophisticated investors, and most people require help. Going to the internet or dialing a toll-free number from a TV ad will not help much and could leave you without assistance when you need it most. There are simply too many variables to consider for purchasing insurance. It is best to find a qualified financial advisor who has the experience and the knowledge to help protect your wealth and who will provide ongoing service as your family, the tax laws, and other needs change over time.

CHOOSING A FINANCIAL ADVISOR

You can protect yourself and get the best underwriting by working with a qualified, trained expert in financial planning and insurance. It is usually not a good idea to rely on a stockbroker, accountant, or banker for the planning of your estate and the purchase of insurance. Providing quality advice on financial planning and insurance strategies requires knowledge that can be obtained only through specific schooling, constant updating, and years of experience. You should work with specialists who have taken the time to obtain the requisite knowledge, as indicated by attainment of industry-recognized designations, such as chartered life underwriter (CLU), chartered financial consultant (ChFC), and certified financial planner (CFP). Such experts can analyze your situation and give you the best choices of companies and products to reach your goals. This is a situation for which, as estate planning authors and attorneys Renno Peterson and Robert Esperti put it, "to use less than the best is to invite disaster."

CHOOSING AN INSURANCE COMPANY

To purchase an insurance policy, you and your professional advisors should analyze not only the products of several insurance companies but also the companies themselves to determine the *financial strength* and *rating* of the company, the company's dividend or interest-crediting *history,* the level of policy *guarantees,* and the company's interest rate and expense *assumptions* used in determining the policy premiums. You may also want to use more than one type of policy from two or more insurance companies to give you the best diversified portfolio with the most flexibility (see the section "Insurance Diversification," below).

RATING SERVICES

To help protect consumers, rating agencies evaluate insurance companies according to financial strength and longevity. The agencies do this by analyzing financial information available in public records, auditing the companies' books and records, analyzing each company's management and sales force, and evaluating overall performance and future growth potential. Several firms provide ratings for life and health insurance companies:

- *A.M. Best* rates the financial and operating performance of virtually all life and health insurance companies.
- *Standard & Poor's* rates the financial strength of those insurers who request a rating. It also provides financial strength ratings from public information for other insurers.

- *Moody's* and *Fitch* both provide ratings for those insurers who request a rating. Therefore, ratings from these two services are not available for all insurance companies.
- *Weiss Research* rates the safety of over 1700 insurance companies.
- *The Comdex* is a composite index based on the ratings received by a company from one or more of the above ratings services. It is the average percentile ranking for all ratings received by a company. As such, it is not another rating but an objective scale (from 1 to 100) that can be used to compare the ratings of different companies from the various rating agencies listed above.
- *VitalSigns* is a life insurance reporting system that has detailed financial information on over 400 U.S. and Canadian life insurance companies. VitalSigns features current ratings from the above five major insurance rating services, the Comdex ranking, and year-end financial data, including assets, investments, operating income, financing, and other indicators of life insurance carrier viability. While VitalSigns by no means offers a complete picture, the third-party ratings, the Comdex ranking, and the numerous financial barometers together provide a starting point to begin analyzing the financial health of the insurance companies you are considering.

Table 48-1 (in Chapter 48) is a summary of the scoring systems of A.M. Best, Standard & Poor's, Moody's and Fitch.

QUALIFYING FOR INSURANCE

Your age and your health play important roles in determining whether you qualify for life insurance, but do not assume that your age and/or current health condition precludes you from obtaining insurance coverage. Most insurance companies offer insurance up to age 90 (and, in special circumstances, some companies go beyond age 90), and all companies have a rating system tied to various health factors. This rating system is designed to determine your "insurance age," which is based on your health. For example, if you are 70 years old and have a ratable health condition, such as heart disease or diabetes, the company may determine that your expected life span is more consistent with someone who is 75 years old. Thus, the premium would be based not on your chronological age of 70 but on your insurance age of 75. Conversely, if you are in excellent health with a good medical history and longevity in your family, you may qualify for a preferred rating that would effectively treat you as if you were younger than you were and, therefore, qualify you for a lower premium.

Not all insurance companies treat specific health factors the same way. Some consider health-related issues (such as smoking, diabetes, occupational hazard, or family history) to be more severe than others do, and the level of their concern is reflected in the prices they quote. Thus, it is prudent to obtain offers of insurance from more than one company when shopping for insurance.

The company with the lowest published premiums may end up with the highest premium offer on the basis of your medical history. Another company, with seemingly high premiums, may be more willing to overlook certain conditions and offer the most insurance coverage per premium dollar. You'll never know unless your insurance professional submits your medical exam report and medical history to several companies to obtain offers. By having your application and medical records examined by more than one company, you have a better opportunity to receive the optimum coverage at the best price.

Purchasing life insurance is not as simple as many people believe. Your medical history, physical exam report, and financial data must be reviewed in order to obtain an offer of insurance. The insurance company must be convinced that there is an insurable interest on the part of your beneficiaries as well as a legitimate need for the coverage amount to ensure that you are not worth more dead than alive. The health and background investigation that takes place after you sign an application is normal, and you can expect at least one phone interview and time delays to evaluate your health and personal data. In short, you must qualify for insurance, but, as discussed above, do not assume that because of one or more health factors, you do not qualify. Also, be aware that no premium quoted to you by an insurance salesperson is correct until you have had a physical exam and the insurance companies have offered a premium price based on your application, the findings of their examination, and a review of your personal medical history.

In addition to health, your age makes a difference. To fully comprehend the difference between levels of qualification based on age, consider a male nontobacco user in good health who applies for $1 million of universal life insurance. At age 55, the cost for $1 million of coverage is approximately $15,200 per year, based on current assumptions of interest and mortality costs, with an enhanced guarantee (guaranteeing coverage for life). Ten years later, when he is 65 years old, that same insurance premium will cost him approximately $24,200 per year—almost 60% more. When he is 75, it costs approximately $42,300, almost three times as much as for a 55-year-old.

According to statistics, women live longer than men. So from the perspective of insurance companies, women represent a better risk and can get a better rate (or lower premium) than men of the same age and health. For a healthy 55-year-old, nontobacco-using female, the cost for $1 million of insurance is approximately $12,000 per year, based on current assumptions with a lifetime guarantee. The cost is approximately $19,100 per year when she is 65—a significant difference from her male counterpart's cost. When she is 75, the cost is approximately $33,300 per year, nearly 22% lower than the cost a 75-year-old male would pay.

If one insurance policy is used to cover two people, such as a husband and wife, and pays on the second death, it is known as a *second-to-die* policy, and the risk to the insurance company is lower. To give you a picture of how the cost of a $1 million second-to-die policy compares to the above, the premium for a couple who are both age 55, nonsmokers, and in good health is approximately $7400 per year, based on current assumptions with a lifetime guarantee. For a couple who are both age 65, the cost is closer to $12,000 per year, and for a 75-year-old couple, the premium is approximately $21,800 per year. This is $11,500 per year lower than that of a 75-year-old, single female and $20,500 per year lower than a single, 75-year-old male, based on the same assumptions.

The premium cost varies by your age, your health, the insurance company and its mortality experience, the rating assigned you, which may vary with each company, the product you choose, the level of guarantees desired, and any additional options that you select.

INSURANCE DIVERSIFICATION

After you have been examined and have obtained several offers, your initial reaction may be to choose the one policy that provides the lowest premium for the coverage you need. However, a better and more prudent course of action could provide both a good premium rate and better long-term results. Just as you would not put all your investment dollars into one stock or bond no matter how secure it seemed, you should also consider diversifying your insurance portfolio by splitting coverage between two or more companies and averaging the cost. Even though no family in the United States has ever failed to collect on a legitimate death claim because of the failure of an insurance company, you can reduce the risk that a higher premium may be required because of changes in interest rates, mortality costs, and expenses—to sustain the death benefit—by diversifying your life insurance.

If several million dollars of coverage is needed, more than one insurance company may be required because of the limited capacity individual carriers have to supply such large amounts of coverage. Even the larger life insurance carriers are limited in the amount of insurance they can cover on one individual. (In fact, most companies retain only $1 to $3 million on a single insurance policy.) The risk on amounts above the basic retention is often shared with *reinsurance* companies in a joint coverage arrangement. The reinsurance is usually transparent to the policy owner but may introduce additional scrutiny of your insurance application and could affect an insurance company's offer. While some companies can bind their reinsurers to coverage at a certain level, above that level the reinsurer makes its own medical determination on the insured, and the determination take precedence over any medical rating by the primary insurance company.

Because insurance company rates are based on current assumptions of expenses, interest rates, and mortality charges and may change over the life of the policy, a single company's quote may not give you the best rate protection. Periodic changes in expenses, interest rates, and mortality are not consistent from one company to another, and changes in costs and interest-crediting rates does not occur unilaterally across the industry. The company that offers the best interest-crediting rate today may not credit your policy with that rate in the future. By using more than one insurance carrier, you are likely to achieve the best long-term average rate available.

(*figure* 47-5)

A diversified life insurance portfolio.

DUDLEY & VEE HOUSE
$30 million estate

Gifts (insurance premiums)

Irrevocable life
insurance trust

Diversification

COMPANY A	COMPANY B	COMPANY C
$4 million	$10 million	$2 million
2d-to-die insurance	2d-to-die insurance	2d-to-die insurance
	+ $ 2 million	
	1st-to-die rider	

47

In addition, you will enjoy a certain level of safety that could only be achieved by using more than one company.

There is yet another reason why diversifying your insurance coverage is a smart idea. Although some investments are clearly safer than others, no investment is absolutely guaranteed. No one can foresee the future. The solidity of your life insurance "investment" is based both on the assumptions used in determining the premium and on the overall solvency of the company carrying your policy.

Although you should insist on quotes from only the highest-rated firms, there are still risks. Even the largest, most reputable firms can suffer setbacks. With so much at stake in your wealth plan, it is a good idea to spread your risk by dividing coverage over more than one quality insurance company. You should have your medical information reviewed by at least three highly rated insurance carriers in order to obtain the best offer of insurance based on each company's evaluation of your health status.

EXAMPLE

Dudley and Vee Smith needed $16 million of life insurance to offset the taxes on their $30 million estate. They were examined by five companies and received offers based on the findings of the examinations. Dudley and Vee have some health issues, so the evaluation of their insurability varied somewhat between the companies. Following sound advice, Dudley and Vee took the three best companies and purchased $4 million of insurance from one, $10 million from another, and the balance from the third. On one of the policies, they purchased a first-to-die rider to produce enough funds at the first death to pay off the balance of the premiums on all three policies. In this way, their cost was averaged and their portfolio protected through diversification. (See Figure 47-5 for a diagram of their plan.)

For Dudley and Vee Smith, the total of their annual premiums was only slightly higher than it would have been if they had selected the company with the lowest premium for all their insurance. The size of the premium, while important, was not the only consideration. The most important factor was the peace of mind and increased protection diversification offered.

LIFE SETTLEMENT

In recent years a whole new industry, known as life settlements, has developed which allows policyholders to sell an existing policy—which is no longer needed or wanted—for *more than* the policy's current cash surrender value. The history of life settlement as an industry can be traced back to the 1980s with the early AIDs victims, who were considered terminally ill. The names *viatical* and viatical settlement were chosen to describe the sale of an insurance policy by a terminally ill insured for a percentage of the death benefit. The viatical sale transaction resulted in the insured receiving some cash to use while still living and the purchaser making a profit of the death benefit less the purchase price at the death of the terminally ill insured who, typically, had a short life expectancy. The term *viatical* now refers to the purchase of a life insurance policy from someone with less than a two-year life expectancy. The newer terms life settlement, *lifetime settlement,* and *senior settlement* refer to the purchase of a life insurance policy from someone who has generally more than a two- but less than a 15-year life expectancy.

On creating the pools of funds needed to purchase existing insurance policies, institutions and other investors found themselves with a limited supply of terminally ill insureds with a two-year or less life expectancy and a large demand for this type of investment. Thus, the industry expanded to purchase policies of those who are not terminally ill but fit within certain criteria, such as age, policy size, longevity, and so on.

Besides the difference regarding terminal illness, the proceeds from a life settlement sale are taxed differently from that of a viatical settlement. In a viatical settlement, the proceeds are treated as insurance proceeds and are free of federal income tax and state income tax (in some states), whereas only the recovery of a policy owner's basis goes untaxed in a life settlement. According to the opinion of tax experts, the portion of the gain representing the difference between the policy owner's basis and cash value is taxed as ordinary income, and the balance is considered a capital gain and taxed as such. Since the IRS has not issued any guidelines for the taxation on the gain from the sale of a life insurance policy, it is best to seek an opinion from your tax advisors on any such transaction.

Criteria for purchasing policies of insurance via a life settlement vary to some degree between investors, which consist primarily of institutions and other corporate entities—some of which are owned or backed by life insurance companies. However, most investors are interested in policies with the following characteristics:

- Insureds who are over age 65
- Face amount of the policy or policies of $250,000 or more
- Insureds who have experienced a change of health since the policy was issued
- Single-life policies (but some second-to-die policies may qualify)
- Policies that are beyond the "contestability" period (two years or older)
- Policies that are no longer wanted or needed

(figure 47-6)

CHECKLIST

Please rate each category, and add the points for a total score. Compare the score with the table below for the probability of a life settlement.

1. Age and sex:

☐ 1 point   Male age 74 or less/Female age 77 or less

☐ 2 points   Male age 75—78/Female age 78—82

☐ 3 points   Male age 79—83/Female age 82—86

☐ 4 points   Male age 84+/Female age 87+

2. Medical condition:

☐ 1 point   Healthy senior

☐ 2 points   Has a minor health problem

☐ 3 points   Health has changed considerably since policy issue

☐ 4 points   Client has developed a terminal illness

3. Policy type:

☐ 1 point   Joint survivorship or whole life

☐ 2 points   Term life

☐ 3 points   Universal life

☐ 4 points   Joint survivorship with one deceased

4. Current cash surrender value of the policy as a percentage of the death benefit:

☐ 1 point   30%+

☐ 2 points   20—30%

☐ 3 points   10—20%

☐ 4 points   0—10%

5. Outstanding loans as a percentage of the death benefit:

☐ 1 point   30%+

☐ 2 points   20—30%

☐ 3 points   10—20%

☐ 4 points   0—10%

6. Current premiums as a percentage of the death benefit:

☐ 1 point   4%+

☐ 2 points   3—4%

☐ 3 points   2—3%

☐ 4 points   1—2%

(*figure* 47-6 *continued*)

SCORE	LIFE SETTLEMENT PROBABILITY
6	Highly unlikely
7—12	Unlikely, but possible
13—18	Likely
19—24	Highly likely

Many life settlement companies have a scoring system to help you evaluate whether your policy is sellable. Figure 47-6 is an example of such a scoring system.

Following are some of the reasons why someone would consider selling an existing insurance policy:

- Universal life policy in jeopardy of lapsing for lack of cash value
- Change in estate size (i.e., stock portfolio value dropped because of market conditions)
- Change in health condition
- Universal life policy not performing as anticipated
- Term policy getting too expensive
- Business policies no longer needed—from old buy-sell and key-person agreements or the sale of a business
- Income needs for retirement
- Divorce or bankruptcy
- Premiums that are no longer affordable
- A policy that is about to be surrendered for its cash value
- Change in the tax law
- Funds needed for an alternative investment
- Desire to make cash gifts to family members or children
- Desire to liquefy an otherwise dormant asset
- To help fund the sale of a business that owns the policy
- To terminate a corporate split-dollar insurance agreement
- Desire to fund a new, more cost-effective life insurance policy
- Outright gift to charity
- Funding for the purchase of permanent life insurance insuring a spouse or second-to-die policy to cover estate taxes
- Purchasing a minority interest in a closely held business
- To facilitate the transfer of a business to the next generation
  To fund the purchase of long term care insurance

If you need insurance but one or more of your existing policies are not working well, a life settlement can provide the fuel to drive a replacement policy with improved economics.

EXAMPLE

For example, Peter and Ann had a second-to-die universal life policy with a death benefit of $9 million and cash surrender value of approximately $880,000. Because rates had come down substantially from the time the policy was first issued nine years before, the policy's cash value was lower than originally estimated. Thus, the policy was projected to terminate at their ages 82 and 79, respectively, unless Peter and Ann were to pay a significant amount of additional premium. Peter had suffered a heart attack since the policy was issued, so the economics of exchanging their policy using their existing cash surrender value for a new policy did not look promising. However, using a life settlement, they were able to sell their existing policy for $1.2 million (approximately $230,000 more than their cash surrender value) and apply these funds to a new second-to-die universal life policy, which provided coverage to age 100, based on current assumptions, much stronger guarantees, and no additional premium.

STEPS TO COMPLETE A LIFE SETTLEMENT

Selling a life insurance policy requires no medical exam, but there are various steps required for a successful transaction:

- The seller submits the necessary paperwork to the life settlement investor, including an application, a copy of the life insurance policy, an in-force illustration ledger (an annual schedule of policy details) projected to maturity, an authorization form, a copy of any trust agreement if the policy is owned by a trust, and the insured's medical records for the prior two years.
- The buyer extends an offer to buy the policy, and the seller accepts.
- A closing occurs with all documents signed.
- The funds are deposited in escrow.
- When the policy transfer is official, the funds in escrow are wired or sent in the form of a cashier's check to the policy owner.
- Payment terms are generally flexible to meet the seller's needs. The most common payment method is in a lump sum. However, some companies offer installments (to defer any taxes) and annuities.

SUMMARY

Life insurance is simply the sharing of risk among a group of insureds with the common goal of providing money to beneficiaries when the insured dies. An insurance policy is a contract between an insurance company and a policy owner. Three factors affect the insurance premium: (1) mortality rates, which vary in accordance with each insurance company's mortality experience, (2) interest-crediting rates, which depend on the performance of each company's general investment account, and (3) company expenses. Your age, sex, and health also affect the amount of your premium. The older and sicker the person, the higher the premium; but do not assume that you are uninsurable because of age or health problems. Insurance companies may rate you rather than deny coverage and charge a larger premium to offset the increased risk from one or more health issues.

Of the five different types of insurance policies—whole life, universal life, variable life, indexed life, and term life—the type of policy best for you depends upon your unique goals, circumstances, and purpose for the insurance. The complexity of each of the various types of insurance is good reason to seek help from a professional who has spent time and energy learning the many variables, is focused on insurance and wealth strategy planning, and can assist you in determining the best choice for your goals.

While you and your investment advisor have no hesitation diversifying your investments (such as stocks, bonds, and the like) for safety, the idea of diversifying your insurance is a relatively new concept. The question really boils down to this: Why not diversify to add a layer of protection for your family wealth transfer plan if, in doing so, you will not significantly increase the cost of insurance?

By seeking help from a trained professional and taking the time to understand how life insurance works, you will not only be able to obtain the most protection for your premium dollar but also have the peace of mind that comes from knowing you have done all you can to protect your loved ones.

WHAT YOU NEED TO KNOW

▶ Life insurance is a versatile tool that has many benefits during life as well as after death, often with a tax advantage.

▶ The cost of life insurance depends on many variables, which can differ considerably between insurance companies. Always shop more than one company.

▶ There are five basic types of life insurance policies: whole life, universal life, variable life, indexed life, and term life. Each has a distinct purpose, and the decision regarding which one will work best for you depends on your personal situation and risk tolerance.

▶ Virtually all insurance companies offer options and riders to their policies that have significant additional benefits. It is important to find out the options available and their cost.

▶ To protect yourself, your family, and your estate plan and get the best underwriting, you should only work with qualified, trained experts who specialize in financial planning and insurance.

▶ You and your professional advisors should analyze not only the products of several insurance companies but also the companies themselves, including their financial strength and their ratings by the major rating agencies.

▶ Not all insurance companies look at your health and age in the same way, so do not assume that your age and/or current health problems preclude you from obtaining insurance coverage. Encourage your insurance professional to present your medical information to various companies and obtain offers of insurance.

▶ You should consider diversifying your insurance portfolio to add safety by splitting coverage between two or more companies and averaging the cost.

▶ If you have one or more existing insurance policies that you no longer need or want, it may be possible to sell the policy for more than its current cash value via a transaction known as life settlement.

FOR MORE INFORMATION

Kilbourn Associates
Web: kilbournassociates.com
Good source for information on estate planning and insurance, with web links to Mike Kilbourn's "Wealth Strategies" column, Naples Sun Times, and the Estate and Wealth Strategies Institute at Michigan State University, at which you can access the world's only "Q&A" estate planning encyclopedia.

AARP
Web: www.aarp.com
General resource that includes some great web links and all types of information for seniors.

American Council of Life Insurers (ACLI)
Web: www.acli.com
Helpful information for both insurance professionals and the general public.

A.M. Best Company
Web: www.ambest.com
Insurance companies and their ratings.

Financial Planning Association (FPA)
Web: www.fpanet.org
Helpful if you need more information on your investments or are looking for a financial planner in your area.

Insurance Information Institute (III)
Web: www.iii.org
Information for both insurance professionals and the general public; many useful references and statistics.

Insure.com
Web: Insure.com
For consumers considering the purchase of various types of insurance.

SUGGESTED READING

▷ Cliffsnotes: Understanding Life Insurance.
Hungry Minds.
Bart Astor. 1999.

▷ New Life Insurance Investment Advisor:
Achieving Financial Security for You and Your
Family through Today's Insurance Products.
Ben G. Baldwin. 2002.
New York: McGraw-Hill.

SOURCE NOTE

Material in this chapter has been adapted from E. Michael Kilbourn's Disinherit the IRS *(2003), revised edition, with permission of the publisher. Published by Career Press, Franklin Lakes, New Jersey. E. Michael Kilbourn wishes to thank Guy E. Baker and Jeff Oberholtzer for the portion of material in this chapter adapted from their booklet, "The Box."*

Long-term care will be the burning health care issue of the 21st century, as baby boomers struggle to prepare for their own needs and take care of their parents as well. We must begin to prepare now for those challenges.

—*Congressman Pete Stark, 1999*

THE AUTHOR

48   *Carlos C. Whaley*

CARLOS C. WHALEY is the chief executive officer of Innovative Consumers Insurance Services, an agency that is focused on senior financial planning and long-term care financing. Since retiring from General Electric Financial Assurance as an executive vice president in 1998, he has worked with several leading insurance companies to bring long-term care insurance and retirement income products to market. He has served on the President's Council for the Assisted Living Federation of America and provided numerous presentations to the long-term care industry, including the American College of Health Care Administrators and the Disability and Long-Term Care Symposium.

48 | INSURANCE PRODUCTS FOR LONG-TERM CARE

Within the array of health insurance concerns facing the United States today, increasing attention is being brought to the issue of paying for long-term care.

As an owner of an insurance agency that serves seniors throughout the United States, I have seen firsthand the financial devastation of both individuals and families who failed to plan for the financial challenges of the longer life spans that our society is experiencing in the 21st century.

This chapter is designed to familiarize you with the long-term care environment, present some financial and emotional risks associated with long-term care, and provide a summary of the highlights of long-term care insurance protection.

THE LONG-TERM CARE ENVIRONMENT

Although the challenges and needs that comprise long-term care are not new, the extent of the problem is. The reason for this lies in six major forces at play in the United States: demographics, advances in medicine and public health, changing social patterns, rising costs, tax policy, and the availability of a rapidly expanding and diversifying set of long-term care services.

Aging population: In 1950, those over 65 represented 8% of the total population. Today, they represent 13%, and in 30 years that percentage is projected to grow to 18%. In raw numbers, over 34 million people are over the age of 65 today, and that number will double over the next 30 years to over 70 million. Since the older population is the segment most at risk for long-term care, these sheer numbers define the size of the problem.

Longer life spans: Advances in medical care and improved nutrition and public health care contribute to people living longer and therefore more likely to need long-term care.

Social changes: Families today are more widely separated than they were in the past. In addition, more women are participating in the workforce, and many couples are having children later in life. This has given rise to what is known as the "sandwich generation," which, in turn, has dramatically limited the historic options of caring for a family member at home. The result is that more people who need long-term care will have no choice but to turn to, in whole or in part, private services rather than relying on care provided by family members.

Rising costs: Compounding the increased need to rely on private services is the rising cost of those services. The average cost for nursing home care is in a range of $50,000 to $100,000, depending on where you live. Home care can also be expensive, ranging from $20,000 to $50,000 and more for around-the-clock care. While the initial cost of graduated levels of care in an assisted living facility is lower, as the infirmities of aging progress, the costs reach the same level as nursing home care.

Tax policy: In 1996, Congress looked at the problem of paying for the country's long-term care and recognized that we do not have the

resources to fund a social insurance program to meet those costs. The outcome was legislation, known as the Health Insurance Portability and Accountability Act (HIPAA) of 1996, which provided favorable tax clarification for private *qualified* long-term care insurance. In passing this law, Congress sent a message to the country that paying for long-term care, for all but the most economically vulnerable, would have to met by private means.

Senior care: Today's seniors have many options for long-term care services, including home care, community programs such as adult day care, continuing care retirement communities, assisted living residences, and nursing homes. These senior care options support independent living while seniors enjoy good health and then provide graduated levels of assistance as needed. Reviewing senior care living alternatives and costs in a geographic area of your choice is essential for considering long-term care insurance protection.

UNDERSTANDING INDIVIDUAL LONG-TERM CARE RISKS

DEFINING LONG-TERM CARE

At an individual level, we associate health care with treatment for acute, short-term conditions resulting from injuries or illness that typically require hospitalization, physician services, and outpatient care. Long-term care, on the other hand, encompasses custodial and health services directed at chronic, long-term conditions associated with long-lasting diseases, disabilities, and the infirmities of aging.

Long-term care that can be covered by insurance is related to the inability to perform certain activities of daily living or cognitive impairment that endangers an individual. *Activities of daily living* are defined as bathing, continence, dressing, eating, toileting, and transferring. Cognitive impairment refers to a loss of mental capacity, as measured by a decline in short- or long-term memory; orientation to people, places, or time; or the capacity for deductive or abstract reasoning. The best-known example of cognitive impairment is Alzheimer's disease.

In practice, long-term care is provided in a wide variety of settings, including an individual's home, the community, or a long-term care facility. Depending on the setting, the care can be either formal or informal, which is to say, paid or unpaid. Much long-term care in this country is provided informally by family and friends in the home and consists of meeting the basic daily needs of a family member or loved one. The majority of formal, or paid care, is provided in the community, such as at home, in adult day care centers, and in facilities, such as assisted living residences and nursing homes.

Though long-term care is usually associated with the elderly, studies show that it all too often affects the young as well. A report by the U.S. General Accounting Office found that of the 12.8 million people who needed help in caring for themselves on a regular basis, 40% were between the ages 18 and 64.

48

Coming to terms with long-term care, whether for oneself or for a family member, is never a pleasant topic. However, because today's medical technology is able to extend life, the prospect of needing long-term care at some point in one's life or that of a family member's has become all too real.

ISSUES OF LONG-TERM CARE

Long-term care is an issue today for four simple reasons: there is a high lifetime risk of needing it, it's expensive, it's not covered by health insurance, and it can have a devastating effect on individuals and families.

It is estimated that the lifetime risk of needing some amount of long-term care is over 60%, and of those needing nursing home care, 20% stay five years or more.

When compared to common risks requiring a claim on homeowner's insurance (1 in 88) or on an automobile policy (1 in 47) to be filed, the risk for long-term care is significant and, surprisingly, not covered by the insurance of most people.

The expenses associated with long-term care can also be very significant: more than $50,000 a year for nursing home care, on average, with costs much higher in some areas. Care at home is also expensive, depending on whether care is needed periodically or full time. Medicare and Medicare supplements do not cover long-term care. In addition, disability insurance or private health insurance likewise does not provide such coverage.

In fact, according to "A Shoppers Guide to Long-Term Care Insurance," produced by the National Association of Insurance Commissioners, one-third of all long-term care costs are paid out of pocket by individuals and their families. The majority of the remaining costs are paid by welfare programs, including Medicaid, that typically become available only after private resources have been depleted. And none of that includes the unmeasured cost of informal care provided by family and friends, estimated to be 80% of all in-home care.

Added to this cost is the burden associated with providing long-term care to a family member or other loved one in the absence of outside support. A study published in *USA Today* documents that, on average, individual caregivers spend 18 hours a week helping a parent or elderly loved one in need of long-term care. Over time, the competing demands of work and home under such circumstances often result in missed business opportunities, forgone promotions, reduced hours, and unpaid leave. It has been estimated that the average lifetime loss in earnings of such caregivers is in excess of half a million dollars. And that doesn't measure the indirect emotional toll, which, at its worst, can be devastating. Without regular, supplemental services, these situations often create stresses that affect family, work, and health.

As a measure of the national importance of long-term care, Congress passed HIPAA in 1996, so that long-term care became a medical expense for tax purposes. The same legislation also set standards for long-term care insurance by providing favorable tax status for premiums paid and benefits received under such plans. The legislation sent the message that the problem is not going away and that individuals should look to private solutions and not public programs to protect themselves.

OPTIONS

Generally, there are four options for long-term care: depending on family, using personal savings, counting on government programs, or the purchase of insurance or annuity products.

Depending on family can work when care needs are limited and can be met in the home on a scheduled basis, but this rarely works for extended periods. Not unsurprisingly, it is the stress placed on caregivers, typically a wife or daughter, that ultimately requires outside services or institutionalization. Sadly, the emotional, financial, and time burdens that develop rarely equate to the loving picture that many have in mind when they think that their family will care for them.

Using personal savings is equivalent to self-insuring, in that personal funds are used in order to cover the costs. This is the position that most individuals are in, though few would choose to characterize it this way. Given how rarely people self-insure against the risk of large medical expenses or auto or homeowner loss, it's curious how many seem willing to accept the long-term care risk.

If the need for long-term care never arises, then accepting the risk is a bet that will have paid off. But the same could be true of other more commonly insured risks, with the exception that they typically have a lower chance of occurrence and therefore represent a smaller risk. The real difference is that most people see long-term care as a distant concern that they will deal with later. Unfortunately, "later" is often too late.

Counting on the government is hardly more encouraging. Medicare pays around 17% of the nation's long-term care costs and provides only limited benefits for skilled services following treatment for an illness or injury. On average, Medicare pays for 23 days of care under its nursing home benefit, and benefits are not available after 100 days (A copayment is required for days 21 through 100.) Home health care benefits under Medicare are similarly limited, as they have strict requirements and limitations that relate to the need for skilled, rehabilitative care of homebound individuals.

Medicaid holds even less promise. Under current rules, single individuals are allowed to keep less than $2000 in assets in order to qualify for Medicaid nursing home benefits. Married couples are allowed to retain additional assets for the at-home spouse although state rules on this vary. There are also limits as to how much income you can have and still qualify for Medicaid in many states. Estate planning tactics, in which assets are transferred in order to qualify, are being subjected to ever-tightening rules, and today the government can recover anything transferred within three years of establishing Medicaid eligibility. A provision under HIPAA attempted, unsuccessfully, to criminalize the practice known as "Medicaid estate planning," but clearly showed Congress's position toward using a

48

welfare program for middle-class purposes. Add to that a declining base of taxpayers to fund benefits for future retirees, and it's difficult to make a case for this, or any government program, as a payer for long-term care. Also, once someone does qualify for Medicaid, long-term care options are limited; Medicaid pays primarily for nursing home care and pays little or nothing for care at home or in an assisted living facility. Not all nursing homes accept Medicaid payments, further limiting your choices if you rely on Medicaid.

The last option is private insurance or annuity funding. Some life insurance policies allow for the acceleration of a death benefit to pay for long-term care. There are also large deposit-based plans that essentially prepay expenses and return a portion of the premium if long-term care is not needed. But the most direct and efficient way to protect against the risk is with long-term care insurance or annuities.

PURCHASING LONG-TERM CARE INSURANCE

Long-term care insurance is a form of individual health insurance that has been available in roughly its present form since the late 1980s. Originally conceived in 1974 as an extension of Medicare's skilled nursing benefit, it has, over the last 25 years, become a comprehensive form of coverage meant to relieve the burden of long-term care expenses while preserving independence, choice, and economic well-being. It has also expanded well beyond its earlier market of Medicare-eligible seniors and is now regarded as an integral part of financial and retirement planning for an increasingly younger audience.

SELECTING INSURANCE COMPANIES

Contact insurance agents to obtain information about long-term care insurance. It is wise to gather information about several companies and their products even if you must deal with more than one insurance agent.

Ask each agent to provide financial ratings for the insurers you are considering. Table 48-1 is a chart of financial ratings from five of the top insurance company rating services in the United States. After you have narrowed the field of companies based on financial strength, contact your state's insurance department to check on each company's track record with regard to long-term care insurance rate increases. Each agent is required by law to provide you with "A Shopper's Guide to Long-Term Care Insurance," published by the National Association of Insurance Commissioners (www.naic.org), or a state-specific version published by your state insurance department. This booklet has telephone numbers for your state insurance department and information about long-term care insurance.

A variety of products provide long-term care insurance protection. The following paragraphs cover the most widely sold products in the long-term care insurance marketplace today. As you review specific policies or policy riders, you should ask for copies of your actual contract to give

(table 48-1)

FINANCIAL RATINGS FOR INSURANCE COMPANIES

DESCRIPTION OF RATING	STANDARD & POOR'S	MOODY'S	A.M. BEST	FITCH
Superior	AAA	Aaa	A++ A+	AAA
Excellent	AA+ AA AA-	Aa1 Aa2 Aa3	A A-	AA+ AA AA-
Very good			B++ B+	
Good	A+ A A-	A1 A2 A3	B B-	A+ A A-
Adequate	BBB+ BBB BBB-	Baa1 Baa2 Baa3		BBB+ BBB BBB-
Fair			C++ C+	
Below average	BB+ BB BB-	Ba1 Ba2 Ba3		BB+ BB BB-
Marginal			C C-	
Financially weak	B+ B B-	B1 B2 B3		B+ B B-
Highly vulnerable or nonviable	CCC CC C	Caa Ca C		
Below minimum standards			D	
Under state supervision			E	
In liquidation			F	

you the opportunity to examine all the provisions relating to benefits and exclusions.

Because long-term care insurance constitutes a fairly complex legal contract that is purchased over the course of several consultations with an agent, you have the right to return the policy within 30 days after purchase in exchange for a full refund of premiums.

UNDERWRITING CONSIDERATIONS

Do not be surprised if your first encounter with an agent involves discussing your health. These initial discussions might save you a lot of time if your medical condition disqualifies you for long-term care insurance with a particular company.

While the agent continues the sales process, eventually you will be fully underwritten and will complete an application that requires detailed medical information.

Additional underwriting information may be collected through medical records, interviews over the telephone, and interviews in your home.

Some companies have multiple underwriting risk categories, such as "preferred" for very healthy applicants and "standard" for someone with some well-controlled medical conditions. Other companies offer coverage on a "substandard" basis to someone with a more complicated medical history or higher risk profile. Coverage might be limited, there might be an additional premium charge, or both.

If you are unable obtain long-term care insurance because of a medical condition, read the section of this chapter entitled "Annuities," below.

COMPREHENSIVE LONG-TERM CARE INSURANCE

Comprehensive policies are the most widely sold long-term care insurance coverage today. The most comprehensive of today's policies cover the full spectrum of care and services available in the United States, including home health care; community-based services, such as adult day health care; and a wide array of facility-based providers, such as assisted living facilities, Alzheimer's care facilities, and nursing homes. Policies generally do not pay for care provided by family members; care received in hospitals, drug and alcohol clinics, and Veterans Administration facilities; or care outside the United States.

COMPREHENSIVE POLICY FEATURES

BENEFITS

Benefits should be payable for all levels of care in any setting. It is particularly important that benefits are payable for both *standby* and *hands-on* assistance.

More than 1 million people reside in assisted living residences. Assisted living residences typically offer a wide range of services, accommodate the highest levels of independent living, and provide graduated levels of assistance as needed. Most long-term care policies pay for care in an assisted living facility if you need help with personal care (like bathing and dressing) but don't pay your rent if you are able to live independently, even if you are living in an assisted living facility. It's important to understand that benefits are paid if you need care and not based on where you are living.

Home benefits are usually not designed to pay for care 24 hours a day, although most policies allow you to select a benefit amount for home care that is equal to the amount you could receive if you needed care in a nursing home. Home care is ideal for people that need help with some activities of daily living, such as bathing and dressing. The need for constant care and supervision is usually only possible in a nursing home or full-service assisted living facility.

MAXIMUM DAILY BENEFIT AND BENEFIT PERIOD

One of the most important decisions relating to the long-term care insurance selection involves the maximum daily benefit payable for

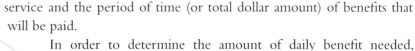

service and the period of time (or total dollar amount) of benefits that will be paid.

In order to determine the amount of daily benefit needed, research must be done. It is advisable to gather current daily costs for home care, nursing homes, and assisted living residences in a geographic area that is satisfactory to the long-term care insurance buyer.

According to a GE long-term care insurance survey, published March 4, 2002, the national average cost for a year in a nursing home is $54,900. The survey also revealed that costs varied widely around the country, from a low of $52.14 per day at one nursing facility in Montana to a high of $704 per day at a facility located on an island in Alaska. Hopefully, you can readily see why your research is a critical ingredient for this decision.

Once you have established the daily benefit you are comfortable with, the period of time over which benefits will be paid must be determined.

Some companies offer lifetime benefits, which means that as long as you qualify for benefits, they will be paid.

Most companies offer limited benefit periods that vary from 2 to 10 years. More often than not, the time period in days, multiplied by the daily benefit, creates a "pool of money" that is the actual lifetime maximum benefit. For days on which the cost of services is less than the maximum daily benefit, the unused portion of the daily benefit is preserved within the lifetime pool, allowing the benefits to continue longer than they otherwise might. In designs that limit the total number of days for which benefits can be received, there is no such "banking" mechanism. Many statistics provide information about length of stays in nursing homes. However, there are no comparable statistics that provide reliable measures of the average duration for all the various long-term care services in combination that one might use throughout an illness or disability. As mentioned earlier, 80% of all long-term care services are provided outside of nursing homes.

When benefits are paid, they are done so as either a *reimbursement* of actual costs up to the maximum daily benefit or as an *indemnity,* which pays the maximum daily benefit regardless of the cost of services. The latter feature is sometimes offered as an optional upgrade to a reimbursement-based policy, with an increase in premium.

Some companies offer shared or pooled benefits. The most common form of shared benefit policies allows more than one person (i.e., husband and wife) to share a pool of benefits for long-term care. This typically reduces the premium required for protecting both people. However, if one of the covered individuals collects benefits, that amount is subtracted from the total policy benefit that is available to either individual in the future.

INFLATION PROTECTION

Once you have determined the maximum daily and lifetime benefit amounts you should purchase today, you must consider the effect of inflation on long-term care in the future.

Annual inflation increase riders are offered by most companies. The rider automatically increases the maximum daily benefit by 5%, compounded or simple, for life. If you purchase the 5% compounded increase, your maximum daily benefit will grow faster and double about every 15 years. If you choose the 5% simple increase, your maximum daily benefit will double in about 20 years and then double more slowly after that. Compound inflation protection riders keep up better with the rising costs of care, but they cost more than the simple inflation increases.

Future purchase options are offered by some companies. This option allows you to purchase increases for the maximum daily benefit at specified intervals (i.e., every one to three years). Typically, the increase offered is determined by changes in the consumer price index.

ELIMINATION PERIOD

The *elimination period* is the initial amount of time during which covered services are received but for which the policy does not pay benefits.

Many companies offer optional periods of time, such as 0, 30, 60, 90, 100, or more days as an elimination period. (You are selecting a period of time that you intend to pay out of pocket for long-term care needs.)

Read elimination period policy provisions carefully because some companies allow you to count calendar days from the day of the first covered service. Some companies require that covered services be provided in order for the day to be counted toward the elimination period. There are other variations that you may encounter as you review specific policies.

WAIVER OF PREMIUM

When benefits are being paid, nearly all policies will waive the requirement to pay premiums. Policies vary in how they structure this benefit, but most require benefits to have been paid for a certain period of time before premiums are waived.

QUALIFYING FOR BENEFITS

The inability to do activities of daily living is the most common way insurance companies determine whether you are eligible for benefits. Remember, most companies define *activities of daily living* as bathing, continence, dressing, eating, toileting, and transferring. Most policies also include eligibility for cognitive impairment or mental incapacity if you can't pass certain tests of mental function. This means that benefit eligibility accommodates the need for care due to Alzheimer's disease and other forms of dementia. Be aware that certain mental illnesses are not covered.

(table 48-2)

DIFFERENCES BETWEEN TAX- AND NON-TAX-QUALIFIED POLICIES

TAX-QUALIFIED POLICIES*	NON-TAX-QUALIFIED POLICIES
Premiums can be included with other annual uncompensated medical expenses for deductions from your income in excess of 7.5% of adjusted gross income up to a maximum amount adjusted for inflation.	You can't deduct any part of your annual premiums.
Benefits that you may receive will not be counted as income.	Benefits that you may receive may or may not count as income. The U.S. Department of the Treasury has not yet ruled on this issue.
Benefit triggers must comply with certain requirements. Must use at least five of the six activities of daily living and cannot require loss of more than three activities of daily living as the basis for paying benefits	Policies can offer different combinations of benefit triggers. Benefit triggers may not be restricted to activities of daily living. They can be broader or more limited in defining benefit triggers.
"Medical necessity" can't be used as a trigger for benefits.	"Medical necessity" and/or other measures of disability can be offered as benefit triggers.
Disability must be expected to last for at least 90 days.	Policies don't have to require that the disability be expected to last for at least 90 days.
For cognitive impairment to be covered, a person must require "substantial supervision."	Policies don't have to require "substantial supervision" to trigger benefits for cognitive impairments.

*The vast majority of policies sold today (about 85%) are tax-qualified.

Please refer to Table 48-2 to understand the overall differences between *tax-qualified policies* and *non-tax-qualified policies.* In a tax-qualified policy, the most prevalent eligibility requirement is the loss of two activities of daily living. However, tax-qualified policies can require the loss of one, two, or three activities of daily living to be eligible for benefits. You may also be eligible for benefits for cognitive impairment if you require substantial supervision. Also, the disability must be expected to last at least 90 days.

Non-tax-qualified policies can have a different combination of benefit triggers, such as medical necessity or other measures of disability. In order to be eligible for benefits with most policies, a licensed health care practitioner (a doctor, nurse, or social worker) must certify that the individual meets the eligibility requirements.

OTHER COMPREHENSIVE POLICY OPTIONS TO CONSIDER

Many comprehensive policies incorporate additional benefits as an integral part of the policy or allow the purchase of riders for optional benefits.

Caregiver training: The caregiver training benefit pays to train an informal caregiver to provide care for the insured person at home. Most companies limit the amount paid to a few days at the maximum daily benefit.

Supportive equipment: The benefit provides supportive equipment and devices to help the insured person remain independent in his or her own home. Most companies specify a lifetime limit for the amount paid for this benefit.

Care advisory: The benefit pays for a care advisor to help the insured person identify care needs and select and arrange appropriate services to best meet those needs. The care advisor can also help on an ongoing basis by ensuring the quality and appropriateness of the services provided.

Respite care: Respite care provides time off for family or friends who are providing care for the insured person. This benefit can be used to pay for care in various settings specified in the policy. Most companies specify an annual limit for this benefit.

Hospice care: The hospice care benefit provides long-term care and support to terminally ill patients. The benefit typically coordinates with hospice care benefits under Medicare and private health insurance.

Restoration of benefits: The benefit provides for restoration of the maximum lifetime benefit after you have been paid benefits. Most companies specify that you must be fully independent and not require or receive any long-term care for six months before restoring the maximum lifetime benefit. If you do not fully recover for at least six months, benefits you have used are never restored.

Bed reservation: The bed reservation benefit pays to reserve a nursing home or assisted living facility bed during a temporary absence for some specified period of time.

Alternative plan of care: The benefit is used to authorize payment for providers, treatment, or services not otherwise covered, but acceptable to the insurance company and the insured, to provide an appropriate, cost-effective alternative for care. This benefit ensures that coverage keeps pace with the ever-changing long-term care system and is flexible to accommodate individual needs and circumstances.

Survivor benefits: Some companies do not require a surviving spouse to pay premiums after the death of an insured spouse if the policy has been held for a specified period of time (typically 7 to 10 years). Other companies allow the purchase of a spousal waiver of premium rider to have this benefit.

Return of premium: Some companies offer one or more riders that return a percentage of premiums paid in the event of death. The riders usually differ in the percentage of total premiums paid that are returned, whether that percentage varies by the age at death and whether reductions are made for any paid benefits. Some options return 100% of premiums paid upon death, no matter what the age. Others return a scheduled percentage of premiums that varies depending on the age at death. Under the latter variety, the percentage is usually greatest for younger ages and declines to zero at later ages. Each design may have a provision that reduces the death benefit by the amount of paid benefits.

Weekly or monthly benefits: Individuals receiving long-term care at home or in the community often incur expenses in an irregular pattern. They may receive 10 hours of care and services one day and none the next. This is particularly true if they are being treated by members of more than one profession, such as therapists, home health aid, and a nurse and receive more than one visit on a single day.

Most long-term care policies do not accommodate irregular expense patterns, as they reimburse the cost of services up to a daily limit. This can create a situation in which someone would not have all their costs covered on one day but not use any of their available benefit the next day. To remedy this, many policies have a weekly limit (equal to seven times the maximum daily limit) or a monthly limit (equal to 30 times the maximum daily limit). The added flexibility of a weekly or monthly maximum is usually in the form of a rider with an additional premium.

Facility-only benefits policy: Many companies offer a policy that only pays for long-term care in a nursing home or assisted living facility. These facility-only policies are limited because they do not cover care at home, but they are also more affordable and do cover the most costly type of care.

Exclusions, limitations, and regulatory requirements: Long-term care, like most all other forms of insurance, contains standard provisions imposed by the insurer meant to (1) prevent inappropriate or uncontrolled use of the policy, (2) limit use of the policy when other primary forms of payment are available, and (3) guard against use of the policy in circumstances that far exceed the insurer's ability to underwrite or control. Examples of exclusions and limitations include the following:

- Payment for services provided by family members or for which no charge is made in the absence of insurance
- Care covered by Medicare, workers' compensation, or similar benefits
- Care required as the result of war, attempted suicide, alcoholism, drug addiction, involvement in a felony, or care delivered outside the United States

PAYING FOR LONG-TERM CARE INSURANCE

Long-term care insurance premiums are designed to remain level and are determined by the age of the insured. All policies sold today are guaranteed renewable, which means that as long as you pay the required premium in accordance with policy provisions, your policy cannot be canceled. Insurance companies can raise the premiums on their policies but only if they raise the premiums on all covered persons in the same class (e.g., age) for all policies of the same type in a particular state. They are not allowed to raise the rates of a single individual.

While premiums for most policies offered are payable for life, some companies offer "limited pay" options that allow the policyholder to pay premiums for a set period, such as 10 years, or a set age, such as 65. Spousal

(table 48-3)

AVERAGE ANNUAL PREMIUMS FOR LEADING LONG-TERM CARE INSURANCE SELLERS, IN 2001*

WITH 5% COMPOUNDED

AGE	BASE	IP†	WITH NFB‡	WITH IP & NFB
COVERAGE AMOUNT: $100 DAILY BENEFIT, 4 YEARS OF COVERAGE, AND 20-DAY ELIMINATION PERIOD				
40	$ 310	$ 641	$ 387	$ 786
50	$ 401	$ 849	$ 502	$ 1022
65	$ 996	$ 1726	$ 1219	$ 2261
79	$ 4180	$ 5821	$ 5087	$ 7002
COVERAGE AMOUNT: $150 DAILY BENEFIT, 4 YEARS OF COVERAGE, AND 90-DAY ELIMINATION PERIOD				
40	$ 396	$ 834	$ 498	$ 1001
50	$ 510	$ 1009	$ 642	$ 1369
65	$ 1263	$ 2273	$ 1554	$ 2988
79	$ 5265	$ 7588	$ 6379	$ 8883

*Eleven sellers were identified as having sold 80% of all individual and group association long-term care insurance policies in 2001.
†IP = inflation protection. ‡NFB = nonforfeiture benefit.
Source: Health Insurance Association of America Long-Term Care Insurance Market Surveys, January 2003.

discounts are offered by most companies if both members of a couple purchase a long-term care insurance policy. Discounts range from a low of 10% to a high of 50%.

Table 48-3 shows average annual premiums for leading long-term care insurance sellers in 2001.

STOPPING PREMIUM PAYMENTS

In many states, the department of insurance requires that a policyholder be provided the option to purchase a benefit that pays a reduced long-term care benefit in the event the policyholder voluntarily allows the policy to lapse through nonpayment of premiums. The amount of the residual benefit is typically equal to 30 times the daily benefit amount chosen or an amount equal to the total premiums paid at the time the policy lapses. This reduced coverage amount, called *a nonforfeiture benefit amount,* is available if you elect this option (for an additional premium charge) at the time you first obtain coverage and if you maintain your coverage for at least three years before it lapses. In addition, some states also require that a similar residual benefit be offered to policyholders in the event the insurer raises premiums on all policyholders and an insured individual decides not to pay further premiums.

TAX BENEFITS FOR TAX-QUALIFIED POLICIES

Individual taxpayers can deduct the premium charge for tax-qualified, long-term care policies as an itemized medical expense, subject to IRS medical deduction limitations and subject to annual caps based on your age. C corporations can deduct 100% of the cost of long-term care insurance premiums for employees.

Beginning in 2003, long-term care insurance premiums are 100% deductible by self-employed individuals and by 2% or more interest owners in partnerships, S corporations, and limited liability companies, subject to annual caps based on the age of the insured person.

All tax-qualified policy benefits paid for long-term care expenses are not subject to federal income taxes.

LONG-TERM CARE ALTERNATIVES

LIFE INSURANCE

Combined life insurance and long-term care protection: New life insurance policies include a level of long-term care benefits. If an individual can qualify for life insurance coverage through normal life underwriting requirements, combination policies can provide a substantial death benefit if the individual requires little or no long-term care benefits while living.

Accelerated death benefit riders: Accelerated death benefit riders are being sold with a variety of life insurance policies. If this rider is designed to provide long-term care, a specified schedule of benefits will be paid out over a period of time until the death benefit of the policy is exhausted. Benefit eligibility is normally very similar to the benefit triggers previously described in Table 48-2.

Single-premium life with long-term care protection: A very popular combination policy uses a single-premium universal life policy combined with riders to provide long-term care benefits greater than the death benefit. The cash value of the policy provides a death benefit if long-term care benefits do not exhaust the cash values during the insured's lifetime.

ANNUITIES

Deferred annuities: Some companies offer savings *annuities* that are designed to provide easy access to funds and in some cases offer a better rate of return for long-term care needs. Most of these deferred annuities do not require any underwriting; however, there are some that have medical questions and impose limitations based on medical conditions. (See also Chapter 50 for a longer discussion of annuities.)

Annuities paying for long-term care services: Single-premium immediate annuities can help finance long-term care needs by providing a lifetime income. As the name implies, *single-premium immediate annuities* are purchased with a single lump-sum premium and typically start income payments within 30 days. Also referred to as *income annuities,* the amount of income is based on your age at purchase and the payout option chosen. Simply put, the older you are, the lower the premium required for a specific lifetime income stream.

Some companies have an impaired risk option that offers individuals with specific medical conditions increased benefits or a reduced premium for a specified payment amount. Individuals with medical conditions should shop for an insurance company that offers an impaired risk, single-premium immediate annuity and provide their medical records to the insurance company for evaluation.

Purchasing an income annuity can be a safeguard against the possibility of running out of money while paying for long-term care during the annuitant's lifetime.

Many payout options are available, including refund options for portions of the premium not received in benefits during the lifetime of the annuitant. For example, if you purchased an income annuity with a cash refund option and you died before receiving a total income at least equal to the premium paid, your beneficiary receives the difference in a lump-sum payment.

CONCLUSION

This chapter has presented important basic information about long-term care needs and insurance options to help people begin planning. While it's difficult to think about a time when you or a loved one might need long-term care, by thinking about it today, you can ensure a more financially secure future with more options for yourself.

WHAT YOU NEED TO KNOW

▶ Increased life spans expose more retirees to the need for long-term care.

▶ Long-term care is available in a variety of desirable settings, including your own home.

▶ Long-term care insurance can protect you and your family from financial ruin.

▶ Annuities are one alternative for financing long-term care if you do not qualify for long-term care insurance.

FOR MORE INFORMATION

▷ **Center for Long-Term Care Financing**
Web: www.centerltc.org

▷ **American Association for Home Care**
Web: www.aahomecare.org

▷ **American Association of Homes and Services for the Aging**
Web: www.aahsa.org

▷ **American College of Health Care Administrators**
Web: www.achca.org

▷ **Assisted Living Federation of America**
Web: www.alfa.org

▷ **National Association of Insurance Commissioners**
816-842-3600
Web: www.naic.org

SUGGESTED READING

▷ **Long-Term Care Planning: The Complete Idiot's Guide**
Marilee Driscoll. 2003.

▷ **Long-Term Care: Your Financial Planning Guide**
Phyllis Shelton. 2003.
Kensington Publishing Company

▷ **"A Shopper's Guide to Long-Term Care Insurance."** Booklet available from the National Association of Insurance Commissioners.
www.naic.com

48

My interest is in the future . . . because I'm going to spend the rest of my life there.

—Charles Kettering, 1876–1958

THE AUTHOR

49

SCOT W. OVERDORF, JD, CPA, is a nationally recognized speaker in the areas of estate planning and retirement plans. For over a decade Mr. Overdorf has taught innumerable attorneys, accountants, insurance agents, and financial advisors across the country. He has written numerous articles and is coeditor of *Ways and Means: Maximizing Your Retirement Plans* (Esperti Peterson Institute, 1998). He is a founder of the National Network of Estate Planning Attorneys and its former director of education. As director of education, Mr. Overdorf was responsible for the creation and implementation of training courses for estate planning attorneys. He is a fellow of the Esperti Peterson Institute Masters Fellowship Program. He is also the founder, president, and CEO of TrustIt, LLC, a consulting and coaching organization providing paperless solutions for small business owners. He also maintains his own law firm and has concentrated in estate planning for over 15 years. He graduated cum laude from Indiana University School of Law, at Indianapolis, and graduated summa cum laude from Ball State University, Muncie, Indiana, with a bachelor of science degree in accounting. A certified public accountant and a licensed life and health insurance agent (inactive status), Mr. Overdorf is past treasurer and director of New Paradigm Christian Church and resides in Indianapolis, Indiana, with his wife, Tanya, and his two children, Victoria and Allison.

49 RETIREMENT PLANNING

Retirement plans are a relatively new concept in our country. Before the 1900s we were largely an agrarian society. Everything we had evolved around land. We were all more or less land entrepreneurs. Our land was our retirement! It wasn't until the 20th century that our country changed.

Perhaps it is this background that has caused so many of us to overlook the need to provide for our retirement. But like it or not, the need is there, and continues to grow larger and larger with each generation. A study from the Social Security Administration published in 2000 (and updated in 2002) revealed the following sources of income for the average retiree, age 65 and older, with a median income of $16,099:

Pensions and retirement savings	18%
Social Security	38%
Personal investments and savings	18%
Earned income	23%
Miscellaneous	3%

Two observations can be made. First, many retirees use part-time employment to supplement nearly 25% of their retirement income. Second, Social Security accounts for less than 40% of all retirement income. Given the fact that many experts suggest that retirement income should be between 70 and 80% of preretirement income, there is one undeniable conclusion. It is up to you, and you alone, to provide for your retirement.

SOURCES OF RETIREMENT INCOME

Do you know the source of your retirement income? Your three main possibilities are earned income, personal investments and savings, and retirement plans.

With regard to *earned income,* isn't that the antithesis of retirement? Isn't the American dream to "do nothing" in retirement, or is that a dream of the past? For personal reasons, some of us will never retire from work. Our work is our life. Retirement is a foreign concept of which we want no part. For financial reasons, others will never retire. They just can't afford to—for a variety of reasons. Years of undisciplined spending, inflation, employer insolvency (e.g., the collapse of Enron and Worldcom), or stock market crashes have made retirement "not an option." Therefore, like it or not, many of us will continue to rely on earned income well past our retirement years.

The second source of retirement income is *personal investments and savings.* Hopefully your response isn't, "What personal savings and investments?" But unfortunately for many that is reality. This is the most overlooked and neglected source of our retirement dollars. Why? Because it's hard to save! Like it or not, our society doesn't promote saving; it promotes spending . . . and lots of it, whether you have it or not. Therefore, in reality, many of us will not be able to rely on our personal investments and savings to live comfortably in our retirement years.

The final source of retirement income is your *retirement plans.* For the vast majority of Americans, these represent the "well" from which retirement dollars will flow. It is therefore critical to understand how retirement plans work and how to tap into this reserve when the time comes. But there is the risk that one day the well may run dry. You must plan for this contingency. You must be able to answer the question: How deep is your well?

This chapter concentrates on this third source of retirement income: retirement plans. In essence there are three types of retirement plans: government, individual, and employer. Each type of plan is discussed below.

GOVERNMENT RETIREMENT PLANS

Government retirement plans are established by the federal government. The three main federal programs that provide retirement benefits are Social Security, Civil Service Retirement System, and Federal Employees Retirement System.

SOCIAL SECURITY

Chances are you are part of Social Security. The amount of your Social Security retirement benefits will generally be based on the amount of your "contributions" during your lifetime. If you are an employee, then your contributions are automatically withheld from your paycheck. If you are self-employed, then you must remit your contributions with your federal income tax return.

As you work and make contributions to Social Security, you earn *credits* that count toward your eligibility to receive retirement benefits. You can earn a maximum of four credits per year. One credit represents a certain amount of your earnings. For 2003, one credit is awarded for every $890 of earnings. If you were born in 1929 or later, you need 40 credits (or 10 years of work) in order to be eligible for Social Security retirement benefits. You are eligible for benefits at full retirement age. Full retirement age depends on when you were born. Refer to Table 49-1.

(table 49-1)

AGE TO RECEIVE FULL SOCIAL SECURITY BENEFITS

YEAR OF BIRTH	FULL RETIREMENT AGE
1937 or earlier	65 years
1938	65 years, 2 months
1939	65 years, 4 months
1940	65 years, 6 months
1941	65 years, 8 months
1942	65 years, 10 months
1943–1954	66 years
1955	66 years, 2 months
1956	66 years, 4 months
1957	66 years, 6 months
1958	66 years, 8 months
1959	66 years, 10 months
1960 and later	67 years

(table 49-2)

INCREASES FOR DELAYED RETIREMENT

YEAR OF BIRTH	YEARLY RATE OF INCREASE
1917–1924	3.0%
1925–1926	3.5%
1927–1928	4.0%
1929–1930	4.5%
1931–1932	5.0%
1933–1934	5.5%
1935–1936	6.0%
1937–1938	6.5%
1939–1940	7.0%
1941–1942	7.5%
1943 or later	8.0%

You may also elect to receive reduced benefits at age 62. If you elect to receive Social Security at age 62, your monthly benefits are reduced, but the overall benefits paid during your lifetime will roughly be the same. For example, if you were born in 1960 or later, your monthly benefit will be reduced by about 30% if you start at age 62, by 25% if you start at age 63, by 20% if you start at age 64, by 13% if you start at age 65, and by 7% if you start at age 66.

Conversely, if you postpone distributions after your full age of retirement, then you receive a special credit for every month up to the age of 70. The amount of your credit depends on your age. Refer to Table 49-2.

Once you begin receiving Social Security benefits, your benefits are automatically increased each year based on a cost-of-living adjustment (COLA). The COLA increase is calculated in December of each year and applied beginning the following January.

If you have not yet reached your retirement age, you may be wondering about your estimated social security benefits. Beginning in 1999, Social Security is required to send you, each year, your Social Security statement. You should receive this statement if you are at least 25 years of age, you have ever contributed to Social Security, and you are not currently receiving benefits. You should receive this annual statement about three months prior to your birth date. In addition, you can request this statement from the Social Security Administration. Carefully review this statement to ensure that your record of earnings and other personal information are accurate.

CIVIL SERVICE RETIREMENT SYSTEM

If you were a full-time federal employee prior to January 1, 1984, you were covered under the *Civil Service Retirement System (CSRS)*. By law, you were excluded from Social Security taxes and coverage. Instead you paid CSRS deductions and your retirement benefits would be calculated under CSRS and not under Social Security.

Generally you may retire voluntarily with full and immediate annuity payments if you are (1) age 62 and have 5 years of service; (2) age 65 and have 20 years of service; or (3) age 55 and have 30 years of service. On your retirement you are entitled to a monthly annuity that is determined by a formula based on factors including your years of service and your highest three years of compensation. Your monthly annuity check comes from the U.S. Office of Personal Management (OPM). Your monthly benefits are increased periodically based on cost-of-living adjustments.

Finally, your monthly annuity may be reduced if you are a "CSRS offset employee." You are a CSRS offset employee if you are covered under both CSRS and Social Security at the same time. In this circumstance your CSRS annuity will be reduced by your Social Security benefits. "For More Information" has links for discovering more about CSRS.

FEDERAL EMPLOYEES RETIREMENT SYSTEM

On January 1, 1987 the new *Federal Employees Retirement System (FERS)* was created. Federal employees who were employed prior to January 1, 1994, were given the option of staying of CSRS or switching to FERS. After January 1, 1994, any new federal employee is automatically covered by FERS.

FERS is a three-tier retirement package consisting of Social Security, an annuity, and a personal savings plan (thrift savings plan). You pay Social Security taxes and FERS basic benefit deductions. You receive an automatic 1% government contribution to your thrift savings plan account. In addition, you have the option to contribute up to 10% of your pay to your thrift account, and the government would provide an equal match not to exceed 4%.

Generally you may retire voluntarily with full and immediate annuity payments if you are (1) age 62 and have 5 years of service; (2) age 65 and have 20 years of service; or (3) have reached a minimum retirement age with 30 years of service (the minimum retirement age varies between 55 and 57, depending on when you were born).

On your retirement you are entitled to a monthly annuity that is determined by a formula based on factors including your years of service and your highest three years of compensation. Your monthly annuity check comes from the U.S. Office of Personal Management (OPM). Your monthly benefits are increased periodically based on cost-of-living adjustments.

INDIVIDUAL RETIREMENT PLANS

Individual retirement plans are established by you. They are known as individual retirement accounts (IRAs). The government allows you this personal retirement vehicle with the hope that the money will help supplement your government retirement plan. Since the government wants you to use this money for your retirement, there are certain rules that you agree to "live by" once you establish an IRA.

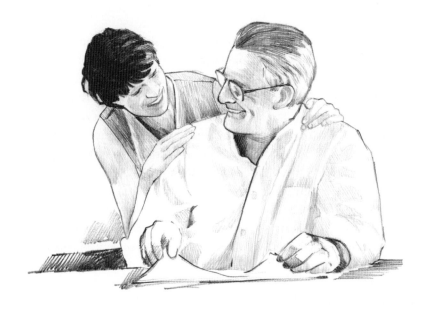

You establish an IRA by a written agreement between you and a *qualified institution*. The written agreement is known as a custodial or trust agreement and the qualified institution is known as the IRA custodian. Institutions qualifying under the law to be an IRA custodian include most banks, savings and loans, credit unions, brokerage firms, and insurance companies.

Once you establish an IRA, you can make, within limits, yearly contributions. The only form of contribution you may make to an IRA is cash. The law allows three different types of IRAs: deductible IRAs, nondeductible IRAs, and Roth IRAs.

TYPES OF IRAS

Historically, IRAs fell within the two categories of deductible and nondeductible. The main difference between the two types involved contribution deduction and distribution taxation.

With a deductible IRA, you receive an income tax deduction for each contribution. Normally this results in an immediate income tax savings, which in turn helps "finance" the cost of your contribution. Each year, the earnings inside your IRA accumulate on a tax-deferred basis: you do not pay current income tax on those earnings. This tax-deferred growth allows your IRA to grow much faster than a normal investment subject to income tax each year. Once you begin withdrawing money from your deductible IRA, both your original contributions and all accumulated earnings are subject to ordinary income tax.

With a nondeductible IRA, you do not receive an income tax deduction for your contributions, but the earnings are tax-deferred just like a deductible IRA. On withdrawal, your contributions are not subject to income tax (since you did not get a deduction when you made the contribution), but all earnings are subject to ordinary income tax.

In 1998 Congress established the Roth IRA, named after Senator Roth who introduced the legislation for this type of IRA. In essence the

(table 49-3)

TOTAL ANNUAL IRA CONTRIBUTION LIMITS

YEAR	OVERALL CONTRIBUTION LIMIT: DEDUCTIBLE, NONDEDUCTIBLE, AND ROTH IRA (UNDER AGE 50)	OVERALL ADDITIONAL CATCH-UP CONTRIBUTIONS: DEDUCTIBLE, NONDEDUCTIBLE, AND ROTH IRA (OVER AGE 50)
2003	$ 3000	$ 500
2004	$ 3000	$ 500
2005	$ 4000	$ 500
2006	$ 4000	$ 1000
2007	$ 4000	$ 1000
2008	$ 5000	$ 1000
2009	$ 5000*	$ 1000

*Indexed for inflation

Roth IRA is a hybrid between a deductible IRA and a nondeductible IRA. You receive no income tax deduction for contributions to a Roth IRA, but the earnings are tax-deferred and maybe even tax-free. You may withdraw your contributions at any time, tax-free. In fact, all distributions are first deemed to be from your original contributions and only thereafter your earnings. But here is the best part: If you do not make a distribution of earnings until you are either 59½ or 5 years from the establishment of your first Roth IRA, whichever is later, then *all* your earnings are tax-free!

CONTRIBUTIONS BY YOU

As a general rule, you decide which type of IRA you want: deductible, nondeductible, and Roth. In fact you may be able to establish more than one type in a given year. However, the government is concerned that such money should be set aside for retirement, not as a wealth accumulation and transfer vehicle for your family when you die. Therefore, the law limits your overall contributions and further reduces your ability to make contributions based on your income and your participation in an employer retirement plan.

In order to be eligible to make contributions to an IRA you must meet a series of tests. In the year of your contribution, you must have earned income equal to or greater than the amount of your contributions to an IRA. *Earned income* includes money from salary, tips, commissions, and self-employment, but does not include interest, dividends, capital gain, or rental income. If you are married and file a joint income tax return, you can consider the earned income of both you and your spouse.

Assuming you have sufficient earned income, you are limited to a maximum contribution amount each year. The maximum contribution limit is shown in Table 49-3 and applies to all IRAs in a given year (deductible, nondeductible, and Roth). For example, if you contribute $2000 to a deductible IRA in 2003, then the most you could contribute to a Roth IRA for 2003 is $1000 (assuming you could meet the other tests provided below). If you are married, this limit applies to each of you.

(table 49-4)

REDUCTION OR ELIMINATION OF DEDUCTIBLE IRA CONTRIBUTION FOR
THOSE WITH EMPLOYER RETIREMENT PLAN

YEAR	CONTRIBUTION LIMIT BEGINS REDUCTION WHEN AGI REACHES	CONTRIBUTION LIMIT ELIMINATED IF AGI REACHES
SINGLE OR HEAD OF HOUSEHOLD		
2003	$ 40,000	$ 50,000
2004	$ 45,000	$ 55,000
2005 and later	$ 50,000	$ 60,000
MARRIED FILING JOINT RETURN		
2003	$ 60,000	$ 70,000
2004	$ 65,000	$ 75,000
2005	$ 70,000	$ 80,000
2006	$ 75,000	$ 85,000
2007	$ 80,000	$ 90,000

Note that a contribution to any IRA must be made no later than April 15 following the contribution year.

Beginning in 2003, if 50 or older, you can make extra contributions each year. Known as *catch-up contributions,* these additional contributions allow you to set aside more for retirement, since your retirement years are quickly approaching. Again, the amount of the catch-up contribution allowed is the total cumulative amount for all IRAs for a given year.

As shown in Table 49-4, your contribution limit to a deductible IRA could be reduced and even eliminated if either you or your spouse participate in an employer retirement plan. If both you and your spouse are participants, Table 49-4 also reflects the reduction or elimination of each of your contributions. If one spouse is not a participant, the nonparticipant spouse's contributions begin to be phased out when your combined *adjusted gross income (AGI)* reaches $150,000.

Your contribution limit to a Roth IRA is first reduced by contributions to a deductible IRA for the same year. Furthermore, your contribution limit could be reduced or eliminated if your modified AGI exceeds certain limits. See Table 49-5. Your contribution limit to a nondeductible IRA is reduced by contributions to a deductible or Roth IRA in the same year. There are no income limits on contributions to a nondeductible IRA.

Finally, you are not allowed to make contributions to a deductible or nondeductible IRA beginning in the year you reach 70½. However, you may continue to make contributions to a Roth IRA (assuming the other tests are met), regardless of your age.

VOLUNTARY WITHDRAWALS BY YOU

Generally, you are allowed to withdraw any money from your IRA at any time. However, if you are under 59½, then the 10% penalty tax will apply unless you meet one of the exceptions.

By law, you may not borrow from, sell, or give away your IRA. Any such transaction would be deemed to be a distribution of the IRA and subject to income taxation.

At any time, you may transfer your IRA tax-free to another IRA of the same type which is owned by you. Two methods accomplish this. The first method is known as a *direct trustee-to-trustee transfer,* in which the institution that holds your current IRA directly transfers the funds to the institution that holds (or will hold) your new IRA. Under this method, you never receive the money directly from the institution (i.e., a check is not cut to you). The second method (known as a *rollover)* involves withdrawing your IRA proceeds from one institution and then within 60 days delivering an equal amount of cash to another institution. You are allowed to rollover an IRA once per year.

MANDATORY WITHDRAWALS

Deductible and nondeductible IRAs are subject to minimum distribution rules, and you must begin withdrawals by April 1 of the year following the year in which you turn 70½. On your death, your beneficiary is subject to after-death minimum distribution rules. Your Roth IRA is not subject to minimum distribution rules during your lifetime. You are never required to withdraw any money from your Roth IRA while you are alive. However, on your death, your beneficiary is subject to after-death minimum distribution rules.

INVESTMENT CHOICES

Normally you are free to invest in most types of assets, such as mutual funds, stocks and bonds, annuities, government securities, and real estate. However, the law does not allow investments in collectibles, such as antiques, stamps, artwork, and coins other than U.S.-minted gold and silver coins. Furthermore, your IRA custodian may limit your types of investments.

CONVERSION BETWEEN REGULAR AND ROTH IRAS

You may convert a deductible or nondeductible IRA to a Roth IRA during any year in which (1) your modified adjusted gross income is not more than $100,000 and (2) you are either single or married filing jointly. In the year of the conversion you will generally report as taxable income the full amount of the IRA. However, provided you meet the five-year holding test, all withdrawals after that date will be income tax–free.

(table 49-5)

REDUCTION OR ELIMINATION OF ROTH IRA CONTRIBUTION

YEAR	CONTRIBUTION LIMIT BEGINS REDUCTION WHEN MODIFIED AGI REACHES	CONTRIBUTION LIMIT ELIMINATED IF MODIFIED AGI REACHES
SINGLE OR HEAD OF HOUSEHOLD		
2003 and later	$ 95,000	$ 110,000
MARRIED FILING JOINT RETURN		
2003 and later	$ 150,000	$ 160,000
MARRIED FILING SEPARATELY		
2003 and later	0	$ 10,000

Your decision to convert from a regular IRA to a Roth IRA depends on a number of factors:

- How long will the money be kept in the Roth IRA?
- Do you have other assets from which to pay the income tax in the year of conversion?
- Will your expected future income tax brackets be higher or lower than today?

There is no right or wrong answer, and it depends on your personal goals. Prior to making any conversion decision, consult with your retirement planning advisors.

EMPLOYER RETIREMENT PLANS

Your employer can establish many types of retirement plans to provide benefits for you. The two main categories for employer retirement plans are qualified plans and nonqualified plans.

In order to have a qualified plan, your employer must comply with federal laws. In exchange for meeting these legal requirements, your employer is allowed deductible contributions. Thus on contributing money to a qualified retirement plan, your employer is entitled to an income tax deduction in the year of contribution.

Furthermore, qualified plans can be divided into two main types: account plan (also known as a *defined contribution plan*) and annuity plan (also known as a *defined benefit plan*). Under an account plan, a separate account is established for you, the employee. Contributions made by you or your employer are deposited directly into your separate account. Normally you are entitled to the money in your account after you leave your employer or you retire. If you die, your named beneficiary will receive any money remaining in your account. Within limits, you are allowed to select how the money in your account will be invested and can periodically change the investment mix of the assets in your account. Since you control how the money is invested, all investment risk is borne solely by you.

An annuity plan holds all money in one fund; a separate account is not established for you. You are normally entitled to receive benefits if you become disabled or reach a certain retirement age. The amount of your benefits is generally tied to your annual salary, number of years employed, and other factors. Your benefits will generally be paid to you in the form of a monthly annuity.

A lifetime annuity is a guaranteed payment for the rest of your life. When you die, the annuity payments stop. You may have the option of having the annuity paid during your lifetime *(single annuity)* or the lifetimes of you and another individual, usually your spouse (joint annuity). A joint annuity has a lower monthly benefit than a single annuity. Furthermore, you generally have the option of electing a term certain. A *term certain*

(table 49-6)

EMPLOYER RETIREMENT PLANS

ANNUITY PLAN QUALIFIED PLANS	ACCOUNT PLANS	NONQUALIFIED PLANS
Pension plan	Money purchase pension plan Profit sharing plan 401(k) SIMPLE 401(k) SIMPLE IRA SEP IRA Stock bonus plan ESOP	Deferred compensation plans Stock option plan 457 plan 403(b) plan

guarantees payment for a specific period of time, regardless of whether you are alive. Thus if you elect a 5-year term certain and die after two years, the annuity payments continue to your beneficiary for another three years. Unless you have elected a term certain, annuity payments stop when you die (for a single annuity) or when both of you die (for a joint annuity). There are no remaining benefits to leave to your family.

Under an annuity plan, you cannot choose how the assets are invested. Your employer is "guaranteeing" your future annuity payments. Since you have no control over how the money is invested, all investment risk is borne by your employer.

Historically, most if not all qualified plans were annuity plans. The most common was the pension plan. Unfortunately, pension plans are not easy to establish and maintain. They have many complex rules that employers must follow each year, and the administrative costs can be very high. For these reasons and others, employers have turned to account plans. Today, most qualified plans are account plans. They are also known as defined contribution plans. Table 49-6 includes the most common qualified account plans.

In a nonqualified retirement plan, an employer is not required to comply with as many federal laws as in a qualified plan; however, contributions made by your employer are generally not deductible. Most nonqualified plans are designed to entice executives and other highly compensated employees to continue working for their employer. Table 49-6 includes the most common nonqualified account plans.

QUALIFED PLANS

The following covers various types of qualified plans. Because the laws vary depending on the type of plan, we have divided the discussion of each plan into seven areas. Keep in mind that many of these areas set forth the requirements provided by law. However, the law often allows your employer to be more lenient. Therefore, you should always review the documentation provided by your employer to ascertain your rights under a particular plan.

First is a general *overview* of the particular plan. The second area involves *your participation*—when you, the employee, are eligible to begin participating in the plan. Many plans provide that you must attain a certain age (age requirement) and be employed for a certain length of time (service requirement). The third area deals with your vesting in the plan. Vesting refers to your ownership rights in the plan should you terminate your employment, die, or become disabled. A vesting period is the amount of time before you are entitled to 100% of your retirement benefits. The two types of vesting periods are known as *graduated vesting* and *cliff vesting*. Under graduated vesting, each year your percentage of ownership increases. With cliff vesting, you become 100% vested after a certain number of years. Thus a three-year cliff vesting means you are entitled to your entire account after three years of service. If you leave prior to the three-year term, you forfeit all your retirement benefits. In addition, your employer can have different vesting periods for different events. Many employers allow 100% vesting in the event of your death or disability. Finally, the law requires 100% vesting on you reaching normal retirement age (as defined in the plan) or on termination of the plan.

The fourth area sets forth whether *contributions* by your employer are mandatory or discretionary and the dollar limits imposed by law. The fifth area mentions whether contributions by you, as employee, are allowed, and if so, the dollar limits imposed by law. The sixth area describes when you are allowed to make *voluntary withdrawals* from your plan. Note that a hardship withdrawal is a voluntary withdrawal and that in the following descriptions, hardship means you have an immediate and heavy financial need, the withdrawal is necessary to satisfy that financial need, and you have exhausted all other resources, including other distributions available under the plan. Generally, hardship includes medical care expenses or post–high school education (for the next 12 months) for you, your spouse, or your dependents; the purchase of a principal residence; or payments to prevent foreclosure on your principal residence. The seventh area describes when you are required to begin taking *mandatory withdrawals* from your plan.

PENSION PLAN

A pension plan is an annuity plan that requires annual mandatory contributions by your employer that are tied to a formula based on something other than profits. Usually mandatory contributions are based solely on employee compensation. Under a pension plan, an individual account is not established for your benefit. All moneys are held in one trust fund.

Your benefits are in the form of an annuity payment and are guaranteed. Furthermore, pension plans are subject to the Pension Benefit Guaranty Corporation (PBGC). The PBGC ensures that your benefits will be paid in the event your employer is unable to make the payments (i.e., your employer files bankruptcy).

Your participation: Generally you must be allowed to participate in your employer's pension plan if you are at least 21 years of age, with one year of service (defined to be at least 1000 hours). If your employer has a vesting schedule that provides 100% vesting after two years, then the service requirement can be extended to two years.

Once you meet the age and service requirements, you must be allowed to begin participation by the earlier of the first day of the plan year beginning after you met the above requirements or six months from the date you met the above requirements.

Your vesting: Generally, a pension plan has a vesting period. By law, the maximum period for graduated vesting is seven years, and the maximum period for cliff vesting is five years. Many employers have a shorter vesting period and different vesting periods for different events, such as death, disability, or termination of employment.

Contributions by your employer: Your employer must make annual contributions to a pension plan until there is enough money to ensure that all current and future benefits to its employees can be paid. The amount of the contribution your employer makes on your behalf is based on calculations to ensure that your employer will have enough money to pay your future annuity payments. However, the law provides that in determining its contribution, your employer cannot consider more than $200,000 of your compensation (adjusted for inflation). In general, the older you are when you begin employment, the larger the contribution your employer must make on your behalf.

Contributions by you: Generally under a pension plan you are not allowed to make contributions.

Voluntary withdrawals by you: A pension plan cannot allow withdrawals by you except for retirement or termination of employment.

Mandatory withdrawals: Your pension plan is subject to the minimum distribution rules, and you must begin withdrawals by April 1 of the year following the year in which you turn 70½. However, if you are still employed and your plan allows, you may postpone distributions until April 1 of the year following your separation from service. This exception only applies if you do not own more than 5% of your employer. However, keep in mind that your pension plan might require mandatory withdrawals prior to the above-mentioned times.

MONEY PURCHASE PENSION PLAN

A money purchase pension plan is an account plan that requires annual mandatory contributions by your employer that are tied to a formula based on something other than profits. Usually mandatory contributions are based solely on employee compensation.

Under prior law, money purchase pension plans were popular because your employer's annual limit on contributions was higher than other account plans. However the contribution limits are now the same, and therefore most money purchase pension plans are being merged into other qualified plans.

Your participation: Generally you must be allowed to participate in your employer's money purchase pension plan if you are at least 21 years of age, with one year of service (defined to be at least 1000 hours). If your employer has a vesting schedule that provides 100% vesting after two years, then the service requirement can be extended to two years.

Your vesting: Generally, a money purchase pension plan has a vesting period. By law, the maximum period for graduated vesting is seven years, and the maximum period for cliff vesting is five years. Many employers will provide a shorter vesting period and can provide different vesting periods for different events, such as death, disability, or termination of employment.

Contributions by your employer: Your employer must make annual contributions to a money purchase pension plan. The maximum contribution that can be made by your employer on your behalf is the lesser of $40,000 (adjusted for inflation) or 100% of your compensation.

Contributions by you: You are not allowed to make contributions to a money purchase pension plan.

Voluntary withdrawals by you: Since a money purchase pension plan is like a pension plan, generally it cannot allow withdrawals by you except for retirement or termination of employment.

Mandatory withdrawals: Your money purchase pension plan is subject to the minimum distribution rules, and you must begin withdrawals by April 1 of the year following the year in which you turn 70½. However, if you are still employed and your plan allows, you may postpone distributions until April 1 of the year following your separation from service. This exception only applies if you do not own more than 5% of your employer. However, keep in mind that your money purchase pension plan might require mandatory withdrawals prior to the above-mentioned times.

PROFIT SHARING PLAN

A profit sharing plan is an account plan and is the most simplistic form of qualified plan. Historically, it was a retirement plan that allowed your employer to "share" a percentage of the company's profits with its employees. Under current law there is no requirement that your employer make a profit in order to contribute to a profit sharing plan. Generally employer contributions are allocated to accounts for employees based on a percentage of their compensation.

Your participation: Generally you must be allowed to participate in your employer's profit sharing plan if you are at least 21 years of age, with one year of service (defined to be at least 1000 hours). If your employer has a vesting schedule that provides 100% vesting after two years, then the service requirement can be extended to two years.

Your vesting: Generally, a profit sharing plan will have a vesting period. By law, the maximum period for graduated vesting is seven years, and the maximum period for cliff vesting is five years. Many employers will provide a shorter vesting period and can provide different vesting periods for different events, such death, disability, or termination of employment.

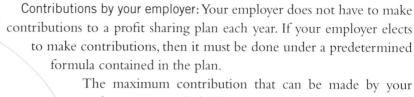

Contributions by your employer: Your employer does not have to make contributions to a profit sharing plan each year. If your employer elects to make contributions, then it must be done under a predetermined formula contained in the plan.

The maximum contribution that can be made by your employer on your behalf is the lesser of $40,000 (adjusted for inflation) or 100% of your compensation.

Contributions by you: Under a profit sharing plan, you are not allowed to make contributions.

Voluntary withdrawals by you: By law, a profit sharing plan must provide you the ability to take withdrawals after a certain number of years or on a certain event, such as your severance from employment, death, or disability. Hardship withdrawals and loans are permitted if allowed by the plan.

Mandatory withdrawals: Your profit sharing plan is subject to the minimum distribution rules, and you must begin withdrawals by April 1 of the year following the year in which you turn 70½. However, if you are still employed and your plan allows, you may postpone distributions until April 1 of the year following your separation from service. This exception only applies if you do not own more than 5% of your employer. However, keep in mind that your profit sharing plan might require mandatory withdrawals prior to the above-mentioned times.

401(K) PLAN

In simplest terms, a 401(k) plan is a profit sharing plan with the added feature of allowing employees to "set aside" some of their compensation. It is also known as a cash or deferred arrangement (CODA) plan, because the plan must allow you, the employee, the option of receiving the compensation (cash) or deferring that part of your compensation on a pretax basis. Thus, the portion of your compensation that you elect to place in the 401(k) plan ("your elective contribution") is not subject to income tax. It is, however, subject to Social Security and Medicare tax.

Undoubtedly the 401(k) is becoming the most popular retirement plan for employers.

Your participation: Generally you must be allowed to participate in your employer's 401(k) plan if you are at least 21 years of age, with one year of service (defined to be at least 1000 hours). If your employer has a vesting schedule that provides 100% vesting after two years, then the service requirement can be extended to two years.

Your vesting: There is no vesting period for your elective contributions. Your elective contributions are automatically 100% vested.

With regard to your employer's contributions, many 401(k) plans have a vesting period. By law, the maximum period for graduated vesting is seven years and the maximum period for cliff vesting is five years. However, if your employee makes matching contributions, then the maximum period for graduated vesting is reduced to six years and maximum period for cliff vesting is reduced to three years.

Contributions by your employer: Your employer does not have to make contributions.

If your employer chooses to make contributions, then they are normally in the form of a matching or nonelective contribution.

With a matching contribution, your employer agrees to set aside a certain amount in your 401(k) account based on the amount of your elective contribution. This match is usually expressed as a certain percentage of your contribution with a cap based on your compensation. For example, your employer might agree to match 100% of your contributions up to 3% of your total compensation. Thus if you elected to set aside $5000 and your total compensation was $60,000, your employer's match would be $1800 (3% of $60,000). On the other hand, if you elected to set aside $1000 and your total compensation was $60,000, your employer's match would be $1000.

If you choose not to participate in the 401(k) plan, then your employer is not required to make any contributions on your behalf. Therefore, as a rule of thumb, it is always wise to make your elective contribution large enough so that your employer's matching contribution is maximized. In essence your employer's match is "free money"!

If your employer makes nonelective contributions, then your employer must make contributions to all eligible employees, regardless of whether they have chosen to make any elective contributions. The amount of nonelective contributions is normally stated as a percentage of your compensation.

The maximum contribution that can be made by your employer on your behalf is the lesser of $40,000 (adjusted for inflation) or 100% of your compensation.

Contributions by you: You may choose to make elective contributions to a 401(k) plan. In addition if you are age 50 or older you may make additional catch-up contributions (see Table 49-7 for contribution and catch-up limits). You are not allowed to make any other contributions to your 401(k) plan.

Voluntary withdrawals by you: By law, a 401(k) plan must generally limit your ability to take withdrawals until the earlier of your severance from employment, death, or disability, the termination of the plan, or on your hardship.

Depending on the terms of your 401(k) plan, you may be able to make loans from your account. Many small companies prohibit loans due to the extra administrative costs. By law the total amount of all loans cannot exceed the lesser of 50% of your vested balance or $50,000. Generally, loans must be repaid quarterly, with interest, and within five years unless the loan is for the purchase of your principal residence.

Mandatory withdrawals: Your 401(k) plan is subject to the minimum distribution rules, and you must begin withdrawals by April 1 of the year following the year in which you turn 70½. However, if you are still employed and your plan allows, you may postpone distributions until April 1 of the year following your separation from service. This exception

(table 49-7)

EMPLOYEE MAXIMUM CONTRIBUTION LIMITS

| YEAR | CONTRIBUTION LIMIT | | ELECTIVE DEFERRAL LIMIT | | | |
| | DEDUCTIBLE, NONDEDUCTIBLE, AND ROTH IRAS (UNDER AGE 50)* | REGULAR AND ROTH IRAS CATCH-UP (AGE 50+)* | 401(K), 403(B), & 457 PLANS | | SIMPLE 401(K) & SIMPLE IRA | |
			UNDER AGE 50†	CATCH-UP (AGE 50+)†	UNDER AGE 50‡	CATCH-UP (AGE 50+)‡
2003	$ 3000	$ 500	$ 12,000	$ 2000	$ 8,000	$ 1000
2004	$ 3000	$ 500	$ 13,000	$ 3000	$ 9,000	$ 1500
2005	$ 4000	$ 500	$ 14,000	$ 4000	$ 10,000	$ 2000
2006	$ 4000	$ 1000	$ 15,000	$ 5000	$ 10,000§	$ 2500
2007	$ 4000	$ 1000	$ 15,000§	$ 5000§	$ 10,000§	$ 2500§
2008	$ 5000	$ 1000	$ 15,000§	$ 5000§	$ 10,000§	$ 2500§
2009	$ 5000§	$ 1000	$ 15,000§	$ 5000§	$ 10,000§	$ 2500§

*Total yearly limit for all IRAs. Subject to reduction or elimination based on income limits and whether you or your spouse participate in a qualified plan.
†Total yearly limit for all 401(k)s and 403(b)s in which you are a participant. Total yearly limit applies separately for 457 plans, which must be combined with other 457 plans but not 401(k) plans or 403(b) plans. Thus for 2003, if under 50, you could defer up to a maximum of $12,000 for all your 401(k)s and 403(b) plans and, in addition, elect to defer up to a maximum of $12,000 for all your 457 plans.
‡Your employer cannot maintain any other qualified plan.
§Amount subject to adjustment for inflation.

only applies if you do not own more than 5% of your employer. However, keep in mind that your 401(k) might require mandatory withdrawals before the above–mentioned times.

Investment choices: Your employer determines your investment choices. By law there is no minimum or maximum number of investment choices that your employer is required to provide. In reality, most employers hire professionals to assist them in this area, and you should have several different investment choices that normally include mutual funds. With regard to your contributions, you do have the right to select among the various investment options available, but your plan can limit the number of times you can make changes in a given year. Depending on the plan, your employer may retain the right to choose the investment choice for its contributions made on your behalf. In fact, some plans require that the employer's contributions be invested in its own stock.

SAVINGS INCENTIVE MATCH PLAN FOR EMPLOYEES (SIMPLE) 401(K)

A savings incentive match plan for employees (SIMPLE) 401(k) is a simplified 401(k) plan. Like a 401(k) plan, it is a retirement plan that allows you, as the employee, to defer a portion of your compensation on a pretax basis. Thus, the portion of your compensation that you elect to place in the SIMPLE 401(k) ("your elective contribution") is not subject to income tax. It is, however, subject to Social Security and Medicare tax. Generally, your employer must have 100 or fewer employees and cannot maintain any other qualified plan. Your employer has little flexibility in designing a SIMPLE 401(k).

Your participation: Generally, you must be included in your employer's SIMPLE 401(k) if you are at least 21 years of age and have been with your employer for one year.

Your vesting: There is no vesting period for contributions. Both your and your employer's contributions are automatically 100% vested.

Contributions by your employer: Your employer must make either (1) a matching contribution that does not exceed 3% of your compensation or (2) a nonelective contribution of 2% for each employee eligible to participate.

Contributions by you: You may make elective contributions to a SIMPLE 401(k). If you are age 50 or older, you may make additional catch-up contributions. (See Table 49-7 for contribution and catch-up limits.) You are not allowed to make any other contributions to your SIMPLE 401(k) plan.

Voluntary withdrawals by you: By law, a SIMPLE 401(k) plan must limit your ability to take withdrawals until the earlier of your severance from employment, death, or disability; the termination of the plan; or on your hardship.

Once you allowed to take withdrawals, you may roll over your SIMPLE 401(k) into a regular IRA or another qualified retirement plan. However, you may not rollover your SIMPLE 401(k) into a SIMPLE IRA, another SIMPLE 401(k), or a 403(b).

Mandatory withdrawals: Your SIMPLE 401(k) plan is subject to the minimum distribution rules, and you must begin withdrawals by April 1 of the year following the year in which you turn 70½. However, if you are still employed and your plan allows, you may postpone distributions until April 1 of the year following your separation from service. This exception only applies if you do not own more than 5% of your employer. However, keep in mind that your SIMPLE 401(k) might require mandatory withdrawals before the above-mentioned times.

SAVINGS INCENTIVE MATCH PLAN FOR EMPLOYEES IRA

A savings incentive match plan for employees (SIMPLE) IRA is another simplified 401(k) plan. Like a SIMPLE 401(k) plan, a SIMPLE IRA is preferred by small employers who do not want to go to the expense or administrative hassle associated with a traditional 401(k). Between the 401(k), SIMPLE 401(k), and the SIMPLE IRA, the SIMPLE IRA provides the least administrative burden and paperwork on your employer. With a SIMPLE IRA, the account established by your employer for you is actually an IRA. Therefore, it is subject to the normal IRA rules, as well as a few special rules noted below.

Generally, your employer must have 100 or fewer employees and cannot maintain any other qualified plan. Your employer has little flexibility in designing a SIMPLE IRA.

Your participation: Generally, you must be included in your employer's SIMPLE IRA if you have received compensation of at least $5000 from your employer during any two previous years and it is anticipated that you will earn at least $5000 in the current year.

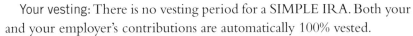

Your vesting: There is no vesting period for a SIMPLE IRA. Both your and your employer's contributions are automatically 100% vested.

Contributions by your employer: Your employer must make contributions to a SIMPLE IRA. However, your employer can select one of two options: matching contributions or nonelective contributions. With matching contributions, your employer contributes on your behalf only if you choose to make contributions. In that circumstance, your employer must match 100% of your contribution up to a maximum of 3% of your compensation. Furthermore, your employer is allowed to reduce its match to 1% for any given year but cannot make this reduction for more than twice in any five-year period.

With nonelective contributions, your employer is required to contribute 2% of the first $200,000 of your compensation (adjusted for inflation) each year, regardless of whether you make any contributions.

These are the only contributions your employer may make.

Contributions by you: You may elect to make salary reduction contributions to your SIMPLE IRA. If age 50 or older, you may make additional catch-up contributions. (See Table 49-7 for contribution and catch-up limits.) You are not allowed to make any other contributions to your SIMPLE IRA.

Voluntary withdrawals by you: Your employer cannot place limits on your ability to withdraw money from your SIMPLE IRA. However, because your SIMPLE IRA is an IRA, you would be subject to a 10% penalty if you withdraw money prior to age 59½, unless an exception applies. Furthermore, if you withdraw money from your SIMPLE IRA during the first two years and the 10% penalty would apply, then the penalty is increased to 25%.

You may not borrow from your SIMPLE IRA. You may roll over your SIMPLE IRA into another SIMPLE IRA at any time. You may roll over your SIMPLE IRA into a regular IRA only after two years. You may not rollover your SIMPLE IRA into a qualified plan.

Mandatory withdrawals: Your SIMPLE IRA is subject to the minimum distribution rules, and you must begin withdrawals by April 1 of the year following the year in which you turn 70½.

SIMPLIFIED EMPLOYEE PENSION PLAN

A simplified employee pension (SEP) plan, which is also known as a SEP IRA, is an account plan under which your employer makes a contribution to an IRA established on your behalf. SEPs are generally used by small employers who do not want to go to the expense or administrative hassle associated with more formal qualified plans. Your employer has little flexibility in designing a SEP. From your standpoint, a SEP is almost identical to your individual IRA, except that the contribution limits are higher.

A SEP can also be established by you if you are self-employed.

Your participation: Generally you must be included in a SEP if you are at least 21 years of age, have been with your employer for at least three out of the last five years, and have at least $450 in compensation for the current year. In addition, all employees who meet this criteria must be included. Your employer cannot discriminate among employees.

Your vesting: There is no vesting period for a SEP. Once a contribution is made to your SEP IRA, you are automatically 100% vested.

Contributions by your employer: Your employer can elect to make or not make contributions on a year-by-year basis. However, once elected, your employer must make contributions for all covered employees during that year. The maximum contribution your employer may make on your behalf each year is limited to the lesser of $40,000 (adjusted for inflation) or 25% of your compensation up to $200,000 (adjusted for inflation).

This maximum limit is reduced by the amount of any contributions you make.

Contributions by you: You are allowed to make contributions to your SEP IRA, and your contribution limits are the same as for a 401(k). However your ability to contribute to another IRA in the same year may be reduced or eliminated since your SEP is considered an employer-sponsored plan. (See discussion on IRAs in the section "Individual Retirement Accounts," above.)

Generally, you are only allowed to make elective deferrals (through salary reduction) under a special type of SEP known as a *SARSEP.* SARSEPs were replaced by the SIMPLE plans, and therefore no new SARSEPs have been allowed since 1996.

Voluntary withdrawals by you: Your employer cannot place limits on your ability to withdraw money from your SEP. However, because your SEP is an IRA, you would be subject to a 10% penalty if you withdraw money prior to 59½, unless an exception applies.

You may not borrow from your SEP IRA.

Mandatory withdrawals: Your SEP IRA is subject to the minimum distribution rules, and you must begin withdrawals by April 1 of the year following the year in which you turn 70½.

STOCK BONUS PLAN

A stock bonus plan is a profit sharing plan in which your employer is authorized, but not required, to invest in its own securities. As with any profit sharing plan, your employer is not required to make a contribution each year. For more information, see the description in the section "Profit Sharing Plan," above.

EMPLOYEE STOCK OWNERSHIP PLANS

An employee stock ownership plan (ESOP) is a stock bonus plan that is mandated to invest primarily in the stock of your employer. It is a trust for the benefit of the employees, the purpose of which is to allow the employees to own some or eventually all of the stock. Normally, the trust borrows money and then uses that money to purchase the stock directly from your employer. Your employer then makes annual contributions to the trust in order for the trust to repay the loan.

If your employer is a public traded company, the ESOP must allow you to vote any stock allocated to your account. If your employer is a private company, then the trustee of the ESOP trust normally votes all shares of stock except for such unusual circumstances as merger or liquidation.

Generally, the only assets permitted to be held by an ESOP are the stock of your employer and cash necessary to buy out employees nearing retirement.

One of the perceived benefits of an ESOP is that you have a stake in the success of your employer. As the value of your company's stock increases, so does the value of your interest in the ESOP. There is an incentive for you, the employee, to work hard, reduce waste, and increase efficiency. On the other hand, the biggest disadvantage of an ESOP is its inherent lack of diversity. Virtually all the assets of the ESOP are in one investment: your company's stock. The old adage "don't put all of your eggs in one basket" doesn't work well with an ESOP. While historically, most ESOPs have probably performed well over time, recent business failures, such an Enron and Worldcom, have cast doubt on the continued reliance on an ESOP for your total retirement investments.

It has been estimated that about 11,000 companies have ESOPs, covering over 8.5 million employees.

NONQUALIFIED PLANS

DEFERRED COMPENSATION PLANS

Deferred compensation plans are used for highly paid executives or other key employees. The goal is to provide you an incentive to continue to work for your employer. The incentive is the company's promise to pay you in the future, usually on your retirement or death. Your employer can chose to set aside funds to pay this future benefit to you (a funded plan) or can simply pay this benefit out of its cash flow once you are entitled to receive benefits (an unfunded plan). If your employer makes contributions each year into a funded plan for your benefit, the contributions are not deductible by your employer. For this reason alone, most employees are not offered deferred compensation benefits.

Your main benefit of a deferred compensation plan is the money is not taxable income until received by you. However, in order to postpone the income taxation, the plan must provide that you have a "substantial risk of forfeiture." In other words, if you leave your employer prior to the agreed-on time, then you lose all benefits under the plan. Furthermore, since you have no legal rights in the plan until the agreed-on time, any funds that your employer has set aside for your benefit are subject to the general creditors of your employer. Therefore, your likelihood of receiving deferred compensation benefits in the future depends on the financial stability of your employer.

EMPLOYER STOCK OPTION PLANS

Another benefit that some employers give their employees is an option to purchase stock in the employer, known as an employer stock option plan. This is also known as a *stock option*. A stock option is the right to buy stock in the future, normally for a predetermined price. The purpose of a stock option to you, the employee, is the ability to participate in the future growth in the value of your employer. If, when you exercise the option, the price you pay for the stock of your employer is less than the fair market value of the stock, then you will have shared in the appreciation in value. There are two types of stock options: qualified (also known as incentive or statutory stock options) and nonqualified.

The taxation of stock options to you largely depends on whether the option is qualified or nonqualified. In essence there are three different times when a stock option could represent taxable income to you: (1) on your initial receipt of the option from your employer (receipt); (2) on your purchase of the stock through the exercise of the option (purchase); and (3) on your sale of the stock (sale).

With a qualified stock option, you do not pay regular income tax on your receipt (or grant) of the option from your employer or on your purchase of the stock. However, your purchase may be subject to alternative minimum income tax, so please consult your tax advisor. Provided you have held the stock for a certain period of time, when you sell the stock you would pay capital gain tax as opposed to ordinary income tax. The holding period is two years after your receipt of the option or one year after your purchase of the stock, which is later.

With a nonqualified stock option, you normally would not pay regular income tax on your receipt of the option unless it has a readily marketable value and is freely transferable. For example, if your stock option is traded on the stock market and you can transfer your option, then the option would be taxable to you on receipt. Unlike qualified stock options, nonqualified stock options are taxable to you on your purchase of the stock. Any gain is ordinary income regardless of how long you have held the option. Finally, on your sale of the stock, any gain from the date of your purchase to the date of sale would be ordinary income or capital gain, depending on how long you held the stock.

457 PLAN

A 457 plan is a nonqualified plan that can be established only by state and local governmental entities or tax-exempt organizations. Under the law, a state or local governmental entity (other than a public school or university) is not allowed to have a 401(k) or a 403(b) plan. Therefore, a 457 plan becomes an attractive alternative.

Although not a qualified plan, a 457 plan provides many of the same tax benefits. For instance, contributions are generally excludable from your gross income and accumulate tax-deferred inside the plan. If you are employed by a governmental entity, then amounts set aside in a 457 plan must be in the form of a trust, custodial account, or annuity contract exclusively for the benefit of you and your beneficiaries.

However, if you are employed by a tax-exempt entity, there is no requirement that amounts set aside be for your exclusive benefit. In fact, the law provides that all amounts set aside in a nongovernmental 457 plan must remain the sole property of your employer and be subject to your employer's creditors. Thus you run the risk that your employer may not have sufficient funds in the future to pay your benefits.

Your participation: A 457 plan is not required to be made available to all employees and therefore can discriminate among certain employees. In many circumstances your ability to participate in a 457 plan depends on your employer. If your employer is a governmental entity, then the 457 plan is usually available to all employees. On the other hand, if your employer is a nongovernmental entity, your participation usually depends on whether you are one of a select group of employees that your employer wants to be eligible for benefits.

As of 2002, you may participate in both a 457 plan and a 403(b) plan at the same time.

Your vesting: The assets of a nongovernmental 457 plan are held in trust by your employer for your benefit but are subject to the creditors of your employer. Unlike an IRA or qualified plan, your rights in a nongovernmental 457 plan are subject to a substantial risk of forfeiture. Therefore, your rights are not vested until your death or until you are entitled to voluntary withdrawals (generally your severance from employment or attaining 70½).

With regard to a governmental 457 plan, the funds must be set aside exclusively for your benefit.

There is no vesting period for your elective contributions. Your elective contributions are automatically 100% vested.

With regard to your employer's contributions, your governmental 457 plan may have a vesting period. Since a 457 plan is a nonqualified plan, the vesting period may be longer than required for a qualified plan.

Contributions by your employer: Your employer is not required to make contributions. There is no tax incentive for your employer to make contributions since your employer is a tax-exempt organization. If your employer makes contributions, then the total of all contributions by both you and your employer cannot exceed the contribution limit (see Tables 49-7 and 49-8 for contribution limits).

Contributions by you: You may be able to make contributions to your 457 plan provided that the plan allows elective contributions. If your 457 plan allows elective contributions, then the total amount of your contributions and your employer's contributions cannot exceed the contribution limit. With regard to a governmental 457 plan, if you are age 50 or older, you may make additional catch-up contributions (See Table 49-7 for contribution and catch-up limits.)

Also, a preretirement, catch-up provision applies to a 457 plan. You are allowed to make additional contributions during your last three years prior to retirement. The additional contribution is generally limited to twice your normal contribution. For any year you elect this preretirement, catch-up contribution, you are not allowed to also make your age 50 or older catch-up contribution.

You are not allowed to make any other contributions to your 457 plan.

Before 2002, your maximum contribution to a 457 plan was dependent on your contributions to other retirement plans. Furthermore, the total contribution limits to your 457 plan were lower than for other retirement plans. Beginning in 2002, your contributions to a 457 plan are not reduced by your contributions to other qualified plans during the same year. For example, for 2004, you could contribute up to $13,000 to your 457 plan and another $13,000 to your 401(k) plan.

Voluntary withdrawals by you: By law, a 457 plan must limit your ability to take withdrawals until the earlier of the calendar year in

(table 49-8)

EMPLOYER MAXIMUM CONTRIBUTION LIMITS FOR 2003

PLAN	CONTRIBUTION LIMIT
Defined benefit	Amount needed to provide annual retirement benefit no larger than smaller of $160,000* or average of three highest compensation years
Defined contribution, including money purchase pension, profit sharing, and 401(k)	Lesser of compensation† or $40,000*
SIMPLE 401(k) and SIMPLE IRA	Either nonelective contribution of 2% of compensation† for all employees; or dollar for dollar matching contribution up to 3% of compensation† for participating employees
SEP IRA	Lesser of 25% of compensation† or $40,000*
457	Combined contributions of employer and employee cannot exceed employee's maximum elective deferral limit
403(b)	Lesser of compensation or $40,000*, reduced by contributions to other qualified plans and 403(b) plans. If employee makes elective deferrals, then further reduced by amount of elective deferrals

*Amount subject to adjustment for inflation.
†Compensation generally limited to $200,000 (subject to inflation).

which you reach 70½, your severance from employment, or an unforeseeable emergency.

Distributions for an unforeseeable emergency are different from distributions for hardship under a 401(k) plan and the requirements are much harder to meet. Generally, an unforeseeable emergency is a severe financial hardship resulting from a sudden and unexpected illness or accident involving you, your spouse, or your dependents. It requires that you have exhausted all other financial means.

Loans may be permitted under a governmental 457 plan, but are prohibited under a nongovernmental 457 plan.

If you leave your employer, any withdrawals prior to 59½ are not subject to the 10% penalty for early withdrawals.

If you change employers, your funds in a governmental 457 plan can be rolled into an IRA. Alternatively, your governmental 457 plan can be rolled into another 457 plan, a qualified plan, or a 403(b) plan, provided the new plan accepts rollovers from 457 plans.

If you leave your employer, your funds in a nongovernmental 457 plan cannot be rolled over to any other type of retirement plan.

Mandatory withdrawals: Your 457 plan is subject to the minimum distribution rules, and you must begin withdrawals by April 1 of the year following the year in which you turn 70½.

403(B) PLAN

A 403(b) plan is a nonqualified plan that can only be established by employees of public education systems (e.g., schools, colleges, and universities); employees of tax-exempt charitable organizations (e.g., churches, hospitals, museums, and zoos); self-employed ministers; and employees of Native American tribal governments.

Historically, a 403(b) plan's only form of benefit was an annuity purchased through an insurance company, and therefore they were often called *tax-sheltered annuities (TSAs)*.

Generally a 403(b) plan will be funded in one of three ways:

1. Only with your elective contributions through salary deductions
2. Only with your employer's contributions
3. With your elective contributions and your employer's matching contributions

Your participation: A 403(b) plan is not required to be made available to all employees. In many circumstances your ability to participate in a 403(b) plan depends on whether you are one of a select group of employees that your employer wants to be eligible for benefits. However, if the 403(b) plan allows employee elective deferrals, then it must be made available to all employees.

Your vesting: There is no vesting period for your elective contributions. Your elective contributions are automatically 100% vested.

With regard to your employer's contributions, your 403(b) plan may have a vesting period. Since a 403(b) plan is a nonqualified plan, the vesting period may be longer than required for a qualified plan.

Contributions by your employer: Your employer is not required to make contributions, but may opt to make nonelective contributions, which can be in the form of a matching contribution, a discretionary contribution, or a mandatory contribution. The maximum annual contribution is limited by annual additions and elective deferrals. The *limit on annual additions* is the lesser of $40,000 (adjusted for inflation) or 100% of your compensation for your most recent year of service. It is further reduced by any contributions to other qualified plans for your benefit.

The *limit on elective deferrals* is the amount described in the next section "Contributions by You" and is shown on Table 49-7. It is further reduced by any elective deferrals you have made to other qualified plans and 403(b) plans in the same year.

- If the only form of contribution is your employer's nonelective contribution, then the maximum amount that can be made by your employer is the limit on annual additions.
- If the only form of contribution is your elective contribution, then the annual maximum amount is the lesser of the limit on annual additions or your limit on elective deferrals.
- If the form of contribution is both your employer's nonelective contribution and your elective contribution, then the combined contributions cannot exceed the limit on annual additions and your elective contributions cannot exceed your limit on elective deferrals.

Contributions by you: You may make elective contributions to a 403(b) plan through salary deductions. If age 50 or older, you may make additional catch-up contributions. (See Table 49-7 for contribution and catch-up limits.) Conversely, your limit on elective deferrals is further reduced by all elective contributions to other qualified plans and 403(b) plans in the same year.

Finally, if you have at least 15 years of service with a public school system, hospital, home health service agency, health and welfare service agency, or church, you may be eligible for a special increase in your elective deferral contributions.

Voluntary withdrawals by you: By law, a 403(b) plan must limit your ability to take withdrawals until age 59½, severance from employment, disability, or financial hardship, whichever occurs first. You may roll over your 403(b) plan into other qualified retirement plans, a regular IRA, or a governmental 457 plan. Within certain limits, you may borrow from your TSA custodial account (but not your TSA annuity contract). However, all loans must be repaid within five years.

Mandatory withdrawals: Your 403(b) plan is subject to the minimum distribution rules. For all contributions and earnings after 1986, you must begin withdrawals by April 1 of the year following the year in which you turn 70½.

Furthermore, all contributions and earnings prior to 1987 can be postponed until age 75 or separation from service, which is later.

Investment choices: Your investment choices are severely limited in a 403(b) plan. Generally, a 403(b) plan can invest only in tax-deferred annuities (a TSA annuity contract) or mutual funds (a TSA custodial account).

DISTRIBUTIONS FROM RETIREMENT PLANS

As stated earlier, the government has provided qualified plans and IRAs as an incentive for you to save for retirement. This money is designed to be used during your retirement years, not before retirement and certainly not as a wealth accumulation and transfer device after your death. In order to curtail any perceived abuses, penalties are imposed if you withdraw money before your retirement or fail to start withdrawing money during your retirement. The penalties take the form of two excise taxes: the premature distribution excise tax and the minimum distribution excise tax.

PREMATURE DISTRIBUTION EXCISE TAX

If you withdraw money from your IRA or qualified retirement plan prior to age 59½ you can be subject to a 10% *premature distribution excise tax*. In addition, all amounts withdrawn can become subject to ordinary income tax. However, exceptions are provided under the law. If you meet an exception, then you are not subject to the 10% excise tax. Most of the exceptions are provided below, but you should always consult with your tax advisor before taking an early distribution from your IRA or qualified plan.

Your separation from service: If you have separated from service (i.e., left your employer) and in the year of termination you are age 55 or older, then distributions from the qualified plan maintained with that employer are exempt from the penalty tax. This exception does not apply to IRAs or qualified plans of other employers.

Distributions not included in your gross income: If any distribution is not included in your gross income, then it is not subject to the 10% penalty. Normally this would include withdrawals of nondeductible contributions or rollovers.

Your death: If you die, all distributions to your beneficiaries are exempt from the 10% penalty tax.

Your disability: If you become disabled, you are not subject to the penalty tax. You meet the definition of *disability* if you are "unable to engage in any substantial gainful activity by reason of any medically determinable physical or mental impairment which can be expected to result in death or to be of long-continued and indefinite duration."

Substantially equal payments: If you begin to take distributions that are part of a series of substantially equal payments based on your life or life expectancy, then the 10% penalty tax does not apply. Generally, the law provides three methods to determine the payments: the life expectancy method, the amortization method, and the annuity method. Be aware that

49

the payments must continue for five years or until age 59½, whichever is later. If payments are stopped prior to that time, the 10% penalty will apply. Also, in order for the penalty not to apply to your qualified plan, you must have left your employment.

Your divorce: Distributions from your qualified plan to your ex-spouse pursuant to a divorce are not subject to the 10% penalty tax. However, caution must be maintained since only distributions pursuant to a qualified domestic relations order (QDRO) issued by the divorce court escapes the penalty. The law also allows the transfer of your IRA to your ex-spouse if it is pursuant to a divorce decree.

Your unreimbursed medical expenses: Distributions that are less than the amount of your unreimbursed medical expenses for a given year (after subtracting 7.5% of your adjusted gross income) are not subject to the penalty.

Your health insurance if you are unemployed: Distributions from your IRA that do not exceed the cost of medical insurance premiums for you, your spouse, and your dependents during a period of your unemployment may be exempt from the penalty tax.

Qualified higher education expenses: Distributions from your IRA for certain qualified higher education expenses for you, your spouse, children, or grandchildren are not subject to the penalty tax. These expenses generally include tuition, fees, books, supplies, equipment, and room and board for post-high school institutions.

First-time home purchasers: Distributions from your IRA for the first-time purchase of a home for you, your spouse, or your descendants or ancestors, are exempt from the penalty tax, as long as the funds are used within 120 days of your receipt. Furthermore, your lifetime limit is $10,000. *First-time purchase* is defined as not owning a home within two years from the date of the purchase of the new home.

MINIMUM DISTRIBUTION EXCISE TAX

If you do not start withdrawing money from your qualified plan or IRA during your retirement, then you will be subject to the *minimum distribution excise tax*. Unfortunately, this excise tax is larger than the premature distribution excise tax. The penalty is 50%. For example, if you are supposed to withdraw $1000 from your IRA and you only withdraw $100, then the penalty is $450 (50% of the $900 shortfall). In addition, the full $1000 will generally be subject to income tax!

BEGINNING DATE FOR DISTRIBUTIONS

The latest date that you can postpone distributions from your IRA or qualified plan is know as the *required beginning date*. For all IRAs, your required beginning date is *always* April 1 of the year following the year in which you turn 70½. For qualified plans, the beginning date is the same;

however, there is an exception if you are still working. With regard to plans maintained by your employer, you can postpone distributions until April 1 of the year following the year in which you separate from service (provided that the plan allows this exception). This exception only applies if you are an employee and you own 5% or less of the employer. If you are an employee and you also own more than a 5% interest in the employer, the IRS is concerned that you could manipulate your retirement date and thus indefinitely postpone your required beginning date.

In addition, the ability to postpone your required beginning date only applies to qualified plans maintained by *your current employer*. The required beginning date for qualified plans from your former employer is the same as that for all IRAs: April 1 of the year following the year in which you turn 70½.

FREQUENCY OF DISTRIBUTIONS

Once you reach your required beginning date, distributions from the IRA or qualified plan must be made at least annually. Each calendar year in which a distribution is required to be withdrawn is known as a distribution year.

The amount required to be withdrawn for a given distribution year is known as a required minimum distribution. The amount of each required minimum distribution is generally based on the balance of your IRA or qualified plan as of December 31 of the previous year and must be withdrawn by December 31 of the current distribution year.

The *first* distribution year is actually the year in which you turn 70½ (or the year in which you separate from service if the exception for qualified plans described above applies). The *first* required minimum distribution will therefore be based on the value of your IRA or qualified plan as of December 31 of the previous year. The normal rule that a required minimum distribution must be made by December 31 of the distribution year does not apply to the first required minimum distribution. The first required minimum distribution can be postponed until your required beginning date (April 1 of the following year). However, for the second and all subsequent distribution years, the required minimum distribution must be made by December 31 of that distribution year.

If you postpone your first required minimum distribution until the calendar year of your required beginning date, you will have to take two required minimum distributions in one taxable year. This could be bad or good depending on your other taxable income. In many circumstances, stacking income into one taxable year could force you into a higher income tax bracket, resulting in higher marginal rates and possibly the loss of itemized deductions. If, however, you anticipate a significant drop in taxable income in the next calendar year (for example, you retire), postponing your first required minimum distribution could result in an overall reduction of income taxes.

Obviously there is no one answer as to whether you should postpone your first required minimum distribution until the calendar year of your required beginning date. This decision should only be made after you have consulted your income tax advisor.

ACCOUNTS SUBJECT TO DISTRIBUTIONS

Once you reach your required beginning date, required minimum distributions must be determined for each IRA or qualified plan. Thus a separate calculation must be made for each of your IRAs or qualified plans. With regard to each qualified plan, you must withdraw your required minimum distribution each year from that plan by the annual due date (normally December 31 of the distribution year).

This is not the case with IRAs. You can total your required minimum distributions from all your IRAs and then choose from which IRAs to take the combined required minimum distributions.

THE DISTRIBUTION METHODS

In general there are two distribution methods: the annuity method and the life expectancy method.

The annuity method: With the *annuity method,* you receive a guaranteed monthly amount for the rest of your life (single life annuity) or for the joint lives of you and another individual (joint and survivor annuity). In addition, you can often elect a term-certain period that guarantees payment for a length of time in the event that you (in a single life annuity) or you and another individual (in a joint and survivor annuity) die before the fixed term. The fixed term ranges from 5 to 10 years.

The life expectancy method: With the *life expectancy method,* you could elect to receive distributions over your own life expectancy or over the joint life expectancy of you and another individual.

The life expectancy method involves tables published by the IRS. These tables are in IRS Publication 590. For single life expectancy, you determine your current age and the table (single life) shows the number of years before you are expected to die. Of course, in reality you will either die before, at, or after your life expectancy. For joint life expectancy, you determine your current age and the age of another individual, and the table (joint and last survivor) shows the number of years before both you and the other individual are expected to die.

The following shows single and joint life expectancies taken from the IRS life expectancy tables.

- The single life expectancy of a 70-year-old is 17 years.
- The joint life expectancy of a 70-year-old and a 60-year-old is 27.4 years.
- The joint life expectancy of a 70-year-old and an 80-year-old is 18.7 years.

Note that the joint life expectancy of two individuals is always longer than the single life expectancy of one individual, even in the circumstance where the one individual is older (e.g., the 80-year-old). The ability to use joint life expectancy is significant because it can reduce the amount of the annual required minimum distribution.

Knowing your options: It is crucial to find out, for each of your plans, whether your distribution options include the annuity method, the life expectancy method, or both. The options available depend on the type of plan. Almost all IRAs will allow either the annuity method or the life expectancy method.

As previously discussed, qualified plans are divided into two main types: account plans and annuity plans. Generally, account plans allow either the annuity method or the life expectancy method. Annuity plans normally have the annuity method as your only option.

REQUIRED MINIMUM DISTRIBUTIONS DURING YOUR LIFETIME

THE ANNUITY METHOD

With the annuity method, as long as the periodic payments are made in intervals not longer than one year and any term-certain period is not longer than 20 years, the minimum distribution rules is satisfied if the first periodic payment begins by your required beginning date. However, if the annuity does not meet the those requirements, then an amount totaling the annuity payments for one year (the *annual amount*) must be withdrawn by the required beginning date, and the annual amount must be withdrawn by December 31 of each subsequent distribution year.

THE LIFE EXPECTANCY METHOD

With the life expectancy method, the required minimum distribution is determined by dividing the account balance as of December 31 of the prior year by the life expectancy number obtained from the IRS tables. The life expectancy number is also known as the *divisor*.

Before January 1, 2003, you had the option of taking your lifetime required minimum distributions based on either your single life expectancy or a joint life expectancy if certain conditions were met. Normally, the ability to use joint life expectancy was quite complicated. It involved the following factors:

- The contractual options available under your IRA or qualified plan
- Your beneficiary designation as of your required beginning date
- Whether you had elected joint life expectancy

As of January 1, 2003, for purposes of determining your lifetime required minimum distributions under the life expectancy method, you are now automatically entitled to receive the benefit of a joint life expectancy calculation. With one exception, you determine your *lifetime* required

49

minimum distributions based solely on a uniform table. Table 49-9 shows the uniform table.

USING THE UNIFORM TABLE

As can be seen from the uniform table, you only need to know your age for the given distribution year. Based on your age, the uniform table provides a number of years of life expectancy. You simply divide your account balance (as of December 31 of the prior year) by the number provided in the uniform table (the divisor) to determine the required minimum distribution for that distribution year.

The required use of the uniform table results in the smallest required minimum distributions during your lifetime that would have been possible under the old law but without the complexities. The uniform table is actually a joint life expectancy table based on your age and an individual 10 years younger than you.

EXCEPTION TO USING THE UNIFORM TABLE

There is one exception to using the uniform table for calculating your lifetime required minimum distributions. If the only beneficiary of your plan during the entire calendar year is your spouse and if your spouse is more than 10 years younger than you, then you must use your actual joint life expectancy to determine the required minimum distribution for that year. Note that the ability to use the actual joint life expectancy of you and your young spouse is determined on an annual basis.

If your spouse dies or you divorce your spouse during a distribution year, the law allows you to continue to use the actual joint life expectancy table for that distribution year. However, for each subsequent year you must revert back to the uniform table (unless you again marry a spouse more than 10 years younger than yourself).

The following examples illustrate the use of the uniform table.

EXAMPLE

Example: You are 70, and you name your spouse, age 65, as the beneficiary of your IRA. Your actual joint life expectancy is 24.3 years. Your required minimum distribution is based on the uniform table for a 70-year-old (27.4 years), not your actual joint life expectancy of 24.3 years. This results in a 12% reduction of your required minimum distribution under the uniform table.

Example: You are 70, and you name your son, age 45, as the beneficiary of your IRA. Your actual joint life expectancy is 39.4 years. However, because your beneficiary is someone other than your spouse, you must take lifetime required minimum distributions under the uniform table. Your required minimum distribution under the uniform table is based on 27.4 years.

Example: You are 70, and your spouse is 55. As of January 1 your spouse was the sole beneficiary of your IRA. You do not change the beneficiary during the entire year. Your actual joint life expectancy is 31.1 years. Your required minimum distribution, based on the uniform table for a 70-year-old is 27.4. However, because you named your spouse as the sole beneficiary of your

(table 49-9)

THE UNIFORM TABLE

AGE	DIVISOR
70	27.4
71	26.5
72	25.6
73	24.7
74	23.8
75	22.9
76	22.0
77	21.2
78	20.3
79	19.5
80	18.7
81	17.9
82	17.1
83	16.3
84	15.5
85	14.8
86	14.1
87	13.4
88	12.7
89	12.0
90	11.4
91	10.8
92	10.2
93	9.6
94	9.1
95	8.6
96	8.1
97	7.6
98	7.1
99	6.7
100	6.3
101	5.9
102	5.5
103	5.2
104	4.9
105	4.5
106	4.2
107	3.9
108	3.7
109	3.4
110	3.1
111	2.9
112	2.6
113	2.4
114	2.1
115+	1.9

IRA for the entire year and your spouse is more than 10 years younger than you, you must use your actual joint life expectancy of 31.1 years to determine your required minimum distribution for that year.

REQUIRED MINIMUM DISTRIBUTIONS AFTER YOUR DEATH

The minimum distribution rules apply both during your lifetime and after your death. To the extent that there are benefits remaining in the IRA or qualified plan at your death, required minimum distributions must continue to your beneficiary until all benefits have been distributed from your account.

The amount of each required minimum distribution will depend on the person named as the beneficiary of the qualified plan or IRA.

WHO IS ENTITLED TO YOUR ACCOUNT BALANCE?

With regard to your IRAs, you normally have the freedom to choose who will receive any remaining funds at the date of your death. This is done through a beneficiary designation form that must be completed, signed by you, and delivered to your IRA custodian prior to the date of your death. You have the right to choose one or more **primary beneficiaries** and one or more contingent beneficiaries. **Contingent beneficiaries** are those who are entitled to your account balance in the event that all primary beneficiaries die before you. Normally, you are not restricted as to whom you can name as a beneficiary. You can name your spouse, your children, or other individuals. In addition, you can name entities, such as a corporation, a charity, a trust, or your own estate.

The same is usually true with regard to your qualified plans. As a general rule, you have the freedom to decide who will receive any remaining funds at the date of your death. A beneficiary designation form can be obtained from your employer or its human resources (HR) department.

However, sometimes there are legal restrictions on naming a beneficiary of your IRA or qualified plan. Most restrictions on IRAs are based on state law. If you are married and live in a community property state, state law may provide that you must name your spouse as your beneficiary or obtain your spouse's consent if you name someone else.

Most restrictions on qualified plans are based on federal law. The Employee Retirement Income Security Act of 1974 (ERISA) and the Retirement Equity Act of 1984 (REA) are two federal laws that govern most qualified plans. These laws were enacted to protect both employees and their spouses. If you are an employee, the main protection is found in the "antialienation" rules. These rules prevent you from transferring your interest in your plan during your lifetime and also prevent others (such as creditors) from gaining access to your benefits. In addition, these rules protect your spouse by providing default provisions in the event of your death.

In general, if you die before distributions have begun, then your spouse must receive some or all of your remaining benefits either outright or in the form of a qualified preretirement survivor annuity. Once you start taking distributions, your remaining benefits must be paid to you in the form of a qualified joint and survivor annuity. On your death, the continuing annuity amount paid to your spouse must be at least 50% and not more than 100% of the annuity amount paid to you during your lifetime.

However, you can waive the right to receive benefits in the form of a qualified preretirement survivor annuity or qualified joint and survivor annuity provided that your spouse consents. Thus if you want to name a beneficiary apart from your spouse, your spouse must agree. Your spouse's consent must be in writing and must be notarized or signed in the presence of a plan representative. You employer (again, generally, the human resources department) can assist you with regard to obtaining spousal consent forms.

CATEGORIZING YOUR BENEFICIARY

Under the law, your beneficiary falls into one of three special categories: surviving spouse, designated beneficiary, and all others (nondesignated beneficiary). Each category has its own set of minimum distribution rules. Determining whether your beneficiary fits within the designated beneficiary category is usually easy. In simple terms, a beneficiary is classified as a designated beneficiary if the beneficiary is an individual. Thus your child, grandchild, parent, sibling, relative, friend, or any other individual is a designated beneficiary. A class of individuals capable of expansion or contraction may also fit within the category of designated beneficiary. Thus a beneficiary designation such as "my children" or "my grandchildren" falls within the category.

By default, if your beneficiary does not fit within the category of spouse or designated beneficiary, then it is classified as a nondesignated beneficiary. *Nondesignated beneficiaries* are generally entities. Thus if you name a corporation, a charity, a trust, or your own estate, your beneficiary is a nondesignated beneficiary.

Whether your beneficiary is a designated or nondesignated beneficiary greatly affects the length of the payout period after your death. In general, if your beneficiary is a designated beneficiary, then he or she is allowed to take after–death required minimum distribution based on his or her single life expectancy. See Table 49-10 for determining the life expectancy of an individual.

If your beneficiary is a nondesignated beneficiary, the after–death required minimum distributions are based on a five-year payout or your remaining hypothetical life expectancy, depending on whether you die before or after your required beginning date. In either event, distributions are generally paid out much more quickly.

(table 49-10)

SINGLE LIFE EXPECTANCY

AGE	LIFE EXPECTANCY	AGE	LIFE EXPECTANCY	AGE	LIFE EXPECTANCY	AGE	LIFE EXPECTANCY
0	82.4	29	54.3	58	27.0	87	6.7
1	81.6	30	53.3	59	26.1	88	6.3
2	80.6	31	52.4	60	25.2	89	5.9
3	79.7	32	51.4	61	24.4	90	5.5
4	78.7	33	50.4	62	23.5	91	5.2
5	77.7	34	49.4	63	22.7	92	4.9
6	76.7	35	48.5	64	21.8	93	4.6
7	75.8	36	47.5	65	21.0	94	4.3
8	74.8	37	46.5	66	20.2	95	4.1
9	73.8	38	45.6	67	19.4	96	3.8
10	72.8	39	44.6	68	18.6	97	3.6
11	71.8	40	43.6	69	17.8	98	3.4
12	70.8	41	42.7	70	17.0	99	3.1
13	69.9	42	41.7	71	16.3	100	2.9
14	68.9	43	40.7	72	15.5	101	2.7
15	67.9	44	39.8	73	14.8	102	2.5
16	66.9	45	38.8	74	14.1	103	2.3
17	66.0	46	37.9	75	13.4	104	2.1
18	65.0	47	37.0	76	12.7	105	1.9
19	64.0	48	36.0	77	12.1	106	1.7
20	63.0	49	35.1	78	11.4	107	1.5
21	62.1	50	34.2	79	10.8	108	1.4
22	61.1	51	33.3	80	10.2	109	1.2
23	60.1	52	32.3	81	9.7	110	1.1
24	59.1	53	31.4	82	9.1	111+	1.0
25	58.2	54	30.5	83	8.6		
26	57.2	55	29.6	84	8.1		
27	56.2	56	28.7	85	7.6		
28	55.3	57	27.9	86	7.1		

MULTIPLE BENEFICIARIES

What happens if at your death, more than one beneficiary is entitled to receive your account balance? Each beneficiary must be classified into one of the three categories. If any beneficiary falls within the nondesignated beneficiary category, then the general rule is that all your beneficiaries are deemed to be nondesignated beneficiaries. One bad apple spoils the whole bunch!

On the other hand, if all the beneficiaries fall within the category of designated beneficiary, another problem arises. As mentioned above, a designated beneficiary is allowed to take after-death distributions based on his or her single life expectancy. If you have multiple designated beneficiaries, then whose life expectancy do you use? Fortunately, the IRS provides a clear-cut answer, but it is not in your family's favor. Each beneficiary must take after-death required minimum distributions based on the life expectancy of the oldest designated beneficiary. This is known as the "oldest heart" rule.

EXCEPTION FOR CERTAIN TRUSTS

A trust is a legal entity. Therefore, the general rule is that a trust does not qualify as a designated beneficiary since a trust is not an individual. However, under the law, there is an exception for certain trusts. A trust can qualify as a designated beneficiary if it meets a five-part test.

1. The trust must be valid under state law. In many states this means that the trust must be in writing and signed by the creator (i.e., you).
2. All beneficiaries of the trust must be individuals.
3. All beneficiaries of the trust must be identifiable. Classes of beneficiaries capable of expansion (e.g., "my children" or "my descendants") are allowed provided that it is possible to ascertain the trust beneficiary with the shortest life expectancy.
4. A copy of the trust must be delivered to the plan administrator. In lieu of providing a copy of the whole trust document, a certification of trust is allowed. In general, a copy of the trust does not have to be delivered to the plan administrator during your lifetime. However, if your spouse is the sole beneficiary of the trust and your spouse is more than 10 years younger than you, you have to provide a copy of the trust (or the certified information) to the plan administrator by your required beginning date. On your death, a copy of the trust (or the certified information) must be delivered to the plan administrator by October 31 of the year following your death.
5. The trust must become irrevocable no later than your death.

If a trust meets this five-part test, then all beneficiaries of the trust are designated beneficiaries for purposes of the minimum distribution rules. If there are multiple individual beneficiaries of the trust, the oldest heart rule applies, and the trust beneficiary with the shortest life expectancy is the designated beneficiary for purposes of determining all after-death required minimum distributions.

Qualifying a trust as a designated beneficiary is no easy task. With the changes in the law after 2002, the ability of a trust to meet parts 2 and 3 of the five-part test is more difficult. If you want to name a trust as the beneficiary of your qualified plan and IRA and you want that trust to meet the designated beneficiary test after your death, you must plan carefully. You should consult with an estate planning attorney who is familiar with the minimum distribution rules in order to ensure that all your estate planning goals are accomplished.

DEATH BEFORE YOUR REQUIRED BEGINNING DATE

As previously discussed, after your death, your beneficiaries fall within one of three special categories: surviving spouse, designated beneficiary, and nondesignated beneficiary. The distribution period for after-death required minimum distribution varies depending on the category and also depending on whether you die before or after your required beginning date.

The following distribution periods apply if you die before your required beginning date.

Surviving Spouse: If your beneficiary is your spouse, then he or she has two options: rollover or leave funds in your plan.

Rollover: Your spouse can roll over all (or any part of) your account balance into his or her own IRA. The rollover is available even if your spouse has reached his or her required beginning date. Once the funds are rolled over, your spouse is treated as the owner of the IRA and can name new beneficiaries to receive any remaining funds on his or her death.

If your spouse has not reached his or her required beginning date, your spouse can postpone distributions until that time. However, if your surviving spouse has not reached 59½, any distributions by your spouse prior to that date will be subject to the 10% penalty for early withdrawal, unless an exception applies.

If your spouse has already reached his or her required beginning date, then for purposes of the rollover IRA, his or her required beginning date will be December 31 of the year following the year the IRA was rolled over.

Leave funds in your plan: Alternatively, your spouse can choose to leave the funds in your IRA or qualified plan. In that circumstance, required minimum distributions must begin by December 31 of the year following your death or by December 31 of the year in which you would have turned 70½, whichever is later.

Each annual required minimum distribution during your spouse's lifetime is based on his or her recalculated single life expectancy using the single life table. On your spouse's death, any remaining benefits must be distributed over your spouse's hypothetical remaining (fixed-term) life expectancy.

If, on the other hand, your spouse dies before distributions are required to commence (as provided above), then for purposes of required minimum distributions after your spouse's death, your spouse is deemed to be the participant and is deemed to have died before his or her required beginning date. In that circumstance, the beneficiaries must take required minimum distributions based on whether they are designated or nondesignated beneficiaries.

Designated beneficiary: If your beneficiary falls within the category of designated beneficiary, then required minimum distributions must commence by December 31 of the year following the year of your death.

The required minimum distributions are normally based on the life expectancy of the designated beneficiary. The life expectancy of the designated beneficiary is determined from the single life table and based on the actual age of the designated beneficiary in the year in which distributions must begin (the year following your death) and are reduced by one for each subsequent withdrawal year.

There is one possibility that a designated beneficiary will not be allowed to use his or her life expectancy. The law allows the IRA or qualified plan to specify whether the five-year rule or the life expectancy rule applies to designated beneficiaries. The *five-year rule* requires that all funds remaining in your IRA or qualified plan must be distributed by December 31 of the fifth year following your death. If the plan does not specify either rule, then the life expectancy rule is mandatory.

If the plan provides for the election by the beneficiary of either rule but does not state which rule applies in the event of the failure of the beneficiary to make the election, then the life expectancy rule is mandatory. Once made, an election by the beneficiary is irrevocable and applies to all subsequent distribution years.

The following example illustrates the determination of after-death required minimum distributions for a designated beneficiary if you die before your required beginning date.

EXAMPLE

You are 58, die on March 4, 2004, and own one IRA. The sole beneficiary of your IRA is your son. The terms of the IRA allow a designated beneficiary to take distributions based on his or her single life expectancy. Your son's first required minimum distribution must be withdrawn by December 31, 2005. Your son's age in the year following your death is 32. Based on the single life table, the life expectancy of a 32-year-old is 51.4. Therefore, the amount of the first required minimum distribution is determined by dividing the account balance as of December 31, 2004, by 51.4. The second required minimum distribution must be withdrawn by December 31, 2006. The amount of the distribution is determined by dividing the account balance as of December 31, 2005, by 50.4. And so on until the account balance has been completely distributed.

Nondesignated beneficiary: If you die before your required beginning date and your beneficiaries fall within the nondesignated category, then the five-year rule applies. Under that rule, all funds remaining in your

IRA or qualified plan must be distributed by December 31 of the fifth year following your death. There is no requirement of any minimum annual distribution, as long as all the benefits are withdrawn by that December 31 deadline.

DEATH AFTER YOUR REQUIRED BEGINNING DATE

The following distribution periods apply if you die after your required beginning date.

Surviving spouse: If you die after your required beginning date, the distribution options for your surviving spouse are essentially the same as if you died before your required beginning date, with one exception. If, as of the date of your death, you have not withdrawn your required minimum distribution for that year, then your required minimum distribution must be withdrawn by December 31 of the year of your death. Your spouse cannot roll over this amount into his or her own IRA. Your spouse is, however, allowed to roll over the remainder.

Designated beneficiary: If your beneficiary falls within the category of designated beneficiary, then required minimum distributions must commence by December 31 of the year following your death. The required minimum distributions are normally based on either the life expectancy of the designated beneficiary or your remaining hypothetical life expectancy, whichever is longer. The life expectancy of the designated beneficiary is taken from the single life table and based on the actual age of the designated beneficiary in the year in which distributions must begin (the year following your death) and will be reduced by one for each subsequent withdrawal year.

Your hypothetical life expectancy is determined from the single life table and based on your actual age in the year of your death and will be reduced by one for each subsequent withdrawal year.

Nondesignated beneficiary: If you die after your required beginning date and your beneficiary falls within the nondesignated category, then the after-death distribution period is your remaining hypothetical life expectancy determined in the year in which you die and reduced by one for each subsequent year.

POSTPONEMENT OF DETERMINATION DATE

As previously discussed, after your death, your beneficiaries fall within one of three special categories: surviving spouse, designated beneficiary, and nondesignated beneficiary. However, for purposes of determining your after-death distribution period, this classification is not made at the moment of your death. Rather the IRS postpones this classification until September 30 of the year following your death. This is known as the *determination date*. Based on when you die in a given year, the determination date can be anywhere from 12 to 21 months after your date of death.

The postponement of the determination date can work in favor of your beneficiaries. If you have named multiple beneficiaries and some are designated beneficiaries and others are nondesignated beneficiaries, the general rule is that you have no designated beneficiaries. However, there are at least three planning opportunities that can be utilized to overcome this situation: disclaimer, distribution, and division.

Disclaimer: The first opportunity involves the ability of your beneficiary to disclaim part or all of the plan benefits. Under the law, a person cannot be forced to accept an inheritance. This includes your beneficiary entitled to IRA or qualified plan benefits. Your beneficiary can always refuse to accept your plan benefits.

This refusal is accomplished through the use of a disclaimer. In simple terms, a disclaimer is a legal no thank you. It is an irrevocable written refusal to accept property. If the beneficiary of your plan benefits disclaims his, her, or its right to those benefits, then the benefits will be distributed as if that beneficiary has died before you. Normally the proceeds would then pass to your contingent beneficiary. If there is no contingent beneficiary, the proceeds are distributed under the default provisions of your IRA or qualified plan.

Disclaimers allow after-death income tax, estate tax, and personal planning flexibility. This is accomplished by naming primary and contingent beneficiaries and then "targeting" the proceeds to the appropriate beneficiary.

In summary, once a beneficiary disclaims your retirement benefits, that beneficiary is deemed to have died before you and is no longer a beneficiary on the determination date.

Distribution: The second opportunity involves the ability to make after-death distributions before the determination date. If a beneficiary has received all of his or her share of plan benefits prior to the determination date, that beneficiary is no longer considered a "beneficiary" as of the determination date.

Division: The third after-death planning opportunity involves the ability to divide the IRA or qualified plan into separate accounts or shares before December 31 of the year following your death.

If you have named multiple beneficiaries and if all the named beneficiaries are designated beneficiaries, then for purposes of determining after-death required minimum distributions, the beneficiary with the shortest life expectancy (the oldest beneficiary) is the designated beneficiary. However, if separate accounts or shares are formed for each beneficiary before December 31 of the year following your death, each designated beneficiary is allowed to take after-death required minimum distributions based on his or her remaining individual life expectancy.

SUMMARY OF MINIMUM DISTRIBUTION RULES

You must begin taking distributions from your account as of your required beginning date. Once you reach your required beginning date, you must take a required minimum distribution at least annually.

The amount of your required minimum distribution depends on one of two distribution methods: the annuity method or the life expectancy method. Under the life expectancy method, your required minimum distribution is generally determined by using the IRS uniform table. To determine the amount of your required minimum distribution, you divide the plan balance as of December 31 of the prior year into the divisor found on the uniform table.

After your death, your beneficiaries are classified as being a surviving spouse, designated beneficiary, or nondesignated beneficiary. In order for a beneficiary to be a designated beneficiary, the beneficiary must be an individual. A designated beneficiary is generally allowed to take after-death required minimum distributions over his or her remaining single life expectancy. If you have named more than one beneficiary, you must look to the oldest beneficiary. If all your beneficiaries are classified as designated beneficiaries, then all beneficiaries must take after-death distributions based on the oldest beneficiary. If any beneficiary is classified as a nondesignated beneficiary, you are deemed not to have any designated beneficiary.

Even though a trust is not an individual, it can qualify as a designated beneficiary if it meets a five-part test. Be careful on naming trusts as beneficiaries of your IRA and qualified plans.

If you die *before* your required beginning date, after-death distributions depend on your beneficiary's classification. If your beneficiary is your surviving spouse, he or she can roll over your account balance into his or her own IRA or leave the proceeds in your account and start distributions when you would have reached 70½. If your beneficiary is a designated beneficiary, then generally distributions can be made over the life expectancy of the designated beneficiary. If your beneficiary is a nondesignated beneficiary, the five-year rule applies, and the entire account must be distributed by December 31 of the fifth year following your death.

If you die *after* your required beginning date, after-death distributions depend on your beneficiary's classification. If your beneficiary is your surviving spouse, he or she can roll over your account balance into his or her own IRA or leave the proceeds in your account and start distributions by December 31 of the year following your death. If your beneficiary is a designated beneficiary, then generally distributions can be made over the longer of the life expectancy of the designated beneficiary or your remaining hypothetical life expectancy. If your beneficiary is a nondesignated beneficiary, distributions can be made over your remaining hypothetical life expectancy.

The classification of your beneficiary is not made immediately at the date of your death. It is postponed until the determination date, which is September 30 of the year following your death. Before the determination date, three strategies can be used to eliminate or isolate beneficiaries: (1) A beneficiary can disclaim his or her rights to your account proceeds to allow distribution to contingent beneficiaries, (2) all account proceeds can be distributed, and (3) separate shares or accounts can be formed for each beneficiary before December 31 of the year following your death.

WHAT YOU NEED TO KNOW

▶ It is your responsibility to plan for your retirement.

▶ The three main sources of retirement income are earned income, personal savings and investments, and retirement plans.

▶ Retirement plans include government, individual, and employer plans. The main government retirement plan is Social Security. Unfortunately for many retirees, Social Security accounts for less than 40% of all retirement income; therefore, you must take advantage of individual and employer retirement plans.

▶ Most individual and employer retirement plans are designed to provide you with an incentive to save in the form of tax-deductible contributions and tax-deferred growth. Because of these incentives, money inside a retirement plan will generally grow much faster than money outside of a retirement plan. The most common type of individual plan is the deductible IRA, and the most common type of employer plan is the 401(k). In order to maximize your retirement savings, you should take full advantage of both individual and employer plans. You must determine your ability to participate in these plans, your maximum contribution limits, and other features of the various plans.

▶ Both your individual and employer retirement plans are subject to a 10% penalty tax if you take money prior to retirement (premature distribution excise tax). Once you reach your required beginning date (usually April 1 of the year in which you reach 70½), you must take annual minimum distributions from your retirement plans in order to avoid a 50% penalty tax (minimum distribution excise tax). Although a complex task under prior law, determining your lifetime annual minimum distribution amount is a now a simple calculation.

▶ After your death, your beneficiaries must continue to take annual minimum distributions until your retirement plan has been exhausted. The amount of the after-death annual minimum distributions will depend on the beneficiary you have named and whether you die before or after your required beginning date. Therefore, you should consult your estate planning professional before naming the beneficiary of your retirement plan.

FOR MORE INFORMATION

▷ Social Security Administration
800-772-1213
Web: www.ssa.gov

▷ Civil Service Retirement System
Web: www.opm.gov/retire/html/library/csrs.asp
Web: www.seniors.gov/fedcalc.html
The first site has general information; the latter can calculate your estimated CSRS benefits.

▷ Federal Employees Retirement System
Web: www.opm.gov/retire/html/library/fers.asp
Web: www.seniors.gov/fedcalc.html
The first site has general information; the latter can calculate your estimated FERS benefits.

▷ Internal Revenue Service
Web: www.irs.gov/formspubs
For small business retirement plans (SEP, SIMPLE, and qualified plans), download IRS Publication 560; for 403(b) plans, download IRS Publication 571; for IRAs, download IRS Publication 590.

▷ CCH Financial Planning Toolkit
Web: www.finance.cch.com
General information on financial, retirement, and estate planning.

Frugality includes all other virtues.

    —Cicero

THE AUTHOR

50

RICHARD W. DUFF has marketing and law degrees from the State University of Iowa. He is an insurance and financial advisor in Denver, Colorado, and author of the consumer-friendly books *Keep Every Last Dime, Money Magic with Annuities,* and *Take Charge of Your IRA.* Dick has been quoted by *USA Today* and *Mutual Fund Magazine,* and has appeared on CNN, PBS, WGN, CBS, and numerous radio talk shows. Since 1996, his imaginative monthly columns have appeared in the *Journal of Financial Planning, Senior Market Advisor,* and *Broker World* magazines. Dick is a popular speaker at seminars and workshops for consumers and financial planners. He is also an expert witness and advisor in litigation in which annuity and life insurance values are in dispute. To explore his publications and services, see "For More Information" at the end of this chapter.

50 PERSONAL ANNUITIES DU JOUR

Annuity comes from a Latin word, annuus, or yearly. The concept of annuity income dates to A.D. 225 and was developed by a Roman jurist named Ulpian. Sometimes referred to as upside-down life insurance (where the insurance company pays you for life instead of the other way around), Webster's defines annuity as "a series of periodic payments over one's lifetime or a period of years."

In this chapter, I take the mystery out of what can be a very complex subject. To begin, I trace briefly the history of annuities and straighten out terms like *premium, annuitant, annuitizing,* and *beneficiary.* Afterward I outline the thinking and strategies that make annuities so compelling—truly the cornerstone to any sound financial plan.

Note: This chapter is about *personal* annuities—policies issued by U.S commercial insurance companies to or for individual policy owners. It is not about *private, charitable gift,* or *group* annuities. Facts and figures about personal annuities are based on data provided by the American Council of Life Insurers (ACLI) in its *Life Insurance Fact Books.*

HISTORY

RENAISSANCE ANNUITIES

In the 1600s, Renaissance mathematicians defined length of life, laws of probability, and a theory of gambling involving actuarial thinking. Most of our early information about these concepts is traced to Newton, Gallileo, Pascal, and even Rembrandt. Interestingly, the Dutch and English financed themselves in the 17th, 18th, and 19th centuries by offering "the promise of an income for life" in exchange for up-front cash.

During the 1600s, the French were fascinated with *tontines* that involved annuities. In return for lump sums, purchasers received lifelong incomes; as payees died one by one, the survivors' annuity payments increased until a single person received all the remaining cash—sort of a "you lose, I win" financial plan. For obvious reasons, this potential windfall at someone's expense is no longer legal in most civilized societies.

ANNUITIES IN THE UNITED STATES

The first annuity here was offered in 1759, to a group of Presbyterian ministers. But annuities flourished mostly after the Great Depression, when insurance companies were seen as especially stable institutions. (Even Babe Ruth became an enthusiast after being steered into annuities, a strategy that enabled him to weather 1929's stock market crash.) Indeed, at the end of the 20th century, over 44 million personal annuities were in force and worth about $900 billion. There was an additional $900 billion in group annuities held by employer-sponsored pension plans. This $1.8 trillion was nearly three times the amount on hand in 1990. (Actually, the dollar amounts refer to industry "reserves," a complicated safety net maintained by insurance companies to back up their policies. If in 2000 all annuities were cashed in, it's likely that surrender values would be somewhat less than the amount of the reserves behind them.)

From the 1930s into the 1970s, insurers normally sold personal annuities (in units of $10 income monthly usually starting at age 65), to augment workers' pensions and Social Security. Most policies had guaranteed cash values that could be withdrawn or borrowed by the policy owner along the way. Since the 1970s, policy owners have put cash in annuity contracts for a variety of reasons (and not so much to guarantee a stream of income at retirement).

Today, personal annuities come in many shapes, and you need to do your homework to know which policy is best for you. It's also important to obtain copies of insurance company ratings from A.M. Best, Moody, and Standard & Poor. (See Chapters 47 and 48 for additional discussion on insurance rating companies.) To learn more on what others say about annuities and how to use them in your financial planning, see "For More Information," at the end of this chapter.

KEY TERMS, PARTIES, AND PHRASES

In casual conversation, everyone understands when a friend has "come into an annuity," slang for good fortune. But if you look into actual annuities issued by insurance companies, it can get confusing. This is largely due to the industry's lingo; let's clarify some of this.

TYPES OF POLICIES

You pay cash deposits *(premiums)* into annuities. It can purchase a personal contract with a view to receiving income later in life, or simply to stash money for a rainy day. Call these accumulation annuities, during the buildup phase. If converted eventually to an income stream, the policy is *annuitized* and becomes a *payout* policy; if it pays "as long as you live," it is said to have a life contingency. Of course, if you want income right away, you can acquire an *immediate payout annuity* policy, which can make payments as early as next month.

You may acquire a personal annuity (1) in your name *(nonqualified policies)* or (2) in your IRA, 401(k), Keogh, tax-sheltered annuity (TSA), or profit sharing account *(qualified policies)*.

EXAMPLE

At age 65, you acquire a personal annuity with lifetime payments beginning next month—a nonqualified, immediate payout annuity with a life contingency. Or when you reach 55, your IRA purchases an annuity for income at age 70½—a qualified, accumulation annuity policy. Get the idea?

All annuities are regulated by the states and are either fixed or variable. Insurance agents sell them, and are licensed under your state insurance department's rules. To market variable policies, agents must also have an appropriate securities license.

Fixed personal policies safeguard your principal and had cash values in 2000 of about $300 billion. Fixed accumulation annuities have a guaranteed minimum rate of interest, usually 3 or 4% each year or a current rate, if higher. There may even be stock market–like upside (an *indexed* fixed annuity), by which the insurance company credits interest based on, say, the Standard & Poor's (S&P) 500 index.

Variable personal policies are regulated by the Securities and Exchange Commission (SEC) and the National Association of Securities Dealers (NASD), and these had cash values in 2000 of $600 billion. You receive a prospectus before the sales process of a variable personal annuity begins. Usually, your upside is unlimited and depends on the performance of selected mutual funds. Of course, there can be unlimited downside too. Variable accumulation annuities have a variety of death benefits that add extra value for your beneficiary. Some newer policies have guaranteed minimum lifetime values for you as well.

Both fixed and variable accumulation policies can be annuitized into payout policies with income streams. If fixed, the insurance company guarantees your income; if variable, the payments rise or fall with values in the mutual funds.

IMPORTANT PEOPLE IN ANNUITY POLICIES

Marriage is great institution, but I'm not ready for an institution.
—*Mae West*

Policy owners have the right to name beneficiaries and annuitants, surrender for cash, or turn accumulation policies into streams of income. *Insurers* write the policy in which their guarantees and promises are spelled out.

The term **annuitant** doesn't mean much in an annuity's accumulation period. However, during the payout phase, his or her life expectancy measures the income the payee receives.

SOMEDAY SON, THIS WILL ALL BE HERS.

Courtesy of Mark Fiore.

EXAMPLE

As a male age 50, you purchase an accumulation annuity naming a sister, age 55, your annuitant. Fifteen years later when you annuitize the policy, the insurance company assumes it will pay over the life expectancy of a female age 70—or 18 years. (If, instead, you are the annuitant, any income would be based on your own life expectancy of a male age 65—perhaps 20 years).

The payee in most policies is the annuitant or policy owner; occasionally, the policy owner names another person to take the annuity payments. The beneficiary receives what's left at an annuitant's or policy owner's death.

EXAMPLE

You annuitize a policy to receive income guaranteed for 20 years. If you die after 10 years, your beneficiary receives "your payments" for the remaining 10 years.

ADDITIONAL TERMS

The policy's maturity date, usually is the annuitant's age 80, 85, or 90, when an income stream begins automatically. In most policies, insurers assess surrender charges that decline in percentages, usually after a penalty-free withdrawal is determined.

There are two main reasons for surrender charges: First, insurers commit annuity money into long-term investments, and the charges discourage short-term withdrawals. Second, there are commissions and startup costs that surrender fees can recoup. *The bottom line:* Don't be too surprised if there is a charge to surrender your annuity in the early years; certificates of deposit, securities, and most other investments also incur fees, charges, and commissions when reduced to cash.

ACCUMULATION ANNUITY POLICIES DU JOUR

More people should learn to tell their dollars where to go instead of asking them where they went.
—Roger W. Babson

In 2000, $140 billion was paid into personal annuities. There were 44 million personal accumulation policies in force—one for about every six U.S. citizens—worth over $800 billion. This certainly indicates that annuities are popular when it comes to saving money.

But accumulation policies are more than a place to park cash for a rainy day. They are a great way to defer taxes, protect assets (in some states) from creditors and lawsuits, pass property to loved ones, and save taxes on Social Security income payments. Let's look at some of these strategies one by one.

BUILDING CAPITAL FOR RETIREMENT

An income tax form is like a laundry list—either way you lose your shirt.
—Fred Allen

For many, the really good news about accumulation annuities is that the buildup isn't taxed as long as it stays in the policy. That's why they are sometimes called **tax-deferred annuities**.

These possibilities demonstrate the potency of tax advantages in annuities. In effect, Congress permits policy owners to keep their tax money as long as the buildup stays in the policy.

PROTECTING CAPITAL FROM LAWSUITS AND CREDITORS

A fool and her money are soon courted.
　　　　—Helen Rowland

Since the Great Depression, states have uniformly given annuity policyholders and payees some measure of creditor protection for their policies. Some of these laws are out of date, and you need to review them carefully before assuming that annuity values are safe from others. Here is a summary:

Group A consists of about 15 states that clearly protect a policy owner's annuity cash values. For instance, Texas law says that the proceeds of annuity contracts "are fully exempt from creditors and from all demands

THE POPULARITY OF ANNUITIES

Here are just a few reasons why personal, nonqualified annuities should be a part of most financial plans:

- Annuity policies are unilateral contracts written by the insurer which make promises to you. If there are ambiguities or disputes, a court should resolve matters in your favor.
- You can determine when to pay taxes on profit in a policy. Let's say $10,000 interest has accrued in an accumulation annuity. When your tax bracket is high, leave this profit in the policy. If your tax bracket is low, you might take out $10,000.
- Unlike an IRA, a 401(k), a Keogh, or a tax-sheltered annuity, there are no limits on premiums into a nonqualified annuity. You don't take a tax deduction when you pay a premium; only the growth portion is taxed later when taken from the policy.
- Unlike a traditional IRA that has mandatory distributions at your age 70½, you can leave everything intact until the annuity's maturity date— perhaps at age 90 or beyond.
- If married and you die, your spouse-beneficiary can continue your accumulation policy until the maturity date or when he or she dies.

- If an insurer gets into financial difficulty, it is common for another carrier to acquire the assets and assume all obligations of the troubled company. If a company is liquidated eventually, all states guarantee your values in a fixed policy, up to a limit of usually $100,000 or more.
- Although virtually all annuities have charges for early withdrawals, some companies don't penalize withdrawals for nursing home expenses or a terminal illness. And some policies give more income for long-term care or extra values at death.
- Accumulation policies are 100% liquid, and your insurer will get you your cash within days or even hours. If you assign a policy to a lender, it will be prime collateral, and the interest rate should be favorable.
- In some states, annuity income paid to a healthy spouse avoids her unhealthy spouse's Medicaid claims.
- Some policies credit bonuses on annuity premiums paid in the early years.
- Annuities have a free-look period, typically 10 to 30 days after you receive a policy, when you can take a full refund without paying any charges.

in any bankruptcy and from execution, attachment, garnishment, or other legal process." How much clearer can it be? You'd think all Texas residents would have some of their nest egg in one or more annuity policies. And one well-known Texas person apparently did exactly that! In February 2000, former Enron chairman, Ken Lay (and his wife Linda) reportedly paid about $4 million to buy variable annuities set up to pay an income in 2007. *Imagine:* Conventional investments such as stocks and savings accounts aren't safeguarded under Texas law, but every single dollar in annuities can be sheltered from litigation by creditors.

A word of caution: There is one problem with purchasing annuities to withhold cash from creditors. Virtually all state laws void their protection if premiums are paid to defraud anyone. Therefore, if a specific claim is threatened, real, or, possibly, just imagined, don't count on immunity under your state's law. Under these circumstances, an adversary will surely argue there was fraudulent intent behind your actions.

There is a group B of about 20 states that also safeguards your cash in an annuity, but their laws have limitations and can be a little vague. For example, Alaska, Illinois, Maryland, and Tennessee give protection only if your beneficiary is a spouse or dependent. North Dakota has a $100,000 shelter limit per policy. Hawaii, Louisiana, and Michigan offer protection from creditors of "insureds" (presumably annuitants).

Group C consists of another 15 states that offer virtually no immunity for annuity cash values or lump sums at death. However, most will protect beneficiaries of annuity income after a policy owner dies.

To check your state's law, go to a public library and ask for the "Revised Statutes." In the index volume, check out "Bankruptcy Exemptions, "Debtor and Creditor," and "Life Insurance," and you'll be directed to law on whether annuities are protected where you live.

NAMING AN INDIVIDUAL BENEFICIARY OF YOUR POLICY

Be awful nice to 'em goin' up, because you're gonna meet 'em all comin' down.
     —Jimmy Durante

Unlike life insurance purchased for protection at death, most annuities are for use while alive. Nonetheless, all annuities have a beneficiary section; you specify who gets anything left when you die. A **primary beneficiary** is first in line. If he or she isn't alive, the **contingent beneficiary** receives everything. Once either owns the annuity, then a successor takes what remains when the first beneficiary dies.

EXAMPLE

You name as cash beneficiary "my wife Mary, if surviving; otherwise my son, Tommy." Mary is your primary beneficiary, and Tommy is the contingent beneficiary. Another option would be to set up a payout plan that gives either Mary or Tommy an income for 20 years. You state, "If my beneficiary dies, any remaining amounts are paid as follows: If Mary is payee, then to Tommy; if Tommy is payee, then to his children equally." Consequently, Tommy is Mary's successor beneficiary, and Tommy's children are his successor beneficiaries.

A word of caution: All sorts of bitter lawsuits are fought over people included in beneficiary designations for annuities, life insurance, 401(k) accounts, and IRAs. There are always marriages, newborns, deaths, divorce—and circumstances that change. It definitely pays to keep your beneficiaries designations current. Ask your financial planner and lawyer periodically to update and coordinate the wording.

Here's an additional pointer: In the above example, I assumed Tommy was an only child. If there are additional children, you usually name them as a group—say, "my lawful surviving children, equally." The problem here is that if one of them dies before you, only other children share in the policy; your deceased child's children (your grandchildren), if any, would be included. You solve this by naming "lawful surviving issue, per stirpes," as beneficiary. Here the children of a deceased child "step up" and take the portion he or she would have received. If your grandchildren are underage, a guardian manages it until they are adults. Be aware: It's always possible this manager could be an outsider, even an estranged son- or daughter-in-law.

A solution: Have your lawyer write a trust that covers every possibility, such as providing for the surviving spouse of a child or grandchild, and then name its trustee beneficiary of the policy. This should give everyone much more flexibility over your annuity values.

I hope you see the importance of naming the right beneficiary. Someone will be thankful later if everything goes smoothly.

NAMING A TRUST BENEFICIARY OF YOUR POLICY

The reason grandparents and grandchildren get along so well is that they have a common enemy.
> —*Sam Levinson*

When you name an individual cash beneficiary of an annuity, the money is under control of that person. It's also subject to the system and others who want it. A well-crafted trust offers more protection and covers a variety of changed circumstances. However, trust beneficiaries have some problems in the area of income taxes.

EXAMPLE

Let's say you have paid $100,000 in premiums to a policy worth $200,000 at your death. It is paid to a trust for your wife, Mary, then to your children at her death. Here's what happens:

Mary's trust cannot continue the policy's tax deferral. (If Mary were an individual beneficiary, she could keep it until the maturity date.) The result is a definite tax disadvantage. Since the policy now matures at your death, Mary's trustee has 60 days to annuitize the policy or all $100,000 of its profit is taxed at once. And 60 days goes by rather quickly.

Some insurers will only pay lump sums to trustees. Consequently, it helps to check first whether your company permits a trustee to annuitize and spread out the taxes.

In any event, Mary's trust will pay high taxes on the annuity profit. In 2004, for example, a trust's federal tax rate was a flat 35% on taxable income over $9550. As a single person, Mary wouldn't incur the 35% bracket until her taxable income reached $319,100.

The bottom line: Definitely, trust beneficiaries of annuities have an edge with flexibility, management, and protection. Definitely, individual annuity beneficiaries have advantages when it comes to income taxes. Ask your annuity advisor to do some calculations and work out what's best with your financial planner and estate planning lawyer.

A CONTINUING ANNUITY POLICY FOR A SURVIVING SPOUSE

I haven't spoken to my wife in years—I didn't want to interrupt her.
    —Rodney Dangerfield

You are married and about to purchase a personal annuity. It's important to get the owner, annuitant, and beneficiary issues straight.

In most cases, you should be both owner and annuitant and name your spouse beneficiary. This way, if you die, he or she can "step into your shoes" to own the policy and continue its tax deferral. If you are owner and name your spouse annuitant, there can be tax problems: For instance, if she dies first and the policy matures, you cannot continue it. Consequently, you would have 60 days to annuitize or pay taxes on all profit at once.

If you are married, take care in choosing the parties to your annuity policy. Uninformed people can make choices that cause surprises eventually.

EXCHANGING AN OLD ANNUITY FOR A NEW ANNUITY TAX-FREE

The point to remember is what the government gives it must first take away.
    —John S. Coleman

Let's say in a period of declining interest rates that you own ABC Insurance Company's annuity policy. There are no surrender charges, and the interest rate is lowered to 3% while XYZ offers a policy paying 5%. Or XYZ comes out with a new annuity that has features which ABC's policy doesn't have. You decide to cash in ABC's policy and replace it with XYZ's contract, even though XYZ does charge if you make an early withdrawal.

There is one stumbling block, however. You paid $100,000 for the ABC policy, and it's now worth $200,000. You don't want to pay income taxes on the profit.

Fortunately, there is a solution. Assign ABC's policy to XYZ in exchange for its newer contract. Then XYZ surrenders your ABC policy. As long as you follow the rules, the law makes this a so-called 1035 exchange (and defers any built-in gain until taken from XYZ's policy). Following is a summary of the key points in this type of exchange:

- It's best to assign the entire ABC policy to XYZ. And if there is an existing policy loan, repay it before making the transfer.
- The annuitant, owner, and maturity dates should be the same in both policies. I recommend that the beneficiary—at least initially—be the same, too.
- Finally, do not cash in your ABC policy and endorse ABC's check to XYZ. The only safe way is the assignment approach that I've described.

EXCHANGING A LIFE INSURANCE POLICY FOR AN ANNUITY TAX-FREE

You can also trade a life insurance contract for an annuity without paying taxes on profit in your present policy. Let's say you want to terminate a life policy with ABC Company. You've paid in a total of $90,000 in premiums (your basis), and the cash value is $120,000. On surrender, you would pay taxes on a profit of $30,000.

If, instead, you assign ABC's life contract to XYZ Company (which cashes in the policy and issues an annuity policy), you defer taxes on any profit until the annuity policy is surrendered or annuitized. For example, if you cash in the annuity later when it is worth $200,000, the taxable profit is $110,000, or $200,000 less the $90,000 in the premiums from the old insurance policy.

Here's another interesting idea. This time your insurance policy has a "loss"; you've paid net premiums of $90,000, and the cash value is only $70,000. If you surrender it, there is no deduction for a $20,000 loss on your tax return. However, if you exchange it for an annuity, your $90,000 basis in the insurance policy becomes the annuity's basis. The result: The first $20,000 of annuity cash value is tax-free—a great example of tax planning in action! Then any additional growth isn't taxed as long as it stays in the policy.

The bottom line: Before canceling any life insurance, be absolutely sure its death benefit no longer plays a role in your financial planning. If your decision still is to cancel, then consider an exchange for an annuity that transfers your basis in the older policy.

SHELTERING A SOCIAL SECURITY CHECK FROM INCOME TAXES

The income tax has made liars out of more Americans than golf.
    —Will Rogers

Before 1994, Social Security income was either not taxable or a maximum of 50% of the payments was counted for income tax purposes. It was relatively easy to compute this taxable amount, if any, with a worksheet and a pocket calculator. Now, more of your Social Security check is taxable, and it's difficult to do the analysis. The key is understanding a term called *provisional income*, which is basically your adjusted gross income *plus* tax-exempt interest, plus 50% of your Social Security benefits. *The bottom line:* If your provisional income in 2004 exceeds $34,000 for unmarried single taxpayers, or for $44,000 for married taxpayers filing jointly, you'll pay tax on potentially 85% of your Social Security benefits.

Determining the tax due could require a conference with your tax advisor. But one thing for certain is that Congress has decided that most Social Security payments are includable in the taxable income base.

If you are receiving Social Security, accumulation annuities can help. By eliminating or reducing taxable income or tax-exempt interest in the equation, the amount of provisional income on your tax return is less. Let's say you replace your municipal bonds or certificates of deposits with tax-deferred annuity contracts. The accrued income in the policy doesn't count as provisional income, and you will gain financially as follows:

- There are no current taxes on any annuity profit that builds up.
- You may save taxes on most of your Social Security income since tax-deferred interest is not included in the definition of provisional income.

Indeed, these tax savings possibilities are intriguing. Of course, the switch requires some financial maneuvering since there will be a reduction in your current cash flow. (Annuities *accumulate* interest; bonds pay interest currently.) However, it may be possible to gain back money by spending invested capital while the annuity is accumulating interest. In other words, deplete some other asset in an amount equal to the policy's buildup.

EXAMPLE

You own a $100,000 bond that pays interest of $4000, which counts as provisional income. You might take $50,000 from the bond and put it into an accumulation annuity. Then deplete the remaining $50,000 gradually so that most of what you receive is tax-paid money (which isn't included as provisional income).

PAYOUT ANNUITIES DU JOUR

Growing old isn't so bad when you consider the alternative.
                    —*Maurice Chevalier*

By some estimates, only 1% of all accumulation annuity policies are ever annuitized. That's amazing! And only about 5% of all insurance death proceeds are annuitized (the rest is paid in cash). That's surprising! Finally, only 1 in 13 of these annuitized policies in 1999 had life contingencies. (The rest were for a fixed period, such as 10 or 20 years, which can come up short.) That's appalling!

Here lies a dilemma. According to Webster's, *annuities* are "a series of payments over a lifetime." Yet we seem to look at them to park money for an emergency, someday. Even when we annuitize, many take the money merely over a fixed period of years.

The bottom line: For at least two or three decades, we've paid very little attention to payout annuities and how these can promise incomes that can't be outlived.

WHY ARE THERE SO FEW PAYOUT ANNUITIES?

A nickel ain't worth a dime anymore.
        —*Yogi Berra*

Most people not thinking seriously about retirement: In 2003, when 35 million or so Americans were over age 65, there were twice as many baby boomers ages 39 to 57 still accumulating for retirement. Unfortunately, studies indicate that many are saving blindly and have seriously misjudged what's necessary for those decades that will be the "golden years." Most people have probably never heard about a payout annuity, which is the last thing that comes to mind.

The belief that it's more about what capital is than what capital does: It's just not that easy psychologically to exchange a nest egg for monthly checks sometime in the future. Besides, most people believe that if money is spent for a lifetime annuity, there won't be anything left for the heirs. (Of course, that's not true if annuities with life contingencies have a minimum payout period as well.)

Employers not promising pension incomes anymore: Up until the 1970s, the retirement program of choice was a defined benefit plan, by which workers often received an income for life and perhaps a gold watch. Since the 1970s, employers have routinely canceled these programs and shifted the risk to employees via 401(k)s and IRA arrangements. Now,

---

NEGATIVE ASPECTS OF PERSONAL ANNUITIES

Here are 10 reasons often listed by articles that try to cast doubt on annuities as staples in financial planning. Alone, each is true, but taken in an overall context, you and a good annuity advisor can counter most of them, especially after you've read this chapter.

1. The profit in annuities is taxed at full ordinary income rates—unlike most dividends and capital gains presently taxed at 15%.
2. There is no step up in basis for annuities at death.
3. Annuities are more complicated than are CDs, bonds, or mutual funds.
4. Since there are often early surrender charges, annuities are not good short-term investments.

5. Some annuities charge for long-term care and death benefits that some people don't want.
6. Annuities aren't attractive if you want all your property to pass in trust.
7. A market value adjustment (MVA) in fixed annuities can catch you and your beneficiaries by surprise.
8. In an IRA, a Keogh, or a 401(k), annuities aren't that appealing because they are already tax-deferred.
9. Some "bonuses" in annuities are forfeited unless the policy is annuitized eventually.
10. Withdrawals before the age of 59½ can attract a 10% penalty tax assessed by the IRS.

the idea is to accumulate a bunch of cash, and everything will surely work out at retirement. Surely?

Many financial advisors not being familiar with annuities: After being annuitized, cash can no longer go into other investments. This means no more commissions, fees, or "money under management." Unfortunately, that's probably excuse enough for many financial advisors to discourage annuitizing.

Everything is about accumulation. It seems infinitely compelling to counsel others on how to become millionaires and then pass everything to the family at death. It's not so interesting to advise on how to spend everything and "die broke," as they say. *The bottom line:* Many financial planners are well informed on building and preserving an estate, but they aren't that familiar with cutting-edge strategies for making income last a lifetime.

Insurers indirectly discouraging the purchase of payout policies: Personal accumulation annuity premiums increased by a factor of 19 from $6 billion in 1980 to nearly $116 billion in 1999, when only $7 billion went into payout policies. Obviously, companies have the tax-deferred buildup part right. But they've forgotten that annuities guarantee incomes which can't be outlived.

Beneficiaries not annuitizing death benefits: Surely, beneficiaries know better when it comes to annuitizing life insurance proceeds paid at death. Not so! Only 5% of all insurance and annuity lump sums are turned into streams of income; the rest is paid in cash. Obviously, insurance companies compete feverishly for new money to come in house. But they don't put the same effort into keeping what's already on the books; they simply release the cash. That's incredible!

Beneficiaries annuitizing but not choosing a lifelong payout: You'd think those who annuitize would at least choose policies with life contingencies. Figures show that about 85 to 90% of the time beneficiaries who elect supplementary contracts choose a payout for fixed periods only. (Supplementary contracts transform the death benefit from a life insurance policy into an annuity stream of income for the beneficiary. Of the 130,228 supplementary contracts issued in 1999, only 9551 had life contingencies.)

My prediction for years to come is that everything is about to change. As the emphasis shifts to managing money in retirement, payout annuities will shine, especially those that guarantee an income for life.

WHY PAYOUT ANNUITIES WILL EXPLODE IN POPULARITY

It's hard to believe that someday I'll be an ancestor.
　　　—Robert Half

Changing U.S. demographics: In 2002 one out of eight Americans was over age 65. It's estimated that by 2030 nearly one out of four Americans will be over age 65. The graying of America will bring a heightened awareness about managing money in retirement.

Living longer: In 2000, there were 9.2 million Americans over age 80 (up from 7 million in 1990). Centenarians are the fastest-growing age segment of the American population. (In 2000, there were about 50,000 U.S. persons over age 100, and 45,000 were women.) The second fastest

(figure 50-1)

CHECKLIST

A checklist to determine whether you might run out of money.

Assume you have a nest egg and want to maximize its cash flow. Using a scale of 1 to 10, classify yourself on each of the following. There are no right answers, but a high score indicates that a payout annuity (with a life contingency) is particularly worth considering.

- People in my family live to a ripe old age.
- On average, I have a healthy lifestyle.
- I'm worried about outliving my money.
- I don't have a "bedrock" pension income to rely on.
- I have other assets to leave to family.
- I'm more concerned about my retirement income than what others will receive when I die.
- I'm not interested in record keeping anymore.
- I understand pretty well how annuities work.
- I don't want to rely on the government for financial security.
- My financial advisor is familiar with payout annuities.
- My children really want me to spend what's mine.
- I want to simplify my financial affairs.
- I have a line of credit, savings fund, or family to fall back on in an emergency.
- I can live with the financial decisions that I make.
- In retirement, I'm more interested in not becoming poor than in getting rich.

⬅ TOTAL

SCORE	RANK	OPPORTUNITY
15—50	Low	Unless there is a right of commutation, payout annuities should not be a significant part of your retirement income planning.
51—90	Average	At least 25% of your retirement income should come from annuities with a lifetime contingency
91—150	High	You will benefit from a well-arranged payout annuity plan that provides 50% or more of your retirement income.

Courtesy of Mark Fiore.

segment is the 85-plus age group (4.8 million persons in 2004), which increased by 37% between 1990 and 2000.

Someday, we may routinely live to age 90, 100, or beyond. If so, it could become risky not to have lifelong incomes as part of a financial plan.

Not looking to the public sector for financial security in retirement: In 2003, the median income of seniors was pitifully low—about $20,000 annually for men and $11,000 for women. Surely, most retirees depend on Social Security, a public program scheduled to go broke by 2042. Then baby boomers will be from 78 to 96 years old and probably in no position to fend for themselves financially.

Only Social Security and insurance companies guarantee incomes that can't be outlived. If Social Security falters or fails, commercial insurers will get better at marketing their payout annuities, especially if Congress has the insurance industry bail out the system. To learn more about Social Security and to obtain the status of your personal account, go to the Social Security Administration listing in "For More Information."

Government promotion of payout annuities: In July 2003, the General Accounting Office (GAO) proposed that Congress amend the Employee Retirement Security of 1974 (ERISA) and require that employers tell retirees about the risk of outliving their savings. This is nearly an "advertisement" for commercial payout annuities. It also alerts insurance companies to get ready for what's ahead.

In addition, Congress is considering favorable legislation for annuities. One bill taxes any income in payout annuities as merely capital gains. Other proposals exclude from income tax IRAs and employer retirement plan payments up to $2500 or $3000 annually. Personally, I would defer or exclude capital gain on proceeds from real estate or securities transferred directly into a payout annuity.

Private studies recommending payout annuities: In 2000, the National Association for Variable Annuities (NAVA) asked PricewaterhouseCoopers (PwC) to research lifetime annuitization. In a variety of circumstances, PwC compared after-tax returns from nonqualified variable payout annuities with systematic withdrawals from mutual funds. The clear winner is payout annuities. See "For More Information" to purchase the PwC report or find out more about NAVA.

Popular columnists more enthusiastic about payout annuities: Jonathan Clements (*Wall Street Journal,* March 9, 2003) advises placing 25 to 50% of your retirement nest egg in a payout annuity "if you think you or your spouse will live past 82." I'd say the chances are pretty good. Even IRS tables say that if you are age 65, your life expectancy is another 20 years.

Humberto Cruz (*The Savings Game,* August 25, 2003) writes: "The primary appeal of income annuities—the reason many advisers recommend many retirees consider them for a portion of their savings—is that you cannot outlive your income."

A favorite is *Money's* Walter Updegrave, who writes, "Can you say annuitization?" Although he believes buying annuities can be "mind numbing" and that most of the emphasis is on accumulation policies, Updegrave gives good information about annuitizing. An example is his July 2002 article, "Income for Life."

When you read what these and other columnists are writing, listen up! Their columns succeed only if they research their topics thoroughly and give well-conceived opinions.

Better payout annuities showing up every day: As mentioned, it's natural to recoil at the thought of giving up permanently a nest egg merely for a lifetime income. A few insurers are doing something about this and have included a "right of commutation" after annuitizing. This allows payees to change their mind and get the money back. If the money can become liquid once again, why wouldn't anyone want to give payout annuities a try?

In addition, look for cost-of-living income increases and more income if there is a terminal illness or need for long-term care.

Note: When insurers give a right to commute or cancel, there may be a charge to get your money back. Or there could be a slight reduction in the annuity income you receive. Read the fine print, and work out what's best with your annuity advisor.

In tomorrow's payout policies, look for more options, including cost-of-living income increases and more income if there is a terminal illness or need for long-term care.

Financial planners promoting income planning: For decades, professional periodicals on investing have mainly promoted such accumulation strategies as asset allocation and market timing. Now, financial planners are advised to "get good at income planning." At the next conference, your financial planner may even ask about your health and whether to risk outliving your income.

Insurers paying insurance agents extra commissions on payout annuities: Some carriers are paying insurance agents periodic bonuses and annual "trailers" to sell their payout annuities. This change recognizes that competent advisors need to be compensated for giving ongoing advice. That's a good thing.

Lump sums not lasting: After 9-11, an uncertain stock market, and a dose of corporate wrongdoing, there could be more of the same in years ahead. A large sum of capital just isn't a sure thing anymore. Instead, many people will prefer streams of steady annuity income. These come on time every time and follow you anywhere in the world.

REAL-LIFE PAYOUT ANNUITY PLANNING OPPORTUNITIES

You can live to be a hundred, if you give up all the things that make you want to be a hundred.
> —*Woody Allen*

Payout annuities are more than a stream of income, possibly for life. They can improve your finances in a number of ways. Following are descriptions for an improved cash flow and for a creative IRA payout plan.

HOW A PAYOUT ANNUITY IS TAXED

The Internal Revenue Code has numerous illustrations of how the taxation of payout annuities are taxed. Here's one example:

Let's say you are age 65, have $100,000 in cash, and are looking to liquidate money for optimum cash flow in retirement. One possibility is a payout annuity that gives $600 per month (or $7200 per year) for 20 years: a total of $144,000. The results: In each of the 20 years that you receive $7200, a twentieth of $100,000 (or $5000) is a partial tax-free return from your $100,000 investment. The balance of $2200 is taxed as ordinary income.

A second possibility is to liquidate $100,000 gradually, without acquiring the annuity. Assuming you can take out $7200 annually and everything lasts for 20 years, you have the following results:

- Unlike a commercial annuity that spreads out taxes evenly over the 20 years, you pay taxes on income as credited. (The first year, for example, if your cash earns $4000 interest, $4000 is taxed and $3200 is tax-free.)
- You'll have a rather daunting task of managing this self-amortizing plan. You may run out of money, too, in the meantime.

In summary, if you are considering spending what's yours, it's both tax-favored and simpler if you acquire a payout annuity.

To maximize cash flow from your investments: Let's say you have a $500,000 nest egg, and it's a struggle to attain both optimum income and growth. At last look, your cash flow is only $20,000, most of it is fully taxable, and the record keeping is becoming burdensome.

Place one-half, or about $250,000, in a payout annuity that gives a steady monthly income and is liquidated over a certain timeframe. (A reasonable amount over 18 years, in mid-2003, could be about $20,000.) Then invest the second $250,000 in an accumulation annuity, life insurance policy, or something that has a tax-deferred buildup along the way. The advantages include that most of your annuity payment is a tax-free return of principal, you eliminate some record keeping, and the second $250,000 has a good chance of building back to at least $500,000 during the next 18 years.

This is called a *split-annuity* or *split-investment plan*—a two-direction cash-flow philosophy that beats traditional planning hands down. (For more about these strategies, see the Map Plan, listed in "For More Information.")

To bolster a creative IRA payout plan: Suppose that most of your retirement kitty is in a large, traditional IRA. On your reaching age 70, the IRS forces you to take some money each year and add this to other taxable income. If you don't manage this well, you'll pay a 50% tax penalty on any shortfall not taken.

Use a payout annuity to make these distributions automatically. It can pay you the minimums imposed by law, or you can annuitize the policy and take an income with a life contingency. Or your financial planner can arrange several annuity payout approaches approved in recent regulations offered by the IRS.

Another suggestion: When forced to take taxable IRA distributions, you can opt to defer taxes on your non-IRA investments by converting them into accumulation annuities. It's just a matter of crunching the numbers.

CHOOSING THE RIGHT PAYOUT ANNUITY

Basically, you have three choices of payout annuity: (1) a life annuity, which pays merely for as long as you live; (2) a period certain annuity, for which payments stop after, say, 20 years; or (3) a life annuity with period certain, which pays for a number of years or life, whichever is longer. A life annuity and a life annuity with period certain have life contingencies, and I recommend having a life annuity with period certain in most instances. Following are some single premiums for each type of payout annuity in February 2004.

EXAMPLE

For a healthy male at age 65 who wants a monthly annuity of $1000, (1) a life annuity costs $150,000, but all income stops the minute he dies; (2) a 20-year period certain annuity costs about $160,000, but since it doesn't have a life contingency, payments will stop at age 85; and (3) a life annuity with a 20-year period certain costs $170,000, but its payments are for 20 years or life, whichever is longer. The life annuity with period certain costs a little more, but in my book it's worth it. (To obtain a personal fixed annuity income quote online, check out "For More Information.")

SPECIAL FEATURES IN PAYOUT POLICIES

Look for insurance companies to start becoming more creative in their payout policies. Shortly, you'll see more payout annuities with cost-of-living adjustments; commutation privileges; upside (but no downside) possibilities; and increased benefits for nursing home, terminal illness, and much more. Right now, there are special policies that even pay more annuity income if you have a health issue (and a shortened life expectancy).

Which policy is best? This is where you'll need help from annuity professionals who can ask insurers the right questions to get answers on your behalf. Give them a copy of *Optimal Aging* when you ask what to do.

GETTING FUNDS INTO A PAYOUT ANNUITY

It's one thing to think about payout annuities in your financial plan. It's another matter to find money for the premiums. *My suggestion:* Save regularly, and look to lump sums during the preretirement years. For instance, let's assume good fortune appears and any of the following occurs:

- A bonus or large commission
- An unexpected gift or inheritance
- A lump sum from a 401(k)
- A cash settlement in divorce or other legal action
- A life insurance death benefit
- The lottery or a wager
- Cash from the sale of real estate or a business

If any of the above occur, put the money into an accumulation annuity that has good payout features when you are ready to annuitize. It's okay if you end up with several policies. I have five annuities that pay lifelong incomes to my bank account. And the insurance company keeps all the records for me.

CONCLUSION

To sum up, annuities du jour truly are an investment or savings plan whose time has come.

Surely, some of your serious money should be inside an annuity policy. Take heed from the following endorsement from John E. Chopoton, former assistant secretary of the U.S. Treasury, in testifying before the Senate Finance Committee on March 30, 1980: "To the extent that annuities can be fashioned to offer interest rates that are competitive with rates paid by other financial instruments, there is little reason why a potential investor should purchase anything but a deferred annuity."

WHAT YOU NEED TO KNOW

In the simplest of terms, annuity policies are contracts issued by insurance companies that give policy owners and beneficiaries certain rights and promises. I've explained and defined most of the terms in this chapter.

Today's accumulation annuities still get most of the emphasis. They offer income tax deferral, creditor protection, and a variety of financial planning situations. These include protecting Social Security income from taxation and two-direction, split-investment thinking.

There aren't many payout annuities in force. But this is about to change—and for good reasons. We are living longer, and traditional pensions and Social Security are no longer dependable sources of lifelong retirement income. Payout annuities stand tall as perhaps your last chance to have an income that can't be outlived.

Insurers are getting more creative in providing policy owner options. These include extra death benefits, nursing home income, cost-of-living increases, and rights of commutation in payout policies.

It's important to structure your annuity properly. Get familiar with who should be the policy owner, annuitant, and, especially, the beneficiary. Since there are so many policies, it's essential to get the right one. Annuities are not commodities or a do-it-yourself financial plan. It's here that a professional annuity advisor can ask the right questions and get you answers based on your unique circumstances.

FOR MORE INFORMATION

AARP
601 East Street NW
Washington, DC 20049
800-424-3410
Web: www.aarp.org
Search for "annuities."

Richard W. Duff, JD, CLU
303-756-3599
Fax: 303-691-0474
E-mail: rwduffclu@aol.com
Web: www.rwduff.com

You can order Dick's consumer books *Keep Every Last Dime, Money Magic with Annuities,* and *Take Charge of Your IRA* via the website. You'll also see a number of his publications and manuals for professionals listed here.

The Map Plan
Web: www.PerfectSolution.org

For those seriously interested in (1) never running out of money, (2) never losing money, (3) increasing their cash flow, and (4) significantly reducing income taxes. It is an educational experience where you design a personal financial planning solution that really makes sense.

A Personal Annuity Income Quote
Web: www.annuityinfo.com

Obtain a personal annuity quotation that calculates a fixed guaranteed monthly income based on your age and the premium amount contributed—numerous quality insurers listed.

Social Security Administration
Web: www.ssa.gov/retirement

Obtain your personal Social Security benefits. It gives guidelines to plan for retirement and a lot of good information regarding Social Security.

Your Personal Lifespan

Web: www.livingto100.com

Lots of fun: A computer calculates your own life expectancy based on truthful responses to a number of questions. Perhaps you'll even make some changes based on the results.

National Association for Variable Annuities (NAVA)

Web: www.navanet.org

This extensive website is about all kinds of annuities. There are a number of interesting publications (including the PwC report I mentioned) which you can order from NAVA. You should spend some time on this site.

Mark Fiore

Web: www.markfiore.com

Email: mark@markfiore.com

Mark's cartoons are featured in this chapter.

Big checkbooks or little checkbooks, they're all empty at the end of the month!

—*John Bresler*

THE AUTHOR

51

DAVID C. PARTHEYMULLER, is a certified financial planner, a certified estate planner, a fellow of the Esperti Peterson Institute, and a founding member and principal of the Normandy Group. Mr. Partheymuller is an adjunct professor for the Estate and Wealth Strategies Institute at Michigan State University and has served as chairman on the board of trustees for the Argyle Foundation in Denver, Colorado. He is a contributing author to *Dynasty IRA* (1998), *Ways and Means: Maximize the Value of Your Retirement Savings* (1998), *21st Century Wealth: Essential Financial Planning Principles* (2000), and *Strictly Business: Planning Strategies for Privately Owned Businesses* (2001).

He manages an office of supervisory jurisdiction for and offers securities through Multi Financial Securities Corp., a member of the ING Advisors Network, a member of the NASD, SIPC, and a registered investment advisor. Mr. Partheymuller lives in Colorado with his wife and children.

51 INVESTING FOR RETIREMENT

It took me a few years to fully realize the sheer simplicity and brilliance of John Bresler's words. At the time I first heard them, I was a complete neophyte in the financial services industry. Even though his little quip made me laugh, Bresler wasn't trying to be funny. Sometimes laughter is the best way to cover ignorance, but I still suspected that John Bresler could see right through me. I was young, essentially irresponsible, and, until that point in my life, had never even thought of saving more than a few hundred dollars anywhere, let alone in 403(b) annuities. I felt relatively comfortable because I was in exceptionally good company. Most of my friends were in that same canoe—and paddles? Well, paddles could be obtained. We could get jobs doing mostly anything if we had to in order to sustain our standard of living, and I already had this great new job under Bresler's tutelage. But now, here, in my new career in financial services, I was preparing to educate others, the public, on the intricacies of investing for retirement. Wasn't retirement something older folks did? Retirement seemed decades away for me, or at least many years away for the people I considered to be "older" at the time. Succinctly, before my financial education truly began, my friends and I were way too young and independent to think about aging and that sort of thing.

CHANGING TIMES

Well the times, they are a changin'!
    —Bob Dylan

I'm standing here staring right in the face of the cost of a college education for my two children while I'm entering the youth of my old age. Skydiving is no longer something I might try. Some things seem to be falling apart, and if it hasn't fallen off, it just hurts! These days I go to bed by 9 P.M. to try and get up at 5 A.M. for the extra time it takes me to find all my parts and dangling participles. I'm not kidding! Excuse me, but *what happened!?* There are huge demands on my time, physical stamina, and money. Stretching? Who ever needed to stretch? Could it be that my paddle is growing smaller, or is it that there is so much more water to tread?

Okay, okay, I can see, taste, and feel it! There will come a time in the not too distant future when I will need my money to work for me rather than having me work for my money. Who'd ever thought? Retirement?

In the last 20 years I've participated in some very stimulating and some very boring conversations about money, wealth, and investing. You know? It isn't that big a deal. It's actually quite simple. Investing for anything has to do with what you need, what feels right, whom you trust, what you want to accomplish, having a few smarts, and exercising a large amount of discipline above all else. If we do our homework, our emotions will have little weight in any investment decision. It's that simple . . . isn't it?

EPIPHANY

The older I get, the more wisdom I find in the ancient rule of taking first things first, a process which often reduces the most complex human problems to manageable proportions.
—Dwight D. Eisenhower

When an epiphany occurs, it can present a huge quandary because of the many insights that can result from having one. For example, *epiphany:* "Wow, now I see it; how simple is that?" *Insight one:* "Gee, I must be really bright." *Insight two:* "If I'm so bright, why did it take me so darn long to see something a child would understand?" In any case, rather than sharing an epiphany that I've experienced, please allow me to share a *process* which helped me have one.

Of course, we'll need to set a ground rule and then implement three small steps to prepare. But now, I did say it is "a process."

Ground rule: Let's not be in a rush. Like every other great thing in life, this may take a little time. We need to find a quiet place where we can reflect.

STEP ONE

We begin by trying to understand who we are and what we stand for. Let's take a close look at our personal composition, our makeup, our experiences, both great and ugly, what we've learned, what we think about what we've learned, and from whom. Call this "a concoction of the soul," or, more simply, our personal wealth! Personal wealth drives our train. Think of personal wealth as the engineer or the little voice that we hear in our head and in our hearts. Personal wealth is our compass and our cognitive recognition of it and its value is an inextricable part of the investing process.

STEP TWO

We need to identify for whom or for what we care. Our spouse? children? grandchildren? siblings? friends? colleagues? church? causes? And . . .

SOMETHING EXTRA FROM RETIREMENT SAVINGS?

Did you know that under current rules a parent's investment in qualified and nonqualified retirement plans—any 401(k), IRA, Keogh, SEP, SIMPLE, 403(b), 457 deferred compensation plan, or tax-deferred annuity in general—as well as the cash values in life insurance policies are not counted, that's right, not counted, in the calculation by the federal government to establish your "expected family contribution" for financial aid for college? Further, all investments, savings accounts, and Uniform Gifts to Minors Act (UGMA), Uniform Transfers to Minors Act (UTMA), and 529 plans in the child's name, and/or under the child's Social Security number are counted!

Many variables should be considered with this issue; however, those who would like their children to take advantage of federal and state scholarships, grants, student work-study programs, and preferred loans and who also have sizable investment accounts outside the types of retirement plans mentioned above might want to rethink their investment strategy. As with most planning, the earlier you start the better.

why? These are our people, our community, our tribe, our village, our place and space in which we live outside ourselves. These people and causes can be referred to as our *social wealth,* and as you might guess, cognitive recognition of both social wealth and personal wealth is equally important.

STEP THREE

More specific to this chapter's topic of investing for retirement has to do with identifying all our "stuff," or our *financial wealth.* Not only the monetary values, but also how we hold title to these financial assets for "accessibility" in the case of disability or an emergency. The importance of proper titling is rudimentary if our ultimate goal is to use our retirement assets most effectively for ourselves. Further, as we proceed with this financial inventory and a healthy desire to invest prudently, we want to reintroduce ourselves to that basic premise that there are some things an individual does well and some things that an individual does not do well. The point being to focus on those things we do well and delegate, or stand clear of, those things we do not.

Nearly two decades have past since I entered the financial services industry, and during the years I've often talked with my children about these issues of personal, social, and financial wealth. We discuss the importance of educating ourselves and creatively implementing what we've learned. In one of our conversations I shared an ongoing discussion that my colleagues and mentors have with regard to financial wealth. "Financial wealth is like rocket fuel," they say, "and rocket fuel can be very unstable if it isn't handled respectfully." In that one particular conversation, my children's ears peaked at the "rocket fuel" aspect of our discussion, and the conversation quickly turned to the space shuttle, by which they assisted in helping develop the following metaphor: Personal wealth is the guidance system within the shuttle, and the commander programs the guidance system. It's the commander's personal wealth that pinpoints the shuttle's ultimate destination. Social wealth is the crew. The people that got us to where we are today, and those that will to continue to help us get where we are going tomorrow. Social wealth includes those people that we love or for whom we care and those that will help us continue on our mission even if we are unable to do so for ourselves. Social wealth includes specialists, advisors, and ground people. We agreed that financial wealth could in fact be the rocket fuel and is most efficient, stable, and effective if all the other elements and systems communicate and interact with the flight commander.

And then, while everything works in harmony, something powerful and wonderful occurs. The point being we want to include our children and talk about our financial wealth before it is beyond our ability to do so. It's important not to put it off. Our children's ability to understand our feelings about money and the power of money is important for a smooth transition in all aspects of our wealth when that time arrives.

How are we doing? So far so good? Let's go!

MAKE CORE PLANNING FUN!

America was built and runs on the best model of capitalism in the world. Unfortunately, the marketing experts and advertisers found that our capitalistic model is most profitable when people are afraid. Fear sells! As a matter of fact, if you don't use XYZ Mouthwash, no one will kiss you. If you don't brush your teeth with brand G, your teeth will have cavities or, worse, fall out, oh no! And if you don't buy life insurance, you will be a poor provider (read as SOB), and your loved ones will suffer greatly. How about this? So what?!

Obviously, the message is clear, and it proliferates everywhere. Stay above the noise by grounding yourself with your core values. Your core values can and will support your core plan. Take, no, *make* the time to understand what you need to be comfortable and safe during this important process, and then create that reality for yourself and your loved ones. Common sense, trusted advisors, a sense of purpose, a willingness to discuss the issues that motivate you, an open mind, and, most important, a sense of humor will go a long way in helping you design your plan based on your values and needs, the needs of your loved ones, and, ultimately, the causes you want to support and the legacy that you want to leave. Make it fun! Definitely, don't skirt the issues, but the next time a fear monger infers something ridiculous, point at them and laugh out loud.

WHY INVEST AT ALL?

The safe way to double your money is to fold it over once and put it in your pocket.
—*Frank "Kin" Hubbard*

Why incur the risk of investing? Why experience the stress, heartburn, or worse? Is it the exhilaration, or excitement, the gambling element, the hope of getting something for nothing, or just the thrill of winning or losing? Is it the conversations at the cocktail parties and the exaggerated stories of gain and loss that we're drawn to? Is it a need to be part of the conversation? Or is there a real and absolute financial need to invest? If we were confident that our retirement income pool (all of our sources of retirement income) contained enough hard assets to provide retirement income throughout our retirement time horizon (how long we will live) without taking risk, why would we subject our portfolio to any risk at all? Why not stash our assets in a "safe" place and forget about them? Is it because in addition to leaving a personal legacy, we may want to leave a financial legacy? Or is it because of the answers to some of the questions above? At any rate, it's a known fact that if we don't consume our assets during our life, they will transfer after our death. Whether or not our assets reach our intended beneficiaries in an efficient manner is another issue and beyond the scope of this chapter, but we do know that our financial wealth will transfer at death. *Note:* There is often a huge disconnect between personal, social, and financial wealth, and many people find their self worth inexplicably tied to their net worth. We know that by honestly exploring these issues, we can become better investors.

Therefore, we do need to understand what it is we need. But how do we learn whether our retirement income pool is deep enough? What assumptions should we use to determine the answer? If we discover that we don't have a deep enough pool of assets from which to draw, which changes would we make or which risks would we take to increase or stabilize the depth of our retirement income pool? What probability for success will we need to feel comfortable with the risks we are willing to take? Most people are not strangers to taking risk, but at what cost? The first step in investing for retirement is to "quantify the available resources," so that we can qualify the standard of living that can potentially be available to us during retirement. Then we have to decide whether that standard of living is acceptable.

WHAT DO WE NEED?

There is no dignity quite so impressive, no independence quite so important, as living within your means.
      —Calvin Coolidge

Qualifying our standard of living throughout a *retirement time horizon* can be many times more difficult than qualifying a current standard of living because of the effects of inflation over time. The **consumer price index (CPI)** is based on a market basket of goods and services and is disseminated by the U.S. Bureau of Labor Statistics on a monthly and annual basis. The index has its foundation in the average price of that market basket of goods over the years 1982 to 1984. The standard at that time was set at $100 for the basket. In 1990 that same basket of goods cost $152. However, the market basket is just a token sampling of expenses, relative and different for most people. For example, today, if we have children, the escalating costs of raising and educating them are definitely more important to us than for those people who do not have children. In addition, the costs of long-term health care is going to be more important for adults who are caring for aged parents or relatives. So it's extremely important to examine and understand our own personal CPI. Inflationary pressures on the costs of raising children today will most likely be replaced with the inflationary pressures of our own medical care tomorrow. In addition, we need to realize that using an inflation rate like 3% across the board can be as misleading and ill-fated as using a 10% annual rate of return for a retirement income portfolio or an income tax rate that is too low. Figure 51-1 is from the Bureau of Labor Statistics website and illustrates the fluctuations in price, on a U.S. citywide basis from January 1993 to June 2003, of one of my favorites: chocolate chip cookies. Price fluctuations on almost anything can be obtained on its website.

Consequently, in order to better understand how price fluctuations may influence cash flows, we have to gather and analyze information. At this point it's important to remember a maxim to which most financial analysts adhere: Garbage in equals garbage out! We respectfully recommend that you subscribe to this maxim as well. Somewhere, maybe "over the rainbow," the huge energy broker Enron loss sight of this rule and the results as we all know were catastrophic. Parallels can be drawn between household finances and the finances and operation of a public company. Just as in a corporation, tracking the income and expense data of our household is a mission critical exercise. More important, it is a

(figure 51-1)
Fluctuations in the price of chocolate chip cookies.

SERIES ID: APU0000702421
AREA: U.S. city average
ITEM: Cookies, chocolate chip, per lb (453.6 gm)

YEAR	JAN	FEB	MAR	APR	MAY	JUN	JUL	AUG	SEP	OCT	NOV	DEC
1993	$ 2.504	$ 2.520	$ 2.447	$ 2.421	$ 2.496	$ 2.564	$ 2.583	$ 2.408	$ 2.445	$ 2.325	$ 2.377	$ 2.426
1994	$ 2.378	$ 2.411	$ 2.468	$ 2.464	$ 2.641	$ 2.675	$ 2.704	$ 2.601	$ 2.611	$ 2.537	$ 2.502	$ 2.541
1995	$ 2.320	$ 2.535	$ 2.444	$ 2.489	$ 2.415	$ 2.485	$ 2.453	$ 2.471	$ 2.464	$ 2.479	$ 2.489	$ 2.576
1996	$ 2.582	$ 2.615	$ 2.628	$ 2.754	$ 2.625	$ 2.557	$ 2.513	$ 2.464	$ 2.526	$ 2.504	$ 2.554	$ 2.614
1997	$ 2.553	$ 2.636	$ 2.647	$ 2.582	$ 2.632	$ 2.643	$ 2.614	$ 2.612	$ 2.536	$ 2.612	$ 2.667	$ 2.633
1998	$ 2.502	$ 2.607	$ 2.499	$ 2.505	$ 2.512	$ 2.563	$ 2.541	$ 2.588	$ 2.560	$ 2.517	$ 2.519	$ 2.577
1999	$ 2.610	$ 2.594	$ 2.607	$ 2.564	$ 2.573	$ 2.540	$ 2.609	$ 2.602	$ 2.583	$ 2.584	$ 2.627	$ 2.673
2000	$ 2.607	$ 2.525	$ 2.567	$ 2.523	$ 2.685	$ 2.555	$ 2.558	$ 2.628	$ 2.587	$ 2.691	$ 2.618	$ 2.537
2001	$ 2.388	$ 2.485	$ 2.475	$ 2.503	$ 2.379	$ 2.372	$ 2.371	$ 2.423	$ 2.448	$ 2.408	$ 2.518	$ 2.511
2002	$ 2.491	$ 2.604	$ 2.531	$ 2.578	$ 2.627	$ 2.514	$ 2.579	$ 2.534	$ 2.574	$ 2.595	$ 2.765	$ 2.736
2003	$ 2.774	$ 2.672	$ 2.729	$ 2.777	$ 2.908	$ 2.921						

good idea to keep it a living and breathing analysis, rather than a snapshot of a moment in time. We all know that there is nothing as constant as change. How much easier and more comforting would it be if we could regularly view our present and future cash flows as changes occur in our life? Updating changes on the fly, in real time, year to year, or at any time interval we deem necessary, can provide a feeling of control and security. Conversely, it is not very comforting to close our eyes, ignore it, fly blind, or by the seat of our pants. Most of us find that peace of mind is closely tied to our quality of life, and that is why peace of mind is a primary objective. Finally, the numbers are what they are, and within that data lay our greatest opportunity to create the retirement we envision.

PLANNING IN ACTION

Associates, you have to realize what we're talking about here! It's not about selling 403(b) annuities . . . it's about giving people the opportunity to maintain their dignity during their retirement years.
— Harry Copeland

Tyler and Leslie came to our firm with their plans for retirement. Like so many investors they were worried about market conditions. They were so emotionally tied to their investment portfolios that they felt paralyzed and unable to respond in a constructive manner. Moreover they needed to know if their retirement income pool was deep enough to accommodate their plans. Our answer was, maybe. The "maybe" depended on several issues. Their ability to control spending, their understanding of their personal inflation factor or personal CPI, their understanding of the inherent risks within their current portfolio, and their chances, or probability, for achieving their target rate of return. Target rate of return is the before-tax assumption for the return on investment, which is used in modeling annual cash flows throughout a retirement time horizon. Target rate is different and usually a lower rate of return from the expected rate of return to allow for deviations in investment performance. **Expected rate of return** is the return which an investor expects as compensation for the risk he or she is willing to accept for making an investment. It is usually greater than the target rate of return.

With regard to retirement cash flows, investment returns are never static so it is advisable to include some years of negative investment performance in our retirement cash-flow projections. Including negative performance scenarios can add a degree of confidence that, even in adverse market environments, we will not drain our retirement income pool. *Note:* There are other ways to lose money than investing in the capital markets; for example, if the local bank is paying us 1% on our savings and our personal CPI is 4%, we are losing purchasing power of 3% annually.

Albeit, once we were invited to learn about Tyler and Leslie's personal and social wealth, it was our task to help analyze what it would cost on an annual and inflated basis to support those values and maintain their desired lifestyle. We began by identifying all of the potential income sources and then separated the sources that they could control from those that they could not. Examples of income sources for which we have typically little or no control would be Social Security, defined benefit pensions, and inheritances. Examples of a few sources over which we would exercise more control include rental income from property, individual retirement accounts (IRAs), defined contribution retirement plans, saving accounts in general, and part-time employment income. To illustrate this point further, the difference between defined benefit retirement plans and defined contribution retirement plans is that for the same level of contributions, defined benefit plans offer more certainty and a fixed level of benefits; defined contribution plans can offer the potential for higher benefits, at the cost of reduced certainty, as well as the risk of potentially lower benefits.

A WEIRD PHENOMENON

There are several references included in this chapter, which you might access for further research. Be aware that as investors learn more about investing, especially the trading of individual stocks, they can often be deceived by the performance of the hypothetical portfolios that they create. It seems so easy, and I know because I speak from experience.

Please remember that investing takes an organized plan or strategy and focused discipline to maximize the potential for success. Monitoring a hypothetical or model portfolio to gain confidence is truly more fun than helpful. This is because of an emotional phenomenon, which occurs when using your own money. It can be compared to musical virtuosity, in that until a virtuoso is tempered by the experience of playing his or her instrument in Carnegie Hall or before a large and discerning audience, true expertise, virtuosity, and talent are never really tested.

So when it's time for the curtain to come up and you're ready to lay your money down, how easy will it be to stick to the score, or your strategic chart? It's the same with golf. Until you actually leave the driving range, you never really know how good you are—or could be. Be assured that committing your own money, even to a well-conceived strategic investment policy, takes discipline, a strong belief in your plan, and regular doses of perseverance. To sleep better at night, be sure your plan contains entrance and exit strategies even when, or particularly when, you seek professional assistance.

Upon our review of Tyler and Leslie's income, expense, and investment allocations, we found that outside of their Social Security and corporate pensions, their potential for growth within their combined investment portfolios could be *expected* to provide the desired supplemental retirement income. However, they discovered that the risk they had assumed for their expected rate of return and the fluctuations to principal that they were experiencing as a result of their current portfolio allocations were far greater than they had truly realized or ever anticipated. In essence, they were extremely uncomfortable with the recent consequences.

Just as in identifying our own individual inflation rate, it is as important to identify our need in a *target rate of return* in order to understand what it will take to attain and maintain our lifestyle during retirement. When Tyler and Leslie came to us, their combined portfolio's expected rate was somewhere north of 11.6%. One of our first questions had been, "Why take such risk if you can have your lifestyle supported with something less?" They couldn't answer why they had invested the way they did other than to say that they were not comfortable with the approach they had taken. Anyway, it's important to know what our target rate of return should be in order to minimize our investment risk.

Once we are in the know, should adjustments be made? If so, are we capable of making them today (i.e., spending less or saving more)? Are we able to keep our target rate of return lower than our expected rate of return to cushion the fluctuations occurring in the investment universe in which our money is in play? Do we have a handle on everything we can know about? Are we protected as best we can be from anything that can derail any investment plan? What about debt, disability, death, and so forth? Are we properly situated and comfortable with everything we can know about before venturing into the financial markets, in which we can anticipate little in advance of the volatility inherent to them? *Note:* After saving for years toward a goal like retirement, it is often very difficult for people like Tyler and Leslie to begin depleting their savings. "Most times it just doesn't feel right." This is a normal and sometimes debilitating psychological aspect of investing for and after retirement. Cheerfully, with a little thought and planning the difficulty can be overcome!

FUNDAMENTAL ANALYSIS, TECHNICAL ANALYSIS, MARKET TIMING, AND MODERN PORTFOLIO THEORY

Thousands upon thousands are yearly brought into a state of real poverty by their great anxiety not to be thought poor.
  —*William Cobbett*

Company risk is the risk associated with investing in an individual corporation, and **market risk** is the risk associated with investing in the financial markets. Statistical analysts believe that company risk can be minimized by diversification: holding approximately 28 different, equally weighted security or investment positions. It is believed that holding more than 28 different positions does not reduce company risk to any greater extent for an investor. In fact, holding significantly more than 28 positions can increase this risk because of the difficulty in following each position effectively. Market risk, on the other hand, cannot be diversified away.

In the early part of the last century Benjamin Graham made his impact on the investment community with his work on **fundamental analysis**. Graham states that it is critical to fully research a company before adding it to a portfolio. By thoroughly understanding the company's current and potential for future cash flows; its management team, products, assets, and liabilities; and everything else that can be known about a particular company, one can derive its **intrinsic value**. If the company's intrinsic value is greater than the price per share for which its stock is selling, then that would present a buying opportunity. Superior research, investigation, and analysis make this method of stock selection viable. It would be wise to review Graham's material before making any investment for retirement or otherwise. The famed investment guru Warren Buffet says he believes in "owning companies," not just stocks as so many people do. Buffet's method of **focus investing** is a model in tireless research, holding concentrated positions and making big bets, bets that are long-term in nature and focus on intrinsic value. He believes knowing the companies you own fundamentally reduces risk and increases the potential for beating the market. Buffet says he doesn't invest in technology or internet companies because he doesn't understand them. Wow, now there's a concept!

In March 1952 Harry Markowitz developed what is known as *portfolio theory*. His thesis ultimately became the cornerstone and the most widely accepted investment theory of the 20th century. Today, most institutional investment advisors around the world rely on it. Markowitz theorized that the rational investor seeks the most return for the risk incurred. The graph that illustrates this portfolio theory is known as the **efficient frontier**, and Figure 51-2 is an example. The curved line represents the greatest return one can receive from a portfolio given the acceptable risk. The farther out on this line (or frontier) that one travels, the greater the risk (as measured by standard deviation) and the greater the potential return. Portfolios that fall below the curved line are "inefficient," since they receive less return for the risk associated with the underlying investments. Markowitz further theorized that by combining assets that did not correlate with each other (assets that moved independently or in opposite directions concurrently), one could reduce the risk in a portfolio. His analysis of the characteristics of individual asset classes is a method for valuing risk. Examples of an asset class would include stocks, bonds, cash, real estate, and natural resources. Subclasses of these would be small capitalization stocks, large capitalization stocks, quality bonds, junk bonds, residential or commercial real estate, and

(figure 51-2)

An example of the efficient frontier. The curved line represents the greatest return one can receive from a portfolio given the acceptable risk.

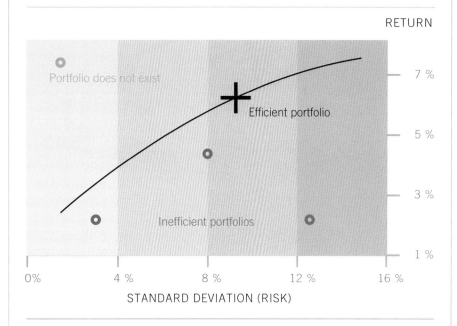

RETURN

Portfolio does not exist

Efficient portfolio

7 %

5 %

3 %

Inefficient portfolios

1 %

0%   4 %   8 %   12 %   16 %

STANDARD DEVIATION (RISK)

so forth. Markowitz's work included a model of the efficient frontier and a method for identifying expected rates of returns and price fluctuations for various combinations of specific asset classes.

In theory Markowicz's investment strategy was exciting; however, it didn't become fully applicable until after Bill Sharpe and his associates added their insight in the *capital asset pricing model (CAPM)*. The CAPM added perspective by introducing the concept of a *risk-free rate of return* and a method to ascertain the risk premium investors might enjoy over and above the risk-free rate for accepting ever-increasing amounts of risk. Markowicz and Sharpe shared the Nobel Prize in Economics for their contribution to investment theory and their development of **modern portfolio theory**. Their work lends some of the greatest support for not putting all your eggs in one basket.

Graham wrote the book on fundamental analysis; Buffet, following in Graham's footsteps, on focus investing; and Markowicz and Sharpe on modern portfolio theory. However, we would be remiss if we didn't mention *technical analysis,* which is the study of trends, price, and volume movements of individual securities and financial market indexes in general. Technical analysis has its basis in following momentum and trends, or, in other words, the herd. Ride ahead of the herd, and let it push you along. For example, if price movements are dramatic and supported by significant increases in volume (buying or selling), then theoretically a signal may be generated for the investor to buy in or sell out, depending on which side he or she is participating. Technical analysis can confirm the other investment analyses, theories, and strategies. For instance, market timers tend to use technical analysis as a signal-generating engine.

However, from our experience market timing does not work for most people. It can be exciting and profitable, but a significant problem remains at the points of entry, exit, and reentry into the markets. For example, with market timing, if we divest at a point in time that we believe is good, when do we reinvest? The optimum point of reinvestment is usually missed or vice versa. Some interesting statistics researched by Standard & Poor's addresses an investor's potential for missing significant days in the market over a 10-year period ending December 31, 2001. The statistics reveal that individuals who stayed fully invested during the aforementioned 10-year time period were rewarded with a 12.94% annual return. Those who missed the top 10 days of market gains over this same period received only 8.18%. Those individuals who missed the top 20 days received 4.71%, and those that missed the top 40 days received minus 0.56%. If you consider that there were 2522 trading days in this 10-year period, it is clear that having money on the sidelines during any of the these top performance days could be extremely detrimental to the long-term objectives of any portfolio. Remember that no one can invest directly in any index, but we are confident that Standard & Poor's research regarding investment discipline and market timing is not lost.

Capturing the best ideas from all these various strategies and molding them into a personalized, integrated investment policy statement is, in our opinion, the best way to approach investing for retirement. However, if as individuals we are not confident in our capability for building, managing, and monitoring our portfolios *unemotionally,* then we need to delegate the responsibility to professionals. Our quality of life and peace of mind may depend on it.

MONTE CARLO

Experience is the name everyone gives to their mistakes.
    – Oscar Wilde

Another analytical tool that we can employ in deciding how we might invest for our retirement is known as the *Monte Carlo simulation*. Monte

Carlo provides insight as to our probabilities of success, that is, achieving our *target rate of return*. Remember, target rate of return is the annual rate of return that we need to generate the required cash from our retirement income pool to maintain our lifestyle, while our *expected rate of return* is the return we expect given the level of risk we are willing to assume from a specific composition of assets in our investment portfolio. Again, and with any luck, our *target* rate of return and our *expected* rate of return should be very different. In general, identifying a target rate of return is a function of the depth of our retirement income pool, our retirement time horizon, and the annual cost of living for which we are planning. Shallow retirement income pools, high expenses (i.e., medical), and potentially longer retirement time horizons typically dictate a higher expected rate of return in order to increase the probability of achieving our target rate of return. Consequentially, if we determine that we need a higher expected rate of return to increase our probability for success, we usually incur a higher level of risk to do so. However, greater risk can equal increased portfolio volatility with potentially greater price fluctuations. Essentially, these circumstances will move the portfolio farther out on the efficient frontier.

The Monte Carlo simulation calculates, as a percentage, all the potential outcomes for a particular portfolio in a given year or number of years and estimates the portfolio's probability for exceeding various target rates of return over those periods. Tyler and Leslie's new expected rate of return for their combined portfolios is somewhere in the neighborhood of 8.75%. We can see from Table 51-1 that if their two portfolios are combined, the probability of exceeding just 5% as a target rate of return in the first year leaves them with an almost 25% probability of achieving something less. *Note:* Even though Leslie has a much greater disposition to tolerate risk than Tyler does, we believe it is important for them as a couple to see the probabilities of success as a household, in addition to individually. Today as a result of constructing a living, breathing analysis which can be monitored and modified at will, Tyler and Leslie have a

(table 51-1)

PROBABILITY OF EXCEEDING TARGET RETURN (AS A PERCENTAGE)

	YEAR 1	YEAR 2	YEAR 3	YEAR 5	YEAR 10
TARGET RETURN 5%					
Combined	76.86	85.04	89.82	94.97	98.99
Leslie	76.28	84.42	89.24	94.52	98.82
Tyler	79.90	88.20	92.67	96.95	99.60
TARGET RETURN 6%					
Combined	73.27	81.01	85.89	91.75	97.52
Leslie	73.06	80.76	85.64	91.53	97.40
Tyler	74.16	82.03	86.92	92.64	97.98
TARGET RETURN 7%					
Combined	69.45	76.41	81.09	87.24	94.62
Leslie	69.66	76.66	81.36	87.50	94.81
Tyler	67.73	74.24	78.73	84.82	92.72

(figure 51-3)

Probability of exceeding target return if Tyler and Leslie's two portfolios are combined.

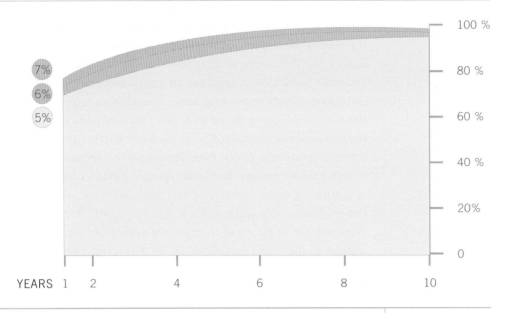

much better understanding of what they need, what they can tolerate in investment risk, and a reasonable expectation of their probabilities for a successful retirement.

Figure 51-3 also makes it clear that after defining a suitable portfolio, maintaining that portfolio throughout the time horizons we have established for ourselves can be critical, since it would seem the longer we hold a suitable portfolio, the greater our potential or probability for success. We must emphasize the operative words here: *suitable portfolio.* As we have discussed, understanding our needs, our personal tolerance for uncertainty, our ability to withstand investment losses, and our ability to fully understand all the risks associated with making any investment help determine whether a particular investment portfolio is suitable for us. Beyond that, it is just a matter of taking responsibility for our investment choices. Therefore, if we choose to delegate our investment responsibilities to someone else, that is, a professional, we must realize then that we cannot delegate the responsibility to do our homework in order to ensure that we have maximized our potential for having made the right choice in delegates.

CHOOSING A WEALTH PLANNING PROFESSIONAL

Learn to unlearn.
   —Benjamin Disraeli

If it is our objective to build a financial house as strong as the third little piggy's, that is, one that cannot be easily blown away, it will take a team. Whatever our net worth, a well-conceived and efficiently implemented wealth strategies design can best be created in a team environment with the appropriate professional advisors. For example, if we picture a surgeon, it would be unimaginable for the surgeon to perform an operation alone. It would be conceivably worse if we called upon an in-law or friend to help with the anesthesia simply because our in-law or friend had surgery before or "knows something" about the subject. The prudent course is to call upon professionals and build a team with which we are comfortable. After all, if we are committed to doing things well, we will be sharing our most personal dreams, hopes, and aspirations. Just as in a surgical team, it makes sense to maximize our own set of unique abilities by finding professionals whose unique abilities complement our own.

From our discussion we can surmise that *investing* is but a small part of the overall process of preparing for retirement. Therefore, in choosing a financial professional to add to our team, we begin by interviewing advisors that have experience and work regularly in collaborative environments with attorneys, CPAs, and other wealth professionals. Finding an investment professional that meets our needs should not be a difficult task if we appropriate the necessary resources.

1. For maximum benefit, as we discussed, we must explore and be able to teach our advisors about our families and ourselves.
2. While we are able today, we want to protect our loved ones, as well as ourselves, by picking the people who can and are willing to act on our behalf when necessary. By identifying those who will take over if we can no longer perform the investment analysis and allocations ourselves, we can be prepared when the time arrives. In fact, establishing those relationships today can have the added benefit of allowing us to test the water and receive additional insights and second opinions with regard to our current investment strategy.
3. Third, we need to do our homework, research beyond the brochures, and check the advisor's credentials.

Here are a few ideas as to how to check an advisor's record. Check with the state insurance department, the National Association of Securities Dealers (NASD), the Certified Financial Planner Board of Standards, the community chamber of commerce, and better business bureau. After the preliminary check, here are some questions we like to see asked:

- *How are they compensated?*
- *Are they independent or captive agents of an insurance company and/or a broker-dealer?* A simple way of checking for independence is to ask if they receive a 1099 or a W-2 for tax purposes. A W-2 points to an employee relationship, whereas a 1099 represents an independent contractor. Independent advisors can receive both; however, truly captive agents receive only a W-2.
- *Do they have to sell a financial product in order to be paid?* In itself, whether they are fee based, commission, or both is not good or bad, however, we will want to understand motivations as best we can.

- *How do they report performance and fees, and how often?* Is it flexible? Can they roll up all your investments in a concise, easily understandable format, without reams of unintelligible statements?
- *Do they provide a clearly defined and written investment policy statement?* An investment policy statement is an excellent tool to help with the monitoring process, and it is meant to protect both the client and the advisor from misunderstandings.
- *Do they demonstrate a commitment to the financial field in which they practice?* Do they have years of dedicated service and experience, certifications, and/or advanced degrees? Are they in good standing with the applicable regulatory bodies and with the associations to which they belong?

There are a great number of highly skilled financial professionals who will place your interests far and away above their own. All we need to do is a little legwork to find them.

INVESTMENT POLICY STATEMENTS AND MONITORING

Excellence is to do a common thing in an uncommon way.
    —Booker T. Washington

After implementing our investment policy, we want to monitor the investment to maintain control and remain confident that we can support the lifestyle we have chosen over our retirement time horizon.

The basic investment policy statement defines such aspects as the time horizon for which we are investing, our expected rate of return, the distributions and contributions which will be made over our time horizon, and our ability to withstand risk. The investment policy statement is a written document that is customized for us. It describes all the parameters for investing our capital assets and can be constructed as

HOW LONG WILL I LIVE?

The following are U.S. life expectancy statistics from a report by the National Center for Health Statistics.

FINAL DATA YEAR 2000	
All Americans, at birth	76.9
All Americans, at age 65	17.9
All males, at birth	74.1
All males, at age 65	16.3
All females, at birth	79.5
All females, at age 65	19.2

The year 2000 report, released in December 2002, states that out of 100,000 men and 100,000 women born alive in the United States, 27,265 men and 42,145 women survived their 85th birthday and 13,045 men and 23,936 women survived their 90th birthday.

(table 51-2)

CASH FLOW SHEET DURING RETIREMENT
Tyler and Leslie: Annual Income and Expense

AGE	TOTAL INCOME*	TAXES & EXPENSES†	BANK & INVESTMENTS‡		
			EXCESS OR SHORTAGE	AFTER-TAX ASSETS	BALANCE RETIREMENT PLAN ASSETS§
67	$ 44,212	$ 74,297	–$ 30,084	$ 18,283	$ 763,804
68	$ 69,694	$ 81,088	–$ 11,394	$ 7,096	$ 801,994
69	$ 74,405	$ 81,501	–$ 7,096	0	$ 811,131
70	$ 85,187	$ 85,188	0	0	$ 809,834
71	$ 87,250	$ 87,250	0	0	$ 806,767
72	$ 89,276	$ 89,276	0	0	$ 801,886
73	$ 91,512	$ 91,512	0	0	$ 794,884
74	$ 93,824	$ 93,824	0	0	$ 785,580
75	$ 96,235	$ 96,235	0	0	$ 773,761
76	$ 98,746	$ 98,746	0	0	$ 759,198
77	$ 101,366	$ 101,366	0	0	$ 741,646
78	$ 104,101	$ 104,101	0	0	$ 720,841
79	$ 106,955	$ 106,955	0	0	$ 696,498
80	$ 109,934	$ 109,934	0	0	$ 668,315
81	$ 113,042	$ 113,042	0	0	$ 635,969
82	$ 94,052	$ 94,052	0	0	$ 622,461
83	$ 97,193	$ 97,193	0	0	$ 605,500
84	$ 100,449	$ 100,449	0	0	$ 584,797
85	$ 103,863	$ 103,863	0	0	$ 560,004
86	$ 104,363	$ 104,363	0	0	$ 533,983
87	$ 102,449	$ 102,449	0	0	$ 509,213
88	$ 106,320	$ 106,320	0	0	$ 479,687
89	$ 110,337	$ 110,337	0	0	$ 445,018
90	$ 114,531	$ 114,531	0	0	$ 404,770

*Includes Social Security benefits, payouts from pensions, interest generated by investments in the nonqualified capital account, payouts from IRAs, and other income including earnings. Doesn't include growth in undistributed qualified retirement assets.

†Includes line item inflation rates (minimum 2.6%) and all other expected expenses over the retirement time horizon.

‡3% target rate.

§5% target rate.

Source: Adapted with permission from software by Lumen Systems.

easily for cash and certificates of deposits (CDs), or mutual funds, as it can be for individual stocks, bonds, or derivatives. We believe it is important that each portfolio have a written investment policy statement and that we have full access and availability to the financial markets. (Figure 51-4 is a sample investment policy statement for review.)

Once our investment policy statement is in force, it is much easier to monitor investment progress. As a side note, it is easy to forget that all investments of principal in all portfolios fluctuate over time. Cash, CDs, or our investment capital are not static assets. Even if we invest in a federally insured bank, our principal can lose purchasing power because of inflation. For instance, if inflation is said to average 3% annually, our principal investment will be worth less than 87% of its initial value in five years. Our principal investment would be worth less than 79% of its original value if inflation is reported to be 5%, and for 10 years at that rate we may have lost as much as 38% by using a perceived "safe" investment. There is no escaping principal fluctuation in any portfolio over time. In fairness the interest we earn in our traditional savings accounts and CDs offsets that fluctuation to some extent; however, inflation and purchasing power is to be taken seriously. We will always have the potential for loss in the principal of our investment capital; it is only a question of whether or not we want to see it on our statements.

HOW LONG WILL MY PORTFOLIO LAST?

The trick is to make sure you don't die waiting for prosperity to come.
— Lee Iacocca

Monitoring our cash flows is as important as monitoring our investment results, and that is why keeping our cash flows "living and breathing" is an excellent exercise. Keeping our investment policy statement and a living, breathing cash-flow analysis side by side can be excellent tools for monitoring our total financial picture during retirement. The roll up examples in Table 51-2 are simplistic; however, any line item that supports the data can be updated on the fly as it changes or is expected to change over time, and therefore we can more easily gauge how we are doing in relation to our original assumptions.

In many cases assumptions are changed to model what-if scenarios going forward. That is, what if the market or our investment portfolio sustains losses for three or four years in a row? What if our retirement time horizon is lengthened? Will we outlive our money, or do we have estate tax issues? What is the impact on our cash flows if we sell our present residence and buy a new home? How much can or should we spend? In any case, monitoring our investments and cash flows can be crucial in obtaining and maintaining the lifestyle we seek during our retirement years (see Table 51-3). Staying on track and in the know in a world for which nothing is as constant as change can provide peace of mind.

(table 51-3)

PORTFOLIO CONSUMPTION DURING RETIREMENT

ANNUAL RETURN	ANNUAL DISTRIBUTIONS							
	18%	16%	14%	12%	10%	8%	6%	5%
10%	9	11	14	19				
9%	9	10	12	17	27			
8%	8	10	12	15	21			
7%	8	9	11	13	18	31		
6%	7	9	10	12	16	24		
5%	7	8	10	12	15	21	37	
4%	7	8	9	11	14	18	29	42

Note: Blue represents potential years of distribution and green potentially unlimited distributions.

PREPARING IN ADVANCE OF THE TRANSITION

One of the hardest things to teach our children about money matters is that it does.
—*William Randolph Hearst*

In an airliner people are better suited to assist others if they put their own oxygen mask on first. Therefore, it is probably safe to assume that in life people should focus initially on themselves and then their spouse, family, friends, causes, and so on, not necessarily in that order. Further, investment allocations, titling, or funding of their financial assets typically mirror these priorities. If we "begin with the end in mind," as Steven Covey suggests in his book, *The 7 Habits of Highly Effective People,* we may want to take our eventual incapacity and/or death into account as we develop our retirement strategies and add an element of continuity to our planning. For instance, who will take over investment management responsibilities? Will it be our spouse, son, or daughter? Do they handle their own personal finances well? Do they have experience with investing potentially large sums of assets? On the subject of incapacity there are a great number of issues to review, but for purposes of this chapter we have focused on investments and how they will be maintained and by whom, when we no longer can manage the responsibility. Basic discussions about our money and investment strategy with our successors is a start, but since we have no way of knowing when we may be incapacitated or need assistance, open conversations followed by letters of instruction about our investments, along with our short- and long-term objectives with our successors, may be a much better idea. Our families will have enough to do caring and supporting us in the event of our disability or incapacity. Do we want them to have to monitor and manage our investment assets too? Possibly, but as we plan for our future, open discussions with the people that are closest to us in combination with dedicated professionals may help us and our families to better understand our goals for our personal, social, and financial wealth.

Good luck and be well!

(figure 51-4)

A SAMPLE INVESTMENT POLICY STATEMENT

Many of the figures in this plan involve the use of numbers because they are the most effective means of illustrating a financial picture. These illustrations can lend an aura of false accuracy. Groups of numbers dealing with investments, and cash flow five years (and longer) into the future are not intended to be viewed as predictive but rather represent projections, based on a certain set of assumptions. Although real life events can rarely be predicted with precision, these projections are useful in comparing the likely results of different strategies and plans of action. Please bring any questions regarding the data and assumptions enclosed in this statement to our attention.

INVESTMENT POLICY SUMMARY

PREPARED FOR	Jane A.	
DATE	5/17/2001	
TYPE OF ASSETS	Qualified	
CURRENT ASSETS	Approximately $ 875,000	
INVESTMENT TIME HORIZON	Greater than 25 years	
EXPECTED RETURN	6.68% above the expected inflation rate of approximately 3.1% (9.78% Gross)	
RISK TOLERANCE	Moderate \ High for short-term	
	Moderate \ High for the intermediate-term	
	Moderate \ High for the long-term	
	Losses not to exceed -14.7% per year with a 90% confidence level	
ASSET ALLOCATION	See following pages for portfolio allocations	
ALLOCATION VARIANCE LIMIT	Quarterly	10 %
BROAD CLASSES	Annually	5 %
REPRESENTATIVE BENCHMARKS*	Cash equivalent	Federal 3Mo T-Bill
	Fixed Income	LEHB Mortgaged Backed
		FIRB High Yield Bond
	Equity	WILS Large Value
		WILS Large Growth

* Subject To Change

OVERVIEW

The primary objective of this investment policy is to identify and adopt an investment strategy that demonstrates the potential to consistently grow capital assets for and during retirement. These assets are intended for supplemental retirement income over the retirement time horizon of greater than 25 years.

Our strategy for accomplishing these objectives is based on the concept of diversification, which we call asset allocation. It is a long-term strategy, designed to suit individual aspirations, personal values, and circumstances, which provides a durable framework within which to make specific investment decisions. This investment program does not attempt to consider the active management of short-term investment fluctuations. We constructed this asset allocation as a long-term strategy for the management of retirement assets.

In designing your personal investment strategy, we began by reviewing your objectives and constraints and from this perspective; we developed our specific recommendations, which we believe to be appropriate for you.

INVESTMENT & OTHER OBJECTIVES

1. Consolidate current assets for ease of monitoring, management, and accessibility.
2. Construct, balance, and manage this portfolio for growth in line with expected returns, personal risk tolerance, target returns, and income needs over an estimated retirement time horizon of more than 25 years.
3. Maintain account registration and beneficiary designations in accordance with disability and estate plans provided by your legal counsel to maximize the value of these retirement assets.
4. Minimize income tax liabilities collaboratively with your Certified Public Accountant (CPA) whenever possible and especially with regards to future issues such as IRD (Income in Respect of a Decedent).

RISK TOLERANCE

Based on our discussions and an analysis of your investment preferences and income needs you will need to continue to make investments in the stock and fixed income securities markets. Therefore, it is important to remember that these types of investments *will* lose money when the markets go down, and the financial markets *will* go down at points in the future! For example, equity markets typically rise and fall with each business cycle.

In establishing your risk tolerance, we have considered your ability to withstand short-, intermediate-, and long-term volatility. Your responses to our query and risk-profiling questionnaire, lead us to believe that you can accept the price fluctuations inherent to a moderately high volatile investment portfolio. Our recommendation is to reduce your current exposure to portfolio volatility (as measured by standard deviation) and reallocate your portfolio assets accordingly. Your current portfolio is more aggressively positioned further out on the scale of the "Efficient Frontier." Through repositioning your current assets into a broader group of asset classes it is our goal to align your investments within your risk tolerance and give your portfolio the potential for increased efficiency. Theoretically, by reducing portfolio volatility, we can increase your comfort with the underlying investments, which in turn, should allow you to remain comfortable enough to leave the assets invested over the prescribed investment time horizon.

ASSET ALLOCATION

We believe that your portfolio's risk and return are in large part, a function of the combination of asset classes, or asset mix. We have reviewed the long-term characteristics of various asset classes, in order to balance the risks and rewards of market performance. Five major asset classes were originally considered, however, due to your preferences, we have eliminated from the proposed portfolio mix international equities and bonds:

- Cash equivalents
- Domestic equities
- Domestic bonds

While covered call writing may be utilized to increase the potential for portfolio income, we did not consider the following securities and transactions: commodities, commodity contracts, venture capital, and short sales.

EXPECTED RETURN

During your investment time horizon, your recommended portfolio will hold varying percentages of cash, equity, and debt instruments. While the allocations among these major asset classes and their related subclasses will vary, it is our goal to have your investment portfolio remain consistent with your personal values, financial objectives, risk tolerance, need for income, and time horizon. You will find your financial objectives, risk tolerance, and time horizons, as you have stated them to us, in the appropriate sections of this investment policy statement.

A reasonable expectation for the long term rate of return of the recommended portfolio is approximately 6.68% greater than the rate of inflation as measured by the consumer price index (CPI). This anticipated return is based on the expected long-term total return for each asset class and its percentage weighting in your portfolio. This recommended portfolio is different from your current portfolio because it implements a broader diversification across many asset classes. This should result in a reduction of risk, (measured by standard deviation) and of return, which when combined, should be more commensurate with your anticipated or expected return. The portfolio return may also be reduced by the deduction of advisory, money management, custodial, and transaction fees. Since this portfolio is constructed for your risk tolerance and time horizon it is our belief that it demonstrates the potential to be more efficient and more suitable to your personal values, income needs, and overall financial objectives.

INVESTMENT RECOMMENDATIONS

We review our recommended Portfolio for your Individual Retirement Account (IRA) in the following pages:

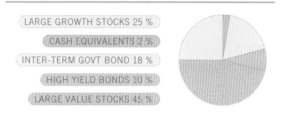

LARGE GROWTH STOCKS 25 %
CASH EQUIVALENTS 2 %
INTER-TERM GOVT BOND 18 %
HIGH YIELD BONDS 10 %
LARGE VALUE STOCKS 45 %

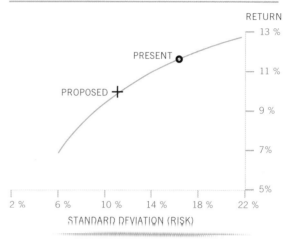

	PRESENT	PROPOSED
Expected Return	11.63 %	9.78 %
Std Deviation (Risk)	16.63 %	10.98 %
Sharpe Ratio	0.55 %	0.66 %
Yield	1.77 %	3.76 %

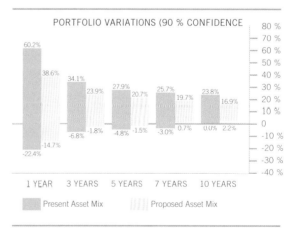

PORTFOLIO VARIATIONS (90 % CONFIDENCE

Present Asset Mix   Proposed Asset Mix

PROBABLITY OF FALLING BELOW TARGET RETURN
TARGET RETURN: 5.00 %

PORTFOLIO	1 YEAR	3 YEARS	5 YEARS	7 YEARS	10 YEARS
Present	29.50 %	25.00 %	21.00 %	18.00 %	14.5 %
Proposed	32.00 %	25.00 %	18.50 %	14.50 %	12.50 %

51

SELECTION & RETENTION CRITERIA

Generally, investment products used to implement the investment program shall be subject to selection criteria*. At a minimum, the investment product must be registered, have sufficient historical performance, and provide timely compliant information. In addition, it will provide necessary details about the firm (personnel, clients, fees, etc.), and strictly adhere to a clearly articulated investment philosophy. This selection and retention process will generally include:

- Past Performance
- Costs Relative to Other Investments within the Asset Class
- The Size of the Mutual Fund, or Security
- Length of Time the Security Has Been In Existence & Length of Time the Security Has Been Under the Direction of the Current Management
- Historical Volatility
- How Well Each Proposed Investment Compliments Other
- Assets within the Portfolio

Any investment alternative or security held at your request will not be subject to the selection and retention criteria stated above.

MONITORING AND REVIEW

We will monitor and report investment performance to you on a quarterly basis. We will compare the investment performance of your investment program against the appropriate benchmarks and review your portfolio's status at least annually to make sure that it continues to achieve your stated objectives. Since this investment program is long-term in nature, the periodic adjustments made to your portfolio are expected to be relatively minor.

OPTIMIZATION

The long-term risk, return, and correlation characteristics associated with individual asset classes, can change over time. Therefore, over your investment time horizon it may be necessary to optimize your investment portfolio and adjust for these potential changes as they occur. Optimization is a method for updating the percentage weighting of asset classes within a portfolio in order to maximize that portfolio's position on the efficient frontier. All optimization adjustments are made in an attempt to increase portfolio efficiency and to limit the potential

for portfolio "drift" as it pertains to your stated risk tolerance and expected return. This means that the complexion, asset allocation or physical makeup of your portfolio can change over time. Typically, optimization modifications occur infrequently.

REBALANCING

The percentage weighting in each asset class within the investment portfolio will vary. We will allow the percentage weighting within each asset class to vary within a reasonable range of +/- 5% to 10% depending upon the market conditions. When rebalancing is required, we will use investment yield, and net cash inflows to meet the strategic asset allocation targets. If cash flow is not sufficient to meet the target allocation for an asset class, we will decide whether to effect transactions in order to rebalance the asset allocation.

I acknowledge reading, and understanding, the above investment policy. I accept the recommendations contained herein and will notify you in writing if any of the pertinent information that you utilized to create this investment policy statement change.

ADVISORY CLIENT

REGISTERED INVESTMENT ADVISOR

HISTORICAL RETURNS

ASSET CLASS	1926–2002		1993–2002	
	ROR	REAL ROR	ROR	REAL ROR
U.S. T-Bills	3.8	.08	4.4	1.9
Intermediate Govt. Bonds	5.4	2.3	7.3	4.7
Long Term Govt. Bonds	5.5	2.4	9.7	7.0
Long Term Corp. Bonds	5.9	2.8	8.8	6.1
Common Stock	10.2	7.0	9.3	6.7
Small Company Stock	12.1	8.8	11.6	8.9
Inflation	3.0		2.5	

Source: Ibbotson Associates

FINANCIAL MARKET PROJECTIONS

FIXED INCOME INVESTMENTS	RATE OF RETURN %	STD DEVIATION %
Cash Equivalents	3.25 %	2.0 %
T-Notes/CDs	3.75 %	3.0 %
Inter-Term Gov't Bonds	6.0 %	6.0 %
Long Term Gov't Bonds	6.5 %	8.0 %
Municipal Bonds	5.0 %	8.0 %
Corporate Bonds	6.75 %	8.5 %
Mortgage Backed Bonds	6.25 %	7.5 %
High Yield Bonds	9.5 %	16.0 %
International Bonds	7.25 %	13.0 %
GROWTH INVESTMENTS	RATE OF RETURN %	STD DEVIATION %
Large Value Stocks	9.75 %	13.25 %
Large Growth Stocks	10.75 %	16.25 %
Small-Cap Value Stocks	11.25 %	18.25 %
Small-Cap Growth Stocks	12.25 %	22.25 %
International Developed	11.25 %	22.25 %
International–Emerging Equities	11.75 %	40.25 %
Real Estate	7.75 %	14.0 %

Source: Frontier Analytics, Inc.

WHAT YOU NEED TO KNOW

▶ *Aspects of wealth:* Of the many aspects of wealth, we explored the three main categories of personal, social, and financial.

▶ *What you need and core planning:* In-depth discovery, mapping, and charting constitute the essential process that increases one's potential for success in investing.

▶ *Investment theory and strategy:* Taking the best ideas and incorporating them into our own personal investment policy can be the best way to build a suitable investment portfolio.

▶ *Monte Carlo and probabilities for success:* Mathematically calculating our probabilities for success can assist us

to better understand the risks inherent in most any potential portfolio.

▶ *Choosing a wealth professional:* If we need professional investment help, the right professionals are available to us. We just need to know how to find them.

▶ *Monitoring and adjustments:* No different from the itinerary we might receive from an auto or travel club. We need to reference often enough to know if we are going in the right direction so we can make course corrections as necessary.

FOR MORE INFORMATION

▷ Certified Financial Planner Board of Standards
Web: www.ctp-board.org
Check an advisor's status.

▷ National Association of Securities Dealers (NASD)
Web: www.nasdr.com
Check an advisor's status.

▷ The Normandy Group
1675 Larimer Street, Suite 675
Denver, CO 80202
303-893-8700 ext. 3505
E mail: david@rgsnormandy.com

▷ U.S. Bureau of Labor Statistics
Web: www.bls.gov
Information on the consumer price index.

SUGGESTED READING

▷ The Intelligent Investor, rev. ed.
Benjamin Graham. 1997.
New York: HarperCollins.

▷ The Warren Buffet Portfolio: Mastering the Power of the Focus Investment Strategy
Robert Hagstrom. 1999.
New York: Wiley.

▷ Investments: An Introduction
Herbert B. Mayo. 1980.
Fort Worth, TX: Dryden Press, Harcourt Brace.

▷ Stan Weinstein's Secrets for Profiting in Bull and Bear Markets
Stan Weinstein. 1992.
New York: McGraw-Hill.

SOURCE NOTE

The artwork in this chapter has been adapted, with permission, from illustrations produced from software by SunGard Online Investment Systems.

It is not how old you are, but how you are old.

—*Marie Dressler*

THE AUTHOR

52

IRA STEWART WIESNER is a nationally recognized elder law attorney and founder of Advocates in Aging, a multidimensional elder law firm in Sarasota, Florida. He is a former president of the National Academy of Elder Law Attorneys, as well as past chair of the Elder Law Section of the Florida Bar. Mr. Wiesner is board-certified as a specialist in taxation, as well as elder law. He is a fellow of the National Academy of Elder Law Attorneys and of the American College of Trust and Estate Counsel. He is a past member of the Florida State Long Term Care Ombudsman and frequent lecturer, consultant, and resource on issues of long-term care financing and aging.

Mr. Wiesner is graduate of the State University of New York (SUNY) at Buffalo, with a Bachelor of Arts in philosophy and political science, cum laude. He received his juris doctor from SUNY at Buffalo Law School and holds a master of laws in taxation from the University of Florida. He has earned a graduate certificate in gerontology from the University of South Florida and is pursuing graduate studies in hospice, palliative care, and end-of-life issues. As an intern with the Spiritual Eldering Institute, Mr. Wiesner works to aid older persons in transforming their aging into saging.

52 | LONG-TERM CARE AND MEDICAID

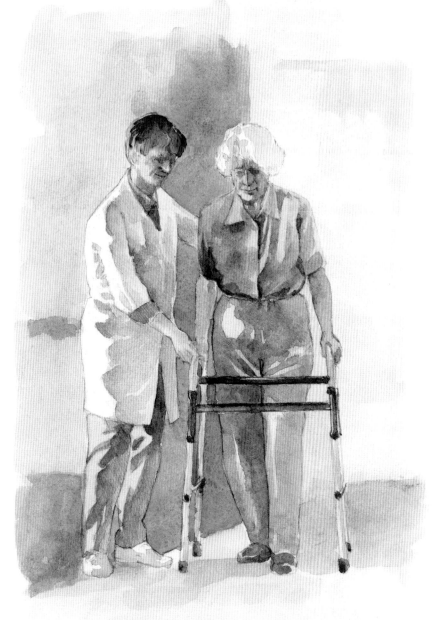

Legal issues take on special significance to aging individuals. Seniors, by and large, are concerned with financing the costs of growing older while preserving self-dignity and control. One of the most critical concerns facing the aging population is financing the costs of long-term care.

LONG-TERM CARE

THE SHEAR NUMBERS

In 2000 the 65- to 84-year-old age group included 30.5 million people. This is expected to climb to 47 million by 2020 and 63 million by 2040. Those over 85 numbered 4.3 million in 2000 and are expected to double to 8.6 million in 2030 and triple to 13.6 million by 2040. In 1990, there were 1.8 million older persons in nursing homes, an increase of 24% from 1980. This figure is projected to increase to 4.6 million by the year 2040. Sixty % of nursing home residents are women. It is estimated that 63% of all nursing home residents suffer from cognitive dysfunctioning. Two-thirds of those persons have some form of senile dementia.

COST

One out of every four persons over the age of 65 will spend time in a skilled nursing facility; for those over 80, that figure increases to one out of two. For the individuals and their families, the costs of such long-term care are shocking: the average cost exceeds $5000 per month. Often, families are even more shocked to learn that unless they purchased long-term care insurance, they may have no choice but to deplete their life savings to pay such costs.

Paying for long-term care has become a crisis in our country, but the price tag of a solution has intimidated politicians from constructively addressing the crisis.

LIMITATIONS OF MEDICARE COVERAGE

Contrary to what many believe, Medicare only pays for about 2% of annual nursing home costs. At most, it will pay for 100 days of skilled care, as long as the following four conditions are met:

1. The patient must be hospitalized for medically necessary inpatient hospital care for at least three consecutive calendar days, not counting the day of discharge (thus, *four days, three nights*). For example, if the patient goes into the emergency room Friday evening, is admitted to the hospital Saturday morning, stays Saturday night and Sunday night, and is discharged Monday morning, Medicare will not cover the nursing home stay because Friday was not an admit day; emergency room and outpatient stays do not count.

2. The patient must be eligible for Part A benefits in the month of discharge from the hospital.

3. Admission to the skilled nursing facility (SNF) must occur within 30 days of discharge unless SNF admission would be medically inappropriate during that time.

4. The patient must continue to demonstrate a need for skilled care, ordered by a physician, the type of care which can be only provided in an SNF. The level-of-care requirements are so strict that many patients cannot meet them. As soon as the patient has rehabilitated as much as possible, eligibility ends.

Even when the above conditions are met, Medicare Part A only covers the full costs of the first 20 days in a benefit period. (A *benefit* period begins when the patient first enters the hospital and continues until no inpatient or extended care services are rendered for 60 days.) For each day from day 25 to day 100, the patient must pay a coinsurance amount. The coinsurance amount in 2003 was $105 per day.

MEDICAID: THE PAYER OF LAST RESORT

Medicaid is a financial assistance program jointly funded by federal and state governments and established in 1965 in order to pay for the health care of the "categorically needy and medically needy." The federal government sets basic rules for the states, but allows the states great latitude in defining the income and asset criteria to follow. As a result, Medicaid programs and eligibility requirements vary considerably from state to state. Each participating state must follow the general eligibility criteria set forth under federal law. States may broaden that criteria but may not promulgate rules that are more restrictive than their federal counterparts.

BASIC ELIGIBILITY CRITERIA

Medicaid programs vary greatly from state to state. In most states, there are at least two categories of needy individuals who may qualify for benefits: the *mandatory categorically needy* and the *optionally categorically needy*. The mandatory categorically needy, who are individuals receiving

MEDICAID JARGON

- *Applicant.* Person applying for benefits.
- *Assets.* Resources and income for purposes of computing a period of ineligibility for dispositions without adequate consideration.
- *Community spouse (CS).* The at-home spouse of an institutionalized spouse (IS). A spouse residing in an assisted living facility, but not receiving his or her own Medicaid benefits, is still considered a community spouse.
- *Community spouse resource allowance (CSRA).* The amount of resources allowed to be retained by a CS without affecting the eligibility of the IS.
- *Income.* Cash, payments, wages, in-kind items, inheritances, rents, dividends, interest, pension payments, and so on, received on a monthly or otherwise periodic basis, received between the first and last day of a month. For example, if income in received on July 31, it is income for July, but on August 1, it becomes a resource.
- *Institutionalized spouse (IS).* A spouse who is in a nursing home.
- *Minimum monthly maintenance needs allowance (MMMNA).* The amount of income a CS may retain each month for his or her own living expenses.
- *Recipient.* Person receiving benefits.
- *Resources.* Assets of an individual or family as of the first day of any calendar month or as of the date of application if not counted as income for the month of application.

Supplemental Security Income (SSI) or Aid to Families with Dependent Children (AFDC), are automatically eligible for Medicaid programs. States may also elect to cover individuals who are optionally categorically needy. The optionally categorically needy include the aged, blind, or disabled. SSI-related Medicaid programs for the optionally categorically needy include the Institutional Care Program (nursing home Medicaid), the medically needy, emergency Medicaid for aliens, home- and community-based care, working disabled, and others.

The basic eligibility criteria for most SSI-related Medicaid programs, including nursing home Medicaid, are as follows:

1. Either 65 years of age or older, blind, or disabled
2. A U.S. resident
3. A state's resident
4. A U.S. citizen or resident alien admitted for permanent residence
5. Provided or filed a Social Security number
6. Filed for all other benefits to which may be entitled
7. Assigned to the state all rights to collect private health insurance

ELIGIBILITY CRITERIA FOR NURSING HOME MEDICAID BENEFITS

The nursing home Medicaid benefit, in many states referred to as the *Institutional Care Program,* provides Medicaid benefits for persons who need institutionalized care. Benefits include payment to nursing homes. In addition to the basic criteria set forth above, nursing home Medicaid applicants must also meet the requirements for level of care, income, and resource eligibility.

Level of care: The applicant must require either intermediate or skilled nursing care in a nursing home or other skilled nursing facility. The nursing home must be a facility capable of providing the care needed. If the applicant is living in an assisted living facility and his or her care needs can be adequately met (both as to the needs and compliance with state licensing laws) in that facility, he or she will not be considered needing a nursing home level of care. The states recognize that some seniors who are frail, but may not need a nursing home, might desire nursing home care because of the Medicaid coverage (which reduces their financial expense) and use this criteria to decide who receives the nursing home benefit. Many states have been given permission to cover limited assisted living care under Medicaid waivers. Ordinarily, however, in order to secure waiver benefits, a similar level of care as for nursing home benefits is required.

Income: In most states, an individual must have too little income to cover his or her care. Income includes both earned and unearned income, unless specifically excluded. Social Security, pensions, dividends, annuity payments, alimony, veteran's benefits, interest income, and any income received at regular intervals are included.

A minority of states have imposed an income cap. Regardless of available assets and resources, an applicant whose income exceeds an amount equal to three times the federal SSI benefit—even by as little as 10 cents—is not eligible for benefits. The income cap of 2003 was $1635 per month. However, individuals who otherwise qualify for nursing home benefits, except for income in excess of the cap, are entitled to establish a special trust, called a qualified income trust or Miller trust, to get around this limitation.

Note: When an applicant's income is examined, a spouse's income is generally *ignored*—there is no deeming of income from one spouse to the other.

Resources: Resources are categorized as either exempt or nonexempt. Nonexempt resources are limited as follows:

- For an individual $2,000
- For a couple $3,000

Note: An applicant's resources include those owned by the applicant, owned jointly by the applicant and another (including the spouse), and resources owned exclusively by the spouse.

A spouse who does not live in a nursing home is called the community spouse (CS) and is allowed to retain a minimum amount of nonexempt resources in order to avoid impoverishment. (See the section "Protecting a Community Spouse," below.) The protected amount is one-half of the couple's combined assets, with a minimum of $14,532 and a maximum of $90,960 (for 2003), although some states allow the maximum without the one-half limitation. It is important to verify the exempt amount on a state-by-state basis. To reach an acceptable figure, spouses may freely transfer assets between themselves without fear of penalty.

Exempt resources: The following resources may be retained:

- *Residence.* The applicant's home is exempt as long as it is the principal place of residence of the applicant or his or her spouse. If the applicant lives alone, he or she must express an intent to return to the home, even if circumstances make that a very remote and highly unlikely possibility.
- *Household furnishings and personal effects.* For individuals, personal property and household furnishings of reasonable value are generally excluded as assets. However, household furnishings are exempt only as long as they are being used in the home.
- *Automobile.* One automobile is excluded, regardless of value or use. In addition, most automobiles over seven years old are also excluded.
- *Income-producing property.* Income-producing property owned by an applicant and essential to that applicant's self-support is excluded if the property is producing income consistent with the property's fair market value.
- *Life insurance.* Life insurance having no cash surrender value is excluded in determining available assets. All other policies are considered to the extent of their cash surrender value and are considered as an available

resource to the extent that the total face value of all policies exceeds an exempt amount.

- *Burial funds.* Certain burial exclusion policies exist. The value of an irrevocable burial contract is excluded from consideration regardless of its amount. A revocable burial contract is excluded from accountability up to a value set by the state.

DETERMINATION OF ELIGIBILITY AND RETROACTIVE BENEFITS

Federal law requires that a determination of Medicaid eligibility must be made within 45 days of the first day of the month in which the application for assistance was filed and all eligibility criteria were met. Extensions of the 45-day period are only permitted for good cause, including delay on the part of the applicant. Nevertheless, in many areas of the country, disposition of an application within the 45-day period is the exception rather than the rule.

One difficulty encountered by nursing home residents is that facilities expect payment while the Medicaid application is pending. If the resident has reduced his or her assets to the Medicaid eligibility level, there will be insufficient resources to pay the nursing home bill until the Medicaid is approved. Even if Medicaid is approved effective as of the date of application, a family may have been required to pay for the cost of care during the extended application period at the higher private-pay rate and not be refunded that payment for the months in which the individual was in fact eligible for Medicaid.

An applicant who is determined to be entitled for Medicaid benefits will be eligible from the first day of the month in which the application for assistance was filed. Benefits may also be available retroactively to the first day of the third month before the month of application if the applicant applies for and meets all the eligibility criteria on any day in each of those months.

PROTECTING THE COMMUNITY SPOUSE

Because of Medicaid's status as payer of last resort, applicants who are subsequently approved for Medicaid are expected to use their net income to pay for the care being provided. As a result, if the institutionalized spouse (IS) has been the primary source of support for his or her family, the community spouse (CS) can be left with insufficient income for daily living. The CS must then spend down any "protected" resources for his or her self-support. The consequence of that policy would be to defeat the intention of the CSRA and increase the possibility that the CS will eventually require government assistance.

To avoid such spousal impoverishment, the CS is permitted to receive or retain a portion of the IS's income and resources which would otherwise have gone to pay the costs of long-term care.

INCOME PROTECTION

The portion which the spouse is permitted to retain is known as the minimum monthly maintenance needs allowance (MMMNA). This allowance has two parts. First is an income allowance sufficient to raise the CS's income to 150% of the federal poverty level for a two-person household. In 2003, the minimum allowance was $1493. Second is an excess shelter allowance to cover unusually high housing costs. The shelter allowance is calculated by adding the CS's expenses for rent or mortgage payments (including principal, interest, taxes, and insurance), condominium maintenance fees, and utility costs. If the sum of these items exceeds 30% of the income allowance (30% of the 2003 amount $1493 equals $448), any excess is an additional amount which the CS may retain or receive from the IS's income.

The first step in determining how much of the IS's income the CS will be allowed to receive is to calculate the amount by which the MMMNA exceeds the CS's actual income. The CS will be entitled to receive from the IS's income an amount equal to that difference, plus any excess shelter allowance available. By federal law, the total MMMNA (income allowance plus excess shelter allowance) cannot exceed $2267 for 2003.

RESOURCE PROTECTION

In order to prevent the community spouse from becoming impoverished by the costs of nursing home care for the institutionalized spouse, the community spouse is allowed a resource allowance. To the extent the assets needed to secure this allowance is in the name of or owned jointly with the institutionalized spouse, the community spouse is granted 90 days from the eligibility determination to transfer title of the assets from the institutionalized spouse to the community spouse.

If the community spouse's income is lower than the minimum monthly needs allowance, the spouse can request a fair hearing to obtain a greater portion of the resources, sufficient to generate the income minimum. For example, if the community spouse has $500 of Social Security and generates $1000 from all assets which total $400,000 (for a 3% return), the spouse could request to retain the entire funds.

ASSET TRANSFER

Medicaid estate planning frequently involves the transfer of assets owned by the applicant in order to meet income and/or asset eligibility requirements. Transfers of assets for Medicaid purposes is defined as a transfer of an asset for which no payment is made. For example, if Albert purchases Barbara's home for its fair market value, Barbara is fully compensated by Albert. However, if Barbara gives Albert the home or only charges Albert $1, the value that Albert receives but didn't pay for is considered the Medicaid transfer. These kinds of uncompensated transfers are subject to strict regulations that must be fully understood in order for the applicant to qualify. *Note:* Failure to comply with the transfer regulations can result in unnecessary and financially damaging penalties to the applicant and his or her family.

THE LOOK-BACK PERIOD

The **look-back period** is how far back, from the date of application, Medicaid looks for identifying uncompensated transfers of assets. Generally, this is 36 months except in the case of payments to or from a trust, which are subject to a 60-month look-back period. Individuals who hold their assets in living trusts and make gifts from the trust funds may be penalized by a longer look-back period than if they'd given away nontrust assets.

CALCULATING THE WAITING PERIOD

With respect to assets transferred after August 11, 1993, the period of ineligibility will be a number of months. The number is obtained by dividing the uncompensated value of the assets transferred from the applicant's name by the statewide monthly average for nursing home care without limit. For example, if the average cost of care is $4281 per month, a transfer of $428,100 would trigger a 100-month period of ineligibility.

Transfers from husband to wife, or vise versa, are exempt from the transfer penalty. In addition, Medicaid treats the following transfers also as exempt:

- transfers to or to a trust for a blind or disabled child
- transfers for fair market value or other valuable considerations
- transfers exclusively for a purpose other than to qualify for medical assistance
- any transfer where denial of eligibility would work an undue hardship on the applicant

Special rules apply to any transfer of the home. These are only exempt if they are transfers to:

- a spouse
- a blind or disabled child
- a dependent child
- a sibling with an equity interest who has resided in the home for one year prior to the applicant's admission to the nursing facility
- the son or daughter of an applicant who has lived in the home for two years prior to the institutionalization and who had cared for that individual

TRUSTS

Issues relating to trusts frequently play a critical role for elders who are planning to establish eligibility for Medicaid. Understanding the importance of the rules and regulations relating to trusts is an essential part of long-term planning.

The existence of a trust, the terms of which identify the applicant or recipient as a beneficiary, raises a red flag for state eligibility specialists.

Because the availability of trust income or principal can potentially result in complete disqualification of the applicant, it is *essential* to be guided by a professional who is versed in eligibility planning and who clearly understands both federal and state regulations relating to trusts. In addition, some points should be highlighted, to help you understand the complexities and hidden traps of these rules.

ESTABLISHING A TRUST

A Medicaid applicant is considered to have established a trust if assets of that individual (which include assets of the individual's spouse) were used to form all or part of the trust and if the trust is established by any of the following individuals:

- The individual
- The individual's spouse
- A person, including a court or administrative body, with legal authority to act in place of or on behalf of the individual or the individual's spouse
- A person, including a court or administrative body, acting at the direction or on the request of the individual or the individual's spouse

RESTRICTING A TRUST

A trust cannot be restricted to get past these rules. The trust rules apply regardless of (1) the purposes for which the trust was established, (2) whether the trustees have or exercise any discretion under the trust, (3) any restrictions on when or whether distributions may be made from the trust, or (4) any restrictions on the use of distributions from the trust.

REVOCABLE AND IRREVOCABLE TRUSTS

The rules also apply to revocable and irrevocable trusts. In the case of a revocable trust, the entire trust principal is considered resources available to the individual or the spouse. Since the individual is considered to own the trust, transfers from the trust to others, such as family member, are scrutinized under the transfer of assets rules. When a part of a revocable trust is treated as a transfer of assets, the look-back period is extended to 60 months.

With respect to an irrevocable trust, if there are any circumstances under which payments from the trust could be made to or for the benefit of the applicant, the portion of the principal of the trust from which payment to that individual could be made is considered resources available to the individual.

EXEMPT TRUSTS

Three kinds of trusts are excluded from application of the new rules:

1. A trust which contains the assets of a disabled individual under the age

of 65 and which was established for the benefit of such individual by the parent, grandparent, legal guardian of the individual, or a court

2. A qualified income trust or Miller Trust
3. A pooled asset trust established for purposes of investment and management by a nonprofit association that maintains separate accounts for each beneficiary of the trust

MEDICAID ESTATE RECOVERIES

States are mandated to have "estate" recovery programs. This enables the state to be repaid at the death of the Medicaid recipient. Since each state has dealt with this in a different manner, professional guidance should be sought. In some states, only probate assets are used to repay Medicaid. In others, anything paid as a result of death, such as annuities and life insurance proceeds, can be taken. Also, in many states, under a variety of circumstances that need to be professionally assessed, the home may be in jeopardy to the state.

NEW DEVELOPMENTS

As of the writing of this chapter, the stability and future of the Medicaid program is in question. President Bush has proposed a restructuring of Medicaid: changing it from a federal entitlement program to a program run by the states as they see fit. That means Medicaid rules won't be uniform, and, more importantly, all the rules that individuals have relied upon will be eliminated.

Even if the Medicaid program is not changed in that manner, many states are seeking permission from the federal government to impose their own rules for transfer penalties, trust rules, and eligibility. Connecticut, Massachusetts, and New York are in that process, and it is expected many states will follow. For those reasons, it is important to seek appropriate guidance from a knowledgeable professional as to how the rules change over the course of the next few years.

WHAT YOU NEED TO KNOW

▶ Life expectancies have increased not only the number of individuals who experience ages beyond the proverbial three score and ten but also the numbers who are forced to deal with extended years of reduced physical and mental capacities. The expectation is that one out of every four seniors over the age of 65 will require nursing home care and half the growing numbers of people over 85 will require long-term care. The problem is that few understand the real costs of this care, and fewer have prepared financially for the future.

▶ Medicare, as structured, provides inconsequential financial coverage for nursing home costs. If a person does not precede nursing home placement by a hospital stay of at least three nights and four days, Medicare will pay nothing. If the necessary hospital stay occurs, Medicare only pays for a maximum of 20 days (in full) and a maximum of 80 days (with the patient paying for the first $100± per day). In all cases, after three months, you're on your own.

▶ Medicaid pays for nursing home care (and, in relatively few situations, a portion of assisted living care). There are many myths surrounding Medicaid eligibility, which can result in families waiting too long to apply for assistance or trying to protect their assets in ways that could permanently exclude them from coverage.

▶ Very often, Medicaid can be accessed in order to cover some or all of the costs of nursing home care, but understanding the rules and the ways these rules can change can mean the difference between a family's financial security and impoverishment.

52

FOR MORE INFORMATION

▢ **National Academy of Elder Law Attorneys**
Web: www.naela.com
The National Academy of Elder Law Attorneys is a nonprofit association that assists lawyers, bar organizations, and others who work with older clients and their families. Established in 1987, the academy has information, education, networking, and assistance for those who must deal with the many specialized issues involved with legal services for the elderly and disabled.

▢ **National Association of Geriatric Care Managers (GCM)**
Web: www.caremanager.org
GCM is a nonprofit, professional organization of practitioners whose goal is the advancement of dignified care for the elderly and their families. With more than 1500 members, GCM is committed to maximizing the independence and autonomy of elders while striving to ensure that the highest quality and most cost-effective health and human services are used when and where appropriate.

No one's death comes to pass without making some impression, and those close to the deceased inherit part of the liberated soul and become richer in their humanness.

—*Hermann Broch*

THE AUTHOR

53   *J. David Kerr*

J. DAVID KERR, JD was born in East Chicago, Indiana and grew up in southwest Michigan and Plattsburgh, New York. He received his juris doctor in 1965 from the University of Michigan. After several years of private practice, he became a university attorney at Central Michigan University and later served as chair of Michigan College and University Legal Officers. Returning to private practice in 1983, he started and runs Kerr and Associates PLLC.

In addition to writing and teaching a course on estate planning at Central Michigan University, David Kerr has given many presentations, including ones for the National Network Collegium Presentation, "When the Plan Matures: Helping Clients Who Are in the Grieving Process," and for the Faculty Academy Multidisciplinary Practice, "Irrevocable Life Insurance Trusts: The Unified Credit and Income Taxation."

David Kerr is a member of the National Network of Estate Planning Attorneys (since 1995), the NNEPA Member Advisory Board, and the American Bar Association Probate and Real Estate Section (since 1966). He is also a past president of the Michigan Forum of Estate Planning Attorneys.

HANDLING LEGAL ASPECTS OF DISABILITY AND DEATH

On our disability or death, the plans we made must be implemented.

Establishing an estate plan is only a beginning. On our disability or death, other people have to do the work. Instructions left in wills and/or other planning documents usually make the work easier and often less expensive. If there are no plans, we must start where we are and move forward. In this chapter, we discuss the work to be done and the legal pitfalls to be avoided.

Note: Title refers to how assets are owned. How assets are owned affects what can be done with those assets on disability and/or death.

IF A LOVED ONE BECOMES DISABLED

It is five times more likely for a loved one to become disabled than to die. Of course, some people become disabled and get better.

It is our experience that disability problems sneak up on people. By the time they begin to deal with the problems, they feel overwhelmed. It is like a gentle breeze which increases in intensity ever so gradually until a gale is blowing. When a loved one is at home or in a facility being cared for, the cash outlay to pay for care becomes clear, hospital and care provider bills are strewn about, and those concerned about the loved one are not feeling chipper because of the condition of the loved one.

Here is an idea to help. When do you start paying attention to what you should be doing because someone is disabled? People who like to sail ask the question: As the wind's speed increases, when do you pay attention to reducing the size of the sail to protect the boat? The answer: Do it the first time you think of it. If a loved one is having any health difficulty, the time to start begin using the suggestions in this chapter for implementing disability procedures is the first time it comes to your mind about whether you should do something.

RECORDS

When a loved one is disabled, records are necessary to protect your legal rights. Setting up a record-keeping system will make life much easier. Advisors who are there to help, government agencies, and insurance carriers all want to see paper.

Set up file folders to hold records in chronological order from the following sources:

- Bills from physicians, hospitals, laboratories, and other health care providers
- Payment vouchers and correspondence from health insurance companies
- Payments made or declined by Medicare, Medicaid, and/or other government providers, such as the Veterans Administration
- Correspondence from attorneys and other advisors

From an office supply store, purchase a cabinet to hold the folders. The folders will then all be in one location and easily accessed when more important things are on your mind.

Billings by health care providers and payments by insurance companies, health care administrative companies, and government agencies are handled on a mass basis. The employees who make the entries are interrupted, have their own problems, or may not be well trained: *Mistakes happen.* You have to review and keep the records if you want to investigate and perhaps receive a correction for improper billings or denied payments.

You may wish to consider software to assist you. An example of software available is Medicare Software (see "For More Information").

TRACKING BILLING CODES

The payments from insurance companies and government payers are driven by codes that represent the diagnosis and procedures of health care providers. There are diagnosis codes. There are procedure codes. Different payers use different systems for determining codes, and different health care providers have different levels of competence in assigning and documenting codes. It is critical that the health care provider's notes conform to the diagnosis and procedure codes used for billing. At times, billing clerks use broad category codes for the diagnosis and procedures which often are not paid by payers. However, a more appropriate subcode, supported by the health care provider's notes, may result in payment. If you keep track of the codes used, you will become familiar with what they mean. You can then compare them to codes which have been used before and have been paid. You will be able to ask meaningful questions if payments do not seem to be properly made. In addition, some payers maintain unpublicized customer service offices where you can bring in your records. Learn what the payer is doing, find these offices, and possibly receive assistance in obtaining a valid payment.

Whenever talking on the phone to a health care provider or a payer, write down:

1. The day and hour you called
2. The first and last name of the person you spoke to
3. The extension number of that person
4. Notes about your conversation
5. The time frame for getting the matter resolved

And always remember to follow up.

COVERAGE OF HEALTH INSURANCE OR GOVERNMENT ASSISTANCE

Health insurance is a contract. The breadth of the coverage you receive is determined by the contract. The contract terms must be read to understand what is covered. The days are gone when we can say we have hospital and medical insurance and rest easy. We have to know ourselves the coverage we have. Health insurance providers furnish booklets describing benefits and benefit offices to help.

Government benefits are determined by government agencies and usually are administered by private companies under a contract with the

53

agency. Government providers or their private administrative companies provide benefit descriptions.

Whether an insurance company or a government provider covers you, benefit descriptions need to be reviewed. Many insurance policies and government programs contain appeal procedures. Appeal procedures can be useful for chronic conditions if the benefit language is general and not specific.

The very first matter to check is the maximum amount the insurance will pay. Many health policies have an absolute maximum, such as $1 million or $4 million. One of our clients was at $750,000 for cancer treatment in September for an illness first diagnosed in May. What a shock! If the maximum were not known and if records had not been kept, there would have been an even more shocking surprise in a short time. As a result of the knowledge, the spouse was able to use an open enrollment period at the spouse's place of work and was able to have new health insurance which provided coverage just as the first policy reached its $1 million coverage maximum.

Next, check for maximums for different kinds of diagnosis and treatment. For example, most policies limit the number of outpatient mental health visits and limit the amount paid annually for outpatient visits.

Check for what is actually covered. To reduce the expense of coverage, some policies eliminate some kinds of treatment completely. Some treatments are considered experimental and are not covered. For example, at one time Medicare classified lung reductions, which were very helpful to severe asthma patients, as experimental. The *experimental* designation resulted in no payment by Medicare. Some policies require the use of a formulary for prescription medicines, and either do not cover or pay less for those medicines outside the formulary.

STAYING IN NETWORK

Some insurance coverage and some government programs require that you be referred by a physician who manages your care and may require that all referrals be to those who have contracts with a particular payer. Review your plan's paperwork. Many are shocked at the large bill they receive after going to a provider who is outside the network. Having the knowledge of what you need to do will help you ask the right questions while health care recommendations for treatment and providers are being made.

HEALTH CARE POWERS

Many states have legislation providing a system for people to designate a person to make health care decisions for them if they are unable to make their own health care decisions. The people authorized to act are called by a variety of names such as: health care agents or patient advocates. A common requirement for a health care agent to have power is the inability of the patient to make health care decisions for himself or herself.

(figure 53-1)
Certification empowering a health care agent. Note: This is only an example. The actual certification needed in your circumstance depends on the health care agent document and your state law.

PHYSICIANS' DETERMINATION OF PATIENT'S INABILITY TO MAKE MEDICAL DECISIONS

Initial Determination
We determine that THOMAS BRADLEY DOE is unable to participate in medical treatment decisions.

Dated:

Dated:

Attending Physician

Another Physician or Licensed Psychologist

The requirement that empowers a health care agent power is described in the document appointing the person who is to make the health care decisions. When the condition for the agent to have power is met, then that person is empowered to make the decisions. Many people confuse this authority with the instructions in a do not resuscitate order or a living will, which indicates when life support should be withdrawn. A better way to think about these documents is to think about the power to make a decision to save someone's life. The same document may also provide power to remove life support.

You may want to include in the health care powers, a designation of *personal representative* under the Health Insurance Portability and Accountability Act (HIPAA) of 1996 and its regulations. If that designation is made, the health providers must generally treat the HIPAA personal representative the same as the patient would be treated with respect to health care information.

The documents delegating power set forth when the power is to be delegated and whether there must be certification of the patient's condition. If there must be certification, the documents usually define the certification and name who must provide that certification. The certification must match the requirements of the document before the agent has power. Figure 53-1 is an example of the certification required by a particular document.

HEALTH CARE INFORMATION
Many family members want to know the condition of their loved one. Privacy of a patient's health information is protected by the Health Insurance Portability and Accountability Act of 1996 and its regulations. If you want designated family members and, perhaps friends, to have access to your physician's opinions and medical records, it is wise to sign a "patient authorization" naming all those whom you want to have access to health opinions, information, and records. Such an authorization gives permission to receive the information whether or not you are disabled.

LONG-TERM CARE

Some people are concerned about the possibility that a loved one or they themselves may have to enter a nursing home for long-term care. Long-term care insurance may provide sufficient funds to pay for long-term care, so examine your long-term care policy to determine the daily amount it will pay toward care, the maximum total amount it will pay, and whether it will provide for care at home.

If you do not have long-term care insurance, government assistance in the form of Medicaid or Veterans Administration benefits may be available. Qualification for Medicaid may be more possible than you realize. The Medicaid program has two sets of rules: federal and state. Federal law creates the Medicaid program and establishes some of the rules. State law creates additional standards and guidelines. Every state is different. State law rules may change often. Chapter 52 goes into detail about qualifying for Medicaid coverage.

DOING BUSINESS AND MANAGING ASSETS

A person with a serious health condition does not usually feel like taking care of the business or managing assets. In Chapter 44, Renno Peterson and Robert Esperti discuss durable power of attorney and trusts. If assets are owned in the name of the patient or if business rights of the patient are involved, you will be using your power of attorney, for example, endorsing an income tax refund check made directly payable to the patient. If assets are owned in the name of a trustee of a trust, the trustee will be signing and managing those assets. You will need an affidavit of trust saying you have authority as successor trustee, if you are, to act on behalf of the trust.

In most states, no one has legal authority to act for another person in business or in health matters in the absence of court orders unless the person has left written instructions in the form of powers of attorney, trust, and health care delegations.

Often many people want to help if a loved one is disabled. They start to do things which may or may not be consistent with instructions the disabled person has left in a trust, instructions in a durable power of attorney, or in a health care directive. Those appointed to do the work in the documents need to step forward and do what they were appointed to do, or they need to resign.

If there are no documents providing for management of a person's assets and for making decisions concerning health care, then it may be necessary to petition the probate court, or comparable court, for a guardian and conservator. The court generally demonstrates its delegation of power to act on behalf of an individual through *letters of authority.* People with whom business is done and health care providers will want to see these letters from the court before relying on anyone telling them what to do. Usually there is a reporting requirement to the court, and if the reports are not made in a timely manner, the court may remove the person appointed.

WHEN DEATH IS NEAR

The health care powers (appointing an agent for those who cannot make their own health care decisions), living wills, and do not resuscitate orders come into play as death nears.

A health care power appointing an agent gives the instruction that if the patient cannot make his or her own health care decisions, the agent is to make the decisions. The document may give the agent the power to remove life support, but the document itself is not a directive to those providing treatment. Only the agent can give direction if the patient is unable to give a direction.

It is wise to take precautions to assure that health care providers understand whether a physician (if inside a health care facility) or an individual (if outside a health care facility) has given a do not resuscitate order as contrasted with delegating another person to make a health care decision. When health care personnel are handling an emergency, a do not resuscitate order issued in a hospital setting is generally an order issued by a physician. However, in at least one state, a do not resuscitate order may be made by an individual from outside a health care facility to give instructions to emergency health care personnel. Once the order is given, it is not necessary for the patient's agent to do or say anything. The health care providers are instructed not to resuscitate the patient.

WHEN A LOVED ONE DIES

GRIEF

Most of us have experienced grief following a person's death, and Chapter 40 is devoted to the grieving process. Here we are concerned with the legal ramifications that can occur if grief turns to anger. The anger may exacerbate making arrangements for funerals, disposing of personal property, and other matters. When long-standing disputes between children, conclusions that one parent favored a child over another, blended families in remarriage situations, and many others add to the stress of the grieving process for all involved, emotions and feelings can run high. The section "Litigation Following Death," below, covers legal issues that anger can instill. Sensitivity and patience can go a long way toward heading off the road to litigation. People are not always rational or logical in times of grief.

TISSUE AND ORGAN DONATION

Some people have signed papers or organ and tissue donation donor cards or endorsed their driver's license indicating their desire for organ and tissue donation. If you know about these instructions, you should notify the health care organization about the instructions. Time is of the essence in such situations.

DISPOSITION OF THE BODY

Most states have legislation addressing what can happen to a person's body following death. However, some are not specific as to which person

BODY RIGHTS

There is no property right in a dead body under the Michigan constitution, and Michigan courts have gone both ways on the issue.

In Dampier v. Wayne County, a claim against a county morgue alleging that it negligently allowed a body to decompose was not cognizable under the state constitution, whereas in Whaley v. County of Tuscola, the court ruled that the plaintiffs had a constitutionally protected property right in the deceased's body, which was violated when a county allowed it to decompose.

has the authority to give direction with respect to disposition of a body. Legislation may be written in terms of receiving an authorization from a "person who has authority to make arrangements for a dead human body" and never define who has that authority. Moreover, court decisions are inconsistent as to whether there is any property right in a human body. The services of a funeral director can be invaluable during the time when a loved one's body is in need of preparation and disposition. Unfortunately, clarifying rights pertaining to disposition of human remains is not apt to catch the attention of legislators when so many other issues are also pressing. The assistance of a professional funeral director can help during these times.

FUNERAL ARRANGEMENTS

Sensitivity is essential in making funeral arrangements. This can be a celebration of the person who passed on. Focusing on a positive goal will help all involved make more positive contributions.

Funeral arrangements are made by contract. The person signing is going to be responsible for payment if the funeral is not paid for another way. Generally, children, the spouse, and others are not legally required to pay for a funeral. Payment comes from the assets titled in the name of the deceased person or a trust established by that person. Because of love or caring, one or more people come forward to make arrangements and pay for the funeral.

What kind of funeral arrangements should be made? If the deceased person left instructions, the task for those making final arrangements is eased. If no instructions are left, remember all the influences coming to bear on this difficult task. If you start to find difficulty with others while doing the task, breathe a little, walk around the block, and consider the celebration of the deceased person. Do not expect those making the arrangements to be rational—including you. If possible, have some fun with your irrationality if it surfaces.

STOPPING AND CHANGING BENEFIT, RETIREMENT, AND PENSION PAYMENTS

Social Security: When people pass on, their right to Social Security, pension, and disability benefits stops. Often, Social Security, pension, and disability benefits are paid by electronic fund transfer to a bank account.

For a time, the funds will just keep coming if those making payments are not informed. If there are overpayments, those making payment will look unkindly on those who took the money if it is not repaid. The easier thing to do is notify those making payments about the death.

To notify the Social Security Administration, telephone its toll-free number (see "For More Information"). If funds are being received by electronic funds transfer, notify the bank of the death. If benefits were being paid by check, *do not cash* any checks received for the month in which the beneficiary died or thereafter. Return the checks to Social Security as soon as possible.

Lump-sum payment to surviving spouse and some children: A one-time payment of $255 is payable to the surviving spouse if he or she was living with the beneficiary at the time of death or, if living apart, the surviving spouse was eligible for Social Security benefits on the beneficiary's earning record for the month of death. If there is no surviving spouse, the payment is made to a child who was eligible for benefits on the beneficiary's earning record in the month of death. Otherwise, no lump-sum amount is available.

Survivor benefits: Monthly survivor benefits can be paid to family members, including the beneficiary's widow or widower, dependent children, and dependent parents. The Social Security Administration provides booklets which describe these benefits (see "For More Information").

You should carefully review benefits and determine how they are taken. For example, if you are under 65, you can draw benefits on your spouse's account beginning at your age 60. You will receive a reduced benefit. At the age that you can draw a full benefit (currently 65) on your own account, you will be entitled to that full benefit and can then start recieving the benefit on your account. You need to make sure at that time that your full benefit (on your account) exceeds the benefit you will receive on your deceased spouse's account.

Full benefits under Social Security are available at different ages, depending on when you were born.

If you are not already receiving Social Security benefits, the Social Security administration requires the following:

- Proof of death—either from funeral home or death certificate
- Your Social Security number, as well as the deceased's Social Security number
- Your birth certificate
- Your marriage certificate if you're a widow or widower
- Your divorce papers if you are applying as a surviving divorced spouse
- Dependent children's Social Security numbers and birth certificates
- Deceased's W-2 forms or federal self-employment tax return for the most recent year
- The name of your bank and your account number so your benefits can be directly deposited into your account

(table 53-1)

AGE TO RECEIVE FULL SOCIAL SECURITY BENEFITS

YEAR OF BIRTH	FULL RETIREMENT AGE	AGE 62 REDUCTION MONTHS	MONTHLY % REDUCTION	TOTAL % REDUCTION
1937	65 years	36	0.555	20.00
1938	65 years, 2 months	38	0.548	20.83
1939	65 years, 4 months	40	0.541	21.67
1940	65 years, 6 months	42	0.535	22.50
1941	65 years, 8 months	44	0.530	23.33
1942	65 years, 10 months	46	0.525	24.17
1943–1954	66 years	48	0.520	25.00
1955	66 years, 2 months	50	0.516	25.84
1956	66 years, 4 months	52	0.512	26.66
1957	66 years, 6 months	54	0.509	27.50
1958	66 years, 8 months	56	0.505	28.33
1959	66 years, 10 months	58	0.502	29.17

Full benefits no longer start at age 65, and the reduction in the Social Security benefit received at age 62 reduces as time passes. Table 53-1 shows the present situation.

Pension and retirement benefits: Pension benefits are usually received as a result of employment. When people pass on, their right to the benefit ends. There may be survivor benefits, but the rights of the person dying end. Often these benefits are paid by electronic fund transfer to a bank account. The funds will keep coming if those making payments are not informed. If there are overpayments, those making payments will look unkindly on those who took the money if the funds are not returned. Notification of the death needs to be made to the organization making payments as soon after death as is practical.

If an individual retirement account (IRA), 401(k), 503(b), or 457 deferred compensation plan is being paid, the beneficiary stands to lose significant benefits if continued payments are received before elections are made (see Chapter 49). We cannot emphasize enough the prompt stopping of these payments and making correct elections before taking any more payments. Thousands and even hundreds of thousands of dollars of additional benefits can be at stake.

Annuity benefits: Annuity benefits are usually received as a result of a contract purchased from an insurance company. An annuity benefit needs to be distinguished from a retirement benefit which has been annuitized. If you are not sure, then this is a matter on which you should get prompt professional help.

Whether annuity benefits will continue depends on what the contract says and the election made by the person benefited by the annuity. The organization administering the annuity should be able to inform you. If you have to make additional choices as to how you will receive funds, it may be appropriate to contact a financial planner who can give you an independent opinion.

IF A LOVED ONE DIES

If a loved one dies, you have four logical steps:

1. The assets of the deceased have to be collected and protected.
2. The legitimate bills and taxes have to be paid.
3. Contractual rights such as life insurance and retirement benefits need attention.
4. The assets must be properly distributed.

That is all.

Why, then, do we hear so many stories about horrible experiences after a person passes on? There are three reasons:

1. Unfortunate things happen as a result of failure to attend to the grieving process or family dysfunction.
2. There was a lack of appreciation of what is involved in handling assets.
3. Greed.

Administration of a will or a trust involves administering each asset on an asset-by-asset basis. If done in this way, administration proceeds logically and is understandable. Figure 53-2 is an example of a form you can use to make a list of assets.

Record keeping is critical. There are some simple rules to follow regarding record keeping. If these rules are followed, administration of the deceased's affairs will be much, much easier. For the deceased's affairs, use one checking account to the extent possible. If a probate is necessary and a trust is also being administered, then use one checking account for the probate and one checking account for the trust. Everything coming in goes into the one appropriate checking account. Everything going

INHERITED BENEFITS

Without Election: June's husband Frank died at age 73 with a $750,000 balance in his individual retirement account which he had rolled over from his company's 401(k) retirement plan. Frank named June as his beneficiary of the IRA. June is age 68. June only needs to take required minimum distributions from the retirement account. She does not elect to rollover the benefit as she is allowed to do as a spouse. Assuming a 4% growth rate, the benefit exhausts in 2030 and June and her children take a total of $2,888,113 in distributions.

With Election: June could have rolled over the IRA. If she did this, she could have used her life expectancy and could have designated her children as her own beneficiaries. At her death, the children could have used, at the very least, the life expectancy of the oldest child to establish required minimum distributions and, if properly arranged, could have used the life expectancy of each child for that child's required minimum distributions. If June had done this, and assuming a 4% growth rate, the family would have received $5,638,996 in distributions ending in 2050.

All agreed Mom favored the three girls, and Dad favored the three boys. Mom and Dad held most of their property jointly, but had identical wills which made equal distribution to the six children. Mom died first. Dad's will named the oldest son and oldest daughter as co-personal representatives to administer his estate. Dad had also placed a significant bank account jointly with his oldest son from which the son wrote checks to pay the bills. When Dad died, the oldest son made distributions of personal property to those he said "Dad would have wanted to have" and claimed ownership of the joint bank account which he said he was going to distribute the way "Dad would have wanted it." The distributions weren't equal, and the boys tended to benefit more than the girls from the oldest son's distribution.

A successful court action was brought to remove the oldest son as personal representative and to include the joint bank account in the estate. Before the matter went further, a family meeting was held with the attorney in which it was explained that additional disputes within the family might best be settled by agreement, even if people felt there were a few thousand dollars sliding one way or the other, because the attorney fees—paid by the estate—to resolve the disputes would make everyone's share smaller. The members of the family fought anyway, usually boys versus the girls or girls versus the boys.

The attorney fee was large. At the hearing to approve the attorney fee, the oldest son testified that the documented attorney fee should not be paid because the attorney had stated at the family meeting that if the members of the family continued to fight, there would be a large attorney fee reducing everyone's share. "Now he's done exactly what he said he would, Judge," testified the oldest son. In approving the large attorney fee, the court referred to that testimony, and to the decision by the members of the family to fight about so many matters, resulting in a large legal bill.

(figure 53-2)*

Example of a form for listing assets.

ASSET LIST

Name of Deceased:		Date of Death:	
REAL PROPERTY ADDRESS	Title (I, JT, RLT)	Estimated Value	Actual Value
BANK ACCOUNTS	Title (I, JT, RLT)	Estimated Value	Actual Value
BROKERAGE AND MUTUAL FUND ACCOUNTS	Title (I, JT, RLT)	Estimated Value	Actual Value
IRA AND OTHER RETIREMENT ACCOUNTS	Benef. (I, RLT)	Estimated Value	Actual Value
MOTOR VEHICLES	Title (I, JT, RLT)	Estimated Value	Actual Value
LIFE INSURANCE	Benef. (I, RLT)	Estimated Value	Actual Value
TANGIBLE PERSONAL PROPERTY	Title (I, RLT)	Estimated Value	Actual Value

out or being reinvested, even to a savings account, goes out of that one appropriate checking account. If assets from a savings account or stock account are needed to pay bills or provide a distribution, take them from savings or the stock account, place them in the one appropriate checking account, and then pay bills or make distribution from that one appropriate account. Never vary from this procedure. You may want to engage a CPA or the attorney assisting with administration to keep the checkbooks.

The date of death is a very important date. Records should be kept in the deceased's name up to the date of death. Records should be kept in the name of the probate, trust, or both—as appropriate—after the date of death.

If there is probate or if the trustee is a person managing the trust (the trustee) and is not one of the people who made the trust, then the trust is seen as a new taxpayer. Since the Social Security number of the deceased person is no longer be used, a new taxpayer identification number must be obtained. This is done with Internal Revenue Service (IRS) Form SS-4. Your accountant or attorney can help you obtain the taxpayer identification number.

WHAT NOT TO DO

Immediately following death, it is usually unwise for anyone other than those appointed in the documents of the deceased or designated by law to do anything. Sometimes there is a person who uses his or her own sense of what the deceased would have wanted to guide direction rather than following the instructions of the deceased or those institutions provided by law if the deceased left no instructions. Any such person needs to be given a firm, but gentle, *no!*

Early distribution of personal property is fraught with danger. Personal property and pictures may have little economic value, but the actual emotional value to many in the family is immeasurable.

WHO DOES WHAT?

The people who wind up the affairs of a deceased person are called fiduciaries. The fiduciary is generally personally liable to the extent of the value held for the legitimate bills and taxes of the deceased.

Limiting the fiduciary's liability: A person serving as a fiduciary may be liable if bills or taxes are not paid, if investments turn sour, or if beneficiaries do not receive what they were to receive. See the sections "Bills," "Collecting and Managing Assets," and "Beneficiaries," below.

Who will be the fiduciary?: If the deceased left instructions in the form of a will or a trust, those documents should identify who is responsible for the work. If there is a will, the person will be referred to as a personal *representative, executor,* or *executrix.* If a trust is involved, the person will be called a trustee. If there is no will or trust, the person will be called an *administrator,* an *administratrix,* or a *personal representative.*

If a will is the primary planning instrument, then a probate court must first issue *letters of administration* before the person who is supposed to do the work is allowed to do the work. The letters of administration inform third parties that the person appointed by the court can access and act on the assets of the deceased. If a trust is the primary planning tool, the successor trustee should prepare an affidavit or *certificate of trust* to show to third parties and then can start doing the trustee's work right away. Probate court procedures should be unnecessary if all assets are titled in the name of the trust.

Rights under life insurance contracts, retirement plans, pensions, and annuity contracts are exercised by the legal person named as beneficiary in the beneficiary designation made by the owner of the life insurance and by the participant in the retirement or pension plan. The beneficiary is usually not a fiduciary unless a trust or estate is named as the beneficiary. Then the fiduciary of the trust or estate will be the fiduciary, since that person is administering the beneficiary of the contract. If the deceased did not designate a beneficiary, many retirement and pension plans and life insurance contracts set forth a beneficiary in the absence of a designated beneficiary.

BENEFICIARY INFORMATION

As early as possible, the fiduciary should obtain information about beneficiaries and heirs. Beneficiaries are people named in a will, trust, retirement plan, pension plan, annuity, or life insurance contract designated to receive a benefit. Heirs are people who, in the absence of a different designation in a will, receive the estate and property of another on that other person's death.

It may be necessary to send notices, papers to sign, accountings, IRS K-1 tax forms, letters, and proposed distributions to beneficiaries and heirs. Collect the following information for each beneficiary and heir:

- Correct legal name
- Relationship to the deceased
- Current address
- Date of birth
- Social Security number
- Telephone numbers—home, work, cell
- Fax number
- E-mail address

THE PROCESSES USED

Ownership (or title) of assets or use of assets changes when a person passes on. Because of the human condition, there is a concern that the assets or use of assets go to the correct people.

Depending on how title is held, three processes are used which are not mutually exclusive: probate, trust settlement, and implementation of beneficiary designations in contracts, such as life insurance, retirement plans, pension plans, and annuities.

Probate: Probate is a court process. States have adopted a wide variety of legislation for probate. In some states this results in a host of choices for probate. The particular processes used in probate are described in legislation and rules of the court.

If there is no legal will, then we say there is an intestacy, and the assets of the deceased person are distributed to those persons as directed by state legislation. For example, in Michigan, the intestate statute directs that when a spouse dies survived by a spouse and three children (of any age), the first $150,000 goes to the surviving spouse and the balance would be divided with half for the spouse and a sixth for each of the three children regardless of age.

EXAMPLE

A man dies intestacy and, after bills and administration expenses are paid, leaves an estate of $500,000 in assets titled in his name alone. The spouse receives $325,000, and each child receives $58,333.33. If a child were a minor, the probate court would have to appoint a person to manage that child's share and there would likely be annual reporting to the court.

If there is a will and assets are titled only in the name of the deceased person, probate follows. The provisions contained in the will are the instructions which are to be implemented for those assets titled only in the name of the deceased.

If there is probate, the authority of the person managing the estate will be shown by letters or an order of the probate court.

Trusts: A trust is an arrangement in which, under an agreement, title is held by one person for the benefit of another person. Figure 53-3 shows the operation of a trust. The objective is to transfer or arrange the assets in the trust, according to the instructions in the trust agreement,

(figure 53-3)
The dynamics of a trust.

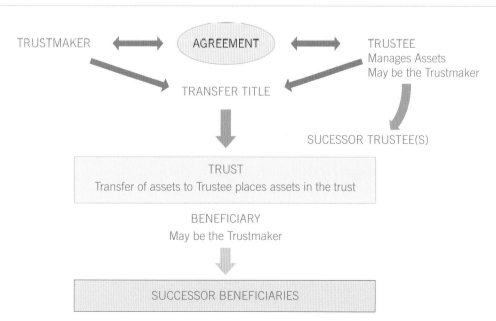

so that the assets benefit the successor beneficiaries as provided in the trust instructions.

Often the deceased person was the trustee of the trust, so we must let those in the world who deal with the trust know that there is a change in who is managing the trust. We do this with a document called an **affidavit of trust** or a **certificate of trust**. The affidavit or certificate is presented to people who deal with the trust assets so that they will know a new person is taking over management of the trust.

Other arrangements: Title may be held other than only in the name of the deceased person or in a trust. Title may be held as a life estate (life lease), jointly, or jointly with right of survivorship. The dangers in these types of ownership are discussed by Renno Peterson and Robert Esperti in Chapter 44.

At death, the people who are to take over after the end of the life estate have possession and usually full ownership of the asset without probate. If a joint tenant or a joint tenant with right of survivorship dies, then the remaining joint tenants continue their possession without the possessor rights of the deceased because those rights are extinguished.

EXAMPLE

Fred Smith and his three friends own a hunting lodge as joint tenants with right of survivorship. Fred dies. The three friends are now the full owners, as joint tenants with right of survivorship, of the hunting lodge. Fred's widow and children have no rights in the hunting lodge.

Business interests (such as a family limited partnership, family limited liability company, S corporation, C corporation, partnership, or joint venture) may need administration. Sophisticated planning techniques (such as charitable remainder trusts, charitable lead trusts, grantor retained annuity trusts, or qualified personal residence trusts) may be involved. The administration of these business interests and planning techniques is beyond the scope of this chapter, and professional assistance is recommended.

BILLS

Bills fall into two categories: those before the loved one died and those after the loved one died.

Bills before death: For probate, the bills arising before death are called *claims against the estate*. For a trust, the bills may or may not be referred to as a claim.

Cutting off the potential bills from the creditors of the deceased can be a good thing. Most probate procedures require publication of a notice to creditors and actual notice to known creditors. The creditors then have a limited period of time—typically four to six months—to make their claims in writing or lose the claim. If trusts are involved, some practitioners open an empty probate and publish a notice to creditors in order to cut off potential creditor's claims. Newer state statutes provide that a trustee must publish a notice to creditors and give notice to known creditors.

Bills after death: Bills arising after death are usually referred to as expenses of administration. Examples include:

- Expenses to manage, maintain, and safeguard the assets
- Fees and expenses of the persons managing the assets
- Professional fees, such as attorneys, CPAs, tax preparers, certified financial planners (CFPs), and appraisers

COLLECTING AND MANAGING ASSETS

Collecting and managing assets are among the primary responsibilities of the fiduciary. The fiduciary can have personal liability if this function is not performed appropriately. These responsibilities include locating and obtaining possession of the assets, protecting assets, managing investments, managing the business of the estate or trust, and distributing assets.

A key decision must be made very shortly after the loved one dies. Are significant assets to be transformed into liquid assets (which are relatively free from market forces)? This protects the estate or trust from potential market declines so that the values to fund the various trusts are available when needed. On the other hand, investing in very conservative investments removes the potential for substantial gain if the markets go up.

FINDING AND COLLECTING ASSETS

You need to identify and list every asset of the deceased person in which that person had any interest, including individual ownership, joint ownership, and an interest in a trust. The following are suggestions on locating assets.

Income tax returns for the last three years: The deceased's income tax returns for the last three years should be reviewed. Real property taxes will likely show up as deductions. If these returns cannot be located, the IRS has Form 4506, on which you can request a copy of a filed return. It costs $23 for each requested return, and a separate form must be used for each return requested.

Check register and canceled checks: The deceased's check register and canceled checks are helpful in locating real estate and other assets for which taxes were paid.

Real estate assessment records: If you are not sure whether you have located all the real and personal property which might be subject to property taxes, check with the county or parish assessor or treasurer to determine whether a computer search can be run using the deceased's name to find parcels of real property.

Banks and stockbrokers: Write to banks and stockbrokers in any region where the deceased lived and request information about any accounts the deceased may have had.

Forward mail: Unless you live at the address where the deceased had lived, request that the post office forward the deceased's mail and any mail to a trust of the deceased to your address. As pieces of mail arrive, you will be alerted to various assets held by the deceased or the deceased's trust.

Physical search: You have to make a physical search of the deceased's effects. Be inventive when you do this. Remember that some people hide assets on purpose, for example, in the pockets of clothing, between and inside mattresses, behind loose boards, behind ceiling moldings and above ceiling tiles, in garages and garden houses, or taped to the bottom of a desk top inside a drawer.

Assets for which you are searching include real estate, bank accounts, brokerage and mutual fund accounts, individual stocks and bonds, collectibles, retirement and pension accounts, business interests, accounts receivable, promissory notes, mortgages, trust deeds, life insurance, annuities, safe-deposit box keys, royalty interests, residual payments (such as commissions and trailing fees), and rental payments.

PROTECTING ASSETS

Immediately following a person's passing, it is important to protect assets.

Real property: If the deceased's residence is vacant, it needs to be secured. Consider changing locks, hiring a private security firm, installing an internal security system, maintaining lawn and garden, and removing important personal items.

Have the premises checked or monitored for environmental controls and maintenance. Request that mail be forwarded to you. Determine if any of the utilities should be shut off, if domestic help is appropriate for maintenance of the condition of the premises, and if a periodic inspection is appropriate.

Property and casualty insurance: Notify carriers of property and casualty insurance of the death. Most insurance contracts have a requirement that this be done within 30 days. Failure to do so can result in loss of coverage. Often, there is a higher premium for unoccupied houses. Premiums on motor vehicle insurance will vary depending on whether the vehicle is driven. *Note:* After the funeral is a time when a decision is often made to allow another to drive the motor vehicle in anticipation of a future transfer of title. Unless immediate attention is given to the details of title transfer and insurance, significant liability can arise.

Credit cards: Cancel credit cards. By letter, request from each credit card company a statement showing the date-of-death balance. Send a copy of the death certificate with the letter, and inquire as to whether there was any credit life insurance.

If the assets of the deceased are insufficient to pay the debts of the deceased, including credit card debt, and if the spouse or partner of the deceased did not sign the credit card application or did not sign a document stating he or she would be liable for the debts resulting from the use of the credit card, then there may be no liability by the spouse or partner for the credit card debt. An attorney should be contacted to determine how your state law addresses this issue. To end harassing phone calls and letters, it may be efficient to go through a probate and give notice to known creditors as well as publish a notice for unknown creditors in order to cause the limitation period for claims to pass and to obtain a court order as to credit card companies which file claims. Adverse credit reports are first dealt with by communicating directly with the three credit reporting companies. A knowledgeable attorney should be contacted.

Pets: Do arrangements need to be made for the care of pets?

Perishable assets: If there is no one living in the residence of the deceased, the refrigerator has to be cleaned. Also, is there any danger that small children are able to access the refrigerator? If so, proper steps should be taken to ensure they do not harm themselves. There can be considerable liability if a child dies in a refrigerator. The premises, inside and out, must be inspected for items which need care or are perishable, such as plants.

GUARDIANSHIPS OR CONSERVATORSHIPS

If there are minor or disabled beneficiaries, guardianships or conservatorships may have to be established unless the deceased's estate plan addressed these issues appropriately. For example, if a minor or an incompetent person is the beneficiary of a trust, a will, or an intestate estate, it may be necessary to appoint a guardian or conservator for that person. If a trust created during the life of the deceased is involved, the trust may address this situation, which makes appointment of a guardian or conservator unnecessary.

IMMEDIATE NEEDS

Determine the level of concern of a surviving spouse or dependents of the deceased for immediate needs. If the deceased managed the money, such as the checkbook, bank deposits, and investment decisions, then the surviving spouse or dependents may have anxiety about money. Anxiety may exist over obtaining food or transportation. The issues need prompt attention.

If there is a totally dependent beneficiary, that beneficiary's cash-flow needs may need the same attention as that of a surviving spouse. Most beneficiaries do not have an immediate need, and wisdom dictates that the administration of the estate is better served by planned and orderly distribution.

Bank safe-deposit box: Determine if there are any bank safe-deposit boxes and if the fiduciary has access. In the presence of a bank officer or credible third party (e.g., a CPA), take a written inventory of the contents of the box. Have the bank officer or third party sign the inventory and keep a copy for himself or herself. Only after the written inventory is completed should contents be removed.

Personal records and income tax returns: Gather personal records, income tax returns, broker statements, and other financial information for the last three years. This helps identify assets and sources of income.

Monies owed to the deceased: If the deceased was owed money, contact those who are responsible for payment and arrange for receiving their payment.

Life insurance: Assemble all policies of life insurance and accident insurance. Remember that annuities, disability income policies, travel clubs, alumni associations, trade associations, and any other organizations might make a death benefit or have life insurance available.

Decedent's business: Did the deceased have a business interest which needs immediate attention? If the deceased made most of the decisions for a business, the fiduciary may have to make immediate business decisions.

There may be a buy-sell agreement or other transition agreements. These should be reviewed by competent counsel and implemented.

INCOME TAX ISSUES

Generally, there is neither income tax on assets received from a deceased person nor income tax on life insurance received on the life of the insured. However, there is income tax on funds received from individual retirement accounts, retirement funds (see Chapter 49), pension funds, unpaid current compensation, deferred compensation, company death benefits payable to beneficiaries of deceased employees (not life insurance), accrued interest and rents owed to the deceased, amounts due on installment sales contracts, and payments from some annuity contracts. All the amounts subject to income tax are generally items for which the deceased had not been subject to income tax and would have had to pay income tax on if he or she were alive.

If there is a probate estate or if the deceased left a separate trust, at least one new taxpayer exists. New taxpayers need a tax identification number, which is obtained by filing IRS Form SS-4.

The regular 1040 income tax return for the deceased is due on April 15 of the year following death. The tax is due on income from the period January 1 to the date of death. Either the probate estate, the deceased's trust, or both, files fiduciary income tax 1041 returns for their respective fiscal years. If additional time is needed to file income tax returns, an extension can be requested on IRS Form 4868.

You must be clear with the professionals doing the tax-related work on the person responsible for particular tasks. If a tax preparer or CPA is to be responsible for the 1040 return and the 1041 return, you should place this instruction in writing.

It is wise to examine income tax returns for the last three years. If not available, they can be requested using IRS Form 4506 at a cost of $23 per return.

IRS Form 56 can be used to advise the IRS that a fiduciary will be filing returns, and IRS Form 4810 can be filed requesting a prompt assessment for any income tax period which is open. These forms assist in limiting the personal liability of the fiduciary.

Discuss with your CPA, tax preparer, or attorney whether it is wise for the probate estate, if there is one, or the deceased's trust to choose a fiscal year or a calendar year for income tax purposes.

"Trapped Income" can be a problem in estate and trust administration. Being alert to the problem can avoid any surprises. This is how trapped income comes about: Some wills and trusts provide that income will be distributed to a beneficiary. Income for income tax purposes is often defined differently from income for estate and trust administration purposes. Income for estate and trust administration purposes is usually defined by state legislation, and different states have different legislation. For example, a distribution from a retirement plan might be considered 10% income for distribution purposes under an estate or a trust but might be 100% taxable as income under IRS rules. The 10% might be distributed to beneficiaries under a will or trust which directed distribution of income. That 10% would usually be taxed at the beneficiary's income tax rates. However, 90% of the distribution might remain trapped in an estate or trust and be taxed to the estate or trust at high income tax rates. (See Table 53-2.)

The fiduciary managing an estate or trust has a duty to send beneficiaries a K-1 form advising them of the nature of any distributions they have received. The distributions may have been principal which is not subject to income tax, tax-free income, capital gain, or ordinary income. The K-1 should inform the beneficiary as to the allocation of the distribution among these categories. The beneficiary then enters the amounts on his or her income tax return.

After a person dies, the assets subject to estate tax receive a new basis (or the cost for tax purposes) equal to the value used for federal estate tax purposes even if no federal estate tax is paid. Under current law, this is true for all years except 2010.

EXAMPLE

Fred owned 1000 shares of General Moors stock purchased for $10.50 per share many years ago. At his death, the shares were worth $53.25 per share. Date-of-death values are used to determine an estate for federal estate tax purposes. Those receiving the shares of stock after Fred's death had a basis of $53.25 per share and could sell the shares of stock at that price without any income tax effect. There would be no capital gain tax.

Under current law, there is no federal estate tax in 2010, and capital gain tax will apply to the assets in estates of people dying in 2010 when those assets are sold. It is very important to keep a record of basis of assets in case a person does die in 2010 and to make a record of the value of assets on the date the loved one passes on because this is more easily done when the information is recent.

(table 53-2)

TAX RATES FOR INCOME RETAINED IN TRUSTS

TAXABLE INCOME	TAX
Not over $1500	15% of taxable income
Over $1500 but not over $3500	$225, plus 28% of the excess over $1500
Over $3500 but not over $5500	$785, plus 31% of the excess over $3500
Over $5500 but not over $7500	$1405, plus 36% of the excess over $5500
Over $7500	$2125, plus 39.6% of the excess over $7500

EXAMPLE

Under current law, if Fred died in 2010, there would be no step up in basis for capital gain which exceeded $1,300,000. In addition, the adjusted basis of assets transferred to a surviving spouse, either outright or in certain other ways, may be increased by an additional $3 million. The result is that if Fred is survived by a spouse, $4.3 million of basis increase is potentially available to assets acquired from Fred in 2010: $1.3 million to nonspouse beneficiaries and $3 million to the spouse. Adjustments are made on an asset-by-asset basis, for example, a block of stock or a single share of stock.

FEDERAL AND STATE DEATH TAXES

Federal and state death taxes are not necessarily tied together in any logical fashion. Each state has its own death tax pattern. Generally, a tax on the transfer of assets at death is called an estate tax. The tax is usually calculated on the total value of the estate of the deceased person. An inheritance tax is a tax on the receipt of assets by beneficiaries. Generally, the tax is calculated based on the amount the beneficiary receives and the amount exempt from tax, and the rate of tax may vary, depending on the relationship of the beneficiary to the deceased.

FEDERAL ESTATE TAX

Table 53-3 shows how the federal estate tax is applied. The federal estate tax covers all assets owned by the deceased or his or her revocable trust. Assets not included in the deceased's probate estate are included in the deceased's estate for federal estate tax purposes. It includes real property, bank accounts, investments, insurance owned by the deceased, joint property for which the deceased paid, tangible personal property, retirement accounts, stock options, deferred compensation, and more. If an estate tax return is due for federal or state estate tax, use a competent professional to prepare the return.

(table 53-3)

CHANGES INCLUDED IN THE ECONOMIC GROWTH AND TAX RELIEF RECONCILIATION ACT OF 2001

YEAR	ESTATE TAX EXEMPTION	TOP RATE, %	GIFT TAX EXEMPTION	STATE DEATH TAX CREDIT	OTHER
2002	$1,000,000	50%	$1,000,000	Reduced 25%	5% bubble eliminated*
2003	$1,000,000	49%	$1,000,000	Reduced 50%	
2004	$1,500,000	48%	$1,000,000	Reduced 75%	
2005	$1,500,000	47%	$1,000,000	Changed to deduction	
2006	$2,000,000	46%	$1,000,000	Changed to deduction	
2007	$2,000,000	45%	$1,000,000	Changed to deduction	
2008	$2,000,000	45%	$1,000,000	Changed to deduction	
2009	$3,500,000	45%	$1,000,000	Changed to deduction	
2010	0†	35% (gift tax only)	$1,000,000	Changed to deduction	Full step up in basis repealed
2011	$1,000,000	55%	$1,000,000	Full credit	Full step up in basis and 5% bubble restored

*On estates over $10 million.
†Estate tax repealed.

A husband and wife can make a living trust or a trust in a will which divides the assets of the first to die into two (or more) trusts. One trust preserves the exemption amount of the deceased person, and the other obtains the marital deduction available because there is a surviving spouse.

Two basic formulas can create the two trusts: pecuniary and fractional share. There are several variations of each which are used, based on what the clients want to accomplish and the experience of the practitioner drafting the clauses. After one of the spouses dies, whatever formula is included in the documents is the one which is used. To determine what to do, read the documents. The division of the assets into the two (or more) trusts is sometimes an intricate exercise and requires the assistance of competent professionals.

The *generation-skipping tax* is an additional tax to the federal estate tax designed to discourage skipping generations as a means of avoiding federal estate tax. If assets are transferred to grandchildren, grandnieces, grandnephews, and so forth, or to persons 35 or more years younger than the deceased, there may be a generation-skipping tax if the deceased transfers more than $1,100,000. If there is a question about the application of the generation-skipping tax, contact a competent professional.

LITIGATION FOLLOWING DEATH

If estates are well planned, the chances of litigation are lower than if they were not planned. Whether planned or not, people do find ways to attempt to influence the distribution of assets.

SPOUSE'S FORCED SHARE

Most states have legislation which provides that the surviving spouse must receive a minimum amount from the probate estate of the deceased spouse. The legislated minimum amount is often taken instead of what is provided in a will but, under some circumstances, may be in addition to what is left in a will. This is called the *forced share*. A state's forced share can be composed of different elements, for example, a minimum amount of the probate estate, something to live on for a year, a homestead amount, or an exemption.

TANGIBLE PERSONAL PROPERTY AND PICTURES

Tangible personal property and pictures have value far beyond their economic value. When someone passes on, the tangible personal property and pictures bring back important memories. Those who remain are often emotionally tied to these reminders.

IS IT REALLY THE DECEASED'S WILL?

If there are substantial assets titled in the name of the deceased and if there is a document offered as the will, is it the real last will?

Was the deceased competent to make the document will?

Claims can be made that the deceased was incompetent at the time the will was written. If the claim is successful, then the assets go to those named in a previous will or named by the intestate legislation of the state in which the deceased resided.

If the document offered as a will does not reflect the intent of the deceased person because that person did not have the mental ability to set forth what he or she wanted, then the document is not a will. Generally a person making a will must know (1) that he or she is creating a document to dispose of his or her property, (2) the nature and extent of his or her property, (3) those people to whom most people give their property, such as spouse, children, and parents, and (4) what the document being signed does with the property. Generally, to make a will, a person may be less than able to make a contract. Even if a conservator has been appointed to manage a person's financial matters, that appointment itself is not necessarily a determination that the person could not make a will.

If mental illness causes a person to believe facts which are not in existence, then the individual may not have the capacity to make a will.

Was there a mistake?: Suppose the document states that "my 50 shares of General Motors are to go to my nieces Jane and Dawn." The deceased owned 500 shares. The mistake can be corrected.

Was there undue influence or coercion?: If a person does not have free will when signing documents, those documents become suspect. Undue influence is behavior by third parties which overcomes volition, destroys free agency, and impels the maker of the document to act against his or her inclination. These behaviors include threats, misrepresentation, undue flattery, fraud, or coercion by physical or moral coercion. Relationships can raise a presumption of undue influence: the existence of a confidential or fiduciary relationship with the document maker, the person with that relationship benefits from the documents, or the person with the relationship had an opportunity to influence the document maker in the transaction.

Forgotten heir: If a person left a child out of a will because of forgetting the child or the mistaken belief the child was dead, some states provide relief.

Document revocation and conditional revocation: A will can be revoked by a subsequent will that explicitly revokes the earlier one. A will can be revoked by its physical destruction: tearing, burning, canceling, or obliterating. The maker might have in his or her presence another person destroy the will. The defining question is, When the act occurred, what was the intent of the maker?

IMPACT OF FORCED SHARE AND ELECTIONS

Most states permit a spouse to elect to take a statutory forced share rather than that which is (or is not) provided in a will. In addition, a spouse may have a right to homestead, exemptions, and a living allowance for a year.

The following chart shows what happened, in Michigan, to Tom's estate of $1 million, for which his will specified equal shares among his four children (from a first marriage) and Alice (his spouse from a second marriage). Tom's intent, obviously, was that each beneficiary should receive $200,000. Let's see what actually occurred:

ASSET	VALUE	PROBATE ESTATE		
House	$ 500,000	$ 500,000		
Market fund	$ 300,000	$ 300,000		
Automobile	$ 10,000	$ 10,000		
Brokerage account	$ 200,000	$ 200,000		
TOTAL PROBATE ESTATE			$ 1,010,000	
Expenses			– $10,000	
Balance for beneficiaries			$ 1,000,000	
Family allowance		$ 18,000		
Homestead		$ 15,000		
Exempt property		$ 10,000		
TOTAL ALLOWANCE, HOMESTEAD, AND EXEMPT PROPERTY			$ 43,000	
SPOUSE ELECTS AGAINST THE WILL				
First $ 150,000		$ 150,000		
Remaining from $ 1,000,000		$ 807,000		
1/2 amount remaining		$ 403,500		
Total normal intestate share for spouse ($150,000 + $403,500)			$ 553,500	
1/2 of normal share			$ 276,750	
Elect against will = 1/2 spouse intestate share				$ 276,750.00
Add family allowance, exempt property and homestead				$ 43,000.00
TOTAL TO ELECTING SPOUSE				$ 319,750.00
Left to divide among 4 children				$ 680,250.00
EACH CHILD				$ 170,062.50

Tom had previously given Alice $1 million while he was living. That did not prevent Alice from grabbing as much as she could, depriving each child of about $30,000.

If Tom had used a trust, instead of a will, Alice would have only been able to claim family allowance, exempt property, and homestead of $43,000, leaving a much fairer distribution for Tom's children.

It might be argued that the maker revoked the will on the mistaken condition that an old document would take effect or a new document would come into existence which did not occur. Other conditions might be raised.

Requirements not met: Each state has its own requirements for the proper execution of a will or trust. These requirements are primarily intended to prevent fraud. Attacks can be made that the signature is not that of the purported maker, the document is not properly witnessed, or its format does not meet legal requirements.

In many states, a will written completely in the hand of the maker setting for the maker's intent would be accepted as a will even though it does not meet the formal requirements.

MEANING OF THE DOCUMENT

Once a document has been determined to be genuine, the issue can arise as to the meaning of the document. If the document says to divide the assets equally among "my children," is a child adopted after the document was written included? Is an illegitimate, unacknowledged child included? If the document says that "my grandchildren shall take the share of deceased parents equally" and one deceased parent had three children and one deceased parent had two children, do the grandchildren each take a fifth of the two deceased parents' shares or do the children of each deceased parent take the share of the parent equally?

Different states deal with these issues differently. Over the centuries, many ambiguities and disputes have arisen because of the poor use of language.

CREDITOR CLAIMS

All bills received are not necessarily valid. The fiduciary determines which is valid or invalid. If the person submitting a bill does not agree, litigation may arise.

EXAMPLE

A detail shop in a metropolitan area is rumored to have checked the death records regularly and reviewed the inventory of the estates. Usually, the entire description of the automobile was present, including its vehicle identification number. A bill would be sent for detailing the automobile. Presumably many of the bills were paid because the sum was not large and the bill looked legitimate.

BREACH OF FIDUCIARY DUTY

The person managing the assets has a duty to arrange the assets for the benefit of the creditors and beneficiaries. If the fiduciary allows people who are not beneficiaries to take personal property from the residence, there may be an allegation of breach of fiduciary duty. If the fiduciary holds onto assets which have been good investments in the past but which decline significantly in value, there may be a charge of breaching the investment duty of the fiduciary.

FEES

The fees of attorneys, fiduciaries, appraisers, and others may be challenged. Hearings determine the reasonableness of the fees.

APPORTIONMENT OF TAXES AND EXPENSES

The manner of apportioning taxes, expenses, and fees among the beneficiaries' shares or with respect to assets passing outside of trusts and wills affects the amount each beneficiary receives.

EXAMPLE

The deceased's estate for probate purposes is $2,250,000 after expenses and claims and is $2,500,000 for federal estate tax purposes after expenses and claims in 2004. The federal estate tax is $465,000. The will leaves $1,500,000 to specific individuals and the balance of everything left to his sister. For federal estate tax purposes, $250,000 of his estate passes under a transfer-on-death designation with his broker. If the entire weight of the tax falls on the sister's share, she would receive $285,000. However, if the person receiving the $250,000 outside the estate has to pick up a proportionate share of the estate tax, the sister would receive $331,500.

Documents or legislation may resolve the issue. But if they do not resolve the issue, then litigation may arise.

BENEFICIARIES

LEGAL AND FINANCIAL PLANNING OPPORTUNITIES

Consider the following list of opportunities. You should consult your professional advisors on whether to implement any of them.

1. If the deceased had a trust, that trust may be able to adopt the fiscal year of any probate which is needed. If there is no probate estate, the trust may be able to adopt a fiscal year for its tax reporting.* Use of a fiscal year for the trust can result in postponing a beneficiary's obligation to pay income tax for many months if payments are made under the guidance of a competent professional. In addition, you can avoid some mismatches of income and deductions through the use of a fiscal year.

2. There is some discretion as to whether some deductions should be taken on the IRS Form 706 federal estate tax return or the IRS Form 1041 fiduciary income tax return. If there is a reduce to zero formula for establishing the marital trust, then the deductions will likely be taken on the Form 1041. However, if there is a large estate tax at a rate in excess of what the beneficiaries will have to pay, a choice may be made to take the appropriate deductions on the IRS Form 706.

3. One or more disclaimers may be used. (A **disclaimer** is the written unqualified and irrevocable refusal to accept an interest in property.) A disclaimer is like having a potential distribution bounce off the person who disclaims. Under the law a disclaimer is treated as though the person died without receiving the distribution. Properly disclaimed property is not subject to gift tax and is not in the estate of the person disclaiming. After a person passes on, a review of the situation can be made, and property can be passed on sooner to children and other beneficiaries if that makes sense. This concept is not just for the rich. Depending on state law, a disclaimer might be used to prevent a person from receiving assets which would otherwise cause that person to be ineligible for Medicaid for long-term nursing home care.

* Unless the correct process is followed, IRC Section 644 would prohibit a trust from using a fiscal year. The use of a fiscal year is limited to the administration following death and not permitted for ongoing trusts such as the family trust and marital trust.

4. If sophisticated planning is being used, attention to proper valuation using very competent appraisers can result in favorable results for estate tax and future income tax.

5. Estate tax payments can be deferred under certain circumstances. When those circumstances apply, a review should be made of the consequences of deferral against the expense of borrowing or selling to pay estate tax.

6. Careful review of opportunities regarding business entities, such as partnerships, limited liability companies, and corporations, is in order to make sure the opportunities are not missed.

7. The surviving spouse may have elections which can be made that will impact what she receives and which may impact estate and income taxes.

8. The investments made affect the amount of ordinary income received and capital gains   realized. These decisions affect the amount of income a beneficiary receives as well as the amount received by those who receive assets at the death of a beneficiary. The decisions also affect the amount of income tax paid by income tax beneficiaries. The assistance of a certified financial planner (CFP) or other qualified financial planner can help with investments which help a family reach its income goals and minimize income taxes.

9. If "skip" beneficiaries receive distributions or if beneficiary designations might result in generation-skipping tax, proper allocations of generation-skipping exclusions and exemptions can be beneficial to a family.

REPORTING TO BENEFICIARIES

Reporting to beneficiaries falls between the desirable and the required. Usually state law or the instructions in documents require that beneficiaries receive copies of the will, trust, or other disposition instruments. Sometimes, the instruction in an instrument prohibits beneficiaries from seeing all but a portion of a document, and unless that instruction violates state law, it must be obeyed.

Beneficiaries are interested in knowing when they will receive their share of the estate or trust. After you determine whether a spouse or dependent beneficiary has any immediate needs (see the section "Immediate Needs," above), a letter outlining the process which will be used and setting expectations is desirable. If a probate estate is the primary administrative vehicle, then a description of the probate process is desirable. If a trust is the primary administrative vehicle, then a description of the trust settlement process is desirable.

It is usually best to set the first expectation that a more comprehensive report will be made to the beneficiaries about four or five months after the date of death. At that time the fiduciary would know many more details and can more accurately estimate the time period for administration. During that fourth or fifth month, a report needs to be sent which plugs in

(figure 53-4)

Example of a form for listing assets at the beginning of administration.

ASSETS AT BEGINNING OF ADMINISTRATION

LOCATION OBTAINED OR RECEIVED FROM	DATE	ASSET DESCRIPTION	AMOUNT
Total Beginning Assets			
Income Received			

RECEIPTS	DATE	PURPOSE	AMOUNT
Received From			
Total Income			$0.00

EXPENSES

PAYEE	DATE	PURPOSE	CHK. #	AMOUNT
Total Expenses				$ 0.00

DISTRIBUTIONS TO BENEFICIARIES DURING ACCOUNTING PERIOD

DISTRIBUTEE	DATE	PURPOSE	CHK. # ITEM #	VALUE
Total Distributions in this accounting				$ 0.00

CHANGES IN ASSET VALUES DURING ADMINISTRATION

ASSET	REASON FOR VALUE CHANGE	VALUE
Total Adjustment for Value Changes		$0.00

ASSETS ON HAND AT THE TIME OF THIS ACCOUNT

Total Assets On Hand	$0.00

approximate dates to the description of the process which was in the first communication. This second communication should not make definite promises but only set approximate time frames. Those time frames should probably be made a little long to take into account unforeseen difficulties. Beneficiaries will be pleased with distributions which are earlier than they expected and distraught if the distributions are later than they expected.

The critical accomplishment for the letter is to set expectations. Initially, the personal representative or trustee has the first opportunity to establish expectations. Since administration involves work which is asset by asset, a problem with any asset can delay the process.

EXAMPLE

The first spouse died and left a well-planned estate using two separate revocable living trusts. During life, the deceased spouse determined not to transfer to either trust title held by the deceased to eight lots in the Bahamas. An unresolved dispute has been pending pertaining to representations made when the lots were sold. The value of the lots affects the funding of the family and marital trusts, and those values are, in part, dependent on how quickly the matters can be resolved. This matter may delay what otherwise would be a speedy settlement of the deceased spouse's trust.

The will, trust, or state law usually requires some type of financial reporting, called an accounting. The accounting is a financial report to the beneficiaries (and to the court if there is probate or a registered trust) of the assets and income received; the bills, taxes, and expenses paid; partial or full distributions made; and the remaining amount held by the fiduciary. Unless a document or state law requires that the financial accounting to beneficiaries be in a particular format, you can choose a format which is comfortable for you. Figure 53-4 shows an accounting format you might like to use.

When the trust, estate, or both are ready for final distribution, a final accounting is compiled. It may be necessary to estimate the final expenses for the final account so that you can determine the final distribution. The format shown in Figure 53-5 might be used.

MAKING DISTRIBUTION

The final step in settlement of a trust or an estate is to distribute the assets to those who should receive them. The trust, will, or state statute directs

(figure 53-5)

Example of a form for estimating final expenses.

ESTIMATED FINAL EXPENSES

Attorney Fee	$ 0.00
Fiduciary Fee	$ 0.00
CPA Prepare Tax Return	$ 0.00
Estimated "Extra" Fee	$ 0.00
Total Estimated Expenses	$ 0.00

(figure 53-6)

Example of a form showing how assets are to be distributed.

ASSETS ON HAND FOR DISTRIBUTION	
ASSET	DISTRIBUTION VALUE
	$ 0.00
	$ 0.00
	$ 0.00
Total to be Distributed from Fiduciary	$ 0.00

53

how the final distribution is made. Making a chart as to which trust or person receives which asset (and that asset's value) is very helpful.

If the instruments create subtrusts or separate trusts, those trusts will need to obtain their tax identification numbers using IRS Form SS-4 and should consider using IRS Form 56 to notify the IRS that tax reporting is about to start.

If the administration follows the death of the first spouse, distribution may be to the surviving spouse or to subtrusts created in the trust of the deceased spouse. If outright distribution to a spouse or spouse and children is instructed, the distribution may not require extensive analysis. If distribution is to subtrusts, the assistance of competent professionals is recommended so that the subtrusts are properly established and so that assets are properly distributed to those trusts. Falling and rising markets can affect which assets are distributed to the respective trusts.

A chart showing how a distribution is made can be very helpful. Figure 53-6 is a suggested format for such a chart. The distribution schedule proposed by the fiduciary is shown in Figure 53-7.

You may wish to request that the beneficiaries consent to the proposed distribution. If a beneficiary does not consent, you may wish to request a court having jurisdiction to approve the proposed distribution. Assistance of competent professionals is advised for this step in the process.

(figure 53-7)

Example of a form showing a schedule of distribution.

SCHEDULE OF DISTRIBUTION		
ASSET DESCRIPTION	DOLLAR AMOUNT OF VALUE	NAME OF RECIPIENT
	$0.00	
	$0.00	
	$0.00	
Total Distribution	$0.00	

COMPLETING LEGAL MATTERS

The tasks which must be completed after distribution vary greatly on the estate or trust which was administered and depend on matters which arose during administration. Often the following have to be completed after distribution:

- Final income tax returns need to be filed for the trusts and/or estates used during administration. If beneficiaries received distributions for which a K-1 is required, send them the forms.
- IRS Form 56 should be filed for each entity which obtained a tax identification number.
- The banks, brokerage firms, and financial organizations which provided accounts for administration need to be informed that those particular accounts are no longer necessary. They will probably all have a balance of zero at the time of notification.
- There may be small items which will have to be managed, such as unexpected interest or an unexpected dividend. Consult with competent professionals on how to handle small details.
- If there was an estate, the final papers need to be filed with the probate court, and the final closing orders obtained and received.

If administration of the deceased's affairs was a smooth experience, then it probably was well planned before the person died. If you participated in that planning, congratulations on being farsighted and making things run smoothly. If you have an estate plan, be sure to keep it maintained by consulting your planning professionals every one to three years.

If administration did not go well, consider planning your matters with competent professionals so that your affairs will be more easily administered on becoming disabled or dying.

WHAT YOU NEED TO KNOW

■ Professional legal help should be sought immediately if a loved one is disabled or dies.

■ Managing the affairs of a disabled or deceased person is a great deal of work.

■ Gain an understanding of the basis of medical billing and payment.

■ If you act on behalf of another person, third parties will want to see the documents authorizing you to act. These documents may be private or court documents depending on whether prior planning was completed.

■ Even if no planning has been done, professional legal help may lead to a better result.

■ A person managing the assets of another person, estate, or trust needs to keep good records and account for what he or she has done.

■ You will receive a great deal of information from well-meaning people who may be in error.

■ Document everything you do.

■ After a person dies, assets must be collected and preserved, debts and taxes paid, and assets distributed to those who should receive them.

■ Title (ownership) of every asset is key information necessary to good administration.

FOR MORE INFORMATION

Internal Revenue Service
Web: www.irs.gov/formspubs
Introductory page to all the IRS forms and publications.

Tom Scott Enterprises
2109 Seaman Circle, NE
Atlanta, GA 30341
Phone: (770) 457-1223
Fax: (770) 457-0755
Web: www.mindspring.com/~tscotent
Sells the software for tracking your medical expenses.

Social Security Administration
800-772-1213
We recommend its booklets "Survivors Benefits" (publication 05-10084) and "Social Security: Understanding the Benefits" (publication 05-10024).

APPENDIX A
WEIGHTS
AND MEASURES

A.A

Medical measurements require precision, and the metric system is used. Note that the metric system is used throughout this book. If you live in the United States, you may not be that familiar with this system, so this appendix helps you understand metric equivalents.

LENGTH

The most common length measurement in this book is the millimeter (mm) or centimeter (cm). Body parts, skin blemishes, and tumors are measured by millimeter or centimeter, so it helps if you have a basic concept of the length of a millimeter or centimeter.

2.54 cm = 1 in

1 cm = 10 mm = 0.39 in

As you can see, a millimeter is a tenth of a centimeter. Thus a millimeter is very small, approximately four-hundredths of an inch. A meter (m) equals 100 centimeters and therefore is quite large, roughly a yard and 3 inches. A kilometer (km) is 1000 meters, approximately six-tenths of a mile.

If you are mathematically inclined (or have a calculator!), use the following conversion table to figure things out for yourself:

Millimeters to inches	Multiply by 10; divide by 254.
Inches to millimeters	Multiply by 254; divide by 10.
Centimeters to feet	Multiply by 10; divide by 307.
Feet to centimeters	Multiply by 307; divide by 10.
Meters to yards	Multiply by 70; divide by 64.
Yards to meters	Multiply by 64; divide by 70.
Kilometers to miles	Multiply by 5; divide by 8.
Miles to kilometers	Multiply by 8; divide by 5.

WEIGHT

The basic weight measurement is the gram (g), a small weight indeed. A gram is approximately four-hundredths of an ounce. It takes 28.4 grams to make 1 ounce and 454 grams to make 1 pound. Most drug measurements are by milligram (mg), which is a thousandth of a gram. A kilogram (kg) is 1000 grams, approximately 2.2 pounds.

For the mathematicians:

Kilograms to pounds	Multiply by 1000; divide by 454.
Pounds to kilograms	Multiply by 454; divide by 1000.
Grams to ounces	Multiply by 20; divide by 567.
Ounces to grams	Multiply by 567; divide by 20.

VOLUME

The basic unit of volume is the liter (L), which is slightly larger than a quart. A milliliter (mL) or cubic centimeter (cc) is a thousandth of a liter. A deciliter (dL) is a tenth of a liter. A common dose for some medicines, such as cough syrup, is 30 cc, or roughly 1 ounce. A gallon is 3.78 liters.

Get your calculator:

Liters to gallons	Multiply by 264; divide by 1000.
Gallons to liters	Multiply by 1000; divide by 264.
Liters to pints	Multiply by 21; divide by 10.
Pints to liters	Multiply by 10; divide by 21.

Celsius to Fahrenheit	Multiply by 1.8, and add 32.
Fahrenheit to Celsius	Subtract 32; then multiply by 0.555.

TEMPERATURE

Body temperature is usually recorded in degrees Fahrenheit (F) in the United States. However, more and more hospitals report the temperature in degrees Celsius (C). Since case reports in medical journals are distributed throughout the world, temperature in degrees Celsius is the standard. Normal body temperature is generally reported as 98.6°F, which is 37°C. Minor variations from this range are considered normal. A temperature above 37.5°C (99.5°F) would prompt closer observation, and a temperature above 38°C (100.4°F) would generally warrant investigation for the source of the fever.

APPENDIX B
PRESCRIPTION DRUGS
AND MEDICAID

MEDICARE PRESCRIPTION DRUG BENEFIT

As this book was being finished, the 2003 Medicare Modernization Act was passed. The legislation allows a Medicare prescription drug benefit, but many people have expressed confusion over what the benefit covers.

Beginning in 2004, a discount card with the Medicare mark is being offered through private companies that will entitle the holder to a discount of 10 to 25% off the retail price of a prescription drug (according to the Medicare website www.medicare.gov).The maximum cost for the card will be $30, but many cards have lower or no fees. Enrollment will continue through December 2005. If your monthly income in 2004 is less than $1047 (or less than $1404 if you are a married couple), you may qualify for $600 to pay for prescription drugs. If you are covered under Medicaid, you are not eligible to receive this card.

In 2006, the Medicare prescription drug benefit will go into effect. This benefit is available to all Medicare beneficiaries, but the program is voluntary. The premium will be $35 per month, and there will be a $250 deductible. This means that you will have to bear the cost of the first $250 for your prescription drugs. After you meet the deductible, Medicare will pay 75% of the cost of your prescription medications up to $2250. You will then pay the drug costs between $2250 and $5100. Medicare will pay 95% of drug costs above $5100. Additional assistance will be provided for those with limited income and assets. For example, Medicare beneficiaries who also qualify for Medicaid with incomes below 100% of the federal poverty level will receive subsidies for the premium and deductible, as well as minimal copays and no gap in coverage. There will be copays of $1 for generic drugs and $3 for brand name drugs. The copay is waived for nursing home residents.

As you can see, the persons who will get the most benefit out of this legislation are those with very low incomes and those with very high drug costs. What if your income is above these limits or you have other circumstances that make the cost of prescription drugs a source of financial stress? Read on.

PRESCRIPTION DRUGS FROM FOREIGN OR ONLINE PHARMACIES

The issue of importation of prescription drugs from Canada and the use of online pharmacies has caused tremendous controversy. This controversy has been fueled by the belief that prescription drug prices in the United States are too high. In fact, the governors of four states (Illinois, Iowa, Minnesota, and Wisconsin) are looking into the possibility of obtaining prescription drugs from Canada in order to reduce the health care budget for state employees and retired persons and thus save money for taxpayers. AARP has supported legislation that allows reimportation of drugs from Canada as long as certain safety standards are met.

Although the cost of drugs is an important consideration to most of us, safety is an even greater concern. In this book, we suggested that you develop a relationship with a pharmacist or pharmacy so that potentially serious adverse drug interactions could be avoided. Your primary care doctor and pharmacist are greatly concerned about the possibility of such interactions. But what happens if you procure prescription medications from foreign or online sources? An important safeguard in this system has been removed. Your pharmacist can't monitor you for problems caused by drugs that he or she doesn't know you take. Your pharmacist should function as an important consultant on your health care team, which requires that he or she monitor all the medicines you take.

Another important aspect of the safety of medicines that you take is their quality. Many people are now buying prescription medication from foreign or online sources with little knowledge of the safety of those products. In June 2003, William Hubbard, associate commissioner for policy and planning at the U.S. Food and Drug Administration (FDA), testified before the Subcommittee on Human Rights and Wellness of the U.S. House of Representatives. The FDA works diligently to maintain high standards for prescription drugs in the United States. However, the FDA cannot guarantee the quality or safety of medications procured from foreign or online sources. Hubbard's comments reflect the serious concerns of health professionals in the United States:

For public health reasons, FDA remains concerned about the importation of prescription drugs into the U.S. In our experience, many drugs obtained from foreign sources that either purport to be or appear to be the same as U.S.-approved prescription drugs are, in fact, of unknown quality. FDA cannot assure the American public that drugs imported from foreign countries are the same as products approved by FDA.

FDA has long taken the position that consumers are exposed to a number of risks when they purchase drugs from foreign sources or from sources that are not operated by pharmacies licensed under state pharmacy law. These outlets may dispense expired, subpotent, contaminated or counterfeit product, the wrong or a contraindicated product, an incorrect dose, or medication unaccompanied by adequate directions for use. The labeling of the drug may not be in English and therefore important information regarding dosage and side effects may not be available to the consumer. The drugs may not have been packaged and stored under appropriate conditions to avoid degradation. There is no assurance that these products were manufactured under current good manufacturing practice standards. When consumers take such unsafe or inappropriate medications, they face risks of dangerous drug interactions and other serious health consequences.

And what happens if you experience a serious adverse event? In addition to the safety concerns, what about the legal issues? What recourse do you have if an imported drug harms you? Most of the sources for these drugs have you sign a waiver of liability. Where do you go if you needed to take legal action? You may find it very difficult to find out who actually owns the pharmacy or online service and where it is actually located.

Finally, there is another legal issue. Currently, it is illegal to import prescription medication into the United States. Some websites for Canadian pharmacies indicate that they provide these prescriptions when rewritten by a Canadian physician in order to comply with Canadian law. The code of ethics of the Canadian Medical Association indicates that it is the responsibility of a physician to perform a history and physical examination, as well as discuss the benefits and risks of drug treatment. Obviously, this seldom occurs. Hubbard makes the issue clear:

In addition to these safety concerns, it is also important to point out that it is illegal, under the Federal Food, Drug, and Cosmetic (FD&C) Act, to import unapproved, misbranded, and adulterated drugs into the U.S. This includes foreign versions of U.S.-approved medications. It is also illegal for anyone other than the drug's manufacturer to re-import a prescription drug that was originally manufactured in the U.S.

This issue is certainly still open to debate. In July, a House bill passed that proposes measures to ensure the safety of prescription drugs imported from foreign sources. These measures include tamper-proof containers and devices to prevent counterfeiting. The FDA has assembled a task force to closely examine these safety measures. However, it may be a few years before the safety and legal implications are fully defined.

Many persons go to Canada and bring back medications for personal use. Medicines obtained from Canadian pharmacies in this fashion are generally considered safe. Although there are laws in the United States against doing this, the FDA and U.S. Customs Service have generally been permissive as long as the person has a prescription and buys drugs only for himself or herself and no more than a month's supply. However, significant concerns exist about the safety of drugs obtained from websites purporting to sell Canadian drugs. The following is quoted from the *Medical Letter on Drugs and Therapeutics* in the December 8, 2003, issue:

> Questions have been raised in the US press recently about the safety of Canadian drugs. The process of drug approval in Canada is similar to that in the US (D. Paul, *Int J Med Marketing* 2001; 1:224). More than 90% of drugs available in Canada have also been approved by the FDA. Most of these drugs come from the same manufacturers as drugs in the US. Health Canada takes longer on average to release drugs than the FDA does; more than half the drugs discontinued for safety reasons by the FDA between 1992 and 2001 had not been approved for use in Canada (NS Rawson and Kl Kaitin, *Ann Pharmacother* 2003; 37:1043). Websites claiming to sell Canadian drugs, however, may be selling counterfeit drugs from unregulated sources.

OTHER OPTIONS

Many pharmaceutical companies have recognized that the limited income of some senior citizens makes purchasing prescription drugs a significant financial hardship and have programs to help such seniors. Check out Table B-1 to see if you qualify for any of their programs.

Another helpful program is ScriptSave (800-262-7136), which offers a discount on medicines from over 30,000 participating pharmacies. There is no enrollment fee or monthly fee, and there is no waiting period. In addition, some companies offer free medicines to qualified enrollees.

The following websites may also help you identify programs that can provide assistance:

- www.needymeds.com
- www.medicinebridge.com
- www.freemedicinefoundation.com
- www.medicare.gov
- www.helpingpatients.org

(table B-1)

PARTIAL LIST OF DRUG PROGRAMS BY PHARMACEUTICAL COMPANIES FOR SENIORS EXPERIENCING FINANCIAL HARDSHIP

COMPANY	PROGRAM	DRUGS COVERED (PARTIAL LIST)	QUALIFICATIONS	APPLICATION INFORMATION
Boehringer-Ingerlhelm	3 months of free medication per request	Aggrenox, Atrovent, Catapres, Combivent, Flomax, Micardis, Mirapex, Mobic	Requests reviewed in case by case basis	800-556-8317
GlaxoSmithKline	Orange card. Average savings of 30%, but possibly up to 40% or more.	Advair, Augmentin, Avandia, Bactroban, Combivir, Coreg, Epivir, Eskalith, Flonase, Flovent, Imitrex, Lamictal, Lanoxin, Paxil, Requip, Serevent, Trizivir, Valtrex, Wellbutrin, Ziagen, Zofran	Medicare eligible; have no private or public insurance covering prescription drugs; annual income less than $26,000 (individual) or $35,000 (a couple)	Your physician or pharmacist, or write to Orange Card Program, P.O. Box 7812, Ocala, FL 34478

COMPANY	PROGRAM	DRUGS COVERED (PARTIAL LIST)	QUALIFICATIONS	APPLICATION INFORMATION
Novartis, AstraZeneca, Janssen, Abbott, Bristol-Myers Squibb, GlaxoSmithKline, OrthoMcNeil, Aventis	Together card. Multiple companies offer many drugs and programs in one card. Savings average 20-40% and sometimes even more.	Accolate, Aciphex, Allegra, Amaryl, Biaxin, BuSpar, Coumadin, Crestor, Coreg, Diovan, Ditropan, Exelon, Glucophage, Lotrel, Mavik, Monopril, Nexium, Paxil, Pravachol, Risperdal, Sinemet, Synthroid, Toprol, Ultracet	Enrolled in Medicare; have no private or public insurance covering prescription drugs; annual income less than $28,000 (individual) or $38,000 (a couple)	Your physician or pharmacist, or call 800-865-7211
Merck	Patient assistance program. Free medicine for up to one year.	Fosamax, Indocin, Maxalt, Moduretic, Pepcid, Propecia, Proscar, Singulair, Vioxx, Zocor	Live in the U.S. (but do not need to be a U.S. citizen) and have a prescription for a Merck medicine from a doctor licensed in the U.S.; have no private or public insurance covering prescription drugs; annual income less than $18,000 (individual), $24,000 (a couple), or $35,000 (a family of four)	Your physician; write Merck Patient Assistance Program, P.O. Box 690, Horsham, PA 19044; or call 800-727-5400
Pfizer	Share card. You pay $15 per medicine for up to a 30-day supply.	Accupril, Aricept, Geodon, Glucotrol/Glucotrol XL, Lipitor, Norvasc, Viagra, Zithromax, Zoloft, Zyrtec	Enrolled with Medicare; have no prescription drug coverage; not eligible for Medicaid or any drug benefitplan funded by the state; have an annual gross income less than $18,000 (individual) or $24,000 (a couple)	Your physician or pharmacist, or call 800-717-6005
Proctor & Gamble	3 month supply of free medication for up to one year.	Actonel, Asacol, Didronel, Macrobid, Macrodantin	Requests reviewed on case by case basis	800-830-9049
Schering-Plough	3 month supply of free medication at a time. Up to one year	Clarinex, Foradil, Imdur, Nasonex	Requests reviewed on case by case basis	800-656-9485
Wyeth	3 month supple of free medication	Cordarone, Effexor, Inderal, Lodine, Phenergan, Premarin, Prempro	U.S. residents, no government or private insurance to pay for the requested medication. Earnings less than 20% of the current Health and Human services (HHS) poverty guidelines	Wyeth Patient Assistance Program P.O. Box 1759 Paoli, PA 19301-0859

Refer to www.helpingpatients.org for an extensive and an up-to-date list.

APPENDIX C
MEDICATIONS

This appendix is an alphabetical listing of drugs mentioned in Optimal Aging. The first column has the generic, or nonproprietary, name of the drug. The second column has the brand name, which is often the name you will hear when you talk with your doctor. The third column has information on the drug's usage.

Some drugs are made by more than one manufacturer and therefore have two or even more brand names, which occasionally causes some confusion. The prescription label on your medicine bottle will often have the generic name, since most pharmacists are allowed to use the generic equivalent for the drug that is prescribed unless the doctor writes on the prescription "medically necessary" or "dispense as written." A generic drug is not a different medicine from the one you are taking but is made by a manufacturer different from the original developer and manufacturer of the drug. Generally, generic drugs are considerably less expensive than their brand name equivalents. However, it is important to understand some of the reasons why this difference exists.

On drugs they develop, pharmaceutical companies generally have patents for 20 years, which allows them to recover the costs of the research and development and make a profit from the sale of the drug. The cost of bringing a drug to market may be as high as $700 to $800 million, and there is no guarantee that the drug will be successful. In some cases, as you know, a drug has to be pulled from the shelves because problems are reported after it becomes more widely used. One example is Rezulin, a medication for diabetes. Within a few years after introduction, a higher than expected incidence of liver problems was reported in those using the drug, and the manufacturer pulled it from the market. Some drugs never even make it through clinical trials. As you can see, the whole process can be extremely expensive. The major pharmaceutical companies employ many research scientists, and the cost for research and development can be staggering.

In addition, by the time the drug actually becomes available for purchase, several years may have passed on the patent. A generic manufacturer can produce the same drug within perhaps 18 years or even 12 years, in some cases, of the original manufacturer's release to the public. The whole question of drug patent protection is being hotly debated. However, it is important for us to look at both sides of the issue. Yes, we want affordable medications. On the other hand, we don't want to cripple the ability of the pharmaceutical companies to produce new drugs that will improve our health and quality of life. If you are truly financially challenged by the cost of your medication, let your doctor know. Perhaps you qualify for one of the cards provided by many of the major pharmaceutical companies that will give you steep discounts on the usual drug price. Many of these companies even provide free medication for those in need (see Appendix B).

GENERIC NAME	BRAND NAME	USES
abarelix	*	Prostate cancer (rapidly reduces serum testosterone to castrate levels). Neither the generic abarelix nor any brand available yet
acarbose	Precose	Diabetes
acetaminophen	Tylenol	Pain, fever
acetazolamide	Diamox	A diuretic; to treat glaucoma and to prevent and treat altitude sickness
acyclovir	Zovirax	Shingles, cold sores, genital herpes
adalimumab	Humira	Rheumatoid arthritis
albuterol	Proventil, Ventolin	Asthma
alendronate	Fosamax	Osteoporosis, Paget's disease
alfuzosin	Uroxatral	Relieves obstructive symptoms of benign prostatic hypertrophy with less risk of ejaculation back into the bladder
allopurinol	Zyloprim	Gout
alprazolam	Xanax	Tranquilizer; helpful in panic disorder
alprostadil	Caverject, Edex	Male erectile dysfunction
amantadine	Symmetrel	Parkinson's disease; influenza prevention and treatment
amifostine	Ethyol	Protects normal tissue from radiation
amikacin	Amikin	Antibiotic
amiodarone	Cordarone, Pacerone	Heart rhythm disturbances
amitriptyline	Elavil, Endep	Depression, chronic pain, migraine prophylaxis
amlodipine	Norvasc	High blood pressure
amoxicillin	Amoxil, Trimox	Antibiotic
amphetamine	Adderall	Attention deficit disorder, narcolepsy
ampicillin	Omnipen, Principen	Antibiotic
anakinra	Kineret	Rheumatoid arthritis
anastrozole	Arimidex	Breast cancer
apomorphine	*	Being studied as a possible treatment for sexual dysfunction in men and women
atenolol	Tenormin	High blood pressure, angina, heart rhythm disturbances
atorvastatin	Lipitor	High blood cholesterol
atropine	*	Accelerates a slow heart rate; relieves airway congestion in dying patients
azathioprine	Imuran	Rheumatoid arthritis, ulcerative colitis, Crohn's disease, transplant rejection, myasthenia gravis
azelastine	Astelin	Rhinitis
azithromycin	Zithromax	Antibiotic
baclofen	Lioresal	Muscle spasm, hiccups
beclomethasone	Beclovent, QVAR, Beconase, Vancenase	Asthma; nasal spray for rhinitis
bicalutamide	Casodex	Antiandrogen to treat prostate cancer
bromocriptine	Parlodel	Parkinson's disease, acromegaly
budesonide	Pulmicort, Rhinocort	Asthma, nasal spray for rhinitis
bumetanide	Bumex	Diuretic (water pill)
bupropion	Zyban, Wellbutrin	Antidepressant; smoking cessation aid
buspirone	BuSpar	Anxiety
cabergoline	Dostinex	Prolactin tumors of the pituitary
calcitriol	Rocaltrol	Low blood calcium (due to kidney failure)
captopril	Capoten	High blood pressure, congestive heart failure, diabetic kidney disease
carbamazepine	Carbatrol, Tegretol	To prevent seizures; to treat trigeminal neuralgia and bipolar disorder

*Only generic drugs available or not yet named.

GENERIC NAME	BRAND NAME	USES
carboplatin	Paraplatin	Cancer treatment
carvedilol	Coreg	A beta-blocker for congestive heart failure and hypertension
celecoxib	Celebrex	Arthritis, pain
cetirizine	Zyrtec	Rhinitis, hives
chlorazepate	Tranxene	Anxiety, alcohol withdrawal
chlordiazepoxide	Librium	Tranquilizer; to manage alcohol withdrawal
chlorpromazine	Thorazine	Antipsychotic; nausea or vomiting; intractable hiccups
cilostazol	Pletal	Blockages in the leg arteries (contraindicated in persons with congestive heart failure)
cimetidine	Tagamet	Peptic ulcers, GERD
ciprofloxacin	Cipro	Antibiotic
cisplatin	Platinol	Cancer treatment
citalopram	Celexa	Antidepressant
sulindac	Clinoril	Arthritis, pain
clomipramine	Anafranil	Obsessive-compulsive disorder
clonazepam	Klonopin	Seizures, panic disorder, neuralgia, periodic limb movement
clonidine	Catapres	High blood pressure
clopidogrel	Plavix	To reduces risk of blood clots
clozapine	Clozaril	Antipsychotic
codeine	*	Pain reliever
colchicine	*	Acute gout, primary biliary cirrhosis
cyclophosphamide	Cytoxan	Cancer, rheumatoid arthritis
cyclosporine	Sandimmune, Neoral	To prevent transplant rejection by suppressing the immune system
dalteparin	Fragmin	Anticoagulant
dehydroepiandrosterone	DHEA	Adrenal insufficiency
demeclocycline	Declomycin	Syndrome of inappropriate antidiuretic hormone secretion
desipramine	Norpramin	Antidepressant
desloratadine	Clarinex	Rhinitis, hives
desmopressin	DDAVP	Diabetes insipidus, hemophilia, von Willebrand's disease
dexamethasone	Decadron	Potent steroid for adrenal insufficiency, brain swelling from tumors, severe lung disease, shock, etc.
dextroamphetamine	*	See amphetamine
diazepam	Valium	Muscle relaxant, sedative, seizures, alcohol withdrawal
diethylstilbestrol	DES	Estrogen for metastatic prostate cancer
digoxin	Lanoxin, Lanoxicaps, Digitek	Congestive heart failure, heart rhythm disturbances
diltiazem	Cardizem, Cartia, Dilacor, Tiazac	High blood pressure, angina, heart rhythm disturbances
dimenhydrinate (OTC)	Dramamine	Motion sickness
diphenoxylate-atropine	Lomotil	Antidiarrheal
disulfiram	Antabuse	Alcohol dependence
donepezil	Aricept	Alzheimer's disease, vascular dementia
doxazosin	Cardura	Antihypertensive; obstructive symptoms due to BPH
doxepin	Sinequan	Antidepressant
doxorubicin	Adriamycin	Cancer treatment
dutasteride	Avodart	Relieves obstructive symptoms from benign prostatic hypertrophy
edrophonium	Tensilon	Diagnostic test for myasthenia gravis
enalapril	Vasotec	ACE inhibitor for congestive heart failure and heart attack
enoxaparin	Lovenox	Anticoagulant

GENERIC NAME	BRAND NAME	USES
entacapone	Comtan	Parkinson's disease
ephedrine	In many OTC cold preparations	Decongestant; as a dietary aid complications have been reported; being investigated for female sexual arousal
epoetin alpha	Epogen, Procrit	Anemia secondary to kidney disease, chemotherapy, or HIV infection
erythromycin	E-mycin, Erythrocin, EES, Ery-Tab, Ilosone	Antibiotic
escitalopram	Lexapro	Antidepressant
esomeprazole	Nexium	Peptic ulcers, GERD
estazolam	ProSom	Insomnia
etanercept	Enbrel	Rheumatoid arthritis, ankylosing spondylitis, psoriatic arthritis
etoposide	*	Cancer treatment
exemestane	Aromasin	Advanced breast cancer
famciclovir	Famvir	Shingles, cold sores, genital herpes
famotidine	Pepcid	Peptic ulcer disease, GERD
felodipine	Plendil	High blood pressure
fentanyl	Duragesic (skin patch)	Pain
fexofenadine	Allegra	Rhinitis, hives
finasteride	Proscar	Benign prostatic hypertrophy
5-fluorouracil	Adrucil (intravenous) Efudex (topical)	Cancer treatment; topical treatment for actinic keratoses and superficial basal cell carcinoma
fluconazole	Diflucan	Yeast infections
fludrocortisone	Florinef	Orthostatic hypotension, adrenal insufficiency
flunisolide	AeroBid	Asthma
fluoxetine	Prozac	Antidepressant, obsessive-compulsive disorder, panic disorder
fluoxymesterone	Halotestin	Low testosterone (in males); palliative treatment for breast cancer
fluphenazine	Prolixin	Antipsychotic
flurazepam	Dalmane	Insomnia
flutamide	Eulexin	Antiandrogen for prostate cancer
fluticasone	Flovent, Flonase Nasal	Asthma; nasal spray for rhinitis
fluvastatin	Lescol	High blood cholesterol
fluvoxamine	Luvox	Obsessive-compulsive disorder
formoterol	Foradil	Asthma; COPD
furosemide	Lasix	Diuretic (water pill)
gabapentin	Neurontin	Seizures, nerve pain, periodic limb movement disorder, mood stabilization
galantamine	Reminyl	Alzheimer's disease, vascular dementia
gefitinib	Iressa	Cancer treatment
gemfibrozil	Lopid	High blood cholesterol and/or triglycerides
gentamicin	Garamycin	Antibiotic
glimepiride	Amaryl	Diabetes
glipizide	Glucotrol	Diabetes
glyburide	DiaBeta, Micronase, Glynase	Diabetes
goserelin	Zoladex	Prostate cancer; reduces testosterone to castrate levels
haloperidol	Haldol	Antipsychotic, Tourette's syndrome
heparin	*	Intravenous anticoagulant
hydrochlorothiazide	Esidrix, HydroDIURIL, Microzide, Oretic	Diuretic, antihypertensive

*Only generic drugs available or not yet named.

GENERIC NAME	BRAND NAME	USES
hydrocodone	Lortab, Lorcet, Vicodin	Narcotic pain reliever
hydrocortisone	Cortef	Steroid to treat adrenal insufficiency and inflammatory disorders
hydromorphone	Dilaudid	Narcotic pain reliever
hydroxychloroquine	Plaquenil	Rheumatoid arthritis, systemic lupus, malaria prevention
hydroxyurea	Hydrea	Cancer, chronic myelocytic leukemia, polycythemia vera, essential thrombocythemia
ibuprofen	Motrin, Advil, Nuprin	Arthritis, pain
imatinib	Gleevec	Chronic myelocytic leukemia
imipramine	Tofranil	Antidepressant
indomethacin	Indocin	Arthritis, pain
infliximab	Remicade	Rheumatoid arthritis, Crohn's disease;
ipratropium	Atrovent	Asthma, COPD, nasal spray for rhinitis
	*	
isocarboxazid	Marplan	Antidepressant
isoniazid (INH)	*	Tuberculosis treatment
labetalol	Normodyne, Trandate,	High blood pressure
lactulose	*	Laxative
lamotrigine	Lamictal	Partial seizures, mood stabilization
leflunomide	Arava	Rheumatoid arthritis
leuprolide	Lupron	Prostate cancer; reduces testosterone to castrate levels
levodopa-carbidopa	Sinemet	Parkinson's disease, periodic limb movement disorder
levothyroxine	Synthroid, Levoxyl, Levothroid	Hypothyroidism
lidocaine	Xylocaine, Lidoderm,	Topical anesthesia, heart rhythm problems, refractory epilepsy
lithium	Eskalith, Lithobid, Lithonate	Bipolar disorder, acute mania
loperamide (OTC)	Imodium	Laxative
loratadine	Claritin	Rhinitis, hives
lorazepam	Ativan	Tranquilizer; insomnia; seizures; alcohol withdrawal; nausea due to chemotherapy
losartan	Cozaar	Hypertension
maprotiline	Ludiomil	Antidepressant
meclizine (OTC)	Antivert, Bonine	Motion sickness, vertigo
meperidine	Demerol	Narcotic pain reliever
metaproterenol	Alupent	Asthma
metformin	Glucophage	Diabetes
methadone	Dolophine	Narcotic pain reliever
methimazole	Tapazole	Hyperthyroidism
methotrexate	Rheumatrex	Rheumatoid arthritis, certain cancers
methylphenidate	Ritalin, Concerta	Attention deficit disorder, narcolepsy
methylprednisolone	Medrol, Solu-Medrol, Depo-Medrol	See prednisone
methyltestosterone	Android	Low testosterone level in males
metoclopramide	Reglan	Nausea or vomiting, GERD, diabetic gastroparesis
metoprolol	Lopressor, Toprol-XL	Hypertension, angina, heart rhythm disturbances, congestive heart failure
metronidazole	Flagyl	Antibiotic; topical treatment for trichomonas vaginitis
midazolam	Versed	Sedative before surgery or for such medical procedures as colonoscopy; may provide palliative sedation for dying patients
midodrine	ProAmatine	Orthostatic hypotension, urinary incontinence

GENERIC NAME	BRAND NAME	USES
minocycline	Minocin	Antibiotic for treatment of acne, gonorrhea, syphilis, and rheumatoid arthritis
mirtazapine	Remeron	Antidepressant
modafinil	Provigil	Narcolepsy; fatigue related to multiple sclerosis
montelukast	Singulair	Asthma, allergic rhinitis
morphine	MS Contin, Roxanol, Avinza	Narcotic pain reliever
mycophenolate	CellCept	To prevent transplant rejection; lupus nephritis
nabumetone	Relafen	Arthritis
N-acetylcysteine	Mucomyst	May protect the kidneys during X-ray or angiogram procedures that require contrast dye
naloxone	Narcan	To treat narcotic overdose
naltrexone	ReVia	Alcohol dependence, opiate addiction
naproxen	Naprosyn, Naprelan, Anaprox, Aleve	Arthritis, pain
nefazodone	Serzone	Antidepressant
nifedipine	Procardia, Adalat	Calcium channel blocker for hypertension, coronary spasm (Prinzmetal's angina); may help prevent altitude sickness
nilutamide	Nilandron	Antiandrogen to treat prostate cancer
nitroglycerin	Nitrostat, NitroQuick	Angina
nortriptyline	Pamelor	Antidepressant
nystatin	Mycostatin, Nilstat	Antifungal
octreotide	Sandostatin	Diarrhea, carcinoid tumors, acromegaly
olanzapine	Zyprexa	Antipsychotic; bipolar disorder
olmesartan	Benicar	High blood pressure
omeprazole	Prilosec	Ulcers, GERD
orlistat	Xenical	Weight loss
oseltamivir	Tamiflu	Influenza prevention and treatment
oxandrolone	Oxandrin	Low testosterone in males; to enhance weight gain in patients with AIDS, cancer, etc.
oxazepam	Serax	Anxiety, alcohol withdrawal
oxybutynin	Ditropan (tablets), Oxytrol (skin patch)	Urge incontinence, overactive bladder
oxcarbazepine	Trileptal	Seizures, tic douloureux, painful peripheral neuropathy
oxymetazoline nasal spray (OTC)	Afrin	Nasal decongestant
pamidronate	Aredia	Elevated blood calcium caused by cancer; Paget's disease; cancer involving the bones
pantoprazole	Protonix	Peptic ulcers, GERD
papaverine	Pavabid	Erectile dysfunction
paroxetine	Paxil	Antidepressant, panic disorder, obsessive-compulsive disorder, social anxiety disorder, posttraumatic stress disorder, diabetic neuropathy
PC Spes	*	Prostate cancer (dietary supplement of extracts from eight Chinese herbs; see also Chapter 11)
pegvisomant	Somavert	Acromegaly
pentoxifylline	Trental	Blockages in the leg arteries
perphenazine	Trilafon	Antipsychotic
phenelzine	Nardil	Antidepressant
phentermine	Fastin	Weight loss
phentolamine	Regitine	Severe hypertension; prior to surgery for pheochromocytoma
phenytoin	Dilantin	To prevent seizures

*Only generic drugs available or not yet named.

GENERIC NAME	BRAND NAME	USES
pioglitazone	Actos	Diabetes
pirbuterol	Maxair	Asthma
pneumococcal vaccine	Pneumovax	Vaccine to help prevent infections by Streptococcus pneumoniae
polyethylene glycol	MiraLax	Laxative
potassium citrate	Urocit-K	To prevent kidney stones
pramipexole	Mirapex	Parkinson's disease
pravastatin	Pravachol	High blood cholesterol
prednisolone	Orapred, Prelone	See prednisone
prednisone	Deltasone, Sterapred	Anti-inflammatory in disorders such as asthma, skin disorders, arthritis
primidone	Mysoline	Seizures, tremor
probenecid	Benemid	Gout
procaine	Novocain	Anesthetic
propantheline	Pro-Banthine	Peptic ulcer, drooling
propoxyphene	Darvon, Darvocet	Pain reliever
propranolol	Inderal	Hypertension, rapid heart rhythms, angina, tremor, migraines
propylthiouracil	*	Hyperthyroidism
protriptyline	Vivactil	Antidepressant; also central sleep apnea and narcolepsy
pseudoephedrine (OTC)	Sudafed	Nasal decongestant
pyridostigmine	Mestinon	Myasthenia gravis
quetiapine	Seroquel	Antipsychotic
quinine	*	Antimalarial, nocturnal leg cramps
raloxifene	Evista	Osteoporosis
rabeprazole	Aciphex	Peptic ulcers, GERD
ramipril	Altace	High blood pressure, congestive heart failure
ranitidine	Zantac	Peptic ulcers, GERD
rimantadine	Flumadine	Influenza prevention and treatment
risedronate	Actonel	Osteoporosis, Paget's disease
risperidone	Risperdal	Antipsychotic, schizophrenia
rivastigmine	Exelon	Alzheimer's disease, vascular dementia
rofecoxib	Vioxx	Arthritis, acute pain, painful menstrual cramping
ropinirole	Requip	Parkinson's disease
rosiglitazone	Avandia	Diabetes
St. John's wort (OTC)	*	Depression
salmeterol	Serevent	Asthma, COPD
salmon calcitonin	Miacalcin (nasal spray)	Osteoporosis, Paget's disease, elevated blood calcium
scopolamine	Transderm Scop (skin patch)	Motion sickness; airway congestion in terminally ill persons
selegiline	Eldepryl	Parkinson's disease
sertraline	Zoloft	Antidepressant, obsessive-compulsive disorder, posttraumatic stress disorder, panic disorder, social anxiety disorder
sibutramine	Meridia	Weight loss
sildenafil	Viagra	Male erectile dysfunction
simvastatin	Zocor	High blood pressure
sodium bicarbonate tablets	Neut	Neutralizes excess acid in the blood in kidney failure
sodium citrate solution	Bicitra	Neutralizes excess acid in the blood in kidney failure
sotalol	Betapace	Heart rhythm disturbances
spironolactone	Aldactone	A diuretic (water pill) for hypertension, congestive heart failure, liver disease, hyperaldosteronism
sulfasalazine	Azulfidine	Ulcerative colitis, Crohn's disease, rheumatoid arthritis

GENERIC NAME	BRAND NAME	USES
sulindac	Clinoril	Arthritis; to prevent or reduce recurrence of colon polyps in familial adenomatous polyposis
tacrine	Cognex	Alzheimer's disease, vascular dementia (rarely used now due to side effects and need for careful monitoring of liver function)
tadalafil	Cialis	Male erectile dysfunction
tamoxifen	Nolvadex	Breast cancer
tamsulosin	Flomax	To relieve obstructive symptoms of benign prostatic hypertrophy
telmisartan	Micardis	High blood pressure
temazepam	Restoril	Insomnia
terazosin	Hytrin	Antihypertensive; also relieves obstructive symptoms due to benign prostatic hypertrophy
terbutaline	Brethine, Brethaire, Bricanyl	Asthma
teriparatide	Forteo	Osteoporosis
testosterone	Depo-Testosterone (injectable); Androderm, AndroGel, Testoderm, Testim (topical); Striant (tablet applied to gums)	Low testosterone in males
thioridazine	Mellaril	Antipsychotic, refractory schizophrenia
thiothixene	Navane	Antipsychotic
tolmetin	Tolectin	Arthritis, pain
tolterodine	Detrol	Urge incontinence, overactive bladder
topiramate	Topamax	Seizure disorders, tremor, mood stabilization
tramadol	Ultram, Ultracet	Pain
tranylcypromine	Parnate	Antidepressant
trastuzumab	Herceptin	Breast cancer
trazodone	Desyrel	Antidepressant (may be helpful for sleep problems associated with depressed mood)
triamcinolone	Azmacort, Aristocort, Kenalog, Nasacort	asthma; injectable form for arthritis; nasal spray for rhinitis; topical form for skin rashes
triazolam	Halcion	Insomnia
trihexyphenidyl	Artane	Parkinson's disease
trimethoprim-sulfamethoxazole	Bactrim, Septra	Antibiotic
valacyclovir	Valtrex	Shingles, cold sores, genital herpes
valdecoxib	Bextra	Arthritis, pain
valproic acid	Depakene, Depakote	Seizure disorders, mania, migraine prophylaxis
vardenafil	Levitra	Male erectile dysfunction
venlafaxine	Effexor	Antidepressant
verapamil	Calan, Verelan	High blood pressure, angina, heart rhythm disturbance
vincristine	Oncovin	Cancer treatment
warfarin	Coumadin	Anticoagulant
yohimbine (OTC)	Yocon, Yohimex	Aphrodisiac (has multiple potential adverse drug interactions with prescription medications)
zaleplon	Sonata	Insomnia
zanamivir	Relenza (inhaled)	Influenza
ziprasidone	Geodon	Antipsychotic, schizophrenia, acute agitation.
zolpidem	Ambien	Insomnia

*Only generic drugs available or not yet named.

MEDICAL GLOSSARY

A

ABG See arterial blood gas.

ABI See ankle/brachial index.

ACE inhibitors See angiotensin-converting enzyme inhibitors.

acetylcholine Chemical material released from nerve cells that allows them to stimulate each other, as well as the muscles and certain organs.

acetylcholine receptor antibody Antibody responsible for myasthenia gravis. This antibody can be measured with a blood test.

Achilles tendon Large tendon that originates in the calf muscle and inserts on the heel bone.

acquired immune deficiency syndrome (AIDS) A clinical syndrome caused by the human immunodeficiency virus (HIV), characterized by a disturbance of the body's immune system.

acromegaly A condition in which the individual produces too much growth hormone from the pituitary gland.

ACTH See adrenocorticotropic hormone.

action tremor A tremor that occurs at the end of a muscle movement.

acupuncture The insertion of very skinny steel needles into specific points in order to treat various health conditions, most commonly pain.

acute adrenal insufficiency A serious medical condition associated with extreme fatigue, weakness, low blood pressure and dizziness, loss of appetite, nausea and vomiting, abdominal pains, and joint pains—due to insufficient production of cortisol by the adrenal glands. The adrenal glands can be damaged due to shock, cancer, or infection. If a patient has been on steroids for a long time, sudden withdrawal can produce acute adrenal insufficiency. Acute adrenal insufficiency is considered a medical emergency.

acute coronary syndrome (ACS) Another name for unstable angina, in which discomfort due to heart disease occurs at rest or with increasing frequency or severity.

acute kidney failure Sudden and often unpredictable loss of kidney function.

acute nonlymphocytic leukemia Malignant conditions of the bone marrow caused by abnormal production of immature white blood cells called myeloblasts.

acute urinary retention Complete inability to urinate, requiring immediate medical attention.

Addison's disease A disease of the adrenal glands that leads to deficient production of cortisol, the body's stress hormone, and/or aldosterone.

adenocarcinoma A type of cancer in which glandular cells (cells that produce secretions or hormones) predominate.

adenoids Part of the lymph system associated with the tonsils.

adenomyosis A condition in which the lining of the uterus grows into the wall of the uterus.

ADH See antidiuretic hormone.

adjuvant therapy Treatment to reduce the risk of recurrence of cancer.

adrenal crisis A sudden, overwhelming, and life-threatening episode of adrenal insufficiency, in which the body's production of cortisol, the body's stress hormone, is deficient. May be precipitated by severe infection, emergency surgery, and trauma.

adrenergic stimulants Drugs that are often used to treat congestion due to colds.

adrenocorticotropic hormone (ACTH) The pituitary hormone that stimulates the adrenal glands to produce cortisol, the body's stress hormone.

adult-onset diabetes mellitus A disease that has its onset in adults and is associated with high blood sugar. Also called type 2 diabetes mellitus.

agnosia Difficulty with visual and spatial skills so that it may be difficult to recognize objects.

agoraphobia Fear of going out, often in response to panic attacks. May also be due to fear of crime or falls.

AIDS See acquired immune deficiency syndrome.

air quality index (AQI) A guide that indicates air pollution levels.

alcoholic dementia Cognitive decline caused by chronic alcohol abuse.

aldosterone A hormone made in the adrenal gland that plays an important role in salt and water metabolism.

allergic rhinitis Inflammation of the nasal passages due to allergies.

allograft Tissue that is transplanted from one person to another.

alpha antagonists 1. Drugs used to treat high blood pressure. 2. Drugs used to treat decreased urinary flow rates in men with prostatic enlargement.

alpha1-antitrypsin deficiency A genetic disorder that may lead to early emphysema and liver failure.

alpha1-blockers Drugs that block the alpha1-adrenergic receptors in the prostate resulting in decreased smooth muscle tension and relief of obstruction to urine flow. Examples include terazosin (Hytrin), doxazosin (Cardura), tamsulosin (Flomax), and alfuzosin (Uroxatral).

alpha-reductase inhibitors A class of drugs used to treat benign prostatic hyperplasia. They inhibit the enzyme alpha-reductase and prevent the conversion of testosterone to its active ingredient, dihydrotestosterone, the major male sex hormone. This results in a decrease in prostate size. Examples include finasteride (Proscar) and dutasteride (Avodart).

alveolar bone The bone surrounding erupted teeth.

alveoli Air sacs in the lungs.

Alzheimer's disease A disease characterized by progressive degeneration of brain cells leading to memory loss, confusion, and disorientation.

amalgam The most common kind of filling, made of an alloy of silver, copper, and mercury.

amaurosis Visual loss or blindness.

aminoglycosides Potent antibiotics, which can sometimes have adverse effects on the kidneys.

amnesia Loss of memory for events that happened in the more remote past, as opposed to loss of short-term memory.

amputee A person who has lost a limb, either an arm or leg or both.

amyloid A protein material that can accumulate in certain tissues leading to disease.

amyloidosis A disorder in which an abnormal protein is deposited in various organs and tissues of the body.

ANA See antinuclear antibody.

androgen A male sex hormone, such as testosterone, found in higher levels in males than in females.

andropause The male counterpart to menopause. Deficient production of testosterone leads to a constellation of symptoms including decreased energy, diminished libido, erectile dysfunction, muscle weakness, and depression.

Anemia The deficiency of an adequate amount of oxygen-carrying hemoglobin in the bloodstream to allow normal functioning of the body's organs

anergy The absence of a response to skin testing due to problems with the immune system.

anesthesiologist A physician who specializes in the administration of anesthetic agents.

aneurysm A weakening in the wall of a blood vessel causing a balloonlike dilatation of the arterial wall.

angina Pain, pressure, or squeezing in the chest due to coronary artery disease. Also called angina pectoris.

angiogram See arteriogram.

angioplasty Procedure by which a blocked artery is opened with a balloon catheter.

angiostatin A protein that is being studied for its potential to deny cancers their source of nutrition with the hope of arresting the disease.

angiotensin-converting enzyme (ACE) inhibitors Medications that can be used to control blood pressure. They have shown benefits in many other situations, especially in diabetics.

angiotensin receptor blockers (ARBs) Medications used to control high blood pressure, but may be used in other situations, such as diabetic kidney disease. They are often used as substitutes for ACE inhibitors if the latter cause coughing or other undesirable side effects.

angle closure glaucoma The sudden rise in eye pressure that causes redness, eye pain, and blurred vision. It is a medical emergency due to blockage of the normal drainage system by the iris.

angular cheilitis "Cracking" at the corners of the mouth, with reddening and oozing. Usually caused by candidiasis and often associated with the use of dentures that have outlived their usefulness. Less commonly, it is caused by nutritional deficiencies of B vitamins or iron.

ankle/brachial index (ABI) A test to screen for arterial disease.

anosmia Loss of smell.

antiandrogens Substances that bind to the androgen receptor and prevent testosterone from acting on the prostate cell.

antiangiogenesis Treatment aimed at reducing the blood flow to tumors in the hope of arresting cancer growth.

antidiuretic hormone (ADH) Produced by the posterior part of the pituitary gland and helps regulate water balance. Also called vasopressin.

antinuclear antibody (ANA) An antibody detected in the blood that may indicate disorders of the immune system, such as systemic lupus erythematosus. However, results need to be interpreted with caution, as the ANA can be positive in healthy older persons and in individuals on certain drugs.

antioxidant An agent that inhibits oxidation and therefore the deterioration of some tissues or materials.

antiphospholipid antibody syndrome A disorder that can lead to blood clotting problems and strokes. This syndrome can be associated with systemic lupus erythematosus. However, antiphospholipid antibodies can be found in otherwise healthy people and can be detected with a blood test. Strokes and blood clots associated with this condition require long-term use of anticoagulants (blood thinners).

antipsychotics Drugs that are used to treat schizophrenia and some problem behaviors in dementia patients. Also called neuroleptics.

antithrombin III One of the body's natural "blood thinners," which prevent clots. Deficiencies can lead to blood clots in the legs and pulmonary embolism.

anxiety Unpleasant, vague feeling which signals an impending danger. An anxiety disorder is characterized by excessive worry that is out of proportion to an event and interferes with daily activities.

aorta The large blood vessel that carries blood from the heart to the rest of the body.

aortic regurgitation (AR) Backflow of blood through the aortic valve, the valve through which blood leaves the heart to enter the circulation.

aortic stenosis Narrowing of the heart's aortic valve. Can lead to angina, shortness of breath, and fainting. Severe cases require heart surgery.

apathy Not caring; unemotional.

aphasia A problem with either understanding words or expressing oneself that is usually caused by a stroke.

aphthous stomatitis A small, circular, isolated white sore that can form on almost any part of the mouth. Also called canker sores.

aplastic anemia A potentially fatal condition in which the bone marrow fails to make cells properly.

apomorphine A derivative of morphine that has been used to treat male sexual dysfunction; has also been used for upset stomach, insomnia, and as an expectorant.

apraxia Disorder of voluntary movement.

AQI See air quality index.

aqueous humor The fluid (not tears) that circulates around the front chamber of the eye. If drainage is impaired, glaucoma results.

ARBs See angiotensin receptor blockers.

arcus senilis A white band around the periphery of the iris that can occur normally with aging but in younger individuals may signify a problem with cholesterol or triglycerides.

areola The area in the center of the breast on which the nipple sits.

arterial blood gas (ABG) A measurement of the oxygen and carbon dioxide content of the blood that is taken from a sample of blood drawn from an artery, usually near the wrist.

arteriogram A test in which dye is injected into the body and X-rays are taken to visualize the blood vessels. Also called an angiogram.

arteriovenous malformations (AVMs) Small collections of abnormal blood vessels that can be found almost anywhere in the body. They are commonly found in the intestines of the elderly, which may bleed and cause anemia that can occasionally be severe.

arthrocentesis Aspiration of a joint with a needle and syringe to obtain fluid for examination.

arthrodesis The surgical fusion of a joint.

arthroplasty The surgical creation of an artificial joint.

arthroscope An instrument through which a doctor can visualize the inside of a joint to diagnose and surgically treat joint problems.

arthrotomy Surgically cutting into a joint.

ascites Swelling of the abdomen with fluid. Cirrhosis, congestive heart failure, and cancers within the abdomen can cause it.

aseptic meningitis Inflammation of the lining of the brain unrelated to bacterial infection. Most cases are caused by viruses.

aspiration pneumonia Pneumonia caused by oral and stomach contents going into the lungs.

asthma A condition characterized by spasm and inflammation of the breathing passages.

asymptomatic Not associated with symptoms.

atherosclerosis Process leading to "hardening of the arteries."

athlete's foot Fungal infection (tinea pedis) that causes redness and cracking of the skin of the feet and between the toes.

atria The upper chambers of the heart.

atrial fibrillation A heart rhythm disturbance in which the atria do not contract properly, usually causing a rapid and irregular heart beat.

atrioventricular (AV) node An electrical "relay station" situated between the atria and the ventricles.

atrophy Thinning or wasting of the body's tissues.

audiologist A person (not a physician) who specializes in the evaluation of hearing disorders; may also fit you for an appropriate hearing aid.

audiometry A test of hearing thresholds, ability to understand the spoken word, and the mobility of the eardrum.

auditory nerve Hearing or acoustic nerve.

AUR See acute urinary retention.

autoantibodies Antibodies that develop against a person's own tissue due to disorders of the immune system.

autoimmune disease Disorders caused by abnormalities in the body's defense system.

autologous graft Any tissue (e.g., bone, blood, tendon, or skin) removed and used elsewhere in the same patient.

autonomic nervous system The part of the nervous system that regulates body functions without your conscious effort.

AV node See atrioventricular node.

AVMs See arteriovenous malformations.

axillary dissection Removal of the lymph nodes under the arm as part of the evaluation of breast cancer. Treatment protocols depend on whether these nodes are involved with cancer.

axonal neuropathy A disorder of the peripheral nerves due to damage to the core of the nerve.

B

bacteremia Bacterial infection in the bloodstream.

balloon angioplasty A technique in which a catheter with a small balloon is inflated to open a blocked artery.

barium swallow X-ray An X-ray examination in which the patient is instructed to swallow a liquid mixture containing barium, and X-ray images are taken of the esophagus and stomach as the barium mixture passes from the mouth to the stomach.

barotitis The condition that causes the discomfort in your ears with a sudden change in altitude.

Barrett's epithelium An abnormal lining to the esophagus related to chronic acid reflux from the stomach into the esophagus. The normal lining of the esophagus is replaced with a lining more typical of that found in the intestine. It is associated with a higher risk of esophageal cancer.

basal cell carcinoma A type of skin cancer.

basal ganglia The area of the brain where dopamine deficiency results in Parkinson's disease.

benign prostatic hyperplasia (BPH) Noncancerous enlargement of the prostate gland due to an increase in the number of prostate cells.

benzodiazepines A class of sedative agents including diazepam (Valium), lorazepam (Ativan), and alprazolam (Xanax). They may be associated with physical and/or psychological dependency with prolonged use.

beta-blockers Drugs used for high blood pressure and heart disease, as well as many other uses.

bicarbonate tablets Pills used to counter acid retention when the kidneys do not function properly.

biceps The large muscles of the upper arms that allow you to bend the elbow.

bilevel positive airway pressure (BiPAP) A technique that delivers positive pressure to the airways. May be useful in certain lung disorders and in some individuals with obstructive sleep apnea.

biofeedback A technique that utilizes muscle monitoring to give a person information about the state of tension or relaxation of the muscles. It may be used to treat stress, migraine headaches, tinnitus, urinary incontinence, and other conditions.

biologics A group of medicines that influence the body's normal biological processes.

biopsy The surgical removal of all or a part of some tissue to permit examination and diagnosis with the use of a microscope.

bipolar disorder A mental illness characterized by fluctuating mood swings. Mood may alternate between depression and excessive excitability. Also called manic-depression.

bisphosphonates A class of drugs that are potent inhibitors of bone resorption and therefore serve an important role in the treatment of osteoporosis. Examples include alendronate (Fosamax) and risedronate (Actonel).

bite registration A record of how the upper and lower jaw relate to each other, obtained by biting into a softened material. After the materials sets, the registration is used to position upper and lower casts in a manner that mimics the situation in the patient.

blepharitis Inflammation of the margins of the eyelids.

blepharoplasty Removal of excess skin, soft tissue, and fat from either the upper or lower eyelid.

BMI See body mass index.

BNP See brain natriuretic peptide.

body mass index (BMI) The most common method used by health professionals and researchers to determine whether an individual is normal, overweight, or underweight.

The calculation is done by dividing weight in kilograms by height in meters squared.

bone densitometry A test that evaluates the density of bone. Helpful in establishing a diagnosis of osteoporosis.

bone marrow The soft inner part of bone where blood cells are made.

bone remodeling unit The area in bone where osteoclasts (bone-resorbing cells) create a cavity and then new bone is laid down by osteoblasts (bone-forming cells).

bone scan A test in which a radioactive isotope is injected into the body and is picked up where bone is being repaired. May help identify fractures, bone tumors, or infections.

Borg scale A means of guiding you on the extent of exercise. Rather than using heart rate or other measures to determine your activity level, you adjust your activities based on how hard you think you are working.

Botox Purified botulinum toxin. Injectable medication used to temporarily block muscular activity. Used to diminish wrinkles around the forehead and eyes. Also used to treat muscle spasticity after a stroke and for migraines. Duration of action is approximately four months.

BPH See benign prostatic hyperplasia.

brachytherapy Delivery of radiation to a short distance, such as prostate seed implants.

bradycardia Slow heart rate.

bradykinesia Slowness of movement.

brain natriuretic peptide (BNP) A blood marker that is elevated in congestive heart failure.

bronchial tubes Breathing passages from the trachea to the lungs.

bronchioles Small breathing passages that lead to the air sacs in the lungs.

bronchitis Infection or inflammation of the breathing passages.

bronchodilators Medications used to open the breathing passages in patients with asthma and COPD.

bruit A noise heard with a stethoscope over an artery due to harsh blood flow caused by a partial blockage.

bundle branch block A delay or blockage of the electrical impulses in the bundle of His.

bundle of His The fibers that carry electrical impulses to the heart's ventricular muscle to stimulate it to contract.

bunion A bony enlargement over the joint at the base of the big toe.

bunionectomy The surgical removal of a bony joint enlargement at the base of the big toe.

bunionette A bony enlargement over the joint at the base of the small toe.

bursitis A painful condition associated with inflammation of a bursa.

bypass A surgical technique in which a piece of vein or an artificial graft is used to carry blood around a blocked artery.

C

CABG See coronary artery bypass graft.

cadaver A corpse; dead body.

calcitriol The active form of vitamin D that is synthesized by the kidneys.

calcium channel blockers Drugs used to treat high blood pressure. They are also used to treat angina, migraine headaches, esophageal spasm, and other conditions.

candidiasis Infection with a fungus called Candida (usually Candida albicans).

cannula A hollow tube that can be inserted into a body cavity. A metal cannula with side holes is used in liposuction to suction fat. A nasal cannula is a flexible plastic tube that delivers oxygen into the nasal passages.

capillaries The very smallest of blood vessels.

carcinogen A substance that causes cancer.

carcinoma insitu Cancer that is well localized and usually readily treated by removal.

cardiac Relating to the heart.

cardiac catheterization A procedure in which a small flexible catheter is inserted through a groin artery and advanced to the coronary circulation where a dye is inserted to visualize the coronary arteries. This term is often used synonymously with coronary angiography.

cardiogenic shock Severe low blood pressure and unstable vital signs due to a heart attack. Without urgent treatment, death results.

cardiomyopathy A disease of the heart muscle. The heart muscle may be weak causing the heart to dilate, or the muscle may be thick impeding the normal function of the heart.

cardioprotective Protects the heart.

caries The result of organic acid dissolving a hole into enamel, cementum, or dentin, and the hole subsequently being occupied and enlarged by oral bacteria. Also called dental decay.

carotid endarterectomy Surgical removal of plaque from the carotid artery.

carotid sinus syndrome Fainting due to a drop in blood pressure and/or heart rate when pressure is applied to the neck arteries, such as by tight collars or ties.

carpal tunnel syndrome A condition characterized by numbness in the thumb and the index, middle, and half of the ring finger due to compression of the main nerve (median nerve) to the hand at the wrist. As the condition progresses, handgrip may be weakened.

castration Elimination of testosterone from the body.

cataplexy Transient loss of muscle tone.

cataract A density that clouds the lens and can eventually impair vision.

catheter A plastic or rubber tube that allows fluid to pass into or from a body cavity (such as the bladder) or blood vessel.

catheterization A procedure in which a tube is inserted into a blood vessel or organ to introduce a dye or fluid or to drain the organ. Bladder catheterization is the removal of fluid from the bladder with a flexible rubber tube. See also cardiac catheterization.

cavernosa Spongy areas of the penis (males) or clitoris (females) that fill with blood when sexually stimulated.

CBC See complete blood count.

cementum The thin layer of mineralized material covering the dentin of the root of the tooth.

central sleep apnea A sleep disorder associated with disordered breathing due to disorders of the central nervous system, heart, or kidneys.

cerebellum The area at the base of the brain that plays a major role in motor control.

cerebral hemorrhage Bleeding into the brain.

cerebral infarction Death of brain cells in the brain, usually due to blockage of a brain blood vessel.

cerebrovascular accident (CVA) A stroke.

cerumen Earwax.

cervicitis Inflammation or infection of the cervix.

cervix The neck of the womb (uterus). The cervix is the part of the uterus that protrudes into the vagina, and the opening in the cervix leads to the inside of the womb.

Charcot's joint A joint that becomes damaged and deformed due to multiple small fractures that occur due to nerve injury and impaired sensation in the affected joint.

charlatan A quack; someone who claims that he or she can cure or treat diseases with worthless remedies.

chelation A technique promoted to remove plaque from the arteries but has been proved worthless. However, chelation is useful in conditions associated with an excess of iron or copper in the body.

chemotherapy Drugs used to treat cancer.

cherry angioma Cherry-red spot on the skin, considered normal with aging.

CHF See congestive heart failure.

chiropractic A health discipline that focuses on misalignments in the spine as a cause of various medical conditions.

chiropractor A person who specializes in chiropractic. The professional degree is a doctor of chiropractic (DC).

Chlamydia An organism that causes many different types of infection, including sexually transmitted disease.

cholesteatoma Cystlike growth of skin cells in the middle ear.

cholinesterase inhibitors Medications that interfere with the breakdown of acetylcholine, in the hope that nerve function, memory, etc., will be improved. Examples include donepezil (Aricept), rivastigmine (Exelon), and galantamine (Reminyl).

chondrocalcinosis Calcification of joint cartilage due to deposition of calcium pyrophosphate. In many cases, this condition is asymptomatic and is discovered on an X-ray. However, joint swelling and pain, called pseudogout, may develop in other cases.

chronic lymphocytic leukemia (CLL) A malignant condition of the bone marrow characterized by overproduction of a white blood cell called a lymphocyte.

chronic myelogenous leukemia (CML) A malignant condition of the bone marrow characterized by abnormal production of a precursor to the white blood cell called a myeloblast.

chronic obstructive pulmonary disease (COPD) A group of disorders associated with narrowing of the breathing passages leading to obstruction of air flow. Includes asthma, emphysema, and chronic bronchitis.

chronic venous insufficiency Permanent damage to the valves in the veins, causing slow movement of the blood in the veins, swelling of the legs, and often discoloration of the skin of the legs.

cilia Hairlike projections of a cell.

cirrhosis of the liver A condition characterized by progressive damage to the liver, ultimately leading to liver failure.

claudication A heaviness, cramping, or pain that occurs in the buttocks or legs while walking and caused by blockages in the leg arteries.

claustrophobic Fear of confined places.

clinical depression A common illness associated with depressed mood, tiredness, lack of interest in activities, diminished libido, appetite changes, concentration difficulties, and, in severe cases, suicidal thoughts.

clitoral Referring to the female's clitoris.

clitoris In females, an appendage in the upper folds of the labia minor analogous to the penis in the male. It is part of the organ complex which contains erectile tissue that becomes engorged with blood during sexual arousal.

CLL See chronic lymphocytic leukemia.

CML See chronic myelogenous leukemia.

cochlea Snail-shaped organ of hearing in the middle ear.

cochlear implant A device surgically implanted in the ear to help those with profound hearing loss.

cochleitis Inflammation of the cochlea.

cognitive function Ability to think and reason.

coitus Sexual intercourse.

collagen 1. The basic structural support of the body's connective tissues. 2. Processed bovine (cow) protein packaged to be injected through a small needle for the purpose of diminishing skin wrinkles.

Colles' fracture A break in the forearm bone (radius) that results in an s-shaped deformity at the wrist.

colostomy Opening of the colon to the abdominal wall. A special bag is used to collect stool.

common bile duct The main duct that forms after the duct from the gallbladder (cystic duct) and duct from the liver (hepatic duct) join together. Carries bile from the liver and gallbladder to the small intestine.

complete blood count (CBC) A blood test to determine the level of red blood cells, white blood cells, and platelets. The CBC helps in the diagnosis of numerous conditions, including anemia, leukemia, and bleeding disorders.

computed tomography (CT) scan A special X-ray procedure that allows the physician interpreting the study to view images of serial sections from the area being examined.

conductive hearing loss Hearing loss due to blockage of sound transmission in the ear canals.

condyle The rounded knob at the end of a bone.

condyloma acuminata Venereal warts; sexually transmitted warty growths that develop on the external genitalia.

congestive heart failure (CHF) A syndrome in which the heart can no longer keep up with the body's demands.

Symptoms often include shortness of breath, tiredness, and leg swelling.

contact dermatitis Allergic reaction to something that contacts the skin and produces an itchy rash.

continuous ambulatory peritoneal dialysis (CAPD) Exchange of fluid from the abdomen 4 times a day in persons with advanced kidney failure.

continuous cycling peritoneal dialysis (CCPD) In persons with advanced kidney failure, a machine exchanges fluid from the abdomen intermittently at night while sleeping.

continuous positive airway pressure (CPAP) A technique to prevent the airway from closing during sleep in those with obstructive sleep apnea.

contraception Prevention of pregnancy.

contraceptive An agent that prevents pregnancy.

contracture Short, tight muscle that results from lack of use and resulting in loss of flexibility. A contracture of muscles around a joint will limit motion of that joint.

COPD See chronic obstructive pulmonary disease.

corn Excessive skin tissue that forms over a toe in response to repetitive pressure over a bony prominence.

cornea Crystal-clear dome in front of the iris.

coronary artery bypass graft (CABG) Involves taking small pieces of leg veins to bypass blocked coronary arteries. An artery inside the chest (internal mammary) is used to bypass blockages in the left anterior descending coronary artery.

coronary artery disease Blockages in the coronary arteries due to atherosclerotic plaque.

coronary catheterization A dye study to evaluate the arteries around the heart. Also called cardiac catheterization or coronary angiography.

corticosteroids Anti-inflammatory substances produced in the body or synthesized to make drugs; its abbreviation is steroids. The body's natural steroids function as "stress hormones" to help fight infection and inflammation. Steroid medications are used in a wide variety of medical conditions.

cortisol A steroid hormone produced by the adrenal glands that functions as the body's main "stress hormone."

cortisone Hormone closely related to cortisol.

costochondritis Inflammation of the cartilages that join the ribs with the breastbone. The symptoms can occasionally mimic those of a heart attack or pulmonary embolism.

COX-2 inhibitors See cyclooxygenase-2 inhibitors.

CPAP See continuous positive airway pressure.

C-reactive protein A blood test that suggests inflammation or infection when elevated. Many disorders can cause elevated C-reactive protein levels.

creatinine A blood test that reflects the kidney's function. It is often elevated as the kidneys fail.

Crohn's disease An inflammatory condition of the gastrointestinal tract that can be associated with ulcers of the intestine, strictures, and abnormal communications between different segments of the intestine or between the intestine and other organs including the skin.

crown A dental restoration that covers the outside of a tooth rather than being surrounded by tooth structure, like a filling. Also called a cap.

cryotherapy 1. Cold therapy, such as an ice pack. 2. Freezing of tissue in order to destroy it. Cryotherapy is used in dermatology to destroy precancers caused by sun damage and in urology to destroy prostate cancer cells.

cryptogenic peripheral neuropathy A disorder of the peripheral nerves for which no explanation can be found.

CT angiogram A test in which a dye is injected and a CT scan of the blood vessels is obtained. It is very helpful in the diagnosis of pulmonary embolism.

CT scan See computed tomography scan.

Cushing's disease A condition produced by overproduction of ACTH by the pituitary gland and resulting in an overproduction of cortisol by the adrenal glands.

Cushing's syndrome A syndrome caused by excessive production of cortisol by the adrenal glands. It may be produced by Cushing's disease or by enlargement or tumors of the adrenal gland, as well as by the use of steroids to treat inflammatory conditions. It is associated with weight gain, a "moon face," a "buffalo hump" on the back, purple stretch marks of the abdomen, and often elevated blood pressure and diabetes.

CVA See cerebrovascular accident.

cyclooxygenase-2 (COX-2) inhibitors A newer class of arthritis drugs in the NSAID class that were designed to cause less adverse effects, such as ulcers.

cystic duct The small tubelike structure that carries bile from the gallbladder to the common bile duct.

cystometrogram (CMG) A study of bladder pressure, flow, and volume with bladder filling and voiding.

D

D&C See dilatation and curettage.

D-dimer A blood test that can help determine if blood clots are present.

debridement Removal of dead or infected tissue.

decibel (dB) A measurement of sound levels.

decubitus ulcer A break in the skin, usually over a bony prominence, due to prolonged pressure that interferes with the blood supply to the skin. Also called a bedsore or pressure ulcer.

deep brain stimulation A treatment for movement disorders in which electric impulses are sent via small wires to areas deep within the brain.

deep vein thrombosis A clot in the veins inside the legs. Also called thrombophlebitis or phlebitis.

dehydroepiandrosterone (DHEA) A hormone made mainly by the adrenal glands but also by the testes. DHEA has been marketed as a supplement and touted to reverse or slow aging, although scientific proof is lacking. Its usage may be associated with serious side effects, including hair loss or growth, high blood pressure, acne, and liver dysfunction.

delirium A sudden state of confusion.

deltoid Large, outermost muscle of the shoulder.

delusions Believing things that are not true.

dementia General mental deterioration, characterized by disorientation and impairment of memory, judgment, and intellect.

dementia with Lewy bodies A form of cognitive dysfunction characterized by features of Parkinson's disease and by visual hallucinations.

demyelinating neuropathy A disorder of the peripheral nerves due to damage to the lining or sheath around the nerve fibers.

dentin The dominant mineralized material in the tooth, lying beneath enamel and cementum.

dentinal tubules Thousands of microscopic channels filled with parts of cells, traversing the dentin from the pulp chamber outward.

denture Any replacement tooth or teeth. Most commonly refers to a removable acrylic appliance that replaces all the upper teeth or all the lower teeth.

denture adhesive A soluble, usually synthetic material, sold without a prescription in a paste (cream) or powder form, to help removable dentures adhere to the gums.

denture reline A procedure in which the internal surfaces of removable dentures that no longer fit acceptably are modified to better conform to the patient's mouth.

deoxyribonucleic acid (DNA) Basic genetic material of the cells.

dermatomyositis A condition in which polymyositis is associated with skin rashes.

dermis The deeper layer of skin which contains the hair follicles, sweat glands, superficial blood vessels, nerve endings, and the pores.

detrusor muscle Smooth muscles of the urinary bladder that pump urine out through the urethra.

DHEA See dehydroepiandrosterone.

DHT See dihydrotestosterone.

diabetes mellitus See adult-onset diabetes mellitus and insulin-dependent diabetes mellitus.

diabetic ketoacidosis A potential life-threatening complication of insulin-dependent diabetes mellitus in which deficiency of insulin leads to loss of the body water and electrolytes, resulting in accumulation of acids that can produce a host of serious derangements of the body's metabolism.

diabetic retinopathy Damage to the blood vessels in diabetics that leads to problems in the retina.

dialysis A process to remove waste products, as well as extra salt and water, from the body.

diaphragm Large muscle separating the chest from the abdominal cavity; the principal muscle of respiration.

diastole Interval while the heart relaxes.

DIC See disseminated intravascular coagulation.

differential diagnosis A number of possible diagnoses considered after a doctor obtains a medical history and performs a physical examination; the doctor then narrows down the possibilities based on further tests.

diffusion capacity A test of the movement of gasses within the lungs.

digit A finger or toe.

digital rectal examination (DRE) An examination in which a physician inserts a lubricated gloved finger into the patient's rectum to assess prostate size, consistency, and sphincter tone. Also used to check for rectal cancer.

dihydrotestosterone (DHT) Active metabolite of testosterone. Testosterone is not active in prostate cells but needs to be converted to DHT, its active metabolite.

dilatation and curettage (D&C) Dilating the opening of the cervix and then scraping the lining of the uterus to look for cancer cells.

diphtheria-tetanus booster An immunization that can prevent serious illness due to diphtheria and tetanus. Recommended that adults receive the booster every 10 years.

disease-modifying antirheumatic drugs (DMARDs) Drugs that interfere with the immune response and are very helpful in the treatment of rheumatoid arthritis.

disseminated intravascular coagulation (DIC) A potentially life-threatening condition in which another serious problem, such as a bloodstream infection or cancer, causes diffuse clotting of blood within the small blood vessels. Interestingly, this process uses up clotting factors, and serious bleeding can result. Treatment involves an attempt to correct the underlying problem, but temporary use of fresh frozen plasma and platelet transfusions may be required.

diuretics Medicines that remove water from the body. Often called water pills.

diverticular disease Symptoms related to small pockets (actually small hernias of the intestinal lining through the wall of the bowel) in the colon called diverticula. Diverticula may become inflamed (diverticulitis), or sometimes massive bleeding can occur.

DMARDs See disease-modifying antirheumatic drugs.

dopamine One of the brain chemicals that help nerve cells communicate with each other. Dopamine deficiency is responsible for Parkinson's disease.

doppler An instrument that generates sounds over an artery. Sounds are diminished or absent if blockages are severe.

double amputee A person who has had both legs removed.

DRE See digital rectal examination.

drug-induced lupus A clinical syndrome that looks identical to systemic lupus erythematosus but is caused by a drug. Generally, the symptoms are reversible on discontinuance of the drug.

duplex scan An instrument that generates pictures of arteries and veins, as well as their blood flow.

dysarthria Inability to pronounce words properly. There are many causes of dysarthria in the elderly, including stroke and other neurological diseases.

dysphagia Difficulty with swallowing. May be associated with coughing or choking while swallowing food or a sensation that food is sticking in the throat or esophagus.

dysplasia Cells that are not normal but have not yet become cancerous.

dystonic tremor A head tremor with pulling to one side. Also called torticollis or wry neck.

E

early detection The discovery of a disease at an early stage before it has grown large or spread to other sites. For example, mammography can help detect breast cancer early, and the PSA blood test can help find prostate cancer early.

ECG See electrocardiogram.

echocardiography Ultrasound examination of the heart.

ECT See electroconvulsive therapy.

ectopic pregnancy The egg implants in the fallopian tube, rather than the uterus. Also called tubal pregnancy.

ectropion Turning out of the eyelid.

ED See erectile dysfunction.

effusion A buildup of fluid. A joint effusion causes swelling of a joint. A pleural effusion is a buildup of fluid under the lung.

ejaculate 1. To release semen during orgasm. 2. Semen.

electrical stimulation A physical therapy modality in which a low-voltage electric current is passed through a muscle to make it contract. It is often used to prevent muscle wasting after a stroke until nerve control is restored or improved.

electrocardiogram (ECG) A tracing of the heart's electrical activity. Also called an EKG.

electrocautery Process by which an instrument applies electricity through a metal probe to stop bleeding from blood vessels or to destroy skin lesions such as warts.

electroconvulsive therapy (ECT) A form of psychiatric treatment in which a seizure is induced after a patient has been medicated. Its usual purpose is to treat severe depression.

electromyogram (EMG) A test in which small needle electrodes are placed in muscles to evaluate their activity.

embolectomy Surgical removal of a clot that has traveled from somewhere else.

embolism A clot that travels from one site to another.

embryo The first stage of development of an organism. In humans, the embryonic period is from the moment of conception until the end of the eighth week of gestation.

EMG See electromyogram.

emphysema Lung disease in which air sacs are destroyed.

enamel Hard, crystalline, translucent outer covering of the part of the tooth that can be seen in the mouth.

encephalopathy A condition characterized by confusion, disorientation, and, occasionally, seizures and coma. It may have many causes and requires a careful history, physical examination, and usually special testing.

endarterectomy Surgical removal of plaque within an artery.

endocrine Refers to the hormone system.

endocrinologist A physician who specializes in the diagnosis and treatment of disorders of the body's hormone system.

endometrial biopsy Surgical sampling of the lining of the uterus to look for cancer.

endometrial carcinoma Cancer of the lining of the uterus.

endometrial hyperplasia A condition in which the lining of the uterus builds up. It may be a premalignant condition leading to uterine cancer.

endometriosis A condition in which cells normally found in the uterus implant on structures outside the uterus, such as the ovaries, fallopian tubes, and intestines.

endometrium Lining of the uterus.

endorphins Substances produced in the central nervous system that may act like the body's own "morphine." They may play an important role in relief of pain and in enhancing a sense of well-being.

endoscopic retrograde cholangiopancreatography (ERCP) A procedure in which dye is passed through a flexible endoscope into the bile ducts and pancreatic ducts and then X-rays are taken. It can be helpful in evaluation of diseases of the bile ducts and pancreas.

endoscopy A procedure usually done with flexile fiberoptic scopes to visualize the inside of a passageway, such as the nose or esophagus.

endostatin A protein that is being studied for its potential to deny cancers their source of nutrition with the hope of arresting the disease.

endothelium Cells that line the inside wall of a blood vessel.

endovascular Within the blood vessel.

entropion Turning in of the eyelid.

epidermis The most superficial layer of skin.

epinephrine A hormone produced in the adrenal gland that triggers the body's fight-or-flight response to a stressful event. Also called adrenaline.

ERCP See endoscopic retrograde cholangiopancreatography.

erectile dysfunction (ED) An inability to sustain an erection satisfactory for sexual intercourse. Also known as impotence.

erythropoietin A hormone made by the kidney that stimulates the production of red blood cells by the bone marrow. The hormone is available by injection to treat anemia related to chronic kidney disease.

esophageal stricture A narrowed area in the esophagus, usually due to chronic acid reflux.

essential tremor Shaking or rhythmic movements about a joint or joints. Essential tremor is the most common tremor in older adults and is characterized most commonly by shaky hands.

estradiol Body's estrogen produced by the ovaries, but also by the adrenal glands, testes, and placenta.

estrogen Female hormone.

eustachian tube A small tube that connects the middle ear with the back of the throat.

euthanasia Deliberate termination of an ill person's life.

executive functions Organization and planning.

exophthalmos Bulging of the eyes, usually due to hyperthyroidism but occasionally a normal anatomic variation.
exostosis A bony growth that occurs most commonly in the ear canals and in the mouth.

external beam radiation A treatment for prostate cancer using high-energy irradiation to the prostate from an X-ray machine.

external carotid artery Artery that supplies blood flow to the face.

F

facelift Surgical procedure to elevate the skin and soft tissues of the face and neck through inconspicuous incisions around the ear and under the chin.

Factor V Leiden A genetic disorder that increases the risk of developing blood clots.

fallopian tubes The tubes that transport eggs from the ovaries to the uterus.

fascia Tough fibrous tissue that wraps around the body under the skin and surrounds muscles.

fecal impaction A bowel obstruction caused by hard stool.

fecal incontinence Involuntary loss of stool.

femoral artery An artery that leads from the groin into the leg.

femoral neck Area of the femur (thighbone) between the "ball" that forms the head of the femur and the main shaft.

femur Thigh bone which extends from the hip to the knee.

ferritin Storage form of iron. Ferritin levels can be measured by a blood test.

fetus Unborn child from about two months following conception to birth.

fiberoptic bronchoscopy A procedure in which a lung specialist looks into the breathing passages via a flexible instrument.

fiberoptic endoscopy A procedure in which a doctor looks at images of internal organs via a flexible instrument.

fibrates Drugs used to lower cholesterol and triglycerides.

fibroadenoma A benign glandular tumor.

fibrocystic Cysts surrounded by ample, fibrous connective tissue.

fibroids Benign muscular tumors of the uterus.

fibromyalgia A condition associated with muscle tenderness and fatigue. There are multiple symmetric tender "trigger points" in various muscles where pressure will produce pain.

fistula 1. An abnormal communication between an organ and the skin or between two organs. In Crohn's disease, there may be fistulas between the skin and the intestines or between different parts of the intestine. 2. A connection that is surgically created between an artery and a vein for the purpose of hemodialysis in patients with kidney failure.

fixed bridge A partial denture that attaches to natural teeth in a manner that the patient is not able (or expected) to remove for cleaning.

flexion contracture Limitation of motion of a joint due to tightening of the tendons and muscles around the joint.

fluorescein angiogram A dye study to evaluate the blood vessels in the retina.

follicle-stimulating hormone (FSH) Hormone made in the pituitary gland in the brain that promotes sperm production in men and enables ovulation in women.

folliculitis An infection of a hair follicle.

Folstein Mini-Mental State Exam (MMSE) A screening test for dementia.

fracture Any disruption in bone or cartilage, whether a crack or break.

frontotemporal dementia A form of dementia that affects mainly the frontal and temporal lobes of the brain, causing personality and behavioral changes.

frostbite Permanent damage to body tissues due to cold exposure.

frozen shoulder A stiff shoulder with limited motion, usually due to lack of use, possibly as a result of previous tendonitis or bursitis.

FSH See follicle-stimulating hormone.

G

ganglion A cystic swelling of the lining of a joint that produces a lump near the joint.

gangrene Death of skin, muscle, or other body tissues due to obstruction of blood flow.

gastroesophageal reflux disease (GERD) Movement of stomach contents back into the esophagus, often causing acid irritation of the esophagus and leading to pain in the chest, heartburn, or, in some cases, hoarseness and asthma symptoms.

general anesthesia Method of anesthesia whereby patients are rendered unconscious by a combination of drugs administered through their veins and inhalation of an anesthetic gas mixed with oxygen. The anesthetic-oxygen mixture is administered through a tube placed by an anesthesiologist or nurse anesthetist into the windpipe through the mouth.

generalized anxiety disorder Excessive anxiety and worry about many things that are hard to control and cause impairment in functioning. People may feel restless, on edge, fatigued, inattentive, irritable, or tense and/or have trouble sleeping.

GERD See gastroesophageal reflux disease.

geriatric rehabilitation The rehabilitation of an elderly person following a serious condition, such as stroke, amputation, or heart attack.

geriatrician A physician who specializes in the medical care of the elderly.

gerontologists Professionals who specialize in the study of aging. May include psychologists, social workers, physicians, etc.

gestational diabetes Diabetes associated with pregnancy.

gingiva The light-pink (if healthy) soft tissue normally covering the alveolar bone and the roots of teeth. Also known as the gums.

gingival hyperplasia A condition in which the amount of gingival tissue actually increases, most commonly in response to plaque in a person receiving certain medications, such as phenytoin (Dilantin) or cyclosporin (Imuran), or one of the calcium channel–blocking agents, such as nifedipine (Procardia).

gingival sulcus Invisible, empty area between the gingiva and the tooth that is not filled with periodontal ligament.

gingivitis An inflammatory condition of the gingiva, usually in response to plaque, but heals within a matter of days once the plaque is removed. The gingiva becomes red, puffy, and bleeds easily.

ginkgo biloba Herbal supplement utilized for a variety of conditions, including memory loss, dizziness, and ringing in the ears. It may interact adversely with aspirin and warfarin. Concentration of active ingredients varies widely between products.

glands A cell or group of cells that produce and release substances used nearby or in other parts of the body.

glaucoma A disease caused by high pressure within the eye.

Gleason grade Popular grading system for prostate cancer. A grade ranging from 1 through 5 is assigned based on how much the arrangement of the cancer cells looks like the way the normal prostate cells are arranged in the prostate gland. The Gleason grade ranges from 1 to 5, where 1 is the best-behaved cancer and 5 is the most aggressive, vicious cancer.

Gleason score A method of classifying prostate cancer cells on a scale of 2 to 10. The higher the Gleason score (also called the Gleason sum), the faster the cancer is likely to grow, the less likely it is to respond to treatment, and the more likely it is to spread beyond the prostate.

glioma A malignant tumor of the brain.

global aphasia A condition in which the individual does not understand what is said or written and also cannot express himself or herself properly, usually caused by a stroke.

glomerulonephritis Inflammation of the filtering units of the kidney.

glottis The structure in the throat that blocks the windpipe when one swallows.

glucose tolerance test A test for diabetes in which a sweet drink rich in glucose is given and then blood glucose is checked periodically thereafter.

gonorrhea A sexually transmitted disease that usually causes a yellowish discharge from the penis in males and the vagina in females.

gout An inflammatory joint disorder due to deposition of uric acid crystals in the joint.

graft 1. A surgical connection between an artery and a vein created by artificial tubing. 2. Transplantation of a structure. For example, a kidney or liver transplant is considered a graft to the person receiving it. Skin grafts involve removing skin from one area to apply somewhere else. Bone grafts are pieces of bone taken from the hip region and used for spinal fusions.

Grave's disease A form of hyperthyroidism in which bulging of the eyes is common (exophthalmos).

growth hormone A hormone made in the pituitary gland that regulates growth in childhood but in adulthood still plays an important role in maintaining a healthy body mass, muscle, and bone density.

Guillain-Barré syndrome A neurological disorder that starts with weakness and numbness in the legs and then progresses to the arms. It may be associated with paralysis and respiratory failure.

gynecologic Refers to the female genital and reproductive tracts.

H

halitosis A persistent, unpleasant odor coming from the mouth. It can be due to a wide variety of causes, including poor oral hygiene, periodontitis, dental caries, medications (e.g., ferrous sulfate or lithium carbonate), foods (e.g., onions, garlic, or alcohol), dry mouth, diseases (e.g., diabetes, kidney dysfunction, or pneumonia).

hallucination Seeing or hearing something that is not there.

heart block The delay or failure of an electrical impulse from the atria to reach the ventricles. Graded as first, second, or third degree based on the severity. First-degree heart block is usually found incidentally on an electrocardiogram and usually requires no treatment. Second- and third-degree heart block are more serious and often will require a pacemaker.

heat exhaustion A condition caused by exposure to extreme heat that results in dehydration. It may be associated with fatigue, confusion, and collapse. It usually responds to fluids and lying down.

heat stroke A medical emergency associated with an extreme rise in body temperature due to heat exposure and an inability to dissipate heat properly. Untreated, it may cause organ failure, mental confusion, coma, and death.

Heberden's nodes Bony lumps that develop at the end of fingers affected by osteoarthritis.

Helicobacter pylori An organism commonly associated with ulcers of the stomach and duodenum. Treatment with antibiotics and medicine to reduce stomach acid reduces the risk of recurrence of ulcers.

hematologist A physician who specializes in diseases of the blood.

hematoma A collection of blood under the skin or in muscle usually caused by an injury; literally, "blood tumor." It may occur spontaneously in individuals with hemophilia.

hemianopsia Blindness that affects one-half of the visual field, either right or left.

hemipelvectomy Removal of a leg and half of the pelvis.

hemiplegia Paralysis of one side of the body.

hemodialysis The use of a machine that cleanses the blood of waste products, as well as extra salt and fluid.

hemoglobin Protein in the red blood cells that binds oxygen in the lung to be transported to the body's tissues.

hemoglobin A1C A blood test used to determine the average blood sugar over the previous 2 or 3 months. Helpful in monitoring diabetes. Also called glycohemoglobin.

hemolysis Breakdown of red blood cells.

hemophilia A hereditary bleeding disorder due to deficiency of clotting factor VIII that almost exclusively affects males. The condition usually manifests itself in childhood by excessive bleeding.

hemorrhage Excessive bleeding.

heparin An anticoagulant given intravenously to treat or prevent blood clots.

hepatitis Inflammation of the liver.

herpes simplex Small, circular, clustered blisters, with yellowish centers and red borders, that break and combine into painful, irregular sores. If they form on the outside of the lips, they will crust. Herpes is caused by a virus and is very contagious when a sore is visible. Also called cold sores.

herpes zoster See shingles.

hertz (Hz) A measurement of frequency or pitch.

hiatus hernia A protrusion of part of the stomach through the opening (hiatus) in the diaphragm through which the esophagus passes.

hip disarticulation Removal of the leg at the hip joint.

hippocampus An area located deep within the brain. Major changes may occur here in Alzheimer's disease.

hirsutism Excessive hair, often in such undesirable places as the face and chest, especially in women.

HIV See human immunodeficiency virus.

Hodgkin's disease One of the major categories of lymphatic malignancies. The most common initial sign of the disease is a single enlarged lymph node, usually in the neck, armpit, or groin. Other symptoms may include fever, night sweats, fatigue, weight loss, and anemia. New advances have resulted in cure for many patients with Hodgkin's disease.

homocysteine An amino acid which has been linked to a higher incidence of heart disease when elevated in the blood.

hormone A chemical substance released into the body by the endocrine glands, such as the thyroid, adrenal, testes, or ovaries. A hormone travels through the bloodstream and sets in motion various body functions. Testosterone and estrogen are examples of male and female hormones, respectively.

hormone therapy Treatment with drugs that interfere with hormone production, utilization, or action.

hospice An organization that provides services to persons terminally ill with cancer or other serious diseases, such as severe heart failure, COPD, cirrhosis, or advanced kidney disease.

hot flashes Sudden rush of body heat causing redness of the face and sweating, a common side effect of some types of hormone therapy. Also commonly seen at menopause, with the decline of estrogen production by the ovaries.

human immunodeficiency virus (HIV) Virus that causes AIDS. See also acquired immune deficiency syndrome.

human papilloma virus (HPV) Virus responsible for venereal warts.

hydrocephalus A condition in which excessive fluid accumulates within the inner chambers of the brain where cerebrospinal fluid is made.

hydrogen peroxide Mild antiseptic for cuts and rashes.

hydrotherapy Water therapy, such as a whirlpool bath.

hymenal membrane A thin layer of tissue partly occluding the opening to the vagina in the virgin. Also called the virginal membrane.

hyperacusis A condition in which ordinary sounds seem loud or painful.

hypercholesterolemia Elevated blood cholesterol, a major risk factor for coronary artery disease.

hyperglycemia Elevated blood glucose.

hyperlipidemia Elevated blood cholesterol, triglycerides, or both.

hyperplasia An increase in the number of normal cells in an organ.

hypertension High blood pressure.

hyperthyroidism An overactive thyroid gland which can result in rapid heart beat, tremor, weight loss, etc. See also Grave's disease.

hypertrophic cardiomyopathy A condition in which the muscles of the heart thicken and enlarge, resulting in impairment of normal function.

hypertrophy Enlargement or thickening of a tissue or organ.

hypnagogic hallucinations A condition in which one sees, feels, or hears things while conscious. Comparable to dreaming while awake.

hypoactive Underactive.

hypochondriac A person who mistakenly believes he or she has a disease or who has an excessive concern about his or her own health and a preoccupation with bodily or mental functions.

hypoglycemia Low blood sugar.

hypogonadism Deficient production of testosterone in men and estrogen in women.

hypoparathyroidism Deficient production of parathyroid hormone which results in low blood calcium and inadequate mineralization of bone. Symptoms may include muscle weakness; tingling around the mouth or in the hands and feet; muscle cramps; tiredness; and seizures.

hypotension Low blood pressure.

hypothalamus A specialized area of the brain that transmits signals from the brain to the pituitary gland through a small stalk containing a unique network of blood vessels and nerves.

hypothermia Low body temperature, usually caused by cold exposure.

hypothyroidism Underactivity of the thyroid gland, which can result in weight gain, tiredness, intolerance to cold, etc.

hysterectomy Surgical removal of the uterus.

hysteroscopy A procedure in which a gynecologist examines the inside of the uterus with a scope.

iatrogenic tremor Tremor that occurs due to medications.

I

ICD See implantable cardioverter defibrillator.

idiopathic The cause is unknown.

idiopathic thrombocytopenic purpura (ITP) A condition characterized by low platelet counts and associated with minute reddish spots on the skin called petechiae. It can be caused as a reaction to certain drugs, or it may be associated with some cancers, viral infections, or immune disorders.

iliac artery The artery that leads from the aorta to the legs.

immune system Body's defense system against infection and cancer.

immunization Administration of a vaccine to prevent or reduce the risk of infection.

immunoglobulin Proteins in the blood that help fight infection but that may also play a harmful role in certain diseases of immunity, such as rheumatoid arthritis and systemic lupus erythematosus.

impaired glucose tolerance Elevated blood glucose not severe enough to warrant treatment to restore the glucose to normal.

impedance plethysmography (IPG) A noninvasive test to screen for blood clots in the legs.

implant 1. A synthetic device that is attached permanently to a jaw and to which some sort of fixed or removable denture may be attached. 2. Any synthetic device that is used in the body, such as an intraocular lens following cataract surgery or an artificial hip prosthesis.

implantable cardioverter defibrillator (ICD) A surgically implanted device that can deliver an electric shock to convert a serious and life-threatening heart rhythm disturbance, such as ventricular fibrillation or ventricular tachycardia, to a normal rhythm.

impotence Inability to achieve erection firm enough for intercourse.

impression A record made of the anatomic shape of some internal part of the mouth. A soft material is placed in a rigid tray over a tooth, teeth, or a whole jaw. After the material sets, it can be removed and a resinous material is poured into the impression, resulting in a replica (a "cast") of the part of the mouth of interest to the dentist. In this way, certain appliances (like braces) or dental restorations (like crowns, bridges, and dentures) can be fabricated using materials and methods that would be unsuitable in the mouth.

incision A cut into the skin or deeper tissues.

incontinence Loss of bladder or bowel control.

incus One of the three bones (ossicles) of the middle ear.

infectious endocarditis Infection of the heart valves.

infectious hepatitis Liver inflammation, usually caused by a virus.

inferior vena cava A large vein that brings blood back to the heart.

inferior vena cava (IVC) filter An umbrella-like device that is inserted into the large vein going back to the heart in order to prevent blood clots from traveling to the lungs.

influenza The virus responsible for the flu.

infusion Introduction of a medicine or fluid into a vein or artery.

injection sclerotherapy A technique in which a chemical is injected into a varicose vein, causing its wall to close down and the vein to disappear.

INR See international normalized ratio.

insomnia The perception of not falling asleep or not getting enough sleep.

Insulin A hormone made in the pancreas that plays an important role in carbohydrate, protein, and fat metabolism.

insulin-dependent diabetes mellitus Condition caused by failure of the pancreas to produce adequate amounts of insulin to control blood sugar. Insulin must be given by injection for control of the elevated blood sugar. Also called type 1 diabetes mellitus.

intercostal muscles Muscles in between the ribs and used for breathing.

internal carotid artery One of the main arteries leading to the brain.

international normalized ratio (INR) A blood test used to monitor treatment with warfarin.

intraocular lens An artificial lens that an eye surgeon uses to replace the lens removed with cataract surgery.

intravenous (IV) contrast dye Fluid that is injected into the veins in order to enhance the contrast of tissues for certain X-ray procedures, such as intravenous pyelograms (IVP) and CT scans.

intravenous infusion Fluids given through a needle into a vein.

introitus An opening, such as the opening of the vagina.

iris The colored part of the eye.

iron deficiency anemia A low red blood cell count due to deficiency of iron, which is necessary for red blood cell synthesis. May be due to deficiency of iron in the diet, poor absorption of iron in the intestine, or to iron blood loss most commonly in the intestines.

irritative symptoms These are urinary symptoms arising from bladder muscle instability and loss of storage function. They include such symptoms as urgency, frequency, getting up at night to urinate, and urge incontinence.

ischemia Poor blood flow.

ischemic colitis Inflammation of the colon related to poor blood flow as a result of blockages in the arteries that carry blood to the colon.

islet cells Cells in the pancreas that produce insulin.

isometric exercise Stressing a muscle against resistance without movement of the joint.

ITP See idiopathic thrombocytopenic purpura.

IV contrast dye See intravenous contrast dye.

IVC filter See inferior vena cava filter.

J

jaundice Yellowing of the skin, usually due to liver disease.

jet lag An uncomfortable feeling of fatigue, disorientation, and fuzziness that may persist for days after arriving at your destination by jetliner. It usually occurs only after crossing over three or more time zones.

K

Kegel's exercises Exercises to strengthen the pelvic floor musculature.

kidney biopsy A sample of tissue taken from the kidney, usually done with a needle inserted through the back after local anesthesia.

kidney transplant A human kidney from a living donor or a recently deceased organ donor that is surgically connected to the blood vessels and bladder of a person with advanced kidney disease.

kilocalorie A unit of energy or heat.

kyphoplasty A procedure similar to vertebroplasty, but a special balloon is inserted and gently inflated inside the fractured vertebrae prior to injecting a cementing material, in order to restore the height of the vertebra and reduce the curvature of the spine.

kyphosis A forward curve in the spine.

L

labia majora Large folds of protective skin and fatty tissue around the vagina.

labia minora Smaller and less prominent folds or lips outside the vagina.

lactose intolerance Dietary intolerance to milk and milk products. Symptoms might include diarrhea, abdominal bloating and gas, and abdominal pain.

L-arginine A treatment for male sexual dysfunction. No reported clinical trials in women.

larynx Voice box.

laser ablation (EVLT or ELVS) A technique in which a laser is used to treat varicose veins or to destroy tissue.

laser hair removal Reduction in hair growth and density by treating the skin with a specific wavelength of light that damages the hair follicles from which the hair grows.

LEEP See loop electrosurgical excision procedure.

left anterior descending coronary artery Originates from the left main coronary artery and supplies blood to the front wall of the heart.

left ventricle The main pumping chamber of the heart.

left ventricular hypertrophy Enlargement of the main pumping chamber of the heart.

leprosy An infection that affects nerves and results in numbness and ulceration of the skin, ultimately resulting in gangrene and mutilation of body parts. Also called Hansen's disease.

leukemia A malignant condition of the bone marrow characterized by overproduction of white blood cells.

leukocytes See white blood cells.

leukorrhea A discharge from the vagina that is usually yellow or white and contains pus cells.

leukotriene modifiers Medicines for asthma that help reduce inflammation and spasm in the breathing passages.

levodopa A precursor of dopamine, a chemical neurotransmitter in the brain. Levodopa is the active ingredient in a frequently used medicine (Sinemet) for Parkinson's disease.

Leydig cells The cells in the testes responsible for secretion of the male hormone testosterone.

LH See luteinizing hormone.

LHRH See luteinizing hormone–releasing hormone.

LHRH agonist See luteinizing hormone–releasing hormone agonist.

libido Sexual desire.

lichen planus A condition of the mouth, as well as the extremities, in which a layer of mucosa or skin is sloughed. In the mouth, a spiderweb appearance of white lines on reddened mucosa is typical. May be due to a drug reaction or emotional stress.

ligation Tying a blood vessel to stop bleeding or blood flow.

lipids Blood fats such as cholesterol and triglycerides.

lipoprotein A protein in the blood that carries fat.

liposuction A procedure that removes deep fat deposits between the muscle layer and the skin to improve the external body shape.

lobules Glandular structures. In the breast, the lobules are responsible for production of milk.

local anesthesia with sedation Numbing medication is injected under the skin by the surgeon after the patient has been given medication through a vein to create a state of relaxation without the need for mechanical ventilation.

loop electrosurgical excision procedure (LEEP) Procedure whereby a thin wire loop electrode emits a painless electric current which excises the abnormal tissue in the cervix or vagina.

low-density lipoprotein (LDL) The "bad cholesterol"; the cholesterol fraction that is associated with atherosclerosis.

lower urinary tract symptoms (LUTS) A combination of irritative and obstructive voiding. LUTS is associated with but not always purely the result of BPH.

lumpectomy Removal of a lump, such as a breast tumor.

lung abscess A walled cavity of pus in the lung caused by certain infections and sometimes by cancer.

lung volume reduction surgery (LVRS) Surgical removal of sections of the lungs, usually the upper lobes, to help improve airflow in the lungs of persons with severe emphysema.

luteinizing hormone (LH) A pituitary hormone that stimulates the Leydig cells in the testes to produce and release testosterone into the circulation.

luteinizing hormone–releasing hormone (LHRH) A hormone released by the hypothalamus that stimulates the pituitary gland to produce luteinizing hormone.

luteinizing hormone–releasing hormone (LHRH) agonist Medications for prostate cancer with a chemical structure similar to natural LHRH. They cause an initial rise in luteinizing hormone and testosterone followed by complete suppression of luteinizing hormone and testosterone to castrate levels. They do so by blocking the release of luteinizing hormone from the pituitary gland. Also called superagonist.

LUTS See lower urinary tract symptoms.

lymphatic system Consists of lymph nodes, lymphatic vessels, and specialized lymphatic tissue in the bone marrow, spleen, and elsewhere. It plays an important role in the body's defense against infection and cancer.

M

macrophages Special cells that help fight infection, but they may also play a harmful role in the development of atherosclerosis.

macula Central part of the retina and location of central vision.

macular degeneration Damage to the macula either due to the "dry" type, in which the cells break down and die, or the "wet" type, in which fragile blood vessels may bleed and cause sudden and severe visual loss.

magnetic resonance angiogram (MRA) A noninvasive test by which magnetic resonance is used to visualize blood flow.

magnetic resonance imaging (MRI) A scan using magnets to generate pictures of the inside of the body.

malaria A febrile illness transmitted by mosquitoes. Also called jungle fever or swamp fever.

malignant lymphoma Cancer which may originate in the lymph nodes but which often involves the bone marrow and other components of the blood system.

malleus One of the three bones (ossicles) of the middle ear.

mandible Jawbone.

mastectomy Removal of a breast.

master cast A cast that is used to fabricate a dental device that the patient will keep, such as a crown, bridge, or denture.

mastitis Inflammation or infection of the breast.

mediastinoscopy Examination of the center of the chest with a scope inserted just above the breastbone.

mediastinum Central cavity of the chest between both lungs.

medical castration Medication which when taken acts to suppress circulating testosterone to castrate levels.

melanoma Cancer of the pigment-producing cells in the skin.

melatonin A supplement used most commonly for insomnia and jet lag. It should be avoided if receiving chemotherapy or if one has liver disease or seizures. Melatonin may interact with numerous prescription medications.

menarche The onset of menstrual bleeding.

Ménière's disease A condition characterized by recurrent bouts of dizziness, ringing in the ears, and hearing loss.

meninges Membranes lining the brain and spinal cord.

meningioma Benign tumor of the membranes lining the brain.

meningitis Infection and/or inflammation of the membranes lining the brain and spinal cord.

menopause The cessation of menstruation correlating with the time of ovarian failure.

menstruation The bleeding that occurs each month with shedding of the lining of the uterus. Popularly called the menstrual period.

metabolism Rate at which a body burns calories.

metastasis Cancer cells that have spread to another part of the body.

metatarsalgia Pain over the ball of the foot due to pressure over the head of the metatarsal bones.

methyltestosterone A male hormone.

MI See myocardial infarction.

microdermabrasion Outpatient and salon treatment using ultrafine crystals blown against the skin to gently abrade away the outer epidermis, giving the skin a younger glow and improving the appearance of sun-damaged skin.

microphlebectomy A surgical technique in which varicose veins are removed through very small cuts in the skin that do not require stitches. Also called ambulatory stab avulsion phlebectomy (ASAP).

microvascular decompression A neurosurgical procedure in which the pressure imposed by a blood vessel against the trigeminal nerve is relieved by placing a piece of Teflon between the artery and nerve.

microwave diathermy A form of deep-heat therapy using electromagnetic waves.

middle ear effusion Fluid within the middle ear.

mitral regurgitation Backflow of blood through the mitral valve.

mitral stenosis (MS) Narrowing of the mitral valve, thus impeding forward blood flow through the valve.

mixed apnea A combination of central and obstructive sleep apnea.

Mohs' surgery A technique for removing skin cancer that limits the extent of removal of normal tissue. The surgeon carefully examines small sections of skin until all the cancer is removed.

monoclonal gammopathy of undetermined significance (MGUS) The finding of an elevated level of one of the gamma globulins in the blood but not associated with bone marrow or blood findings typical of multiple myeloma. Only 20% of patients with this finding will progress in future years to develop multiple myeloma.

monosymptomatic rest tremor A rest tremor that does not progress to Parkinson's disease.

mons pubis Fatty prominence over the pubic bone that protects the clitoris and opening of the vagina.

Morton's neuroma Not truly a neuroma (nerve tumor) but the development of scar tissue about the nerve as it passes between the third and fourth toes (or less commonly between the second and third toes) due to repeated irritation of the nerve. Pain under the affected toes is common, and occasionally numbness may occur.

MRA See magnetic resonance angiogram.

MRI See magnetic resonance imaging.

mucocele A blocked minor salivary gland of the cheek, lip, or roof of mouth. Its characterized by a small translucent bluish or pale pink swelling with a reddened border, which may or may not be uncomfortable.

mucosa The tissue that lines certain body parts. The oral mucosa lines the inside of the mouth. The gastric mucosa lines the inside of the stomach. The intestinal mucosa lines the inside of the small and large intestines.

multi-infarct dementia Dementia caused by multiple strokes.

multiple myeloma A form of bone cancer in which there is an abnormal proliferation of cells in the bone marrow called plasma cells.

murmur A whooshing noise heard over the heart with a stethoscope due to turbulent blood flow across a heart valve.

mutation A spontaneous change in a gene that may result in disease, cancer, or birth defects.

myasthenia gravis A neurological disorder in which an antibody develops to the muscle receptor for acetylcholine. The typical symptoms that this produces in the older adult are most often double vision that may get better and worse, difficulty swallowing and speaking, and easy tiring of the muscles.

myelin The lining or sheath of a nerve fiber, comparable to the insulation around an electric wire.

myeloblast The precursor of the white blood cell. It may be overproduced in some types of leukemia.

myocardial infarction (MI) A heart attack. Blockage of a coronary artery due to plaque or a ruptured plaque with an adherent clot leads to death of heart muscle cells.

myositis ossificans The formation of bone within muscle as an abnormal response to injury.

myxedema An advanced form of hypothyroidism, associated with slow thinking, weight gain, dryness of skin and hair, swelling of the legs, and muscle weakness.

N

N-acetylcysteine Often used to protect the kidneys when X-ray procedures that require dye are required. Also called Mucomyst.

narcolepsy A disorder characterized by excessive daytime sleepiness and possibly "sleep attacks." Other features may include sudden loss of muscle tone, sleep paralysis, and hallucinations while trying to fall asleep or shortly after waking up.

nasal cannula Small prongs used to deliver oxygen into the nasal passages.

nasal polyps Benign growths caused by allergy or infection. They may be association with blockage of the nose and sinus passageways, bleeding, and pain.

nasal septum The flexible, rubbery tissue that divides nostrils into right and left.

nasal vestibulitis An infection of the skin surrounding the nostrils.

nasopharyngeal carcinoma Cancer of the upper part of the throat in back of the nasal passage. The Epstein-Barr virus may play a role.

neoplasm A new growth or tumor, which may be benign or malignant.

nephrocalcinosis Calcification of the kidneys.

nephrologist A physician who specializes in kidney diseases.

nerve conduction velocity (NCV) A neurological test in which small needle electrodes are placed in nerves to evaluate their activity.

neuritic plaques Material that deposits in the brain when nerve cells break down. Also called senile plaques.

neurofibrillary tangles Tangled filaments that appear in degenerating nerve cells.

neurofibroma A tumor of the lining sheath of a nerve.

neuroleptic malignant syndrome A rare syndrome that can be caused by antipsychotic drugs. It is characterized by fever, muscular rigidity, confusion, and unstable vital signs. It is a medical emergency.

neuroleptics See antipsychotics.

neurologist A physician who specializes in disorders of the brain and nervous system.

neuron A nerve cell.

neuropathic arthropathy See Charcot's joint.

neuropsychologist A specialist in the relationships between the brain and behavior.

nitric oxide (NO) A gas that plays an important role in the dilatation or relaxation of blood vessels.

nocturia The necessity to void during the night, measured in frequency of such urination.

nocturnal leg cramps Painful spasms of the muscles of the legs and feet that occur at night and can disrupt sleep.

noncompliance Failure to follow the doctor's directions.

non-Hodgkin's lymphoma (NHL) One of the major classifications of lymphatic malignancies. Many different types of NHL can be identified by the pathologist, and treatment and prognosis vary depending on the type.

non-rapid eye movement (NREM) sleep Four stages of sleep from a transitional phase to very deep.

nonsteroidal anti-inflammatory drugs (NSAIDs) Medications used to treat arthritis, tendonitis, and many other painful conditions.

norepinephrine A chemical that plays a role in nerve function in a variety of tissues. It is also released from the adrenal gland into the circulation in response to stress.

norovirus Virus that can cause nausea, vomiting, and diarrhea. It has been found in seasonal outbreaks and has been the culprit responsible for some well-publicized outbreaks on cruise ships. Formerly called the Norwalk virus.

nosocomial infection An infection acquired in the hospital.

NREM sleep See non-rapid eye movement sleep.

NSAIDs See nonsteroidal anti-inflammatory drugs.

O

OA See osteoarthritis.

obesity Excessively overweight.

obsessive-compulsive disorder (OCD) A disorder characterized by obsessions and compulsions. Obsessions are unwanted thoughts, impulses, or images that pop into a person's mind and cause distress. People know these are just thoughts, but they cause great anxiety. Compulsions are repetitive behaviors or mental acts that reduce distress.

obstructive sleep apnea (OSA) A sleep disorder caused by obstruction of the upper air passage, often leading to excessive snoring and perhaps periods of absent breathing.

obstructive symptoms Symptoms arising from the obstruction to the outflow of urine, such as a diminished flow, hesitancy, interruption, and urinary retention.

occupational therapist (OT) Person on the rehabilitation team responsible for improving the function of the hands and fingers.

OCD See obsessive-compulsive disorder.

odontoblasts The outermost cells of the pulp that line the pulp chamber and continuously form chemicals which become additional dentin.

olfactory cells Specialized cells in the nose for smell.

olfactory system System for smell. It comprises special sensory cells and nerve cells in the nose that transmit signals which the brain interprets.

oncogene Genes that promote cancer.

oncologist A physician who specializes in the evaluation and treatment of cancer.

oncology The study of cancer.

onychomycosis Fungal infection of fingernails or toenails.

open angle glaucoma Impairment of drainage of the fluids in the front chamber of the eye leading to increased pressure within the eye that can eventually cause damage to the optic nerve. It is the most common type of glaucoma.

ophthalmologist A medical doctor who has completed special training in eye diseases. An ophthalmologist can perform eye examinations, prescribe eyeglasses, and perform eye surgery.

opiates Powerful, narcotic pain relievers.

optic nerve The nerve to the eye that carries images from the retina to the brain, so that they can be interpreted as the things one sees (a sunrise, a person's face, the words on a page).

optometrist An eye doctor who can examine the eyes to determine the presence of vision problems and eye disorders. An optometrist can prescribe eyeglasses, but cannot perform surgery. The designation after the name of an optometrist is OD.

oral cancer Uncontrolled growth of abnormal tissue in the lips, mouth, and/or throat. Over 95% of oral cancers form from oral mucosa and are termed squamous cell carcinoma.

oral mucosa Skin on the inside of the lips and mouth, which takes one of three forms: a stiff form (such as the gums next to the teeth and the roof of the mouth), a specialized form (such as the upper surface of the tongue), and the movable form (everything else, e.g., inside of cheeks and beneath tongue).

orgasm Sexual climax.

oropharynx The anatomic area bounded by the walls of the throat on the sides, the back of the tongue above, and the voice box below.

orthopedic surgery Surgery that deals with problems of the bones, joints, and muscles.

orthostatic hypotension A drop in blood pressure on standing.

orthotic An orthopedic appliance.

orthotist A person who makes and fits orthopedic appliances.

ossicles Bones of the middle ear.

osteoarthritis (OA) The process of wear and tear causing thinning and fissuring of the smooth cartilage at the end of a bone. Eventually the bone does not glide freely. OA may cause pain and limitation of joint motion. Also called degenerative joint disease (DJD).

osteoblast Cell that makes new bone.

osteoclast Cell that resorbs or breaks down bone.

osteogenesis imperfecta A hereditary disorder associated with brittle bones that break easily.

osteolysis Breakdown of bone.

osteoma Benign bone tumor.

osteomalacia Soft bones as a result of vitamin D deficiency. Also called adult rickets.

osteomyelitis Infection of bone.

osteopath A physician of osteopathy. These professionals have training very similar to traditional medical doctors, perhaps with slightly more emphasis on the role of the musculoskeletal system in disease. An osteopath receives a doctor of osteopathy (DO) degree and often pursues specialty training in the same programs as an MD.

osteopenia A borderline decrease in bone density, not severe enough to qualify as osteoporosis.

osteophytes Bony spurs that develop around joints affected by osteoarthritis.

osteoporosis Severe thinning of the bones. Also called brittle bone disease.

osteotomy Surgical removal of bone.

otolaryngologist A physician who specializes in ears, nose, and throat disorders.

ovaries Paired structures in a woman's pelvis that contain the eggs.

ovulation Release of an egg from the ovary.

P

PAD See peripheral arterial disease.

Paget's disease A disease of bone metabolism that usually produces no symptoms. However, in some cases, it may cause skull, back, and leg pain. Deformity of the legs and an increase in hat size can occur in more severe cases. A bone enzyme called the alkaline phosphatase is usually very elevated. In rare cases, a bone cancer called osteosarcoma may develop.

palliative treatment Therapy that relieves symptoms such as pain but is not anticipated to cure the disease. Its main purpose is to improve the patient's quality of life. Examples are hormone therapy and radiation therapy to relieve pain from bone cancer.

pallidotomy Surgical destruction of an area of the brain called the globus pallidus. May be useful in the management of some patients with Parkinson's disease.

palpitation An awareness of the heart. Some people feel a flip-flop in the chest. Others may feel that their heart is racing or the rhythm is irregular.

panic attacks Sudden anxiety attacks characterized by an impending feeling of doom, losing control, or going crazy and having several physical symptoms, including palpitations, butterflies in stomach, nausea, numbness in fingers or toes, throat closing, shortness of breath, sweating, and tremors. These symptoms last about 10 minutes, and the person fears having another one and often changes his or her life to try to avoid having them.

Pap smear A screening test for cervical cancer. A sample of cells is taken from the cervix with a wooden spatula and/or brush, smeared onto a microscope slide, and examined for cancer cells by a pathologist.

paraffin bath A form of heat therapy for arthritic hands in order to relieve pain.

parathyroid glands Four pea-sized glands located next to the thyroid gland that regulate calcium and phosphorus metabolism.

parathyroid hormone (PTH) A hormone made by the parathyroid glands and that has an important role in calcium and phosphorus metabolism.

Parkinson's disease A disease resulting from a deficiency (in an area of the brain called the basal ganglia) of a brain chemical called dopamine. The clinical picture is characterized by slowness of movement, muscle rigidity, shuffling gait, blank facial expression, and, often but not always, a coarse tremor.

Parkinson-dementia complex A syndrome associated with cognitive decline in a substantial number of those afflicted with Parkinson's disease.

parotitis Infection (usually bacterial in adults) of the major salivary gland that is located in front of and slightly below the ear. Potentially quite serious and usually painful. The viral form of this disease, usually restricted to children, is called mumps.

partial denture A denture that attaches (permanently or not) to one or more remaining natural teeth in one of the jaws and replaces the other missing teeth in that jaw. Also known as a removable partial denture, which a patient would remove at least daily for hygiene.

patella Kneecap.

pathologist A specialist who studies tissue samples to determine whether they are benign or cancerous.

presbycusis Sensorineural hearing loss caused by the aging process of the hearing apparatus.

penile Referring to the penis.

penis Organ of copulation in men. Analogous to the clitoris in women.

peptic ulcer disease A disorder affecting the lining of the esophagus, stomach, or duodenum and caused by the action of hydrochloric acid and pepsin, a digestive enzyme. Many cases of ulcer are known to be related to infection with an organism called Helicobacter pylori.

pericarditis Inflammation of the lining sac around the heart.

perilymph fistula A break or tear in one of the membranes of the inner ear.

perimenopause The time leading up to menopause.

perineal body Skin between the vagina and rectum.

periodic limb movement disorder (PLMS) A condition associated with abnormal movements in the legs and sometimes the arms while sleeping. Also called nocturnal myoclonus.

periodontal ligament A fibrous sheath surrounding the root of a tooth and anchoring the cementum to the alveolar bone.

periodontitis An inflammatory condition of the periodontium, usually in response to subgingival plaque, that results in loss of alveolar bone. It may not be apparent on sight or may result in pus that forms in the gingival sulcus.

periodontium Attachment apparatus of the tooth: the periodontal ligament, the surrounding alveolar bone, and the gingiva.

peripheral arterial disease (PAD) Atherosclerosis of the arteries outside the heart.

peripheral neuropathy A condition characterized by damage to the peripheral nerves that can result in weakness, numbness, burning, or tingling of the feet and/or hands. It can be caused by diabetes, vitamin B_{12} deficiency, and numerous other conditions.

peritonitis A serious infection of the lining of the abdomen.

pernicious anemia A deficiency of vitamin B_{12} in the body due to deficient or absent production of a factor (intrinsic factor) in the stomach that is necessary for vitamin B_{12} to be absorbed properly in the intestines.

personality disorders A group of disorders characterized by abnormal behavior. People with personality disorders have difficulty seeing their own behavior and how it affects others. Because of their extreme personality characteristics, adapting to the changes of aging can be very difficult.

PET scan See positron emission tomography.

phantom limb pain Pain experienced as if it were in the lost part of an amputated limb.

phantom limb sensation The sensation that an amputated limb is still present.

pharynx Throat.

phlebitis See deep vein thrombosis.

phlebotomy The procedure of drawing blood for testing.

phosphorus An element in the blood required for the proper function of cells. It may accumulate excessively in those with kidney failure.

photocoagulation Use of a laser to stop bleeding or destroy blood vessels.

PhotoDerm light A technique that uses light to treat spider veins, age spots, and tattoos.

photosensitivity Sensitivity to the sun resulting in a rash or blisters. Certain medications may increase the risk for skin problems with sun exposure.

physiatrist A physician specializing in physical medicine and rehabilitation.

physical therapist (PT) The person on the rehabilitation team who is responsible for increasing or maintaining joint mobility, strengthening weak muscles, and maintaining the muscle strength of normal muscles.

physiological Referring to the body's normal internal processes.

pica A compulsive craving for a food that has little or no nutritional value. For example, a craving for ice or carrots may be a manifestation of pica caused by iron deficiency.

Pick's disease Disorder resembling findings noted in frontotemporal dementia, but Pick bodies can be found in the brain cells at autopsy. The cause is unknown and may be difficult to distinguish from Alzheimer's disease during the person's lifetime.

PIN See prostate intraepithelial neoplasia.

pinguecula A yellowish piece of tissue that forms adjacent to the iris and is usually on the same side as the nose. It generally does not cause any problem.

pituitary gland A gland in the brain that regulates production of hormones from such other glands as the thyroid, adrenal glands, testes, and ovaries.

plantar fasciitis Inflammation of the tissues of the sole of the foot resulting in heel pain.

plaque 1. With atherosclerosis, fatty buildup on the wall of the blood vessels. 2. In dentistry, the accumulation of bacteria and their products on the surface of the teeth.

plasma Liquid part of blood, as opposed to the cellular part of blood which contains the red blood cells, white blood cells, and platelets.

plasma exchange Removal of toxic substances from the blood.

platelets Small elements in the blood that are important for clotting.

pleura Refers to the tissue lining the outside of the lung and the inside of the chest cavity.

pleural cavity Chest cavity.

pleural friction rub A grating noise, heard with a stethoscope, due to inflammation of the lining surfaces around the lungs.

PMR See polymyalgia rheumatica.

pneumococcal pneumonia The most frequent type of pneumonia found in older persons living at home. The responsible bacterium is Streptococcus pneumoniae.

pneumococcal vaccine A vaccine given by injection to protect against pneumococcal pneumonia. The brand name for the vaccine is Pneumovax.

pneumonia Infection in the lung.

pneumothorax An abnormal collection of air within the chest cavity; a collapsed lung.

podiatrist A specialist in foot disorders. Their professional degree is a doctor of podiatric medicine (DPM).

polyarteritis nodosa A disease of the body's immunity that causes inflammation and damage to some arteries.

polycythemia An increase in red blood cells. A disorder of the bone marrow that causes an abnormal increase in the number of red blood cells is called polycythemia vera.

polymyalgia rheumatica (PMR) A condition characterized by aching and stiffness of the muscles of the neck, shoulders, and, often, the hips. The sedimentation rate is often markedly elevated. The condition responds dramatically to low doses of steroids. In a small percentage of patients, it may be associated with temporal arteritis.

polymyositis An inflammatory condition of muscles that results in weakness and tenderness.

polyp A growth that projects outward from a tissue.

polypharmacy Multiple medications for one individual.

polysomnogram A sleep test done in a specialized sleep laboratory.

popliteal artery Artery located behind the knee.

positron emission tomography (PET) A scan used to check for cancer since cancer cells will usually take up the isotope used for scanning and produce a "hot spot." It may also help determine whether cancer has spread to other organs, and is also being investigated as a tool in the diagnosis of Alzheimer's disease.

posterior tibial tendon dysfunction Inflammation of a tendon on the inside of the ankle bone that, if untreated, leads to a drop in the arch of the foot, as well as flattening and rolling out of the foot to the side. Walking becomes painful, balance is impaired, and the ability to thrust onto the toes is lost.

postherpetic neuralgia Persistent nerve pain following an attack of shingles.

posttraumatic stress disorder (PTSD) A disorder characterized by a person feeling numb, detached, or dazed after experiencing or witnessing a traumatic event. The person may forget details of the event or feel as if event were unreal.

PPD See purified protein derivative.

presbyopia Nearsightedness.

presbycusis Hearing loss associated with aging.

pressure sore A breakdown of the skin due to pressure against a bony prominence.

priapism A sustained and painful erection requiring immediate treatment.

primary orthostatic tremor A rapid tremor that occurs on standing. This condition can be quite disabling. Also called shaky leg tremor.

progesterone A hormone secreted by the ovaries that prepares the lining of the uterus for implantation of an egg.

prognosis A prediction of the course of the disease; the outlook for the cure of the patient.

progressive supranuclear palsy A neurological disorder which can mimic Parkinson's disease. However, problems with eye muscle movement distinguish this from Parkinson's disease.

prolactin A hormone secreted by the pituitary gland that stimulates breast milk production in a woman after the birth of a child.

prolactinoma A tumor of the prolactin-producing cells in the pituitary. It represents the most common pituitary tumor.

prolapse An organ which has protruded or dropped from its normal position.

prostaglandins Substances having an important role in the development of inflammation and pain. Prostaglandins also play a role in protection of the lining of the stomach.

prostate capsule The outside lining, or "skin," of the prostate.

prostate gland A rubbery walnut-sized gland located at the outlet of a man's bladder and encircling the urethra.

prostate intraepithelial neoplasia (PIN) Possible precursor to prostate cancer.

prostate-specific antigen (PSA) A glycoprotein in the blood which is secreted by the prostate. Its level acts as a marker for prostate tissue. PSA is often used to help detect prostate cancer, but it may be increased in a number of benign disorders, such as BPH and prostatitis. Moreover, although PSA is usually elevated in prostate cancer, this is not always the case.

prostatitis Inflammation of the prostate gland. Infection may be a cause, but there are also noninfectious causes.

prosthesis 1. An artificial replacement for a body part, such as a leg or eye. 2. A surgical implant, such as an artificial hip or knee.

proteins C and S Two of the body's natural "blood thinners," which prevent clots. Deficiencies can lead to blood clots in the legs and pulmonary embolism.

pseudogout An inflammatory joint disorder due to deposition of calcium pyrophosphate crystals in the joint.

pseudohypoparathyroidism A rare condition in which a genetic defect results in a defective receptor on the surface of cells for parathyroid hormone and produces the same problems that occur with hypoparathyroidism, but parathyroid hormone levels are actually increased in the blood in an attempt to compensate for the body's resistance to parathyroid hormone.

psoriasis Skin condition associated with scaly, red plaques.

psychiatrist A physician who specializes in disorders of mental function and emotion.

psychologist A professional responsible for assessment of emotional and psychological state.

psychometrician A professional who specializes in the administration of psychological tests.

pterygium A triangular patch of tissue that extends across the iris toward the pupil. It may adversely affect vision.

pulmonary angiogram An invasive test done by a radiologist to look for pulmonary embolism. It requires inserting a catheter and passing it to the blood vessels of the lung where a dye is injected.

pulmonary embolectomy Surgical removal of large, life-threatening blood clots in the lungs.

pulmonary embolism A clot that has traveled from the legs or pelvic veins and lodged in the lungs.

pulmonary function test Test of the workings of the lung.

pulmonary hypertension Elevated pressure in the arteries to the lungs. In older persons, pulmonary hypertension is caused primarily by such heart problems as congestive heart failure. Primary pulmonary hypertension is a serious condition that usually affects younger women and causes shortness of breath.

pulmonologist A specialist in lung diseases.

pulp Soft tissue inside the tooth that consists of nerves, blood vessels, and connective tissue.

pulp chamber Space within the dentin, open to end of the root, that is occupied by the pulp.

pulse oximeter A finger-clip device that measures the oxygen level in the blood.

pure tone average (PTA) Overall estimate of hearing across all frequencies. Used to grade the severity of hearing loss.

purified protein derivative (PPD) Material used for tuberculosis skin testing.

purpura Purple spots on the skin, usually caused by minor trauma.

pylon A temporary artificial limb used for rehabilitation until the permanent prosthesis is made.

Q

quadriceps The large muscle of the front part of the thigh that allows one to extend the knee and straighten the leg.

R

RA See rheumatoid arthritis.

radiofrequency ablation (VNUS) A technique in which radiofrequency waves are used to heat the tip of a catheter, which is then used to close down or destroy a varicose vein. Also used to destroy abnormal electrical circuits in the heart that may cause heart rhythm disturbances.

radiologist A specialist in reading X-rays, CT scans, ultrasound, and nuclear medicine studies. May do special tests that require the use of dye injections, such as angiograms.

radiotherapy Radiation used to treat cancer.

rapid eye movement (REM) sleep Time during sleep when most dreaming occurs.

Raynaud's phenomenon spasm of the arteries to the fingers causing the fingers to turn white with cold exposure. After blood flow returns, the fingers can turn blue or red. Cold exposure needs to be avoided, not just for the hands but the whole body.

recreation therapist A person that recommends leisure activities that a person would enjoy in order to avoid boredom.

red blood cells (RBC) Cells that circulate in the blood and carry oxygen to the body's tissues.

reflex sympathetic dystrophy (RSD) Wasting of tissue and bone due to the spasm of the blood vessels that occurs as a result of an injury.

regional ileitis See Crohn's disease.

rehabilitation nurse A nurse who specializes in the rehabilitation of disabled patients.

rejection A process in which the immune system causes the body to fail to accept a transplanted organ.

REM sleep See rapid eye movement sleep.

renal artery stenosis Narrowing of a kidney artery.

renal replacement therapy (RRT) Treatment that takes over the function of diseased kidneys. Includes dialysis and kidney transplant.

residual urine Urine retained in the bladder after voiding.

respiratory system Body's breathing system, consisting of the lungs, the nasal passages, sinuses, trachea, bronchi, chest cavity, and diaphragm.

restless leg syndrome (RLS) A disorder characterized by uncomfortable sensations in the legs at night and that can lead to an irresistible urge to move them.

restrictive cardiomyopathy A condition in which the pumping action of the heart is impeded by diseases that infiltrate the heart muscle.

reticuloendothelial system System of tissues dispersed throughout the body that plays an important role in the body's immune system.

retina The innermost layer of the eye on which the images one sees are projected. It is analogous to film in a camera.

retinal detachment The peeling of the retina away from its supporting structures.

retrograde ejaculation Ejaculation of semen into the bladder rather than through the urethra.

revascularization Reestablishment of blood flow through a blocked artery either by angioplasty or surgical bypass.

rheumatoid arthritis (RA) A chronic inflammatory disorder that affects joints, tendons, and bursae. The severity of the condition varies from patient to patient.

rheumatoid factor A blood test for rheumatoid arthritis. However, its usefulness is limited by the fact that it may be negative early in the course of rheumatoid arthritis, and it may be positive in some persons without rheumatoid arthritis, including a small percentage of healthy older people. In some rheumatoid arthritis patients, the rheumatoid factor never turns positive.

rheumatology Study of disorders of the musculoskeletal system.

rhinitis Inflammation of the internal membranes of the nose.

rhinophyma Enlargement and distortion of the nose, often assuming a red and bulbous appearance; also called rum nose or brandy nose.

rhinoplasty Reconstruction of the nose; a "nose job."

rickets A bone disorder from vitamin D deficiency that causes deformed bones, fractures, growth retardation, and muscle weakness in children.

RLS See restless leg syndrome.

root canal A dental treatment for which the pulp is removed and replaced with an inert (usually soft rubber) material. It is usually necessary after decay has invaded the pulp chamber.

root caries Decay attacking any part of the tooth not covered by enamel.

rosacea Adult acne, characterized by redness and pimples around the nose and cheeks.

rose bengal test A special stain used by eye doctors to check for damage to the cornea.

Rosenbaum Pocket Vision Screener A pocket chart that doctors use to check visual acuity.

rotator cuff The four tendons that surround the back, top, and front of the shoulder.

S

SA node See sinoatrial node.

salicylic acid Active ingredient in aspirin.

salvage therapy Treatment given to a patient whose cancer has recurred after primary treatment. For example, if initial treatment for cancer was surgery, then salvage therapy could involve radiation therapy. If the initial treatment was radiation therapy, then salvage therapy could be surgery or chemotherapy.

saphenous vein Large leg vein that travels on the inside of the leg.

sarcoma Cancer of any of the body's connective tissues; for example, involving bone, cartilage, muscle, or fat.

scabies Itchy rash caused by a mite that burrows under the skin.

Schilling test A special test, if vitamin B12 deficiency is found, to determine whether the cause is due to pernicious anemia or due to a problem in the intestine that causes poor absorption of vitamin B12.

Schirmer's test A test of eye dryness. A special filter paper is used and examined for wetness. It is helpful in the diagnosis of Sjögren's syndrome.

schizophrenia A mental illness in which a person cannot distinguish reality from their thoughts. People with schizophrenia have psychotic symptoms and have trouble maintaining close relationships, functioning at work, and taking care of themselves.

scleroderma A disease characterized by firm, tight skin. However, it is often associated with Raynaud's phenomenon, as well as a variety of problems in other internal organs.

sclerosis Thickening of a tissue. For example, aortic sclerosis involves thickening of a heart valve, usually with aging, but without narrowing of the valve; and scleroderma involves thickening of the skin.

scoliosis An S-shaped curve in the spine.

seborrheic keratosis Brown, crusted skin bumps commonly seen on aging skin.

sedimentation rate A blood test that can be abnormal in many conditions, including infections, inflammatory dis-

orders, and cancer. The sedimentation rate can sometimes tip off the doctor that something is wrong; however, its usefulness is limited in that so many diseases can elevate the sedimentation rate.

selective estrogen receptor modulator (SERM) A synthetic estrogen used in the treatment of osteoporosis that stimulates bone but does not have adverse effects on the breast or uterus.

selective serotonin reuptake inhibitors (SSRI) A newer class of antidepressants that are generally safer and better tolerated than the traditional tricyclic antidepressants.

sensorineural hearing loss Hearing loss due to problems in the cochlea or auditory nerve.

sentinel lymph node The closest lymph node to a cancer. If this is negative for cancer, more extensive lymph node dissection may not be necessary. It helps guide treatment decisions.

sepsis Overwhelming infection due to bloodstream invasion by bacteria.

septic arthritis Infection of a joint. Also called infectious arthritis.

septic shock Severe drop in blood pressure and abnormal vital signs associated with serious infection.

serotonin A brain chemical that plays an important role in mood disorders.

serum A straw-colored body fluid that includes protein, white blood cells, and salt.

sexually transmitted disease (STD) A disease transmitted by sexual means, such as AIDS, gonorrhea, Chlamydia, human papilloma virus, and syphilis.

shingles Rash, often painful, caused by the chickenpox virus (herpes zoster) that spreads along the distribution of a nerve.

SIADH See syndrome of inappropriate ADH secretion.

sick sinus syndrome A syndrome characterized by chaotic atrial activity in which the heart rate may be persistently slow or rapid heart rates may alternate with slow heart rates (tachycardia-bradycardia syndrome).

sickle cell anemia A hereditary condition in which the red blood cells become crescent- or sickle-shaped and break down easily. It may be associated with leg ulcers, kidney problems, bone pain, and strokes due to blockage of blood vessels.

sideroblastic anemia A form of anemia that causes small red blood cells. Unlike iron deficiency anemia, which also causes small red blood cells, body iron is actually increased. Although certain drugs and alcohol excess can cause sideroblastic anemia, often no specific cause can be identified.

simple phobia A fear, such as fear of heights, dogs, cats, spiders, snakes, flying, and having blood drawn.

single photon emission computed tomography (SPECT) scan A nuclear scan that may play a role in the evaluation of some diseases.

sinoatrial (SA) node Natural pacemaker of the heart. Electrical impulses to stimulate the heart's contraction are initiated here.

sinuses Air-filled cavities within the bones of the forehead and cheeks.

sinusitis Inflammation or infection of the sinuses.

sitz bath A very warm bath, often used to treat painful hemorrhoids and prostatitis.

Sjögren's syndrome A condition characterized by dry mouth and dry eyes. Caused by inflammation in the glands that produce tears and saliva. Other areas of the body that might be involved include the joints, skin, nerves, and small blood vessels. This disease is related to a disturbance in the body's immune system. It may be associated with a more serious connective tissue disorder, such as systemic lupus erythematosus or rheumatoid arthritis.

skeleton Bony framework of the body.

SLE See systemic lupus erythematosus.

sleep paralysis A condition that occurs just before going to sleep or after waking up in which the affected person is unable to move or speak.

slit lamp An instrument used by eye doctors to examine the inner parts of the eye.

social phobia Fear of being in a social situation where one could be scrutinized by others. Public speaking and performance anxiety are two examples. Some people experience extreme anxiety in daily situations—going to a meeting or answering the phone—because they fear what the other person thinks of them and become greatly limited.

social worker A person who evaluates your overall situation and prepares you for return to your home or community. This work may involve arranging home health services and a home assessment or arranging for assisted living or skilled nursing care.

solar lentigo Brown spot on the skin and related to sun exposure.

SPECT scan See single photon emission computed tomography scan.

speech pathologist The person on the rehabilitation team responsible for evaluating and treating speech and swallowing problems.

spider veins Small dilated blood vessels in the skin.

spirometry A test of lung function by which a person blows into a machine and the force of airflow is measured.

spondylolisthesis forward slippage of a vertebra in relation to the one below it.

sprain An injury to the ligaments of an overstressed joint.

sputum Material that is expectorated from the air passages.

squamous cell carcinoma A type of cancer that can be found in the skin, throat, lung, and many other sites.

SSRI See selective serotonin reuptake inhibitors.

stapes One of the three bones (ossicles) of the middle ear.

stasis dermatitis Inflammation and discoloration of the skin of the legs due to vein problems.

statins Drugs used to lower cholesterol.

STD See sexually transmitted disease.

stem cells Precursor, or "parent," cells for red blood cells, white blood cells, and other bone marrow elements.

stent A small scaffolding device used to prevent arteries that have been dilated by angioplasty from blocking up again.

steroids See corticosteroids.

sternum Breastbone.

stethoscope An instrument used by doctors and nurses to listen to the heart, lungs, etc.

Streptococcus pneumoniae A bacterium that can cause infection in the lungs, sinuses, nervous system, and elsewhere. Also called pneumococcus.

stroke A neurological condition that results from damage to brain cells, usually caused by a blockage of a blood vessel in the brain or bleeding into the brain.

stye A tender, red lump on the eyelid.

subdural hematoma A collection of blood between the brain and skull usually caused by head injury.

subgingival plaque Plaque that forms on the root surface within the gingival sulcus.

sundowning Excitability, agitation, and combativeness that may be seen in persons with Alzheimer's disease and other dementias at night.

superficial phlebitis Inflammation of veins just under the skin.

suppressor genes Genes that inhibit the development of cancer.

surgical castration 1. In men, surgical removal of the testes (also known as orchiectomy). 2. In women, surgical removal of the ovaries (also known as oophorectomy).

suture 1. A stitch or the material used to bring two surfaces together. 2. To unite two ends together by sewing.

syncope Fainting.

syndrome of inappropriate ADH (SIADH) secretion A condition resulting from excessive production of antidiuretic hormone by the pituitary gland that leads to water retention and a drop in blood sodium. Predisposing conditions include major surgery, brain and lung disorders, some cancers, and some medications.

synovectomy Surgical removal of the lining of a joint.

synovial joints Location at which two bones covered with cartilage come together and are held in place by flexible ligaments, so that movement can occur. Fluid within the joint allows the bone surfaces to slide over each other with little friction.

synovitis Inflammation of the lining of a joint.

synovium The special lining of the joint that secretes a fluid that lubricates and nourishes the joint surface.

syphilis A sexually transmitted disease that often starts with an ulcer on the genitals called a chancre. The infection can spread to the heart and nervous system.

systemic lupus erythematosus (SLE) A disorder of the immune system that is often associated with skin rashes and arthritis. In severe cases, the kidneys, brain, and other tissues may be involved.

systole Interval while the heart contracts.

systolic blood pressure The higher number recorded when the blood pressure is taken. Correlates with the pressure generated in the arteries when the heart contracts.

T

tachycardia Rapid heart rate.

tardive dyskinesia A condition characterized by involuntary tongue and mouth movements. It may be caused by some antipsychotic drugs.

tarsal tunnel syndrome A condition that produces numbness or burning of the sole of the foot due to compression of a major foot nerve in the ankle region.

temporal arteritis Inflammation of the temporal artery that often leads to tenderness of the scalp and the area in front of the ear. Discomfort may occur when chewing. Urgent treatment with steroids is needed to prevent blindness. Temporal arteritis may be associated with polymyalgia rheumatica.

temporal lobes Part of the sides of the brain. Their functions include memory, language, and emotion.

temporomandibular joint The jaw joint, where the ascending part of the lower jaw joins the underside of the skull.

tendon The tissue that attaches muscle to bone.

tendonitis Inflammation of a tendon usually associated with pain and tenderness.

tennis elbow A tendon inflammation that causes pain and tenderness on the outside of the elbow, usually as a result of strain. This injury can occur from activities other than tennis.

Tensilon test A test for myasthenia gravis in which edrophonium Tensilon is injected into a peripheral vein. A positive test is indicated by improvement in the patient's symptoms.

testosterone The male hormone, produced in greatest quantities by the testes in the male although the adrenal glands or the ovaries in women may produce smaller amounts.

thalamotomy Surgical destruction of the thalamus. It has limited usefulness in treatment of Parkinson's disease.

thalassemia A hereditary disorder of hemoglobin production, predominantly found in African Americans, Southeast Asians, Greeks, and Italians. Most people diagnosed in adult life have only one gene for this disorder, which may cause small red blood cells and be misdiagnosed as iron deficiency anemia. Thalassemia major (Cooley's anemia) is the serious form of this disorder and requires repeated blood transfusions and iron chelation therapy to remove the excess iron deposited as a result of the transfusions.

thermal ablation Destruction of tissue with heat; for example, removal of prostate tissue that impedes urine flow.

thrombocytopenia A low platelet count.

thrombolytic drug A drug which breaks up clots. Often called clot busters.

thrombolytic therapy See thromboylytic drugs.

thrombophlebitis See deep vein thrombosis.

thrombus A blood clot.

thymectomy Surgical removal of the thymus gland. May be done in some patients to treat myasthenia gravis.

thyroid gland A small butterfly-shaped gland at the base of the neck that secretes a hormone that regulates the body's metabolism.

thyroid-stimulating hormone (TSH) The pituitary hormone that stimulates the thyroid gland to produce thyroid hormone.

TIA See transient ischemic attack.

tibia Shinbone.

tic douloureux A condition characterized by severe sharp pains in the jaw in the distribution of the trigeminal nerve. Also called trigeminal neuralgia.

Tietze syndrome A form of costochondritis (inflammation of the chest cartilage) in which a tender swollen area develops over the left fourth or fifth rib.

tinea pedis See athlete's foot.

tinnitus A noise heard in the ears, often ringing, buzzing, or roaring.

TNM classification system A classification scheme for cancers. T refers to the tumor size; N to lymph node involvement; and M to the presence of metastasis (spread of the cancer).

trabecular meshwork Drainage system for the fluid that circulates in the front chamber of the eye.

trachea Windpipe.

tracheostomy A procedure by which a tube is placed surgically in the neck and directly into the windpipe.

transient ischemic attack (TIA) A neurological condition which resembles a stroke but clears within 24 hours. It suggests a high risk for stroke.

transrectal ultrasonography (TRUS) Images of the prostate obtained by inserting an ultrasound probe into the rectum. Its usual purpose is to evaluate the prostate.

transurethral incision of the prostate (TUIP) A surgical technique for relieving bladder outlet obstruction by making small incisions within the inside part of the prostate.

transurethral microwave therapy (TUMT) A technique that uses heat from microwaves to remove tissue from the inside of the prostate in order to relieve symptoms caused by an enlarged prostate.

transurethral needle ablation (TUNA) of the prostate A technique for relief of symptoms of an enlarged prostate, in which heat from radiofrequency waves removes tissue from the inside of the prostate with a catheter device fitted with adjustable needles.

transurethral resection of the prostate (TURP) Surgical removal of the inside part of the prostate in order to relieve the symptoms of an enlarged prostate. The urologist uses a scope to visualize the urethra and prostate bed. Special cutting instruments are used to remove the obstructing prostate tissue.

traveler's diarrhea A common problem among traveler's to certain regions, especially South America, Asia, and Africa. Associated with frequent watery bowel movements.

tremor An involuntary trembling movement, most commonly of the hands. There are several different types of tremor. The most common is essential tremor. Persons with Parkinson's disease often exhibit a coarse tremor while the hands or legs are at rest.

trial denture A preliminary step in the fabrication of a removable denture that is made of wax and helps the patient and dentist judge whether the appearance and other characteristics of the final device will be suitable.

trigeminal neuralgia See tic douloureux.

TSH See thyroid-stimulating hormone.

TUIP See transurethral incision of the prostate.

TUMT See transurethral microwave therapy.

TUNA See transurethral needle ablation of the prostate.

tuning fork A two-pronged instrument that produces a musical note when struck. May be used to evaluate hearing loss, but also used to evaluate vibration sense in persons with peripheral nerve disorders.

TURP See transurethral resection of the prostate.

tympanic membrane Eardrum.

U

uremia Condition associated with symptoms of kidney failure, such as nausea, tiredness, and itching, which may lead eventually to malnutrition, coma, and death.

ureters Small tubes that carry urine from the kidneys to the bladder.

urethra Canal through which urine is transported from the bladder.

urgency A sudden strong desire to urinate.

urgency incontinence A sudden uncontrolled desire to urinate, resulting in involuntary loss of urine.

uroflowmetry Measurement of urinary flow rate.

urologist A surgical specialist in disorders of the urinary tract.

uterus Womb.

uvula Small appendage that hangs down the back of the throat.

uvulopalatopharyngoplasty (UPPP) Surgical removal of the tissue that blocks the back of the throat in persons with obstructive sleep apnea.

V

vagina Tubelike structure that is the sexual receptor organ of the female.

vaginectomy Surgical removal of the vagina.

valvuloplasty Repair of a deformed heart valve either surgically or with a balloon catheter.

varicose vein A dilated vein due to damage of the valves in the vein.

vascular dementia Cognitive decline due to strokes or other disease of the blood vessels to the brain.

vascular endograft A device inserted through the arteries to stabilize a weak area, such as an aortic aneurysm.

vascular graft A material, often synthetic, that is sewn in place to bypass or replace a diseased segment of a blood vessel.

vascular Pertaining to blood vessels.

vasculitis Inflammation of the blood vessels.

vasodepressor reflex A drop in blood pressure and heart rate, often associated with fainting and/or light-headedness.

vasovagal syndrome Fainting due to a drop in blood pressure and/or heart rate usually triggered by emotional stress, prolonged standing, or trauma.

veins Blood vessels that take blood back to the heart.

venogram an x-ray study of the veins using contrast dye to determine if a blood clot is present.

venous thrombosis A blood clot in a vein, most commonly in a leg vein.

ventilation-perfusion scan A nuclear medicine test used in the diagnosis of pulmonary embolism.

ventricles Main pumping chambers of the heart.

ventricular fibrillation A heart rhythm disturbance in which the electrical activity of the ventricles is chaotic and fragmented. If not promptly treated with electrical cardioversion and medications, death will soon result.

ventricular tachycardia A heart rhythm disturbance in which 3 or more beats originating in the ventricles, rather than the atria, occur in a row. It usually points to serious underlying heart disease.

vertebral Pertaining to the bones of the back (vertebra).

vertebroplasty A procedure in which a vertebra (bone in the spine) is reinforced with a cementing material injected through the skin into the bone.

vestibule A small cavity or space at the entrance to a canal. The vestibule of the vagina is the outer entrance to the vagina penetrated by the urethra.

video-assisted thoracoscopic lung biopsy A procedure by which a chest surgeon looks inside the chest cavity and takes biopsies with the assistance of video imaging.

vitreous humor Gelatinous material that fills the inside of the eyeball.

vocational counselor A person who assesses one's ability to return to previous employment. The counselor may arrange for job retraining if necessary.

von Willebrand's disease The most common inherited bleeding disorder. It may be associated with excessive bleeding from surgery or dental extraction, repeated nosebleeds, excessive bruising, and, in women, heavy menstrual periods. It is a hereditary disorder with different subtypes that may affect men and women.

vulva External female genitals comprised of the labia majora, labia minora, mons pubis, clitoris, and the opening of the urethra and vagina.

vulvovaginitis Inflammation or infection of the vulva and vagina.

W

Waldenström's macroglobulinemia A malignant condition associated with elevated plasma cells in the bone marrow and an increase of a large antibody called immunoglobulin M in the blood that makes the blood thicker and more viscous. As a result, dizziness, nosebleeds, tiredness, and visual problems are more common.

watchful waiting Close monitoring by a physician. As opposed to active treatment for a condition, watchful waiting has the purpose of delaying intervention until the disease progresses beyond a preset threshold.

white blood cells Cells that help in the body's defense against infection. Also called a leukocytes.

X

xerosis Dry skin.

xerostomia Perception of a dry mouth. It may be due to inadequate saliva, but it may also be due to a change in the composition of saliva. Many prescription and nonprescription drugs can cause dry mouth.

LEGAL AND FINANCIAL GLOSSARY

LG

A

account plan A qualified retirement plan that establishes a separate account for each employee under which an employer contributes a certain amount each year, but the benefit the employee receives upon death, disability, or retirement is a prorated share of the total amount contributed and the earnings on it. Also called a defined contribution plan.

accounting For settlement matters, a financial report to the beneficiaries (and to the court if there is probate or a registered trust) of the assets and income received; the bills, taxes and expenses paid; partial or full distributions made; and the remaining amount held by the fiduciary.

accumulation annuity An annuity that accumulates value until such time as the payee begins to take payments.

advanced medical directive Any document that gives direction pertaining to a patient's care or removal. Advance directives, health care powers of attorney, health proxies, patient advocates, do not resuscitate orders, no code orders, and living wills are all forms of advanced medical directives.

affidavit of trust A sworn statement usually setting forth the name of the person who made the trust, the serving trustee, that the trust is in effect, and the state law that applies to the trust.

annuitant A person who buys or creates an annuity and whose life expectancy is used to determine what the payee receives.

annuity A series of periodic payments over one's lifetime or a period of years.

annuity beneficiary The person who receives the balance of an annuity after the death of a payee.

annuity plan A type of qualified retirement plan which holds all the money in one fund and which pays employees a predefined benefit upon retirement, disability, and, in some plans, at death.

applicant For Medicaid, a person applying benefits. See also recipient.

assets For Medicaid, resources and income for purposes of computing a period of ineligibility for dispositions without adequate consideration.

B

basis Cost of a capital asset for income tax purposes. The basis is subtracted from the sale price to determine the amount of gain on a sale or transfer subject to income tax.

beneficiary A person designated to receive a benefit from a will, trust, retirement plan pension plan, annuity, or life insurance contract. See also primary beneficiary and contingent beneficiary.

beneficiary designation property Property, such as life insurance proceeds or retirement plan proceeds, that passes to a named beneficiary upon a certain event.

C

cash or deferred arrangement (CODA) plan See 401(k) plan.

cash surrender value The amount of money that a cash value life insurance policy is worth when it is surrendered (sold back or canceled) to the issuing life insurance company.

certificate of trust See affidavit of trust.

certified financial planner™ (CFP®) A person who has met the professional standards and has agreed to adhere to the principles of integrity, objectivity, competence, fairness, confidentiality, professionalism, and diligence when dealing with clients as required by the Certified Financial Planner Board of Standards.

certified public accountant (CPA) A person who has completed a program of study in accounting at a college or university, passed the Uniform CPA Examination, and, in most states, reached a certain amount of professional work experience in public accounting.

CFP® See certified financial planner™.

COLA See cost-of-living adjustment.

community property Property that is presumed to belong to a husband and wife even if held in one or the other's name. Only ten states allow this type of ownership.

community spouse (CS) For Medicaid, the at-home spouse of an institutionalized spouse. A spouse residing in an assisted living facility, but not receiving his or her own Medicaid benefits, is still considered a community spouse.

community spouse resource allowance (CSRA) The amount of resources allowed to be retained by a community spouse without affecting the Medicaid eligibility of the institutionalized spouse.

company risk The risk associated with investing in an individual company.

comprehensive long-term care insurance policy A long-term care policy that covers the full spectrum of care and services currently available.

conservator A court-appointed person who manages the financial and business affairs of a legally incapacitated person, such as depositing funds, paying bills, making investment decisions, and so forth.

consumer price index (CPI) An index issued by the U.S Department of Labor Statistics that reflects how the cost of various goods and services have changed since the years 1982 through 1984.

contingent beneficiary A beneficiary that receives property if the primary beneficiary dies.

cost-of-living adjustment (COLA) Inflation-adjusted increase for Social Security benefits.

CPA See certified public accountant.

CPI See consumer price index.

D

deductible IRA An IRA for which contributions are deductible, earnings are tax-deferred, and income taxes are paid when money is distributed.

defined benefit plan See annuity plan.

defined contribution plan See account plan.

designated beneficiary A beneficiary (of a retirement plan) that is an individual or a certain type of trust.

disclaimer The written unqualified and irrevocable refusal to accept an interest in property. To be useful, a disclaimer may have to meet the requirements of state law, as well as the separate requirements of the Internal Revenue Code.

do not resuscitate (DNR) order A physician order in a health care facility, which tells the medical staff that if the patient goes into life-threatening distress, the staff is not to try to resuscitate the patient. However, in at least one state, a do not resuscitate order may be made by an individual to apply to emergency personnel acting outside a health care facility. A do not resuscitate order is sometimes called a no code order.

durable power of attorney (DPA) A delegation of power of one person (principal) to another person (agent) authorizing the agent to act on the principal's behalf; the delegation of power continues even if the principal becomes disabled. The delegation of power ends when the death of the principal is known.

durable power of attorney for health care (DPAHC) A document which allows a person, even if disabled, to control his or her health care by putting health care instructions in writing and by designating a surrogate decision maker (agent) to make health care decisions in the event the disabled person cannot.

E

efficient frontier The greatest return an investor can receive from a portfolio given the risk the investor is willing to accept. See also modern portfolio theory.

employee stock ownership plan (ESOP) A stock bonus plan that is mandated to invest primarily in the stock of the employer.

employer stock option plan A fringe benefit (sponsored by an employer) that grants some employees an option to purchase the employer's stock in the future at a predetermined price.

equity-based life insurance See indexed life insurance.

ESOP See employee stock ownership plan.

estate planning Thoughtful, deliberate process to ensure that you and the ones you love, as well as your property, are insulated as much as is legally possible from the uncertainties of a complex society.

estate tax A tax on the transfer of a person's assets at the death of that person.

expected rate of return The annual return expected from an investment portfolio given the risk an investor is willing to take.

F

fee simple Full and outright ownership of property.

fiduciary A person who manages the assets of another for the benefit of persons, at least one of whom is not the fiduciary. A fiduciary is held to a high standard of care because of the special duty of trust that the fiduciary holds.

financial wealth The sum of the assets a person owns and how those assets are titled.

focus investing Holding concentrated positions and betting heavily on those positions.

formulary List of prescription medications generally covered under a pharmacy benefit plan and subject to applicable limits and conditions usually set forth in a health insurance policy or prescription drug policy.

401(k) plan A profit sharing plan with the added feature of allowing employees to set aside some of their compensation on a pretax basis.

403(b) plan A nonqualified deferred compensation plan which is limited to employees of public educational systems, employees of tax-exempt charitable organizations, self-employed ministers, and employees of Indian tribal governments and which allows investments in annuities and some mutual funds.

457 plan A nonqualified deferred compensation retirement plan for state and local governmental agencies and tax-exempt organizations.

fundamental analysis Thorough knowledge of a company's current and potential cash flow, management plan, products, assets, and liabilities.

G

guardian A court-appointed person who makes decisions pertaining to the personal matters of a legally incapacitated person. See also conservator.

H

health care agent See patient advocate designation.

health care power of attorney A durable power of attorney in which the maker appoints someone to make health care decisions on the maker's behalf.

heir An individual who will receive the estate and property of a person upon that person's death.

I

income For Medicaid, value—such as cash payments, wages, in-kind items, inheritances, rents, dividends, interest, and pension payments—received on a monthly or otherwise periodic basis, received between the first and last day of a month.

indexed life insurance A form of universal life insurance that is indexed to the general account earnings of the life insurance company. Also known as equity-based life insurance.

individual retirement account (IRA) A personal retirement account established by federal law. An IRA can be deductible, non-deductible, or a Roth.

inheritance tax A tax on the receipt of assets from the estate of a deceased person.

institutionalized spouse (IS) For Medicaid, a spouse who is in a nursing home. See also community spouse.

intestacy State-mandated distribution of assets of a person who dies without a valid will.

intrinsic value The value of a company that is derived from fundamental analysis, which may be different from the value of its stock in the marketplace.

investment policy statement A document that sets forth an investor's time horizon, expected rate of return, disbursements and contributions which will be made over the time horizon, and risk tolerance.

IRA See individual retirement account.

J

joint annuity An annuity that pays during the lives of two people.

joint tenancy with right of survivorship Property owned by two or more people in which each joint tenant owns 100% of the asset and which passes by law to the surviving joint tenants on the death of a joint tenant.

L

life annuity An annuity that pays during the life of the annuitant.

life annuity with period certain An annuity that pays for a fixed number of years or life, if longer.

life insurance A legal contract (policy) issued by an insurer that guarantees to pay a certain amount of money (death benefit) to a specified person or entity (beneficiary) when the insured dies.

life settlement The purchase of an existing life insurance policy that is no longer wanted or needed for more than the policy's current cash surrender value. See also viatical settlement.

living will A document giving instructions that, in specific circumstances, the maker, if unable to communicate his or her desires, does not want certain measures taken to prolong his or her life.

long-term care A form of health care that encompasses services directed at chronic, long-term conditions usually associated with long-lasting diseases, disabilities, and the infirmities of aging.

long-term care insurance A comprehensive form of individual health insurance that covers long-term care expenses to maintain independence, choice, and economic well-being.

look-back date The date on which the application for Medicaid is filed after a period of long-term care institutionalization of the applicant.

look-back period The period preceding a person's application for Medicaid (beginning at the look-back date and extending back 36 or 60 months). The person's financial records are subject to examination to determine eligibility for Medicaid. The look back is for transfer to individuals in the last 36 months and for transfer to trusts in the last 60 months.

M

market risk The general risk of investing in the financial markets.

maturity date The date mandatory payments are made from an annuity.

Medicaid Federal health insurance that is available to certain low-income individuals and families who fit into an eligibility group as defined by federal and state law.

Medicare The federal health insurance program for elderly persons, usually 65 years and older. Medicare is a safety net of health care coverage for qualifying individuals. It has two parts: A and B. Part A is hospital insurance protection. Part B, which is medical insurance, covers physicians' services, outpatient hospital care, physical therapy, diagnostic tests, and other services.

minimum monthly maintenance needs allowance (MMMNA) For Medicaid, the amount of income a community spouse may retain each month for his or her own living expenses.

modern portfolio theory A theory by which an investor seeks a diversified portfolio of investments to have the most return for the risk he or she is willing to incur. See also efficient frontier.

money purchase pension plan An account plan that requires annual mandatory contributions by an employer that are tied to a formula based on something other than profits.

Monte Carlo simulation A calculation of all the potential outcomes for a particular portfolio in a given year or years to estimate the probability of exceeding various target rates of return.

mortality table A table (created by an insurance company) that predicts the chances of a person's death in any given year.

N

no code order See do not resuscitate order.

nondeductible IRA An IRA in which contributions are not deductible and earnings are tax-deferred. Upon withdrawal, only the earnings are subject to income taxation.

nonqualified retirement plan A plan established by an employer, usually for executives or highly compensated employees, whereby the employer promises to pay income at a future date. The amount owed is not tax-deductible by the employer until paid, at which time the employee must pay income taxes on the amounts received.

P

patient advocate designation A written designation (made when a person is competent) meeting the requirements of state law and naming someone to make medical decisions for the person when that person cannot make his or her own decisions. Also called a health care agent.

payee Person who receives periodic payments from an annuity.

pension plan See annuity plan.

period certain annuity An annuity that pays for a period of time.

personal wealth The sum of a person's experience, knowledge, and thoughts.

pour-over will A will that directs property subject to the probate process to the will maker's trust; these assets pour over from probate to a trust.

primary beneficiary A beneficiary who is first in line to receive property.

probate An administrative process to ensure that a deceased person's will is valid, debts are paid, and property is properly distributed.

profit sharing plan An account plan in which an employer can make discretionary contributions for the benefit of all eligible employees based on a percentage of their compensation.

prudent investor rule In some states, the standard by which a fiduciary is judged in the performance of his or her duties. The fiduciary must, in effect, act in the same manner as a professional fiduciary would act under similar circumstances. See also fiduciary.

Q

qualified retirement plan An employer-sponsored retirement plan for which contributions by the employer are tax-deductible, earnings grow tax-deferred, and the employee pays income taxes when funds are withdrawn.

R

rating service Company that regularly evaluates insurance companies as to their financial strength and longevity.

reasonable person standard In some states, the standard by which a fiduciary is judged in the performance of his or her duties. The fiduciary must act in the same manner as a reasonably prudent person would act under similar circumstances. See also fiduciary.

recipient For Medicaid, person receiving benefits. See also applicant.

required minimum distribution For an IRA or a qualified retirement plan, the amount that must be withdrawn in each calendar year in which a distribution is required.

resources For Medicaid, assets of an individual or family as of the first day of any calendar month, or as of the date of application if not counted as income for the month of application.

retirement income pool All the sources of a person's retirement income.

retirement time horizon The length of time a person will live.

revocable living trust A trust that allows its maker to change its terms, revoke it, and freely transfer assets held in the trust. See also trust.

riders Options that can be added to an insurance policy and that could affect the premium.

Roth IRA An IRA for which contributions are not deductible, the earnings grow tax-deferred, and withdrawals may be entirely tax-free.

S

savings incentive match plan for employees (SIMPLE) 401(k) plan A 401(k) plan for employers with 100 or fewer employees.

savings incentive match plan for employees (SIMPLE) IRA A type of simplified 401(k) plan that allows small employers to set up IRA accounts for employees and to make mandatory contributions.

second-to-die life insurance policy A policy that covers two lives, paying a death benefit only after both insureds have died.

secondary guarantees An insurance company guarantee that the face amount of a universal life insurance policy would not require additional premiums.

SEP IRA See simplified employee pension plan.

simplified employee pension (SEP) plan An account plan under which an employer makes a contribution to an IRA for each eligible employee, except that the contribution limits are higher than in an IRA set up directly by an individual. Employer contributions are optional, unlike a SIMPLE IRA.

snapshot date For Medicaid, the first date on which an applicant was admitted to a health care facility for 30 continuous days and who then applies for benefits.

Social Security A program of the federal government that provides retirement, disability, and survivor benefits, as well as Medicare and supplemental security income benefits.

social wealth The sum of those people or causes that a person cares about.

stock bonus plan A profit sharing plan in which the employer is authorized, but not required, to invest in its own securities.

successor trustee A trustee who takes over administration of a trust if another trustee can no longer serve.

suitable portfolio A portfolio that meets an investor's particular needs and risk tolerance.

surrender charges The amount an insurer assesses for excess withdrawals from an annuity or early termination of an annuity.

survivor life insurance policy See second-to-die life insurance policy.

T

target rate of return The before-tax assumption for the return on investment which is utilized to model annual cash flows throughout a retirement time horizon.

tax-deferred annuity The ability of assets held in annuity to grow free from income tax until paid out.

tax-qualified long-term care policy A form of long-term care insurance policy for which the premiums can be itemized or deducted and for which benefits are not subject to federal income taxes.

tenancy by the entirety Almost identical to joint tenancy with right of survivorship but limited to married couples.

tenancy in common Property that has two or more owners, each owning an equal share in the property, although the percentage of ownership can be changed by agreement.

term life insurance A policy that is beneficial for a specific period of time, with minimal cash value.

title The way in which assets are owned.

trust Generally, a written set of instructions by a trust maker that appoints a trustee or trustees to administer property held in the name of the trustees for the benefit of the trust's beneficiaries.

trust maker One who establishes a trust. Sometimes called a grantor, trustor, or settler.

trustee A person who manages the assets held in a trust according to the instructions in the trust. A trustee is a fiduciary.

U

underwriting An insurance company's process of assessing risk to determine an applicant's eligibility and premium for insurance.

universal life insurance A cash-value-building policy that provides flexibility by giving the policy owner the ability to set and vary premium levels, payment schedules, and death benefits, within certain limits.

variable life insurance A type of universal life insurance that allows the cash value to be invested in a separate account at the policy owner's direction.

V

vesting In a qualified plan, the time by which an employee is entitled to part or all of his or her benefits.

viatical settlement The sale of an insurance policy by a terminally ill insured for a percentage of the death benefit. See also life settlements.

W

whole life insurance A policy having fixed annual premiums, a cash buildup, and a guaranteed death benefit for the insured's entire life. Sometimes called ordinary life, straight life, or permanent insurance.

will A formal set of instructions that control property at the death of its maker. The legal validity of a will is ascertained in the probate process. See also probate.

will maker One who establishes a will. Also known as a testator (if male) or testratrix (if female).

INDEX

A

A1C blood test, 199, 480

Abarelix, 236

Abdominal aortic aneurysm, 146

Abdominal pain, 164–166, 172, 176

Abdominoplasty, 732–733

Abscess, 513, 523

Abuse. *See* Elder abuse

Accumulation annuities, 1009–1017

ACE inhibitors. *See* Angiotensin-converting enzyme (ACE) inhibitors

Acetaminophen, 193, 360–362, 709
  liver injury, 174
    osteoarthritis, 299, 311, 413

Acetazolamide, 745, 755

Acetylcholine, 503, 606

Achilles tendon, 347–348, 408

Acid retention, 198

Acne, 12, 18, 50

Acquired immune deficiency syndrome (AIDS), 257, 524

Acromegaly, 97, 453, 455–456

Actonel, 301, 302, 313, 366, 445

Actos, 481

Acupuncture, 770

Acute adrenal insufficiency, 313

Acute coronary syndrome (ACS), 113

Acute kidney failure, 192–195

Acute myelogenous leukemia (AML), 541

Acute myocardial infarction, 115–119

Acute nonlymphocytic leukemia (ANLL), 541

Acute sinusitis, 55

Acute urinary retention (AUR), 212

Acyclovir, 76

Adalat, 124, 305, 745

Adalimumab, 315

Adderall, 757

Addiction, 360–361

Addison's disease, 472

Adenocarcinoma, 79, 177, 283

Adenoids, 97

Adenoma, 79, 453

Adenomyosis, 285

Adhesions, 372

Adjusted gross income (AGI), 970

Adjuvant therapy, 560

Adipocyte defect, 476

Adrenal glands, 361, 456, 471–476

Adrenal nodular hyperplasia, 474

Adrenaline, 361, 483, 550

Adrenergic stimulants, 262

Adrenocorticotropin (ACTH), 452–453, 456–457, 472, 474

Adriamycin, 100

Adult acne, 12, 18, 50

Adult day care, 838

Adult-onset diabetes, 195

Advanced care directive, 206, 790, 793–794

Adverse drug reactions (ADRs), 717–724
  See also Drug therapy

Advil, 193, 412, 709, 795–796

Aerobic exercise, 649
   cardiovascular disease, 126
   hypertension, 130
   peripheral arterial disease, 145
Afrin, 741
Age spots, 9, 17
Age-Related Eye Diseases Study (AREDS), 26
Aggrenox, 150
Agnogenic myeloid metaplasia (AMM), 542
Agnosia, 613-614
Agoraphobia, 582
Agranulocytosis, 464
AIDS, 257, 524
Air quality index (AQI), 92-93
Air travel, 740-744
Albuterol, 93
Alcohol
   abuse of, 620-625, 815-816
   bone loss, 443
   and dementia, 611
   and driving, 739
   erectile dysfunction (ED), 245
   female sexual dysfunction (FSD), 260
   and hypertension, 130
   liver disease, 173-175
   stomach injury, 163
Aldactone, 121, 198
Aldosterone, 471-472
Alendronate, 301, 302, 366, 445
Aleve, 8, 412, 795-796
Alfuzosin, 216
Alkaline phosphatase, 301
Alkylating agents, 543
Allegra, 54
Allergic contact reaction, 12-13
Allergic rhinitis, 53-54, 91
Allograft, 375
Allopurinol, 300
Alpha-1 antitrypsin deficiency, 175
Alpha-adrenergic blockers, 215-216
Alpha-antagonists, 262
Alpha-reductase inhibitors, 215-216
Alprazolam, 584, 593
Alprostadil, 250
Altace, 131
Altered fractionation, 562

Alternative medicine, 764-772
   acupuncture, 770
   cancer treatment, 770-771
   chiropractic, 769-770
   nonprescription and herbal medication, 597-598, 724, 767-769
Altitude adjustments, 740-741, 744-745
Alveolar bone, 61
Alveoli, 88-89
Alzheimer's disease, 947
   and assisted living facilities, 839
   and behavioral problems, 586-587, 615-617
   and brain changes, 606-607, 609
   and caregiving, 613-617
   diagnosing, 604-605, 609-611
   and sleep disorders, 760
   and smell, 53
   treating, 596, 597, 611-613
   and urinary incontinence, 267
Amantadine, 497, 501, 513
Amaurosis, 149
Ambien, 597
Ambulatory stab avulsion phlebectomy (ASAP), 153
American Urologic Association (AUA)
   symptom score, 212-213
Amifostine, 564
Amikacin, 193
Aminoglycosides, 193
Amitriptyline, 214, 591, 710
Amnesia, 500
Amoxicillin, 13
Amphetamine, 757
Ampicillin, 13
Amputee rehabilitation, 676-681
   acute care, 677-678
   phantom limb, 680
   and prosthesis, 677, 678-679
   stump conditioning and care, 678-679
   and wheelchairs, 680
Amsler grid, 27
Amyloid mutation, 606-607
Amyloidosis, 122, 196
Anafranil, 591
Anakinra, 315
Analgesics, 360-361
Anaplastic cancer cell, 284
Androderm, 487

AndroGel, 487

Androgen replacement, 261-262, 487

Androgens, 236, 472

Andropause, 484-487

Androstenedione, 249, 472

Anemia, 196-197, 535-539
  bone defects, 326
  of chronic disease, 539
  refractory, 543
  types of, 536

Anergy, 514

Anesthesia, 84

Aneurysms, 146-149, 670

Angina pectoris, 113-115

Angiogram, 143
  coronary, 119
  pulmonary, 102

Angioplasty, 117-119, 145, 151

Angiostatin, 561

Angiotensin II, 472

Angiotensin receptor blockers (ARBs), 29, 193, 200

Angiotensin-converting enzyme (ACE) inhibitors,
    29, 115, 121, 131, 143
  and COX-2 inhibitors, 363
  kidney disease, 193, 199-200
  and lithium, 594
  potassium, 198
  scleroderma, 307

Angle closure glaucoma, 27-28

Angular cheilitis, 76

Ankle, 311
  arthritis, 405-407
  sprain, 409

Ankle/brachial index (ABI), 142

Annuitant, 1010

Annuities, 1007-1027
  accumulation, 1009-1017
  advantages/disadvantages, 1012, 1018
  beneficiaries, 1013-1015
  death benefits, 1074, 1084
  defined, 1008
  employer retirement plans, 972-973
  exchanging, 1015-1016
  life contingency, 1009, 1019
  long-term care, 959-960
  payout, 1017-1025
  single-premium immediate, 959

Annuities (continued)
  and Social Security, 1016-1017
  split-annuity plan, 1023
  state protection, 1012-1013
  surrender charges, 1011
  taxation, 1011-1012, 1021, 1023
  tax-sheltered, 987
  types of, 1009-1010, 1024

Annulus fibrosus, 422

Anosmia, 53

Antabuse, 624

Anterior cervical discectomy, 426

Anterior nosebleed, 55

Antiandrogens, 234, 236

Antiangiogenesis, 561

Antianxiety medications, 583-584, 616

Antiarrhythmic medication, 133

Antibiotics, 364-365
  drug reaction, 13
  nasal infections, 52
  prophylaxis, 522
  sinusitis, 55

Anticoagulation medication, 103, 114, 133-134

Antidepressants, 590-592, 597-598
  for chronic pain, 709-710
  and dementia, 616
  and sleep apnea, 755

Antidiuretic hormone (ADH), 453

Antiestrogen therapy, 561

Antifungal creams, 11

Antihistamines, 54

Anti-inflammatory drugs, 361-364
    cyclooxygenase-2 (COX-2) inhibitors, 305, 312, 363-364, 709
    See also Angiotensin-converting enzyme (ACE) inhibtors;
      Nonsteroidal anti-inflammatory drugs (NSAIDs); Steroids

Antinuclear antibodies (ANA), 303

Antioxidants, 612

Antiphospholipid antibody syndrome, 305

Antipsychotic medications, 594-596, 616-617

Anti-resorptive agents, 365-369

Antisocial personality disorder, 589

Antithrombin III (ATIII), 102, 548

Antithyroid drugs, 464-465

Antivert, 741

Anxiety disorder, 581-584
  and depression, 575
  treating, 583-584, 592-593

Aorta, 146

Aortic balloon valvotomy, 123

Aortic dissection, 123-124

Aortic regurgitation (AR), 123-124

Aortic stenosis, 110, 122-123

Apathetic hyperthyroidism, 464

Aphasia, 613-614, 668-669

Aphthous stomatitis, 77

Apnea, 95-97, 754-755

Apomorphine, 249, 262

Appendicitis, 522-523

Appetite, 630, 797-798

Apraxia, 613-614

Aquaporin, 460

Aqueous humor, 27

Arch collapse, 402-403

Arcus senilis, 23-24

Aredia, 301

Areola, 280

Aricept, 501, 596, 612

Arimidex, 561

Arrhythmias, 132-136

Artane, 497

Arterial blood gas (ABG), 92

Arteries, 107-109, 139-151

    aneurysms, 146-149

    arterial system, 139

    peripheral arterial disease, 140-146

    stroke, 149-151

    temporary arteritis, 302-303

    See also Atherosclerosis

Arteriogram, 143

Arteriovenous malformations, 178

Arthopods, 324

Arthritis, 332

    ankle, 405-407

    drugs for, 311-315

    great toe, 394-395

    and oral health, 66

    osteoarthritis, 296-298, 338, 369-370

    osteophytes, 296, 425, 443

    rheumatoid arthritis, 298-299, 314, 337, 410

    septic, 520

    spondylosis, 427, 433

    stomach injury, 162-163

    of TMJ, 82

    See also Joints; Musculoskeletal disorders

Arthrocentesis, 520

Arthrodesis, 391, 422

Arthroplasty, 378

Arthroscope, 372

Arthrotomy, 378

Artificial tears, 23

Ascites, 174, 193

Aseptic meningitis, 305

Aspiration pneumonia, 512-513

Aspirin, 362, 481, 709

    acute coronary syndrome, 114

    acute kidney failure, 193

    asthma symptoms, 91

    benemid, 300

    bruising, 8

    colon cancer, 182

    and COX-2 inhibitors, 364

    peripheral arterial disease, 144, 150

    platelet function, 547

    and rhinitis, 54

    stomach injury, 162-163

    TMJ pain, 83

Assisted living, 839-840

    long-term care insurance, 952

    and Medicaid, 1056

Assistive devices, 682-686, 834-836

    for bathroom tasks, 834-835

    for memory impairment, 686

    for movement, 683-685

    for preventing falls, 683, 834

    for saving energy, 682-683

    for vision and hearing impairment, 685-686

Astelin, 54

Asthma, 89-91, 94

Asystole, 134

Atchley, Robert, 830

Atenolol, 464

Atherosclerosis, 30, 42, 109, 111-113

    and dementia, 610, 613

    and diabetes, 479-480

    kidney failure, 194, 196

    peripheral arterial disease, 140-146

    vascular occlusive disease, 42

Athlete's foot, 11, 18

Ativan, 593

Atrial fibrillation, 110, 132-134

Atrioventricular (AV) node, 136

Atrophic rhinitis, 54

Atrophic vaginitis, 516

Atrophy, 280, 324, 349

Atrovent, 54, 93

Atypia, 227

Audiogram, 36-37

Audiologist, 35, 658

Audiometry, 38

Auditory nerve, 34

Autoantibodies, 303

Autoimmune disease, 42, 195

Autologous graft, 375

Automatic premium loan, 929

Autonomic nervous system, 259

Avandia, 481

Avascular necrosis, 336, 341, 361

Avodart, 210, 215-217

Avoidant personality disorder, 589

Axillary dissection, 560

Axonal neuropathy, 502

Azathioprine, 313, 504

Azelastine, 54

Azithromycin, 747

Azulfidine, 299

B

Bacitracin, 13

Back. *See* Spine

Backbone, 330

Baclofen, 502

Bacteremia, 523

Bacterial meningitis, 518-519

Bacterial vaginosis, 281

Bactroban, 401

"Bad cholesterol," 112

Baggy eyes, 22-23

Balance exercises, 762

Balloon angioplasty, 145, 151

Barium swallow X-ray, 159, 161

Barotitis, 740-741

Barrett, Norman, 161

Barrett's epithelium, 160-161

Basal cell cancer, 282

Basal ganglia, 495

Basophils, 532

BAT ultrasound system, 563

Beclomethasone, 94

Bedsores, 14, 19, 664, 796-797

Behavior therapy, 599

Belching, 167-169

Belladonna, 495

Belly, muscle, 323-324

Benadryl, 597

Beneficiaries
    death, 1078, 1083, 1085-1086, 1090-1095
    retirement plans, 996-1004

Beneficiary designation property, 867

Benemid, 300

Benign keratosis, 9, 10, 17

Benign prostatic hyperplasia (BPH), 210-221
    laser treatment, 218-219
    and lower urinary tract symptoms (LUTS),
    210-212
    medication, 215-217
    phytotherapy, 214-215
    transurethral microwave therapy (TUMT), 218
    transurethral needle ablation (TUNA), 217-218
    transurethral resection of the prostate (TURP),
    216, 220-221

Benzodiazepines
    and anxiety disorder, 584, 592-593
    and dementia, 587

Bereavement, 802-821
    and caregivers, 809-811
    causes of, 806-812
    and clergy, 829-830
    and depression, 577-578
    and doctor-patient relationship, 829-830
    effects of, 804-806
    healthy, 817-818
    length of, 806, 818
    of others, 818-819
    stages of, 805, 806-809

Beta-blockers
    acute coronary syndrome, 114
    aneurysms, 148
    asthma symptoms, 91
    atrial fibrillation, 134
    congestive heart failure, 121
    hypertension, 130-131
    hyperthyroidism, 464

Bextra, 412-413

Bicalutamide, 236

Bicarbonate, 198

Biceps tendon, 348

Bile salts, 172

Bilevel positive airway pressure (BiPAP), 97

Biliary system, 163

Biliary tract, 523

Bilirubin, 172-173

Biofeedback, 711

Biologic agents, 314-315, 366-368

Bionic ears, 44-45

Bioprosthetic valves, 123

Biopsy, 75

    endometrial, 285

    incisional/excisional, 373-374

    kidney, 195

    lung, 99

    prostate, 226-227

Bipolar disorder, 579-581, 593-594, 597

Bisphosphonates, 366, 445

Bite registration, 72

Bladder muscle dysfunction, 210-212

Blepharitis, 23

Blepharoplasty, 728-729

Blieszner, Rosemary, 826

Blindness. *See* Eye

Blood clot, 113, 133, 533

    and air travel, 742

    coronary thrombosis, 113

    pulmonary embolism, 101-104

    superficial phlebitis, 152

    thrombolytic medication, 103

    thrombolytic therapy, 116-117, 145

Blood pressure, high. *See* Hypertension

Blood pressure, low, 192

Blood pressure medication, 13

Blood sugar. *See* Diabetes

Blood system, 531-551

    anemia, 326, 535-539

    bleeding, 546-549

    bone marrow, 534

    coagulation system, 533, 546-549

    components of, 532-533

    leukemia, 540-541

    lymphomas, 509, 545-546

    multiple myeloma, 544-545

    myelodysplastic disorders, 542-544

    myeloproliferative diseases, 542-543

Blood system *(continued)*

    reticuloendothelial and lymphatic systems, 534-535

    transfusion therapy, 549-550

Blood test

    A1C, 199, 480

    CA-125, 287

Blood thinner, 103, 114, 194

Blood typing, 549

Body clock malfunction, 756-757

Body composition, 629-630

Body mass index, 644

Body water, 629-630

Bone densitometry, 327, 331, 443

Bone necrosis, 336

Bone scan, 230, 328, 330

Bone spurs, 333, 425

Bone-forming agents, 365-369

Bones, 197, 320-322, 326-332

    anemia, 326

    and blood flow, 336, 341

    fractures, 329

    grafting, 375-376

    hyperparathyroidism, 470

    infections, 519-521

    marrow, 321, 503, 534, 544

    osteomyelitis, 329, 332

    osteoporosis, 302, 313, 327, 338

    realignment, 377

    remodeling, 441-442

    See also Musculoskeletal disorders

Bonine, 741

Borderline personality disorder, 589

Borg scale, 762

Bosentan, 307

Botox (botulinum toxin), 9, 665

Botulinum A, 272

Bowel function, 169-171, 260, 797-880

Bow-legged deformity, 333, 385

Brachytherapy, 233-235, 561-562

Bradyarrhythmias, 135-136

Bradycardia, 135-136

Bradykinesia, 494

Brain natriuretic peptide (BNP), 121

Brain tumor, 499

Breast, 280

    chemotherapy/radiation therapy, 560-561

    cosmetic surgery, 731-732

Breast *(continued)*
  mastectomy/lumpectomy, 559-560
  self-examination, 288-290, 555
Breastbone, 519
Breathing problems, 799
Brittle bones, 326
  See also Osteoporosis
Bromocriptine, 454
Bronchial tubes, 88
Bronchioles, 88
Bronchitis, 88-90
Bronchodilators, 93-94
Bruising, 8-9, 17
Bruit, 142, 149
Budesonide, 94
Buffalo hump, 475
Buffet, Warren, 1038
Bunionectomy, 394
Bunionette, 398-399
Bunions, 393-394
Bupivacaine, 511
Bupropion, 579, 591-592
Bupropion hydrochloride, 92
Bursa, 296, 309
Bursitis, 309-310
Buspirone (Buspar), 584, 593
Butterfly rash, 304
Bypass surgery, 119, 123, 146, 671

C

CA-125 blood test, 287
Cabergoline, 454
Cadaver, 375
Calcaneus, 404, 407
Calcitonin, 445
Calcitriol, 468-470, 632
Calcium, 321-322, 444, 632, 637
  calcium receptor, 468
  hypocalcemia, 465
  shoulder problems, 351
  thyroid disorders, 470
  and Vitamin D, 442
  and weight loss, 648
Calcium channel blockers, 134, 305
Calcium pyrophosphate, 301
Call options, 925

Cancer, 553-565
  alternative treatments, 564, 770-771
  bone marrow, 503, 544-545
  brain, 499
  breast, 288-290, 555, 559-561
  cervical, 283-284, 562
  colorectal, 179-182, 555
  and depression, 577
  detection, 555-556
  diagnosis and staging, 557-558
  endometrial, 285-286, 556
  esophageal, 161
  growth of, 554
  local/systemic therapy, 559
  lung, 98-101, 556, 563-564
  nasopharyngeal, 55-56
  oral, 70, 74-75, 79
  ovarian, 286-288
  pain management, 711-712
  pancreatic, 177
  papillary, 467
  prostate, 221-237
  quality-adjusted survival, 563-564
  screening, 555-556
  skin, 14-15, 19, 50-51
  TNM system, 100
  treatment options, 559-564
  vulva/vagina, 281-283
Candida albicans, 73, 281
Candidiasis, 75-76
Cane, 297-298
Canker sores, 77
Capillaries, 326
Capital asset pricing model (CAPM), 1039
Capital gains tax, 904
Capsaicin, 511
Captopril, 13
Carbamazepine, 502, 581
Carbidopa, 495
Carbohydrates, 648-649
Carbon dioxide, 168
Carboplatin, 100
Carcinogens, 554
Carcinoma. *See* Cancer
Carcinoma in situ, 281
Cardiac catheterization, 115, 123
Cardiogenic shock, 118

Cardiomyopathy, 120, 122, 134

Cardiovascular exercise, 649

Cardiovascular rehabilitation, 670-673

Cardiovascular system, 108-111
  See also Heart

Cardioversion, 133

Cardizem, 305

Cardura, 210, 216-217

Caregiving
  and dementia, 586-587, 613-617
  difficulties of, 574, 809-811
  and elder abuse, 844-846
  and end-of-life care, 796
  and pain management, 705-706
  and rehabilitation, 661-663, 673
  See also Family

Caries, 62-63

Carotenes, 182

Carotid artery disease, 149-151

Carotid endarterectomy, 150

Carpal tunnel syndrome, 297, 302, 307, 310-311

Cartia, 305

Cash or deferred arrangement (CODA) plans, 977-980

Casodex, 236

Castration, 236

Cataplexy, 757

Cataract, 24-26

Catch-up contribution, 970

Catheter, 202, 515-516, 523

Catheterization, coronary, 194

Cauda equina syndrome, 423-424

Caverject, 250

Cavernosal blood flow, 262

Celecoxib (Celebrex), 412-413, 709, 796

Celiac disease, 169

Cementum, 61

Centrifuge, 533

Cerebral infarction and hemorrhage, 117, 663

Cerebrovascular accident (CVA), 149
  See also Stroke

Cerebrovascular disease. See Stroke

Certified diabetes educator (CDE), 482

Certified financial planner (CFP), 931

Cerumen, 39

Cervical cancer, 283-284, 562

Cervical disc, 424-426

Cervical myelopathy, 425, 433-434

Cervicitis, 283

Cervix, 194, 279, 283-284, 556

Cetirizine, 54

Charcot, Jean Martin, 495

Charcot's joint, 410

Chartered financial consultant (ChFC), 931

Chartered life underwriter (CLU), 931

Chatters, Linda, 827-828

Cheilectomy, 394-395

Chelation, 144

Chemotherapy, 100, 560-561

Cherry angiomas, 9, 17

Chest pain, 113

Chicken pox virus, 329, 510, 525-526

Chiropractic, 769-770

Chlamydia, 257, 283, 286

Chlordiazepoxide, 593

Chlorpromazine, 596

Cholesteatoma, 40

Cholesterol, 112-113, 126-128, 176
  and diabetes, 481
  kidney disease, 200
  stones, 176

Cholinesterase inhibitors, 587, 612

Chondoprotective agents, 366-369

Chondrocalcinosis, 301

Chondroitin sulfate, 367

Chopoton, John E., 1025

Chordae tendineae, 124

Chronic bronchitis, 90

Chronic kidney failure, 195-196

Chronic lymphocytic leukemia (CLL), 540

Chronic myelogenous leukemia (CML), 542, 554

Chronic myelomonocytic leukemia (CMML), 543

Chronic obstructive pulmonary disease (COPD), 89-95, 511
  and air travel, 742
  medications, 93-94
  types of, 89-91
  See also Lungs

Chronic sinusitis, 55

Chronic venous insufficiency, 152

Cialis, 249

Cigarette smoking
  bone loss, 443
  erectile dysfunction (ED), 245
  female sexual dysfunction (FSD), 260
  hypertension, 130

Cigarette smoking (continued)
  kidney disease, 200
  lung cancer, 98, 101
  nicotine replacement therapy, 92
  oral cancer, 79
  peptic ulcer disease, 162
  pulmonary disease, 90
  wrinkles, 8
Cilia, 93, 511
Cilostazol, 144, 347
Ciprofloxacin (Cipro), 745, 747
Circulatory system, 140
  See also Arteries
Cirrhosis, 173-175, 193
Cisplatin, 100
Civil Service Retirement System (CSRS), 966-967
Clarinex, 54
Claritin, 54
Claudication, 142, 427-428, 479
Claw hand, 307
Clements, Jonathan, 1021
Cliff vesting, 974
Clinical breast examination (CBE), 290
Clinical depression, 812
  See also Depression
Clitoris, 259, 279
Clomipramine, 591
Clonazepam, 755
Clonidine, 54, 262
Clopidogrel, 118, 144, 347
Clorazepate, 593
Clostridium difficile, 522
Clot busters, 116-117
Clotting. See Blood clot
Clozapine (Clozaril), 595
Coagulation factors, 533
Coagulation system, 533, 546-549
Cocaine, 51
Cochlea, 34
Cochlear implants, 44-45
Codeine, 360
Coffee intake, 130
Cognex, 596, 612
Cognitive impairment, 501, 947
Cognitive-behavior therapy, 599
Colchicine, 300
Cold sores, 76-77

Cold temperatures, 745-746
Colitis, 178, 181, 337, 522
Collagen, 306, 327
Colles' fracture, 348
Colonic lavage, 171
Colonoscopy, 181, 183-184
Colorectal cancer, 179-182, 555
Colostomy, 148
Columnar epithelium, 160
Comminuted fracture, 329, 375
Common bile duct, 175-176
Community property, 868
Complete blood count (CBC), 536
Compound fracture, 329
Compression fractures, 329, 435-436, 440-441
Computed tomography (CT) scan, 176, 557, 608
  bones and muscles, 330
  brain tumors, 499
  CT angiogram, 102, 193
  lung cancer, 556
  prostate cancer, 230-231
Comtan, 498
Concerta, 596
Condoms, 257
Conductive hearing loss, 38-40
Condyle, 81-82
Condylomata acuminata, 281
Congenital bicuspid valve, 123
Congestive heart failure (CHF), 102, 110, 119-122, 192
  and air travel, 742
  polyuria, 268
Connective tissue diseases (CTDs), 296, 303-311
Conservatorship, 1070, 1083
Constipation, 169-171, 631, 638, 798
Consumer price index (CPI), 1034
Contact dermatitis, 12-13, 19
Continuous ambulatory peritoneal dialysis (CAPD), 203
Continuous cycling peritoneal dialysis (CCPD), 203
Continuous positive airway pressure (CPAP), 97
Contraception, 257
Contracture, 307, 349
Conversion privilege, 929
Cooley's anemia, 326
Cornea, 23
Corns, 399-400
Coronary angiography, 119
Coronary artery bypass graft (CABG), 119, 123, 671

Coronary artery disease, 108, 112-115

Coronary catheterization, 194

Coronary revascularization, 119

Coronary thrombosis, 113

Corpus striatum, 497

Corticosteroids, 94
> See also Steroids

Corticotropin-releasing hormone (CRH), 472

Cortisol, 313, 456, 471, 474

Cortisone, 361, 379

Cosmetic surgery, 726-735
>> body-contouring, 731-734
>> face and skin, 728-731

Costochondritis, 310

Cost-of-living adjustment (COLA), 966

Coumadin, 103, 237, 347, 548-549
>> drug interactions, 594, 598
>> nosebleeds, 55

Counseling, psychological, 578-579, 590, 598-599
>> and grief, 805-806
>> and pain management, 711
> See also Psychological problems

Covey, Steven, 1047

COX-2 inhibitors, 305, 312, 363-364, 709

Cranial arteritis, 303

Craniotomy, 499

C-reactive protein, 299

Creatinine, 190

Crohn's disease, 181, 337, 539

Crosby, Bing, 860

Crown, dental, 70

Cruciate ligament, 386

Cruises, 744

Crustaceans, 324

Cruz, Humberto, 1021

Cryoablation, 235

Cryotherapy, 28, 235, 657

Cryptogenic peripheral neuropathy, 503

Cryptosporidiosis, 522

CT angiogram, 102, 193

CT scan. See Computed tomography (CT) scan

Curettage, 373

Cushing's disease, 454, 456-457, 474

Cushing's syndrome, 474-476

Cyclooxygenase-2 (COX-2) inhibitors, 305, 312, 363-364, 709

Cyclophosphamide, 100

Cyclosporine, 66, 307, 313

Cyst, 10, 17
>> dermoid, 287
>> ganglion, 403
>> ovarian, 286

Cystic duct, 175-176

Cystitis, 516

Cystometrogram (CMG), 213

Cystoscopy, 214, 268

Cytokine, 298

Cytotoxic T cells, 555

D

Dalmane, 593

Dalteparin, 548

Dandruff, 12, 18

Darvocet, 360

Darvon, 360

Daypro, 412

D-dimer, 102

Deafness. See Hearing loss

Death, 1071-1097
>> annuity benefits, 1074
>> beneficiaries, 1078, 1083, 1085-1086, 1090-1095
>> bills, 1080-1081, 1090
>> body rights, 1071-1072
>> collecting and protecting assets, 1081-1084
>> credit card cancellation, 1082-1083
>> death taxes, 1086
>> federal estate tax, 882-883, 1086-1087, 1090-1091
>> income tax, 1077, 1084-1086, 1091-1092
>> insurance, 1082, 1084
>> pension/retirement benefits, 1074
>> probate, 860-864, 1079
>> record-keeping, 1075-1077
>> Social Security benefits, 1072-1074
>> tissue/organ donation, 1071
>> wills and trusts, 1077-1080, 1085-1091
> See also End-of-life care

Debridement, 371-374, 378-379

Decadron, 474

Decibel (dB), 36

Declomycin, 460

Decubitus ulcer, 665, 796-797

Deep brain stimulation, 493, 498

Deferred compensation plans, 983-984

Degenerative joint disease, 296-298

Degenerative spondylolisthesis, 430-432

Dehydration, 192, 629-630

Dehydroepiandrosterone (DHEA), 249, 261, 472-473

Delirium, 608

Deltasone, 302, 312

Deltoid muscle, 372

Delusions. *See* Psychosis

Demeclocycline, 460

Dementia
    alcoholic, 611
    with behavioral problems, 586-587, 615-617
    caregiving, 613-617
    and cognitive deficits, 613-615
    and delirium, 608
    and depression, 608
    diagnosing, 604-605, 608-611
    frontal-temporal, 587, 610
    with Lewy bodies, 587, 596, 610
    oral health, 66
    Parkinson's, 611
    and sleep disorders, 760
    treating, 596, 597, 611-613, 616-617
    and urinary incontinence, 267
    vascular, 610
    See also Alzheimer's disease

Demerol, 360, 592

Demopressin (DDAVP), 458

Demyelinating neuropathy, 502

Dental amalgam, 70

Dental decay, 62-63, 70
    See also Oral health

Dental floss, 68-69

Dentin, 61

Dentinal tubules, 61

Dentists, 69-71

Dentures, 71-74

Deoxyribonucleic acid (DNA), 538

Depakene, 594

Depakote, 594

Dependent personality disorder, 589

Depo-Medrol, 362

Depression, 575-579
    and alcoholism, 624
    and Alzheimer's disease, 586
    and anxiety disorder, 575

Depression *(continued)*
    and grief, 806, 811, 812-816
    and memory loss, 608
    oral health, 66
    and other illnesses, 577-578
    and rehabilitation, 658-659
    treating, 578-579, 590-592, 597-598
    See also Psychological problems

Dermatitis
    contact, 12-13, 19
    seborrheic, 12, 50, 524

Dermatome, 510

Dermatomyositis, 344

Dermis, 7-8

Dermoid cyst, 287

Desipramine, 591

Desloratadine, 54

Desyrel, 592, 597

Detrol-LA, 273

Detrusor, 210

Dexamethasone, 472, 474, 511

Dextroamphetamine, 757

Diabetes, 476-484
    and air travel, 742
    and amputation, 676
    and atherosclerosis, 479-480
    care team, 482-483
    and cholesterol, 126-128
    costs, 479
    and depression, 577
    diabetic ketoacidosis (DKA), 477
    erectile dysfunction (ED), 244
    eye conditions, 25, 29, 479
    foot care, 143-144, 409-410, 480
    hyperglycemia, 476
    hypoglycemia, 261-262, 483-484
    impaired glucose tolerance (IGT), 477-478
    kidney disease, 195, 199, 479
    medications, 481-482
    nerve disease, 337, 350, 479
    oral health, 66
    risk factors, 478
    treatment, 480-482
    type 1/type 2, 476-477
    urinary incontinence, 267

Diabetic retinopathy, 29

Diagnostic laparoscopy, 286

Dialectical-behavior therapy, 599

Dialysis, 190, 200-205

Diamox, 745, 755

Diaphragm, 88, 160

Diarrhea, 518, 522
   and end-of-life care, 798
   traveler's, 746-747

Diastole, 109

Diazepam, 584

Diet, 626-641
   anemia, 538
   and body composition, 629-630
   calcium, 444
   and cholesterol, 126-127
   colon cancer, 180
   constipation, 170-171
   and diabetes, 480
   and digestion, 630-631
   and end-of-life care, 797-798
   evaluating, 633-634
   and hypertension, 130
   and immune function, 632-633
   intestinal gas, 167, 169
   kidney disease, 199
   menu planning, 637-639
   nutritional guidelines, 634-638, 648
   and obesity, 647-648
   oral health, 65-66
   peripheral arterial disease, 143
   phosphorus, 197
   potassium, 198
   prostate cancer, 223
   vitamin D, 444

Diethylstilbestrol (DES), 237

Diffusion capacity, 92

Digestion, 630-631

Digital rectal exam (DRE), 212, 223-224

Digitek, 121

Digoxin, 121-122, 134

Dihydrotestosterone (DHT), 210, 234

Dilacor, 305

Dilantin, 66

Dilatation and curettage (D&C), 285

Dilated cardiomyopathy, 134

Dilaudid, 360

Diltiazem, 13, 199, 305

Dimenhydrinate, 741

Dimethyl sulfoxide (DMSO), 367-368

Diphenhydramine, 597

Diphtheria, 525

Diphtheria-tetanus booster, 746

Dipyridamole, 347

Disability, 654, 1065-1071
   defining, 875
   durable power of attorney (DPA), 877, 1070
   estate planning, 857, 870-871
   health care powers, 1068-1069, 1071
   health insurance, 1067-1068
   long-term care, 1070-1071
   record-keeping, 1066-1067
   retirement plan distributions, 989
   See also Long-term care options; Rehabilitation

Disc, 421

Disclaimer, 1091

Discogram, 421

Disease-modifying antirheumatoid drugs (DMARDs), 299, 311, 313-314

Disjointed ownership, 866

Disseminated intravascular coagulation (DIC), 548

Disulfiram, 624

Ditropan-XR, 273

Diuretic medications
   dehydration, 192
   hearing loss, 42
   hypertension, 130-131

Diverticular disease, 171-172

Diverticulitis, 172

Dividends, insurance, 929-930

Divorce, 990, 994

Dizziness, 504

Do not resuscitate (DNR) order, 793

Doctor-patient relationship, 774-787
   communication, 777-782, 792
   consultations, 783-784
   end-of-life care, 790-792
   evaluating tests and procedures, 782-783
   in hospitals, 784-785
   initial visit, 778-779
   and religion, 829-830
   understanding medications, 783, 785

Domeboro, 13

Donepezil, 501, 596, 612

Dopamine, 495, 497
   and depression, 577

Dopamine *(continued)*
  and schizophrenia, 586
Doppler, 142
Dorsal column stimulator (DCS), 710
Dosimetry, 233-234
Dostinex, 454
Dowager's hump, 435, 440
Doxazosin, 216
Doxepin, 591
Dramamine, 741
Draw sheet, 797
Driving abilities, 738-740
Drug addiction, 360-361
Drug allergy, 13, 19
Drug therapy, 714-725
  adverse reactions, 717-724
  and aging, 716-717
  disease and drug interactions, 720-722
  and driving, 739
  drug expiration dates, 723
  and end-of-life care, 795-796
  inappropriate, 718-719
  and multiple pharmacies and physicians, 722-724
  and multiple prescriptions, 718-721
  nonprescription and herbal medications, 724
  and pain management, 709-710
  patient noncompliance, 721
  photosensitivity, 745
  and sleep disorders, 758
  and substance abuse, 815-816
Drug-induced lupus, 305
Dry eyes, 23, 79, 308
Dry mouth, 65-66, 78-79, 81, 308
Dry skin, 11-12, 18
Dual X-ray absorptiometry (DXA), 443, 471
Duodenitis, 162
Duodenum, 161
Duplex scan, 142, 149
Durable power of attorney (DPA), 876-877
Dutasteride, 215-216
Dyazide, 594
Dysarthria, 669-670
Dyskinesia, 498
Dysphagia, 159, 668
Dysplasia, 281-284
Dyspnea, 120

E

Ear, anatomy of, 33-34
  See also Hearing loss
Echocardiography, 121, 123, 125, 518
ECT (electroconvulsive therapy), 579, 597
Ectopic pregnancy, 286
Ectropion, 23
Edema, 120
Edex, 250
Effexor, 584, 592, 710
Efficient frontier, 1038-1039
Effusion, joint, 337
Efudex, 282
Egg allergy, 528
Ejection function, 125
Elavil, 214, 591, 710
Eldepryl, 496-497
Elder abuse, 842-849
  exploitation, 846
  indications, 844-847
  neglect, 845-846
  physical and emotional, 845
  reporting, 847, 848
Electrical stimulation, rehabilitative, 657
Electrocardiogram (ECG), 114, 132-133, 135
Electrocautery, 12, 56, 400
Electroconvulsive therapy (ECT), 579, 597
Electromyogram (EMG), 503
Electrophysiology testing (EPS), 135
Embolectomy, 146
Embolism, 140, 146
Embryo, 280
Emergency alert response service (EARS), 835
Emphysema, 89-91, 94
Employee Retirement Income Security
  Act of 1974 (ERISA), 996, 1021
Employee stock ownership plan (ESOP), 983
Enamel, 61
Enbrel, 315
Encephalopathy, 175
Endarterectomy, 145-146, 150
Endocarditis, 29, 123, 517
Endocrine system, 260, 450-487
  adrenal glands, 361, 471-476
  gonads, 484-487
  pancreas, 476-484

Endocrine system *(continued)*
   parathyroid glands, 468–471
   pituitary gland, 451–460
   thyroid gland, 460–468
   See also Diabetes
Endocrinologist, 450–451
End-of-life care, 788–801
   advanced care directives, 206, 790, 793–794
   bowel and urinary problems, 798–799
   and communication, 792
   pain management, 795–796
   payment issues, 792
Endometrial biopsy, 285
Endometrial hyperplasia, 285
Endometriosis, 286
Endometrium, 279, 556
Endoscopic enucleation, 219
Endoscopic retrograde cholangiopancreatography
   (ERCP), 176, 183
Endoscopy, 40, 182–184
Endostatin, 561
Endothelial cells, 306
Endothelium, 112
Endovascular procedures, 145, 148–149
Endurance exercise, 761–762
Enoxaparin, 548
Entacapone, 498
Entropion, 23
Eosinophils, 532
Ephedrine, 262
Epidermal growth factor receptor (EGFR), 561
Epidermis, 7–8
Epidural steroid injection, 428–429
Epigastric area, 165
Epinephrine, 483, 550
Epistaxis, 55–56
Epogen, 539
Equity-indexed life insurance, 925–927
Erectile dysfunction (ED), 243–247
Eros-Clitoral Therapy Device, 262
Erythromycin, 144
Erythropoietin, 196, 202, 539
Esophageal motility test, 159
Esophageal stricture, 307
Esophagitis, 162
Esophagus, 158–161
Esperti, Robert, 931

Essential tremor, 491–492
Estate planning, 855–885
   advisors, 872–873
   cost, 878–880
   disability/incapacity, 857, 870–871, 875
   documentation, 868–869
   durable power of attorney (DPA), 876–877
   federal estate and gift tax, 882–883
   guardian/conservator, 857
   health care power of attorney, 878
   intestacy, 858
   living will, 877–878
   parents, 895
   pour-over will, 876
   probate, 860–864
   property ownership, 865–868
   revocable living trust, 874–876, 880–882
   risk factors, 869–870
   steps in, 864
   title, 865, 1080
   vacation/investment homes, 907
   See also Trusts; Wills
Estate tax, 882–883, 1086–1087, 1090–1092
Estradiol, 260
Estrogen, 280, 459
   benign prostatic hyperplasia, 211
   bone loss, 442, 446
   dry eyes, 23
   osteoporosis, 332
   pulmonary embolism, 102
   and rhinitis, 54
   sexual function, 243
   urinary incontinence, 273
Estrogen replacement therapy (ERT), 261
Etanercept, 315
Etiology, 278
Etoposide, 100
Eulexin, 236
Eustachian tube, 40
Euthanasia, 796
Evista, 445
Executive function impairment, 614–615
Executor, 858
Exelon, 501, 596, 612
Exercise, 636, 760–762
   aerobic, 126, 130, 145, 649
   and diabetes, 480–481

Exercise *(continued)*
  and falls, 694
  and joint disease, 339
  osteoarthritis, 297
  osteoporosis, 445
  programs, 761-762
  and pulmonary disease, 95
  rehabilitation, 358-359
  strength training, 629, 649, 762
  and weight loss, 648-650
Exostoses, 39
Expected rate of return, 1035, 1041
External radiation therapy, 233
Eye, 21-31
  adapting to deficits, 685-686
  aging, 22-24
  anatomy, 21
  cataract, 24-26
  cosmetic surgery, 728-729
  and diabetes, 25, 29, 479
  dryness, 23, 79, 308
  glaucoma, 22, 27-28
  hemianopsia, 667-668
  laser treatment, 26-27, 29
  macular degeneration, 25-27
  retinal detachment, 24, 28
Ezetimibe, 128

F

Facelift, 729-730
Facet joint syndrome, 421
Facet rhizotomy, 421
Facets, 420-421
Facial nerve, 511
Factor V Leiden, 102
Fainting, 122, 136
Fallopian tubes, 279-280, 286-288
Falls, 688-695
  head injuries, 500
  incidence and consequences, 690-691
  osteoporosis, 446
  prevention, 683, 693-696, 834
  risk factors, 691-693
  and stroke, 666, 670
  and urinary incontinence, 266
Familial adenomatous polyposis, 181

Familial hypocalciuric hypercalcemia (FHH), 471
Family
  and bereavement, 809-811
  and elder abuse, 844
  life stages of, 890-892
  and long-term care, 836, 838-839
  and pain management, 705-706
  parents, 887-899
  and rehabilitation, 661-663, 673
  See also Caregiving
Fascia, 376
Fastin, 650
Fat, 648-649
  See also Obesity
Fauchard, Pierre, 64
Febrile reaction, 550
Fecal impaction, 798
Fecal incontinence, 169-171, 260
Federal Employees Retirement System (FERS), 967
Federal estate tax, 882-883, 1086-1087, 1090-1092
Fee simple property, 866
Feeding tube, 797-798
Female sexual function, 255-263
  cigarette smoking, 260
  female sexual dysfunction (FSD), 256-260
  menopause, 257, 259
Femoral artery, 143
Femoral head replacement, 379
Femoral neck, 334-335, 443
Femoral nerve, 420, 423
Femur, 366
Ferritin, 539
Fetus, 280
Fever of unknown origin (FUO), 509
Fexofenadine, 54
Fiber, dietary, 170-171, 638
Fiberoptic bronchoscopy, 99
Fiberoptic endoscope, 159
Fibrates, 143
Fibroadenomas, 288
Fibroids, 194, 259, 285
Fibromyalgia, 302, 710
Fibula, 404
Fiduciary, 881, 1077, 1090
Finasteride, 215-216, 222
Fine-needle aspiration (FNA), 467
Fistula, 201

5-fluorouracil, 282

Fixed bridge, 71

Flagyl, 281

Flatfoot, adult-acquired, 403–405

Flatulence, 167–169

Flavor perception, 80–81, 158

Floaters, 28

Flomax, 210, 216–217

Flow cytometry, 545

Flu vaccine, 513, 527–528

Fludrocortisone, 473

Fluid retention, 197

Flumadine, 513

Flunisolide, 94

Fluorescein angiogram, 27

Fluoride, 68–69

Fluoroquinolone, 516

Fluoxetine, 590

Fluoxymesterone, 487

Fluphenazine, 595, 596

Flurazepam, 593

Flutamide, 236

Fluticasone, 94

Focus investing, 1038

Folate, 637

Folic acid, 314, 536, 538–539

Follicle-stimulating hormone (FSH), 453

Follicular neoplasms, 467

Folliculitis, 52

Folstein Mini-Mental State Examination, 607

Food pyramid, 634–635

Food Stamps, 640

Foot, 392–415

    Achilles tendon, 347–348, 408

    ankle arthritis, 405–407

    ankle sprain/fracture, 409

    bumonette, 398–399

    bunions, 393–394

    corns, 399–401

    and diabetes, 143–144, 409–410, 480

    ganglion cyst, 403

    and gout, 410

    great toe arthritis, 394–395

    metatarsalgia, 396–398

    midfoot collapse, 402–403

    Morton's neuroma, 397–398

    orthotics and custom shoes, 393, 411

Foot (continued)

    plantar fasciitis, 407–408

    posterior tibial tendonitis, 403–405

    and rheumatoid arthritis, 410

    synovitis, 399

    terminology, 392

    warts, 400

Foot drop, 665, 666

Foraminal spinal stenosis, 430

Formoterol, 93

Forssman, Werner, 120

Forteo, 445–446

Fosamax, 301, 302, 313, 366, 445

Fossa, 81–82

401(k) plans, 977–980

403(b) plans, 987–989

457 plans, 985–987

Fractures, bone, 329

Fragmin, 548

Frontal sinusitis, 55

Frontal-temporal dementia, 587, 610

Frostbite, 746

Frozen shoulder, 351

Functional incontinence (FI), 267

Fundamental analysis, 1038

Funerals, 1072

Furuncle, 52

Fusion, spinal, 422

G

Gabapentin, 54, 511, 594

Galactorrhea, 454

Galantamine, 501, 596, 612

Gallbladder, 175–176

Gallop rhythm, 123

Gallstone pancreatitis, 176

Gallstones, 175–176

Gamma globulins, 544

Gamma knife, 563

Ganglion cyst, 403

Ganglions, 310–311

Gangrene, 142

Gas, intestinal, 167–169

Gastritis, 162

Gastroesophageal reflux disease (GERD), 159–161

Gastrointestinal system, 157-187
   abdominal pain, 164-166, 172
   Barrett's epithelium, 160-161
   bleeding, 172, 178-179
   colon cancer, 179-182
   constipation/incontinence, 169-171
   diverticulosis, 171-172
   endoscopy, 182-184
   esophageal cancer, 161
   flatulence/gas, 167-169
   gallstones, 175-176
   gastroesophageal reflux disease (GERD), 159-161
   indigestion, 161-162
   infections, 522-523
   jaundice, 172-173
   liver disease, 173-175, 193, 547
   and nutrition, 630-631
   pancreatic cancer, 177
   peptic ulcer disease, 162-164
Gene therapy, 561
Generalized anxiety disorder, 582
   See also Anxiety disorder
Generation-skipping tax, 1087
Gentamicin, 193
Geodon, 596
Geriatric depression scale, 812-813
Geriatric rehabilitation, 659-661
Gestational diabetes mellitus, 477
Giant cell arteritis, 303
Gift tax, 882-883
Gingiva, 61
Gingival hyperplasia, 67
Gingival sulcus, 63
Gingivitis, 63, 66
Ginkgo biloba, 549, 612
Glaucoma, 22, 27-28, 757
Gleason score, 227, 554
Gleevec, 542, 554
Glioma, 499
Glitazones, 481
Globus pallidus, 498
Glomerulonephritis, 193, 195
Glottis, 511
Glucocorticoids, 471
Glucophage, 481
Glucosamine sulfate, 298, 367
Glucose monitoring, 480

Glucose tolerance test (GTT), 478
Goiter, 461, 463, 467
Golfer's elbow, 309
Gonadotroph adenoma, 454, 457
Gonadotropins, 453
Gonads, 484-487
Gonorrhea, 283, 520
Good cholesterol, 127
Gout, 299-301, 337, 410
Government retirement plans, 965-967
Graduating vesting, 974
Graft, bone, 375-376
Graft, dialysis, 201-202
Graham, Benjamin, 1038
Gram stain, 512
Granulomas, 122
Graves disease, 463-464
Greater trochanter, 309
Grief. *See* Bereavement
Growth hormone (GH), 452, 455, 459
Grunzig, Andreas, 120
Guardianship, 857, 1070, 1083
Guillain-Barré syndrome, 503
Gum diseases, 63-64
Gustatory rhinitis, 53-54
Gynecology, 277-293
   breasts, 288-290
   cervix, 283-284
   female anatomy, 279-281
   ovaries and fallopian tubes, 286-288
   uterus, 284-286
   vulva/vagina, 281-283

H

Halcion, 597
Haldol, 595, 596
Halitosis, 64, 69
Hallucinations, 757
   See also Psychosis
Haloperidol, 595, 596
Hamstring, 347
Hand problems, 296-298, 307
   adapting to, 685
   carpal tunnel syndrome, 297, 302, 307, 310-311
Handbook of Religion and Health, 826-827
Havrix, 526

HDL cholesterol, 127-128

Head injuries, 500-501

Headache, 55

Health care power of attorney, 878, 1068-1069, 1071

Health Insurance Portability and Accountability Act (HIPAA), 947-949, 1069

"Healthy Aging Stop Smoking Program," 92

Hearing loss, 33-47, 658

    adapting to, 686

    cochlear implants, 44-45

    conductive, 38-40

    diagnosis, 34-38

    hearing aids, 43-44

    sensorineural, 38-39, 41-43

Heart, 107-137

    acute myocardial infarction, 115-119

    anatomy, 107-109

    arrhythmias, 132-136

    atherosclerosis, 30, 42, 109, 111-113

    cardiovascular system, 108-111

    cholesterol, 126-128

    conduction system, 111

    congestive heart failure (CHF), 102, 110, 119-122, 192

    coronary artery disease, 108, 112-115

    coronary revascularization, 119

    and falls, 694

    hypertension, 128-132

    infections, 517-518

    and kidney disease, 198

    and sexual function, 245, 248-249, 260

    valvular heart disease, 122-126

Heart attack, 115-119, 479-480, 670-673

Heart block, 136

Heart disease, 108, 112-115

    and dementia, 610, 613

    and depression, 577

Heart murmur, 123

Heart Outcomes Prevention Evaluation (HOPE), 131

Heartburn, 159-161, 307

Heat exhaustion and heat stroke, 745

Heberden's nodes, 296

Heel, 407-408

Helicobacter pylori, 162-163

Hematocrit, 536

Hematologist, 532

Hematoma, 347, 519, 547

Hemianopsia, 667-668

Hemipelvectomy, 676

Hemiplegia, 663, 670, 675-676

Hemochromatosis, 122, 175, 301

Hemodialysis, 190, 201-202, 306

Hemoglobin, 532, 535-536

Hemoglobin A1C, 199, 480

Hemolysis, 173

Hemolytic reaction, 550

Hemophilia, 546-547

Hemophilus, 281

Hemophilus influenzae, 519

Hemorrhage, 192

Henry VIII, 863

Heparin, 103, 114, 548

Hepatitis, 173-174, 193, 526

Herbal medication, 597-598, 767-769

    and drug interaction, 724

    for obesity, 650

    See also Alternative medicine

Herceptin, 561

Hereditary nonpolyposis colorectal cancer, 181

Herniated disc, 422-426

Herpes simplex, 76-77, 524

Herpes virus infections, 257

Herpes zoster. See Shingles

Hertz (Hz), 36

Heterotopic ossification, 346

Hiatus hernia, 159-160

High blood pressure. See Hypertension

High-intensity focused ultrasound (HIFU), 219

Hill, Peter, 825

Hip, 297, 334-335

    antiresorptive agents, 365-366

    disarticulation, 676

    fractures, 440, 443

    and hemiplegia, 670, 675-676

    rehabilitation, 673-676

    replacement, 379-384

    and spinal stenosis, 428

Hirsutism, 261

Histrionic personality disorder, 589

HIV infections, 257, 524

Hoarseness, 465

Hodgkin's disease (HD), 545-546

Holmium laser enucleation (HoLEP), 219

Home care, 952

    See also Living at home; Long-term care

Home equity loans, 905

Home health aides, 836–838

Homeostasis, 450

Homocysteine, 637

Hood, Ralph, 825

Hormonal therapy, 561

Hormone replacement therapy (HRT), 261, 284, 291–292, 458–459

Hormones, 450, 452
   See also Endocrine system

Hospice, 205, 791, 792

Hufnagel, Charles, 123

Human immunodeficiency virus (HIV), 257, 524

Human papilloma virus (HPV), 281, 283

Humerus, 330

Humira, 315

Humors, 300

Hunchback, 435

Hyaluronic acid, 368–369

Hydrocephalus, 608

Hydrochlorothiazide, 594

Hydrocodone, 360

Hydrocortisone, 12–13, 458, 472–474

Hydrogen, 168

Hydrogen peroxide, 94

Hydromorphone, 360

Hydrotherapy, 657

Hydroxychloroquine, 299, 313–314

Hymenal membrane, 279

Hypercalcemia, 470–471

Hypercholesterolemia, 112

Hypercortisolism, 474

Hyperglycemia, 476

Hyperlipidemia, 126–128, 481

Hyperparathyroidism, 301, 470–471

Hypersecretion, 453–454

Hypertension
   chronic kidney failure, 196, 198–199
   and heart disease, 120, 128–132
   orthostatic, 129, 216
   peripheral arterial disease, 143
   pulmonary, 29
   and sleep apnea, 96

Hyperthyroidism, 457, 463–466

Hypertrophic cardiomyopathy, 122

Hypertrophy, 324

Hyperviscosity syndrome, 545

Hypoactive sexual desire, 258

Hypocalcemia, 465, 469

Hypochondriac, 165

Hypoglycemia, 261–262, 483–484

Hypogonadism, 484

Hypoparathyroidism, 469–470

Hypopituitarism, 453

Hyposecretion, 454

Hypothalamus, 234, 236, 451–452, 472

Hypothermia, 746

Hypothyroidism, 97, 115, 132, 301, 344, 461–463

Hysterectomy, 259, 282

Hysteroscopy, 285

Hytrin, 210, 215, 217

I

Ibuprofen, 311, 347, 709
   acute kidney failure, 193
   arthritis, 412
   drug allergy, 13
   gastrointestinal system, 162
   TMJ pain, 83

Idiopathic disorder, 502

Idiopathic thrombocytopenic purpura (ITP), 547

Idler, Ellen, 827

Iliac arteries, 146

Imatinib, 542

Imipramine, 214, 591

Immobilization, 358

Immune system, 508, 532
   and diet, 632–633
   immune tolerance, 315

Immunization, 524–528, 746

Immunoglobins, 533–534, 544

Imodium, 747, 798

Impacted fracture, 375

Impaction, fecal, 171

Impaired glucose tolerance (IGT), 477–478

Impedance plethysmography (IPG), 102

Implant, dental, 71

Implantable cardiac defibrillator (ICD), 135, 740, 742

Impotence, 243–244

Imuran, 66, 504

Incision, 371

Income tax, 1077, 1084–1086, 1091–1092

Incontinence, 667
   fecal, 169–171
   overflow, 212, 267
   urinary, 265–275, 799
Incus, 34
Inderal, 464, 493
Indexed life insurance, 925–927
Indigestion, 161–162
Individual retirement plans (IRAs), 967–973
   and annuities, 1009, 1023
   beneficiaries, 996
   contributions/withdrawals, 969–971
   conversions, 971–972
   death benefits, 1075
   distribution options, 992–993
   rollover, 971, 1000, 1075
   Roth, 969–972
   SEP, 981–983
   SIMPLE, 980–981
   types of, 968–969
   See also Retirement plan distributions
Indomethacin, 412
Infarction, 361
Infections, 507–529
   bacteremia, 523
   bone and joint, 519–522
   fever and, 508–509
   gastrointestinal, 522–523
   heart, 517–518
   HIV, 257, 524
   immunization, 524–528
   influenza, 513
   lung, 511–513
   nervous system, 518–519
   nosocomial, 512
   prevention, 746–747
   prostatitis, 516–517
   prosthetic joints, 521–522
   sepsis, 523
   tuberculosis (TB), 513–514
   urinary tract infection (UTI), 514–516, 523
Infectious arthritis, 520
Infectious diarrhea, 522
Infectious hepatitis, 193
Infective endocarditis, 29, 123, 517
Inferior petrosal sinus sampling (IPSS), 457, 475
Inferior vena cava (IVC) filter, 103

Inflammation, 314–315
   See also Musculoskeletal problems
Infliximab, 315
Influenza, 513, 527–528
Inheritance tax, 1086
In-home services, 836–838
Initiated cell, 554
Injection sclerotherapy, 153
Insomnia, 753, 758–759
   See also Sleep disorders
Institutional Care Program, 1056
Insulin, 476, 481
Insulin-dependent diabetes mellitus (IDDM), 477
   See also Diabetes
Insulin-like growth factor (IGF-I), 455
Insurance. *See* Life insurance
Intensity-modulated radiation therapy (IMRT), 233, 563
Intercostal muscles, 88
Intermittent androgen blockade, 237
International Association for Medical Assistance to
Travelers, 743–744
International certificate of vaccination, 744
International normalized ratio (INR), 103, 133
International prostate symptom score (IPSS), 212–213
Interpersonal psychotherapy, 599
Intersocietal Commission on the Accreditation of Vascular
Labs (ICAVL), 142
Interstim, 272
Interstitial laser ablation, 218
Intertrochanteric fracture, 334–335
Interventional radiologist, 103
Intestacy, 858, 1079
Intestinal motility, 631
Intraocular lens, 26
Intraocular pressure, 27
Intravaginal oxybutynin therapy, 273
Intravenous contrast dye, 193
Intravenous (IV) infusion, 192
Intravesical oxybutynin therapy, 273
Intrinsic factor antibody test, 539
Intubation, 122
Investing. *See* Retirement investing
Investment property, 906–907
Iodine, 461, 465
Ipratropium, 54, 93
Iressa, 561
Iris, 23

Iron deficiency anemia, 196-197, 537
Ischemia, myocardial, 113, 120
Ischemic colitis, 178
Islet cells, 482
Isolated systolic hypertension, 129
Isoniazid (INH), 514
Isthmic spondylolisthesis, 430, 432-433

J

Jaipur block, 511
Jaundice, 172-173
Jaw joint, 81-83
Jerky legs, 753, 755
Jet lag, 742-743
Joint life expectancy, 992-996
Joint tenancy property, 866
Joints, 322-323, 332-343
    arthoscopic debridement, 378-379
    avascular necrosis, 336, 341
    bone spurs, 333, 425
    effusions, 521
    and exercise, 339
    foot and ankle, 392-415
    fusion, 391
    hip, 297, 334-335, 365-366, 379-384
    infections, 519-522
    knee, 333, 384-391
    normal functioning, 333-337
    realignment, 377
    steroid injections, 362, 379, 412
    synovial, 322-323
    See also Arthritis; Musculoskeletal disorders

K

Kegel, Arnold, 270
Kegel exercises, 214, 270
Keratosis, 10
Kidneys, 189-207, 631-632
    acute kidney failure, 192-195
    biopsy, 195
    calcium resorption, 468
    and cardiovascular disease, 198
    chronic kidney failure, 195-196
    diabetes, 195, 199, 479
    disease, 190-191, 196-198

Kidneys (continued)
    function, 191-192
    hypertension, 196, 198-199
    hypoparathyroidism, 469-470
    preventive measures, 198-200
    renal replacement therapy, 200-206
    transplant, 190, 204-205, 261
Kidney lupus, 305-306
Killer cells, 553, 555
Kineret, 315
Klebsiella, 512
Klonopin, 755
Knees, 297
    bow-legged/knock-kneed deformity, 333, 385, 387
    prostheses, 387-390
    replacement, 384-391
Knock-knees, 333, 385
Koenig, Harold, 826-827, 828
Krause, Neal, 825-826
Kübler-Ross, Elisabeth, 791
Kyphoplasty, 435-436, 446
Kyphosis, 333, 445

L

Labetalol, 262
Labia majora, 279
Labia minora, 279
Lactase deficiency, 168
Lactation, 280
Lactose intolerance, 631
Lactulose, 798
Lamictal, 502, 594
Lamina, 424
Laminectomy, 429
Lamisil AT, 11
Lamotrigine, 502, 594
Landsteiner, Karl, 549
Language impairment, 613-614
Lanoxin, 121
Laparoscopic cholecystectomy, 176
Laparoscopy, 286
L-arginine, 262
Larson, David, 826-827
Larynx, 88
Laser ablation (EVLT), 153
Laser eye treatment, 26-27, 29

Last Acts Partnership, 794

Lateral epicondylitis, 309

Laxatives, 171

LDL cholesterol, 112-113, 127-128

Lean body mass, 629

Leflunomide, 313

Left ventricular hypertrophy, 109-110

Leg pain, 427

Leg cramps, nocturnal, 755

Leukocyte, 532-533

Leukorrhea, 283

Leukotriene modifiers, 94

Levin, Jeff, 824

Levitra, 249

Levodopa, 495, 497-498, 755

Levothyroxine (L-thyroxine), 458-459, 462

Lewy body dementia, 587, 596, 610

Leydig cell, 234, 236

Librium, 593

Lichen planus, 77-78

Lidocaine, 511

Lidoderm, 511

Life annuity, 1024

Life expectancy, 700

Life expectancy (LE), 700, 1020-1021, 1044

   and life insurance, 919-920

   and retirement planning, 992-996, 998

Life insurance, 868-869, 911-943

   adverse selection, 920

   and annuities, 1016

   beneficiary designation property, 867

   call options, 925-927

   combination long-term care policies, 959

   death benefits, 1082, 1084

   defined, 912

   diversification, 934-936

   first-to-die rider, 930

   indexed life, 925-927

   interest-sensitive, 922

   level premium, 920

   long-term care, 951-959

   makeup provision, 930

   Medicaid exemption, 1057-1058

   mortality tables, 915-917

   multiple life, 928-929

   participating/fixed-premium accumulation, 921

   participation rate, 926-927

Life insurance (continued)

   qualifying for, 932-934

   rating services, 931-932

   reinsurance, 935

   riders/options, 929-930

   secondary guarantees, 923

   survivor/second-to-die, 929-930, 933-934

   and taxation, 904, 913-914, 937

   as tax-free savings plan, 913-914

   term life, 927-928, 930

   types of, 928

   universal life, 922-927, 930

   uses of, 913

   variable life, 924

   viatical settlement, 937

   waiver of premium, 930

   whole life, 920-922

Life settlement, 937-940

Ligaments, 296, 323, 386

Liniments, 368

Liothyronine, 462

Lipoprotein profile, 127

Liposuction, 650, 731-732

Listeria monocytogenes, 519

Lithium, 196, 581, 593-594

Liver disease, 173-175, 193, 476, 547

Liver spots, 9, 17

Living at home, 901-909

   adaptations, 681-686, 834-836

   caretaking, 902

   choosing retirement residence, 834

   companions, 904

   and family members, 903

   financing, 904-906

   in-home services, 836-838

   preventing falls, 693-694, 834

   renting, 903-904

   selling and financing, 907-908

   vacation/investment homes, 906-907

   See also Assistive devices

Living trust, 874-876

Living will, 790, 793, 877-878

Loans, home, 905

Lobules, 280

Lone atrial fibrillation, 132

Long-term care, 945-950

   annuities, 959-960

Long-term care *(continued)*

  assisted living facility, 839-840

  costs, 946, 948, 953, 1054

  defined, 947

  disability, 1070-1071

  living at home, 834-838

  living with family members, 838-839

  Medicare/Medicaid, 949-950, 1054-1055

  nursing facility, 840

  retirement community, 840

  urinary incontinence, 266

Long-term care insurance, 950-959

  benefits, 952-953

  home care, 952

  premiums, 957-958

  purchasing/underwriting, 950-952

  qualifying for, 954-955

  riders/options, 955-957

  tax benefits, 955, 958-959

Loop electrosurgical excision procedure (LEEP), 284

Loperamide, 747, 798

Lopressor, 121, 464

Lorand, Arnold, 824

Loratadine, 54

Lorazepam, 593

Lotrimin, 11

Lovenox, 548

Low back pain, 420-422

Low blood pressure, 192, 523

Low-density lipoprotein (LDL) cholesterol, 112-113, 140-141

Lower urinary tract symptoms (LUTS), 210-212

Ludiomil, 591

Lumbar disc, 422-424

Lumbar puncture, 519

Lumbar spondylosis, 427

Lumbar vertebrae, 422

Lumpectomy, 559

Lung volume reduction surgery (LVRS), 94

Lungs, 87-105

  abscess, 513, 523

  chronic obstructive pulmonary disease, 89-95

  infections, 511-513

  lung cancer, 98-101, 556, 563-564

  obstructive sleep apnea, 95-97

  oxygen use, 94-95

  pulmonary edema, 122

Lungs *(continued)*

  pulmonary embolism, 101-104

  pulmonary function tests, 91-92

  respiratory system, 87-88

  surgery and transplantation, 94, 100-101

Lupron, 236-237

Lupus. *See* Systemic lupus erythematosus (SLE)

Luteinizing hormone (LH), 453

Luteinizing hormone-releasing hormone (LHRH), 234, 236

Lymph nodes, 100, 560

Lymphatic system, 534-535

Lymphocytes, 298, 313, 532

Lymphoid organs, 535

Lymphomas, 509, 545-546

M

McCullough, Michael, 826-827

Macrocytic anemia, 538-539

Macrophage, 112, 141, 298, 535, 542, 555

Macular degeneration, 25-27

Magnetic resonance imaging (MRI), 142-143, 609

  bones, 328, 331

  brain, 454, 499

  hearing loss, 42

  memory loss, 609

  osteoarthritis, 297

  prostate cancer, 230-231

  spinal canal, 434

Major depression. *See* Depression

Malaria, 747

Male sexual function, 241-253

  decline of, 812

  erectile dysfunction (ED), 243-247

  Viagra, 247-249

Malleus, 34

Malnutrition, 344-345

Malunion, 377

Mammography, 290, 555

Mandibular division, 501

Manic depression. *See* Bipolar illness

MAOIs, 591, 592

Maprotiline, 591

Markowitz, Harry, 1038

Marshall, Barry, 163

Massachusetts Male Aging Study, 244

Mastectomy, 559

Master cast, dental, 72

Mastitis, 289

Matching, donor/recipient, 205

Maxilla, 51

Maxillary division, 501

Maxillary sinusitis, 55

Maze procedure, 134

Measles virus, 329

Measures of Religion, 825

Meclizine, 741

Medial malleolus, 403

Median nerve, 310

Mediastinoscopy, 99

Medicaid, 792, 949-950, 1053-1063

    asset transfer, 1059-1060

    community/institutionalized spouse, 1055, 1057-1059

    eligibility, 1055-1058

    estate recovery, 1062

    long-term care, 949-950

    look-back period, 1060

    minimum monthly maintenance needs allowance (MMMNA), 1055, 1059

    terminology, 1055

    and trusts, 1060-1062

Medical Therapy of Prostatic Symptoms (MTOPS), 216-217

Medicare, 1054-1055, 1068

    long-term care, 949

    end-of-life care, 792-793

    in-home services, 838

    while traveling, 743

Medication usage. *See* Drug therapy

Melanoma, 14-15, 19, 56, 282

Melatonin, 742-743

Mellaril, 596

Memory loss, 603-619

    adapting to, 686

    diagnosing, 604-605, 608-611

    and driving, 739

    treating, 596, 597, 611-613, 616-617

    See also Alzheimer's disease; Dementia

Menarche, 280

Menierè's disease, 42

Meninges, 518

Meningioma, 499

Meningitis, 518-519

Meniscus, 378

Menopause, 257, 259, 280-281, 484

Menstruation, 279, 283

Mental illness, 570-602

    adapting to change, 572-574

    anxiety disorder, 581-584

    bipolar disorder, 579-581

    dementia-related, 586-587, 615-617

    depression, 575

    personality disorder, 587-590

    schizophrenia, 584-586

    treating, 578-579, 581, 583-584, 586, 590-599

    See also Psychological problems

Meperidine, 360

Meridia, 650

Mesentery, 165

Mestinon, 504

Metabolism, 476

Metaproterenol, 93

Metastasis, 99, 230, 327, 554

Metatarsal osteotomy, 394

Metatarsalgia, 396-398

Metformin, 481

Methane, 168

Methimazole, 464

Methotrexate, 299, 307, 313-314

Methylphenidate, 501, 596, 757

Methylphenyltetrahydropyridine (MPTP), 496

Methylprednisolone, 94, 362, 474

Methylsulfonal methane (MSM), 367-368

Methyltestosterone, 261, 487

Metoprolol, 464

Metronidazole, 281

Miacalcin, 445

Microcytic anemia, 537-538

Microphlebectomy, 153

Microvascular decompression, 502

Microwave diatherym, 657

Midazolam, 799

Middle ear effusion, 40

Midline granuloma, 56

Miller trust, 1057

Mineral oil, 171

Mineralocorticoids, 471

Minocycline, 313

MiraLax, 798

Mirtazapine, 579, 592

Mitral annulus, 126

Mitral regurgitation, 124–125

Mitral stenosis (MS), 125–126

Mitral valve, 108

Mixed incontinence (MI), 267

Mobic, 412

Modafinil, 757

Mohs' surgery, 51

Moisturizing cream, 12

Molded ankle foot orthosis (MAFO), 405

Mole, 15, 19

Molecular therapy, 561

Money purchase pension plans, 975–976

Monilia, 281

Monoamine oxidase inhibitors (MAOIs), 591, 592

Monoclonal gammopathy, 544

Monosymptomatic rest tremor, 494

Mons pubis, 259, 279

Monte Carlo simulation, 1040–1042

Montelukast, 54

Mood stabilizers, 593–594

    See also Bipolar disorder

Moon facies, 475

Morphine, 360

Mortality tables, 915–917

Mortgages, home, 905–906

Morton's neuroma, 396–398

Motrin, 8, 193, 412, 709, 795–796

Mouth, anatomy of, 59

    See also Oral health

Mouthwash, 69

Movement adaptation, 683–685

Movement impairment, 613–614

MRI. *See* Magnetic resonance imaging (MRI)

Mucinous saliva, 78

Mucocele, 79

Mucomyst, 194

Mucosa, 62, 66, 162

Multiple myeloma, 503, 544–545

Mupirocin, 401

Muscles, 323–324, 343–352

    Achilles tendon, 347–348

    biceps/quadriceps tendon, 348

    deltoid, 372

    hypothyroidism, 344

    myositis ossificans, 346

    nerve defects, 349–350

Muscles *(continued)*

    polymyalgia rheumatica, 343–344

    polymyositis/dermatomyositis, 344

    shoulder problems, 350–351

    tennis elbow, 309, 346–347

Musculoskeletal disorders, 295–317, 325–352

    bone diseases, 326–332

    connective tissue diseases (CTDs), 303–309

    gout/pseudogout, 299–301, 337, 410

    joint diseases, 332–343

    medication, 311–315, 359–369

    muscle diseases, 343–352

    osteoarthritis, 296–298, 338, 369–370

    Paget's disease, 301, 329–332, 369–370

    polymyalgia rheumatica (PMR), 302

    rheumatoid arthritis, 298–299, 314, 337, 410

    soft tissue problems, 308–311

    treatment options, 353–359

    See also Orthopedic surgery

Musculoskeletal system, 320–325

Muse, 250

Myasthenia gravis, 503–504

Mycobacterium tuberculosis, 519

Myelin, 502

Myeloblasts, 541

Myelogram, 429

Myeloma, 196

Myelopathy, 425, 433–434

Myocardial infarction (MI), 115–119, 479–480, 670–673

    See also Heart

Myocardial ischemia, 113

Myocarditis, 120

Myofascial pain syndrome, 420

Myositis ossificans, 346

Mysoline, 493

Myxedema, 538

Myxomatous degeneration, 123

N

N-acetylcysteine, 194

Naltrexone, 624

Naprosyn, 193, 412, 795–796

Naproxen, 83, 193, 311, 795–796

Narcissistic personality disorder, 589

Narcolepsy, 757–758

Narcotic analgesics, 360–361

Narrow angle glaucoma, 27-28

Nasal drip, 53-54

Nasal polyps, 55

Nasal septum, 51

Nasal sprays, 54

Nasal vestibulitis, 52

Nasopharyngeal cancer, 55-56

Nasopharyngoscope, 56

National Cholesterol Education Program (NCEP), 126

National Heart, Lung, and Blood Institute (NHLBI), 128

National Surgical Adjuvant Breast Program (NSABP), 559

Natural killer (NK) cells, 555

Navane, 595

Navicular bone, 404

Neck check, 467-468

Neck problems, 425-426, 433

Needle biopsy, 99

Nefazodone, 592

Neglect, 845-846

   See also Elder abuse

Neisseria gonorrhoeae, 520

Neoadjuvant hormonal therapy, 236-237

Neoplasm, 554

Neoral, 307

Nephrocalcinosis, 470

Nephrologist, 191

Nerve block, 796

Nerve conduction studies, 503

Nerve pain, 796

Nervous system, 491-505

   brain tumors, 499

   infections, 518-519

   myasthenia gravis, 503-504

   Parkinson's disease, 494-499

   peripheral neuropathy, 502-503

   tic douloureux, 501-502

   trauma, 499-501

   tremor, 491-494

Neuritic plaques, 606

Neurofibrillary tangles, 606

Neurofibroma, 499

Neurogenic claudication, 427

Neurologist, 492

Neurons, 585

Neurontin, 54, 511, 594

Neuropathic arthropathy, 336

Neuropathy, 477, 479

Neuropathy, peripheral, 409, 502-503, 710

Neurotransmitters, 577

Neutrophils, 532

Niacin, 143

Nicotine replacement therapy, 92

Nifedipine, 66, 124, 305, 745

Nilandron, 236

Nilutamide, 236

Nipple, 280

Nisseria meningitides, 519

Nitric oxide, 259

Nitrogen, 167

Nitroglycerin, 113-114, 118, 248

Nocturia, 211, 266

Nocturnal leg cramps, 755

Noise-induced hearing loss, 43

Nolvadex, 561

Nonallergic rhinitis, 53-54

Noncompliant patients, 721

Non-Hodgkin's lymphoma (NHL), 545-546

Non-insulin-dependent diabetes mellitus (NIDDM), 477

   See also Diabetes

Nonopiates, 709

Nonprescription medication. *See* Herbal medication;
Over-the-counter medication

Non-Q wave myocardial infarction (NQMI), 116

Nonqualified retirement plans, 973, 983-989

   deferred compensation plans, 983-984

   403(b) plans, 987-989

   457 plans, 985-987

   stock option plans, 984-985

Non-small cell carcinoma, 99-100

Nonsteroidal anti-inflammatory drugs (NSAIDs), 362-364

   acute kidney failure, 193, 300

   and Alzheimer's disease, 612-613

   arthritis, 311-312, 405, 412-413

   asthma symptoms, 91

   bruising, 8

   colon cancer, 182

   COX-2 inhibitors, 305, 312, 363-364

   drug reaction, 13

   and end-of-life care, 795-796

   gout, 300

   lupus, 305

   and photosensitivity, 745

   prostatitis, 517

   and rhinitis, 54

Nonsteroidal anti-inflammatory drugs (NSAIDs) *(continued)*
  stomach injury, 162-163
Norepinephrine, 577
Normocytic anemia, 539
Norovirus, 744
Norpramin, 591
Nortriptyline, 591, 710, 758
Norwalk virus, 522
Nose, 49-57
  anatomy of, 49, 51
  infections, 52
  nasal drip, 53-54
  nasopharyngeal cancer, 55-56
  nosebleeds, 55-56
  sinus infection, 55
  skin conditions, 50-51
  smell, 52-53, 630
Nosocomial infections, 512
Novocain, 421
NSAIDs. *See* Nonsteroidal anti-inflammatory
  drugs (NSAIDs)
Nucleus pulposus, 422
Nursing facilities
  costs, 946, 948, 953
  and elder abuse, 847-848
  for long-term care, 840
  Medicaid coverage, 949-950, 1056-1058
  for rehabilitation, 655-656, 662-663
  See also Long-term care
Nutrition. *See* Diet
Nutritional rickets, 327

O

Oat cell carcinoma, 100
Obesity, 463, 642-651
  causes, 644-645
  central, 478
  diet, 647-648
  health problems, 645-646
  medication and surgery, 481, 650
  treatment, 646-650
  See also Diet
Obsessive-compulsive disorder, 582
Obstructive sleep apnea (OSA), 95-97
Occult blood, 181
Occupational therapy, 657-658

Octreotide, 456
Odontoblasts, 61
Olanzapine, 594, 595
Old Age Deferred, 824
Older Americans Act, 639, 836, 845, 858
Olecranon bursitis, 309-310
Olfaction, 52-53, 80-81
Olfactory cells, 53
Olfactory system. See Nose
On Death and Dying, 791
Onassis, Jackie Kennedy, 860
Oncogenes, 554
Oncologist, 288
Oncology, 559
  See also Cancer
Onychomycosis, 11, 18, 400
Open angle glaucoma, 27-28
Open simple subtotal prostatectomy, 221
Ophthalmic division, 502
Ophthalmologist, 22, 511
Opiates, 709
Optic nerve, 25, 27
Optometrist, 22
Oral health, 59-85
  dentists, 69-71
  dentures, 71-74
  diet, 65-66
  dry mouth, 65-66, 78-79, 81, 308
  jaw joint, 81-83
  and medications, 66, 81
  and nutrition, 630
  oral cancer, 70, 74-75, 79
  oral diseases, 75-78
  oral hygiene, 67-69
  salivary gland disorders, 78-79
  taste and smell disorders, 80-81, 630
  teeth and gums, 61-65
Organ donation, 1071-1072
Orgasm, 242, 258
Origin, muscle, 323
Orlistat, 481
Oropharynx, 74
Orthopedic surgery, 296, 320, 370-392
  bone and tendon repair, 374-376
  choosing a doctor, 355-356
  incision and debridement, 371-374
  infection, 364-365

Orthopedic surgery *(continued)*
    joint reconstruction, 378-391
    passive motion, 372-373
    realignment, 377
    risks, 413-415
    surgical release, 376-377
    See also Musculoskeletal disorders
Orthopnea, 120
Orthostatic hypertension, 129, 216
Orthotics, 393, 411
Orthotist, 393
Oseltamivir, 513
Osler, William, 512, 567, 716
Ossicles, 34
Osteitis fibrosa cystica, 470
Osteoarthritis, 296-298, 338, 369-370
    See also Musculoskeletal disorders
Osteoblast, 441
Osteoclast, 441, 468
Osteogenesis imperfecta, 326
Osteolysis, 366
Osteomalacia, 327, 338, 469
Osteomas, 39
Osteomyelitis, 329, 332, 519-520
Osteonecrosis, 336
Osteopath, 769
Osteopenia, 443
Osteophytes, 296, 425, 443
Osteoporosis, 302, 313, 327, 338, 439-447
    bone densitometry, 443
    bone remodeling, 441-442
    hip/vertebral fractures, 440-441
    medications, 445-446
    prevalence and costs, 440
    risk factors, 442-443
    vertebroplasty/kyphoplasty, 435-436, 446
Osteosarcoma, 301
Osteotomy, 377, 394
Otolaryngologist, 35, 51, 56, 658
Otoscope, 35-36
Outpatient rehabilitation clinics, 655
Ovaries, 280, 286-288
Overactive bladder (OAB), 266-267, 272-273
Overflow incontinence (OI), 212, 267
Over-the-counter medication
    and drug interaction, 724
    and sleep disorders, 757

Over-the-counter medication *(continued)*
    See also Herbal medication
Ovulation, 280
Oxandrolone, 487
Oxazepam, 593
Oxcarbazepine, 502
Oxybutynin, 273
Oxygen, 168
Oxygen, supplemental, 94-95
Oxymetazoline, 741

P

Pacemakers, 135-136, 740, 742
Paget's disease, 301, 329-332
Paid-up additions (PUAs), 930
Pain, 83
    abdominal, 164-166, 172, 176
    back, 420
    biopsychosocial treatment model, 701-706
    cancer, 711-712, 795
    causes of, 701-703
    chronic or recurrent, 701
    and end-of-life care, 795-796
    referred, 165
    somatic, 165
    specialists, 707
    treatments, 700, 706-711
    visceral, 165
Palliative care, 712
    for breathing difficulties, 799
    and hospice, 791, 792
Pallidotomy, 498
Palpitation, 121
Pamelor, 591, 710, 758
Pamidronate, 301
Pancreas, 476-484
Pancreatic cancer, 177
Panhypopituitarism, 458
Panic disorder, 582
    See also Anxiety disorder
Pap smear, 281, 284, 291, 556
Papanicolaou, George Nicolas, 291
Papaverine, 250
Papillary cancer, 467
Papillary muscle, 124
Papilloma virus, 400

Paraffin bath, 657

Paranoid personality disorder, 589

Parathyroid glands, 197, 465, 468–471

Parathyroid hormone (PTH), 197, 445–446

Parents, 887–899

   estate planning, 895

   health care, 896

   stages of family life, 890–892

   talking with, 892–894

Parkinson, James, 495

Parkinson's disease, 494–499

   and dementia, 611

   and depression, 577

Parkinson's tremor, 494

Parlodel, 454

Parotid glands, 78

Parotitis, 79

Paroxysmal atrial fibrillation, 132

Paroxysmal nocturnal dyspnea, 120

Partial hypopituitarism, 458

Passive motion, 372–373

Patella, 348

Pathologist, 99

Pathophysiology, 278

Payout annuities, 1017–1025

PC Spes, 237

Pegvisomant, 456

Pelvic floor exercises, 270

Pelvic mass, 286

Penile implant surgery, 251

Penile self-injection therapy, 250

Pension Benefit Guaranty Corporation (PBGC), 974

Pension plans, 974–976, 1074

Pentoxifylline, 144

Peptic ulcer disease, 162–164

Per anserinus bursitis, 309–310

Perennial rhinitis, 53–54

Pericarditis, 200

Perilymph fistula, 42

Perimenopause, 285

Perineum, 226–227, 279

Periodic limb movement disorder, 755

Periodontal ligament, 61

Periodontitis, 63–64, 66

Periodontium, 61

Peripheral arterial disease, 140–146

Peripheral neuropathy (PN) , 409, 502–503, 710

Peripheral vascular disease (PVD), 140, 196

Peristalsis, 158

Peritoneal dialysis (PD), 190, 203–204

Peritonitis, 203

Periumbilical area, 165

Periurethral adenoma, 219

Pernicious anemia, 539

Persantine, 347

Personality disorders, 587–590

Petechiae, 546

Peterson, Renno, 931

Peyronie, François de la, 244

Peyronie's disease, 244

Pge, 262

Phalen's sign, 311

Phantom limb, 680

Pharynx, 158

Phentolamine, 250, 262

Phenytoin, 66

Phlebitis, 152

Phlebotomy, 543

Phobias, 582

Phosphorus, 197

Photocoagulation, 29

PhotoDerm light, 153

Photoselective vaporization of the prostate (PVP), 218–219

Photosensitivity, 745

Physiatrist, 654, 656

Physical therapy

   and chronic pain, 710–711

   and rehabilitation, 656–657

Physician-assisted suicide, 796

Phytotherapy, 214–215

Pica, 537

Pick's disease, 587, 610

Pig valves, 123

Pigment stones, 176

Pinched nerves, 310–311

Pinguecula, 24

Pioglitazone, 481

Pirbuterol, 93

Pituitary gland, 236, 280, 451–460, 472

   acromegaly, 455–456

   Cushing's disease, 456–457

   hormone replacement therapy, 458–459

   and hormones, 452–453

Pituitary gland *(continued)*
   prolactinoma, 454-455
Plantar condylectomy, 396, 398
Plantar fasciitis, 406-408
Plaque
   arterial, 30, 112-113, 140, 149-150, 194
   dental decay, 62
Plaquenil, 299, 305
Plasma, 532
Plasma cells, 533
Plasma exchange, 503
Plastic surgery, 50
Platelets, 144, 150, 533, 547
Plavix, 118, 144, 150, 347, 481
Pletal, 144, 347
Pleural cavity, 88
Pleural friction rub, 102
Pneumococcal pneumonia, 512
Pneumococcal vaccine, 512, 526-527
Pneumonia, 88, 511-512, 520, 526-527
Pneumovax, 512, 527, 746
Podiatrist, 393
Polio, 336
Polyarteritis nodosa, 141
Polycythemia, 261
Polycythemia vera (PV), 542
Polymyalgia rheumatica (PMR) , 30, 302, 343-344, 509
Polymyositis, 344
Polyps, 555
   cervical, 283
   colonic, 180
   nasal, 55
   vulva/vagina, 281
Polypharmacy, 718-721
Polysomnogram, 96
Polyuria, 268
Popliteal arteries, 146
Portfolio theory, 1038-1039
Positron emission tomography (PET), 99, 557-558
Posterior nosebleed, 55-56
Posterior tibial tendon dysfunction, 351-352
Posterior tibial tendonitis, 403-405
Postherpetic neuralgia, 13, 502, 510
Posttraumatic stress disorder, 582
   See also Anxiety disorder
Postvoid residual (PVR), 268
Potassium, 130, 198

Pour-over will, 876
Power of attorney, 876-878
Prednisolone, 94
Prednisone, 8, 94, 302, 312, 413, 472, 510
Premature ventricular complexes (PVCs), 134
Presbycusis, 43
Presbyopia, 24
Present value amount, 915
Pressure sore, 14, 19, 507, 509-510
Pressure ulcer, 665, 796, 796-797
Priapism, 250
Prilosec, 144
Primary thrombocythemia (PT), 542
Primidone, 493
Primogeniture, 863
Probate, 860-864, 1079
   costs, 862-864
Probate
   spouses' rights, 863
   and wills, 859
Probenecid, 300
Procardia, 66, 124, 305, 745
Procrit, 539
Profit sharing plans, 976-977
Progesterone, 280, 755
Progressive supranuclear palsy, 496
Progressive systemic sclerosis (PSS), 307
Prolactin, 452
Prolactinoma, 453-454
Prolapse, 259
Prolixin, 595, 596
Propoxyphene, 360
Propranolol, 464, 493
Propylthiouracil (PTU), 464
Proscar, 210, 215-217, 222
Prostaglandins, 312
Prostate, 194, 209-239
   benign prostatic hyperplasia, 210-221
   erectile dysfunction (ED), 244-245
   hormonal therapy, 561
   prostatism, 210
   prostatitis, 210, 516-517
   prostatodynia, 517
   screening, 555
   urinary/reproductive system, 209
Prostate cancer, 221-237
   biopsy, 226-227

Prostate cancer *(continued)*
  clinical/latent, 222-223
  diet, 223
  digital rectal exam (DRE), 223-224
  Gleason score, 227
  hormonal therapy, 234-237
  pathology and staging, 227-230
  prostatectomy, 219-221, 232-233
  PSA determination, 224-225
  radiation therapy, 233-235, 562
  3D mapping, 226-227
  transrectal ultrasound (TRUS), 225-226
  treatment options, 228-229, 231-233, 235
Prostate Cancer Prevention Trial (PCPT), 222
Prostate intraepithelial neoplasia (PIN), 227
Prostatectomy, 219-221, 232-233
Prostate-specific antigen (PSA) determination, 213, 216, 224-225, 517, 555
Prosthesis, 657
  after amputation, 677
  and hip surgery, 674
  pylon, 678
Prosthetic joint infections, 521-522
Protein, 636-637, 648-649
Protein C, 102
Protein S, 102
Proteoglycans, 296
Proteomics, 224
Protriptyline, 755, 758
Provigil, 757
Prudent investor rule, 881
Pseudoephedrine, 741
Pseudogout, 301
Pseudohypoparathyroidism, 469
Pseudomembranous colitis, 522
Pseudomonas, 512
Psoriasis, 10, 337
Psychodynamic psychotherapy, 599
Psychological problems
  and Alzheimer's disease, 611
  and chronic pain, 702-706, 711
  and driving, 739
  and end-of-life care, 799-800
  and grief, 804-806
  and rehabilitation, 658-659
  and sleep disorders, 757
  See also Mental illness

Psychosis
  and Alzheimer's disease, 586, 608
  and depression, 575
  treating, 594-596, 597
Psychotherapy, 578-579, 590, 598-599
  and pain management, 711
  types of, 599
  See also Counseling, psychological
Pterygium, 24
Puberty, 280
Pulmonary angiogram, 102
Pulmonary disease. *See* Chronic obstructive pulmonary disease (COPD)
Pulmonary edema, 122, 125
Pulmonary embolism, 101-104, 742
Pulmonary function tests, 91-92
Pulmonologist, 99
Pulp, 61
Pulp chamber, 61
Pulse oximeter, 92
Pure tone average (PTA), 38
Purified protein derivative (PPD), 514
Purpura, 8-9, 17, 546
Pyelonephritis, 516
Pyridostigmine, 504
Pyridoxine, 537

Q

QRS complex, 132-133
Quadriceps tendon, 348
Qualified income trust, 1057
Qualified retirement plans, 972-983
  account/annuity plan, 972-973
  annuities, 1009
  beneficiaries, 996
  distribution options, 992-993
  401(k) plans, 977-980
  IRAs, 980-983
  pension plans, 974-976, 981-983
  profit sharing plans, 976-977
  stock plans, 983
  vesting, 974
  See also Retirement plan distributions
Quetiapine, 595
Quinine, 756

R

Radiation therapy, 561–562

Radiculopathy, 423

Radioactive iodine (RAI) ablation, 465

Radioactive iodine uptake study (RAIU), 464

Radiofrequency ablation (VNUS), 153

Radiofrequency facet denervation, 421

Radiologist, 102

Radiotherapy, 101
  See also X-rays

Raloxifene, 445

Ramipril, 131

Ramsey, Janet, 826

Rapid transcranial magnetic stimulation, 597

Rating agencies, financial, 931–932

Raynaud's phenomenon, 305–307

Reasonable person standard, 881

Receptor, 450

Recreation therapist, 659

Red blood cells (RBCs), 532

Referred pain, 165

Reflex sympathetic dystrophy (RSD), 409

Reflux, 159–161

Refractory anemia (RA), 543

Regional ileitis, 539

Registered dietician, 482

Rehabilitation, 652–687
  adaptations and self-help devices, 681–686
  amputee, 676–681
  cardiovascular, 670–673
  and caregivers, 661–663, 673
  defined, 654
  exercise, 358–359
  facilities for, 654–655
  geriatric, 659–661
  goals, 656, 660
  after hip fracture, 673–676
  length of, 660–661
  and physical therapy, 656–657
  specialists for, 655–659
  after stroke, 663–670

Rejection, kidney, 204

Relafen, 412

Relenza, 513

Religion. See Spirituality

Religious epidemiology, 824

Remeron, 579, 592

Remicade, 315

Reminyl, 501, 596, 612

Renal artery stenosis, 193–194

Renal failure, 192–196, 261

Renal replacement therapy (RRT), 200–206

Renin-angiotensin-aldosterone axis, 472

Renova, 8–9

Resectoscope, 220

Respiratory syncytial virus, 512

Respiratory system, 87–88
  See also Lungs

Rest tremor, 494

Restless leg syndrome, 755

Restoril, 597

Restrictive cardiomyopathy, 122

Reticuloendothelial system, 534–535

Retinal detachment, 24, 28

Retinopathy, 477

Retirement adjustment, 805, 834

Retirement communities, 840

Retirement Equity Act of 1984 (REA), 996

Retirement investing, 1029–1051
  capital asset pricing model (CAPM), 1039
  cash flows, 1034–1037, 1045–1046
  and college scholarships, 1031
  company/market risk, 1037–1038
  focus investing, 1038
  fundamental analysis, 1038
  investment policy statements, 1044–1046, 1048–1050
  Monte Carlo simulation, 1040–1042
  portfolio theory, 1038–1039
  principal fluctuation, 1045–1046
  professional advice, 1042–1044
  risk-free rate of return, 1039
  target/expected rate of return, 1035–1036, 1041
  technical analysis, 1039–1040

Retirement plan, 963–1005
  beneficiary designation property, 867
  deferred compensation plans, 983–984
  defined benefit/defined contribution plans, 1036
  employer plans, 972–973
  401(k) plans, 977–980
  403(b) plans, 987–989
  457 plans, 985–987
  government plans, 965–967
  income sources, 964–965

Retirement plan *(continued)*
    IRAs, 967-973, 980-983
    pension plans, 974-976, 981-983
    profit sharing plans, 976-977
    qualified/nonqualified plans, 972-973
    stock plans, 983-985
Retirement plan distributions, 989-1004
    annuity method, 992-993
    beneficiaries, 996-1004
    death benefits, 1074
    determination date, 1002-1003
    first-time home purchase, 990
    5-year rule, 1001
    frequency, 991-992
    life expectancy method, 992-994
    minimum distribution excise tax, 990
    premature distribution excise tax, 989-990
    required minimum distribution, 992
    uniform table, 994-996
Retrograde ejaculation, 148, 216, 218-219
Revascularization, 113
Reverse mortgage, 905-906
ReVia, 624
Revocable living trust, 874-876
    cost, 879
    funding, 880-881
    trustees, 881-882
Rheumatoid arthritis, 298-299, 314, 337, 410
Rheumatoid factor, 298-299
Rheumatology, 296
Rheumatrex, 307
Rhinitis, 53-54, 91
Rhinophyma, 50
Rhinoplasty, 50
Rhizotomy, facet, 421
Rickets, 327, 469
Rimantadine, 513
Risedronate, 301, 366, 445
Risk-free rate of return, 1039
Risperidone (Risperdal), 595
Ritalin, 501, 596, 757
Rivastigmine, 501, 596, 612
Rofecoxib, 709, 796
Root canal, 70-71
Root caries, 63
Rosacea, 12, 18, 50
Rose bengal stain, 308

Rosenbaum Pocket Vision Screener, 22
Rosiglitazone, 481
Rotator cuff, 350-351
Rotavirus, 522
Roth IRA, 969-972
RTMS, 597
Rubefacients, 368
Ruptured disc, 422
Rusk, Howard A., 654

S

Sacroiliac joints, 520
Sacrum, 509
Saddle nose, 51
Salary reduction simplified employee pension (SASEP)
    plan, 982
Salicylic acid, 10
Saliva, 62, 65, 78-79, 81
Salivary stones, 79
Salmeterol, 93
Salmon calcitonin, 445
Salt intake/removal, 130, 191, 197
    See also Kidney
Sandimmune, 307
Sandostatin, 456
Saphenous veins, 151, 153
Sarcoidosis, 122
Sarcoma, 56
Sarna lotion, 13
Savings incentive match plans for employees (SIMPLE),
    979-981
Saw palmetto, 215
Scabies, 13-14
Schilling test, 539
Schirmer's test, 23, 308
Schizoid personality disorder, 589
Schizophrenia, 584-586, 594-597
Sciatica, 420
Scintigraphy, 467
Sclera, 24
Scleroderma, 306-307
Sclerosis, 110
Scoliosis, 333, 430
Seborrheic dermatitis, 12, 50, 524
Seborrheic keratosis, 10
Sedimentation rate, 299

Seizure, 499

Seizure medications, 13, 710

Selective androgen receptor modulators (SARMs), 487

Selective estrogen receptor modulators (SERMs), 445

Selective serotonin reuptake inhibitors (SSRIs), 97, 579, 590-591

Selegiline, 496-497, 612

Self-blood glucose monitoring (SBGM), 480

Self-help devices. *See* Assistive devices

Sella turcica, 451, 454

Sensorineural hearing loss, 38-39, 41-43

Sentinel lymph node, 560

Sepsis, 192, 510, 523

Septic shock, 523

Serax, 593

Seroquel, 595

Serotonin, 577

Serous saliva, 78

Serzone, 592

7 Habits of Highly Effective People, 1047

Sex hormone-binding globulin (SHBG), 486

Sexual function. *See* Female sexual function; Male sexual function

Sexually transmitted diseases (STDs), 257

Sharpe, Bill, 1039

Shingles, 13, 19, 510-511
   and AIDS, 524
   and chicken pox, 329
   postherpetic neuralgia, 502

Shock, 192

Shock treatment, 579, 597

Shoes, 393, 396, 411

Shoulder, 350-351

Shower chair, 683-684

Sibutramine, 481

Sick sinus syndrome, 135-136

Sickle cell anemia, 326, 535

Sideroblastic anemia, 537-538

Sigmoidoscopy, 181, 183-184

Signal-averaged electrocardiography, 135

Sildenafil, 54, 247-249

Silent ischemia, 113

Simple phobia, 582

Simplified employee pension (SEP) plan, 981-983

Sinemet, 495, 755

Sinequan, 591

Singulair, 54

Sinoatrial (SA) node, 134-135

Sinus infection, 55

Sinus rhythm, 133

Sinuses, 88, 534

Sinusitis, 55

Sitz baths, 517

Sjögren's syndrome, 23, 79, 307-308

Skeleton, 320, 324-325
   See also Musculoskeletal disorders

Skin, 7-19, 631-632
   acne, 12
   allergies, 12-13
   athlete's foot, 11
   cancer, 14-15, 19, 50-51
   changes, 8-9
   composition of, 7
   cosmetic surgery for, 728-731
   cysts and warts, 10
   dandruff, 12
   dermatomyositis, 344
   dry, 11-12, 797
   and end-of-life care, 796-797
   fungal infections, 11
   infections, 509-511
   keratoses, 10
   pressure sores, 14, 19, 507, 509-510
   scabies, 13-14
   scleroderma, 306-307
   self-exam, 15
   shingles, 13, 19, 329, 502, 510-511, 524
   tags, 9, 17
   young/aged, 8

Sleep apnea, 95-97, 754-755

Sleep disorders, 750-760
   evaluating, 753-755
   medications, 596-597, 759-760
   and normal sleep, 752-753
   treatment, 754-759
   types of, 753, 757

Slipped disc, 422

Slit lamp, 23

Small cell carcinoma, 100

Smell, sense of, 52-53, 80-81, 158

Smoking. *See* Cigarette smoking

Snellen chart, 22

Snoring, 753

Social phobia, 582

Social Security, 965-966, 1021, 1072-1074

Social worker, 658

Sodium citrate, 198

Sodium intake, 130, 197

Soft tissue problems, 308-311

Solar lentigos, 9, 17

Solu-Medrol, 474

Somatic pain, 165

Somatic treatment, 578

Somatropin, 459

Somavert, 456

Sonata, 597

Spastic muscles, 336, 665

Speech disorders
  aphasia, 668-669
  dysarthria, 669-670

Speech pathologist, 658

Speech therapy, 658

Sphincter, 267

Sphincter of Oddi, 183

Spider veins, 140, 151-155

Spinal cord, 424, 433

Spinal stenosis, 426-430

Spinal tap, 519

Spine, 333, 419-437
  axial/radicular pain, 420, 422
  cervical myelopathy, 433-434
  compression fractures, 435-436, 440-441
  flexion, 427
  herniated cervical/thoracic disc, 424-426
  herniated lumbar disc, 422-424
  low back pain, 420-422
  spinal stenosis, 426-430
  spondylolisthesis, 429-433
  surgical innovations, 429

Spirituality, 823-831
  and grief, 804
  impact on health, 826-828
  measuring, 825-826
  and religion, 824-825
  and resiliency, 826

Spirometry, 91

Spironolactone, 121, 198

Spleen, 542

Spondylolisthesis, 429-430

Spondylosis, 427, 432

Spouses
  as annuity beneficiaries, 1015
  community/institutionalized, 1055, 1057-1059
  forced share, 1087, 1089
  retirement plan distributions, 997, 1000-1002

Sprain, 335

Sprue, 169

Sputum, 90, 556

Squamocolumnar junction, 283

Squamous cell cancer, 79, 282-283

Squamous epithelium, 160

SSRIs, 579, 590-591

Stapes, 34

Staphylococcus aureus, 52, 512, 520

Stasis dermatitis, 152

Statins, 114, 128, 143, 481

Stem cell therapy, 306

Stenosis, 116
  aortic, 110, 122-123
  mitral, 125-126
  renal artery, 193-194

Stent, 145, 219

Sterapred, 302

Stereotactic radiosurgery, 563

Sternum, 88, 124, 519

Steroids, 94, 302, 361-362
  arthritis, 312-313, 405, 412
  bone loss, 443
  bruising, 8
  hearing loss, 41
  hormone deficiency, 454
  injections, 362, 379, 412, 428-429
  lupus, 305
  sprays, 54
  steroid creams, 13

Stethoscope, 102, 142

Stimulants, 596

Stock bonus plans, 983

Stock option plans, 984-985

Stomach, 630

Stool test, 181

Strength training, 629, 649, 762

Streptococcus, 283

Streptococcus pneumonia, 512, 519-520, 526-527

Stress incontinence (SUI), 267, 271

Stretching exercises, 649, 762

Striant, 487

Stripping, 152
Stroke, 66, 132-133
    defined, 663
    and dementia, 613
    and depression, 577
    periodontitis, 64
Stroke rehabilitation, 663-670
    acute stage care, 664-665
    cerebral infarction and hemorrhage, 663
    dysarthria, 669-670
    dysphagia, 668
    foot drop, 665, 666
    goals, 664
    hemianopsia, 667-668
    hemiplagia, 663, 670, 675-676
    incontinence, 667
    muscle weakness and spasm, 664-665
    nursing facility placement, 662-663
    prevention of recurrence, 670
    psychological problems, 668
    speech disorders, 668-670
    transient ischemic attack (TIA), 149, 663
    and walking, 666-667
Subacromial bursitis, 309
Subdural hematoma, 500, 608
Subgingival plaque, 63
Sublingual gland, 78
Submandibular gland, 78
Sudafed, 741
Sugar, 65-66
Suicide, 816-817
    and alcoholism, 624
    and depression, 578
    physician-assisted, 796
    warning signs, 815
Sulfa drugs, 745
Sulfamethoxazole, 516
Sulfasalazine, 299, 313-314
Sulindac, 182
Sun exposure
    cataracts, 25
    dry skin, 11
    nose, 50
    skin cancer, 14-15
    wrinkles, 8
Sundowning, 760
Supplemental oxygen, 94-95

Support groups, 711
Suppressor genes, 554
Suprapubic area, 165
Suture, 376
Swallowing difficulty, 158-159, 668
Symmetrel, 497, 513
Syncope, 122, 136
Syndrome of inappropriate antidiuretic hormone (SIADH), 459-460
Synovectomy, 378
Synovial joints, 298, 322-323
Synovitis, 399
Synovium, 322, 337
Syphilis, 51, 257, 336
Systemic lupus erythematosus (SLE) , 141, 304-306, 337
Systemic scleroderma, 307
Systole, 109

T

T lymphocytes, 298, 313
Tachycardia, 134
Tachycardia-bradycardia syndrome, 136
Tacrine, 596, 612
Tadalafil, 249
Tailbone, 509
Talk therapy. *See* Counseling, psychological
Tamiflu, 513
Tamoxifen, 445, 561
Tamsulosin, 216
Tapazole, 464
Target rate of return, 1035-1036, 1041
Tarsal tunnel syndrome, 311
Taste
    buds, 81
    perception, 80-81, 158, 630
    thresholds, 80
Taxation
    annuities, 1011-1012, 1021, 1023
    capital gains, 904
    death taxes, 1086
    deceased taxpayer, 1077, 1084-1086, 1091-1092
    federal estate tax, 882-883, 1086-1087, 1090-1091
    generation-skipping tax, 1087
    and life insurance, 904, 913-914, 937
    life/viatical settlement, 937
    long-term care insurance, 955, 958-959

Taxation (*continued*)
    retirement plan distributions, 989-990
    and Social Security, 1016-1017
    stock options, 984-985
    trapped income, 1084-1085
Tax-deferred annuities, 1011, 1017
Tax-sheltered annuities (TSAs), 987
Tears, 23
Technetium, 330
Technical analysis, 1039-1040
Teeth, 61-65
    See also Oral health
Tegretol, 502
Temazepam, 597
Temperature, 508-509
Template-guided transperineal saturation biopsy, 226-227
Temporal arteritis, 30, 302-303, 509
Temporomandibular joint (TMJ), 81-83
Tenancy by the entirety, 867
Tenancy in common, 867
Tendinosis, 408
Tendonitis, 309, 404, 408
Tendons, 296, 323-324, 376
Tennis elbow, 309, 346-347
Tenormin, 464
Tensilon test, 504
Terazosin, 215
Terbutaline, 93
Teriparatide, 445-446
Term life insurance, 927-928, 930
Terminal ileum, 183
Terminal illness. *See* End-of-life care
Testator, 858
Testim, 487
Testoderm, 487
Testosterone, 210, 234-236, 459
    andropause, 484-487
    bone loss, 442
    erectile dysfunction (ED), 247
    female sexual dysfunction (FSD), 260
Tetanus, 525
Tetracycline, 745
Thalamotomy, 498
Thalassemia major, 326
Theophylline, 755
Thermal ablation, 217
Thiazide diuretics, 745

Thionamides, 464
Thioridazine, 596
Thiothixene, 595
Third-party beneficiary property, 867
Thoracic disc, 424-426
Thoracic myelopathy, 434
Thoracoscopic lung biopsy, 99
Thoracotomy, 434
Thorazine, 596
Thrombocytopenia, 547
Thromboembolic event. See Blood clot
Thrombolytic drugs, 103
Thrombolytic therapy, 116-117, 145
Thrombus, 113
Thrush, 524
Thymus gland, 504
Thyroid gland, 460-468
Thyroid nodules, 466-468
Thyroid-stimulating hormone (TSH), 453, 457-462
Thyroxine (T4), 460
TIA, 149, 663
    See also Stroke
Tiazac, 305
Tibia, 309
Tic douloureux, 501-502
Tietze syndrome, 310
Tinactin, 11
Tinea pedis, 11
Tinel's sign, 311
Tinnitus, 38
TNM classification system, 100, 230, 557
Tobacco. *See* Cigarette smoking
Toenails
    infection, 400-401
    ingrown, 401-402
Toes
    bunionette, 398-399
    great toe arthritis, 394-395
    hammertoe/claw toe, 395-396
    synovitis, 399
    See also Foot
Tofranil, 214, 591
Tolterodine, 273
Tooth loss, 64-65
    See also Oral health
Toothbrushing, 67-68
Toothpastes, 68

Topamax, 594

Tophi, 300

Topiramate, 594

Toprol, 121, 464

Toxoid, 525

Trabecular meshwork, 27

Tracheostomy, 97

Tracleer, 307

Tramadol, 361

Transdermal oxybutynin therapy, 273

Transdermal scopolamine patches, 741

Transesophageal echocardiogram (TEE), 133-134

Transfusion, blood, 549-550

Transient ischemic attack (TIA), 149, 663

   See also Stroke

Transrectal untrasound (TRUS), 225-226

Transsphenoidal microsurgery, 455

Transurethral incision of the prostate (TUIP), 221

Transurethral microwave therapy (TUMT), 218

Transurethral needle ablation (TUNA), 217-218

Transurethral resection of the prostate (TURP),
   216, 220-221

Transurethral therapy, 250-251

Transurethral vaporization of the prostate, 221

Tranxene, 593

Trauma, 499-501

Traut, Herbert F., 291

Travel, 736-749

   air travel, 740-744

   cruises, 744

   driving, 738-740

   to higher altitudes, 744-745

   and infections, 746-747

   supplies for, 747-748

   and temperature changes, 745-746

Trazodone, 592, 597

Tremor, 491-494

Trental, 144

Triamcinolone, 94

Triazolam, 597

Tricuspid valve, 108, 122

Tricyclic antidepressants, 97, 591

Trigeminal neuralgia, 501-502, 511

Trigger finger, 297, 309

Triglycerides, 127

Trihexyphenidyl, 497

Trileptal, 502

Trimethoprim, 516

Trimethoprim-sulfamethoxazole, 13

Triple arthrodesis, 405

Trochanteric bursitis, 309

Trusts, 983, 1079-1080

   affadavit/certificate of trust, 1080

   as designated beneficiary, 999-1000, 1014-1015

   distributions, 1094-1095

   and federal estate tax, 1087, 1091

   income tax, 1085-1086, 1091

   and Medicaid, 1060-1062

   qualified income, 1057

   successor trustee, 1077-1078

   and wills, 859, 863

   See also Revocable living trust

Tuberculosis (TB), 513-514

Tuberculous pericarditis, 514

Tummy tuck, 732-733

Tumor necrosis factor-alpha (TNF-alpha), 298, 312-313

Tumors

   bone, 327-328

   hearing loss, 42-43

   lung, 91, 98-101

   nasal, 56

   ovarian, 286

   squamous cell, 79

   See also Cancer

Tuning fork, 36

Tunnel vision, 454

Tylenol, 174, 193, 362

   arthritis, 298, 311, 709

   liver injury, 360, 413

Tympanic membrane, 34, 40

U

Ulcer

   oral, 66

   peptic ulcer disease, 162

Ulcerative colitis, 181, 337

Ulpian, 1008

Ultracet, 361

Ultrasound, 102-103, 142, 213

   BAT system, 563

   high-intensity focused ultrasound (HIFU), 219

   rehabilitative treatment, 657

   thyroid, 464, 466-467

   transrectal ultrasound (TRUS), 225-226

Universal life insurance, 922-927, 930

Unstable angina, 113

Updegrave, Walter, 1021-1022

Uremia, 200

Ureters, 194

Urethra, 194, 212, 267, 279

Urge incontinence (UI), 266

Uric acid, 299-301

Urinary incontinence, 265-275

    costs, 266

    and end-of-life care, 799

    and falls, 266

    Kegel exercises, 270

    surgery and medication, 271-273

    types of, 266-267

Urinary tract infection (UTI), 514-516, 523

Urine

    acute urinary retention (AUR), 212

    protein in, 191, 199

    ureter obstruction, 194-195

    voiding problems, 211-212, 268-269

Urodynamics, 271

Uroflowmetry, 213

Uroxatral, 210, 216-217

Uterus, 194, 279, 284-286, 556

Uvula, 97

Uvulopalatopharyngoplasty (UPPP), 97

V

VA QTA, 526

Vaccination, 524-528

Vacation homes, 906-907

Vacuum erection devices (VEDs), 249-250

Vagina, 258-259, 279, 281-283

Vaginectomy, 283

Vaginitis, 516

Vagus nerve stimulation, 597

Valium, 584

Valproic acid, 581, 594

Valvular heart disease, 122-126

Valvular regurgitation, 110-111, 123-125

Valvuloplasty, 126

Vardenafil, 249

Variable life insurance, 924

Varicella virus, 329, 510, 525-526

Varicose veins, 101, 140, 151-155

Vascular claudication, 428

Vascular dementia, 610-611

Vascular graft, 148

Vascular nervous system, 259

Vascular occlusive disease, 42

Vasculitis, 195, 308

Vasodepressor reflex, 122

Vasopressin, 453, 458

Veins, 151-154

Venereal warts, 281

Venlafaxine, 584, 592, 710

Venogram, 102

Ventilation-perfusion (VQ) scan, 102

Ventricles, 110

Ventricular arrhythmias, 134-135

Ventricular fibrillation, 134

Ventricular flutter, 134

Ventricular premature beats (VPBs), 134

Ventricular tachycardia, 134

Versed, 799

Vertebrae, 420

Vertebrates, 324

Vertebroplasty, 435-436, 446

Vertigo, 504

Vestibule, 279

Vesting, 974

Viagra, 54, 247-249

Viatical settlement, 937

Video-assisted thoracoscopic lung biopsy, 99

Vincristine, 100

Vioxx, 412-413, 709, 796

Viral cochleitis, 41

Visceral pain, 165

Vision. *See* Eye

Visiting nurse organizations, 655

Visual-spatial impairment, 613-614

Vitamin B12, 536, 538-539, 630-631

Vitamin C, 367

Vitamin D, 7, 197, 322, 327

    bone loss, 637

    calcium absorption, 442, 444

    skin's ability to synthesize, 631-632

Vitamin E, 496, 612

Vitamins

    and digestion, 630

    and drug interaction, 724

    essential, 637

Vitamins *(continued)*
   macular degeneration, 26
   supplements, 632
Vitreous humor, 24
Vivactil, 755, 758
VNS (Vagus nerve stimulation), 597
Vocational counselor, 659
Voiding diary
Voiding problems, 211-212, 268-269
Voltaren, 412
Von Willebrand's disease, 546-547
Vulva, 279, 281-283
Vulvovaginitis, 281

W

Waldenström's macroglobulinemia, 544-545
Walking
   and amputee rehabilitation, 677
   and stroke rehabilitation, 666-667
Warfarin, 103, 347, 548
   atrial fibrillation, 133
   drug interactions, 594, 598
   mechanical heart valves, 123
   nosebleeds, 55
Warren, Robin, 163
Warts, 10, 17-18, 281, 400
Water, 629-630
Weight loss
   and exercise, 648-650
   and hypertension, 129
   hypothyroidism, 463
   sleep apnea, 97
   See also Obesity
Wellbutrin, 92, 579, 591-592
Wells, Horace, 84
Wheelchairs, 657-658, 680
White blood cells (WBCs), 532-533, 540-541
Whole life insurance, 920-922
Wills, 858-860
   cost, 879
   execution of, 1077-1079
   litigation, 1087-1090
   pour-over, 876
   taxes, 1085-1087
   and trusts, 859, 863
Wilson's disease, 175

Wintergreen oil, 368
Womb, 194, 279, 284-286
Wrinkles, 8, 17
Wrist, 348, 441

X

Xanax, 237, 584, 593
Xenical, 481, 650
Xerosis, 11-12, 18
Xerostomia, 65-66, 78-79, 81
X-ray
   bones and muscles, 330-331
   dual X-ray absorptiometry (DXA), 443, 471
   pituitary tumors, 458
   spine, 434
Xylocaine, 511

Y

Yeast infection, 73, 281, 524
Yellow card, 744
Yohimbine, 262

Z

Zaleplon, 597
Zanamivir, 513
Zetia, 128
Zinc, 53
Ziprasidone, 596
Zithromax, 747
Zoladex, 236-237
Zolpidem, 597
Zyban, 92
Zyloprim, 300
Zyprexa, 594, 595
Zyrtec, 54

Designed by Cynthia Mason and Doug Bell
Ringling School Design Center, 2004

Printed and bound in China through Asia Pacific Offset
Composed in Bembo, Trade Gothic and Letter Gothic

Printed on 82 gsm Japanese matt

Photo credits: Mary McCulley
figures: 2-5, 3-10, 6-4, 6-6, 6-8, 8-12, 16-3, 16-4, 16-5, 16-8, 17-7,
17-10, p. 354, p. 359, p. 361, p. 390, 17-25, 17-37, 17-47, 19-6,
21-3, 21-7, 23-2, 23-5, 25-2, 25-3, 25-4, 25-7, 26-5, 27-1, 28-1,
28-4, 29-1, 29-2, 29-4, 29-5, 29-6, p. 656, 30-2, 30-3, 30-4,
30-5, 30-6, 30-7, 30-8, 30-9, 30-11, 30-12, 30-13, 30-15, 30-16,
30-18, 32-2, 35-1, 35-5, 36-2, 36-3, p. 760, 36-4, 36-5, 37-2,
37-3, 38-1, 38-4, 39-2, 40-1, p.826, 42-1, and 43-2.